MediaShare for Business offers a curated collection of business videos that provide customizable, auto-scored assignments. MediaShare for Business helps students understand why they are learning key concepts and how they will **apply** those in their careers.

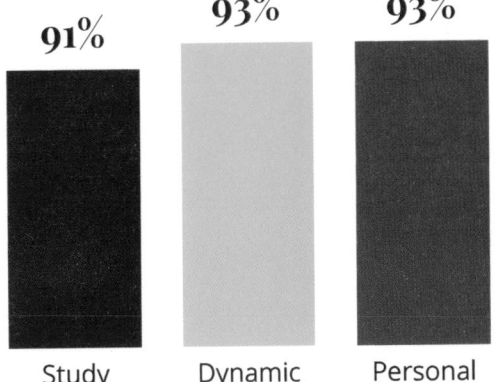

91% — Study Plan
93% — Dynamic Study Modules
93% — Personal inventory assessment

% of students who found learning tool helpful

Pearson eText enhances student learning—both in and outside the classroom. Take notes, highlight, and bookmark important content, or engage with interactive lecture and example videos that bring learning to life (available with select titles). Accessible anytime, anywhere via MyLab or the app.

89%

of students would tell their instructor to keep using MyLab Intro to Business

The **MyLab Gradebook** offers an easy way for students and instructors to view course performance. Item Analysis allows instructors to quickly see trends by analyzing details like the number of students who answered correctly/incorrectly, time on task, and median time spend on a question by question basis. And because it's correlated with the AACSB Standards, instructors can track students' progress toward outcomes that the organization has deemed important in preparing students to be **leaders.**

For additional details visit: www.pearson.com/mylab/Intro-to-Business

business
essentials

business

essentials

TWELFTH EDITION

Ronald J. Ebert

Ricky W. Griffin

 Pearson

New York, NY

Vice President, Business, Economics, and UK Courseware: Donna Battista

Director of Portfolio Management: Stephanie Wall

Portfolio Manager: Nicole Sam

Editorial Assistant: Courtney Paganelli

Vice President, Product Marketing: Roxanne McCarley

Product Marketer: Kaylee Carlson

Product Marketing Assistant: Marianela Silvestri

Manager of Field Marketing, Business Publishing: Adam Goldstein

Field Marketing Manager: Nicole Price

Vice President, Production and Digital Studio, Arts and Business: Etain O'Dea

Director of Production, Business: Jeff Holcomb

Managing Producer, Business: Melissa Feimer

Content Producer: Michelle Zeng

Operations Specialist: Carol Melville

Design Lead: Kathryn Foot

Manager, Learning Tools: Brian Surette

Content Developer, Learning Tools: Sarah Peterson

Managing Producer, Digital Studio and GLP, Media Production and Development: Ashley Santora

Managing Producer, Digital Studio: Diane Lombardo

Digital Studio Producer: Monique Lawrence

Digital Studio Producer: Alana Coles

Project Management: Thistle Hill Publishing Services

Composition: Cenveo® Publisher Services

Interior Design: Cenveo® Publisher Services

Cover Design: Cenveo® Publisher Services

Cover Art: Cenveo® Publisher Services

Printer/Binder: LSC Communications, Inc.

Cover Printer: Phoenix Color/Hagerstown

Library of Congress Cataloging-in-Publication Data

Names: Ebert, Ronald J., author. | Griffin, Ricky W., author.

Title: Business essentials/Ronald J. Ebert, Ricky W. Griffin.

Description: Twelfth Edition. | New York, NY : Pearson, [2019] | Revised edition of the authors' Business essentials, 2015. | Includes bibliographical references and index.

Identifiers: LCCN 2017045717 | ISBN 9780134728391 (hardcover) | ISBN 0134728394 (hardcover)

Subjects: LCSH: Industrial management—United States. | Business enterprises—United States.

Classification: LCC HD70.U5 E2 2019 | DDC 658—dc23

LC record available at https://lccn.loc.gov/2017045717

6 2022

 Pearson

ISBN 10: 0-13-472839-4

ISBN 13: 978-0-13-472839-1

For Griffin Grace, Sutton Sloane, and Andrew Preston—I do this for them.
—R. W. G.

brief contents

contents

Part 5 Managing Information for Better Business Decisions

14 Information Technology (IT) for Business 442

15 The Role of Accountants and Accounting Information 476

Ronald J. Ebert is Emeritus Professor at the University of Missouri–Columbia, where he lectures in the Management Department and serves as advisor to students and student organizations. Professor Ebert draws on more than thirty years of teaching experience at such schools as Sinclair College, University of Washington, University of Missouri, Lucian Blaga University of Sibiu (Romania), and Consortium International University (Italy). His consulting alliances have included such firms as Mobay Corporation, Kraft Foods, Oscar Mayer, Atlas Powder, and John Deere. He has designed and conducted management development programs for such diverse clients as the American Public Power Association, the U.S. Savings and Loan League, and the Central Missouri Manufacturing Training Consortium.

His experience as a practitioner has fostered an advocacy for integrating concepts with best business practices in business education. The five business books he has coauthored have been translated into Spanish, Chinese (Simplified), Chinese (Traditional), Malaysian, Bahasa Indonesian, and Romanian languages. Professor Ebert has served as the Editor of the *Journal of Operations Management*. He is a Past President and Fellow of the Decision Sciences Institute. He has served as consultant and external evaluator for *Quantitative Reasoning for Business Studies*, an introduction-to-business project sponsored by the National Science Foundation.

Ricky Griffin joined the faculty at Texas A&M University in 1981. During his career at Texas A&M, he has taught undergraduate and graduate courses in management, organizational behavior, human resource management, and international business. Professor Griffin's research interests include workplace aggression and violence, organizational security, workplace culture, and leadership. His work has been published in such journals as *Academy of Management Review*, *Academy of Management Journal*, *Administrative Science Quarterly*, and *Journal of Management*. He served as Associate Editor and then as Editor of *Journal of Management*.

In addition, Professor Griffin has also authored or coauthored several leading textbooks and coedited three scholarly books. His books have been used at more than 500 colleges and universities on five continents and have been translated into Spanish, Russian, Polish, and Chinese. He has served the Academy of Management as Chair of the Organizational Behavior Division and as Program Chair of the Research Methods Division. He also has served as President of the Southwest Division of the Academy of Management and on the Board of Directors of the Southern Management Association. Professor Griffin is a Fellow of both the Academy of Management and the Southern Management Association. He has also won several awards for research and has been supported by more than $400,000 in federal research funding. Professor Griffin has served as Director of the Center for Human Resource Management and Head of the Department of Management at Texas A&M University. He has also served as Executive Associate Dean and Interim Dean at the Mays Business School.

preface

New to This Edition

Chapter Opening Cases

All cases have been updated or replaced. Covering a wide variety of topics and organizations, including Netflix and Wegmans, these real-world cases introduce relatable topics that draw students into the content.

Current Events

The author has added new coverage of the likely impact of Donald Trump's election as president of the United States, the looming withdrawal of Great Britain from the European Union, the increasing diversity of the labor force, the continuing impact of social media, and the slow but steady growth of the U.S. economy. He has also added coverage on the emerging new relationship between the United States and Cuba. All data and statistics have also been updated to the most current information available.

The Door Opens

In July 2015, the United States officially restored diplomatic relations with Cuba after 54 years of hostility. President Barack Obama, who was born the year Eisenhower severed ties with the Communist country, urged Congress to reopen the borders, reasoning that, "Instead of supporting democracy and opportunity for the Cuban people, our efforts to isolate Cuba despite good intentions increasingly had the opposite effect—cementing the status quo and isolating the United States from our neighbors in this hemisphere."[1]

End-of-Chapter Activities

Five kinds of chapter-ending involvement activities—to reinforce and practice the use of chapter concepts—are back by popular demand!

questions & exercises

QUESTIONS FOR REVIEW

4-1. What are the advantages and disadvantages of globalization?

4-2. What are the three possible levels of involvement in international business? Give examples of each.

4-3. What are the elements of national competitive advantage? Give a current, real-world example of each condition.

4-4. Describe the five international organizational structures.

4-7. Research and identify a protectionist tariff imposed by the United States. Do you support that tariff? If so, why?

4-8. Do you think that a firm operating internationally is better advised to adopt a single standard of ethical conduct or to adapt to local conditions? What are the advantages and disadvantages of adapting to local conditions?

APPLICATION EXERCISES

4-9. The World Bank uses per-capita income to make distinctions among countries. Use Web or database research to

Solving Teaching and Learning Challenges

Many students who take Introduction to Business courses have difficulty seeing the relevance of course topics to their lives and future careers. This reduces the willingness of many students to prepare for class and to be engaged during class. We use the following resources to engage students with the content and to highlight how Introduction to Business is relevant and important for their employability and careers.

Applied Learning Opportunities Throughout Business Cases & Features

Managing in Turbulent Times

- Students learn from disappointments and challenges real companies face.

- New features look at recent IPOs, leadership in a virtual world, and workplace bullying.

managing in turbulent times

The Ups and Downs of Globalization

As markets move toward globalization, many countries are experiencing an identity crisis of sorts. The U.S. is rethinking its relationship with the World Trade Organization and NAFTA and reconsidering trade embargos with countries like Myanmar and Cuba. In Britain, after 43 years of strained relations with the European Union (EU), a large portion of the citizens pushed for the United Kingdom to exit the union. This movement took on the name "Brexit."

The European Union was formed after World War II to foster economic cooperation, and has grown to become a "single market," essentially allowing goods and people to move around as if the member states were one country. It has its own currency, the euro, which is used by 19 of the member countries (but not Great Britain), and its own parliament. Being part of the single market gave UK businesses easy access to all 500 million customers in the member countries and allowed UK consumers and companies to purchase goods and services from across the continent free of most tariffs and restrictions. It also allowed the relatively free movement of people across borders, much as the people of the US are free to move from state to state. Still, the British people continued to voice concerns over continued participation in the EU.

In 2015, as part of his campaign for re-election, Prime Minister David Cameron promised to put a referendum on the ballot asking voters to decide if they wanted to stay in the EU or exit. The expected logical outcome was to remain with the EU,

but the pivotal issues turned out to be a British desire for sovereignty and a fear of immigrants pouring into the country. On the day of the vote, with a 72 percent turnout, 51.9 percent of voters opted to leave.[12] Cameron, who had relied on the benefits of belonging to the EU as the cornerstone of his administration, resigned the day of the vote. The actual exit is a two-year process that is expected to culminate in 2019.

What does this mean for businesses around the world? As the economy and political climates change, expect to see traditional, long-standing relationships, treaties, and trade organizations struggle to keep up with the ups and downs of globalization.

Finding a Better Way

- This boxed feature reveals examples of organizations that are "finding a better way" to meet business challenges and describes how they are doing it.

finding a better way

Too Much of a Good Thing? China's Success Creates More Jobs in Mexico

In today's competitive global economy, businesses strive for every possible advantage. Many manufacturers, for example, locate their factories in countries that have an ample supply of low-cost skilled labor. During the 1980s and 1990s, the place to be was Mexico. Hundreds of factories were built just across the U.S.–Mexican border, and workers streamed to the region from other parts of Mexico for stable and well-paying jobs. But in the late 1990s, the world started to shift.

Mexican prosperity, fueled in part by its role as a center of manufacturing, led to increases in the cost of living, followed quickly by wage increases so workers could keep up. At about that same time, China began to emerge as an attractive manufacturing alternative. For instance, in 2003, wages in China were only one-third of the wages in Mexico. And there was certainly no shortage of workers eager to take steady jobs in factories making products for other countries. China's boom was Mexico's bust, as one company after another reduced or eliminated manufacturing there and moved to Asia.

In recent years, things have started to tilt back in Mexico's favor. As China's economy has flourished, its labor costs have crept higher and higher, so it's less of a bargain than it used to be. Whereas Mexican wages were once three times higher than wages in China, Mexican wages today are more than 40 percent less than those in China, according to research by Merrill Lynch.[7] When manufacturers factor in shipping costs (which have increased because of fuel prices), producing in Mexico may cost the same or less than in China. Time differences between the United States and China also can make it difficult to schedule videoconferences and telephone calls.

Several companies have also been burned by China's lack of protection for industrial and intellectual property.

Mexico is making enormous gains in the automobile sector. Companies such as Nissan, Honda, Volkswagen, and Mazda have invested billions of dollars in Mexican production vehicles, with over 3.4 million vehicles produced in 2016.[8] Eighty percent of these cars are exported to other countries, with the bulk being sent to the United States. Because of NAFTA, as well as other trade agreements, Mexico can export cars without tariffs to North and South America as well as Europe and Japan. According to Volkswagen's Vice President of Corporate Affairs in Mexico, "There's not another country in the world where you can do that."[9] However, the future is uncertain, as the U.S. moves to renegotiate NAFTA and puts pressure on U.S. companies to dissuade them from investing in more projects in Mexico.

Entrepreneurship and New Ventures

● This updated boxed feature shows students entrepreneurs who have really made a difference, some in large firms, others in smaller start-up companies.

entrepreneurship and new ventures

A Better Coconut Water

Founded in 2009, Harmless Harvest is the manufacturer and distributor of a popular line of organic coconut water that is available in stores across the United States. Douglas Riboud and Justin Guilbert saw an opportunity with the sudden popularity of coconut water, but they were troubled by environmental and economic concerns. After extensive research, Riboud and Guilbert concluded that the best-tasting coconut water could be produced from a single species of coconut from Thailand, in spite of lower yields and more complex cultivation. Unlike other producers, their coconut water is pasteurized through high-pressure treatment rather than heat, creating a raw, better-tasting product. According to Riboud, "The most important thing for us is taste. And the best we can do, the hardest job you can do as a manufacturer who works in food, is not screw up the ingredient you had in the first place."[15]

Harmless Harvest has addressed environmental concerns by making sure that their product is organic. They made an early commitment to working with farmers to make sure that no harmful pesticides or synthetic fertilizers were used and worked to obtain organic certification. Although this process was time-consuming and costly, it assured Riboud and Guilbert that their entire supply chain was built upon their vision of sustainability.

Finally, Harmless Harvest has contributed to economic change in a number of ways. In 2015, Harmless Harvest combined its Nam Hom coconut water with organic coffee, creating a drink with 50 mg of naturally occurring caffeine, the equivalent of a shot of espresso. The Peruvian cooperative that harvests Harmless Harvest's organic coffee beans has a focus on empowering women and the impoverished, with over 50 percent of members located in areas of extreme poverty. The organization has seen a significant decrease in domestic abuse against women, as well as an increased priority on educating children to strengthen the community as a whole. Guilbert notes that, "Sourcing from this cooperative is just another proof that better products can be made to benefit everyone involved. It's worth the extra effort."[16]

Brent T. Madison/Alamy Stock Photo

Reach Every Student with MyLab Intro to Business

MyLab is the teaching and learning platform that empowers you to reach every student. By combining trusted author content with digital tools and a flexible platform, MyLab personalizes the learning experience and improves results for each student. Learn more at www.pearson.com/mylab/intro-to-business.

● **Deliver trusted content:** You deserve teaching materials that meet your own high standards for your course. That's why we partner with highly respected authors to develop interactive content and course-specific resources that you can trust—and that keep your students engaged.
  ○ **Problem-Based Learning Assignments** make it easy for you to break your students' habit of memorization by challenging them to think critically about timely real-world situations. For example, after students learn about import-export balances, the Problem-Based Learning Assignment asks students to recommend whether Walmart should continue to expand globally even if it's struggled to do so in the past. Working individually or in a group, students think deeper about how to apply the concepts they've learned, and communicate their ideas via writing assignments and in-class discussion. You can assign these within MyLab via auto-graded questions or open-ended writing assignments.
  ○ **Mini Sims** put students in professional roles and give them the opportunity to apply course concepts and develop decision-making skills through real-world business challenges.

- **Empower each learner:** Each student learns at a different pace. Personalized learning pinpoints the precise areas where each student needs practice, giving all students the support they need—when and where they need it—to be successful.
  - The **Study Plan** gives students personalized recommendations, practice opportunities, and learning aids to help them stay on track.
  - **Dynamic Study Modules** help students study chapter topics on their own by continuously assessing their knowledge application and performance in real time.

- **Teach your course your way:** Your course is unique. So, whether you'd like to build your own assignments, teach multiple sections, or set prerequisites, MyLab gives you the flexibility to easily create *your* course to fit *your* needs..

- **Improve student results:** When you teach with MyLab, student performance improves. That's why instructors have chosen MyLab for over 15 years, touching the lives of over 50 million students.

Wearing the Hats

There's an old adage about people wearing different "hats." In general, this means that people usually have different roles to play in different settings. For example, your roles may include student, child, spouse, employee, friend, or parent. You could think of each of these roles as needing a different hat—when you play the role of a student, for example, you wear one hat, but when you leave campus and go to your part-time job, you put on a different hat. From the perspective of studying and interfacing with the world of business, there are a variety of different hats that you might wear:

- The Employee Hat. One hat is as an employee working for a business. Many people wear this hat during the early stages of their career. To wear the hat successfully, you will need to understand your place in the organization—your job, how to work with your co-workers and boss, and so on. You'll begin to see how to best wear this hat as you learn more about organizing business enterprises in Chapter 6 and how organizations manage people in Chapter 10, as well as in several other places in this book.

- The Employer or Boss Hat. It is also very likely that one day other people will be working for you. You'll still need to know your own job responsibilities, of course. But you'll now also need to understand how to manage other people— how to understand, lead, and motivate them and the social and legal parameters that affect how you deal with them. Chapters 3, 5, 8, and 9 provide a lot of information about how you can best wear this hat, although the role of manager runs throughout the entire book.

- The Consumer Hat. Even if you don't work for a business, you will still wear the hat of a consumer. Whenever you fill your car at Shell, buy an airline ticket from Delta and charge it on Visa, order a new backpack from Amazon, bid for something on eBay, buy clothes at H&M, or download a song from iTunes, you're consuming products created by business. To wear this hat effectively, you need to understand how to assess the value of what you're buying, your rights as a consumer, and so on. We discuss how you can best wear this hat in Chapters 4, 7, 11, 12, and 13.

- The Investor Hat. The final business hat is that of an investor. You may buy a business or work for a company that lets you buy its stock. You may also invest in other companies by buying their stock or shares of a mutual fund. For you to invest wisely, you must understand some basics, such as financial markets, business earnings, and the basic costs of investment. Chapters 4, 15, 16, 17, and Appendix III will help you learn how to best wear this hat.

Many people wear more than one of these hats at the same time. Regardless of how many hats you wear or when you may be putting them on, it should be clear that you have in the past, do now, and will in the future interface with many businesses in different ways. Knowing how to best wear all these hats is what this book is all about.

Developing Skills for Your Career

For students to succeed in a rapidly changing job market, they should be aware of their career options and how to go about developing a variety of skills. In this book and MyLab, we focus on developing these skills in the following ways:

Communication: Communication is covered in several places throughout the book. For example, Chapter 5 discusses how leaders communicate the corporate culture, while Chapter 6 discusses how managers communicate the delegation process and how managers can use communication to offset errors in the grapevine.

Critical Thinking: Chapter 9 devotes specific attention to the decision-making process. Chapter 11 discusses the research process and research methods. Collaboration teams and team-based methods of organizing are discussed in Chapters 6 and 8. At the end of each chapter, there is also a continuing team exercise.

Business Ethics and Social Responsibility: Chapter 2 is entirely devoted to ethics and social responsibility.

Information Technology Application and Computing Skills: Chapter 14 is devoted to information technology application and computing skills for business.

Instructor Teaching Resources

This program comes with the following teaching resources.

Supplements available to instructors at www.pearsonhighered.com	Features of the Supplement
Instructor's Manual authored by Carol Davis Wright from California State University, Monterey Bay	• Chapter-by-chapter summaries • Examples and activities not in the main book • Teaching outlines • Teaching tips • Solutions to all questions and problems in the book
Test Bank authored by Susan Schanne from Eastern Michigan University	4,000 multiple-choice, true/false, short-answer, and graphing questions with these annotations: • Difficulty level (1 for straight recall, 2 for some analysis, 3 for complex analysis) • Type (Multiple-choice, true/false, short-answer, essay) • Topic (The term or concept the question supports) • Learning outcome • AACSB learning standard (Ethical Understanding and Reasoning, Analytical Thinking Skills, Information Technology; Diverse and Multicultural Work, Reflective Thinking, Application of Knowledge) • Page number in the text
Computerized TestGen	TestGen allows instructors to: • Customize, save, and generate classroom tests • Edit, add, or delete questions from the test item files • Analyze test results • Organize a database of tests and student results
PowerPoints authored by Jeffrey Anderson from Ohio University	Slides include all the graphs, tables, and equations in the textbook. PowerPoints meet accessibility standards for students with disabilities. Features include, but are not limited to: • Keyboard and screen reader access • Alternative text for images • High color contrast between background and foreground colors

acknowledgments

This book bears the names of two authors. In reality, however, it reflects the combined efforts of many different people in what can only be called a team effort. First of all, we'd like to thank our reviewers and users who provided valuable feedback on the current strengths of the book and how we could make it better. The content and subject matter reviewers are highlighted earlier in the preface. In addition, we would also like to thank the following individuals for their contributions to the MyLab. We are truly appreciative of their hard work and important contributions.

Joe Cooke, Walla Walla Community College
Susan Gall
Storm Russo, Valencia College
Susan Schanne, Eastern Michigan University

I would also like to acknowledge the outstanding professionalism of our team at Pearson Education. Nicole Sam, Portfolio Manager; Angela Urquhart, Project Manager; Michelle Zeng, Content Producer; and Andrea Archer, Project Manager; have been instrumental in helping me continue to elevate the quality of my work and make this book even stronger.

I would also like to welcome Joe Cooke to the team. Joe is a professor at Walla Walla Community College. Joe helped update or replace the boxes and cases throughout the book and revised and enhanced all of the end-of-chapter pedagogy. I would also like to acknowledge and express my gratitude to Ron Ebert. Ron and I worked on this book together for many years and his imprint can still be found in many different places.

Finally, we would like to acknowledge our families. Their contributions to our work are far too extensive and personal to list. Suffice it to say that our wives, children, and grandchildren are the bedrocks of our lives. We are continually reminded by them of the fragility of life, the joy of being, and the importance of living every day to the fullest.

Ricky W. Griffin

P.S. (from Ricky)

I would also like to take a few lines here to personally acknowledge and express my gratitude to Ron Ebert. Ron retired from the University of Missouri–Columbia a few years ago after a long and distinguished career but continued to work with me on revisions of this book. However, he recently made the decision to retire from this work as well.

Ron was Chair of the Department of Management at Missouri when I completed my doctorate in 1978 and recruited me to join his department. Simply put, it was one of the best decisions of my life. I learned many lessons from Ron about scholarship, teaching, professionalism, and life and credit him for being one of my most significant mentors throughout my career. More importantly, though, he has been a wonderful friend. Ron, I'll miss working with you but will always treasure our friendship.

Ricky W. Griffin
2017

business
essentials

chapter 1

The U.S. Business Environment

The best way to make money is to sell products that

consumers want or need. While this

sounds simple,

only   a   few   strike   gold.

After reading this chapter, you should be able to:

1-1 **Define** the nature of U.S. business, describe the external environments of business, and discuss how these environments affect the success or failure of organizations.

1-2 **Describe** the different types of global economic systems according to the means by which they control the factors of production.

1-3 **Show** how markets, demand, and supply affect resource distribution in the United States, identify the elements of private enterprise, and explain the various degrees of competition in the U.S. economic system.

1-4 **Explain** the importance of the economic environment to business and identify the factors used to evaluate the performance of an economic system.

1-5 **Learn** about the skills you will gain through this text.

Doing Business in the Global Marketplace

You may have heard that China is a communist country, but what does that mean exactly? The terminology can be confusing. In 1978, China moved away from its socialist roots, where the government (in the form of the Chinese Communist Party) owned the factories and farms, toward a more free-market economy that China itself calls a "socialist market economy." This relatively new version of China allows individuals to own property and to take risks, as Jack Ma did when he started Alibaba. You may not have heard of his company, but in 2016 Alibaba accounted for 80 percent of China's online shopping and total sales dwarfed other e-commerce companies like Amazon and eBay.

Ma's story isn't one of overnight success, even though it may seem that way in hindsight. It took Ma Yun, aka Jack Ma, four years to pass the stringent entrance exams for college in China, but he persevered and finally received a degree in English. Shortly after that, he worked his way through graduate school, teaching English, to earn a degree in business. Still, he couldn't land a job in the tough Chinese job market. In the mid-1990s, he took a trip to the United States and experienced the Internet for the first time. Back in China, he started building rudimentary websites for Chinese companies and in 1999 he founded what is now known as the Alibaba Group, a family of online wholesale and retail companies.

The empire began with Alibaba.com, a business-to-business platform that allowed even small businesses access to a vast network of sellers. Building upon this success, Ma launched Taobao and Tmall.com, retail sites targeting the burgeoning Chinese middle class. One of the keys to the success of these sites is Alipay, a financial services firm that provides safe transactions, accounting for as much as 80 percent of online sales. Through Alipay, money is held in escrow until quality of goods is confirmed. This protection has helped to overcome concerns about subpar and fake goods and inadequate remedies through the Chinese legal system.

Jack took the company public in September of 2014, raising $25 billion overnight and making Jack Ma one of the richest men in the world, despite the fact that he is a Chinese citizen, and the influx of capital from selling stock in the United States has allowed Alibaba to expand almost exponentially. For the fiscal year ended March 31, 2016, Alibaba reported sales of almost $24 billion, and, counting third party sales through its websites (known as Gross Merchandise

what's in it for me?

Political, technological, cultural, and economic forces created enormous challenges for Jack Ma as he built his business. Even though the details change, these are the same general forces that will challenge you as you enter today's business world. All businesses are subject to the influences of economic forces. But these same economic forces also provide astute managers and entrepreneurs with opportunities for profits and growth. By understanding these economic forces and how they interact, you'll be better able to (1) appreciate how managers must contend with the challenges and opportunities resulting from economic forces from the standpoint of an employee and a manager or business owner, and (2) understand why prices fluctuate from the perspective of a consumer. You should have a deeper appreciation of the environment in which managers work and a better understanding of why the prices you pay for goods and services go up and down.

In this chapter, we'll first introduce the concepts of profit and loss and then describe the external environments of businesses. As we will see, the domestic business environment, the global business environment, and the technological, political-legal, sociocultural, and economic environments are also important. Next, we'll look at some basic elements of economic systems and describe the economics of market systems. We'll also introduce and discuss several indicators that are used to gauge the vitality of our domestic economic system.

Volume, or GMV), the company surpassed $485 billion. For comparison, e-Bay reported GMV of $84 billion for the year ended December 31, 2016 and revenues of $9 billion.

Marketing has played a big part in the company's success. China is experiencing a high volume of unmarried citizens, and Alibaba managed to usurp an informal holiday, called Singles Day, on November 11th of each year (11.11), that is similar to the American Valentine's Day. In 2009, marketing gurus at Alibaba began launching Double 11 deals to bolster sales during the lull before Christmas, and they hit a magic button. Sales went through the roof, and Alibaba trademarked "Singles Day." On Single's Day 2016, in just one 24-hour period, Alibaba posted $17.8 billion in GMV.

China is a giant, growing market. In 2015, General Motors sold 3.6 million cars in China and 3 million in the United States, with Buicks and Cadillacs leading the charge. It should be no surprise that sales in China are robust, since China's population is now almost 1.4 billion (roughly 18.5 percent of the world population). Compare that to a population in the United States of less than 330 million in about the same land area. The middle class consumers in China are still a small proportion of the total population, but they are growing in power and size and are consuming more and more goods, as evidenced by Alibaba's sales volume and that of General Motors and the many other international businesses selling to the Chinese markets. Some experts estimate that right now the United States accounts for about half of total world consumptions of goods and services, with only 5 percent of the total population. What happens to the world economy when China catches up with and maybe even surpasses the American per capita rate of consumption? Will there be enough goods and services to supply that amount of demand? Will there be enough natural resources? One of the great challenges of this generation of business people will be to find the socio-economic balance between global demand and supply.

Meanwhile, future opportunities for entrepreneurs are limited only by the imagination as the economy becomes worldwide and borders—both physical and political—continue to disappear.

(After studying the content in this chapter, you should be able to answer the set of discussion questions found at the end of the chapter.)

Jack Ma

Business, Profit, and the External Environment

OBJECTIVE 1-1
Define
the nature of U.S. business, describe the external environments of business, and discuss how these environments affect the success or failure of organizations.

What do you think of when you hear the word *business*? Does it conjure up images of large, successful corporations, such as Apple, Starbucks, and Amazon? Or of once-great but now struggling companies like Sears and Yahoo!? Do you think of multinational giants such as Honda, General Electric, or Nestle? Are you reminded of smaller firms, such as your local supermarket or favorite chain restaurant? Or do you think of even smaller family-owned operations, such as your neighborhood pizzeria, dry cleaners, or the florist down the street?

Business and Profit

All these organizations are **businesses**, organizations that provide goods or services that are then sold to earn profits. Indeed, the prospect of earning **profits**, the difference between a business's revenues and its expenses, is what encourages people to open and expand businesses. After all, profits are the rewards owners get for risking their money and time. The right to pursue profits distinguishes a business from those organizations—such as most universities, hospitals, and government agencies—that run in much the same way but that generally don't seek profits.[1]

Business *organization that provides goods or services to earn profits*

Profits *difference between a business's revenues and its expenses*

Consumer Choice and Demand In a capitalistic system, such as that in the United States, businesses exist to earn profits for owners; within certain broad constraints, an owner is free to set up a new business, grow that business, sell it, or even shut it down. But consumers also have freedom of choice. In choosing how to pursue profits, businesses must take into account what consumers want or need. No matter how efficient a business is, it won't survive if there is no demand for its goods or services. Neither a snowblower shop in Florida nor a beach umbrella store in Alaska is likely to do well.

Opportunity and Enterprise If enterprising businesspeople can spot a promising opportunity and then develop a good plan for capitalizing on it, they can succeed. For example, when large businesses such as Circuit City, Linens-N-Things, and Blockbuster Video close their doors, other firms profit from these closings by handling the inventory liquidations of these failed companies. And as oil prices recently dropped, gasoline producers like Exxon Mobile and BP have seen their profits decline. But food distributors like Sysco and delivery services such as FedEx saw their expenses drop and hence their profits grow. In general, then, business opportunity involves goods or services that consumers need or want—especially if no one else is supplying them or if existing businesses are doing so inefficiently or incompletely.

The Benefits of Business So what are the benefits of businesses? Businesses produce most of the goods and services we consume, and they employ most working people. They create most innovations and provide a vast range of opportunities for new businesses, which serve as their suppliers. A healthy business climate also contributes to the quality of life and standard of living of people in a society. Business profits enhance the personal incomes of millions of owners and stockholders, and business taxes help to support governments at all levels. Many businesses support charities and provide community leadership. However, some businesses also harm the Earth's environment, and their decision makers sometimes resort to unacceptable practices for their own personal benefit.

We now turn our attention to the environment in which businesses operate. Understanding the environment provides a foundation for our subsequent discussions dealing with economic forces that play a major role in the success and failure of businesses everywhere.

The External Environments of Business

All businesses, regardless of their size, location, or mission, operate within a larger external environment. This **external environment** consists of everything outside an organization's boundaries that might affect it. (Businesses also have an *internal environment*, more commonly called *corporate culture*; we discuss this in Chapter 5.) Not surprisingly, the external environment plays a major role in determining the success or failure of any organization. Managers must, therefore, have a thorough and accurate understanding of their environment and then strive to operate and compete within it. Businesses can also influence their environments. Figure 1.1 shows the major dimensions and elements of the external environment as it affects businesses today. As you can see, these include the *domestic business environment*, the *global business environment*, the *technological environment*, the *political-legal environment*, the *sociocultural environment*, and the *economic environment*.

Domestic Business Environment The **domestic business environment** refers to the environment in which a firm conducts its operations and derives its revenues. In general, businesses seek to be close to their customers, to establish strong relationships with their suppliers, and to distinguish themselves from their competitors. Take Urban Outfitters, for example. The firm initially located its stores near urban college campuses; it now locates stores in other, often more upscale, areas as well. The company also has a strong network of suppliers and is itself a wholesale

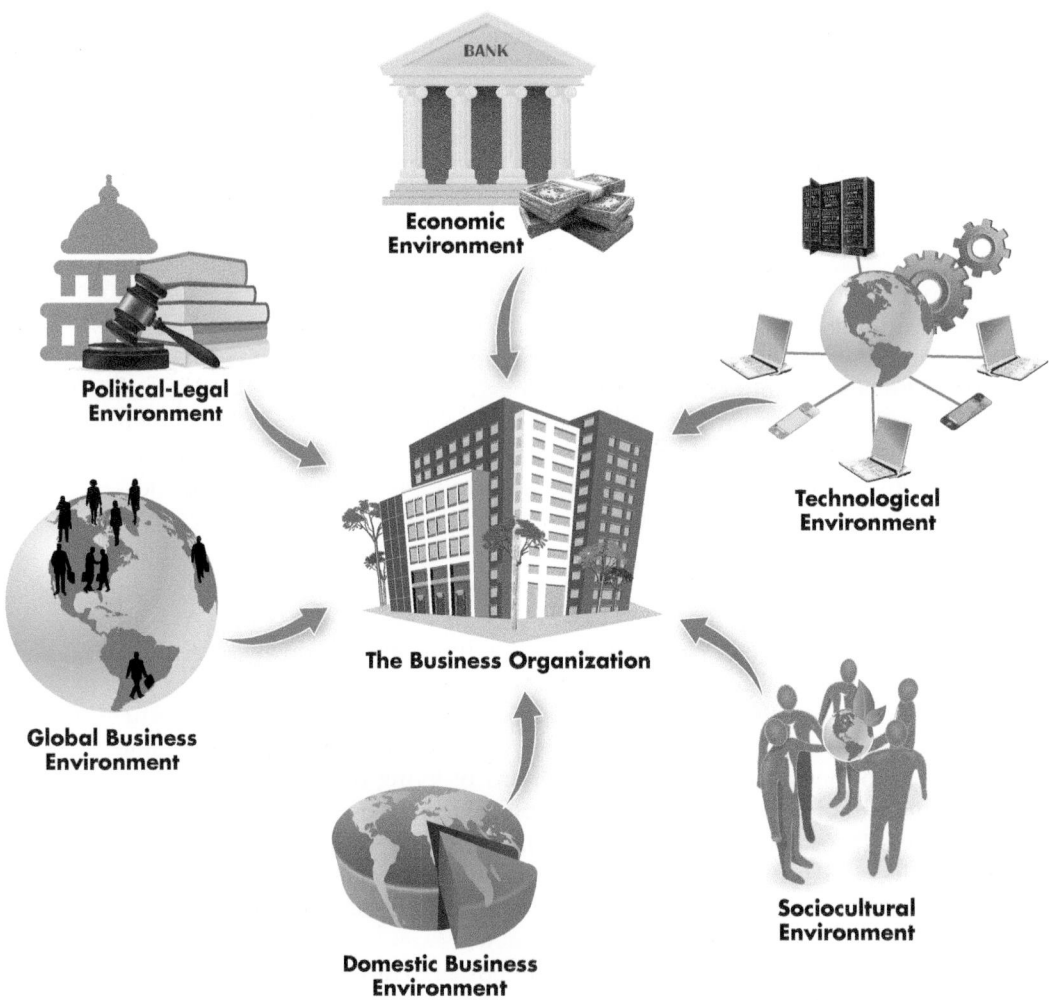

FIGURE 1.1 Dimensions of the External Environment

finding a better way

The B Team

As a general rule, we would say that the goal of every business is to achieve and maximize profits. The executives of the organization also have a responsibility to shareholders and investors to seek profits, making this their goal in decision making. On the other hand, many nonprofit organizations, such as the Red Cross, American Cancer Society, and the Appalachian Heritage Museum, work to serve the public good or solve social problems. B (or Benefit) Corporations fall in the space between the two.

B corporations are businesses—each is an organization that seeks to earn profits—but performance is measured not only by profits or growth in stock price but also by the organization's impact on society and the environment. Portland, Oregon-based EcoZoom is a B corporation that began in 2011 with a goal of generating a profit as well as concern for the health of their customers, economic development, and environmental awareness. Founder Ben West left his successful career in the transportation industry to earn an MBA. One of his professors was on the board of directors of Aprovecho, a nonprofit that designed cookstoves for use in developing countries. Although Aprovecho had developed great technology, they didn't know how to get the product to the market. This is where EcoZoom entered the story. EcoZoom manufactures the stoves in China and sells them in the United States for camping and other outdoor uses.[2] However, their primary market is developing countries, such as Kenya, Somalia, and Nigeria, where women and children are being exposed to toxic smoke from inefficient stoves that make them more susceptible to acute illnesses such as pneumonia, lung cancer, and heart disease.[3]

EcoZoom produces several models of low-emissions cookstoves, each very energy-efficient. Because the cookstoves reduce fuel use and cooking time, women have more time to spend with their families and on other tasks, such as

EcoZoom

maintaining their gardens. Their stoves can burn traditional biomass fuels, such as corncobs and cow dung, as well as wood and charcoal. Since fuel costs can run up to 30 percent of a family's monthly income, the simple addition of an efficient stove can make a huge difference.

The company recently partnered with micro-lending and crowd-funding sites like Trine and Kiva in order to fund distribution, as well as local entrepreneurs and even quasi-government organizations such as the Savings and Credit Cooperative Societies (Saccos) in Kenya that provide credit to families that can't afford to pay cash. EcoZoom, and other B corporations, continue to seek out and find better ways to do business and benefit society.

supplier to other retailers through its Free People division. It has established a clear identity for itself within the domestic business environment that enables it to compete effectively with such competitors as American Eagle and J. Crew.

Global Business Environment The **global business environment** refers to the international forces that affect a business. Factors affecting the global environment at a general level include international trade agreements, international economic conditions, political unrest, and so forth. For example, as political protests spread through much of the Middle East in 2014, oil prices began to surge and companies with operations in the region took emergency measures to protect their employees. But in 2015, a global oil surplus caused oil prices to plunge. At a more immediate level, any given business is likely to be affected by international market opportunities, suppliers, cultures, competitors, and currency values. For instance, Urban Outfitters currently has stores in the United States, Canada, Belgium, France, Denmark, Germany, Ireland, Scotland, Sweden, and several others and ships to

Global Business Environment *the international forces that affect a business*

customers in 133 countries. But as it has expanded into other parts of the world, it has to contend with different languages, more diverse cultures, different forms of technology, different currencies, and many other factors. Complicating things further, many of its suppliers are foreign companies.

Technological Environment *all the ways by which firms create value for their constituents*

Technological Environment

The **technological environment** generally includes all the ways by which firms create value for their constituents. Technology includes human knowledge, work methods, physical equipment, electronics and telecommunications, and various processing systems that are used to perform business activities. For instance, Urban Outfitters relies on a sophisticated information system that tracks sales and inventory levels to be highly responsive to its customers. The firm also enjoys considerable success with its e-commerce websites. Urban Outfitters has developed a strong market presence in Japan, for example, even though it has no traditional brick-and-mortar retail outlets in that country.

Political-Legal Environment *the relationship between business and government*

Political-Legal Environment

The **political-legal environment** reflects the relationship between business and government, usually in the form of government regulation of business. This environment is important for several reasons. First, the legal system defines in part what an organization can and cannot do. For instance, Urban Outfitters is subject to a variety of political and legal forces, including product identification laws, employee hiring restrictions, and local zoning requirements. Likewise, various government agencies regulate important activities, such as advertising practices, safety and health considerations, and acceptable standards of business conduct. Pro- or anti-business sentiment in government and political stability are also important considerations, especially for international firms. For instance, shortly after President Barack Obama first took office, a number of new regulations were imposed on businesses. Among other things, he signed legislation that imposed new restrictions on lobbying and on political action committees (these regulations are discussed in Chapter 2). But, shortly after Donald Trump was elected president in 2016, he pledged to reduce what he called excessive government regulation.

Sociocultural Environment *the customs, mores, values, and demographic characteristics of the society in which an organization functions*

Sociocultural Environment

The **sociocultural environment** includes the customs, mores, values, and demographic characteristics of the society in which an organization functions. Sociocultural processes also determine the goods and services, as well as the standards of business conduct, that a society is likely to value and accept. For example, a few years ago, Urban Outfitters introduced a Monopoly-like game called *Ghettopoly*. The company received a lot of unfavorable publicity about the game, based on critics' charges that it made light of poverty and other social problems. In response, Urban Outfitters pulled it from shelves and discontinued its sale. But the firm continues to push the limits. For instance, in recent years, Urban Outfitters has been criticized for selling t-shirts with a pocket patch resembling the yellow stars Jews were forced to wear during the Nazi regime in Germany, for clothing items with a color option listed as Obama Black, and for a holiday catalog with numerous items containing words and images that some people saw as offensive.[4]

Economic Environment *relevant conditions that exist in the economic system in which a company operates*

Economic Environment

The **economic environment** refers to relevant conditions that exist in the economic system in which a company operates. For example, if an economy is doing well enough that most people have jobs and wages are high, a growing company may find it necessary to pay even higher wages and offer more benefits to attract workers from other companies. But if many people in an economy are looking for jobs, a firm may be able to pay less and offer fewer benefits. Like many retailers, Urban Outfitters experienced some financial pressures during the recent recession, but its revenues and profits stabilized again when the economy began to rebound. But, like many other brick-and-mortar retailers, Urban Outfitters is also facing intense competition from online retailers like Amazon and Alibaba

Urban Outfitters is affected by the external environment in many different ways. The domestic business environment, global business environment, technological environment, political-legal environment, sociocultural environment, and economic environment all interact to provide Urban Outfitters with both opportunities and challenges.

and has recently closed several underperforming stores. The rest of this chapter is devoted to the economic environment; the other environments of business are covered throughout the rest of the book.

Economic Systems

A U.S. business operates differently from a business in France or the People's Republic of China, and businesses in those countries differ from those in Japan or Brazil. A key factor in these differences is the economic system of a firm's *home country*, the nation in which it does most of its business. An **economic system** is a nation's system for allocating its resources among its citizens, both individuals and organizations.

Factors of Production

A basic difference between economic systems is the way in which a system manages its **factors of production**, the resources that a country's businesses use to produce goods and services. Economists have long focused on four factors of production: *labor, capital, entrepreneurs,* and *physical resources*. In addition to these traditional four factors, many economists now include *information resources*. Note that the concept of factors of production can also be applied to the resources that an individual organization *manages* to produce tangible goods and intangible services.

Labor People who work for businesses provide labor. **Labor**, sometimes called **human resources** or *human capital*, includes the physical and intellectual contributions people make while engaged in economic production. Starbucks, for example, employs more than 238,000 people.[5] The firm's workforce includes the baristas who prepare coffees for customers, store managers, regional managers, coffee tasters, quality control experts, coffee buyers, marketing experts, financial specialists, and other specialized workers and managers.

OBJECTIVE 1-2
Describe
the different types of global economic systems according to the means by which they control the factors of production.

Economic System *a nation's system for allocating its resources among its citizens*

Factors of Production *resources used in the production of goods and services—labor, capital, entrepreneurs, physical resources, and information resources*

Labor (Human Resources) *physical and mental capabilities of people as they contribute to economic production*

Capital *funds needed to create and operate a business enterprise*

Capital Obtaining and using labor and other resources requires **capital**, the financial resources needed to operate a business. You need capital to start a new business and then to keep it running and growing. For example, when Howard Schultz decided to buy the fledgling Starbucks coffee outfit back in 1987, he used personal savings and a loan to finance his acquisition. As Starbucks grew, he came to rely more on Starbucks's profits. Eventually, the firm sold stock to other investors to raise even more money. Starbucks continues to rely on a blend of current earnings and both short- and long-term debt to finance its operations and fuel its growth. Moreover, even when the firm decided to close several hundred coffee shops a few years ago, it employed capital to pay off leases and provide severance pay to employees who lost their jobs.

Entrepreneur *individual who accepts the risks and opportunities involved in creating and operating a new business venture*

Entrepreneurs An **entrepreneur** is a person who accepts the risks and opportunities entailed in creating and operating a new business. Three individuals founded Starbucks back in 1971 and planned to emphasize wholesale distribution of fresh coffee beans. However, they lacked the interest or the vision to see the retail potential for coffee. Schultz, however, was willing to accept the risks associated with retail growth and, after buying the company, he capitalized on the market opportunities for rapid growth. Had his original venture failed, Schultz would have lost most of his savings. Most economic systems encourage entrepreneurs, both to start new businesses and to make the decisions that allow them to create new jobs and make more profits for their owners.

Physical Resources *tangible items that organizations use in the conduct of their businesses*

Physical Resources **Physical resources** are the tangible things that organizations use to conduct their business. They include natural resources and raw

Starbucks uses various factors of production, including (a) labor, such as this Starbucks barista; (b) entrepreneurs, such as CEO Howard Schultz; and (c) physical resources, including coffee beans.

materials, offices, storage and production facilities, parts and supplies, computers and peripherals, and a variety of other equipment. For example, Starbucks relies on coffee beans and other food products, the equipment it uses to make its coffee drinks, and paper products for packaging, as well as office equipment and storage facilities for running its business at the corporate level.

Information Resources The production of tangible goods once dominated most economic systems. Today, **information resources**, data and other information used by businesses, play a major role. Information resources that businesses rely on include market forecasts, the specialized knowledge of people, and economic data. In turn, much of what businesses do with the information results either in the creation of new information or the repackaging of existing information for new users. For example, Starbucks uses various economic statistics to decide where to open new outlets. It also uses sophisticated forecasting models to predict the future prices of coffee beans. And consumer taste tests help the firm decide when to introduce new products.

Information Resources *data and other information used by businesses*

Types of Economic Systems

Different types of economic systems view these factors of production differently. In some systems, for example (and in theory), the ownership of both the factors of production and the actual businesses is private; that is, ownership is held by entrepreneurs, individual investors, and other businesses. As discussed next, these are market economies. In other systems, though (and also in theory), the factors of production and all businesses are owned or controlled by the government. These are called *planned economies*. Note that we described these kinds of systems as being "in theory." Why? Because in reality, most systems fall between these extremes.

Economic systems also differ in the ways decisions are made about production and allocation. A **planned economy** relies on a centralized government to control all or most factors of production and to make all or most production and allocation decisions. In a **market economy**, individual producers and consumers control production and allocation by creating combinations of supply and demand. Let's look at each of these types of economic systems as well as mixed market economies in more detail.

Planned Economy *economy that relies on a centralized government to control all or most factors of production and to make all or most production and allocation decisions*

Market Economy *economy in which individuals control production and allocation decisions through supply and demand*

Planned Economies There are two basic forms of planned economies: *communism* (discussed here) and *socialism* (discussed later as a form of mixed market economy). As envisioned by nineteenth-century German economist Karl Marx, **communism** is a system in which the government owns and operates all factors of production. Under such a system, the government would assign people to jobs; it would also own all business and control business decisions—what to make, how much to charge, and so forth. Marx proposed that individuals would contribute according to their abilities and receive benefits according to their needs. He also expected government ownership of production factors to be temporary; once society had matured, government would wither away, and workers would take direct ownership of the factors of production.

Communism *political system in which the government owns and operates all factors of production*

The former Soviet Union and many Eastern European countries embraced communism until the end of the twentieth century. In the early 1990s, however, one country after another renounced communism as both an economic and a political system. Today, North Korea, Vietnam, Laos, Cuba, and the People's Republic of China are the only nations remaining that are controlled by communist parties. However, China in particular now functions much more like a mixed market economy (discussed below) than a pure communist-based economy.

Market Economies A **market** is a mechanism for exchange between the buyers and sellers of a particular good or service. (Like *capital*, the term *market* can have multiple meanings.) Market economies rely on capitalism and free enterprise

Market *mechanism for exchange between buyers and sellers of a particular good or service*

entrepreneurship and new ventures

The Lucrative Business of App Development

Snap, Inc., the maker of Snapchat, joins the ranks of notable companies started by individuals who have resisted the allure of quick riches offered by Facebook , which offered $3 billion for the company back in 2013. Started in 2011 by Stanford college roommates and headed up now by Evan Spiegel, the company sold shares instead to the general public in the form of an Initial Public Offering (IPO) of stock (listed as SNAP:NYSE), raising almost $5 billion and establishing a market value of $33 billion for the entire company.

Jack Dorsey, who founded Twitter, turned down a paltry offer of $500 million from Facebook in 2008, and then went public on November 7, 2013. By the end of the day, the company had reached a value of over $32 billion.

But not everyone takes their company public in order to reap the rewards of innovation. At about the same time Jack Ma was starting up Alibaba, two former employees of *Yahoo!* quit their jobs, took a sabbatical, and then applied for jobs with Facebook but got turned down. Ever the entreprenuers, Jan Koum and Brian Acton saw future opportunities in mobile apps and so they designed WhatsApp—one of the first messaging applications for the smartphone. In an ironic turn of events, Facebook bought WhatsApp for a whopping $19.3 billion in 2014.

In early 2017, *The Economist* reported that approximately 41 percent of Americans aged 18 to 34 use Snapchat every day, and 150 million people globally spend time on it every day.[6] However, Snapchat's data intensive app is costly to

Tanuha2001/Shutterstock

access for people in emerging markets, and it doesn't have as wide an appeal to the public or advertisers as do Facebook or even Twitter. Will Snap be able to withstand the competition from Facebook-owned Instagram and Google subsidiary YouTube? Only time will tell.

to create an environment in which producers and consumers are free to sell and buy what they choose (within certain limits). As a result, items produced and prices paid are largely determined by supply and demand. The underlying premise of a market economy is to create shared value—in theory, at least, effective businesses benefit because they earn profits on what they sell, and customers also benefit by getting what they want for the best price available.[7]

To understand how a market economy works, consider what happens when you go to a fruit market to buy apples. One vendor is selling apples for $1 per pound; another is charging $1.50. Both vendors are free to charge what they want, and you are free to buy what you choose. If both vendors' apples are of the same quality, you will buy the cheaper ones. If the $1.50 apples are fresher and healthier looking, you may buy them instead. In short, both buyers and sellers enjoy freedom of choice; that is, the vendors are free to charge whatever price they choose for their apples, and the customer is free to decide whether to buy the $1 apples, the $1.50 apples, someone else's apples, or no apples at all.

Taken to a more general level of discussion, individuals in a market system are free to not only buy what they want but also to work where they want and to invest, save, or spend their money in whatever manner they choose. Likewise, businesses are free to decide what products to make, where to sell them, and what prices to charge. This process contrasts markedly with that of a planned economy, in which individuals may be told where they can and cannot work, companies may be told what they can and cannot make, and consumers may have little or no choice in what they purchase or how much they pay. The political basis of market processes is called **capitalism**, which allows the private ownership of the factors of production and encourages entrepreneurship by offering profits as an incentive. The economic basis of market processes is the operation of demand and supply, which we discuss in the next section.

Capitalism *system that sanctions the private ownership of the factors of production and encourages entrepreneurship by offering profits as an incentive*

Mixed Market Economies   In reality, there are really no "pure" planned or "pure" market economies. Most countries rely on some form of **mixed market economy** that features characteristics of both planned and market economies. Even a market economy that strives to be as free and open as possible, such as the U.S. economy, restricts certain activities. Some products can't be sold legally, others can be sold only to people of a certain age, advertising must be truthful, and so forth. And the People's Republic of China, the world's most important planned economy, is increasingly allowing private ownership and entrepreneurship (although with government oversight). Indeed, it is probably more accurate today to describe China as a mixed market economy in a country controlled by the communist party.

Mixed Market Economy *economic system featuring characteristics of both planned and market economies*

When a government is making a change from a planned economy to a market economy, it usually begins to adopt market mechanisms through **privatization**, the process of converting government enterprises into privately owned companies. In Poland, for example, the national airline was sold to a group of private investors. In recent years, this practice has spread to many other countries as well. For example, the postal system in many countries is government owned and government managed. The Netherlands, however, privatized its TNT Post Group N.V. (now called Post NL), and it is among the world's most efficient post office operations. Canada has also privatized its air traffic control system. In each case, the new enterprise reduced its payroll, boosted efficiency and productivity, and quickly

Privatization *process of converting government enterprises into privately owned companies*

Geoff A Howard/Alamy Stock Photo

Many formerly planned economies have moved toward a more mixed economic model. For example, the People's Republic of China has used a planned economic model for decades but is now moving more toward a mixed market economy. Hong Kong, meanwhile, has been using the mixed market model for years. These signs on a busy Hong Kong street, for instance, are promoting a variety of goods and services provided by merchants along the street.

became profitable. More recently, the government of Iran has privatized numerous oil refineries and petrochemical plants that were previously state owned (although they have not revealed their productivity data).

In the partially planned system called **socialism**, the government owns and operates selected major industries. In such mixed market economies, the government may control banking, transportation, or industries producing basic goods such as oil and steel. Smaller businesses, such as clothing stores and restaurants, though, are privately owned. Many Western European countries, including England and France, allow free market operations in most economic areas but keep government control of others, such as health care.

Socialism *planned economic system in which the government owns and operates only selected major sources of production*

OBJECTIVE 1-3
Show

how markets, demand, and supply affect resource distribution in the United States, identify the elements of private enterprise, and explain the various degrees of competition in the U.S. economic system.

The Economics of Market Systems

Understanding the complex nature of the U.S. economic system is essential to understanding the environment in which U.S. businesses operate. In this section, we describe the workings of the U.S. market economy. Specifically, we examine the nature of *demand and supply, private enterprise,* and *degrees of competition.* We will then discuss private enterprise and forms of competition.

Demand and Supply in a Market Economy

A market economy consists of many different markets that function within that economy. As a consumer, for instance, the choices you have and the prices you pay for gas, food, clothing, and entertainment are all governed by different sets of market forces. Businesses also have many different choices about buying and selling their products. Dell Computer, for instance, can purchase keyboards from literally hundreds of different manufacturers. In addition to deciding where to buy supplies, its managers also have to decide what inventory levels should be, at what prices they should sell their goods, and how they will distribute these goods. Similarly, online retailers like Amazon can decide to use FedEx, UPS, or the U.S. Postal Service to deliver products bought by customers. Literally billions of exchanges take place every day between businesses and individuals; between businesses; and among individuals, businesses, and governments. Moreover, exchanges conducted in one area often affect exchanges elsewhere. For instance, when gas prices are high, this may also lead to prices going up for other products, ranging from food to clothing to delivery services. Why? Because each of these businesses relies heavily on gas to transport products.

The Laws of Demand and Supply On all economic levels, decisions about what to buy and what to sell are determined primarily by the forces of demand and supply.[8] **Demand** is the willingness and ability of buyers to purchase a product (a good or a service). **Supply** is the willingness and ability of producers to offer a good or service for sale. Generally speaking, demand and supply follow basic laws:

Demand *the willingness and ability of buyers to purchase a good or service*

Supply *the willingness and ability of producers to offer a good or service for sale*

Law of Demand *principle that buyers will purchase (demand) more of a product as its price drops and less as its price increases*

Law of Supply *principle that producers will offer (supply) more of a product for sale as its price rises and less as its price drops*

Demand and Supply Schedule *assessment of the relationships among different levels of demand and supply at different price levels*

- The **law of demand:** Buyers will purchase (demand) *more* of a product as its price *drops* and *less* of a product as its price *increases.*

- The **law of supply:** Producers will offer (supply) *more* of a product for sale as its price *rises* and *less* of a product as its price *drops.*

THE DEMAND AND SUPPLY SCHEDULE To appreciate these laws in action, consider the market for pizza in your town (or neighborhood). If everyone is willing to pay $25 for a pizza (a relatively high price), the town's only pizzeria will produce a large supply. But if everyone is willing to pay only $5 (a relatively low price), it will make fewer pizzas. Through careful analysis, we can determine how many pizzas will be sold at different prices. These results, called a **demand and supply schedule,** are obtained from marketing research, historical data, and other studies of the market.

Properly applied, they reveal the relationships among different levels of demand and supply at different price levels.

DEMAND AND SUPPLY CURVES The demand and supply schedule can be used to construct demand and supply curves for pizza in your town. A **demand curve** shows how many products—in this case, pizzas—will be demanded (bought) at different prices. A **supply curve** shows how many pizzas will be supplied (baked or offered for sale) at different prices.

Figure 1.2 shows demand and supply curves for pizzas. As you can see, demand increases as price decreases; supply increases as price increases. When demand and supply curves are plotted on the same graph, the point at which they intersect is the

Demand Curve *graph showing how many units of a product will be demanded (bought) at different prices*

Supply Curve *graph showing how many units of a product will be supplied (offered for sale) at different prices*

DEMAND AND SUPPLY SCHEDULES

Price	Quantity of Pizzas Demanded	Quantity of Pizzas Supplied
$2	2,000	100
$4	1,900	400
$6	1,600	600
$8	1,200	800
$10	1,000	1,000
$12	800	1,200
$14	600	1,300
$16	400	1,600
$18	200	1,800
$20	100	2,000

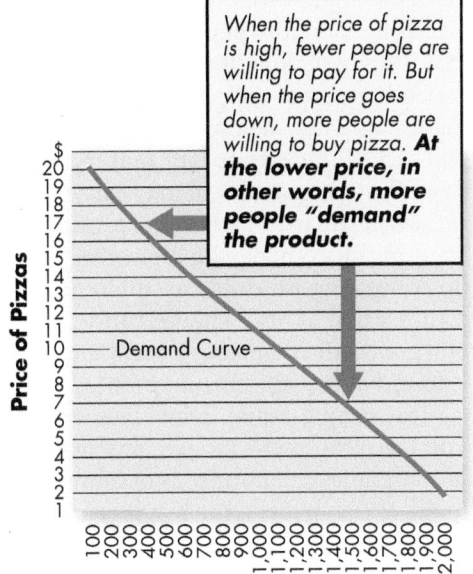

*When the price of pizza is high, fewer people are willing to pay for it. But when the price goes down, more people are willing to buy pizza. **At the lower price, in other words, more people "demand" the product.***

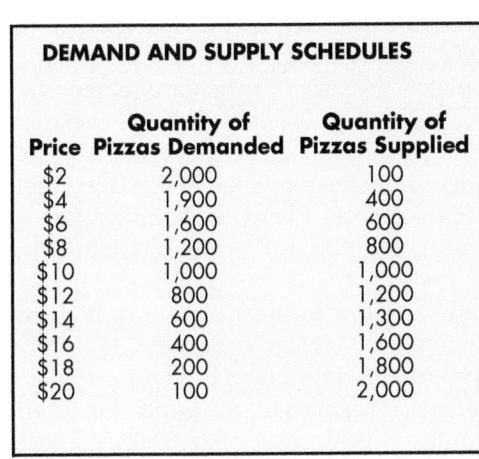

*When the price of pizza is low, more people are willing to buy pizza. Pizza makers, however, do not have the money to invest in making pizzas and so they make fewer. Supply, therefore, is limited, and **only when the price goes up will pizza makers be willing and able to increase supply.***

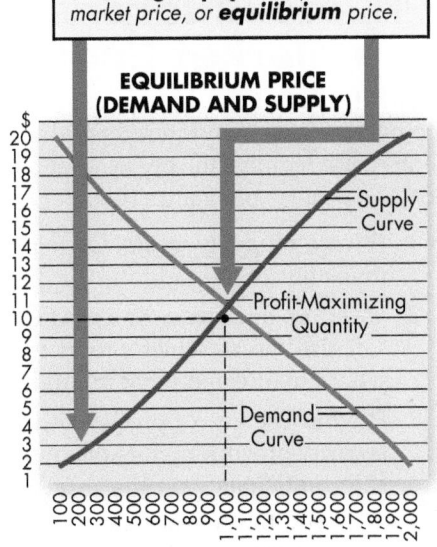

*When the pizza makers increase supply to satisfy demand, there will be **a point at which the price that suppliers can charge is the same as the price that a maximum number of customers is willing to pay**. That point is the market price, or **equilibrium** price.*

FIGURE 1.2 Demand and Supply

Market Price (Equilibrium Price) *profit-maximizing price at which the quantity of goods demanded and the quantity of goods supplied are equal*

market price (also called the **equilibrium price**), the price at which the quantity of goods demanded and the quantity of goods supplied are equal. In Figure 1.2, the equilibrium price for pizzas in our example is $10. At this point, the quantity of pizzas demanded and the quantity of pizzas supplied are the same: 1,000 pizzas per week.

SURPLUSES AND SHORTAGES What if the pizzeria decides to make some other number of pizzas? For example, what would happen if the owner tried to increase profits by making *more* pizzas to sell? Or what if the owner wanted to lower overhead, cut back on store hours, and *reduce* the number of pizzas offered for sale? In either case, the result would be an inefficient use of resources and lower profits. For instance, if the pizzeria supplies 1,200 pizzas and tries to sell them for $10 each, 200 pizzas will not be bought. Our demand schedule shows that only 1,000 pizzas will be demanded at this price. The pizzeria will therefore have a **surplus**, a situation in which the quantity supplied exceeds the quantity demanded. It will lose the money that it spent making those extra 200 pizzas.

Surplus *situation in which quantity supplied exceeds quantity demanded*

Shortage *situation in which quantity demanded exceeds quantity supplied*

Conversely, if the pizzeria supplies only 800 pizzas, a **shortage** will result, meaning the quantity demanded will be greater than the quantity supplied. The pizzeria will "lose" the extra profit that it could have made by producing 200 more pizzas. Even though consumers may pay more for pizzas because of the shortage, the pizzeria will still earn lower total profits than if it had made 1,000 pizzas. It will also risk angering customers who cannot buy pizzas and encourage other entrepreneurs to set up competing pizzerias to satisfy unmet demand. Businesses should seek the ideal combination of price charged and quantity supplied so as to maximize profits, maintain goodwill among customers, and discourage competition. This ideal combination is found at the equilibrium point.

This simple example involves only one company, one product, and a few buyers. The U.S. economy—indeed, any market economy—is far more complex. Thousands of companies sell hundreds of thousands of products to millions of buyers every day. In the end, however, the result is much the same: Companies try to supply the quantity and selection of goods that will earn them the largest profits. For example, most families vacation during the summer months when children are out of school. As a result, airlines increase their capacity to popular travel destinations and hotels, and resorts, and car rental agencies at those destinations adjust their rates to account for the increased demand. But when September rolls around, airlines adjust their routes to other destinations and many resorts start to lower their rates. Adjustments continue throughout the year to account for fluctuations during ski season, spring break, long weekends, and other times that people may decide to take vacations.

Private Enterprise and Competition in a Market Economy

Private Enterprise *economic system that allows individuals to pursue their own interests without undue governmental restriction*

Market economies rely on a **private enterprise** system—one that allows individuals to pursue their own interests with minimal government restriction. In turn, private enterprise requires the presence of four elements: private property rights, freedom of choice, profits, and competition.

1 *Private property rights.* Ownership of the resources used to create wealth is in the hands of individuals.

2 *Freedom of choice.* You can sell your labor to any employer you choose. You can also choose which products to buy, and producers can usually choose whom to hire and what to produce.

3 *Profits.* The lure of profits (and freedom) leads some people to abandon the security of working for someone else and to assume the risks of entrepreneurship. Anticipated profits also influence individuals' choices of which goods or services to produce.

4 *Competition.* If profits motivate individuals to start businesses, competition motivates them to operate those businesses efficiently. **Competition** occurs when two or more businesses vie for the same resources or customers. To gain

Competition *vying among businesses for the same resources or customers*

an advantage over competitors, a business must produce its goods or services efficiently and be able to sell at a reasonable profit. To achieve these goals, it must convince customers that its products are either better or less expensive than those of its competitors. Competition, therefore, forces all businesses to make products better or cheaper. A company that produces inferior, expensive products is likely to fail.

Degrees of Competition Even in a free enterprise system, not all industries are equally competitive. Economists have identified four degrees of competition in a private enterprise system: *perfect competition, monopolistic competition, oligopoly,* and *monopoly*. Note that these are not always truly distinct categories but instead tend to fall along a continuum; perfect competition and monopoly anchor the ends of the continuum, with monopolistic competition and oligopoly falling in between. Table 1.1 summarizes the features of these four degrees of competition.

PERFECT COMPETITION For **perfect competition** to exist, two conditions must prevail: (1) all firms in an industry must be small, and (2) the number of firms in the industry must be large. Under these conditions, no single firm is powerful enough to influence the price of its product. Prices are, therefore, determined by such market forces as supply and demand.

> **Perfect Competition** *market or industry characterized by numerous small firms producing an identical product*

In addition, these two conditions also reflect four principles:

1   The products of each firm are so similar that buyers view them as identical to those of other firms.

2   Both buyers and sellers know the prices that others are paying and receiving in the marketplace.

3   Because each firm is small, it is easy for firms to enter or leave the market.

4   Going prices are set exclusively by supply and demand and accepted by both sellers and buyers.

U.S. agriculture is a good example of perfect competition. The wheat produced on one farm is the same as that from another. Both producers and buyers are aware of prevailing market prices. It is relatively easy to start producing wheat and relatively easy to stop when it's no longer profitable.

MONOPOLISTIC COMPETITION In **monopolistic competition**, numerous sellers are trying to make their products at least seem to be different from those of competitors. Although many sellers are involved in monopolistic competition, there tend to be

> **Monopolistic Competition** *market or industry characterized by numerous buyers and relatively numerous sellers trying to differentiate their products from those of competitors*

table 1.1 Degrees of Competition

Characteristic	Perfect Competition	Monopolistic Competition	Oligopoly	Monopoly
Example	Local farmer	Stationery store	Steel industry	Public utility
Number of competitors	Many	Many, but fewer than in perfect competition	Few	None
Ease of entry into industry	Relatively easy	Fairly easy	Difficult	Regulated by government
Similarity of goods or services offered by competing firms	Identical	Similar	Can be similar or different	No directly competing goods or services
Level of control over price by individual firms	None	Some	Some	Considerable

fewer than in pure competition. Differentiating strategies include brand names (Tide versus Cheer versus in-store house brands of detergent), design or styling (Diesel versus Lucky versus True Religion jeans), and advertising (Coke versus Pepsi versus Dr. Pepper). For example, in an effort to attract weight-conscious consumers, Kraft Foods promotes such differentiated products as low-fat Cool Whip, low-calorie Jell-O, and sugar-free Kool-Aid.

Monopolistically competitive businesses may be large or small, but they can still enter or leave the market easily. For example, many small clothing stores compete successfully with large apparel retailers, such as Abercrombie & Fitch, Banana Republic, and J. Crew. A good case in point is bebe stores. The small clothing chain controls its own manufacturing facilities and can respond just as quickly as firms such as the Gap to changes in fashion tastes. Likewise, many single-store clothing businesses in college towns compete by developing their own T-shirt and baseball cap designs with copyrighted slogans and logos.

Product differentiation also gives sellers some control over prices. For instance, even though Target shirts may have similar styling and other features, Ralph Lauren Polo shirts can be priced with little regard for lower Target prices. But the large number of buyers relative to sellers applies potential limits to prices; although Polo might be able to sell shirts for $20 more than a comparable Target shirt, it could not sell as many shirts if they were priced at $200 more.

Oligopoly *market or industry characterized by a handful of (generally large) sellers with the power to influence the prices of their products*

OLIGOPOLY When an industry has only a handful of sellers, an **oligopoly** exists. As a general rule, these sellers are quite large. The entry of new competitors is hard because large capital investment is needed. Thus, oligopolistic industries (automobile, airline, and steel industries) tend to stay that way. Only two companies make large commercial aircraft: Boeing (a U.S. company) and Airbus (a European consortium). Furthermore, as the trend toward globalization continues, most experts believe that oligopolies will become increasingly prevalent.

Oligopolists have more control over their strategies than do monopolistically competitive firms, but the actions of one firm can significantly affect the sales of every other firm in the industry. For example, when one firm cuts prices or offers incentives to increase sales, the others usually protect sales by doing the same. Likewise, when one firm raises prices, others generally follow suit. Therefore, the prices of comparable products are usually similar. When an airline announces new fare discounts, others adopt the same strategy almost immediately. Just as quickly, when discounts end for one airline, they usually end for everyone else.

Monopoly *market or industry in which there is only one producer that can therefore set the prices of its products*

Natural Monopoly *industry in which one company can most efficiently supply all needed goods or services*

MONOPOLY A **monopoly** exists when an industry or market has only one producer (or else is so dominated by one producer that other firms cannot compete with it). A sole producer enjoys complete control over the prices of its products. Its only constraint is a decrease in consumer demand as a result of increased prices. In the United States, laws, such as the Sherman Antitrust Act (1890) and the Clayton Act (1914), forbid many monopolies and regulate prices charged by **natural monopolies**, industries in which one company can most efficiently supply all needed goods or services. Many electric companies are natural monopolies because they can supply all the power needed in a local area. Duplicate facilities—such as two power plants and two sets of power lines—would be wasteful.

OBJECTIVE 1-4
Explain
the importance of the economic environment to business and identify the factors used to evaluate the performance of an economic system.

Economic Indicators

Because economic forces are so volatile and can be affected by so many things, the performance of a country's economic system varies over time. Sometimes it gains strength and brings new prosperity to its members (this describes the U.S. economy during the early years of the twenty-first century); other times, it weakens and damages fortunes (as was the case during 2009–2010). And, at still other times, it provides moderate growth, helping some members of society but not others (as is the case at present). Clearly, then, knowing how an economy is performing is useful for business owners and investors alike. Most experts look to various **economic indicators**— statistics that show whether an economic system is strengthening, weakening, or remaining stable—to help assess the performance of an economy.

Economic Indicators *statistics that help assess the performance of an economy*

Economic Growth, Aggregate Output, and Standard of Living

At one time, about half the U.S. population was involved in producing the food that we needed. Today, less than 1 percent of the U.S. population claim farming as their occupation.[9] But agricultural efficiency has actually improved because the industry has devised better ways of producing products with more efficient technology. We can say that agricultural productivity has increased because we have been able to increase total output in the agricultural sector.

We can apply the same concepts to a nation's economic system, although the computations are more complex. Fundamentally, how do we know whether an economic system is growing or not? Experts call the pattern of short-term ups and downs (or, better, expansions and contractions) in an economy the **business cycle**. The primary measure of growth in the business cycle is **aggregate output**, the total quantity of goods and services produced by an economic system during a given period.[10]

Business Cycle *short-term pattern of economic expansions and contractions*

Aggregate Output *the total quantity of goods and services produced by an economic system during a given period*

To put it simply, an increase in aggregate output is growth (or economic growth). When output grows more quickly than the population, two things usually follow:

1 Output per capita—the quantity of goods and services per person—goes up.

2 The system provides more of the goods and services that people want.

When these two things occur, people living in an economic system benefit from a higher **standard of living**, which refers to the total quantity and quality of goods and services that they can purchase with the currency used in their economic system. To know how much your standard of living is improving, you need to know how much your nation's economic system is growing (see Table 1.2).[11] For instance, although the U.S. economy reflects overall growth in most years, in 2009 the economy actually shrank by 2.6 percent due to the recession.

Standard of Living *the total quantity and quality of goods and services people can purchase with the currency used in their economic system*

Gross Domestic Product **Gross domestic product (GDP)** refers to the total value of all goods and services produced within a given period by a national economy through domestic factors of production. GDP is a measure of aggregate output. Generally speaking, if GDP is going up, aggregate output is going up; if aggregate output is going up, the nation is experiencing *economic growth*.

Gross Domestic Product (GDP) *total value of all goods and services produced within a given period by a national economy through domestic factors of production*

Sometimes, economists also measure **gross national product (GNP)**, which refers to the total value of all goods and services produced by a national economy within a given period regardless of where the factors of production are located. What, precisely, is the difference between GDP and GNP? Consider a General Motors automobile plant in Brazil. The profits earned by the factory are included in U.S. GNP—but not in GDP—because its output is not produced domestically (that is, in the United States). Conversely, those profits are included in Brazil's GDP—but not GNP— because they are produced domestically (that is, in Brazil). Calculations quickly become complex because of different factors of production. The labor, for example, will be mostly Brazilian but the capital mostly American. Thus, wages paid to Brazilian workers are part of Brazil's GNP even though profits are not.

Gross National Product (GNP) *total value of all goods and services produced by a national economy within a given period regardless of where the factors of production are located*

table 1.2 U.S. GDP and GDP per Capita

2015 GDP (\$ Trillion)	2015 GDP: Real Growth Rate (%)	2015 GDP per Capita: Purchasing Power Parity
\$17.95	2.4%	\$55,800

GDP (gross domestic product)

REAL GROWTH RATE GDP and GNP usually differ by less than 1 percent, but economists argue that GDP is a more accurate indicator of domestic economic performance because it focuses only on domestic factors of production. With that in mind, let's look at the middle column in Table 1.2. Here, we find that the real growth rate of U.S. GDP—the growth rate of GDP *adjusted for inflation and changes in the value of the country's currency*—was 2.4 percent in 2015. But what does this number actually mean? Remember that *growth depends on output increasing at a faster rate than population.* The U.S. population is growing at a rate of 0.70 percent per year.[12] The *real growth rate* of the U.S. economic system, therefore, has been modest since 2011.

GDP PER CAPITA The number in the third column of Table 1.2 is a reflection of the standard of living: **GDP per capita** means GDP per individual person. We get this figure by dividing total GDP ($17.95 trillion) by total population, which happens to be a bit over about 322 million.[13] In a given period (usually calculated on an annual basis), the United States produces goods and services equal in value to $55,800 for every person in the country. Figure 1.3 shows both GDP and GDP per capita in the United States between 1950 and 2015. GDP per capita is a better measure than GDP itself of the economic well-being of the average person.

REAL GDP **Real GDP** means that GDP has been adjusted to account for changes in currency values and price changes. To understand why adjustments are necessary, assume that pizza is the only product in a hypothetical economy. In 2017, a pizza cost $10; in 2018, a pizza cost $11. In both years, exactly 1,000 pizzas were produced. In 2017, the local GDP was $10,000 ($10 × 1,000); in 2018, the local GDP was $11,000 ($11 × 1,000). Has the economy grown? No. Because 1,000 pizzas were produced in

GDP per Capita *gross domestic product divided by total population*

Real GDP *GDP adjusted to account for changes in currency values and price changes*

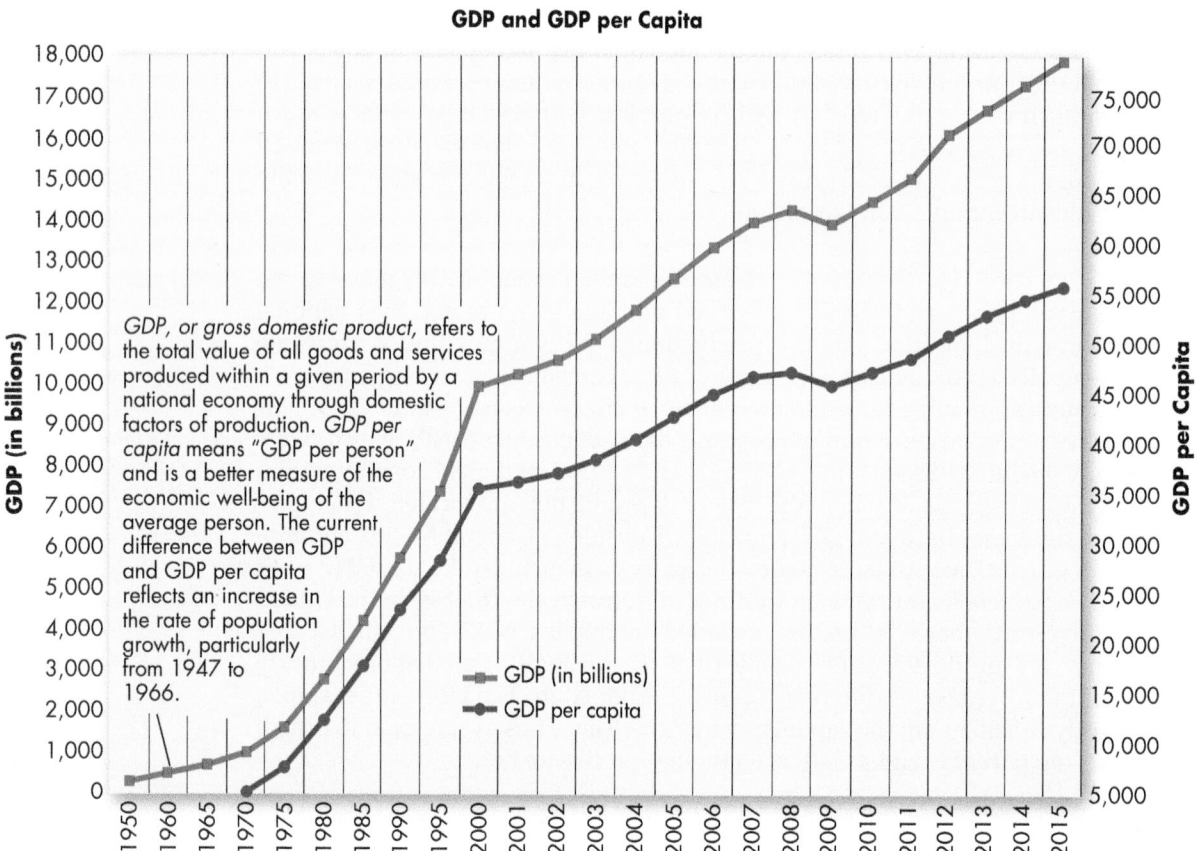

FIGURE 1.3 GDP and GDP per Capita

Sources: Based on http://www.bea.gov/iTable/index_nipa.cfm and http://www.census.gov/popest/data/historical/index.html; http://bea.gov/national/index.htm#gdp; and http://data.worldbank.org/indicator/NY.GDP.PCAP.CD

both years, *aggregate output* remained the same. The point is to not be misled into believing that an economy is doing better than it is. If it is not adjusted, local GDP for 2018 is **nominal GDP**—GDP measured in current dollars or with all components valued at current prices.[14]

Nominal GDP *GDP measured in current dollars or with all components valued at current prices*

PURCHASING POWER PARITY In the example, *current prices* would be 2018 prices. On the other hand, we calculate real GDP when we adjust GDP to account for changes in *currency values and price changes*. When we make this adjustment, we account for both GDP and **purchasing power parity**, the principle that exchange rates are set so that the prices of similar products in different countries are about the same. Purchasing power parity gives us a much better idea of *what people can actually buy with the financial resources allocated to them by their respective economic systems*. In other words, it gives us a better sense of standards of living across the globe. Figure 1.4 illustrates a popular approach to see how purchasing power parity works in relation to a Big Mac. For instance, the figure pegs the price of a Big Mac in the United States at $5.04. Based on currency exchange rates, a Big Mac would cost $6.59 in Switzerland and $5.51 in Norway. But the same burger would cost only $2.79 in China and $2.41 in India.

Purchasing Power Parity *the principle that exchange rates are set so that the prices of similar products in different countries are about the same*

Productivity A major factor in the growth of an economic system is **productivity**, which is a measure of economic performance that compares how much a system produces with the resources needed to produce it. Let's say that it takes 1 U.S. worker and 1 U.S. dollar to make 10 soccer balls in an 8-hour workday. Let's also say that it takes 1.2 Mexican workers and the equivalent of 1.5 dollars in pesos, the currency of Mexico, to make 10 soccer balls in the same 8-hour workday. We can say that the U.S. soccer-ball industry is more productive than the Mexican soccer-ball industry. The two factors of production in this extremely simple case are labor and capital.

Productivity *a measure of economic growth that compares how much a system produces with the resources needed to produce it*

If more products are being produced with fewer factors of production, the prices of these products will likely go down. As a consumer, therefore, you would need less of your currency to purchase the same quantity of these products. In short, your standard of living—at least with regard to these products—has improved. If your entire economic system increases its productivity, then your overall standard of living improves. In fact, standard of living improves *only* through increases in productivity.[15] Real growth in GDP reflects growth in productivity.

Productivity in the United States is generally increasing, and as a result, so are GDP and GDP per capita in most years (excluding the 2009 recession). Ultimately,

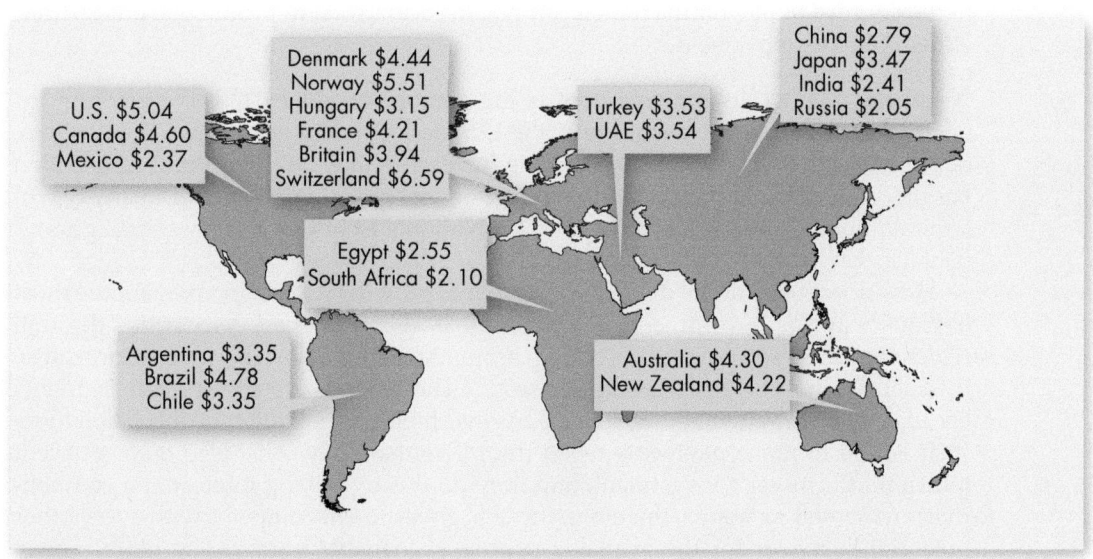

FIGURE 1.4 Price of a Big Mac in U.S. Currency in July 2015
Source: Based on The Big Mac index. Published by the Economist Newspaper Limited. http://www
.economist.com/content/big-mac-index

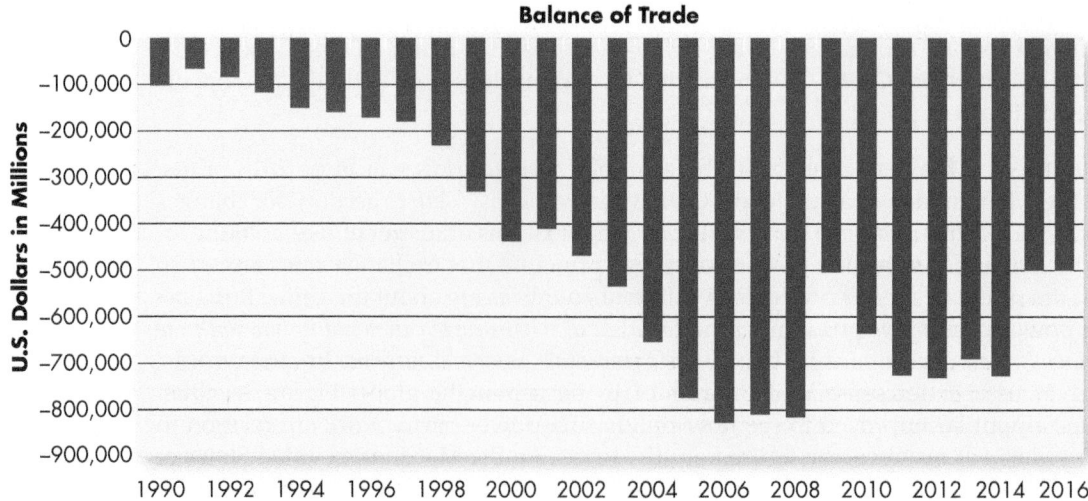

FIGURE 1.5 Balance of Trade
Source: http://www.census.gov/foreign-trade/balance/c0004.html#2008

increases in these measures of growth mean an improvement in the standard of living. However, things don't always proceed so smoothly. Several factors can inhibit the growth of an economic system, including *balance of trade* and the *national debt*.

Balance of Trade *the economic value of all the products that a country exports minus the economic value of all the products it imports*

BALANCE OF TRADE A country's **balance of trade** is the economic value of all the products that it exports minus the economic value of its imported products. The principle here is quite simple:

● A *positive* balance of trade results when a country exports (sells to other countries) more than it imports (buys from other countries).

● A *negative* balance of trade results when a country imports more than it exports.

A negative balance of trade is commonly called a *trade deficit*. In 2015, the U.S. trade deficit was about $746 billion. The United States is a *debtor nation* rather than a *creditor nation*. Recent trends in the U.S. balance of trade are shown in Figure 1.5.

Trade deficit affects economic growth because the amount of money spent on foreign products has not been paid in full. Therefore, it is, in effect, borrowed money, and borrowed money costs more in the form of interest. The money that flows out of the country to pay off the deficit can't be used to invest in productive enterprises, either at home or overseas.

National Debt *the amount of money the government owes its creditors*

NATIONAL DEBT Its **national debt** is the amount of money that the government owes its creditors. As of this writing, the U.S. national debt is around $19.48 trillion, or about $60,200 per U.S. citizen, and is increasing at a rate of around $2.4 billion per day. You can find out the national debt on any given day by going to any one of several Internet sources, including the U.S. National Debt Clock at www.brillig.com/debt_clock.

How does the national debt affect economic growth? Although taxes are the most obvious way the government raises money, it also sells *bonds*—securities through which it promises to pay buyers certain amounts of money by specified future dates. (In a sense, a bond is an IOU with interest.[16]) These bonds are attractive investments because they are extremely safe: The U.S. government is not going to default on them (that is, fail to make payments when due). Even so, they must also offer a decent return on the buyer's investment, and they do this by paying interest at a competitive rate. By selling bonds, therefore, the U.S. government competes with every other potential borrower for the available supply of loanable money. The more money the government borrows, the less money is available for the private borrowing and investment that increase productivity.

Economic Stability

Stability is a condition in which the amount of money available in an economic system and the quantity of goods and services produced in it are growing at about the same rate. A chief goal of an economic system, stability can be threatened by certain factors.

Inflation **Inflation** occurs when an economic system experiences widespread price increases. Instability results when the amount of money injected into an economy exceeds the increase in actual output, so people have more money to spend but the same quantity of products available to buy. As supply and demand principles tell us, when people compete with one another to buy available products, prices go up. These high prices will eventually bring the amount of money in the economy back down. However, these processes are imperfect—the additional money will not be distributed proportionately to all people, and price increases often continue beyond what is really necessary. As a result, purchasing power for many people declines.

Keeping in mind that our definition of inflation is the occurrence of widespread price increases throughout an economic system, it stands to reason that we can measure inflation by measuring price increases. Price indexes such as the **consumer price index (CPI)** measure the prices of typical products purchased by consumers living in urban areas.[17] The CPI is expressed as a percentage of prices as compared to a base period. The current base period used to measure inflation is 1982–1984, which is set at 100 (indicating a percentage). For comparison purposes, the CPI index was 172.2 in 2000, 195.3 in 2005, 218.1 in 2010, 229.6 in 2012, and 240.7 in late 2016. So, prices in 2010 reached more than double the level in the 1982–1984 base period.

Although we tend to view inflation as bad, in most ways it is better than *deflation*, which happens when there are widespread price cuts. Whereas inflation creates instability, it also generally indicates the overall economy is growing (just in an erratic manner). But deflation generally means the overall economy is shrinking, a more serious problem from most perspectives.

Unemployment Finally, we need to consider the effect of unemployment on economic stability. **Unemployment** is the level of joblessness among people actively seeking work in an economic system. When unemployment is low, there is a shortage of labor available for businesses to hire. As businesses compete with one another for the available supply of labor, they raise the wages they are willing to pay. Then, because higher labor costs eat into profit margins, they raise the prices of their products. Although consumers have more money to inject into the economy, this increase is soon undone by higher prices, so purchasing power declines.

At least two problems are related to unemployment:

1 If wage rates get too high, businesses will respond by hiring fewer workers and unemployment will go up.

2 Businesses could raise prices to counter increased labor costs, but they won't be able to sell as many of their products at higher prices. Because of reduced sales, they will cut back on hiring and, once again, unemployment will go up.

What if the government tries to correct this situation by injecting more money into the economic system—say by cutting taxes or spending more money? Prices in general may go up because of increased consumer demand. Again, purchasing power declines and inflation may set in.[18] During the recession of 2009 and its aftermath, millions of workers lost their jobs as businesses such as Circuit City closed their doors, and others, such as General Motors and Kodak, cut thousands of jobs in an effort to stem losses. Indeed, in early 2010, unemployment in the United States reached a 25-year high of 10.2 percent. By November 2011, as the economy was gradually pulling out of recession, unemployment had dropped to around 8.7 percent,

Stability *condition in which the amount of money available in an economic system and the quantity of goods and services produced in it are growing at about the same rate*

Inflation *occurs when widespread price increases occur throughout an economic system*

Consumer Price Index (CPI) *a measure of the prices of typical products purchased by consumers living in urban areas*

Unemployment *the level of joblessness among people actively seeking work in an economic system*

managing in turbulent times

Financial Turmoil—Is the Worst Behind Us?

In 2005, the global economy was booming. In the United States, for example, business profits were soaring, jobs were plentiful, and home ownership was at an all-time high. The stock market reached unprecedented heights, pension plan assets were growing exponentially, and new business opportunities were plentiful, but some economists, citing the historical *business cycle*, warned that the economy was headed for trouble because during extended periods of prosperity, people sometimes start to act as though good times will last forever. They continue to bid up stock prices, for instance, far beyond rational value. They also take on too much debt, save too little money, and spend beyond their means. Businesses, too, start taking more risks, carrying larger inventories, expanding too quickly, and hiring too many people. But things have a way of correcting themselves.

In 2008, gross domestic product (GDP), which is a broad measure of economic health, began to tumble. Consumers got nervous and stopped spending. As a result, businesses, like Ford Motor Company, had to curtail production and lay off workers as profits suffered. Between 2007 and 2009, hundreds of thousands of jobs were lost and unemployment claims soared. Banks had over-extended their ability to grant credit and now people couldn't repay what they had borrowed. It became a vicious downward spiral that may not look like much on a chart of GDP, but it was catastrophic in terms of standard of living in the United States. Unemployment, which had hovered around 5 percent of the workforce for years (considered *frictional*, or normal unemployment due to changes in jobs and the mobile workforce), suddenly doubled to 10 percent by mid-2009.

The stock market felt the pinch as well. In the 16 months between October 2007 and February 2009, the S&P 500, a broad indicator of prices on the New York Stock exchange, fell by 50 percent. For investors, this meant that 12 years of gains had been wiped out in just over a year.

The government intervened quickly, based on the economic data, and poured over $800 billion into the economy in the form of government projects that put people back to work. Some of the spending was controversial, such as $600,000 in grant money to the city of Denver to plant trees in wealthy neighborhoods, but overall, the Economic Recovery Act of 2009 stabilized the economy, along with monetary policy implemented by the Federal banking system.

Recovery was slow though, and the economy never got back on its pre-recession track. However, by mid-2011, the stock market was inching back up, continued to slowly recover throughout 2012, and was at nearly triple the 2009 low by early 2015. Even so, 2015 was a flat year for the market as investors reacted to uncertainty in global markets and the domestic political environment, but by late 2016 the market was making up for lost time and unemployment had dropped back into the 5 percent, pre-recession level.[19]

As the economy has slowly started to grow again and businesses are gaining confidence in the future, hiring is on the upswing and the stock market is making up for lost time. This is good news for both investors and entrepreneurs, but we should all remember, of course, that even when the good times are rolling again, another correction will likely take place somewhere down the road.

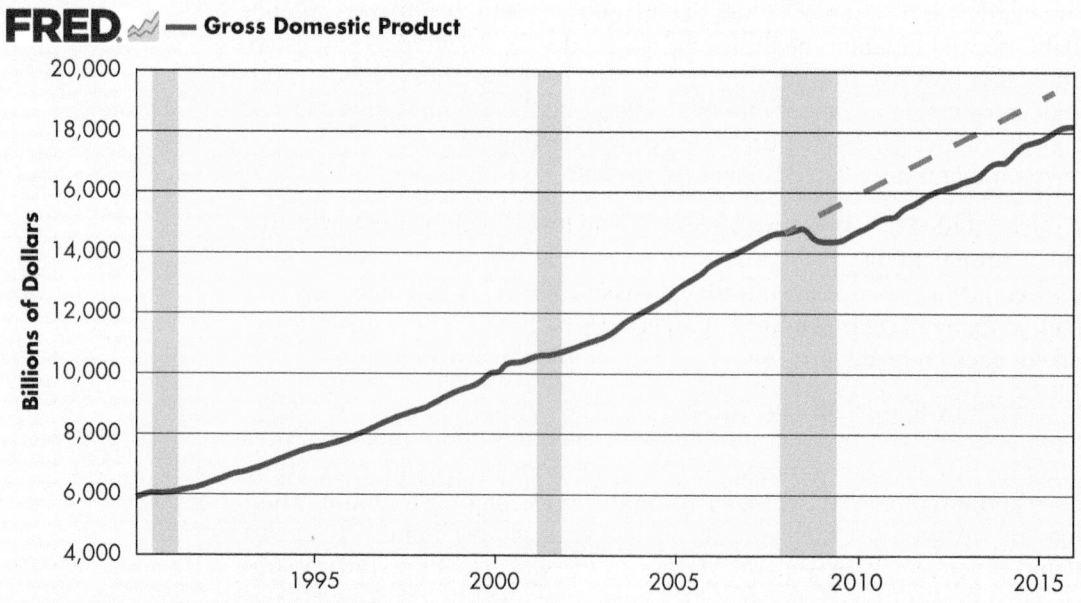

FIGURE 1.6 GDP, United States 1990–2015
Source: Based on Gross Domestic Product (GDP). Published by FRED. https://fred.stlouisfed.org/series/GDP

and by November of 2012, official unemployment was 7.7 percent. By the end of 2016, it had dropped even further, to 4.9 percent.[20]

RECESSIONS AND DEPRESSIONS Unemployment is sometimes a symptom of a system-wide disorder in the economy. During a downturn in the business cycle, people in different sectors may lose their jobs at the same time. As a result, overall income and spending may drop. Feeling the pinch of reduced revenues, businesses may cut spending on the factors of production—including labor. Yet more people will be put out of work, and unemployment will only increase further. Unemployment that results from this vicious cycle is called *cyclical unemployment*.

If we look at the relationship between unemployment and economic stability, we are reminded that when prices get high enough, consumer demand for goods and services goes down. We are also reminded that when demand for products goes down, producers cut back on hiring and, not surprisingly, eventually start producing less. Consequently, aggregate output decreases. When we go through a period during which aggregate output declines, we have a recession. During a *recession*, producers need fewer employees—less labor—to produce products. Unemployment, therefore, goes up.

To determine whether an economy is going through a recession, we start by measuring aggregate output. Recall that this is the function of real GDP, which we find by making necessary adjustments to the total value of all goods and services produced within a given period by a national economy through domestic factors of production. A **recession** is more precisely defined as a period during which aggregate output, as measured by real GDP, declines. As noted previously, most economists agree that the U.S. economy went into recession in 2008; most also agree that we were gradually emerging from that recession in 2011. A prolonged and deep recession is a **depression**. The last major depression in the United States started in 1929 and lasted more than 10 years. Most economists believe that the 2008–2011 recession, although the worst in decades, was not really a depression. However, it has come to be popularly known as the Great Recession, and we will use this phrase in this book.

Recession *a period during which aggregate output, as measured by GDP, declines*

Depression *a prolonged and deep recession*

Managing the U.S. Economy

The government acts to manage the U.S. economic system through two sets of policies: fiscal and monetary. It manages the collection and spending of its revenues through **fiscal policies**. Tax rates, for example, can play an important role in fiscal policies helping to manage the economy. One key element of President Obama's presidential platform was an overhaul of the U.S. tax system. Among other things, he proposed cutting taxes for the middle class while simultaneously raising taxes for both higher-income people and businesses. For a variety of reasons, however, little ever gets accomplished in the area of comprehensive tax reform.

Fiscal Policies *policies used by a government regarding how it collects and spends revenue*

Monetary policies focus on controlling the size of the nation's money supply. Working primarily through the Federal Reserve System (the nation's central bank, often referred to simply as "the Fed"), the government can influence the ability and willingness of banks throughout the country to lend money. For example, to help combat the Great Recession, the government injected more money into the economy through various stimulus packages. On the one hand, officials hoped that these funds would stimulate business growth and the creation of new jobs. On the other hand, though, some experts feared that increasing the money supply might also lead to inflation.

Monetary Policies *policies used by a government to control the size of its money supply*

Taken together, fiscal policy and monetary policy make up **stabilization policy**, government economic policy in which the goal is to smooth out fluctuations in output and unemployment and to stabilize prices. In effect, the Great Recession was a significant departure from stabilization as business valuations dropped and jobs were eliminated. The various government interventions, such as financial bailouts, represented strategies to restore economic stability.

Stabilization Policy *government economic policy intended to smooth out fluctuations in output and unemployment and to stabilize prices*

OBJECTIVE 1-5
Learn
about the skills you will gain
through this text.

Developing Skills in Your Career

If you haven't yet decided on a major, you may be thinking that this section isn't relevant to you. Let me assure you it is. Whether or not you plan on a career in business, the lessons you learn in this course will help you (in business and/or in your life). Moreover, it is only through the aggregate of your educational experience that you will have the opportunity to develop many of the skills that employers have identified as critical to success in the workplace. In this course, and specifically in this text, you'll have the opportunity to develop and practice these skills in the following places:

Communication Communication is covered in several places throughout the book. For example, Chapter 5 discusses how leaders communicate the corporate culture, while Chapter 6 discusses how managers communicate the delegation process and how managers can use communication to offset errors in the grapevine.

Critical Thinking Chapter 9 devotes specific attention to the decision-making process. Chapter 11 discusses the research process and research methods.

Collaboration Teams and team-based methods of organizing are discussed in Chapters 6 and 8. At the end of each chapter, there is also a continuing team exercise.

Business Ethics and Social Responsibility Chapter 2 is entirely devoted to ethics and social responsibility.

Information Technology Application and Computing Skills Chapter 14 is devoted to information technology application and computing skills for business.

summary of learning objectives

Define the nature of U.S. business, describe the external environments of business, and discuss how these environments affect the success or failure of organizations. (pp. 7–11)

A *business* is an organization that sells goods or services to earn profits. The prospect of earning *profits*, the difference between a business's revenues and expenses, encourages people to open and expand businesses. Businesses produce most of the goods and services that Americans consume and employ most working people. A healthy business environment supports innovation and contributes to the quality of life and standard of living of people in a society.

The *external environment* of business refers to everything outside its boundaries that might affect it. Both the *domestic* and the *global business environment* affect virtually all businesses. The domestic business environment is the environment in which a business conducts its operations and derives its revenues. The global business environment also refers to the international forces that affect a business, for example, international trade agreements, economic conditions, and political unrest.

The *technological, political-legal, sociocultural,* and *economic environments* are also important. The technological environment includes all of the ways by which firms create value for their constituents. Technology includes human knowledge, work methods, physical equipment, electronics, telecommunications, and various processing systems that are used to perform business functions. The political-legal environment reflects the relationship between business and government, usually in the form of government regulation of business. The sociocultural environment includes the customs, mores, values, and demographic characteristics of the society in which an organization functions. Sociocultural processes also determine the goods and services that a society is likely to value and accept. The economic environment refers to the relevant conditions that exist in the economic system in which an organization functions.

Describe the different types of global economic systems according to the means by which they control the factors of production. (pp. 11–16)

Economic systems differ in the ways in which they manage the five *factors of production:* (1) *labor,* or *human resources,* (2) *capital,* (3) *entrepreneurship,* (4) *physical resources,* and (5) *information resources.* Labor, or human resources, includes the physical and intellectual contributions people make while engaged in business. Capital includes all financial resources needed to operate a business. Entrepreneurs are an essential factor of production. They are the people who accept the risks and opportunities associated with creating and operating businesses. Virtually every business will rely on physical resources, the tangible things organizations use to conduct their business. Physical resources include raw materials, storage and production facilities, computers, and equipment. Finally, information resources are essential to the success of a business enterprise. Information resources include data and other information used by business.

Economic systems can be differentiated based on the way that they allocate the factors of production. A *planned economy* relies on a centralized government to control factors of production and make decisions. Under *communism,* the government owns and operates all sources of production. In a *market economy,* individuals—producers and consumers—control production and allocation decisions through supply and demand. A *market* is a mechanism for exchange between the buyers and sellers of a particular product or service. Sellers can charge what they want, and customers can buy what they choose. The political basis of market processes is *capitalism,* which fosters private ownership of the factors of production and encourages entrepreneurship by offering profits as an incentive. Most countries rely on some form of *mixed market economy*—a system featuring characteristics of both planned and market economies. *Socialism* may be considered a planned economy or a mixed economy, with government ownership of selected industries but considerable private ownership, especially among small businesses.

OBJECTIVE 1-3

Show how markets, demand, and supply affect resource distribution in the United States, identify the elements of private enterprise, and explain the various degrees of competition in the U.S. economic system. (pp. 16–20)

Decisions about what to buy and what to sell are determined by the forces of demand and supply. *Demand* is the willingness and ability of buyers to purchase a product or service. *Supply* is the willingness and ability of producers to offer a product or service for sale. A *demand and supply schedule* reveals the relationships among different levels of demand and supply at different price levels. The point at which the demand and supply curves intersect is called the market or equilibrium price. If a seller attempts to sell above the market price, he or she will have a surplus where the quantity supplied exceeds the demand at that price. Conversely, a shortage occurs when a product is sold below the equilibrium price and demand outstrips supply.

Market economies reflect the operation of a *private enterprise system*, a system that allows individuals to pursue their own interests without government restriction. Private enterprise requires the presence of four elements: (1) private property rights, (2) freedom of choice, (3) profits, and (4) competition. Economists have identified four degrees of competition in a private enterprise system: (1) *perfect competition*, (2) *monopolistic competition*, (3) *oligopoly*, and (4) *monopoly*. Perfect competition exists when all firms in an industry are small, there are many of them, and no single firm is powerful enough to influence prices. In monopolistic competition, numerous sellers try to differentiate their product from that of the other firms. An oligopoly exists when an industry has only a few sellers. It is usually quite difficult to enter the market in an oligopoly and the firms tend to be large. A monopoly exists when there is only one seller in a market. A firm operating in a monopoly has complete control over the price of its products.

OBJECTIVE 1-4

Explain the importance of the economic environment to business and identify the factors used to evaluate the performance of an economic system. (pp. 20–28)

Economic indicators are statistics that show whether an economic system is strengthening, weakening, or remaining stable. The overall health of the economic environment—the economic system in which businesses operate—affects organizations. The two key goals of the U.S. system are *economic growth* and *economic stability*. Growth is assessed by *aggregate output, the total quantity of goods and services produced by an economic system*. Although gains in productivity can create growth, the *balance of trade* and the *national debt can inhibit growth*. While growth is an important goal, some countries may pursue economic stability. *Economic stability* means that the amount of money available in an economic system and the quantity of goods and services produced in it are growing at about the same rate. The two key threats to stability are *inflation* and *unemployment*. The government manages the economy through two sets of policies: *fiscal policies* (such as tax increases) and *monetary policies* that focus on controlling the size of the nation's money supply.

key terms

aggregate output (p. 21)
balance of trade (p. 24)
business (p. 7)
business cycle (p. 21)
capital (p. 12)
capitalism (p. 15)
communism (p. 13)
competition (p. 18)
consumer price index (CPI) (p. 25)
demand (p. 16)
demand and supply schedule (p. 16)

demand curve (p. 17)
depression (p. 27)
domestic business environment (p. 8)
economic environment (p. 10)
economic indicators (p. 21)
economic system (p. 11)
entrepreneur (p. 12)
external environment (p. 8)
factors of production (p. 11)
fiscal policies (p. 27)
global business environment (p. 9)

gross domestic product (GDP) (p. 21)
GDP per capita (p. 22)
gross national product (GNP) (p. 21)
inflation (p. 25)
information resources (p. 13)
labor (human resources) (p. 11)
law of demand (p. 16)
law of supply (p. 16)
market (p. 13)
market economy (p. 13)
market price (equilibrium price) (p. 18)

mixed market economy (p. 15)
monetary policies (p. 27)
monopolistic competition (p. 19)
monopoly (p. 20)
national debt (p. 24)
natural monopoly (p. 20)
nominal GDP (p. 23)
oligopoly (p. 20)
perfect competition (p. 19)
physical resources (p. 12)

planned economy (p. 13)
political-legal environment (p. 10)
private enterprise (p. 18)
privatization (p. 15)
productivity (p. 23)
profits (p. 7)
purchasing power parity (p. 23)
real GDP (p. 22)
recession (p. 27)
shortage (p. 18)

socialism (p. 16)
sociocultural environment (p. 10)
stability (p. 25)
stabilization policy (p. 27)
standard of living (p. 21)
supply (p. 16)
supply curve (p. 17)
surplus (p. 18)
technological environment (p. 10)
unemployment (p. 25)

MyLab Intro to Business

To complete the problems with the ✪, go to EOC Discussion Questions in the MyLab.

questions & exercises

QUESTIONS FOR REVIEW

1-1. What are the benefits of businesses? Can a business negatively affect society? Give one example of a business that is benefiting society and one example of a negative effect.

✪ 1-2. What are the factors of production? Is one factor more important than the others? If so, which one? Why?

1-3. What is a demand curve? A supply curve? How are they related?

✪ 1-4. Why is inflation both good and bad? How does the government try to control demand and supply curves?

QUESTIONS FOR ANALYSIS

1-5. Identify and describe at least three factors in the external environment that affect college enrollment. Explain how each trend affects colleges and universities. Explain how each factor may affect college and university enrollment, either by bolstering it or reducing it.

1-6. Give an example of a situation in which a surplus of a product led to decreased prices. Similarly, give an example of a situation in which a shortage led to increased prices. What eventually happened in each case? Why?

1-7. Explain how current economic indicators, such as inflation and unemployment, affect you personally. Explain how they may affect you as a manager.

✪ 1-8. How are the overall economic goals of stability and growth related? Can they be reconciled to each other? If so, how?

APPLICATION EXERCISES

1-9. Visit a local shopping mall or shopping area. List each store that you see and determine what degree of competition it faces in its immediate environment. For example, if only one store in the mall sells shoes, that store represents a "local" monopoly. Note businesses that have direct competitors (for instance, two gas stations right next to each other) and show how they compete with one another. Also consider why they might have located right next to each other.

1-10. Interview a business owner or senior manager. Ask this individual to describe for you the following things: (1) how demand and supply affect the business, (2) what essential factors of production are most central to the firm's operations, and (3) how fluctuations in economic indicators affect his or her business.

building a business: continuing team exercise

Build a team of three to five classmates. You will be working with this team throughout the semester to make decisions about the launch of a new product.

Assignment

Meet with your team members and develop specific responses to the following:

1-11. Have each team member work individually to identify at least three trends in the external environment that will create business opportunities. Come together as a group and create a master list of trends.

1-12. Which trend do you think creates the greatest opportunity for success? Why?

1-13. Identify a product, either a good or a service, that will take advantage of this opportunity. Although you will refine this throughout the semester, write a four- to six-sentence description of your product and how it will spark buyer interest.

1-14. Who is your competition for this product, either direct competition or substitute products? Is competition a good sign for your business?

team exercise

COMPETITION IN THE NEW MOBILE ECONOMY

Background Information

You are one of two owners of the Red Hot Coffee Pot. Your establishment is on a side street right off the main street through town. Your customer base is largely university students, artists, writers, and other locals who prefer your cozy atmosphere with its overstuffed couches, fireplace, outdoor seating in the summer, shelves full of books to borrow and browse, locally roasted coffees, and, of course, free Wi-Fi. Within a five-block radius there are at least three other coffee houses with slightly less ambiance but otherwise similar perks, and prices are consistent for all the drinks and pastries across the range of competitors. However, you've become concerned because one of your competitors (the national chain store right around the corner) is promoting its new mobile app and customer loyalty program. Customers can order and pay online, pick up the drinks without having to wait in line, and earn points toward future purchases. Your profit margin is very narrow and you are already seeing a slight decline in business, although you can't directly attribute that to the new app. Your partner is worried and has shown you a quick graph, drawn on a napkin during a lunch break, of the relationship between supply and demand, and that a reduction of price would theoretically increase quantity demanded, and therefore, according to your partner, market share and ultimately, profits. You've decided to assemble a team to address this issue proactively.

Team Activity

Assemble a group of four or five people. Each group should develop a general strategy for responding to competitors' marketing strategies. Be sure to consider the following factors:

- How price changes affect the demand for your product and profits
- The number of competitors selling the same or a similar product
- The methods you can use—other than price—to attract new customers and retain current customers

FOLLOW-UP QUESTIONS

1-15. What form of competition best characterizes this market? What characteristics did you identify that led you to that conclusion?

1-16. Develop specific strategies based on each of the following situations:

- The average cup of coffee sells for $3 in your area. Right now you are selling 10,000 cups of coffee a month, and your fixed costs, including your own salary and that of your partner, are about $30,000 per month.
- The big chain store around the corner reduces their average sales price per cup to $2.80. As a result, your business falls off by 25 percent.

1-17. Discuss the role that various inducements other than price might play in affecting demand and supply in this market.

1-18. Is it always in a company's best interest to feature the lowest prices?

exercising your ethics

GETTING CAUGHT OUT IN THE COLD

The Situation

You are the owner of a small company that provides heating oil to residential and business customers in a rural Midwest county. The business has been in your family for several generations and you are a well-respected member of the community. Although the business had once provided a steady income for you and your family, increased energy efficiency and a move away from oil heat have cut your profits to almost nothing in recent years.

The Dilemma

After the retirement of your long-time marketing manager, you've hired a recent college graduate, Huma. Huma has analyzed your firm's financial position, as well as the most up-to-date demographic and market information. In the prior heating season, oil prices were quite high and your customers became accustomed to paying more than $2.60 per gallon. You've done your research, though, and know that it's very likely that the price that you must pay suppliers will be much lower this winter due to an increase in the supply of heating oil as more and more customers in other geographic areas switch to natural gas. While you're hoping to pass these cost savings on to your customers, Huma is recommending just the opposite. Huma proposes that you send out a "special offer" to your customers, allowing them to lock into a price of $2.40 per gallon for the upcoming heating season, in spite of the fact that you think that you could sell profitably at a much lower price. She believes that many of your customers will jump at the opportunity and you will be able to make a significant profit during the upcoming winter. On one hand, it would be nice to generate a large profit and rebuild your savings, but you're wondering if this is really the right thing to do.

QUESTIONS TO ADDRESS

1-19. What are the roles of supply and demand in this scenario?

1-20. What are the underlying ethical issues?

1-21. What would you do if you were actually faced with this situation?

cases

DOING BUSINESS IN THE GLOBAL MARKETPLACE

At the beginning of this chapter, you read about the Alibaba Group. Using the information presented in this chapter, you should now be able to answer these questions.

QUESTIONS FOR DISCUSSION

1-22. What is the difference between a market economy and a planned economy?

1-23. Explain how managers of Alibaba, eBay, Amazon.com, and other online retailers might view the concepts of supply and demand.

1-24. What economic indicators would a business owner be most likely to watch, and why?

1-25. Does Jack Ma's success increase or decrease your confidence in a capitalistic system based on private enterprise?

1-26. Should there be more government intervention in the markets and business dealings? Why, or why not?

GAME THEORY IN THE VIDEO GAME CONSOLE INDUSTRY

Nintendo, Sony, and Microsoft have been going head-to-head-to-head in the gaming industry ever since the demise of the Sega Dreamcast in 2000, the last of the old-school game consoles. Now the three major console manufacturers own 100 percent of the market share.

Sony leads the pack with its PS4, priced between $250–$300 (depending on options and features), with Microsoft's Xbox One in close second, also priced in the $250–$300 range. Nintendo's retired its innovative but aging Wii system in favor of Wii U and Wii Switch, which also comes in at $250–$300.

Video gamers can be militantly loyal to their brand. Sony and Microsoft allocate large amounts of their advertising and promotional budgets to differentiating their products, trying to get users to switch, but it wasn't until the introduction of the Wii in November 2006 by Nintendo that a game console was actually different. Nintendo focused on revolutionizing its product through new and different game play and by introducing the motion-sensor controller. As Nintendo president Reggie Fils-Aimé put it, "Nintendo has a quite appropriate reputation of doing its own thing, so whatever Microsoft and Sony decide to do, that's for them to manage."[21]

In 2013, entrepreneur Julie Uhrman brought the $100 list price Ouya game console to market with Kickstarter funds, but with only a few original games and a limited capacity to produce and promote, the company failed and the product was pulled from the market in 2015. So, currently there are still only three players in the market and it looks to stay that way for the foreseeable future.

QUESTIONS FOR DISCUSSION

1-27. Is it surprising that innovations, breakthroughs, and pricing strategies in the game console market seem to be coordinated? Why, or why not?

1-28. How hard would it be for a new company to get started in the game console industry? Has anyone tried, and if so, what was the result? What are the barriers to entry?

1-29. In terms of degrees of competition, how would you describe the market for game consoles? Do you think that this will change in the next five years? If so, how?

1-30. In 2006, Nintendo broke new ground in the video industry with the introduction of the Wii. Sony recently unveiled a virtual reality version of the PS4. If you were a member of the Microsoft marketing and R&D (research and development) team, what advice would you be giving your teammates?

1-31. Do you think that having only three manufacturers in this industry is positive or negative? Why?

1-32. Which game console do you think is superior? Why?

Writing Assignments

1-33. Research Gross Domestic Product (GDP) for two countries, both by country and per capita, choosing one country with a high standard of living and one with a low standard of living. Compare and contrast the two countries, taking into account GDP, factors of production, and the economic and political environments of each. What makes one country thrive while another seems to struggle? What other factors, besides economic quality of life, might make one country a better place to live than another?

1-34. Two of the most common leading indicators of economic health are unemployment and inflation. Look up current measures and trends and briefly explain what these measures mean and how they are relevant to business owners, managers, and other stakeholders. What do these indicators mean to you as a citizen and a consumer?

endnotes

[1] See Paul Heyne, Peter J. Boetke, and David L. Prychitko, *The Economic Way of Thinking*, 12th ed. (Upper Saddle River, NJ: Pearson, 2010), 171–176.

[2] Baker, Linda. 2012. "Cooking Clean." *Oregon Business Magazine 35*, no. 9: 9. Business Source Premier, EBSCOhost (accessed April 18, 2015).

[3] United Nations Foundation. "Health." Global Alliance for Clean Cookstoves. Accessed April 19, 2015. http://cleancookstoves.org/impact-areas/health/

[4] See "Urban Outfitters Swears by Naughty Holiday Catalog," *USA Today*, December 12, 2012, p. 1B.

[5] *Hoover's Handbook of American Business.* 2017 (Austin: Hoover's, 2017), pp. 790–791.

[6] "Snap's IPO Will Be the Largest in Years." *The Economist.* Accessed February 15, 2017. http://www.economist .com/news/business/21716070-app-company-has-pioneered-distinctive-vision-internet-snaps-ipo-will-be-largest

[7] Porter, Michael, and Kramer, Mark. "Creating Shared Value," *Harvard Business Review*, January–February 2011, pp. 62–77.

[8] See Karl E. Case and Ray C. Fair, *Principles of Economics*, 10th ed., updated (Upper Saddle River, NJ: Prentice Hall, 2011), 103–105.

[9] http://www.epa.gov/agriculture/ag101/demographics.html (January 10, 2015)

[10] Case and Fair, *Principles of Economics*, 432–433.

[11] https://www.cia.gov/library/publications/the-world-factbook/geos/us.html, accessed on January 2, 2017

[12] http://www.census.gov/popest/data/historical/2010s/vintage_2011/index.html, accessed on January 2, 2017

[13] http://www.census.gov/popest/data/historical/2010s/vintage_2011/index.html, accessed on January 2, 2017

[14] See Olivier Blanchard, *Macroeconomics*, 6th ed. (Upper Saddle River, NJ: Pearson, 2013), 24–26.

[15] See Jay Heizer and Barry Render, *Operations Management*, 11th ed. (Upper Saddle River, NJ: Prentice Hall, 2014).

[16] Heyne, Paul, Boetke, Peter J., and Prychitko, David L. *The Economic Way of Thinking*, 12th ed. (Upper Saddle River, NJ: Pearson, 2010), 491–493.

[17] Ayers, Ronald M., and Collinge, Robert A. *Economics: Explore and Apply*. (Upper Saddle River, NJ: Prentice Hall, 2004), 163–167.

[18] See Heyne, Boetke, and Prychitko, *The Economic Way of Thinking*, 403–409, 503–504.

[19] United States Department of Labor. "Employment Situation Summary." Bureau of Labor Statistics. Accessed February 17, 2017. https://www.bls.gov/news.release/empsit.nr0.htm

[20] http://www.ncsl.org/research/labor-and-employment/national-employment-monthly-update.aspx, accessed on January 3, 2015

[21] Gaudiosi, John. "How Sony, Microsoft, and Nintendo Are Preparing for Their Gaming Future" *Fortune*. Accessed February 13, 2017. http://fortune.com/2016/12/23/sony-microsoft-nintendo-future.

chapter 2

Understanding Business Ethics and Social Responsibility

How do companies that care about society balance social welfare with profits? Should we punish those that don't?

After reading this chapter, you should be able to:

2-1 **Explain** how individuals develop their personal codes of ethics and why ethics are important in the workplace.

2-2 **Distinguish** social responsibility from ethics, identify organizational stakeholders, and characterize social consciousness today.

2-3 **Show** how the concept of social responsibility applies both to environmental issues and to a firm's relationships with customers, employees, and investors.

2-4 **Identify** four general approaches to social responsibility and note the role of social responsibility in small business.

2-5 **Explain** the role of government in social responsibility in terms of how governments and businesses influence each other.

2-6 **Discuss** how businesses manage social responsibility in terms of both formal and informal dimensions and how organizations can evaluate their social responsibility.

Simply Divine

More than 70 percent of the world's supply of cacao beans comes from small farms scattered throughout the West African nations, including Ivory Coast and Ghana. In the past decade, consumers have become increasingly aware of a particularly disturbing business practice—the use of child slave labor in the cocoa industry.

In countries such as Ivory Coast, one-half of the country's exports are cocoa. Cocoa farmers often earn less than the poverty level, even with the use of child and slave labor.[1] Cocoa is an extremely unstable commodity—global prices fluctuate significantly. Along with price instability, profitability depends upon factors over which farmers have no control, such as drought and crop disease. To improve their chances of making a profit, cocoa farmers look for ways to cut costs, and the use of slave and child labor is the most effective money-saving measure.

This is where the idea of "fair trade" comes in. *Fair trade* refers to programs designed to ensure that export-dependent farmers in developing countries receive fair prices for their crops. Organizations such as TransFair USA certify that farmers supplying cocoa products are paid fair prices, while paying their employees reasonable wages and providing a safe and environmentally friendly workplace. While many fair-trade products are also organic, this is not a requirement for certification by TransFair. However, the organization bans the use of genetically modified organisms (GMOs) and encourages farmers to limit their use of pesticides and fertilizers.[2]

A 3.5-ounce candy bar labeled *fair trade* may sell for $3.49, compared to about $1.84 for one that's not. Why so much? Because the fair-trade candy bar, says TransFair USA spokesperson Nicole Chettero, occupies a niche market. She predicts, however, that, "as the demand and volume of Fair Trade–certified products increase, the market will work itself out…. [R]etailers will naturally start to drop prices to remain competitive." Ultimately, she concludes, "there is no reason why fair-trade [products] should cost astronomically more than traditional products."

Some critics of fair-trade practices and prices agree in principle but contend that consumers don't need to pay such excessive prices, even under *current* market conditions. They point out that, according to TransFair's own data, cocoa farmers get only 3 cents of the

Andres Rodriguez/Fotolia

what's in it for me?

Suppose you were the owner of a convenience store that carries the same candy lines sold everywhere—Snickers, Hershey's, and so forth—and three new candy distributors want you to start selling their products as well. You know that one distributor's candy is made by standard methods in which ingredients are bought for the lowest price possible and all profits go to the manufacturer. Another distributor is promoting a line of candy labeled "fair trade" that costs a dollar more per candy bar, and the supplier of the cacao bean gets about a quarter of that dollar. The third distributor's products cost two dollars more than the first item, but you know the grower of the cacao bean would get half of the extra—a dollar more. Because of the price differences, you know that you can sell more of the first distributor's candy, a little less of the second distributor's candy, and even less of the third distributor's candy. Which product would you choose to sell in your store?

Business practices today are under more scrutiny than ever before. Business owners and managers are often torn between doing what makes sense for the bottom line (such as increasing profit) versus doing what makes sense for general social welfare. By understanding the material in this chapter, you'll be better able to assess ethical and socially responsible issues facing you as an employee and as a boss or business owner and understand the ethical and socially responsible actions of businesses you deal with as a consumer and as an investor.

In this chapter, we'll look at ethics and social responsibility—what they mean and how they apply to environmental issues and to a firm's relationships with customers, employees, and investors. Along the way, we look at general approaches to social responsibility, the steps businesses must take to implement social responsibility programs, how issues of social responsibility and ethics affect small businesses, and how businesses attempt to manage social responsibility programs. But first, we begin this chapter by discussing ethics in the workplace—individual, business, and managerial.

$3.49 that a socially conscious consumer pays for a Fair Trade–certified candy bar. "Farmers often receive very little," reports consumer researcher Lawrence Solomon. "Often fair trade is sold at a premium," he charges, "but the entire premium goes to the middlemen."

Critics like Solomon suggest that sellers of fair-trade products are taking advantage of consumers who are socially but not particularly price conscious. They point out that if sellers priced that $3.49 candy bar at $2.49, farmers would still be entitled to 3 cents. The price, they contend, is inflated to $3.49 simply because there's a small segment of the market willing to pay it. Fair-trade programs, advises English economist Tim Harford, "make a promise that the producers will get a good deal. They do not promise that the consumer will get a good deal. That's up to you as a savvy shopper."[3]

Divine Chocolate is a company that is taking fair-trade cocoa to the next level. Unlike other companies selling fair-trade chocolates, Divine returns a share of their profits to the farmers in their supply chain. Divine's largest shareholder group is Kuapa Kokoo, a fair-trade cocoa cooperative. Cocoa farmers who belong to this group not only receive a fair-trade price for their cocoa but also receive dividends from the profits of Divine Chocolate.[4] (After studying the content in this chapter, you should be able to answer the set of discussion questions found at the end of the chapter.)

OBJECTIVE 2-1
Explain
how individuals develop their personal codes of ethics and why ethics are important in the workplace.

Ethics *beliefs about what is right and wrong or good and bad in actions that affect others*

Ethical Behavior *behavior conforming to generally accepted social norms concerning beneficial and harmful actions*

Unethical Behavior *behavior that does not conform to generally accepted social norms concerning beneficial and harmful actions*

Business Ethics *ethical or unethical behaviors by employees in the context of their jobs*

Ethics in the Workplace

Just what is ethical behavior? **Ethics** are beliefs about what's right and wrong or good and bad. An individual's values and morals, plus the social context in which his or her behavior occurs, determine whether behavior is regarded as ethical or unethical. In other words, **ethical behavior** is behavior that conforms to individual beliefs and social norms about what's right and good. **Unethical behavior** is behavior that conforms to individual beliefs and social norms about what is defined as wrong and bad. **Business ethics** is a term often used to refer to ethical or unethical behaviors by employees and managers in the context of their jobs.

Individual Ethics

Because ethics are based on both individual beliefs and social concepts, they vary from person to person, from situation to situation, and from culture to culture. Social standards are broad enough to support differences in beliefs. Without violating general standards, people may develop personal codes of ethics reflecting a wide range of attitudes and beliefs.

Thus, ethical and unethical behaviors are determined partly by the individual and partly by the culture. For instance, virtually everyone would agree that if you see someone drop $20, the ethical thing to do would be to return it to the owner. But there'll be less agreement if you find $20 in an empty room but don't know who dropped it. Should you turn it in to the lost-and-found department? Or, because the rightful owner isn't likely to claim it, can you just keep it?

The Law and the Real World

Societies generally adopt formal laws that reflect prevailing ethical standards or social norms. For example, because most people regard stealing as unethical, we have laws against stealing and ways of punishing those who steal. Those who write laws try to make them as clear and unambiguous as possible, but interpreting and applying them can still lead to ethical ambiguities. Real-world situations can often be interpreted in different ways, and it isn't always easy to apply statutory standards to real-life behavior. For instance, during the aftermath of natural disasters like hurricanes or earthquakes, desperate survivors sometimes break into grocery stores for food and water. These actions are, of course, illegal, but most law enforcement agencies will not press charges because of the circumstances.

Unfortunately, the epidemic of scandals that dominated business news over the past several years shows how willing people can be to take advantage of potentially ambiguous situations—and even create them. For example, Burger King, based in Florida, bought a Canadian fast-food chain and considered moving its corporate offices there simply to take advantage of lower Canadian taxes. Walgreens, headquartered in Illinois, bought a Swiss firm and could also have legally moved its corporate headquarters to Switzerland. However, in the face of adverse publicity and government pressure, both firms reversed course and decided to not relocate.[5] Similarly, in 2016 some drug manufacturers were criticized when they raised certain drug prices by several hundred percent. A few dropped some of those prices back to their previous levels, but others kept them at higher levels even in the wake of public outrage.

Individual Values and Morals

How should we deal with business situations that are ambiguous in terms of both ethics and the law? No doubt we have to start with the values and morals of people in a business, its managers, employees, and other legal representatives. Each person's individual values and morals help determine his or her personal code of ethics. Values and morals, in turn, are determined by a combination of factors. We start to form values and morals as children in response to our perceptions of the behavior of parents and other adults. Soon, we enter school, where we're influenced by peers, and as we grow into adulthood, experience shapes our lives and contributes to our ethical beliefs and our behavior. If you put financial gain at the top of your priority list, you may develop a code of ethics that supports the pursuit of material comfort. If you set family and friends as a priority, you'll no doubt adopt different standards.

Business and Managerial Ethics

Managerial ethics are the standards of behavior that guide individual managers in their work.[6] Although your ethics can affect your work in any number of ways, it's helpful to classify them in terms of three broad categories.

Managerial Ethics standards of behavior that guide individual managers in their work

Behavior Toward Employees This category of managerial ethics relates to such matters as hiring and firing, wages and working conditions, and privacy and respect. Ethical guidelines suggest and legal standards require that hiring and firing decisions should be based solely on a person's ability to perform a job. A manager who discriminates against African Americans or women in hiring exhibits both unethical and illegal behavior. But what about the manager who hires a friend or relative who is qualified for the job when someone else might be equally qualified? Or slightly more qualified? Although such decisions may not be illegal, they may be questionable on ethical grounds.

Wages and working conditions, although regulated by law, are also areas for potential controversy. A manager may pay a worker less than he deserves, for example, because the manager knows that the employee can't afford to quit or risk his job by complaining. While it is hard to judge whether some cases are clearly ethical or unethical, others are fairly clear-cut. Consider the behavior of Enron management toward company employees. Enron management encouraged employees to invest retirement funds in company stock and then, when financial problems began to surface, refused to permit them to sell the stock (even though top officials were allowed to sell). Ultimately, the firm's demise caused thousands of employees to lose their jobs and much of their pensions.

Behavior Toward the Organization Ethical issues can also arise from employee behavior toward employers, especially in such areas as conflict of interest, confidentiality, and honesty. A *conflict of interest* occurs when an activity may benefit the individual to the detriment of his or her employer. Most companies have policies that forbid buyers from accepting gifts from suppliers, for instance, because such gifts might be construed as a bribe or an attempt to induce favoritism. Businesses in highly competitive industries—software and fashion apparel, for example—have safeguards against designers selling company secrets to competitors.

Relatively common problems in the general area of honesty include stealing supplies, padding expense accounts, calling in sick just to stay home and relax, and using a business phone to make personal, long-distance calls.[7] Most employees are honest, but many organizations remain vigilant. Again, Enron is a good example of employees' unethical behavior toward an organization; top managers not only misused corporate assets but they often also committed the company to risky ventures to further their own personal interests.

Behavior Toward Other Economic Agents Ethics also come into play in the relationship of a business and its employees with so-called *primary agents of interest*, mainly customers, competitors, stockholders, suppliers, dealers, and unions. In dealing with such agents, there is room for ethical ambiguity in just about every activity—advertising, financial disclosure, ordering and purchasing, bargaining and negotiation, and other business relationships. Bernard Madoff's investment scams cost hundreds of his clients their life savings. He led them to believe their money was safe and that they were earning large returns when in fact their money was being hidden and used to support his own extravagant lifestyle. He then used funds from new clients to pay returns to older clients (this is called a *Ponzi scheme*). Madoff's actions showed a blatant disregard for his investors.

As previously mentioned, businesses in the pharmaceutical industry are often criticized because of the rising prices of drugs. Critics argue that pharmaceutical companies reap huge profits at the expense of the average consumer. In its defense, the pharmaceutical industry argues that prices must be set high to cover the costs of research and development programs to develop new drugs. Similarly, oil companies are sometimes criticized for reaping big prices when gas supplies are low and prices are high. The solution to such problems seems obvious: Find the right balance between reasonable pricing and price gouging (responding to increased demand with overly steep price increases). But like so many questions involving ethics, there are significant differences of opinion about the proper balance.

Another problem is global variations in business practices. In many countries, bribes (sometimes called "expediting payments") are a normal part of doing business. U.S. law, however, forbids bribes, even if rivals from other countries are paying them. A U.S. power-generating company once lost a $320 million contract in the Middle East because it refused to pay bribes (although not called that, of course) that a Japanese firm used to get the job. Walmart's Mexico subsidiary has been charged with paying $24 million in bribes to local officials to sidestep regulations and obtain construction permits for new stores.[8] Although these bribes are illegal in Mexico, local experts note that they are also common practice. We'll discuss some of the ways in which social, cultural, and legal differences among nations affect international business in Chapter 4.

Assessing Ethical Behavior

What distinguishes ethical from unethical behavior is often subjective and subject to differences of opinion. So how can we decide whether a particular action or decision is ethical? The following three steps set a simplified course for applying ethical judgments to situations that may arise during the course of business activities:

1 Gather the relevant factual information.

2 Analyze the facts to determine the most appropriate moral values.

3 Make an ethical judgment based on the rightness or wrongness of the proposed activity or policy.

Unfortunately, the process doesn't always work as smoothly as these three steps suggest. What if the facts aren't clear-cut? What if there are no agreed-on moral values? Nevertheless, you must make the judgment and decide how to go forward. Experts point out that judgments and decisions made in a moral and ethical manner lead to increased trust among all parties concerned. And trust is indispensable in any business transaction.

To fully assess the ethics of specific behavior, we need a more complex perspective. Consider a common dilemma faced by managers with expense accounts. Companies routinely provide managers with accounts to cover work-related expenses, hotel bills, meals, and rental cars or taxis when they're traveling on company business or entertaining clients for business purposes. They expect employees to claim only work-related expenses.

If a manager takes a client to dinner and spends $100, submitting a $100 reimbursement receipt for that dinner is accurate and appropriate. But suppose that this manager has a $100 dinner the next night with a good friend for purely social purposes. Submitting that receipt for reimbursement would be unethical, but some managers rationalize that it's okay to submit a receipt for dinner with a friend when they are on a business trip. Perhaps they tell themselves that they're underpaid and just "recovering" income due to them. (Most companies would allow reimbursement for the manager's meal, just not for the friend's meal.)

Ethical *norms* also come into play in a case like this. Consider four such norms and the issues they entail:[9]

1 *Utility.* Does a particular act optimize the benefits to those who are affected by it? (That is, do all relevant parties receive "fair" benefits?)

2 *Rights.* Does it respect the rights of all individuals involved?

3 *Justice.* Is it consistent with what's fair?

4 *Caring.* Is it consistent with people's responsibilities to each other?

Figure 2.1 incorporates the consideration of these ethical norms into a model of ethical judgment making.

Now let's return to our case of the inflated expense account. Although the utility norm acknowledges that the manager benefits from a padded account, others, such as coworkers and owners, don't. Most experts would also agree that the act doesn't respect the rights of others (such as investors, who have to indirectly foot the bill). Moreover, it's clearly unfair and compromises the manager's responsibilities to other stakeholders by violating their trust. This particular act, then, appears to be clearly unethical.

Figure 2.1, however, also provides mechanisms for dealing with unique circumstances. Suppose, for example, that our manager loses the receipt for the legitimate dinner but retains the receipt for the social dinner. Some people will now argue that it's okay to submit the illegitimate receipt because the manager is only doing so to get proper reimbursement. Others, however, will reply that submitting the alternative receipt is wrong under any circumstances. We won't pretend to arbitrate the case, and we will simply make the following point: Changes in most situations can make ethical issues either more or less clear-cut.

Company Practices and Business Ethics

As unethical and even illegal activities by both managers and employees plague more companies, many firms have taken additional steps to encourage ethical behavior in the workplace. Many set up codes of conduct and develop clear ethical positions on how the firm and its employees will conduct business. An increasingly controversial area regarding business ethics and company practices involves the privacy of e-mail and other communication that take place inside an organization. For instance, some companies monitor the Web searches conducted by their employees; the appearance of certain key words may trigger a closer review of how an employee is using the company's computer network. Although some companies argue they do this for business reasons, some employees claim that it violates their privacy.

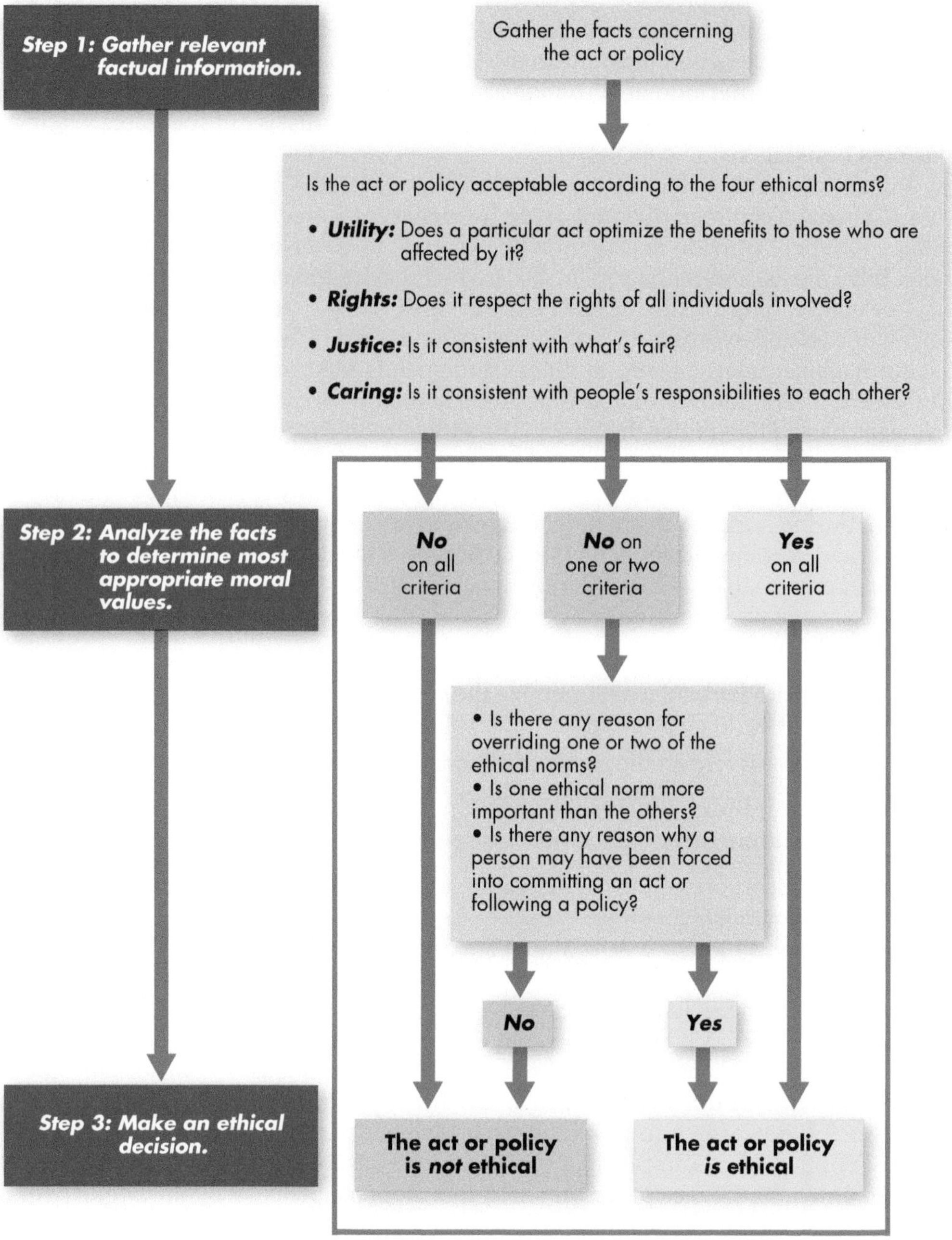

Step 1: Gather relevant factual information.

Gather the facts concerning the act or policy

Is the act or policy acceptable according to the four ethical norms?

- *Utility:* Does a particular act optimize the benefits to those who are affected by it?

- *Rights:* Does it respect the rights of all individuals involved?

- *Justice:* Is it consistent with what's fair?

- *Caring:* Is it consistent with people's responsibilities to each other?

Step 2: Analyze the facts to determine most appropriate moral values.

No on all criteria

No on one or two criteria

Yes on all criteria

- Is there any reason for overriding one or two of the ethical norms?
- Is one ethical norm more important than the others?
- Is there any reason why a person may have been forced into committing an act or following a policy?

No

Yes

Step 3: Make an ethical decision.

The act or policy is *not* ethical

The act or policy *is* ethical

FIGURE 2.1 Model of Ethical Judgment Making

Perhaps the single most effective step that a company can take is to demonstrate top management support of ethical standards. This policy contributes to a corporate culture that values ethical standards and announces that the firm is as concerned with good citizenship as with profits. For example, when United Technologies (UT), a Connecticut-based industrial conglomerate, published its 21-page code of ethics, it also named a vice president for business practices to ensure that UT conducted business ethically and responsibly. By formulating a detailed code of ethics and employing a senior official to enforce it, the firm sent a signal that it expects ethical conduct from its employees. Two of the most common approaches to formalizing top management commitment to ethical business practices are *adopting written codes* and *instituting ethics programs*.

Adopting Written Codes Like UT, many other businesses (Starbucks, Texas Instruments, Boeing, Apple, and Microsoft among them) have written codes

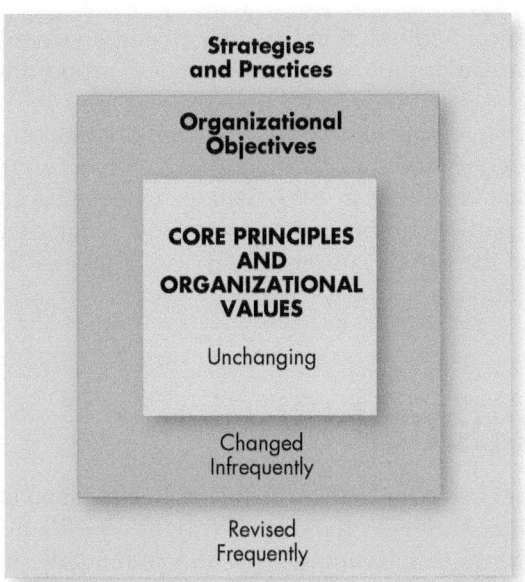

FIGURE 2.2 Core Principles and Organizational Values

that formally announce their commitment to do business in an ethical manner. The number of such companies has risen dramatically in the last three decades, and today almost all major corporations have written codes of ethics. Even Enron had a code of ethics, but managers must follow the code if it's going to work. On one occasion, Enron's board of directors voted to set aside the code to complete a deal that would violate it; after the deal was completed, they then voted to reinstate the code!

Figure 2.2 illustrates the role that corporate ethics and values should play in corporate policy. You can use it to see how a good ethics statement might be structured. Basically, the figure suggests that although strategies and practices can change frequently and objectives can change occasionally, an organization's core principles and values should remain steadfast. Hewlett-Packard, for example, has had the same written code of ethics, called *The HP Way*, since 1957. Its essential elements are the following:

- We have trust and respect for individuals.

- We focus on a high level of achievement and contribution.

- We conduct our business with uncompromising integrity.

- We achieve our common objectives through teamwork.

- We encourage flexibility and innovation.

Instituting Ethics Programs Many examples suggest that managers can learn ethical responses through experience. Businesses that sincerely stress the importance of ethical behavior and that consistently promote ethical cultures tend to have fewer ethical scandals than businesses that only pay lip service to ethics. But can business ethics be taught, either in the workplace or in schools? Not surprisingly, business schools have become important players in the debate about ethics education. Most analysts agree that even though business schools must address the issue of ethics in the workplace, companies must take the chief responsibility for educating employees. In fact, more and more firms are doing so.

For example, both ExxonMobil and Boeing have major ethics programs. All managers must go through periodic ethics training to remind them of the importance of ethical decision making and to update them on the most current laws and regulations that might be particularly relevant to their firms. Interestingly, some of the more popular ethics training programs today are taught by former executives who

Social Responsibility *the attempt of a business to balance its commitments to groups and individuals in its environment, including customers, other businesses, employees, investors, and local communities*

Organizational Stakeholders *those groups, individuals, and organizations that are directly affected by the practices of an organization and who therefore have a stake in its performance*

OBJECTIVE 2-2
Distinguish
social responsibility from ethics, identify organizational stakeholders, and characterize social consciousness today.

have spent time in prison for their own ethical transgressions.[10] Others, such as Texas Instruments, have ethical hotlines, numbers that an employee can call, either to discuss the ethics of a particular problem or situation or to report unethical behavior or activities by others.

Businesses must also recognize how quickly strong reputations can be tarnished. For decades Wells Fargo was considered to be above reproach, but its reputation suffered when a major scandal broke in 2016. Bankers were being incentivized to open false accounts for the bank's current customers in order to falsely build market share and make it look like the bank's customer base was growing. In fact, the reported growth was mostly fictitious.

Social Responsibility

Ethics affect individual behavior in the workplace. **Social responsibility**, meanwhile, is a related concept that addresses the overall way in which a business attempts to balance its commitments to relevant groups and individuals in its environment. These groups and individuals are often called **organizational stakeholders**, who are groups, individuals, and other organizations that are directly affected by the practices of an organization and, therefore, have a stake in its performance. Major corporate stakeholders are identified in Figure 2.3.

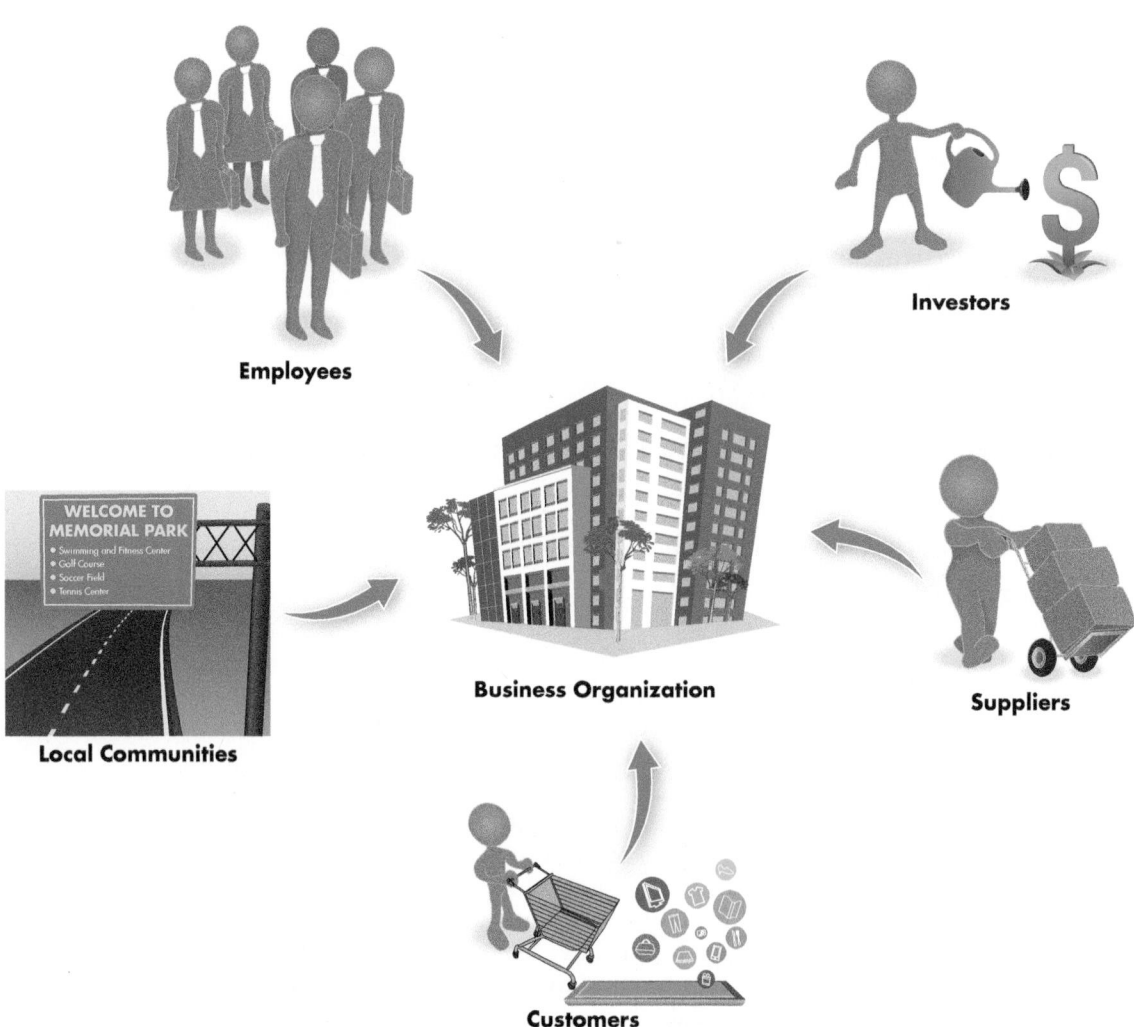

FIGURE 2.3 Major Corporate Stakeholders

The Stakeholder Model of Responsibility

Most companies that strive to be responsible to their stakeholders concentrate first and foremost on five main groups: (1) *customers*, (2) *employees*, (3) *investors*, (4) *suppliers*, and (5) the *local communities* where they do business. They may then select other stakeholders that are particularly relevant or important to the organization and try to address their needs and expectations as well.

Customers Businesses that are responsible to their customers strive to treat them fairly and honestly. They also seek to charge fair prices, honor warranties, meet delivery commitments, and stand behind the quality of the products they sell. L.L. Bean, Orvis, Starbucks, and Johnson & Johnson are among those companies with excellent reputations in this area. In recent years, many smaller banks have prospered by offering much stronger customer service than the large national banks (such as Wells Fargo and Bank of America). For instance, some offer their customers free coffee and childcare while they're in the bank conducting business. These smaller banks simply seem to have a better sense of what customers want and often promote the fact that they are local, neighbors, and so forth. And as a result, their profits have grown at a faster rate than have the profits of larger national banks.

Together, these companies are combining social consciousness with venture capital and lending practices to lift communities out of poverty and to make the world a better place.

Employees Businesses that are socially responsible in their dealings with employees treat workers fairly, make them a part of the team, and respect their dignity and basic human needs. Organizations such as The Container Store, Nucor Steel,

entrepreneurship and new ventures

Social Capital Is Making the World a Better Place

While big banks strive for profitability, sometimes through seemingly questionable lending practices, smaller companies like not-for-profit Kiva strive to reduce poverty by connecting people through micro-lending. The loans are crowdfunded by accumulating donations as small as $25. Since its founding ten years ago, Kiva's micro-lending platform has helped entrepreneurs in emerging markets in 82 countries borrow $945 million with a 97 percent repayment rate, and most of the borrowers are women.[11] In addition, organizations such as the International Rescue Committee (IRC) are making microloans and providing training and support for refugees in order to help them get a fresh start, and Women's Empowerment International is making micro-loans worldwide to help lift women from poverty. One commonality these organizations share is reliance on character, trust, and potential community benefits to determine who gets a loan, rather than credit reports and financial statements.

Micro-lending isn't limited to crowdfunded sources. There are small, community-based micro-lenders who receive their funding from state and local governments and are monitored by the Small Business Administration. However, where the crowdfunded micro-lenders rely on social capital to determine the borrower's creditworthiness, traditional lenders rely on a

Commerceandculturestock/Moment Open/Getty Images

more traditional underwriting process. Even so, with small loan amounts and short payback periods, these micro-loans are designed for entrepreneurs who have limited credit history and personal funds.

Crowdfunding sites such as KickStarter and GoFundMe can also help start-ups get product to market, but they tend to favor more commercial products rather than the smaller entrepreneurial ventures that the micro-lenders target. Even so, there is some evidence that the crowdfunding sites favor women entrepreneurs over men.[12]

Starbucks, Microsoft, and American Express go to great lengths to find, hire, train, and promote qualified minorities. Each year, *Fortune* magazine publishes lists of the "Best Companies to Work for in America" and the "Best Companies for Minorities." These lists bring great publicity and also help attract more individuals who are eager to work for such highly regarded employers.

Investors To maintain a socially responsible stance toward investors, managers should follow proper accounting procedures, provide appropriate information to shareholders about financial performance, and manage the organization to protect shareholder rights and investments. Managers should also strive to be accurate and candid in assessing future growth and profitability, and they should avoid even the appearance of impropriety in such sensitive areas as insider trading, stock-price manipulation, and the withholding of financial data. Indeed, many of today's accounting scandals have stemmed from similarly questionable practices. For example, Diamond Foods, distributor of nuts and popcorn snacks, recently had to restate its earnings twice after acknowledging it had improperly accounted for $80 million in payments to almond growers.[13] Similarly, Hewlett-Packard had to address an accounting scandal involving how it handled various transactions when it bought a British software developer for $11.1 billion.[14]

Suppliers Businesses and managers should also manage their relations with suppliers with care. For example, it might be easy for a large corporation to take advantage of suppliers by imposing unrealistic delivery schedules and reducing profit margins by constantly pushing for lower prices. At one time, Walmart had a bad reputation for doing this. Many firms now recognize the importance of mutually beneficial partnership arrangements with suppliers. Thus, they keep suppliers informed about future plans, negotiate delivery schedules and prices that are acceptable to both firms, and so forth. Toyota and Amazon.com are among the firms acknowledged to have excellent relationships with their suppliers.

Local and International Communities Most businesses also try to be socially responsible to their local communities. They may contribute to local programs, such as Little League baseball, get actively involved in charitable programs, such as the United Way, and strive to simply be good corporate citizens by minimizing their negative impact on communities. Target, for example, donates a percentage of sales to the local communities where it does business. The company says it also gives over $4 million each week to neighborhoods, programs, and schools across the country.[15]

The stakeholder model can also provide some helpful insights into the conduct of managers in international business. In particular, to the extent that an organization acknowledges its commitments to its stakeholders, it should also recognize that it has multiple sets of stakeholders in each country where it does business. Daimler-Benz (maker of Mercedes Benz automobiles), for example, has investors not only in Germany but also in the United States, Japan, and other countries where its shares are publicly traded. It also has suppliers, employees, and customers in multiple countries; its actions affect many different communities in dozens of different countries. Similarly, international businesses must also address their responsibilities in areas, such as wages, working conditions, and environmental protection, across different countries that have varying laws and norms regulating such responsibilities. ExxonMobil, for instance, has helped build hospitals and expand schools in the West African nation of Angola, where it has established a growing oil business. The firm also supports a local anti-malaria program.

Contemporary Social Consciousness

Social consciousness and views toward social responsibility continue to evolve. Early business leaders like John D. Rockefeller, J. P. Morgan, and Cornelius Vanderbilt created huge businesses and amassed large fortunes but also raised concerns about abuses of power. These concerns led to the nation's first laws regulating basic business practices. In the 1930s, many people blamed the Great Depression on a climate of business greed and lack of restraint. Out of this economic turmoil emerged new laws that dictated an expanded role for business in protecting and enhancing the general welfare of society. Hence, the concept of *accountability* was formalized. The new laws and regulations contributed to a sense of *laissez-faire* feelings about business during the growing economic prosperity of the late 1940s and 1950s.

In the 1960s and 1970s, however, business was again characterized as a negative social force. Some critics even charged that defense contractors had helped promote the Vietnam War to spur their own profits. Eventually, increased social activism prompted increased government regulation in a variety of areas. Health warnings were placed on cigarettes, for instance, and stricter environmental protection laws were enacted.

During the 1980s and 1990s, the general economic prosperity most sectors of the economy enjoyed led to another period of laissez-faire attitudes toward business. Although the occasional scandal or major business failure occurred, for the most part people seemed to view business as a positive force in society and one that was generally able to police itself through self-control and free-market forces. This view shifted again, though, during the Great Recession. Many observers faulted the mortgage lending practices of large banks for the crisis that started in 2008. Critics were also unhappy that the U.S. government bailed out both these same banks and other large businesses like General Motors and Chrysler.

Amid growing concerns about climate change and calls for more sustainable business practices, many businesses at least appear to have again moved toward a more responsible approach to doing business. Recycling programs are flourishing, for instance, within firms like Best Buy, DuPont, and General Motors. Many businesses also continue to operate in enlightened and socially responsible ways in other areas. For example, retailers such as Sears and Target have policies against selling handguns and other weapons. GameStop refuses to sell mature-rated games to minors and Anheuser-Busch promotes the concept of responsible drinking in some of its advertising.

Firms in numerous other industries have also integrated socially conscious thinking into their production plans and marketing efforts. The production of environmentally safe products has become a potential boom area, and many companies introduce products designed to be environmentally friendly. Electrolux, a Swedish appliance maker, has developed a line of water-efficient washing machines, a solar-powered lawn mower, and ozone-free refrigerators. Ford and General Motors are both aggressively studying and testing ways to develop and market low-pollution vehicles fueled by electricity, hydrogen, and other alternative energy sources. The Company Store donates a comforter or blanket to a homeless child for every one it sells. Warby Parker sells sunglasses and glasses frames and donates half of the profits on each pair to nonprofit organizations.

Areas of Social Responsibility

OBJECTIVE 2-3
Show
how the concept of social responsibility applies both to environmental issues and to a firm's relationships with customers, employees, and investors.

When defining its sense of social responsibility, a firm typically confronts four areas of concern: responsibilities toward the *environment*, its *customers*, its *employees*, and its *investors*.

Responsibility Toward the Environment

The topic of global climate has become a major issue for business and government alike. However, although most experts agree that the Earth is warming, the causes, magnitude, and possible solutions are all subject to widespread debate. It appears that climate change is occurring at a relatively mild pace, and we are experiencing few day-to-day changes in the weather. We are, however, increasing the likelihood of having troublesome weather around the globe—droughts, hurricanes, winter sieges, and so forth.[16] Indeed, 2016 was the warmest year on Earth since records have been kept. The charges leveled against greenhouse emissions are disputed, but as one researcher puts it, "The only way to prove them for sure is to hang around 10, 20, or 30 more years, when the evidence would be overwhelming. But in the meantime, we're conducting a global experiment. And we're all in the test tube." The movie *The Day After Tomorrow* portrayed one possible scenario of rapid climate changes wrought by environmental damage, and 2011's *Contagion* and 2013's *World War Z* illustrated the possible effects of a global pandemic.

Controlling *pollution*, the injection of harmful substances into the environment, is a significant challenge for contemporary business. Although noise pollution is now attracting increased concern, air, water, and land pollution remain the greatest problems in need of solutions from governments and businesses alike. In the following sections, we focus on the nature of the problems in these areas and on some of the current efforts to address them.

Air Pollution Air pollution results when several factors combine to lower air quality. Carbon monoxide emitted by cars contributes to air pollution, as do smoke and other chemicals produced by manufacturing plants. Air quality is usually worst in certain geographic locations, such as the Denver area and the Los Angeles basin, where pollutants tend to get trapped in the atmosphere. For this reason, the air

finding a better way

Mission Zero

In 1970, Nobel Prize-winning economist Milton Friedman espoused his view that a business has only one responsibility, and that is to maximize profits for the owners. It's a deceptively simple rule, and it has been a guiding force in corporate culture for almost 50 years. However, there are business leaders who see it differently, like Interface, Inc.'s Ray Anderson, who said, "There is no more strategic issue for a company, or any organization, than its ultimate purpose. For those who think business exists to make a profit, I suggest they think again. Business makes a profit to exist. Surely it must exist for some higher, nobler purpose than that."

Anderson founded Interface in 1973, and by 1994 it had grown into the largest provider of modular carpet in the world. In 1994, Anderson was asked to speak to a small task force organized to answer questions customers were asking about the company's stance on environmental issues. Stymied by the request, he came upon a book called *The Ecology of Commerce*, by Paul Hawken. It was the antithesis of Friedman's position, and it convinced Anderson that the current industrial system was destroying the planet, and only leaders of industry had the power to turn the tide. Anderson became an outspoken proponent for social responsibility and set Interface on a quest to become 100 percent sustainable by 2020.

As he put it, "I stand convicted by me, myself alone, not by anyone else, as a plunderer of the earth, but not by our civilization's definition. By our civilization's definition, I'm a captain of industry. In the eyes of many a kind of modern day hero.

Rob245/Fotolia

But really, really, the first industrial revolution is flawed; it is not working. It is unsustainable. It is the mistake and we must move on to another and better industrial revolution and get it right this time."

Anderson was diagnosed with cancer in 2010 and passed away on August 8, 2011, but the corporate culture he established and his vision for the company live on. In 2016, Interface was awarded Best Company at the Ethical Corporation's Responsible Business Awards and, as it approaches the achievement of its sustainability goal, the company has adopted a new mission called Climate Take Back, focusing on driving positive impacts in the world to create a climate fit for life.

around Mexico City and Beijing is generally considered to be among the most polluted in the world.

Legislation has gone a long way toward controlling air pollution. Under current laws, many companies must use special equipment to limit the pollutants they expel into the air, but such efforts are costly. Air pollution is compounded by such problems as acid rain—which occurs when sulfur is pumped into the atmosphere, mixes with natural moisture, and falls to the ground as rain. Much of the damage to forests and streams in the eastern United States and Canada has been attributed to acid rain originating in sulfur from manufacturing and power plants in the midwestern United States. The North American Free Trade Agreement (NAFTA) also includes provisions that call for tight controls on air pollution, especially targeting areas that affect more than one member nation.

Water Pollution Water becomes polluted primarily from chemical and waste dumping. For years, businesses and cities dumped waste into rivers, streams, and lakes with little regard for the consequences. Cleveland's Cuyahoga River was once so polluted that it literally burst into flames one hot summer day.

Thanks to new legislation and increased awareness, water quality in many areas of the United States is improving. The Cuyahoga River is now home to fish and used for recreation. Laws in New York and Florida forbidding dumping of phosphates (an ingredient found in many detergents) have helped to make Lake Erie and other major waters safe again for fishing and swimming. Both the Passaic River in New Jersey and the Hudson River in New York are much cleaner now than they were just a few years ago as a result of these new laws.

Land Pollution Two key issues characterize land pollution. The first is how to restore the quality of land that has already been damaged. Land and water damaged by toxic waste, for example, must be cleaned up for the simple reason that people still need to use them. The second problem is the prevention of future contamination. New forms of solid-waste disposal constitute one response to these problems. Combustible wastes can be separated and used as fuels in industrial boilers, and decomposition can be accelerated by exposing waste matter to certain microorganisms.

TOXIC WASTE DISPOSAL An especially controversial problem in land pollution is toxic waste disposal. Toxic wastes are dangerous chemical or radioactive by-products of manufacturing processes. U.S. manufacturers produce between 40 and 60 million tons of such material each year. As a rule, toxic waste must be stored; it cannot be destroyed or processed into harmless material. Few people, however, want toxic waste storage sites in their backyards. A few years ago, American Airlines pled guilty—and became the first major airline to gain a criminal record—to a felony charge that it had mishandled some hazardous materials packed as cargo in passenger airplanes. Although fully acknowledging the firm's guilt, Anne McNamara, American's general counsel at the time, argued that, "This is an incredibly complicated area with many layers of regulation. It's very easy to inadvertently step over the line."

RECYCLING Recycling is another controversial area in land pollution. Recycling, the reconversion of waste materials into useful products, has become an issue not only for municipal and state governments but also for many companies engaged in high-waste activities. Certain products, such as aluminum cans and glass, can be efficiently recycled, whereas others are more troublesome. For example, brightly colored plastics, such as some detergent and juice bottles, must be recycled separately from clear plastics, such as milk jugs. Most plastic bottle caps, meanwhile, contain a vinyl lining that can spoil a normal recycling batch. Nevertheless, many local communities actively support various recycling programs, including curbside pickup of aluminum, plastics, glass, and pulp paper. Unfortunately, consumer awareness and interest in this area—and the policy priorities of businesses—are more acute at some times than at others.

One of today's more contentious business practices related to the natural environment is fracking. Fracking involves injecting water and chemical compounds into underground rock formations in order to break them apart. After this has been done, oil companies can then extract petroleum more easily and in areas where drilling was previously impossible. Fracking has led to a dramatic increase in the supply of oil and has resulted in lower energy prices. At the same time, though, environmentalists have expressed concerns that the chemical compounds used in fracking may be polluting underground water sources and causing instability in nearby towns and residential areas.[17]

Responsibility Toward Customers

A company that does not act responsibly toward its customers will ultimately lose their trust and business. To encourage responsibility, the Federal Trade Commission (FTC) regulates advertising and pricing practices, and the Food and Drug Administration (FDA) enforces labeling guidelines for food products. These government-regulating bodies can impose penalties against violators, who may also face civil litigation. For example, the FTC fined the social networking site Xanga $1 million for allowing children under the age of 13 to create accounts, in clear violation of the Children's Online Privacy Protection Act.[18] Table 2.1 summarizes the central elements of so-called "green marketing," the marketing of environmentally friendly goods.

Consumer Rights Interest in business responsibility toward customers can be traced to the rise of **consumerism**, social activism dedicated to protecting the rights of consumers in their dealings with businesses. The first formal declaration of consumer rights protection came in the early 1960s, when President John F. Kennedy identified four basic consumer rights. Since then, general agreement on two additional rights has emerged; these rights are described in Figure 2.4. The Consumer Bill of Rights is backed by numerous federal and state laws.

Merck provides an instructive example of what can happen to a firm that violates one or more of these consumer rights. For several years, the firm aggressively marketed a painkiller under the brand name Vioxx. When clinical trials linked the drug to an increased risk of heart attacks and strokes, Merck was forced to discontinue sales of Vioxx and recall supplies that it had already shipped. During the course of

Consumerism *form of social activism dedicated to protecting the rights of consumers in their dealings with businesses*

table 2.1 The Elements of Green Marketing

- Production Processes Businesses, such as Ford Motors and General Electric, modify their production processes to limit the consumption of valuable resources such as fossil fuels by increasing energy efficiency and reducing their output of waste and pollution by cutting greenhouse gas emissions.
- Product Modification Products can be modified to use more environmentally friendly materials, a practice S. C. Johnson encourages with its Greenlist of raw materials classified according to their impact on health and the environment. Committed to only using the safest materials on this list, S. C. Johnson eliminated 1.8 million pounds of volatile organic compounds from its glass cleaner Windex.[19]
- Carbon Offsets are used by some companies that are committed to replenishing, repairing, or restoring those parts of the environment that are damaged by their operations, especially those that produce carbon dioxide (CO_2). In 2007, Volkswagen began a program of planting trees in the so-called VW Forest in the Lower Mississippi Alluvial Valley to offset the CO_2 emissions of every car it sells.[20]
- Packaging Reduction, for example, reducing and reusing materials used in packaging products, is another important strategy of green marketing, which Starbucks has pioneered. In 2004, the FDA gave the coffee retailer the first-ever approval to use recycled materials in its food and beverage packaging. Starbucks estimates that using cups composed of 10 percent recycled fibers reduces its packaging waste by more than 5 million pounds per year.[21]
- Sustainability, using renewable resources and managing limited resources responsibly and efficiently, is an important goal for any business pursuing a green policy. For example, Whole Foods Market is committed to buying food from farmers who use sustainable agriculture practices that protect the environment and agricultural resources, such as land and water.

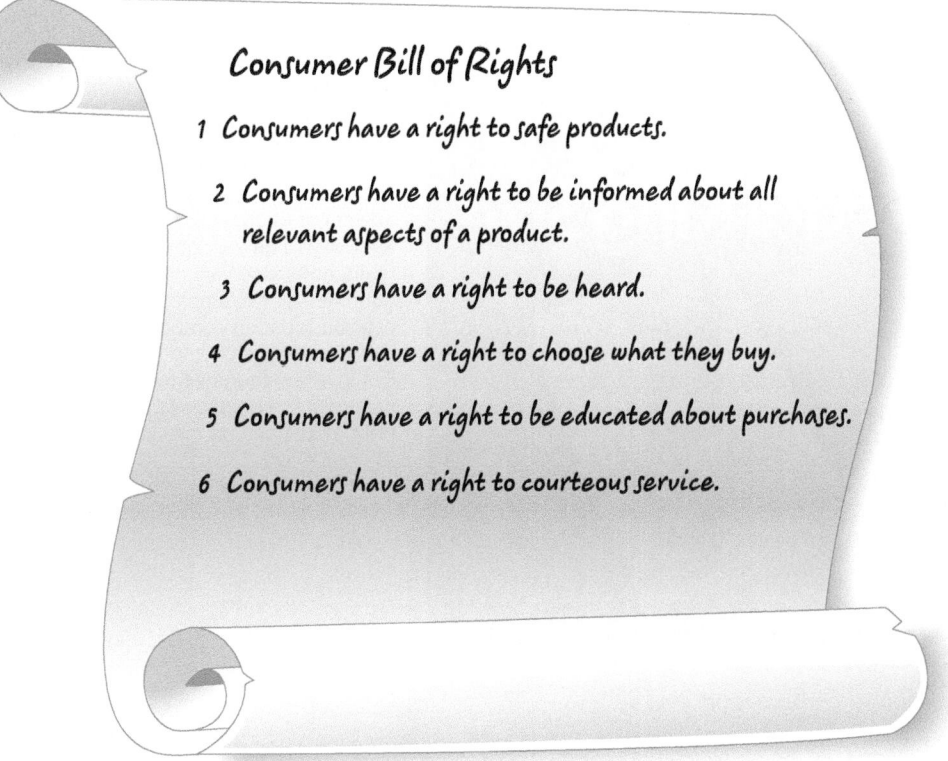

Consumer Bill of Rights

1 Consumers have a right to safe products.

2 Consumers have a right to be informed about all relevant aspects of a product.

3 Consumers have a right to be heard.

4 Consumers have a right to choose what they buy.

5 Consumers have a right to be educated about purchases.

6 Consumers have a right to courteous service.

FIGURE 2.4 Consumer Bill of Rights

the recall, documents also surfaced that showed that Merck had known about these risks for at least four years before it was forced to suspend sales. Merck subsequently agreed to pay $4.85 billion to individuals or families of those who were injured or died as a result of taking the drug.

Unfair Pricing Interfering with competition can take the form of illegal pricing practices. **Collusion** occurs when two or more firms collaborate on such wrongful acts as price fixing. Two European airlines, Virgin Atlantic and Lufthansa, admitted to colluding with rivals to raise the prices of fuel surcharges on passenger flights as much as 12 times the regular price during one 18-month period. British Airways and Korean Air Lines were heavily fined for doing the same thing, but in exchange for turning them in, Virgin and Lufthansa were not penalized.[22] The U.S. Justice Department has charged Apple with price fixing and collusion related to its pricing of e-books.

Collusion illegal agreement between two or more companies to commit a wrongful act

Firms can also come under attack for *price gouging*, responding to increased demand with overly steep (and often unwarranted) price increases. For example, during threats of severe weather, people often stock up on bottled water and batteries. Unfortunately, some retailers take advantage of this pattern by marking up the prices of these items. Reports were widespread of gasoline retailers doubling or even tripling prices immediately after the events of September 11, 2001. Similar charges were made following the U.S. invasion of Iraq, after hurricanes Katrina and Rita damaged oil refineries along the Gulf Coast, and still again after the BP drilling accident shut down petroleum operations in that same area.

Ethics in Advertising Attention is also often focused on ethics in advertising and product information. Controversy arose when *Newsweek* magazine reported that Sony had literally created a movie critic who happened to be particularly fond of movies released by Sony's Columbia Pictures. When advertising its newest theatrical releases, the studio had been routinely using glowing quotes from a fictitious critic.

Advertising standards in different countries vary in many different ways. Some of the differences are attributable to sociocultural norms. For instance, ads and billboards in some parts of Europe occasionally feature nudity and may be much more provocative than might be accepted in the United States, while ads in the Middle East and parts of Asia are likely to be very conservative. Legal restrictions also vary across different countries. For example, U.S. regulations prohibit tobacco companies from advertising on television and most magazines. But in other countries tobacco companies may still be allowed to advertise in print media and on television.

Jeff Morgan 02/Alamy Stock Photo

After the story broke, Sony hastily stopped the practice and apologized. Some critics also point to misleading labeling and advertising in the agricultural sector. Egg and chicken producers sometimes label their products "free range." That term connotes certain images, but in reality it only means that the chickens are not kept in cages; it says nothing about how densely they are packed into open pens.

Another issue concerns advertising that some consumers consider morally objectionable—for products such as underwear, condoms, alcohol, tobacco products, and firearms. Laws regulate some of this advertising (for instance, tobacco cannot be promoted in television commercials but can be featured in print ads in magazines), and many advertisers use common sense and discretion in their promotions. But some companies, such as Calvin Klein and Victoria's Secret, have come under fire for being overly explicit in their advertising. GoDaddy and Arby's also have reputations for the same thing.

Responsibility Toward Employees

In Chapter 10, we will show how a number of human resource management activities are essential to a smoothly functioning business. These activities—recruiting, hiring, training, promoting, and compensating—are also the basis for social responsibility toward employees.

Legal and Social Commitments By law, businesses cannot discriminate against people in any facet of the employment relationship for any reason not related to performance. For example, a company cannot refuse to hire someone because of ethnicity or pay someone a lower salary than someone else on the basis of gender. A company that provides its employees with equal opportunities without regard to race, sex, or other irrelevant factors is meeting both its legal and its social responsibilities. Firms that ignore these responsibilities risk losing good employees and leave themselves open to lawsuits.

Most would also agree that an organization should strive to ensure that the workplace is physically and socially safe. Companies with a heightened awareness of social responsibility also recognize an obligation to provide opportunities to balance work and life pressures and preferences, help employees maintain job skills, and when terminations or layoffs are necessary, treat them with respect and compassion.

Ethical Commitments: The Special Case of Whistle-Blowers Respecting employees as people also means respecting their behavior as ethical individuals. Ideally, an employee who discovers that a business has been engaging in illegal, unethical, or socially irresponsible practices should be able to report the problem to higher-level management and feel confident that managers will stop the questionable practices. However, if no one in the organization will take action, the employee may inform a regulatory agency or the media and become what is known as a **whistle-blower**, an employee who discovers and tries to put an end to a company's unethical, illegal, or socially irresponsible actions by publicizing them.

Unfortunately, whistle-blowers are sometimes demoted, fired, or, if they remain in their jobs, treated with mistrust, resentment, or hostility by coworkers. One study found that about half of all whistle-blowers eventually get fired, and about half of those who get fired subsequently lose their homes or families.[23] The law offers some recourse to employees who take action. The current whistle-blower law stems from the False Claims Act of 1863, which was designed to prevent contractors from selling defective supplies to the Union Army during the Civil War. With revisions to the law in 1986, the government can recover triple damages from fraudulent contractors. If the Justice Department does not intervene, a whistle-blower can proceed with a civil suit. In that case, the whistle-blower receives 25 to 30 percent of any money recovered. Unfortunately, however, the prospect of large cash awards has generated a spate of false or questionable accusations.[24] In the wake of the Madoff investment scams, news broke that a Boston fraud investigator had been trying to convince the Securities and Exchange Commission (SEC) for years that Madoff was engaging in illegal and unethical practices. His warnings, though, had been ignored. This embarrassing revelation led to the SEC's recent announcement that it was reviewing all of its procedures regarding whistle-blowing and a pledge from the SEC chairman that new procedures would be put into place to safeguard against future problems.

> **Whistle-Blower** *employee who detects and tries to put an end to a company's unethical, illegal, or socially irresponsible actions by publicizing them*

Responsibility Toward Investors

Managers can abuse their responsibilities to investors in several ways. As a rule, irresponsible behavior toward shareholders means abuse of a firm's financial resources so that shareholder owners do not receive their due earnings or dividends. Companies can also act irresponsibly toward shareholder owners by misrepresenting company resources. Blatant financial mismanagement, such as paying excessive salaries to senior managers, sending them on extravagant "retreats" to exotic resorts, and providing frivolous perks, may be unethical but not necessarily illegal. In such situations, creditors and stockholders have few options for recourse. Forcing a management changeover is a difficult process that can drive down stock prices—a penalty that shareholders are usually unwilling to impose on themselves. However, insider trading and the misrepresentation of finances are clearly illegal as well as unethical.

Insider Trading **Insider trading** is using confidential information to gain from the purchase or sale of stocks. Suppose, for example, that a small firm's stock is currently trading at $50 a share (this means that $50 is the current price at which people are buying and selling the stock). If a larger firm is going to buy the smaller one, it might have to pay as much as $75 a share for a controlling interest. Individuals aware of the impending acquisition before it is publicly announced, such as managers of the two firms or the financial institution making the arrangements, could gain by buying the stock at $50 in anticipation of selling it for $75 after the proposed acquisition is announced.

> **Insider Trading** *illegal practice of using special knowledge about a firm for profit or gain*

Informed executives can also avoid financial loss by selling stock that's about to drop in value. Legally, stock can only be sold on the basis of public information available to all investors. Potential violations of this regulation were at the heart of an insider trading scandal involving Martha Stewart. Sam Waksal, president of ImClone, learned that the company's stock was going to drop in value and hastily tried to sell his own stock. He also allegedly tipped off close friend Stewart, who subsequently sold her stock as well. Stewart, who argued that she never received Waksal's call and sold her stock only because she wanted to use the funds elsewhere, eventually pled guilty to other charges (lying to investigators) and served several months in prison. Waksal, meanwhile, received longer jail time (over seven years) and a larger fine (over $4 million) because his own attempts to dump his stock were well documented.

Misrepresentation of Finances In maintaining and reporting its financial status, every corporation must conform to generally accepted accounting principles (GAAP, see Chapter 14). Unethical managers might project profits in excess of what they actually expect to earn, hide losses or expenses to boost paper profits, or slant financial reports to make the firm seem stronger than is really the case. In 2002, the U.S. Congress passed the *Sarbanes-Oxley Act*, which requires an organization's chief financial officer to personally guarantee the accuracy of all financial reporting (see Chapter 14).

Implementing Social Responsibility Programs

OBJECTIVE 2-4
Identify

four general approaches to social responsibility and note the role of social responsibility in small business.

Opinions differ dramatically concerning social responsibility as a business goal. Although some oppose any business activity that threatens profits, others argue that social responsibility must take precedence. Some skeptics fear that businesses will gain too much control over the ways social projects are addressed by society as a whole or that they lack the expertise needed to address social issues. Still, many believe that corporations should help improve the lives of citizens because they are citizens themselves, often control vast resources, and may contribute to the problems that social programs address.

Approaches to Social Responsibility

Given these differences of opinion, it is little wonder that corporations have adopted a variety of approaches to social responsibility. As Figure 2.5 illustrates, the four stances that an organization can take concerning its obligations to society fall along a continuum ranging from the lowest to the highest degree of socially responsible practices.

Obstructionist Stance *approach to social responsibility that involves doing as little as possible and may involve attempts to deny or cover up violations*

Obstructionist Stance The few organizations that take an **obstructionist stance** to social responsibility usually do as little as possible to solve social or environmental problems, have little regard for ethical conduct, and will go to great lengths to deny or cover up wrongdoing. For example, IBP, a leading meat-processing firm, has a long record of breaking environmental protection, labor, and food-processing laws and then trying to cover up its offenses. Similarly, a Georgia peanut-processing plant owned by Peanut Corporation of America recently shipped products contaminated with salmonella. The firm's top manager allegedly knew that the products had failed

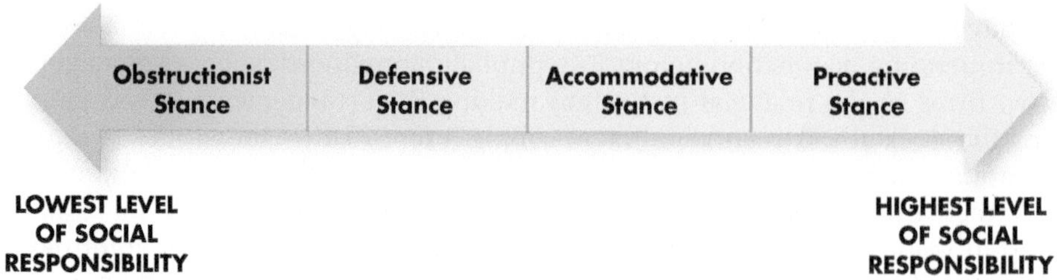

| Obstructionist Stance | Defensive Stance | Accommodative Stance | Proactive Stance |

LOWEST LEVEL OF SOCIAL RESPONSIBILITY   **HIGHEST LEVEL OF SOCIAL RESPONSIBILITY**

FIGURE 2.5 Spectrum of Approaches to Corporate Social Responsibility

safety tests but shipped them anyway to avoid losing money. The plant manager and three other officials subsequently served time in jail. Volkswagen was found guilty of knowingly and intentionally misreporting emissions data in order to make its automobiles look more environmentally friendly. In the wake of this scandal, VW paid billions of dollars in fines and suffered significant damage to its reputation.

Defensive Stance Organizations that take a **defensive stance** will do everything that is legally required, including admitting to mistakes and taking corrective actions, but nothing more. Defensive stance managers insist that their job is to generate profits and might, for example, install pollution-control equipment dictated by law but not higher-quality equipment to further limit pollution. Tobacco companies generally take this position in their marketing efforts. In the United States, they are legally required to include product warnings and to limit advertising to prescribed media. Domestically, they follow these rules to the letter of the law, but in many Asian and African countries, which don't have these rules, cigarettes are heavily promoted, contain higher levels of tar and nicotine, and carry few or no health warning labels.

> **Defensive Stance** *approach to social responsibility by which a company meets only minimum legal requirements in its commitments to groups and individuals in its social environment*

Accommodative Stance A firm that adopts an **accommodative stance** meets and, in certain cases, exceeds its legal and ethical requirements. Such firms will agree to participate in social programs if solicitors convince them that given programs are worthy of their support. Both Shell and IBM, for example, will match contributions made by their employees to selected charitable causes.

> **Accommodative Stance** *approach to social responsibility by which a company, if specifically asked to do so, exceeds legal minimums in its commitments to groups and individuals in its social environment*

Proactive Stance Firms with the highest degree of social responsibility exhibit the **proactive stance**: They take to heart the arguments in favor of social responsibility, view themselves as citizens in a society, indicate sincere commitment to improve the general social welfare, and surpass the accommodative stance by proactively seeking opportunities to contribute. The most common—and direct—way to implement this stance is to set up a foundation for providing direct financial support for various social programs. Table 2.2, using the most recent data, lists the top 25 corporate foundations.

> **Proactive Stance** *approach to social responsibility by which a company actively seeks opportunities to contribute to the well-being of groups and individuals in its social environment*

An excellent example of a proactive stance is the McDonald's Corporation's Ronald McDonald House program. These houses, located close to major medical centers, can be used for minimal cost by families while their sick children are receiving medical treatment nearby. However, these categories are not sharply distinct; organizations do not always fit neatly into one category or another. The Ronald McDonald House program has been widely applauded, but McDonald's has also been accused of misleading consumers about the nutritional value of its food products.

Social Responsibility and the Small Business

As the owner of a garden supply store, how would you respond to a building inspector's suggestion that a cash payment will speed your application for a building permit? As the manager of a liquor store, would you call the police, refuse to sell, or sell to a customer whose identification card looks forged? As the owner of a small laboratory, would you call the state board of health to make sure that it has licensed the company with whom you want to contract to dispose of medical waste? Who will really be harmed if a small firm pads its income statement to help it get a much-needed bank loan? Many of the examples in this chapter illustrate big business responses to ethical and social responsibility issues, but small businesses must answer many of the same questions. Differences between the two types of businesses are primarily differences of scale.

At the same time, the ethical issues are largely questions of *individual* ethics. What about questions of social responsibility? Can a small business, for example, afford a social agenda? Should it sponsor youth soccer teams, make donations to the United Way, and buy light bulbs from the Lion's Club? Do joining the chamber of commerce and supporting the Better Business Bureau cost too much? Clearly, ethics and social responsibility are decisions faced by all managers in all organizations, regardless of rank or size. One key to business success is to decide in advance how to respond to the issues that underlie all questions of ethical and social responsibility.

table 2.2 Top 25 Corporate Foundations

Rank	Name/(State)	Total Giving	As of Fiscal Year End Date
1.	Novartis Patient Assistance Foundation, Inc. (NJ)	$456,825,176	12/31/2014
2.	Wells Fargo Foundation (CA)	189,380,780	12/31/2014
3.	The Bank of America Charitable Foundation, Inc. (NC)	175,729,430	12/31/2014
4.	The Wal-Mart Foundation, Inc. (AR)	168,582,621	01/31/2014
5.	The JPMorgan Chase Foundation (NY)	130,855,483	12/31/2013
6.	GE Foundation (CT)	108,401,652	12/31/2014
7.	The Coca-Cola Foundation, Inc. (GA)	90,518,700	12/31/2014
8.	Citi Foundation (NY)	78,000,000	12/31/2014
9.	ExxonMobil Foundation (TX)	75,212,563	12/31/2014
10.	Bayer U.S. Patient Assistance Foundation (PA)	58,474,547	11/30/2014
11.	George Lucas Family Foundation (CA)	55,486,655	12/31/2014
12.	Caterpillar Foundation (IL)	49,640,075	12/31/2014
13.	The PNC Foundation (PA)	48,597,927	12/31/2014
14.	Johnson & Johnson Family of Companies Foundation (NJ)	46,445,669	12/31/2013
15.	The UPS Foundation (GA)	42,895,860	12/31/2013
16.	MetLife Foundation (NY)	41,068,034	12/31/2014
17.	Intel Foundation (OR)	39,047,597	12/31/2014
18.	Publix Super Markets Charities (FL)	38,602,791	12/31/2014
19.	The Goldman Sachs Foundation (NY)	37,245,807	12/31/2014
20.	Emerson Charitable Trust (MO)	36,181,743	09/30/2014
21.	The Prudential Foundation (NJ)	34,835,423	12/31/2014
22.	General Motors Foundation, Inc. (MI)	30,821,026	12/31/2014
23.	The Merck Company Foundation (NJ)	30,691,387	12/31/2014
24.	Verizon Foundation (NJ)	30,628,914	12/31/2014
25.	Ford Motor Company Fund (MI)	30,222,388	12/31/2014

Source: Data from Foundation Center, www.fcpubhub.net/findfunders/topfunders/top50giving.html.

The Government and Social Responsibility

OBJECTIVE 2-5
Explain
the role of government in social responsibility in terms of how governments and businesses influence each other.

An especially important element of social responsibility is the relationship between business and government. In planned economies, for example, the government heavily regulates business activities, ostensibly to ensure that business supports some overarching set of social ideals. And even in market economies, there is still considerable government control of business, much of it directed at making sure that business interests do not damage social interests. Alternatively, businesses also attempt to influence the government by attempting to offset or reverse government restrictions. Businesses and the government use several methods in their attempts to influence each other.

How Governments Influence Business

The government (national, state, or local) attempts to shape social responsibility practices through both direct and indirect channels. Direct influence most frequently is manifested through *regulation*, whereas indirect influence can take a number of forms, most notably taxation policies.[25]

Direct Regulation The government most often directly influences organizations through **regulation**, the establishment of laws and rules that dictate what organizations can and cannot do. This regulation usually evolves from social beliefs about how businesses should conduct themselves. To implement legislation, the government generally creates special agencies to monitor and control certain aspects of business activity. For example, the Environmental Protection Agency handles environmental issues; the FTC and the FDA focus on consumer-related concerns; the Equal Employee Opportunity Commission, the National Labor Relations Board, and the Department of Labor help protect employees; and the SEC handles investor-related issues. These agencies have the power to levy fines or bring charges against organizations that violate regulations.

Regulation *the establishment of laws and rules that dictate what organizations can and cannot do*

Another approach that governments can use to regulate business practices is through legislation. For instance, the U.S. Foreign Corrupt Practices Act provides for financial sanctions against businesses or business officials who engage in bribery. Siemens AG, a large German engineering firm, was investigated for practices that included routine bribery of foreign officials to win infrastructure construction projects. All told, the firm was alleged to have spent more than $1 billion in bribing officials in at least 10 different countries. Siemens recently agreed to pay the U.S. government a fine of $800 million. (The U.S. government had the authority to fine Siemens because the German firm has a class of stock listed on the New York Stock Exchange and was thus subject to the Foreign Corrupt Practices Act.[26]) Similarly, another German firm, Daimler-Benz AG, was charged with bribery in 22 countries, which helped the company earn more than $50 million in profit. The company was alleged to have given millions of dollars in bribes to foreign officials to win contracts supplying their governments with vehicles. Charges included conspiracy and falsifying records. Daimler agreed to pay $185 million in its settlement. An American entrepreneur named Joseph Sigelman launched a successful oilfield service company in the Columbian rainforest called PetroTiger but was recently charged with six counts of bribery, accepting kickbacks, and laundering money.[27]

Indirect Regulation Other forms of regulation are indirect. For example, the government can indirectly influence the social responsibility of organizations through its tax codes. In effect, the government can influence how organizations spend their social responsibility dollars by providing greater or lesser tax incentives. For instance, suppose that the government wanted organizations to spend more on training the chronically unemployed, people who lack most basic job skills and who routinely have trouble finding jobs. Congress could then pass laws that provided tax incentives to companies that opened new training facilities, and as a result of the tax break, more businesses would probably do so. Of course, some critics argue that regulation is already excessive. They maintain that a free market system would eventually accomplish the same goals as regulation, with lower costs to both organizations and the government.

How Business Influences Government

Just as governments can influence businesses, so, too, can businesses influence the government. Businesses have four main methods of addressing governmental pressures for more social responsibility: (1) personal contacts, (2) lobbying, (3) political action committees, and (4) favors. (During the early days of President Barack Obama's administration, he implemented several measures designed to restrict or regulate business influence on the government, especially through lobbying.[28])

Personal Contacts Because many corporate executives and political leaders travel in the same social circles, personal contacts and networks offer one method of influence. For instance, a business executive may be able to contact a politician directly and present his or her case regarding a piece of legislation being considered.

Lobbying *the use of persons or groups to formally represent an organization or group of organizations before political bodies*

Lobbying **Lobbying**, or the use of persons or groups to formally represent an organization or group of organizations before political bodies, is also an effective way to influence the government. The National Rifle Association (NRA), for example, has a staff of lobbyists in Washington with a substantial annual budget. These lobbyists work to represent the NRA's position on gun control and to potentially influence members of Congress when they vote on legislation that affects the firearms industry and the rights of gun owners. As noted previously, President Obama took steps to control or limit lobbying. For instance, any discussion between a lobbyist and a member of Congress that goes beyond general conversation has to be written in the form of a letter and posted online. It remains to be seen if President Trump will maintain these efforts or not.

Political Action Committees (PACs) *special organizations created to solicit money and then distribute it to political candidates*

Political Action Committees Companies themselves cannot legally make direct donations to political campaigns, so they influence the government through *political action committees*. **Political action committees (PACs)** are special organizations created to solicit money and then distribute it to political candidates. Employees of a firm may be encouraged to make donations to a particular PAC because managers know that it will support candidates with political views similar to their own. PACs, in turn, make the contributions themselves, usually to a broad slate of state and national candidates. For example, FedEx's PAC is called FedExpac. FedExpac makes regular contributions to the campaign funds of political candidates who are most likely to work in the firm's best interests. As with lobbying, President Obama implemented measures to limit the influence of PACs.

Favors Finally, organizations sometimes rely on favors and other influence tactics to gain support. Although these favors may be legal, they are still subject to criticism. A few years back, for example, two influential members of a House committee attending a fund-raising function in Miami were needed in Washington to finish work on a piece of legislation that FedEx wanted passed. The law being drafted would allow the company and its competitors to give their employees standby seats on airlines as a tax-free benefit. As a favor, FedEx provided one of its corporate jets to fly the committee members back to Washington. FedEx was eventually reimbursed for its expenses, so its assistance was not illegal, but some people argue that such actions are dangerous because of how they might be perceived.

OBJECTIVE 2-6
Discuss
how businesses manage social responsibility in terms of both formal and informal dimensions and how organizations can evaluate their social responsibility.

Managing Social Responsibility

The demands for social responsibility placed on contemporary organizations by an increasingly sophisticated and educated public are stronger than ever. As we have seen, there are pitfalls for managers who fail to adhere to high ethical standards and for companies that try to circumvent their legal obligations. Organizations need to fashion an approach to social responsibility in the same way that they develop any other business strategy. In other words, they should view social responsibility as a major challenge that requires careful planning, decision making, consideration, and evaluation. They may accomplish this through both formal and informal dimensions of managing social responsibility.

Formal Organizational Dimensions

Some dimensions of managing social responsibility involve a formal and planned activity on the part of the organization. Indeed, some businesses are approaching social responsibility from a strategic perspective.[29] Formal organizational dimensions that can help manage social responsibility are (1) legal compliance, (2) ethical compliance, and (3) philanthropic giving.

Legal Compliance **Legal compliance** is the extent to which the organization conforms to local, state, federal, and international laws. The task of managing legal compliance is generally assigned to the appropriate functional managers. For example, the organization's top human resource executive is responsible for ensuring compliance with regulations concerning hiring, pay, and workplace safety and health. Likewise, the top financial executive generally oversees compliance with securities and banking regulations. The organization's legal department provides general oversight and answers queries from managers about the appropriate interpretation of laws and regulations. Unfortunately, though, legal compliance may not be enough; in some cases, for instance, perfectly legal accounting practices have still resulted in deception and other problems.[30]

Legal Compliance the extent to which the organization conforms to local, state, federal, and international laws

Ethical Compliance **Ethical compliance** is the extent to which the members of the organization follow basic ethical (and legal) standards of behavior. We noted previously that organizations have increased their efforts in this area by providing training in ethics and developing guidelines and codes of conduct. These activities serve as vehicles for enhancing ethical compliance. Many organizations also establish formal ethics committees. These committees might review proposals for new projects, help evaluate new hiring strategies, or assess a new environmental protection plan. They might also serve as a peer review panel to evaluate alleged ethical misconduct by an employee.[31]

Ethical Compliance the extent to which the members of the organization follow basic ethical (and legal) standards of behavior

Philanthropic Giving Finally, **philanthropic giving** is the awarding of funds or gifts to charities or other worthy causes. Target Corporation routinely gives 5 percent of its taxable income to charity and social programs. Omaha Steaks gives more than $100,000 per year to support the arts.[32] Giving across national boundaries is also becoming more common. For example, Alcoa gave $112,000 to a small town in Brazil to build a sewage treatment plant. And Japanese firms such as Sony and Mitsubishi make contributions to a number of social programs in the United States. However, in the current climate of cutbacks, many corporations have also had to limit their charitable gifts over the past several years as they continue to trim their own budgets.[33] And many firms that continue to make contributions are increasingly targeting them to programs or areas where the firm will get something in return. For example, firms today are more likely to give money to job training programs than to the arts. The logic is that they get more direct payoff from the former type of contribution—in this instance, a better-trained workforce from which to hire new employees.[34] Indeed, corporate donations to arts programs declined 29 percent between 2008 and 2010 and have only recently returned to pre-recession levels.[35]

Philanthropic Giving the awarding of funds or gifts to charities or other worthy causes

Informal Organizational Dimensions

In addition to these formal dimensions for managing social responsibility, there are also informal ones. Organization leadership and culture and how the organization responds to whistle-blowers all help shape and define people's perceptions of the organization's stance on social responsibility.

Organization Leadership and Culture Leadership practices and organizational culture can go a long way toward defining the social responsibility stance an organization and its members will adopt.[36] Ethical leadership often sets the tone for the entire organization. For example, for years, Johnson & Johnson executives provided a consistent message to employees that customers, employees, communities where the company did business, and shareholders were all important—and primarily in that order. Thus, when packages of poisoned Tylenol showed up on store shelves in the 1980s, Johnson & Johnson employees did not need to wait for orders from headquarters to know what to do; without considering how this act would affect the shareholders, they immediately pulled all the packages from shelves before any other customers could buy them.[37]

Whistle-Blowing As we noted previously, whistle-blowing is the disclosure by an employee of illegal or unethical conduct on the part of others within the organization.[38] How an organization responds to this practice often illustrates its stance on social responsibility. Whistle-blowers may have to proceed through a number of channels to be heard, and they may even get fired for their efforts.[39] Many organizations, however, welcome their contributions. A person who observes questionable behavior typically first reports the incident to his or her boss. If nothing is done, the whistle-blower may then inform higher-level managers or an ethics committee, if one exists. Eventually, the person may have to go to a regulatory agency or even the media to be heard. For example, Charles W. Robinson, Jr., worked as a director of a GlaxoSmithKline lab in San Antonio. One day, he noticed a suspicious billing pattern that the firm was using to collect lab fees from Medicare; the bills were considerably higher than the firm's normal charges for the same tests. He pointed out the problem to higher-level managers, but they ignored his concerns. He subsequently took his findings to the U.S. government, which sued SmithKline and eventually reached a settlement of $325 million.[40]

More recently, David Magee, a former employee of Mississippi's Stennis Space Center, reported to superiors and federal agents that government employees conspired with Lockheed Martin and Science Applications International Corporation to ensure they would win the contract to work on the Naval Oceanographic Office Major Shared Resource Center, violating the False Claims Act. Allegedly, the defendants shared secret information about the bidding process, ensuring a successful bid. For filing the suit, Magee will receive $560,000 of the $2 million settlement against Lockheed.[41]

Evaluating Social Responsibility

To make sure their efforts are producing the desired benefits, any business that is serious about social responsibility must apply the concept of control to social responsibility. Many organizations now require all employees to read their guidelines or code of ethics and then sign a statement agreeing to abide by it. A business should also evaluate how it responds to instances of questionable legal or ethical conduct. Does it follow up immediately? Does it punish those involved? Or does it use delay and cover-up tactics? Answers to these questions can help an organization form a picture of its approach to social responsibility.

More formally, an organization may sometimes actually evaluate the effectiveness of its social responsibility efforts. For example, when BP Amoco established a job-training program in Chicago, it allocated additional funds to evaluate how well the program was meeting its goals. In addition, some businesses occasionally conduct a **corporate social audit**, a formal and thorough analysis of the effectiveness of a firm's social performance. A task force of high-level managers from within the firm usually conducts the audit. It requires that the organization clearly define all of its social goals, analyze the resources it devotes to each goal, determine how well it is achieving the various goals, and make recommendations about which areas need additional attention. Recent estimates suggest that around 80 percent of the world's 250 largest firms now issue annual reports summarizing their efforts in the areas of environmental and social responsibility.

Corporate Social Audit systematic analysis of a firm's success in using funds earmarked for meeting its social responsibility goals

managing in turbulent times

Shredding the Electronic Paper Trail

In 2015, the company that hosted Hillary Clinton's private e-mail server used a simple program called BleachBit to delete a storage file (.pst file) of personal e-mails, bringing the issue of electronic mail retention to national prominence. Even before that, however, many of the major corporate scandals of the last few years have involved the discovery of incriminating personal e-mails. Citigroup analyst Jack Grubman changed stock recommendations in exchange for favors from CEO Sandy Weill and then sent an e-mail to confirm the arrangement.[42] Investigators found that David Duncan, Arthur Andersen's head Enron auditor, had attempted to delete incriminating e-mails shortly after the start of the Justice Department's investigation.[43] After Tim Newington, an analyst for Credit Suisse First Boston, refused to give in to pressure to change a client's credit rating, an e-mail circulated on the problem of Newington's troublesome integrity: "Bigger issue," warned an upper manager, "is what to do about Newington in general. I'm not sure he's salvageable at this point."[44]

More recently, Daniel Donovan, a former information manager for Volkswagen, filed a whistle-blower lawsuit when he was fired for informing his superiors that his co-workers had been deleting electronic data and correspondence shortly after the Environmental Protection Agency (EPA) filed a Notice of Violation against the car manufacturer for installing software in certain diesel autos that cheated emissions tests.[45]

Volkswagen employees claimed they were deleting data due to a shortage of storage space, but other than freeing up space on a hard drive, are there other justifiable reasons to delete business e-mails? If so, what is a reasonable amount of time to keep those data files, and is it necessary to remove every trace of the e-mail? The BleachBit website asserts that you can use the product to, "...free cache, delete cookies, clear Internet history, shred temporary files, delete logs, and discard junk you didn't know was there. ... Beyond simply deleting files, BleachBit includes advanced features such as shredding files to prevent recovery, wiping free disk space to hide traces of files deleted by other applications..." It also notes that there's no money trail, since the program is free, but as companies are finding, e-mails, even shredded ones, have a haunting way of resurfacing.

Stephen Clarke/123RF

summary of learning objectives

OBJECTIVE 2-1

Explain how individuals develop their personal codes of ethics and why ethics are important in the workplace. (pp. 40–46)

Ethics are beliefs about what's right and wrong or good and bad. *Ethical behavior* conforms to individual beliefs and social norms about what's right and good, and *unethical behavior* is behavior that individual beliefs and social norms define as wrong and bad. Though ethical behavior and the law are often the same, there can also be ambiguity. *Managerial ethics* are standards of behavior that guide managers. Managerial ethics can affect people's work in three broad categories: (1) *behavior toward employees*, (2) *behavior toward the organization*, and (3) *behavior toward other economic agents*.

One model for applying ethical judgments to business situations recommends the following three steps: (1) Gather relevant factual information, (2) analyze the facts to determine the most appropriate moral values, and (3) make an ethical judgment based on the rightness or wrongness of the proposed activity or policy. Perhaps the single most effective step that a company can take is to *demonstrate top management support*. In addition to promoting attitudes of honesty and openness, firms can also take specific steps to formalize their commitment: (1) *adopting written codes* and (2) *instituting ethics programs*.

OBJECTIVE 2-2

Distinguish social responsibility from ethics, identify organizational stakeholders, and characterize social consciousness today. (pp. 46–49)

Ethics affect individual behavior. *Social responsibility* is a related concept that refers to the way a firm attempts to balance its commitments to organizational stakeholders—those groups, individuals, and organizations that are directly affected by the practices of an organization and, therefore, have a stake in its performance. Many companies concentrate on five main groups: (1) *customers*, (2) *employees*, (3) *investors*, (4) *suppliers*, and (5) *local communities*.

Attitudes toward social responsibility have changed. The late nineteenth century, though characterized by the entrepreneurial spirit and the laissez-faire philosophy, also featured labor strife and predatory business practices. Concern about unbridled business activity was soon translated into laws regulating business practices. Out of the economic turmoil of the 1930s, when greed was blamed for business failures and the loss of jobs, came new laws protecting and enhancing social well-being. During the 1960s and 1970s, activism prompted increased government regulation in many areas of business. The economic prosperity of the 1980s and 1990s marked a return to the laissez-faire philosophy, but the recent epidemic of corporate scandals threatens to revive the 1930s call for more regulation and oversight.

OBJECTIVE 2-3

Show how the concept of social responsibility applies both to environmental issues and to a firm's relationships with customers, employees, and investors. (pp. 49–56)

A firm confronts four primary areas of concern when addressing social responsibility:

1. Responsibility toward the environment (including issues associated with climate change and air, water, and land pollution)
2. Responsibility toward customers (largely stemming from issues about consumer rights, unfair pricing, ethics in advertising, and green marketing)
3. Responsibility toward employees (including legal and social commitments and the special case of the whistle-blower)
4. Responsibility toward investors (including concerns about improper financial management, insider trading, and misrepresentation of finances)

OBJECTIVE 2-4

Identify four general approaches to social responsibility and note the role of social responsibility in small business. (pp. 56–58)

A business can take one of four stances concerning its social obligations to society: (1) *obstructionist stance*, (2) *defensive stance*, (3) *accommodative stance*, or (4) *proactive stance*. The few organizations that take an *obstructionist stance* to social responsibility usually do as little as possible to solve social or environmental problems, have little regard for ethical conduct, and will go to great lengths to deny or cover up wrongdoing. Organizations that take a *defensive stance* will do everything that is legally required, including admitting to mistakes and taking corrective actions, but nothing more. A firm that adopts an *accommodative stance* meets and, in certain cases exceeds, its legal and ethical requirements. Firms with the highest degree of social responsibility exhibit the *proactive stance*; they take to heart the arguments in favor of social responsibility, view themselves as citizens in a society, indicate sincere commitment to improve the general social welfare, and surpass the accommodative stance by proactively seeking opportunities to contribute.

For small business owners and managers, ethical issues are questions of individual ethics. But in questions of social responsibility, they must ask themselves if they can afford a social agenda. They should also realize that managers in *all* organizations face issues of ethics and social responsibility.

OBJECTIVE 2-5

Explain the role of government in social responsibility in terms of how governments and businesses influence each other. (pp. 58–60)

An especially important element of social responsibility is the relationship between business and government. The government (national, state, or local) attempts to shape social responsibility practices through direct and indirect channels. The government most often directly influences organizations through *regulation*, or the establishment of rules that dictate what organizations can and cannot do. To implement these rules and regulations, the government often creates special agencies to monitor and control certain aspects of business activity. Governments may also use legislation to forbid unethical practices such as bribery. Other forms of regulation are indirect, such as using tax codes that may encourage or discourage certain business decisions.

Businesses have four main methods of addressing governmental pressures for more social responsibility. Personal contacts and networks offer one method of influence. *Lobbying*, or the use of persons or groups to formally represent an organization or group of organizations before political bodies, is another. Companies themselves cannot legally make direct donations to political campaigns, so they influence the government through *political action committees (PACs)*, special organizations created to solicit money and then distribute it to political candidates. Finally, organizations sometimes rely on favors and other influence tactics to gain support.

OBJECTIVE 2-6

Discuss how businesses manage social responsibility in terms of both formal and informal dimensions and how organizations can evaluate their social responsibility. (pp. 60–63)

Organizations need to fashion an approach to social responsibility in the same way that they develop any other business strategy. Formal organizational dimensions that can help manage social responsibility are legal compliance, ethical compliance, and philanthropic giving. *Legal compliance* is the extent to which the organization conforms to local, state, federal, and international laws, and *ethical compliance* is the extent to which the members of the organization follow basic ethical (and legal) standards of behavior. Finally, *philanthropic giving* is the awarding of funds or gifts to charities or other worthy causes.

Informal methods of managing social responsibility include an organization's thoughts on leadership and culture and how organizations respond to whistle-blowers. Leadership practices and organization culture can go a long way toward defining the social responsibility stance an organization and its members will adopt. Ethical leadership often sets the tone for the entire organization. A key issue in social responsibility is how the organization handles whistle-blowers. Whistle-blowing is the disclosure by an employee of illegal or unethical conduct on the part of others within the organization. Although some organizations welcome the contributions of whistle-blowers, it is not uncommon for managers to ignore concerns.

To ascertain whether their efforts are producing the desired benefits, a business should evaluate how it responds to instances of questionable legal or ethical conduct. More formally, an organization may sometimes actually evaluate the effectiveness of its social responsibility efforts. A *corporate social audit* is a formal and thorough analysis of the effectiveness of a firm's social performance.

key terms

accommodative stance (p. 57)
business ethics (p. 40)
collusion (p. 53)
consumerism (p. 52)
corporate social audit (p. 62)
defensive stance (p. 57)
ethical behavior (p. 40)
ethical compliance (p. 61)

ethics (p. 40)
insider trading (p. 55)
legal compliance (p. 61)
lobbying (p. 60)
managerial ethics (p. 41)
obstructionist stance (p. 56)
organizational stakeholders (p. 46)
philanthropic giving (p. 61)

political action committees (PACs)
    (p. 60)
proactive stance (p. 57)
regulation (p. 59)
social responsibility (p. 46)
unethical behavior (p. 40)
whistle-blower (p. 55)

MyLab Intro to Business

To complete the problems with the ✪, go to EOC Discussion Questions in the MyLab.

questions & exercises

QUESTIONS FOR REVIEW

2-1. What factors determine an individual's ethics? For you, which factor has been most significant?

✪ **2-2.** When making decisions, who are the stakeholders that a business should consider?

2-3. What are the major areas of social responsibility with which businesses should be concerned?

2-4. What are the four basic approaches to social responsibility?

2-5. How does government shape the social responsibility of organizations?

QUESTIONS FOR ANALYSIS

2-6. In your opinion, which area of social responsibility is most important? Why? Are there areas other than those noted in the chapter that you consider important?

✪ **2-7.** What role should government play in social responsibility? Should government create more regulations to encourage businesses to uphold their responsibility to stakeholders? Or, should government take a laissez-faire approach and allow businesses to be only as socially responsible as they choose?

✪ **2-8.** The Foreign Corrupt Practices Act makes it illegal for U.S. firms to bribe government officials in other countries. What challenges could this create for a company doing business abroad?

APPLICATION EXERCISES

2-9. Describe your personal code of ethics. Be sure to include what you think is right and wrong, as well as your ethical framework for making decisions.

2-10. Using newspapers, magazines, and other business references, identify at least one company that takes each of the four stances to social responsibility: obstructionist, defensive, accommodative, and proactive. For each company, highlight its actions that support your conclusion.

building a business: continuing team exercise

Assignment

Meet with your team members and discuss your new business venture within the context of this chapter. Develop specific responses to the following:

2-11. Thinking about your business venture, identify at least three ethical issues that could potentially arise.

2-12. Should your venture have a formal statement of company practices and business ethics or simply rely on your own individual ethical standards? What are the pros and cons of each approach?

2-13. Who are the primary stakeholders in your new venture? Rank them in order of their relative importance.

2-14. Does it make sense for a new business to develop a formal social responsibility program? Why, or why not?

team exercise

TO LIE OR NOT TO LIE: THAT IS THE QUESTION

Background Information

It seems that workplace lying has become business as usual. According to one survey, one-quarter of working adults in the United States said that they had been asked to do something illegal or unethical on the job; 4 in 10 did what they were told. Another survey of more than 2,000 secretaries showed that many employees face ethical dilemmas in their day-to-day work.

Method

STEP 1

Working with a small group of other students, discuss how you would respond to the following ethical dilemmas. When there is a difference of opinion among group members, try to determine the specific factors that influence different responses.

- Would you lie about your supervisor's whereabouts to someone on the phone? Would it depend on what the supervisor was doing?
- Would you lie about who was responsible for a business decision that cost your company thousands of dollars to protect your own or your supervisor's job?
- Would you inflate sales and revenue data on official company accounting statements to increase stock value? Would you do so if your boss ordered it?
- Would you say that you witnessed a signature when you did not if you were acting in the role of a notary?
- Would you keep silent if you knew that the official minutes of a corporate meeting had been changed? Would the nature of the change matter?

- Would you destroy or remove information that could hurt your company if it fell into the wrong hands?

STEP 2

Research the commitment to business ethics at Johnson & Johnson (www.jnj.com; search for ethics) and Duke Energy (www.duke-energy.com/about-us/our-commitment-to-ethics.asp) by checking out their respective websites. As a group, discuss ways in which these statements are likely to affect the specific behaviors mentioned in Step 1.

STEP 3

Working with group members, draft a corporate code of ethics that would discourage the specific behaviors mentioned in Step 1. Limit your code to a single printed page, but make it sufficiently broad to cover different ethical dilemmas.

FOLLOW-UP QUESTIONS

2-15. What personal, social, and cultural factors do you think contribute to lying in the workplace?

2-16. Do you agree or disagree with the following statement: "The term *business ethics* is an oxymoron"? Support your answer with examples from your own work experience or that of someone you know.

2-17. If you were your company's director of human resources, how would you ensure compliance with your company's code of ethics?

2-18. Choose an ethical dilemma from Step 1. How would you handle it? How far would you go to maintain your personal ethical standards?

exercising your ethics

THE CASE OF ORPHAN DRUGS

The Situation

You are an executive at a major U.S. pharmaceutical firm. A team of your employees has been conducting research into new drugs for acid reflux, a common ailment. The researchers were surprised to discover that one of the investigational pharmaceuticals was effective at treating a rare neurological disorder, although it was completely ineffective at treating acid reflux. The research team is elated with their discovery and would like the company to move forward with clinical trials, FDA approval, and commercialization.

The Dilemma

You are the financial manager for the pharmaceutical company and the CEO is asking for your recommendation about moving ahead with clinical trials of this new drug. There are many things to consider. On one hand, advocacy groups have made you aware of the great suffering of children afflicted with this rare neurological disorder. They even organized a rally encouraging your company to move toward making the drug commercially available. Doing so could create a lot of great press for the company and could ease the suffering of those afflicted with the disorder.

However, despite all the arguments for moving ahead with clinical trials, you are concerned that there is little potential for profit with this new drug. Clinical trials are required for FDA approval and are extremely expensive. The costs associated with trials, FDA approval, and production of the drug are much greater than the potential revenues from sales. Although your company's mission is to produce drugs that make people's lives better, you also have a responsibility to stockholders to be as profitable as possible. From the perspective of maximizing profits, it just doesn't make sense to go ahead with this drug.

The CEO is pressing you for a recommendation and you are torn. You must recommend moving ahead with clinical trials with the goal of commercialization or refocusing the company's efforts on new drugs that could generate profits.

QUESTIONS TO ADDRESS

2-19. Putting yourself in the shoes of the financial manager, which course of action would you recommend?

2-20. Are the short-term consequences of your decision different from the long-term consequences? Describe the short- and long-term impacts.

2-21. How could the government encourage companies to commercialize "orphan" drugs that treat or cure rare conditions but are not economically desirable? If you were a member of Congress, would you support or oppose government intervention in this situation? Explain.

cases

SIMPLY DIVINE

At the beginning of this chapter, you read about fair-trade practices, especially as they apply to the market for cacao beans and the company Divine Chocolate. Using the information presented in this chapter, you should now be able to respond to these questions.

QUESTIONS FOR DISCUSSION

2-22. While Divine Chocolate has embraced the concept of fair trade, their products are not organic. On their website, they argue that purely organic production methods could result in greater instability in production because cocoa is very disease-prone. Do you think that Divine has an ethical obligation to require farmers to become organic? Why or why not?

2-23. How would you describe Divine Chocolate's approach to social responsibility? How do they balance their responsibilities to their stakeholders?

2-24. Do you pay attention to fair-trade products in your own purchasing behavior? For what kinds of products might you be willing to pay a premium price to help those who produce the ingredients?

2-25. Under what circumstances might fair trade actually cause harm? To whom? At what point would fair-trade trade-offs no longer be acceptable?

WHEN MOTHER NATURE STORMS IN

On October 25, 2012, Hurricane Sandy began a devastating path through the Caribbean and eastern United States. The storm roared through Haiti, Jamaica, and Cuba, killing 72 residents and displacing millions. In Haiti, still recovering from a 2010 earthquake, severe flooding compromised the safety of the food supply, exposing at least 1.5 million residents to cholera and other waterborne illnesses.

The massive storm continued up the east coast of the United States, making landfall in New Jersey on October 29. Sandy collided with a winter weather system, creating the "perfect storm." The storm was so large that its impact was felt as far south as Tennessee and as far west as Lake Michigan. The famous Jersey Shore was devastated by destructive winds, heavy rain, and unprecedented flooding. Power outages lasted for weeks after Sandy passed. Estimates of U.S. losses exceeded $50 billion, making Hurricane Sandy one of the worst natural disasters to hit the country.

The impact on businesses along the Jersey Shore was immediate and profound. Hard-working entrepreneurs saw their businesses leveled and their customer base washed away. Large home improvement stores, such as Lowe's and Home Depot, were forced to close their doors, just when customers needed them the most.

Just as rapid as the devastation, however, was the response from the business community. Home improvement giant Lowe's immediately shipped truckloads of batteries, generators, and flashlights to reopened stores in the most highly impacted areas. In addition, the company made a commitment to freeze the price of these emergency goods and others, in spite of the opportunity to reap substantial profits.[46]

The Home Depot Foundation, the charitable arm of the big box retailer, pledged one million dollars to support Hurricane Sandy relief, recovery, and reconstruction, disbursing money to organizations such as the American Red Cross, Team Rubicon, and Operation Homefront.[47]

Appliance manufacturer Whirlpool stepped up to the plate, donating 30 household appliances. Volunteers from Discovery Communications and Habitat for Humanity rebuilt homes along the Jersey Shore and installed the donated appliances. The company highlighted their donation in vignette advertisements on Discovery's TLC.[48]

Although the recovery effort will take years, if not decades, the contributions of these and other businesses have helped ease the suffering of those affected by this natural disaster and speed the healing and rebuilding process.

QUESTIONS FOR DISCUSSION

2-26. After Hurricane Sandy hit, Lowe's committed to maintaining prices on emergency goods. Do you think that other retailers acted similarly? Why, or why not?

2-27. Do you think that social responsibility is good for business? What would motivate a profit-seeking company like Whirlpool to incur the expense of donating appliances to the rebuilding effort?

2-28. How would you characterize Home Depot's approach to social responsibility? Support your conclusion.

2-29. Do you think that U.S. businesses have a greater responsibility to support rebuilding in New Jersey or Haiti? Defend your answer.

2-30. What is the appropriate role of government in the event of a natural disaster such as Hurricane Sandy?

Writing Assignments

2-31. In a capitalist economy, we assume that the market plays a major role in monitoring and regulating the business environment. Businesses that act irresponsibly often lose customers and are unprofitable. However, government regulations can require businesses to act in a socially responsible manner, even when market mechanisms would not result in the same decisions. On the other hand, excessive regulation has driven many U.S. businesses to move some or all of their operations offshore, resulting in lost jobs and tax revenues. When does government regulation work in the best interests of society? In what areas do you believe there is excessive and unnecessary government regulation? Support your conclusion with examples.

2-32. Explain the concept of ethics and then compare and contrast that concept to social responsibility. Can a company be moral and ethical? What market forces drive a company to adopt socially responsible positions? What market forces drive a company to be socially irresponsible? Give examples of each.

endnotes

[1] "Child Labor and Slavery in the Chocolate Industry." Food Empowerment Project. Accessed April 12, 2015. http://www.foodispower.org/slavery-chocolate

[2] "Frequently Asked Questions." Fair Trade USA. Accessed April 12, 2015. http://fairtradeusa.org/what-is-fair-trade/faq

[3] North, Rodney. "V-Day's Dark Side," *Equal Exchange*, February 2010, at www.equalexchange.com, accessed on March 30, 2013; "Cocoa's Bitter Child Labour Ties," *BBC News*, March 30, 2013, at http://newsvote.bbc.co, accessed on March 30, 2013; Baue, Bill. "Abolishing Child Labor on West African Cocoa Farms," *Social Funds*, April 24, 2008, at www.socialfunds.com, accessed on March 30, 2013; Fairtrade International, "Our Vision," "Aims of Fairtrade Standards," "Cocoa," 2010, at www.fairtrade.net, accessed on March 30, 2013; TransFair USA, "What Is Fair Trade?" "Cocoa," 2010, at www.transfairusa.org, accessed on March 30, 2013; Josephs, Leslie. "Selling Candy with a Conscience," *Wall Street Journal*, December 24, 2010, at http://online.wsj.com, accessed on March 30, 2013; Alsever, Jennifer. "Fair Prices for Farmers: Simple Idea, Complex Reality," *New York Times*, March 19, 2006, at www.nytimes.com, accessed on March 30, 2013.

[4] Klein, Karen E. 2011. "Sharing Profits with 45,000 Farmers." Businessweek.Com 6. Business Source Premier, EBSCOhost (accessed April 12, 2015).

[5] See "In Dixon, an Uproar Over Walgreens Going Swiss," *USA Today*, July 30, 2014, p. 5B.

[6] This section follows the logic of Gerald F. Cavanaugh, *American Business Values: A Global Perspective*, 5th ed. (Upper Saddle River, NJ: Prentice Hall, 2006), Chapter 3.

[7] "CareerBuilder Releases Annual List of the Most Unusual Excuses for Calling in Sick, According to U.S. Employers," CareerBuilder.com, accessed on January 8, 2017.

[8] "Walmart's Discounted Ethics," *Time*, May 7, 2012, p. 19.

[9] Velasquez, Manuel G. *Business Ethics: Concepts and Cases*, 6th ed. (Upper Saddle River, NJ: Prentice Hall, 2006), Chapter 2. See also John R. Boatright, *Ethics and the Conduct of Business*, 4th ed. (Upper Saddle River, NJ: Prentice Hall, 2003), 34–35, 57–59.

[10] Harrison, Jeffrey S., and Freeman, R. Edward. "Stakeholders, Social Responsibility, and Performance: Empirical Evidence and Theoretical Perspectives," *Academy of Management Journal*, 1999, vol. 42, no. 5, 479–485. See also David P. Baron, *Business and Its Environment*, 5th ed. (Upper Saddle River, NJ: Prentice Hall, 2006), Chapter 18.

[11] Kiva. "About Kiva." Kiva.com https://www.kiva.org/about (accessed February 24, 2017).

[12] Spors, Kelly. "Why Crowdfunding Favors Women-Owned Businesses." American Express, https://www.americanexpress.com/us/small-business/openforum/articles/why-crowdfunding-favors-women-owned-businesses/ (accessed February 24, 2017).

[13] "Diamond Foods Restating Profits After an Audit," *Bloomberg Businessweek*, February 13–February 19, 2012, p. 28.

[14] See "Whitman Dinged for HP Write-Down," *USA Today*, November 21, 2012, p. 7B.

[15] http://target.com/target_group/community_giving/index .jhtml, accessed January 8, 2017

[16] For a recent summary of these questions, see "Can Geoengineering Put the Freeze on Global Warming?" *USA Today*, February 25, 2011, pp. 1B, 2B.

[17] See "Frack Fluid Tracer," *Bloomberg Businessweek*, December 1–7, 2014, p. 37.

[18] Sullivan, Bob. "FTC Fines Xanga for Violating Kids' Privacy," (September 7, 2006), at http://www.msnbc.msn.com/id/14718350

[19] http://money.cnn.com/galleries/2007/fortune/0703/gallery.green_giants.fortune/7.html, accessed May 30, 2008; http://www.scjohnson.com/environment/growing_1.asp, accessed May 30, 2008

[20] http://www.nytimes.com/2008/01/09/business/09offsets .html?_r=1&ex=1357707600&en=05dc8be5247f9737&ei= 5088&partner=rssnyt&emc=rss&oref=slogin, accessed May 30, 2008

[21] http://www.starbucks.com/csrnewsletter/winter06/csrEnvironment.asp, accessed May 30, 2008

[22] "British Airways and Korean Air Lines Fined in Fuel Collusion," *New York Times* (August 2, 2007), at http://www.nytimes.com/2007/08/02/business/worldbusiness/02air.html?scp=2&sq=british+airways+price+fixing&st=nyt

[23] Daniels, Cora. "It's a Living Hell," *Fortune* (April 15, 2002), 367–368.

[24] http://www.usdoj.gov/usao/iln/pr/chicago/2008/pr03 18_01.pdf, accessed May 30, 2008; Goldstein, Jacob. "CVS to Pay $37.5 Million to Settle Pill Switching Case," *Wall Street Journal* (March 18, 2008), at http://blogs.wsj.com/health/2008/03/18/cvs-to-pay-375-million-to-settle-pill-switching-case

[25] Easton, Nina, and Demos, Telis. "The Business Guide to Congress," *Fortune*, May 11, 2012, pp. 72–75.

[26] "Siemens to Pay Huge Fine in Bribery Inquiry," *Wall Street Journal*, December 15, 2011, pp. B1, B5.

[27] "Felon or Mark?" *Bloomberg Businessweek*, January 19–25, 2015, pp. 64–69.

[28] Easton, Nina, and Demos, Telis. "The Business Guide to Congress," *Fortune*, May 11, 2012, pp. 72–75.

[29] Heslin, Peter A., and Ochoa, Jenna. "Understanding and Developing Strategic Corporate Social Responsibility," *Organizational Dynamics*, 2008, Vol. 37, No. 2, pp. 125–144.

[30] "Legal—But Lousy," *Fortune*, September 2, 2009, p. 192.

[31] Paine, Lynn Sharp. "Managing for Organizational Integrity," *Harvard Business Review*, March–April 2004, pp. 106–115.

[32] "To Give, or Not to Give," *Time*, May 11, 2012, p. 10.

[33] "Battling 'Donor Dropsy,'" *Wall Street Journal*, July 19, 2010, pp. B1, B4.

[34] "A New Way of Giving," *Time*, July 24, 2010, pp. 48–51. See also Michael Porter and Mark Kramwe, "The Competitive Advantage of Corporate Philanthropy," *Harvard Business Review*, December 2009, pp. 57–66.

[35] "To Give, or Not to Give," *Time*, May 11, 2012, p. 10.

[36] Messick. David M., and Bazerman, Max H. "Ethical Leadership and the Psychology of Decision Making," *Sloan Management Review*, Winter 1996, pp. 9–22; see also Muel Kaptein, "Developing and Testing a Measure for the Ethical Culture of Organizations," *Journal of Organizational Behavior*, 2008, Vol. 29, pp. 923–947.

[37] "Ethics in Action: Getting It Right," *Selections*, Fall 2012, pp. 24–27.

[38] For a thorough review of the literature on whistle-blowing, see Janet P. Near and Marcia P. Miceli, "Whistle-Blowing: Myth and Reality," *Journal of Management*, 1996, Vol. 22, No. 3, pp. 507–526. See also Michael Gundlach, Scott Douglas, and Mark Martinko, "The Decision to Blow the Whistle: A Social Information Processing Framework," *Academy of Management Review*, 2003, Vol. 28, No. 1, pp. 107–123.

[39] For instance, see "The Complex Goals and Unseen Costs of Whistle-Blowing," *Wall Street Journal*, November 25, 2012, pp. A1, A10.

[40] "A Whistle-Blower Rocks an Industry," *Businessweek*, June 24, 2002, pp. 126–130.

[41] "Lockheed to Pay $2 Million to Settle Lawsuit," *Washington Post*, January 25, 2011, p. B1; "Feds Intervening in Mississippi Bid-Rigging Lawsuit at Stennis Space Center," *Associated Press Wire Story*, July 3, 2009, ap.com, accessed on September 5, 2009.

[42] Beckett, Paul. 2002. "Despite Best Efforts of Citigroup's Chief, Cleanup Stretches On." *Wall Street Journal–Eastern Edition*, November 15. C1. Business Source Premier, EBSCOhost (accessed April 9, 2015).

[43] Brown, Ken, Hitt, Greg, Liesman, Steve, Weil, Jonathan, Emshwiller, John R., and Tom Hamburger. 2002. "Andersen Fires Partner It Says Led Shredding of Enron Documents (cover story)." *Wall Street Journal–Eastern Edition*, January 16. A1. Business Source Premier, EBSCOhost (accessed April 9, 2015).

[44] Kahn, Jeremy. 2002. "Frank Quattrone's Heavy Hand." *Fortune 146*, no. 13: 78. Business Source Premier, EBSCOhost (accessed April 9, 2015).

[45] https://mobile.nytimes.com/2016/03/15/business/energy-environment/vw-diesel-emissions-scandal-whistleblower.html

[46] "The Home Depot Foundation Supports Recovery Efforts after Hurricane Sandy." *JustMeans*. JustMeans, 20 Nov. 2012. Web. 13 June 2013.

[47] "Hurricane Sandy." *Center for Disaster Philanthropy*. N.p., n.d. Web. 13 June 2013.

[48] Lafayette, Jon. "Whirlpool Brings TLC to Sandy Relief Efforts." *Broadcasting & Cable* 3 June 2013: 16. *EBSCO Business Source Premier*. Web. 13 June 2013.

What makes entrepreneurs tick? What drives

them to succeed even if they first fail?

The lessons they

offer often pave the road to business success.

After reading this chapter, you should be able to:

3-1 **Define** *small business*, discuss its importance to the U.S. economy, and explain popular areas of small business.

3-2 **Explain** entrepreneurship and describe some key characteristics of entrepreneurial personalities and activities.

3-3 **Describe** distinctive competence, the business plan, and the start-up decisions made by small businesses and identify sources of financial aid available to such enterprises.

3-4 **Discuss** the trends in small business start-ups and identify the main reasons for success and failure among small businesses.

3-5 **Explain** sole proprietorships, partnerships, and cooperatives and discuss the advantages and disadvantages of each.

3-6 **Describe** corporations, discuss their advantages and disadvantages, and identify different kinds of corporations; explain the basic issues involved in managing a corporation and discuss special issues related to corporate ownership.

It All Started With a Late Fee

In the 1980s and 1990s, consumers who wanted to watch movies at home headed to their neighborhood movie rental store. Blockbuster was the clear leader in the market. Consumers were able to rent a movie for a flat fee of several dollars, but late fees were steep. In 1997, California entrepreneur Reed Hastings incurred a $40 late fee at Blockbuster. "It was six weeks late," he admits. "I had misplaced the cassette [and] I didn't want to tell my wife.... I was embarrassed about it." After locating the *Apollo 13* movie that he had rented several weeks before, he dropped off the VHS cassette and paid the late fee on his way to the gym. As it turns out, his itinerary for the day was quite opportune: In the middle of his workout, he recalls, "I realized [the gym] had a much better business model. You could pay $30 or $40 a month and work out as little or as much as you wanted."

Thus, the idea for Netflix was born. But Hastings knew he needed to start slowly. So, when Netflix was launched in 1997, its only innovations involved the convenience of ordering movies over the Internet and receiving and returning them by mail; Netflix merely rented movies for $4 apiece plus $2 for postage (and, yes, it charged late fees). Basically, the customer base consisted of people who wanted to watch movies without having to leave the house. But Hastings and co-founder Marc Randolph quickly decided to test a subscription-based model, unlimited rentals by mail for a flat fee and, perhaps most important, no due dates (and thus no late fees). Current customers were first offered the opportunity to shift from their pay-per-rental plans to subscription plans on a free-trial basis and then given the chance to renew the subscription plan on a paid basis. "We knew it wouldn't be terrible," says Hastings, "but we didn't know if it would be great." In the first month, however, 80 percent of Netflix users who'd tried the no-cost subscription plan had renewed on a paid basis.

"Having unlimited due dates and no late fees," said Hastings back in 2003, "has worked in a powerful way and now seems obvious, but at that time, we had no idea if customers would even build and use an online queue." The "queue," as any Netflix user will tell you, is the list of movies that the customer wants to watch. Netflix maintains your queue, follows your online directions in keeping it up to date, and automatically sends you the next movie you want each time you send one back.

The essence of queuing—and of the Netflix business model—is clearly convenience. Although the ability to enhance customer convenience, even when combined with cost savings, often gives a company a competitive advantage in its industry, it doesn't always have the industry-wide effect that it's had in the case of Netflix.

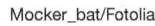

what's in it for me?

A recent Gallup poll suggests that almost half of the young people in the United States today are interested in entrepreneurship.[1] Even if you are not among that number, you will still be called on to interact with small businesses and entrepreneurs as a customer, as an investor, or as a client. You may also be trying to sell products or services to small businesses and entrepreneurs. One key to understanding entrepreneurship is to understand entrepreneurs themselves and what it takes for them to succeed. Reed Hastings displays many of the characteristics key to entrepreneurial success. Netflix also highlights some of the problems inherent in converting a great business idea into a profitable enterprise. If you ever aspire to start and run your own business, you can learn valuable lessons from the experiences of Hastings and his management team. As an investor, you should also be better prepared to assess the market potential for new and up-and-coming businesses. This chapter will discuss these and additional issues important for starting and owning a business, including the business plan, reasons for success and failure, and the advantages and disadvantages of different kinds of ownership. First, we'll start by defining a small business and identifying its importance in the U.S. economy.

Not only did the Netflix subscriber model improve the service provided by the industry in an unexpected way but ultimately it also weakened the competitive positions of companies already doing business in the industry—notably, Blockbuster. By 2010, Blockbuster had declared bankruptcy, and Dish Network acquired the company the following year. In the years since, all of Blockbuster's retail stores have been closed as well as its DVD rental-by-mail operation, although Dish Network still retains rights to the name. Investors who had purchased a share of Netflix stock in early 2009 for $36 found that their stock had grown to more than $440 by the beginning of 2015.

How had Hastings's upstart company managed to put itself in such an enviable position? For one thing, it got off to a fast start. In 1997, when DVDs were just being test-marketed in the United States, Hastings and Randolph decided that the new medium would eventually overtake videocassettes as the format of choice for both the home-movie industry and the home-movie renter. They were right, of course, and by 2002, one in four U.S. households owned a DVD player. As the first company to rent movies by mail, Netflix was the first to establish a rental-by-mail customer base. At first, says Hastings, "people thought the idea was crazy. But it was precisely because it was a contrarian idea that [it] enabled us to get ahead of our competitors." As Netflix continued to expand and nurture its subscriber base, it also generated both brand recognition and brand loyalty. "Netflix has customer loyalty. It's a passion brand," explains Hastings, who hastens to add that keeping customers happy is crucial "because the more someone uses Netflix, the more likely they are to stay with us."

More importantly, Netflix continues to be at the forefront of innovation. After the fizzling demise of Blockbuster, Redbox became the rental kiosk of choice, but as streaming video became more and more common, Redbox faced the same fate as its predecessors. Netflix, on the other hand, evolved, offering more streaming content, including an ever-increasing array of high-quality original content. Despite competition from companies such as Dish Network, Apple, HBO, CBS, and Amazon, the company saw a 47 percent increase in international streaming revenues in 2016 while the domestic subscription base added 10 million new users, nearing the 50 million mark.[2] In addition, the company garnered 54 Emmy nominations for the 2016 season. According to Hastings, the company plans to continue to focus on movies and TV on a global basis for the foreseeable future.[3] Perhaps the next conquest for Netflix will be the eclipse of cable networks like HBO and FX. And beyond that, only Hastings and time will tell. (After studying this chapter, you should be able to respond to the set of discussion questions found at the end of the chapter.)

OBJECTIVE 3-1
Define

small business, discuss its importance to the U.S. economy, and explain popular areas of small business.

Small Business Administration (SBA) *government agency charged with assisting small businesses*

Small Business *independently owned business that has relatively little influence in its market*

What Is a Small Business?

The term *small business* is not easy to define. Locally owned-and-operated restaurants, dry cleaners, and hair salons are obviously small businesses, and giant corporations, such as Nike, Starbucks, Apple, Target, and Netflix, are clearly big businesses. Between these two extremes, though, fall thousands of companies that cannot be easily categorized.

The U.S. Department of Commerce has traditionally considered a business to be small if it has fewer than 500 employees. The U.S. **Small Business Administration (SBA)**, a government agency that assists small businesses, has different standards based on industry. For instance, a manufacturer is considered to be small if it has 1,000 or fewer employees. A wholesaling firm is small if it has between 100 and 500 employees. Other industries, though, such as services, retailing, and construction, are generally classified based on revenue. Because strict numerical terms sometimes lead to contradictory classifications, we will consider a **small business** to be one that is independent (that is, not owned by or a unit of a larger business) and that has relatively little influence in its market. A small neighborhood grocer would be small, then, assuming it is not part of a chain and that market forces largely set the prices it pays to wholesalers and that it can charge its customers. Dell Computer was a small business when founded by Michael Dell in 1984, but today it's one of the world's largest computer companies and is not small in any sense of the term. Hence, it can negotiate from a position of strength with its suppliers and can set its prices with less consideration for what other computer firms are charging.

The Importance of Small Business in the U.S. Economy

As Figure 3.1 shows, most U.S. businesses employ fewer than 100 people, and most U.S. workers are employed by small business. Moreover, this same pattern exists across most free-market economies.

Figure 3.1(a) shows that 89.59 percent of all businesses employ 20 or fewer people. Another 8.58 percent employ between 20 and 99 people, and 1.52 percent employ between 100 and 499 people. Only about .16 of 1 percent employ 1,000 or more people. Figure 3.1(b) shows that 17.86 percent of all workers are employed by firms with fewer than 20 people, and 17.14 percent are employed by firms with between 20 and 99 people. Another 14.49 percent are employed by firms with between 100 and 499 people. So, around half of all workers are employed by firms with 500 or fewer employees and the other half work for larger organizations. We can measure the contribution of small business in terms of its impact on key aspects of the U.S. economic system, including *job creation, innovation*, and its *contributions to big business*.

Job Creation Small businesses—especially in certain industries—are an important source of new (and often well-paid) jobs. In recent years, small businesses have accounted for around 40 percent of all new jobs in high-technology sectors of

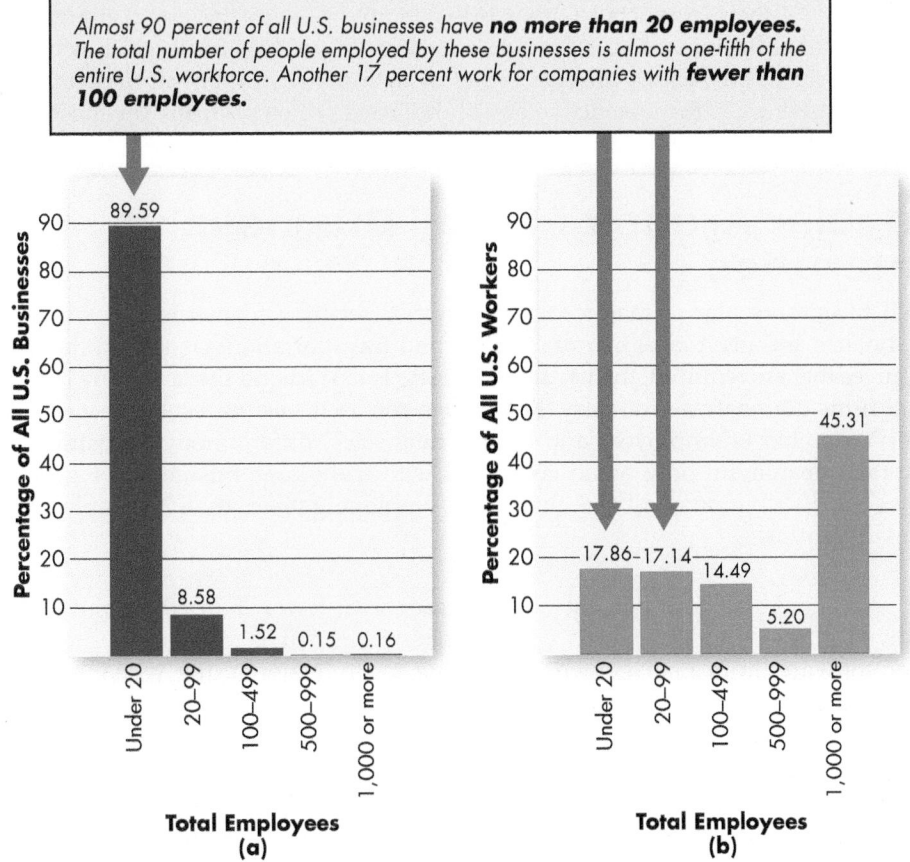

FIGURE 3.1 The Pervasiveness of Small Business in the United States
Source: Data from www.census.gov/

the economy.[4] Jobs are created by companies of all sizes, all of which hire and lay off workers. Although small firms often hire at a faster rate, they also tend to cut jobs at a higher rate. They are generally the first to hire in times of economic recovery, and big firms are generally the last to lay off workers during downswings.

However, relative job growth among businesses of different sizes is not easy to determine. For one thing, when a successful small business starts adding employees at a rapid clip, it may quickly cease being small. For example, Dell Computer had exactly 1 employee in 1984 (Michael Dell himself). But the payroll grew to around 100 employees in 1986; over 2,000 in 1992; more than 39,000 in 2004; 94,300 in 2010; and over 100,000 in 2016. Although there was no precise point at which Dell turned from "small" into "large," some of the jobs it created would have been counted in the small business sector and some in the large.

Innovation History reminds us that major innovations are as likely to come from small businesses (or individuals) as from big ones. Small firms and individuals invented the PC, the stainless-steel razor blade, the photocopier, and the jet engine and launched Facebook, Amazon, Starbucks, Instagram, and eBay. Innovations are not always new products, though. Dell didn't invent the PC; he developed an innovative way to build it (buying finished components and then assembling them) and an innovative way to sell it (directly to consumers, first by telephone and now online). Similarly, Reed Hastings invented neither the DVD nor the DVD rental business, but he did introduce revolutionary new payment and delivery models. In general, small businesses produce 16 times as many patents per employee as large patenting firms.[5]

Contributions to Big Business Most of the products made by big businesses are sold to consumers by small ones. For example, most dealerships that sell Chevrolets, Toyotas, and Hondas are independently operated. Even as more shoppers turn to online shopping, smaller businesses still play critical roles. For instance, most larger online retailers actually outsource the creation of their websites and the distribution of their products to other firms, many of them small or regional companies. Smaller businesses also provide data storage services for larger businesses. Moreover, small businesses provide big ones with many of their services and raw materials. Microsoft, for instance, relies on hundreds of small firms for most of its routine code-writing functions.

Popular Areas of Small Business Enterprise

Small businesses play a major role in services, retailing, construction, wholesaling, finance and insurance, manufacturing, and transportation. Generally, the more resources that are required, the harder a business is to start and the less likely it is that small firms dominate an industry. Remember, too, that *small* is a relative term. The criteria (number of employees and total annual sales) differ among industries and are often meaningful only when compared with truly large businesses. Figure 3.2 shows the distribution of all U.S. businesses employing fewer than 20 people across industry groups.

Services About 56.2 percent of businesses with fewer than 20 employees are involved in the service industry, which ranges from marriage counseling to computer software, from management consulting to professional dog walking. Partly because they require few resources (and hence don't cost as much to start), service providers are the fastest growing segment of small business.

Retailing Retailers, which sell products made by other firms directly to consumers, account for about 11.9 percent of small businesses. Usually, people who start small retail businesses favor specialty shops, such as big men's clothing or gourmet coffees that let the owners focus limited resources on narrow or small market segments.

New businesses often emerge in response to emerging opportunities. For instance, an increase in the number of working families with pets has created an opportunity for professional dog walkers. Most dog walkers, in turn, are individual entrepreneurs.

Construction About 11.9 percent of all U.S. businesses are involved in construction. Because many construction jobs are small local projects, such as a homeowner adding a garage or remodeling a room, local contractors are often best suited to handle them.

Wholesaling Small business owners often do well in wholesaling, which accounts for about 5.0 percent of businesses with fewer than 20 employees. Wholesalers buy products in bulk from manufacturers or other producers and store them in quantities and locations convenient for selling them to retailers.

Finance and Insurance Financial and insurance firms account for about 4.1 percent of small businesses. Most of these businesses, such as local State Farm Insurance offices, are affiliates of or agents for larger national firms. Small locally owned banks are also common in smaller communities and rural areas.

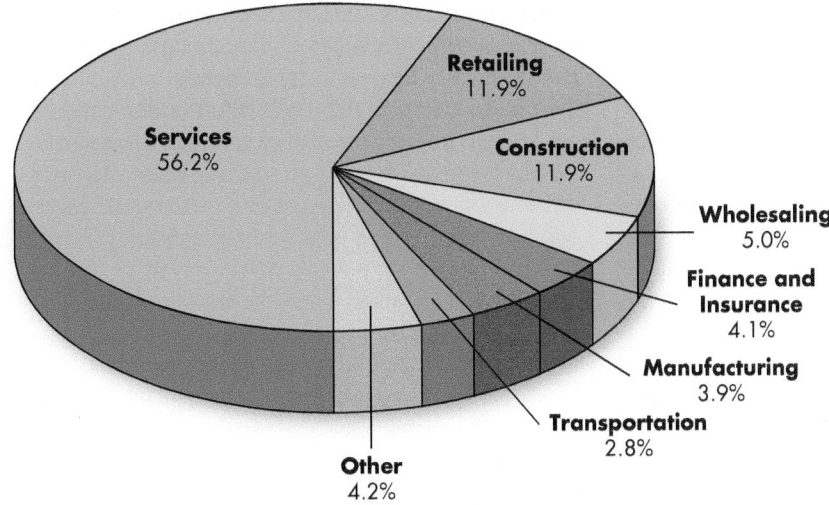

FIGURE 3.2 Small Business by Industry
Source: www.census.gov/

finding a better way

The Rise of Services

Manufacturing is a form of business that combines and transforms resources into tangible outcomes that are then sold to others. Goodyear is a manufacturer because it combines rubber and chemical compounds and uses blending equipment and molding machines to create tires. Broyhill is a manufacturer because it buys wood and metal components, pads, and fabric and then combines them into furniture. And Apple is a manufacturer because it uses electronic, metal, plastic, and composite components to build smartphones, computers, and other digital products.

Manufacturing was once the dominant technology in the United States. During the 1970s, though, manufacturing entered a long period of decline, primarily because of foreign competition. U.S. firms had grown lax and sluggish, and new foreign competitors came onto the scene with better equipment, much higher levels of efficiency, and employees willing to work for lower wages. For example, steel companies in Asia were able to produce high-quality steel for much lower prices than large U.S. steel companies such as Bethlehem Steel and U.S. Steel. Faced with a battle for survival, some companies disappeared, but many others underwent a long and difficult period of change by eliminating waste and transforming themselves into leaner, more efficient, and responsive entities. They reduced their workforces dramatically, closed antiquated or unnecessary plants, and modernized their remaining plants. Over the last decade or so, however, their efforts have started to pay dividends because U.S. manufacturing has regained a competitive position in many different industries. Although low wages continue to center a great deal of global manufacturing in Asia, once-strong manufacturers are once again thriving in the United States.

During the decline of the manufacturing sector, a tremendous growth in the service sector, often fueled by visionary entrepreneurs, kept the overall U.S. economy from declining at the same rate. A service organization is one that transforms resources into an intangible output and creates time or place utility for its customers. For example, Netflix provides video rentals through mail order and online streaming. Facebook offers its members a venue for networking and interacting with others. And your local hairdresser cuts your hair. In 1947, the service sector was responsible for less than half of the U.S. gross national product (GNP). By 1975, however, this figure was nearly 65 percent, and by 2016, it had reached approximately 80 percent. The service sector has been responsible for almost 90 percent of all new jobs created in the United States since 1990.

Moreover, employment in service occupations is expected to continue to represent a larger share of employment in the

Gemenacom/Shutterstock

U.S. economy. In 2002, 76.3 percent of U.S. workers were employed in the service sector, and this grew to 79.9 percent in 2012. By 2022, it is expected that 80.9 percent of workers in this country will be employed in service jobs. Among all service jobs, it is expected that professional and business services and health care and social assistance will represent an increased share. Looking at the Bureau of Labor Statistics list of the fastest-growing occupations between 2012 and 2022, we see that almost all of these occupations are in the service sector, largely in the areas of professional and business services and health care and social assistance.

Managers have come to see that many of the tools, techniques, and methods that are used in a factory are also useful to a service firm. For example, managers of automobile plants and hair salons each have to decide how to design their facility, identify the best location for it, determine optimal capacity, make decisions about inventory storage, set procedures for purchasing raw materials, and set standards for productivity and quality. At the same time, though, service-based firms must hire and train employees based on a different skill set than is required by most manufacturers. For instance, consumers seldom come into contact with the Toyota employee who installs the seats in their car, so that person can be hired based on technical skills. But Toyota must also recruit people for sales and customer service jobs who not only know how to do a job but who can also effectively interface with a variety of consumers. In addition, most services are simultaneously produced and consumed, so traditional models of quality control need to be revisited. As the service economy grows, managers will need to learn more about how to effectively recruit, train, and reward employees in service jobs.[6]

Manufacturing More than any other industry, manufacturing lends itself to big business, but it still accounts for about 3.9 percent of firms with fewer than 20 employees. Indeed, small manufacturers sometimes outperform big ones in such innovation-driven industries as electronics, equipment and machine parts, and computer software.

Transportation About 2.8 percent of small companies are in transportation and related businesses, including many taxi and limousine companies, charter airplane services, and tour operators.

Other The remaining 4.2 percent or so of small businesses are in other industries, such as small research-and-development laboratories and independent media companies—start-up web channels, small-town newspapers, and radio broadcasters.

Entrepreneurship

OBJECTIVE 3-2
Explain
entrepreneurship and describe some key characteristics of entrepreneurial personalities and activities.

Entrepreneur *businessperson who accepts both the risks and the opportunities involved in creating and operating a new business venture*

Entrepreneurship *the process of seeking business opportunities under conditions of risk*

We noted previously that Dell Computer started as a one-person operation and grew into a giant corporation. Dell's growth was spurred by the imagination and skill of Michael Dell, the entrepreneur who founded the company. **Entrepreneurs** are people, like Dell, who assume the risk of business ownership.[7] **Entrepreneurship** is the process of seeking business opportunities under conditions of risk. However, not all entrepreneurs have the same goals.

Entrepreneurship Goals

People may decide to pursue entrepreneurship for a variety of reasons. Many entrepreneurs seek to launch a new business with the goal of independence—independence from working for someone else, coupled with some reasonable degree of financial security. Such entrepreneurs want to achieve a safe and secure financial future for themselves and their families but do not necessarily aspire to grow their business beyond their capacity to run it. Consider Jack Matz, a former corporate executive in Houston who lost his job when his firm merged with another. Rather than look for another management position, Matz opened a photocopying and custom printing business near a local university. His goal was to earn enough money to lead a comfortable life until he retires in 10 years. The term *small business* is most closely associated with these kinds of enterprises.

Other entrepreneurs, however, launch new businesses with the goal of growth and expansion—that is, to transform their venture into a large business. This was Dell's vision when he started his business; likewise, when Howard Schultz took over Starbucks, he also had plans to grow and develop the fledgling coffee company into a much larger enterprise. Terms such as *new ventures* and *start-ups* are often used to refer to these kinds of businesses.

In still other cases, the goals of an entrepreneur may not always be clear in the early stages of business development. For instance, one entrepreneur might launch a business with little or no expectation that it will have huge growth potential but then find that it can grow dramatically. Mark Zuckerberg, for example, had no idea that his Facebook firm would grow to its present size. Another entrepreneur might start out with ambitious growth plans but find that expected opportunities cannot be realized: Perhaps there is no large market or another firm established dominance over that market first.

Entrepreneurial Characteristics

Regardless of their goals, many successful entrepreneurs share certain characteristics. Among these characteristics are resourcefulness and a concern for good, often personal, customer relations. Most of them also have a strong desire to be their own bosses. Many express a need to "gain control over my life" or "build for the family" and believe that building successful businesses will help them do it. They can also deal with uncertainty and risk.

Yesterday's entrepreneur was often stereotyped as "the boss"—self-reliant, male, and able to make quick, firm decisions. Today's entrepreneur is seen more often as an open-minded leader who relies on networks, business plans, and consensus. Past and present entrepreneurs also have different views on such topics as how to succeed, how to automate business, and when to rely on experience in the trade or on basic business acumen.[8]

Consider Yoshiko Shinohara, who had lost her father by the age of 8, was divorced by the age of 28, and never received a college education. At the age of 70, she is Chairman and Director of Tempstaff, a Japanese temp agency that she started out of her one-room apartment more than 35 years ago. Fueled by Japan's need for temps during a period of stagnation in the 1990s and Shinohara's ambition, Tempstaff is now a $3.1 billion company with a high-rise headquarters in Tokyo.[9]

Among other things, Shinohara's story illustrates what is almost always a key element in entrepreneurship: risk. Interestingly, most successful entrepreneurs seldom see what they do as risky. Whereas others may focus on possibilities for failure and balk at gambling everything on a new venture, most entrepreneurs are so passionate about their ideas and plans that they see little or no likelihood of failure. For example, when Shinohara started Tempstaff, few Japanese businesses understood or had even heard of the temporary worker concept. But Shinohara felt that she "had nothing to lose anyway" and preferred taking that risk to ending up "serving tea or just being a clerical assistant."[10]

OBJECTIVE 3-3
Describe
distinctive competence, the business plan, and the start-up decisions made by small businesses and identify sources of financial aid available to such enterprises.

Starting and Operating a New Business

First the Internet and more recently social media have dramatically changed the rules for starting and operating a small business. Setting up is easier and faster than ever, there are more potential opportunities than at any other time, and the ability to gather and assess information is at an all-time high. Today, for example, many one-person retailers do most of their business—both buying and selling—on Internet auction sites, such as eBay.

Even so, would-be entrepreneurs must make the right start-up decisions. For instance, they need to have a clear vision of why their business will succeed. They must also decide how to get into business—should they buy an existing business or build from the ground up? They must know when to seek expert advice and where to find sources of financing. If, for example, a new firm needs financial backing from investors or a line of credit from vendors or distributors, the entrepreneur must have in place a comprehensive, well-crafted business plan. Creating a business plan, in turn, begins with understanding the potential firm's distinctive competencies.

Understanding Distinctive Competencies

An organization's distinctive competencies are the aspects of business that the firm performs better than its competitors. The distinctive competencies of small business usually fall into three areas: (1) the ability to identify new niches in established markets, (2) the ability to identify new markets, and (3) the ability to move quickly to take advantage of new opportunities.

Established Market *one in which many firms compete according to relatively well-defined criteria*

Identifying Niches in Established Markets An **established market** is one in which many firms compete according to relatively well-defined criteria. For example, the video rental market was well established when Hastings decided to launch Netflix. Blockbuster was the dominant firm, but many independent video rental firms were also prospering. Retail outlets kept an inventory of video products available for rent. Customers drove or walked to the stores, paid a fee, and took a video home. They kept it for a defined period of time and then returned it to the store (with a late fee, if they kept it too long). A **niche** is simply a segment of a market that is not currently being exploited. In general, small entrepreneurial businesses are better at discovering these niches than are larger organizations. Large organizations usually have so many resources committed to older, established business practices that they may be unaware of new opportunities. Entrepreneurs can see these opportunities and move quickly to take advantage of them. Hastings's decision to rent by mail allowed Netflix to develop and exploit a niche.

Niche a segment of a market that is not currently being exploited

Entrepreneurs Dave Gilboa and Neil Blumenthal founded Warby Parker, a business that sells prescription eyewear through the mail. The entrepreneurs realized that most consumers disliked the experience of going to an optical shop to try on glasses and then were irritated at the price of those glasses. So, Warby Parker offers lower-priced glasses with contemporary designs and a money-back guarantee. Astute marketing then allowed them to get a quick start with their niche business, selling more than 50,000 pairs of glasses and generating profits after only a single year of operation.[11] Warby Parker has now established itself as a leading eyewear retailer.

Identifying New Markets Successful entrepreneurs also excel at discovering whole new markets. Discovery can happen in at least two ways. First, an entrepreneur can transfer a product or service that is well established in one geographic market to a second market. This is what Marcel Bich did with ballpoint pens, which occupied a well-established market in Europe before Bich introduced them in the United States more than 50 years ago. Bich's company, Société Bic, eventually came to dominate the U.S. market.

Second, entrepreneurs can sometimes create entire industries. Entrepreneurial inventions of the dry paper copying process and the semiconductor have created vast new industries. Not only were the first companies to enter these markets successful (Xerox and National Semiconductor, respectively) but their entrepreneurial activity also spawned the development of hundreds of other companies and hundreds of thousands of jobs. Again, because entrepreneurs are not encumbered with a history of doing business in a particular way, they are usually better at discovering new markets than are larger, more mature organizations.

First-Mover Advantages A **first-mover advantage** is any advantage that comes to a firm because it exploits an opportunity before any other firm does. Sometimes large firms discover niches within existing markets or new markets at just about the same time as small entrepreneurial firms, but they cannot move as quickly as small companies to take advantage of these opportunities. Many of the "app" developers for smartphones exploit first-mover advantage.

First-Mover Advantage any advantage that comes to a firm because it exploits an opportunity before any other firm does

There are numerous reasons for the difference. For example, many large organizations make decisions slowly because each of their many layers of hierarchy has to approve an action before it can be implemented. Also, large organizations may sometimes put a great deal of their assets at risk when they take advantage of new opportunities. Every time Boeing decides to build a new model of a commercial jet, it is making a decision that could literally bankrupt the company if it does not turn out well. The size of the risk may make large organizations cautious. The dollar value of the assets at risk in a small organization, in contrast, is quite small. Managers may be willing to "bet the company" when the value of the company is only $100,000. They might be unwilling to "bet the company" when the value of the company is $1 billion.

Crafting a Business Plan

After the would-be entrepreneur has defined a potential distinctive competence and made the decision to proceed, the next step is formulating a **business plan** in which the entrepreneur describes his or her business strategy for the new venture and demonstrates how it will be implemented.[12] A real benefit of a business plan is the fact that in the act of preparing it, the would-be entrepreneur is forced to develop the

Business Plan document in which the entrepreneur summarizes his or her business strategy for the proposed new venture and how that strategy will be implemented

business idea on paper and firm up his or her thinking about how to launch it before investing time and money in it. The idea of the business plan isn't new. What is new is the use of specialized business plans, mostly because creditors and investors demand them as tools for deciding whether to finance or invest.

Setting Goals and Objectives A business plan describes the match between the entrepreneur's abilities and experiences and the requirements for producing or marketing a particular product. It also defines strategies for production and marketing, legal elements and organization, and accounting and finance. In particular, a business plan should answer three questions: (1) What are the entrepreneur's goals and objectives? (2) What strategies will be used to obtain them? (3) How will these strategies be implemented?

Sales Forecasting Although a key element of any business plan is sales forecasts, plans must carefully build an argument for likely business success based on sound logic and research. Entrepreneurs, for example, can't forecast sales revenues without first researching markets. Simply asserting that the new venture will sell 100,000 units per month is not credible; the entrepreneur must demonstrate an understanding of the current market, of the strengths and weaknesses of existing firms, and of the means by which the new venture will compete. Without the sales forecast, no one can estimate the required size of a plant, store, or office or decide how much inventory to carry and how many employees to hire.

Financial Planning Financial planning refers to the entrepreneur's plan for turning all other activities into dollars. It generally includes a cash budget, an income statement, balance sheets, and a breakeven chart. The cash budget shows how much money you need before you open for business and how much you need to keep the business going before it starts earning a profit.

Starting the Small Business

A Chinese proverb says that a journey of a thousand miles begins with a single step. This is also true of a new business. The first step is the individual's commitment to becoming a business owner. In preparing a business plan, the entrepreneur must choose the industry and market in which he or she plans to compete. This choice means assessing not only industry conditions and trends but also one's own abilities and interests. Like big business managers, small business owners must understand the nature of the enterprises in which they are engaged.

Buying an Existing Business After an entrepreneur has forecast sales and completed the financial planning, then he or she must decide whether to buy an existing business or start from scratch. Many experts recommend the first approach because, quite simply, the odds are better: If it's successful, an existing business has already proven its ability to attract customers and generate profit. It has also established relationships with lenders, suppliers, and other stakeholders. Moreover, an existing track record gives potential buyers a much clearer picture of what to expect than any estimate of a start-up's prospects.

Ray Kroc bought McDonald's as an existing business, added entrepreneurial vision and business insight, and produced a multinational giant. Both Southwest Airlines and Starbucks were small but struggling operations when entrepreneurs took over and grew them into large businesses. About 35 percent of all new businesses that were started in the past decade were bought from someone else.

Franchising Most McDonald's, Subway, 7 Eleven, RE/Max, Holiday Inn, and Dunkin' Donuts outlets are franchises operating under licenses issued by parent companies to local owners. A **franchise** agreement involves two parties, a *franchisee* (the local owner) and a *franchiser* (the parent company).[13]

Franchise *arrangement in which a buyer (franchisee) purchases the right to sell the good or service of the seller (franchiser)*

Franchisees benefit from the parent corporation's experience and expertise, and the franchiser may even supply financing. It may pick the store location, negotiate the lease, design the store, and purchase equipment. It may train the first set of employees and managers and issue standard policies and procedures. Once the business is open, the franchiser may offer savings by allowing the franchisee to purchase from a central location. Marketing strategy (especially advertising) may also be handled by the franchiser. In short, franchisees receive—that is, invest in—not only their own ready-made businesses but also expert help in running them.

Franchises have advantages for both sellers and buyers. Franchises can grow rapidly by using the investment money provided by franchisees. The franchisee gets to own a business and has access to big-business management skills. The franchisee does not have to build a business step by step, and because each franchise outlet is probably similar to other outlets, failure is less likely. Recent statistics show that franchising is on the upswing. For instance, franchise businesses added 247,000 jobs in 2015 and generated economic output of $868 billion. The franchise sector contributed an estimated 3.4 percent of the U.S. GDP in 2015.[14]

Perhaps the most significant disadvantage in owning a franchise is the start-up cost. Franchise prices vary widely. The fee for a Fantastic Sam's hair salon is $185,000; however, the franchisee must also invest additional funds in building and outfitting the salon. A McDonald's franchise has an initial fee of at least $1 million, but again requires the additional funds to construct and outfit a restaurant; the costs generally run the total outlay to over $2 million. And professional sports teams (which are also franchises) can cost several hundred million dollars. Franchisees may also be obligated to contribute a percentage of sales to parent corporations. From the perspective of the parent company, some firms choose not to franchise to retain more control over quality and earn more profits for themselves. Starbucks, for instance, does not franchise its coffee shops. (Starbucks does have licensing agreements where other firms operate Starbucks kiosks and other niche outlets; it does not, though, franchise individual free-standing coffee shops to individuals.)

Starting from Scratch Despite the odds, some people seek the satisfaction that comes from planting an idea and growing it into a healthy business. There are also practical reasons to start from scratch. A new business doesn't suffer the ill effects of a prior owner's errors, and the start-up owner is free to choose lenders, equipment, inventories, locations, suppliers, and workers. Of all new businesses begun in the past decade, about 64 percent were started from scratch. Dell Computer, Walmart, Microsoft, Amazon, and Twitter are among today's most successful businesses that were started from scratch by an entrepreneur.

But as we have already noted, the risks of starting a business from scratch are greater than those of buying an existing firm. New business founders can only make projections about their prospects. Success or failure depends on identifying a genuine opportunity, such as a product for which many customers will pay well but which is currently unavailable. To find openings, entrepreneurs must study markets and answer the following questions:

- Who and where are my customers?
- How much will those customers pay for my product?
- How much of my product can I expect to sell?
- Who are my competitors?
- Why will customers buy my product rather than the product of my competitors?

Financing the Small Business

Although the choice of how to start a business is obviously important, it's meaningless unless you can get the money to finance your ideas. Among the more common sources for funding are family and friends, personal savings, lending institutions, investors, and governmental agencies. Lending institutions are more likely to help finance the purchase of an existing business because the risks are better understood. Individuals starting new businesses will probably have to rely on personal resources. One of the many causes of the 2008–2011 recession was a sharp reduction in the availability of credit, including funds to help start new businesses. This credit crunch, in turn, limited both new start-up funding and funding for existing businesses wanting to make new investments.

According to the National Federation of Independent Business, personal resources, not loans, are the most important sources of money. Including money borrowed from friends and relatives, personal resources account for more than two-thirds of all money invested in new small businesses, and one-half of that is used to purchase existing businesses. Getting money from banks, independent investors, and government loans requires extra effort. At a minimum, banks and private investors will want to review business plans, and government loans have strict eligibility guidelines.

Venture Capital Company *group of small investors who invest money in companies with rapid growth potential*

Venture capital companies are groups of small investors seeking to make profits on companies with rapid growth potential. Most of these firms do not lend money. They invest it, supplying capital in return for partial ownership (like stocks, discussed later in this chapter). They may also demand representation on boards of directors. In some cases, managers need approval from the venture capital company before making major decisions. In most cases, venture capitalists do not provide money to start a new business; instead, once a business has been successfully launched and its growth potential established, they provide the funds to fuel expansion. Of all venture capital currently committed in the United States, about 30 percent comes from true venture capital firms. Steve Case, co-founder of AOL, operates a successful venture capital company. He looks to invest in new start-ups that have a great business idea, a passionate entrepreneur, and a solid and well-crafted business plan.[15]

Small Business Investment Company (SBIC) *government-regulated investment company that borrows money from the SBA to invest in or lend to a small business*

Small business investment companies (SBICs) also invest in companies with potential for rapid growth. They are federally licensed to borrow money from the SBA and to invest it in or lend it to small businesses, and they are themselves investments for their shareholders. Past beneficiaries of SBIC capital include Apple Computer, Intel, and FedEx. The government also sponsors *minority enterprise small business investment companies (MESBICs)*. As the name suggests, MESBICs target minority-owned businesses.

SBA Financial Programs Since its founding in 1953, the SBA has sponsored financing programs for small businesses that meet standards in size and independence. Eligible firms must be unable to get private financing at reasonable terms. The most common form of SBA financing, its *7(a) loans programs*, allows small businesses to borrow from commercial lenders and guarantees to repay up to 85 percent of loans of up to $150,000 and 75 percent of loans of more than $150,000.[16] The SBA's *special purpose loans* target businesses with specific needs, such as meeting international demands or implementing pollution-control measures. For loans under $50,000, the SBA offers the *micro loan program*. The *Certified Development Company (504) program* offers fixed interest rates on loans from nonprofit community-based lenders to boost local economies.[17]

The SBA also helps entrepreneurs improve their management skills. The Service Corps of Retired Executives (SCORE) is made up of retired executives who volunteer to help entrepreneurs start new businesses. The **Small Business Development Center (SBDC)** program consolidates information from various disciplines and institutions for use by new and existing small businesses.

Small Business Development Center (SBDC) *SBA program designed to consolidate information from various disciplines and make it available to small businesses*

Other Sources of Financing Some entrepreneurs find financing from overseas investors. James Buck developed a new implantable heart device to treat certain heart conditions but could not find adequate funding to start his business. He ended up looking to investors in Asia and obtained $5 million from the government of Malaysia.[18]

The Internet has also opened doors to new financing options. For instance, Kabbage.com is an online company that provides cash advances to small business.[19]

Trends, Successes, and Failures in New Ventures

For every Sam Walton, Mark Zuckerberg, Mary Kay Ash, or Bill Gates—entrepreneurs who transformed small businesses into big ones—there are many entrepreneurs who fail. Each year, generally between 610,000 and 835,000 new businesses are launched in the United States. On the other hand, between 605,000 and 805,000 businesses fail each year.[20] In 2016, for instance, approximately 665,000 new firms started operations and another 690,000 closed down. In this section, we look first at a few key trends in small business start-ups. Then we examine some of the reasons for success and failure in small business undertakings.

Trends in Small Business Start-Ups

As noted previously, thousands of new businesses are started in the United States every year. Several factors account for this trend, and in this section, we focus on five of them.

Emergence of E-Commerce The most significant recent trend is the rapid emergence of e-commerce. Because the Internet provides fundamentally new ways of doing business, savvy entrepreneurs have created and expanded new businesses faster and easier than ever before. Such leading-edge firms as Google, Amazon, and eBay owe their existence to the Internet. Figure 3.3 underscores this point by summarizing the growth in e-commerce from 2005 through 2016.

Crossovers from Big Business More businesses are being started by people who have opted to leave big corporations and put their experience to work for themselves. In some cases, they see great new ideas that they want to develop.

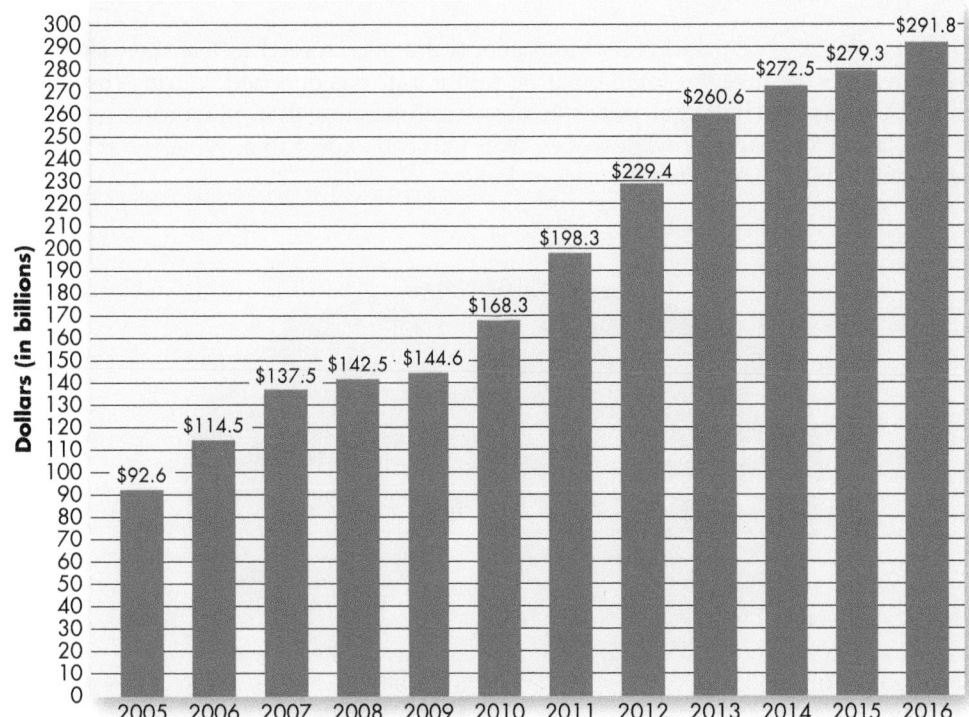

FIGURE 3.3 Growth of Online Retail Spending
Source: http://www.census.gov/retail/

Others get burned out in the corporate world. Some have lost their jobs, only to discover that working for themselves was a better idea anyway. John Chambers spent several years working at IBM and Wang Laboratories/GLOBAL before he decided to try his hand at entrepreneurship. After resigning from Wang in 1991, he signed on to help Cisco, then a small and struggling firm. Under his leadership and entrepreneurial guidance, Cisco has become one of the largest and most important technology companies in the world.

Opportunities for Minorities and Women More small businesses are also being started by minorities and women.[21] The number of businesses owned by African Americans increased by 60 percent during the most recent five-year period for which data are available and now is about 2 million. The number of Hispanic-owned businesses has grown 44 percent and now is about 2.25 million. Ownership among Asians has increased 41 percent and among Pacific Islanders 35 percent.[22]

Almost 9.4 million businesses are also now owned by women, and they generate a combined $1.6 trillion in revenue a year and employ about 9 million workers.[23] Figure 3.4 shows some of the reasons women cite for starting their own businesses. Anne Beiler bought a small Amish-owned pretzel stand to support her family when her husband decided to become a no-fee marriage counselor. She worked long hours and continued to tinker with both her menu and pretzel recipes until things began to take off. Today, her firm is known as Auntie Anne's Soft Pretzels, has 1,600 locations, and generates over $400 million in annual revenues.[24]

Global Opportunities Many entrepreneurs are also finding new opportunities in foreign markets. Doug Mellinger founded PRT Group, a software development company. One of Mellinger's biggest problems was finding trained programmers. There aren't enough U.S.-based programmers to go around, and foreign-born programmers face strict immigration quotas. So Mellinger set up shop on Barbados, a Caribbean island where the government helped him attract foreign programmers and did everything it could to make things easier. Today, PRT (now enherent Corp.) has customers and suppliers from dozens of nations.

Better Survival Rates More people are encouraged to test their skills as entrepreneurs because the small business failure rate has declined. During the 1960s and 1970s, less than half of all new start-ups survived more than 18 months; only one in five lasted 10 years. Now, however, over half can expect to survive for at least 4 years and a third survive for 10 years or longer.[25]

FIGURE 3.4 Reasons Women Give for Starting Businesses

managing in turbulent times

The Wide World of Risk

When a well-established individual or business needs a loan, they generally head to the bank. Armed with a credit score and a financial history, they are generally able to borrow money to grow their business. But what happens when someone needs just a little money to get started, but they lack any type of credit history or even a banking relationship? It's exactly this situation that has created the new world of micro-lending—very small loans made to individuals to start a new business. The challenge is particularly pronounced in developing nations, where budding entrepreneurs need just one or two hundred dollars to get their business off the ground. The concept of micro-lending has caught on, but lenders still look for some kind of data to determine who is the best candidate for even the smallest of loans. In Chapter 1 you read about Kiva, a micro-lender based on crowd funding, but there are even more innovations in micro-lending, such as the work that Tala is doing.

As a researcher for an investment back, Shivani Siroya became aware of micro-finance and the challenges that both borrowers and lenders faced. Micro-finance became her passion, and she went back to school to study health economics and econometrics at Columbia University. From there she dived fully into the issues as a United Nations researcher working in nine different countries in Africa, where she determined the real problem was simply lack of data. In April 2011, she founded InVenture, now called Tala, a California-based tech company that leverages mobile technology to create credit scores for unbanked individuals in India, Kenya, and South Africa.

To collect data that could be used for credit decisions on micro-loans, Tala developed a mobile app that monitors the length of users' phone calls and tracks their financial transactions. Using a proprietary algorithm, Tala evaluates over 10,000 indicators of responsibility. For example, applicants whose average phone calls were longer than four minutes were thought to have stronger relationships, making them a better credit risk. Using this and other more complex data, Tala accepted half

Alison Buck/Stringer/Getty Images

of its applicants, making small loans, often between $20 and $100, and charging just 5 percent interest. Even more impressive was the repayment rate of 85 percent in the company's first year of operation.

In early 2017, Tala received more than $30 million in venture capital to expand its services into new markets by accelerating product development and building its internal team. But Siroya hasn't lost sight of the original vision. "From day one, Tala's mission has been to change global financial systems so that people have more access, choice, and control," she said in a recent press release. "With this new round and team of phenomenal investors and advisors, we are positioned to connect millions of underserved people to financial services that can advance their lives."[26]

Reasons for Failure

Unfortunately, even though survival rates have improved, almost half of all new businesses still will not enjoy long-term success. Why do some succeed and others fail? Although no set pattern has been established, four general factors contribute to failure:

1 *Managerial incompetence or inexperience.* Some entrepreneurs put too much faith in common sense, overestimate their own managerial skills, or believe that hard work alone ensures success. If managers don't have a sound business plan, don't know how to make basic business decisions, or don't understand basic management principles, they aren't likely to succeed in the long run.

2 *Neglect.* Some entrepreneurs try to launch ventures in their spare time, and others devote only limited time to new businesses. But starting a small business demands an overwhelming time commitment. If you aren't willing to put in the time and effort that a business requires, you aren't likely to survive.

3 *Weak control systems.* Effective control systems keep a business on track and alert managers to potential trouble. If your control systems don't signal impending problems, you may be in serious trouble before you spot more obvious difficulties. For instance, some businesses fail because they do a poor job of managing their credit collection policies. Anxious to grow, they may be too liberal in extending credit to their customers and then end up not being able to collect all the money that is owed to them.

4 *Insufficient capital.* Some entrepreneurs are overly optimistic about how soon they'll start earning profits. In most cases, it takes months or even years. Amazon didn't earn a profit for 10 years but obviously still required capital to pay employees and to cover other expenses. Experts say you need enough capital to operate at least six months without earning a profit; some recommend enough to last a year.[27]

Reasons for Success

Four basic factors are also typically cited to explain small business success:

1 *Hard work, drive, and dedication.* Small business owners must be committed to succeeding and willing to spend the time and effort to make it happen. Tai Lee wanted to open a restaurant in College Station, Texas, but did not have sufficient capital. He partnered with a local investor and opened Veritas Wine and Bistro in 2009. In the early days, he typically spent 14 hours a day managing the restaurant, handling the cooking, and greeting customers. His wife also worked beside him, waiting on customers and taking reservations. This schedule persisted for over three years. Eventually, though, Veritas took off and became a big success. Today, Tai owns three restaurants and has a gourmet food truck that has received national acclaim.

2 *Market demand for the products or services being provided.* Careful analysis of market conditions can help small business owners assess the probable reception of their products. Attempts to expand restaurants specializing in baked potatoes, muffins, and gelato often struggle, but hamburger and pizza chains continue to expand. In the case of Veritas, College Station had relatively few fine dining options and that segment of the market was clearly underserved.

3 *Managerial competence.* Successful owners may acquire competence through training or experience or by drawing on the expertise of others. Few, however, succeed alone or straight out of college. Most spend time in successful companies or partner with others to bring expertise to a new business. Tai Lee studied both business and culinary arts before opening Veritas. He also sought advice from other successful entrepreneurs.

4 *Luck.* After Alan McKim started Clean Harbors, an environmental cleanup firm in New England, he struggled to keep his business afloat and was running low on capital. Before his funding was exhausted, though, the U.S. government committed $1.6 billion to toxic waste cleanup—McKim's specialty. He quickly landed several large government contracts and put his business on solid financial footing. Had the government fund not been created at just the right time, McKim might well have failed. Similarly, Netflix might not have succeeded if it had not started just as customers were shifting away from video cassettes to DVDs.

OBJECTIVE 3-5
Explain
sole proprietorships, partnerships, and cooperatives and discuss the advantages and disadvantages of each.

Noncorporate Business Ownership

Whether they intend to launch a small local business or a new venture projected to grow rapidly, all entrepreneurs must decide which form of legal ownership best suits their goals: *sole proprietorship, partnership,* or *corporation.* Because this choice affects a host of managerial and financial issues, few decisions are more critical. Entrepreneurs

table 3.1 Comparative Summary: Three Forms of Business Ownership

Business Form	Liability	Continuity	Management	Sources of Investment
Proprietorship	Personal, unlimited	Ends with death or decision of owner	Personal, unrestricted	Personal
General Partnership	Personal, unlimited	Ends with death or decision of any partner	Unrestricted or depends on partnership agreement	Personal by partner(s)
Corporation	Capital invested	As stated in charter, perpetual or for specified period of years	Under control of board of directors, which is selected by stockholders	Purchase of stock

must consider their own preferences, their immediate and long-range needs, and the advantages and disadvantages of each form. Table 3.1 compares the most important differences among the three major ownership forms.

Sole Proprietorships

The **sole proprietorship** is owned and usually operated by one person. About 74 percent of all U.S. businesses are sole proprietorships; however, they account for only about 4 percent of total business revenues. Though usually small, they may be as large as steel mills or department stores.

Sole Proprietorship *business owned and usually operated by one person who is responsible for all of its debts*

Advantages of Sole Proprietorships Freedom may be the most important benefit of sole proprietorships. Because they own their businesses, sole proprietors answer to no one but themselves. Sole proprietorships are also easy to form. Sometimes, you can go into business simply by putting a sign on the door. The simplicity of legal setup procedures makes this form appealing to self-starters and independent spirits, as do low start-up costs.

Another attractive feature is the tax benefits extended to businesses that are likely to suffer losses in their early stages. Tax laws permit owners to treat sales revenues and operating expenses as part of their personal finances, paying taxes based on their personal tax rate. They can cut taxes by deducting business losses from income earned from personal sources other than the business.

Disadvantages of Sole Proprietorships A major drawback is **unlimited liability**; a sole proprietor is personally liable for all debts incurred by the business. If the company fails to generate enough cash, bills must be paid out of the owner's pocket. Another disadvantage is lack of continuity; a sole proprietorship legally dissolves when the owner dies. Although the business can be reorganized by a successor, executors or heirs must otherwise sell its assets.

Unlimited Liability *legal principle holding owners responsible for paying off all debts of a business*

Finally, a sole proprietorship depends on the resources of one person whose managerial and financial limitations may constrain the business. Sole proprietors often find it hard to borrow money to start up or expand. Many bankers fear that they won't be able to recover loans if owners become disabled or insolvent.

Partnerships

The most common type of partnership, the **general partnership**, is similar to a sole proprietorship but is owned by more than one person. Partners may invest equal or unequal sums of money. In most cases, partners share the profits equally or in proportion to their investment. In certain cases, though, the distribution of profits may be based on other things. A locally prominent athlete, for instance, may lend her or

General Partnership *business with two or more owners who share in both the operation of the firm and the financial responsibility for its debts*

his name to the partnership and earn profits without actually investing funds. And sometimes one partner invests all of the funds needed for the business but plays no role in its management. This person is usually called a *silent partner*. Another partner might invest nothing but provide all the labor. In this case, the financial investor likely owns the entire business, and the labor partner owns nothing. But over time, and as specified in a contract, the labor partner gradually gains an ownership stake in the business (usually called *sweat equity*).

Advantages of Partnerships The most striking advantage of general partnerships is the ability to grow by adding new talent and money. Because banks prefer to make loans to enterprises that are not dependent on single individuals, partnerships find it easier to borrow money when compared to sole proprietorships. They can also invite new partners to join by investing money.

Like a sole proprietorship, a partnership can be organized by meeting only a few legal requirements. Even so, all partnerships must begin with an agreement of some kind. In all but two states, the Revised Uniform Limited Partnership Act requires the filing of specific information about the business and its partners. Partners may also agree to bind themselves in ways not specified by law. In any case, an agreement should answer questions such as the following:

- Who invested what sums?

- Who will receive what share of the profits?

- Who does what, and who reports to whom?

- How may the partnership be dissolved? In the event of dissolution, how will assets be distributed?

- How will surviving partners be protected from claims made by a deceased partner's heirs?

The partnership agreement is strictly a private document. No laws require partners to file agreements with any government agency. Nor are partnerships regarded as legal entities. In the eyes of the law, a partnership is just two or more people working together. Because partnerships have no independent legal standing, the Internal Revenue Service (IRS) taxes partners as individuals.

Disadvantages of Partnerships For general partnerships as for sole proprietorships, unlimited liability is the greatest drawback. Each partner may be liable for all debts incurred by the partnership. If any partner incurs a business debt, all partners may be liable, even if some of them did not know about or agree to the new debt.

Partnerships also share with sole proprietorships the potential lack of continuity. When one partner dies or leaves, the original partnership dissolves, even if one or more of the other partners want it to continue. But dissolution need not mean a loss of sales revenues. Survivors may form a new partnership to retain the old firm's business.

A related disadvantage is difficulty in transferring ownership. No partner may sell out without the consent of the others. A partner who wants to retire or to transfer interest to a son or daughter must have the other partners' consent.

Limited Partnership *type of partnership consisting of limited partners and a general (or managing) partner*

Limited Partner *partner who does not share in a firm's management and is liable for its debts only to the limits of said partner's investment*

General (or Active) Partner *partner who actively manages a firm and who has unlimited liability for its debts*

Alternatives to General Partnerships Because of these disadvantages, general partnerships are among the least popular forms of business. Roughly 3.5 million U.S. partnerships generate only 15 percent of total sales revenues.[28] To resolve some of the problems inherent in general partnerships, especially unlimited liability, some partners have tried alternative agreements. The **limited partnership** allows for **limited partners** who invest money but are liable for debts only to the extent of their investments. They cannot, however, take active roles in business operations. A limited partnership must have at least one **general (or active) partner**, mostly for liability purposes. This is usually the person who runs the business and is responsible for its survival and growth.

Under a **master limited partnership**, an organization sells shares (partnership interests) to investors on public markets such as the New York Stock Exchange. Investors are paid back from profits. The master partner retains at least 50 percent ownership and runs the business, and minority partners have no management voice. (The master partner differs from a general partner, who has no such ownership restriction.) The master partner must regularly provide minority partners with detailed operating and financial reports.

Master Limited Partnership *form of ownership that sells shares to investors who receive profits and that pays taxes on income from profits*

Cooperatives

Sometimes, groups of sole proprietorships or partnerships agree to work together for their common benefit by forming cooperatives. **Cooperatives** combine the freedom of sole proprietorships with the financial power of corporations. They give members greater production power, greater marketing power, or both. On the other hand, they are limited to serving the specific needs of their members. Although cooperatives make up only a minor segment of the U.S. economy, their role is still important in agriculture. Ocean Spray, the Florida Citrus Growers, Riceland, and Cabot Cheese are among the best-known cooperatives.

Cooperatives *form of ownership in which a group of sole proprietorships or partnerships agree to work together for common benefits*

Corporations

There are about 6 million corporations in the United States. As you can see from Figure 3.5, they account for about 17 percent of all U.S. businesses but generate about 81 percent of all sales revenues.[29] Almost all large businesses use this form, and corporations dominate global business. As we will see, corporations need not be large; many small businesses also elect to operate as corporations.

According to the most recent data, Walmart, the world's largest corporation, posted annual revenue of over $482 billion, with total profits of more than $16 billion. Even "smaller" large corporations post huge sales figures. The New York Times Company, though five hundredth in size among U.S. corporations, posted a profit of $38 million on revenues of $1.6 billion. Given the size and influence of this form of ownership, we devote a great deal of attention to various aspects of corporations.

OBJECTIVE 3-6
Describe corporations, discuss their advantages and disadvantages, and identify different kinds of corporations; explain the basic issues involved in managing a corporation and discuss special issues related to corporate ownership.

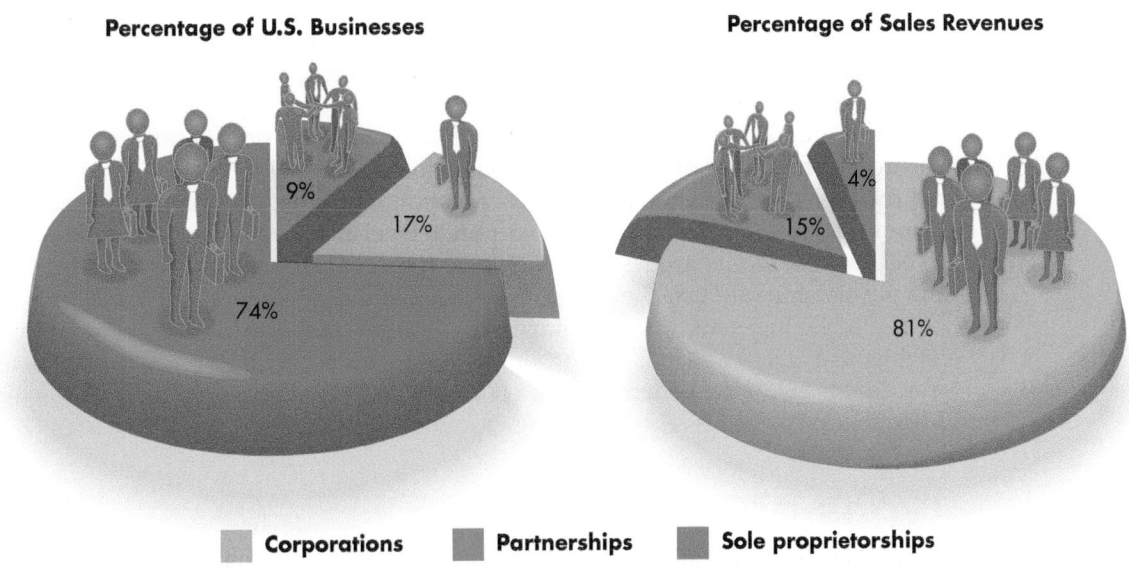

Percentage of U.S. Businesses

9%
17%
74%

Percentage of Sales Revenues

4%
15%
81%

■ **Corporations**   ■ **Partnerships**   ■ **Sole proprietorships**

FIGURE 3.5 Proportions of U.S. Firms in Terms of Organization Type and Sales Revenue
Sources: Based on http://www.census.gov/

The Corporate Entity

When you think of corporations, you probably think of giant operations such as Walmart, Google, or Apple. The very word *corporation* inspires images of size and power. In reality, however, your corner newsstand has as much right to incorporate as a giant automaker. Moreover, the newsstand and Apple would share the characteristics of all **corporations**: legal status as separate entities, property rights and obligations, and indefinite life spans.

Corporation *business that is legally considered an entity separate from its owners and is liable for its own debts; owners' liability extends to the limits of their investments*

In 1819, the U.S. Supreme Court defined a corporation as "an artificial being, invisible, intangible, and existing only in contemplation of the law." The court defined the corporation as a legal person. Corporations may, therefore, perform the following activities:

- Sue and be sued

- Buy, hold, and sell property

- Make and sell products

- Commit crimes and be tried and punished for them

Advantages of Incorporation The biggest advantage of corporations is **limited liability**; investor liability is limited to personal investment (through stock ownership, covered later) in the corporation. In the event of failure, the courts may seize and sell a corporation's assets but cannot touch the investors' personal possessions. If, for example, you invest $1,000 in stock in a corporation that ends up failing, you may lose your $1,000, but no more. In other words, your liability is limited to the $1,000 you invested.

Limited Liability *legal principle holding investors liable for a firm's debts only to the limits of their personal investments in it*

Another advantage is continuity. Because it has a legal life independent of founders and owners, a corporation can, at least in theory, continue forever. Shares of stock may be sold or passed on to heirs, and most corporations also benefit from the continuity provided by professional management. Finally, corporations have advantages in raising money. By selling stock, they expand the number of investors and the amount of available funds. Continuity and legal status tend to make lenders more willing to grant loans.

Disadvantages of Incorporation Although a chief attraction is ease of transferring ownership, this same feature can create complications. For example, using a legal process called a **tender offer**, an offer to buy shares made by a prospective buyer directly to a corporation's shareholders, a corporation can be taken over against the will of its managers. Another disadvantage is start-up cost. Corporations are heavily regulated, and incorporation entails meeting the complex legal requirements of the state in which the firm is chartered.

Tender Offer *offer to buy shares made by a prospective buyer directly to a target corporation's shareholders, who then make individual decisions about whether to sell*

The biggest disadvantage of incorporation, however, is **double taxation**. In addition to income taxes on company profits, stockholders also pay taxes on income returned by their investments in the corporation. Thus, the profits earned by corporations are taxed twice—once at the corporate level and then again at the ownership level. Because profits are treated as owners' personal income, sole proprietorships and partnerships are taxed only once.

Double Taxation *situation in which taxes may be payable both by a corporation on its profits and by shareholders on dividend incomes*

The advantages and disadvantages of corporate ownership have inspired laws establishing different kinds of corporations. Most are intended to help businesses take advantage of the benefits of the corporate model without assuming all the disadvantages. We discuss these corporate forms next.

Types of Corporations

We can classify corporations as either *public* or *private*. But within these broad categories, we can identify several specific types of corporations, some of which are summarized in Table 3.2.

table 3.2 Types of Corporations

Type	Distinguishing Features	Examples
Closely Held	Stock held by only a few people Subject to corporate taxation	Blue Cross/Blue Shield MasterCard PrimeStar
Publicly Held	Stock widely held among many investors Subject to corporate taxation	Apple Starbucks Texas Instruments
Subchapter S	Organized much like a closely held corporation Subject to additional regulation Subject to partnership taxation	Minglewood Associates EnTech Pest Systems Frontier Bank
Limited Liability	Organized much like a publicly held corporation Subject to additional regulation Subject to partnership taxation	Pacific Northwest Associates Global Ground Support Ritz Carlton
Professional	Subject to partnership taxation Limited business liability Unlimited professional liability	Norman Hui, DDS & Associates B & H Engineering Anderson, McCoy & Orta
Multinational	Spans national boundaries Subject to regulation in multiple countries	Toyota Nestlé General Electric

- The most common form of U.S. corporation is the **closely held (or private) corporation**. Stock is held by only a few people and is not available for sale to the public. The controlling group of stockholders may be a family, a management group, or even the firm's employees. Most smaller corporations fit this profile.

- When shares are publicly issued, the firm becomes a **publicly held (or public) corporation**. Stock is widely held and available for sale to the public. Many large businesses are of this type.

- The **S corporation** (more fully called the *Subchapter S corporation*) is a hybrid of a closely held corporation and a partnership. It is organized and operates like a corporation, but it is treated like a partnership for tax purposes. To qualify, firms must meet stringent legal conditions. For instance, stockholders must be individual U.S. citizens.

- Another hybrid is the **limited liability corporation (LLC)**. Owners are taxed like partners, each paying personal taxes only. However, they also enjoy the benefits of limited liability accorded to publicly held corporations. LLCs have grown in popularity in recent years, partially because of IRS rulings that allow corporations, partnerships, and foreign investors to be partial owners.

- **Professional corporations** are most likely composed of doctors, lawyers, accountants, or other professionals. Although the corporate structure means protection from unlimited financial liability, members are not immune from unlimited liability. Professional negligence by a member can entail personal liability on an individual's part.

Closely Held (or Private) Corporation *corporation whose stock is held by only a few people and is not available for sale to the general public*

Publicly Held (or Public) Corporation *corporation whose stock is widely held and available for sale to the general public*

S Corporation *hybrid of a closely held corporation and a partnership, organized and operated like a corporation but treated as a partnership for tax purposes*

Limited Liability Corporation (LLC) *hybrid of a publicly held corporation and a partnership in which owners are taxed as partners but enjoy the benefits of limited liability*

Professional Corporation *form of ownership allowing professionals to take advantage of corporate benefits while granting them limited business liability and unlimited professional liability*

entrepreneurship and new ventures

More Than Just a Burger and Fries

In 2001, restauranteur Danny Meyer opened a hot dog cart in New York City's Madison Square Park. He hoped to attract more people to the area and provide additional opportunities for employees at his nearby restaurant. That little hot dog cart quickly grew into the fast-casual restaurant Shake Shack. According to Meyer, "We entertained a bunch of names for the kiosk (most of them pretty bad—like Custard's First Stand, Dog Run, and Madison Mixer) and ultimately settled on Shake Shack." The company website explains their niche: "This modern-day 'roadside' burger stand serves up the most delicious burgers, hot dogs, frozen custard, shakes, beer, wine and more. An instant neighborhood fixture, Shake Shack welcomed people from all over the city, country, and world who gathered together to enjoy fresh, simple, high-quality versions of the classics in a majestic setting. The rest, as they say, is burger history." The company prides itself by using only Angus beef that has been vegetarian fed, humanely raised, and antibiotic-free.

From this single location, the restaurant grew. Meyer took on investors to fuel the expansion, including two limited partnerships, Green Equity Investors and Select Equity Group, and a private equity backer, Jonathan Sokoloff. Expansion was focused in several key U.S. locations: New York, Massachusetts, Chicago, and Washington, DC. The only restaurant west of the Mississippi is located in Las Vegas, Nevada. Internationally, the company had 13 locations by the beginning of 2015, including London, Moscow, and Dubai. The restaurants are so popular that people often line up for more than an hour in hopes of getting one of their famed burgers and crinkle-cut fries.

John Angelillo/UPI/Newscom

With an eye on expanding from 63 restaurants to 450 locations, the company had an initial public offering of stock in January 2015. At the time of the IPO, Danny Meyer owned 21 percent of the company's stock, with two limited partnerships, Green Equity Investors and Select Equity Group, owning 38.3 percent. Jonathan Sokoloff (a private equity backer) owned 26 percent. The company offered 5 million new shares of stock for sale at a price of $21 per share. Through this IPO, Shake Shack raised $105 million to fuel expansion. Days after the IPO, the company's stock had more than doubled from its issue price and Meyer's stock alone was worth more than $340 million. Select Equity Group, one of the initial investors, sold their interest of more than 4 million shares just days after the IPO, realizing millions of dollars of return on their investment. On the form 10-Q report to the SEC on September 28, 2016, the company reported 105 Shacks in operation, of which 41 were international licensees. And all of this started with a hot dog cart in the park.[30]

Multinational (or Transnational) Corporation *form of corporation spanning national boundaries*

- As the term implies, the **multinational (or transnational) corporation** spans national boundaries. Stock may be traded on the exchanges of several countries, and managers are likely to be of different nationalities.

Managing a Corporation

Creating any type of corporation can be complicated because of the various legal conditions that must be met. In addition, once the corporate entity comes into existence, it must be managed by people who understand the principles of **corporate governance**, the roles of shareholders, directors, and other managers in corporate decision making and accountability. In this section, we discuss the principles of *stock ownership* and *stockholders' rights* and describe the role of *boards of directors*. We then examine some special issues related to corporate ownership.

Corporate Governance *roles of shareholders, directors, and other managers in corporate decision making and accountability*

Corporate governance is established by the firm's bylaws and usually involves three distinct bodies. **Stockholders (or shareholders)** are the owners of a corporation, investors who buy ownership shares in the form of stock. The *board of directors* is a group elected by stockholders to oversee corporate management. Corporate *officers* are top managers hired by the board to run the corporation on a day-to-day basis.

Stockholder (or Shareholder) *owner of shares of stock in a corporation*

Stock Ownership and Stockholders' Rights Corporations sell shares, called *stock*, to investors who then become stockholders, or shareholders. Profits are distributed among stockholders in the form of *dividends*, and corporate managers serve at stockholders' discretion. In a closely held corporation, only a few people own stock. Shares of publicly held corporations are widely held.

Boards of Directors The governing body of a corporation is its **board of directors**. Boards communicate with stockholders and other stakeholders through such channels as an annual report, a summary of a firm's financial health. They also set policy on dividends, major spending, and executive compensation. They are legally responsible and accountable for corporate actions and are increasingly being held personally liable for them.

Board of Directors *governing body of a corporation that reports to its shareholders and delegates power to run its day-to-day operations while remaining responsible for sustaining its assets*

Officers Although board members oversee operations, most do not participate in day-to-day management. Rather, they hire a team of managers to run the firm. This team, called **officers**, is usually headed by the firm's **chief executive officer (CEO)**, who is responsible for overall performance. Other officers typically include a *president*, who is responsible for internal management, and *vice presidents*, who oversee various functional areas such as marketing and operations.

Officers *top management team of a corporation*

Chief Executive Officer (CEO) *the top manager of an organization*

Special Issues in Corporate Ownership

In recent years, several issues have grown in importance in the area of corporate ownership, including *joint ventures and strategic alliances, employee stock ownership plans*, and *institutional ownership*. Other important issues in contemporary corporate ownership involve *mergers, acquisitions, divestitures*, and *spin-offs*.

Joint Ventures and Strategic Alliances In a **strategic alliance**, two or more organizations collaborate on a project for mutual gain. When partners share ownership of what is essentially a new enterprise, it is called a **joint venture**. The number of strategic alliances has increased rapidly in recent years on both domestic and international fronts. For example, General Motors and Ford recently announced a new strategic alliance to jointly develop 10-speed transmissions for automobiles.[31] Ford also has joint ventures with Volkswagen (in South America) and Mazda (in Japan).

Strategic Alliance *strategy in which two or more organizations collaborate on a project for mutual gain*

Joint Venture *strategic alliance in which the collaboration involves joint ownership of the new venture*

Employee Stock Ownership Plans An **employee stock ownership plan (ESOP)** allows employees to own a significant share of the corporation through trusts established on their behalf. Current estimates count about 11,500 ESOPs in the United States. The growth rate in new ESOPs has slowed a bit in recent years, but they still are an important part of corporate ownership patterns in the United States.

Employee Stock Ownership Plan (ESOP) *arrangement in which a corporation holds its own stock in trust for its employees, who gradually receive ownership of the stock and control its voting rights*

Institutional Ownership Most individual investors don't own enough stock to exert influence on corporate managers. In recent years, however, more stock has been purchased by **institutional investors**. Because they control enormous resources, these investors—especially mutual and pension funds—can buy huge blocks of stock. The national teachers' retirement system (TIAA CREF) has assets of more than $480 billion, much of it invested in stocks. Institutional investors own almost 55 percent of all the stock issued in the United States.

Institutional Investor *large investor, such as a mutual fund or a pension fund, that purchases large blocks of corporate stock*

Mergers, Acquisitions, Divestitures, and Spin-Offs Another important set of issues includes mergers, acquisitions, divestitures, and spin-offs. Mergers and acquisitions involve the legal joining of two or more corporations. A divestiture occurs when a corporation sells a business operation to another corporation; with a spin-off, it creates a new operation.

Mergers and Acquisitions (M&As) A **merger** occurs when two firms combine to create a new company. For example, United Airlines and Continental merged

Merger *the union of two corporations to form a new corporation*

to create one of the world's largest airlines. The new airline bears the United name but retains the equipment design of Continental. Continental's CEO assumed control of the new company. The firm took more than two years to integrate their respective operations into a unified new firm. Even more recently, American Airlines and US Airways announced that they, too, were merging and as of this writing are finalizing their integration plans.

Acquisition *the purchase of one company by another*

In an **acquisition**, one firm buys another outright. Many deals that are loosely called mergers are really acquisitions. Why? Because one of the two firms will usually control the newly combined ownership. In general, when the two firms are roughly the same size, the combination is usually called a merger even if one firm is taking control of the other. When the acquiring firm is substantially larger than the acquired firm, the deal is really an acquisition. So-called M&As are an important form of corporate strategy. They let firms increase product lines, expand operations, go international, and create new enterprises. Halliburton Corporation recently acquired Boots and Coots, an oilfield firefighting business.

Divestiture *strategy whereby a firm sells one or more of its business units*

Spin-off *strategy of setting up one or more corporate units as new, independent corporations*

DIVESTITURES AND SPIN-OFFS Sometimes, a corporation decides to sell a part of its existing business operations or set it up as a new and independent corporation. There may be several reasons for such a step. A firm might decide, for example, that it should focus more specifically on its core businesses, and thus it will sell off unrelated or underperforming businesses. Such a sale is called a **divestiture**. When a firm sells part of itself to raise capital, the strategy is known as a **spin-off**. A spin-off may also mean that a firm deems a business unit more valuable as a separate company.

summary of learning objectives

OBJECTIVE 3-1

Define *small business*, discuss its importance to the U.S. economy, and explain popular areas of small business. (pp. 76–81)

A *small business* is independently owned and managed and has relatively little influence in its market. Most U.S. businesses are small businesses and employ fewer than 20 people. Small businesses are vitally important to the economy because of (1) *job creation*, (2) *innovation*, and (3) *contributions to big business*. The most common types of small businesses are firms engaged in (1) *services*, (2) *retailing*, and (3) *construction*. Services comprise the largest sector, in part because most service businesses require relatively little capital to start. In contrast, there are relatively fewer small businesses who manufacture products because the start-up costs are often high.

OBJECTIVE 3-2

Explain entrepreneurship and describe some key characteristics of entrepreneurial personalities and activities. (pp. 81–82)

Entrepreneurs are people who assume the risk of business ownership. Some entrepreneurs have a goal of independence and financial security, and others want to launch a new venture that can be grown into a large business. Most successful entrepreneurs are resourceful and concerned for customer relations. They have a strong desire to be their own bosses and can handle ambiguity and surprises. Today's entrepreneur is often an open-minded leader who relies on networks, business plans, and consensus and is just as likely to be female as male. Finally, although successful entrepreneurs understand the role of risk, they do not necessarily regard what they do as being risky.

OBJECTIVE 3-3

Describe distinctive competence, the business plan, and the start-up decisions made by small businesses and identify sources of financial aid available to such enterprises. (pp. 82–86)

A new business must first understand its potential distinctive competence, such as the ability to identify a niche (or unmet need) in an established market. Another distinctive competence is the ability to serve a new unexploited market. Still another is the ability to move quickly to take advantage of new opportunities, often called "first-mover advantage."

After identifying a potential distinctive competence, the next step in entrepreneurship is developing a business plan. A *business plan* summarizes business strategy for the new venture and shows how it will be implemented. The key elements of a business plan are setting goals and objectives, sales forecasting, and financial planning. Business plans are increasingly important because creditors and investors demand them as tools for deciding whether to finance or invest.

Entrepreneurs must also decide whether to buy an existing business, operate a franchise, or start from scratch. Entrepreneurs who choose to buy an existing business have better chances for success compared to those who start from scratch because of existing relationships with vendors and customers. Franchises provide considerable support in setup and operation, but franchise costs can be high and severely cut into profits. Starting a business from scratch can be the most risky, yet rewarding, way to start a new business.

To start a new business, it is essential to have money to finance the operation. Common funding sources include personal funds, family and friends, savings, lenders, investors, and governmental agencies. Lending institutions are more likely to finance an existing business than a new business because the risks are better understood. *Venture capital companies* are groups of small investors seeking to make profits on companies with rapid growth potential. Most of these firms do not lend money but rather invest it, supplying capital in return for partial ownership. New businesses may also seek funding from small business investment companies (SBICs) as well as through Small Business Administration (SBA) programs.

OBJECTIVE 3-4

Discuss the trends in small business start-ups and identify the main reasons for success and failure among small businesses. (pp. 87–90)

Five trends have helped facilitate the growth in new businesses started in the United States every year. These trends are: (1) *the emergence of e-commerce*, (2) *crossovers from big business*, (3) *increased opportunities for minorities and women*, (4) *new opportunities in global enterprise*, and (5) *improved rates of survival among small businesses*.

However, more than half of all small businesses fail. Four basic factors contribute to most small business failure: (1) *managerial incompetence or inexperience*, (2) *neglect*, (3) *weak control systems*, and (4) *insufficient capital*. Likewise, four basic factors explain most small business success: (1) *hard work, drive, and dedication*, (2) *market demand for the products or services being provided*, (3) *managerial competence*, and (4) *luck*.

OBJECTIVE 3-5

Explain sole proprietorships, partnerships, and cooperatives and discuss the advantages and disadvantages of each. (pp. 90–93)

A *sole proprietorship* is a business that is owned by one person. The most significant advantage to organizing as a sole proprietorship is the freedom to make decisions. In addition, it is relatively easy to form and operate a sole proprietorship. There are tax benefits for new businesses that are likely to suffer losses in early stages because these losses can offset income from another business or job on the tax return of a sole proprietor. A major drawback is *unlimited liability*, which is the legal concept that makes the owners of a sole proprietorship personally responsible for all its debts. Another disadvantage is that a sole proprietorship lacks continuity; when the owner dies or leaves the business, it does not continue to exist. Finally, a sole proprietorship depends on the resources of a single individual.

A *general partnership* is a sole proprietorship multiplied by the number of partner owners. The biggest advantage is its ability to grow by adding new talent and money. Partners report their share of the partnership's income and it is taxed on their individual tax return. Like a sole proprietorship, *unlimited liability* is a drawback. Partnerships may lack continuity, and transferring ownership may be hard. No partner may sell out without the consent of the others. There are also special forms of partnerships, most notably limited partnerships and master limited partnerships.

Cooperatives combine the freedom of sole proprietorships with the financial power of corporations. A cooperative is a group of sole proprietorships or partnerships working together to gain greater production or marketing power.

OBJECTIVE 3-6

Describe corporations, discuss their advantages and disadvantages, and identify different kinds of corporations; explain the basic issues involved in managing a corporation and discuss special issues related to corporate ownership. (pp. 93–98)

All *corporations* share certain characteristics: legal status as separate entities, property rights and obligations, and indefinite life spans. They may sue and be sued; buy, hold, and sell property; make and sell products; and commit crimes and be tried and punished for them. The biggest advantage of incorporation is *limited liability*: Investor liability is limited to one's personal investments in the corporation. Another advantage is continuity; a corporation can last indefinitely and does not end with the death or withdrawal of an owner. Finally, corporations have advantages in raising money. By selling stock, they expand the number of investors and the amount of available funds. Continuity and the ability to sell stock tend to make lenders more willing to grant loans.

One disadvantage is that a corporation can be taken over against the will of its managers. Another disadvantage is start-up cost. Corporations are heavily regulated and must meet complex legal requirements in the states in which they're chartered. The greatest potential drawback to incorporation is *double taxation* of profits. Profits are taxed first at the level of the corporation and then taxed as dividends when distributed to the stockholders. Corporations may be either private or public. A private, or closely held, corporation has only a small number of owners and shares of stock are not available to the general public. Public corporations are able to sell their stock on the stock exchanges and have the ability to raise large amounts of capital. Special forms of ownership, such as S corporations, LLCs, and professional corporations, combine the limited liability of a corporation with the tax treatment of partnerships.

Corporations sell shares, called *stock*, to investors who then become *stockholders* (or shareholders) and the real owners. Profits are distributed among stockholders in the form of *dividends*, and managers serve at their discretion. The governing body of a corporation is its *board of directors*. Most board members do not participate in day-to-day management but rather hire a team of managers. This team, called *officers*, is usually headed by a *chief executive officer (CEO)* who is responsible for overall performance.

Several issues have grown in importance in the area of corporate ownership. In a *strategic alliance*, two or more organizations collaborate on a project for mutual gain. When partners share ownership of a new enterprise, the arrangement is called a *joint venture*. An *employee stock ownership plan (ESOP)* allows employees to own a significant share of the corporation through trusts established on their behalf. More stock is now being purchased by *institutional investors*. A *merger* occurs when two firms combine to create a new company, and in an *acquisition*, one firm buys another outright. A *divestiture* occurs when a corporation sells a part of its existing business operations or sets it up as a new and independent corporation. When a firm sells part of itself to raise capital, the strategy is known as a *spin-off*.

key terms

acquisition (p. 98)
board of directors (p. 97)
business plan (p. 83)
chief executive officer (CEO) (p. 97)
closely held (or private) corporation (p. 95)
cooperative (p. 93)
corporate governance (p. 96)
corporation (p. 94)
divestiture (p. 98)
double taxation (p. 94)
employee stock ownership plan (ESOP) (p. 97)
entrepreneur (p. 81)
entrepreneurship (p. 81)
established market (p. 82)
first-mover advantage (p. 83)

franchise (p. 84)
general (or active) partner (p. 92)
general partnership (p. 91)
institutional investor (p. 97)
joint venture (p. 97)
limited liability (p. 94)
limited liability corporation (LLC) (p. 95)
limited partner (p. 92)
limited partnership (p. 92)
master limited partnership (p. 93)
merger (p. 97)
multinational (or transnational) corporation (p. 96)
niche (p. 83)
officers (p. 97)
professional corporation (p. 95)

publicly held (or public) corporation (p. 95)
S corporation (p. 95)
small business (p. 76)
Small Business Administration (SBA) (p. 76)
Small Business Development Center (SBDC) (p. 86)
small business investment company (SBIC) (p. 86)
sole proprietorship (p. 91)
spin-off (p. 98)
stockholder (or shareholder) (p. 96)
strategic alliance (p. 97)
tender offer (p. 94)
unlimited liability (p. 91)
venture capital company (p. 86)

MyLab Intro to Business

To complete the problems with the ⭐, go to EOC Discussion Questions in the MyLab.

questions & exercises

QUESTIONS FOR REVIEW

3-1. Why are small businesses important to the U.S. economy?

3-2. Which industries are easiest for a small business to enter? Which are hardest? Why?

3-3. What are the primary reasons for new business failure and success?

⭐ **3-4.** What are the basic forms of noncorporate business ownership? What are the key advantages and disadvantages of each?

QUESTIONS FOR ANALYSIS

3-5. After considering the characteristics of entrepreneurs, do you think that you would be a good candidate to start your own business? Why or why not?

3-6. If you were going to open a new business, what type would it be? Why?

⭐ **3-7.** Would you prefer to buy an existing business or start from scratch? Why?

⭐ **3-8.** Why might a closely held corporation choose to remain private? Why might it choose to be publicly traded?

APPLICATION EXERCISES

3-9. Interview the owner/manager of a sole proprietorship or a general partnership. What characteristics of that business form led the owner to choose it? Does he or she ever contemplate changing the form of the business?

3-10. Although more than half of all small businesses don't survive five years, franchises have a much better track record. However, it can be difficult to buy a franchise. Research a popular food industry franchise, such as Panera Bread, Sonic, California Tortilla, or Subway, and detail the requirements for net worth and liquid cash for the franchisee as well as up-front and annual fees.

building a business: continuing team exercise

Assignment

Meet with your team members and discuss your new business venture within the context of this chapter. Develop specific responses to the following:

3-11. To what extent do each of you really want to be an entrepreneur?

3-12. For the specific business you are starting (in this exercise), does it make more sense to start from scratch, to buy an existing business, or to buy a franchise? Why?

3-13. How will you most likely finance your new venture?

3-14. What factors will most likely contribute to your success? What factors might cause your business to fail? Is there a way to minimize or eliminate these risk factors?

3-15. What form of ownership will your group use? What are the advantages and disadvantages of this approach?

team exercise

A TASTY IDEA

Background Information

Suppose that you and three friends from college would like to open a new restaurant. Collectively, you have almost 20 years of experience in the restaurant industry and, with lots of new houses in the area, you think that there's an opportunity to make a lot of money if you can offer interesting food at good prices. You've even identified a great location, but you realize that it's going to take a lot of money to get this business off the ground. As recent college graduates, you don't have a lot of money, so you're looking for the best source of funding. Realistically, you realize that you're going to need at least $100,000 to sustain operations until your business starts to return a profit.

Team Activity

STEP 1

Individually or in a group of two or three students, brainstorm a list of options for financing. You'll want to do some online research to find out more about some of the loan programs identified in the text.

STEP 2

For each of the funding options, develop a list of pros and cons. Be sure to consider all the implications of each form of financing, including interest rates, repayment options, and eligibility requirements.

FOLLOW-UP QUESTIONS

3-16. Before getting financing, what will be expected of you and your business partners?

3-17. Which source of financing would be best for you and your partners? Why?

3-18. What form of business ownership would be most appropriate for your new restaurant and why?

exercising your ethics

BREAKING UP IS HARD TO DO

The Situation

Connie and Mark began a 25-year friendship after finishing college and discovering their mutual interest in owning a business. Established as a general partnership, their home furnishings center is a successful business sustained for 20 years by a share-and-share-alike relationship. Start-up cash, daily responsibilities, and profits have all been shared equally. The partnership agreement was general and doesn't require specific work hours. The partners both average four days a week in the store except in particularly busy seasons. Shared goals and compatible personalities have led to a solid give-and-take relationship that helps them overcome business problems while maintaining a happy interpersonal relationship.

The division of work is a natural match and successful combination because of the partners' different but complementary interests. Mark is a natural salesman and has most of the face-to-face contact with customers; he also handles personnel matters (hiring and training employees). Connie manages the inventory, buys shipping supplies, keeps the books, and oversees the finances. Both partners share in decisions about advertising and promotions.

The Dilemma

Things began changing two years ago when Connie became less interested in the business and got more involved in other activities. Whereas Mark's enthusiasm remained high, Connie's time was increasingly consumed by travel, recreation, and community service activities. At first, she reduced her work commitment from four to three days a week. Although not physically present as many hours, she was attentive to e-mails and often worked from home ordering inventory and paying bills. Then she indicated that she wanted to cut back further, to just two days. At first, the store continued to operate pretty well, but problems began to arise. With Connie spending less time managing the inventory, Mark found that they often had empty spaces on the showroom floor. Furthermore, Connie had less time to focus on their financial situation and suppliers started complaining about late payments on invoices. While Connie feels that her contributions are still substantial, Mark feels that their 50/50 is no longer fair. Connie, on the other hand, believes that she's keeping up her end of the bargain and doesn't want to make any changes to the partnership agreement.

QUESTIONS TO ADDRESS

3-19. What are the reasons the business has been successful? How did each partner contribute to the success?

3-20. Looking ahead, what are the biggest risks to their venture?

3-21. Is it fair for Connie to work fewer hours than Mark? What changes could they make to create equity and fairness in their agreement?

cases

IT ALL STARTED WITH A LATE FEE

Continued from page 76

At the beginning of this chapter, you read about how the idea for Netflix came about and how the company chose its business model. Using the information presented in this chapter, you should now be able to answer the following questions:

QUESTIONS FOR DISCUSSION

3-22. What are some of the primary reasons Netflix has been successful?

3-23. Netflix is a corporation. Why do you think the firm uses this form of ownership?

3-24. What threats might derail Netflix's success? What steps might the firm take today to thwart those threats?

3-25. Suppose Reed Hastings asked you for advice on how to make Netflix better. What would you tell him?

ICE CREAM HEADACHE

If you have ever visited a Cold Stone Creamery, you are familiar with the seemingly endless list of ice creams and toppings, as well as prepared cakes and other confections. You may not be aware, however, that Cold Stone is a franchise sold by Kahala Brands, whose other franchisee opportunities include Blimpie's sandwich shops and Samurai Sam's Teriyaki Grills.[32]

In case you are considering opening your own Cold Stone, you might be interested in the conditions of ownership. Those who wish to purchase a Cold Stone franchise must show that they are financially sound, with at least $125,000 of cash available and a $250,000 net worth. The up-front franchise fee is $27,000 and the franchise is good for a ten-year term. Cold Stone provides plenty of assistance in selecting a location and opening a store, but start-up costs are estimated to be as much as $467,525. The company estimates that the average time to open a location is four to twelve months, which presents a real challenge for a new franchise owner. Once in operation, franchisees will pay a royalty fee of 6 percent of gross sales and an advertising fee of 3 percent of gross sales.[33]

Cold Stone's parent organization provides support in site selection, lease terms, and equipment selection. It provides 11 days of training at the company's headquarters and three additional days of training at the franchisee's location. Once the business is up and running, it provides continued support through newsletters and annual meetings, cooperative advertising arrangements, and a toll-free hotline.

Revenues for Cold Stone franchises have declined in recent years. In 2005, the typical location earned approximately $400,000 in revenues, but this number dipped to $352,000 in 2011. Tough economic times cut into discretionary spending, hurting the ice cream business, and by 2016 Cold Stone's 1,500 locations worldwide had dropped to approximately 1,300, with a majority of the decline attributed to U.S. franchises. In 2012, a group of Cold Stone Creamery franchise owners threatened to file suit against the company, alleging that the company was not delivering on promised marketing campaigns. In addition, there was an ongoing dispute over revenue and interest from unused gift cards. Tensions between franchisors and franchisees are becoming increasingly common. Eric Stites, managing director of *Franchise Business Review,* reflects, "When franchises aren't making money, that's when you see them form associations and sue the franchiser." Franchises in the food industry seem to have been hit especially hard. Although the initial investment is often more than $450,000, annual profits average only $88,382. Although a bowl of ice cream will brighten almost anyone's day, a Cold Stone Franchise may not be a sure thing.[34]

QUESTIONS FOR DISCUSSION

3-26. What would be the advantages of buying a Cold Stone Creamery franchise as opposed to starting a business from scratch?

3-27. What are the disadvantages of buying a Cold Stone Creamery franchise?

3-28. While franchise owners must have at least $125,000 of cash available, average start-up costs are more than double this amount. What are the most likely sources of funding for a franchise?

3-29. How would you research a franchise purchase before making the decision to invest?

3-30. Do you think that you would be interested in owning a Cold Stone Creamery franchise? Why or why not?

Writing Assignments

3-31. Research suggests that entrepreneurs share certain characteristics. Pick three common entrepreneurial mindsets and explain how they are relevant. Also explain how these same traits may hinder an entrepreneur's success. Which of these traits do you think you exhibit?

3-32. What are the three primary forms of business ownership? Provide a description of each as well as the most significant advantages and disadvantages. When is each form most appropriate or desirable?

endnotes

1 "Oh, To Be Young, and An Entrepreneur," *USA Today*, February 8, 2013, p. 8B.

2 "Why We Revised Our Price Estimate for Netflix to $137." Forbes.com, February 22, 2017, at https://www.forbes.com/sites/greatspeculations/2017/02/22/why-we-revised-our-price-estimate-for-netflix-to-137/#ff94fe18be1d, accessed on February 24, 2017.

3 "What's Next for Netflix?" *wsj.com*, 10/24/2016 at http://www.wsj.com/video/what-next-for-netflix/6DE2938D-BEF0-49AA-B1E1-DAA3CD22052C.html, accessed February 24, 2017.

4 See http://www.sba.gov

5 See http://www.sba.gov/aboutsba

6 *Employment Projections: 2012–2022 Summary*, U.S. Bureau of Labor Statistics, March 14, 2015.

7 Byrne, John. "The 12 Greatest Entrepreneurs of Our Time," *Fortune*, April 9, 2012, pp. 68–86.

8 "A New Generation Rewrites the Rules," *Wall Street Journal* (May 22, 2002), R4; See also Mark Henricks, "Up to the Challenge," *Entrepreneur* (February 2006), 64–67.

9 "Special Report—Stars of Asia," *BusinessWeek* (July 12, 2004), p. 18; see also https://www.tempstaff.co.jp/english/corporate/, accessed on January 27, 2015.

10 "Special Report—Stars of Asia," p. 18.

11 "A Startup's New Prescription for Eyewear," *Businessweek,*, July 4–10, 2011, pp. 49–51.

12 See Thomas Zimmerer and Norman Scarborough, *Essentials of Entrepreneurship and Small Business Management*, 5th ed. (Upper Saddle River, NJ: Prentice Hall, 2008).

13 Combs, James, Ketchen, David, Shook, Christopher, and Jeremy Short. "Antecedents and Consequences of Franchising: Past Accomplishments and Future Challenges, *Journal of Management*, January 2011, pp. 99–126.

14 See http://www.franchise.org/Franchise-News-Detail.aspx?id=63438, accessed on January 30, 2015.

15 "Case Looks for Passion in Start-Ups," *USA Today*, March 26, 2013, p. 3B.

16 See https://www.sba.gov/content/7a-loan-amounts-fees-interest-rates, accessed on January 28, 2015.

17 http://www.census.gov/ces/dataproducts/bds/data_firm.html

18 "To Fund a Startup, Go to Kuala Lumpur," *Bloomberg Businessweek*, February 25–March 3, 2012.

19 "Small Businesses Go Alternative for Loans," *USA Today*, November 14, 2012, p. 1B. See also "Alternative Online Lenders Fill Funding Needs for Small Businesses," *Forbes*, September 23, 2014, accessed at forbes.com on January 20, 2015.

[20] http://www.census.gov/ces/dataproducts/bds/data_firm.html

[21] U.S. Census Bureau, "1997 Economic Census Surveys of Minority and Women Owned Business Enterprises," at http://www.census.gov/csd/mwb

[22] Hoy, Peter. "Minority and Women Owned Businesses Skyrocket," *Inc.* (May 1, 2006), pp. 20–24.

[23] Zimmerer and Scarborough, *Essentials of Entrepreneurship and Small Business Management*, 20; see also http://nawbo.org/section_103.cfm http://nawbo.org/pdfs/2014_State_of_Women-owned_Businesses.pdf, accessed on January 20, 2015.

[24] "Soft Pretzels out of Hard Times," *Fortune*, July 22, 2014, pp. 23–26.

[25] See U.S. Small Business Administration, "Frequently Asked Questions," at http://app1.sba.gov/faqs/faqIndex-All.cfm?areaid=24, accessed on February 20, 2011; see also https://www.sba.gov/sites/default/files/FAQ_March_2014_0.pdf, accessed on January 20, 2015.

[26] Based on Tala, "Tala Raises Over $30 Million In New Financing Led By IVP." News Release. Accessed February 24, 2017. http://tala.co/press-releases

[27] Ibid.

[28] www.sba.gov

[29] Ibid.

[30] De La Merced, Michael. "Shake Shack More Than Doubles Its I.P.O. Price in Market Debut." *DealBook*, January 30, 2015. Accessed March 22, 2015. http://dealbook.nytimes.com/2015/01/30/shake-shack-more-than-doubles-its-i-p-o-price-in-market-debut/?_r=2: "Investor Overview." Shake Shack Inc. Accessed March 22, 2015. http://investor.shakeshack.com/investors-overview/overview/default.aspx; Williams, Trey. "6 things to know about Shake Shack with IPO set to start trading." MarketWatch. Last modified January 30, 2015. Accessed March 22, 2015. http://www.marketwatch.com/story/6-things-to-know-about-shake-shack-ahead-of-its-ipo-2015-01-20

[31] "GM, Ford Team to Develop 10-Speed Transmissions," *USA Today*, April 16, 2013, p. 2B.

[32] "Benefits of Franchising." *Cold Stone Creamery*. Kahala Franchising, LLC, n.d. Web. 13 June 2013.

[33] "Cold Stone Creamery Franchise Information." *Entrepreneur.com*. Entrepreneur Media, Inc, n.d. Web. 23 June 2017.

[34] Needleman, Sarah E. "Tough Times for Franchising." *Wall Street Journal*. Dow Jones Company, Inc., 9 Feb. 2012. Web. 13 June 2013.

chapter 4

Understanding the Global Context of Business

Diego Grandi/Shutterstock

No matter where in the world a firm does

business, management drives its success.

International

businesses create unique management

challenges in

markets scattered

around the globe.

After reading this chapter, you should be able to:

4-1 **Discuss** the rise of international business and describe the major world marketplaces, trade agreements, and alliances.

4-2 **Explain** how differences in import–export balances, exchange rates, and foreign competition determine the ways in which countries and businesses respond to the international environment.

4-3 **Discuss** the factors involved in deciding to do business internationally and in selecting the appropriate levels of international involvement and international organizational structure.

4-4 **Explain** the role and importance of the cultural environment in international business.

4-5 **Describe** some of the ways in which economic, legal, and political differences among nations affect international business.

The Door Opens

In July 2015, the United States officially restored diplomatic relations with Cuba after 54 years of hostility. President Barack Obama, who was born the year Eisenhower severed ties with the Communist country, urged Congress to reopen the borders, reasoning that, "Instead of supporting democracy and opportunity for the Cuban people, our efforts to isolate Cuba despite good intentions increasingly had the opposite effect—cementing the status quo and isolating the United States from our neighbors in this hemisphere."[1]

The re-opening of borders creates a number of opportunities for U.S. businesses. One of the most significant impacts is the ability of U.S. citizens to travel to Cuba. In the past, travel to Cuba was limited to certain educational or humanitarian efforts. However, travel to Cuba is now authorized under 12 broad categories, including athletic competitions and people-to-people programs, and travelers do not have to apply for any special licenses before they travel.

In Cuba's socialist economy, most hotels are partially or completely government owned and often lack the amenities desired by American travelers. In addition, hotel capacity is limited and no new hotels are under construction. However, many private homes are available for short-term stays, and San Francisco Airbnb has stepped in to fill the void. For as little as $25 per night, travelers can arrange a stay in a private home in Cuba, soaking up the warm weather and Caribbean sunshine.[2] And Starwood Hotels & Resorts was able to negotiate a license with the Cuban government to renovate and manage three government-owned hotels in Havana.

Restoring diplomatic relations and easing travel and financial restrictions have created inroads for the tourist and hospitality industry, but the U.S. embargo on Cuban exports remains, and only Congress can repeal those restrictions. The embargo, which was first imposed in 1960 in response to the revolutionary communist government's appropriation of U.S. land holdings in the country, prevents "U.S. persons" and entities "owned or controlled" by "U.S. persons" from engaging in any transactions in which Cuba has an "interest of any nature whatsoever, direct or indirect." Cuba, therefore, has no access to the U.S. market, does without U.S. imports, and amasses substantial debts to other trading partners. But observers also point out that if the embargo were repealed, the effects may not be dramatic. Cubans now buy ice cream and soft drinks from Swiss-based Nestlé, soap and shampoo from Anglo-Dutch Unilever, and cigarettes from Brazil's Souza Cruz. The fact that the United States is the world's largest market for rum did not deter French-owned Pernod-Ricard from building a new distillery in Cuba, and Britain's Imperial Tobacco expects to double sales when Americans can once again purchase premium hand-rolled Cuban cigars.

Minerva Studio/Fotolia

what's in it for me?

As we will see in this chapter, global forces—business as well as political—affect each and every one of us on a daily basis. As you begin your business career, regardless of whether you see yourself living abroad, working for a big company, or starting your own business, the global economy will affect you in a variety of ways. Exchange rates for different currencies and global markets for buying and selling are all of major importance to everyone, regardless of their role or perspective. As a result, this chapter will better enable you to (1) understand how global forces affect you as a customer, (2) understand how globalization affects you as an employee, and (3) assess how global opportunities and challenges can affect you as a business owner and an investor. You will also gain insights into how wages and working conditions in different regions are linked to what we buy and the prices we pay.

This chapter explores the global context of business. We begin with an exploration of the major world marketplaces and trade agreements that affect international business. Next, we examine several factors that help determine how countries and businesses respond to international opportunities and challenges. We then direct our attention to some of the decisions managers must make if they intend to compete in international markets. Finally, we conclude with a discussion of some of the social, cultural, economic, legal, and political factors that affect international business.

Paul Katzeff, founder of Thanksgiving Coffee Company, a California producer of specialty coffees, regards the U.S. embargo as impractical (on the grounds that it hasn't achieved its goals) and immoral (on the grounds that it punishes Cuban people rather than their government). Katzeff is thinking the same thing that many U.S. businesspeople are undoubtedly thinking: Repeal of the embargo will create new business opportunities. As he sees it, Cuban coffee has a promising post-embargo future. Its potential is enormous because of the quality of the coffee beans. Although Katzeff's geopolitics may rankle some people, his business sense seems sound. At present, of course, he can't actually do business with Cuban coffee growers, but he has figured out a way to lay a solid foundation. He has already established working relationships with coffee cooperatives—groups of individual growers who pool their crops to enter the export market and secure higher prices—in Latin America and Africa. His longer-term goal is to invest the same capital and acquired know-how in relationships with Cuban growers. The director of Thanksgiving's Cuba project, Nick Hoskins, has already developed contacts in Cuba's coffee-growing regions, and Katzeff hopes to establish a *twinning agreement*, an exchange of people-to-people programs, with cooperatives in the coffee-growing province of Santiago de Cuba. (After studying this chapter, you should be able to respond to the set of discussion questions found at the end of the chapter.)

OBJECTIVE 4-1
Discuss
the rise of international business and describe the major world marketplaces, trade agreements, and alliances.

Globalization *process by which the world economy is becoming a single interdependent system*

Import *product made or grown abroad but sold domestically*

Export *product made or grown domestically but shipped and sold abroad*

The Contemporary Global Economy

The total volume of world trade is immense—more than $19.3 trillion in merchandise is traded each year. Foreign investment in the United States exceeds $225 billion, and U.S. investment abroad is more than $395 billion.[3] As more firms engage in international business, the world economy is fast becoming an interdependent system through a process called **globalization**.

We often take for granted the diversity of products we can buy as a result of international trade. Your television, your shoes, and even your morning coffee or juice are probably **imports**, products made or grown abroad and sold domestically in the United States. At the same time, the success of many U.S. firms depends on **exports**, products made or grown here, such as machinery, electronic equipment, and grains, and shipped for sale abroad.

Firms such as McDonald's, Microsoft, Apple, and Starbucks have found international markets to be a fruitful area for growth. But firms sometime stumble when they try to expand abroad. Home Depot first opened and then closed dozens of stores in China, for example, because labor costs are so low there that few homeowners are interested in "do-it-yourself" projects. Similarly, Best Buy also closed its stores in China because consumers there tend to buy their electronics goods at lower prices from local or online merchants.[4] When Disney first opened a theme park in Hong Kong it performed poorly because Disney managers made the park too "American" and bungled the park's advertising campaign.

The impact of globalization doesn't stop with firms looking to open locations abroad or having to close locations that fail. Small firms with no international operations (for example, an independent coffee shop) may still buy from international suppliers, and even individual contractors or self-employed people can be affected by fluctuations in exchange rates.

Indeed, international trade is becoming increasingly important to most nations and their businesses. Many countries that once followed strict policies to protect domestic business now encourage trade just as aggressively. They are opening borders to foreign businesses, offering incentives for domestic businesses to expand internationally, and making it easier for foreign firms to partner with local firms. Likewise, as more industries and markets become global, so, too, are the firms that compete in them.

Several forces have combined to spark and sustain globalization. For one thing, governments and businesses are more aware of the benefits of globalization to

Some globalization protestors, like this man, fear that multinational companies will wipe out small domestic businesses like family farms.

businesses and shareholders. These benefits include the potential for higher standards of living and improved business profitability. New technologies have made international travel, communication, and commerce faster and cheaper than ever before. Finally, there are competitive pressures: Sometimes a firm must expand into foreign markets simply to keep up with competitors.

Globalization is not without its detractors. Some critics charge that globalization allows businesses to exploit workers in less-developed countries and bypass domestic environmental and tax regulations. For example, businesses pay workers in Vietnam and Indonesia lower wages than their counterparts in the United States. Factories in China are not subject to the same environmental protection laws as are firms in Europe. And businesses that headquarter their corporate offices in the Cayman Islands pay lower taxes. Critics also charge that globalization leads to the loss of cultural heritages and often benefits the rich more than the poor. For instance, as the English language becomes increasingly widespread throughout the world, some local languages are simply disappearing. Similarly, local residents in Africa receive relatively few economic benefits when oil or precious minerals are discovered on their land; prosperous investors buy the rights from landowners, who often don't realize the value of these resources. As a result, many international gatherings of global economic leaders are marked by protests and demonstrations.

The Major World Marketplaces

Managers involved with international businesses need a solid understanding of the global economy, including the major world marketplaces. This section examines some fundamental economic distinctions among countries based on wealth and then looks at some of the world's major international marketplaces.

Distinctions Based on Wealth The World Bank, an agency of the United Nations, uses per-capita income, average income per person, to make distinctions among countries. Its current classification method consists of four different categories of countries:[5]

1 *High-income countries:* Those with annual per-capita income greater than $12,476

2 *Upper-middle-income countries:* Those with annual per-capita income of $12,475 or less but more than $4,036

3 *Lower-middle-income countries:* Those with annual per-capita income of $4,035 or lower but more than $1,026

4 *Low-income countries* (often called *developing countries):* Those with annual per-capita income of $1,025 or less

Geographic Clusters The world economy generally revolves around three major marketplaces: North America, Europe, and Pacific Asia. In general, these clusters include relatively more of the upper-middle- and high-income nations but relatively few low- and lower-middle-income countries.

NORTH AMERICA As the world's largest marketplace and most stable economy, the United States dominates the North American market. Canada also plays a major role in the international economy, and the United States and Canada are among each other's largest trading partners.

Mexico has been a major manufacturing center, especially along the U.S. border, where cheap labor and low transportation costs have encouraged many firms from the United States and other countries to build factories. However, Mexico's role as a low-cost manufacturing center is in flux. Just a few years ago, many experts believed that the emergence of China as a low-cost manufacturing center would lead companies to begin to shift their production from Mexico to China.[6] (Drug-related violence along the northern Mexican border also contributed to this shift.)

EUROPE Europe is often regarded as two regions—Western and Eastern. Western Europe, dominated by Germany, the United Kingdom, and France, has long been a mature but fragmented marketplace. The transformation of this region via the European Union (discussed later in this chapter) into an integrated economic system has further increased its importance. E-commerce and technology have also become increasingly important in this region. There has been a surge in Internet start-ups in southeastern England, the Netherlands, and the Scandinavian countries; Ireland is now one of the world's largest exporters of software; Strasbourg, France, is a major center for biotech start-ups; Barcelona, Spain, has many flourishing software and Internet companies; and the Frankfurt region of Germany is dotted with software and biotech start-ups.

Eastern Europe, once primarily communist, has also gained in importance, both as a marketplace and as a producer. Such multinational corporations as Daewoo, Nestlé, General Motors, and ABB Asea Brown Boveri have all set up operations in Poland. Ford, General Motors, Suzuki, and Volkswagen have built new factories in Hungary. On the other hand, governmental instability, corruption, and uncertainty have hampered development in parts of Russia, Bulgaria, Albania, Romania, and other countries.

PACIFIC ASIA Pacific Asia is generally agreed to consist of Japan, China, Thailand, Malaysia, Singapore, Indonesia, South Korea, Taiwan, the Philippines, and Australia. Fueled by strong entries in the automobile, electronics, and banking industries, the economies of these countries grew rapidly in the 1970s and 1980s. After a currency crisis in the late 1990s that slowed growth in virtually every country of the region, Pacific Asia showed clear signs of revitalization until the global recession in 2009. As the global economy begins to regain its momentum, Pacific Asia is expected to again be in the forefront. This is especially true of Japan, which, led by firms such as Toyota, Toshiba, and Nippon Steel, dominates the region. South Korea (home to firms Samsung and Hyundai, among others), Taiwan (owner of Chinese Petroleum and the manufacturing home of many foreign firms), and Hong Kong (a major financial center) are also successful players in the international economy.

China, one of the world's most densely populated countries, has emerged as an important market and now boasts one of the world's largest economies. Although its per-capita income remains low, the sheer number of potential consumers makes it an important market. India, though not part of Pacific Asia, is also rapidly emerging as one of the globe's most important economies. As in North America and Europe, technology promises to play an increasingly important role in the future of this region. In some parts of Asia, however, poorly developed electronic infrastructures,

finding a better way

Too Much of a Good Thing? China's Success Creates More Jobs in Mexico

In today's competitive global economy, businesses strive for every possible advantage. Many manufacturers, for example, locate their factories in countries that have an ample supply of low-cost skilled labor. During the 1980s and 1990s, the place to be was Mexico. Hundreds of factories were built just across the U.S.–Mexican border, and workers streamed to the region from other parts of Mexico for stable and well-paying jobs. But in the late 1990s, the world started to shift.

Mexican prosperity, fueled in part by its role as a center of manufacturing, led to increases in the cost of living, followed quickly by wage increases so workers could keep up. At about that same time, China began to emerge as an attractive manufacturing alternative. For instance, in 2003, wages in China were only one-third of the wages in Mexico. And there was certainly no shortage of workers eager to take steady jobs in factories making products for other countries. China's boom was Mexico's bust, as one company after another reduced or eliminated manufacturing there and moved to Asia.

In recent years, things have started to tilt back in Mexico's favor. As China's economy has flourished, its labor costs have crept higher and higher, so it's less of a bargain than it used to be. Whereas Mexican wages were once three times higher than wages in China, Mexican wages today are more than 40 percent less than those in China, according to research by Merrill Lynch.[7] When manufacturers factor in shipping costs (which have increased because of fuel prices), producing in Mexico may cost the same or less than in China. Time differences between the United States and China also can make it difficult to schedule videoconferences and telephone calls.

Vario images GmbH & Co.KG/Alamy Stock Photo

Several companies have also been burned by China's lack of protection for industrial and intellectual property.

Mexico is making enormous gains in the automobile sector. Companies such as Nissan, Honda, Volkswagen, and Mazda have invested billions of dollars in Mexican production vehicles, with over 3.4 million vehicles produced in 2016.[8] Eighty percent of these cars are exported to other countries, with the bulk being sent to the United States. Because of NAFTA, as well as other trade agreements, Mexico can export cars without tariffs to North and South America as well as Europe and Japan. According to Volkswagen's Vice President of Corporate Affairs in Mexico, "There's not another country in the world where you can do that."[9] However, the future is uncertain, as the U.S. moves to renegotiate NAFTA and puts pressure on U.S. companies to dissuade them from investing in more projects in Mexico.

slower adoption of computers and information technology, and a higher percentage of lower-income consumers hamper the emergence of technology firms.

Trade Agreements and Alliances

Various legal agreements have sparked international trade and shaped the global business environment. Virtually every nation has formal trade treaties with other nations. A *treaty* is a legal agreement that specifies areas in which nations will cooperate with one another. Among the most significant treaties is the *North American Free Trade Agreement*. The *European Union*, the *Association of Southeast Asian Nations*, and the *World Trade Organization*, all governed by treaties, are also instrumental in promoting international business activity.

North American Free Trade Agreement The **North American Free Trade Agreement (NAFTA)** removed most tariffs and other trade barriers among the United States, Canada, and Mexico and includes agreements on environmental issues and labor abuses.

North American Free Trade Agreement (NAFTA) *agreement to gradually eliminate tariffs and other trade barriers among the United States, Canada, and Mexico*

Most observers agree that NAFTA is achieving its basic purpose—to create a more active and unified North American market. It has created several hundred thousand new jobs, although this number is smaller than NAFTA proponents had hoped. One thing is clear, though; the flood of U.S. jobs lost to Mexico predicted by NAFTA critics, especially labor unions, has not occurred. (It is also worth noting that during the 2016 presidential campaign Donald Trump said that NAFTA was one of the worst treaties ever signed and that, if elected, he would seriously consider cancelling it. It remains to be seen, however, if he will carry through on this statement.)

European Union (EU) *agreement among major European nations to eliminate or make uniform most trade barriers affecting group members*

The European Union The **European Union (EU)** includes most European nations, as shown in Figure 4.1. These nations have eliminated most quotas and set uniform tariff levels on products imported and exported within their group. In 1992, virtually all internal trade barriers went down, making the EU the largest free marketplace in the world. The adoption of a common currency, the *euro*, by most member nations further solidified the EU's position in the world economy. In early 2016 the citizens of the United Kingdom, one of the most important members of the EU, voted to withdraw from the Union. The withdrawal process was formally initiated by the government of the United Kingdom in March 2017 and is scheduled to be completed by April 2019. However, its complete impact won't be fully understood for several years.

Note: Citizens of the United Kingdom voted in 2016 to withdraw from the European Union (shown in purple). This process formally began in March 2017 and is expected to be completed by April 2019.

FIGURE 4.1 The Nations of the European Union
Source: European Union, http://europa.eu/eurpean-union/index_en, accessed April 5, 2013.

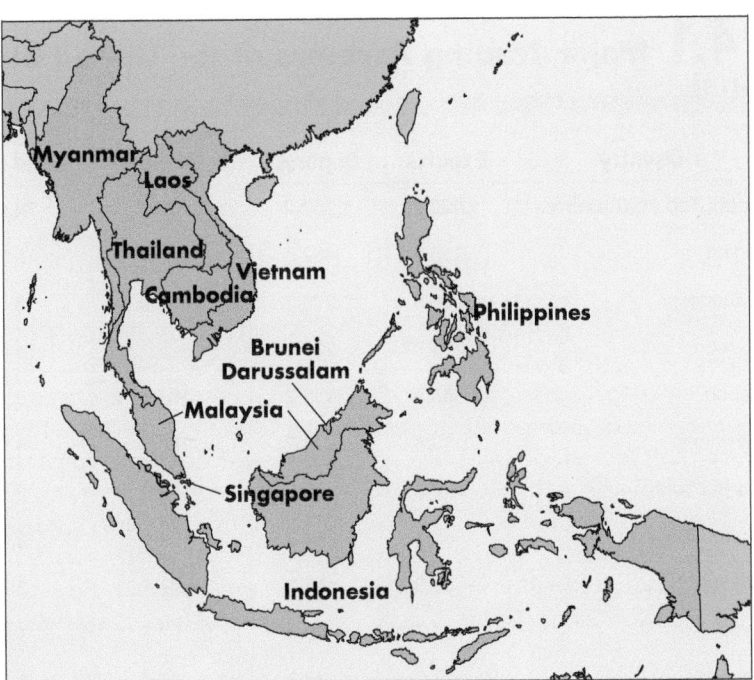

FIGURE 4.2 The Nations of the Association of Southeast Asian Nations (ASEAN)

The Association of Southeast Asian Nations The **Associa-tion of Southeast Asian Nations (ASEAN)** was founded in 1967 as an organization for economic, political, social, and cultural cooperation. In 1995, Vietnam became the group's first communist member. Figure 4.2 shows a map of the ASEAN countries. Because of its relative size, the ASEAN does not have the same global economic significance as NAFTA and the EU.

> **Association of Southeast Asian Nations (ASEAN)** *organization for economic, political, social, and cultural cooperation among Southeast Asian nations*

The World Trade Organization The **General Agreement on Tariffs and Trade (GATT)** was signed in 1947. Its purpose was to reduce or eliminate trade barriers, such as tariffs and quotas. It did so by encouraging nations to protect domestic industries within agreed-on limits and to engage in multilateral negotiations. The GATT proved to be relatively successful. So, to further promote globalization, most of the world's countries joined to create the **World Trade Organization (WTO)**, which began on January 1, 1995. (The GATT is the actual treaty that governs the WTO.) The 160 member countries are required to open markets to international trade, and the WTO is empowered to pursue three goals:[10]

> **General Agreement on Tariffs and Trade (GATT)** *international trade agreement to encourage the multilateral reduction or elimination of trade barriers*

> **World Trade Organization (WTO)** *organization through which member nations negotiate trading agreements and resolve disputes about trade policies and practices*

1 Promote trade by encouraging members to adopt fair-trade practices.

2 Reduce trade barriers by promoting multilateral negotiations.

3 Establish fair procedures for resolving disputes among members.

International Trade

The global economy is essentially defined by international trade. International trade occurs when an exchange involving goods, services, and/or currency takes place across national boundaries. Although international trade has many advantages, it can also pose problems if a country's imports and exports don't maintain an acceptable balance. Table 4.1 lists the United States's 15 largest trading partners. However, the United States also does business with many more countries. For instance, in 2013, the United States exported $5.1 billion to Egypt, $2.4 billion to Kuwait, $3.0 billion

> **OBJECTIVE 4-2**
> **Explain**
> how differences in import–export balances, exchange rates, and foreign competition determine the ways in which countries and businesses respond to the international environment.

table 4.1 Major Trading Partners of the United States (in Millions)

Rank	Country	Exports	Imports	Total Trade	Percent of Total Trade
	Total, Top 15 Countries	1,022.2	1,707.2	2,729.4	74.9%
1	China	115.8	462.8	578.6	15.9%
2	Canada	266.8	278.1	544.9	15.0%
3	Mexico	231.0	294.2	525.1	14.4%
4	Japan	63.3	132.2	195.5	5.4%
5	Germany	49.4	114.2	163.6	4.5%
6	Korea, South	42.3	69.9	112.2	3.1%
7	United Kingdom	55.4	54.3	109.7	3.0%
8	France	30.9	46.8	77.7	2.1%
9	India	21.7	46.0	67.7	1.9%
10	Taiwan	26.0	39.3	65.4	1.8%
11	Italy	16.8	45.2	62.0	1.7%
12	Switzerland	22.7	36.4	59.1	1.6%
13	Netherlands	40.4	16.2	56.5	1.6%
14	Brazil	30.3	26.2	56.5	1.5%
15	Ireland	9.6	45.5	55.1	1.5%

Source: http://www.census.gov/foreign-trade/statistics/highlights/top/top1512yr.html

to Poland, and $132.9 million to Zambia; imports from those same countries were $2.8 billion, $12.2 billion, $4.2 billion, and $62 million, respectively. In deciding whether an overall balance exists between imports and exports, economists use two measures: *balance of trade* and *balance of payments*.

Balance of Trade

Balance of Trade *economic value of all products a country exports minus the economic value of all products it imports*

A country's **balance of trade** is the total economic value of all the products that it exports minus the economic value of all the products that it imports. A *positive balance of trade* results when a country exports (sells to other countries) more than it imports (buys from other countries). A *negative balance of trade* results when a country imports more than it exports.

Relatively small trade imbalances are common and are unimportant. Large imbalances, however, are another matter. The biggest concern about trade balances involves the flow of currency. When U.S. consumers and businesses buy foreign products, dollars flow from the United States to other countries; when U.S. businesses are selling to foreign consumers and businesses, dollars flow back into the United States. A large negative balance of trade means that many dollars are controlled by interests outside the United States.

Trade Deficit *situation in which a country's imports exceed its exports, creating a negative balance of trade*

Trade Surplus *situation in which a country's exports exceed its imports, creating a positive balance of trade*

A **trade deficit** occurs when a country's imports exceed its exports, when it has a negative balance of trade. When exports exceed imports, the nation enjoys a **trade surplus**. Several factors, such as general economic conditions and the effect of trade agreements, influence trade deficits and surpluses. For example, higher domestic costs, greater international competition, and continuing economic problems among some of its regional trading partners have slowed the tremendous growth in exports

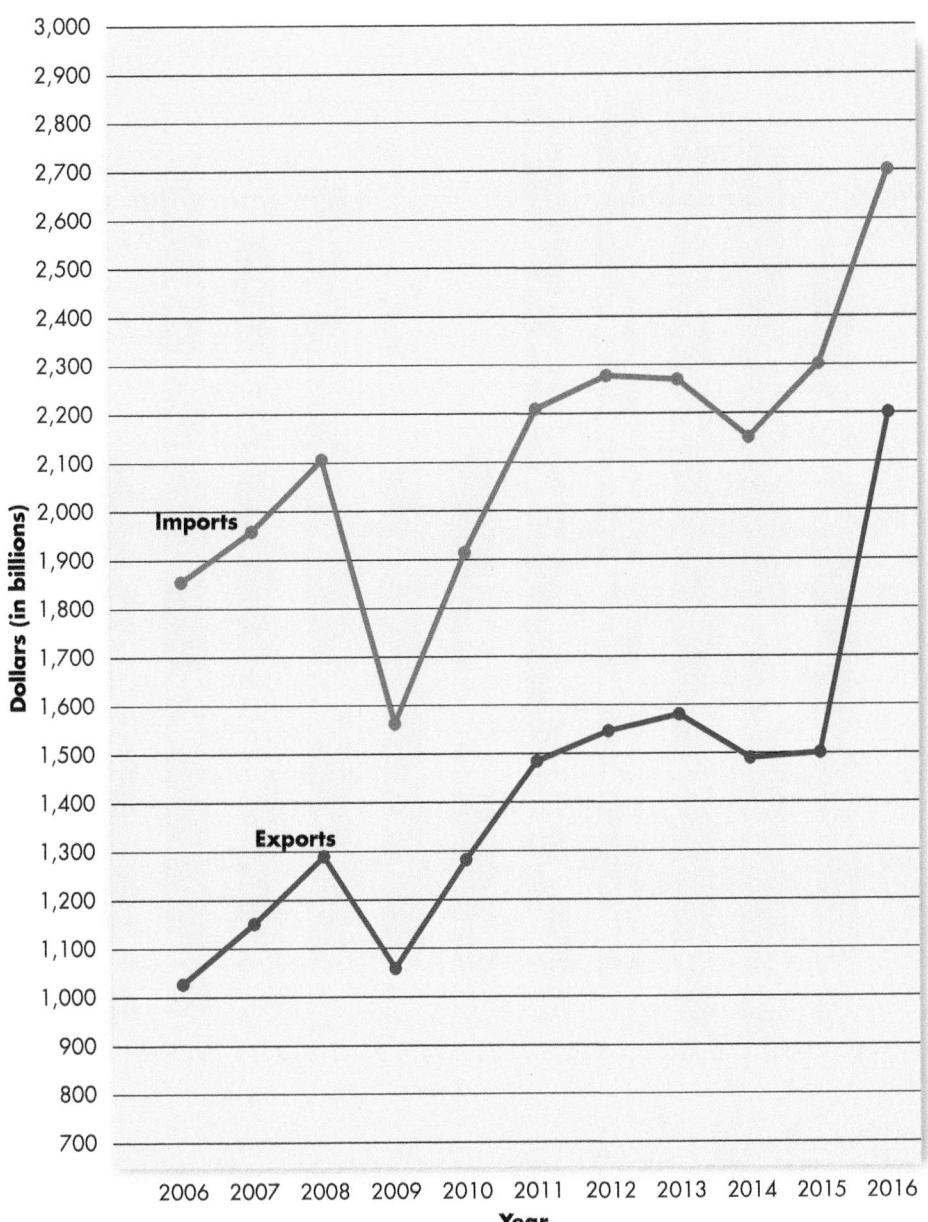

FIGURE 4.3 U.S. Imports and Exports
Source: http://www.census.gov/foreign-trade/

that Japan once enjoyed. But rising prosperity in China and India has led to strong increases in both exports from and imports to those countries.

Figures 4.3 and 4.4 highlight two series of events: (1) recent trends in U.S. exports and imports and (2) the resulting trade deficit. As Figure 4.3 shows, both U.S. imports and U.S. exports, with minor variations, have been generally increasing—a trend that's projected to continue.

Trade deficits between 2005 and 2016 are shown in Figure 4.4. There was a deficit in each of these years because more money flowed out to pay for foreign imports than flowed in to pay for U.S. exports. For example, in 2016, the United States exported $2.2 trillion in goods and services and imported $2.7 trillion in goods and services. Because imports exceeded exports, the United States had a *trade deficit* of $500 billion (the difference between exports and imports). Note also that both exports and imports declined in 2009 from the previous year. This was a result of the global economic slowdown during that period.

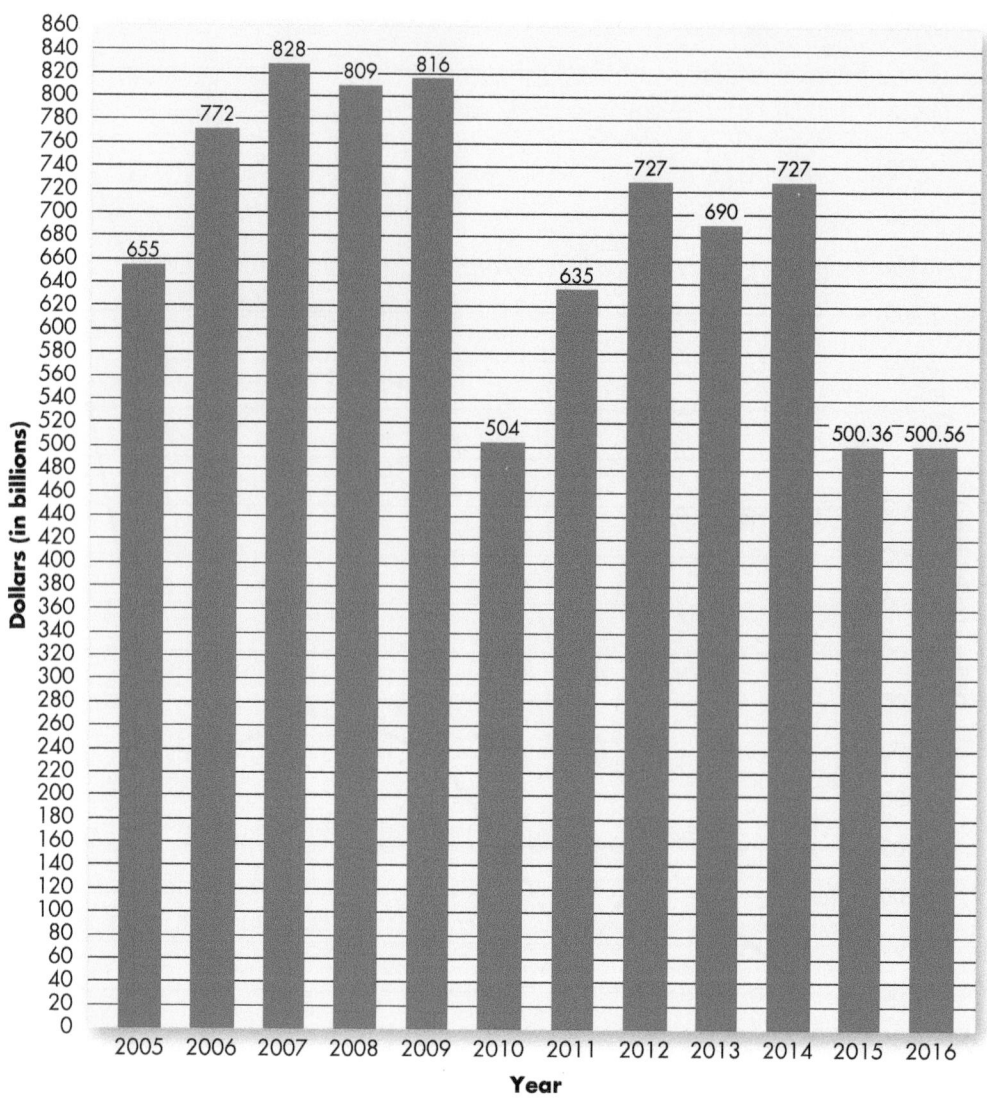

FIGURE 4.4 U.S. Trade Deficit
Source: U.S. Census Bureau: Foreign Trade Statistics, at http://www.census.gov/foreign-trade/statistics/highlights/annual.html, accessed 2016

Balance of Payments

Balance of Payments *flow of all money into or out of a country*

The **balance of payments** refers to the flow of *money* into or out of a country. The money that a country pays for imports and receives for exports, its balance of trade, accounts for much of its balance of payments. Other financial exchanges are also factors. Money spent by tourists in a country, money spent by a country on foreign-aid programs, and money exchanged by buying and selling currency on international money markets affect the balance of payments.

For instance, suppose that the United States has a negative balance of trade of $1 million. Now, suppose that this year, U.S. citizens travel abroad as tourists and spend a total of $200,000 in other countries. This amount gets added to the balance of trade to form the balance of payments, which is now a negative $1.2 million. Now, further suppose that tourists from other countries come to the United States and spend the equivalent of $300,000 while they are here. This has the effect of reducing the negative balance of payments to $900,000. Then, further suppose that the United States then sends $600,000 in aid to help the victims of a tsunami-ravaged country in Asia. Because this represents additional dollars leaving the United States, the balance of payments is now a negative $1.5 million. For many years, the United States enjoyed a positive balance of payments. Recently, however, the overall balance has become negative.

Exchange Rates

The balance of imports and exports between two countries is affected by the rate of exchange between their currencies. An **exchange rate** is the rate at which the currency of one nation can be exchanged for that of another. Suppose, for example, that the exchange rate between the U.S. dollar and the British pound was $2 to £1. This means that it costs £1 to "buy" $2 or $1 to "buy" £0.5. Stated differently, £1 and $2 have the same purchasing power, or £1 = $2.

At the end of World War II, the major nations of the world agreed to set *fixed exchange rates*. The value of any country's currency relative to that of another would remain constant. The goal was to allow the global economy to stabilize. Today, however, *floating exchange rates* are the norm, and the value of one country's currency relative to that of another varies with market conditions. For example, when many British citizens want to spend pounds to buy U.S. dollars (or goods), the value of the dollar relative to the pound increases. Demand for the dollar is high, and a currency is strong when demand for it is high. It's also strong when there's high demand for the goods manufactured with that currency. On a daily basis, exchange rates fluctuate very little. Significant variations usually occur over longer time spans. Highly regulated economic systems such as in China are among the few that still use fixed exchange rates. The Chinese government regulates the flow of currency—its own as well as all others—into and out of China and determines the precise rate of exchange within its borders.

Exchange-rate fluctuation can have an important impact on balance of trade. Suppose you want to buy some English tea for £10 per box. At an exchange rate of $2 to £1, a box will cost you $20 (£10 × 2 = 20). But what if the pound is weaker? At an exchange rate of, say, $1.25 to £1, the same box would cost you only $12.50 (£10 × 1.25 = 12.50). If the dollar is strong in relation to the pound, the prices of all U.S.-made products will rise in England, and the prices of all English-made products will fall in the United States. The English would buy fewer U.S. products, and Americans would be prompted to spend more on English-made products. The result would probably be a U.S. trade deficit with England.

One of the most significant developments in foreign exchange has been the introduction of the **euro**, the common currency of the EU. The euro was officially introduced in 2002 and has replaced several other currencies, such as the German Deutsche Mark, the Italian lira, and the French franc. In the years since its debut, the euro has become one of the world's most important currencies. When it was first introduced, the euro's value was pegged as being equivalent to the dollar: €1 = $1. But because the dollar was relatively weak in the years that followed, its value eroded relative to that of the euro. At one point in the late 1990s, $1 was worth only about half a euro. In the aftermath of the Great Recession, though, the dollar has strengthened relative to the euro and the exchange in early 2017 was $1 = €.94.

Companies with international operations must watch exchange-rate fluctuations closely because changes affect overseas demand for their products and can be a major factor in competition. In general, when the value of a country's currency rises—becomes stronger—companies based there find it harder to export products to foreign markets and easier for foreign companies to enter local markets. It also makes it more cost-efficient for domestic companies to move operations to lower-cost foreign sites. When the value of a currency declines—becomes weaker—the opposite occurs. As the value of a country's currency falls, its balance of trade usually improves because domestic companies should experience a boost in exports. There should also be less reason for foreign companies to ship products into the domestic market and less reason to establish operations in other countries.

Exchange Rate *rate at which the currency of one nation can be exchanged for the currency of another nation*

Euro *a common currency shared among most of the members of the EU (excluding Denmark, Sweden, and the United Kingdom)*

Forms of Competitive Advantage

Before we discuss the fundamental issues involved in international business management, we must consider one last factor: forms of *competitive advantage*. Because no country can produce everything that it needs, countries tend to export what they can produce better or less expensively than other countries and use the proceeds to import what they can't produce as effectively. This principle doesn't fully explain why nations export and import what they do. Such decisions hinge partly on the advantages that a particular country enjoys regarding its abilities to create or sell certain products and resources.[11] Economists traditionally focused on absolute and comparative advantage to explain international trade. But because this approach focuses narrowly on such factors as natural resources and labor costs, a more contemporary view of national competitive advantage has emerged.

Absolute Advantage *the ability to produce something more efficiently than any other country can*

Absolute Advantage An **absolute advantage** exists when a country can produce something that is cheaper or of higher quality than any other country. Saudi Arabian oil, Brazilian coffee beans, and Canadian timber come close (because these countries have such abundant supplies of these resources), but examples of true absolute advantage are rare. For example, many experts say that the vineyards of France produce the world's finest wines. But the burgeoning wine business in California demonstrates that producers there can also make good wines—wines that rival those from France but come in more varieties and at lower prices.

Comparative Advantage *the ability to produce some products more efficiently than others*

Comparative Advantage A country has a **comparative advantage** in goods that it can produce more efficiently or better than other nations. If businesses in a given country can make computers more efficiently than they can make automobiles, then that nation has a comparative advantage in computer manufacturing.

managing in turbulent times

The Ups and Downs of Globalization

As markets move toward globalization, many countries are experiencing an identity crisis of sorts. The U.S. is rethinking its relationship with the World Trade Organization and NAFTA and reconsidering trade embargos with countries like Myanmar and Cuba. In Britain, after 43 years of strained relations with the European Union (EU), a large portion of the citizens pushed for the United Kingdom to exit the union. This movement took on the name "Brexit."

The European Union was formed after World War II to foster economic cooperation, and has grown to become a "single market," essentially allowing goods and people to move around as if the member states were one country. It has its own currency, the euro, which is used by 19 of the member countries (but not Great Britain), and its own parliament. Being part of the single market gave UK businesses easy access to all 500 million customers in the member countries and allowed UK consumers and companies to purchase goods and services from across the continent free of most tariffs and restrictions. It also allowed the relatively free movement of people across borders, much as the people of the US are free to move from state to state. Still, the British people continued to voice concerns over continued participation in the EU.

In 2015, as part of his campaign for re-election, Prime Minister David Cameron promised to put a referendum on the ballot asking voters to decide if they wanted to stay in the EU or exit. The expected logical outcome was to remain with the EU,

Creativa Images/Shutterstock

but the pivotal issues turned out to be a British desire for sovereignty and a fear of immigrants pouring into the country. On the day of the vote, with a 72 percent turnout, 51.9 percent of voters opted to leave.[12] Cameron, who had relied on the benefits of belonging to the EU as the cornerstone of his administration, resigned the day of the vote. The actual exit is a two-year process that is expected to culminate in 2019.

What does this mean for businesses around the world? As the economy and political climates change, expect to see traditional, long-standing relationships, treaties, and trade organizations struggle to keep up with the ups and downs of globalization.

In general, both absolute and comparative advantages translate into competitive advantage. Brazil, for instance, can produce and market coffee beans knowing full well that few other countries have the right mix of climate, terrain, and altitude to enter the coffee bean market. The United States has comparative advantages in the computer industry (because of technological sophistication) and in farming (because of large amounts of fertile land and a temperate climate). South Korea has a comparative advantage in electronics manufacturing because of efficient operations and cheap labor. As a result of each country's comparative advantage, U.S. firms export computers and grain to South Korea and import DVD players from South Korea. South Korea can produce food, and the United States can build DVD players, but each nation imports certain products because the other holds a comparative advantage in the relevant industry.

National Competitive Advantage In recent years, a theory of national competitive advantage has become a widely accepted model of why nations engage in international trade.[13] **National competitive advantage** derives from four conditions:

1   *Factor conditions* are the factors of production we discussed in Chapter 1— *labor, capital, entrepreneurs, physical resources*, and *information resources*.

2   *Demand conditions* reflect a large domestic consumer base that promotes strong demand for innovative products.

3   *Related and supporting industries* include strong local or regional suppliers or industrial customers.

4   *Strategies, structures, and rivalries* refer to firms and industries that stress cost reduction, product quality, higher productivity, and innovative products.

National Competitive Advantage
international competitive advantage stemming from a combination of factor conditions, demand conditions, related and supporting industries, and firm strategies, structures, and rivalries

When all attributes of national competitive advantage exist, a nation is likely to be heavily involved in international business. Japan, for instance, has an abundance of natural resources and strong domestic demand for automobiles. Its carmakers have well-oiled supplier networks, and domestic firms have competed intensely with one another for decades. These circumstances explain why Japanese car companies such as Toyota and Honda are successful in foreign markets.

International Business Management

OBJECTIVE 4-3
Discuss
the factors involved in deciding to do business internationally and in selecting the appropriate levels of international involvement and international organizational structure.

Regardless of where a firm is located, its success depends largely on how well it's managed. International business is so challenging because basic management tasks— planning, organizing, directing, and controlling—are much more difficult when a firm operates in markets scattered around the globe.

Managing means making decisions. In this section, we examine the three basic decisions that a company must make when considering globalization. The first decision is whether to go international. Once that decision has been made, managers must decide on the level of international involvement and on the organizational structure that will best meet the firm's global needs.

Going International

As the world economy becomes increasingly globalized, more and more firms are expanding their international operations. U.S. firms are aggressively expanding abroad, and foreign companies such as BP and Nestlé continue to expand into foreign markets as well, including the U.S. market. This route, however, isn't appropriate for every company. If you buy and sell fresh fish, you'll probably find it more profitable to confine your activities to limited geographic areas because storage and transport costs may be too high to make international operations worthwhile. As Figure 4.5 shows, several factors affect the decision to go international.

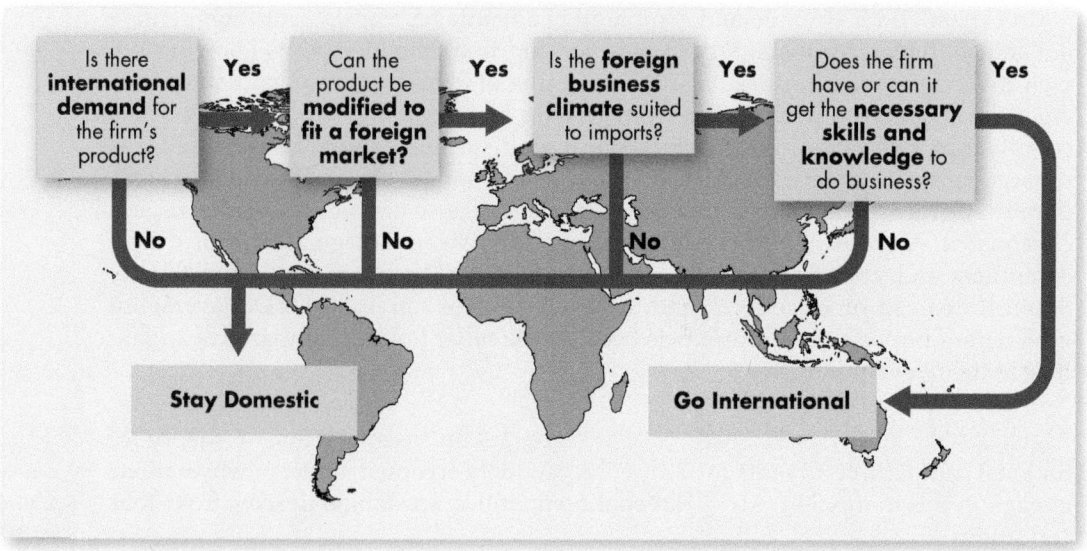

FIGURE 4.5 Going International

Gauging International Demand In considering international expansion, a company must determine whether there is a demand for its products abroad. Products that are successful in one country may be useless in another. Even when there is demand, advertising and promotion may still need to be adjusted. For example, bicycles are largely used for recreation in the United States but are seen as basic transportation in China. Hence, a bicycle maker would need to use different marketing strategies in each of these countries. Market research or the prior market entry of competitors may indicate whether there's an international demand for a firm's products.

Adapting to Customer Needs If its product is in demand, a firm must decide whether and how to adapt it to meet the special demands of foreign customers. For example, to satisfy local tastes, McDonald's sells wine in France, beer in Germany, gazpacho in Spain, and some vegetarian sandwiches in India. Likewise, consumer electronics companies have to be aware that different countries use different kinds of electric sockets and different levels of electric power. Therefore, regardless of demand, customer needs must still be considered.

Outsourcing *the practice of paying suppliers and distributors to perform certain business processes or to provide needed materials or services*

Offshoring *the practice of outsourcing to foreign countries*

Outsourcing and Offshoring **Outsourcing**, the practice of paying suppliers and distributors to perform certain business processes or to provide needed materials or services, has become a popular option for going international. It has become so popular because (1) it helps firms focus on their core activities and avoid getting sidetracked on secondary activities, and (2) it reduces costs by locating certain business functions in areas where relevant costs are low.[14]

The practice of outsourcing to foreign countries is more specifically referred to as **offshoring**. Many companies today contract their manufacturing to low-cost factories in Asia. Similarly, many service call centers today are outsourced to businesses located in India. The Oscar-winning movie *Slumdog Millionaire* featured a young Indian man who worked for an international call center in Mumbai. In real life, DirecTV, Chase Bank Credit Card Services, and several home mortgage support businesses have established call centers in India and have enjoyed considerable success. On the other hand, though, the network of FTD florists opened a call center in India but subsequently closed it. As it turns out, many people who call to order flowers need more personal assistance—advice on types of flowers, colors of arrangements, and so forth—than can be provided by someone from a different culture on the other side of the world.

entrepreneurship and new ventures

A Better Coconut Water

Founded in 2009, Harmless Harvest is the manufacturer and distributor of a popular line of organic coconut water that is available in stores across the United States. Douglas Riboud and Justin Guilbert saw an opportunity with the sudden popularity of coconut water, but they were troubled by environmental and economic concerns. After extensive research, Riboud and Guilbert concluded that the best-tasting coconut water could be produced from a single species of coconut from Thailand, in spite of lower yields and more complex cultivation. Unlike other producers, their coconut water is pasteurized through high-pressure treatment rather than heat, creating a raw, better-tasting product. According to Riboud, "The most important thing for us is taste. And the best we can do, the hardest job you can do as a manufacturer who works in food, is not screw up the ingredient you had in the first place."[15]

Harmless Harvest has addressed environmental concerns by making sure that their product is organic. They made an early commitment to working with farmers to make sure that no harmful pesticides or synthetic fertilizers were used and worked to obtain organic certification. Although this process was time-consuming and costly, it assured Riboud and Guilbert that their entire supply chain was built upon their vision of sustainability.

Finally, Harmless Harvest has contributed to economic change in a number of ways. In 2015, Harmless Harvest combined its Nam Hom coconut water with organic coffee, creating a drink with 50 mg of naturally occurring caffeine, the equivalent of a shot of espresso. The Peruvian cooperative that harvests Harmless Harvest's organic coffee beans has a focus on empowering women and the impoverished, with over 50 percent of members located in areas of extreme poverty. The organization has seen a significant decrease in domestic abuse against women, as well as an increased priority on educating children to strengthen the community as a whole. Guilbert notes that, "Sourcing from this cooperative is just another proof that better products can be made to benefit everyone involved. It's worth the extra effort."[16]

Brent T. Madison/Alamy Stock Photo

Levels of International Involvement

After deciding to go international, a firm must determine the level of its involvement. Several levels are possible: A firm may act as an exporter or importer, organize as an international firm, or (like most of the world's largest industrial firms) operate as a multinational firm.

Exporters and Importers An **exporter** makes products in one country to distribute and sell in others. An **importer** buys products in foreign markets and brings them home for resale. Both conduct most of their business in their home nations. Both entail the lowest level of involvement in international operations, and both are good ways to learn the fine points of global business. Many large firms entered international business as exporters. General Electric and Coca Cola, among others, exported to Europe for several years before setting up production sites there. It is also useful to remember that most import–export transactions involve both activities. A bottle of French wine sold in New York, for instance, was exported by the French winery but simultaneously imported by a U.S. wine distributor.

Exporter *firm that distributes and sells products to one or more foreign countries*

Importer *firm that buys products in foreign markets and then imports them for resale in its home country*

International Firm *firm that conducts a significant portion of its business in foreign countries*

International Firms As exporters and importers gain experience and grow, many move to the next level of involvement. **International firms** conduct a meaningful amount of their business abroad and may even maintain overseas manufacturing facilities. An international firm may be large, but it's still basically a domestic company with international operations. Hershey, for instance, buys ingredients for its chocolates from several foreign suppliers and makes all of its products in the United States, but it has one plant in Mexico. Moreover, although it sells its products in approximately 70 other countries, it generates most of its revenues from its domestic market.[17]

Multinational Firm *firm that designs, produces, and markets products in many nations*

Multinational Firms Most **multinational firms**, firms that design, produce, and market products in many nations, such as ExxonMobil, Nestlé, Honda, and Ford, don't think of themselves as having domestic and international divisions. Headquarters locations are almost irrelevant, and planning and decision making are geared to international markets. The world's largest non-U.S. multinationals in 2016 based on sales, profits, and employees, are shown in Table 4.2.

We can't underestimate the economic impact of multinational firms. Consider just the impact of the 500 largest multinationals: In 2015, these 500 firms generated $27.6 trillion in revenues and $1.5 trillion in owner profits.[18] They employed tens of millions of people, bought materials and equipment from literally thousands of other firms, and paid billions in taxes. Moreover, their products affected the lives of hundreds of millions of consumers, competitors, investors, and even protestors.

International Organization Structures

Different levels of international involvement entail different kinds of organizational structures. A structure that would help coordinate an exporter's activities would be inadequate for those of a multinational. In this section, we consider the spectrum of

table 4.2 The World's Largest Non-U.S. Companies by Sales, Profits, and Number of Employees (2016)

Company	Sales ($millions)	Profits ($billions)	Employees
State Grid	329, 601		
China Nat'l Petro.	299,271		
Sinopec	294,344		
Royal Dutch Shell	272,156		
Volkswagen	236,592		
Industrial and Commercial Bank of China		44.2	
China Construction Bank		36.4	
Bank of China		27.2	
Agricultural Bank of China		28.8	
HSBC		13.5	
Hon Hai Precision Industries			1,290,000
Volkswagen			593,000
Petro China			535,000
Compass Group			515,000
Tesco			510,000

Sources: The Fortune 2016 Global 500 (fortune.com); The World's Most Profitable Companies (forbes.com)

organizational strategies, including *independent agents, licensing arrangements, branch offices, strategic alliances,* and *foreign direct investment.*

Independent Agents An **independent agent** is a foreign individual or organization that represents an exporter in foreign markets. Independent agents often act as sales representatives: They sell the exporter's products, collect payment, and make sure that customers are satisfied. They often represent several firms at once and usually don't specialize in a particular product or market. Peter So operates an import–export office in Hong Kong. He and his staff of three handle imports from about 15 foreign companies into Hong Kong and about 10 Hong Kong firms that export products abroad.

Independent Agent *foreign individual or organization that agrees to represent an exporter's interests*

Licensing Arrangements Companies seeking more involvement may opt for licensing arrangements. A **licensing arrangement** is a contract under which one firm allows another to use its brand name, operating procedures, or proprietary technology. Firms give foreign individuals or companies exclusive rights (called *licensing agreements*) to manufacture or market their products in that market. In return, the exporter receives a fee plus ongoing payments (royalties) that are calculated as a percentage of the license holder's sales. Franchising is a popular form of licensing. For example, McDonald's, Pizza Hut, and Hertz Car Rental have franchises around the world.

Licensing Arrangement *arrangement in which firms choose foreign individuals or organizations to manufacture or market their products in another country*

Branch Offices Instead of developing relationships with foreign agents or licensing companies, a firm may send its own managers to overseas branch offices, where the firm has more direct control than it does over agents or license holders. **Branch offices** also furnish a more visible public presence in foreign countries, and foreign customers tend to feel more secure when there's a local branch office. Halliburton, a Houston-based oil field supply and services company, opened a branch office in Dubai to more effectively establish relationships with customers in the Middle East.

Branch Office *foreign office set up by an international or multinational firm*

Strategic Alliances In a **strategic alliance**, a company finds a partner in the country in which it wants to do business. Each party agrees to invest resources and capital into a new business or to cooperate in some mutually beneficial way. This new business, the alliance, is owned by the partners, who divide its profits. Such alliances are sometimes called *joint ventures,* but the term *strategic alliance* has arisen because such partnerships are playing increasingly important roles in the strategies of major companies. Ford and Russian automaker Sollers have a joint venture in Russia. Sollers manufactures Ford products in Russia and the two partners work together on marketing them.[19] In many countries, such as Mexico, India, and China, laws make alliances virtually the only way to do international business. Mexico, for example, requires that all foreign firms investing there have local partners. Likewise, local interests own the majority of both Disney theme parks in China; Disney is the minority owner but also collects management and licensing fees.

Strategic Alliance *arrangement (also called joint venture) in which a company finds a foreign partner to contribute approximately half of the resources needed to establish and operate a new business in the partner's country*

In addition to easing the way into new markets, alliances give firms greater control over foreign activities than agents and licensees. Alliances also allow firms to benefit from the knowledge and expertise of foreign partners. Microsoft, for example, relies heavily on alliances when it expands into new international markets. This approach has helped the firm learn the intricacies of doing business in China and India, two of the hardest emerging markets to crack.

Foreign Direct Investment **Foreign direct investment (FDI)** involves buying or establishing tangible assets in another country. Dell Computer, for example, has built assembly plants in Europe and China. Volkswagen has built a factory in Brazil, and Coca-Cola has built bottling plants in dozens of different countries. FedEx has a major distribution center in Paris. Each of these activities represents FDI by a firm in another country.

Foreign Direct Investment (FDI) *arrangement in which a firm buys or establishes tangible assets in another country*

Understanding the Cultural Environment

A major factor in the success—or failure—of international business activity is having a deep understanding of the cultural environment and how it affects business. As mentioned earlier, Disney's Hong Kong theme park struggled after it first opened, in large part because Disney made the mistake of minimizing all elements of Chinese culture in the park—essentially making it a generic miniature reproduction of the original Disneyland in California. Disney also confused potential visitors with ads showing a father, mother, and two children walking hand-in-hand toward the theme park, overlooking China's laws that restrict many families to a single child. Only after a refurbishment to make the park more Chinese and a revised ad campaign did attendance begin to improve.[20] A country's culture includes all the values, symbols, beliefs, and language that guide behavior.

Values, Symbols, Beliefs, and Language

Cultural values and beliefs are often unspoken; they may even be taken for granted by those who live in a particular country. Cultural factors do not necessarily cause problems for managers when the cultures of two countries are similar. Difficulties can arise, however, when there is little overlap between the home culture of a manager and the culture of the country in which business is to be conducted. For example, most U.S. managers find the culture and traditions of England relatively familiar. The people of both countries speak the same language and share strong historical roots, and there is a history of strong commerce between the two countries. When U.S. managers begin operations in Japan or the Middle East, however, most of those commonalities disappear.

In Japanese, the word *hai* (pronounced "hi") means "yes." In conversation, however, this word is used much like people in the United States use "uh-huh"; it moves a conversation along or shows the person with whom you are talking that you are paying attention. So when does *hai* mean "yes" and when does it mean "uh-huh"? This turns out to be a relatively difficult question to answer. If a U.S. manager asks a Japanese manager if he agrees to some trade arrangement, the Japanese manager is likely to say, "Hai"—but this may mean "Yes, I agree," "Yes, I understand," or "Yes, I am listening." Some U.S. managers become frustrated in negotiations with the Japanese because they believe that the Japanese continue to raise issues that have already been settled (because the Japanese managers said "Yes"). What many of these managers fail to recognize is that "yes" does not always mean "yes" in Japan.

Cultural differences between countries can have a direct impact on business practice. For example, the religion of Islam teaches that people should not make a living by exploiting the misfortune of others; as a result, charging interest payments is seen as immoral. This also means that in Saudi Arabia there are few businesses that provide auto-towing services to take stalled cars to a garage for repair (because that would be capitalizing on misfortune), and in the Sudan, banks cannot pay or charge interest. Given these cultural and religious constraints, those two businesses—automobile towing and banking—do not seem to hold great promise for international managers in those particular countries!

Some cultural differences between countries can be even subtler and yet have a major impact on business activities. For example, in the United States, most managers clearly agree about the value of time. Most U.S. managers schedule their activities tightly and then try to adhere to their schedules. Other cultures do not put such a premium on time. In the Middle East, managers do not like to set appointments, and they rarely keep appointments set too far into the future. U.S. managers interacting with managers from the Middle East might misinterpret the late arrival of a potential business partner as a negotiation ploy or an insult, when it is rather a simple reflection of different views of time and its value.[21]

Language itself can be an important factor. Beyond the obvious and clear barriers posed by people who speak different languages, subtle differences in meaning can also play a major role. For example, Imperial Oil of Canada markets gasoline under the brand name Esso. When the firm tried to sell its gasoline in Japan, it learned that *esso* means "stalled car" in Japanese. Likewise, when Chevrolet first introduced a U.S. model called the Nova in Latin America, General Motors executives could not understand why the car sold poorly. They eventually learned, though, that, in Spanish, *no va* means "It doesn't go." The color green is used extensively in Muslim countries, but it signifies death in some other countries. The color associated with femininity in the United States is pink, but in many other countries, yellow is the most feminine color.

Employee Behavior Across Cultures

Managers in international business also have to understand that there are differences in what motivates people in different cultures. Although it's impossible to predict exactly how people from different cultures will react in the workplace, some insights have been developed from research on individual behaviors and attitudes across different cultures. This research, conducted by Geert Hofstede, identifies five important dimensions along which people seem to differ across cultures. These dimensions are illustrated in Figure 4.6.

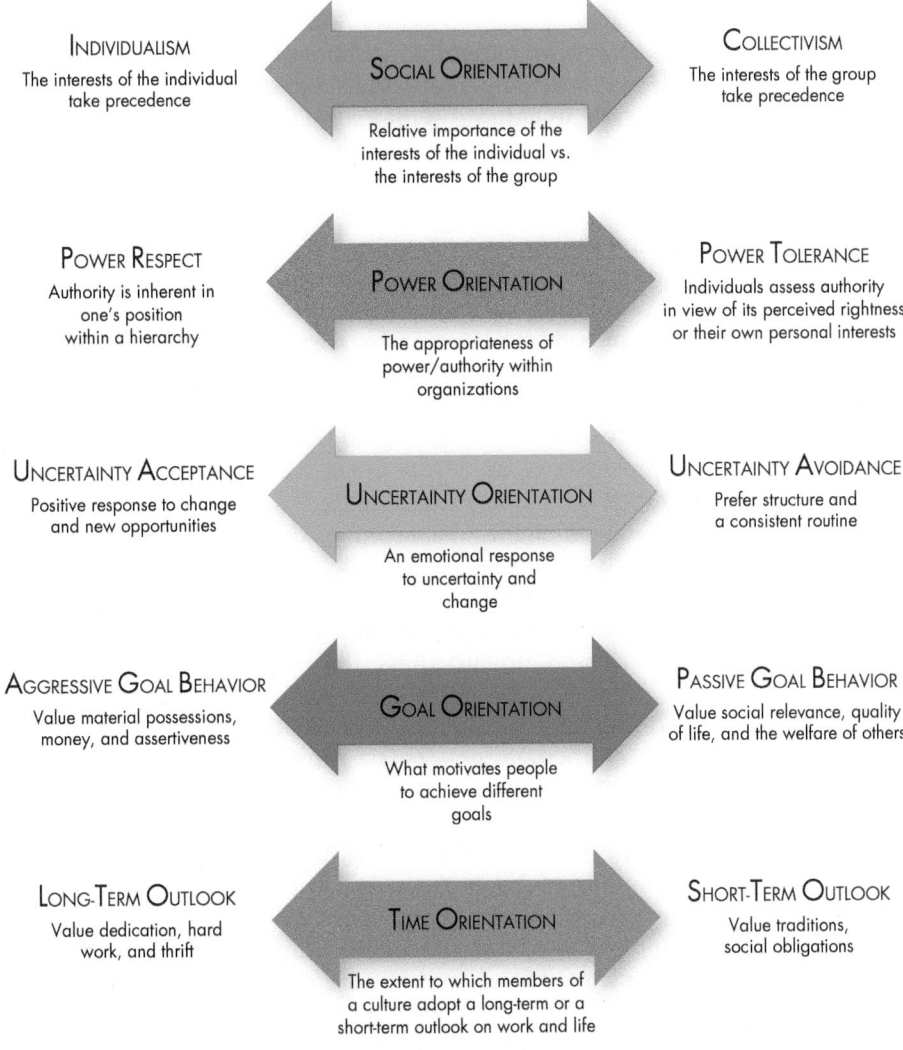

FIGURE 4.6 Hofstede's Five Dimensions of National Culture

Social Orientation *a person's beliefs about the relative importance of the individual versus groups to which that person belongs*

The first dimension is **social orientation**. Social orientation is a person's beliefs about the relative importance of the individual versus groups to which that person belongs. The two extremes of social orientation are individualism and collectivism. *Individualism* is the cultural belief that the person comes first. Research suggests that people in the United States, the United Kingdom, Australia, Canada, New Zealand, and the Netherlands tend to be relatively individualistic. *Collectivism* is the belief that the group comes first. Research has found that people from Mexico, Greece, Hong Kong, Taiwan, Peru, Singapore, Colombia, and Pakistan tend to be relatively collectivistic in their values. In countries with higher levels of individualism, many workers may prefer reward systems that link pay with the performance of individual employees. In a more collectivistic culture, such a reward system may in fact be counterproductive.

Power Orientation *the beliefs that people in a culture hold about the appropriateness of power and authority differences in hierarchies such as business organizations*

A second important dimension is **power orientation**, the beliefs that people in a culture hold about the appropriateness of power and authority differences in hierarchies such as business organizations. Some cultures are characterized by *power respect*. This means that people tend to accept the power and authority of their superiors simply on the basis of their position in the hierarchy and to respect their right to hold that power. Research has found that people in France, Spain, Mexico, Japan, Brazil, Indonesia, and Singapore are relatively power accepting. In contrast, people in cultures with a *power tolerance* orientation attach much less significance to a person's position in the hierarchy. These individuals are more willing to question a decision or mandate from someone at a higher level or perhaps even refuse to accept it. Research suggests that people in the United States, Israel, Austria, Denmark, Ireland, Norway, Germany, and New Zealand tend to be more power tolerant.

Uncertainty Orientation *the feeling individuals have regarding uncertain and ambiguous situations*

The third basic dimension of individual differences is *uncertainty orientation*. **Uncertainty orientation** is the feeling individuals have regarding uncertain and ambiguous situations. People in cultures with *uncertainty acceptance* are stimulated by change and thrive on new opportunities. The research suggests that many people in the United States, Denmark, Sweden, Canada, Singapore, Hong Kong, and Australia are among those in this category. In contrast, people with *uncertainty avoidance* tendencies dislike and will avoid ambiguity whenever possible. The research found that many people in Israel, Austria, Japan, Italy, Columbia, France, Peru, and Germany tend to avoid uncertainty whenever possible.

Goal Orientation *the manner in which people are motivated to work toward different kinds of goals*

The fourth dimension of cultural values is goal orientation. In this context, **goal orientation** is the manner in which people are motivated to work toward different kinds of goals. One extreme on the goal orientation continuum is *aggressive goal behavior*. People who exhibit aggressive goal behaviors tend to place a high premium on material possessions, money, and assertiveness. On the other hand, people who adopt *passive goal behavior* place a higher value on social relationships, quality of life, and concern for others. According to the research, many people in Japan tend to exhibit relatively aggressive goal behaviors, whereas many people in Germany, Mexico, Italy, and the United States reflect moderately aggressive goal behaviors. People from the Netherlands and the Scandinavian countries of Norway, Sweden, Denmark, and Finland all tend to exhibit relatively passive goal behaviors.

Time Orientation *the extent to which members of a culture adopt a long-term versus a short-term outlook on work, life, and other elements of society*

A fifth dimension is called time orientation. **Time orientation** is the extent to which members of a culture adopt a long-term versus a short-term outlook on work, life, and other elements of society. Some cultures, such as Japan, Hong Kong, Taiwan, and South Korea, have a longer-term orientation. One implication of this orientation is that people from these cultures are willing to accept that they may have to work hard for many years before achieving their goals. Other cultures, such as Pakistan and West Africa, are more likely to have a short-term orientation. As a result, people from these cultures may prefer jobs that provide more immediate rewards. Research suggests that people in the United States and Germany tend to have an intermediate time orientation.[22]

Barriers to International Trade

Whether a business is truly multinational or sells to only a few foreign markets, several factors will affect its international operations. Success in foreign markets will largely depend on the ways a business responds to *social and cultural forces* (as described previously) and *economic, legal, and political barriers* to international trade.

Economic Differences

Although cultural differences are often subtle, economic differences can be fairly pronounced. As we discussed in Chapter 1, in dealing with mixed-market economies like those of France and Sweden, firms must know when—and to what extent—the government is involved in a given industry. The French government, for instance, is heavily involved in all aspects of airplane design and manufacturing. The impact of economic differences can be even greater in planned economies such as those of China and Vietnam, where the government owns and operates many factors of production.

Legal and Political Differences

Governments can affect international business in many ways. They can set conditions for doing business within their borders and even prohibit doing business altogether. They can control the flow of capital and use tax legislation to discourage or encourage activity in a given industry. They can even confiscate the property of foreign-owned companies. In this section, we discuss some of the more common legal and political issues in international business: *quotas, tariffs,* and *subsidies; local content laws;* and *business practice laws.*

Quotas, Tariffs, and Subsidies Even free market economies, such as the United States, have some quotas or tariffs, both of which affect prices and quantities of foreign-made products. A **quota** restricts the number of products of a certain type that can be imported and, by reducing supply, raises the prices of those imports. The United States has imposed quotas on ice cream and timber: Belgian ice-cream makers can't ship more than 922,315 kilograms to the United States each year, and Canada can ship no more than 14.7 billion board feet of softwood timber per year. Quotas are often determined by treaties. Better terms are often given to friendly trading partners, and quotas are typically adjusted to protect domestic producers.

Quota *restriction on the number of products of a certain type that can be imported into a country*

The ultimate quota is an **embargo**, a government order forbidding exportation or importation of a particular product—or even all products—from a specific country. Many nations control bacteria and disease by banning certain agricultural products. Since the days of the Cold War, the United States had an embargo against Cuba, and it wasn't until 2015 that this embargo started to be lifted. The United States also has embargoes against trade with Libya, Iran, and North Korea. When the United States imposes an embargo, it means that U.S. firms can't invest in these countries, and their products can't legally be sold in U.S. markets.

Embargo *government order banning exportation or importation of a particular product or all products from a particular country*

Tariffs are taxes on imported products. They raise the prices of imports by making consumers pay not only for the products but also for tariff fees. Tariffs take two forms: revenue and protectionist. Revenue tariffs are imposed to raise money for governments, but most tariffs, called protectionist tariffs, are meant to discourage particular imports. Did you know that firms that import ironing-board covers into the United States pay a 7 percent tariff on the price of the product? Firms that import women's athletic shoes pay a flat rate of $0.90 per pair plus 20 percent of the product price. Such figures are determined through a complicated process designed to put foreign and domestic firms on competitive footing (that is, to make the foreign goods cost about the same as the domestic goods).

Tariff *tax levied on imported products*

Quotas and tariffs are imposed for numerous reasons. The U.S. government aids domestic automakers by restricting the number of Japanese cars imported into this country. Because of national security concerns, we limit the export of technology (for example, computer and nuclear technology to China). The United States isn't the only country that uses tariffs and quotas. To protect domestic firms, Italy imposes high tariffs on electronic goods. As a result, Asian-made DVD players are very expensive in Italy.

Subsidy *government payment to help a domestic business compete with foreign firms*

A **subsidy** is a government payment to help a domestic business compete with foreign firms. They're actually indirect tariffs that lower the prices of domestic goods rather than raise the prices of foreign goods. For example, many European governments subsidize farmers to help them compete against U.S. grain imports.

Protectionism *practice of protecting domestic business against foreign competition*

The Protectionism Debate In the United States, **protectionism**, the practice of protecting domestic business at the expense of free market competition, is controversial. Supporters argue that tariffs and quotas protect domestic firms and jobs as well as shelter new industries until they're able to compete internationally. They contend that we need such measures to counter steps taken by other nations. During the 2012 London Olympics, critics were outraged when it was discovered that Ralph Lauren, provider of official U.S. team uniforms, had outsourced the production of those uniforms to firms in China. These critics charged that the jobs of making the uniforms should have gone to U.S. workers. On the other hand, Ralph Lauren pointed out that the uniforms would have cost a lot more if they had been made in the United States. Other advocates justify protectionism in the name of national security. A nation, they argue, must be able to produce efficiently the goods needed for survival in case of war.

Critics cite protectionism as a source of friction between nations. They also charge that it drives up prices by reducing competition. They maintain that although jobs in some industries would be lost as a result of free trade, jobs in other industries (for example, electronics and automobiles) would be created if all nations abandoned protectionist tactics.

Protectionism sometimes takes on almost comic proportions. Neither Europe nor the United States grows bananas, but both European and U.S. firms buy and sell bananas in foreign markets. Problems arose a few years ago when the EU put a quota on bananas imported from Latin America, a market dominated by two U.S. firms, Chiquita and Dole, to help firms based in current and former European colonies in the Caribbean. To retaliate, the United States imposed a 100 percent tariff on certain luxury products imported from Europe, including Louis Vuitton handbags, Scottish cashmere sweaters, and Parma ham.

Local Content Law *law requiring that products sold in a particular country be at least partly made there*

Local Content Laws Many countries, including the United States, have **local content laws**, requirements that products sold in a country be at least partly made there. Firms seeking to do business in a country must either invest there directly or take on a domestic partner. In this way, some of the profits from doing business in a foreign country stay there rather than flow out to another nation. In some cases, the partnership arrangement is optional but wise. In Mexico, for instance, Radio Shack de México is a joint venture owned by Tandy Corporation (49 percent) and Mexico's Grupo Gigante (51 percent). This allows the retailer to promote a strong Mexican identity; it also makes it easier to address certain import regulations that are easier for Mexican than for U.S. firms. Both China and India currently require that when a foreign firm enters into a joint venture with a local firm, the local partner must have the controlling ownership stake.

Business Practice Law *law or regulation governing business practices in given countries*

Business Practice Laws Many businesses entering new markets encounter problems in complying with stringent regulations and bureaucratic obstacles. Such practices are affected by the **business practice laws** by which host countries govern business practices within their jurisdictions. As part of its entry strategy in Germany several years ago, Walmart had to buy existing retailers rather than open brand-new stores because, at the time, the German government was not issuing new licenses to sell food products. Walmart also was not allowed to follow its normal practice of refunding price differences on items sold for less by other stores because the practice is illegal in Germany. In addition, Walmart had to comply with business-hour restrictions: Stores can't open before 7:00 A.M., must close by 8:00 P.M. on week-nights and 4:00 P.M. on Saturday, and must remain closed on Sunday. After a few years, Walmart eventually decided its meager profits in Germany didn't warrant the effort it required to generate them and closed all of its stores there.

Sometimes, a legal—even an accepted—practice in one country is illegal in another. In some South American countries, for example, it is sometimes legal to bribe business and government officials. These bribes are generally called "expediting fees" or something similar. The existence of **cartels**, associations of producers that control supply and prices, also gives tremendous power to some nations, such as those belonging to the Organization of Petroleum Exporting Countries (OPEC). U.S. law forbids both bribery and cartels.

Cartel *association of producers whose purpose is to control supply and prices*

Finally, many (but not all) countries forbid **dumping**, selling a product abroad for less than the cost of production at home. U.S. antidumping legislation sets two conditions for determining whether dumping is being practiced:

Dumping *practice of selling a product abroad for less than the cost of production*

1 Products are being priced at "less than fair value."
2 The result unfairly harms domestic industry.

Just a few years ago, the United States charged Japan and Brazil with dumping steel at prices 70 percent below normal value. To protect local manufacturers, the U.S. government imposed a significant tariff on steel imported from those countries.

summary of learning objectives

OBJECTIVE 4-1

Discuss the rise of international business and describe the major world marketplaces, trade agreements, and alliances. (pp. 110–115)

Importing and exporting products from one country to another greatly increases the variety of products available to consumers and businesses. Several forces have combined to spark and sustain globalization. Governments and businesses have become aware of the potential for higher standards of living and increased profits. New technologies make international travel, communication, and commerce faster and less expensive. In addition, some companies expand into foreign markets just to keep up with their competitors.

North America, Europe, and Pacific Asia represent three geographic clusters that are the major marketplaces for international business activity. These major marketplaces include relatively more of the upper-middle-income and high-income nations but relatively few low-income and low-middle-income countries.

Trade treaties are legal agreements that specify how countries will work together to support international trade. The most significant treaties are (1) the *North American Free Trade Agreement (NAFTA)*, (2) the *European Union (EU)*, (3) the *Association of Southeast Asian Nations (ASEAN)*, and (4) the *General Agreement on Tariffs and Trade (GATT)*.

OBJECTIVE 4-2

Explain how differences in import–export balances, exchange rates, and foreign competition determine the ways in which countries and businesses respond to the international environment. (pp. 115–121)

Economists use two measures to assess the balance between imports and exports. A nation's *balance of trade* is the total economic value of all products that it exports minus the total economic value of all products that it imports. When a country's imports exceed its exports, it has a *negative balance of trade* and it suffers a *trade deficit*. A *positive balance of trade* occurs when exports exceed imports, resulting in a *trade surplus*.

The *balance of payments* refers to the flow of money into or out of a country. Payments for imports and exports, money spent by tourists, funding from foreign-aid programs, and proceeds from currency transactions all contribute to the balance of payments.

Exchange rates, the rates at which one nation's currency can be exchanged for that of another, are a major influence on international trade. Most countries use *floating exchange rates*, in which the value of one currency relative to that of another varies with market conditions.

Countries *export* what they can produce better or less expensively than other countries and use the proceeds to *import* what they can't produce as effectively. Economists once focused on two forms of advantage to explain international trade: *absolute advantage* and *comparative advantage*. Today, the theory of *national competitive advantage* is a widely accepted model of why nations engage in international trade. According to this theory, comparative advantage derives from four conditions: (1) factor of production conditions, (2) demand conditions, (3) related and supporting industries, and (4) strategies, structures, and rivalries.

OBJECTIVE 4-3

Discuss the factors involved in deciding to do business internationally and in selecting the appropriate levels of international involvement and international organizational structure. (pp. 121–125)

Several factors enter into the decision to go international. A company wishing to sell products in foreign markets should consider the following questions: (1) Is there a *demand* for its products abroad? (2) If so, must it *adapt* those products for international consumption? Companies may also go international through outsourcing and offshoring.

After deciding to go international, a firm must decide on its level of involvement. Several levels are possible: (1) *exporters and importers*, (2) *international firms*, and (3) *multinational firms*. Different levels of involvement require different kinds of organizational structure. The spectrum of international organizational strategies includes the following: (1) *independent agents*, (2) *licensing arrangements*, (3) *branch offices*, (4) *strategic alliances* (or *joint ventures*), and (5) *foreign direct investment (FDI)*. Independent agents are foreign individuals or organizations that represent an exporter in foreign markets. Another option, licensing arrangements, represents a contract under which one firm allows another to use its brand name, operating procedures, or proprietary technology. Companies may also consider establishing a branch office by sending managers overseas to set up a physical presence. A strategic alliance occurs when a company seeking international expansion finds a partner in the country in which it wishes to do business. Finally, FDI is the practice of buying or establishing tangible assets in another country.

OBJECTIVE 4-4

Explain the role and importance of the cultural environment in international business. (pp. 126–128)

A country's culture includes all the values, symbols, beliefs, and language that guide behavior. Cultural values and beliefs are often unspoken; they may even be taken for granted by those who live in a particular country. Cultural factors do not necessarily cause problems for managers when the cultures of two countries are similar. Difficulties can arise, however, when there is little overlap between the home culture of a manager and the culture of the country in which business is to be conducted. Cultural differences between countries can have a direct impact on business practice. Some cultural differences between countries, such as the meaning of time, can be even subtler and yet have a major impact on business activities. Language itself can be an important factor. Beyond the obvious and clear barriers posed by people who speak different languages, subtle differences in meaning can also play a major role.

Managers in international business also have to understand that there are differences in what motivates people in different cultures. Social orientation is a person's beliefs about the relative importance of the individual versus groups to which that person belongs. A second important dimension is power orientation, the beliefs that people in a culture hold about the appropriateness of power and authority differences in hierarchies, such as business organizations. Uncertainty orientation is the feeling individuals have regarding uncertain and ambiguous situations. Goal orientation is the manner in which people are motivated to work toward different kinds of goals. Time orientation is the extent to which members of a culture adopt a long-term versus a short-term outlook on work, life, and other elements of society.

OBJECTIVE 4-5

Describe some of the ways in which economic, legal, and political differences among nations affect international business. (pp. 129–131)

Economic differences among nations can be fairly pronounced and can affect businesses in a variety of ways. Common legal and political issues in international business include *quotas, tariffs, subsidies, local content laws*, and *business practice laws*. Quotas restrict the number of certain products that can be imported into a country, and a tariff is a tax that a country imposes on imported products. Subsidies are government payments to domestic companies to help them better compete with international companies. Another legal strategy to support a nation's businesses is implementing local content laws that require that products sold in a country be at least partially made there. Business practice laws control business activities within their jurisdiction and create obstacles for businesses trying to enter new markets.

The term *protectionism* describes the practice of protecting domestic businesses at the expense of free market competition. Although some economists argue that legal strategies such as quotas, tariffs, and subsidies are necessary to protect domestic firms, others argue that protectionism ultimately hurts consumers because of the resulting higher prices.

A final obstacle to international business is that business practices that are legal in one country may not be legal in another. Bribery, the formation of cartels, and dumping are forbidden in the United States, but legal in other countries, which is challenging for U.S. companies trying to enter some foreign markets.

key terms

absolute advantage (p. 120)
Association of Southeast Asian Nations (ASEAN) (p. 115)
balance of payments (p. 118)
balance of trade (p. 116)
branch office (p. 125)
business practice law (p. 130)
cartel (p. 131)
comparative advantage (p. 120)
dumping (p. 131)
embargo (p. 129)
euro (p. 119)
European Union (EU) (p. 114)
exchange rate (p. 119)
export (p. 110)
exporter (p. 123)

foreign direct investment (FDI) (p. 125)
General Agreement on Tariffs and Trade (GATT) (p. 115)
globalization (p. 110)
goal orientation (p. 128)
import (p. 110)
importer (p. 123)
independent agent (p. 125)
international firm (p. 124)
licensing arrangement (p. 125)
local content law (p. 130)
multinational firm (p. 124)
national competitive advantage (p. 121)
North American Free Trade Agreement (NAFTA) (p. 113)

offshoring (p. 122)
outsourcing (p. 122)
power orientation (p. 128)
protectionism (p. 130)
quota (p. 129)
social orientation (p. 128)
strategic alliance (p. 125)
subsidy (p. 130)
tariff (p. 129)
time orientation (p. 128)
trade deficit (p. 116)
trade surplus (p. 116)
uncertainty orientation (p. 128)
World Trade Organization (WTO) (p. 115)

MyLab Intro to Business

To complete the problems with the ✪, go to EOC Discussion Questions in the MyLab.

questions & exercises

QUESTIONS FOR REVIEW

4-1. What are the advantages and disadvantages of globalization?

4-2. What are the three possible levels of involvement in international business? Give examples of each.

✪ **4-3.** What are the elements of national competitive advantage? Give a current, real-world example of each condition.

4-4. Describe the five international organizational structures.

QUESTIONS FOR ANALYSIS

✪ **4-5.** Make a list of five things you own, such as an item of furniture, a vehicle, electronics, and other consumer goods, making sure that each one was made in a different country. Develop a hypothesis about why each product was made in that particular country.

4-6. Describe the United States in terms of the five cultural orientations.

✪ **4-7.** Research and identify a protectionist tariff imposed by the United States. Do you support that tariff? If so, why?

4-8. Do you think that a firm operating internationally is better advised to adopt a single standard of ethical conduct or to adapt to local conditions? What are the advantages and disadvantages of adapting to local conditions?

APPLICATION EXERCISES

4-9. The World Bank uses per-capita income to make distinctions among countries. Use Web or database research to identify at least three countries in the following categories for last year: high-income countries, upper-middle-income countries, lower-middle-income countries, and lower-income countries. In addition, identify the source of the data that you used to draw these conclusions.

4-10. China is one of the fastest-growing markets in the world. Use Web or database research to uncover how to best describe China according to the five cultural dimensions. Cite the sources for your information.

building a business: continuing team exercise

Assignment

Meet with your team members and discuss your new business venture within the context of this chapter. Develop specific responses to the following:

4-11. Are you likely to acquire any of your materials, products, or services from abroad? Why, or why not?

4-12. Are there likely to be any export opportunities for your products or services? Why, or why not? If you are able to export your product, will it need to be adapted to sell in foreign markets?

4-13. To what extent, if any, will your new venture be affected by social and cultural differences, economic differences, and/or legal and political differences across cultures?

team exercise

WEIGHING THE TRADE-OFFS

The Situation

Able Systems is a software company specializing in technology solutions for the food industry, including supermarkets and restaurants. All of your customers are located in the United States and operate nearly 24 hours a day. You provide excellent phone support for customers who have an issue, but your expenses are increasing and you're looking for ways to contain costs.

The Dilemma

Able Systems has tried to stem escalating phone support costs by limiting the number of specialists working on each shift, but long wait times have angered customers. Because of the technical and problem-solving skills needed to provide remote support, hiring less-qualified employees is just not an option. You're looking at your competitors and you've noticed that many have offshored their operations—hiring employees in other countries to provide support. Because of a large number of English speakers and an adequate supply of applicants with the education needed for a support position, you are considering setting up a phone support center in Jamaica.

This solution is not without concerns. If you offshore your support operation, you will have to lay off most of the U.S. support employees. You're willing to provide outplacement services to make sure that they can find new jobs, but you're still concerned about the impact of layoffs on your remaining employees. A group of programmers who caught wind of this proposal have begun to wonder if their jobs are next. In addition, local elected officials are concerned about the impact of layoffs on the local economy. Your boss is pressuring you for a recommendation and you're weighing the pros and cons of both options.

Team Activity

4-14. Have each member of the team create a list of the pros and cons of offshoring the phone support. As you develop your list, be sure to consider all of the stakeholders in this decision—the company's executives, employees, customers, and community.

4-15. Gather your group together and reveal, in turn, each member's lists of pros. Narrow the list to the three or four most commonly cited and important advantages of offshoring phone support.

4-16. In similar fashion, have each member of the team read his or her list of disadvantages. Identify the most significant disadvantages based on your team's assessment.

4-17. Considering the interests of all stakeholders, what is the best option in this situation?

exercising your ethics

PAYING HEED TO FOREIGN PRACTICES

The Situation

Assume that you're an up-and-coming manager at a medium-sized manufacturing company. Your company is one of only a few companies making certain components for radiant floor-heating systems. The primary advantage of these systems is that they are energy efficient and can result in significantly lower heating costs. Although radiant floor heating is just catching on in the United States, there is a lot of potential in foreign markets where energy is expensive. You've been assigned to head up your company's new operations in a Latin American country. Because at least two of your competitors are also trying to enter this same market, your boss wants you to move as quickly as possible. You also sense that your success in this assignment will likely determine your future with the company.

You would like to build a production facility and have just completed meetings with local government officials. However, you're pessimistic about your ability to get things moving quickly. You've learned, for example, that it will take 10 months to get a building permit for a needed facility. Moreover, once the building's up, it will take another 6 months to get utilities. Finally, the phone company says that it may take up to 2 years to install the phone lines that you need for high-speed Internet access.

The Dilemma

Various officials have indicated that time frames could be considerably shortened if you were willing to pay special "fees." You realize that these fees are bribes, and you're well aware that the practice of paying such fees is both unethical and illegal in the United States. In this foreign country, however, it's not illegal and not even considered unethical. Moreover, if you don't pay and one of your competitors does, you'll be at a major competitive disadvantage. In any case, your boss isn't likely to understand the long lead times necessary to get the operation running. Fortunately, you have access to a source of funds that you could spend without the knowledge of anyone in the home office.

QUESTIONS TO ADDRESS

4-18. What are the key ethical issues in this situation?

4-19. What do you think most managers would do in this situation?

4-20. What would you do?

cases

THE DOOR OPENS

Continued from page 110

At the beginning of this chapter, you read about the historic changes to restrictions on travel to Cuba, as well as the continued embargo on U.S. exports to this island nation. Using the information presented in this chapter, you should now be able to respond to these questions.

QUESTIONS FOR DISCUSSION

4-21. How has opening Cuba to international travel affected the travel industry in the United States and other countries? What are the potential benefits of virtually open travel to Cuba to Cuban citizens as well as the Cuban government?

4-22. How have changes in the *structure of the global economy* affected the U.S. embargo, which has been in effect for around 50 years? More specifically, how can U.S. companies deal with changing *environmental challenges— economic, political and legal*, and *cultural*—in their relations not only with Cuba but also with other countries in Latin America?

4-23. How might U.S. businesses best prepare themselves for a possible elimination of the embargo?

NOT MY CUP OF TEA

China is a country famous for tea. Over thousands of years, tea has been the beverage of choice in China. This, however, did not deter Starbucks from entering one of the fastest-growing consumer markets in the world. The first Starbucks opened in Taipei, Taiwan, in 1998 and the first mainland store was opened in Beijing in 1999. In an interview with CNN, Starbucks CEO Howard Schultz discussed the initial road bumps the company encountered in the tea-obsessed country. "We had to educate and teach many Chinese about what coffee was—the coffee ritual, what a latte was … So in the early years, we did not make money." However, by late 2016 there were over 2,300 stores in China, and Starbucks announced a goal of 5,000 by 2021, opening one new store every day for the next five years.[23]

Starbucks analyzed the Chinese market and found that their brand was valued not only for their food and beverage offerings but also for the atmosphere of Starbucks stores. Chinese consumers enjoyed the opportunity to meet with friends and business partners in a comfortable location and appreciated the upbeat music and chic interiors. While kiosks have become popular in the United States, some Chinese Starbucks locations are as large as 3,800 square feet.

Starbucks has customized its product offerings, introducing the Green Tea Frappuccino® Blended Crème beverage in 2002 and Starbucks bottled Frappuccino® coffee drinks into Chinese markets in 2007. Not all Chinese consumers are fans of Starbucks coffee. Cheng Xiaochen, an English teacher who likes to meet students at Starbucks, exclaims, "It's a good place to meet people, but the coffee is so bitter it tastes like Chinese medicine." Responding to Mr. Cheng and others like him, the company offers mint hot chocolate and red bean frappuccinos. Food offerings have also been customized to the Chinese market, with Hainanese chicken sandwiches and rice wraps.[24]

Starbucks has also worked to enter the ready-to-drink market, teaming up with Chinese Company Tingyi Holding, a leader in ready-to-drink teas and instant noodles. Starbucks hopes to expand its sales of bottled beverages, which were available in approximately 6,000 retail locations in 2014. The ready-to-drink market is especially appealing because it is projected to grow at a rate of 20 percent over the next three years in the very large Chinese market. Through this partnership, Starbucks will provide "coffee expertise, brand development, and future product innovation," while Tingyi will manufacture and distribute the product.[25]

Starbucks acknowledges that employees are at the center of its success and makes a considerable investment in training, developing, and retaining these employees. However, Starbucks faced a challenge in an achievement-oriented Chinese culture, where parents aspire for their children to take jobs in traditionally successful fields such as financial services and banking. In response, Starbucks launched a family forum in 2012, which provided stories from managers who have worked their way up the career ladder with Starbucks.[26]

Starbucks has worked to extend every component of its corporate culture into its Chinese expansion. The company has a long-established tradition of community commitment, and it has brought this to China. Through a $5 million grant to the Starbucks China Education Project, the company aims to help students and teachers in rural China, increase access to clean drinking water, and provide relief from the 2008 Sichaun earthquake.[27] Starbucks has demonstrated that a long-term commitment and sensitivity to international market conditions are the keys to success.[28]

QUESTIONS FOR DISCUSSION

4-24. What motivates companies like Starbucks to expand into international markets with little perceived interest for their product?

4-25. How has Starbucks adapted to Chinese culture?

4-26. How will expansion in the ready-to-drink market help or hinder sales in China's Starbucks stores?

4-27. China has a collectivist culture. How do you believe that this will affect managers in a Starbucks store?

4-28. Would you describe Starbuck's model as multinational or global? Why? How would you differentiate the two different approaches to marketing?

crafting a business plan

PART 1: THE CONTEMPORARY BUSINESS ENVIRONMENT

Goal of the Exercise

In Chapter 3, we discussed how the starting point for virtually every new business is a *business plan*. Business plans describe the business strategy for any new business and demonstrate how that strategy will be implemented. One benefit of a business plan is that in preparing it, would-be entrepreneurs must develop their idea on paper and firm up their thinking about how to launch their business before investing time and money in it. In this exercise, you'll get started on creating your own business plan.

Exercise Background: Part 1 of the Business Plan

The starting point for any business plan is coming up with a "great idea." This might be a business that you've already considered setting up. If you don't have ideas for a business already, look around. What are some businesses with which you come into contact on a regular basis? Restaurants, childcare services, and specialty stores are a few examples you might consider. You may also wish to create a business that is connected with a talent or interest you have, such as crafts, cooking, or car repair. It's important that you create a company from "scratch" rather than use a company that already exists. You'll learn more if you use your own ideas.

Once you have your business idea, your next step is to create an "identity" for your business. This includes determining a name for your business and an idea of what your business will do. It also includes identifying the type of ownership your business will take, topics we discussed in Chapter 3. The first part of the plan also briefly looks at who your ideal customers are as well as how your business will stand out from the crowd. Part 1 of the plan also looks at how the business will interact with the community and demonstrate social responsibility, topics we discussed in Chapter 2. Finally, almost all business plans today include a perspective on the impact of global business.

Your Assignment

STEP 1

To complete this assignment, you first need to download the *Business Plan Student Template* file from the book's Companion website at www.pearsonhighered.com/ebert. This is a Microsoft Word file you can use to complete your business plan. For this assignment, you will fill in "Part 1" of the plan.

STEP 2

Once you have the *Business Plan Student Template* file, you can begin to answer the following questions in "Part 1: The Contemporary Business Environment."

4-29. What is the name of your business?

   Hint: When you think of the name of your business, make sure that it captures the spirit of the business you're creating.

4-30. What will your business do?

   Hint: Imagine that you are explaining your idea to a family member or a friend. Keep your description to 30 words or fewer.

4-31. What form of business ownership (sole proprietorship, partnership, or corporation) will your business take? Why did you choose this form?

   Hint: For more information on types of business ownership, refer to the discussion in Chapter 3.

4-32. Briefly describe your ideal customer. What would he or she be like in terms of age, income level, and so on?

   Hint: You don't have to give too much detail in this part of the plan; you'll provide more details about customers and marketing in later parts of the plan.

4-33. Why will customers choose to buy from your business instead of your competition?

   Hint: In this section, describe what will be unique about your business. For example, is the product special or will you offer the product at a lower price?

4-34. All businesses have to deal with ethical issues. One way to address these issues is to create a code of ethics. List three core principles your business will follow.

   Hint: To help you consider the ethical issues that your business might face, refer to the discussion in Chapter 2.

4-35. A business shows social responsibility by respecting all of its stakeholders. What steps will you take to create a socially responsible business?

   Hint: Refer to the discussion of social responsibility in Chapter 2. What steps can you take to be a "good citizen" in the community? Consider also how you may need to be socially responsible toward your customers and, if applicable, investors, employees, and suppliers.

4-36. Will you sell your product in another country? If so, what countries and why? What challenges will you face?

   Hint: To help you consider issues of global business, refer to Chapter 4. Consider how you will expand internationally (e.g., independent agent, licensing, etc.). Do you expect global competition for your product? What advantages will foreign competitors have?

   Note: Once you have answered the questions, save your Word document. You'll be answering additional questions in later chapters.

Writing Assignments

4-37. Some countries have more national competitive advantages than others. Based on the four conditions described to create national competitive advantage, what are some national competitive advantage opportunities in the United States? In China? In India? Provide examples of businesses utilizing these advantages. How can each of these countries benefit from the national competitive advantage of the other?

4-38. What are some of the cultural barriers, concessions, and challenges for companies expanding into global markets? Choose a company, like Starbucks, Papa Johns, Microsoft, or even Alibaba. Research current and past globalization successes and failures, and document some of the recurrent issues. Also explain how the company dealt with the challenge(s).

endnotes

[1] The White House, Office of the Press Secretary. (2015) Statement by the President on the Re-Establishment of Diplomatic Relations with Cuba, https://obamawhitehouse.archives.gov/the-press-office/2015/07/01/statement-president-re-establishment-diplomatic-relations-cuba, accessed March 1, 2016

[2] Sampson, Hannah. "U.S.-based Airbnb adding private Cuban homes to listings." Miami Herald, April 2, 2015. Accessed April 7, 2015. www.miamiherald.com/news/business/article17152853.html

[3] See http://www.bea.gov/newsreleases/international/intinv/intinvnewsrelease.htm, accessed on January 14, 2017.

[4] "Best Buy, Home Depot Find China Market a Tough Sell," *USA Today*, February 23, 2011, p. 5B.

[5] See http://blogs.worldbank.org/opendata/new-country-classifications-2016), accessed on January 14, 2017; see also Griffin, Ricky W., and Pustay, Michael W. *International Business: A Managerial Perspective*, 8th ed. (Upper Saddle River, NJ: Prentice Hall, 2015).

[6] Friedman, Thomas. *The World Is Flat* (New York: Farrar, Straus, and Giroux, 2005).

[7] Yuk, Paul Kwan. "Want cheap labour? Head to Mexico, not China." Financial Times. Accessed March 1, 2017. https://www.ft.com/content/bddc8121-a7a0-3788-a74c-cd2b49cd3230

[8] Morely, Hugh R. 2017. "Mexican port growth outpaces U.S., Canada." http://www.joc.com/port-news/international-ports/port-lázaro-cárdenas/mexican-port-growth-outpaces-us-canada_20170215.html (accessed March 1, 2017)

[9] Muller, Joann. 2014. "America's Car Capital Will Soon Be ... Mexico." Forbes 194, No. 3: 128-134. Business Source Premier, EBSCOhost (accessed April 6, 2015).

[10] World Trade Organization, at www.wto.org/English/thewto_e/whatis_e/tif_e/org6_e.htm, accessed on January 10, 2015.

[11] Griffin and Pustay, *International Business: A Managerial Perspective*; see also Steven Husted and Michael Melvin, *International Economics*, 5th ed. (Boston: Addison Wesley Longman, 2001), 54–61; and Karl E. Case and Ray C. Fair, *Principles of Economics*, 8th ed. (Upper Saddle River, NJ: Prentice Hall, 2007), 700–708.

[12] The Electoral Commission. "Official result of the EU Referendum is declared by Electoral Commission in Manchester," press release, June 24, 2016, http://www.electoralcommission.org.uk/i-am-a/journalist/electoral-commission-media-centre/news-releases-referendums/official-result-of-the-eu-referendum-is-declared-by-electoral-commission-in-manchester (Accessed March 2, 2017)

[13] Porter, Michael. *The Competitive Advantage of Nations* (Boston: Addison-Wesley Longman, 2001), 54–61; see also Case and Fair, *Principles of Economics*, 669–677.

[14] Krajewski, Lee J., Malhotra, Manoj, and Ritzman, Larry P. *Operations Management: Processes and Value Chains*, 8th ed. (Upper Saddle River, NJ: Prentice Hall, 2007), 401–403.

[15] Peters, Adele. "Can This Startup Help Lead the Booming Coconut Water Industry to Sustainability?" *Fast Company*, February 19, 2015. Accessed April 7, 2015. www.fastcoexist.com/3042078/can-this-startup-help-lead-the-booming-coconut-water-industry-to-sustainability

[16] Harmless Harvest. "Harmless Harvest Launches the World's First 100% Raw Coconut Water with Fair Trade Coffee," press release, http://www.harmlessharvest.com/press-releases/ (Accessed March 2, 2017)

[17] *Hoover's Handbook of American Business 2014* (Austin, Texas: Hoover's Business Press, 2014), 432–433.

[18] http://money.cnn.com/magazines/fortune/global500/2012/full_list/index.html, accessed on January 12, 2015.

[19] "Ford, Russian Automaker Make Deal," *USA Today*, February 21, 2011, p. 1B.

[20] "Main Street, H.K.—Disney Localizes Mickey to Boost Its Hong Kong Theme Park," *Wall Street Journal*, January 23, 2008, pp. B1, B2.

[21] "What If There Weren't Any Clocks to Watch?" *Newsweek*, June 30, 1997, p. 14.

[22] Hofstede, Geert. *Culture's Consequences: International Differences in Work-Related Values* (Beverly Hills, CA: Sage, 1980); Hofstede, Geert. "The Business of International Business Is Culture," *International Business Review*, 1994, Vol. 3, No. 1, pp. 1–14.

[23] Jethro Mullen and Mallika Kapur, "China will get a new Starbucks every day for 5 years," CNN Money, October 19, 2016, http://money.cnn.com/2016/10/19/investing/starbucks-howard-schultz-china-growth/ (Accessed March 2, 2017.)

[24] Burkitt, Laurie. "Starbucks Plays to Local Chinese Tastes." *Wall Street Journal*. Dow Jones Company, Inc., 26 Nov. 2012. Web. 13 June 2013.

[25] Flannery, Russell. 2015. "Starbucks Takes Aim At 'Massive' China Ready-To-Drink Market Through Pact With Tingyi." *Forbes.Com* 16. *Business Source Premier*, EBSCOhost (accessed April 6, 2015).

[26] Peterson, Hayley. "5 Ways Starbucks Is Different in China." *Business Insider*, August 8, 2014. Accessed April 6, 2015. www.businessinsider.com/how-starbucks-is-different-in-china-2014-8

[27] "Greater China." *Starbucks.com*. Starbucks Corporation, n.d. Web. 13 June 2013.

[28] Wang, Helen H. "Five Things Starbucks Did to Get China Right." *Forbes*. Forbes.com, LLC, 10 Aug. 2012. Web. 13 June 2013.

Managing the Business

chapter 5

Science and statistics don't hold all the answers; managers must rely on their gut—on

the basis of

intuition, experience, instinct, and

personal insight.

After reading this chapter, you should be able to:

5-1 **Describe** the nature of management and identify the four basic functions that constitute the management process.

5-2 **Identify** different types of managers likely to be found in an organization by level and area.

5-3 **Describe** the basic roles and skills required of managers.

5-4 **Explain** the importance of strategic management and effective goal setting in organizational success.

5-5 **Discuss** contingency planning and crisis management in today's business world.

5-6 **Describe** the development and explain the importance of corporate culture.

Google

✱✱✱✱✱✱✱✱✱✱✱✱✱✱✱✱✱✱✱✱✱✱✱✱

I'm Feeling Lucky

Alphabet Soup

Sergey Brin and Larry Page chose the name Alphabet for their new company because they felt that it held a dual meaning, both as a collection of letters that represent language and as a reference

to the investment term alpha (returns above a benchmark). The two met at Stanford University in 1995, where they were graduate students in computer science. At the time, Page was working on a software-development project designed to create an index of websites by scouring sites for key words and other linkages. Brin joined him on the project, and when they were satisfied that they'd developed something with commercial value, they tried to license the technology to other search companies. As luck would have it, they couldn't find a buyer and settled instead for procuring enough investment capital to keep refining and testing their product.

In 2000, Brin and Page ran across the description of a business model based on the concept of selling advertising in the form of sponsored links and search-specific ads. They adapted it to their own concept and went into business for themselves, eventually building Google into the world's largest search engine. But their ambitions and innovations didn't stop there. By the end of 2016, they had purchased over 200 companies, such as Android, YouTube, and DoubleClick, always striving to further their mission: to organize the world's information and make it universally accessible and useful. In October of 2015, in order to better separate all of the different directions the business had taken, Brin and Page created a holding company, called Alphabet, and turned the helm of Google over to an up-and-coming star manager named Sundar Pichai. By the end of 2016, the company was worth over $578 billion and Google, its major subsidiary, provided over 80 percent of the world's search market.

How did two young computer scientists build this astoundingly successful company, and where will they take it in the future? Brin and Page have been remarkably successful in attracting talented and creative employees, like Pichai, and providing them with a work environment and culture that foster the kind of productivity and innovation for which they were hired. They've also remained in the forefront of Alphabet's search for technological innovations, but nobody knows for sure what Brin and Page have on the drawing board. In fact, outsiders—notably potential investors—often criticized Google

what's in it for me?

Sergey Brin and Larry Page clearly are effective managers, and they understand what it takes to build a business and then keep it at the forefront of its industry. A **manager** is someone whose primary responsibility is to carry out the management process. In particular, a manager is someone who plans and makes decisions, organizes, leads, and controls human, financial, physical, and information resources. Today's managers face a variety of interesting and challenging situations. The average executive works more than 60 hours a week, has enormous demands placed on his or her time, and faces increased complexities posed by globalization, domestic competition, government regulation, shareholder pressure, and Internet-related uncertainties. The job is complicated even more by rapid changes (such as the recession of 2008–2011 and the recovery that really began to take hold in 2015), unexpected disruptions, exciting new opportunities, and both minor and major crises. The manager's job is unpredictable and fraught with challenges, but it is also filled with opportunities to make a difference. Good managers can propel an organization into unprecedented realms of success, whereas poor managers can devastate even the strongest of organizations.[1] After reading this chapter, you'll be better positioned to carry out various management responsibilities yourself. And from the perspective of a consumer or investor, you'll be able to more effectively assess and appreciate the quality of management in various companies.

In this chapter, we explore the importance of strategic management and effective goal setting to organizational success. We also examine the functions that constitute the management process and identify different types of managers likely to be found in an organization by level and area. Along the way, we look at basic management skills and roles and explain the importance of corporate culture.

for being a "black box" when they want a few more details on the company's long-range strategy. "We don't talk about our strategy," explains Page, "... because it's strategic. I would rather have people think we're confused than let our competitors know what we're going to do."[2]

One of the considerations for creating Alphabet was to provide greater transparency, but the company seems to have missed that mark. Alphabet's semi-secret research facility "X," also known as the "moonshot factory," has its own website and is currently working on a self-driving car, fuel from seawater, and other long-shot, innovative projects that may or may not pan out. If there is a long-term strategic vision, it may be simply to provide the resources and freedom to some of the best and brightest dreamers in the world, and then to let their ideas develop into the reality of the future. (After studying this chapter, you should be able to answer a set of discussion questions found at the end of this chapter.)

OBJECTIVE 5-1
Describe

the nature of management and identify the four basic functions that constitute the management process.

Manager *someone whose primary work responsibilities are a part of the management process*

The Management Process

All corporations depend on effective management. Whether they run a multibillion-dollar business such as Google or Apple or a small local fashion boutique or corner taco stand, **managers** perform many of the same functions and have many of the same responsibilities. These include analyzing their competitive environments and planning, organizing, directing, and controlling the day-to-day operations of their business. Ultimately, they are also responsible for the performance and effectiveness of the teams, divisions, or companies that they head.

Although our focus is on managers in business settings, remember that the principles of management apply to other kinds of organizations as well. Charitable enterprises, churches, the military, educational institutions, and government agencies all need to be managed and therefore need managers. The prime minister of Canada, curators at the Museum of Modern Art, the dean of your college, and the chief administrator of your local hospital are all managers (although they may have different titles, of course). Remember, too, that managers bring to small organizations much the same kinds of skills—the ability to make decisions and respond to a variety of challenges—that they bring to large ones. Regardless of the nature and size of an organization, managers are among its most important resources.

Basic Management Functions

Management *process of planning, organizing, leading, and controlling an organization's resources to achieve its goals*

Management itself is the process of planning, organizing, leading, and controlling an organization's financial, physical, human, and information resources to achieve its goals. Managers oversee the use of all these resources in their respective firms. All aspects of a manager's job are interrelated. Any given manager is likely to be engaged in each of these activities during the course of any given day. Consider the management process at Google. Sergey Brin and Larry Page founded Google shortly after graduating from Stanford and still run the company today. To do so effectively they must first create goals and plans that articulate what they want the company to accomplish. Then they rely on effective organization to help make those goals and plans reality. Brin and Page also pay close attention to the people who work for the company, and they keep a close eye on how well the company is performing. Each of these activities represents one of the four basic managerial functions: (1) Setting goals is part of planning, (2) setting up the organization is part of organizing, (3) managing people is part of leading, and (4) monitoring performance is part of controlling (see Figure 5.1).

Kristoffer Tripplaar/Alamy Stock Photo

Slaven Vlasic/Everett Collection Inc./Alamy Stock Photo

Dpa Picture Alliance/Alamy Stock Photo

Planning Determining what the organization needs to do and how best to get it done requires *planning*. **Planning** has three main components. It begins when managers determine the firm's goals. Next, they develop a comprehensive *strategy* for achieving those goals. After a strategy is developed, they design *tactical and operational plans* for implementing the strategy. We discuss these three components in more detail later in this chapter. Howard Schultz is the President and CEO of Starbucks. He is responsible for developing strategies and strategic plans to keep Starbucks growing while simultaneously maintaining quality. He must also ensure that the firm's strategic, tactical, and operational planning efforts are all integrated and consistent with one another.

Organizing Managers must also organize people and resources. For example, some businesses prepare charts that diagram the various jobs within the company and how those jobs relate to one another. These *organization charts* help everyone understand roles and reporting relationships, key parts of the **organizing** function. Some businesses go so far as to post their organization chart on an office wall. But in most larger businesses, roles and reporting relationships, although important, may be too complex to draw as a simple box-and-line diagram. Starbucks has over 18,000 coffee shops in more than 60 countries. In addition, the firm also owns 250 Teavana retail stores and the Evolution Fresh fruit and vegetable juice company, and has

Kenneth Chenault (CEO of American Express), Indra Nooyi (Chairman and CEO of PepsiCo), and Tim Cook (President and CEO of Apple) are all senior managers responsible for overseeing the planning, organizing, leading, and controlling functions in their businesses.

Planning *management process of determining what an organization needs to do and how best to get it done*

Organizing *management process of determining how best to arrange an organization's resources and activities into a coherent structure*

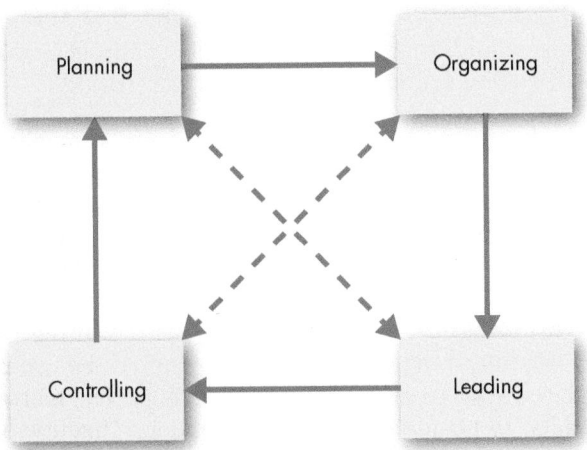

FIGURE 5.1 The Management Process

myriad licensing and joint venture agreements with PepsiCo, Dreyer's, Beam, and other companies. Schultz is responsible for creating and managing an organization structure for Starbucks to facilitate coordination across these various products and divisions and promote faster decision making. We explore organizing in more detail in Chapter 6.

Leading *management process of guiding and motivating employees to meet an organization's objectives*

Leading Managers have the power to give orders and demand results. Leading, however, involves more complex activities. When **leading**, a manager works to guide and motivate employees to meet the firm's objectives. Legendary management figures such as Walt Disney, Sam Walton (of Walmart), and Herb Kelleher (of Southwest Airlines) had the capacity to unite their employees in a clear and targeted manner and motivate them to work in the best interests of their employer. Their employees respected them, trusted them, and believed that by working together, both the firm and themselves as individuals would benefit. Howard Schultz has been a very effective leader at Starbucks. Starbucks was the first privately owned business to offer stock options to its employees, and among the first to provide benefits to part-time employees. The company has an excellent reputation for communicating with all of its employees, and those employees, in turn, generally hold Schultz in high regard. Leading involves a number of different processes and activities, which are discussed in Chapter 9.

Controlling *management process of monitoring an organization's performance to ensure that it is meeting its goals*

Controlling **Controlling** is the process of monitoring a firm's performance to make sure that it is meeting its goals. All CEOs must pay close attention to costs and performance. Managers at United Airlines, for example, focus almost relentlessly on numerous indicators of performance that they can constantly measure and adjust. Everything from on-time arrivals to baggage-handling errors to the number of empty seats on an airplane to surveys of employee and customer satisfaction are regularly and routinely monitored. If on-time arrivals start to slip, managers focus on the problem and get it fixed. If customers complain too much about the food, catering managers figure out how to improve it. As a result, no single element of the firm's performance can slip too far before it's noticed and fixed. At Starbucks, new products are generally tested in a limited number of coffee shops before they are rolled out on a large scale. But if products don't meet expectation and forecasts, the company is also willing to drop them.

Figure 5.2 illustrates the control process that begins when management establishes standards, often for financial performance. If, for example, a company sets a goal of increasing its sales by 20 percent over the next 10 years, an appropriate standard to assess progress toward the 20-percent goal might be an increase of about 2 percent a year.

Managers then measure actual performance each year against standards. If the two amounts agree, the organization continues along its present course. If they vary significantly, however, one or the other needs adjustment. If sales have increased 2.1 percent by the end of the first year, things are probably fine. If sales have dropped 1 percent, some revision in plans may be needed. For example, managers can decide to lower the original goal or spend more money on advertising.

The Science and the Art of Management

Given the complexity inherent in the manager's job, one may ask whether management is more of a science or an art. In fact, effective management is a blend of both science and art. And successful executives recognize the importance of combining both the science and the art of management as they practice their craft.[3]

The Science of Management Many management problems and issues can be approached in ways that are rational, logical, objective, and systematic. Managers can gather data, facts, and objective information. They can use quantitative models and decision-making techniques to arrive at "correct" decisions. They need to take such a scientific approach to solving problems whenever possible, especially

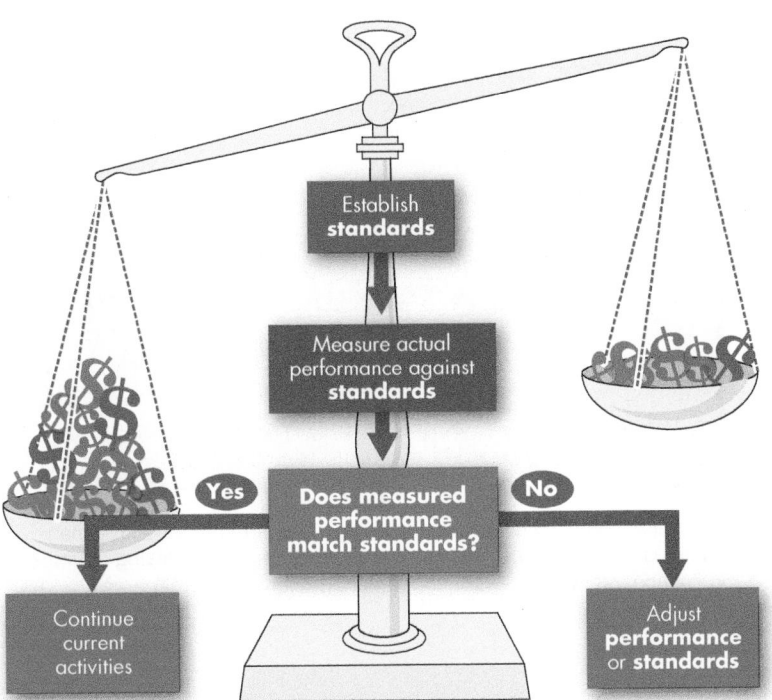

FIGURE 5.2 The Control Process

when they are dealing with relatively routine and straightforward issues. When Starbucks considers entering a new market, its managers look closely at a wide variety of objective details as they formulate their plans. Technical, diagnostic, and decision-making skills (which we will discuss later in the chapter) are especially important when approaching a management task or problem from a scientific perspective.

The Art of Management Even though managers may try to be scientific as often as possible, they must frequently make decisions and solve problems on the basis of intuition, experience, instinct, and personal insights. Relying heavily on conceptual, communication, interpersonal, and time-management skills, for example, a manager may have to decide among multiple courses of action that look equally attractive. And even "objective facts" may prove to be wrong. When Starbucks was planning its first store in New York City, market research clearly showed that New Yorkers preferred drip coffee to more exotic espresso-style coffees. After first installing more drip coffeemakers and fewer espresso makers than in their other stores, managers had to backtrack when New Yorkers lined up, clamoring for espresso. Starbucks now introduces a standard menu and layout in all its stores, regardless of presumed market differences, and then makes necessary adjustments later. Thus, managers must blend an element of intuition and personal insight with hard data and objective facts.[4]

Becoming a Manager

How does one acquire the skills necessary to blend the science and art of management and become a successful manager? Although there are as many variations as there are managers, the most common path involves a combination of education and experience.[5]

The Role of Education Many of you reading this book right now are doing so because you are enrolled in a management course at a college or university. You are already acquiring management skills in an educational setting. When you complete the course (and this book), you will have a foundation for developing your management skills in more advanced courses. A college degree has become almost a

Education plays a vital role in becoming a manager. Prospective managers usually complete at least one degree in business, taking courses in finance, marketing, accounting, management, and other areas.

requirement for career advancement in business, and virtually all CEOs in the United States have a college degree. MBA degrees are also common among successful executives today. Most foreign universities also offer academic programs in management.

Even after obtaining a degree, most prospective managers have not seen the end of their management education. Many middle and top managers periodically return to campus to participate in executive or management development programs, ranging in duration from a few days to several weeks. First-line managers also take advantage of extension and continuing education programs offered by institutions of higher education or through online media. A recent innovation in extended management education is the executive MBA program offered by many top business schools, in which middle and top managers with several years of experience complete an accelerated program of study on weekends.[6] Finally, many large companies have in-house training programs for furthering managers' education. Indeed, some firms have even created what are essentially corporate universities to provide the specialized education they feel is required for their managers for them to remain successful.[7] McDonald's, General Electric, and Shell Oil are among the leaders in in-house courses. Alongside formal education routes, there is also a distinct trend toward online educational development for managers.[8]

The primary advantage of education as a source of management skills is that, as a student, a person can follow a well-developed program of study, becoming familiar with current research and thinking on management. Many college students can devote full-time energy and attention to learning. On the negative side, management education is often general and meets the needs of a wide variety of students; specific know-how may be hard to obtain. Further, although many aspects of the manager's job can be discussed in a book, it is hard to appreciate and understand them until you have experienced them.

The Role of Experience This book will help provide you a solid foundation for enhancing your management skills. Even if you were to memorize every word in every management book ever written, however, you could not then step into a top management position and immediately be effective. Why not? Management skills must also be learned through experience. Most managers advanced to their present positions from other jobs. Only by experiencing the day-to-day pressures a manager faces and by meeting a variety of managerial challenges can an individual develop insights into the real nature and character of managerial work.

For this reason, most large companies, and many smaller ones as well, have developed management-training programs for their prospective managers. People are hired from college campuses, from other organizations, or from the ranks of the organization's first-line managers and operating employees. These people are systematically assigned to a variety of jobs. Over time, the individual is exposed to most, if not all, of the major aspects of the organization. In this way, the manager learns by experience. The training programs at some companies, such as Procter & Gamble, General Mills, and Shell Oil, are so good that other companies try to hire people who have graduated from them.[9] Even without formal training programs, managers can achieve success as they profit from varied experiences. For example, Herb Kelleher was a practicing attorney before he took over at Southwest Airlines and led it to become one of the most successful and admired businesses in the United States. Of course, natural ability, drive, and self-motivation also play roles in acquiring experience and developing management skills.

The majority of effective managers learn their skills through a combination of education and experience. Some type of college degree, even if it is not in business administration, usually provides a foundation for a management career. The individual then gets his or her first job and subsequently progresses through a variety of management situations. During the manager's rise in the organization, occasional education "updates," such as management-development programs, may supplement on-the-job experience. Increasingly, managers also need to acquire international expertise as part of their personal development. As with general managerial skills, international expertise can be acquired through a combination of education and experience.[10]

Types of Managers

OBJECTIVE 5-2
Identify
different types of managers likely to be found in an organization by level and area.

Although all managers plan, organize, lead, and control, not all managers have the same degree of responsibility for these activities. It is helpful to classify managers according to levels and areas of responsibility.

Levels of Management

The three basic levels of management are *top, middle,* and *first-line* management. As summarized in Table 5.1, most firms have more middle managers than top managers and more first-line managers than middle managers. Both the power of managers and the complexity of their duties increase as they move up the ladder.

Top Managers Like Brin, Page, and Schultz, the fairly small number of executives who get the chance to guide the fortunes of most companies are top managers. Common titles for top managers include *president, vice president, treasurer, chief executive officer* (CEO), and *chief financial officer* (CFO). **Top managers** are responsible for the overall performance and effectiveness of the firm. They set general policies, formulate strategies, approve all significant decisions, and represent the company in dealings with other firms and with government bodies. Indra Nooyi, Chairman and CEO of PepsiCo, is a top manager.

Top Manager *manager responsible for a firm's overall performance and effectiveness*

Middle Managers Just below the ranks of top managers is another group of managers who also occupy positions of considerable autonomy and importance and who are called middle managers. Titles such as *plant manager, operations manager,* and *division manager* designate middle-management slots. In general, **middle managers** are responsible for implementing the strategies and working toward the goals set by top managers.[11] For example, if top management decides to introduce a new product in 12 months or to cut costs by 5 percent in the next quarter, middle managers are primarily responsible for determining how to meet these goals. The manager of an American Express service center or a regional sales manager of Frito-Lay snack products (a division of PepsiCo) will likely be a middle manager.

Middle Manager *manager responsible for implementing the strategies and working toward the goals set by top managers*

table 5.1 The Three Levels of Management

Level	Examples	Responsibilities
Top managers	President, vice president, treasurer, CEO, chief financial officer (CFO)	• Responsible for the overall performance and effectiveness of the firm • Set general policies, formulate strategies, and approve all significant decisions • Represent the company in dealings with other firms and with government bodies
Middle managers	Plant manager, operations manager, division manager, regional sales manager	• Responsible for implementing the strategies and working toward the goals set by top managers
First-line managers	Supervisor, office manager, project manager, group leader, sales manager	• Responsible for supervising the work of employees who report to them • Ensure employees understand and are properly trained in company policies and procedures

First-Line Managers Those who hold such titles as *supervisor, office manager, project manager*, and *group leader* are **first-line managers**. Although they spend most of their time working with and supervising the employees who report to them, first-line managers' activities are not limited to that arena. At a building site, for example, the project manager not only ensures that workers are carrying out construction as specified by the architect but also interacts extensively with materials suppliers, community officials, and middle- and upper-level managers at the home office. The supervisor of delivery drivers for Frito-Lay products in Cleveland would be considered a first-line manager.

First-Line Manager *manager responsible for supervising the work of employees*

Areas of Management

In any large company, top, middle, and first-line managers work in a variety of areas, including human resources, operations, marketing, information, and finance. For the most part, these areas correspond to the types of basic management skills described later in this chapter and to the wide range of business principles and activities discussed in the rest of this book.

Human Resource Managers Most companies have *human resource managers* who hire and train employees, evaluate performance, and determine compensation. At large firms, separate departments deal with recruiting and hiring, wage and salary levels, and labor relations. A smaller firm may have a single department—or even a single person—responsible for all human resource activities. (We discuss the key issues in human resource management in Chapter 10.)

Operations Managers As we will see in Chapter 7, the term *operations* refers to the systems by which a firm produces goods and services. Among other duties, *operations managers* are responsible for production, inventory, and quality control. Manufacturing companies such as General Electric, Ford, and Caterpillar have a strong need for operations managers at many levels. Such firms typically have a *vice president for operations* (top manager), *plant managers* (middle managers), and *production supervisors* (first-line managers). In recent years, sound operations management practices have become increasingly important to a variety of service organizations.

entrepreneurship and new ventures

Innovations in Management

In 2004 Sal Khan made a series of rudimentary Web videos that went viral, and by 2009 Khan had quit his day job as a hedge fund manager to keep up with demand. Today, the Khan Academy website draws over 10 million unique visitors every month and has evolved into an international adaptive learning system providing a free education to anyone with Web access.

In an interview with Stephen Meyer of *Forbes* magazine, Khan identified his three core management strategies:

1 Motivate managers by linking talent development to their compensation. Even though as a not-for-profit Khan Academy can't offer big bonuses and stock options, Khan's pays well—commensurate with the upper-quartile of Silicon Valley. He's a firm believer in rewarding good work with adequate pay, and the productivity of his team proves his point.

2 Make it easier for managers by giving them tools. One of his goals is to create a library of internal videos that capture the Khan approach to every imaginable challenge, from how to read a financial statement to delegation, stating, "It would be very hypocritical if we're out there trying to make tools and resources for the rest of the world to learn, but we weren't doing that with our own people."

3 Set an example. Khan is just discovering management for himself. He'd rather be making videos and coding, but

as the organization has grown, so has his role, and he's begun to develop a whole new generation of managers, leading and teaching by example.

Khan's perspective is that the role of management is mentoring rather than motivating. "It's an eighteenth- or nineteenth-century phenomenon to say the role of a manager is to get someone to do work," he explains. "That's wrong. The role of a modern manager is, 'How do I develop my people?'"[12]

Marketing Managers As we will see in Chapter 11, marketing encompasses the development, pricing, promotion, and distribution of goods and services. *Marketing managers* are responsible for getting products from producers to consumers. Marketing is especially important for firms that manufacture or sell consumer products, such as Under Armour, Frito-Lay, and Apple. Such firms often have large numbers of marketing managers at several levels. For example, a large consumer products firm is likely to have a *vice president for marketing* (top manager), several *regional marketing managers* (middle managers), and several *district sales managers* (first-line managers).

Information Managers Occupying a fairly new managerial position in many firms, *information managers* design and implement systems to gather, organize, and distribute information. Huge increases in both the sheer volume of information and the ability to manage it have led to the emergence of this important function. Although still relatively few in number, the ranks of information managers are growing at all levels. Some firms have a top-management position for a *chief information officer (CIO)*. Middle managers help design information systems for divisions or plants. Computer systems managers within smaller businesses are usually first-line managers. We'll discuss information management in more detail in Chapter 13.

Financial Managers Nearly every company has *financial managers* to plan and oversee its accounting functions and financial resources. Levels of financial management may include *CFO* or *vice president for finance* (top), a *division controller* (middle), and an *accounting supervisor* (first-line manager). Some financial institutions, such as Wells Fargo and State Farm Insurance, have even made effective financial management the company's reason for being. We'll discuss financial management in more detail in Chapters 14 and 15.

Other Managers Some firms also employ other specialized managers. Many companies, for example, have public relations managers. Chemical, pharmaceutical, and technology companies such as Dow Chemical, Merck, and HP have research and development managers. The range of possibilities is wide, and the areas of management are limited only by the needs and imagination of the firm.

OBJECTIVE 5-3
Describe
the basic roles and skills
required of managers.

Management Roles and Skills

Regardless of their levels or areas within an organization, all managers must play certain roles and exhibit certain skills if they are to be successful. The concept of a role, in this sense, is similar to the role an actor plays in a theatrical production. A person does certain things, meets certain needs, and has certain responsibilities in the organization. In the sections that follow, first we highlight the basic roles managers play and then discuss the skills they need to be effective.

Managerial Roles

Research offers a number of interesting insights into the nature of managerial roles.[13] Based on detailed observations of what executives do, it appears that many of their activities fall into 10 different roles. These roles, summarized in Table 5.2, fall into three basic categories: interpersonal, informational, and decisional.

Interpersonal Roles *a category of managerial roles, including figurehead, leader, and liaison*

Interpersonal Roles Three **interpersonal roles** are inherent in the manager's job. First, the manager is often expected to serve as a *figurehead*—taking visitors to dinner, attending ribbon-cutting ceremonies, and the like. These activities are typically more ceremonial and symbolic than substantive. The manager is also expected to serve as a *leader*—hiring, training, and motivating employees. A manager who formally or informally shows subordinates how to do things and how to perform under pressure is leading. Finally, managers can have a *liaison* role. This role often involves serving as a coordinator or link among people, groups, or organizations. For example, companies in the computer industry may use liaisons to keep other companies informed about their plans. This enables Microsoft, for example, to create software for interfacing with new Canon printers at the same time those printers are being developed. And, at the same time, managers at Canon can incorporate new Microsoft features into the printers they introduce.

table 5.2 Basic Managerial Roles

Category	Role	Sample Activities
Interpersonal	Figurehead	Attending ribbon-cutting ceremony for new plant
	Leader	Encouraging employees to improve productivity
	Liaison	Coordinating activities of two project groups
Informational	Monitor	Scanning industry reports to stay abreast of developments
	Disseminator	Sending memos outlining new organizational initiatives
	Spokesperson	Making a speech to discuss growth plans
Decisional	Entrepreneur	Developing new ideas and fostering innovation
	Disturbance handler	Resolving conflict between two subordinates
	Resource allocator	Reviewing and revising budget requests
	Negotiator	Reaching agreement with a key supplier or labor union

Informational Roles The three **informational roles** flow naturally from the interpersonal roles just discussed. The process of carrying out the interpersonal roles places the manager at a strategic point to gather and disseminate information. The first informational role is that of *monitor*, one who actively seeks information that may be of value. The manager questions subordinates, is receptive to unsolicited information, and attempts to be as well informed as possible. The manager is also a *disseminator* of information, transmitting relevant information back to others in the workplace. When the roles of monitor and disseminator are viewed together, the manager emerges as a vital link in the organization's chain of communication. The third informational role focuses on external communication. The *spokesperson* formally relays information to people outside the unit or outside the organization. For example, a plant manager at Dow Chemical may transmit information to top-level managers so that they will be better informed about the plant's activities. The manager may also represent the organization before a chamber of commerce or consumer group. Although the roles of spokesperson and figurehead are similar, there is one basic difference between them. When a manager acts as a figurehead, the manager's presence as a symbol of the organization is what is of interest. In the spokesperson role, however, the manager carries information and communicates it to others in a formal sense.

Informational Roles a category of managerial roles, including monitor, disseminator, and spokesperson

Decisional Roles The manager's informational roles typically lead to the **decisional roles**. The information acquired by the manager as a result of performing the informational roles has a major bearing on important decisions that he or she makes. There are four decisional roles. First, the manager has the role of *entrepreneur*, the voluntary initiator of change. A manager at 3M Company developed the idea for the Post-it Note but had to "sell" it to other skeptical managers inside the company. A second decisional role is initiated not by the manager but by some other individual or group. The manager responds to her role as *disturbance handler* by handling such problems as strikes, copyright infringements, or problems in public relations or corporate image.

Decisional Roles a category of managerial roles, including entrepreneur, disturbance handler, resource allocator, and negotiator

The third decisional role is that of *resource allocator*. As resource allocator, the manager decides how resources are distributed and with whom he or she will work most closely. For example, a manager typically allocates the funds in the unit's operating budget among the unit's members and projects. A fourth decisional role is that of *negotiator*. In this role, the manager enters into negotiations with other groups or organizations as a representative of the company. For example, managers may negotiate

Managers play a variety of important roles. One key interpersonal role is that of figurehead. These managers, for example, are cutting a ribbon symbolizing the opening of a new business.

a union contract, an agreement with a consultant, or a long-term relationship with a supplier. Negotiations may also be internal to the organization. The manager may, for instance, mediate a dispute between two subordinates or negotiate with another department for additional support.

Basic Management Skills

In addition to fulfilling numerous roles, managers also need a number of specific skills if they are to succeed. The most fundamental management skills are *technical, interpersonal, conceptual, diagnostic, communication, decision-making*, and *time-management* skills.[14] Global and technology skills are also becoming increasingly important.

Technical Skills skills needed to perform specialized tasks

Technical Skills The skills needed to perform specialized tasks are called **technical skills**. A programmer's ability to write code, an animator's ability to draw, and an accountant's ability to audit a company's records are all examples of technical skills. People develop technical skills through a combination of education and experience. Technical skills are especially important for first-line managers. Many of these managers spend considerable time helping employees solve work-related problems, training them in more efficient procedures, and monitoring performance.

Human Relations Skills skills in understanding and getting along with people

Human Relations Skills Effective managers also generally have good **human relations skills**, skills that enable them to understand and get along with other people. A manager with poor human relations skills may have trouble getting along with subordinates, cause valuable employees to quit or transfer, and contribute to poor morale. Although human relations skills are important at all levels, they are probably most important for middle managers, who must often act as bridges between top managers, first-line managers, and managers from other areas of the organization. Managers should possess good communication skills. Many managers have found that being able both to understand others and to get others to understand them can go a long way toward maintaining good relations in an organization.

Conceptual Skills abilities to think in the abstract, diagnose and analyze different situations, and see beyond the present situation

Conceptual Skills **Conceptual skills** refer to a person's ability to think in the abstract, to diagnose and analyze different situations, and to see beyond the present situation. Conceptual skills help managers recognize new market opportunities and threats. They can also help managers analyze the probable outcomes of their decisions. The need for conceptual skills differs at various management levels. Top managers depend most on conceptual skills, first-line managers least. Although the purposes and everyday needs of various jobs differ, conceptual skills are needed in almost any job-related activity. In many ways, conceptual skills may be the most important ingredient in the success of executives in e-commerce businesses. For example, the ability to foresee how a particular business application will be affected by or can be translated to the Internet is clearly conceptual in nature.

Decision-Making Skills skills in defining problems and selecting the best courses of action

Decision-Making Skills **Decision-making skills** include the ability to effectively define a problem and to select the best course of action. These skills involve gathering facts, identifying solutions, evaluating alternatives, and implementing the chosen alternative. Periodically following up and evaluating the effectiveness of the choice are also part of the decision-making process. These skills allow some managers to identify effective strategies for their firm, such as Michael Dell's commitment to direct marketing as the firm's primary distribution model. But poor decision-making skills can also lead to failure and ruin. Indeed, poor decision making played a major role in the demise of such major U.S. businesses as Montgomery Ward, American Motors, Circuit City, and Enron and the decline of firms like Sears and Motorola. We'll discuss decision making more fully in Chapter 9.

Time Management Skills skills associated with the productive use of time

Time Management Skills **Time management skills** are the productive use that managers make of their time. Suppose, for example, that a CEO is paid $2 million in base salary (this is not an especially large CEO salary, by the way!).

Assuming that she works 50 hours a week and takes two weeks' vacation, our CEO earns $800 an hour—a little more than $13 per minute. Any amount of time that she wastes clearly represents a large cost to the firm and its stockholders. Most middle- and lower-level managers receive much smaller salaries than this, of course, but their time is still valuable, and poor use of it still translates into costs and wasted productivity.

To manage time effectively, managers must address four leading causes of wasted time:

1 *Paperwork.* Some managers spend too much time deciding what to do with letters and reports. Most documents of this sort are routine and can be handled quickly. Managers must learn to recognize those documents that require more attention.

2 *Telephone calls.* Experts estimate that managers get interrupted by the telephone every five minutes. To manage this time more effectively, they suggest having an assistant screen all calls and setting aside a certain block of time each day to return the important ones. Unfortunately, the explosive use of cell phones seems to be making this problem even worse for many managers.

3 *Meetings.* Many managers spend as much as four hours a day in meetings. To help keep this time productive, the person handling the meeting should specify a clear agenda, start on time, keep everyone focused on the agenda, and end on time.

4 *E-mail.* Increasingly, managers are relying heavily on e-mail and other forms of digital communication. Time is wasted when managers have to sort through spam and a variety of electronic folders, inboxes, and archives.

Global Management Skills Tomorrow's managers must equip themselves with the special tools, techniques, and skills needed to compete in a global environment—in other words, they need *global management skills*. They will need to understand foreign markets, cultural differences, and the motives and practices of foreign rivals. They also need to understand how to collaborate with others around the world on a real-time basis.

On a more practical level, businesses will need more managers who are capable of understanding international operations. In the past, most U.S. businesses hired local managers to run their operations in the various countries in which they operated. More recently, however, the trend has been to transfer U.S. managers to foreign locations. This practice helps firms transfer their corporate cultures to foreign operations. In addition, foreign assignments help managers become better prepared for international competition as they advance within the organization. The top management teams of large corporations today are also likely to include directors from other countries.

Management and Technology Skills Another significant issue facing tomorrow's managers is technology, especially as it relates to communication. Managers have always had to deal with information. In today's world, however, the amount of information has reached staggering proportions. In the United States alone, people exchange hundreds of millions of e-mail messages every day. New forms of technology have added to a manager's ability to process information while simultaneously making it even more important to organize and interpret an ever-increasing wealth of input and to develop effective *technology skills*.

Technology has also begun to change the way the interaction of managers shapes corporate structures. Elaborate networks control the flow of a firm's lifeblood— information. This information no longer flows strictly up and down through hierarchies. It now flows to everyone simultaneously. As a result, decisions are made quicker, and more people are directly involved. With e-mail, videoconferencing, and other forms of communication, neither time nor distance—nor such corporate boundaries as departments and divisions—can prevent people from working more closely together. More than ever, bureaucracies are breaking down, and planning, decision making, and other activities are beginning to benefit from group building and teamwork. We discuss the effects technology has on business in more detail in Chapter 13.

Strategic Management: Setting Goals and Formulating Strategy

As we noted previously, planning is a critical part of the manager's job. Managers today are increasingly being called on to think and act strategically. **Strategic management** is the process of helping an organization maintain an effective alignment with its environment. For instance, if a firm's business environment is heading toward fiercer competition, the business may need to start cutting its costs and developing more products and services before the competition really starts to heat up. Likewise, if an industry is globalizing, a firm's managers may need to start entering new markets and developing international partnerships during the early stages of globalization rather than waiting for its full effects.

The starting point in effective strategic management is setting **goals**—objectives that a business hopes and plans to achieve. Every business needs goals. Remember, however, that deciding what it intends to do is only the first step for an organization. Managers must also make decisions about what actions will and will not achieve company goals. Decisions cannot be made on a problem-by-problem basis or merely to meet needs as they arise. In most companies, a broad program underlies those decisions. That program is called a **strategy**, which is a broad set of organizational plans for implementing the decisions made for achieving organizational goals. Let's begin by examining business goals more closely.

Setting Business Goals

Goals are performance targets, the means by which organizations and their managers measure success or failure at every level. Different organizations, of course, pursue different goals. And the goals of any given organization change over time. At AmEx, for example, CEO Kenneth Chenault is currently focusing on revenue growth, the firm's stock price, and digital technology. At Pepsi, CEO Indra Nooyi's goals include keeping abreast of changing consumer tastes and leveraging the firm's current products into new markets. And CEO Oscar Munoz's goals at United Airlines are to continue the smooth integration of Continental and United into one of the world's largest airlines while also overcoming some of the negative imagery created by his predecessor, Jeff Smisek.

Purposes of Goal Setting An organization functions systematically when it sets goals and plans accordingly. An organization commits its resources on all levels to achieve its goals. Specifically, we can identify four main purposes in organizational goal setting:

1 *Goal setting provides direction and guidance for managers at all levels.* If managers know precisely where the company is headed, there is less potential for error in the different units of the company. Starbucks, for example, has a goal of increasing capital spending by 10 percent, with all additional expenditures devoted to opening new stores. This goal clearly informs everyone in the firm that expansion into new territories is a high priority for the firm.

2 *Goal setting helps firms allocate resources.* Areas that are expected to grow will get first priority. The company allocates more resources to new projects with large sales potential than it allocates to mature products with established but stagnant sales potential. Thus, Starbucks is primarily emphasizing new

store expansion, and its e-commerce initiatives are currently given a lower priority. "Our management team," says recently retired CEO Howard Schultz, "is 100 percent focused on growing our core business without distraction … from any other initiative."

3 *Goal setting helps to define corporate culture.* For years, the goal at General Electric has been to push each of its divisions to first or second in its industry. The result is a competitive (and often stressful) environment and a corporate culture that rewards success and has little tolerance for failure. At the same time, however, GE's appliance business, medical technology, aircraft engine unit, and financial services business are each among the best in their respective industries. Eventually, the firm's CEO set an even higher companywide standard: to make the firm the most valuable one in the world.

4 *Goal setting helps managers assess performance.* If a unit sets a goal of increasing sales by 10 percent in a given year, managers in that unit who attain or exceed the goal can be rewarded. Units failing to reach the goal will also be compensated accordingly. GE has a long-standing reputation for evaluating managerial performance, richly rewarding those who excel—and getting rid of those who do not.

Kinds of Goals Goals differ from company to company, depending on the firm's purpose and mission. Every enterprise has a purpose, or a reason for being. Businesses seek profits, universities seek to discover and transmit new knowledge, and government agencies seek to set and enforce public policy. Many enterprises also have missions and **mission statements**, statements of how they will achieve their purposes in the environments in which they conduct their businesses.

Mission Statement *organization's statement of how it will achieve its purpose in the environment in which it conducts its business*

A company's mission is usually easy to identify, at least at a basic level. Starbucks sums up its mission succinctly: The firm intends to "establish Starbucks as the premier purveyor of the finest coffee in the world while maintaining our uncompromising principles while we grow." But businesses sometimes have to rethink their strategies and mission as the competitive environment changes. A few years ago, for example, Starbucks announced that Internet marketing and sales were going to become core business initiatives. Managers subsequently realized, however, that this initiative did not fit the firm as well as they first thought. As a result, they scaled back this effort and made a clear recommitment to their existing retail business. The demands of change force many companies to rethink their missions and revise their statements of what they are and what they do.

In addition to its mission, every firm also has *long-term*, *intermediate*, and *short-term goals*:

- **Long-term goals** relate to extended periods of time, typically five years or more. For example, AmEx might set a long-term goal of doubling the number of participating merchants during the next 10 years. Canon might adopt a long-term goal of increasing its share of the digital camera market by 10 percent during the next eight years.

Long-Term Goal *goal set for an extended time, typically five years or more into the future*

- **Intermediate goals** are set for a period of one to five years. Companies usually set intermediate goals in several areas. For example, the marketing department's goal might be to increase sales by 3 percent in two years. The production department might want to reduce expenses by 6 percent in four years. Human resources might seek to cut turnover by 10 percent in two years. Finance might aim for a 3 percent increase in return on investment in three years.

Intermediate Goal *goal set for a period of one to five years into the future*

- **Short-term goals** are set for perhaps one year and are developed for several different areas. Increasing sales by 2 percent this year, cutting costs by 1 percent next quarter, and reducing turnover by 4 percent over the next six months are examples of short-term goals.

Short-Term Goal *goal set for the near future*

After a firm has set its goals, it then focuses attention on strategies to accomplish them.

Types of Strategy

As shown in Figure 5.3, the three types of strategy that are usually considered by a company are *corporate strategy, business* (or *competitive) strategy,* and *functional strategy.*

Corporate Strategy *strategy for determining the firm's overall attitude toward growth and the way it will manage its businesses or product lines*

Corporate Strategy The purpose of **corporate strategy** is to determine what business or businesses a company will own and operate. Some corporations own and operate only a single business. The makers of WD-40, for example, concentrate solely on that brand. Other corporations own and operate many businesses. A company may decide to *grow* by increasing its activities or investment or to *retrench* by reducing them.

Sometimes a corporation buys and operates multiple businesses in compatible industries as part of its corporate strategy. For example, the restaurant chains operated by YUM! (KFC, Pizza Hut, and Taco Bell) are clearly related to one another. This strategy is called *related diversification.* However, if the businesses are not similar, the strategy is called *unrelated diversification.* Samsung, which owns electronics, construction, chemicals, catering, and hotel businesses, is following this approach. Under Kenneth Chenault, AmEx corporate strategy calls for strengthening operations through a principle of growth called *e-partnering,* buying shares of small companies that can provide technology that AmEx itself does not have.

Business (or Competitive) Strategy *strategy, at the business-unit or product-line level, focusing on improving a firm's competitive position*

Business (or Competitive) Strategy When a corporation owns and operates multiple businesses, it must develop strategies for each one. **Business (or competitive) strategy,** then, takes place at the level of the business unit or product line and focuses on improving the company's competitive position. For example, at this level, AmEx makes decisions about how best to compete in an industry that includes Visa, MasterCard, and other credit card companies. In this respect, the company has committed heavily to expanding its product offerings and serving customers through new technology. Pepsi, meanwhile, has one strategy for its soft drink business as it competes with Coca-Cola, a different strategy for its sports drink division, and yet another strategy for its juice beverages division. It has still other strategies for its snack foods businesses.

Functional Strategy *strategy by which managers in specific areas decide how best to achieve corporate goals through productivity*

Functional Strategy At the level of **functional strategy,** managers in specific areas such as marketing, finance, and operations decide how best to achieve corporate goals by performing their functional activities most effectively. At AmEx, for

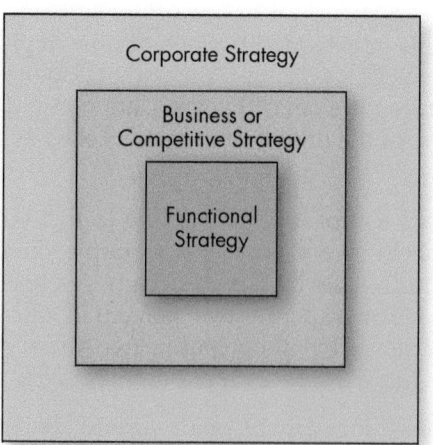

FIGURE 5.3 Hierarchy of Strategy
Source: Based on Thomas L. Wheelen and J. David Hunger, *Strategic Management and Business Policy,* 8th ed. (Upper Saddle River, NJ: Prentice Hall, 2002), 14.

finding a better way

Standing Firm on Social Consciousness

Strategic planning isn't something a company does once. Goals and objectives are moving targets as market forces, mergers and acquisitions, and leadership changes shape and reshape the business environment. Companies have to learn to adapt and to create new strategies to survive and thrive, as was the case with SolarCity in 2016.

Lyndon Rive and his brother Peter created SolarCity in 2006 based on a suggestion by their cousin, Tesla's Elon Musk, who provided venture capital funding. By 2007, the company had become the leading provider of residential solar power in California. In December 2012 the company raised $92 million in its initial public offering, pricing shares at $8. By 2014, the company employed more than 7,500 employees and was the nation's largest installer of solar equipment, with more than 140,000 customers. Sales were skyrocketing and the share price hit a high of almost $85 in February. Both Google and Musk's company SpaceX invested heavily in the business and SolarCity issued over $200 million in bonds to further finance operations.

Rive's strategy to make solar panels more affordable was paying off. The company offered attractive financing and leasing options and leadership changed the focus of their management control model from accounting revenues to cash flow. However, investment analysts began to suspect that most of the growth in the price of the stock was due to investors overvaluing the potential for future growth. SolarCity was leading the way in solar energy, but at a high cost. It had borrowed heavily and had tapped out the capital market.

By mid-2016, the stock price had slumped to less than $20, and big utility companies were fighting back against the idea that consumers could basically live off the grid when the sun was shining, selling back excess energy, and then re-access the power grid again when the weather turned bad.

This is when Musk stepped in and convinced shareholders of Tesla Motors to acquire all of SolarCity's outstanding stock for $2.6 billion. In addition, Musk announced a new Tesla mission statement: "To accelerate the world's transition to sustainable energy," replacing the word *transport* with the word *energy* and, in the process, expanding the vision of the company to bring solar energy into the fold of electric automobiles and

The Bakersfield Californian/ZUMA Press, Inc./Alamy Stock Photo

batteries. In late 2016, as SolarCity was being folded into Tesla, Musk announced in a blog post that he had revised his original overall strategy for the parent company:

"The first master plan that I wrote 10 years ago is now in the final stages of completion. It wasn't all that complicated and basically consisted of: (a) create a low volume car, which would necessarily be expensive; (b) use that money to develop a medium volume car at a lower price; (c) use that money to create an affordable high volume car; and, (d) provide solar power."[15]

Going forward, he lays out his new overall strategy as follows:

- Create stunning solar roofs with seamlessly integrated battery storage.

- Expand the electric vehicle product line to address all major segments.

- Develop a self-driving capability that is 10 times safer than manual via massive fleet learning.

- Enable your car to make money for you when you aren't using it.

In an interview with Sal Khan, founder of Khan Academy, in his *Interview with Entrepreneurs* series, Musk summarized his vision, stating, "Our goal—It's not to become a big brand or to compete with Honda Civics, rather to advance the cause of electric vehicles. And I think the point at which we're approaching half of all new cars made are electric, then I think I would consider that to be the victory condition."[16]

example, each business unit has considerable autonomy in deciding how to use the single website at which the company has located its entire range of services. Pepsi, meanwhile, develops functional strategies for marketing its beverage and snack foods products and operations strategies for distributing them. The real challenges—and opportunities—lie in successfully creating these strategies. Therefore, we now turn our attention to the basic steps in strategy formulation.

Formulating Strategy

Planning is often concerned with the nuts and bolts of setting goals, choosing tactics, and establishing schedules. In contrast, *strategy* tends to have a wider scope. By definition, it is a broad concept that describes an organization's intentions. Further, a strategy outlines how the business intends to meet its goals and includes the organization's responsiveness to new challenges and new needs. Because a well-formulated strategy is so vital to a business's success, most top managers devote substantial attention and creativity to this process. **Strategy formulation** involves the three basic steps summarized in Figure 5.4 and discussed next.

Strategy Formulation *creation of a broad program for defining and meeting an organization's goals*

Strategic Goal *goal derived directly from a firm's mission statement*

Step 1: *Setting Strategic Goals*—**Strategic goals** are derived directly from a firm's mission statement. For example, Disney continually focuses on expanding its dominance of the family entertainment industry. The company continues to invest in its existing properties (expanding its theme parks in Orlando, for example, in 2017 and 2018) and opening new theme parks (Shanghai in 2016, for instance). In addition, Disney has also made a number of strategic acquisitions in recent years, including Pixar, Marvel, and Lucas Films. Each of these initiatives has allowed the firm is add to its revenue base and increase its profit.

Step 2: *Analyzing the Organization and the Environment: SWOT Analysis*—After strategic goals have been established, managers usually attempt to assess both their organization and its environment. A common framework for this assessment is called a **SWOT analysis**. This process involves assessing organizational strengths and weaknesses (the S and W) and environmental opportunities and threats (the O and T). In formulating strategy, managers attempt to capitalize on organizational strengths and take advantage of environmental opportunities. During this same process, they may seek ways to overcome or offset organizational weaknesses and avoid or counter environmental threats. Scanning the business environment for threats and opportunities is often called **environmental analysis**. Changing consumer tastes and hostile takeover offers are threats, as are new government regulations that will limit a firm's opportunities. Even more important threats come from new products and new competitors. For example, online music services such as iTunes dramatically reduced consumer demand for CDs and CD players. Now, however, streaming music services like Spotify and SoundCloud have emerged as threats to iTunes. Likewise, the emergence of digital photography has dramatically weakened companies tied to print photography. Opportunities, meanwhile, are areas in

SWOT Analysis *identification and analysis of organizational strengths and weaknesses and environmental opportunities and threats as part of strategy formulation*

Environmental Analysis *process of scanning the business environment for threats and opportunities*

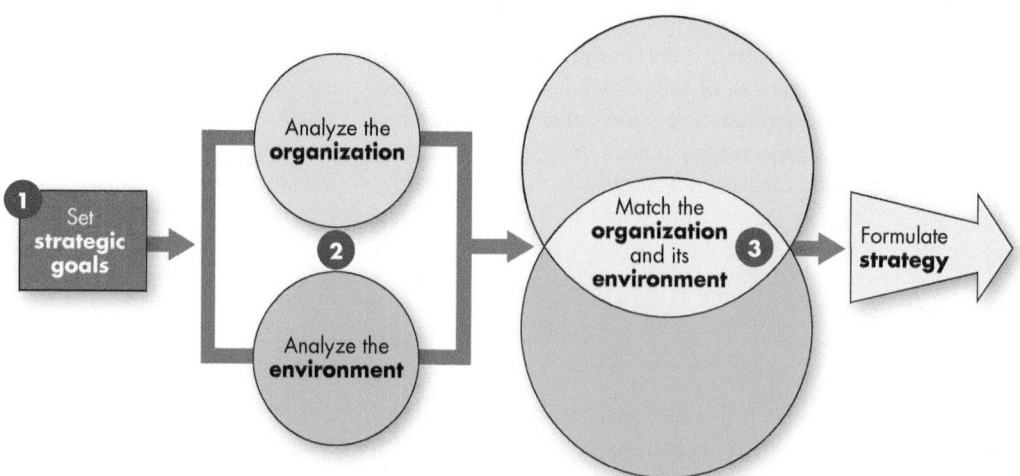

FIGURE 5.4 Strategy Formulation
Source: Adapted from Stephen P. Robbins and Mary Coulter, *Management*, 12th ed. (Upper Saddle River, NJ: Prentice Hall, 2014), 242.

which the firm can potentially expand, grow, or take advantage of existing strengths. For example, when Pepsi managers recognized the growing market potential for bottled water, they moved quickly to launch their Aquafina brand and to position it for rapid growth.

In addition to analyzing external factors by performing an environmental analysis, managers must also examine internal factors. The purpose of such an **organizational analysis** is to better understand a company's strengths and weaknesses. Strengths might include surplus cash, a dedicated workforce, an ample supply of managerial talent, technical expertise, or little competition. For example, Pepsi's strength in beverage distribution through its network of soft drink distributors was successfully extended to distribution of bottled water. A cash shortage, aging factories, a heavily unionized workforce, and a poor public image can all be important weaknesses.

Organizational Analysis *process of analyzing a firm's strengths and weaknesses*

Step 3: *Matching the Organization and Its Environment*—The final step in strategy formulation is matching environmental threats and opportunities against corporate strengths and weaknesses. This matching process is at the heart of strategy formulation. That is, a firm should attempt to leverage its strengths so as to capitalize on opportunities and counteract threats. It should also attempt to shield its weaknesses, or at least not allow them to derail other activities. For instance, knowing how to distribute consumer products (a strength) allows Pepsi to add new businesses and extend existing ones that use the same distribution models. But a firm that lacked a strong understanding of consumer product distribution would be foolish to add new products whose success relied heavily on efficient distribution.

Understanding strengths and weaknesses may also determine whether a firm typically takes risks or behaves more conservatively. Either approach can be successful. For example, Google's reputation as an innovator, its cadre of creative product designers and engineers, and strong cash reserves all allow the firm to constantly look for new product ideas and quickly test them in the market. On the other hand, Apple has many of the same strengths but because its products require longer design and manufacturing cycles, and in most cases more financial investment, the firm is more deliberate and systematic in rolling out new products.

A Hierarchy of Plans

The final step in formulating strategy is translating the strategy into more operational language. This process generally involves the creation of actual plans. Plans can be viewed on three levels: *strategic, tactical,* and *operational*. Managerial responsibilities are defined at each level. The levels constitute a hierarchy because implementing plans is practical only when there is a logical flow from one level to the next (see Figure 5.5).

- **Strategic plans** reflect decisions about resource allocations, company priorities, and the steps needed to meet strategic goals. They are usually created by the firm's top management team but, as noted previously, often rely on input from others in the organization. So, the fundamental outcome of the strategic planning process is the creation of a strategic plan. General Electric's decision that viable businesses must rank first or second within their respective markets is a matter of strategic planning.

Strategic Plan *plan reflecting decisions about resource allocations, company priorities, and steps needed to meet strategic goals*

- **Tactical plans** are shorter-term plans for implementing specific aspects of the company's strategic plans. That is, after a strategic plan has been created, managers then develop shorter-term plans to guide decisions so they are consistent with the strategic plan. They typically involve upper and middle management. Dell's effort to extend its distribution expertise into the markets for televisions and other home electronics is an example of tactical planning.

Tactical Plan *generally short-term plan concerned with implementing specific aspects of a company's strategic plans*

- **Operational plans**, which are developed by mid-level and lower-level managers, set short-term targets for daily, weekly, or monthly performance. Starbucks, for instance, has operational plans dealing with how its stores must buy, store, and brew coffee.

Operational Plan *plan setting short-term targets for daily, weekly, or monthly performance*

FIGURE 5.5 The Hierarchy of Plans

Contingency Planning and Crisis Management

OBJECTIVE 5-5
Discuss
contingency planning and crisis management in today's business world.

Because business environments are often difficult to predict and because the unexpected can create major problems, most managers recognize that even the best-laid plans sometimes simply do not work out. For instance, when The Walt Disney Company first announced plans to launch a cruise line replete with familiar Disney characters and themes, managers also began aggressively developing and marketing packages linking cruises with visits to Disney World in Florida. The inaugural sailing was sold out more than a year in advance, and the first year was booked solid six months before the ship was launched. Three months before the first sailing, however, the shipyard constructing Disney's first ship (the *Disney Magic*) notified the company that it was behind schedule and that delivery would be several weeks late. When similar problems befall other more established cruise lines, they can generally offer to rebook passengers on alternative itineraries. Because Disney had no other ship, it had no choice but to refund the money it had collected as prebooking deposits for its first 15 cruises.

The 20,000 displaced customers were offered big discounts if they rebooked on a later cruise. Many of them, however, could not rearrange their schedules and requested full refunds. Moreover, quite a few blamed Disney for the problem and expressed outrage at what they saw as poor planning by the entertainment giant. Fortunately for Disney, however, the *Disney Magic* was eventually launched and has now become popular and profitable. Because managers know such things can happen, they often develop alternative plans in case things go awry. Two common methods of dealing with the unknown and unforeseen are *contingency planning* and *crisis management*.

Contingency Planning

Contingency Planning *identifying aspects of a business or its environment that might entail changes in strategy*

Contingency planning seeks to identify in advance important aspects of a business or its market that might change. It also identifies the ways in which a company will respond to changes. Suppose, for example, that a company develops a plan to create a new division. It expects sales to increase at an annual rate of 10 percent for the

managing in turbulent times

When Disaster Strikes

From exploding Samsung smartphones to Wells Fargo fraud, companies had their share of bungles in 2016. But sometimes crisis arises from external events. For instance, insurance companies paid out billions of dollars to settle business and personal claims in 2016 due to wildfires like the Soberanes fire in Monterey County, California. In addition to safeguarding a company from internal woes, a good strategic plan includes both contingency planning and a crisis management plan that enables a company to recover from other disasters such as fire, flood, computer or network failure, and data loss.

While most businesses never see a fire outside their door, network failure and data loss are fairly common. On October 21, 2016, major websites such as Twitter, Netflix, Spotify, and Airbnb were shut down by a cyber-attack on Dyn, a company whose servers monitor and reroute Internet traffic. Dyn is one of many hosts for the Domain Name System, or DNS, which translates user-friendly Web addresses like amazon.com into numerical addresses. Without the DNS servers operated by Internet service providers, the Internet could not operate.

The attack was identified as a Distributed Denial-of-Service (DDoS) attack used on hundreds of thousands of Internet-connected devices like cameras, baby monitors, and home routers—all infected with malware to flood the company's servers with traffic until it collapsed under the load. Such attacks are becoming more and more common, and there is evidence that they are also becoming more powerful, more sophisticated, and increasingly aimed at core Internet infrastructure providers.

Security researchers have long warned that the increasing number of devices being hooked up to the Internet—the so-called Internet of Things—would present an enormous security issue. In this case, the attack was aimed at the Dyn

Matejmo/iStock/Getty Images Plus/Getty Images

infrastructure that supports Internet connections. While the attack did not affect the websites themselves, it blocked or slowed users trying to gain access to those sites.

Strategists note that these assaults are the reason so many companies are pushing at least parts of their infrastructure to cloud computing networks, to decentralize their systems and make them harder to attack. Even so, in March 2017, Amazon's Web servers, the largest and most secure in the world and serving such notable companies as Airbnb, the Securities and Exchange Commission, Adobe, and Amazon itself, suffered an hours-long outage that affected Internet functionality across the world. The cause? A typo in a coding update. The giant S3 storage system had grown beyond Amazon's capacity to serve, and the single innocuous command issued during a routine debugging attempt caused a series of cascading failures that shut down the cloud storage service for hours, costing unknown millions of dollars of business interruption.

next five years, and it develops a marketing strategy for maintaining that level. But suppose that sales have increased by only 5 percent by the end of the first year. Does the firm (1) abandon the venture, (2) invest more in advertising, or (3) wait to see what happens in the second year? Whichever choice the firm makes, its efforts will be more efficient if managers decide in advance what to do in case sales fall below planned levels.

Contingency planning helps them do exactly that. Disney learned from its mistake with its first ship; when the second ship was launched a year later, managers allowed for an extra two weeks between when the ship was supposed to be ready for sailing and its first scheduled cruise.

Crisis Management

A crisis is an unexpected emergency requiring immediate response. **Crisis management** involves an organization's methods for dealing with emergencies. Seeing the consequences of poor crisis management after the California wildfires in 2010, the impact of Hurricane Sandy in 2012, and the Carnival cruise ship debacle in 2013 that left thousands of passengers floating in the Gulf of Mexico for days without power and toilet facilities, many firms today are working to create new and better crisis management

Crisis Management *organization's methods for dealing with emergencies*

plans and procedures. One of the most recent areas for crisis management is the growing threat of terrorism. Businesses are being challenged to consider how they might best respond if one of their facilities is bombed by terrorists or if an employee is taken hostage by a terrorist group.[17]

For example, both Reliant Energy and Duke Energy rely on computer trading centers where trading managers actively buy and sell energy-related commodities. If a terrorist attack or natural disaster were to strike their trading centers, they would essentially be out of business. Consequently, Reliant and Duke have created secondary trading centers at other locations. In the event of a shutdown at their main trading centers, these firms can quickly transfer virtually all their core trading activities to their secondary centers within 30 minutes or less.[18] However, many firms do not have comprehensive crisis management strategies. For example, as concerns grew about the outbreak of Ebola in 2015 and some officials warned of a possible pandemic, a survey found that only about 57 percent of U.S. businesses had plans in place to deal with a viral or bacterial pandemic.

Management and the Corporate Culture

OBJECTIVE 5-6
Describe
the development and explain the importance of corporate culture.

Corporate Culture *the shared experiences, stories, beliefs, and norms that characterize an organization*

Every organization—big or small, more successful or less successful—has an unmistakable "feel" to it. Just as every individual has a unique personality, every company has a unique identity, or a **corporate culture**, the shared experiences, stories, beliefs, and norms that characterize an organization. This culture helps define the work and business climate that exists in an organization.

A strong corporate culture serves several purposes. For one thing, it directs employees' efforts and helps everyone work toward the same goals. Some cultures, for example, stress financial success to the extreme, whereas others focus more on quality of life. In addition, corporate culture helps newcomers learn accepted behaviors. If financial success is the key to a culture, newcomers quickly learn that they are expected to work long, hard hours, and that the "winner" is the one who brings in the most revenue. But if quality of life is more fundamental, newcomers learn that it's more acceptable to spend less time at work and that balancing work and nonwork is encouraged.

Building and Communicating Culture

Where does a business's culture come from? In some cases, it emanates from the days of an organization's founder. Firms such as Disney, Walmart, and Starbucks, for example, still bear the imprint of their founders. In other cases, an organization's culture is forged over a long period of time by a constant and focused business strategy. Pepsi, for example, has an achievement-oriented culture tied to its long-standing goal of catching its biggest competitor, Coca-Cola. Similarly, Google has a sort of "work hard, play hard" culture stemming from its constant emphasis on innovation and growth coupled with lavish benefits and high pay.

Corporate culture influences management philosophy, style, and behavior. Managers, therefore, must carefully consider the kind of culture they want for their organizations and then work to nourish that culture by communicating with everyone who works there.

To use a firm's culture to its advantage, managers must accomplish several tasks, all of which hinge on effective communication. First, managers themselves must have a clear understanding of the culture. Second, they must transmit the culture to others in the organization. Thus, training and orientation for newcomers in an organization often include information about the firm's culture. A clear and meaningful statement of the organization's mission is also a valuable communication tool.

Sam Walton honed his craft as a retailer at Walton's Five and Dime. He then used his experience to create a unique corporate culture when he founded Walmart.

Finally, managers can maintain the culture by rewarding and promoting those who understand it and work toward maintaining it.

Changing Culture

Organizations must sometimes change their cultures. In such cases, they must also communicate the nature of the change to both employees and customers. According to the CEOs of several companies that have undergone radical change in the last decade or so, the process usually goes through three stages:

1   *At the highest level, analysis of the company's environment highlights extensive change as the most effective response to its problems.* This period is typically characterized by conflict and resistance.

2   *Top management begins to formulate a vision of a new company.* Whatever that vision, it must include renewed focus on the activities of competitors and the needs of customers.

3   *The firm sets up new systems for appraising and compensating employees who enforce the firm's new values.* The purpose is to give the new culture solid shape from within the firm.

Continental and United Airlines recently merged into a single, much larger airline. Top managers then developed a plan for creating one new unified corporate culture drawing from the best of the cultures at the two individual airlines. The entire process took more than three years.[19]

summary of learning objectives

OBJECTIVE 5-1

Describe the nature of management and identify the four basic functions that constitute the management process. (pp. 144–149)

Management is the process of planning, organizing, leading, and controlling a firm's resources to achieve its goals. *Planning* is determining what the organization needs to do and how best to get it done. The process of arranging resources and activities into a coherent structure is called *organizing.* When *leading*, a manager guides and motivates employees to meet the firm's objectives. *Controlling* is the process of monitoring performance to make sure that a firm is meeting its goals.

Effective management is a blend of both science and art. Many management problems and issues can be approached in ways that are rational, logical, objective, and systematic. Managers can gather data, facts, and objective information and use quantitative models and decision-making techniques to arrive at "correct" decisions. But even though managers may try to be scientific as often as possible, they must frequently make decisions and solve problems on the basis of intuition, experience, instinct, and personal insights.

The most common path to becoming a successful manager involves a combination of education and experience. A college degree has become almost a requirement for career advancement in business, and virtually all CEOs in the United States have a college degree. Management skills must also be learned through experience. Most managers advanced to their present positions from other jobs. Only by experiencing the day-to-day pressures a manager faces and by meeting a variety of managerial challenges can an individual develop insights into the real nature and character of managerial work.

OBJECTIVE 5-2

Identify different types of managers likely to be found in an organization by level and area. (pp. 149–152)

The three levels of management are top, middle, and first-line. The few executives who are responsible for the overall performance of large companies are *top managers.* Just below top managers are *middle managers*, including plant, operations, and division managers, who implement strategies, policies, and decisions made by top managers. Supervisors and office managers are the *first-line managers* who work with and supervise the employees who report to them.

In any large company, most managers work in one of five areas. *Human resource managers* hire and train employees, evaluate performance, and determine compensation. *Operations managers* are responsible for production, inventory, and quality control. *Marketing managers* are responsible for getting products from producers to consumers. *Information managers* design and implement systems to gather, organize, and distribute information. Finally, *financial managers*, including the chief financial officer (top), division controllers (middle), and accounting supervisors (first-line), oversee accounting functions and financial resources.

OBJECTIVE 5-3

Describe the basic roles and skills required of managers. (pp. 152–156)

Most managerial activities fall into 10 different roles. These roles fall into three basic categories: interpersonal, informational, and decisional. Three interpersonal roles inherent in the manager's job are *figurehead, leader,* and *liaison.* The three informational roles are *monitor, disseminator,* and *spokesperson.* The four decisional roles are *entrepreneur, disturbance handler, resource allocator,* and *negotiator.*

Effective managers must develop a number of important skills. Traditionally, five managerial skills have been identified: technical skills, human relations skills, conceptual skills, decision-making skills, and time management skills. *Technical skills* are skills needed to perform specialized tasks, including a programmer's ability to write code or an animator's ability to draw. *Human relations skills* are skills in understanding and getting along with other people. *Conceptual skills* refer to the ability to think abstractly, diagnose and analyze different situations, and see beyond the present. *Decision-making skills* include the ability to define a problem and select the best course of action. *Time management skills* refer to the productive use of time, including managing e-mail, telephone calls, and meetings. In the twenty-first century, several new skills have become increasingly important to managers. *Global management skills* include understanding foreign markets, cultural differences, and the motives and practices of foreign rivals. *Technology management skills* include the ability to process, organize, and interpret an ever-increasing amount of information.

OBJECTIVE 5-4

Explain the importance of strategic management and effective goal setting in organizational success. (pp. 156–162)

Strategic management is the process of helping an organization maintain an effective alignment with its environment. It starts with setting *goals*, objectives that a business hopes (and plans) to achieve. Goal setting is vitally important to the organization for several reasons. Goal setting provides direction and guidance for managers at all levels. Goal setting also helps firms to allocate resources and define corporate culture. Finally, goal setting is essential to managers who wish to assess performance. Most companies will create mission statements and long-term, intermediate, and short-term goals.

Strategy refers to a broad set of organizational plans for achieving organizational goals. The three types of strategy that are usually considered by a company are *corporate strategy*, *business* (or *competitive*) *strategy*, and *functional strategy*. Formulating strategy involves setting strategic goals, analyzing the organization and its environment, and then matching the organization to its environment. Most organizations have a hierarchy of strategic, tactical, and operational plans.

OBJECTIVE 5-5

Discuss contingency planning and crisis management in today's business world. (pp. 162–164)

Companies often develop alternative plans in case things go awry. There are two common methods of dealing with the unforeseen, *contingency planning* and *crisis management*. Contingency planning is planning for change. It seeks to identify in advance important aspects of a business or its market that might change. It also identifies the ways in which a company will respond to changes. Crisis management involves an organization's methods for dealing with emergencies.

OBJECTIVE 5-6

Describe the development and explain the importance of corporate culture. (pp. 164–165)

Every company has a unique identity called *corporate culture*: its shared experiences, stories, beliefs, and norms. It helps define the work and business climate of an organization. A strong corporate culture directs efforts and helps everyone work toward the same goals. Corporate culture can also help new employees learn acceptable behaviors. Managers must carefully consider the kind of culture they want for their organizations and then work to nourish that culture by communicating it with everyone who works there. If an organization must change its culture, it must communicate the nature of the change to both employees and customers.

key terms

business (or competitive) strategy (p. 158)
conceptual skills (p. 154)
contingency planning (p. 162)

controlling (p. 146)
corporate culture (p. 164)
corporate strategy (p. 158)
crisis management (p. 163)

decisional roles (p. 153)
decision-making skills (p. 154)
environmental analysis (p. 160)
first-line manager (p. 150)

MyLab Intro to Business

To complete the problems with the ✪, go to EOC Discussion Questions in the MyLab.

questions & exercises

QUESTIONS FOR REVIEW

5-1. Describe the roles and responsibilities of top, middle, and first-line managers.

5-2. What are the four main purposes of setting goals in an organization?

5-3. Identify and explain the three basic steps in strategy formulation.

✪ **5-4.** What is corporate culture? How is it formed? How is it sustained? How does it relate to the corporate mission and vision?

QUESTIONS FOR ANALYSIS

5-5. Relate the five basic management skills (technical, human relations, conceptual, decision-making, and time management) to the four activities in the management process (planning, organizing, leading, and controlling). For example, which skills are most important in leading?

✪ **5-6.** Describe the difference between leadership and management.

5-7. What contingencies would a major retailer of home improvement supplies need to consider in planning? How do you think the organization would address those risks?

✪ **5-8.** Some business people claim that "culture trumps mission." What do you think that statement means and how would that affect the corporate strategy?

APPLICATION EXERCISES

5-9. Interview a manager at a local company or read a published interview of a manager. What are the strategies and skill sets identified? How are that manager's background, education, and experience relevant to the job?

5-10. Critique three mission statements from various companies. Describe how the mission relates to vision, values, strategies, and culture. How effective do you think the mission statements are? How useful? How clearly do they reflect the identity of the company?

building a business: continuing team exercise

Assignment

Meet with your team members and discuss your new business venture within the context of this chapter. Develop specific responses to the following:

5-11. What areas of management will be most important in your business? Will these change over time?

5-12. What basic management skills will be most important to your business? Will these change over time?

5-13. What are the specific business goals of your new venture?

5-14. For your venture, is there a difference between your corporate and business strategies?

5-15. Does your management team need to develop any contingency plans? Why, or why not?

5-16. What sort of corporate culture do you want to create for your venture? What steps will you take to do so?

team exercise

DREAMS CAN COME TRUE

The Situation

Arturo Juarez has years of experience in the travel industry as a manager at a high-end hotel as well as sales director at a large travel agency. He is ready to start his own business, Dream Vacations, offering travel-planning services for individuals and families. His company will research destinations, hotels, and activities and help its customers make travel memories by providing top-notch service and creative solutions. To achieve this goal, Arturo is working to develop contracts with resorts in the Caribbean, South America, and the Mediterranean to get better pricing for his customers. He hopes that his business will grow at least 10 percent per year over the first five years through advertising and referrals. Initially, Arturo plans to operate out of office space in Atlanta, but his goal is to have offices in South Carolina, Alabama, and Tennessee within two years.

Team Activity

Arturo has asked for a team of students to provide him with assistance getting his company going. Form a group of three to five students to provide guidance to Arturo.

ACTION STEPS

5-17. Working with your group, develop a mission statement for Dream Vacations. Why is developing a mission statement important?

5-18. Considering Dream Vacations's mission statement and the information provided in the case, what are the company's long-term goals? How should Arturo measure these goals?

5-19. What intermediate goals will help Dream Vacations meet its long-term goals and realize its mission? What types of corrective action should Arturo take if the company fails to meet these goals?

5-20. Identify Dream Vacations's short-term goals. Are short-term goals more or less important than long-term goals?

exercising your ethics

TIME FOR THE AX?

The Situation

You are the sales manager for Que, Inc., a new pharmaceutical company that has recently purchased the license to sell an allergy medicine that comes in a unique dispenser. Before the acquisition of the license, the product, called PediPlume, sold for $10 per dose, but the owner and CEO of the company, Betty Scheckt, has increased the price to $40 over the past year with no noticeable decline in demand. In fact, due to a new law that requires the presence of such a device in every public school, Scheckt is predicting an increase in demand and is asking you to increase the price by another 15 percent. In addition, the only other real competitor just pulled their product off the market, so Que now commands a 90 percent market share. Scheckt is certain the market will bear the new price and intends to continue increasing the sales price until the market reaches equilibrium—the point at which supply and demand are equal.

The Dilemma

Recalling that in the free-market system, equilibrium price is the ideal balance between supply and demand, and it is consumer behavior that determines the equilibrium point, it makes sense to increase the price as long as demand is steady or increasing. However, you are worried about the effect that pricing might have on the market mix, as lower-income consumers who have relied on an inexpensive, critical drug are now priced out of the market. Profits are soaring and the CEO is paid a bonus on profits, having earned over $92 million last year. In addition, her father was a major sponsor of the bill requiring the product in schools. Scheckt has called a meeting for tomorrow morning to discuss the price increase.

QUESTIONS TO ADDRESS

5-21. What areas of management functions are involved in this scenario? What skills? What strategies?

5-22. What are the ethical issues in this situation?

5-23. What is the logical, business-based approach for a manager to take in this situation? Explain your position.

5-24. What would you do, and why?

5-25. How would you describe the culture of this company, based on the limited information in the scenario?

cases

ALPHABET SOUP

Continued from page 144

At the beginning of this chapter, you read about how Alphabet's founders manage their employees and plan for the future. Using the information presented in this chapter, you should now be able to answer the following questions:

QUESTIONS FOR DISCUSSION

5-26. Describe examples of each of the management functions illustrated in this case.

5-27. Which management skills seem to be most exemplified in Sergey Brin and Larry Page?

5-28. What role have goals and strategy played in the success of Alphabet?

5-29. How would you describe the corporate culture at Alphabet?

WHEN OLD IS NEW AND NEW IS OLD

Late in 2011, JCPenney made a dramatic move, ousting CEO Myron Ullman and bringing in Ron Johnson. Johnson was perceived as a change agent who could reinvent the company as a new, hip place to shop, just as he had transformed the Apple Store from a run-of-the-mill mall store to an entertainment destination.[20] His vision was clear, stating, "In the United States, the department store has a chance to regain its status as the leader in style, the leader in excitement. It will be a period of true innovation for this company." Johnson proposed offering new products and interesting product lines, such as Martha Stewart and Joe Fresh, to lure in high-end customers. He also envisioned JCPenney as a destination, where shoppers would look forward to spending time browsing the store, similar to the excitement one often finds in an Apple Store.

Unfortunately for JCPenney, Johnson's new vision was a near complete failure. Penney's loyal customer base was unhappy with the new store and pricing strategies. The company failed to attract new customers and sales fell by 25 percent in one year. Even the major shareholder who championed Johnson's recruitment, Bill Ackman, realized that the company had made a new fatal error, lamenting, "One of the biggest mistakes was perhaps too much change too quickly without adequate testing on what the impact would be." Notre Dame marketing Professor Carol Phillips points out that the company failed to understand the buyer with its new value pricing, no sale strategy. "JCP's CEO Ron Johnson was … clueless about what makes shopping fun for women. It's the thrill of the hunt, not the buying." The new strategy was a mismatch with the company's existing managers, product lines, pricing strategies, and customer base. Sadly, the company moved too quickly without carefully analyzing the steps needed to implement the new vision. According to Virgin

America CEO David Cush, "Don't destroy your old revenue model before you have proved your new revenue model. That's the box that JCPenney has put themselves in."[21]

In April 2013, JCPenney's board reinstated former CEO Ullman, whose number one priority was reconnecting with the company's former customer base. Matthew Boss, an analyst at JPMorgan Chase, reports, "He talked about having the right product, but more importantly having the price and the value perception, something that he believes was lost over the past year." This means returning to the company's prior pricing strategy of marking up prices, then offering heavy discounts and abundant coupons and other promotional offers. Ullman planned to begin a slow process of analyzing the company's environment and adjusting the company's strategy to increase sales and profitability.[22] Many were optimistic that Ullman would be able to restore Penney as a stronger, more diverse company. However, the stock price continued to tumble and investors became concerned.

In 2015, Ullman resigned and Marvin Ellison stepped into the CEO position. Ellison had joined the company as president in late 2014, with prior experience at both Home Depot and Target. But Ellison is facing a heavy lift. Shoppers are flocking away from once stalwart department store chains like Macy's and Sears toward alternatives like online sellers and niche retailers. In 2017, the company announced plans to close down 130 to 140 stores and to offer buyouts to 6,000 workers, while at the same time offering new product lines, such as toys, beauty products, appliances, and home goods designed to appeal to their identified customer base that is 70 percent women and 70 percent homeowners. Along with shifting product lines, the company added online sales and a mobile app, and is even considering regional pricing. Along with a new business model, the company also adopted a new mission: Help our customer find what she loves for less time, money, and effort. Even though JCPenney turned a profit in 2016 for the first time since 2010, the question still remains: Does Ellison have the secret to turning around JCPenney? Only time will tell.[23]

QUESTIONS FOR DISCUSSION

5-30. As CEOs, both Ullman and Johnson were involved in each of the four management functions. Briefly describe the types of decisions that the CEO of JCPenney must make as they relate to each of the four functions.

5-31. The text describes a variety of skills that are essential to management. Which two skills do you think will be most important for CEO Ellison?

5-32. Do you think that Ron Johnson changed the mission of JCPenney or just implemented new strategies? Be sure to support your conclusion.

5-33. What do you think were Ron Johnson's biggest mistakes?

5-34. Do you think that Ellison will be successful in rescuing JCPenney, or is it too late?

Writing Assignments

5-35. What is corporate culture and why is it important? How is corporate culture created? Is it possible to change an organization's culture? If so, how?

5-36. Imagine that you are the CEO of a major company. Write a memo to your upper-level management team describing your management philosophy and your expectations of them as managers.

endnotes

[1] See "The Best (& Worst) Managers of the Year," *Businessweek*, January 22, 2014, pp. 50–72.

[2] Google, "Corporate Information," April 11, 2013, at http://www.google.com; "The Secret to Google's Success," *BusinessWeek*, March 6, 2008, http://www.businessweek.com; "In Search of the Real Google," *Time*, February 20, 2007, http://www.time.com; http://www.google.com/competition/howgooglesearchworks.html

[3] Hamel, Gary, and Prahalad, C. K. "Competing for the Future," *Harvard Business Review*, July–August 1994, pp. 122–128; see also Joseph M. Hall and M. Eric Johnson, "When Should a Process Be Art, Not Science?" *Harvard Business Review*, March 2009, pp. 58–65.

[4] Waldroop, James, and Butler, Timothy. "The Executive as Coach," *Harvard Business Review*, November–December 1996, pp. 111–117.

[5] See Steven J. Armstrong and Anis Mahmud, "Experiential Learning and the Acquisition of Managerial Tacit Knowledge," *Academy of Management Learning & Education*, 2008, Vol. 7, No. 2, pp. 189–208.

[6] "The Executive MBA Your Way," *Businessweek*, October 18, 1999, pp. 88–92.

[7] "Despite Cutbacks, Firms Invest in Developing Leaders," *Wall Street Journal*, February 9, 2009, p. B4.

[8] "Turning B-School into E-School," *Businessweek*, October 18, 1999, p. 94.

[9] See "Reunion at P&G University," *Wall Street Journal*, June 7, 2000, pp. B1, B4, for a discussion of Procter & Gamble's training programs.

[10] For an interesting discussion of these issues, see Rakesh Khurana, "The Curse of the Superstar CEO," *Harvard Business Review*, September 2002, pp. 60–70.

[11] Raes, Anneloes, Heijltjes, Mrielle, Glunk, Ursula, and Row, Robert. "The Interface of the Top Management Team and Middle Managers: A Process Model," *Academy of Management Review*, January 2011, pp. 102–126.

[12] Meyer, Stephen J. "Salman Khan: The World's Best-Known Teacher Is Learning to Lead." *Forbes*. N.p. December 3, 2014. Web. December 16, 2016.

[13] Mintzberg, Henry. *The Nature of Managerial Work* (Englewood Cliffs, NJ: 1973).

[14] See Robert L. Katz, "The Skills of an Effective Administrator," *Harvard Business Review*, September–October 1974, pp. 90–102, for a classic discussion of several of these skills. For a recent perspective, see J. Brian Atwater, Vijay R. Kannan, and Alan A. Stephens, "Cultivating Systemic Thinking in the Next Generation of Business Leaders," *Academy of Management Learning & Education*, 2008, Vol. 7, No. 1, pp. 9–25.

[15] Musk, Elon. "Master Plan, Part Duex," tesla.com (July 20, 2016). https://www.tesla.com/blog/master-plan-part-deux (Accessed March 2, 2017).

[16] From interview with Elon Musk, https://www.khanacademy.org/economics-finance-domain/entrepreneurship2/interviews-entrepreneurs/copy-of-khan-academy-living-room-chats/v/elon-musk (Accessed March 2, 2017)

[17] "Business World Must Be 'Watchful'," *USA Today*, January 24, 2015, p. 5T.

[18] Jones, Del. "Next Time," *USA Today* (October 4, 2005), 1B, 2B.

[19] "Marriage at 30,000 Feet," *Bloomberg Businessweek*, February 6–February 12, 2012, pp. 36–40.

[20] Clifford, Stephanie. "J.C. Penney's New Plan Is to Reuse Its Old Plans." *New York Times*. N.p., 16 May 2013. Web. 17 June 2013.

[21] Denning, Steve. "J.C. Penney: Was Ron Johnson's Strategy Wrong?" *Forbes*, 09 Apr. 2013. Web. 17 June 2013.

[22] "Saving JCPenney: New CEO Ullman Plans Coupons, Discounts." *CNBC.com*. N.p., 10 Apr. 2013. Web. 17 June 2013.

[23] Bomey, Nathan. "J.C. Penney to close up to 140 stores, offer buyouts," (2017). USA Today, http://www.usatoday.com/story/money/2017/02/24/jc-penney-store-closures/98344540/ (Accessed March 6, 2017)

chapter 6

Organizing the Business

The secret to success lies with the people behind

the products. The relationship between

managers and

employees can make or break

any company.

After reading this chapter, you should be able to:

6-1 **Discuss** the factors that influence a firm's organizational structure.

6-2 **Explain** specialization and departmentalization as two of the building blocks of organizational structure.

6-3 **Describe** centralization and decentralization, delegation, and authority as the key ingredients in establishing the decision-making hierarchy.

6-4 **Explain** the differences among functional, divisional, matrix, and international organizational structures and describe the most popular new forms of organizational design.

6-5 **Describe** the informal organization and discuss intrapreneuring.

Organizing for
Success

One of the key determinants of organizational structure is the mission and strategy of the business. Entrepreneurs must be particularly conscious as they begin to define an organizational structure that is appropriate to their goals and strategy, and it's possible that the organization will outgrow its initial structure as time goes by. Even so, it can be difficult to disentwine structure from culture. As Matthew Yglesias of Vox asks about tech-giant Apple: "If GE can build jet engines, tidal energy farms, freight rail data systems, mining equipment, and medical devices, how is it that the world's most valuable company can't find the time to make a full line of personal computers and PC peripherals alongside its market-leading smartphones and tablets? The answer goes back to Apple's corporate structure, which, though fairly common for a startup, is extremely unusual for an enormous company."[1]

In an entrepreneurial organization, simple, flat organizational structures with very few top managers usually work well. Unlike more complex companies, an entrepreneurial organization would ideally be relatively unstructured and informal. The advantage of this structure is that decisions can be made quickly and the structure is flexible enough to adapt to a rapidly changing market. However, with very few top managers, it's easy to become overwhelmed with decision-making.[2]

Perhaps one of the most iconic examples of a simple entrepreneurial structure is Valve Software, the company that created the Half-Life, Counter-Strike, and Portal video games series. While Valve has 300 employees, they have no managers—none. According to the employee handbook, "Of all the people at this company who aren't your boss, Gabe [the co-founder] is the MOST not your boss, if you get what we're saying." In an interview with Bloomberg Business, Gabe Newell explained it this way:

"When we started Valve [in 1996], we thought about what the company needed to be good at. We realized that here, our job was to create things that hadn't existed before. Managers are good at institutionalizing procedures, but in our line of work that's not always good. Sometimes the skills in one generation of product are irrelevant to the skills in another generation. Our industry is in such technological, design, and artistic flux that we need somebody who can recognize that. It's pretty rare for someone to be in a lead role on two consecutive projects."

Employees at Valve move from project to project, often taking on different roles from one project to the next. A "group contributor" is responsible for helping others be more productive, although their ability to think creatively is often limited by this role. At other times, Valve employees may work

Se Media/Fotolia

what's in it for me?

All managers need the assistance of others to succeed and so must trust the members of their team to do their jobs and carry out their responsibilities. The team members themselves need the support of their boss and a clear understanding of their role in the organization. The working relationship between managers and their subordinates is one of the most critical elements comprising an organization. As you will see in this chapter, managing the basic frameworks that organizations use to get their work done, *structure*, is a fundamental part of the management process.

Imagine asking a child to build a castle with a set of building blocks. She selects a few small blocks and other larger ones. She uses some square ones, some round ones, and some triangular ones. When she finishes, she has her own castle, unlike any other. Another child, presented with the same task, constructs a different castle. He selects different blocks, for example, and combines them in different ways. The children's activities, choosing certain combinations of blocks and then putting them together in unique ways, are in many ways analogous to the manager's job of organizing. Managers at similar companies competing in the same industries may create structures that are nearly identical to one another, completely different from one another, or somewhere in between.

Organizing is deciding how best to group organizational elements. Just as children select different kinds of building blocks, managers can choose a variety of structural possibilities. And just as the children can assemble the blocks in any number of ways, so, too, can managers put the organization together in many different ways. Understanding the nature of these building blocks and the different ways in which they can be configured can have a powerful impact on a firm's competitiveness.

By understanding the material in this chapter, you'll also be prepared to understand your "place" in the organization that employs you. Similarly, as a boss or owner, you'll be better equipped to create the optimal structure for your own organization. This chapter examines factors that influence a firm's organizational structure. We discuss the building blocks of organizational structure as well as the differences among decision making in different types of organizations. Along the way, we look at a variety of organizational structures and describe the most popular new forms of organizational design.

on a more individual project, where they are allowed to work more independently.[3]

During the development of their iconic PC-based video game, Half-Life, the company developed cross-discipline teams called "cabals" to design the final product and bring it to market. Even though the company has grown to over 360 employees and billions of dollars in revenue, it's still privately held and the organizational structure is flat.

It's not surprising that Gabe Newell and Mike Harrington adopted a family-like work environment when they started Valve in 1996. Both had worked for Bill Gates as Microsoft engineers during the early years when the structure was still relatively flat. However, by 2010, Microsoft was in the throes of becoming more divisional, by necessity, although in fits and starts. In 2015, Microsoft completed a corporate re-organization that left it looking classically divisional after a previous reorganization effort in 2013 that attempted to align the business functionally.

So, what has happened to Apple in the years since Steve Jobs founded it? Large companies often develop a divisional organizational structure. When Google mutated into Alphabet, its structure became more divisional and less based on function, with Google and division "X" being the most prominent, each focused on a specific market segment or sub-mission. In a divisional organization, people work for units, like Google, and they are responsible for particular lines of business. There are still some areas that are aligned functionally, like accounting, but for the most part, large businesses seem to do better with a divisional, rather than a functional, structure. Apple, however, is still clinging to its functional roots. Functional structures allow for more collaboration. At Apple, top managers are responsible for broad areas such as software engineering, hardware, and marketing. These areas cross each other and cross markets as well. It may seem like a fuzzy distinction, but where the CEO for Google is responsible for the success of the search engine functionality and not the success of the mobile phone division, a manager at Apple may be responsible for chip development across the board, from the Apple Watch to the iPhone to the MacBook and the iPad, and another manager may be responsible for across the board marketing. This structure can make product management an extremely complicated process for a large company, and it may not provide any single person as a point of accountability for the final product. (After studying this chapter, you should be able to answer the set of questions found at the end of the chapter.)

OBJECTIVE 6-1
Discuss
the factors that influence a firm's organizational structure.

Organizational Structure *specification of the jobs to be done within an organization and the ways in which they relate to one another*

What Is Organizational Structure?

One key decision that business owners and managers must address is how best to structure their organization. Stated differently, they must decide on an appropriate organizational structure. We can define **organizational structure** as the specification of the jobs to be done within an organization and the ways in which those jobs relate to one another.[4] Perhaps the easiest way to understand structure is in terms of an *organization chart*.

Organization Charts

Organization Chart *diagram depicting a company's structure and showing employees where they fit into its operations*

Chain of Command *reporting relationships within a company*

Most small businesses create an **organization chart** to clarify structure and to show employees where they fit into a firm's operations. Figure 6.1 is an organization chart for Contemporary Landscape and Lawn Services, a small but growing business in a small Texas community. Each box in the chart represents a specific job. The solid lines define the *chain of command*. The **chain of command**, in turn, refers to *reporting relationships* within the company. In theory, such reporting relationships follow a "chain" from the highest level in the organization to the lowest. For example, the retail shop, nursery, and landscape operations managers all report to the owner and president. Within the landscape operation is one manager for residential accounts and another for commercial accounts. Similarly, there are other managers in the retail shop and the nursery.

The organization charts of large firms are far more complex and include individuals at many more levels than those shown in Figure 6.1. Size prevents many large firms from even having charts that include all their managers. Typically, they create one organization chart showing overall corporate structure, separate charts for each division, and even more charts for individual departments or units.

Recall our definition of organizational structure: the specification of the jobs to be done within an organization and the ways in which those jobs relate to one another. The boxes in the organization chart represent the jobs, and the lines connecting the boxes show how the jobs are related. As we will see, however, even though organizational structure can be broken down into a series of boxes and lines, virtually no two organizations will have the same structure. What works for Microsoft will not work for Google, Jet Blue, Exxon Mobil, Amazon, or the U.S. Department of Commerce. Likewise, the structure of the American Red Cross will probably not work for Urban Outfitters, Target, Starbucks, or the University of Nebraska.

Determinants of Organizational Structure

How is an organization's structure determined? Ideally, managers carefully assess a variety of important factors as they plan for and then create an organizational structure that will allow their organization to function most efficiently effectively.

Many factors play a part in determining an organization's optimal structure. Chief among them are the organization's *mission* and *strategy*. A dynamic and rapidly growing business, for example, needs an organizational structure that allows it to be flexible, to respond quickly to changes in its environment and strategy, and to grow. A stable organization with only modest growth goals and a more conservative strategy will most likely function best with a different organizational structure.

Size of the company and elements of the organization's environment also affect organizational structure. As we saw in Chapter 5, organizing is a key part of the management process. As such, it must be conducted with an equal awareness of both a firm's external and internal environments. A large services provider or manufacturer operating in a strongly competitive environment, such as American Airlines or Hewlett-Packard, requires a different organizational structure than a local hair salon or clothing boutique. Even after an organizational structure has been created, it is rarely free from tinkering—or even outright re-creation. Most organizations change their structures on an almost continuing basis.

Since it was first incorporated in 1903, Ford Motor Company has undergone literally dozens of major structural changes, hundreds of moderate changes, and

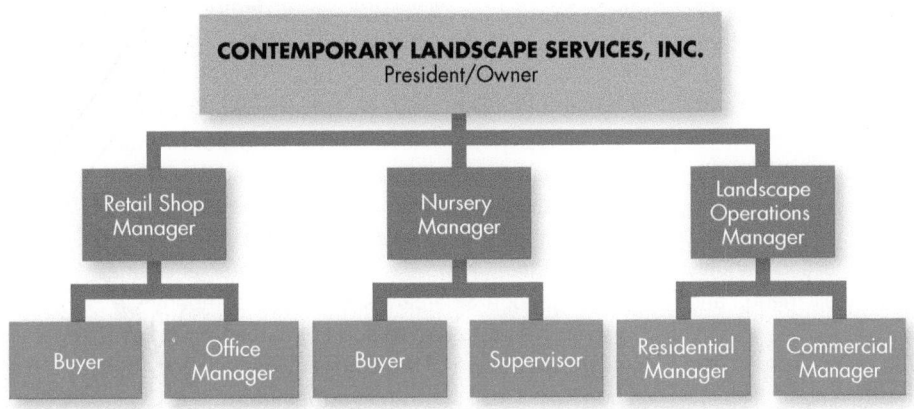

FIGURE 6.1 The Organization Chart

thousands of minor changes. In the last 25 years alone, Ford has initiated several major structural changes. In 1995, for instance, the firm announced a major restructuring plan called Ford 2000, which was intended to integrate all of Ford's vast international operations into a single, unified structure by the year 2000.

By 1998, however, midway through implementation of the grand plan, top Ford executives announced major modifications, indicating that (1) additional changes would be made, (2) some previously planned changes would not be made, and (3) some recently realigned operations would be changed again. In early 1999, managers announced another set of changes intended to eliminate corporate bureaucracy, speed decision making, and improve communication and working relationships among people at different levels of the organization. Early in 2001, Ford announced yet more sweeping changes intended to boost the firm's flagging bottom line and stem a decline in product quality. More significant changes followed in both 2003 and 2004, and in 2006, the firm announced several plant closings, resulting in even more changes. Not surprisingly, yet another major reorganization was announced in 2010 as the firm sought to deal with a global recession and a major slump in automobile sales. In 2011 the firm announced even more restructuring to gain more international market share, and other changes were announced in 2015 as global auto sales began to increase and Ford needed additional manufacturing capacity.

entrepreneurship and new ventures

Organizing for Growth

Nine out of ten new businesses fail. For a successful startup, the entrepreneur needs a great product or service and a lot of business savvy, and that means building a great team, which means that some kind of arrangement of people and ideas is necessary. However, for most start-ups, organizational structure is the last thing the owner is thinking about.

Does structure grow organically, or is it developed? For Gauri Nanda, creator of Clocky, the perky little robot alarm clock marketed by her company Nanda Home, organizational structure wasn't an issue. Nanda designed Clocky as a graduate student project for her MIT Media Lab class in 2004, but having no entrepreneurial leanings at the time, she threw it in the back of her closet and continued with her master's degree. However, Clocky had already gained a tiny online presence, and in 2005 she suddenly discovered that she had unearthed a potential goldmine. Rather than going big though, with production facilities and employees and all the risks and headaches that might provide, she found a manufacturer in Hong Kong (via AliBaba.com) and outsourced production. Her first run of 500 clocks sold out overnight.

Since then, she's incorporated Nanda Home, but as of early 2017 the nascent store still sports only the one product. Not to be deterred, she's started a new venture, this time with a partner and a larger scope. In 2013, she and a partner, Audry Hill, launched a company called Toymail. The eponymous product has two parts—an app, for the parents, and the Talkies, vaguely bat-shaped stuffed toys that connect kids to their friends and family via voice chat.

They started small, selling over 20,000 units on a limited marketing campaign while beta-testing with real families to

Toymail/Rex Features/AP Images

develop the most useful and marketable Talkies. By late 2016, the company had raised $1.5 million from Amazon, Verizon, and a venture capital company called Y Combinator when they received an invitation from the television show *Shark Tank* to pitch their idea. The appearance landed them a $600,000 co-investment from sharks Lori Greiner and Chris Sacca in exchange for a 5 percent stake in the company.

Now it's up to Nanda and Hill to turn their creative attention toward the design of the company itself as they begin the transition from small start-up to a member of the 10 percent club.

The Building Blocks of Organizational Structure

OBJECTIVE 6-2
Explain
specialization and departmentalization as two of the building blocks of organizational structure.

The first step in developing the structure of any business, large or small, involves three activities:

1 *Specialization.* Determining who will do what
2 *Departmentalization.* Determining how people performing certain tasks can best be grouped together
3 *Establishment of a Decision-Making Hierarchy.* Deciding who will be empowered to make which decisions and who will have authority over others

These three activities are the building blocks of all business organizations. In this section, we discuss specialization and departmentalization. Because the decision-making hierarchy actually includes several elements, we cover it in more detail in the next section.

Job Specialization

The process of identifying the specific jobs that need to be done and designating the people who will perform them leads to **job specialization**. In a sense, all organizations have only one major job, such as making cars (Ford), selling finished goods to consumers (Lenova), or providing telecommunications services (Sprint). Usually, that job is more complex in nature. For example, the "job" of Nucor Corporation is converting scrap steel (such as wrecked automobiles) into finished steel products (such as beams and reinforcement bars). Similarly, the "job" of American Airlines is to transport passengers and their luggage from one airport to another.

Job Specialization *the process of identifying the specific jobs that need to be done and designating the people who will perform them*

To perform this one overall job, managers actually break it down, or specialize it, into several smaller jobs. Thus, some workers at Nucor transport the scrap steel to the company's mills. Others operate shredding equipment before turning raw materials over to the workers who then melt them into liquid form. Other specialists oversee the flow of the liquid into molding equipment, where it is transformed into new products. Finally, other workers are responsible for moving finished products to a holding area before they are shipped out to customers. At American, some specialists schedule flights, others book passengers, others fly the planes, and still others deal with passenger luggage and other cargo. When the overall job of the organization is broken down like this, workers can develop real expertise in their jobs, and employees can better coordinate their work with that done by others.

In a small organization, the owner may perform every job. As the firm grows, however, so does the need to specialize jobs so that others can perform them. To see how specialization can evolve in an organization, consider the case of the Walt Disney Company. When Walt Disney first opened his animation studio, he and his brother Roy did everything. For example, when they created their first animated feature, *Steamboat Willy*, they wrote the story, drew the pictures, transferred the pictures to film, provided the voices, and went out and sold the cartoon to theater operators.

Today, however, a Disney animated feature is made possible only through the efforts of thousands of people. The job of one animator may be to create the face of a single character throughout an entire feature. Another artist may be charged with coloring background images in certain scenes. People other than artists are responsible for the subsequent operations that turn individual computer-generated images into a moving picture or for the marketing of the finished product.

Job specialization is a natural part of organizational growth. It also has certain advantages. For example, specialized jobs are learned more easily and can be performed more efficiently than nonspecialized jobs, and it is also easier to replace people who leave an organization if they have highly specialized jobs. However, jobs at lower levels of the organization are especially susceptible to overspecialization. If such jobs become too narrowly defined, employees may become bored and careless, derive less

When Walt Disney was just starting out, he did most of the work on his animated features all by himself. But today's features like *Zootopia, Frozen, Coco*, and *Inside Out* all require the work of thousands of people.

satisfaction from their jobs, and lose sight of their roles in the organization. These conditions, in turn, may prompt people to look for more interesting jobs elsewhere.

Departmentalization

Departmentalization *process of grouping jobs into logical units*

After jobs are specialized, they are then grouped into logical units, which is the process of **departmentalization**. Departmentalized companies benefit from this division of activities; control and coordination are narrowed and made easier, and top managers can see more easily how various units are performing.

Profit Center *separate company unit responsible for its own costs and profits*

Departmentalization allows the firm to treat each department as a **profit center**, a separate company unit responsible for its own costs and profits. Thus, Macy's can calculate the profits it generates from men's clothing, home furnishings, cosmetics, women's shoes, and every other department within a given store separately. Managers can then use this information in making decisions about advertising and promotional events, space allocation adjustments, budgeting, and so forth.

Managers do not departmentalize jobs randomly, of course. They group them logically, according to some common thread or purpose. In general, departmentalization may occur along *functional, product, process, customer,* or *geographic* lines (or any combination of these).

Functional Departmentalization *dividing an organization according to groups' functions or activities*

Functional Departmentalization Many service and manufacturing companies, especially smaller ones just getting started, use **functional departmentalization** to create departments according to a group's functions or activities. Most new start-up firms, for instance, use functional departmentalization. Such firms typically have production, marketing and sales, human resources, and accounting and finance departments. Departments may be further subdivided. For example, the marketing department might be divided into separate groups for market research, advertising, and sales promotions.

Product Departmentalization *dividing an organization according to specific products or services being created*

Product Departmentalization Both manufacturers and service providers often opt for **product departmentalization**, dividing an organization according to the specific product or service being created. This becomes especially true when a firm grows and starts to offer multiple products or services. Kraft Foods uses this approach to divide departments. For example, the Oscar Mayer division focuses on hot dogs and lunch meats, the Kraft Cheese division focuses on cheese products, and the Maxwell House and Post division focus on coffee and breakfast cereal, respectively.[5] Because

finding a better way

Blending the Old with the New

In 1883, the great composer and piano virtuoso Franz Liszt wrote Henry (Heinrich) Steinway, founder of Steinway & Sons, to praise the Steinway grand piano. In particular, Liszt had good things to say about the tonal effect of the piano's *scale*, the arrangement of its strings. Thirty years earlier, Henry Steinway Jr., had patented a technique for scaling called *overstringing*: Instead of running them parallel to the piano's treble strings, he taught his workers to fan the bass strings above and diagonally to create a second tier of strings. As a result, he was able to improve the instrument's tone by using longer strings with superior vibratory quality.

Another feature developed by Steinway and his employees in the mid-nineteenth century made it possible to use strings that were also bigger—and thus louder. If you look under a piano, you'll see a cast-iron plate. This component was once made of wood fortified by metal braces, but Steinway had made the cast-iron plate a regular feature by the 1840s. The metal plate, of course, is much stronger and allowed the piano maker to apply much greater tension to the strings; in turn, the ability to increase string tension made it possible to tune the piano to more exacting standards of pitch.

Steinway was the first piano maker to combine the cast-iron plate with the technique of overstringing, and little has changed in the construction of a grand piano since these and a few other facets of traditional technology were first introduced. In effect, just as the job of a Disney animator has changed as the firm and its technology have changed, so too have the jobs at Steinway. Indeed, Steinway's workers still perform specialized jobs, but the jobs have also changed dramatically over the years. Take, for example, the soundboard, which you'll see if you open up a grand piano and look inside. A solid wooden "diaphragm" located between the strings and the metal plate; the *soundboard* is a marvel of deceptively simple design that vibrates to amplify the sound of the strings while withstanding the 1,000 pounds of pressure that they place on it. Because they're constructed by hand, no two soundboards are exactly the same size. Nor is any one piano *case*, the curved lateral surface that runs around the whole instrument, the same size as any other. The important thing is that the case is fitted—and fitted *precisely*—to a soundboard.

Because the soundboard is measured first and the case then fitted to it, there's only one case for each soundboard. To ensure a satisfactory fit between case and soundboard, the case must be *frazed*, sawed and planed to specification. Performed by hand, this task took 14 hours, but today it's done in 1 1/2 hours by a *computer numerically controlled* (CNC) milling machine, a system in which a computerized storage medium issues programmed commands to a variety of specialized tools. Steinway workers, then, must be masters of their craft to perform effectively.

Granted, CNC technology is fairly new at Steinway—the million-dollar milling machine and several other pieces of CNC technology were introduced only in the last 10 years or so. Most

Ulrich Perrey/Picture-Alliance/Dpa/Dpaweb/Newscom

of Steinway's CNC tools are highly specialized, and the company custom-built many of them. Obviously, such technology leads to a lot of labor savings, but Steinway officials are adamant about the role of technology in maintaining rather than supplanting Steinway tradition: Some people, says Director of Quality Robert Berger, "think that Steinway is automating to save on labor costs or improve productivity. But these investments are all about quality. We're making a few specific technology investments in areas where we can improve the quality of our product."[6]

Steinway has gone through many organizational changes over the past several decades. After going public in 1996, it struggled as the recession hit sales of luxury items especially hard. In 2013, billionaire John Paulson purchased the company for over $500 million, taking it private and turning it around, and in 2015 the company produced its 600,000th piano. As Paulson explains it, Steinway's legacy of high quality was the motivation behind his investment decision: "I've always been enamored with the product. You have Mercedes in cars and top brands in every other area. But no one has such a high share of the high end."

Despite its deep roots in the past, Steinway continues to innovate. In 2016, the company introduced the Spirio player piano—a high-tech combination of acoustic instrument and digital technology that captures the essence of great musicians and reproduces it on demand. The company sees great potential for international sales, with robust interest by cultural institutions in China. And, for Steinway, it's the people behind that product that make all the difference. According to *Forbes* magazine, it's an ideal export—"a luxury product produced with U.S. skilled labor, packed with prestige that can't be outsourced."[7]

each division represents a defined group of products or services, managers at Kraft Foods are able—in theory—to focus on *specific* product lines in a clear and defined way.

Process Departmentalization Other manufacturers favor **process departmentalization**, in which the organization is divided according to production processes used to create a good or service. This principle is logical for Vlasic, which has three separate departments to transform cucumbers into either fresh-packed pickles, pickles cured in brine, or relishes. Cucumbers destined to become fresh-packed pickles must be packed into jars immediately, covered with a solution of water and vinegar, and prepared for sale. Those slated to be brined pickles must be aged in brine solution before packing. Relish cucumbers must be minced and combined with a host of other ingredients. Each process requires different equipment and worker skills, and different departments were created for each. Some service providers also use this approach as well. For instance, an automobile insurance company might use one department to receive claims from policy holders, another to review coverage, and another to issue payments.

Customer Departmentalization Retail stores actually derive their generic name, department stores, from the manner in which they are structured—a men's department, a women's department, a luggage department, a lawn and garden department, and so on. Each department targets a specific customer category (men, women, people who want to buy luggage, people who want to buy a lawn mower) by using **customer departmentalization** to create departments that offer products and meet the needs of identifiable customer groups. Thus, a customer shopping for a baby's crib at Walmart can bypass lawn and garden supplies and head straight for children's furniture. In general, the store is more efficient, and customers get better service because salespeople tend to specialize and gain expertise in their departments. Another illustration of customer departmentalization is reflected in most banks. An individual wanting a consumer loan goes to the retail banking office, whereas a small business owner goes to the commercial banking office and a farmer goes to the agricultural loan department.

Geographic Departmentalization Geographic **departmentalization** divides firms according to the areas of the country or the world that they serve. Levi Strauss, for instance, has one division for North and South America; one for Europe, the Middle East, and North Africa; and one for the Asia Pacific region.[8] Within the United States, geographic departmentalization is common among utilities. For example, Southern Company organizes its power subsidiaries into four geographic departments—Alabama, Georgia, Gulf, and Mississippi Power.[9]

Process Departmentalization
dividing an organization according to production processes used to create a good or service

Customer Departmentalization
dividing an organization to offer products and meet needs for identifiable customer groups

Geographic Departmentalization
dividing an organization according to the areas of the country or the world served by a business

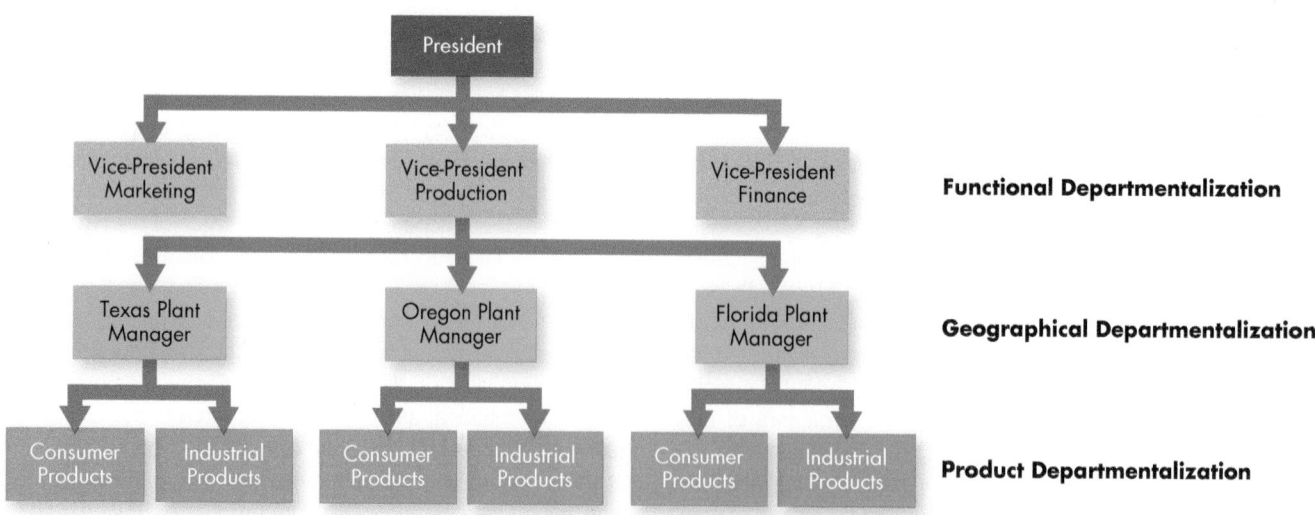

FIGURE 6.2 Multiple Forms of Departmentalization

Multiple Forms of Departmentalization Because different forms of departmentalization have different advantages, as firms grow in size they tend to adopt different types of departmentalization for various levels. The company illustrated in Figure 6.2 uses functional departmentalization at the top level. At the middle level, production is divided along geographic lines. At a lower level, marketing is departmentalized by product group. Larger firms are certain to use all of these different forms of departmentalization in various areas.

Establishing the Decision-Making Hierarchy

OBJECTIVE 6-3
Describe
centralization and decentralization, delegation, and authority as the key ingredients in establishing the decision-making hierarchy.

The third major building block of organizational structure is the establishment of a decision-making hierarchy. This is usually done by formalizing reporting relationships. When the focus is on the reporting relationships among individual managers and the people who report to them, it is most commonly referred to as delegation. However, when the focus is on the overall organization, it becomes a question of decentralization versus *centralization*.

Distributing Authority: Centralization and Decentralization

Some managers make the conscious decision to retain as much decision-making authority as possible at the higher levels of the organizational structure; others decide to push authority as far down the hierarchy as possible. Although we can think of these two extremes as anchoring a continuum, most companies fall somewhere between the middle of such a continuum and one end point or the other.

Centralized Organizations In a **centralized organization**, most decision-making authority is held by upper-level managers.[10] McDonald's practices centralization as a way to maintain standardization. All restaurants must follow precise steps in buying products and making and packaging menu items. Most advertising is handled at the corporate level, and any local advertising must be approved by a regional manager. Restaurants even have to follow prescribed schedules for facilities' maintenance and upgrades such as floor polishing and parking lot cleaning. Centralized authority is most commonly found in companies that face relatively stable and predictable environments and is also typical of small businesses.

Centralized Organization
organization in which most decision-making authority is held by upper-level management

Decentralized Organizations As a company gets larger and more decisions must be made, the company tends to adopt **decentralized organization**, in which much decision-making authority is delegated to levels of management at various points below the top. Decentralization is typical in firms that have complex and dynamic environmental conditions. It is also common in businesses that specialize in customer services. Decentralization makes a company more responsive by allowing managers increased discretion to make quick decisions in their areas of responsibility. For example, Urban Outfitters practices relative decentralization in that it allows individual store managers considerable discretion over merchandising and product displays. Whole Foods Market takes things even further in its decentralization. Stores are broken up into small teams, which are responsible for making decisions on issues such as voting on which new staff members to hire and which products to carry based on local preferences. This practice taps into the idea that the people who will be most affected by decisions should be the ones making them.[11]

Decentralized Organization
organization in which a great deal of decision-making authority is delegated to levels of management at points below the top

Tall and Flat Organizations Decentralized firms tend to have relatively fewer layers of management, resulting in a **flat organizational structure** like that of

Flat Organizational Structure
characteristic of decentralized companies with relatively few layers of management

managing in turbulent times

Keeping the Organizational Tools Sharp

There's been quite a bit of news about the death of manufacturing jobs in the United States, but Illinois Tool Works (ITW), headquartered in Glenview, Illinois, is out to prove the critics wrong. Established in 1912 to manufacture metal cutting tools, the company has grown over the last century to more than 48,000 employees around the globe. Beginning in 1980, ITW grew through the acquisition of hundreds of smaller companies, acquiring their product lines and distinctive competencies. Today, the company is organized into seven segments or operating divisions: Automotive OEM; Test & Measurement and Electronics; Food Equipment; Polymers & Fluids; Welding; Construction Products; and Specialty Products. Its products and services are quite diverse—in its Automotive OEM division, it produces plastic and metal components for automobiles and light trucks, while its Polymers and Fluids division produces industrial adhesives, cleaning and lubrications fluids, and polymers and fillers for automotive repairs and maintenance.

ITW's structure is built around a highly decentralized philosophy. Each of the seven operating divisions is designed to operate as a smaller, more flexible and entrepreneurial organization, maintaining its own revenue and cost centers. Decision-making is highly decentralized, with most decisions about strategy made within the divisions. The company believes that this ITW business model not only responds effectively to customer needs, but it also maximizes economic performance.

Another key to Illinois Tool Work's success is its 80/20 Business Process. This is an operating philosophy that states that 80 percent of its revenues and profits should come from just 20 percent of its customers. In a company where innovation is the key, this philosophy has helped ITW to focus its energies on product lines that will create the most synergy. ITW

Kristoffer Tripplaar/Alamy Stock Photo

also emphasizes *customer back innovation*, a term it uses to describe that innovation is customer centered and focuses on the key needs of its most important constituents.

Illinois Tool Works has a strong global presence, operating in 57 countries, with major operations in Australia, Belgium, Brazil, Canada, China, Czech Republic, Denmark, France, Germany, Ireland, Italy, the Netherlands, Spain, Switzerland, and the United Kingdom. Though the United States is its biggest market, more than one-quarter of its revenues are in Europe, and more than ten percent in Asia. This geographic diversification helps to mitigate the risk associated with a downturn in any regional economy.

These strategies have paid off for Illinois Tool Works. Like most companies, it was hit hard by the recession, but it has rebounded strongly. Its stock price has increased nearly five-fold in the eight years from 2008 to 2016. So far, ITW's strategy and organizational structure have allowed the company to weather tough times and have positioned it for success in the future.[12]

Tall Organizational Structures *characteristic of centralized companies with multiple layers of management*

the hypothetical law firm shown in Figure 6.3(a). Centralized firms typically require multiple layers of management and thus **tall organizational structures**, as in the U.S. Army example in Figure 6.3(b). Because information, whether upward or downward bound, must pass through so many organizational layers, tall structures are prone to delays in information flow.

As organizations grow in size, it is both normal and necessary that they become at least somewhat taller. For instance, a small firm with only an owner-manager and a few employees is likely to have two layers, the owner-manager and the employees who report to that person. As the firm grows, more layers will be needed. A manager must ensure that he or she has only the number of layers his or her firm needs. Too few layers can create chaos and inefficiency, whereas too many layers can create rigidity and bureaucracy.

Span of Control As you can see in Figure 6.3, the distribution of authority in an organization also affects the number of people who work for any individual manager. In a flat organizational structure, the number of people directly managed

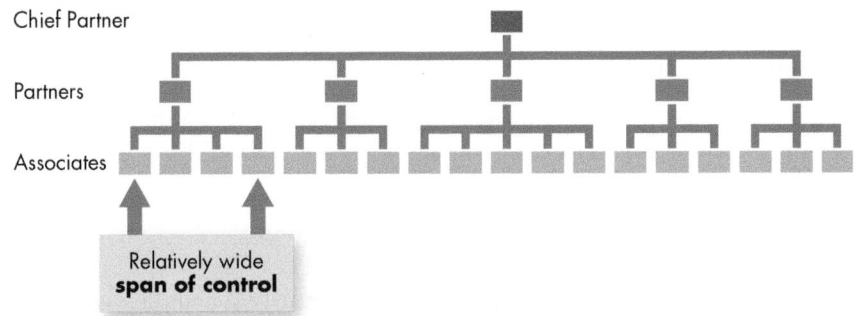

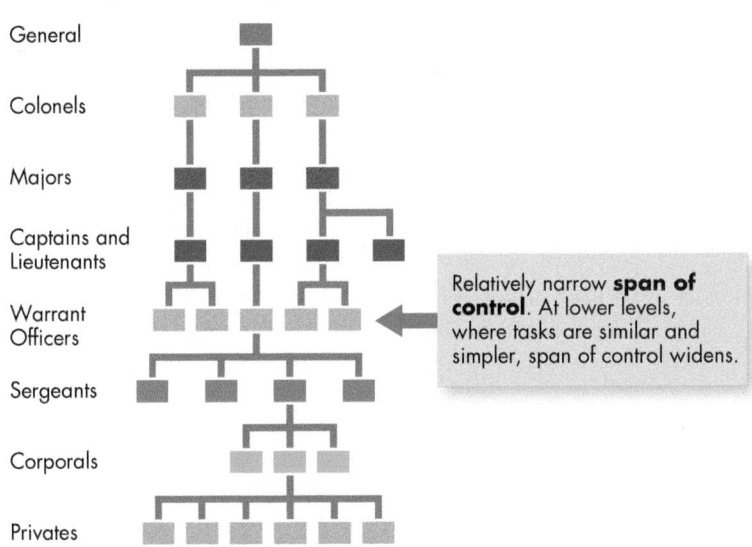

FIGURE 6.3 Organizational Structures and Span of Control

by one supervisor, the manager's **span of control**, is usually wide. In tall organizations, span of control tends to be narrower. Employees' abilities and the supervisor's managerial skills influence how wide or narrow the span of control should be, as do the similarity and simplicity of tasks and the extent to which they are interrelated.

If lower-level managers are given more decision-making authority, their supervisors will have fewer responsibilities and may then be able to take on a widened span of control. Similarly, when several employees perform either the same simple task or a group of interrelated tasks, a wide span of control is possible and often desirable. For instance, because of the routine and interdependent nature of jobs on an assembly line, one supervisor may well control the entire line.

In contrast, when jobs are more diversified or prone to change, a narrow span of control is preferable. Consider how Electronic Arts develops video games. Design, art, audio, and software development teams have specialized jobs whose products must come together in the end to create a coherent game. Although related, the complexities involved with and the advanced skills required by each job mean that one supervisor can oversee only a small number of employees.

The Delegation Process

Delegation is the process through which a manager allocates work to subordinates. In general, the delegation process involves:

1 Assigning **responsibility**, the duty to perform an assigned task.

Span of Control number of people supervised by one manager

Delegation process through which a manager allocates work to subordinates

Responsibility duty to perform an assigned task

Authority *power to make the decisions necessary to complete a task*

Accountability *obligation employees have to their manager for the successful completion of an assigned task*

2 Granting **authority**, or the power to make the decisions necessary to complete the task.

3 Creating **accountability**, the obligation employees have for the successful completion of the task.

For the delegation process to work smoothly, responsibility and authority must be equivalent. Table 6.1 lists some common obstacles that hinder the delegation process, along with strategies for overcoming them.

Three Forms of Authority

As individuals are delegated responsibility and authority, a complex web of interactions develops in the forms of *line, staff,* and *committee and team* authorities.

Line Authority *organizational structure in which authority flows in a direct chain of command from the top of the company to the bottom*

Line Department *department directly linked to the production and sales of a specific product*

Line Authority The type of authority that flows up and down the chain of command is **line authority**. Most companies rely heavily on **line departments** linked directly to the production and sales of specific products. For example, in the division of Clark Equipment that produces forklifts and small earthmovers, line departments include purchasing, materials handling, fabrication, painting, and assembly (all of which are directly linked to production) along with sales and distribution (both of which are directly linked to sales).

As the doers and producers, each line department is essential to an organization's ability to sell and deliver finished goods. A bad decision by the manager in one department can hold up production for an entire plant. For example, suppose the painting department manager at Clark Equipment changes a paint application on a batch of forklifts, which then show signs of peeling paint. The batch will have to be repainted (and perhaps partially reassembled) before the machines can be shipped.

Staff Authority *authority based on expertise that usually involves counseling and advising line managers*

Staff Members *advisers and counselors who help line departments in making decisions but who do not have the authority to make final decisions*

Staff Authority Some companies also rely on **staff authority**, which is based on special expertise and usually involves advising line managers in areas such as law, accounting, and human resources. A corporate attorney, for example, may advise the marketing department as it prepares a new contract with the firm's advertising agency, but it will not typically make decisions that affect how the marketing department does its job. **Staff members** help line departments make decisions but do not usually have the authority to make final decisions.

Typically, the separation between line authority and staff responsibility is clearly delineated and is usually indicated in organization charts by solid lines (line authority) and dotted lines (staff responsibility), as shown in Figure 6.4. It may help to understand this separation by remembering that whereas *staff members* generally

table 6.1 Learning to Delegate Effectively

I'm afraid to delegate because ...	Solution
My team doesn't know how to get the job done.	If members of your team are exhibiting opportunities for improved performance, offer them the training necessary for them to become more effective at their jobs.
I like controlling as many things as possible.	Recognize that trying to accomplish everything yourself while your team does nothing only sets you up for burnout and failure. As you begin to relinquish control, you will come to trust your team more as you watch your team members succeed.
I don't want anyone on my team outperforming me.	High-performing team members are a reflection of your success as a manager. Encourage them to excel, praise them for it, and share the success of your team with the rest of the organization.
I don't know how to delegate tasks effectively.	Consider taking a management training course or reading some books on the topic of delegating effectively.

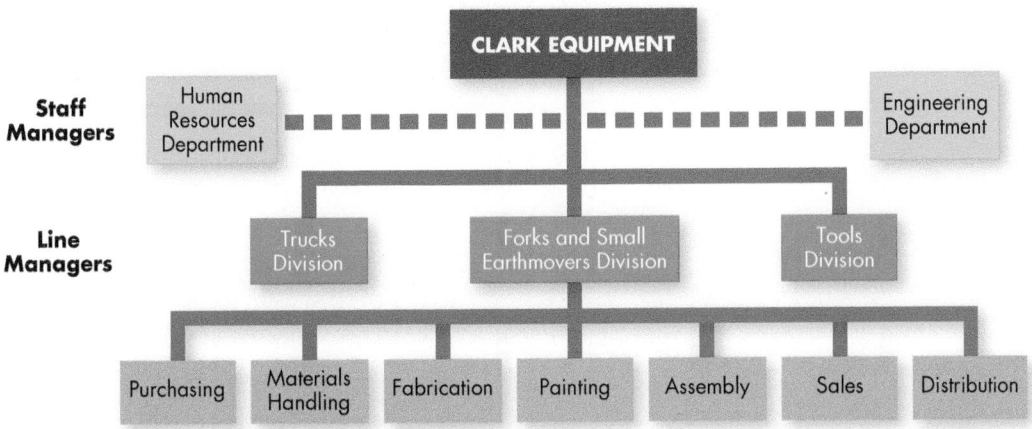

FIGURE 6.4 Line and Staff Organization

provide services to management, *line managers* are directly involved in producing the firm's products.

Committee and Team Authority In recent times, many organizations have started to grant *committee and team authority* to groups that play central roles in daily operations. A committee, for example, may consist of top managers from several major areas. If the work of the committee is especially important and if the committee members will be working together for an extended time, the organization may grant it **committee and team authority**, special authority as a decision-making body beyond the individual authority possessed by each of its members.

At the operating level, many firms today use **work teams** that are empowered to plan, organize, and perform their work with minimal supervision and often with special authority as well. Most U.S. companies today use teams in at least some areas; some make widespread use of teams throughout every area of their operations.

Committee and Team Authority *authority granted to committees or teams involved in a firm's daily operations*

Work Team *groups of operating employees who are empowered to plan and organize their own work and to perform that work with a minimum of supervision*

Basic Forms of Organizational Structure

Organizations can structure themselves in an almost infinite number of ways; according to specialization, for example, or departmentalization, or the decision-making hierarchy. Nevertheless, it is possible to identify four basic forms of organizational structure that reflect the general trends followed by most firms: (1) *functional*, (2) *divisional*, (3) *matrix*, and (4) *international*.

OBJECTIVE 6-4
Explain
the differences among functional, divisional, matrix, and international organizational structures and describe the most popular new forms of organizational design.

Functional Structure

Under a **functional structure**, relationships between group functions and activities determine authority. Functional structure is used by most small- to medium-sized firms, which are usually structured around basic business functions: a marketing department, an operations department, and a finance department. The benefits of this approach include specialization within functional areas and smoother coordination among them.

In large firms, coordination across functional departments becomes more complicated. Functional structure also fosters centralization (which can be desirable but is usually counter to the goals of larger businesses) and makes accountability more difficult. As organizations grow, they tend to shed this form and move toward one of the other three structures. Figure 6.5 illustrates a functional structure.

Functional Structure *organization structure in which authority is determined by the relationships between group functions and activities*

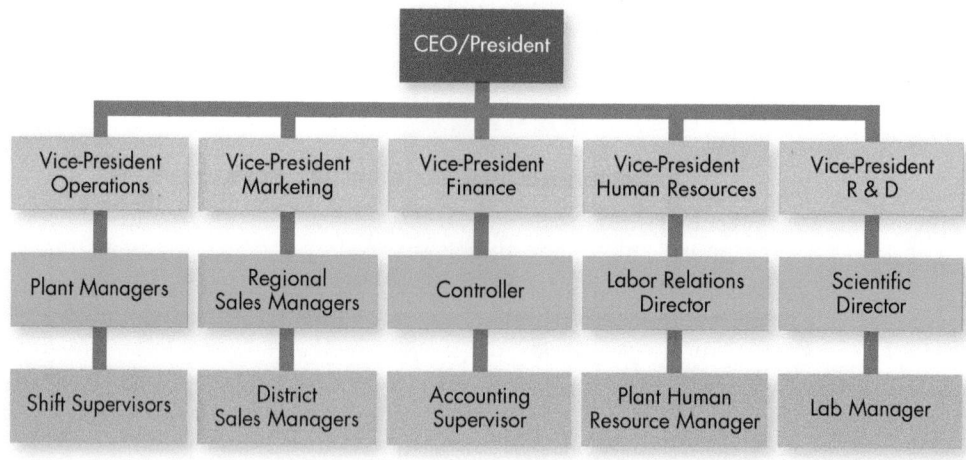

FIGURE 6.5 Functional Structure

Divisional Structure *organizational structure in which corporate divisions operate as autonomous businesses under the larger corporate umbrella*

Division *department that resembles a separate business in that it produces and markets its own products*

Divisional Structure

A **divisional structure** relies on product departmentalization. Organizations using this approach are typically structured around several product-based **divisions** that resemble separate businesses in that they produce and market their own products. The head of each division may be a corporate vice-president or, if the organization is large enough, a divisional president. In addition, each division usually has its own identity and operates as a relatively autonomous business under the larger corporate umbrella. Figure 6.6 illustrates a divisional structure.

Johnson & Johnson, one of the most recognizable names in healthcare products, organizes its company into three major divisions: consumer healthcare products, medical devices and diagnostics, and pharmaceuticals. Each major division is then broken down further. The consumer healthcare products division relies on product departmentalization to separate baby care, skin and hair care, topical health care, oral health care, women's health, over-the-counter medicines, and nutritionals. These divisions reflect the diversity of the company, which can protect it during downturns, such as the recession in 2008–2010, which showed the slowest pharmaceutical growth in four decades. Because they are divided, the other divisions are protected from this decline and can carry the company through it.

Consider also that Johnson & Johnson's over-the-counter pain management medicines are essentially competition for their pain management pharmaceuticals. Divisions can maintain healthy competition among themselves by sponsoring separate advertising campaigns, fostering different corporate identities, and so forth. They can also share certain corporate-level resources (such as market research data). However, if too much control is delegated to divisional managers, corporate

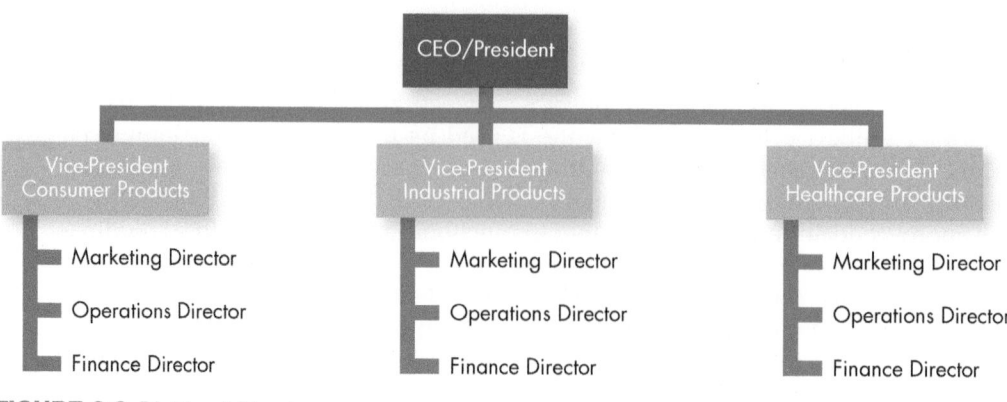

FIGURE 6.6 Divisional Structure

managers may lose touch with daily operations. Also, competition between divisions can become disruptive, and efforts in one division may duplicate those of another.[13]

Matrix Structure

Sometimes a **matrix structure**, a combination of two separate structures, works better than either simpler structure alone. This structure gets its matrix-like appearance, when shown in a diagram, by using one underlying "permanent" organizational structure (say, the divisional structure flowing up-and-down in the diagram), and then superimposing a different organizing framework on top of it (e.g., the functional form flowing side-to-side in the diagram). This highly flexible and readily adaptable structure was pioneered by NASA for use in developing specific space programs.

Suppose a company using a functional structure wants to develop a new product as a one-time special project. A team might be created and given responsibility for that product. The project team may draw members from existing functional departments, such as finance and marketing, so that all viewpoints are represented as the new product is being developed; the marketing member may provide ongoing information about product packaging and pricing issues, for instance, and the finance member may have useful information about when funds will be available.

In some companies, the matrix organization is a temporary measure installed to complete a specific project and affecting only one part of the firm. In these firms, the end of the project usually means the end of the matrix—either a breakup of the team or a restructuring to fit it into the company's existing line-and-staff structure. Ford, for example, uses a matrix organization to design new models, such as the 2017 Mustang. A design team composed of people with engineering, marketing, operations, and finance expertise was created to design the new car. After its work was done, the team members moved back to their permanent functional jobs.[14]

In other settings, the matrix organization is a semipermanent fixture. Figure 6.7 shows how Martha Stewart Living Omnimedia has created a permanent matrix organization for its lifestyle business. As you can see, the company is organized broadly into media and merchandising groups, each of which has specific products and product groups. For instance, there is an Internet group housed within the media group. Layered on top of this structure are teams of lifestyle experts led by area specialists organized into groups, such as cooking, entertainment, weddings, crafts, and so forth. Although each group targets specific customer needs, they all work, as necessary, across all product groups. An area specialist in weddings, for example, might contribute to an article on wedding planning for an Omnimedia magazine, contribute a story idea for an Omnimedia cable television program, and supply content for an Omnimedia site. This same individual might also help select fabrics suitable for wedding gowns that are to be retailed.

Matrix Structure *organizational structure created by superimposing one form of structure onto another*

International Structure

Several different **international organizational structures** are also common among firms that actively manufacture, purchase, and sell in global markets. These structures also evolve over time as a firm becomes more globalized. For example, when Walmart opened its first store outside the United States in 1992, it set up a special projects team. In the mid-1990s, the firm created a small international department to handle overseas expansion. Several years later, international sales and expansion had become such a major part of operations that a separate international division headed up by a senior vice-president was created. International operations have now become so important to Walmart that the international division has been further divided into geographic areas, such as Mexico and Europe. And as the firm expands into more foreign markets, such as Russia and India, new units have been created to oversee those operations.

International Organizational Structures *approaches to organizational structure developed in response to the need to manufacture, purchase, and sell in global markets*

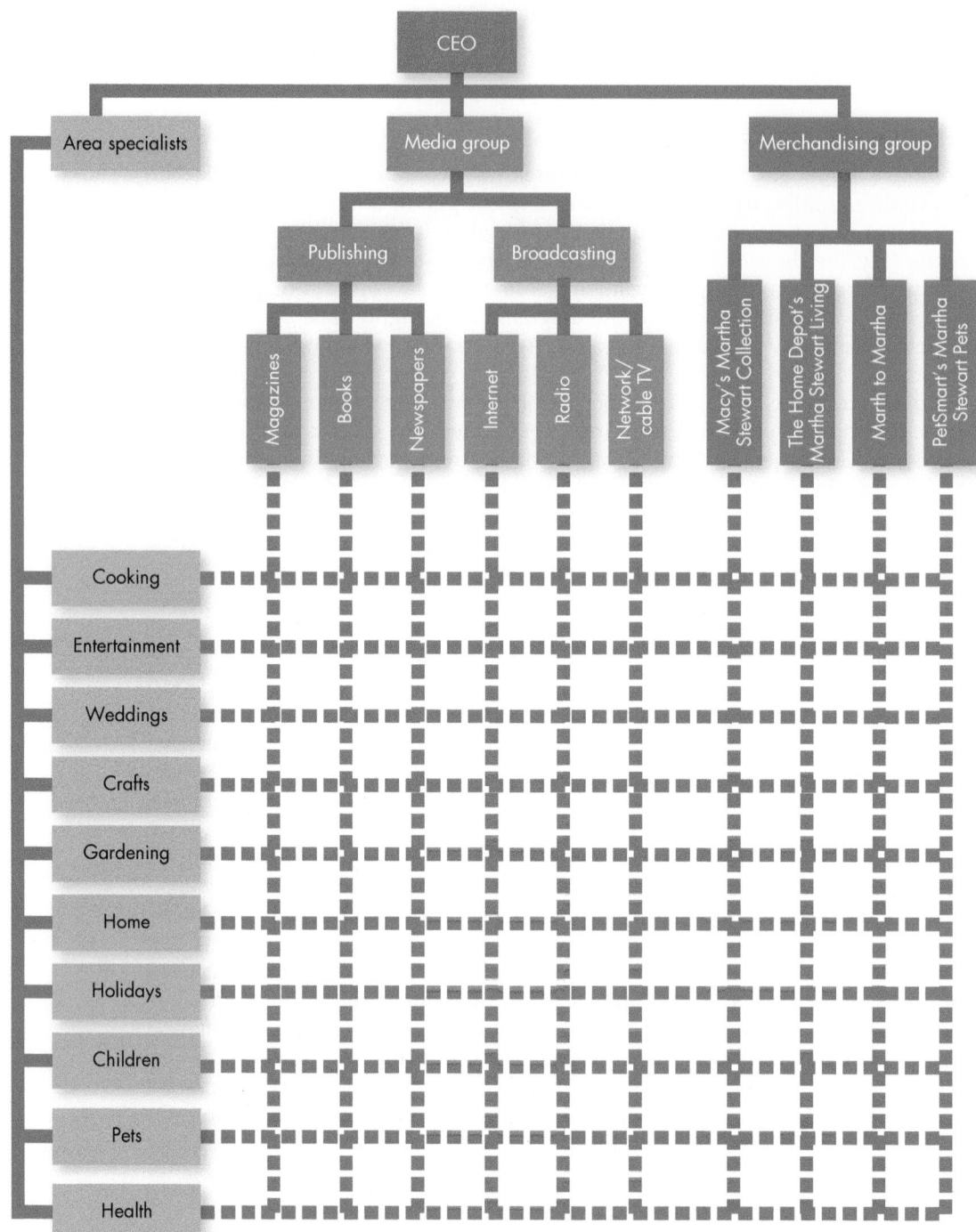

FIGURE 6.7 Matrix Organization of Martha Stewart Living Omnimedia

Some companies adopt a truly global structure in which they acquire resources (including capital), produce goods and services, engage in research and development, and sell products in whatever local market is appropriate, without consideration of national boundaries. Until a few years ago, General Electric (GE) kept its international business operations as separate divisions, as illustrated in Figure 6.8. Now, however, the company functions as one integrated global organization. GE businesses around the world connect and interact with each other constantly, and managers freely move back and forth among them. This integration is also reflected in GE's executive team, which includes executives from Spain, Japan, Scotland, Ireland, and Italy.

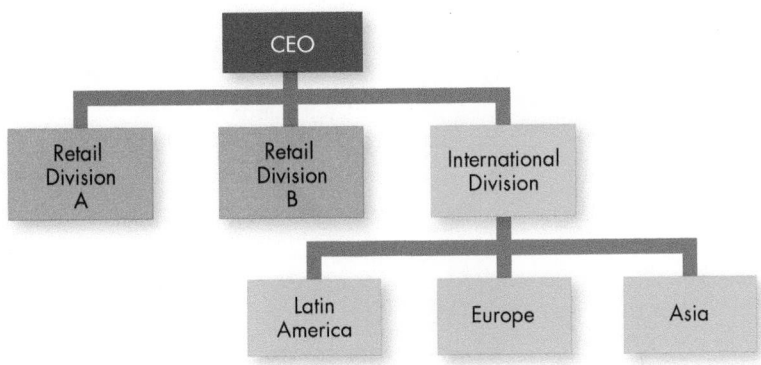

FIGURE 6.8 International Division Structure

New Forms of Organizational Structure

As the world grows increasingly complex and fast-paced, organizations also continue to seek new forms of organization that permit them to compete effectively. Among the most popular of these new forms are the *team organization*, the *virtual organization*, and the *learning organization*.

Team Organization *Team organization* relies almost exclusively on project-type teams, with little or no underlying functional hierarchy. People float from project to project as dictated by their skills and the demands of those projects. As the term suggests, team authority is the underlying foundation of organizations that adopt this organizational structure.

Virtual Organization Closely related to the team organization is the *virtual organization*. A virtual organization has little or no formal structure. Typically, it has only a handful of permanent employees, a small staff, and a modest administrative facility. As the needs of the organization change, its managers bring in temporary workers, lease facilities, and outsource basic support services to meet the demands of each unique situation. As the situation changes, the temporary workforce changes in parallel, with some people leaving the organization and others entering. Facilities and the subcontracted services also change. In other words, the virtual organization exists only in response to its own needs. This structure would be applicable to research or consulting firms that hire consultants based on the specific content knowledge required by each unique project. As the projects change, so too does the composition of the organization. Figure 6.9 illustrates a hypothetical virtual organization.

Learning Organization The so-called *learning organization* works to integrate continuous improvement with continuous employee learning and development. Specifically, a learning organization works to facilitate the lifelong learning and personal development of all of its employees while continually transforming itself to respond to changing demands and needs.

Although managers might approach the concept of a learning organization from a variety of perspectives, the most frequent goals are superior quality, continuous improvement, and performance measurement. The idea is that the most consistent and logical strategy for achieving continuous improvement is to constantly upgrade employee talent, skill, and knowledge. For example, if each employee in an organization learns one new thing each day and can translate that knowledge into work-related practice, continuous improvement will logically follow. Indeed, organizations that wholeheartedly embrace this approach believe that only through constant employee learning can continuous improvement really occur. Shell Oil's Shell Learning Center boasts state-of-the-art classrooms and instructional technology,

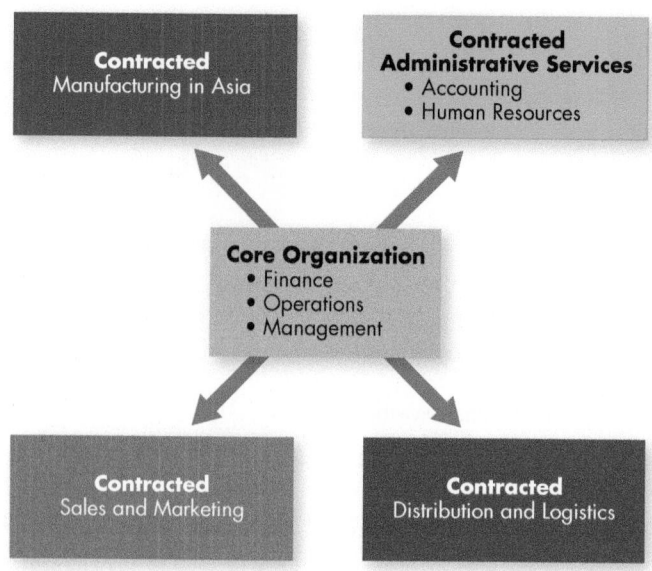

FIGURE 6.9 The Virtual Organization

lodging facilities, a restaurant, and recreational amenities. Line managers rotate through the center to fulfill teaching assignments, and Shell employees routinely attend training programs, seminars, and related activities.

OBJECTIVE 6-5
Describe
the informal organization and discuss intrapreneuring.

Informal Organization *network, unrelated to the firm's formal authority structure, of everyday social interactions among company employees*

Informal Organization

The structure of a company, however, is by no means limited to the *formal organization* as represented by the organization chart and the formal assignment of authority. Frequently, the **informal organization**, everyday social interactions among employees that transcend formal jobs and job interrelationships, effectively alters a company's formal structure.[15] This level of organization is sometimes just as powerful—if not more powerful—than the formal structure. When Hewlett-Packard fired its CEO, Carly Fiorina, a few years ago, much of the discussion that led to her firing took place outside formal structural arrangements in the organization. Members of the board of directors, for example, held secret meetings and reached confidential agreements among themselves before Fiorina's future with the company was addressed in a formal manner.[16]

On the negative side, the informal organization can reinforce office politics that put the interests of individuals ahead of those of the firm and can disseminate distorted or inaccurate information. For example, if the informal organization is highlighting false information about impending layoffs, valuable employees may act quickly (and unnecessarily) to seek other employment.

Informal Groups

Informal groups are simply groups of people who decide to interact among themselves. They may be people who work together in a formal sense or who just get together for lunch, during breaks, or after work. They may talk about business, the boss, or nonwork-related topics such as families, movies, or sports. Their impact on the organization may be positive (if they work together to support the organization), negative (if they work together in ways that run counter to the organization's interests), or irrelevant (if what they do is unrelated to the organization).

Informal groups can be a powerful force that managers cannot ignore.[17] One writer described how a group of employees at a furniture factory subverted their boss's efforts to increase production. They tacitly agreed to produce a reasonable amount of work but not to work too hard. One man kept a stockpile of completed work hidden as a backup in case he got too far behind. In another example, auto workers described how they left out gaskets and seals and put soft-drink bottles inside doors to cause customer complaints.[18] Of course, informal groups can also be a positive force, as when people work together to help out a colleague who has suffered a personal tragedy. For example, several instances of this behavior were reported in the wake of devastating tornadoes that swept through Alabama and Missouri in 2011, after hurricane Sandy devastated parts of the northeast in 2012, and during the Ebola virus outbreak in 2014–2015.

In recent years, the Internet has served as a platform for the emergence of more and different kinds of informal or interest groups. As one example, Chevron uses its internal network to facilitate a wide array of interest groups that bring together people with common interests. And increasingly, workers who lose their jobs as a result of layoffs band together electronically to offer moral support to one another and to facilitate networking as they all look for new jobs.[19] Indeed, social media plays a major role in informal groups today.

Organizational Grapevine

The **grapevine** is an informal communication network that can permeate an entire organization. Grapevines are found in all organizations except the smallest, but they do not always follow the same patterns as, nor do they necessarily coincide with, formal channels of authority and communication. Research has identified two kinds of grapevines.[20] One such grapevine, the gossip chain, occurs when one person spreads the message to many other people. Each one, in turn, may either keep the information confidential or pass it on to others. The gossip chain is likely to carry personal information. The other common grapevine is the cluster chain, in which one person passes the information to a selected few individuals. Some of the receivers pass the information to a few other individuals; the rest keep it to themselves.

> **Grapevine** *informal communication network that runs through an organization*

There is some disagreement about how accurate the information carried by the grapevine is, but research is increasingly finding it to be fairly accurate, especially when the information is based on fact rather than speculation. One study found that the grapevine may be between 75 percent and 95 percent accurate.[21] That same study also found that informal communication is increasing in many organizations for several basic reasons. One contributing factor is the recent increase in merger, acquisition, and takeover activity. Because such activity can greatly affect the people within an organization, it follows that they may spend more time talking about it.[22] The second contributing factor is that as more and more corporations move facilities from inner cities to suburbs, employees tend to talk less and less to others outside the organization and more and more to one another. Yet another contributing factor is simply the widespread availability of information technology that makes it easier than ever before for people to communicate quickly and easily. Much like in informal groups, social media plays a growing role in the grapevine.

More recently, another study looked at the effects of the recent recession and large-scale job losses on informal communication. More than half of the survey participants reported a sharp increase in gossip and rumors in their organizations. The same survey also reported an increase in the amount of eavesdropping in most businesses.[23] Further, in another recent survey, 32 percent of people claimed to use their work e-mail inappropriately and 48 percent admitted gossiping with other employees through their e-mail.[24] In 2014, a poll found that 47 percent of those responding indicated that they gossiped at work and 18 agreed that no topics were "off-limits." And yet another study reported that 55 percent of conversations in the workplace between men and 67 percent of conversations among women involved at least some gossip.[25]

Attempts to eliminate the grapevine are fruitless, but fortunately the manager does have some control over it. By maintaining open channels of communication and responding vigorously to inaccurate information, the manager can minimize the damage the grapevine can do. The grapevine can actually be an asset. By learning who the key people in the grapevine are, for example, the manager can partially control the information they receive and use the grapevine to sound out employee reactions to new ideas, such as a change in human resource policies or benefit packages. The manager can also get valuable information from the grapevine and use it to improve decision making.[26]

Intrapreneuring

<aside>
Intrapreneuring *process of creating and maintaining the innovation and flexibility of a small-business environment within the confines of a large organization*
</aside>

Good managers recognize that the informal organization exists whether they want it or not and can use it not only to reinforce the formal organization, but also to harness its energy to improve productivity.

Many firms, including Rubbermaid, DreamWorks Animation, 3M, and Xerox, support **intrapreneuring**, creating and maintaining the innovation and flexibility of a small-business environment within a large, bureaucratic structure. Historically, most innovations have come from individuals in small businesses. As businesses increase in size, however, innovation and creativity tend to become casualties in the battle for more sales and profits. In some large companies, new ideas are even discouraged, and champions of innovation have been stalled in midcareer. At Lockheed Martin, the Advanced Development Programs (ADP) encourages intrapreneurship in the tradition of Skunk Works, a legendary team developed in 1943 as engineer Kelly Johnson's response to Lockheed's need for a powerful jet fighter. Johnson's innovative organization approach broke all the rules, and not only did it work, but it also taught Lockheed the value of encouraging that kind of thinking.[27]

There are three intrapreneurial roles in large organizations.[28] To successfully use intrapreneurship to encourage creativity and innovation, the organization must find one or more individuals to perform these roles. The *inventor* is the person who actually conceives of and develops the new idea, product, or service by means of the creative process. Because the inventor may lack the expertise or motivation to oversee the transformation of the product or service from an idea into a marketable entity, however, a second role comes into play. A *product champion* is usually a middle manager who learns about the project and becomes committed to it. He or she helps overcome organizational resistance and convinces others to take the innovation seriously. The product champion may have only limited understanding of the technological aspects of the innovation. Nevertheless, product champions are skilled at knowing how the organization works, whose support is needed to push the project forward, and where to go to secure the resources necessary for successful development. A *sponsor* is a top-level manager who approves of and supports a project. This person may fight for the budget needed to develop an idea, overcome arguments against a project, and use organizational politics to ensure the project's survival. With a sponsor in place, the inventor's idea has a much better chance of being successfully developed.

summary of learning objectives

OBJECTIVE 6-1

Discuss the factors that influence a firm's organizational structure. (pp. 176–178)

Each organization must develop an appropriate *organizational structure*—the specification of the jobs to be done and the ways in which those jobs relate to one another. Most organizations change structures almost continuously. Firms prepare *organization charts* to clarify structure and to show employees where they fit into a firm's operations. Each box represents a job, and solid lines define the *chain of command*, or *reporting relationships*. The charts of large firms are complex and include individuals at many levels. Because size prevents them from charting every manager, they may create single organization charts for overall corporate structure and separate charts for divisions. An organization's structure is determined by a variety of factors, including the organization's mission and strategy, size, environment, and history. Structure is not static but is changed and modified frequently.

OBJECTIVE 6-2

Explain specialization and departmentalization as two of the building blocks of organizational structure. (pp. 179–183)

The process of identifying specific jobs and designating people to perform them leads to *job specialization*. After they're specialized, jobs are grouped into logical units—the process of *departmentalization*. Departmentalization follows one (or any combination) of five forms:

1 *Functional departmentalization* based on functions or activities
2 *Product departmentalization* based on products or services offered
3 *Process departmentalization* based on production processes used to create goods and services
4 *Customer departmentalization* based on customer types or customer groups
5 *Geographic departmentalization* based on geographic areas

Larger companies may take advantage of different types of departmentalization for various levels.

OBJECTIVE 6-3

Describe centralization and decentralization, delegation, and authority as the key ingredients in establishing the decision-making hierarchy. (pp. 183–187)

After jobs have been specialized and departmentalized, firms establish decision-making hierarchies. One major issue addressed through the creation of the decision-making hierarchy involves whether the firm will be relatively *centralized* or relatively *decentralized*. In a centralized organization, decision-making authority is retained at the top levels of the organization. Centralized authority systems typically require multiple layers of management and thus *tall organizational structures*. Conversely, in a decentralized organization, most decision-making authority is delegated to lower levels of management. A related concept is *span of control*, which refers to the number of people who report to a manager. Tall, centralized organizations tend to have a narrow span of control, whereas flat, centralized organizations tend to have wider spans of control.

Decentralized firms tend to have relatively fewer layers of management, resulting in a *flat organizational structure*. *Delegation* is the process through which a manager allocates work to subordinates. In general, the delegation process involves three steps:

1 The assignment of *responsibility*
2 The granting of *authority*
3 The creation of *accountability*

As individuals are delegated responsibility and authority in a firm, a complex web of interactions develops.

These interactions may take one of three forms of authority: line, staff, or committee and team. Line authority follows the chain of command, and staff authority relies on expertise in areas such as law, accounting, and human resources.

OBJECTIVE 6-4

Explain the differences among functional, divisional, matrix, and international organizational structures and describe the most popular new forms of organizational design. (pp. 187–192)

Most firms rely on one of four basic forms of organizational structure: (1) *functional*, (2) *divisional*, (3) *matrix*, or (4) *international*. A functional structure is based on organizational functions, such as marketing, finance, or operations. A divisional structure, in contrast, groups activities in terms of distinct product or service groups. A matrix structure, a combination of two structures, imposes one type of structure on top of another. Several different international organizational structures have emerged in response to the need to manufacture, purchase, and sell in global markets. A company may start with a small international department that may grow into an international division. As global competition becomes more complex, companies may experiment with ways to respond. Some adopt truly global structures, acquiring resources and producing and selling products in local markets without consideration of national boundaries.

Organizations also continue to seek new forms of organization that permit them to compete effectively. The most popular new forms include:

1 *Team organizations*, which rely almost exclusively on project-type teams with little or no underlying functional hierarchy.

2 *Virtual organizations*, which have little or no formal structure and just a handful of employees.

3 *Learning organizations*, which work to integrate continuous improvement with ongoing employee learning and development.

OBJECTIVE 6-5

Describe the informal organization and discuss intrapreneuring. (pp. 192–194)

The *formal organization* is the part that can be represented in chart form. The *informal organization*, everyday social interactions among employees that transcend formal jobs and job interrelationships, may alter formal structure. There are two important elements in most informal organizations. *Informal groups* consist of people who decide to interact among themselves. Their impact on a firm may be positive, negative, or irrelevant. The *grapevine* is an informal communication network that can run through an entire organization. Because it can be harnessed to improve productivity, some organizations encourage the informal organization. Many firms also support *intrapreneuring*—creating and maintaining the innovation and flexibility of a small business within the confines of a large, bureaucratic structure. In large organizations, intrapreneurship requires the participation of individuals who will serve roles as inventors, product champions, and sponsors.

key terms

accountability (p. 186)
authority (p. 186)
centralized organization (p. 183)
chain of command (p. 176)
committee and team authority (p. 187)
customer departmentalization (p. 182)
decentralized organization (p. 183)

delegation (p. 185)
departmentalization (p. 180)
division (p. 188)
divisional structure (p. 188)
flat organizational structure (p. 183)
functional departmentalization (p. 180)
functional structure (p. 187)

geographic departmentalization (p. 182)
grapevine (p. 193)
informal organization (p. 192)
international organizational structures (p. 189)
intrapreneuring (p. 194)
job specialization (p. 179)

MyLab Intro to Business

To complete the problems with the ⭐, go to EOC Discussion Questions in the MyLab.

questions & exercises

QUESTIONS FOR REVIEW

⭐ **6-1.** Describe the five basic forms of departmentalization. Give examples of each.

6-2. What are the advantages and disadvantages of a decentralized organizational structure?

6-3. What is the difference between responsibility and authority?

6-4. Why do some managers have difficulties in delegating authority? Of these reasons, which do you think would be the most significant issue for you?

6-5. Why is a company's informal organization important?

QUESTIONS FOR ANALYSIS

⭐ **6-6.** Draw a high-level organization chart for your college or university.

⭐ **6-7.** Describe a hypothetical organizational structure for a start-up Internet marketing firm. Describe changes that might be necessary as the business grows.

6-8. Do you think that you would want to work in a matrix organization, such as Martha Stewart Living Omnimedia, where you were assigned simultaneously to multiple units or groups? Why, or why not?

APPLICATION EXERCISES

6-9. Interview the manager of a local service business, such as a fast-food restaurant. What types of tasks does this manager typically delegate? Is the appropriate authority also delegated in each case?

6-10. Select a company where you would like to work one day. Using online research, determine if the company has a functional, divisional, matrix, international, team, virtual, or learning organization. Explain how you arrived at this conclusion. Do you believe that their organizational structure is consistent with the organization's mission? Do you think that organizational structure is well-suited to your working style and preferences?

building a business: continuing team exercise

Assignment

Meet with your team members and discuss your new business venture within the context of this chapter. Develop specific responses to the following:

6-11. Thinking ahead one year, how many employees do you expect that you will have in your business? How did you come to this conclusion?

6-12. Draw a sample organization chart for your business in one year. Although you won't know the names of all

your employees, your organization chart should include job titles.

6-13. Will decision-making in your business be centralized or decentralized? Be sure to support your conclusion.

6-14. How do you think that your organizational structure will change over time? Will it be the same in 10 years?

team exercise

GETTING WITH THE PROGRAM

Background Information

You are the founder of a small but growing high-tech company that develops new computer software. With your current

workload and new contracts in the pipeline, your business is thriving, except for one problem: You cannot find computer programmers for product development. Worse yet, current staff members are being lured away by other high-tech firms. After suffering a particularly discouraging personnel raid in which competitors captured three of your most valued employees, you schedule a meeting with your director of human resources to plan organizational changes designed to encourage worker loyalty. You already pay top dollar, but the continuing exodus tells you that programmers are looking for something more.

Method

Working with three or four classmates, identify some ways in which specific organizational changes might improve the working environment and encourage employee loyalty. As you analyze the following factors, ask yourself the obvious question: If I were a programmer, what organizational changes would encourage me to stay?

- *Level of job specialization.*   With many programmers describing their jobs as tedious because of the focus on detail in a narrow work area, what changes, if any, would you make in job specialization? Right now, for instance, few of your programmers have any say in product design.
- *Decision-making hierarchy.*   What decision-making authority would encourage people to stay? Is expanding employee

authority likely to work better in a centralized or decentralized organization?

- *Team authority.*   Can team empowerment make a difference? Taking the point of view of the worker, describe the ideal team.
- *Intrapreneuring.*   What can your company do to encourage and reward innovation?

FOLLOW-UP QUESTIONS

6-15. With the average computer programmer earning nearly $80,000, and with all competitive firms paying top dollar, why might organizational issues be critical in determining employee loyalty?

6-16. If you were a programmer, what organizational factors would make a difference to you? Why?

6-17. As the company founder, how willing would you be to make major organizational changes in light of the shortage of qualified programmers?

exercising your ethics

I HEARD IT THROUGH THE GRAPEVINE

The Situation

Assume that you are a divisional manager at a large high-tech company. The company has just lost a large contract, and the human resources director has just advised company executives that they must cut the workforce by 10 percent within three months to preserve their financial position. You are distressed at the prospect of losing long-time employees, especially those nearing retirement or with young families.

The Dilemma

As you ponder the situation, another regional member has brought up a potential solution that will spare you from actually

laying off employees. "The grapevine has worked against us in the past, so let's make it work for us this time. If we leak word that the company is planning to cut pay by 15 percent for most of the workforce as a result of the loss of this contract, people will get scared. They'll start looking for jobs or reevaluating retirement and the layoff will take care of itself. Once we've reached the desired level of resignations, we will reassure the remaining employees that their jobs are secure."

QUESTIONS TO ADDRESS

6-18. What are the ethical issues in this situation?

6-19. What do you think most people would do in this situation?

6-20. What would you do in this situation?

cases

PUSHING THE PRODUCT

Continued from page 176

At the beginning of this chapter you read about both Apple and Valve's corporate organizational strategies. Using the information presented in this chapter, you should now be able to answer the following questions.

QUESTIONS FOR DISCUSSION

6-21. Describe the organizational structure of your college or university. Is it more functional or divisional?

6-22. In what ways does this structure help and hurt the mission of the college?

6-23. If you were hired by the college to help reorganize for better efficiency and better provision of service, what tangible advice could you offer?

HEARD IT THROUGH THE GRAPEVINE

When you think of the word *gossip*, it's most likely that the term has negative connotations. Take it one step farther, into the workplace, and you almost certainly have concerns. However, there is considerable research to support the claim that gossip, or the grapevine, is an important part of organizational culture. According to Professor Kathleen Reardon of the USC Marshall School of Business, "We learn who we are through what people say to us and about us."[29] Managing the office grapevine and your role in this informal communication can be tricky.

Several guidelines can help you understand when to participate in gossip as a sender or receiver. First, you should understand the benefits of gossip. Gossip, or the office grapevine, may be the first place that you hear important information, such as a new job opening up or a major contract that the company is about to sign. However, as you pass along information, you must remember that what you say will reflect upon you. If you share negative information about a coworker, it is very likely that others may come to distrust you. In addition, you should carefully consider the people with whom you share gossip and information, making sure that they will keep confidential information private. Your supervisor may be particularly uncomfortable if you develop a reputation as a gossip, as your comments may be perceived as threatening. Finally, be very careful about the medium that you choose to share information. An email is never private and should not be used for any communication that you would not want shared publicly.[30]

As a manager, you may have a slightly different perspective on gossip or the office grapevine. You may be concerned that gossip limits your ability to control how information is shared and may limit your power. Holly Green, in an article in *Fortune* magazine, shares several suggestions about managing the office grapevine.[31] A vigorous grapevine is often the sign of boredom. Rather than having employees spend hours a week gossiping about others, find other outlets for their creative abilities. You should also realize that grapevines grow most quickly when information is scarce. Employees turn to the grapevine when they believe that they are not getting enough information from formal channels of communication. Therefore, to control rampant gossip, a manager should work towards intentionally sharing as much information as possible. Managers should also keep their ear to the grapevine, as it may convey important information, such as manageable concerns of employees. Managed correctly, the grapevine can be a powerful tool for employees and managers.

QUESTIONS FOR DISCUSSION

6-24. Thinking about your office or college, what types of information are conveyed through the grapevine? How often is the information accurate?

6-25. Does a flat organization encourage or discourage office gossip? What leads you to this conclusion?

6-26. Do you think that the grapevine would be more or less active in a matrix organization? Why?

6-27. Many companies encourage their employees to form social relationships outside of work to build a sense of camaraderie. How would these informal groups feed or limit the grapevine?

Writing Assignments

6-29. Each organization's structure is unique, but most structures can be grouped into four basic forms. There are advantages and disadvantages to each form of organization structure. Which of the four basic forms of organizational structure would you rather work in? Write an essay: (a) Explaining your choice, including the advantages and disadvantages of that form of organizational structure, and (b) Describing under what conditions that structure might work best.

6-30. Choose a company to research. Determine whether or not the company is centralized or decentralized, and how the company might be departmentalized. Describe your findings in a short essay. Include an analysis of the underlying reasons for the apparent organizational structure, and whether or not it is the best structure for that type of business. How might the company reorganize to be more effective and efficient?

endnotes

[1] Yglesias, Matthew, "Apple May Have Finally Gotten too Big for Its Unusual Corporate Structure," vox.com, November 27, 2016, http://www.vox.com/new-money/2016/11/27/13706776/apple-functional-divisional (Accessed March 8, 2017)

[2] Henry Mintzberg, "Structure in 5's: A Synthesis of the Research on Organization Design," *Management Science*, March 1980, p. 322–341.

[3] Claire Suddath, "Why There Are No Bosses at Valve," *Bloomberg Business*, April 27, 2012, at http://www.bloomberg.com/bw/articles/2012-04-27/why-there-are-no-bosses-at-valve#p1, accessed April 26, 2015.

[4] See Royston Greenwood and Danny Miller, "Tackling Design Anew: Getting Back to the Heart of Organizational Theory," *Academy of Management Perspectives*, November 2010, pp. 78–88.

[5] AllBusiness.com, "Kraft Foods North America Announces New Management Structure," September 28, 2000 (March 5, 2011), at http://www.allbusiness.com/food-beverage/food-beverage-overview/6505848-1.html.

[6] Steinway & Sons, "Steinway History: Leadership Through Craftsmanship and Innovation," 2012, at www.steinway.com, accessed on April 11, 2013; Steinway & Sons, "Online Factory Tour," 2012, at http://archive.steinway.com, accessed on April 11, 2013; Victor Verney, "88 Keys: The Making of a Steinway Piano," *All About Jazz*, June 18, 2012, at www.allaboutjazz.com, accessed on April 11, 2013; WGBH (Boston), "*Note by Note*: The Making of Steinway L1037," 2010, at www.wgbh.org, accessed on April 11, 2013; M. Eric Johnson, Joseph Hall, and David Pyke, "Technology and Quality at Steinway & Sons," Tuck School of Business at Dartmouth, May 13, 2005, at http://mba.tuck.dartmouth.edu, accessed on April 11, 2013.

[7] O'Malley Greenburg, Zack. 2014. "Piano Forte: Inside Steinway's Century-Spanning Business." Forbes.Com

17. Business Source Premier, EBSCOhost (accessed April 27, 2015).

8 See Levi Strauss & Co., at http://www.levistrauss.com/Company/WorldwideRegions.aspx.

9 "Blowing Up Pepsi," *BusinessWeek*, April 27, 2009, pp. 32–36; *Hoover's Handbook of American Business 2015* (Austin, Texas: Hoover's Business Press, 2015), pp. 638–639.

10 Michael E. Raynor and Joseph L. Bower, "Lead From the Center," *Harvard Business Review*, May 2001, 93–102.

11 Gary Hamel, "What Google, Whole Foods Do Best," *Fortune*, September 27, 2007, p. 59.

12 2014. "Illinois Tool Works Inc. SWOT Analysis." Illinois Tool Works, Inc. SWOT Analysis 1-8. Business Source Premier, EBSCOhost (accessed April 27, 2015).

13 *Hoover's Handbook of American Business 2013* (Austin, Texas: Hoover's Business Press, 2013), pp. 58–60; Brian Dumaine, "How I Delivered the Goods," *Fortune Small Business*, October 2002, pp. 78–81; Charles Haddad, "FedEx: Gaining on the Ground," *Businessweek*, December 16, 2002, pp. 126–128; Claudia H. Deutsch, "FedEx Has Hit the Ground Running, but Will Its Legs Tire?" *New York Times*, October 13, 2002, p. BU7; http://www.Forbes.com/finance (February 16, 2006); PBS.org, "Who Made America" (June 19, 2008), at http://www.pbs.org/wgbh/theymadeamerica/whomade/fsmith_hi.html.

14 phx.corporate-ir.net/phoenix.zhtml?c=96022&p=irol-newsArticle&ID=1489110&highlight=.

15 "The Office Chart That Really Counts," *Businessweek*, February 27, 2006, pp. 48–49.

16 Carol Loomis, "How the HP Board KO'd Carly," *Fortune*, March 7, 2005, pp. 99–102.

17 Rob Cross, Nitin Nohria, and Andrew Parker, "Six Myths about Informal Networks—And How to Overcome Them," *Sloan Management Review*, Spring 2002, pp. 67–77.

18 Robert Schrank, *Ten Thousand Working Days* (Cambridge, MA: MIT Press, 1978); Bill Watson, "Counter Planning on the Shop Floor," in Peter Frost, Vance Mitchell, and Walter

Nord (eds.), *Organizational Reality*, 2nd ed. (Glenview, IL: Scott, Foresman, 1982), pp. 286–294.

19 "After Layoffs, More Workers Band Together," *Wall Street Journal*, February 26, 2002, p. B1.

20 Keith Davis, "Management Communication and the Grapevine," *Harvard Business Review*, September–October 1953, pp. 43–49.

21 "Spread the Word: Gossip Is Good," *Wall Street Journal*, October 4, 1988, p. B1.

22 See David M. Schweiger and Angelo S. DeNisi, "Communication with Employees Following a Merger: A Longitudinal Field Experiment," *Academy of Management Journal*, March 1991, pp. 110–135.

23 "Job Fears Make Offices All Fears," *Wall Street Journal*, January 20, 2009, p. B7.

24 Institute of Leadership and Management, "32% of People Making Inappropriate Use of Work Emails," April 20, 2011; accessed on April 12, 2013.

25 www.valuewalk.com/2014/05/avoid-office-gossip/, accessed on February 10, 2015.

26 Nancy B. Kurland and Lisa Hope Pelled, "Passing the Word: Toward a Model of Gossip and Power in the Workplace," *Academy of Management Review*, 2000, Vol. 25, No. 2, pp. 428–438.

27 Lockheed Martin, "Skunk Works" (June 19, 2008), at http://www.lockheedmartin.com/aeronautics/skunkworks/index.html.

28 See Gifford Pinchot III, *Intrapreneuring* (New York: Harper & Row, 1985).

29 Gallo, Amy. "Go Ahead and Gossip." *Harvard Business Review*. N.p., 21 Mar. 2013. Web. 19 June 2013.

30 Spiers, Carole. "Managing Office Gossip." Gulfnews.com. Al Nisr Publishing LLC, 7 Jan. 2013. Web. 19 June 2013

31 Green, Holly. "How to Prune Your Organizational Grapevine." Forbes. *Forbes Magazine,* 22 May 2012. Web. 19 June 2013.

chapter 7

Operations Management and Quality

Paul Morigi/Stringer/Getty Images Entertainment/Getty Images

There isn't a "perfect" way to produce a product

or service; just be flexible. An

open mind and

the willingness to try new things drive efficient

operations

and lead to innovation.

After reading this chapter, you should be able to:

7-1 **Explain** the meaning of *operations* and discuss the growth in the services and goods sectors of the U.S. economy.

7-2 **Identify** the three kinds of utility created by operations and the characteristics that distinguish service operations from goods production.

7-3 **Explain** how companies with different business strategies are best served by having different operations capabilities.

7-4 **Identify** the major factors that are considered in operations planning.

7-5 **Discuss** the information contained in four kinds of operations schedules—the master operations schedule, detailed schedule, staff schedule, and project schedule.

7-6 **Discuss** the two key activities required for operations control.

7-7 **Identify** the activities and underlying objectives involved in total quality management.

7-8 **Explain** how a supply chain strategy differs from traditional strategies for coordinating operations among firms.

Dessert Is Always a Great Idea

In 1972, Evelyn and Oscar Overton took the last of their savings and moved from Detroit, Michigan, to Los Angeles, California, to try their hand, one last time, at entrepreneurship. Evelyn had been selling cheesecakes from a small kitchen in her basement for almost 30 years, but she dreamed of something bigger. It wasn't until 1978 that their son, David, opened the first restaurant dedicated to showcasing his mother's creations. With an extensive menu of both meals and desserts, the first Cheesecake Factory was a huge success. The family incorporated the business and took it public in 1992 with plans to open 3–4 new restaurants every year, but just 13 years later, in 2005, the company had 103 locations and had surpassed $1 billion in revenue. By 2016, the Cheesecake Factory Incorporated owned and operated over 200 full-service, casual dining restaurants throughout the United States and Puerto Rico, and 15 more restaurants operated internationally under licensing agreements. Their mission: creating an environment where absolute guest satisfaction is the highest priority.

The Cheesecake Factory's kitchen is organized like a production line. Orders, with the recipes, appear on computer monitors above the food prep stations, where prep staff chop veggies, meat, and seasonings while a timer counts down. The cook assembles the final product and it is quality checked by the head cook before going out to the customer. The system is streamlined, efficient, and highly replicable. Every Cheesecake Factory follows the same formula and uses the same system, ensuring both quality of food and quality of service.

The Cheesecake Factory's lunch and dinner menus include seafood, pasta, burgers, and more, designed to appeal to a broad audience, and most of the food is made from scratch. The only thing not made on demand, ironically, is the cheesecake. The iconic dessert comes from the Company's bakery division, which operates two bakery production facilities, one in Calabasas Hills, California, and one in Rocky Mount, North Carolina, that produce quality cheesecakes and other baked products for its restaurants, international licensees, and third-party bakery customers.

Atul Gawande wrote a piece for the *New Yorker* in 2012, praising the operations management of the Cheesecake Factory and musing about why his own industry, health care, couldn't seem to integrate some of the obvious operational efficiencies that the restaurant chain had implemented to combine both profit and service.

In addition to quality control, Atul noticed that "the managers monitored the pace, too—scanning the screens for a station stacking up red flags, indicating orders past the target time, and deciding whether to give the cooks at the station a nudge or an extra

what's in it for me?

Perhaps you have been pleasantly surprised by a new product you purchased or smiled at excellent service. In either case, you'll find it easy to relate to the topics in this chapter. We'll explore the numerous ways companies align their operations processes with their business plans, and we will discuss how these decisions contribute to a firm's ability to create a high-quality product. Gaining an appreciation for the many steps it takes to bring high-quality goods and services to market will help make you a smarter consumer and more effective employee. And if you're a manager, understanding that production activities are pliable and should be reoriented to better support new business strategies will help you redefine your company and its marketplace over time.

pair of hands. They watched for waste—wasted food, wasted time, wasted effort. The formula was Business 101: Use the right amount of goods and labor to deliver what customers want and no more. Anything more is waste, and waste is lost profit."[1]

The company uses data analytics to forecast not only how many guests to expect on a given night but also what they will likely order. The model allows each restaurant to order the right kinds and the right amount of groceries, and to have just the right number of staff on board.

However, according to David Overton, who is still running the company as CEO, his focus is on people. In an interview with *Fortune* magazine in 2011, he boiled his operational philosophy down into three main points:

- Focus on people: "You have to devote resources to training, from the cooks to customer service. In this business, it's all location, location, location. But once you grow, it's all people, people, people."

- Let some things go: "Don't limit your business for the sake of control. Whether building our infrastructure or thinking about growth, I focused on allowing us to be as successful as we could be, not trying to control everything."

- Prevent copycats: "I created a unique concept with the broadest and deepest menu in casual dining. It's a big part of what attracts guests, but it's also highly complicated, which makes it a huge barrier to entry."[2]

Overton claims that people are his greatest asset, and his employees back him up on that. In 2017, the Company was named to the *Fortune* magazine "100 Best Companies to Work For" list for the fourth consecutive year. The stock, which went public at $20, was trading above $60 by the end of 2016, and, according to Overton, "We delivered our 28th consecutive quarter of positive comparable sales, marking seven years of strong financial performance and meaningful shareholder value creation."[3] (After studying the content in this chapter, you should be able to answer a set of discussion questions found at the end of the chapter.)

OBJECTIVE 7-1
Explain
the meaning of *operations* and discuss the growth in the services and goods sectors of the U.S. economy.

Service Operations (or Service Production) *activities producing intangible and tangible products, such as entertainment, transportation, and education*

What Does *Operations* Mean Today?

Although you may not always think about it, you are constantly involved in business activities that provide goods and services to customers. You wake up to the sound of your favorite digital music, and on your bus ride to work or school, you message on a smartphone. Your instructors, the bus driver, the messaging provider, and the music provider all work in **service operations (or service production)**. They provide intangible and tangible service products, such as entertainment, transportation,

Some businesses focus solely on service operations and others solely on goods operations. General Electric (GE) uses both service operations (in its financial services businesses) and goods operations (in its electric turbine business).

education, and communications services. Firms that make only tangible products—digital recordings or radios, smartphones, buses, textbooks—are engaged in activities for **goods operations (or goods production)**.

The term **operations (or production)** refers to all the activities involved in making products—goods and services—for customers. In modern societies, much of what we need or want, from health care to fast food, is produced by service operations. As a rule, managers in the service sector give more consideration to the human element in operations (as opposed to the equipment or technology involved), because success or failure often depends on provider-customer contact. As we will see, a key difference between goods and services operations is the customer's involvement in service operations.

Although companies are typically classified as either goods producers or service providers, the distinction is often blurred. Consider General Electric (GE). When you think of GE, you may first think of appliances and jet engines. However, GE is not just a goods producer. According to its annual report, GE's "growth engines"—its most vibrant business activities—are service operations, including insurance and real estate, consumer and commercial finance, investment, transportation services, and healthcare information, which account for around 70 percent of the company's revenues.[4]

Growth in the Services and Goods Sectors

Historically, agriculture was the dominant economic sector in the early years of the United States. Eventually, though, manufacturing began to grow in importance and became the economic core of the U.S. economy from the nineteenth century into the mid-twentieth century. Services then began a rapid climb in economic importance in terms of both number of employees and percentage of gross domestic product (GDP)—the value of all goods and services produced by the economy, excluding foreign income. The outsourcing of U.S. manufacturing to other countries became a major concern in recent decades, so that by the year 2000, employment in the goods-producing sector (mining, construction, and manufacturing) was only about 20 percent of private sector employment versus 80 percent in services. Still, as recently as 2016 the United States remained the world's second largest exporter of manufactured goods, trailing only China and ahead of both Germany and Japan.

Of course, both goods and service industries are important, but as you can see from Figure 7.1, employment has risen significantly in the service sector and has

Goods Operations (or Goods Production) *activities producing tangible products, such as radios, newspapers, buses, and textbooks*

Operations (or Production) *activities involved in making products—goods and services—for customers*

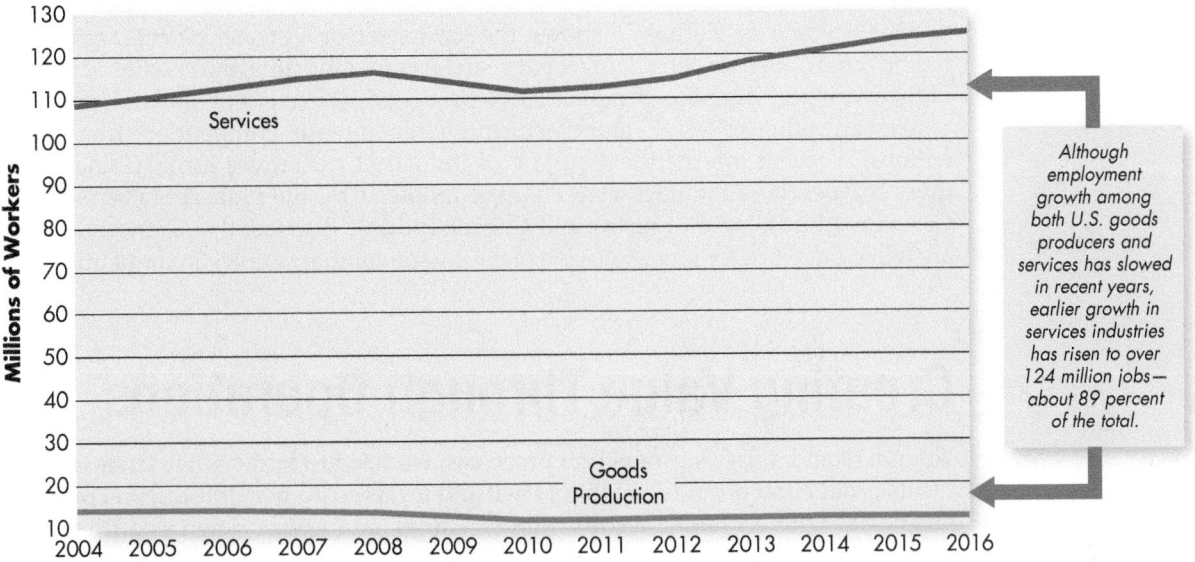

Although employment growth among both U.S. goods producers and services has slowed in recent years, earlier growth in services industries has risen to over 124 million jobs—about 89 percent of the total.

FIGURE 7.1 Employment in Goods and Services Sectors
Source: http://data.bls.gov/timeseries/CES0700000001?data_tool=XGtable http://www.data.bls.gov/cgi-bin/surveymost, accessed June 26, 2017.

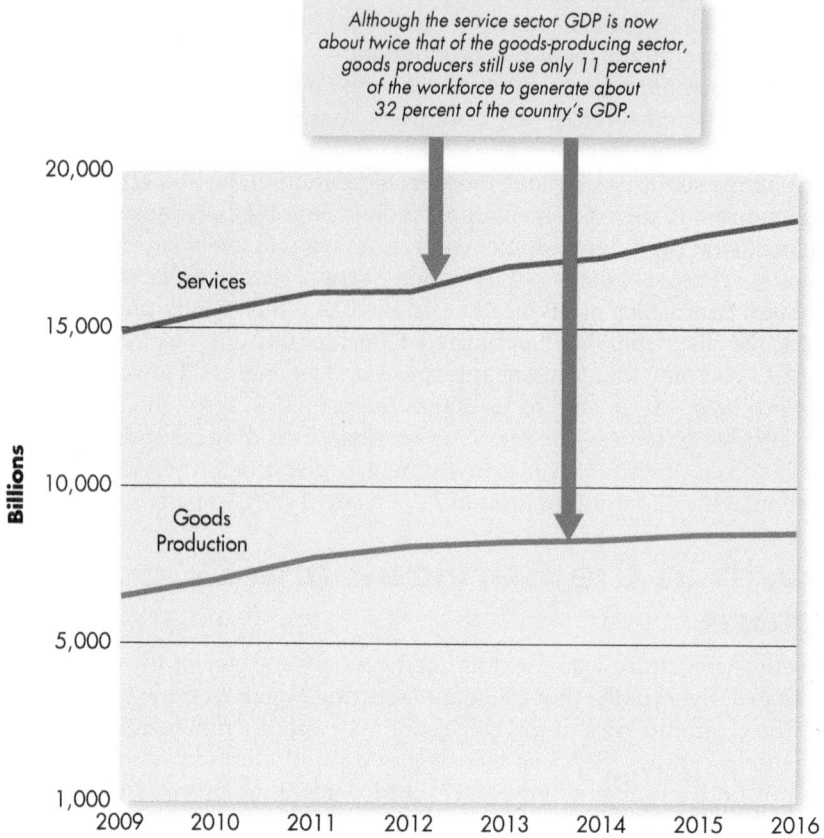

> Although the service sector GDP is now about twice that of the goods-producing sector, goods producers still use only 11 percent of the workforce to generate about 32 percent of the country's GDP.

FIGURE 7.2 GDP from Goods and Services
Source: http://useconomy.about.com/od/grossdomesticproduct/f/GDP_Components. htm, accessed June 26, 2017.

leveled off at just 11 to 12 percent in goods-producing industries for years 2003 through 2016. Much of this growth comes from e-commerce, business services, health care, amusement and recreation, and education.

By 2016, the service sector's growth generated about 68 percent of private-sector national income. As Figure 7.2 shows, the service sector's greater percentage of GDP has hovered above 65 percent in recent years. At the same time, the smaller 11 percent of the workforce in goods-producing jobs produced 32 percent of national income.

Globally, though, U.S. manufacturing faces intense competition from other nations. A recent international survey of industrial executives ranks China as the most competitive manufacturing country, followed by the United States (second), Germany (third), Japan (fourth), and Canada (ninth).[5] The fact that Chinese workers are willing to work for low wages is a major reason for that country's competitiveness.

OBJECTIVE 7-2
Identify

the three kinds of utility created by operations and the characteristics that distinguish service operations from goods production.

Utility *product's ability to satisfy a human want or need*

Creating Value Through Operations

To understand a firm's production processes, we need to know what kinds of benefits its production provides, both for itself and for its customers. Production provides businesses with economic results: profits, wages, and goods purchased from other companies. At the same time, it adds customer value by providing **utility**—the ability of a product to satisfy a want or need—in terms of form, time, and place:

● Production makes products available: By converting raw materials and human skills into finished goods and services, production creates *form utility*, as when

Cinemark combines building materials, theater seats, and projection equipment to create an entertainment venue.

- When a theater offers midday, afternoon, and evening shows seven days a week, it creates *time utility*; that is, it adds customer value by making products available when different consumers want them.

- When a theater offers a choice of 15 movies, all under one roof, at a popular location, it creates *place utility*: It makes products available where they are convenient for consumers.

Creating a product that customers value is no accident; it results from organized effort. **Operations (production) management** is the systematic direction and control of the activities that transform resources into finished services and goods that create value for and provide benefits to customers. In overseeing production, operations (production) managers are responsible for ensuring that operations activities create what customers want and need.

As Figure 7.3 shows, **operations (production) managers** draw up plans to transform resources into products. First, they bring together basic resources: knowledge, physical materials, information, equipment, the customer, and human skills. Then, they put them to effective use in a facility where the service is provided or the physical good is produced. As demand for a product increases, operations managers schedule and control work to produce the required amount. Finally, they control costs, quality levels, inventory, and facilities and equipment. In some businesses, often in small startup firms such as sole proprietorships, the operations manager is one person. Typically, however, different employees work together to complete these different responsibilities.

Some operations managers work in service "factories," such as FedEx package-sorting depots, whereas others work in production factories making smartphones; still others work in offices, restaurants, hospitals, and stores. Farmers are operations managers who create utility by transforming soil, seeds, fuel, and other inputs into soybeans, milk, and other outputs. They may hire crews of workers to plant and harvest, opt instead for automated machinery, or prefer some combination of workers and machinery. These types of decisions affect costs and determine the kinds of buildings and equipment farmers include in their operations and the quality and quantity of the goods they produce.

Operations (Production) Management *systematic direction and control of the activities that transform resources into finished products that create value for and provide benefits to customers*

Operations (Production) Managers *managers responsible for ensuring that operations activities create value and provide benefits to customers.*

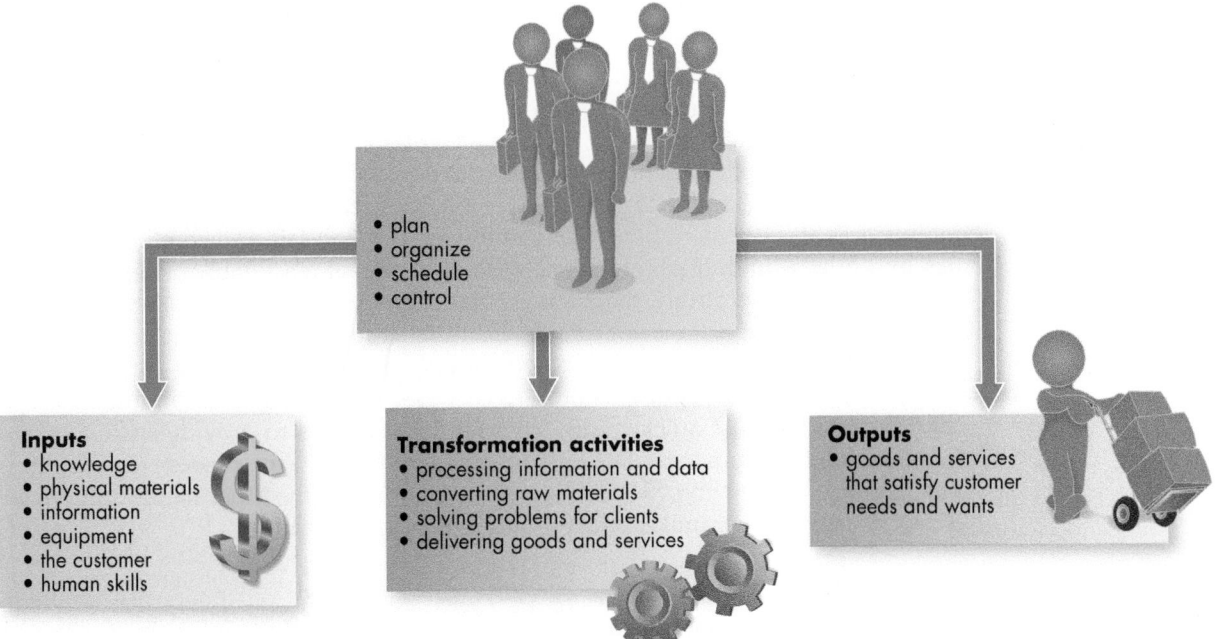

Inputs
- knowledge
- physical materials
- information
- equipment
- the customer
- human skills

- plan
- organize
- schedule
- control

Transformation activities
- processing information and data
- converting raw materials
- solving problems for clients
- delivering goods and services

Outputs
- goods and services that satisfy customer needs and wants

FIGURE 7.3 The Resource Transformation Process

Differences between Service and Goods Manufacturing Operations

Both service and manufacturing operations transform raw materials into finished products. In service operations, however, the raw materials, or inputs, are not things like glass or steel. These service inputs are people who have either unsatisfied needs or possessions needing care or alteration. In service operations, finished products or outputs are people with needs met and possessions serviced.

There are several obvious differences between service and manufacturing operations. Four aspects of service operations can make service production more complicated than simple goods production: (1) interacting with customers, (2) the intangible and unstorable nature of some services, (3) the customer's presence in the process, and (4) service quality considerations.

Interacting with Customers   Manufacturing operations emphasize outcomes in terms of physical goods, like a new jacket. But the products of most *service* operations are really combinations of goods and services—both making a pizza *and* delivering (serving) it. Service workers need different skills. For example, gas company employees may need strong interpersonal skills to calm frightened customers who have reported gas leaks. In contrast, factory workers who install gas pipes in manufactured homes without any customer contact don't need such skills.

Services Can Be Intangible and Unstorable   Two prominent characteristics—*intangibility* and *unstorability*—set services apart from physical goods:

- *Intangibility.* Services often can't be touched, tasted, smelled, or seen, but they're still there. An important satisfier for customers, therefore, is the *intangible* value they receive in the form of pleasure, gratification, or a feeling of safety. For example, if you hire an attorney to handle a legal matter, you purchase not only the intangible quality of legal expertise but also the equally intangible reassurance that help is at hand.

- *Unstorability.* Many services, such as trash collection, transportation, child care, and house cleaning, can't be produced ahead of time and then stored for high-demand periods. If a service isn't used when available, it's usually wasted. Services, then, are typically characterized by a high degree of *unstorability*.

Customers' Presence in the Operations Process   Because service operations transform customers or their possessions, the customer is often present in the operations process. To get a haircut, for example, most of us have to go to a hair salon. As participants in the operations process, customers can affect it. As a customer, you expect the salon to be conveniently located (place utility), to be open for business at convenient times (time utility), to provide safe and comfortable facilities, and to offer high-quality grooming (form utility) at reasonable prices (value for money spent). Accordingly, the manager sets hours of operation, available services, and an appropriate number of employees to meet her customer requirements. But what happens if a customer, scheduled for only a haircut, also asks for additional services, such as color highlights or a shave, when she or he arrives? In this case, the service provider must quickly adjust the service activities to provide customer satisfaction. High customer contact has the potential to affect the process significantly. The manufacturers who produce the salon's scissors, on the other hand, don't have to worry if a customer makes a last-minute change in demands.

Intangibles Count for Service Quality   Consumers use different measures to judge services and goods because services include intangibles, not just physical objects. Most service managers know that quality of work and quality of service are not necessarily the same thing. Your car, for example, may have been flawlessly repaired (quality of work), but you'll probably be unhappy with the service if you're forced to pick it up a day later than promised because the work wasn't finished on time (quality of service).

Operations Processes

To better understand the diverse kinds of production in various firms and industries, it is helpful to classify production according to differences in operations processes. An **operations process** is a set of methods and technologies used to produce a good or a service. Banks, for example, use two processes—document shredding and data encryption—to protect confidential information. Automakers use precision painting methods (equipment and materials) to produce a glittering paint finish.

Operations Process *set of methods and technologies used to produce a good or a service*

We can classify goods production into broad groupings by asking whether its operations process has a "make-to-order" or a "make-to-stock" emphasis. We can classify services according to the extent of customer contact required.

Goods Production Processes: Make-to-Order versus Make-to-Stock Processes

Clothing, such as evening gowns, is available either off-the-shelf in department stores or custom-made at a designer or tailor shop. The designer or tailor's **make-to-order operations** respond to one-of-a-kind gown requirements, including unique patterns, materials, sizes, and shapes, depending on customers' characteristics. **Make-to-stock operations**, in contrast, produce standard gowns in large quantities to be stocked on store shelves or in displays for mass consumption. The production processes are quite different for the two settings, including procedures for designing gowns; planning for materials purchases; equipment and work methods for cutting, sewing, and assembling gowns; and employee skills for production.

Make-to-Order Operations *activities for one-of-a-kind or custom-made production*

Make-to-Stock Operations *activities for producing standardized products for mass consumption*

Service Production Processes: Extent of Customer Contact

In classifying services, we may ask whether we can provide a service without the customers' being present in the production system. In answering this question, we classify services according to *extent of customer contact*.

LOW-CONTACT SYSTEMS Consider the postal delivery operations at your local U.S. post office. Postal employees gather mail from mailboxes, sort it, and send it on its delivery journey to addressees. This operation is a **low-contact system**: Customers

Low-Contact System *level of customer contact in which the customer need not be part of the system to receive the service*

Peathegee Inc/Blend Images/Getty Images

Because service operations transform customers or their possessions, the customer is often present in the operations process. For example, customers who want their hair cut or colored must go in person to a hair salon in order to receive this service.

are not in contact with the post office while the service is performed. They can receive the service—mail sent and mail received—without setting foot in the processing center. Gas and electric companies, auto repair shops, and lawn-care services are other examples of low-contact systems.

HIGH-CONTACT SYSTEMS Think about your local public transit system. The service is transportation; when you purchase transportation, you board a bus or train. For example, the Bay Area Rapid Transit (BART) system, which connects San Francisco with outlying suburbs, is, like all public transit systems, a **high-contact system**: To receive the service, the customer must be part of the system. Thus, managers must worry about the cleanliness of trains, safety of passengers, and the usability of its ticket kiosks. By contrast, a firm that ships coal is less concerned with the appearance of its trains since no paying passengers are riding on them. A coal-shipping firm is a low-contact system.

High-Contact System *level of customer contact in which the customer is part of the system during service delivery*

Business Strategy as the Driver of Operations

OBJECTIVE 7-3
Explain

how companies with different business strategies are best served by having different operations capabilities.

There is no one standard way for doing production, either for services or for goods. Rather, it is a flexible activity that can be molded into many shapes to give quite different operations capabilities for different purposes. How, then, do companies go about selecting the kind of production that is best for them? They aim to adopt the kind of production that achieves the firm's larger business strategy in the most efficient way possible.

The Many Faces of Production Operations

Consider the four firms listed in Table 7.1. Two are in goods production (Toyota and 3M), and the other two (Save-a-Lot and FedEx) are in services. These successful companies have contrasting business strategies and, as we shall see, they have chosen different operations capabilities. Each company has identified a business strategy that it uses for attracting customers in its industry. More than 40 years ago, Toyota chose *quality* as the strategy for competing in selling autos. Save-A-Lot grocery stores, in contrast to others in the grocery industry, offer customers *lower prices*. The *flexibility* strategy at 3M emphasizes new product development in an ever-changing line of products for home and office. FedEx captures the overnight delivery market by emphasizing delivery *dependability*.

table 7.1 Business Strategies that Win Customers for Four Companies

Company	Strategy for Attracting Customers	What the Company Does to Implement Its Strategy
Toyota	Quality	Cars perform reliably, have an appealing fit and finish, and consistently meet or exceed customer expectations at a competitive price
Save-A-Lot	Low price	Foods and everyday items offered at savings up to 40 percent less than conventional food chains
3M	Flexibility	Innovation, with more than 55,000 products in a constantly changing line of convenience items for home and office
FedEx	Dependability	Every delivery is fast and on time, as promised

Business Strategy Determines Operations Capabilities

Successful firms design their operations to support the company's business strategy.[6] In other words, managers adjust production operations to support the firms' target markets. Because our four firms use different business strategies, we should expect to see differences in their operations, too. The top-priority **operations capability (production capability)**—the special ability that production does especially well to outperform the competition—is listed for each firm in Table 7.2, along with key operations characteristics for implementing that capability. Each company's operations capability matches up with its business strategy so that the firm's activities—from top to bottom—are focused in a particular direction.

For example, because Toyota's top priority focuses on quality, its operations, the resource inputs for production, the transformation activities, and the outputs from production are devoted first and foremost to that characteristic. Its car designs and production processes emphasize appearance, reliable performance, and desirable features at a reasonable price. All production processes, equipment, and training are designed to build better cars. The entire culture supports a quality emphasis among employees, suppliers, and dealerships. Had Toyota instead chosen to compete as the low-price car in the industry, as some successful car companies do, then a cost-minimization focus would have been appropriate, giving Toyota's operations an altogether different form. Toyota's operations support its chosen business strategy, and did it successfully until quality problems arose in 2008. Soon thereafter, the commitment to quality intensified. By 2012, Toyota had regained its position as the world's top-selling auto maker. Before the 2008 downturn, the company had more than 35 consecutive years of increasing sales for which quality was the foundation for greatness.

Operations Capability (Production Capability) *special ability that production does especially well to outperform the competition*

table 7.2 Operations Capabilities and Characteristics for Four Companies

Operations Capability	Key Operations Characteristics
Quality (Toyota)	• High-quality standards for materials suppliers • Just-in-time materials flow for lean manufacturing • Specialized, automated equipment for consistent product buildup • Operations personnel are experts on continuous improvement of product, work methods, and materials
Low Cost (Save-A-Lot)	• Avoids excessive overhead and costly inventory (no floral departments, sushi bars, or banks that drive up costs) • Limited assortment of products (staples), in one size only for low-cost restocking, lower inventories, and less paperwork • Many locations; small stores—less than half the size of conventional grocery stores—for low construction and maintenance costs • Reduces labor and shelving costs by receiving and selling merchandise out of custom shipping cartons
Flexibility (3M)	• Maintains some excess (expensive) production capacity available for fast startup on new products • Adaptable equipment and facilities for production changeovers from old to new products • Hires operations personnel who thrive on change • Many medium- to small-sized manufacturing facilities in diverse locations, which enhances creativity
Dependability (FedEx)	• Customer automation: uses electronic and online communications tools with customers to shorten shipping time • Wireless information system for package scanning by courier, updating of package movement, and package tracking by customer • Maintains a company air force, global weather forecasting center, and ground transportation for pickup and delivery, with backup vehicles for emergencies • The 25 automated regional distribution hubs process 3.5 million packages per day for next-day deliveries

Expanding into Additional Capabilities Finally, it should be noted that excellent firms learn, over time, how to achieve more than just one competence. The firms in Table 7.1 eventually became excellent in several capabilities. Aside from dependability, FedEx is also noted for world-class service quality and cost containment. Regarding quality, FedEx was honored in the "2016 Customer Service Hall of Fame," ranking 9th for service quality among 150 companies in *MSN Money*'s annual survey. To reduce costs, the company eliminates jobs that become unnecessary with advances in technology, sells off its older inefficient airplanes, and reduces the number of flights by re-routing its air and ground fleets.

OBJECTIVE 7-4
Identify

the major factors that are considered in operations planning.

Operations Planning

Let's turn now to a discussion of production activities and resources that are considered in every business organization. Like all good managers, we start with planning. Managers from many departments contribute to decisions about operations. As Figure 7.4 shows, however, no matter how many decision makers are involved, the process is a logical sequence of decisions.

The business plan and forecasts developed by top managers provide guidance for long-term operations plans. Covering a two- to five-year period, the operations plan anticipates the number of plants or service facilities and the amount of labor, equipment, transportation, and storage needed to meet future demand for new and existing products. The planning activities fall into five categories: *capacity, location, layout, quality*, and *methods planning*.

Capacity Planning

Capacity *amount of a product that a company can produce under normal conditions*

The amount of a product that a company can produce under normal conditions is its **capacity**. A firm's capacity depends on how many people it employs and the number and size of its facilities. A supermarket's capacity for customer checkouts,

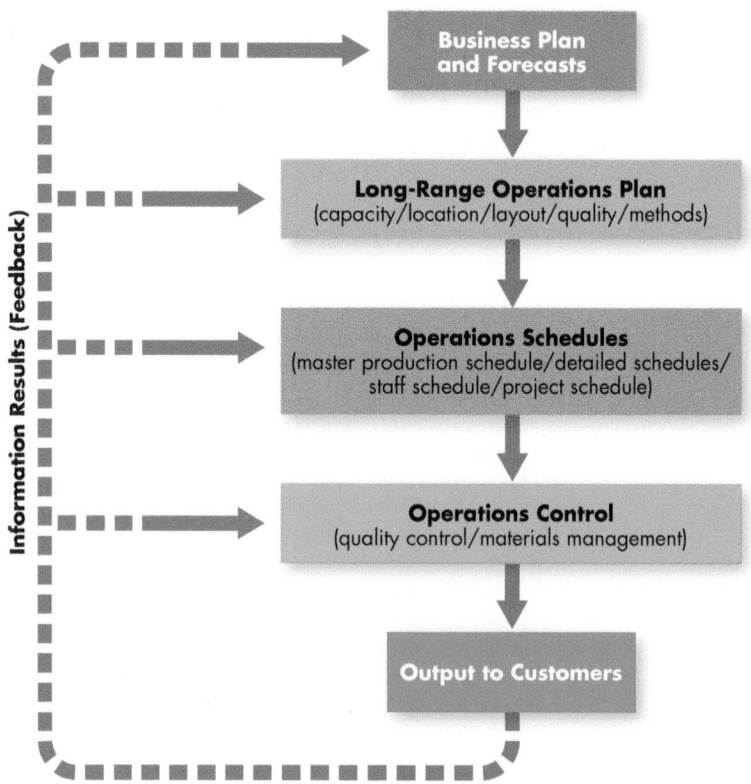

FIGURE 7.4 Operations Planning and Control

for instance, depends on its number of checkout stations. A typical store has excess capacity—more cash registers than it needs—on an average Tuesday, but on Saturday morning or during the three days before Thanksgiving, they'll all be running at full capacity.

Long-range capacity planning considers both current and future requirements. If capacity is too small for demand, the company must turn away customers, a situation that cuts into profits and alienates both customers and salespeople. If capacity greatly exceeds demand, the firm is wasting money by maintaining facilities that are too large, keeping excess machinery online, or employing too many workers.

The stakes are high in capacity decisions: While expanding fast enough to meet future demand and to protect market share from competitors, managers must also consider the costs of expanding. When markets are growing, greater capacity is desirable. In troubled times, however, existing capacity may be too large and too expensive to maintain, requiring a reduction in size.

Location Planning

Because location affects production costs and flexibility, sound location planning is crucial for factories, offices, and stores. Depending on its site, a company may be able to produce low-cost products, or it may find itself at a cost disadvantage relative to its competitors.

Consider the reasons why Slovakia has become known as "Detroit East." Even during the worldwide slowdown in car sales resulting from the Great Recession, Slovakia's

entrepreneurship and new ventures

Nothing Like a Home-Cooked Meal

It wasn't that long ago that families sat down at the dinner table every night for a home-cooked meal. Restaurant dining was reserved for special occasions and even prepared meals were the exception. Well, those days are long gone. Today, many families eat out or bring home takeout several nights a week. And singles and couples without children are even more likely to do so. This is the economic reality that drives success in the restaurant industry, opening the way for profits and growth like that experienced by the Cheesecake Factory. But not every venture has to be that large. Even the Cheesecake Factory started small, and when a person with an idea can find a need and create a product or service to fill that need, a business is born.

Stephanie Allen, a caterer from Washington state, found herself in exactly this situation. Allen and a friend started to get together one Saturday a month to prepare a bunch of freezable meals that they could heat up with little preparation. Word of their strategy spread and Allen, along with partner Tina Kuna, started Dream Dinners in 2002. The company quickly expanded in the Seattle area and became a franchise the following year. A little more than 14 years later, they have 86 locations in 25 states.

Interested? Well, having a healthy, nutritious, and tasty dinner is easier than you think. Each location establishes a list of monthly menu options catering to a wide variety of palates. For example, you can choose between making herb crusted flank steak, sweet cider bbq chicken, pizza burger sliders on pretzel buns, soy glazed salmon, Rio Grande chicken fajitas, or terracotta chicken with pita and hummus. All the shopping is done

Monkey Business/Fotolia

ahead of time by Dream Dinners, with special attention to price and quality. Ingredients have been chopped and sliced, and laminated recipe cards tell would-be chefs how to assemble a tasty meal in a zippered bag or foil pan. Depending upon the store location, there may be one or more work stations with ingredients, and patrons move around the workstation selecting the items on their recipe cards in the prescribed quantities. When you're all done, just load your meals into a cooler and head home to put them in the freezer, where they will wait until you are ready for a delicious home-cooked meal. The cost of a meal varies based on the ingredients, but an average meal is less than $5 per person, far less than a restaurant meal, and right in your own kitchen.[7]

auto production held constant. And during the 2012 Euro-zone economic crisis it produced more cars per capita—including Volkswagen SUVs, Peugeot Citroens, and Kias—than most other Euro-zone countries. Its auto factories remain well-positioned to increase volume as the worldwide economy improves. The central European country is an ideal place to produce cars. It has a good railroad system and nearby access to the Danube River, meaning economical transportation for incoming materials and outgoing cars once auto factories are in operation. The area also has skilled, hard-working laborers, and wages lower than those of surrounding countries.[8]

In contrast to manufacturing, consumer services concentrate on being located near customers. Thus, fast-food restaurants, such as Taco Bell and McDonald's, are located near areas with high traffic, such as busy highways, college campuses, hospital cafeterias, and shopping malls. At retail giant Walmart, managers of the company's huge distribution centers regard Walmart outlets as their customers. To ensure that truckloads of merchandise flow quickly to stores, distribution centers are located near the hundreds of Walmart stores that they supply, not near the companies that supply them.

Layout Planning

Layout is the physical location or floor plan for service centers, machinery, equipment, customers, and supplies. It determines whether a company can respond efficiently to demand for more and different products or whether it finds itself unable to match competitors' speed and convenience. Among the many layout possibilities, three well-known alternatives—*(1) process layouts (or custom-product layouts), (2) product layouts (or same-steps layouts)*, and *(3) fixed-position layouts*—are presented here to illustrate how different layouts serve different purposes for operations.

Process Layout (Custom-Product Layout) *physical arrangement of production activities that groups equipment and people according to function*

Process Layouts In a **process layout** (also called **custom-product layout**), which is well suited to *make-to-order shops* (or *job shops*) specializing in custom work, equipment and people are grouped according to function. FedEx Office stores (formerly Kinko's Copy Centers), for example, use custom-products layouts to accommodate a variety of custom jobs. Specific activities or processes, such as photocopying, faxing, computing, binding, and laminating, are performed in separate, specialized areas of the store. Walk-in customers—local individuals and small-business clients—move from area to area using the self-service they need.

The main advantage of process layouts is flexibility—at any time, the shop can process individual customer orders, each requiring different kinds of work. Depending on its work requirements, a client being served or a job being processed may flow through three activity areas, another through just one area, and still others through four or more work zones. Figure 7.5 shows the process layout of a service provider—a medical clinic. The path taken through the facility reflects the unique treatments for one patient's visit. Goods producers such as machine shops, woodworking and print shops, and dry cleaning stores, as well as health clinics and physical fitness studios are among the many facilities using custom-product layouts.

Product Layout (Same-Steps Layout) *physical arrangement of production steps designed to make one type of product in a fixed sequence of activities according to its production requirements*

Assembly Line Layout *a same-steps layout in which a product moves step by step through a plant on conveyor belts or other equipment until it is completed*

Product Layouts A **product layout** (also called **a same-steps layout** or **assembly line layout**) is set up to provide one type of service or make one type of product in a fixed sequence of production steps. All units go through the same set of steps. It is efficient for large-volume make-to-stock operations that mass-produce many units of a product quickly: A partially finished product moves step by step through the plant on conveyor belts or other equipment, often in a straight line, as it passes through each stage until the product is completed. Automobile, food-processing, and television-assembly plants use same-steps layouts, as do mail-processing facilities, such as UPS or FedEx.

Figure 7.6 shows a product layout at a service provider—an automatic car wash. Figure 7.7 is a goods-producer assembling parts needed to make storm windows. Same-steps layouts are efficient because the work skill is built into the equipment, allowing unskilled labor to perform simple tasks. But they are often inflexible, especially where they use specialized equipment that's hard to rearrange for new applications.

Example patient flow for one customer

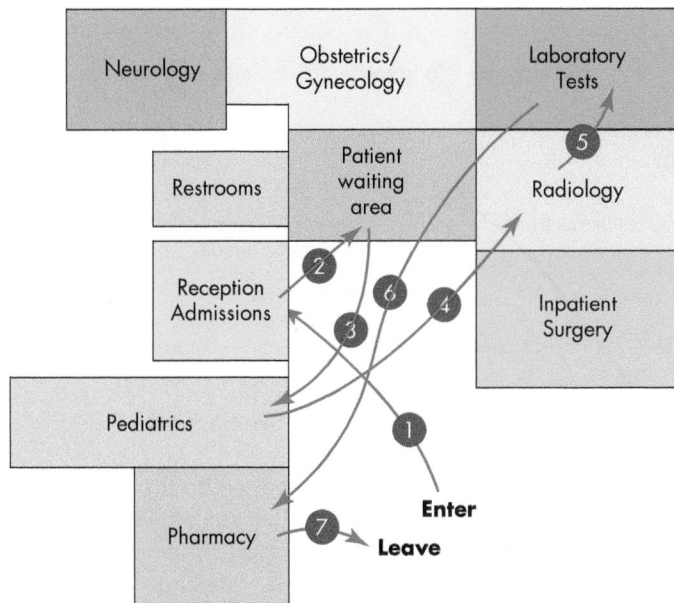

FIGURE 7.5 Process Layout for a Service Provider—a Medical Clinic

Fixed Position Layouts A **fixed-position layout** is often used when size, shape, or other factors make it difficult to move the service to another production facility. In fixed-position layouts the product or client remains at one location; equipment, materials, and human skills are moved to that location, as needed, to perform the service or to build the product. While recovering at home from a knee replacement, for example, physical rehabilitation specialists come to the patient's home for rehab services. When home plumbing goes bad or the roof leaks, repair services are brought to that home—at its fixed position—where the services are performed. Such layouts are used for building huge ships that can't be moved, for constructing buildings, and for agricultural operations—plowing, fertilizing, and harvesting—at farm sites.

Fixed-Position Layout *labor, equipment, materials, and other resources are brought to the geographic location where all production work is done*

Quality Planning

Every operations plan includes activities for ensuring that products meet the firm's and customers' quality standards. The American Society for Quality defines **quality** as a subjective term, the combination of "characteristics of a product or service that bear on its ability to satisfy stated or implied needs."[9] Such characteristics may include a reasonable price and dependability in delivering the benefits it promises.

Quality *combination of "characteristics of a product or service that bear on its ability to satisfy stated or implied needs"*

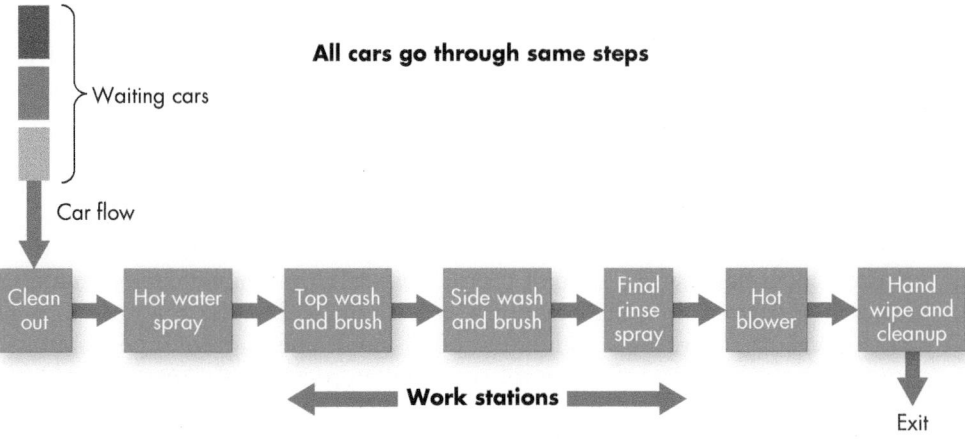

FIGURE 7.6 Product Layout for a Service—Automated Car Wash

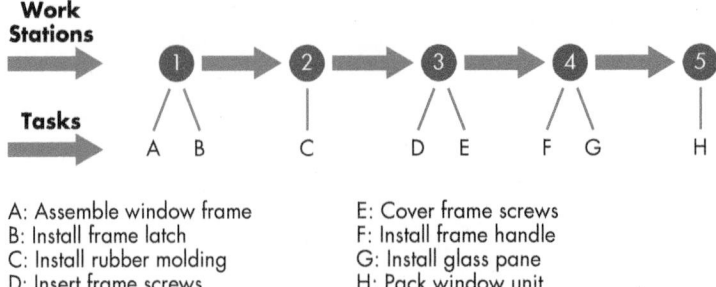

A: Assemble window frame
B: Install frame latch
C: Install rubber molding
D: Insert frame screws

E: Cover frame screws
F: Install frame handle
G: Install glass pane
H: Pack window unit

FIGURE 7.7 Product Layout for Goods Production—Storm Window Assembly

Planning for quality begins when products are being designed. As we will see later, product design is a marketing responsibility, but it involves operations managers, too. Early in the process, goals are established for both performance and consistency. **Performance** refers to how well the product does what it is supposed to do. For loyal buyers of Godiva premium chocolates, performance includes such sensory delights as aroma, flavor, color, and texture. "Truly fine chocolates," observes master chocolatier Thierry Muret, "are always fresh, contain high-quality ingredients like cocoa beans and butter … and feature unusual textures and natural flavors." The recipe was designed to provide these features. Superior performance helps Godiva remain one of the world's top brands.[10]

In addition to performance, quality also includes **consistency**, the sameness of product quality from unit to unit. Business travelers using Courtyard by Marriott, for example, enjoy high consistency with each overnight stay, which is one reason Courtyard by Marriott is among the best-selling brands in the lodging industry. Courtyard by Marriot achieved this status by maintaining the same features at all of Marriott's more than 967 Courtyard hotels in 38 countries. Designed for business travelers, most guest rooms include a Courtyard Suite with high-speed Internet access, meeting space, and access to an exercise room, restaurant and lounge, and a swimming pool, and 24-hour access to food. The layout of the suites is identical at many locations, the rooms are always clean, and check-in/checkout procedures are identical so that lodgers know what to expect with each overnight stay. This consistency is achieved by monitoring for uniformity of materials and supplies, encouraging conscientious work, training employees, and maintaining equipment.

In addition to product design, quality planning includes employees deciding what constitutes a high-quality product—for both goods and services—and determining how to measure these quality characteristics.

Methods Planning

In designing operations systems, managers must identify each production step and the specific methods for performing it. They can then reduce waste and inefficiency by examining procedures on a step-by-step basis by using an approach called *methods improvement*.

Improving Process Flows Improvements for operations begin by documenting current production practices. A detailed description, often using a diagram called a *process flowchart*, is helpful in organizing and recording information. The flowchart identifies the sequence of production activities, movements of materials, and work performed at each stage of the process. It can then be analyzed to isolate wasteful activities, sources of delay, and other inefficiencies in both goods and services operations. The final step is implementing improvements.

Improving Customer Service Consider, for example, the traditional checkout method at hotels. The process flowchart in Figure 7.8 shows five stages of

Performance *dimension of quality that refers to how well a product does what it is supposed to do*

Consistency *dimension of quality that refers to sameness of product quality from unit to unit*

Step   Guest Activity

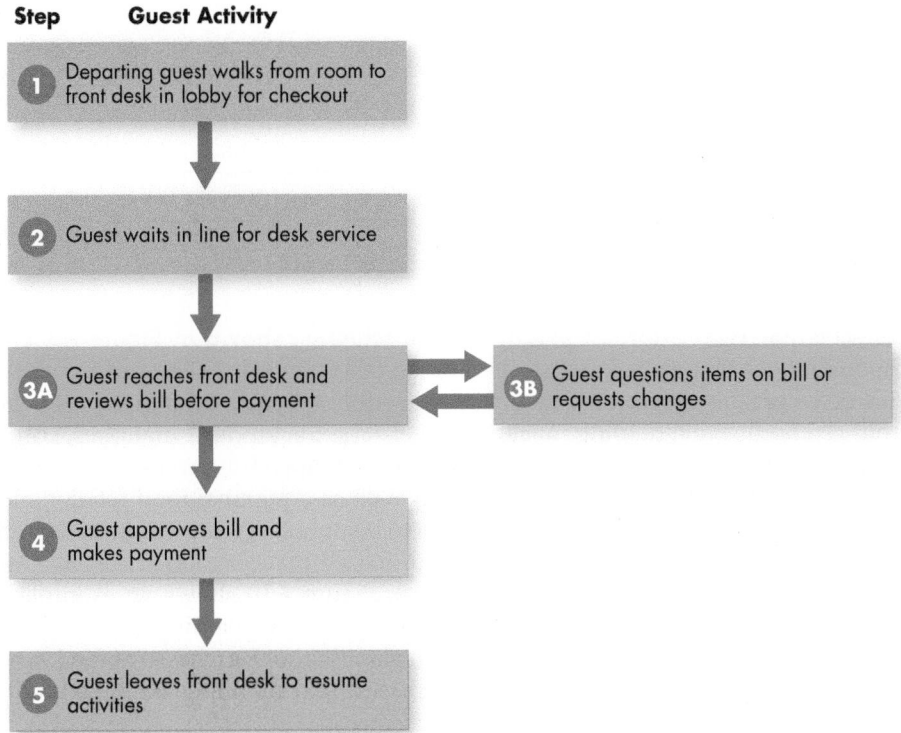

FIGURE 7.8 Flowchart of Traditional Guest Checkout

customer activities. Hotel checkout can be time consuming for customers standing in line to pay. They become impatient and annoyed, especially during popular checkout times when lines are long. Other hotel tasks are disrupted, too, as managers are forced to reassign employees to the front desk to assist with surging checkout lines. Hotel managers developed an improved checkout method that avoids wasting time in line for customers and reduces interruptions of other staff duties as well. It saves time by eliminating steps 1, 2, 3A, and 5. On the morning of departure customers find a copy of charges delivered under their room door. Or, they can scan their bills on television in the privacy of their rooms anytime before departure. If the bill is correct, no further checkout is required, and the hotel submits the charges against the credit card that the customer submitted during check-in.

Operations Scheduling

OBJECTIVE 7-5
Discuss
the information contained in four kinds of operations schedules—the master operations schedule, detailed schedule, staff schedule, and project schedule.

Continuing with the flow of activities in Figure 7.4, once managers and their teams have determined the operations plans, they then develop timetables for implementing the plans. This aspect of operations, called *operations scheduling*, identifies times when specific activities will occur. In this section we consider four general kinds of schedules. (1) The *master schedule* is "the game plan" for deciding the volume of upcoming activities for months ahead. (2) *Detailed schedules* show day-to-day activities that will occur in production. (3) *Staff schedules* identify who and how many employees will be working, and when. (4) Finally, *project schedules* provide coordination for completing large-scale projects.

The Master Operations Schedule

Scheduling of operations occurs at different levels. First, a top-level **master operations schedule** shows which services or products will be produced and when, in upcoming time periods. Logan Aluminum, for example, makes coils of aluminum that it supplies to customer companies that use it to make beverage cans. Logan's

Master Operations Schedule *schedule showing which products will be produced, and when, in upcoming time periods*

Coil # (Product)	8/4/19	8/11/19	8/18/19	...	11/3/19	11/10/19
TC016	1,500	2,500			2,100	600
TC032	900		2,700		3,000	
TR020	300		2,600			1,600

FIGURE 7.9 Example of Partial Master Operations Schedule

master schedule, with a format like the partial schedule shown in Figure 7.9, covers production for 60 weeks in which more than 300,000 tons will be produced. For various types of coils (products), the master schedule specifies how many tons will be produced each week, helping managers determine the kinds of materials, equipment, and other resources that will be needed for each upcoming week.

The master schedule for a service provider, such as a regional food retailer, may begin with the planned number of retail stores to be operating in each quarter of the coming two years. Then, key resources needed in each quarter to provide customer services for all stores are identified (estimated). Figure 7.10 shows an example of such a partial master schedule. It provides information for planning on how many people the company will have to hire and train, planning for purchases of food products and the financing needed for those purchases, and planning for construction requirements of new stores.

Detailed Schedules

Detailed Schedule schedule showing daily work assignments with start and stop times for assigned jobs

Although the master production schedule is the backbone for overall scheduling, additional information comes from **detailed schedules**, schedules showing daily work assignments with start and stop times for assigned jobs at each work station. Logan's production employees need to know the locations of all coils in the plant and their various stages of completion. Managers must assign start and stop times,

Quarter/Year

KEY RESOURCES		1/2019	2/2019	3/2019	4/2019	1/2020	2/2020	3/2020	4/2020
	Number of Stores	17	17	18	19	20	20	21	22
	Staffing Level (no. of Employees)	1,360	1,360	1,530	1,615	1,700	1,700	1,653	1,827
	Fresh Vegetables (tons)	204	204	192	228	240	240	230	260
	Canned Goods (case loads)	73,950	77,350	80,100	80,100	83,000	84,500	88,600	90,200
	Fresh Meats Etc.	–	–	–	–	–	–	–	–
	– – –								

FIGURE 7.10 Food Retailer's Partial Operations Schedule

and employees need scheduled work assignments daily, not just weekly. Detailed short-term schedules allow managers to use customer orders and information about equipment status to update sizes and the variety of coils to be made each day.

Staff Schedules and Computer-Based Scheduling

Scheduling is useful for employee staffing in service companies, too, including restaurants, hotels, and transportation and landscaping companies. **Staff schedules**, in general, specify assigned working times in upcoming days—perhaps for as many as 30 days or more—for each employee on each work shift. Staff schedules consider employees' needs and the company's efficiency and costs, including the ebbs and flows of demand for production.

Staff Schedule *assigned working times in upcoming days for each employee on each work shift*

Computer-based scheduling, using tools such as the *ABS Visual Staff Scheduler® PRO* (VSS Pro) software, can easily handle multishift activities for many employees—both part-time and full-time. It accommodates vacation times, holiday adjustments, and daily adjustments in staffing for unplanned absences and changes in production schedules.

Project Scheduling

Special projects, such as new business construction or redesigning a product, require close coordination and precise timing among many activities. In these cases, project management is facilitated by project scheduling tools, including Gantt charts and PERT.

The Gantt Graphical Method Named after its developer, Henry Gantt, a **Gantt chart** breaks down large projects into steps to be performed and specifies the time required to perform each one. The project manager lists all activities needed to complete the work, estimates the time required for each step, records the progress on the chart, and checks the progress against the time scale on the chart to keep the project moving on schedule. If work is ahead of schedule, some employees may be shifted to another project. If it's behind schedule, workers may be added or completion delayed.

Gantt Chart *production schedule that breaks down large projects into steps to be performed and specifies the time required to perform each step*

Figure 7.11 shows a Gantt chart for the renovation of a college classroom. It shows progress to date and schedules for remaining work and that some steps can

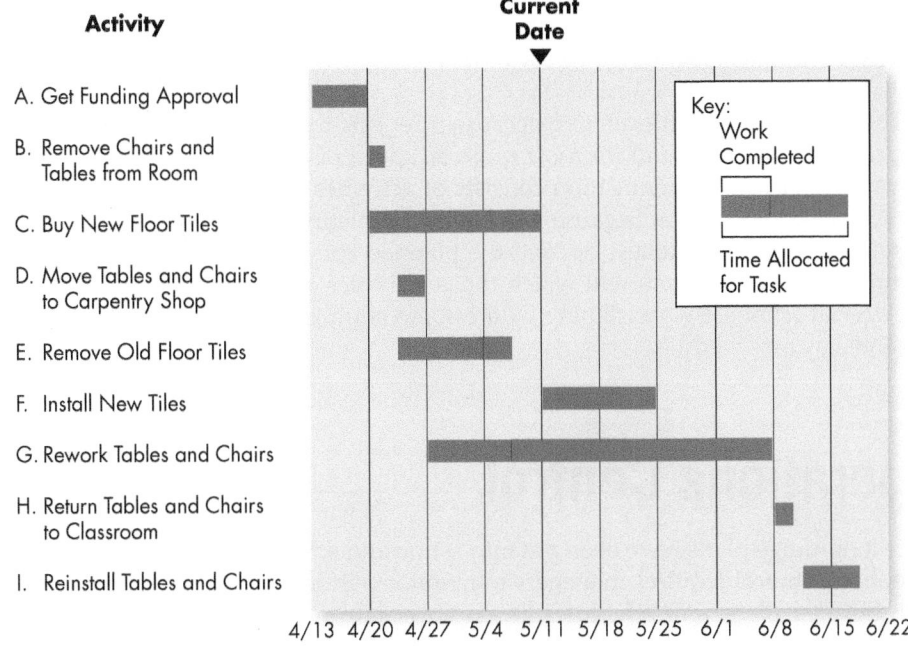

FIGURE 7.11 Gantt Chart

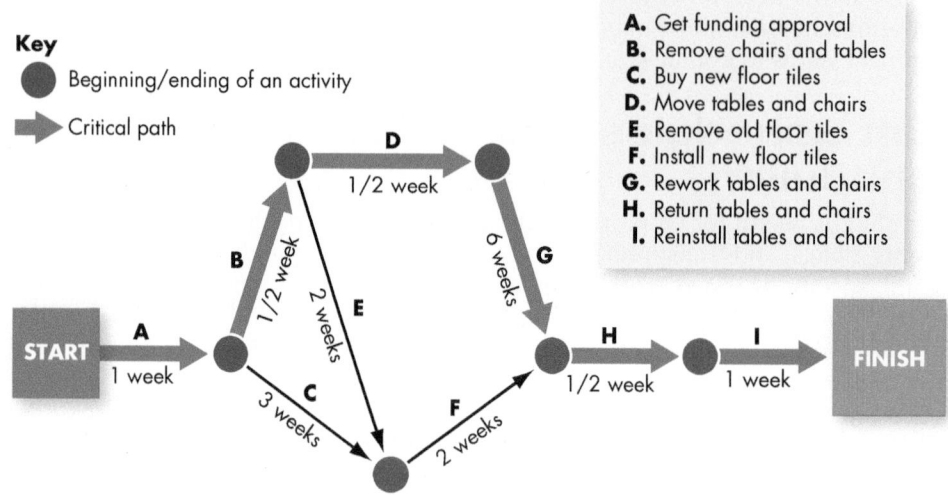

Key

● Beginning/ending of an activity

➤ Critical path

A. Get funding approval
B. Remove chairs and tables
C. Buy new floor tiles
D. Move tables and chairs
E. Remove old floor tiles
F. Install new floor tiles
G. Rework tables and chairs
H. Return tables and chairs
I. Reinstall tables and chairs

FIGURE 7.12 PERT Chart

be performed at the same time (e.g., step D can be performed during the same time as steps C and E), but others cannot (e.g., step A must be completed before any of the others can begin). Step E is behind schedule; it should have been completed before the current date.

Project Scheduling with PERT Charts

The *Program Evaluation and Review Technique* (*PERT*) provides even more information for controlling the progress of large projects. Along with times required to perform the activities, the layout of the **PERT chart** uses arrows to show the necessary *sequence* among activities, from start to finish, for completing the project. It also identifies the *critical path*, the most time-consuming set of activities, for completing the project.

Figure 7.12 shows a PERT chart for renovating the college classroom. The project's nine activities and the times required to complete them are identified. Each activity is represented by an arrow. The arrows are positioned to show the required sequence for performing the activities. For example, chairs and tables can't be returned to the classroom (H) until after they've been reworked (G) and after new floor tiles are installed (F). Accordingly, the diagram shows arrows for G and F coming before activity H. Similarly, funding approval (A) has to occur before anything else can get started.

The critical path is informative because it reveals the most time-consuming path for project completion, and for most projects, speed of completion is vital. The critical path for classroom renovation consists of activities A, B, D, G, H, and I, requiring 9.5 weeks. It's critical because a delay in completing any of those activities will cause corresponding lateness beyond the planned completion time (9.5 weeks after startup). Project managers will watch those activities and, if potential delays arise, take special action—by reassigning workers and equipment—to speed up late activities and stay on schedule.

PERT Chart *production schedule specifying the sequence of activities, time requirements, and critical path for performing the steps in a project*

Discuss
the two key activities required for operations control.

Operations Control *process of monitoring production performance by comparing results with plans and taking corrective action when needed*

Operations Control

Once long-range plans have been put into action and schedules have been drawn up, **operations control** requires managers to monitor performance by comparing results with detailed plans and schedules. If employees do not meet schedules or quality standards, managers can take corrective action. **Follow-up**, checking to ensure that production decisions are being implemented, is a key and ongoing facet of operations.

Operations control includes *materials management* and *quality control*. Both activities ensure that schedules are met and products delivered, both in quantity and in quality.

Follow-Up *operations control activity for ensuring that production decisions are being implemented*

Materials Management

Some of us have difficulty keeping track of personal items now and then—clothes, books, smartphones, and so on. Imagine keeping track of thousands, or even millions, of things at any one time. That's the challenge in **materials management**, the process by which managers plan, organize, and control the flow of materials from sources of supply through distribution of finished goods. For manufacturing firms, typical materials costs make up 50 to 75 percent of total product costs.

Materials Management *process of planning, organizing, and controlling the flow of materials from sources of supply through distribution of finished goods*

Materials Management Activities for Physical Goods Once a product has been designed, successful materials flows depend on five activities. From selecting suppliers on through the distribution of finished goods, materials managers engage in the following areas that compose materials management:

- **Supplier selection** is the process of finding and choosing suppliers of services and materials. This step includes evaluating potential suppliers, negotiating terms of service, and maintaining positive buyer–seller relationships.

Supplier Selection *process of finding and choosing suppliers from whom to buy*

- **Purchasing** (sometimes called *procurement*) is the acquisition of all the raw materials and services that a company needs to produce its products. Most large firms have purchasing departments to buy proper services and materials in the amounts needed.

Purchasing *acquisition of the materials and services that a firm needs to produce its products*

- **Transportation** is the means of transporting resources to the producer and finished goods to customers.

Transportation *activities in transporting resources to the producer and finished goods to customers*

- **Warehousing** is the storage of both incoming materials for production and finished goods for distribution to customers.

Warehousing *storage of incoming materials for production and finished goods for distribution to customers*

- **Inventory control** includes the receiving, storing, handling, and counting of all raw materials, partly finished goods, and finished goods. It ensures that enough materials inventories are available to meet production schedules, while at the same time avoiding expensive excess inventories.

Inventory Control *process of receiving, storing, handling, and counting of all raw materials, partly finished goods, and finished goods*

Lean Production Systems Managers must take timing into consideration when managing materials as well. Pioneered by Toyota, **lean production systems** are designed for smooth production flows that avoid inefficiencies, eliminate unnecessary inventories, and continuously improve production processes. **Just-in-time (JIT) production**, a type of lean system, brings together all needed materials at the precise moment they are required for each production stage, not before, thus creating fast and efficient responses to customer orders. All resources flow continuously—from arrival as raw materials to final assembly and shipment of finished products.

Lean Production System *production system designed for smooth production flows that avoid inefficiencies, eliminate unnecessary inventories, and continuously improve production processes*

JIT production reduces the number of goods in process (goods not yet finished) to practically nothing. It minimizes inventory costs, reduces storage space requirements for inventories, and saves money by replacing stop-and-go production with smooth movement. Once smooth flow is the norm, disruptions are more visible and employees can resolve them more quickly. Finding and eliminating disruptions by the continuous improvement of production is a major objective of JIT production.

Just-in-Time (JIT) Production *type of lean production system that brings together all materials at the precise time they are required at each production stage*

Inventory Management Is Crucial for Producing Services For many service firms, too, the materials stakes are high. UPS delivers 18 million packages every day and promises that all of them will arrive on schedule. It keeps this promise by tracking the locations, schedules, and on-time performance of 542 aircraft and 104,926 vehicles. However, the most important "inventory" used for many high-contact services is not physical goods but exists in the form of information about

Quality control means taking action to ensure that operations produce products that meet specific quality standards. These quality control inspectors are checking finished goods before shipment to make sure they meet or surpass the standards set by their customers.

service product offerings, clients, their interests, needs, activities, and even their plans for interactions with other clients.

Consider, as an example, the *inventories of information* at Collette Vacations where the *management of information* is a vital activity. Collette offers three product lines, Classic Touring, Explorations (for smaller groups), and Family Vacations, that collectively offer more than 150 escorted tours on seven continents including more than 50 countries. Each tour (the product), designed by a professional tour planner, includes a complete itinerary, duration, advanced arrangements for accommodations, and pricing. Vacationers select from among land tours, river cruises, and rail journeys that include sightseeing, meals, entertainment, and accommodations to experience new places, people, history, and culture.

As a tour begins, one of the company's more than 100 Professional Tour Managers interacts face-to-face with clients as friend and guide for the entire duration, often 8 to 14 days, while handling all day-to-day details—confirming meal availabilities, ensuring hotel room accommodations, arranging local transportation, helping with sight-seeing selections, providing knowledge of local culture, assisting each tourist with any questions or problems, and handling emergencies.

As you can see, these many activities create vast amounts of information—the *inventory of information*—that must be accurate and accessible for success with current tours and clients, and for all the thousands of clients booked on hundreds of future tours. It is also vital for contacting many thousands of potential customers with advance information about tours that will be offered a year or two in the future.[11]

Quality Control

Quality Control *action of ensuring that operations produce products that meet specific quality standards*

Quality control is taking action to ensure that operations produce goods or services that meet specific quality standards. Consider, for example, service operations in which customer satisfaction depends largely on the employees who provide the service. By monitoring services, managers and other employees can detect mistakes and make corrections. First, however, managers or other personnel must establish specific standards and measurements. At a bank, for example, quality control for teller services might require supervisors to observe employees periodically and evaluate their work according to a checklist. Managers would review the results with employees and either confirm proper performance or indicate changes for bringing performance up to standards.

The high quality of customer-employee interactions is no accident in firms that monitor customer encounters and provide training for employee skills development. Many managers realize that without employees trained in customer-relationship skills, quality suffers, and businesses, such as airlines and hotels, can lose customers to better-prepared competitors.

Quality Improvement and Total Quality Management

OBJECTIVE 7-7
Identify
the activities and underlying objectives involved in total quality management.

It is not enough to *control* quality by inspecting products and monitoring service operations as they occur, as when a supervisor listens in on a catalog sales service representative's customer calls. Businesses must also consider *building* quality into goods and services in the first place. Hospitals, such as St. Luke's Hospital of Kansas City, for example, use employee teams to design quality-assured treatment programs and patient-care procedures. Learning from past problems of staff and patients, teams continuously redesign treatments, work methods, and procedures to eliminate the sources of quality problems, rather than allowing existing conditions to continue. That is, they insist that every job be done correctly without error ("do it right the first time"), rather than relying on inspection to catch mistakes and make corrections after they occur. To compete on a global scale, U.S. companies continue to emphasize a quality orientation. All employees, not just managers, participate in quality efforts, and firms have embraced new methods to measure progress and to identify areas for improvement. In many organizations, quality improvement has become a way of life.

Now, with a bit of lift beneath their wings, airlines are investing record profits back into their operations. In a consolidated, highly competitive industry, it's not possible for airlines to differentiate on price and schedule alone. The companies seem to have realized that they must shift focus to customer satisfaction initiatives like on-time performance and bag handling, and that operational efficiencies are just as important in boom times as they are in the doldrums.

The Quality-Productivity Connection

It's no secret that *quality* and *productivity* are watchwords in today's competitive environment. Companies are not only measuring productivity and insisting on improvements; they also are requiring that quality brings greater satisfaction to customers, improves sales, and boosts profits.

Productivity is a measure of economic performance: It compares how much we produce with the resources we use to produce it. The formula is fairly simple. The more services and goods we can produce while using fewer resources, the more productivity grows and the more everyone—the economy, businesses, and workers—benefits. At the national level, the most common measure is called *labor productivity*, because it uses the amount of labor worked as the resource to compare against the benefits, the country's GDP, resulting from using that resource:

Productivity the amount of output produced compared with the amount of resources used to produce that output

$$\text{Labor productivity of a country} = \frac{\text{GDP for the year}}{\text{Total number of labor hours worked for the year}}$$

This equation illustrates the general idea of productivity. We prefer the focus on labor, rather than on other resources (such as capital or energy), because most countries keep accurate records on employment and hours worked. Thus, national labor productivity can be used for measuring year-to-year changes and to compare productivities with other countries. For 2015, for example, U.S. labor productivity was $64.12 of output per hour worked by the nation's labor force. By comparison, Norway was $86.61, Ireland was $71.31, and Belgium was $60.17. In contrast, the Republic of Korea was $26.83, lowest among the 20 measured countries.[12]

managing in turbulent times

Leaner Operations Restore Balance in the Airline Industry

In 2011, rising fuel prices, along with earthquakes, a tsunami, nuclear power meltdowns, and political strife, sent the airline industry into a tailspin. Historically, airlines operate on a very thin margin of profitability even in a good year, so when oil prices soared above $120 per gallon and demand for travel dropped, the industry suffered.

In addition to cutting services and adopting surcharges for items that had once been included in airfare, such as luggage, the economic slump forced the airline industry to create and adopt operational improvements, from the fuel-efficient Boeing 787 Dreamliner to microchips embedded in luggage tags that allow them to be automatically scanned as they are checked in and then tracked through the system.

By 2016, fuel prices had dropped and demand was robust again, yet the airline companies still have operational issues to deal with, both internal and external. In late 2016, Delta, the company that led the way in chip-enabled baggage control, experienced an early morning data outage in Atlanta that crippled its mission control center. The contingency plan was ineffective. By that afternoon, Delta was still only able to operate

T.W. van Urk/Shutterstock

about a third of its usual 6,000 flights. In March of 2017, a snowstorm pounded the east coast of the U.S., shutting down airports and grounding thousands of flights. That's why United Airlines, operating more than 4,500 flights per day on over 730 aircraft, is now working to cut expenses by over $4.8 billion by 2020 in an operational strategy designed to stabilize the company for the next inevitable crisis, economic or otherwise.

However, focusing on just the amount of output is a mistake because productivity refers to both the *quantity and quality* of what we produce. When resources are used more efficiently, the quantity of output is certainly greater. But experience has shown businesses that unless the resulting products are of satisfactory quality, consumers will reject them. And when consumers don't buy what is produced, GDP suffers and productivity falls. Producing quality, then, means creating fitness for use—offering features that customers want.

Managing for Quality

Total Quality Management (TQM) *all activities involved in getting high-quality goods and services into the marketplace*

Total quality management (TQM) includes all the activities necessary for getting high-quality goods and services into the marketplace. TQM begins with leadership and a desire for continuously improving both processes and products. It must consider all aspects of a business, including customers, suppliers, and employees. To marshal the interests of all these stakeholders, TQM first evaluates the costs of poor quality. TQM then identifies the sources causing unsatisfactory quality, assigns responsibility for corrections, and ensures that those who are responsible take steps for improving quality.

The Cost of Poor Quality As seen prominently in the popular press, Toyota recalled more than 24 million cars in 2009–2013, costing the world's then-number-one automaker billions of dollars and a severe blemish to its high-quality image. Problems ranging from sticking gas pedals to stalling engines and malfunctioning fuel pumps were dangerous and costly not only to Toyota, but also to many consumers.

As with goods producers, service providers and customers suffer financial distress from poor-quality service products. The banking industry is a current example.

As a backbone of the U.S. financial system, banks and their customers are still suffering because of bad financial products, most notably home mortgage loans. Lenders during "good times" began relaxing (or even ignoring altogether) traditional lending standards for determining whether borrowers were creditworthy. Lenders in some cases intentionally overstated property values so customers could borrow more money than the property justified. Borrowers were sometimes encouraged to overstate (falsify) their incomes and were not required to present evidence of income or even employment. Some borrowers, unaware of the terms of their loan agreements, were surprised after an initial time lapse when a much higher interest rate (and monthly payment) suddenly kicked in. Unable to meet their payments, borrowers had to abandon their homes. Meanwhile, banks were left holding foreclosed properties, unpaid (defaulted) loans, and no cash. With shortages of bank funds threatening to shut down the entire financial system, the entire nation felt the widespread costs of poor quality—loss of equity by homeowners from foreclosures, a weakened economy, high unemployment, and loss of retirement funds in peoples' savings accounts.

Quality Ownership: Taking Responsibility for Quality To ensure high-quality goods and services, many firms assign responsibility for some aspects of TQM to specific departments or positions. These specialists and experts may be called in to assist with quality-related problems in any department, and they keep everyone informed about the latest developments in quality-related equipment and methods. They also monitor quality-control activities to identify areas for improvement.

The backbone of TQM, however, and its biggest challenge, is motivating all employees and the company's suppliers to achieve quality goals. Leaders of the quality movement use various methods and resources to foster a quality focus, such as training, verbal encouragement, teamwork, and tying compensation to work quality. When those efforts succeed, employees and suppliers will ultimately accept **quality ownership**, the idea that quality belongs to each person who creates it while performing a job.

> **Quality Ownership** *principle of total quality management that holds that quality belongs to each person who creates it while performing a job*

With TQM, everyone—purchasers, engineers, janitors, marketers, machinists, suppliers, and others—must focus on quality. At Saint Luke's Hospital of Kansas City, for example, every employee receives the hospital's "balanced scorecard" showing whether the hospital is meeting its goals: fast patient recovery for specific illnesses, 94 percent or better patient-satisfaction rating, every room cleaned when a patient is gone to X-ray, and the hospital's return on investment being good enough to get a good bond rating in the financial markets. Quarterly scores show the achievement level reached for each goal. Every employee can recite where the hospital is excelling and where it needs improvement. In recognition of its employees' dedication to quality performance, Saint Luke's received the Malcolm Baldrige National Quality Award, the prestigious U.S. award for excellence in quality, and is a five-time winner of the Missouri Quality Award.[13]

Tools for Total Quality Management

Hundreds of tools have proven useful for quality improvement, ranging from statistical analysis of product data, to satisfaction surveys of customers, to **competitive product analysis**, a process by which a company analyzes a competitor's products to identify desirable improvements. Using competitive analysis, for example, Canon might take apart a Xerox copier and test each component. The results would help managers decide which Canon product features are satisfactory, which features should be upgraded, and which operations processes need improvement. In this section, we survey five of the most commonly used tools for TQM: (1) *value-added analysis*, (2) *quality improvement teams*, (3) *getting closer to the customer*, (4) *the ISO series*, and (5) *business process reengineering*.

> **Competitive Product Analysis** *process by which a company analyzes a competitor's products to identify desirable improvements*

Value-Added Analysis **Value-added analysis** refers to the evaluation of all work activities, materials flows, and paperwork to determine the value that they add

> **Value-Added Analysis** *process of evaluating all work activities, materials flows, and paperwork to determine the value that they add for customers*

for customers. It often reveals wasteful or unnecessary activities that can be eliminated without jeopardizing customer service. The basic tenet is so important that Tootsie Roll Industries, the venerable candy company, employs it as a corporate principle: "We run a trim operation and continually strive to eliminate waste, minimize cost, and implement performance improvements."[14]

Quality Improvement Teams Companies throughout the world have adopted **quality improvement teams**, which are patterned after the successful Japanese concept of *quality circles*, collaborative groups of employees from various work areas who meet regularly to define, analyze, and solve common production problems. The teams' goal is to improve both their own work methods and the products they make. Quality improvement teams organize their own work, select leaders, and address problems in the workplace. For years, Motorola has sponsored company-wide team competitions to emphasize the value of the team approach, to recognize outstanding team performance, and to reaffirm the team's role in the company's continuous-improvement culture.

Quality Improvement Team *total quality management tool in which collaborative groups of employees from various work areas work together to improve quality by solving common shared production problems*

Getting Closer to the Customer Successful businesses take steps to know what their customers want in the products they consume. On the other hand, struggling companies have often lost sight of customers as the driving force behind all business activity. Such companies waste resources by designing products that customers do not want. Sometimes, they ignore customer reactions to existing products. For instance, some airlines seem to disregard customer complaints about poor service. Or companies fail to keep up with changing customer preferences. BlackBerry mobile devices, for example, fell behind competing products because they did not offer customers the features that Samsung, Motorola, and Apple provided.

Successful firms take steps to know what their customers want in the products they consume. Caterpillar's (CAT) financial services department, for example, received the Malcolm Baldrige National Quality Award for high ratings by its customers (that is, dealers and buyers of Caterpillar equipment). Buying and financing equipment from Cat Financial became easier as CAT moved its services increasingly online. Customers now have 24/7 access to information on how much they owe on equipment costing anywhere from $30,000 to $2 million, and they can make payments around the clock, too. In the past, the 60,000 customers had to phone a CAT representative, who was often unavailable, resulting in delays and wasted time. The improved online system is testimony to Cat Financial's dedication in knowing what customers want, and then providing it.[15]

IDENTIFYING CUSTOMERS—INTERNAL AND EXTERNAL Improvement projects are undertaken for both external and internal customers. Internal suppliers and internal customers exist wherever one employee or activity relies on others. For example, marketing managers rely on internal accounting information—costs for materials, supplies, and wages—to plan marketing activities for coming months. The marketing manager is a customer of the firm's accountants, the information user relies on the information supplier. Accountants in a TQM environment recognize this supplier–customer connection and take steps to improve information for marketing.

The ISO Series Perhaps you've driven past companies proudly displaying large banners announcing, "This Facility Is ISO Certified." The ISO (pronounced ICE-oh) label is a mark of quality achievement that is respected throughout the world, and, in some countries, it's a requirement for doing business.

ISO 9000 ISO 9000 is a certification program attesting that a factory, a laboratory, or an office has met the rigorous quality management requirements set by the International Organization for Standardization (ISO). Today, more than 170 countries have adopted ISO 9000 as a national standard. Over 1 million certificates have been issued to organizations worldwide meeting the ISO standards.

ISO 9000 *program certifying that a factory, laboratory, or office has met the quality management standards set by the International Organization for Standardization*

The standards of *ISO 9000* allow firms to show that they follow documented procedures for testing products, training workers, keeping records, and fixing defects. It allows international companies to determine (or be assured of) quality of product (or the business) when shipping for, from, and to suppliers across borders. To become certified, companies must document the procedures followed by workers during every stage of production. The purpose is to ensure that a company's processes can create products exactly the same today as it did yesterday and as it will tomorrow.

ISO 14000 The **ISO 14000** program certifies improvements in environmental performance by requiring a firm to develop an *environmental management system*: a plan documenting how the company has acted to improve its performance in using resources (such as raw materials) and in managing pollution. A company must not only identify hazardous wastes that it expects to create, but it must also stipulate plans for treatment and disposal.

ISO 14000 certification program attesting to the fact that a factory, laboratory, or office has improved its environmental performance

Business Process Reengineering Every business consists of processes, activities that it performs regularly and routinely in conducting business, such as receiving and storing materials from suppliers, billing patients for medical treatment, filing insurance claims for auto accidents, and filling customer orders from Internet sales. Any business process can increase customer satisfaction by performing it well. By the same token, any business process can disappoint customers when it's poorly managed.

Business process reengineering focuses on improving a business process—rethinking each of its steps by starting from scratch. *Reengineering* is the fundamental rethinking and radical redesign of business processes to achieve dramatic improvements as measured by cost, quality, service, and speed. The discussion of CAT's changeover to an online system for customers is an example. CAT reengineered the whole payments and financing process by improving equipment, retraining employees, and connecting customers to CAT's databases. As the example illustrates, redesign is guided by a desire to improve operations and thereby provide higher-value services for customers.

Business Process Reengineering *rethinking and radical redesign of business processes to improve performance, quality, and productivity*

Adding Value Through Supply Chains

OBJECTIVE 7-8
Explain
how a supply chain strategy differs from traditional strategies for coordinating operations among firms.

The term *supply chain* refers to the group of companies and stream of activities that work together to create a product. A **supply chain (or value chain)** for any product is the flow of information, materials, and services that starts with raw-materials suppliers and continues adding value through other stages in the network of firms until the product reaches the end customer.

Figure 7.13 shows the chain of activities for supplying baked goods to consumers. Each stage adds value for the final customer. This bakery example begins with raw materials (grain harvested from the farm). It also includes storage and transportation activities, factory operations for baking and wrapping, and distribution to retailers. Each stage depends on the others for success in getting freshly baked goods to consumers. However, a failure by any link can spell disaster for the entire chain.

Supply Chain (or **Value Chain**) *flow of information, materials, and services that starts with raw-materials suppliers and continues adding value through other stages in the network of firms until the product reaches the end customer*

The Supply Chain Strategy

Traditional strategies assume that companies are managed as individual firms rather than as members of a coordinated supply system. Supply chain strategy is based on the idea that members of the chain will gain competitive advantage by working as a coordinated unit. Although each company looks out for its own interests, it works closely with suppliers and customers throughout the chain. Everyone focuses on the entire chain of relationships rather than on just the next stage in the chain.

A traditionally managed bakery, for example, would focus simply on getting production inputs from flour millers and paper suppliers, and then on supplying

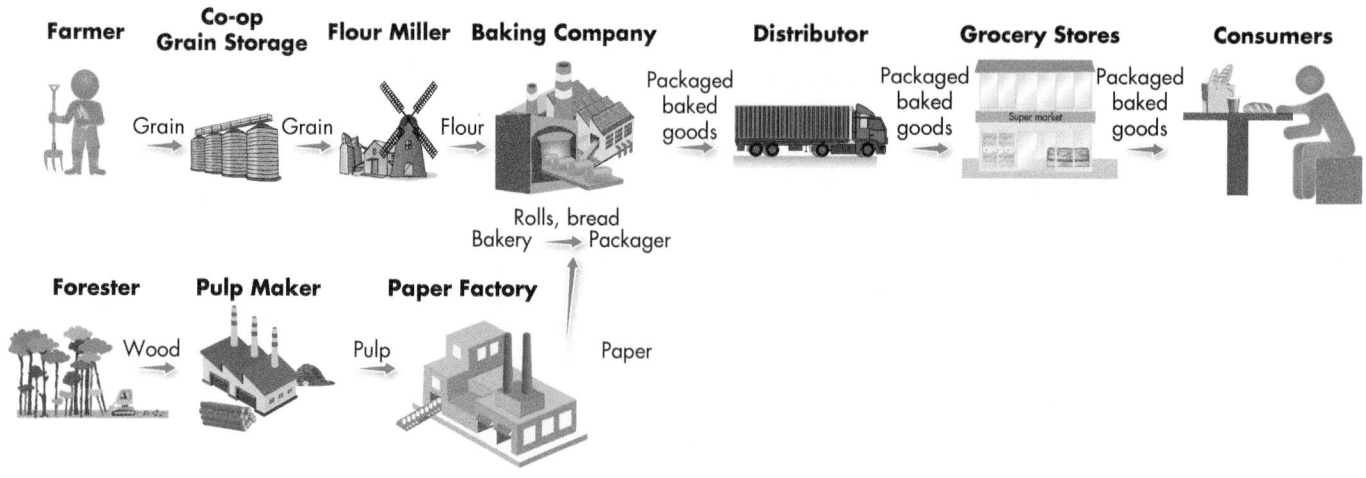

FIGURE 7.13 Supply Chain for Baked Goods

baked goods to distributors. Unfortunately, this approach limits the chain's performance and doesn't allow for possible improvements when activities are more carefully coordinated. Proper management and better coordination among supply chain activities can provide fresher baked goods at lower prices.

Supply Chain Management (SCM) *principle of looking at the supply chain as a whole to improve the overall flow through the system*

Supply Chain Management **Supply chain management (SCM)** looks at the chain as a whole to improve the overall flow through a system composed of companies working together. Because customers ultimately get better value, supply chain management gains competitive advantage for each of the chain's members.

An innovative supply chain strategy was the heart of Michael Dell's vision when he established Dell Inc. Dell's concept improves performance by sharing information among chain members. Dell's long-term production plans and up-to-the-minute sales data are available to suppliers via the Internet. The process starts when customer orders are automatically translated into updated production schedules in the factory. These schedules are used not only by operations managers at Dell but also by such parts suppliers as Sony, which adjust their own production and shipping activities to better meet Dell's production needs. In turn, parts suppliers' updated schedules are transmitted to their materials suppliers, and so on up the chain. As Dell's requirements change, suppliers up and down the chain synchronize their schedules to produce only the right materials and parts. As a result, Dell's prices are low and turnaround time for shipping PCs to customers is reduced to a matter of hours instead of days.

Reengineering Supply Chains for Better Results Process improvements and reengineering often are applied in supply chains to lower costs, speed up service, and coordinate flows of information and material. Because the smoother flow of accurate information along the chain reduces unwanted inventories and transportation, avoids delays, and cuts supply times, materials move faster to business customers and individual consumers. SCM offers faster deliveries and lower costs than customers could get if each member acted only according to its own operations requirements.

Outsourcing and Global Supply Chains

Outsourcing *replacing internal processes by paying suppliers and distributors to perform business processes or to provide needed materials or services*

Outsourcing is the strategy of paying suppliers and distributors to perform certain business processes or to provide needed materials or services. The decision to outsource expands supply chains. The movement of manufacturing and service operations from the United States to countries such as China, Mexico, and India has reduced U.S. employment in traditional jobs. It has also created new operations jobs for SCM. Maytag, for example, had to develop its own internal global operations

finding a better way

Too Good to Waste

In 2013, the Food and Agriculture Organization (FAO) of the United Nations released a report on the impact of food waste. Among its more disturbing findings was that approximately one-third of all food produced is wasted or lost. According to FAO Director-General José Graziano da Silva, "We simply cannot allow one-third of all the food we produce to go to waste or be lost because of inappropriate practices, when 870 million people go hungry every day." According to this study, food waste occurs along the supply chain, with 54 percent occurring during production, post-harvest handling, and storage. However, there are some differences among low-income countries and their middle- and high-income counterparts. "Downstream" waste, at the retail or consumer level, is much higher in developed economies, creating additional opportunities for consumer education in these areas.

In addition to the human impacts of food wastage, there are dire environmental consequences. For example, meat wastage has the most severe environmental consequences as the land use and carbon footprint associated with meat production is much higher. Unused grain and cereal products, such as rice, impact both land use and methane emissions (which are particularly high in rice production). On the other hand, the impact of fruit waste tends to be primarily associated with excess water consumption. Given the increasing scarcity of water supplies, this concern is not easily dismissed.

The key to minimizing food waste falls in supply chain management. Beginning with the producer, it is essential that predictive analytics are employed to balance production with downstream demand for the product. Even with better modeling, food surpluses will continue to occur, but they could be

Kaliantye/123RF

better managed. Rather than disposing of excess food in the supply chain, intermediaries need to be more diligent about finding alternative uses, whether it is donating it to food programs or diverting it for livestock feed. Consumers must also be educated about the importance of planning their food spending to avoid over-purchasing as well as the actual meaning of "best-before-dates," which often lead retailers and consumers to discard healthy and nutritious foods because they fail to meet certain aesthetic standards. Each member of the supply chain, from producer to consumer, has a role in reducing food waste, becoming better stewards of our planet and resources.[16]

In 2015, the UN announced an ambitious agenda to end poverty, promote prosperity, and protect the environment. One of the key objectives of that agenda is to "halve per capita global food waste at the retail and consumer level, and reduce food losses along production and supply chains by 2030."[17]

---

expertise before it could decide to open a new refrigerator factory in Mexico, import refrigerators from South Korea's Daewoo, and get laundry appliances from South Korea's Samsung Electronics. In departing from a long-standing practice of domestic production, Maytag adopted new supply chain skills for evaluating prospective outsourcing partners.

Skills for coordinating Maytag's domestic activities with those of its cross-border partners didn't end with the initial decision to get appliances from Mexico and Korea. Maytag personnel in their Newton, Iowa, headquarters have near-constant interaction with their partners on a host of continuing new operations issues. Product redesigns are transferred from the United States and used at remote manufacturing sites. Arrangements for cross-border materials flows require compliance with each country's commerce regulations. Production and global transportation scheduling are coordinated with U.S. market demand so that outsourced products arrive in the right amounts and on time without tarnishing Maytag's reputation for high quality. Although manufacturing operations are located remotely, they are closely integrated with the firm's home-base activities. That tightness of integration demands on-site operations expertise on both sides of the outsourcing equation. Global communication technologies are essential. The result for outsourcers is a greater need of operations skills for integration among dispersed facilities.

summary of learning objectives

OBJECTIVE 7-1

Explain the meaning of *operations* and discuss the growth in the services and goods sectors of the U.S. economy. (pp. 206–208)

Operations (or *production*) refers to all the activities involved in making products—goods and services—for customers. In modern societies, much of what we need or want is produced by service operations, where success or failure depends on provider-customer contact. Many companies, such as General Electric, provide both goods and services. Employment has risen significantly in the service sector over the past 10 years. However, the 11 percent of the U.S. workforce employed in producing goods generate 32 percent of national income.

Production or operations adds customer value by providing *utility*—the ability of a product to satisfy a want or need—in terms of form, time, and place: (1) *Form utility*: By turning raw materials and human skills into finished goods and services, production adds customer value by making products available. (2) *Time utility*: Production provides customer value by making products available when customers want them. (3) *Place utility*: Production adds customer value by making products available where they are convenient for customers.

Operations management is the systematic direction and control of the activities that transform resources into finished goods and services that create value for and provide benefits to customers. Through their operations processes—using resources that include knowledge, physical materials, information, equipment, the customer, and human skills—firms provide benefits for themselves and for their customers.

OBJECTIVE 7-2

Identify the three kinds of utility created by operations and the characteristics that distinguish service operations from goods production. (pp. 208–212)

Although the creation of both goods and services involves resources, transformations, and finished products, service operations differ from goods manufacturing in several important ways. In service production, the raw materials are not things such as glass or steel, but rather people who choose among sellers because they have unsatisfied needs or possessions in need of care or alteration. Therefore, whereas services are typically performed, goods are physically produced. In addition, services are largely *intangible* and more *unstorable* than most physical goods. It is difficult, as an example, to store a supply (an inventory) of childcare services. If the services are not consumed when available, they are lost forever.

Service businesses, therefore, focus explicitly on the intangibility and unstorable nature of their products. Because services are intangible, for instance, providers work to ensure that customers receive value in the forms of pleasure, satisfaction, or a feeling of safety. Often they also focus on both the transformation process and the final product (such as making the loan interview a pleasant experience as well as providing the loan itself). As part of the transformation process, service providers typically focus on *customer-provider contact*. This requires service workers who, because they interact with customers, possess different skills than workers producing physical goods.

An *operations process* is a set of methods and technologies used to produce a good or service. Goods production can be classified as *make-to-order* or *make-to-stock*. Make-to-order operations respond to specific customer specifications, and make-to-stock operations produce standardized goods for mass consumption.

Service operations can be classified according to the extent of customer contact. In a *low-contact system*, customers have a limited presence as the service is performed. Low-contact systems include mail and package delivery, auto repair, lawn care services, and gas and electric providers. On the other hand, in a *high-contact system*, the customer is present as the service is delivered. Examples of high-contact systems include airlines and hair salons.

OBJECTIVE 7-3

Explain how companies with different business strategies are best served by having different operations capabilities. (pp. 212–214)

Production is a flexible activity that can be molded into many shapes to give different operations capabilities (production capabilities) for different purposes. Its design is best driven from above by the firm's larger business strategy. When firms adopt different strategies for winning customers in specific target markets, they should also adjust their *operations capabilities*—what production must do especially well—to match the chosen strategy. That is, different target markets have different desires or expectations for the products—services and goods—that they seek. Accordingly, operations managers must clarify and understand their target market's most-preferred product characteristic from among the following: Do they want low-cost products? The highest quality products? Dependability of product performance? A wide variety of offerings rather than just a few? To meet any chosen strategy, then, they adopt an operations capability that is geared toward meeting the target customers' needs. The operations capability that is appropriate for a low-cost strategy, for example, is different than the kind of competence that is best for a dependability strategy. Accordingly, the operations characteristics, such as number and size of production facilities, employee skills, kinds of equipment, and its operations activities, will be different, resulting in different operations capabilities to better support their different purposes.

OBJECTIVE 7-4

Identify the major factors that are considered in operations planning. (pp. 214–219)

Operations planning includes five major considerations: (1) *Capacity planning* considers current and future capacity requirements for meeting anticipated customer demand. The amount of a product that a company can produce under normal conditions is its *capacity*, and it depends on how many people it employs and the number and sizes of its facilities. (2) *Location planning* is crucial because a firm's location affects costs of production, ease of transportation, access to skilled workers, and convenient accessibility for customers. (3) *Layout planning* determines the physical location of service teams, machinery, equipment, and facilities and affects how efficiently a company can respond to customer demand. A *process (custom-products) layout* is effective for make-to-order production specializing in custom designed services or goods. A *product (same-steps) layout*, such as an assembly line, is often used for large-volume, make-to-stock production of services or goods. A *fixed-position layout* is necessary when, because of size, shape, or any other reason, the service to be provided cannot be moved to another facility. Instead, the product or client remains at one location; equipment, materials, and human skills are moved to that location, as needed, to perform the service or to build the product. (4) *Quality planning* begins when products are being designed and extends into production operations for ensuring that the desired performance and consistency are built into products. Quality is defined as the combination of "characteristics of a product or service that bear on its ability to satisfy stated or implied needs." Quality planning involves setting goals for both *performance* and *consistency*. (5) *Methods planning* considers each production step and the specific methods for performing it for producing services and goods. The purpose is to reduce waste and inefficiency by methods improvement procedures.

OBJECTIVE 7-5

Discuss the information contained in four kinds of operations schedules—the master operations schedule, detailed schedule, staff schedule, and project schedule. (pp. 219–222)

Operations scheduling identifies times when specific operations activities will occur. The *master schedule*, the top-level schedule for upcoming production, shows how many of which products (services or goods) will be produced in each time period, in weeks or months ahead, to meet upcoming customer demand. Thereafter, the schedule shows how many units of each major resource—materials, employees, equipment—will be required. By identifying these future resource requirements, managers can develop plans for acquiring the resources on time for upcoming time periods.

Detailed schedules take a shorter-range perspective by specifying daily work assignments with start and stop times for assigned jobs at each workstation. Detailed schedules allow managers and other employees to make last-minute adjustments so that resources are available and matched to meet immediate customer service requirements.

Staff schedules identify who and how many employees will be working and their assigned working times on each work shift for the upcoming month or months. Staff scheduling considers the needs of employees as well as the company's goals of maximizing efficiency and controlling costs.

Finally, *project schedules* provide information for completing large-scale projects using project scheduling tools, such as *Gantt* and *PERT charts*. A Gantt chart breaks down special large projects into the sequence of steps to be performed and specifies the time required to perform each. Gantt charts help managers to assess if work is ahead or behind schedule so that adjustments can be made. PERT charts show the necessary sequence among activities, and identify the critical path—the most time-consuming set of activities for completing the project.

OBJECTIVE 7-6

Discuss the two key activities required for operations control. (pp. 222–225)

Materials management and quality control are two key activities of operations control. Once plans and schedules have been drawn up, operations control requires managers to monitor performance by comparing results against those plans and schedules. If schedules or quality standards are not met, managers take corrective action. Follow-up—checking to ensure that decisions are being implemented—is an essential facet of operations control. Materials management—including supplier selection, purchasing, transportation, warehousing, and inventory control—facilitates the flow of materials. Materials management is the process by which managers plan, organize, and control the flow of materials and services from sources of supply through distribution of finished products to customers. For producing and delivering physical goods, it may use lean production systems, such as just-in-time operations, for smooth production flows that avoid inefficiencies, comply with schedules, eliminate unnecessary inventories, and continuously improve production processes. For high-contact services, such as tourism and vacation services, inventory exists in the forms of information about service offerings, facilities arrangements, clients, client interests, activities schedules, and plans for interactions among and with clients. Quality control means taking action to ensure that operations produce goods and services that meet specific quality standards. By monitoring products and services, managers and other employees can detect mistakes, identify potential quality failures, and make corrections to avoid poor quality. Both materials management and quality control are essential to ensure that schedules are met and products delivered, both in quality and quantity.

OBJECTIVE 7-7

Identify the activities and underlying objectives involved in total quality management. (pp. 225–229)

Successful companies focus on productivity, which measures both the quantity and quality of the products produced or delivered. Productivity compares the level of production with the amount of resources used to produce it. *Total quality management* (TQM) is a customer-driven culture for offering products with characteristics that customers want. It includes all the activities necessary for getting customer-satisfying goods and services into the marketplace and, internally, getting every job to give better service to internal customers (other departments) within the organization. TQM begins with leadership and a desire for continuously improving both processes and products. It considers all aspects of a business, including customers, suppliers, and employees. The TQM culture fosters an attitude of *quality ownership* among employees and suppliers, the idea that quality belongs to each person who creates it while performing a job, so that quality improvement becomes a continuous way of life. It identifies the *costs of poor quality*, including all forms of financial distress resulting from poor-quality products, and uses cost-of-poor-quality information as a guide for process improvement to prevent such costs in the future.

Numerous quality-improvement tools can then be used to gain those improvements and reduce those costs. Some process improvement tools of TQM include competitive product analysis, value-added analysis, the use of quality improvement teams, business process reengineering, and "getting closer to the customer" to gain valid information about what customers really want, so that improved products more closely meet customer desires.

ISO 9000 is a certification program attesting that a factory, laboratory, or office has met the rigorous quality management requirements set by the International Organization for Standardization. Similarly, *ISO 14000* certifies improvements in environmental performance. Finally, business process reengineering focuses on the radical redesign of business processes to achieve improvements in cost, quality, service, and speed.

OBJECTIVE 7-8

Explain how a supply chain strategy differs from traditional strategies for coordinating operations among firms. (pp. 229–231)

The supply chain strategy is based on the idea that members of the *supply chain*, the stream of all activities and companies that add value in creating a product, will gain competitive advantage by working together as a coordinated unit. The supply chain for any product, be it a service or a physical good, is the flow of information, materials, and services that starts with raw-materials suppliers and continues adding value through other stages in the network of firms until the product reaches the end customer. In contrast, traditional strategies assume that companies are managed as individual firms, each acting in its own interest. By managing the chain as a whole—using *supply chain management*—companies can more closely coordinate activities throughout the chain. Because accurate information is shared between companies along the chain, they can reduce unwanted materials and transportation, avoid delays in deliveries to cut supply times, quickly add service centers to meet upsurges in demand, and move materials faster through the chain. By sharing information across all stages in the chain, overall costs and inventories can be reduced, quality can be improved, and overall flow through the system can be improved, thus providing customers higher value from faster deliveries and lower costs.

Outsourcing, the strategy of paying suppliers and distributors to perform certain business processes or to provide needed materials or services, expands supply chains. The prevalence of outsourcing has created new operations jobs in supply chain management.

key terms

MyLab Intro to Business

To complete the problems with the ⭐, go to EOC Discussion Questions in the MyLab.

questions & exercises

QUESTIONS FOR REVIEW

⭐ **7-1.** Describe, in your own words, the meaning and significance of business operations. What do we mean when we talk about operations? What does it encompass? What does it exclude?

7-2. What are the major differences between goods-production operations and service operations?

7-3. What are the major differences between high-contact and low-contact service systems? Give an example of each, comparing and contrasting them.

⭐ **7-4.** Identify the three kinds of utility and describe each one briefly.

QUESTIONS FOR ANALYSIS

7-5. Apply the five major categories of operations planning to your college or to a local business.

7-6. What type of business strategy does Disney use to attract customers to its theme parks? What does the company do to implement its strategy? What are the key operational characteristics?

⭐ **7-7.** Choose three different businesses that you frequent and rate the quality of their service or product on a scale of 1–5, with 1 being poor quality and 5 being high quality. Explain the standard that you applied for each business to determine quality. Was it the same standard, or did you apply a different standard to each one? If so, why?

7-8. If you were a member of a quality improvement team at your college, what would be five specific high-impact recommendations that you would support? Of those five, which two would be the most important, and briefly explain what strategies you might employ as a college administrator to implement those two recommendations.

APPLICATION EXERCISES

7-9. Map out the process for enrolling in classes at your school by drawing a process flowchart that shows the stages in the activity, and then tell how you would use that flowchart as part of a methods improvement approach to operations planning.

7-10. Interview the manager of a local service business, such as a restaurant or hair salon. Identify the major decisions involved in planning that business's service operations.

building a business: continuing team exercise

Assignment

Meet with your team members to consider your new business venture and how it relates to the operations management and quality topics in this chapter. Develop specific responses to the following:

7-11. In what ways is your business connected with service operations? Identify the ways it is connected with goods production. Which of these, service operations or goods production, is more important to your business? Why?

7-12. Explain what must be done to ensure that your operations capabilities are consistent with your business strategy. How does your mission statement support operations? What kinds of quality control measures should you consider?

7-13. Discuss how your team is going to identify the key operations characteristics that best provide support for accomplishing your business strategy. Based on the discussion, what are the key characteristics that seem to be most prominent at this stage of development of your business?

7-14. Analyze the planned production activities for your business to determine the operations processes for which total quality management will be important.

7-15. In what ways, if any, will supply chains be of concern for your business? Explain.

team exercise

CALCULATING THE COST OF CONSCIENCE

The Situation

Product quality and cost affect every firm's reputation and profitability, as well as the satisfaction of customers. As director of quality for a major appliance manufacturer, Ruth was reporting to the executive committee on the results of a program for correcting problems with a newly redesigned compressor (the motor that cools the refrigerator) that the company had recently begun using in its refrigerators. Following several customer complaints, the quality lab had determined that some of the new compressor units ran more loudly than expected, although they still effectively cooled the units.

The Decision

Faced with this information, Ruth has been asked to recommend a strategy for the company. One corrective option was simply waiting until customers complained and responding to each complaint if and when it occurred. Fixing noisy units could be expensive, but the company wishes to maintain its high-quality image.

Ruth, however, decided that this approach was inconsistent with the company's policy of being the high-quality leader in the industry. Insisting on a proactive, "pro-quality" approach, Ruth suggests a program for contacting all customers who had purchased refrigerators containing the new compressor. Unfortunately, the "quality-and-customers-first" policy will be expensive. Service representatives nationwide will have to phone every customer, make appointments for home visits, and replace original compressors with a newer model. Because replacement time is only 30 minutes, customers will hardly be inconvenienced, and food will stay refrigerated without interruption.

Others have even suggested that the company require consumers to pay a part of the cost of repairing the noisy compressor because the compressors still meet all expectations with respect to cooling, and this is the primary function of the refrigerator. Advocates of this position argue that the new compressors will extend the life of the refrigerator and customers will benefit.

FOLLOW-UP QUESTIONS

7-16. If you were a customer, what would you hope that the company would do? Would your answer be different if you were an investor or stockholder?

7-17. How might Ruth's boss, the vice president for operations, view the situation differently than Ruth?

7-18. Which is the best of the three options in the short-term? What about in the long-term?

7-19. How could the company have avoided this situation?

exercising your ethics

PROMISES, PROMISES

The Situation

Unfortunately, false promises are not uncommon when managers feel pressure to pump up profits. Many operations managers no doubt recall times when excited marketing managers asked for unrealistic commitments from production to get a new customer contract. This exercise will introduce you to some ethical considerations pertaining to such promises and commitments.

The Dilemma

You are an operations manager for a factory that makes replacement car mufflers and tailpipes. Your products are distributed throughout the country to muffler-repair shops that install them on used vehicles. After several years of modest but steady growth, your company recently suffered a downturn and shut down 5 percent of the factory's production capacity. Two supervisors and 70 production workers were laid off.

After returning from lunch, you get a phone call from the general manager of King Kong Mufflers, one of the nation's top three muffler-repair chains, who says the following:

I suppose you know that we're about to sign a contract for your firm to supply us with replacement parts in large volumes, *beginning two months from now. Your sales manager assures me that you can reliably meet my needs, and I just want to confirm that promise with you before I sign the contract.*

This is the first you've heard about this contract. While your potential customer is talking, you realize that meeting his needs will require a 20 percent increase in your current production capacity. Two months, however, isn't enough time to add more equipment, acquire tools, hire and train workers, and contract for supplies. An increase this large might even require a bigger building (which would take considerably more than two months to arrange). On the other hand, you also know how much your firm needs the business. The caller waits in silence while you gather your thoughts.

QUESTIONS TO ADDRESS

7-20. What are the underlying ethical issues in this situation?

7-21. From an ethical standpoint, what is an appropriate response to the customer's question? What steps should you take in responding to it? Explain.

7-22. What would you say on the phone at this time to this customer?

cases

DESSERT IS ALWAYS A GREAT IDEA

Continued from page 206

At the beginning of this chapter you read about the operational philosophy of the Cheesecake Factory. Using the information presented in this chapter, you should now be able to answer these questions.

QUESTIONS FOR DISCUSSION

7-23. How would you define *quality* and how is quality measured in the restaurant industry? Are some measurements more useful than others? Explain.

7-24. Would you categorize the Cheesecake Factory as a service provider or a provider of goods, or both? How would your classification affect your quality control decisions? How would it affect the way you approach operations?

7-25. Describe how *process flowcharts* may be helpful for methods improvement in restaurant operations. What kinds of information would you hope to gain from the flowcharts?

7-26. Identify a major U.S. restaurant chain that has recently received *poor quality ratings*. Who are its customers, and what are the basic causes that led to declining quality?

7-27. U.S. restaurants must comply with local health regulations. The results of periodic inspections have to be posted or published, or both. What actions would you recommend be considered by restaurants to overcome negative perceptions from a less-than satisfactory rating?

TELECOMMUTING BOOSTS QUALITY AND PRODUCTIVITY ... OR DOES IT?

Early in 2013, Yahoo CEO Marissa Mayer made the controversial decision to ban employees from working exclusively at home. Her action seemed to run in the face of a years-long trend in the opposite direction by her company and other businesses across many industries. The question, then, that faces many organizations (and employees) is the following: Is telecommuting really beneficial? And if so, who reaps those benefits? Certainly today's information technologies provide telecommuting possibilities on a larger scale than ever before. Yahoo, like many other firms, has an internal Virtual Private Network, into which thousands of employees can log in at remote locations for conducting company business. Mayer's decision suggested that disadvantages outweighed advantages for her company at that time.[18]

And yet, more U.S. employees are working remotely than ever before. For example, a Gallup poll in 2016 indicated that 43 percent of employees were working from home at least part of the time, up from 39 percent in 2012. Because those numbers are growing, the future stakes for businesses and employees will depend even more on decisions about home-based versus office-based employment.[19]

Advocates for telecommuting cite its benefits. A Stanford study indicates a 13 percent productivity increase for call center employees working at home. It also cites greater work satisfaction and less employee turnover. Other studies report home-based employees work up to seven hours longer in their workweek than do those working at the office, have greater productivity, and less absenteeism. At-home employees note that they don't get distracted by co-workers, they avoid unnecessary commute time, take breaks when they prefer, and have a better quality of life, among other benefits.[20]

Critics, in contrast, note telecommuting's downside. Some people simply don't like to work alone. Others are not as productive working alone because better ideas and problem solutions are more forthcoming through face-to-face interactions and being physically nearby for work-related discussions. Also cited are advantages of separating home and workplace, avoiding the many distractions at home, and claims that telecommuting is widely abused. Employers report that having at least some scheduled on-site work time, even if not full-time, provides better performance, including problem solutions for customer service.

Mayer concluded that Yahoo's quality and productivity were at unacceptable levels because of too many employees working exclusively at home. She is reported to favor working at the office, citing benefits of gaining information and ideas from meeting new people, spontaneous conversations in the hallways, and quick accessibility to other face-to-face interactions for solving problems. "Speed and quality are often sacrificed when we work from home." Accordingly, Mayer suspected that Yahoo's telecommuting may be less productive than it should be. Rather than relying on mere suspicions, she wanted some factual basis, preferably backed up by data. So, she turned to Yahoo's Virtual Private Network and looked at the data files showing frequencies of employees' log-ins. She concluded that they were not checking in enough, thus indicating too much inactivity and too little productivity.[21]

Does face-to-face contact among employees really affect quality and productivity? A study of workers in call-center teams at Bank of America found that, yes, it does matter. Productivity was found to be greatest for workers in close-knit teams where workers mingled more frequently, rather than when working alone. Collaboration and spontaneous information sharing seemed to enhance productivity. But what about in other jobs where workers face different kinds of tasks, some more complex and others much simpler? Does either the office setting or the telecommuting setting, in general, always provide more promise for better productivity and quality? The answer is more likely to be situational rather than "one size fits all."[22]

QUESTIONS FOR DISCUSSION

7-28. How would you define *quality* for Yahoo's situation in this case? Explain why.

7-29. To figure out if Yahoo's telecommuting is less productive than it should have been, Mayer looked at the log of Yahoo's Virtual Private Network to see how frequently employees checked in. What do you think of this as a measure of productivity and quality? What other measure(s) would you suggest instead of the one she used?

7-30. Go to Yahoo's career website (https://careers.yahoo.com) and look at the kinds of jobs available at Yahoo. From these, identify two job descriptions that you recommend as appropriate for telecommuting. Identify two others that are appropriate for office-based employment. Explain the reasons for your recommendations.

7-31. Consider businesses such as hotels, television broadcasting, or others that provide services products to consumers. Suppose you want to improve the quality of such a service (choose one or two services). To do so, suppose you are considering allowing telecommuting by some employees, but requiring others to be office-based employees. Identify two kinds of work suitable for telecommuting, and two kinds for office-only jobs. Explain your reasoning.

7-32. How do you feel about telecommuting? Would you rather have a job, like those at Yahoo, where you have set office hours, or would you rather work from home? Do you think that working from home would cause you to be more productive or less productive? Why?

crafting a business plan

PART 2: THE BUSINESS OF MANAGING

Goal of the Exercise

In Part 1 of the business plan project, you formulated a basic identity for your business. Part 2 of the business plan project asks you to think about the goals of your business, some internal and external factors affecting the business, and the organizational structure of the business.

Exercise Background: Part 2 of the Business Plan

As you learned in Chapter 5, every business sets goals. In this part of the plan, you'll define some of the goals for your business.

Part 2 of the business plan also asks you to perform a basic SWOT analysis for your business. As you'll recall from Chapter 5, a SWOT analysis looks at the business's *strengths, weaknesses, opportunities,* and *threats*. The strengths and weaknesses are internal factors—things that the business can control. The opportunities and threats are generally external factors that affect the business:

Sociocultural forces	Will changes in population or culture help your business or hurt it?
Economic forces	Will changes in the economy help your business or hurt it?
Technological forces	Will changes in technology help your business or hurt it?
Competitive forces	Does your business face much competition or very little?
Political-legal forces	Will changes in laws help your business or hurt it?

Each of these forces will affect different businesses in different ways, and some of these may not apply to your business at all.

Part 2 of the business plan also asks you to determine how the business is to be run. Part of this will require you to create an organizational chart to get you thinking about the different tasks needed for a successful business. You'll also examine various factors relating to operating your business.

Your Assignment

STEP 1

Open the saved *Business Plan* file you began working on in Part 1. You will continue to work from the same file you started working on in Part 1.

STEP 2

For the purposes of this assignment, you will answer the questions in "Part 2: The Business of Managing":

7-33. Provide a brief mission statement for your business.

Hint: Refer to the discussion of mission statements in Chapter 5. Be sure to include the name of your business, how you will stand out from your competition, and why a customer will buy from you.

7-34. Consider the goals for your business. What are three of your business goals for the first year? What are two intermediate to long-term goals?

Hint: Refer to the discussion of goal setting in Chapter 5. Be as specific and realistic as possible with the goals you set. For example, if you plan on selling a service, how many customers do you want by the end of the first year, and how much do you want each customer to spend?

7-35. Perform a basic SWOT analysis for your business, listing its main strengths, weaknesses, opportunities, and threats.

Hint: We explained previously what factors you should consider in your basic SWOT analysis. Look around at your world, talk to classmates, or talk to your instructor for other ideas in performing your SWOT analysis.

7-36. Who will manage the business? *Hint*: Refer to the discussion of managers in Chapter 5. Think about how many *levels* of management as well as what *kinds* of managers your business needs.

7-37. Show how the "team" fits together by creating a simple organizational chart for your business. Your chart should indicate who will work for each manager as well as each person's job title.

Hint: As you create your organizational chart, consider the different tasks involved in the business. To whom will each person report? Refer to the discussion of organizational structure in Chapter 6 for information to get you started.

7-38. Create a floor plan of the business. What does it look like when you walk through the door?

Hint: When sketching your floor plan, consider where equipment, supplies, and furniture will be located.

7-39. Explain what types of raw materials and supplies you will need to run your business. How will you produce your good or service? What equipment do you need? What hours will you operate?

Hint: Refer to the discussion of operations in this chapter for information to get you started.

7-40. What steps will you take to ensure that the quality of the product or service stays at a high level? Who will be responsible for maintaining quality standards?

Hint: Refer to the discussion of quality improvement and TQM in this chapter for information to get you started. *Note*: Once you have answered the questions, save your Word document. You'll be answering additional questions in later chapters.

Writing Assignments

7-41. Imagine that you are the newly hired manager for the Quality Control Department of a major food processing operation. During the past two years, there have been two major, and expensive, recalls of product. You have been hired to improve the performance of the department. What questions would you ask? What strategies would you consider?

7-42. Successful business leaders say that any business's success depends on the matchup (or compatibility) between its operations capabilities and its overall business strategy. That is, major competitive weaknesses exist when operations capabilities are not consistent with or conflict with company strategy. In contrast, successful companies ensure that operations are designed to support overall strategy. Compare and contrast two companies that have chosen different strategies for attracting customers, as follows: (a) Describe the differences in their strategies. (b) Identify and describe key operations capabilities and characteristics for each company. (c) Explain for each company how its operations characteristics support its strategy, or how those characteristics do not support its overall strategy.

endnotes

[1] Gawande, Atul, "Big Med: Restaurant chains have managed to combine quality control, cost control, and innovation. Can health care?" *The New Yorker* (2012) http://www.newyorker.com/magazine/2012/08/13/big-med (Accessed March 14, 2017)

[2] Eng, Dinah, "Cheesecake Factory's winning formula," Interview with David Overton of Cheesecake Factory, May 9, 2011, *Fortune*, http://archive.fortune.com/2011/05/02/smallbusiness/cheescake_factory_david_overton.fortune/index.htm (Accessed March 14, 2017)

[3] News release, The Cheesecake Factory, Feb 22, 2017, http://investors.thecheesecakefactory.com/phoenix.zhtml?c=109258&p=irol-newsArticle&ID=2248413 (accessed March 14, 2017)

[4] General Electric Company, *Annual Report for Year Ended Dec. 31, 2015, FORM 10-K*, (U.S. Securities and Exchange Commission, March 1, 2016).

[5] http://www2.deloitte.com/global/en/pages/manufacturing/articles/global-manufacturing-competitiveness-index.html), accessed on January 25, 2017.

[6] Alex Hill and Terry Hill, *Manufacturing Operations Strategy*, 6th edition (Basingstoke, UK: Palgrave Macmillan, 2017); James A. Fitzsimmons, Mona J. Fitzsimmons, *Service Management: Operations Strategy, Information Technology*, 9th edition (Boston: Irwin McGraw-Hill, 2017).

[7] Stein, Joel. 2008. "Outsourcing Home Cooking." *Time* 171, no. 6: 61. Business Source Premier, EBSCOhost (accessed January 26, 2017).

[8] Martin Santa, "Slowing Car Production Prompts Slovak Industrial Output Decline," *Reuters.com*, February 8, 2013, at http://www.reuters.com/article/2013/02/08/slovakia-economy-idUSL5N0B85G120130208; Jack Ewing, "The Auto Slump Hits Slovakia," *SPIEGEL ONLINE*, June 19, 2009 at http://www.spiegel.de/international/business/0,1518,druck-631388,00.html; Gail Edmondson, Willam Boston, and Andrea Zammert, "Detroit East," *Businessweek*, July 25, 2005, at http://www.businessweek.com/print/magazine/content/05_30/b3944003.htm?chan=gl/.

[9] American Society for Quality, "ASQ Glossary of Terms," at asq.org/glossary/q.html, accessed on January 27, 2017.

[10] "How We Make Chocolate," at http://www.godiva.com/experience-godiva/HowWeMakeChocolate_RichArticle,default,pg.html, accessed on January 27, 2017.

[11] "About Collette" and "Ways to Tour," *Collette Vacations* at www.collettevacations.com, accessed January 27, 2017.

[12] "International Comparisons of GDP per Capita and per Hour, 1960–2014," *U.S. Bureau of Labor Statistics*, at http://www.bls.gov/ilc/intl_gdp_capita_gdp_hour.htm#table03, accessed on March 1, 2015.

13 "Missouri Quality Award: Fifth Win for Saint Luke's, Second Time as a Health System," November 2010, at https://www.saintlukeshealthsystem.org/article/missouri-quality-award; Del Jones, "Baldrige Award Honors Record 7 Quality Winners," *USA Today*, November 26, 2003, 6B.

14 Tootsie Roll Industries, Inc., *Annual Report 2014* (Chicago: 2015), p. 1.

15 Del Jones, "Baldrige Award Honors Record 7 Quality Winners," *USA Today*, November 26, 2003, 6B.

16 Food and Agriculture Organization of the United Nations. "Food waste harms climate, water, land and biodiversity—new FAO report." News release. Accessed April 30, 2015. http://www.fao.org/news/story/en/item/196220/icode/.

17 United Nations, "Sustainable Development Goals: 17 goals to transform our world," http://www.un.org/sustainabledevelopment/sustainable-development-goals/ (Accessed March 14, 2017).

18 Nicholas Carlson, "How Marissa Mayer Figured Out Work-At-Home Yahoos Were Slacking Off," *Business Insider*, March 2, 2013, at http://www.businessinsider.com/how-marissa-mayer-figuredout-work-at-home-yahoos-were-slacking-off-2013-3.

19 Neil Shah, "More Americans Working Remotely," *Wall Street Journal*, March 3, 2013, A3.

20 Leanne Italie, "Yahoo Ban Turns Spotlight on Telecommuting," *Fort Worth Star Telegram*, March 9, 2013, at http://www.star-telegram.com/2013/03/09/4671879/yahoo-ban-turns-spotlight-on-telecommuting.html.

21 "Yahoo CEO Marissa Mayer Demands Telecommuters Report to Office," *Huffington Post Business*, February 23, 2013, at http://www.huffingtonpost.com/2013/02/23/yahoo-working-remote_n_2750698.html.

22 Rachel Emma Silverman, "Tracking Sensors Invade the Workplace," *Wall Street Journal*, March 7, 2013, B1–B2.

Employee Behavior and Motivation

chapter 8

Keeping employees involved and invested is the key to a company's bottom line. When **employees stop** caring, everyone suffers.

After reading this chapter, you should be able to:

8-1 **Identify** and discuss the basic forms of behaviors that employees exhibit in organizations.

8-2 **Describe** the nature and importance of individual differences among employees.

8-3 **Explain** the meaning and importance of psychological contracts and the person-job fit in the workplace.

8-4 **Identify** and summarize the most important models and concepts of employee motivation.

8-5 **Describe** some of the strategies and techniques used by organizations to improve employee motivation.

A Living Wage

In January 2015, insurance giant Aetna announced their plans to increase the base wage of their lowest paid employees to at least $16 per hour, more than double the federal minimum wage at that time. That increase affected 12 percent of Aetna's 48,000 employees and had a significant impact on both the employees and the company. The lowest paid employees, who had a base rate of $12 per hour, saw a 33 percent increase in pay, with the average increase of those affected being 11 percent. In addition, the company extended health insurance benefits to nearly 7,000 employees, thus lowering those employees' annual out-of-pocket costs by up to $4,000.

While the employees are, no doubt, delighted, this increase in compensation and benefits comes with a hefty price tag. The total cost of the wage and benefit enhancements was estimated at $14 million in 2015 and more than $25 million in 2016. However, Aetna's operating profit in 2014 was $2.04 billion and for 2015, $2.4 billion, an increase of over 17 percent. Therefore, the fully implemented cost of these changes was only about 1 percent of profit. In addition, the company estimated that employee turnover costs them about $120 million a year. Research has shown that low-wage workers are more likely to quit than their higher paid counterparts. The costs associated with recruiting, hiring, and training new employees are substantial, so a high turnover rate comes with significant hidden costs.

CEO Mark Bertolini is convinced that the pay raise increases productivity. Many of the lowest paid workers are employed in the company's call centers, an extremely stressful environment. Callers are often upset by the events that led to their claim, such as damage to their home or car, or an illness or injury, and may also have questions or disputes about coverage. According to Kally Dunn, a call center supervisor from Fresno, "When they call, … they're angry. And so it's just a lot of de-escalating, calming them down, … reassuring them." On top of the stress of their job, these low-wage workers face the challenges of paying their day-to-day expenses. One of the affected employees from the Fresno call center is Fabian Arredondo. He says, "Finance can be one of the main stresses in people's lives. And when you can pull some relief away from that stress, I definitely think it makes for—you know, a happy employee is a productive employee."

This is exactly the logic that led Aetna to make this bold move. Bertolini was surprised to find that many of his employees were on public assistance, such as food stamps and Medicaid. He was shocked "that we as a thriving organization, as a success company, a *Fortune* 100 company, should have people that were living like that among the ranks of our employees." Aetna was careful to ensure that the raises that they awarded

what's in it for me?

Think about people as jigsaw puzzles. Puzzles consist of various pieces that fit together in precise ways. And of course, no two puzzles are exactly alike. They have different numbers of pieces, the pieces are of different sizes and shapes, and they fit together in different ways. The same can be said of people, their behaviors, and the causes of those behaviors. Each of us is a whole picture, like a fully assembled jigsaw puzzle, but the puzzle pieces that define us and the way those pieces fit together are unique. Every person in an organization is fundamentally different from everyone else. To be successful, managers must recognize that these differences exist, attempt to understand them, and then see if they can harness them in ways that are beneficial to both the individuals themselves and the organization.

They also need to understand why people work. People obviously work for a wide variety of different reasons. Some people want money, others want a challenge. Some want prestige, some want security, and still others want power. What people in an organization want from work and how they think they can achieve it plays an instrumental role in determining their motivation to work. As we see in this chapter, motivation is vital to all organizations. Indeed, the difference between highly effective organizations and less effective ones often lies in the motivations of their members.

Successful managers usually have at least a fundamental understanding of what accounts for employee behavior and motivation in organizations. Thus, managers need to understand the nature of individual motivation, especially as it applies to work situations. By understanding the basic elements of this chapter, you'll be better able to (1) understand your own feelings toward your work from the perspective of an employee and (2) understand the feelings of others toward their work from the perspective of a manager or owner. To start developing your understanding, let's begin by describing the different forms of behaviors that employees exhibit at work. We'll then examine many of the ways that people differ from one another. Later in the chapter, we'll look at some important models and concepts of employee motivation, as well as some strategies and techniques used by organizations to improve employee motivation.

employees were enough to offset any loss of public assistance benefits, so that they truly ended up in a better financial position after the change.

Bertolini also believes that Aetna's shareholders, the owners of the company, are supportive of the change. "We positioned it with them on the economics first, but went to this very notion of 'this isn't fair.' We need to invest in our employees. We need to help restore the middle class, and that should be good for the economy as a whole. And so for us it is as much—probably, for me personally, more—a moral argument than it is a financial one."

Economists Justin Wolfers and Jan Zilinsky recently released a study of the impact of this type of pay increase in private-sector businesses in the United States. Wolfers and Zilinsky found research to support the conclusion that higher wages can improve worker productivity and performance. They cited one study that showed that more than half of the cost of a pay increase can be offset by increases in productivity and decreases in turnover-related costs. In addition, by offering higher wages, companies are able to recruit and hire better employees and decrease disciplinary issues. Famous economists such as Janet Yellen (current Chair of the Board of Governors of the Federal Reserve System), as far back as 1984, asserted that higher wages create the groundwork for employee productivity as a result of "reduced shirking by employees due to a higher cost of job loss; lower turnover; an improvement in the average quality of job applicants and improved morale." The benefits of higher wages also extend to quality and customer service. A number of recent studies found that employers reported improvements in both customer service and the quality of production. There are thousands of variables affecting a company's financial results, but for Aetna, indications are in line with the studies. Even though general and administrative costs increased over 2015 and 2016, revenues increased by a wider margin, increasing operating income by $500 million per year.

However, Bertolini also knows that corporate culture is perhaps an even more important factor in keeping employees and in helping them become more productive. Corporate culture goes beyond the formal mission, vision, and values statements. It's the informal way that people interact. It is implied, rather than expressly defined, and it often grows organically out of the individual behaviors of all of the members of the organization. Leaders can underestimate its power; in fact, many people say that culture trumps mission. It's no wonder then that companies that are concentrating on culture are seeing the biggest payoffs because they are putting their employees first. (After studying the content of this chapter, you should be able to answer the set of discussion questions found at the end of the chapter.)

OBJECTIVE 8-1
Identify

and discuss the basic forms of behaviors that employees exhibit in organizations.

Employee Behavior *the pattern of actions by the members of an organization that directly or indirectly influences the organization's effectiveness*

Forms of Employee Behavior

Employee behavior is the pattern of actions by the members of an organization that directly or indirectly influences the organization's effectiveness. Some employee behaviors, called *performance behaviors*, directly contribute to productivity and performance. Other behaviors, referred to as *organizational citizenship*, provide positive benefits to the organization but in more indirect ways. *Counterproductive behaviors* detract from performance and actually cost the organization. Let's look at each of these types of behavior in a bit more detail.

Performance Behaviors

Performance Behaviors *the total set of work-related behaviors that the organization expects employees to display*

Performance behaviors are the total set of work-related behaviors that the organization expects employees to display. Essentially, these are the behaviors directly targeted at performing a job. For some jobs, performance behaviors can be narrowly defined and easily measured. For example, an assembly-line worker who sits or stands by a moving conveyor and attaches parts to a product as it passes by has relatively few performance behaviors. He or she is expected to remain at the work-station for a predetermined number of hours and correctly attach the parts. Such performance can often be assessed quantitatively by counting the percentage of parts correctly attached. Similarly, sales representatives are expected to promote the firm's products and services, find new customers, and keep existing customers satisfied. Sales revenue and growth, then, are common performance indicators for sales jobs.

For some jobs, however, performance behaviors are more diverse and difficult to assess. For example, consider the case of a research-and-development scientist at Merck Pharmaceuticals. The scientist works in a lab trying to find new scientific breakthroughs that have commercial potential. The scientist must apply knowl-edge and experience gained from previous research. Intuition and creativity are also important. But even with all the scientist's abilities and effort, a new breakthrough may take months or even years to accomplish and validate and even longer to start generating revenue and profit.

Organizational Citizenship

Employees can also engage in positive behaviors that do not directly contribute to the bottom line. Such behaviors are often called **organizational citizenship**.[1] Organi-zational citizenship refers to the behavior of individuals who make a positive overall contribution to the organization. Consider, for example, an employee who does work that is highly acceptable in terms of both quantity and quality. However, she refuses to work overtime, won't help newcomers learn the ropes, and is generally unwill-ing to make any contribution beyond the strict performance requirements of her job. This person may be seen as a good performer, but she is not likely to be seen as a good organizational citizen. Another employee, though, may exhibit a comparable level of performance, but she always works late when the boss asks her to, she takes time to help newcomers learn their way around, and she is perceived as being help-ful and committed to the organization's success. She is likely to be seen as a better organizational citizen.

A number of factors, including individual, social, and organizational variables, play roles in promoting or minimizing organizational citizenship behaviors. For example, the personality, attitudes, and needs of the individual may cause some people to be more helpful than others. Similarly, the individual's work group may encourage or discourage such behaviors. And the organization itself, especially its corporate cul-ture, may or may not promote, recognize, and reward these types of behaviors.

Organizational Citizenship *positive behaviors that do not directly contrib-ute to the bottom line*

Organizational citizenship is the behavior of individuals who make a positive contribution to the organization above and beyond strict job performance. This manager, for example, is helping her col-leagues better understand important organizational processes and customer expectations.

Counterproductive Behaviors

Counterproductive Behaviors
behaviors that detract from organizational performance

Still other work-related behaviors are actually counterproductive. **Counterproductive behaviors** are those that detract from, rather than contribute to, organizational performance. **Absenteeism** occurs when an employee does not show up for work. Some absenteeism, of course, has a legitimate cause, such as illness, jury duty, or death or illness in the family. Other times, the employee may report a feigned legitimate cause that's actually just an excuse to stay home. When an employee is absent, legitimately or not, his or her work does not get done at all, a substitute must be hired to do it, or others in the organization must pick up the slack. In any event, though, absenteeism results in direct costs to a business.

Absenteeism *when an employee does not show up for work*

Turnover *annual percentage of an organization's workforce that leaves and must be replaced*

  Turnover occurs when people quit their jobs. An organization usually incurs costs in replacing workers who have quit, and loses productivity while seeking a replacement and training someone new, and so on. Turnover results from a number of factors, including aspects of the job, the organization, the individual, the labor market, and family influences. In general, a poor person-job fit (which we'll discuss later in the chapter) is also a likely cause of turnover. There are some employees whose turnover doesn't hurt the business, but when productive employees leave an organization, it does reflect counterproductive behavior.

managing in turbulent times

Not Just on the Playground

While we often associate the term *bullying* with childhood behaviors, there's considerable research to suggest that these behaviors can extend into the workplace. In fact, 28 percent of workers surveyed by CareerBuilder said that they had been bullied at work. The impact of bullying is real—19 percent of these workers left their jobs as a result of the bullying. In addition, workplace bullying has been associated with a number of counterproductive attitudes and behaviors such as disengagement, job dissatisfaction, and symptoms of anxiety, depression, burnout, and psychological distress. Rosemary Haefner, vice president of human resources at CareerBuilder, goes on to explain, "One of the most surprising takeaways from the study was that bullying impacts workers of all backgrounds regardless of race, education, income, and levels of authority within the organization. Many of the workers who have experienced this don't confront the bully or elect not to report the incidents, which can prolong a negative work experience that leads some to leave their jobs."

  You might wonder exactly what bullying looks like in the workplace. It can take many forms, but the most common include being falsely accused of mistakes, constant criticism, gossip, belittling comments, purposeful exclusion from projects or meetings, and even physical intimidation. Bullying is generally a long-term, persistent pattern of behavior intended to cause humiliation, offense, or distress. According to the survey, bullies tended to be older than the worker and were most commonly their boss or someone else above them in the organization. Interestingly, workers in governmental organizations reported being bullied nearly twice as often as those in corporate settings. Bullying appears to disproportionately affect racial and ethnic minorities, as well as the disabled. It appears that bullying is slightly

Paula Connelly/E+/Getty Images

less common when a worker has a higher level of education or higher pay, although workers at all levels were generally equally likely to have been bullied at some point in their careers.

  In light of these statistics, there's a very real chance that you may be the victim of a bully in the future. Of those surveyed, nearly half confronted their bully, but this was successful in remedying the situation only about half the time. Unfortunately, contacting the human resources department appears to be even less effective, with no action taken 58 percent of the time. Should you find yourself in this situation, it is important to document incidents of bullying and keep track of what happened and who was present. It may be a good idea to start by speaking directly with the bully—there are many times that a bully may not understand the effects of his or her actions. Finally, it's important to focus on the resolution, rather than dwell on what has already happened.[2]

Other forms of counterproductive behavior may be even more costly for an organization. *Theft and sabotage*, for example, result in direct financial costs for an organization. *Sexual and racial harassment* also cost an organization, both indirectly (by lowering morale, producing fear, and driving off valuable employees) and directly (through financial liability if the organization responds inappropriately). *Workplace aggression and violence* are also a concern in some organizations, as is *bullying*.

Individual Differences Among Employees

OBJECTIVE 8-2
Describe
the nature and importance of individual differences among employees.

What causes some employees to be more productive than others, to be better citizens than others, or to be more counterproductive than others? As we already noted, every individual is unique. **Individual differences** are personal attributes that vary from one person to another. Individual differences may be physical, psychological, and emotional. The individual differences that characterize a specific person make that person unique. As we see in the sections that follow, basic categories of individual differences include *personality* and *attitudes*.[3]

Individual Differences *personal attributes that vary from one person to another*

Personality at Work

Personality is the relatively stable set of psychological attributes that distinguish one person from another. In recent years, researchers have identified five fundamental traits that are especially relevant to organizations. These are commonly called the *"big five" personality traits*. *Emotional intelligence*, although not part of the "big five," also plays a large role in employee personality.

Personality *the relatively stable set of psychological attributes that distinguish one person from another*

The "Big Five" Personality Traits   The **"big five" personality traits** are shown in Figure 8.1 and can be summarized as follows.

"Big Five" Personality Traits *five fundamental personality traits especially relevant to organizations*

- *Agreeableness* is a person's ability to get along with others. A person with a *high* level of agreeableness is gentle, cooperative, forgiving, understanding, and

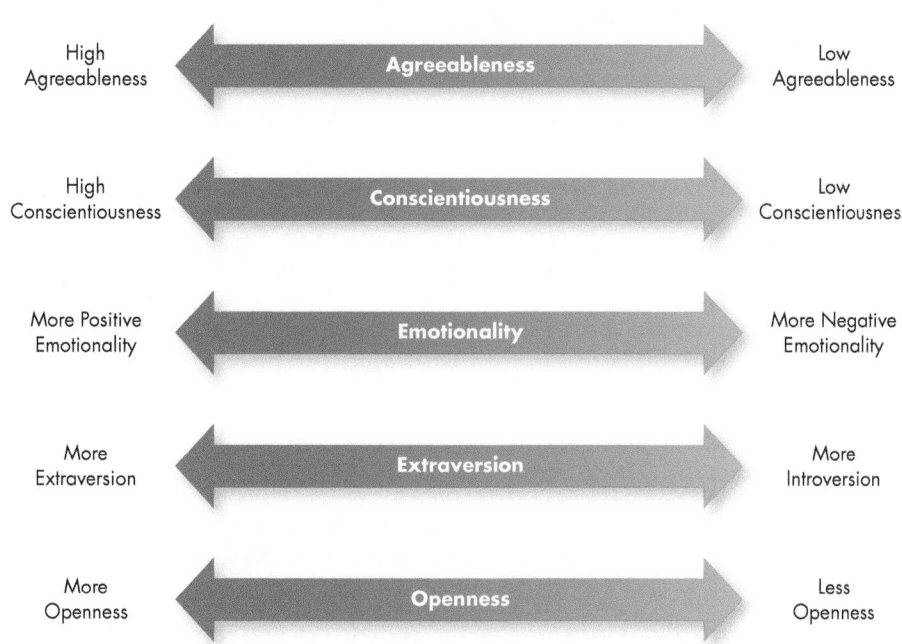

FIGURE 8.1 The "Big Five" Personality Traits

good-natured in dealings with others. A person with a *low* level of agreeableness is often irritable, short-tempered, uncooperative, and generally antagonistic toward other people. Highly agreeable people are better at developing good working relationships with coworkers, whereas less agreeable people are not likely to have particularly good working relationships.

- **Conscientiousness** in this context refers to the individual's persistence, dependability, and orderliness. *Highly conscientious* people tend to focus on relatively few tasks at one time; as a result, they are likely to be organized, systematic, careful, thorough, responsible, and self-disciplined. *Less conscientious* people tend to pursue a wider array of tasks; as a result, they are often more disorganized and irresponsible, as well as less thorough and self-disciplined. Highly conscientious people tend to be relatively higher performers in a variety of different jobs.

- **Emotionality** refers to the degree to which people tend to be positive or negative in their outlook and behaviors toward others. People with *positive* emotionality are relatively poised, calm, resilient, and secure; people with negative emotionality are more excitable, insecure, reactive, and subject to mood swings. People with positive emotionality might be expected to better handle job stress, pressure, and tension. Their stability might also lead them to be seen as being more reliable than their less-stable counterparts.

- **Extraversion** refers to a person's comfort level with relationships. *Extraverts* are sociable, talkative, assertive, and open to establishing new relationships. *Introverts* are much less sociable, talkative, and assertive, and more reluctant to begin new relationships. Extraverts tend to be higher overall job performers than introverts and are more likely to be attracted to jobs based on personal relationships, such as sales and marketing positions.

- **Openness** reflects how open or rigid a person is in terms of his or her beliefs. People with *high* levels of openness are curious and willing to listen to new ideas and to change their own ideas, beliefs, and attitudes in response to new information. People with *low* levels of openness tend to be less receptive to new ideas and less willing to change their minds. People with more openness are often better performers because of their flexibility and the likelihood that they will be better accepted by others in the organization.

The potential value of the "big five" framework is that it encompasses an integrated set of traits that appear to be valid predictors of certain behaviors in certain situations. Thus, managers who can both understand the framework and assess these traits in their employees are in a good position to understand how and why they behave as they do.

The Myers-Briggs Framework Another interesting approach to understanding personalities in organizations is the Myers-Briggs framework. This framework, based on the classical work of Carl Jung, differentiates people in terms of four general dimensions. These are defined as follows.

- **Extraversion (E) Versus Introversion (I).** Extraverts get their energy from being around other people, whereas introverts are worn out by others and need solitude to recharge their energy.

- **Sensing (S) Versus Intuition (N).** The sensing type prefers concrete things, whereas intuitives prefer abstract concepts.

- **Thinking (T) Versus Feeling (F).** Thinking individuals base their decisions more on logic and reason, whereas feeling individuals base their decisions more on feelings and emotions.

- **Judging (J) Versus Perceiving (P).** People who are the judging type enjoy completion or being finished, whereas perceiving types enjoy the process and open-ended situations.

To use this framework, people complete a questionnaire designed to measure their personality on each dimension. Higher or lower scores in each of the dimensions are used to classify people into one of 16 different personality categories. The **Myers-Briggs Type Indicator (MBTI)** is a popular questionnaire that some organizations use to assess personality types. It is among the most popular selection instruments used today, with as many as 2 million people taking it each year. Research suggests that the MBTI is a useful method for determining communication styles and interaction preferences. In terms of personality attributes, however, questions exist about both the validity and the stability of the MBTI.

Myers-Briggs Type Indicator (MBTI) *a popular questionnaire that some organizations use to assess personality types*

Emotional Intelligence The concept of emotional intelligence has been identified in recent years and also provides some interesting insights into personality. **Emotional intelligence, or emotional quotient (EQ)**, refers to the extent to which people are self-aware, can manage their emotions, can motivate themselves, express empathy for others, and possess social skills.[4] These various dimensions can be described as follows:

Emotional Intelligence (Emotional Quotient, EQ) *the extent to which people are self-aware, can manage their emotions, can motivate themselves, express empathy for others, and possess social skills*

- *Self-awareness* refers to a person's capacity for being aware of how they are feeling. In general, more self-awareness allows people to more effectively guide their own lives and behaviors.

- *Managing emotions* refers to a person's capacities to balance anxiety, fear, and anger so that they do not overly interfere with getting things accomplished.

- *Motivating oneself* is a person's ability to remain optimistic and to continue striving in the face of setbacks, barriers, and failure.

- *Empathy* is a person's ability to understand how others are feeling even without being explicitly told.

- *Social skills* help people get along with others and establish positive relationships.

Preliminary research suggests that people with high EQs may perform better than others, especially in jobs that require a high degree of interpersonal interaction (such as a public relations specialist) or that involve influencing or directing the work of others (such as a project manager). Moreover, EQ appears to be something that isn't biologically based but which can be developed.

Other Personality Traits at Work Besides these complex models of personality, several other specific personality traits are also likely to influence behavior in organizations. Among the most important are locus of control, self-efficacy, authoritarianism, Machiavellianism, self-esteem, and risk propensity.

Locus of control is the extent to which people believe that their behavior has a real effect on what happens to them.[5] Some people, for example, believe that if they work hard they will succeed. They may also believe that people who fail do so because they lack ability or motivation. People who believe that individuals are in control of their lives are said to have an internal locus of control. Other people think that fate, chance, luck, or other people's behavior determines what happens to them. For example, an employee who fails to get a promotion may attribute that failure to a politically motivated boss or just bad luck, rather than to his or her own lack of skills or poor performance record. People who think that forces beyond their control dictate what happens to them are said to have an external locus of control.

Locus of Control *the extent to which people believe that their behavior has a real effect on what happens to them*

Self-efficacy is a related but subtly different personality characteristic. A person's **self-efficacy** is that person's belief about his or her capabilities to perform a task. People with high self-efficacy believe that they can perform well on a specific task, whereas people with low self-efficacy tend to doubt their ability to perform a specific task. Coupled with the individual's personality, self-assessments of ability contribute to self-efficacy. Some people simply have more self-confidence than others. This belief in their ability to perform a task effectively results in their being more self-assured and better able to focus their attention on performance.[6]

Self-Efficacy *a person's belief about his or her capabilities to perform a task*

Authoritarianism *the extent to which a person believes that power and status differences are appropriate within hierarchical social systems such as organizations*

Another important personality characteristic is **authoritarianism**, the extent to which a person believes that power and status differences are appropriate within hierarchical social systems such as organizations.[7] For example, a person who is highly authoritarian may accept directives or orders from someone with more authority purely because the other person is "the boss." On the other hand, a person who is not highly authoritarian, although he or she may still carry out reasonable directives from the boss, is more likely to question things, express disagreement with the boss, and even refuse to carry out orders if they are for some reason objectionable. A highly authoritarian manager may be relatively autocratic and demanding, and highly authoritarian subordinates are more likely to accept this behavior from their leader. On the other hand, a less authoritarian manager may allow subordinates a bigger role in making decisions, and less authoritarian subordinates might respond more positively to this behavior.

Machiavellianism is another important personality trait. This concept is named after Niccolo Machiavelli, a sixteenth-century author. In his book *The Prince*, Machiavelli explained how the nobility could more easily gain and use power. The term **Machiavellianism** is now used to describe behavior directed at gaining power and controlling the behavior of others. Research suggests that the degree of Machiavellianism varies from person to person. More Machiavellian individuals tend to be rational and nonemotional, may be willing to lie to attain their personal goals, put little emphasis on loyalty and friendship, and enjoy manipulating others' behavior. Less Machiavellian individuals are more emotional, less willing to lie to succeed, value loyalty and friendship highly, and get little personal pleasure from manipulating others.

Machiavellianism *used to describe behavior directed at gaining power and controlling the behavior of others*

Self-esteem is the extent to which a person believes that he or she is a worthwhile and deserving individual. A person with high self-esteem is more likely to seek higher-status jobs, be more confident in his or her ability to achieve higher levels of performance, and derive greater intrinsic satisfaction from his or her accomplishments. In contrast, a person with less self-esteem may be more content to remain in a lower-level job, be less confident of his or her ability, and focus more on extrinsic rewards (extrinsic rewards are tangible and observable rewards such as a paycheck, job promotion, and so forth). Among the major personality dimensions, self-esteem is the one that has been most widely studied in other countries. Although more research is clearly needed, the published evidence suggests that self-esteem as a personality trait does indeed exist in a variety of countries and that its role in organizations is reasonably important across different cultures.

Self-Esteem *the extent to which a person believes that he or she is a worthwhile and deserving individual*

Risk propensity is the degree to which a person is willing to take chances and make risky decisions. A manager with a high-risk propensity, for example, might experiment with new ideas and gamble on new products. Such a manager might also lead the organization in new and different directions. This manager might be a catalyst for innovation or, if the risky decisions prove to be bad ones, might jeopardize the continued well-being of the organization. A manager with low risk propensity might lead an organization to stagnation and excessive conservatism or might help the organization successfully weather turbulent and unpredictable times by maintaining stability and calm. Thus, the potential consequences of a manager's risk propensity depend heavily on the organization's environment.

Risk Propensity *the degree to which a person is willing to take chances and make risky decisions*

Attitudes at Work

People's attitudes also affect their behavior in organizations. **Attitudes** reflect our beliefs and feelings about specific ideas, situations, or other people. Attitudes are important because they are the mechanism through which we express our feelings. An employee's comment that he feels underpaid reflects his feelings about his pay. Similarly, when a manager says that she likes the new advertising campaign, she is expressing her feelings about the organization's marketing efforts.

Attitudes *a person's beliefs and feelings about specific ideas, situations, or people*

How Attitudes Are Formed
Attitudes are formed by a variety of forces, including our personal values, our experiences, and our personalities. For example,

if we value honesty and integrity, we may form especially favorable attitudes toward a manager whom we believe to be honest and moral. Similarly, if we have had negative and unpleasant experiences with a particular coworker, we may form an unfavorable attitude toward that person. Any of the "big five" or individual personality traits may also influence our attitudes. Understanding the basic structure of an attitude helps us see how attitudes are formed and can be changed.

Attitude Structure Attitudes are usually viewed as stable dispositions to behave toward objects in a certain way. For any number of reasons, a person might decide that he or she does not like a particular political figure or a certain restaurant (a disposition). We would expect that person to express consistently negative opinions of the candidate or restaurant and to maintain the consistent, predictable intention of not voting for the political candidate or not eating at the restaurant. In this view, attitudes contain three components: (1) cognition, (2) affect, and (3) intention.

Cognition is the knowledge a person presumes to have about something. You may believe you like a class because the textbook is excellent, the class meets at your favorite time, the instructor is outstanding, and the workload is light. This "knowledge" may be true, partially true, or totally false. For example, you may intend to vote for a particular candidate because you think you know where the candidate stands on several issues. In reality, depending on the candidate's honesty and your understanding of his or her statements, the candidate's thinking on the issues may be exactly the same as yours, partly the same, or totally different. Cognitions are based on perceptions of truth and reality, and, as we note later, perceptions agree with reality to varying degrees.

Cognition the knowledge a person presumes to have about something

A person's **affect** is his or her feelings toward something. In many ways, affect is similar to emotion; it is something over which we have little or no conscious control. For example, most people react to words such as *love, hate, sex,* and *war* in a manner that reflects their feelings about what those words convey. Similarly, you may like one of your classes, dislike another, and be indifferent toward a third. If the class you dislike is an elective, you may not be particularly concerned about your participation or final grade. But if it is the first course in your chosen major, your affective reaction may cause you considerable anxiety.

Affect a person's feelings toward something

Intention guides a person's behavior. If you like your instructor, you may intend to take another class from him or her next semester. Intentions are not always translated into actual behavior, however. If the instructor's course next semester is scheduled for 8 A.M., you may decide that another instructor is just as good. Some attitudes, and their corresponding intentions, are much more central and significant to an individual than others. You may intend to do one thing (take a particular class) but later alter your intentions because of a more significant and central attitude (fondness for sleeping late).

Intention part of an attitude that guides a person's behavior

Cognitive Dissonance When two sets of cognitions or perceptions are contradictory or incongruent, a person experiences a level of conflict and anxiety called **cognitive dissonance**. Cognitive dissonance also occurs when people behave in a fashion that is inconsistent with their attitudes. For example, a person may realize that smoking and overeating are dangerous yet continue to do both. Because the attitudes and behaviors are inconsistent with each other, the person probably will experience a certain amount of tension and discomfort and may try to reduce these feelings by changing the attitude, altering the behavior, or perceptually distorting the circumstances. For example, the dissonance associated with overeating might be resolved by continually deciding to go on a diet "next week." Cognitive dissonance affects people in a variety of ways. We frequently encounter situations in which our attitudes conflict with each other or with our behaviors. Dissonance reduction is the way we deal with these feelings of discomfort and tension. In organizational settings, people contemplating leaving the organization may wonder why they continue to stay and work hard. As a result of this dissonance, they may conclude that the company is not so bad after all, that they have no immediate options elsewhere, or that they will leave "soon."

Cognitive Dissonance when two sets of cognitions or perceptions are contradictory or incongruent

Key Work-Related Attitudes People in an organization form attitudes about many different things. Employees are likely to have attitudes about their salary, their promotion possibilities, their boss, employee benefits, and so on. Especially important attitudes are *job satisfaction* and *organizational commitment*.

Job Satisfaction *degree of enjoyment that people derive from performing their jobs*

- **Job satisfaction** reflects the extent to which people have positive attitudes toward their jobs. (Some people use the word *morale* instead of job satisfaction.) A satisfied employee tends to be absent less often, to be a good organizational citizen, and to stay with the organization. Dissatisfied employees may be absent more often, may experience stress that disrupts coworkers, and may be continually looking for another job. Contrary to "common sense" and what a lot of managers believe, however, high levels of job satisfaction do not necessarily lead to higher levels of productivity.

Organizational Commitment *an individual's identification with the organization and its mission*

- **Organizational commitment**, sometimes called *job commitment*, reflects an individual's identification with the organization and its mission. A highly committed person will probably see himself or herself as a true member of the firm (for example, referring to the organization in personal terms, such as "we make high-quality products"), overlook minor sources of dissatisfaction, and see himself or herself remaining a member of the organization. A less committed person is more likely to see himself or herself as an outsider (e.g., referring to the organization in less personal terms, such as "they don't pay their employees very well"), to express more dissatisfaction about things, and to not see himself or herself as a long-term member of the organization.

There are a few critical things managers can do to promote satisfaction and commitment. For one thing, if the organization treats its employees fairly and provides reasonable rewards and job security, its employees are more likely to be satisfied and committed. Allowing employees to have a say in how things are done can also promote these attitudes. Designing jobs so that they are stimulating can enhance both satisfaction and commitment. Another key element is understanding and respecting what experts call *psychological contracts*, which we will discuss in the next section.

OBJECTIVE 8-3
Explain
the meaning and importance of psychological contracts and the person-job fit in the workplace.

Matching People and Jobs

Given the array of individual differences that exists across people and the many different forms of employee behaviors that can occur in organizations, it stands to reason that managers would like to have a good match between people and the jobs they are performing. Two key methods for helping to understand how this match can be better understood are *psychological contracts* and the *person-job fit*.

Psychological Contracts

Psychological Contract *set of expectations held by an employee concerning what he or she will contribute to an organization (referred to as contributions) and what the organization will in return provide the employee (referred to as inducements)*

A **psychological contract** is the overall set of expectations held by employees and the organization regarding what employees will contribute to the organization and what the organization will provide in return. Unlike a formal business contract, a psychological contract is not written on paper, nor are all of its terms explicitly negotiated.[8]

Figure 8.2 illustrates the essential nature of a psychological contract. The individual makes a variety of *contributions* to the organization, such as effort, ability, loyalty, skills, and time. These contributions satisfy their obligation under the contract. For example, Jill Henderson, a branch manager for Charles Schwab and Co., uses her knowledge of financial markets and investment opportunities to help her clients make profitable investments. Her MBA in finance, coupled with hard work and motivation, have led her to become one of the firm's most promising young managers. The firm believed she had these attributes when it hired her and expected that she would do well.

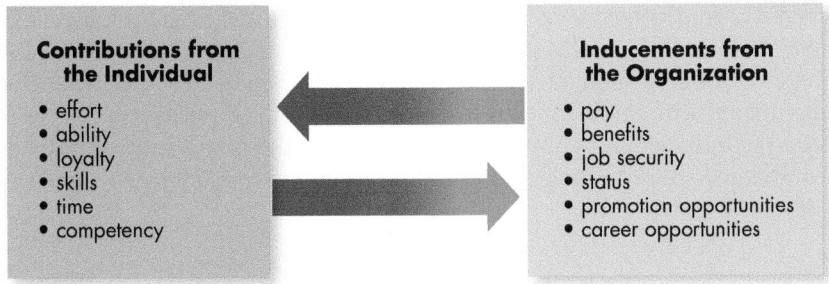

FIGURE 8.2 The Psychological Contract

In return for these contributions, the organization provides *inducements* to the individual. These inducements satisfy the organization's contract obligation. Some inducements, such as pay and career opportunities, are tangible rewards. Others, such as job security and status, are more intangible. Henderson started at Schwab at a competitive salary and has received a salary increase each of the six years she has been with the firm. She has also been promoted twice and expects another promotion in the near future.

In this instance, both Henderson and Schwab apparently perceive that the psychological contract is fair and equitable. Both will be satisfied with the relationship and will do what they can to continue it. Henderson is likely to continue to work hard and effectively, and Schwab is likely to continue to increase her salary and give her promotions. In other situations, however, things might not work out as well. If either party sees an inequity in the contract, that party may initiate a change. The employee might ask for a pay raise or promotion, put forth less effort, or look for a better job elsewhere. The organization can also initiate change by training the worker to improve his or her skills, transferring him or her to another job, or firing him or her.

All organizations face the basic challenge of managing psychological contracts. They want value from their employees, and they need to give employees the right inducements. For instance, underpaid employees may perform poorly or leave for better jobs elsewhere. Similarly, an employee may even occasionally start to steal from the company as a way to balance the psychological contract.

Person-job fit is an important consideration when hiring people to perform specific jobs. For instance, some people might thrive working in extreme weather conditions, performing risky jobs, or traveling most of the time. Other people, in contrast, would balk at any of these opportunities and instead only want to work under mild weather conditions, performing low-risk tasks, or never traveling. Consider, for example, the job of cleaning external windows on high-rise buildings like the person shown here. Some people can handle jobs like this easily while others might be terrified!

When an organization starts to downsize or impose cutbacks the process of managing psychological contracts may become more complicated. For example, many organizations used to offer at least reasonable assurances of job permanence as a fundamental inducement to employees. Now, however, job permanence is less likely, so alternative inducements may be needed. Among the new forms of inducements, some companies are providing additional training opportunities and increased flexibility in working schedules.

The Person-Job Fit

Person-Job Fit *the extent to which a person's contributions and the organization's inducements match one another*

The **person-job fit** refers to the extent to which a person's contributions and the organization's inducements match one another. A good person-job fit is one in which the employee's contributions match the inducements the organization offers. In theory, each employee has a specific set of needs that he or she wants fulfilled and a set of job-related behaviors and abilities to contribute. If the organization can take perfect advantage of those behaviors and abilities and exactly fulfill his or her needs, it will have achieved a perfect person-job fit. Good person-job fit, in turn, can result in higher performance and more positive attitudes. A poor person-job fit, though, can have just the opposite effects.

Basic Motivation Concepts and Theories

OBJECTIVE 8-4
Identify
and summarize the most important models and concepts of employee motivation.

Motivation *the set of forces that cause people to behave in certain ways*

Broadly defined, **motivation** is the set of forces that cause people to behave in certain ways. One worker may be motivated to work hard to produce as much as possible, whereas another may be motivated to do just enough to survive. Managers must understand these differences in behavior and the reasons for them.

Over the years, a steady progression of theories and studies has attempted to address these issues. In this section, we survey the major studies and theories of employee motivation. In particular, we focus on three approaches to human relations in the workplace that reflect a basic chronology of thinking in the area: (1) *classical theory* and *scientific management*, (2) *early behavioral theory*, and (3) *contemporary motivational theories*.

Classical Theory

Classical Theory of Motivation *theory holding that workers are motivated solely by money*

According to the **classical theory of motivation**, workers are motivated solely by money. In his 1911 book, *The Principles of Scientific Management*, industrial engineer Frederick Taylor proposed a way for both companies and workers to benefit from this widely accepted view of life in the workplace. If workers are motivated by money, Taylor reasoned, paying them more should prompt them to produce more. Meanwhile, the firm that analyzed jobs and found better ways to perform them would be able to produce goods more cheaply, make higher profits, and pay and motivate workers better than its competitors.

Taylor's approach was known as *scientific management*. His ideas captured the imagination of many managers in the early twentieth century. Soon, manufacturing plants across the United States were hiring experts to perform time-and-motion studies: Industrial engineering techniques were applied to each facet of a job to determine how to perform it most efficiently. These studies were the first scientific attempts to break down jobs into easily repeated components and to devise more efficient tools and machines for performing them.[9] Two of Taylor's colleagues, Frank and Lillian Gilbreth, wrote a popular book, *Cheaper by the Dozen*, explaining how they used scientific management to manage their large family. The book was later made into a movie.

Ariel Skelley/Blend Images/Alamy Stock Photo

Treating employees with respect and recognizing that they are valuable members of the organization can go a long way toward motivating employees to perform at their highest levels.

Early Behavioral Theory

In 1925, a group of Harvard researchers began a study at the Hawthorne Works of Western Electric outside Chicago. With an eye to increasing productivity, they wanted to examine the relationship between changes in the physical environment and worker output.

The results of the experiment were unexpected, even confusing. For example, increased lighting levels improved productivity. For some reason, however, so did lower lighting levels. Moreover, against all expectations, increased pay failed to increase productivity. Gradually, the researchers pieced together the puzzle. The explanation lay in the workers' response to the attention they were receiving. The researchers concluded that productivity rose in response to almost any management action that workers interpreted as special attention. This finding, known today as the **Hawthorne effect**, had a major influence on human relations theory, although in many cases it amounted simply to convincing managers that they should pay more attention to employees.

Hawthorne Effect *tendency for productivity to increase when workers believe they are receiving special attention from management*

Following the Hawthorne studies, managers and researchers alike focused more attention on the importance of good human relations in motivating employee performance. Stressing the factors that cause, focus, and sustain workers' behavior, most motivation theorists became concerned with the ways in which management thinks about and treats employees. The major motivation theories include the *human resources model*, the *hierarchy of needs model*, and *two-factor theory*.

Human Resources Model: Theories X and Y In one important book, behavioral scientist Douglas McGregor concluded that managers tended to have had radically different beliefs about how best to use the human resources employed by a firm. He classified these beliefs into sets of assumptions that he labeled "Theory X" and "Theory Y." The basic differences between these two theories are shown in Table 8.1.

table 8.1 Theory X and Theory Y

Theory X	Theory Y
People are lazy.	People are energetic.
People lack ambition and dislike responsibility.	People are ambitious and seek responsibility.
People are self-centered.	People can be selfless.
People resist change.	People want to contribute to business growth and change.
People are gullible and not bright.	People are intelligent.

Theory X *theory of motivation holding that people are naturally lazy and uncooperative*

Theory Y *theory of motivation holding that people are naturally energetic, growth-oriented, self-motivated, and interested in being productive*

Hierarchy of Human Needs Model *theory of motivation describing five levels of human needs and arguing that basic needs must be fulfilled before people work to satisfy higher-level needs*

Managers who subscribe to **Theory X** tend to believe that people are naturally lazy and uncooperative and must be either punished or rewarded to be made productive. Managers who are inclined to accept Theory Y tend to believe that people are naturally energetic, growth-oriented, self-motivated, and interested in being productive.

McGregor argued that **Theory Y** managers are more likely to have satisfied and motivated employees. Theory X and Y distinctions are somewhat simplistic and offer little concrete basis for action. Their value lies primarily in their ability to highlight and classify the behavior of managers in light of their attitudes toward employees.

Maslow's Hierarchy of Needs Model Psychologist Abraham Maslow's **hierarchy of human needs model** proposed that people have several different needs that they attempt to satisfy in their work. Maslow classified these needs into five basic types and suggested that they be arranged in the hierarchy of importance, as shown in Figure 8.3. According to Maslow, needs are hierarchical because lower-level needs must be met before a person will try to satisfy higher-level needs.

Once a set of needs has been satisfied, it ceases to motivate behavior. For example, if you feel secure in your job (that is, your security needs have been met), additional opportunities to achieve even more security, such as being assigned to a long-term project, will probably be less important to you than the chance to fulfill social or esteem needs, such as working with a mentor or becoming the member of an advisory board.

If, however, a lower-level need suddenly becomes unfulfilled, most people immediately refocus on that lower level. Suppose, for example, you are seeking to meet your self-esteem needs by working as a divisional manager at a major company. If you learn that your division and, consequently, your job may be eliminated, you might well find the promise of job security at a new firm as motivating as a promotion once would have been at your old company.

Two-Factor Theory After studying a group of accountants and engineers, psychologist Frederick Herzberg concluded that job satisfaction and dissatisfaction

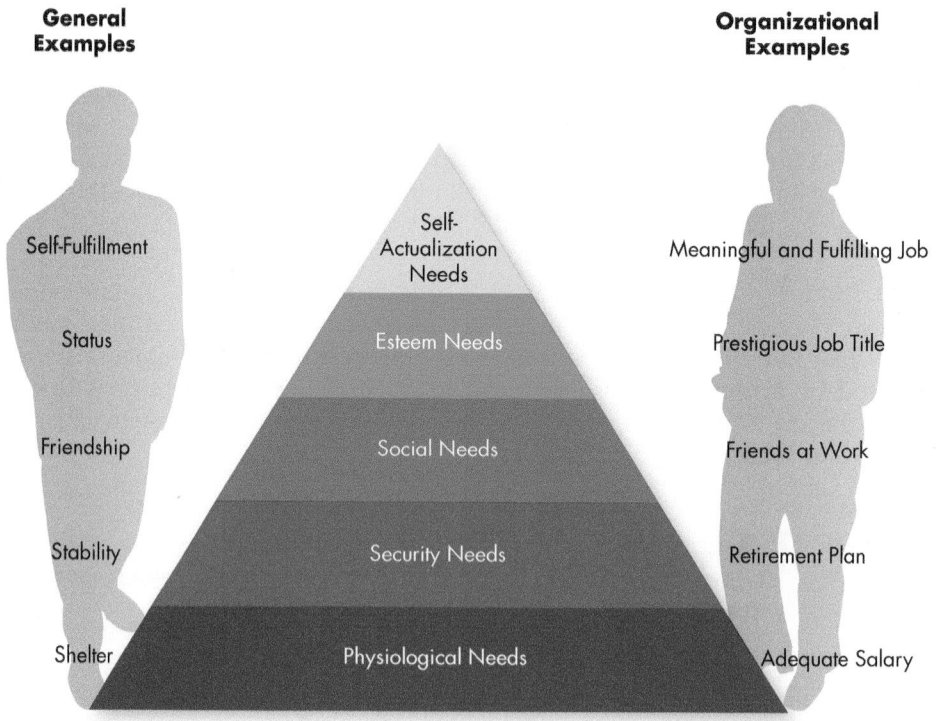

FIGURE 8.3 Maslow's Hierarchy of Human Needs
Source: Maslow, Abraham H.; Frager, Robert D.; Fadiman, James, *Motivation and Personality*, 3rd Ed., © 1987. Adapted and Electronically reproduced by permission of Pearson Education, Inc., Upper Saddle River, NJ.

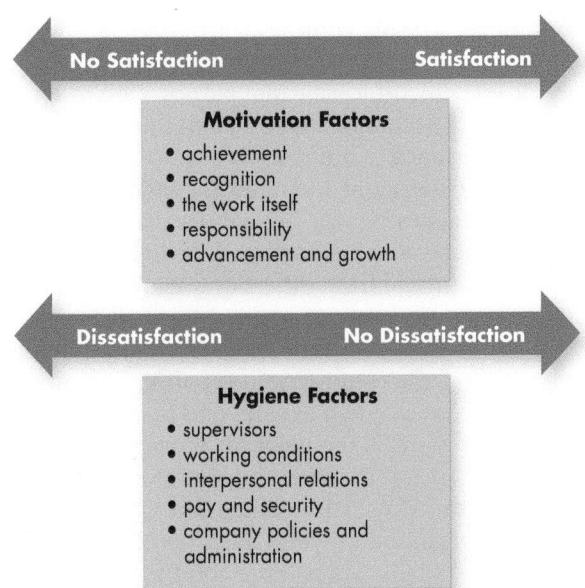

FIGURE 8.4 Two-Factor Theory of Motivation

depend on two factors: *hygiene factors*, such as working conditions, and *motivation factors*, such as recognition for a job well done.

According to Herzberg's **two-factor theory**, hygiene factors affect motivation and satisfaction only if they are absent or fail to meet expectations. For example, workers will be dissatisfied if they believe they have poor working conditions. If working conditions are improved, however, they will not necessarily become satisfied; they will simply not be dissatisfied. If workers receive no recognition for successful work, they may be neither dissatisfied nor satisfied. If recognition is provided, they will likely become more satisfied.

Figure 8.4 illustrates the two-factor theory. Note that motivation factors lie along a continuum from satisfaction to no satisfaction. Hygiene factors, in contrast, are likely to produce feelings that lie on a continuum from dissatisfaction to no dissatisfaction. Whereas motivation factors are directly related to the work that employees actually perform, hygiene factors refer to the environment in which they work.

This theory suggests that managers should follow a two-step approach to enhancing motivation. First, they must ensure that hygiene factors, such as working conditions or clearly stated policies, are acceptable. This practice will result in an absence of dissatisfaction. Then they must offer motivation factors, such as recognition or added responsibility, as a way to improve satisfaction and motivation.

Two-Factor Theory *theory of motivation holding that job satisfaction depends on two factors, hygiene and motivation*

Other Important Needs Each theory discussed so far describes interrelated sets of important individual needs within specific frameworks. McClelland's acquired needs theory hypothesized three other needs: the needs for achievement, affiliation, and power. Most people, however, are more familiar with the three needs as stand-along concepts rather than as part of the original theory itself.

The **need for achievement** arises from an individual's desire to accomplish a goal or task as effectively as possible.[10] Individuals who have a high need for achievement tend to set moderately difficult goals and to make moderately risky decisions. High-need achievers also want immediate, specific feedback on their performance. They want to know how well they did something as quickly after finishing it as possible. For this reason, high-need achievers frequently take jobs in sales, where they get almost immediate feedback from customers, and avoid jobs in areas such as research and development, where tangible progress is slower and feedback comes at longer intervals. Preoccupation with work is another characteristic of high-need achievers. They think about it on their way to the workplace, during lunch, and at home. They find it difficult to put their work aside, and they become frustrated when

Need for Achievement *an individual's desire to accomplish a goal or task as effectively as possible*

they must stop working on a partly completed project. Finally, high-need achievers tend to assume personal responsibility for getting things done. They often volunteer for extra duties and find it difficult to delegate part of a job to someone else. Accordingly, they derive a feeling of accomplishment when they have done more work than their peers without the assistance of others.

Need for Affiliation *an individual's desire for human companionship*

Many individuals also experience the **need for affiliation**—the need for human companionship.[11] Researchers recognize several ways that people with a high need for affiliation differ from those with a lower need. Individuals with a high need tend to want reassurance and approval from others and usually are genuinely concerned about others' feelings. They are likely to act and think as they believe others want them to, especially those with whom they strongly identify and desire friendship. As we might expect, people with a strong need for affiliation most often work in jobs with a lot of interpersonal contact, such as sales and teaching positions.

Need for Power *the desire to control one's environment, including financial, material, informational, and human resources*

A third major individual need is the **need for power**—the desire to control one's environment, including financial, material, informational, and human resources.[12] People vary greatly along this dimension. Some individuals spend much time and energy seeking power; others avoid power if at all possible. People with a high need for power can be successful managers if three conditions are met. First, they must seek power for the betterment of the organization rather than for their own interests. Second, they must have a fairly low need for affiliation because fulfilling a personal

entrepreneurship and new ventures

The Opportunity to Begin Again

At the heart of the definition of an entrepreneur is the willingness to take risks. An entrepreneur will risk his or her financial security and reputation in hopes of a significant reward. We are all too familiar with the rags to riches stories of those who struck it big, but we tend to forget that many entrepreneurs actually have a more humbling start. As Henry Ford once said, "Failure is only the opportunity to begin again more intelligently."

Sophia Amoruso started out selling vintage clothing on eBay and built a customer base around the cool, slightly gritty style that she dubbed "nasty girl." In 2014, Nasty Girl had opened a bricks-and-mortar store in Los Angeles and then another in 2015 in Santa Monica, and *Forbes* magazine predicted gross sales would exceed $300 million that year. In addition, the magazine put Amoruso on its list of America's richest self-made women, and the Council of Fashion Designers of America inducted her into its hall of fame. But growth can bring challenges as well as success.

In 2015, the company faced a series of lawsuits brought by women who had been laid off just before they took maternity leave, as well as a suit brought by an employee who had been laid off after a five-week leave due to kidney disease. Along with employee issues, the company was overextended with debt and overhead costs and had burned through the initial venture capital funds. Without a constant influx of dollars into the marketing budget, sales declined, and the once profitable company quickly became insolvent. By the end of 2016, Nasty Girl was in bankruptcy and Amoruso was out of a job.

There's a fair amount of research that documents the role of failure in entrepreneurial growth and success. Entrepreneurs

Robin Marchant/Getty Images

who experience failure may find themselves discouraged and lack efficacy if they are too focused on their role in the failure. On the other hand, if one is to learn from failure, a certain amount of analysis and introspection is essential. Indeed, in research published by Yamakawa, Peng, and Deeds, entrepreneurs are discouraged from focusing too much on the role of the external environment or luck and advised to take advantage of the opportunity to learn. Entrepreneurs must pick themselves up after failure, dust themselves off, and make wiser and more informed choices about their new venture.[13]

Recently, Amoruso has turned her notoriety into a new career. She's leveraging her experience into a message of strength and inspiration for women entrepreneurs. Who knows? Success may still be on the horizon for the original nasty girl.

Contemporary Motivation Theory

More complex and sophisticated models of employee behavior and motivation have been developed in recent years.[15] Two of the more interesting and useful ones are *expectancy theory* and *equity theory*.

Expectancy Theory **Expectancy theory** suggests that people are motivated to work toward rewards that they want *and* that they believe they have a reasonable chance—or expectancy—of obtaining. A reward that seems out of reach is not likely to be motivating even if it is intrinsically positive. Figure 8.5 illustrates expectancy theory in terms of issues that are likely to be considered by an individual employee.

Consider the case of an assistant department manager who learns that her firm needs to replace a retiring division manager three levels above her in the organization. Even though she might want the job, she does not apply because she doubts she will be selected. In this case, she considers the performance-reward issue: She believes that her performance will not get her the position because it would be such a large promotion. She also learns that the firm is looking for a production manager on the night shift. She thinks she could get this job but does not apply because she does not want to work nights (the rewards–personal goals issue). Finally, she learns of an opening one level higher—department manager—in her own division. She may well apply for this job because she both wants it and thinks that she has a good chance of getting it. In this case, her consideration of all the issues has led to an expectancy that she can reach a goal.

Expectancy theory helps explain why some people do not work as hard as they can when their salaries are based purely on seniority. Paying employees the same whether they work hard or just hard enough to get by removes the financial incentive for them to work harder. In other words, they ask themselves, "If I work harder, will I get a pay raise?" (the performance–reward issue) and conclude that the answer is "no." Similarly, if hard work will result in one or more undesirable outcomes, such as a transfer to another location or a promotion to a job that requires unpleasant travel (the rewards–personal goals issue), employees will not be motivated to work hard.

Equity Theory **Equity theory** focuses on social comparisons, people evaluating their treatment by the organization relative to the treatment of others. This approach suggests that people begin by thinking about their inputs (what they contribute to their jobs in terms of time, effort, education, experience) relative to their outputs (what they receive in return—salary, benefits, recognition, security). At this point, the comparison is similar to the psychological contract as discussed earlier. As viewed by equity theory, though, the result is a ratio of contribution to return. When they compare their own ratios with those of other employees, they ask whether their ratios are comparable to, greater than, or less than those of the people with whom they are comparing themselves. Depending on their assessments, they experience

Expectancy Theory theory of motivation holding that people are motivated to work toward rewards that they want and that they believe they have a reasonable chance of obtaining

Equity Theory theory of motivation holding that people evaluate their treatment by the organization relative to the treatment of others

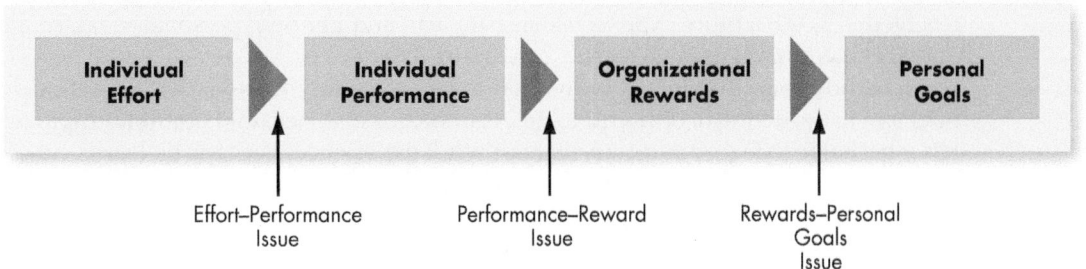

FIGURE 8.5 Expectancy Theory Model

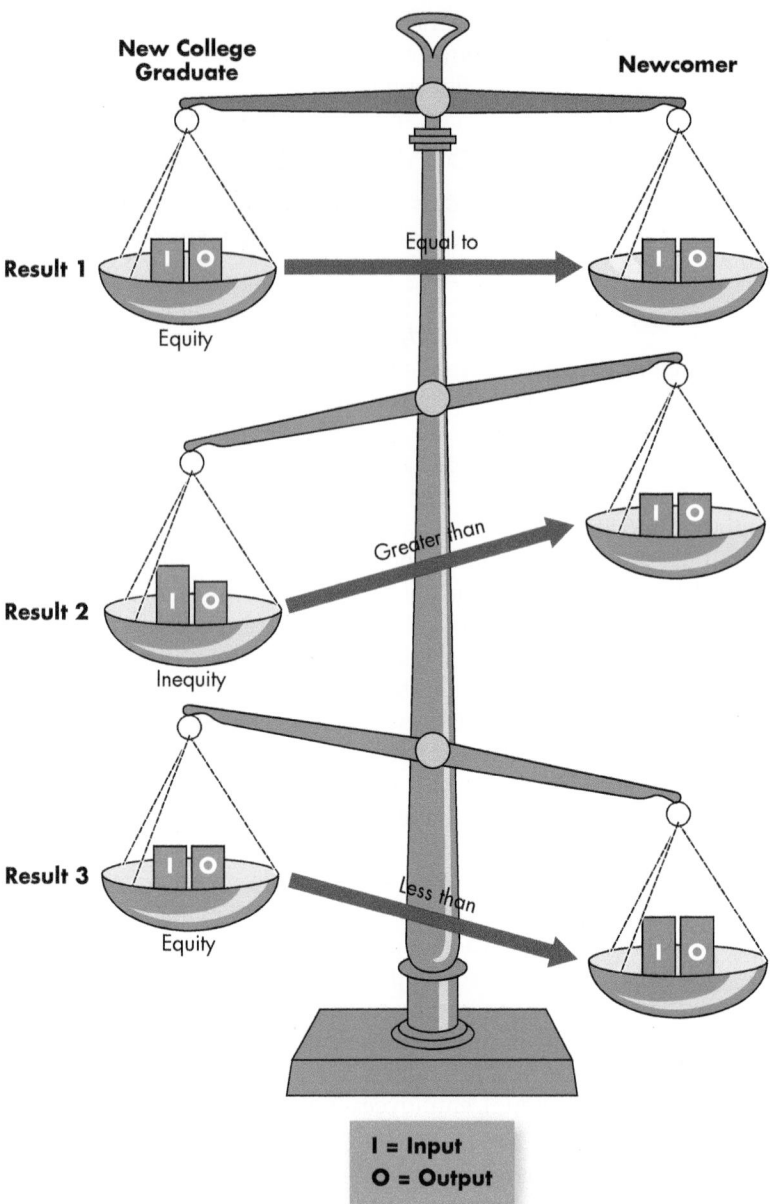

FIGURE 8.6 Equity Theory: Possible Assessments

feelings of equity or inequity. Figure 8.6 illustrates the three possible results of such an assessment.

For example, suppose a new college graduate gets a starting job at a large manufacturing firm. His starting salary is $65,000 a year, he gets an inexpensive company car, and he shares an assistant with another new employee. If he later learns that another new employee has received the same salary, car, and staff arrangement, he will feel equitably treated (result 1 in Figure 8.6). If the other newcomer, however, has received $75,000, a more expensive company car, and her own personal assistant, he may feel inequitably treated (result 2 in Figure 8.6).

Note, however, that for an individual to feel equitably treated, the two ratios do not have to be identical, only equitable. Assume, for instance, that our new employee has a bachelor's degree and two years of work experience. Perhaps he learns subsequently that the other new employee has an advanced degree and 10 years of experience. After first feeling inequity, the new employee may conclude that the person with whom he compared himself is actually contributing more to the organization (more education and experience). That employee is perhaps equitably entitled, therefore, to receive more in return (result 3 in Figure 8.6).

When people feel they are being inequitably treated, they may do various constructive and some not so constructive things to restore fairness. For example, they may speak to their boss about the perceived inequity. Or (less constructively) they may demand a raise, reduce their efforts, work shorter hours, or just complain to their coworkers. They may also rationalize ("management succumbed to pressure to promote a woman/Asian American"), find different people with whom to compare themselves, or leave their jobs.

Strategies and Techniques for Enhancing Motivation

OBJECTIVE 8-5
Describe
some of the strategies and techniques used by organizations to improve employee motivation.

Understanding what motivates workers is only one part of the manager's job. The other part is applying that knowledge. Experts have suggested—and many companies have implemented—a range of programs designed to make jobs more interesting and rewarding, to make the work environment more pleasant, and to motivate employees to work harder.

Reinforcement/Behavior Modification

Some managers try to influence workers' behavior through systematic rewards and punishments for specific behaviors. Such managers first try to define the specific behaviors that they want their employees to exhibit (working hard, being courteous to customers, stressing quality) and the specific behaviors they want to eliminate (wasting time, being rude to customers, ignoring quality). Then they try to shape employee behavior by linking positive reinforcement with desired behaviors and punishment with undesired behaviors.

Positive reinforcement is used when a company or manager provides a reward when employees exhibit desired behaviors, such as working hard, helping others, and so forth. When rewards are tied directly to performance, they serve as positive reinforcement. For example, paying large cash bonuses to salespeople who exceed quotas prompts them to work even harder during the next selling period. John Deere uses a reward system based on positive reinforcement. Among other things, the company gives its workers pay increases when they complete college courses and demonstrate mastery of new job skills.

Positive Reinforcement *reward that follows desired behaviors*

Punishment is designed to change behavior by presenting people with unpleasant consequences if they exhibit undesired behaviors. Employees who are repeatedly late for work, for example, may be suspended or have their pay docked. Similarly, when the National Football League or Major League Baseball fines or suspends players found guilty of substance abuse, the organization is seeking to change players' behavior by punishing them.

Punishment *unpleasant consequences of an undesirable behavior*

Social learning occurs when people observe the behaviors of others, recognize their consequences, and alter their own behavior as a result. A person can learn to do a new job by observing others or by watching videos. Or an employee may learn to avoid being late by seeing the boss chew out fellow workers. Social learning theory, then, suggests that individual behavior is determined by a person's cognitions and social environment. More specifically, people are presumed to learn behaviors and attitudes at least partly in response to what others expect of them.

Social Learning *learning that occurs when people observe the behaviors of others, recognize their consequences, and alter their own behavior as a result*

Using Goals to Motivate Behavior

Performance goals are also commonly used to direct and motivate behavior. The most frequent method for setting performance goals is called **management by objectives (MBO)**, which is a system of collaborative goal setting that extends from the top of an organization to the bottom. MBO involves managers and subordinates in setting goals and evaluating progress. After the program is started, the organization

Management by Objectives (MBO) *set of procedures involving both managers and subordinates in setting goals and evaluating progress*

finding a better way

More Than Just a Paycheck

Fortune magazine ranked Google as the best place to work in 2017 for the eighth time in 11 years, and for the sixth year in a row, citing perks like free gourmet food, haircuts, and laundry services. But the company also takes a more analytical approach to employee satisfaction and productivity, providing generous healthcare benefits, pay equity, and employee resource groups.[16]

Maybe more surprising are the number two and three spots on the list. Wegmans Food Markets ranked second based on the family-like environment. When asked about their mission, they responded: "We are a mission-driven, values-based, family company. Much more than a supermarket, we help people live healthier, better lives through food. Our caring, knowledgeable people provide incredible service and a warm welcoming atmosphere in our one-of-a-kind shopping experience across 90 locations." The company is privately held and based in Rochester, New York, with locations across the state and in nearby areas such as Maryland, Massachusetts, Pennsylvania, and Washington, DC, and although the mission statement indicates 90 locations, the number of U.S. sites was closer to 120 as of the end of 2016, with over 46,800 employees. Wegmans' focus on family includes flexible scheduling, wellness initiatives, employee assistance programs, scholarships, lactation rooms, and, of course, robust health care coverage. The company is looking for employees who are "values-matched" with the company's mission, namely, people who are passionate about food and great service. In addition, the company looks for employees who will stay involved in the process of continuous improvement through Open Door Days, Huddles, Focus Groups, and other means of open communication, including a Q&A blog with the senior vice president of operations.[17]

Surprisingly, the third-ranked company is a management-consulting firm that claims to be "the world's leading advisor on business strategy." Surprising because business consulting is usually a high-stress environment, but The Boston Consulting

Jim West/Alamy Stock Photo

Group (BCG) appears to be doing something right. Lauded for being the best place to work for working parents, Asian Americans, and recent graduates, and as honoring diversity, BCG offers an array of diversity and inclusion networks within the company, and holds diversity as a core value and a business success strategy. BCG employees receive generous health care coverage with no required employee contribution and incredibly low ($5) co-pays. In addition, the company provides a plethora of training opportunities, mentoring, on-the-job coaching, and other personal and professional development tools and opportunities. In addition, BCG offers an option to telecommute and 90 percent of the employees take advantage of flexible scheduling.[18]

Michael C. Bush, CEO of Great Place to Work, says of the *Fortune* list, "The new, largely uncharted business territory is about developing every ounce of human potential, so that organizations can reach their full potential. All companies—including the Best Workplaces—face the challenge of creating an outstanding culture for everyone, no matter who they are or what they do for the organization."[19]

specifies its overall goals and plans. Managers then collaborate with each of their subordinates to set individual goals that will best contribute to the organization's goals. Managers meet periodically to review progress toward individual goals, and then, usually on an annual basis, they evaluate goal achievement and use the results as a basis for starting the cycle over again.

According to many experts, motivational impact is the biggest advantage of MBO. When employees sit down with managers to set upcoming goals, they learn more about companywide objectives, feel that they are an important part of a team, and see how they can improve companywide performance by reaching their own goals. If an MBO system is used properly, employees should leave meetings not only with an understanding of the value of their contributions but also with fair rewards for their performances. They should also accept and be committed to the moderately difficult and specific goals they have helped set for themselves.[20]

Participative Management and Empowerment

When a firm uses **participative management and empowerment** it gives its employees a voice in how they do their jobs and in how the company is managed; they become empowered to take greater responsibility for their own performance. Not surprisingly, participation and empowerment often make employees feel more committed to organizational goals they have helped to shape.

Participation and empowerment can be used in large firms or small firms, both with managers and operating employees. For example, managers at General Electric who once needed higher-level approval for any expenditure more than $5,000 now have the autonomy to make their own expense decisions up to as much as $50,000. At Adam Hats Company, a small firm that makes men's dress, military, and cowboy hats, workers who previously had to report all product defects to supervisors now have the freedom to correct problems themselves or even return products to the workers who are responsible for them. Both Google and 3M allow employees to devote 10 percent of their work time to experimenting with new ideas apart from their normal job duties. And NetFlix allows its employees to take unlimited vacation time so long as they meet their work obligations and perform at a consistently high level.

Although some employees thrive in participative programs, such programs are not for everyone. People may be frustrated by responsibilities they are not equipped to handle. Moreover, participative programs may actually result in dissatisfied employees if workers see the invitation to participate as more symbolic than substantive or if managers never act on their suggestions or ideas. One key, say most experts, is to invite participation only to the extent that employees want to have input and only if participation will have real value for an organization.

Participative Management and Empowerment method of increasing job satisfaction by giving employees a voice in the management of their jobs and the company

Work Teams and Team Structures

We have already noted the increased use of teams in organizations. Yet another benefit that some companies get from using teams is increased motivation and enhanced job satisfaction among those employees working in teams. Although teams are often less effective in traditional and rigidly structured bureaucratic organizations, they frequently help smaller, more flexible organizations make decisions more quickly and effectively, enhance companywide communication, and encourage organizational members to feel more like a part of an organization. In turn, these attitudes usually lead to higher levels of both employee motivation and job satisfaction.[21]

But managers should remember that teams are not for everyone. Levi Strauss, for example, encountered major problems when it tried to use teams. Individual workers previously performed repetitive, highly specialized tasks, such as sewing zippers into jeans, and were paid according to the number of jobs they completed each day. In an attempt to boost productivity, company management reorganized everyone into teams of 10 to 35 workers and assigned tasks to the entire group. Each team member's pay was determined by the team's level of productivity. In practice, however, faster workers became resentful of slower workers because they reduced the group's total output. Slower workers, meanwhile, resented the pressure put on them by faster-working coworkers. As a result, motivation, satisfaction, and morale all dropped, and Levi Strauss eventually abandoned the teamwork plan altogether.

Job Enrichment and Job Redesign

Whereas goal setting and MBO programs and empowerment can work in a variety of settings, *job enrichment* and *job redesign* programs are generally used to increase satisfaction in jobs significantly lacking in motivational properties.

Job Enrichment Programs **Job enrichment** is intended to add one or more motivating factors to job activities. For example, job rotation programs expand growth opportunities by rotating employees through various positions in the same

Job Enrichment method of increasing job satisfaction by adding one or more motivating factors to job activities

firm. Workers gain not only new skills but also a broader overview of their work and their organization. Other programs focus on increasing responsibility or recognition. At United Airlines, for example, flight attendants now have more control over their own scheduling. The jobs of flight service managers were enriched when they were given more responsibility and authority for assigning tasks to flight crew members.

Job Redesign *method of increasing job satisfaction by designing a more satisfactory fit between workers and their jobs*

Job Redesign Programs **Job redesign** acknowledges that different people want different things from their jobs. By restructuring work to achieve a more satisfactory fit between workers and their jobs, job redesign can motivate individuals with strong needs for career growth or achievement. Job redesign is usually implemented in one of three ways: through *combining tasks*, *forming natural work groups*, or *establishing client relationships*.

COMBINING TASKS The job of combining tasks involves enlarging jobs and increasing their variety to make employees feel that their work is more meaningful. In turn, employees become more motivated. For example, the job done by a programmer who maintains computer systems might be redesigned to include some system design and system development work. While developing additional skills, the programmer also gets involved in the overall system development.

FORMING NATURAL WORK GROUPS People who do different jobs on the same projects are candidates for natural work groups. These groups are formed to help employees see the place and importance of their jobs in the total structure of the firm. They are valuable to management because the people working on a project are usually the most knowledgeable about it and the most capable problem solvers.

ESTABLISHING CLIENT RELATIONSHIPS Establishing client relationships means letting employees interact with customers. This approach increases job variety. It gives workers both a greater sense of control and more feedback about performance than they get when their jobs are not highly interactive. For example, software writers at Microsoft watch test users work with programs and discuss problems with them directly rather than receive feedback from third-party researchers.

Modified Work Schedules and Alternative Workplaces

As another way of increasing job satisfaction many companies also use *modified work schedules*, different approaches to working hours and the workweek. Two common forms of modified scheduling are *work-share programs* and *flextime programs*. A related approach is the alternative workplace strategy.[22]

Work-Share Programs At Steelcase, the country's largest maker of office furnishings, two talented people in the marketing division both wanted to work only part-time but the company needed a full-time employee. The solution: They now share a single full-time job. With each working 2.5 days a week, both got their wish and the job gets done—and done well. The practice, known as **work sharing (or job sharing)**, has "brought sanity back to our lives," according to at least one Steelcase employee.

Work Sharing (or Job Sharing) *method of increasing job satisfaction by allowing two or more people to share a single full-time job*

Job sharing usually benefits both employees and employers. Employees, for instance, tend to appreciate the organization's attention to their personal needs. At the same time, the company can reduce turnover and save on the cost of benefits. On the negative side, job-share employees generally receive fewer benefits than their full-time counterparts and may be the first to be laid off when cutbacks are necessary.

Flextime Programs *method of increasing job satisfaction by allowing workers to adjust work schedules on a daily or weekly basis*

Flextime Programs **Flextime programs** allow people to choose their working hours by adjusting a standard work schedule on a daily or weekly basis. That is, employees are allowed to choose when they work as long as they meet certain requirements. In some cases, businesses allow their employees almost total discretion over when they work as long as their jobs get done. At the other extreme, employees may be allowed some options but also have some required work hours. Steelcase, for instance, uses flextime for all of its employees but requires them to work certain core hours. This practice allows everyone to reach coworkers at a specified time of day. Employees can then decide whether to make up the rest of the standard eight-hour day by coming in and leaving early (by working 6:00 A.M. to 2:00 P.M. or 7:00 A.M. to 3:00 P.M.) or late (9:00 A.M. to 5:00 P.M. or 10:00 A.M. to 6:00 P.M.).

In another variation, companies may also allow employees to choose four, five, or six days on which to work each week. Some, for instance, may choose Monday through Thursday, others Tuesday through Friday. By working 10 hours in four workdays, employees still complete 40-hour weeks.

Alternative Workplaces A rapidly growing number of U.S. workers do a significant portion of their work via **telecommuting (or teleworking)**, performing some or all of a job away from traditional office settings. Working from a home office using high-speed Internet and a company intranet connection, telecommuters can keep abreast of everything going on at the office. Almost 80 percent of white collar and other professional workers in the United States performed at least some of their work from a location other than their office. Experts also estimate that more than 5 percent of those workers work exclusively from home or other remote settings.

Telecommuting (or teleworking) *form of flextime that allows people to perform some or all of a job away from standard office settings*

Advantages and Disadvantages of Modified Schedules and Alternative Workplaces Flextime gives employees more freedom in their professional and personal lives. It allows workers to plan around the work schedules of spouses and the school schedules of young children. Studies show that the increased sense of freedom and control reduces stress and improves individual productivity.

Companies also benefit in other ways. In urban areas, for example, such programs can reduce traffic congestion and similar problems that contribute to stress and lost work time. Furthermore, employers benefit from higher levels of commitment and job satisfaction. John Hancock Insurance, Shell Oil, and MetLife are among the major U.S. corporations that have successfully adopted some form of flextime.

Conversely, flextime sometimes complicates coordination because people are working different schedules. In addition, if workers are paid by the hour, flextime may make it difficult for employers to keep accurate records of when employees are actually working.

As for telecommuting, it may not be for everyone. For instance, some people may be attracted to telecommuting because they envision not having to shave or put on makeup and relish the idea of spending the day in their pajamas. But not everyone has the necessary self-discipline to work from home without supervision and others come to miss the social interaction of the workplace. One study has shown that even though telecommuters may be producing results, those with strong advancement ambitions may miss networking and "rubbing elbows" with management on a day-to-day basis.

Another obstacle to establishing a telecommuting program is convincing management that it can be beneficial for all involved. Telecommuters may have to fight the perception from both bosses and coworkers that if they are not being supervised, they are not working. Managers, admits one experienced consultant, "usually have to be dragged kicking and screaming into this. They always ask 'How can I tell if someone is working when I can't see them?'" By the same token, he adds, "that's based on the erroneous assumption that if you can see them, they are working." Most experts agree that re-education and constant communication are requirements of a successful telecommuting arrangement. Both managers and employees must determine expectations in advance.

As we have illustrated in this chapter, employee behavior and motivation are important concepts for managers to understand. They are also complex processes that require careful consideration by managers. For example, a clumsy attempt to motivate employees to work harder without fully considering all factors can actually have just the opposite effect. But managers who do take the time to understand the people with whom they work can better appreciate their efforts. Another important factor that affects employee behavior is *leadership*, the subject of our next chapter.

summary of learning objectives

OBJECTIVE 8-1

Identify and discuss the basic forms of behaviors that employees exhibit in organizations. (pp. 246–249)

Employee behavior is the pattern of actions by the members of an organization that directly or indirectly influences the organization's effectiveness. *Performance behaviors* are the total set of work-related behaviors that the organization expects employees to display. They directly contribute to productivity and performance. *Organizational citizenship*, on the other hand, refers to the behavior of individuals who make a positive overall contribution to the organization, although not directly contributing to the bottom line. A number of factors, including individual and organizational variables, play roles in promoting or minimizing organizational citizenship behaviors. *Counterproductive behaviors* are those that detract from, rather than contribute to, organizational performance. Counterproductive behaviors include absenteeism, turnover, theft and sabotage, sexual and racial harassment, and workplace aggression and violence.

OBJECTIVE 8-2

Describe the nature and importance of individual differences among employees. (pp. 249–254)

Individual differences are personal attributes that vary from one person to another, such as personality and attitudes. *Personality* is the relatively stable set of psychological attributes that distinguish one person from another. The *"big five" personality traits* are *agreeableness, conscientiousness, emotionality, extraversion,* and *openness. Agreeableness* is a person's ability to get along with others. *Conscientiousness,* another of the "big five" traits, refers to the individual's persistence, dependableness, and orderliness. *Emotionality* refers to the degree to which people tend to be positive or negative in their outlook and behaviors toward others. *Extraversion* refers to a person's comfort level with relationships. Extraverts are sociable, talkative, assertive, and open to new relationships and tend to be higher performers. Finally, *openness* is how open or rigid a person is in terms of his or her beliefs. People with a high level of openness are curious and willing to listen to new ideas and are, therefore, often higher performers. The potential value of this framework is that it encompasses an integrated set of traits that appear to be valid predictors of certain behaviors in certain situations. Thus, managers who can both understand the framework and assess these traits in their employees are in a good position to understand how and why they behave as they do.

The Myers-Briggs framework differentiates people in terms of four general dimensions: sensing, intuiting, judging, and perceiving. Higher and lower positions in each of the dimensions are used to classify people into one of 16 different personality categories. Research suggests that the Myers-Briggs Type Indicator is a useful method for determining communication styles and interaction preferences.

Emotional intelligence, or *emotional quotient (EQ),* refers to the extent to which people are self-aware, can manage their emotions, can motivate themselves, can express empathy for others, and possess social skills. Preliminary research suggests that people with high EQs perform better than others. Just as important, it appears that emotional intelligence is not biologically based but can be learned.

Other important personality traits are locus of control, self-efficacy, authoritarianism, Machiavellianism, self-esteem, and risk propensity. *Locus of control* is the extent to which people believe that their behavior has a real effect on what happens to them. People with an internal locus of control believe that they will succeed if they work hard, whereas those with an external locus of control believe that fate, chance, luck, or the behavior of others determines their own success. A similar concept is *self-efficacy.* A person's self-efficacy is their belief about their ability to perform a task. *Authoritarianism* is the extent to which a person believes that power and status differences are acceptable within an organization. A person who is highly authoritarian is more likely to accept direction and orders from a supervisor. *Machiavellianism* is a personality trait related to an individual's desire to gain power and control the behavior of others. *Self-esteem* is a personality trait that refers to the extent to which a person believes that he or she is worthwhile and deserving. Individuals with high self-esteem are more likely to seek higher-status jobs and are more confident in their performance. Finally, *risk propensity* refers to the degree to which a person is willing to take chances and make risky decisions. This characteristic can be a major influence on a manager's decision-making behavior.

Attitudes reflect our beliefs and feelings about specific ideas, situations, or other people. Attitudes are important because they are the mechanism through which we express our feelings. Attitudes are formed by a variety of forces, including our personal values, our experiences, and our personalities. Attitudes are usually viewed as stable dispositions to behave toward objects in a certain way and contain three components: cognition, affect, and intention. *Cognition* is the knowledge a person presumes to have about something. A person's *affect* is his or her feelings toward something, and *intention* guides a person's behavior. When two sets of cognitions or perceptions are contradictory or incongruent, a person experiences a level of conflict and anxiety called *cognitive dissonance*. Especially important work-related attitudes are *job satisfaction* and *organizational commitment*. Job satisfaction, also known as morale, is the extent to which people have positive attitudes toward their jobs. Organizational commitment, in contrast, reflects an individual's identification with the organization and its mission.

OBJECTIVE 8-3

Explain the meaning and importance of psychological contracts and the person-job fit in the workplace. (pp. 254–256)

A *psychological contract* is the overall set of expectations held by employees and the organization regarding what employees will contribute to the organization and what the organization will provide in return. An individual makes a variety of contributions to the organization, such as effort, ability, loyalty, skills, and time. In return, the organization provides inducements such as pay, career opportunities, job security, and status. All organizations must manage psychological contracts, providing the right inducements to retain employees.

A good *person-job fit* is achieved when the employee's contributions match the inducements the organization offers. Having a good match between people and their jobs can help enhance performance, job satisfaction, and motivation.

OBJECTIVE 8-4

Identify and summarize the most important models and concepts of employee motivation. (pp. 256–263)

Motivation is the set of forces that cause people to behave in certain ways. Early approaches to motivation assumed that workers are motivated solely by money. Managers employed this theory through *scientific management* by paying workers for productivity and finding more efficient ways of getting things done. However, the results of a study at Western Electric revealed that worker productivity improves in response to special attention, a phenomenon known as the *Hawthorne effect*.

As a result, researchers focused more on the effect of human relations on employee performance. Abraham Maslow's *hierarchy of human needs* model holds that people at work try to satisfy one or more of five different needs: physiological, security, social, esteem, and self-actualization. According to this theory, people are motivated by their lowest level of unsatisfied need.

Frederick Herzberg's *two-factor theory* argues that satisfaction and dissatisfaction depend on *hygiene factors*, such as working conditions, and *motivation factors*, such as recognition for a job well done. Herzberg suggests that the absence of hygiene factors causes dissatisfaction, but the presence of these same factors does not cause motivation. Employees are motivated by the presence of one or more motivation factors.

McClelland's acquired needs theory hypothesized that workers may have three types of needs: the needs for achievement, affiliation, and power. These needs are shaped over time and influence behavior. Those with high achievement needs are motivated by challenging tasks, whereas those with high affiliation needs desire to develop personal connections with other workers. Employees with high power needs have a desire to control their environment.

Douglas McGregor proposed the human resources model. He described two types of managers. Theory X managers believe that workers are naturally lazy and unmotivated and Theory Y managers believe that people are naturally self-motivated and interested in being productive.

Expectancy theory suggests that people are motivated to work toward rewards that they have a reasonable expectancy of obtaining. *Equity theory* focuses on social comparisons—people evaluating their treatment by the organization relative to its treatment of others.

OBJECTIVE 8-5

Describe some of the strategies and techniques used by organizations to improve employee motivation. (pp. 263–267)

There are several major strategies and techniques often used to make jobs more interesting and rewarding. *Positive reinforcement* is used when a company or manager provides a reward when employees exhibit desired behaviors, whereas *punishment* is designed to change behavior by presenting employees with unpleasant consequences if they exhibit undesired behaviors. *Social learning* occurs when people observe the behaviors of others and recognize their consequences, altering their own behavior as a result.

Management by objectives (MBO) is a system of collaborative goal setting that extends from the top of an organization to the bottom. Managers periodically meet with subordinates to review progress toward goals, increasing satisfaction and commitment. In *participative management and empowerment*, employees are given a voice in how they do their jobs and in how the company is managed. Participative management tends to increase employee commitment to organizational goals.

Using *teams* is another strategy to increase motivation. Job enrichment and job redesign are generally used to increase satisfaction in jobs significantly lacking motivating factors. *Job enrichment* adds motivating factors to job activities. *Job redesign* is a method of increasing job satisfaction by designing a more satisfactory fit between workers and their jobs through combining tasks, forming natural workgroups, or establishing client relationships. Some companies also use *modified work schedules*—different approaches to working hours and the workweek. Common options include *work sharing (job sharing), flextime programs*, and *telecommuting*.

key terms

absenteeism (p. 247)
affect (p. 253)
attitudes (p. 252)
authoritarianism (p. 252)
"big five" personality traits (p. 249)
classical theory of motivation (p. 256)
cognition (p. 253)
cognitive dissonance (p. 253)
counterproductive behaviors (p. 248)
emotional intelligence (emotional quotient, EQ) (p. 251)
employee behavior (p. 246)
equity theory (p. 261)
expectancy theory (p. 261)
flextime programs (p. 266)
Hawthorne effect (p. 257)
hierarchy of human needs model (p. 258)

individual differences (p. 249)
intention (p. 253)
job enrichment (p. 265)
job redesign (p. 266)
job satisfaction (p. 254)
locus of control (p. 251)
Machiavellianism (p. 252)
management by objectives (MBO) (p. 263)
motivation (p. 256)
Myers-Briggs Type Indicator (MBTI) (p. 251)
need for achievement (p. 259)
need for affiliation (p. 260)
need for power (p. 260)
organizational citizenship (p. 247)
organizational commitment (p. 254)

participative management and empowerment (p. 265)
performance behaviors (p. 256)
personality (p. 249)
person-job fit (p. 256)
positive reinforcement (p. 263)
psychological contract (p. 254)
punishment (p. 263)
risk propensity (p. 252)
self-efficacy (p. 251)
self-esteem (p. 252)
social learning (p. 263)
telecommuting (p. 267)
Theory X (p. 258)
Theory Y (p. 258)
turnover (p. 248)
two-factor theory (p. 259)
work sharing (or job sharing) (p. 266)

MyLab Intro to Business

To complete the problems with the ✪, go to EOC Discussion Questions in the MyLab.

questions & exercises

QUESTIONS FOR REVIEW

8-1. Describe the "big five" personality traits and how they contribute to employee performance.

8-2. What are the three structural components of an attitude? Be sure to describe each.

⭐ **8-3.** Describe several strategies and techniques for enhancing employee motivation and give examples of each.

8-4. Make a list of the pros and cons of participative management.

QUESTIONS FOR ANALYSIS

⭐ **8-5.** What is a psychological contract? Describe the psychological contract you currently have or have had in the past with an employer, or describe the psychological contract that you have with the instructor in this class.

⭐ **8-6.** Do you think that most people are relatively satisfied or dissatisfied with their work? What factors do you think most contribute to satisfaction or dissatisfaction?

8-7. Describe your most recent job in terms of your contributions and the organization's inducements.

8-8. What would you tell a worker performing a simple and routine job who wants more challenge and enjoyment from work?

APPLICATION EXERCISES

8-9. Assume you are about to start your own business. What would you do from the beginning to ensure that your employees will be satisfied and motivated?

8-10. Ask an employer what they believe motivates their employees. Identify one or more theories of motivation that seem consistent with this manager's approach.

building a business: continuing team exercise

Assignment

Meet with your team members and discuss your new business venture within the context of this chapter. Develop specific responses to the following:

8-11. Thinking about your new business venture, choose two dramatically different positions in the company and define performance behaviors for each position. What counterproductive behaviors would be most detrimental to your business?

8-12. If you were able to measure the emotional intelligence of prospective employees, which dimension or dimensions will be most important to you?

8-13. There are many theories of motivation. If you believe that Maslow's needs hierarchy best explains motivation in the workplace, how will you motivate your employees to work hard?

8-14. Another popular theory of motivation is Herzberg's two-factor theory. How could you apply this theory to your new business venture?

8-15. In your new company, will employees be able to work from home or work flexible hours? Why, or why not?

team exercise

TOO MUCH OF A GOOD THING

The Situation

For years, working for George Uhe, a small chemicals broker in Paramus, New Jersey, made employees feel as if they were members of a big family. Unfortunately, this family was going broke because too few "members" were working hard enough to make money for it. Employees were happy, comfortable, complacent—and lazy.

With sales dropping in the pharmaceutical and specialty-chemicals division, Uhe brought in management consultants to analyze the situation and to make recommendations. The outsiders quickly identified a motivational problem affecting the sales force: Sales representatives were paid a handsome salary and received automatic, year-end bonuses regardless of performance. They were also treated to bagels every Friday and regular group birthday lunches that cost as much as $200. Employees felt satisfied but had little incentive to work hard. Eager to return to profitability, Uhe's owners waited to hear the consultants' recommendations.

Method

STEP 1

In groups of four, step into the role of Uhe's management consultants. Start by analyzing your client's workforce-motivation problems from the following perspectives and then develop a set of recommendations.

8-16. *Job satisfaction and morale.* As part of a 77-year-old, family-owned business, Uhe employees were happy and loyal, in part because they were treated so well. Can high morale have a downside? How can it breed stagnation, and what can managers do to prevent stagnation from taking hold?

8-17. *Theory X versus Theory Y.* Although the behavior of these workers seems to make a case for Theory X, why is it difficult to draw this conclusion about a company that focuses more on satisfaction than on sales and profits?

8-18. *Two-factor theory.* Analyze the various ways in which improving such motivational factors as recognition, added responsibility, advancement, and growth might reduce the importance of hygiene factors, including pay and security.

8-19. *Expectancy theory.* Analyze the effect on productivity of redesigning the company's sales force compensation structure—namely, by paying lower base salaries while offering greater earnings potential through a sales-based incentive system. Why would linking performance with increased pay that is achievable through hard work motivate employees? Why would the threat of a job loss also motivate greater effort?

8-20. What is your group's most important recommendation? Why do you think it is likely to succeed?

exercising your ethics

TOO MUCH OF A GOOD THING

The Situation

Longines Corporation is a financial services company located in a large urban area. Because of omnipresent traffic issues, Longines has implemented a number of strategies to help employees avoid the heaviest traffic times. For instance, they have implemented alternative work schedules, such as a four-day workweek and flextime. Additionally, many employees are able to telecommute and work from home.

Longines's CEO realizes that the company's biggest asset is its loyal and talented workforce. They have had a low level of turnover because of excellent working conditions and a collaborative work environment. Despite the popularity of flextime, four-day workweeks, and telecommuting, the CEO and board are becoming concerned that these popular programs are actually hurting the company. The CEO has announced that these programs will be discontinued in three months and employees are upset.

The Dilemma

You are the human resource manager for Longines and the CEO has come to you for advice. She understands that her decision is unpopular, but she believes that it is the right one. In recent years, it has become increasingly difficult to organize meetings with employees working from home and on alternate work schedules. The CEO believes that this has impaired the ability of Longines to respond to changes in the market and to solve complex problems. She is asking you to take a strong stance in support of this new plan. However, despite the CEO's concerns, you believe that these alternative work schedules and telecommuting options are actually positive elements. You've had personal experience with this, as you have been able to manage your work and home life because your wife is able to telecommute for her job four days per week. A number of trusted employees have come to you and suggested that this change is a fundamental change in their relationship with the company.

QUESTIONS TO ADDRESS

8-21. What are the ethical issues in this case?

8-22. What do you think most managers would do in this situation?

8-23. What would you do?

cases

A LIVING WAGE

Continued from page 246

At the beginning of this chapter you read about Aetna's decision to increase the pay of its lowest paid employees. Using the information presented in this chapter you should now be able to answer these questions.

QUESTIONS FOR DISCUSSION

8-24. Do you think that higher pay caused higher productivity and lower turnover for Aetna? What leads you to this conclusion?

8-25. What factors motivate you personally?

8-26. Explain Aetna's decision in light of the classical theory of motivation.

8-27. How could Maslow's hierarchy of needs help to explain the relationship between pay and productivity?

8-28. Use equity theory, expectancy theory, or two-factor theory to explain Aetna's decision.

8-29. Do you believe that companies have a social responsibility to pay higher wages? Why, or why not?

SEARCHING FOR A GREAT PLACE TO WORK

BuzzFeed videos often depict a fun, exciting, creative workplace. But how do you assess if that is really true, and how do you assess whether or not you would be a good fit for the company? How do you assess whether or not the company is a good fit for you?

Traditionally, prospective employees would call someone who worked there, or would talk to someone within their social network, hoping for some firsthand knowledge about the company. Job seekers might also reference news and magazine articles, annual reports, employment agencies, and even other companies. The demand for information has given rise to websites such as Glassdoor.com, a website where millions of employees and former employees have anonymously reviewed companies and their management.

BuzzFeed may portray a great company image on their website and videos, but in 2016 they only rated 3.1 out of 5 stars on Glassdoor, based on 128 reviews.[23]

There are other employment related sites as well, such as LinkedIn and Monster, but Glassdoor touts itself as the only employee-generated database. Both LinkedIn and Glassdoor interact with the user's social network to connect job seekers with past and present employees of the prospective company. And social media itself is playing a bigger and bigger part in both the recruiting process for companies and in uncovering and bringing to light the sometimes secret cultures that underlie the public image of an organization. For instance, Susan Fowler wrote an expose on her blog in January of 2017 describing firsthand her "strange, fascinating and slightly horrifying" experience of her year working at Uber, which was then shared and amplified on Twitter, Facebook, and other social media platforms.

In response, Uber CEO Travis Kalanick and the chief human resource officer Liane Hornsey both issued public apologies, the company brought in former attorney general Eric Holder to conduct an internal investigation, and board member Arianna Huffington said she would "hold the leadership team's feet to the fire."[24] It's not clear yet how much influence these heavy hitters will have on the Uber corporate culture, but it is clear that social media is changing the way that prospective employees are able to pry into the inner workings of today's employers.

QUESTIONS FOR DISCUSSION

8-30. What criteria do you have for a great place to work?

8-31. Describe your ideal job or career and list the performance behaviors that you think would make you successful.

8-32. Using Herzberg's two-factor theory, determine which factor is more important to you and describe how you would assess a potential employment situation for those factors.

Writing Assignments

8-33. Although each individual's personality is unique, many personality traits can be summarized in five encompassing traits. Which of the "Big Five" personality traits are more important for first-line, middle, and top managers? Support your answer. How might each of the "Big Five" personality traits affect employee attitudes, such as job satisfaction or organizational commitment, at work?

8-34. Based on your experiences at school and at work, what motivates you the most? What factors de-motivate you? Why do you think that is? Also, describe your ideal work environment. Remember to include things like hours, benefits, locations, organizational structure, culture, and leadership style.

endnotes

[1] Dennis W. Organ, Philip M. Podsakoff, and Nathan P. Podsakoff, "Expanding the Criterion Domain to Include Organizational Citizenship Behavior: Implications for Employee Selection," in Sheldon Zedeck, (Ed.), *Handbook of Industrial and Organizational Psychology* (American Psychological Association: Washington, D.C., 2010).

[2] "Dealing with Workplace Bullying," Teller Vision no. 1453: 4-5. Business Source Premier, EBSCOhost (accessed February 1, 2017). "Dealing with Workplace Bullying," *Teller Vision* no. 1453: 4-5. Business Source Premier, EBSCOhost (February 1, 2017). Trépanier, Sarah-Geneviève, Claude Fernet, and Stéphanie Austin. 2015. "A Longitudinal Investigation of Workplace Bullying, Basic Need Satisfaction, and Employee Functioning." *Journal Of Occupational Health Psychology* 20, no. 1: 105–116. Business Source Premier, EBSCOhost (accessed February 1, 2017).

[3] Oleksandr S. Chernyshenko, Stephen Stark, and Fritz Drasgow, "Individual Differences: Their Measurement and Validity," in Sheldon Zedeck, (Ed.), *Handbook of Industrial and Organizational Psychology* (American Psychological Association: Washington, D.C., 2010).

[4] See Daniel Goleman, *Emotional Intelligence: Why It Can Matter More Than IQ* (New York: Bantam Books, 1995); see also Kenneth Law, Chi-Sum Wong, and Lynda Song, "The Construct and Criterion Validity of Emotional Intelligence and Its Potential Utility for Management Studies," *Journal of Applied Psychology*, 2004, vol 89, no. 3, 483–596.

[5] J. B. Rotter, "Generalized Expectancies for Internal vs. External Control of Reinforcement," *Psychological Monographs,* 1966, vol. 80, pp. 1–28.

[6] See Jeffrey Vancouver, Kristen More, and Ryan Yoder, "Self-Efficacy and Resource Allocation: Support for a Non-monotic, Discontinuous Model," *Journal of Applied Psychology,* 2008, vol. 93, no. 1, pp. 35–47.

[7] T. W. Adorno, E. Frenkel-Brunswick, D. J. Levinson, and R. N. Sanford, *The Authoritarian Personality* (New York: Harper & Row, 1950).

[8] Denise M. Rousseau, "The Individual-Organization Relationship: The Psychological Contract," in Sheldon Zedeck, (Ed.), *Handbook of Industrial and Organizational Psychology* (American Psychological Association: Washington, D.C., 2010).

[9] See Daniel Wren, *The History of Management Thought,* 6th ed. (New York: John Wiley & Sons), 2008.

[10] David McClelland, *The Achieving Society* (Princeton, NJ: Nostrand, 1961). See also David C. McClelland, *Human Motivation* (Cambridge, UK: Cambridge University Press, 1988).

[11] Stanley Schachter, *The Psychology of Affiliation* (Palo Alto: Stanford University Press, 1959).

[12] David McClelland and David H. Burnham, "Power Is the Great Motivator," *Harvard Business Review,* March–April 1976, pp. 100–110.

[13] Yasuhiro, Yamakawa, Mike W. Peng, and David L. Deeds. 2015. "Rising From the Ashes: Cognitive Determinants of Venture Growth After Entrepreneurial Failure." *Entrepreneurship: Theory & Practice* 39, no. 2: 209–235. Business Source Premier, EBSCOhost (accessed May 4, 2015).

[14] Pinder, *Work Motivation in Organizational Behavior,* 2nd ed. (Upper Saddle River, NJ: Prentice-Hall, 2008); McClelland and Burnham, "Power Is the Great Motivator."

[15] Lyman Porter, Gregory Bigley, and Richard Steers, *Motivation and Work Behavior,* 8th ed. (New York: McGraw-Hill), 2008.

[16] "100 Best Companies to Work for 2017," Fortune, http://beta.fortune.com/best-companies/ (Accessed March 15, 2017). Also see http://reviews.greatplacetowork.com/google-inc?utm_source=fortune&utm_medium=referral&utm_content=reviews-link&utm_campaign=2017-fortune100-list, accessed June 26, 2017.

[17] See http://reviews.greatplacetowork.com/wegmans-food-markets-inc?utm_source=fortune&utm_medium=referral&utm_content=reviews-link&utm_campaign=2017-fortune100-list, accessed June 26, 2017.

[18] See http://reviews.greatplacetowork.com/the-boston-consulting-group-inc?utm_source=fortune&utm_medium=referral&utm_content=reviews-link&utm_campaign=2017-fortune100-list, accessed June 26, 2017.

[19] Great Place to Work, "Great Place to Work® Research for 2017 Fortune 100 Best Companies Reveals Great Places to Work FOR ALL Will Be Key to Better Business Performance," PRNewswire, March 9, 2017, http://www.prnewswire.com/news-releases/great-place-to-work-research-for-2017-fortune-100-best-companies-reveals-great-places-to-work-for-all-will-be-key-to-better-business-performance-300420902.html (Accessed March 15, 2017)

[20] Gary P. Latham, "The Importance of Understanding and Changing Employee Outcome Expectancies for Gaining Commitment to an Organizational Goal," *Personnel Psychology*, 2001, vol. 54, 707–720.

[21] Adam M. Grant, Yitzhak Fried, and Tina Juillerat, "Work Matters: Job Design in Classic and Contemporary Perspectives," in Sheldon Zedeck, (Ed.), *Handbook of Industrial and Organizational Psychology* (American Psychological Association: Washington, D.C., 2010). See also Bradley Kirkman and T. Brad Harris, *3D Team Leadership: A New Approach for Complex Teams* (Palo Alto, CA: Stanford University press, 2017).

[22] Stephanie Armour, "Working 9-to-5 No Longer," *USA Today*, December 6, 2004, 1B, 2B.

[23] See https://www.glassdoor.com/Overview/Working-at-BuzzFeed-EI_IE496875.11,19.htm (Accessed March 19, 2017)

[24] Uber, "Update from Arianna Huffington," February 21, 2017, https://newsroom.uber.com/ariannaupdate/ (Accessed March 19, 2017)

chapter 9

Leadership and Decision Making

Not all managers are leaders. But if an organization

can develop capable managers who are

also leaders, they

will be formidable competitors in any market.

After reading this chapter, you should be able to:

9-1 **Define** *leadership* and distinguish it from management.

9-2 **Summarize** early approaches to the study of leadership.

9-3 **Discuss** the concept of situational approaches to leadership.

9-4 **Describe** transformational and charismatic perspectives on leadership.

9-5 **Identify** and discuss leadership substitutes and neutralizers.

9-6 **Discuss** leaders as coaches and examine gender and cross-cultural issues in leadership.

9-7 **Describe** strategic leadership, ethical leadership, and virtual leadership.

9-8 **Relate** leadership to decision making and discuss both rational and behavioral perspectives on decision making.

PRODUCT C   CLAVE
AND EXPO

Authentic Leadership

Brad Smith grew up in the small town of Kenova, West Virginia, in the 1970s. Even today, Kenova has a population of just over 3,000 people and everyone knows everyone else. One of Smith's early memories is watching, from a distance, the fiery aftermath of the plane crash that took the lives of 37 Marshall University football players along with their coach and 27 other staff and community members, all returning from a game in North Carolina. His cousins were up on the hillside helping fight the fires where the aircraft came down.

Smith earned a bachelor's degree in business administration with an emphasis in marketing from Marshall in 1986 and later, while working in sales management and business development for Pepsi, he added a master's degree in management from Aquinas College in Michigan, attending night classes as he worked days. After a few career changes, he landed at Intuit in 2003. He started out working in Plano, Texas, running the accountant relations portion of the professional tax business. Due to his success there, Intuit asked him to move to San Diego to run TurboTax, the company's flagship consumer tax business. In 2005, Smith moved to the Silicon Valley to help lead a team that would fend off an attempt by Microsoft to steal market share from QuickBooks. Having proved that he was more than just a manager, the board of directors named him CEO in 2008.

As a leader, Smith melds innovation with profit-motive. For instance, based on Google's innovative model, he implemented unstructured time where employees can use 10 percent of their time to work on any project they choose. His theory is sound. He says, "… people who focus on things they love will work harder and get more done. We're looking for great ideas that will improve our workers' skills and efficiency. We're also hoping to foster innovation—if someone has an idea for a new product that our customers would love, then we encourage them to go for it." Since introducing unstructured time, Intuit has seen more than 200 initiatives go to market, resulting in $100 million in new revenue.[1]

Another one of Smith's strategies was to focus on design in order to overcome the perception that financial software is boring and dull. He even reconfigured the layout of the physical space within the organization, making fewer cubicles and more open spaces, encouraging collaboration. His goal: to make Intuit one of the most design-driven companies in the world by 2020.

Smith attributes his success as a leader to lessons he gathered along the way: from his parents, who instilled a sense of community, family, and leadership; to his academic career; and his extracurricular experiences, such as teaching martial arts. In high school, he'd played football until his sophomore year when he

Kurhan/Fotolia

what's in it for me?

Is your boss a manager? A leader? What does she or he do to inspire you to work harder? Do you aspire to be a manager or a leader? When you have a leadership position, what will you do to inspire your employees to work harder? Do you think management and leadership are the same thing? These are some of the issues we'll explore in this chapter. In Chapter 8, we described the primary determinants of employee behavior and noted that managers can influence the behavior and enhance the motivation of employees. Now it's time to examine in detail how leaders such as Brad Smith go about influencing employee behavior and motivating employee performance. We will place these strategies and tactics in the context of various approaches to leadership through the years, including the situational perspective accepted today. Understanding these concepts will help you function more effectively as a leader and give you more insight into how your manager or boss strives to motivate you through his or her own leadership.

We start this chapter by taking a look at the nature of leadership. We then describe early approaches to leadership, as well as the situational perspective accepted today. Next, we examine leadership through the eyes of followers as well as alternatives to leadership. The changing nature of leadership and emerging issues in leadership are discussed next. Finally, we describe the important related concept of decision making.

decided to dedicate his time to studying martial arts. By the time he was a senior he had earned his black belt, and soon after, he notes, "I was teaching an entire school, with about 150 students. You get measured on the progress of the students you're teaching. It's no longer about your own abilities; it's about building the capability in others. I fall back on that to this day."

College was formative as well. Of his alma mater, he says, "Marshall has a sense of purpose and values that I love. Look at what it has accomplished since the plane crash. Champions aren't defined by whether they hit the canvas, but by how quickly they get back up. Marshall University just perseveres. It's a university that has been hit with tragedy and fought its way through, and it just keeps coming back. And I think that is the secret to life."

Even more fundamental than those experiences was the effect his parents had on his world-view. He often encapsulates their wisdom in a simple story: "When my mom or dad walked into the room, the first thing you saw was a smile and the last thing you saw when they left was a smile. But, they told me to never mistake kindness for weakness."[2]

Based on his experience, Smith believes that great leaders share five key focal points:

- Strategic Thinking—Strategic thinking is a game of chess and requires focusing on the larger picture. As Stephen Covey would say, "The manager accomplishes the task at hand, slashing through the jungle, overcoming problems and clearing the path, but the leaders are high in the tree tops, studying the lay of the land; they are the ones willing to say, 'Hey, this is the wrong jungle! Let's move on!'"

- Results Orientation—Strategy can enable an idea to make the leap from aspiration to reality, but "Strategies alone don't move mountains—bulldozers do." The best leaders remove barriers and focus on creating an environment where great ideas can come to life.

- Strong Team Building—The role of leaders is to provide the grand challenge, invest in people, and create an environment where their greatness can emerge.

- Adapting and Improving—Great leaders are constantly adapting, improving themselves and their organizations.

- Inspiring both heart and mind, blending a high IQ and a high EQ (emotional quotient).[3]

When he took the helm of Intuit at the age of 43, the company had 8,000 employees and annual revenues of $2.6 billion. Today, as well as being a long-term member of Fortune magazine's 100 Best Places to Work list, the company's revenues have doubled and the stock price has risen from under $25 to over $120 per share. But Smith would be the first to tell you that he didn't do it all on his own, and yet his leadership has certainly played a key role in the company's ongoing success.

One of Smith's favorite quotes comes from Bill Campbell, a well-known business coach and one of Smith's early mentors, who said, "Your title makes you a manager, people decide if you're a leader." (After studying the content of this chapter, you should be able to answer the set of discussion questions found at the end of the chapter.)

OBJECTIVE 9-1
Define
leadership and distinguish it from management.

Leadership *the processes and behaviors used by someone, such as a manager, to motivate, inspire, and influence the behaviors of others*

The Nature of Leadership

Because *leadership* is a term that is often used in everyday conversation, you might assume that it has a common and accepted meaning. In reality, though, the word *leadership* is often misused. We define **leadership** as the processes and behaviors used by someone, such as a manager, to motivate, inspire, and influence the behaviors of others.

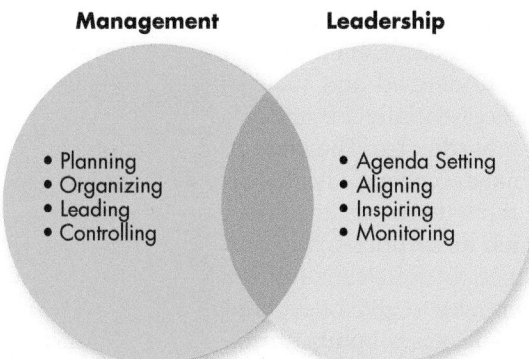

Management   **Leadership**

- Planning
- Organizing
- Leading
- Controlling

- Agenda Setting
- Aligning
- Inspiring
- Monitoring

FIGURE 9.1 Distinctions between Management and Leadership

Leadership and Management

One of the biggest mistakes some people make is assuming that leadership and management mean the same thing, when they are really different concepts. A person can be a manager, a leader, both, or neither.[4] Some of the basic distinctions between the two are summarized in Figure 9.1. As illustrated in the circle on the left, management (as discussed in Chapter 5) focuses primarily on the activities of planning, organizing, leading, and controlling. Leadership, in contrast, is much more closely related to activities such as agenda setting, aligning, inspiring, and monitoring. As also illustrated in the figure, management and leadership may occasionally overlap but each is also a discrete and separate set of activities. Hence, a person may be a manager (but not a leader), a leader (but not a manager), or both a manager and a leader.

Consider the various roles of managers and leaders in a hospital setting. The chief of staff (chief physician) of a large hospital is clearly a manager by virtue of his or her position. However, he or she may not be respected or trusted by others and may have to rely solely on the authority vested in the position to get people to do things. On the other hand, a nurse in the emergency department with no formal authority may be quite effective at taking charge of chaotic situations and directing others in dealing with specific patient problems. The chief of staff is a manager but not really a leader, whereas the nurse is a leader but not really a manager.

Finally, the head of pediatrics, supervising a staff of 20 other doctors, nurses, and attendants, may also enjoy the staff's complete respect, confidence, and trust. They readily take his or her advice, follow directives without question, and often go far beyond what is necessary to help carry out the unit's mission. Thus, the head of pediatrics is both a manager (by virtue of the position he or she occupies) and a leader (by virtue of the respect he or she commands from others and their willingness to follow her direction).

Organizations need both management and leadership if they are to be effective. Management in conjunction with leadership can help achieve planned orderly change, and leadership in conjunction with management can keep the organization properly aligned with its environment.

Leadership and Power

To fully understand leadership, it is also necessary to understand *power*. **Power** is the ability to affect the behavior of others. Of course, one can have power without actually using it. For example, a football coach has the power to bench a player who is not performing up to par. The coach seldom has to use this power because players recognize that the power exists and they work hard to keep their starting positions. In organizational settings, there are usually five kinds of power: legitimate, reward, coercive, referent, and expert power.[5]

Legitimate power is power granted through the organizational hierarchy; it is the power defined by the organization to be accorded to people occupying a particular

Power *the ability to affect the behavior of others*

Legitimate Power *power granted through the organizational hierarchy*

position. A manager can assign tasks to a subordinate, and a subordinate who refuses to do them can be reprimanded or even fired. Such outcomes stem from the manager's legitimate power as defined and vested in her or him by the organization. Legitimate power, then, is essentially the same as authority. All managers have legitimate power over their subordinates. The mere possession of legitimate power, however, does not by itself make someone a leader. Some subordinates follow only orders that are strictly within the letter of organizational rules and policies. If asked to do something not in their job descriptions, they refuse or choose to do a poor job. The manager of such employees is exercising authority but not leadership.

Reward Power *the power to give or withhold rewards*

Reward power is the power to give or withhold rewards. Rewards that a manager may control include salary increases, bonuses, promotion recommendations, praise, recognition, and interesting job assignments. In general, the greater the number of rewards a manager controls and the more important the rewards are to subordinates, the greater is the manager's reward power. If the subordinate values only the formal organizational rewards provided by the manager, then the manager is not a leader. If the subordinate also wants and appreciates the manager's informal rewards, such as praise, gratitude, and recognition, however, then the manager is also exercising leadership.

Coercive Power *the power to force compliance by means of psychological, emotional, or physical threat*

Coercive power is the power to force compliance by means of psychological, emotional, or physical threat. Physical coercion in organizations was once relatively common. In most organizations today, however, coercion is limited to verbal reprimands, written reprimands, disciplinary layoffs, fines, demotion, and termination. Some managers occasionally go so far as to use verbal abuse, humiliation, and psychological coercion in an attempt to manipulate subordinates. (Of course, most people agree that these are not appropriate managerial behaviors.) Prison guards sometimes resort to the use of coercive power. Charlie Ergen, cofounder and Chairman of the Board of Dish Network, has a reputation for yelling at employees, belittling managers in front of their peers, and imposing harsh penalties on those who disagree with him.[6] The more punitive the elements under a manager's control and the more important they are to subordinates, the more coercive power the manager possesses. On the other hand, the more a manager uses coercive power, the more likely he or she is to provoke resentment and hostility and the less likely he or she is to be seen as a leader.[7]

Referent Power *power based on identification, imitation, loyalty, or charisma*

Compared with legitimate, reward, and coercive power, which are relatively concrete and grounded in objective facets of organizational life, **referent power** is abstract. It is based on identification, imitation, loyalty, or charisma. Followers may react favorably because they identify in some way with a leader, who may be like them in personality, background, or attitudes. In other situations, followers might choose to imitate a leader with referent power by wearing the same kind of clothes, working the same hours, or espousing the same management philosophy. Referent power may also take the form of charisma, an intangible attribute of the leader that inspires loyalty and enthusiasm. Thus, a manager might have referent power, but it is more likely to be associated with leadership.

Expert Power *power derived from information or expertise*

Expert power is derived from information or expertise. A manager who knows how to interact with an eccentric but important customer, a scientist who is capable of achieving an important technical breakthrough that no other company has dreamed of, and an administrative assistant who knows how to unravel bureaucratic red tape all have expert power over anyone who needs that information. The more important the information and the fewer the people who have access to it, the greater is the degree of expert power possessed by any one individual. In general, people who are both leaders and managers tend to have a large amount of expert power.

Early Approaches to Leadership

Although leaders and leadership have profoundly influenced history, careful scientific study of them began only about a century ago. Early studies focused on the *traits*, or personal characteristics, of leaders. Later research shifted to examine actual leader *behaviors*.

Pictorial Press Ltd/Alamy Stock Photo

When asked to identify important leaders, people often mention influential historical figures such as Winston Churchill, Abraham Lincoln, Martin Luther King, Jr., and Mother Teresa.

MPVHistory/Alamy Stock Photo

GL Archive/Alamy Stock Photo

B Maiti/Dinodia Photo/AGE Fotostock

Trait Approaches to Leadership

Early researchers believed that notable leaders had some unique set of qualities or traits that distinguished them from their peers and endured throughout history. This **trait approach to leadership** led researchers to focus on identifying the essential leadership traits, including intelligence, dominance, self-confidence, energy, activity (versus passivity), and knowledge about the job. Unfortunately, the list of potential leadership traits quickly became so long that it lost any practical value. In addition, the results of many studies were inconsistent. For example, one argument stated that the most effective leaders were tall, like Abraham Lincoln. But critics were quick to point out that neither Napoleon Bonaparte nor Adolf Hitler was tall, but both were effective leaders in their own way.

Trait Approach to Leadership *focused on identifying the essential traits that distinguished leaders*

Although the trait approach was all but abandoned several decades ago, in recent years, it has resurfaced. For example, some researchers have again started to focus on a limited set of traits. These traits include emotional intelligence, mental intelligence, drive, motivation, honesty and integrity, self-confidence, knowledge of the business, and charisma. However, it is too early to know whether these traits really do relate to leadership.

Behavioral Approaches to Leadership

In the late 1940s, most researchers began to shift away from the trait approach and to look at leadership as a set of actual behaviors. The goal of the **behavioral approach to leadership** was to determine what *behaviors* were employed by effective leaders. These researchers assumed that the behaviors of effective leaders differed somehow from the behaviors of less effective leaders, and that the behaviors of effective leaders would be the same across all situations.

Behavioral Approach to Leadership *focused on determining what behaviors are employed by leaders*

This research led to the identification of two basic forms of leader behavior. Although different researchers applied different names, the following are the basic leader behaviors identified during this period:

- **Task-focused leader behavior**: Task-focused leader behavior occurs when a leader focuses on how tasks should be performed to meet certain goals and to achieve certain performance standards.

Task-Focused Leader Behavior *leader behavior focusing on how tasks should be performed to meet certain goals and to achieve certain performance standards*

- **Employee-focused leader behavior**: Employee-focused leader behavior occurs when a leader focuses on the satisfaction, motivation, and well-being of his or her employees.

Employee-Focused Leader Behavior *leader behavior focusing on satisfaction, motivation, and well-being of employees*

During this period, people believed that leaders should always try to engage in a healthy dose of both behaviors, one to increase performance and the other to increase job satisfaction and motivation. Experts also began to realize that they could train managers to engage in these behaviors in a systematic manner. But they also discovered that other leader behaviors needed to be considered, and that, in some circumstances, different combinations of leader behaviors might be more effective than other combinations.

For instance, suppose a new manager takes over a work site that is plagued by low productivity and whose workers, although perhaps satisfied, are not motivated to work hard. The leader should most likely emphasize task-focused behaviors to improve lagging productivity. But suppose the situation is different—productivity is high, but workers are stressed out about their jobs and have low levels of job satisfaction. In this instance, the manager should most likely concentrate on employee-focused behaviors to help improve job satisfaction. This line of thinking led to the development of *situational theories*.

OBJECTIVE 9-3
Discuss
the concept of situational approaches to leadership.

Situational Approach to Leadership *assumes that appropriate leader behavior varies from one situation to another*

The Situational Approach to Leadership

The **situational approach to leadership** assumes that appropriate leader behavior varies from one situation to another, as shown in Figure 9.2. The trait and behavioral approaches to leadership were both universal in nature. They attempted to prescribe leader behaviors that would lead to a set of universal outcomes and consequences. For instance, proponents of these universal perspectives might argue that tall and intelligent people or people who are consistently employee-focused will always be good leaders. In reality, though, research has found this simply is not true. So, the situational approach to leadership attempts to identify various forms of leader behavior that result in contingent outcomes and consequences. By contingent, we mean that they depend on elements of the situation and characteristics of both the leader and followers.

Consider, for example, how Edward Bastian, CEO of Delta Airlines, has to vary his leadership style when he is interacting with different kinds of people. When he is dealing with investors, he has to convey an impression of confidence about the company's financial picture. When he interacts with union officials, he needs to take a firm stand on cost control combined with collaboration. Bastian often speaks to leaders at other

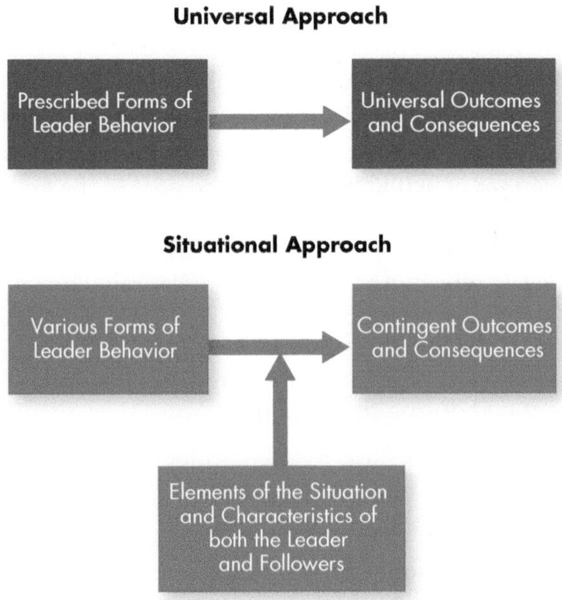

Universal Approach

Prescribed Forms of Leader Behavior → Universal Outcomes and Consequences

Situational Approach

Various Forms of Leader Behavior → Contingent Outcomes and Consequences

↑ Elements of the Situation and Characteristics of both the Leader and Followers

FIGURE 9.2 The Situational Approach to Leadership

airlines and has to balance their mutual interests against Delta's own competitive situation. And when dealing with customers, he has to be charming and respectful.

Leadership characteristics include the manager's value system, confidence in subordinates, personal inclinations, feelings of security, and actual behaviors. Subordinate characteristics include the subordinates' need for independence, readiness to assume responsibility, tolerance for ambiguity, interest in the problem, understanding of goals, knowledge, experience, and expectations. Situational characteristics that affect decision making include the type of organization, group effectiveness, the problem itself, and time pressures. Three important situational approaches to leadership are (1) the *path–goal theory*, (2) the *decision tree approach*, and (3) the *leader–member exchange model*.

The **path–goal theory** of leadership is a direct extension of the expectancy theory of motivation discussed in Chapter 8.[8] Recall that the primary components of expectancy theory include the likelihood of attaining various outcomes and the value associated with those outcomes. The path–goal theory of leadership suggests that the primary functions of a leader are to make valued or desired rewards available in the workplace and to clarify for the subordinate the kinds of behavior that will lead to goal accomplishment and valued rewards. The leader should clarify the paths to goal attainment.

Path–Goal Theory *theory of leadership that is a direct extension of the expectancy theory of motivation*

Path–goal theory identifies four kinds of behaviors that leaders can use, depending on the situation. *Directive leader behavior* lets subordinates know what is expected of them, gives guidance and direction, and schedules work. *Supportive leader behavior* is being friendly and approachable, showing concern for subordinates' welfare, and treating members as equals. *Participative leader behavior* includes consulting with subordinates, soliciting suggestions, and allowing participation in decision making. *Achievement-oriented leader behavior* sets challenging goals, expects subordinates to perform at high levels, encourages subordinates, and shows confidence in subordinates' abilities.

Another major contemporary approach to leadership is the **decision tree approach**. Like the path–goal theory, this approach attempts to prescribe a leadership style appropriate to a given situation. It also assumes that the same leader may display different leadership styles. But the decision tree approach concerns itself with only a single aspect of leader behavior: subordinate participation in decision making. The decision tree approach assumes that the degree to which subordinates should be encouraged to participate in decision making depends on the characteristics of the situation. In other words, no one decision-making process is best for all situations. After evaluating a variety of problem attributes (characteristics of the problem or decision), the leader determines an appropriate decision style that specifies the amount of subordinate participation.

Decision Tree Approach *approach to leadership that provides decision rules for deciding how much participation to allow*

The **leader–member exchange (LMX) model** stresses the importance of variable relationships between supervisors and each of their subordinates.[9] Each superior–subordinate pair represents a "vertical dyad." The model differs from previous approaches in that it focuses on the differential relationship leaders often establish with different subordinates. This model suggests that supervisors establish a special relationship with a small number of trusted subordinates, referred to as "the in-group." The in-group usually receives special duties requiring responsibility and autonomy; they may also receive special privileges. Subordinates who are not a part of this group are called "the out-group," and they receive less of the supervisor's time and attention. However, the key element of this theory is the concept of individual vertical dyads and how leaders have different relationships with each of their subordinates.

Leader–Member Exchange (LMX) Model *approach to leadership that stresses the importance of variable relationships between supervisors and each of their subordinates*

Leadership Through the Eyes of Followers

OBJECTIVE 9-4
Describe
transformational and charismatic perspectives on leadership.

Another recent perspective that has been adopted by some leadership experts focuses on how leaders are seen through the eyes of their followers. The two primary approaches to leadership through the eyes of followers are *transformational leadership* and *charismatic leadership*. Donald Trump's successful bid for the U.S. presidency was fueled in part by many people's perceptions that he was both a transformational and charismatic leader. Indeed, during his campaign, he frequently talked about the need to change the way the United States addressed issues such as health care, immigration, and foreign policy. Many people were attracted to him because of his personal charisma as well.

Transformational Leadership

Transformational leadership focuses on the importance of leading for change (as opposed to leading during a period of stability). According to this view, much of what a leader does involves carrying out what might be thought of as basic management "transactions," such as assigning work, evaluating performance, and making decisions. Occasionally, however, the leader has to engage in transformational leadership to initiate and manage major change, such as managing a merger, creating a new work team, or redefining the organization's culture.

Transformational Leadership *the set of abilities that allows a leader to recognize the need for change, to create a vision to guide that change, and to execute the change effectively*

Transactional Leadership *comparable to management, it involves routine, regimented activities*

Thus, **transformational leadership** is the set of abilities that allows a leader to recognize the need for change, to create a vision to guide that change, and to execute the change effectively. Some experts believe that change is such a vital organizational function that even successful firms need to change regularly to avoid becoming complacent and stagnant. In contrast, **transactional leadership** is very similar to basic management in that it involves routine, regimented activities. Only a leader with tremendous influence can hope to perform both functions successfully. Accordingly, leadership for change is extremely important.

Some leaders are able to adopt either transformational or transactional perspectives, depending on their circumstances. For instance, when Jeff Bezos started Amazon.com, his strategy was to simply sell books through an online "store." When Amazon developed sustainable revenues, he used transactional leadership to slowly grow the business and build cash reserves. Bezos then adopted a transformational style as he led the company to become a major online "retailer" of thousands of different products. He then reverted to a transactional approach to again let the business entrench itself. More recently, Bezos has again been using transformational leadership as Amazon develops new methods for product distribution, explores new product lines and extensions, and tries to position itself as a competitor for Apple and Google.

Charismatic Leadership

Charismatic Leadership *type of influence based on the leader's personal charisma*

Charismatic leadership is a type of influence based on the leader's charisma, a form of interpersonal attraction that inspires support and acceptance. Charismatic leaders are likely to have a lot of confidence in their beliefs and ideals and a strong need to influence people. They also tend to communicate high expectations about follower performance and to express confidence in their followers. Many of the most influential leaders in history have been extremely charismatic, including entrepreneurs Mary Kay Ash, Steve Jobs, and Ted Turner; civil rights leader Martin Luther King, Jr.; and Pope John Paul II. Unfortunately, charisma can also empower leaders in other directions. Adolf Hitler, for instance, had strong charismatic qualities.

Most experts today acknowledge three crucial elements of charismatic leadership:[10]

1 Charismatic leaders envision likely future trends and patterns, set high expectations for themselves and for others, and behave in ways that meet or exceed those expectations.

2 Charismatic leaders energize others by demonstrating personal excitement, personal confidence, and consistent patterns of success.

3 Charismatic leaders enable others by supporting them, empathizing with them, and expressing confidence in them.

Charismatic leadership ideas are quite popular among managers today and are the subject of numerous books and articles.[11] Unfortunately, few studies have specifically attempted to test the meaning and impact of charismatic leadership. Lingering

entrepreneurship and new ventures

"Success Unshared Is Failure"

John Paul DeJoria is the charismatic leader behind John Paul Mitchell Systems, which produces and distributes Paul Mitchell hair care products, and the Patrón Spirits Company. His net worth has been estimated at more than $3 billion. However, unlike many of those on the *Forbes* magazine 400 list of wealthiest Americans, DeJoria did not inherit wealth or privilege. He grew up in a working-class neighborhood and had his first job selling Christmas cards door-to-door at age nine. After graduating from high school and serving in the Navy, DeJoria began selling encyclopedias and quickly moved through 10 jobs in just a couple of years. Eventually, he moved into sales in the beauty industry and quickly found his niche. However, after nine years of success in the industry, he lost his job when his commissions began to exceed the pay of the owner of the company.

In 1980, DeJoria was homeless, living in an old Rolls-Royce in L.A. He had just invested all of his savings—amounting to just $700—in Paul Mitchell, which he cofounded with the company's namesake. With a bare-bones budget, they sold their products door-to-door in hair salons. While others might have given up, DeJoria believed in their products and was persistent. In a 2013 interview with *Forbes* magazine, he advises, "Be prepared for the rejection. No matter how bad it is, don't let it overcome you and influence you—keep on going towards what you want to do—no matter what. You need to be as enthusiastic about door number one hundred as door number one." While the first two years were difficult, they had almost $1 million in annual sales in their third year of operation. Today, the company's products are sold in more than 150,000 beauty salons in 87 countries, and annual sales exceed $1 billion.

DeJoria is a serial entrepreneur, having started more than a dozen businesses, including House of Blues, DeJoria Diamonds, and Gustin Energy Company. Although he started Patrón Spirits in 1989 as a hobby with friend Martin Crowley, the business quickly got more serious. They wanted to create a market for high-end tequila and selected a hand-blown bottle and expensive blue agave as the base. Building on DeJoria's connections, Patrón quickly became a well-recognized brand. DeJoria's good friend Clint Eastwood put Patrón in his movie *In the Line of Fire,* and chef Wolfgang Puck began touting it to his friends and business contacts.

In each of his businesses, DeJoria makes high quality and sustainability a priority. In his interview with *Fortune* magazine, he explains, "A lot of people make things to sell. But when the product is old, the consumer tosses it out and buys something else. If you make things with the highest quality, you'll be in the reorder business, which keeps the sales growing." Sustainability is a common thread, from his investment in environmentally responsible oil and gas exploration with Gustin Energy Company to sales of conflict-free diamonds through

Nicholas Kamm/AFP/Getty Images

DeJoria Diamonds. This theme is also a big part of the Paul Mitchell product line: "We looked at costs in our warehouse system—everything from what doors we can shut to what lights we can change. We found ways to create a 25 percent savings in our power costs. We plant trees to offset our Tea Tree shampoo line to make up for the carbon that we use. It's good for the world and good for business."

While much of DeJoria's success can be attributed to hard work, his charisma and message inspire others. One of his mottos is "Success unshared is failure." He is committed to giving back through organizations such as Habitat for Humanity and Food4Africa. He is also the founder of Grow Appalachia, an organization that helps those in rural areas to overcome food insecurity by growing their own food. Not surprisingly, DeJoria signed Warren Buffett and Bill Gates's Giving Pledge, through which the world's wealthiest citizens commit to giving most of their wealth to philanthropy.[12]

ethical concerns about charismatic leadership also trouble some people. They stem from the fact that some charismatic leaders inspire such blind faith in their followers that they may engage in inappropriate, unethical, or even illegal behaviors just because the leader instructed them to do so. This tendency likely played a role in the unwinding of both Enron and Arthur Andersen because people followed orders from their charismatic bosses to hide information, shred documents, and mislead investigators.

Taking over a leadership role from someone with substantial personal charisma is also a challenge. For instance, the immediate successors to successful and charismatic athletic coaches such as Vince Lombardi (Green Bay Packers) and Phil Jackson (Chicago Bulls) each failed to measure up to their predecessors' legacies and were subsequently fired.

OBJECTIVE 9-5
Identify
and discuss leadership substitutes and neutralizers.

Special Issues in Leadership

Another interesting perspective on leadership focuses on *alternatives* to leadership. In some cases, certain factors may actually *substitute* for leadership, making actual leadership unnecessary or irrelevant. In other cases, factors may exist that *neutralize* or negate the influence of a leader even when that individual is attempting to exercise leadership.

Leadership Substitutes

Leadership Substitutes *individual, task, and organizational characteristics that tend to outweigh the need for a leader to initiate or direct employee performance*

Leadership substitutes are individual, task, and organizational characteristics that tend to outweigh the need for a leader to initiate or direct employee performance. In other words, if certain factors are present, the employee will perform his or her job capably, even without the direction of a leader. Table 9.1 identifies several basic leadership substitutes.

Consider, for example, what happens when an ambulance with a critically injured victim screeches to the door of a hospital emergency department. Do the emergency department employees stand around waiting for someone to take control and instruct them on what to do? The answer is no: They are highly trained, well-prepared professionals who know how to respond and work together as a team without someone playing the role of leader. When a U.S. Airways flight crashed into the Hudson River in 2009, all members of the flight crew knew exactly what to do, without waiting for orders. As a result of their effective and prompt actions, a disaster was averted, and all passengers on the plane were quickly rescued.

table 9.1 Leadership Substitutes and Neutralizers

Individual factors	• Individual professionalism • Individual ability, knowledge, and motivation • Individual experience and training • Indifference to rewards
Job factors	• Structured/automated • Highly controlled • Intrinsically satisfying • Embedded feedback
Organization factors	• Explicit plans and goals • Rigid rules and procedures • Rigid reward system not tied to performance • Physical distance between supervisor and subordinate
Group factors	• Group performance norms • High level of group cohesiveness • Group interdependence

Leadership Neutralizers

In other situations, even if a leader is present and attempts to engage in various leadership behaviors, those behaviors may be rendered ineffective—or neutralized—by various factors that can be called **leadership neutralizers**. Suppose, for example, that a relatively new and inexperienced leader is assigned to a work group composed of experienced employees with long-standing performance norms and a high level of group cohesiveness. The norms and cohesiveness of the group may be so strong that there is nothing the new leader can do to change things.

Leadership Neutralizers factors that may render leader behaviors ineffective

In addition to group factors, elements of the job itself may also limit a leader's ability to "make a difference." Consider, for example, employees working on a moving assembly line. Employees may only be able to work at the pace of the moving line, so performance quantity and quality are constrained by the speed of the line and simplicity of each individual task.

Finally, organizational factors can also neutralize at least some forms of leader behavior. Suppose a new leader is accustomed to using merit pay increases as a way to motivate people. But in his or her new job, pay increases may be dictated by union contracts and based solely on employee seniority and cost of living. The leader's previous approach to motivating people would be neutralized, and new approaches would have to be identified.

The Changing Nature of Leadership

OBJECTIVE 9-6
Discuss
leaders as coaches and examine gender and cross-cultural issues in leadership.

Various alternatives to leadership aside, many settings still call for at least some degree of leadership, although the nature of that leadership continues to evolve. Among the recent changes in leadership that managers should recognize are the increasing role of *leaders as coaches* as well as *gender and cross-cultural patterns* of leader behavior.

Leaders as Coaches

We noted in Chapter 6 and again in Chapter 8 that many organizations today are using teams. Many other organizations are attempting to become less hierarchical by eliminating the old-fashioned command-and-control mentality often inherent in bureaucratic organizations and motivating and empowering individuals to work independently. In each case, the role of leaders is also changing. Whereas leaders were once expected to control situations, direct work, supervise people, closely monitor performance, make decisions, and structure activities, many leaders today are instead being asked to change how they manage people. Perhaps the best description of this new role is for the leader to become more of a *coach* rather than an *overseer*.[13]

From the standpoint of a business leader, a coaching perspective would call for the leader to help select and train team members and other new employees, to provide some general direction, and to help the team get the information and other resources it needs. Coaches from different teams may play important roles in linking the activities and functions of their respective teams. Some leaders may function as *mentors*, helping less experienced employees learn the ropes and better preparing them to advance within the organization; they may also help resolve conflicts among team members and mediate other disputes that arise. But beyond these activities, the leader keeps a low profile and lets the group get its work done with little or no direct oversight, just as during a game, an athletic coach trusts his or her players to execute the plays successfully.

Jeff Bezos, founder and CEO of Amazon.com, often plays the role of coach. He likes to focus on long-term, strategic issues and leave the daily management of Amazon.com to senior managers. But their decisions must also be consistent with his vision for the firm. As a result, he works with them on a regular basis to help them develop their decision-making skills and to equip them with the information they need to help lead the firm in the directions he has set.

Gender and Leadership

Another factor that is clearly altering the face of leadership is the growing number of women advancing to higher levels in organizations. Given that most leadership theories and research studies traditionally focused on male leaders, developing a better understanding of how women lead is clearly an important next step. Some early observers, for instance, predicted that (consistent with prevailing stereotypes) female leaders would be relatively warm, supportive, and nurturing as compared to their male counterparts. But research suggests that female leaders are not necessarily more nurturing or supportive than male leaders. Likewise, male leaders are not systematically harsher, more controlling, or more task focused than female leaders.

finding a better way

Women Leading the Way

In a workforce that has been historically dominated by men, much of the research on leadership has focused on men and the ways in which they lead. As more women entered the workforce, research began to evolve and turned to evaluating the differences between men and women as leaders. Unfortunately, many of the conclusions were focused on ways that women could adapt their innate style to be more like men. Ruzwana Bashir, cofounder of the travel site Peek and former Goldman Sachs employee, would beg to differ. As she began her career in the financial services industry, she felt pressure to act more like her male counterparts. At the Forbes Under 30 summit, she explains, "In that environment as a woman, you can feel crowd-forced to conform." While earning her MBA at Harvard's Business School as a Fulbright Scholar, she realized that traditionally feminine attributes can be an advantage. "Those 'female' traits of empathy and compassion—of being collaborative—are true business strengths."

Bashir has made a huge mark at an early age. Born in Pakistan, she was educated in the United Kingdom and studied at Oxford University. At Oxford, she became president of the Oxford Union, a debating society famed for hosting speakers as famous as Senator John McCain and fashion designer Tom Ford. She was only the second female Asian president of that prestigious society, following in the footsteps of former Pakistani President Benazir Bhutto, who became the union's leader in 1977. It was at Oxford that Bashir first wore Western clothing, and although she excelled in school, she always felt different in race, gender, and class. It was in 2012, after spending over 20 frustrating hours trying to arrange a get-away with friends to Turkey, she and cofounder Oskar Bruening launched Peek.com, adding yet another benchmark to her already impressive social resume—that of a woman-founded tech company. Although there are already several travel websites, Peek occupies a unique space in the market. Peek helps travelers to plan the perfect trip, including itineraries for a "Perfect Day" in your destination.

At Peek.com, the company has maintained a staffing mix of 50 percent men and 50 percent women, with considerable

Nils Jorgensen/FEREX/Shutterstock/AP Images

ethnic diversity. Bashir encourages female employees and introduces them to mentors. She also practices what she preaches—allowing herself to show vulnerability rather than presenting the traditionally male decisive and authoritative style. In addition, she is an outspoken advocate for women's rights worldwide. In 2014, she wrote a groundbreaking essay that drew attention to the abuse of women in the U.K.'s Asian communities. "Growing up the way I did gave me empathy and understanding for different walks of life," Bashir says. "It inspired me to choose the kind of company I wanted to build."[14]

The one difference that has arisen in some cases is that women may be slightly more democratic in making decisions, whereas men have a tendency to be more autocratic.[15] However, much more work needs to be done to better understand the dynamics of gender and leadership. In the meantime, high-profile and successful female leaders, such as Indra Nooyi (CEO of PepsiCo), Sherilyn McCoy (CEO of Avon Products), and Angela Merkel (chancellor of Germany), continue to demonstrate the effectiveness with which women can be exceptional leaders.

Cross-Cultural Leadership

Another changing perspective on leadership relates to cross-cultural issues. In this context, *culture* is used as a broad concept to encompass both international differences and diversity-based differences within one culture. For instance, Japan is generally characterized by *collectivism* (group before individual), whereas the United States is based more on *individualism* (individual before group). So when a Japanese firm sends an executive to head up the firm's operation in the United States, that person will likely find it necessary to recognize the importance of individual contributions and rewards and the differences in individual and group roles that exist in Japanese and U.S. businesses.

For instance, Carlos Ghosn runs both Renault (an Italian car company) and Nissan (a Japanese car company). Ghosn knows that cultural differences cause his European managers to expect him to lead in certain ways, whereas his Japanese managers expect him to lead in slightly different ways. More specifically, in Europe, leaders must often be aggressive, and meetings are often characterized by loud verbal exchanges and arguments. In Japan, though, more emphasis is put on consensus building and polite exchanges of dialogue.

Similarly, cross-cultural factors also play a growing role in organizations as their workforces become more diverse. As African Americans, Asian Americans, Hispanics, and members of other ethnic groups achieve more leadership positions, it may be necessary to reassess how applicable current theories and models of leadership are when applied to an increasingly diverse pool of leaders.

Emerging Issues in Leadership

OBJECTIVE 9-7
Describe
strategic leadership, ethical leadership, and virtual leadership.

Finally, three emerging issues in leadership warrant discussion. These issues are *strategic leadership*, *ethical leadership*, and *virtual leadership*.

Strategic Leadership

Strategic leadership is a somewhat new concept that explicitly relates leadership to the role of top management. **Strategic leadership** is a leader's ability to understand the complexities of both the organization and its environment and to lead change in the organization so as to enhance its competitiveness. Howard Schultz, former CEO and current executive chairman, of Starbucks, is recognized as a strong strategic leader. Not content to continue functioning as "simply" a coffee retailer, Schultz is always on the lookout for new opportunities and how Starbucks can effectively exploit those opportunities.

Strategic Leadership *leader's ability to understand the complexities of both the organization and its environment and to lead change in the organization so as to enhance its competitiveness*

To be effective as a strategic leader, a manager needs to have a thorough and complete understanding of the organization—its history, its culture, its strengths, and its weaknesses. In addition, the leader needs a firm grasp of the organization's external environment. This understanding needs to include current business and economic conditions and circumstances as well as significant trends and issues on the horizon. The strategic leader also needs to recognize the firm's current strategic advantages and shortcomings.

Ethical Leadership

Most people have long assumed that business leaders are ethical people. But in the wake of recent corporate scandals at firms such as Wells Fargo, Volkswagen, Toshiba, and Walmart, faith in business leaders is not as strong as it perhaps once was. As a result, now more than ever high standards of ethical conduct are being held up as a prerequisite for effective leadership. More specifically, business leaders are being called on to maintain high ethical standards for their own conduct, to unfailingly exhibit ethical behavior, and to hold others in their organizations to the same standards—in short, to practice **ethical leadership**.

The behaviors of top leaders are being scrutinized more than ever, and those responsible for hiring new leaders for a business are looking more closely at the backgrounds of those being considered. The emerging pressures for stronger corporate governance models are likely to further increase the commitment to select only those individuals with high ethical standards for leadership positions in business and to hold them more accountable than in the past for both their actions and the consequences of those actions.

Ethical Leadership *leader behaviors that reflect high ethical standards*

Virtual Leadership

Virtual Leadership *leadership in settings where leaders and followers interact electronically rather than in face-to-face settings*

Finally, **virtual leadership** is also emerging as an important issue for organizations. In previous times, leaders and their employees worked together in the same physical location and engaged in face-to-face interactions on a regular basis. But in today's world, both leaders and their employees may work in locations that are far from one another. Such arrangements might include people telecommuting from a home office one or two days a week or people actually living and working far from company headquarters.

managing in turbulent times

The Changing Faces of Leadership

In 2016, after years of lagging behind in the athletic footwear and attire market, Adidas, headquartered in Germany, finally started to close the gap, in no small part due to changes in leadership. Most significantly, after 15 years as the boss of Adidas, Herbert Hainer was asked to leave. After an in-depth search, the job was offered to Kasper Rørsted, who took over in mid-2016. Unlike Hainer, who first went to work for the company in 1987 in its sales department, Rørsted was an industry outsider, coming off a stint as CEO of Henkel, a German consumer packaged goods maker. Investors were optimistic; the stock price increased dramatically in 2016 while competitors faltered.

It wasn't all about the very top leadership, though. Other parts of the organization were responding to the challenges of the marketplace. Mark King came on board in 2014 as the new head of struggling Adidas North America, arriving at his new job only to find internal divisiveness and disorganization. He immediately targeted his efforts toward building a cohesive culture. Since then, Adidas has grown at a faster pace than the overall U.S. market, stealing market share from competitors Nike and Under Armour, the latter still reeling from flops like the all-white Curry 2 Low "Chef" basketball shoe, which Twitter users dubbed the "Seinfeld" sneaker. Then, in 2017, the board accepted the resignation of Chief Financial Officer Robin Stalker and appointed in his place Harm Ohlmeyer, who has been with Adidas since 1998 in various financial leadership roles.

In addition to leadership changes, the company is making strategic operating changes. For instance, it is working with

Daniel Karmann/Dpa Picture Alliance/Alamy Stock Photo

suppliers to increase purchasing flexibility. Instead of ordering a set quantity of shoes or clothing for an entire season, which can result in shortages or overstocking, the company is shifting toward buying limited numbers at the outset and then responding to demand.

Rørsted continues to revamp Adidas's leadership as he implements his strategy of building on sales momentum from classic lines like Stan Smith, adding more modern takes on sportswear fashion, and divesting itself of some non-core businesses like the TaylorMade golf unit. "We are 18 months into our strategy," Rørsted said at a press conference in March 2017. "We still have a lot ahead of us to deliver."

Increasingly, then, communication between leaders and their subordinates happens largely by telephone and e-mail. One implication may be that leaders in these situations must work harder at creating and maintaining relationships with their employees that go beyond words on a computer screen. Although nonverbal communication, such as smiles and handshakes, may not be possible online, managers can instead make a point of adding a few personal words in an e-mail (whenever appropriate) to convey appreciation, reinforcement, or constructive feedback.

Leadership, Management, and Decision Making

OBJECTIVE 9-8
Relate
leadership to decision making and discuss both rational and behavioral perspectives on decision making.

We noted previously the differences and similarities between managing and leading. *Decision making* is another important related concept. Indeed, decision making is a fundamental component of both leadership and management—managers and leaders must frequently make decisions.

The Nature of Decision Making

Decision making can refer to either a specific act or a general process. **Decision making** is the act of choosing one alternative from among a set of alternatives. The decision-making process, however, is much more than this. One step of the process, for example, is that the person making the decision must both recognize that a decision is necessary and identify the set of feasible alternatives before selecting one. Hence, the **decision-making process** includes recognizing and defining the nature of a decision situation, identifying alternatives, choosing the "best" alternative, and putting it into practice.[16]

Decision Making choosing one alternative from among several options

Decision-Making Process recognizing and defining the nature of a decision situation, identifying alternatives, choosing the "best" alternative, and putting it into practice

The word *best* implies effectiveness. Effective decision making requires that the decision maker understand the situation driving the decision. Most people would consider an effective decision to be one that optimizes some set of factors, such as profits, sales, employee welfare, and market share. In some situations, though, an effective decision may be one that minimizes losses, expenses, or employee turnover. It may even mean selecting the best method for going out of business, laying off employees, or terminating a strategic alliance.

We should also note that managers make decisions about both problems and opportunities. For example, making decisions about how to cut costs by 10 percent reflects a problem—an undesirable situation that requires a solution. But decisions are also necessary in situations of opportunity. Learning that the firm is earning higher-than-projected profits, for example, requires a subsequent decision. Should the extra funds be used to increase shareholder dividends, reinvest in current operations, or expand into new markets? Of course, it may take a long time before a manager can know if the right decision was made.

Types of Decisions Managers must make many different types of decisions. In general, however, most decisions fall into one of two categories: *programmed* and *nonprogrammed*.[17] A **programmed decision** is one that is relatively structured or recurs with some frequency (or both). Starbucks uses programmed decisions to purchase new supplies of coffee beans, cups, and napkins, and Starbucks employees are trained in exact procedures for brewing coffee. Likewise, a College Station Ford dealer may make a decision that he or she will sponsor a youth soccer team each year. Thus, when the soccer club president calls, the dealer already knows what he or she will do. Many decisions regarding basic operating systems and procedures and standard organizational transactions are of this variety and can therefore be programmed.[18]

Programmed Decision decision that is relatively structured or recurs with some frequency (or both)

Nonprogrammed decisions, on the other hand, are relatively unstructured and occur much less often. Disney's decision to buy the *Stars Wars* properties from George

Nonprogrammed Decision decision that is relatively unstructured and that occurs with low frequency

Lucas was a nonprogrammed decision. Managers faced with such decisions must treat each one as unique, investing enormous amounts of time, energy, and resources into exploring the situation from all perspectives. Intuition and experience are major factors in nonprogrammed decisions. Most of the decisions made by top managers involving strategy (including mergers, acquisitions, and takeovers) and organization design are nonprogrammed. Nonprogrammed decisions also include those concerning new facilities, new products, labor contracts, and legal issues.

Decision-Making Conditions Just as there are different kinds of decisions, the conditions in which decisions must be made also are different. Managers sometimes have an almost perfect understanding of conditions surrounding a decision, but at other times they have few clues about those conditions. In general, the circumstances that exist for the decision maker are conditions of certainty, risk, or uncertainty.[19]

CERTAINTY When the decision maker knows with reasonable certainty what the alternatives are and what conditions are associated with each alternative, a **state of certainty** exists. Suppose, for example, that managers at Singapore Airlines make a decision to buy five new jumbo jets. Their next decision is from whom to buy them. Because only two companies in the world make jumbo jets, Boeing and Airbus, Singapore Airlines knows its options with certainty. Each has proven products and will guarantee prices and delivery dates. The airline thus knows the alternative conditions associated with each. There is little ambiguity and relatively little chance of making a bad decision.

State of Certainty when the decision maker knows with reasonable certainty what the alternatives are and what conditions are associated with each alternative

Few organizational decisions, however, are made under conditions of true certainty. The complexity and turbulence of the contemporary business world make such situations rare. Even the airplane purchase decision we just considered has less certainty than it appears. The aircraft companies may not be able to guarantee delivery dates, so they may write cost-increase or inflation clauses into contracts. Thus, the airline may be only partially certain of the conditions surrounding each alternative.

State of Risk when the availability of each alternative and its potential pay-offs and costs are all associated with probability estimates

RISK A more common decision-making condition is a state of risk. Under a **state of risk**, the availability of each alternative and its potential payoffs and costs are all associated with probability estimates.[20] Suppose, for example, that a labor contract negotiator for a company receives a "final" offer from the union right before a strike deadline. The negotiator has two alternatives: to accept or to reject the offer. The risk centers on whether the union representatives are bluffing. If the company negotiator accepts the offer, he or she avoids a strike but commits to a relatively costly labor contract. If he or she rejects the contract, he or she may get a more favorable contract if the union is bluffing, but he or she may provoke a strike if it is not.

On the basis of past experience, relevant information, the advice of others, and his or her own judgment, he or she may conclude that there is about a 75 percent chance that union representatives are bluffing and about a 25 percent chance that they will back up their threats. Thus, he or she can base a calculated decision on the two alternatives (accept or reject the contract demands) and the probable consequences of each. When making decisions under a state of risk, managers must reasonably estimate the probabilities associated with each alternative. For example, if the union negotiators are committed to a strike if their demands are not met, and the company negotiator rejects their demands because he or she guesses they will not strike, the miscalculation will prove costly. Decision making under conditions of risk is accompanied by moderate ambiguity and chances of a bad decision.

State of Uncertainty when the decision maker does not know all the alternatives, the risks associated with each, or the likely consequences of each alternative

UNCERTAINTY Most of the major decision making in contemporary organizations is done under a **state of uncertainty**. The decision maker does not know all the alternatives, the risks associated with each, or the likely consequences of each alternative. This uncertainty stems from the complexity and dynamism of contemporary organizations and their environments. The emergence of the Internet as a significant force in today's competitive environment has served to increase both revenue potential and uncertainty for most managers.

To make effective decisions in these circumstances, managers must acquire as much relevant information as possible and approach the situation from a logical and rational perspective. Intuition, judgment, and experience always play major roles in the decision-making process under conditions of uncertainty. Even so, uncertainty is the most ambiguous condition for managers and the one most prone to error.[21] Lorraine Brennan O'Neil is the founder and CEO of 10 Minute Manicure, a quick-service salon located in airports. The company found quick success and experienced rapid growth from its inception. However, the Great Recession required O'Neil to rethink her plans in an attempt to stay afloat through a rocky and unknown future. Knowing that the company no longer had the time to wait and monitor new stores' success, she opted to focus solely on existing stores with profits, shutting down those with losses. Aside from this, she restructured her business plan, seeking nontraditional locations, reducing corporate overhead, cutting products, and developing an online product line as a second source of income.[22]

Rational Decision Making

Managers and leaders should strive to be rational in making decisions. Figure 9.3 shows the steps in the rational decision-making process.

Recognizing and Defining the Decision Situation The first step in rational decision making is recognizing that a decision is necessary; some stimulus or spark must initiate the process. The stimulus for a decision may be either positive or negative. Managers who must decide how to invest surplus funds,

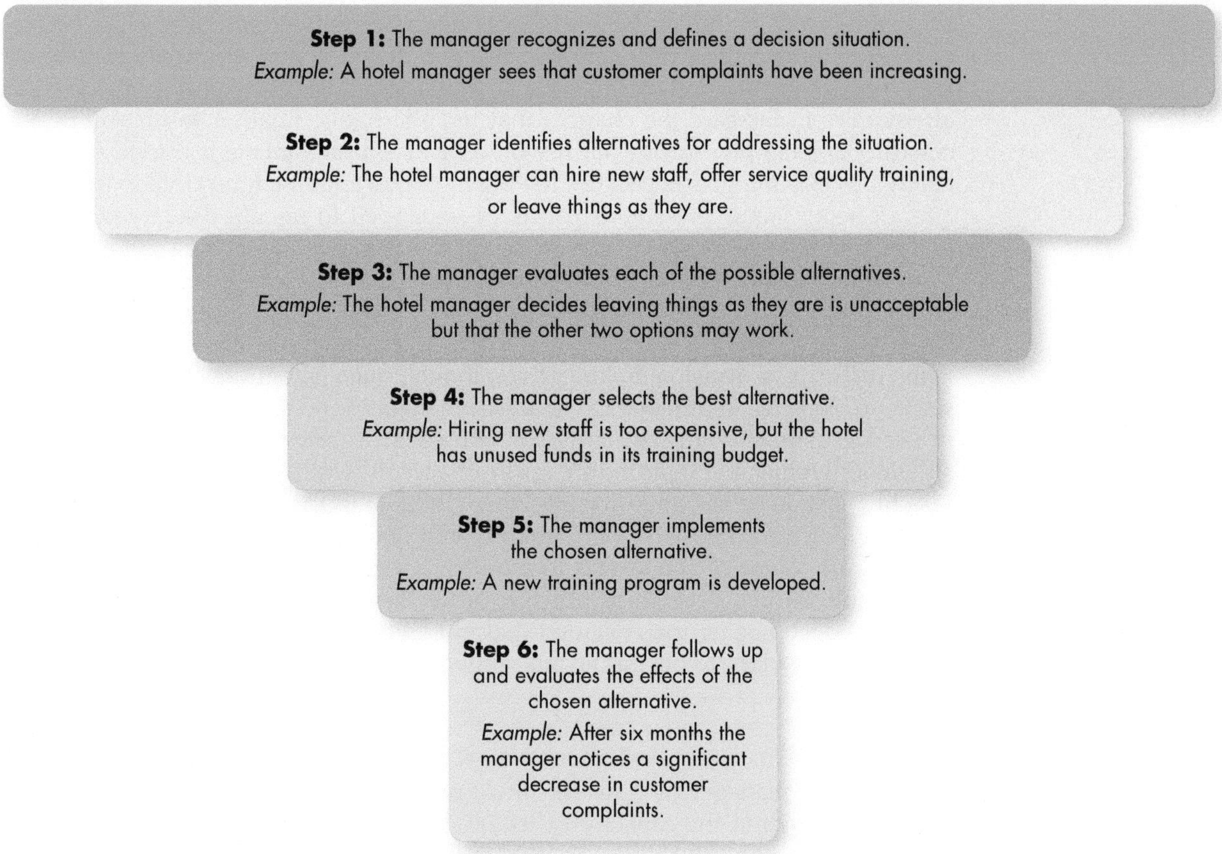

Step 1: The manager recognizes and defines a decision situation.
Example: A hotel manager sees that customer complaints have been increasing.

Step 2: The manager identifies alternatives for addressing the situation.
Example: The hotel manager can hire new staff, offer service quality training, or leave things as they are.

Step 3: The manager evaluates each of the possible alternatives.
Example: The hotel manager decides leaving things as they are is unacceptable but that the other two options may work.

Step 4: The manager selects the best alternative.
Example: Hiring new staff is too expensive, but the hotel has unused funds in its training budget.

Step 5: The manager implements the chosen alternative.
Example: A new training program is developed.

Step 6: The manager follows up and evaluates the effects of the chosen alternative.
Example: After six months the manager notices a significant decrease in customer complaints.

FIGURE 9.3 Steps in the Rational Decision-Making Process
Source: Based on Griffin, *Management* 8e. © 2005 South-Western, a part of Cengage Learning, Inc. Reproduced by permission. www.cengage.com/permissions.

for example, face a positive decision situation. A negative financial stimulus could involve having to trim budgets because of cost overruns.

Inherent in making such a decision is the need to precisely define the problem. Consider the situation currently being faced in the international air travel industry. Because of the growth of international travel related to business, education, and tourism, global carriers need to increase their capacity. Because most major international airports are already operating at or near capacity, adding a significant number of new flights to existing schedules is not feasible. As a result, the most logical alternative is to increase capacity on existing flights. Thus, Boeing and Airbus, the world's biggest manufacturers of large commercial aircraft, recognized an important opportunity and defined their decision situations as how best to respond to the need for increased global travel capacity.[23]

Identifying Alternatives Once the decision situation has been recognized and defined, the second step is to identify alternative courses of effective action. Developing both obvious, standard alternatives and creative, innovative alternatives is useful. In general, the more important the decision, the more attention is directed to developing alternatives. Although managers should seek creative solutions, they must also recognize that various constraints often limit their alternatives. Common constraints include legal restrictions, moral and ethical norms, and constraints imposed by the power and authority of the manager, available technology, economic considerations, and unofficial social norms. After assessing the question of how to increase international airline capacity, Boeing and Airbus identified three different alternatives: They could independently develop new large planes, they could collaborate in a joint venture to create a single new large plane, or they could modify their largest existing planes to increase their capacity.

Evaluating Alternatives The third step in the decision-making process is evaluating each of the alternatives. Some alternatives may not be feasible because of legal or financial barriers. Limited human, material, and information resources may make other alternatives impractical. Managers must thoroughly evaluate all the alternatives to increase the chances that the alternative finally chosen will be successful. For example, Airbus felt it would be at a disadvantage if it tried simply to enlarge its existing planes because the Boeing 747 was at the time already the largest aircraft being made and could readily be expanded to remain the largest. Boeing, meanwhile, was seriously concerned about the risk inherent in building a new and even larger plane, even if it shared the risk with Airbus as a joint venture partner.

Selecting the Best Alternative Choosing the best available alternative is the real crux of decision making. Even though many situations do not lend themselves to objective, mathematical analysis, managers and leaders can often develop subjective estimates and weights for choosing an alternative. Decision makers should also remember that finding multiple acceptable alternatives may be possible; selecting just one alternative and rejecting all the others might not be necessary. For example, Airbus proposed a joint venture with Boeing. Boeing, meanwhile, decided that its best course of action was to modify its existing 747 to increase its capacity. As a result, Airbus decided to proceed on its own to develop and manufacture a new jumbo jet. Boeing then decided that in addition to modifying its 747, it would develop a new plane to offer as an alternative, albeit one not as large as the 747 or the proposed Airbus plane.

Implementing the Chosen Alternative After an alternative has been selected, managers and leaders must put it into effect. Boeing set its engineers to work expanding the capacity of its 747 by adding 30 feet to the plane's body; the firm also began developing another plane intended for international travel, the 787. Airbus engineers, meanwhile, developed design concepts for a new jumbo jet equipped with escalators and elevators and capable of carrying 655 passengers. Airbus's development costs alone were estimated to exceed $12 billion.

Managers must also consider people's resistance to change when implementing decisions. The reasons for such resistance include insecurity, inconvenience, and fear of the unknown. Managers should anticipate potential resistance at various stages of the implementation process. However, even when all alternatives have been evaluated as precisely as possible and the consequences of each alternative have been weighed, unanticipated consequences are still likely. Employees may resist or protest change; they may even quit rather than agree to it. Other factors, such as unexpected cost increases, a less-than-perfect fit with existing organizational subsystems, or unpredicted effects on cash flow or operating expenses, could develop after implementation has begun. Both Boeing and Airbus were plagued by production delays that pushed back delivery of their respective aircrafts by years and ended up costing each company billions of dollars. Airbus got its plane to market first (it began flying in late 2007), but profits have been pushed far into the future because the global recession caused many airlines to cancel or delay orders for several years.

Following Up and Evaluating the Results The final step in the decision-making process requires that managers and leaders evaluate the effectiveness of their decision. They should make sure that the chosen alternative has served its original purpose. If an implemented alternative appears not to be working, they can respond in several ways. Another previously identified alternative (the original second or third choice, for instance) could be adopted. Or they might recognize that the situation was not correctly defined to begin with and start the process all over again. Finally, managers and leaders might decide that the original alternative is in fact appropriate but either has not yet had time to work or should be implemented in a different way.

At this point, both Boeing and Airbus are nearing the crucial period when they will learn whether they made good decisions. Airbus's A380 made its first commercial flight in 2007, though delays continue to push back its production schedule. The plane has also been hampered by technical problems. Meanwhile, Boeing's 787 faced numerous delays, and widespread use of the plane continues to be delayed by technical issues.[24] The expanded 747 was launched on schedule, however, and was in service in 2011. Most airlines have been willing to wait patiently for the 787s, which are designed to be much more fuel efficient than other international airplanes. Given the dramatic surge in fuel costs in recent years, a fuel-efficient option like the 787 could be an enormous success. Indeed, Airbus has begun developing its own fuel-efficient jet, the A350.[25] Qatar Airways took delivery of the first A350 in December 2014.

As time passed, though, demand for the expanded 747 stalled and Boeing decided to suspend production. The A380, meanwhile, proved to be only moderately successful and as of 2017 only the airline Emirates still had active orders for the jumbo jet. The 787 and A350, on the other hand, appear to be on track for long-term success.

Behavioral Aspects of Decision Making

If all decision situations were approached as logically as described in the previous section, more decisions would prove successful. Yet decisions are often made with little consideration for logic and rationality. Some experts have estimated that U.S. companies use rational decision-making techniques less than 20 percent of the time. Of course, even when organizations try to be logical, they sometimes fail. For example, when Starbucks opened its first coffee shops in New York, it relied on scientific marketing research, taste tests, and rational deliberation in making a decision to emphasize drip over espresso coffee. However, that decision proved wrong because it became clear that New Yorkers strongly preferred the same espresso-style coffees that were Starbucks mainstays in the West. Hence, the firm had to reconfigure its stores hastily to meet customer preferences.

On the other hand, sometimes a decision made with little regard for logic can still turn out to be correct.[26] Important ingredients in how these forces work are behavioral aspects of decision making. These include *political forces, intuition, escalation of commitment,* and *risk propensity.*

Political Forces in Decision Making Political forces contribute to the behavioral nature of decision making. One major element of politics, *coalitions*, is especially relevant to decision making. A **coalition** is an informal alliance of individuals or groups formed to achieve a common goal. This common goal is often a preferred decision alternative. For example, coalitions of stockholders frequently band together to force a board of directors to make a certain decision.

Coalition *an informal alliance of individuals or groups formed to achieve a common goal*

The New York Yankees once contacted three major sneaker manufacturers, Nike, Reebok, and Adidas, and informed them that they were looking to make a sponsorship deal. While Nike and Reebok were carefully and rationally assessing the possibilities, managers at Adidas quickly realized that a partnership with the Yankees made a lot of sense for them. They responded quickly to the idea and ended up hammering out a contract while the competitors were still analyzing details.[27]

When these coalitions enter the political arena and attempt to persuade lawmakers to make decisions favorable to their interests, they are called *lobbyists*. Lobbyists may also donate money to help elect a candidate who is more likely to pursue their agendas. A recurring theme in U.S. politics is the damaging influence these special interest groups have on politicians, who may feel unduly obligated to favor campaign donors when making decisions.

Intuition *an innate belief about something, often without conscious consideration*

Intuition **Intuition** is an innate belief about something, often without conscious consideration. Managers sometimes decide to do something because it "feels right" or they have a hunch. This feeling is usually not arbitrary, however. Rather, it is based on years of experience and practice in making decisions in similar situations. Such an inner sense may help managers make an occasional decision without going through a full-blown rational sequence of steps. That said, all managers, but most especially inexperienced ones, should be careful not to rely too heavily on intuition. If rationality and logic are continually flouted for "what feels right," the odds are that disaster will strike one day.

Escalation of Commitment *condition in which a decision maker becomes so committed to a course of action that she or he stays with it even when it appears to have been wrong*

Escalation of Commitment Another important behavioral process that influences decision making is **escalation of commitment** to a chosen course of action. In particular, decision makers sometimes make decisions and then become so committed to the course of action suggested by that decision that they stay with it, even when it appears to have been wrong.[28] For example, when people buy stock in a company, they sometimes refuse to sell it even after repeated drops in price. They choose a course of action, buying the stock in anticipation of making a profit, and then stay with it even in the face of increasing losses. Moreover, after the value drops, they may rationalize that they can't sell at such a low price because they will lose money.

Risk Propensity *extent to which a decision maker is willing to gamble when making a decision*

Risk Propensity and Decision Making The behavioral element of **risk propensity** is the extent to which a decision maker is willing to gamble when making a decision. Some managers are cautious about every decision they make. They try to adhere to the rational model and are extremely conservative in what they do. Such managers are more likely to avoid mistakes, and they infrequently make decisions that lead to big losses. Others are extremely aggressive in making decisions and willing to take risks.[29] They rely heavily on intuition, reach decisions quickly, and often risk big investments on their decisions. As in gambling, these managers are more likely than their conservative counterparts to achieve big successes with their decisions; they are also more likely to incur greater losses.[30] The organization's culture is a prime ingredient in fostering different levels of risk propensity.

summary of learning objectives

Define *leadership* **and distinguish it from management. (pp. 280–282)**

Leadership refers to the processes and behaviors used by someone to motivate, inspire, and influence the behaviors of others. Although leadership and management are often related, they are not the same thing. Leadership involves such things as developing a vision, communicating that vision, and directing change. Management, meanwhile, focuses more on outlining procedures, monitoring results, and working toward outcomes.

Power is the ability to affect the behavior of others. In organizational settings, there are usually five kinds of power: (1) legitimate, (2) reward, (3) coercive, (4) referent, and (5) expert power. *Legitimate power* is power granted through the organizational hierarchy; it is the power defined by the organization to be accorded to people occupying a particular position. *Reward power* is the power to give or withhold rewards. *Coercive power* is the power to force compliance by means of psychological, emotional, or physical threat. *Referent power* is based on identification, imitation, loyalty, or charisma. *Expert power* is derived from information or expertise.

Summarize **early approaches to the study of leadership. (pp. 282–284)**

The *trait approach to leadership* focused on identifying the traits of successful leaders. The earliest researchers believed that important leadership traits included intelligence, dominance, self-confidence, energy, activity (versus passivity), and knowledge about the job. However, this research did not produce conclusive results. More recent researchers have started to focus on traits such as emotional and mental intelligence, drive, motivation, honesty and integrity, self-confidence, knowledge of the business, and charisma.

The *behavioral approach* to leadership sought to determine what behaviors were employed by effective leaders. Research identified two basic and common leader behaviors: *task-focused* and *employee-focused* leader behaviors. It is thought that leaders should engage in both behaviors to increase performance and motivation.

Discuss **the concept of situational approaches to leadership.**
(pp. 284–285)

The *situational approach to leadership* proposes that there is no single best approach to leadership. Instead, situational factors influence the approach to leadership that is most effective. This approach was proposed as a continuum of leadership behavior, ranging from having the leader make decisions alone to having employees make decisions with minimal guidance from the leader. Each point on the continuum is influenced by *characteristics of the leader, his or her subordinates*, and the *situation*.

The path–goal theory of leadership is a direct extension of the expectancy theory of motivation. It suggests that the primary functions of a leader are to make valued or desired rewards available in the workplace and to clarify for the subordinate the kinds of behavior that will lead to goal accomplishment and valued rewards. The leader should clarify the paths to goal attainment. Path–goal theory identifies four kinds of behaviors that leaders can use, depending on the situation: (1) *directive leader behavior*, (2) *supportive leader behavior*, (3) *participative leader behavior*, and (4) *achievement-oriented leader behavior*.

The decision tree approach attempts to prescribe a leadership style appropriate to a given situation. The decision tree approach assumes that the degree to which subordinates should be encouraged to participate in decision making depends on the characteristics of the situation. After evaluating a variety of problem attributes (characteristics of the problem or decision), the leader determines an appropriate decision style that specifies the amount of subordinate participation.

The *leader-member exchange (LMX) model of leadership* stresses the importance of variable relationships between supervisors and each of their subordinates. Each superior–subordinate pair represents a "vertical dyad." The model differs from previous approaches in that it focuses on the differential relationship leaders often establish with different subordinates.

OBJECTIVE 9-4

Describe transformational and charismatic perspectives on leadership. (pp. 285–288)

Transformational leadership (as distinguished from *transactional leadership*) focuses on the set of abilities that allows a leader to recognize the need for change, to create a vision to guide that change, and to execute the change effectively. *Charismatic leadership* is influence based on the leader's personal charisma. The basic concept of charisma suggests that charismatic leaders are likely to have self-confidence, confidence in their beliefs and ideals, and a need to influence people. They also tend to communicate high expectations about follower performance and to express confidence in their followers.

OBJECTIVE 9-5

Identify and discuss leadership substitutes and neutralizers. (pp. 288–289)

Leadership substitutes are individual, task, and organizational factors that tend to outweigh the need for a leader to initiate or direct employee performance. In other words, if certain factors are present, the employee will perform his or her job without the direction of a leader. Examples of leadership substitutes include individual professionalism, highly structured jobs, explicit plans and goals, and group performance norms. Even if a leader attempts to engage in leadership behaviors, *leadership neutralizers* may render the leader's efforts ineffective. Such neutralizers include group cohesiveness as well as elements of the job itself.

OBJECTIVE 9-6

Discuss leaders as coaches and examine gender and cross-cultural issues in leadership. (pp. 289–291)

Many organizations expect their leaders to play the role of *coach*—to select team members, provide direction, train, and develop—but otherwise allow the group to function autonomously. Some leaders may function as mentors, helping less experienced employees learn the ropes and better preparing them to advance in an organization.

Another factor that is altering the face of leadership is the number of women advancing to higher levels. Although there appear to be few differences between men and women leaders, the growing number of women leaders suggests a need for more study. Some evidence indicates that women are more democratic in decision making and have the potential to be excellent leaders, as shown by a number of high-profile, successful female leaders.

Another changing perspective on leadership relates to cross-cultural issues. In this context, *culture* encompasses international differences and diversity-based differences within one culture. For example, the level of collectivism or individualism can affect a manager's leadership style.

OBJECTIVE 9-7

Describe strategic leadership, ethical leadership, and virtual leadership. (pp. 291–293)

Strategic leadership is the leader's ability to lead change in the organization so as to enhance its competitiveness. To be effective as a strategic leader, a manager needs to have a thorough and complete understanding of the organization's history, culture, strengths, and weaknesses. Business leaders are also being called on to practice *ethical leadership*—that is, to maintain high ethical standards for their own conduct, and to hold others in their organizations to the same standards. As more leaders and employees work in different settings, a better understanding of *virtual leadership* is also becoming more important.

OBJECTIVE 9-8

Relate leadership to decision making and discuss both rational and behavioral perspectives on decision making. (pp. 293–298)

Decision making—choosing one alternative from among several options—is a critical management and leadership skill. Decision making can refer to either a specific act or a general process. Most decisions fall into one of two categories: programmed and nonprogrammed. A programmed decision is one that is relatively structured or recurs with some frequency (or both). Nonprogrammed decisions are relatively unstructured and occur much less often. There are three different conditions in which decisions must be made. These are conditions of certainty, risk, or uncertainty. When the decision maker knows what the alternatives are and the likely outcomes, a *state of certainty* exists. Under a *state of risk*, the availability of each alternative and its payoffs and costs are not clear. Finally, in a *state of uncertainty*, the decision maker does not know all the alternatives, risks, or consequences.

The *rational perspective* prescribes a logical process for making decisions. It involves six steps: (1) recognizing and defining the decision situation, (2) identifying alternatives, (3) evaluating alternatives, (4) selecting the best alternative, (5) implementing the chosen alternative, and (6) following up and evaluating the results. The *behavioral perspective* acknowledges that things such as *political forces, intuition, escalation of commitment*, and *risk propensity* are also important aspects of decision making.

key terms

behavioral approach to leadership (p. 283)
charismatic leadership (p. 286)
coalition (p. 298)
coercive power (p. 282)
decision making (p. 293)
decision-making process (p. 293)
decision tree approach (p. 285)
employee-focused leader behavior (p. 283)
escalation of commitment (p. 298)
ethical leadership (p. 292)
expert power (p. 282)
intuition (p. 298)

leader-member exchange (LMX) model (p. 285)
leadership (p. 280)
leadership neutralizers (p. 289)
leadership substitutes (p. 288)
legitimate power (p. 281)
nonprogrammed decision (p. 293)
path–goal theory (p. 285)
power (p. 281)
programmed decision (p. 293)
referent power (p. 282)
reward power (p. 282)

risk propensity (p. 298)
situational approach to leadership (p. 284)
state of certainty (p. 294)
state of risk (p. 294)
state of uncertainty (p. 294)
strategic leadership (p. 291)
task-focused leader behavior (p. 283)
trait approach to leadership (p. 283)
transactional leadership (p. 286)
transformational leadership (p. 286)
virtual leadership (p. 292)

MyLab Intro to Business

To complete the problems with the ✪, go to EOC Discussion Questions in the MyLab.

questions & exercises

QUESTIONS FOR REVIEW

✪ **9-1.** What are the basic differences between management and leadership?

9-2. Summarize the basic premises underlying the trait approach to leadership.

9-3. What are leadership substitutes and neutralizers?

✪ **9-4.** List and briefly explain the steps in rational decision making.

QUESTIONS FOR ANALYSIS

9-5. Describe the five types of power. Which type or types does your current supervisor exercise?

9-6. When is task-focused leader behavior most important? When is it more important for a leader to exhibit employee-focused behavior?

9-7. The impact of virtual leadership is likely to grow in the future. As a potential "follower" in a virtual leadership situation, what issues would be of most concern to you? What would the issues be from the perspective of the "leader" role in such a situation?

★ 9-8. Identify a leader who you believe exhibits charismatic leadership and explain the behaviors that support this conclusion.

APPLICATION EXERCISES

9-9. Overwhelmingly, the CEOs of the largest companies in the United States are white males, but women and minorities are making inroads. Identify a leader who is a member of a minority group and describe the challenges that he or she faced and overcame.

9-10. In 2012, Marissa Mayer was appointed president and CEO of Yahoo!, Inc. In her tenure with Yahoo, she made a number of bold decisions, not all of which were popular, such as eliminating the telecommuting option. Research Mayer's career, especially at Yahoo. What type of leader is Mayer? How would you describe her leadership style? Do you think she is an effective leader? Why?

building a business: continuing team exercise

Assignment

Meet with your team members to consider your new business venture and how it relates to the leadership topics in this chapter. Develop specific responses to the following:

9-11. How will you select a leader for your organization? What traits or characteristics will be most important to you when selecting a leader?

9-12. Which types of power will be most important to the leader of your business venture?

9-13. What leadership substitutes could support your business venture as you get started?

9-14. Are there any leadership neutralizers that could derail your new effort?

9-15. As your business venture gets off the ground, you will have to make many important decisions. Will you rely more heavily on rational decision making or intuition? Why?

team exercise

MANAGING CHANGES IN STRATEGIC DIRECTION

The Situation

Commonwealth Services is a commercial cleaning service, with customers across the state of Virginia. Your company provides cleaning services for office buildings and other commercial customers. Commonwealth is a lean operation, with a flat organizational structure and a small number of managers. The recession took its toll on the company and employees have not had a raise in years. To make matters worse, your employees don't find that cleaning is particularly rewarding work. Customers expect a consistently high level of service and dependability, but you're finding it hard to motivate employees. To expand your customer base, Commonwealth has decided to expand its services and will now offer clean-up services for foreclosed properties being prepared for sale. These properties are often in a great state of disarray and the work can be particularly unappealing. Employees are not excited about these new customers and are not supportive of the change. The company has asked you to come in as a consultant and conduct leadership workshops for the management team. Your job is to develop a set of concrete recommendations about how to lead employees through this change in strategy.

Team Activity

Assemble a group of four students and assign each group member to one of the following approaches to leadership:

- Leader-member exchange (LMX) model
- Path–goal theory
- Task-focused leader
- Employee-focused leader

ACTION STEPS

9-16. Working individually, develop a leadership strategy based on your assigned approach to leadership. What will be most important to your success? How will you communicate with employees and motivate them?

9-17. Assemble your group and share your assignment perspectives. Make sure you define the approach, outline the strategy, and tie it back to the facts of the case.

9-18. As a group, develop a list of advantages and disadvantages of each approach.

9-19. Select the most appropriate leadership style and change management strategy and develop a justification for your decision.

exercising your ethics

EXERCISING CHARISMA

The Situation

You are the chief financial officer (CFO) for Advanced Nutriceuticals, a leading manufacturer of nutritional supplements in the United States. The company's CEO, Jeff Johnson, is passionate about health and the value of nutritional supplements. Jeff has a compelling story—he is a survivor of Stage IV skin cancer, an outcome he attributes to the use of nutritional supplements. He is featured widely in company advertising and is admired by most of the company's employees.

Unlike prescription medications, nutritional supplements are not subject to U.S. Food and Drug Administration regulation, and the company does not have a lot of well-supported research to support the efficacy of its products. In addition, there has been considerable competition from manufacturers outside the United States, who can produce the same products at a much lower cost. The company has spent a year developing a long-term strategy that involves increasing production and expansion into international markets.

The Dilemma

As the CFO, you have been asked to develop a budget for the next three years. The company has plans to expand its operations, and you have projected that there will be a need for a large amount of capital. You have presented your budget to the CEO and board of directors and have discussed various options for raising capital, such as the sale of bonds and a public offering of additional stock. After analyzing each of the alternatives that you have presented, Jeff has come back with a new option: He wants to move all of the employees' retirement funds to stock in Advanced Nutriceuticals and encourage every employee to show "company spirit" by investing as much as possible. Jeff is convinced that he can sell this to the employees based on his charm and charisma. You are concerned that this is a risky move for employees; if the company is not successful, they will be out of a job and a retirement fund. You are also aware that the employees respect Jeff and believe in him, and they will probably follow his recommendations.

QUESTIONS TO ADDRESS

9-20. What are the ethical issues in this situation?

9-21. What do you think most managers would do in this situation?

9-22. What would you do?

cases

AUTHENTIC LEADERSHIP

Continued from page 280

At the beginning of this chapter, you read about Brad Smith's rise through the ranks from marketing manager to CEO of Intuit. Using the information presented in this chapter, you should now be able to respond to these questions.

QUESTIONS FOR DISCUSSION

9-23. What personal traits does Brad Smith possess that aid him as a leader?

9-24. How would you describe Brad Smith's leadership style?

9-25. Do you believe that Smith's gender played a part in his success? Why or why not?

9-26. What are three important lessons from Smith's career path?

THE MAN BEHIND THE GENIUS

There is no doubt that Steve Jobs, cofounder of Apple, was a one-of-a-kind leader. In many ways, Jobs was defined by his passion for innovation and willingness to take risks. As the leader of a company that created the iMac, iPhone, iPod, and iPad, Jobs demonstrated that he could see beyond the present and motivate his employees by sharing his vision clearly and compellingly. According to Apple's current CEO, Tim Cook, "Even though he was running a large company, he kept making bold moves that I don't think that anyone else would have done."[31]

The challenge, however, for Jobs and Apple was this same vision and passion. A visionary leader's strength is an ability to mobilize his or her employees to work toward a goal at superhuman speed. Yet, when the vision is flawed, the employees demonstrate the same commitment and move quickly, and even dangerously, in the wrong direction.[32] Often, these visionary leaders effectively screen out negative chatter, but this is not always positive, particularly when employees discover a fatal flaw.

Jobs had a unique managerial style. According to Joe Nocera of *The New York Times*, he "violated every rule of management. He was not a consensus builder but a dictator who listened mainly to his own intuition. He was a maniacal micromanager. He had an astonishing aesthetic sense, which businesspeople almost always lack…. He never mellowed, never let up on Apple employees, never stopped relying on his singular instincts in making decisions about how Apple products should look and how they should work."[33]

Although inspiring thousands of employees and millions of customers, Jobs could be brutal when dealing with employees who failed to successfully implement his vision. Despite many successes, Apple had its failures. One of the most notable was the MobileMe e-mail system. Jobs was so disappointed by flaws in the system that he fired the employee leading the MobileMe effort in front of a crowd of employees.

Jobs's passion was at the core of his being. When Jobs had a liver transplant in 2009, he found himself in the hospital with an oxygen mask. He pulled off the mask and told the pulmonologist that he was unwilling to suffer through the poor design, though barely able to speak. Ultimately, Jobs succumbed to pancreatic cancer in 2011, but he left an indelible mark on the world.

QUESTIONS FOR DISCUSSION

9-27. Do you think Steve Jobs was a charismatic leader? What leads you to this conclusion?

9-28. Jobs enjoyed almost cult-like loyalty among his employees. Why do you think people clamored to work for Apple under Jobs's leadership?

9-29. What challenges face employees working for a leader such as Jobs?

9-30. Describe Jobs with respect to intuition, escalation of commitment, and risk propensity.

9-31. Do you think that you would have enjoyed working for Apple during Jobs's leadership? Why, or why not?

9-32. How does a leader differ from a manager? Describe the situational approach to leadership and three major theories within this category. How would the path–goal theory help you identify the most appropriate leadership style in a situation?

Writing Assignments

9-33. Many followers prefer to have transformational or charismatic leaders. Do you think that a transformational focus and charisma are guarantees for success? Does being a transformational or charismatic leader indicate successful management? Are there situations where charisma can mislead followers about a leader's ability? Support your answers.

9-34. Imagine that you are the CEO of a major company. Write a memo to your upper level management team describing the differences between management and leadership and your expectations of them in both areas. Also, address how you see the role of leadership in middle management and line staff.

endnotes

1 Houvouras, Jack, "Mr. Smith Goes to Silicon Valley," *Huntington Quarterly*, 2015, http://huntingtonquarterly.com/articles/issue91/mr-smith-goes-to-silicon-valley.php (accessed March 21, 2017).

2 Bryan, Adam, "Brad Smith of Intuit: Follow the Fastest Beat of Your Heart," *The New York Times*, 2014, https://www.nytimes.com/2014/04/13/business/brad-smith-of-intuit-follow-the-fastest-beat-of-your-heart.html (accessed March 21, 2017).

3 Smith, Brad, "Five Keys to Being a Great Leader," BLUEprint by Intuit, December 7, 2016, https://medium.com/blueprint-by-intuit/five-keys-to-being-a-great-leader-7d9fa5edf0e0#.vytl36tte (accessed March 21, 2017).

4 See John Kotter, "What Leaders Really Do," *Harvard Business Review*, December 2001, 85–94.

5 French, John R. P., and Raven, Bertram. "The Bases of Social Power," in Cartwright, Dorwin, (ed.), *Studies in Social Power* (Ann Arbor, MI: University of Michigan Press, 1959), pp. 150–167.

6 "Management Secrets from the Meanest Company in America," *Bloomberg BusinessWeek*, January 2, 2013, pp. 46–51.

7 "Bad Bosses Can Be Bad for Your Health," *USA Today*, August 8, 2012, p. 5B; Tepper, Bennett J. "Abusive Supervision in Work Organizations: Review, Synthesis, and Research Agenda," *Journal of Management*, 2007, vol. 33, no. 3, pp. 261–289.

8 Evans, Martin G. "The Effects of Supervisory Behavior on the Path–Goal Relationship," *Organizational Behavior and Human Performance*, May 1970, pp. 277–298; House, Robert J., and Mitchell, Terence R. "Path-Goal Theory of Leadership," *Journal of Contemporary Business*, Autumn 1974, pp. 81–98; see also Yukl, Gary. *Leadership in Organizations*, 8th ed. (Upper Saddle River: Prentice-Hall, 2013).

9 Graen, George, and Cashman, J. F. "A Role-Making Model of Leadership in Formal Organizations: A Developmental Approach," in Hunt, J. G., and Larson L. L., (eds.), *Leadership Frontiers* (Kent, OH: Kent State University Press, 1975), pp. 143–165; Dansereau, Fred, Graen, George, and Haga, W. J. "A Vertical Dyad Linkage Approach to Leadership Within Formal Organizations: A Longitudinal Investigation of the Role-Making Process," *Organizational Behavior and Human Performance*, 1975, vol. 15, pp. 46–78.

10 Waldman, David A., and Yammarino, Francis J. "CEO Charismatic Leadership: Levels-of-Management and Levels-of-Analysis Effects," *Academy of Management Review*, 1999, vol. 24, no. 2, pp. 266–285.

11 Howell, Jane, and Shamir, Boas. "The Role of Followers in the Charismatic Leadership Process: Relationships and Their Consequences," *Academy of Management Review*, January 2005, pp. 96–112.

12 Canal, Emily. 2014. "FORBES 400: Meet The American Billionaires Attending The Forbes Under 30 Summit." *Forbes.Com* 1. *Business Source Premier*, EBSCOhost (accessed February 3, 2017); Eng, Dinah. 2012. "Adventures of a Serial Entrepreneur." *Fortune* 165, no. 6: 23–26; *Business Source Premier*, EBSCOhost (accessed February 3, 2017); Peterson-Withorn, Chase. 2014. "After Building Two Billion-Dollar Brands, John Paul DeJoria Shares His Success." Forbes.Com 1. Business Source Premier, EBSCOhost (accessed May 13, 2015).

[13] Hackman, J. Richard, and Wageman, Ruth. "A Theory of Team Coaching," *Academy of Management Review*, April 2005, pp. 269–287.

[14] Rao, Leena, "How Ruzwana Bashir Became Silicon Valley's Favorite British Import.'" *Fortune*, 2016, http://fortune.com/2016/11/02/ruzwana-bashir-peek-silicon-valley/ (accessed March 22, 2017).

[15] "How Women Lead," *Newsweek*, October 24, 2005, pp. 46–70.

[16] For a review of decision making, see E. Frank Harrison, *The Managerial Decision Making Process*, 5th ed. (Boston: Houghton Mifflin, 1999). See also Weber, Elke U., and Johnson, Eric J. "Mindful Judgment and Decision Making," in Fiske, Susan T., Schacter, Daniel L., and Sternberg, Robert (eds.), *Annual Review of Psychology 2009* (Palo Alto, CA: Annual Reviews, 2009), pp. 53–86; Gigerenzer, Gerd, and Gaissmaier, Wolfgang. "Heuristic Decision Making," in Fiske, Susan T., Schacter, Daniel L., and and Taylor, Shelley (eds.), *Annual Review of Psychology 2011* (Palo Alto, CA: Annual Reviews, 2011), pp. 451–482.

[17] Huber, George P. *Managerial Decision Making* (Glenview, IL: Scott, Foresman, 1980).

[18] For an example, see Paul D. Collins, Lori V. Ryan, and Sharon F. Matusik, "Programmable Automation and the Locus of Decision-Making Power," *Journal of Management*, 1999, Vol. 25, pp. 29–53.

[19] Huber, George. *Managerial Decision Making*. See also David W. Miller and Martin K. Starr, *The Structure of Human Decisions* (Englewood Cliffs, NJ: Prentice-Hall, 1976); Elbing, Alvar. *Behavioral Decisions in Organizations*, 2nd ed. (Glenview, IL: Scott, Foresman, 1978).

[20] Stulz, Rene M. "Six Ways Companies Mismanage Risk," *Harvard Business Review*, March 2009, pp. 86–94.

[21] Hodgkinson, Gerard P., Bown, Nicola J., Maule, A. John, Glaister, Keith W., and Pearman, Alan D. "Breaking the Frame: An Analysis of Strategic Cognition and Decision Making under Uncertainty," *Strategic Management Journal*, 1999, Vol. 20, pp. 977–985.

[22] "Using Intuition in Your Business Plan," *Forbes*, September 20, 2010, pp. 34–36.

[23] Useem, Jerry. "Boeing vs. Boeing," *Fortune*, October 2, 2000, pp. 148–160; "Airbus Prepares to 'Bet the Company' As It Builds a Huge New Jet," *Wall Street Journal*, November 3, 1999, pp. A1, A10.

[24] "Dreamliner Reliability in Doubt After Failures," *USA Today*, January 9, 2013, pp. 1A, 5A.

[25] "Accommodating the A380," *Wall Street Journal*, November 29, 2005, B1; "Boeing Roars Ahead," *BusinessWeek*, November 7, 2005, pp. 44–45; "Boeing's New Tailwind," *Newsweek*, December 5, 2005, p. 45; Crown, Judith. "Even More Boeing 787 Delays?" *BusinessWeek*, April 4, 2008 (May 27, 2008), at http://www.businessweek.com/bwdaily/dnflash/content/apr2008/db2008043_948354.htm?campaign_id=rss_daily; Aaron Karp, *ATW Daily News*, April 9, 2008 (May 27, 2008), at http://www.atwonline.com/news/story.html?storyID=12338; "Airbus: New Delays for A380 Deliveries," CNNMoney.com, May 13, 2008 (May 27, 2008), at http://money.cnn.com/2008/05/13/news/international/airbus_delay.ap/index.htm?postversion=2008051304; "Airbus A380 Delays Not Disclosed for Months," MSNBC.com, May 29, 2007 (May 27, 2008), at http://www.msnbc.msn.com/id/18918869/.

[26] "Making Decisions in Real Time," *Fortune*, June 26, 2000, 332–334; see also Gladwell, Malcolm. *Blink* (New York: Little, Brown, 2005).

[27] Wallace, Charles P. "Adidas—Back in the Game," *Fortune*, August 18, 1997, pp. 176–182.

[28] Staw, Barry M., and Ross, Jerry. "Good Money After Bad," *Psychology Today*, February 1988, pp. 30–33; Bobocel, D. Ramona, and Meyer, John. "Escalating Commitment to a Failing Course of Action: Separating the Roles of Choice and Justification," *Journal of Applied Psychology*, vol. 79, 1994, pp. 360–363.

[29] McNamara, Gerry, and Bromiley, Philip. "Risk and Return in Organizational Decision Making," *Academy of Management Journal*, vol. 42, 1999, pp. 330–339.

[30] See Brian O'Reilly, "What It Takes to Start a Startup," *Fortune*, June 7, 1999, pp. 135–140, for an example.

[31] Caulfield, Brian. "Steve Jobs Bio: Neither Insane Nor Great." *Forbes Magazine*, October 26, 2011, at http://www.forbes.com/sites/briancaulfield/2011/10/26/steve-jobs-bio-neither-insane-nor-great/, accessed on June 28 2013.

[32] Sherman, Erik. "The Problem with Charismatic Leaders." *Inc.com*. May 6, 2013, at http://www.inc.com/erik-sherman/the-problem-with-charismatic-leaders.html, accessed on February 3, 2017.

[33] Allen, Frederick E. "Steve Jobs Broke Every Leadership Rule. Don't Try It Yourself." *Forbes Magazine*, August 27, 2011, at http://www.forbes.com/sites/frederickallen/2011/08/27/steve-jobs-broke-every-leadership-rule-dont-try-that-yourself/, accessed on May 10, 2017.

Effective human resource management is an organization's lifeblood. Putting people **first is the best** strategy a firm can have.

After reading this chapter, you should be able to:

10-1 **Define** *human resource management*, discuss its strategic significance, and explain how managers plan for their organization's human resource needs.

10-2 **Discuss** the legal context of human resource management and identify contemporary legal issues.

10-3 **Identify** the steps in staffing a company and discuss ways in which organizations recruit and select new employees.

10-4 **Describe** the main components of a compensation and benefits system.

10-5 **Describe** how managers develop the workforce in their organization through training and performance appraisal.

10-6 **Discuss** workforce diversity, the management of knowledge workers, and the use of a contingent workforce as important changes in the contemporary workplace.

10-7 **Explain** why workers organize into labor unions and describe the collective bargaining process.

A Unique Partnership
Drives Wegmans

If you're looking for the best Parmesan cheese for your chicken parmigiana recipe, you might try Wegmans, especially if you happen to live in the vicinity of Pittsford, New York.

Cheese department manager Carol Kent will be happy to recommend the best brand because her job calls for knowing cheese as well as managing some 20 subordinates. Kent is a knowledgeable employee, and Wegmans sees that as a key asset. Specifically, Wegmans believes that its employees are more knowledgeable than are the employees of its competitors.

Wegmans Food Markets, a family-owned East Coast chain with more than 80 stores in six states, prides itself on its commitment to customers, and it shows. It ranks near the top of the latest *Consumer Reports* survey of the best national and regional grocery stores, and in 2017, for the 20th year in a row, the company landed a top spot on *Fortune* magazine's list of 100 Best Companies to Work For. But commitment to customers is only half of Wegmans' overall strategy, which calls for reaching its customers through its employees. "How do we differentiate ourselves?" asks CEO Danny Wegman, who then proceeds to answer his own question: "If we can sell products that require knowledge in terms of how you use them, that's our strategy. Anything that requires knowledge and service gives us a reason to be." That's the logic behind one of Kent's recent assignments—one that she understandably regards as a perk. Wegmans sent her to Italy to conduct a personal study of Italian cheese. "We sat with the families" that make the cheeses, she recalls, "broke bread with them. It helped me understand that we're not just selling a piece of cheese. We're selling a tradition, a quality."

Kent and the employees in her department also enjoy the best benefits package in the industry, including affordable high-quality health insurance. And that includes part-timers, who make up about two-thirds of the company's workforce of nearly 47,000. In part, the strategy of extending benefits to this large segment of the labor force is intended to make sure that stores have enough good workers for crucial peak periods, but there's no denying that the costs of employee-friendly policies can mount up. At 15 to 17 percent of sales, for example, Wegmans' labor costs are well above the 12 percent figure for most supermarkets. But according to one company HR executive, holding down labor costs isn't necessarily a strategic priority: "We would have stopped offering free health insurance [to part-timers] a long time ago," she admits, "if we tried to justify the costs." In addition to its healthcare package, Wegmans offer perks such as fitness center discounts, compressed workweeks, telecommuting, and domestic-partner benefits (which extend to same-sex partners).

what's in it for me?

Do you—or will you in the future—work for someone else as an employee? Do you—or will you in the future—own a business and have employees who work for you? In either case, human resource management is a critical activity for you to understand. Effectively managing human resources is the lifeblood of organizations. A firm that takes this activity seriously and approaches it from a strategic perspective has a much better chance for success than does a firm that simply goes through the motions. By understanding the material in this chapter, you'll be better able to understand (1) the importance of properly managing human resources in a unit or business you own or supervise and (2) why and how your employer provides the working arrangements that most directly affect you.

We start this chapter by explaining how managers plan for their organization's human resource needs. We'll also discuss ways in which organizations select, develop, and appraise employee performance and examine the main components of a compensation system. Along the way, we'll look at some key legal issues involved in hiring, compensating, and managing workers in today's workplace and discuss workforce diversity. Finally, we'll explain why workers organize into labor unions and describe the collective bargaining process. Let's get started with some basic concepts of human resource management.

In an industry in which total turnover hovers around 19 percent (and can approach 100 percent for part-timers) and related costs have been known to outstrip total annual profits by 40 percent, Wegmans employee turnover is about 6 percent. In fact, almost 20 percent of Wegmans employees have been with the company for at least 10 years, and many have logged at least a quarter century. Longevity benefits the company by sustaining a more knowledgeable staff, and it reflects the working environment. Says one 19-year-old college student who works at an upstate-New York Wegmans while pursuing a career as a high school history teacher, "I love this place. If teaching doesn't work out, I would so totally work at Wegmans." Edward McLaughlin, who directs the Food Industry Management Program at Cornell University, understands this sort of attitude: "When you're a 16-year-old kid, the last thing you want to do is wear a geeky shirt and work for a supermarket," but at Wegmans, he explains, "it's a badge of honor. You're not a geeky cashier. You're part of the social fabric."

The company goes above and beyond the minimum benefits offered by most companies. For instance, under the company's Employee Scholarship Program, full-time workers can receive up to $2,200 a year for four years and part-timers up to $1,500. Since its inception in 1984, the program has handed out $100 million in scholarships to more than 32,000 employees. Like most Wegmans policies, this one combines employee outreach with long-term corporate strategy: "This program has made a real difference in the lives of many young people," says president Colleen Wegman, who adds that it's also "one of the reasons we've been able to attract the best and the brightest to work at Wegmans."

Granted, Wegmans, which has remained in family hands since its founding in 1915, has an advantage in being as generous with its resources as its family of top executives wants to be. It doesn't have to do everything with quarterly profits in mind, and the firm likes to point out that taking care of its employees is a long-standing priority. Profit sharing and fully funded medical coverage were introduced in 1950 by Robert Wegman, son and nephew of brothers Walter and John, who opened the firm's original flagship store in Rochester, New York, in 1930. Why did Robert Wegman make such generous gestures to his employees way back then? "Because," he says simply, "I was no different from them."[1] (After studying the content of this chapter, you should be able to answer the set of discussion questions found at the end of the chapter.)

The Foundations of Human Resource Management

OBJECTIVE 10-1
Define

human resource management, discuss its strategic significance, and explain how managers plan for their organization's human resource needs.

Human Resource Management (HRM) *set of organizational activities directed at attracting, developing, and maintaining an effective workforce*

Human Resources (HR) *the people comprising an organization's workforce*

Human resource management (HRM) is the set of organizational activities directed at attracting, developing, and maintaining an effective workforce. In recent years, experts have come to appreciate the strategic importance of HRM as well as the need for systematic human resource planning.

The Strategic Importance of HRM

Human resources (HR) are the people comprising an organization's workforce. Human resources are critical for effective organizational functioning. HRM (or "personnel," as it is sometimes called) was once relegated to second-class status in many organizations, but its importance has grown dramatically in the last several years. Its growing importance stems from increased legal complexities, the recognition that people are a valuable resource for improving productivity, and an increased awareness of the costs associated with poor HRM.[2] For example, during the last decade, Microsoft has announced two different large-scale layoffs (one numbering 5,000 and the other 14,000 employees), mostly individuals working in software development. At the same time, though, the firm has continued to expand and hire thousands of other highly talented people for jobs related to Internet search and network integration, important growth areas for the company. This careful and systematic approach to talent management, reducing employees in areas where they are no longer needed and adding new talent to key growth areas, reflects a strategic approach to HRM.

Indeed, managers now realize that the effectiveness of their HR function has a substantial impact on the bottom-line performance of the firm. Poor HR planning can result in spurts of inefficient hiring followed by costly layoffs, which are expensive in terms of unemployment compensation payments, training, public relations, and employee morale. Haphazard compensation systems do not attract, keep, and motivate good employees, and outmoded recruitment practices can expose the firm to expensive and embarrassing discrimination lawsuits. Consequently, the chief HR executive of most large businesses is a vice president directly accountable to the CEO, and many firms develop sophisticated strategic HR plans and integrate those plans with other strategic planning activities.

Even organizations with as few as 200 employees usually have an HR manager and an HR department charged with overseeing these activities. Responsibility for HR activities, however, is often shared between the HR department and line managers. The HR department may recruit and initially screen prospective new employees, for instance, but the final hiring decisions are usually made by managers in the department where the new employees will work. Similarly, although the HR department may establish performance appraisal policies and procedures, the actual evaluation and coaching of employees are generally done by their immediate superiors.

The growing awareness of the strategic significance of HRM has even led to new terminology to reflect a firm's commitment to people. **Human capital** reflects the organization's investment in attracting, retaining, and motivating an effective workforce. Hence, just as the phrase *financial capital* is an indicator of a firm's financial resources and reserves, so, too, does *human capital* serve as a tangible indicator of the value of the people who comprise an organization.[3] Similarly, some managers today talk about talent management. **Talent management** reflects the view that the people in an organization represent a portfolio of valuable talents and skills that can be effectively managed and tapped in ways best targeted to organizational success.

Human Capital *reflects the organization's investment in attracting, retaining, and motivating an effective workforce*

Talent Management *the view that the people in an organization represent a portfolio of valuable talents that can be effectively managed and tapped in ways best targeted to organizational success*

HR Planning

As you can see in Figure 10.1, the starting point in attracting qualified new employees is planning. Specifically, HR planning involves job analysis and forecasting the demand for, and supply of, labor.

Job Analysis **Job analysis** is a systematic analysis of jobs within an organization; most firms have trained experts who handle these analyses. A job analysis results in two things:

Job Analysis *systematic analysis of jobs within an organization*

- The **job description** lists the duties and responsibilities of a job; its working conditions; and the tools, materials, equipment, and information used to perform it.

- The **job specification** lists the skills, abilities, and other credentials and qualifications needed to perform the job effectively.

Job Description *description of the duties and responsibilities of a job, its working conditions, and the tools, materials, equipment, and information used to perform it*

Job Specification *description of the skills, abilities, and other credentials and qualifications required by a job*

Job analysis information is used in many HRM activities. For instance, knowing about job content and job requirements is necessary to develop appropriate selection methods, create job-relevant performance appraisal systems, and set equitable compensation rates.

Forecasting HR Demand and Supply After managers comprehend the jobs to be performed within an organization, they can start planning for the organization's future HR needs. The manager starts by assessing trends in past HR usage, future organizational plans, and general economic trends.

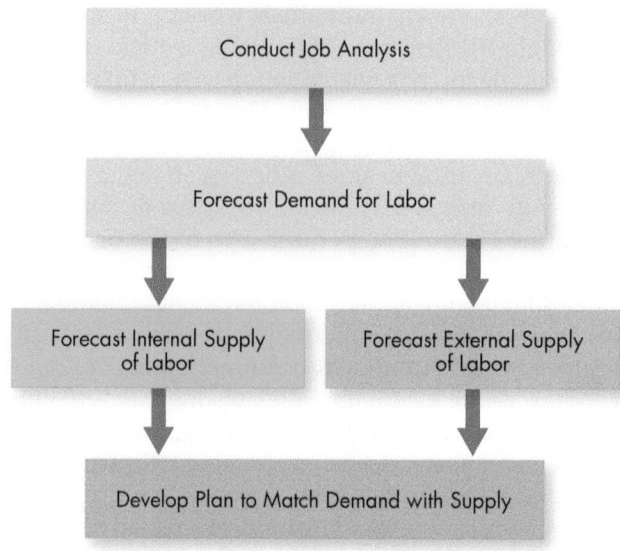

FIGURE 10.1 The HR Planning Process

Forecasting the supply of labor is really two tasks:

1 Forecasting *internal supply*, the number and type of employees who will be in the firm at some future date

2 Forecasting *external supply*, the number and type of people who will be available for hiring from the labor market at large

Replacement Chart *list of each management position, who occupies it, how long that person will likely stay in the job, and who is qualified as a replacement*

REPLACEMENT CHARTS At higher levels of an organization, managers plan for specific people and positions. The technique most commonly used is the **replacement chart**, which lists each important managerial position, who occupies it, how long that person will probably stay in it before moving on (either to another position or to retirement), and who is now qualified or soon will be qualified to move into it. (In most firms today, of course, this information is online.) This technique allows ample time to plan developmental experiences for people identified as potential successors for critical managerial jobs. Halliburton, for instance, has a detailed replacement system that the firm calls its Executive Succession System (ESS). When a manager has his or her performance reviewed each year, notations are placed in the system about the person's readiness for promotion, potential positions for promotion, and what development activities are needed to prepare the individual for promotion. Other managers throughout the firm can access the system whenever they have positions available.

Employee Information System (Skills Inventory) *computerized system containing information on each employee's education, skills, work experiences, and career aspirations*

SKILLS INVENTORIES To facilitate both planning and identifying people for transfer or promotion, some organizations also have **employee information systems (skills inventories)** that contain information on each employee's education, skills, work experience, and career aspirations. Such a system can quickly locate every employee who is qualified to fill a position. Again, although these systems were once handled with charts and files, they are almost always in digital form today.

Forecasting the external supply of labor is a different problem altogether. Planners must rely on information from outside sources, such as state employment commissions, government reports, and figures supplied by colleges on the numbers of students in major fields.

Matching HR Supply and Demand After comparing future demand and internal supply, managers can make plans to manage predicted shortfalls or overstaffing. If a shortfall is predicted, new employees can be hired, present employees can be retrained and transferred into understaffed areas, individuals approaching retirement can be convinced to stay on, or labor-saving or productivity-enhancing systems can be installed. If overstaffing is expected to be a problem, the main options are transferring the extra employees, not replacing individuals who quit, encouraging early retirement, and laying off workers. During the Great Recession of 2008–2011, many firms found it necessary to reduce the size of their workforces through layoffs. Others responded to the economic downturn by reducing the number of hours their employees worked, by imposing pay cuts on their employees, or by some combination of all of these approaches.

The Legal Context of HRM

OBJECTIVE 10-2
Discuss
the legal context of human resource management and identify contemporary legal issues.

A number of laws regulate various aspects of employee–employer relations, especially in the areas of equal employment opportunity, compensation and benefits, labor relations, and occupational safety and health. Several of the most significant ones are summarized in Table 10.1.

Equal Employment Opportunity

Title VII of the Civil Rights Act of 1964 forbids discrimination in all areas of the employment relationship, such as hiring, opportunities for advancement, compensation increases, layoffs, and terminations, against members of certain protected

Title VII of the Civil Rights Act of 1964 *forbids discrimination in all areas of the employment relationship*

table 10.1 Major Laws and Regulations Affecting Human Resource Management

Equal Employment Opportunity

Title VII of the Civil Rights Act of 1964 (as amended by the Equal Employment Opportunity Act of 1972). Forbids discrimination on the basis of race, color, gender, religious beliefs, or national origin in all areas of the employment relationship.

Age Discrimination in Employment Act. Outlaws discrimination against people older than 40 years.

Various executive orders, especially Executive Order 11246 in 1965. Requires employers with government contracts to engage in affirmative action.

Pregnancy Discrimination Act. Specifically outlaws discrimination on the basis of pregnancy.

Vietnam Era Veterans' Readjustment Assistance Act. Extends affirmative action mandate to military veterans who served during the Vietnam War.

Americans with Disabilities Act. Specifically outlaws discrimination against disabled persons.

Civil Rights Act of 1991. Makes it easier for employees to sue an organization for discrimination but also limits punitive damage awards if they win.

Compensation and Benefits

Fair Labor Standards Act. Establishes minimum wage and mandated overtime pay for work in excess of 40 hours per week.

Equal Pay Act of 1963. Requires that men and women be paid the same amount for doing the same job.

Employee Retirement Income Security Act (ERISA) of 1974. Regulates how organizations manage their pension funds.

Family and Medical Leave Act (FMLA) of 1993. Requires employers to provide up to 12 weeks of unpaid leave for family and medical emergencies.

Labor Relations

National Labor Relations Act. Spells out procedures by which employees can establish labor unions and requires organizations to bargain collectively with legally formed unions; also known as the *Wagner Act.*

Labor-Management Relations Act. Limits union power and specifies management rights during a union-organizing campaign; also known as the *Taft-Hartley Act.*

Health and Safety

Occupational Safety and Health Act (OSHA) of 1970. Mandates the provision of safe working conditions.

classes based on factors such as race, color, gender, religious beliefs, or national origin. The intent of Title VII is to ensure that employment decisions are made on the basis of an individual's qualifications rather than on the basis of personal biases. The law has reduced direct forms of discrimination (for example, refusing to promote African Americans into management, failing to hire men as flight attendants, refusing to hire women as construction workers, etc.) as well as indirect forms of discrimination (using employment tests that Caucasians pass at a higher rate than do African Americans, for instance). Note, however, that organizations are free to base employment decisions on such job-related factors as qualifications, performance, seniority, and so forth. For example, an organization can certainly hire a male job applicant instead of a female applicant if he is more qualified (i.e., has more education and/or experience related to the job). However, he cannot be hired simply because of his gender.

Employment requirements such as test scores and other qualifications are legally defined as having an adverse impact on minorities and women when such individuals meet or pass the requirement at a rate less than 80 percent of the rate of majority group members. Criteria that have an **adverse impact** on protected groups can be used only when there is solid evidence that they effectively identify individuals who are better able than others to do the job. The **Equal Employment Opportunity Commission (EEOC)** is charged with enforcing Title VII as well as several other employment-related laws.

The **Age Discrimination in Employment Act**, passed in 1967, amended in 1978 and again in 1986, is an attempt to prevent organizations from discriminating against older workers. In its current form, it outlaws discrimination against people older than 40 years. Both the Age Discrimination in Employment Act and Title VII require passive nondiscrimination, or **equal employment opportunity**. Employers are not required to seek out and hire minorities, but they must treat all who apply fairly.

Several executive orders, however, require that employers holding government contracts engage in **affirmative action**, actively and intentionally seeking and hiring employees from groups that are underrepresented in the organization. These organizations must have a written **affirmative action plan** that spells out employment goals for underused groups and how those goals will be met. These employers are also required to act affirmatively in hiring Vietnam-era veterans (as a result of the Vietnam Era Veterans' Readjustment Assistance Act) and qualified disabled individuals. Finally, the Pregnancy Discrimination Act forbids discrimination against women who are pregnant.

In 1990, Congress passed the **Americans with Disabilities Act**, which forbids discrimination on the basis of disabilities and requires employers to provide reasonable accommodations for disabled employees.

More recently, the **Civil Rights Act of 1991** amended the original Civil Rights Act as well as other related laws by making it easier to bring discrimination lawsuits while simultaneously limiting the amount of punitive damages that can be awarded against employers in those lawsuits.

Compensation and Benefits

Laws also regulate compensation and benefits. The **Fair Labor Standards Act**, passed in 1938 and amended frequently since then, sets a minimum wage and requires the payment of overtime rates for work in excess of 40 hours per week. Salaried professional, executive, and administrative employees are exempt from the minimum hourly wage and overtime provisions. The **Equal Pay Act of 1963** requires that men and women be paid the same amount for doing the same job. Attempts to circumvent the law by having different job titles and pay rates for men and women who perform the same work are also illegal. Basing an employee's pay on seniority or performance is legal, however, even if it means that a man and woman are paid different amounts for doing the same job.

The provision of benefits is also regulated in some ways by state and federal laws. Certain benefits are mandatory, such as workers' compensation insurance

Adverse Impact *when minorities and women meet or pass the requirement for a job at a rate less than 80 percent of the rate of majority group members*

Equal Employment Opportunity Commission (EEOC) *federal agency enforcing several discrimination-related laws*

Age Discrimination in Employment Act *outlaws discrimination against people older than 40 years*

Equal Employment Opportunity *legally mandated nondiscrimination in employment on the basis of race, creed, sex, or national origin*

Affirmative Action *intentionally seeking and hiring employees from groups that are underrepresented in the organization*

Affirmative Action Plan *written statement of how the organization intends to actively recruit, hire, and develop members of relevant protected classes*

Americans with Disabilities Act *forbids discrimination on the basis of disabilities and requires employers to provide reasonable accommodations for disabled employees*

Civil Rights Act of 1991 *amended the original Civil Rights Act*

Fair Labor Standards Act *sets a minimum wage and requires the payment of overtime rates for work in excess of 40 hours per week*

Equal Pay Act of 1963 *requires that men and women be paid the same amount for doing the same job*

for employees who are injured on the job. Employers who provide a pension plan for their employees are regulated by the **Employee Retirement Income Security Act (ERISA) of 1974**. The purpose of this act is to help ensure the financial security of pension funds by regulating how they can be invested. The **Family and Medical Leave Act (FMLA) of 1993** requires employers to provide up to 12 weeks of unpaid leave for family and medical emergencies. President Donald Trump has stated that he believes this leave period should be extended, although as of this writing no action has been taken.

Labor Relations

Union activities and management's behavior toward unions constitute another heavily regulated area. The **National Labor Relations Act** (also known as the **Wagner Act**), passed in 1935, established procedures for employees to vote on whether or not to be represented by a union. If they vote to be represented by a union, management is required to bargain collectively with that union. The **National Labor Relations Board (NLRB)** was established by the Wagner Act to enforce its provisions. Following a series of severe strikes in 1946, the **Labor-Management Relations Act** (also known as the **Taft-Hartley Act**) was passed in 1947 to limit union power. The law increases management's rights during an organizing campaign. The Taft-Hartley Act also contains the National Emergency Strike provision, which allows the president of the United States to prevent or end a strike that endangers national security. Taken together, these laws balance union and management power. Employees can be represented by a legally created and managed union, but the business can make non-employee-related business decisions without interference.

Health and Safety

The **Occupational Safety and Health Act (OSHA) of 1970** directly mandates the provision of safe working conditions. It requires that employers (1) provide a place of employment that is free from hazards that may cause death or serious physical harm and (2) obey the safety and health standards established by the Department of Labor. Safety standards are intended to prevent accidents, whereas occupational health standards are concerned with preventing occupational disease. For example, standards limit the concentration of cotton dust in the air because this contaminant has been associated with lung disease in textile workers. The standards are enforced by OSHA inspections, which are conducted when an employee files a complaint about unsafe conditions or when a serious accident occurs.

Spot inspections of plants in especially hazardous industries such as mining and chemicals are also made. Employers who fail to meet OSHA standards may be fined. A Miami-based company, Lead Enterprises Inc., was cited by OSHA as knowingly failing to protect employees from lead exposure despite knowing the potential hazards (brain damage, kidney disease, and reproductive system damage). The company, which produces various lead products, including fish tackles and lead diving weights, was cited for 32 safety and health violations after multiple inspections and fined more than $307,000 in penalties.[4] More recently, a massive explosion at a fertilizer plant in the town of West, Texas, in 2013 may have been partially caused by unsafe work practices. Moreover, preliminary evidence suggested that OSHA inspectors had also missed some warning signs of a potential disaster at the plant.

Other Legal Issues

In addition to these established areas of HR legal regulation, several other legal issues are also noteworthy.

AIDS in the Workplace Although AIDS is considered a disability under the Americans with Disabilities Act of 1990, the AIDS situation itself is severe enough that it warrants special attention. Employers cannot legally require an HIV test or any other medical examination as a condition for making an offer of employment.

Employee Retirement Income Security Act (ERISA) of 1974 *ensures the financial security of pension funds by regulating how they can be invested*

Family and Medical Leave Act (FMLA) of 1993 *requires employers to provide up to 12 weeks of unpaid leave for family and medical emergencies*

National Labor Relations Act (*also known as the* **Wagner Act**) *sets up a procedure for employees to vote on whether to have a union*

National Labor Relations Board (NLRB) *established by the Wagner Act to enforce its provisions*

Labor-Management Relations Act (*also known as the* **Taft-Hartley Act**) *passed to limit union power*

Occupational Safety and Health Act (OSHA) of 1970 *federal law setting and enforcing guidelines for protecting workers from unsafe conditions and potential health hazards in the workplace*

Organizations must accommodate or make a good-faith effort to accommodate individuals with HIV, maintain the confidentiality of all medical records, and try to educate coworkers about AIDS.

Sexual Harassment *making unwelcome sexual advances in the workplace*

Sexual Harassment

Sexual harassment is defined by the EEOC as unwelcome sexual advances in the work environment. If the conduct is indeed unwelcome and occurs with sufficient frequency to create an abusive work environment, the employer is responsible for changing the environment by warning, reprimanding, or firing the harasser. The courts have defined two types of sexual harassment:

Quid Pro Quo Harassment *form of sexual harassment in which sexual favors are requested in return for job-related benefits*

1 In cases of **quid pro quo harassment**, the harasser offers to exchange something of value for sexual favors. A male supervisor, for example, might tell or suggest to a female subordinate that he will recommend her for promotion or give her a raise in exchange for sexual favors.

Hostile Work Environment *form of sexual harassment deriving from off-color jokes, lewd comments, and so forth*

2 The creation of a **hostile work environment** is a more subtle form of sexual harassment. A group of male employees who continually make off-color jokes and lewd comments and perhaps decorate the work environment with inappropriate photographs may create a hostile work environment for a female colleague, who may become uncomfortable working in that environment.

In recent years, the concept of harassment has been expanded to encompass unwelcome or inappropriate behaviors regarding ethnicity, religion, and age.

Employment at will *principle, increasingly modified by legislation and judicial decision, that organizations should be able to retain or dismiss employees at their discretion*

Employment at Will

The concept of **employment at will** holds that both employer and employee have the mutual right to terminate an employment relationship at any time for any reason, with or without advance notice to the other. Over the last two decades, however, terminated employees have challenged the employment-at-will doctrine by filing lawsuits against former employers on the grounds of wrongful discharge.

In the last several years, such suits have put limits on employment-at-will provisions in certain circumstances. In the past, for example, organizations were guilty of firing employees who filed workers' compensation claims or took "excessive" time off to serve on jury duty. More recently, however, the courts have ruled that employees may not be fired for exercising rights protected by law.

The Patriot Act

In response to the terrorist attacks of September 11, 2001, the U.S. government passed legislation that increases its powers to investigate and prosecute suspected terrorists. This legislation, known as the **Patriot Act**, has several key implications for HRM. For instance, certain "restricted" individuals (including ex-convicts and aliens from countries deemed by the State Department to have "repeatedly provided support for acts of international terrorism") are ineligible to work with potentially dangerous biological agents. More controversial are sections granting government investigators access to previously confidential personal and financial records.

Patriot Act *legislation that increased U.S. government's power to investigate and prosecute suspected terrorists*

In addition to these areas of legal regulation, other issues also continue to emerge. For instance, in recent years, gender identity, sexual orientation, country of origin, and immigration have all taken on renewed social significance in ways that have implications for human resource management.

OBJECTIVE 10-3
Identify

the steps in staffing a company and discuss ways in which organizations recruit and select new employees.

Staffing the Organization

When managers have determined that new employees are needed and understand the legal context in which they operate, they can then turn their attention to recruiting and hiring the right mix of people. This involves two processes: (1) acquiring new employees from outside the company and (2) promoting current employees from within. Both external and internal staffing, however, start with effective *recruiting*.

Recruiting Employees

Recruiting is the process of attracting qualified persons to apply for the jobs that are open.

Internal Recruiting

Internal recruiting means considering present employees as candidates for openings. Promotion from within can help build morale and keep high-quality employees from leaving. For higher-level positions, a digital skills inventory system may be used to identify internal candidates, or managers may be asked to recommend individuals to be considered. Of course, internal promotions also create new openings that then have to be filled.

External Recruiting

External recruiting involves attracting people outside the organization to apply for jobs. External recruiting methods include posting jobs on the company website or other online job sites, such as Monster.com; holding campus interviews for potential college recruits; using employment agencies or executive search firms to scout for potential talent; seeking referrals by present employees; advertising in traditional print publications; and hiring "walk-ins" (unsolicited applicants).

The organization must also keep in mind that recruiting decisions often go both ways—the organization is recruiting an employee, but the prospective employee is also selecting a job. For instance, when unemployment is low (meaning fewer people are seeking work), businesses may have to work harder to attract new employees. But when unemployment is higher (meaning more people are looking for work), organizations may find it easier to recruit prospective employees without having to resort to expensive hiring incentives. But even if a firm can take its pick of the best potential employees, it still should put its best foot forward, treat all applicants with dignity, and strive for a good person–job fit. Hiring the wrong employee can cost the company about half of a low-skilled worker's annual wages or three to five times upper-level employees' annual wages. Therefore, hiring the "wrong" employee for $50,000 per year could cost the company at least $25,000. These costs stem from training, counseling, low productivity, termination, and recruiting and hiring a replacement.

One generally successful method for facilitating a good person–job fit is what is called a **realistic job preview (RJP)**. As the term suggests, the RJP involves providing the applicant with a real picture of what performing the job that the organization is trying to fill would be like.[5] For example, it would not make sense for a firm to tell an applicant that the job is exciting and challenging when in fact it is routine and straightforward, yet some managers do this to hire the best people. The likely outcome is a dissatisfied employee who will quickly start looking for a better job. If the company is more realistic about a job, though, the person hired will be more likely to remain in the job for a longer period of time. Of course, a manager might not want to describe a job as boring and monotonous, even if that is in fact accurate. An effective solution to this dilemma may be to allow a job applicant to observe people performing the job or perhaps watch a short video of the job and then allow the applicants to make their own assessments.

Selecting Employees

Once the recruiting process has attracted a pool of applicants, the next step is to select whom to hire. The intent of the selection process is to gather from applicants the information that will predict job success and then to hire the candidate(s) likely to be most successful.

Application Forms

The first step in selection is usually asking the candidate to fill out an application. An application form is an efficient method of gathering information about the applicant's previous work history, educational background, and other job-related demographic data. Application forms are seldom used for upper-level jobs; candidates for such positions usually provide the same information on their résumé. Most applications are now prepared and submitted online, although some firms still use traditional paper forms.

Tests Employers sometimes ask candidates to take tests during the selection process. Tests of ability, skill, aptitude, or knowledge relevant to a particular job are usually the best predictors of job success, although tests of general intelligence or personality are occasionally useful as well. Some companies use a test of the "Big Five" personality dimensions discussed in Chapter 8 (or other personality measures) to predict success.

Interviews *Interviews* are a popular selection device, although they are actually often a poor predictor of job success. For example, biases inherent in the way people perceive and judge others when they first meet affect subsequent evaluations. Interview validity can be improved by training interviewers to be aware of potential biases and by tightening the structure of the interview. In a structured interview, questions are written in advance, and all interviewers follow the same question list with each candidate. Structured interviews tend to be used for jobs that are relatively routine, such as some administrative assistant positions, data entry jobs, and college admissions processing positions. For interviewing managerial or professional candidates, a somewhat less structured approach can be used. Although question areas and information-gathering objectives are still planned in advance, specific questions vary with the candidates' backgrounds. Sometimes, companies are looking for especially creative employees and may try to learn more about the individual's creativity during an interview.

Other Techniques Organizations also use other selection techniques that vary with circumstances. Polygraph tests, once popular, are declining in popularity. On the other hand, organizations occasionally require applicants to take physical exams (being careful that their practices are consistent with the Americans with Disabilities Act). More organizations are using drug tests, especially in situations in which drug-related performance problems could create serious safety hazards. For example, potential employees who may be handling hazardous chemicals or medical waste or engaging in public transportation activities like driving buses are likely to be drug tested. Some organizations also run criminal background checks on prospective employees. Reference checks with previous employers are also used, but they have been shown to have limited value because individuals are likely to only provide the names of references that will give them positive recommendations. Even worse, some applicants literally make up references.[6]

OBJECTIVE 10-4
Describe
the main components of a compensation and benefits system.

Compensation System *total package of rewards that organizations provide to individuals in return for their labor*

Compensation and Benefits

People who work for a business expect to be paid, of course, and most workers today also expect certain benefits from their employers. Indeed, a major factor in retaining talented employees is a company's **compensation system**, the total package of rewards that it offers employees in return for their contributions to the organization's mission. Creating an effective compensation system requires finding the right balance between offering sufficient inducements to attract and retain employees while also keeping labor costs in line with revenues and competing employers.

Wages *compensation in the form of money paid for time worked*

Salary *compensation in the form of money paid for discharging the responsibilities of a job*

Wages and Salaries

Wages and salaries are the dollar amounts paid to employees for their labor. **Wages** are paid for time worked. For example, if your job pays you $10 an hour, that is your wage. A **salary**, on the other hand, is paid for performing a job. A salaried executive earning $100,000 per year is paid to achieve results even if that means working 5 hours one day and 15 the next. Salaries are usually expressed as an amount paid per month or year.

In setting wage and salary levels, a company may start by looking at its competitors. Firms must also decide how their internal wage and salary levels will compare for different jobs. Some organizations pay everyone doing the same job the same amount. In other organizations, though, an employee with more experience or who consistently performs at a higher level may earn more than another employee doing the same job. This practice is legal and can be motivational so long as the reasons for the pay differential are job-related and not based on bias or favoritism.

The Great Recession of 2008–2011 prompted some firms to reduce the wages and salaries they were paying to lower costs. For example, Hewlett-Packard reduced the salaries of all but its top performers by amounts ranging from 2.5 to 20 percent. CareerBuilder.com reduced all employee pay but also began giving all employees Friday afternoons off to reflect their lower pay.

Incentive Programs

Studies have shown that beyond a certain point, more money will not necessarily result in better performance. Money motivates employees only if it is tied directly to performance. The most common method of establishing this link is the use of **incentive programs**, special pay programs designed to motivate high performance. Some programs are available to individuals, whereas others are distributed on a companywide basis.

A sales bonus is a typical incentive. Employees receive **bonuses**, special payments above their salaries, when they sell a certain number or certain dollar amount of goods for a designated period, such as a week, month, quarter, or year. Employees who fail to reach this goal earn no bonuses. **Merit salary systems** link pay raises to performance levels in nonsales jobs.

Executives commonly receive stock options as incentives. Apple CEO Tim Cook, for example, can buy several thousand shares of company stock each year at a predetermined price. If his managerial talent leads to higher profits and stock prices, he can buy the stock at a price lower than the market value for which, in theory, he is largely responsible. He is then free to sell the stock at market price at a specified future date, keeping the profits for himself.

Another popular incentive plan is called **pay for performance** (or **variable pay**). In essence, middle managers are rewarded for especially productive output with earnings that significantly exceed the cost of bonuses. The number of variable pay programs in the United States has been growing consistently for the last decade, and most experts predict that they will continue to grow in popularity. Many firms say that variable pay is a better motivator than merit raises because the range between generous and mediocre merit raises is usually quite small.

Companywide Incentives Some incentive programs apply to all the employees in a firm. Under **profit-sharing plans**, for example, profits earned above a certain level are distributed to employees. Also, **gainsharing plans** distribute bonuses to employees when a company's costs are reduced through greater work efficiency. **Pay-for-knowledge plans** pay workers to learn new skills and to become proficient at different jobs.

Benefits Programs

Benefits, compensation other than wages and salaries and other incentives offered by a firm to its workers, account for a substantial percentage of most compensation budgets. Most companies are required by law to pay tax for Social Security retirement benefits and provide **workers' compensation insurance**, insurance for compensating workers injured on the job. Most businesses also provide some level of health, life, and disability insurance for their full-time employees, as well as paid time off

Incentive Program *special compensation program designed to motivate high performance*

Bonus *individual performance incentive in the form of a special payment made over and above the employee's salary*

Merit Salary System *individual incentive linking compensation to performance in nonsales jobs*

Pay for Performance (or **Variable Pay**) *individual incentive that rewards a manager for especially productive output*

Profit-Sharing Plan *incentive plan for distributing bonuses to employees when company profits rise above a certain level*

Gainsharing Plan *incentive plan that rewards groups for productivity improvements*

Pay-for-Knowledge Plan *incentive plan to encourage employees to learn new skills or become proficient at different jobs*

Benefits *compensation other than wages and salaries*

Workers' Compensation Insurance *legally required insurance for compensating workers injured on the job*

finding a better way

Holding True at Nucor Steel

For the most part, the watchwords in U.S. business during the 2008–2011 recession were cutting payroll, reducing headcount, and eliminating jobs. But Nucor, the country's largest steelmaker, didn't lay off a single employee. Hit by a 50 percent plunge in output that had begun in September 2008, the U.S. steel industry had laid off some 10,000 workers by January 2009, and the United Steelworkers union projected that the number would double before the recession came to an end. Not only did Nucor retain all of its employees during the recession, the company has not laid off a single employee because of lack of work in more than 40 years.

As far as top management is concerned, the company's ability to weather the recent economic crisis was based on several factors—most important, the firm's employees and culture. What's that culture like? It originated in the 1960s as the result of policies established by Ken Iverson, who brought a radical perspective on how to manage a company's HR to the job of CEO. Iverson figured that workers would be much more productive if an employer went out of its way to share authority with them, respect what they accomplished, and compensate them as handsomely as possible. Today, the basics of the company's HR model are summed up in its "Employee Relations Principles":

1 Management is obligated to manage Nucor in such a way that employees will have the opportunity to earn according to their productivity.

2 Employees should feel confident that if they do their jobs properly, they will have a job tomorrow.

3 Employees have the right to be treated fairly and must believe that they will be.

4 Employees must have an avenue of appeal when they believe they are being treated unfairly.

H. Mark Weidman Photography/Alamy Stock Photo

for vacations and holidays. A few, such as Starbucks and The Container Store, also provide similar benefits, but at a reduced level, to their part-time employees. Some also allow employees to use payroll deductions to buy stock at discounted prices. Counseling services for employees with alcohol, drug, or emotional problems are also provided by some large employers, as are on-site child-care centers. Some companies even provide reduced membership fees at gyms and health clubs, as well as insurance or other protection for identity theft.[7]

Retirement Plans Retirement plans (or pension plans) constitute another important—and sometimes controversial—benefit that is available to many employees. Company-sponsored retirement plans were historically set up to pay pensions to workers when they retire (these are referred to as *defined benefit plans*). In some cases, the company contributed all the money to the pension fund. In others, both the company and employees made contributions. In recent years, though, some companies have run into problems because they have not set aside enough money to cover the retirement funds they have agreed to provide.

The Iverson approach is based on motivation, and the key to that approach is a highly original pay system. Step 1, which calls for base pay below the industry average, probably doesn't seem like a promising start, but the Nucor compensation plan is designed to get better as the results of the work get better. If a shift, for example, can turn out a defect-free batch of steel, every worker is entitled to a bonus that's paid weekly and that can potentially triple his or her take-home pay. In addition, there are one-time annual bonuses and profit-sharing payouts.

However, the system cuts both ways. Take that defect-free batch of steel, for example. If there's a problem with a batch, workers on the shift obviously don't get any weekly bonus. And that's if they catch the problem before the batch leaves the plant. If it reaches the customer, they may *lose* up to three times what they would have received as a bonus. "In average-to-bad years," adds HR vice president James M. Coblin, "we earn less than our peers in other companies. That's supposed to teach us that we don't want to be average or bad. We want to be good." During fiscal year 2009, total pay at Nucor was down by about 40 percent.

Everybody in the company, from janitors to the CEO, is covered by some form of incentive plan tied to various goals and targets. Nucor's profit-sharing plan guarantees that the company will contribute 10 percent of all earnings before taxes to the plan. In addition, there are incentives at the level of the work group for production employees and at the departmental and divisional levels for managers.

The company has an unusually flat organizational structure—another Iverson innovation. There are just four layers of personnel between a janitor and senior management: general managers, department managers, line supervisors, and hourly personnel. Most operating decisions are made at the divisional level or lower, and the company is known for its tolerance of honest mistakes made in the line of decision-making duty. The Nucor website points out that workers are allowed to fail if that failure comes as a result of logical initiative and idea sharing. That is, if a worker approaches a problem in a logical manner and makes a sound decision that is defensible but turns out to be wrong, he or she is not punished. The reasoning behind this approach is that it promotes creativity and initiative.

The Nucor system works not only because employees share financial risks and benefits but also because, in sharing risks and benefits, they're a lot like owners. And people who think like owners are a lot more likely to take the initiative when decisions have to be made or problems solved. What's more, Nucor has found that teamwork is a good incubator for initiative as well as idea sharing. John J. Ferriola, who managed the Nucor mill in Hickman, Arkansas, before becoming CEO in 2013, remembers an afternoon in March 2006 when the electrical grid at his facility went down. His electricians got on the phone to three other company electricians, one in Alabama and two in North Carolina, who dropped what they were doing and went straight to Arkansas. Working 20-hour shifts, the joint team had the plant up and running again in three days (as opposed to an anticipated full week). There was nothing in it (at least financially) for the visiting electricians, but they knew that maintenance personnel get no bonuses when equipment in their facility isn't operating. "At Nucor," says one frontline supervisor, "we're not 'you guys' and 'us guys.' It's all of us guys. Wherever the bottleneck is, we go there, and everyone works on it."

Many companies today are transitioning to what are called defined contributions plans, also called 401(k) plans. Under these plans, contributions from the employee, sometimes matched by the employer, are invested in stock and/or bond funds. The individual's retirement account is subject to greater risk (as well as potentially greater returns) while the employer incurs less risk. Both FedEx and Goodyear have recently made this shift for all of their employees. Other employers who are also making this transition include Anheuser-Busch, Wells Fargo, General Motors, AT&T, General Electric, and Saks.

Containing the Costs of Benefits

As the range of benefits has increased, so has concern about containing the costs of these benefits. Many companies are experimenting with cost-cutting plans while still attracting and retaining valuable employees. One approach is the **cafeteria benefits plan**. A certain dollar amount of benefits per employee is set aside so that each employee can choose from a variety of alternatives.

Another area of increasing concern is healthcare costs. Medical expenses have increased insurance premiums, which have increased the cost to employers of

Cafeteria Benefits Plan *benefit plan that sets limits on benefits per employee, each of whom may choose from a variety of alternative benefits*

maintaining benefits plans. Many employers are looking for new ways to cut those costs. One increasingly popular approach is for organizations to create their own networks of healthcare providers. These providers agree to charge lower fees for services rendered to employees of member organizations. In return, they enjoy established relationships with large employers and, thus, more clients and patients. Insurers also charge less to cover the employees of network members because they make lower reimbursement payments.

OBJECTIVE 10-5
Describe

how managers develop the workforce in their organization through training and performance appraisal.

Developing the Workforce

After a company has hired new employees, it must acquaint them with the firm and their new jobs. Managers also take steps to train and develop employees and to further develop necessary job skills. In addition, every firm has some system for performance appraisal and feedback.

Training and Development

Training *usually refers to teaching operational or technical employees how to do the job for which they were hired*

Development *usually refers to teaching managers and professionals the skills needed for both present and future jobs*

In HRM, **training** usually refers to teaching operational or technical employees how to do the job for which they were hired. It also refers to technical areas such as new software and technology. **Development** refers to teaching managers and professionals the skills needed for both present and future jobs and includes improved decision making, strategic leadership, and so forth.[8] Most organizations provide regular training and development programs for managers and employees. For example, IBM spends more than $620 million annually on programs and has a vice president in charge of employee education. U.S. businesses spend more than $127 billion annually on training and development programs away from the workplace. Over $265 billion is spent annually worldwide. And these figures do not include wages, salaries, and benefits paid to employees while they are participating in such programs.

Assessing Training Needs The first step in developing a training plan is to determine what needs exist. For example, if employees do not know how to operate the machinery necessary to do their job, a training program on how to operate the machinery is clearly needed. On the other hand, when a group of office workers is performing poorly, training may not be the answer. The problem could be motivation, aging equipment, poor supervision, inefficient work design, or a deficiency of skills and knowledge. Only the last could be remedied by training. As training programs are being developed, the manager should set specific and measurable goals specifying what participants are to learn. Managers should also plan to evaluate the training program after employees complete it.

On-the-Job Training *training, sometimes informal, conducted while an employee is at work*

Vestibule Training *off-the-job training conducted in a simulated environment*

Common Training Methods Many different training and development methods are available. Selection of methods depends on many considerations, but perhaps the most important is training content. When the training content is factual material (such as company rules or explanations of how to fill out forms), assigned reading, programmed learning, and lecture methods work well. When the content is interpersonal relations or group decision making, however, firms need to use a method that allows interpersonal contact, such as role-playing or case discussion groups. When employees must learn a physical skill, methods allowing practice and the actual use of tools and materials are needed, as in **on-the-job training** or **vestibule training**. (Vestibule training enables participants to focus on safety, learning, and feedback rather than on productivity.)

Web-based and other digital media-based training are especially popular today. Such methods allow a mix of training content, are relatively easy to update and revise, let participants use a variable schedule, and lower travel costs.[9] On the other hand, they are limited in their capacity to simulate real activities and facilitate face-to-face interaction. Xerox, Massachusetts Mutual Life Insurance, and Ford have all reported tremendous success with these methods. In addition, most training programs rely on a mix of methods. Boeing, for example, sends managers to an intensive two-week training seminar involving tests, simulations, role-playing exercises, and flight-simulation exercises.[10]

Finally, some larger businesses have their own self-contained training facilities, often called *corporate universities*. McDonald's was among the first to start this practice with its so-called Hamburger University in Illinois. All management trainees for the firm attend training programs there to learn exactly how long to grill a burger, how to maintain good customer service, and so on. The cult hamburger chain In-N-Out Burger also has a similar training venue it calls In-N-Out University. Other firms that use this approach include Shell Oil and General Electric.[11]

Evaluation of Training Finally, the effectiveness of training and development programs should always be evaluated. Typical evaluation approaches include measuring one or more relevant criteria (such as attitudes or performance) before and after the training, and determining whether the criteria changed as a result of the training and development. Evaluation measures collected at the end of training are easy to get, but actual performance measures collected when the trainee is on the job are more important. Trainees may say that they enjoyed the training and learned a lot, but the true test is whether their job performance improves after their training.

Performance Appraisal

Once employees are trained and settled into their jobs, one of management's next concerns is performance appraisal.[12] **Performance appraisal** is a formal assessment of how well employees are doing their jobs. Employees' performance should be evaluated regularly for many reasons. One reason is that performance appraisal may be necessary for validating selection devices or assessing the impact of training programs. A second, administrative reason is to aid in making decisions about pay raises, promotions, and training. Still another reason is to provide feedback to employees to help them improve their current performance and plan their future careers.[13]

Performance Appraisal evaluation of an employee's job performance to determine the degree to which the employee is performing effectively

Because performance evaluations often help determine wages and promotions, they must be fair and nondiscriminatory. In the case of appraisals, managers use content validation to show that the appraisal system accurately measures performance on important job elements and does not measure traits or behavior that are irrelevant to job performance.

Common Appraisal Methods Two basic categories of appraisal methods commonly used in organizations are objective methods and judgmental methods. Objective measures of performance include actual output (number of units produced), scrap rate, dollar volume of sales, and number of claims processed. Objective performance measures may be contaminated by "opportunity bias" if some persons have a better chance to perform than others. For example, a sales representative selling snowblowers in Michigan has a greater opportunity than does a colleague selling the same product in Alabama. Fortunately, adjusting raw performance figures for the effect of opportunity bias and thereby arriving at figures that accurately represent each individual's performance is often possible.

Judgmental methods, including ranking and rating techniques, are the most common way to measure performance. Ranking compares employees directly with one another and orders them from best to worst. Ranking has a number of drawbacks. Ranking is difficult for large groups because the individuals in the middle of the distribution may be hard to distinguish from one another accurately. Comparisons of people in different work groups are also difficult. For example, an employee ranked third in a high-performing group may be more valuable than an employee ranked first in a lower-performing group. Another criticism of ranking is that the manager must rank people on the basis of overall performance, even though each person likely

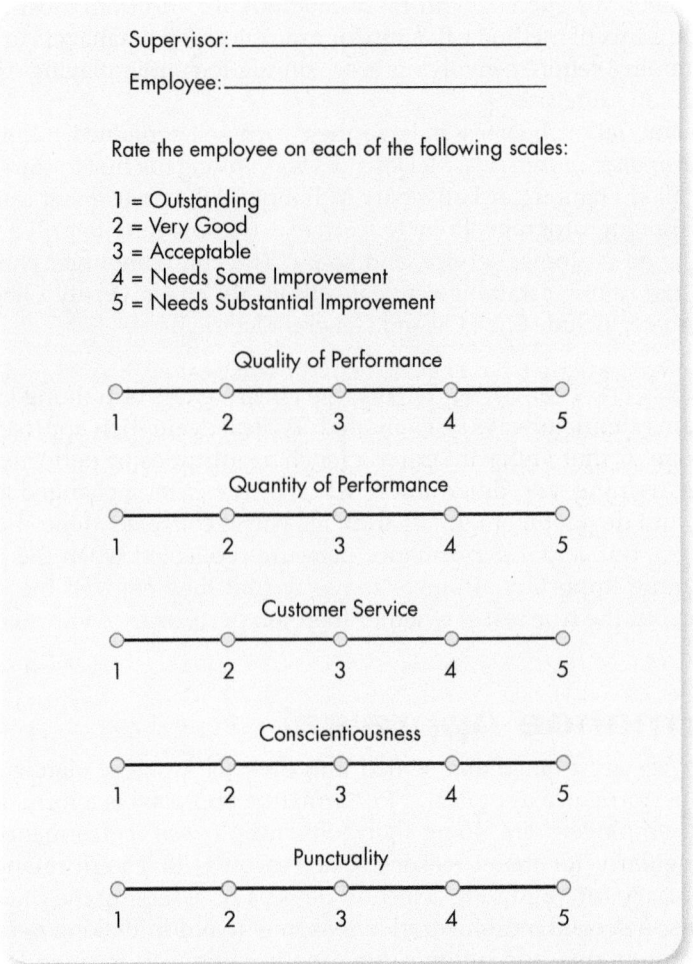

Supervisor:_____

Employee:_____

Rate the employee on each of the following scales:

1 = Outstanding
2 = Very Good
3 = Acceptable
4 = Needs Some Improvement
5 = Needs Substantial Improvement

Quality of Performance
1   2   3   4   5

Quantity of Performance
1   2   3   4   5

Customer Service
1   2   3   4   5

Conscientiousness
1   2   3   4   5

Punctuality
1   2   3   4   5

FIGURE 10.2 Sample Performance Evaluation Form

has both strengths and weaknesses. Furthermore, rankings do not provide useful information for feedback. To be told that one is ranked third is not nearly as helpful as to be told that the quality of one's work is outstanding, its quantity is satisfactory, one's punctuality could use improvement, or one's interpersonal skills are excellent.

Rating differs from ranking in that it compares each employee with a fixed standard rather than with other employees. A rating scale provides the standard. Figure 10.2 gives examples of graphic rating scales for a bank teller. Each consists of a performance dimension to be rated (punctuality, congeniality, and accuracy), followed by a scale on which to make the rating. In constructing graphic rating scales, performance dimensions that are relevant to job performance must be selected. In particular, they should focus on job behaviors and results rather than on personality traits or attitudes.

Errors in Performance Appraisal Errors or biases can occur in any kind of rating or ranking system.[14] One common problem is *recency error*, the tendency to base judgments on the subordinate's most recent performance because it is most easily recalled. Often a rating or ranking is intended to evaluate performance over an entire time period, such as six months or a year, so the recency error does introduce error into the judgment. Other errors include overuse of one part of the scale—being too lenient, being too severe, or giving everyone a rating of "average."

Halo error is allowing the assessment of an employee on one dimension to "spread" to ratings of that employee on other dimensions. For instance, if an employee is outstanding on quality of output, a rater might tend to give her or him higher marks

entrepreneurship and new ventures

Time to Go

Dan Yoo had everything going for him. He graduated cum laude from Georgetown University in 1999 with a degree in management and finance. After working for Merrill Lynch for a year, he moved onto Epoch Investment Partners, a "technology-enabled" investment bank. Within a year, his dream job was gone. The company was acquired by Goldman Sachs and he and several recently hired employees were out of a job. In the years since, he's worked in a series of high-profile positions in the financial services and technology sectors. Most recently, he left his job as vice president for business operations and business analytics at LinkedIn to become COO at NerdWallet, a San Francisco-based provider of customized financial advice and analysis.

Beginning with his unfortunate experience at Epoch Investment Partners, Yoo understands the importance of compassion in every interaction with employees. While very few people go into business because they look forward to conducting performance appraisals and even firing employees, strong human relations skills are essential for an entrepreneur. In an article in *Entreprenuer* magazine, Yoo offers advice on how to fire employees with compassion, whether as a result of poor performance or cost-cutting decisions.

- The first step in firing an employee begins on the day that the employee is hired. Employee behavior must be shaped, and supervisors cannot afford to overlook bad behavior. In the start-up world, one weak performer can make a big difference, so it's important to let employees know where they stand. Yoo explains, "Just as there's a need for decisive action if it's not working out, there needs to be an aggressive onboarding and feedback loop to communicate problems quickly and give an opportunity for corrective action before swinging the axe."

- In the event that you must fire an employee, it's important to plan the discussion in advance, with your goal being to leave the termination meeting on the best terms possible. This is where empathy plays a big role—understanding the situation from the perspective of the terminated employee.

- It's important to be brief and direct because dragging out bad news doesn't really soften the blow. But it's also important to allow the employee to share his or her perspectives

Roman Samborskyi/Shutterstock

and feel that they have been heard. Although it's unlikely to change your decision, it creates the opportunity for the manager to learn and the employee to feel valued.

- Finally, if it's possible, this is the time to be generous. Losing a job is so much more than money, but you can help ease the transition through extended health insurance benefits or outplacement services. When Yoo was fired from Epoch Investment Partners, he and the other fired employees were able to collect their bonuses as well as vest their interests in the company's profit-sharing plan. While there was no legal obligation for the company to do so, it helped them part on good terms.[15]

By the end of 2016, NerdWallet had more than 400 employees—or Nerds, as they call themselves—and like many of the California tech companies, offered perks that were once thought to be unusual, like nap rooms and healthy lunches, but are now more mainstream.

"We have an inclusive, collaborative and casual vibe with open-space offices built for employees to come together, the best technology to equip our employees with what they need to be successful and rooftop hangouts to refresh," says founder and Chief Executive Officer Tim Chen. "We start every week with a company-wide meeting and end the week with a happy hour to celebrate all the great work."[16]

than deserved on other dimensions. Errors can also occur because of race, sex, or age discrimination, intentionally or unintentionally. The best way to offset these errors is to ensure that a valid rating system is developed at the outset and then to train managers in how to use it.

One interesting approach to performance appraisal used in some organizations today is called **360-degree feedback**, in which managers are evaluated by everyone around them—their boss, their peers, and their subordinates. Such a complete and thorough approach provides people with a far richer array of information about their

360-Degree Feedback *performance appraisal technique in which managers are evaluated by everyone around them—their boss, their peers, and their subordinates*

performance than does a conventional appraisal given by just the boss. Of course, such a system also takes considerable time and must be handled so as not to breed fear and mistrust in the workplace.[17]

Performance Feedback The last step in most performance appraisal systems is giving feedback to subordinates about their performances. This is usually done in a private meeting between the person being evaluated and his or her boss. The discussion should generally be focused on the facts: the assessed level of performance, how and why that assessment was made, and how it can be improved in the future. Feedback interviews are not easy to conduct, however. Many managers are uncomfortable with providing candid feedback, especially if the feedback is negative and subordinates are disappointed by what they hear. Properly training managers, however, can help them conduct more effective feedback interviews.[18]

New Challenges in the Changing Workplace

OBJECTIVE 10-6
Discuss
workforce diversity, the management of knowledge workers, and the use of a contingent workforce as important changes in the contemporary workplace.

Workforce Diversity *the range of workers' attitudes, values, beliefs, and behaviors that differ by gender, race, age, ethnicity, physical ability, and other relevant characteristics*

In addition to the challenges we have already considered, HR managers face several new challenges reflecting the changing economic and social environments of business.

Managing Workforce Diversity

One extremely important set of HR challenges centers on **workforce diversity**, the range of workers' attitudes, values, beliefs, and behaviors that differ by gender, race, age, ethnicity, physical ability, and other relevant characteristics. In the past, organizations tended to work toward homogenizing their workforces, getting everyone to think and behave in similar ways. Partly as a result of affirmative action efforts, however, many U.S. organizations are now creating more diverse workforces than ever before.

Figure 10.3 shows recent trends in age and ethnic composition of the U.S. workforce. The picture is clearly one of increasing diversity. The number of Caucasian Americans as a percentage of the total workforce is declining steadily, offset by increases in every other racial group. Most striking are the growing numbers of people of Hispanic origin (who may be members of any racial group). By 2050, the U.S. Department of Labor estimates that nearly a quarter of the workforce will be Hispanic.

Today, organizations are recognizing that diversity can be a competitive advantage. For example, by hiring the best people available from every single group rather than hiring from just one or a few groups, a firm can develop a higher-quality labor force. Similarly, a diverse workforce can bring a wider array of information to bear on problems and can provide insights on marketing products to a wider range of consumers.

Managing Knowledge Workers

Traditionally, employees added value to organizations because of what they did or because of their experience. In the information age, however, employees who add value because of what they know are usually called **knowledge workers**. Knowledge workers, which include computer scientists, engineers, physical scientists, game developers, and software application designers, typically require extensive and highly specialized training. Once they are on the job, retraining and training updates are critical to prevent their skills from becoming obsolete. It has been suggested, for example, that the half-life of a technical education in engineering is about three years.

Knowledge Workers *employees who are of value because of the knowledge they possess*

A firm's failure to update the skills of its knowledge workers not only results in the loss of competitive advantage but also increases the likelihood that those workers will go to other firms that are more committed to updating their skills. Hence,

Ethnic Composition

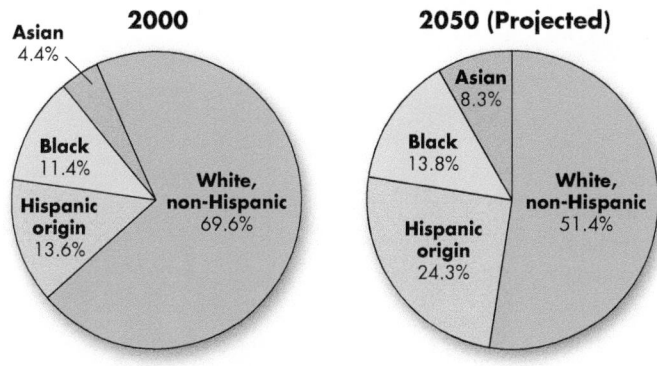

Age Distributions

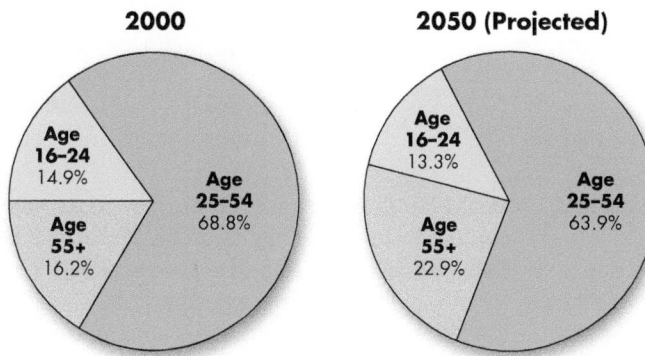

FIGURE 10.3 Changing Composition of the U.S. Labor Force by Ethnicity and Age

Source: Based on U.S. Department of Labor, https://www.bls.gov/emp/ep_pub_labor_force.htm (accessed June 27, 2017).

HR managers must ensure that the proper training is prepared to enable knowledge workers to stay current while also making sure they are compensated at market rates.

A major part of this challenge is recruiting new knowledge workers on a regular basis. Given both the high demand for knowledge workers and their relative short supply, firms often resort to extreme measures to recruit the best and brightest. For example, Google, Facebook, and Zynga often compete head-to-head for programmers and software engineers. To help recruit knowledge workers, these firms offer such lavish perks as free massages, laundry services, gourmet meals and snacks, and premium coffee.[19]

Contingent and Temporary Workers

A final contemporary HR issue of note involves the growing use of contingent and temporary workers. Many employers use contingent and temporary workers to increase their flexibility and, in most cases, lower their costs.

Trends in Contingent and Temporary Employment A **contingent worker** is a person who works for an organization on something other than a permanent or full-time basis. Categories of contingent workers include independent contractors, on-call workers, temporary employees (usually hired through outside agencies), and contract and leased employees. Another category is part-time workers. In recent years, there has been an explosion in the use of such workers by organizations. For instance, in 2017, around 20 percent of employed U.S. workers fell into one of these categories, up from 10 percent in 2008.

Managing Contingent and Temporary Workers One key to managing contingent workers effectively is careful planning and analysis. Rather than having to call in workers sporadically, and with no prior notice, organizations

Contingent Worker *employee hired on something other than a full-time basis to supplement an organization's permanent workforce*

managing in turbulent times

The Talent Gap

Even with unemployment at less than 5 percent, the 2016 U.S. Talent Shortage Survey conducted by ManpowerGroup reported that over 40 percent of employers were having difficulty finding the right talent for the job opening, the highest percentage reported since before the 2008 recession. The likely culprit isn't lack of workers—it's the effects of technological innovation, shifting demographics, an increasing amount of customer sophistication, and the rise of individual choice.

Nearly one in four respondents to the Manpower survey reported a lack of applicants, while another one in five employers said applicants did not have the relevant experience required and lacked technical skills. It may seem strange to hear employers complaining about lack of talent while unemployment is falling, but there is a component of unemployment called "structural unemployment" that is caused by a mismatch between unemployed workers' skills and the needs and demands of the workplace.

"Low unemployment paired with shorter skills cycles due to the speed of technological change means employers across the United States are struggling to fill positions," said Kip Wright, former senior vice president of Manpower North America. "We see this particularly in industries like manufacturing, construction, transportation and education."

Sunny Ackerman, Manpower's vice president and general manager for U.S. field operations, notes that, "With relatively strong job creation over the past few years, individuals simply have more choices about where they work—we are shifting from a talent rich environment to one that is far more competitive."

At the same time, diversity is playing an ever-increasing role in talent development and recruiting by opening more opportunities within the recruitment, hiring, and retention processes. Not surprisingly, employers who integrate diversity into their regular HR functions have higher rates of engagement, satisfaction, and retention than those who do not.

In today's working world, diversity has to do with more than race or ethnicity. Diverse workplaces are composed of employees with varying characteristics including religious and political beliefs, gender, ethnicity, education, socioeconomic background, sexual orientation, and geographic location. As employers struggle to find good talent, they are also struggling to recognize and honor an ever-widening array of diverse employees.

But change comes slowly, as evidenced by the gradual integration of women into the workforce. In the 1950s, women were simply fighting to work. In a 1979 case in which a woman sued three of her supervisors for harassing her, a District Court judge found that "the making of improper sexual advances to female employees [was] standard operating procedure, a fact of life, a normal condition of employment," and refused to

Sakkmesterke/Fotolia

award her any damages. Of course, social norms are changing, but even as recently as 2014, Microsoft's chief executive, Satya Nadella, declared that women should not bother to ask for raises. Instead, he suggested, they should have faith that the system would reward them appropriately. Refraining from asking for a raise, he added, is actually "good karma." Facing a Twitterstorm of backlash, Nadella apologized publicly, but with the company position in the spotlight, it's no wonder that less than a year later, the company was sued by a former employee, Katie Moussouris, claiming that she was only one of a number of women at Microsoft who earned less than their male counterparts. Moussouris also alleged that men received preferential treatment in promotions and systematically received more favorable job reviews.

Money may not be the only motivating factor in employee satisfaction, but it is still the baseline by which most jobs are measured. Free lunches and ping-pong tables will work well to attract younger workers just entering the formal workforce, but more senior workers who have been around long enough to have developed skills and experience value freedom, autonomy, diversity of experience, and the ability to work on projects they're passionate about. And although they demand a premium salary, they can often get the work done faster and better than a cheaper employee (who simply may not even be able to do the same work), and therefore can be a more profitable addition to the company, despite a higher pay scale.

In the 1940s and 1950s, employment issues largely centered around retirement benefits, collective bargaining agreements, and workplace safety. Now, more than ever before, companies are dealing with individuality and quality of life issues. Even so, for today's corporations, solving the talent shortage, whether the approach is in the form of perks or pay or a combination of both, still remains a question of balancing cost against profit.

try to bring in specified numbers of workers for well-defined periods of time. For instance, most retailers hire temporary seasonal employees for the Christmas holiday shopping period. Based on their past experience, they generally know how many people they need to hire and when they need to hire them. Firms should also be able to document the labor-cost savings of using contingent workers.

A second key is recognizing what can and cannot be achieved by using contingent and temporary workers. For instance, these workers may lack the firm-specific knowledge to perform as effectively as a permanent employee would perform. They are also less committed to the organization and less likely to engage in organizational citizenship behaviors.

Finally, managers must make decisions about how to integrate contingent workers into the organization. These decisions may be as simple as whether to invite contingent workers to the holiday party, or they may be more complicated, such as whether to grant contingent workers access to such employee benefits as counseling services and child care.

Dealing with Organized Labor

A **labor union** is a group of individuals working together to achieve shared job-related goals, such as higher pay, shorter working hours, more job security, better benefits, or improved working conditions. **Labor relations** refers to the process of dealing with employees who are represented by a union.

Unionism Today

In the years immediately following World War II and continuing through the mid-1960s, most unions routinely won certification elections. In recent years, however, labor unions have been winning certification only about half the time.[20] As a result, although millions of workers still belong to unions, union membership as a percentage of the total workforce has steadily declined. In 2007, only 12.1 percent of U.S. workers belonged to a labor union, down from 20.1 percent in 1983, when the U.S. Department of Labor first began compiling data.[21] As the recession of 2008–2011 began to increase fears about unemployment and wage cuts, union membership began to increase again, albeit only slightly. By 2010, it had dropped again, falling below prerecession levels. In 2016, union membership was 11.1 percent. These trends are shown in Figure 10.4.

OBJECTIVE 10-7
Explain
why workers organize into labor unions and describe the collective bargaining process.

Labor Union *group of individuals working together to achieve shared job-related goals, such as higher pay, shorter working hours, more job security, greater benefits, or better working conditions*

Labor Relations *process of dealing with employees who are represented by a union*

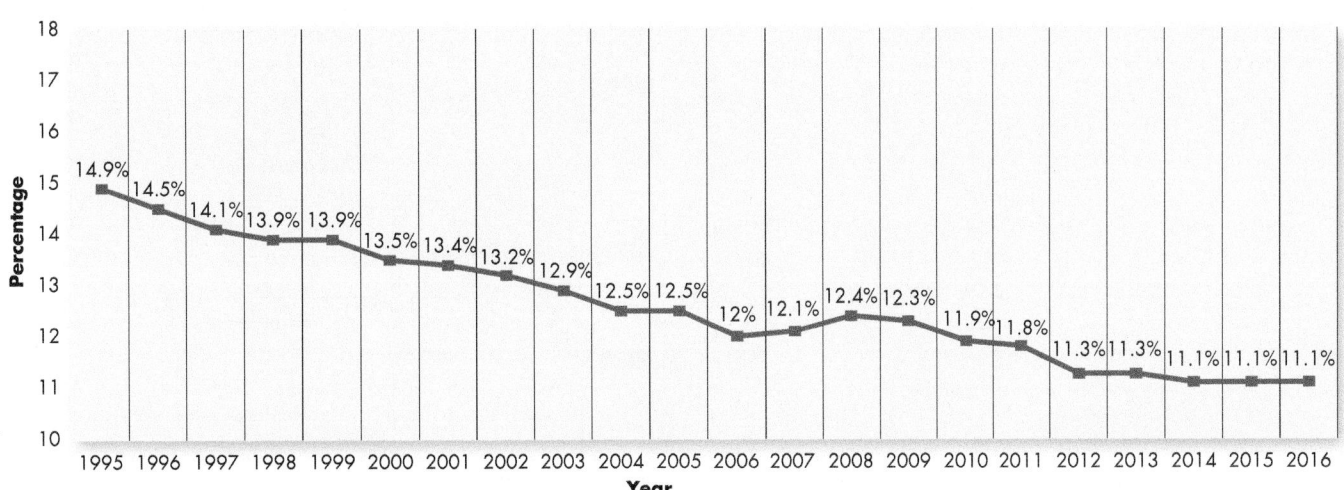

FIGURE 10.4 Percentage of Workers Who Belong to Unions: 1995–2016

Sources: U.S. Department of Labor, Bureau of Labor Statistics, www.aflcio.org/joinaunion/why/uniondifference/uniondiff11.cfm.

The Future of Unions Even though several of its members withdrew from the parent organization in 2005, the American Federation of Labor and Congress of Industrial Organizations (AFL-CIO), as well as independent major unions such as the Teamsters and the National Education Association (NEA), still play a major role in U.S. business. Unions in the traditional strongholds of goods-producing industries continue to wield considerable power as well. The United Automobile Workers (UAW) was for decades one of the largest unions in the United States. But it, too, seems to be entering a period of decline. The traumas experienced by the U.S. auto industry in 2008–2009, for instance, required the UAW to make many major concessions to help Ford, DaimlerChrysler (now Daimler AG), and General Motors survive. In addition, auto plant closures will dramatically reduce the number of auto jobs in the years to come.

Another issue affecting the future of unionism is the geographic shift in the U.S. economy. For the most part, unionism in the United States started in the North and Midwest regions and in cities such as Detroit, Pittsburgh, Cleveland, St. Louis, and Chicago. But over the past several decades, there has been a pronounced shift as businesses have moved their operations to the South and Southwest, areas that do not have a strong union heritage. For instance, Nucor Steel, profiled in Finding a Better Way, locates its facilities in smaller communities in the southern United States in part because it knows these workers are not prone to unionization.

Collective Bargaining

The power of unions comes from collective action, forcing management to listen to the demands of all workers rather than to just the few who speak out. **Collective bargaining** is the process by which labor and management negotiate conditions of employment for union-represented workers and draft a labor contract.

Collective Bargaining process by which labor and management negotiate conditions of employment for union-represented workers

Reaching Agreement on Contract Terms The collective bargaining process begins when the union is recognized as the exclusive negotiator for its members and union leaders meet with management representatives to agree on a labor contract. By law, both parties must sit down at the bargaining table and negotiate in good faith. Figure 10.5 shows what is called the "bargaining zone." For instance, in theory, employers want to pay as little as possible; they will generally pay more than the minimum, but there is also some upper limit beyond which they will not pay. Likewise, unions want the highest pay possible but expect to get less. But they, too, have a limit beyond which they will not go.

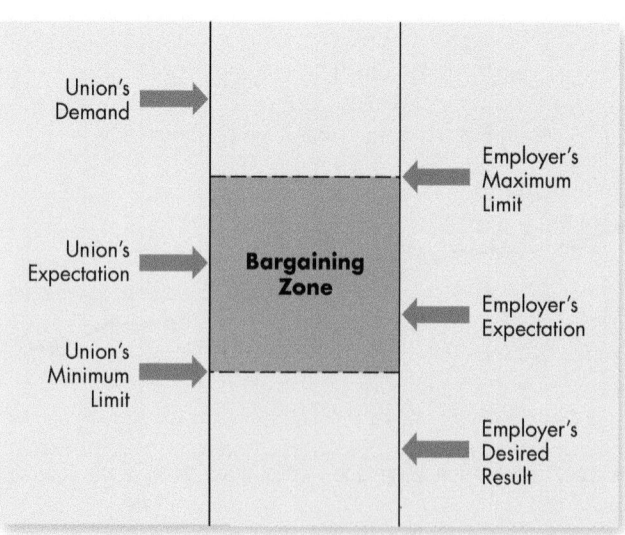

FIGURE 10.5 The Bargaining Zone

For example, suppose the bargaining issue is pay increases. The employer may initially propose a pay increase of 2 percent but (secretly) be willing to offer up to 6 percent. However, under no circumstances can it afford to pay more than 8 percent. The union, meanwhile, may initially demand a 10 percent increase but (secretly) be willing to accept as little as 4 percent. Assuming each party negotiates in good faith and is willing to make concessions to the other, the real bargaining zone falls between the union minimum (4 percent) and the employer maximum (6 percent). The real outcome will then depend on such things as other items being negotiated and the skills of the respective negotiators.

Sometimes, this process goes quite smoothly. At other times, the two sides cannot agree. For instance, the preceding example should result in an agreement because the union minimum and the employer maximum provide a bargaining zone. But if the union demands no less than 8 percent and the employer is unwilling to give more than a 4 percent increase, there is no bargaining zone. Resolving the impasse depends in part on the nature of the contract issues, the willingness of each side to use certain tactics, such as strikes, and the prospects for mediation or arbitration.

Contract Issues The labor contract itself can address an array of different issues. Issues that are typically most important to union negotiators include *compensation, benefits,* and *job security.* Certain management rights, such as control over hiring policies and work assignments, are also negotiated in most bargaining agreements. Other possible issues might include such specific details as working hours, overtime policies, rest period arrangements, differential pay plans for shift employees, the use of temporary workers, grievance procedures, and allowable union activities (dues collection, union bulletin boards, and so forth).

COMPENSATION Compensation includes both current and future wages. One common tool for securing wage increases is a **cost-of-living adjustment (COLA)**. Most COLA clauses tie future raises to the *Consumer Price Index (CPI)*, a government statistic that reflects changes in consumer purchasing power. Almost half of all labor contracts today include COLA clauses.

A union might be uncomfortable with a long-term contract based solely on COLA wage increases. One solution is a **wage reopener clause**, which allows wage rates to be renegotiated at preset times during the life of the contract.

Cost-of-Living Adjustment (COLA) *labor contract clause tying future raises to changes in consumer purchasing power*

Wage Reopener Clause *clause allowing wage rates to be renegotiated during the life of a labor contract*

BENEFITS Employee benefits are also an important component in most labor contracts. Unions typically want employers to pay all or most of the costs of insurance for employees. Other benefits commonly addressed during negotiations include retirement benefits, paid holidays, and working conditions. Because of surging healthcare costs, employee health insurance premiums have become a major point of contention in recent years. For example, many employees have much larger co-pays today when they visit their doctor than was the case a few years ago. (A *co-pay* is the dollar amount a patient pays to the doctor; insurance then pays the remainder.)

JOB SECURITY Job security also remains an important agenda item in many bargaining sessions today. Unions have historically fought for the use of seniority to determine who is retained in the event that job cuts are necessary. Employers, meanwhile, may object to this position because newer workers generally earn lower wages.

Unions have also focused their efforts on preserving jobs for workers in the United States in the face of business efforts to outsource production in some sectors to countries where labor costs are cheaper. For example, the AFL-CIO has been an outspoken opponent of efforts to normalize trade relations with China, fearing that more businesses might be tempted to move jobs there to take advantage of lower wage levels.

When Bargaining Fails An impasse occurs when, after a series of bargaining sessions, management and labor have failed to agree on a new contract or a contract to replace an agreement that is about to expire. Although it is generally agreed that both parties suffer when an impasse is reached and some action by one party againt the other is taken, each side can use several tactics to support its cause until the impasse is resolved.

UNION TACTICS Historically, one of the most common union tactics has been the **strike**, which occurs when employees temporarily walk off the job and refuse to work. The number of major strikes in the United States has steadily declined over the past few decades. From 1960 to 1980, for example, an average of 281 strikes occurred per year. In the 1980s, there was an average of 83 major strikes per year; in the 1990s, this figure fell to an average of 35 per year. Between 2000 and 2010, there was an average of 20 major strikes per year.[22] Since 2011 there have been an average of only 18 major strikes per year in the United States.

To support a strike, a union faced with an impasse has recourse to additional legal activities:

- In **picketing**, workers march at the entrance to the employer's facility with signs explaining their reasons for striking.

- A **boycott** occurs when union members agree not to buy the products of a targeted employer. Workers may also urge consumers to boycott the firm's products.

- Another alternative to striking is a **work slowdown**. Instead of striking, workers perform their jobs at a much slower pace than normal. A variation is the *sickout*, during which large numbers of workers call in sick.

MANAGEMENT TACTICS Like workers, management can respond forcefully to an impasse with the following:

- **Lockouts** occur when employers deny employees access to the workplace. Lockouts are illegal if they are used as offensive weapons to give management a bargaining advantage. However, they are legal if management has a legitimate business need (for instance, avoiding a buildup of perishable inventory). When the National Football League failed to reach a new contract agreement with its players association in 2011, the league owners imposed a lockout until an agreement was reached. More recently, the Toronto Zoo locked out its employees in 2013 over a labor dispute, as did the St. Paul Chamber Orchestra.

- A firm can also hire temporary or permanent replacements called **strikebreakers**. However, the law forbids the permanent replacement of workers who strike because of unfair practices. In some cases, an employer can obtain legal injunctions that either prohibit workers from striking or prohibit a union from interfering with its efforts to use replacement workers.

Mediation and Arbitration Rather than wield these often unpleasant weapons against one another, labor and management can agree to call in a third party to help resolve the dispute:

In **mediation**, the neutral third party (the mediator) can suggest, but cannot impose, a settlement on the other parties.

In **arbitration**, the neutral third party (the arbitrator) dictates a settlement between the two sides, which have agreed to submit to outside judgment. In some disputes, such as those between the government and public employees, arbitration is compulsory, or required by law.

Managing an organization's HR is both a complex and important undertaking. Most businesses can buy the same equipment and use the same technology as their competitors. But differences in employee talent and motivation are not easily copied. Consequently, most well-managed companies today recognize the value provided by their employees and strive to ensure that the HR function is managed as efficiently and effectively as possible.

Strike *labor action in which employees temporarily walk off the job and refuse to work*

Picketing *labor action in which workers publicize their grievances at the entrance to an employer's facility*

Boycott *labor action in which workers refuse to buy the products of a targeted employer*

Work Slowdown *labor action in which workers perform jobs at a slower than normal pace*

Lockout *management tactic whereby workers are denied access to the employer's workplace*

Strikebreaker *worker hired as a permanent or temporary replacement for a striking employee*

Mediation *method of resolving a labor dispute in which a third party suggests, but does not impose, a settlement*

Arbitration *method of resolving a labor dispute in which both parties agree to submit to the judgment of a neutral party*

summary of learning objectives

Define *human resource management*, **discuss its strategic significance, and explain how managers plan for their organization's human resource needs.** (pp. 310–313)

Human resource management (HRM) is the set of organizational activities directed at attracting, developing, and maintaining an effective workforce. Human resources (HR) are critical for effective organizational functioning. HRM was once relegated to second-class status in many organizations, but its importance has grown dramatically in the last two decades. Its new importance stems from increased legal complexities, the recognition that HR are a valuable means for improving productivity, and the awareness today of the costs associated with poor HRM. *Human capital* reflects the organization's investment in attracting, retaining, and motivating an effective workforce. Hence, just as the phrase *financial capital* is an indicator of a firm's financial resources and reserves, so, too, does human capital serve as a tangible indicator of the value of the people who comprise an organization.

Job analysis is a systematic analysis of jobs within an organization resulting in two things: a *job description* and a *job specification*. A job description lists the duties and responsibilities of a job, whereas a job specification identifies the skills, abilities, and qualifications needed to perform the job. Managers must plan for future HR needs by assessing past trends, future plans, and general economic trends. Forecasting labor supply is really two tasks: (1) *forecasting internal supply* and (2) *forecasting external supply*. To analyze internal supply, HR managers often develop *employee information systems* (or skills inventories). The next step in HR planning is matching HR supply and demand.

Discuss the legal context of human resource management and identify contemporary legal issues. (pp. 313–316)

A number of laws regulate various aspects of employee–employer relations, especially in the areas of equal employment opportunity, compensation and benefits, labor relations, and occupational safety and health. *Title VII of the Civil Rights Act of 1964* forbids discrimination in all areas of the employment relationship such as hiring, opportunities for advancement, compensation increases, layoffs, and terminations against members of certain protected classes based on factors such as race, color, gender, religious beliefs, or national origin. In addition to enforcing rules against overt discrimination, the *Equal Employment Opportunity Commission (EEOC)* is also charged with evaluating employment requirements that have *adverse impact*. Several other laws have expanded the scope of antidiscrimination law. The *Age Discrimination in Employment Act*, passed in 1967, amended in 1978, and amended again in 1986, is an attempt to prevent organizations from discriminating against older workers. The *Pregnancy Discrimination Act* forbids discrimination against women who are pregnant. The *Americans with Disabilities Act* forbids discrimination on the basis of disabilities and requires employers to provide reasonable accommodations for disabled employees. The *Civil Rights Act of 1991* amended the original Civil Rights Act as well as other related laws by both making it easier to bring discrimination lawsuits while simultaneously limiting the amount of punitive damages that can be awarded in those lawsuits.

Affirmative action was created through executive order and requires government contractors to make proactive attempts to recruit, hire, and promote employees from groups that are underrepresented in the organization.

The *Fair Labor Standards Act*, passed in 1938 and amended frequently since then, sets a minimum wage and requires the payment of overtime rates for work in excess of 40 hours per week. The *Equal Pay Act of 1963* requires that men and women be paid the same amount for doing the same job. Employers who provide a pension plan for their employees are regulated by the *Employee Retirement Income Security Act (ERISA) of 1974*. The *Family and Medical Leave*

Act (FMLA) of 1993 requires employers to provide up to 12 weeks of unpaid leave for family and medical emergencies.

The *National Labor Relations Act* (also known as the Wagner Act), passed in 1935, sets up a procedure for employees to vote on whether to have a union. The *Labor-Management Relations Act* (also known as the Taft-Hartley Act) was passed in 1947 to limit union power. Taken together, these laws balance union and management power. Employees can be represented by a legally created and managed union, but the business can make non-employee-related business decisions without interference.

The *Occupational Safety and Health Act (OSHA) of 1970* directly mandates the provision of safe working conditions. Under the Americans with Disabilities Act of 1990, AIDS is considered a disability and employers cannot require an HIV test or any other medical examination as a condition of employment. Sexual harassment, both quid pro quo harassment and a hostile work environment, is forbidden under antidiscrimination law as well.

In general, employees work under the legal concept of *employment at will*, which gives both the employee and the employer the right to terminate an employment relationship at any time. However, this concept has been tested in the courts and limited in scope by a variety of legislative provisions.

OBJECTIVE 10-3

Identify the steps in staffing a company and discuss ways in which organizations recruit and select new employees. (pp. 316–318)

Staffing an organization means recruiting and hiring the right mix of people. *Recruiting* is the process of attracting qualified persons to apply for open jobs, either from within the organization or from outside the organization. To help prospective employees understand the job, some employers offer a *realistic job preview (RJP)*.

The next step is the *selection process*, gathering information that will predict applicants' job success and then hiring candidates. Common selection techniques include application forms; tests of ability, aptitude, or knowledge; and interviews.

OBJECTIVE 10-4

Describe the main components of a compensation and benefits system. (pp. 318–322)

A company's *compensation system* is the financial rewards given by the organization to its employees in exchange for their work. *Wages* are the hourly compensation paid to operating employees. *Salary* refers to compensation paid for total contributions, as opposed to pay based on hours worked. A good compensation system can help attract qualified applicants, retain present employees, and stimulate high performance at a cost reasonable for one's industry and geographic area.

Companies may also try to link compensation to performance through *incentive programs*. Individual incentive programs include *bonuses, merit salary systems*, and *variable pay*. Companywide incentives include *profit sharing, gainsharing*, and *pay-for-knowledge plans*.

Benefits are things of value other than wages that the organization provides to its workers. Most employers are required to pay into Social Security on behalf of employees and to maintain workers' compensation insurance, protecting employees injured on the job. Many companies also provide health, life, and disability insurance. Other types of benefits include employee stock ownership plans, counseling services, on-site child care, and reduced-fee memberships at gyms and health clubs. Many companies provide retirement plans for their employees, although many are funded entirely by employee contributions. Companies that offer *cafeteria benefit plans* set aside a certain dollar amount per employee for benefits, allowing the employee to select the benefits most important to his or her individual situation.

OBJECTIVE 10-5

Describe how managers develop the workforce in their organization through training and performance appraisal. (pp. 322–326)

In HRM, *training* usually refers to teaching operational or technical employees how to do the job for which they were hired. *Development* refers to teaching managers and professionals the skills needed for both present and future jobs. Most organizations provide regular training and development programs for managers and employees. The first step in developing a training plan is to determine what needs exist. Many different training and development methods are available—assigned reading, programmed learning, lecture, role-playing, case discussion groups, on-the-job training, vestibule training, web-based training, and other electronic media-based training. Training and development programs should always be evaluated for effectiveness.

Once employees are trained and settled into their jobs, one of management's next concerns is performance appraisal. *Performance appraisal* is a formal assessment of how well employees are doing their jobs. Because performance evaluations often help determine wages and promotions, they must be fair and nondiscriminatory. Two basic categories of appraisal methods commonly used in organizations are objective methods and judgmental methods. Objective measures of performance include actual output (number of units produced), scrap rate, dollar volume of sales, and number of claims processed. Judgmental methods, including ranking and rating techniques, are the most common way to measure performance. Ranking compares employees directly with one another and orders them from best to worst. Rating differs from ranking in that it compares each employee with a fixed standard rather than with other employees, with a rating scale providing the standard. Errors or biases can occur in any kind of rating or ranking system. One common problem is recency error—the tendency to base judgments on the subordinate's most recent performance because it is most easily recalled. Halo error is allowing the assessment of an employee on one dimension to "spread" to ratings of that employee on other dimensions. The last step in most performance appraisal systems is giving feedback to subordinates about their performance, usually done in a private meeting between the person being evaluated and his or her boss.

OBJECTIVE 10-6

Discuss workforce diversity, the management of knowledge workers, and the use of a contingent workforce as important changes in the contemporary workplace. (pp. 326–329)

Workforce diversity refers to the range of workers' attitudes, values, beliefs, and behaviors that differ by gender, race, age, ethnicity, physical ability, and other relevant characteristics. In the past, organizations tended to work toward homogenizing their workforces; however, many organizations are now realizing that diversity can be a competitive advantage.

Employees who add value because of what they know are usually called *knowledge workers*, and managing them skillfully helps determine which firms will be successful in the future. *Contingent workers*, including independent contractors, on-call workers, temporary employees, contract and leased employees, and part-time employees, work for organizations on something other than a permanent or full-time basis. Organizations must understand when it is appropriate to use contingent workers and how to integrate them into the organization.

OBJECTIVE 10-7

Explain why workers organize into labor unions and describe the collective bargaining process. (pp. 329–332)

Labor relations is the process of dealing with employees who are represented by a union. A *labor union* is a group of individuals working together to achieve shared job-related goals, such as higher pay, shorter working hours, more job security, greater benefits, or better working conditions. At one time, almost a third of the entire U.S. labor force belonged to a labor union, with the largest membership following World War II into the mid-1960s. Union membership fell from 20.1 percent of the workforce in 1983 to only 12.1 percent of the workforce in 2007.

The intent of *collective bargaining* is to agree on a labor contract between management and the union that is satisfactory to both parties. The contract contains agreements about such issues as wages, work hours, job security, promotion, layoffs, discipline, benefits, methods of allocating overtime, vacations, rest periods, and the grievance procedure. Sometimes, the process of collective bargaining goes quite smoothly and management and the union agree to the terms of a new contract. However, when bargaining fails, the union has the option to go on *strike*, *picket* the organization, organize a *boycott*, or implement a *work slowdown*. Management has options as well; it may *lock out* employees until an agreement has been reached or hire *strikebreakers*. Rather than wielding these weapons, labor and management can agree to call in a third party, either a *mediator* or *arbitrator*, to help resolve the dispute.

key terms

360-degree feedback (p. 325)
adverse impact (p. 314)
affirmative action (p. 314)
affirmative action plan (p. 314)
Age Discrimination in Employment Act
    (p. 314)
Americans with Disabilities Act (p. 314)
arbitration (p. 332)
benefits (p. 319)
bonus (p. 319)
boycott (p. 332)
cafeteria benefits plan (p. 321)
Civil Rights Act of 1991 (p. 314)
collective bargaining (p. 330)
compensation system (p. 318)
contingent worker (p. 327)
cost-of-living adjustment (COLA) (p. 331)
development (p. 322)
employee information system (skills
    inventory) (p. 312)
employment at will (p. 316)
Employment Retirement Income
    Security Act (ERISA) of 1974 (p. 315)
equal employment opportunity (p. 314)
Equal Employment Opportunity
    Commission (EEOC) (p. 314)
Equal Pay Act of 1963 (p. 314)
external recruiting (p. 317)

Fair Labor Standards Act (p. 314)
Family and Medical Leave Act (FMLA)
    of 1993 (p. 315)
gainsharing plan (p. 319)
hostile work environment (p. 316)
human capital (p. 311)
human resources (p. 310)
human resource management (HRM)
    (p. 310)
incentive program (p. 319)
internal recruiting (p. 317)
job analysis (p. 311)
job description (p. 311)
job specification (p. 311)
knowledge workers (p. 326)
labor relations (p. 329)
labor union (p. 329)
Labor-Management Relations Act
    (Taft-Hartley Act) (p. 315)
lockout (p. 332)
mediation (p. 332)
merit salary system (p. 319)
National Labor Relations Act (Wagner
    Act) (p. 315)
National Labor Relations Board (NLRB)
    (p. 315)
Occupational Safety and Health Act
    (OSHA) of 1970 (p. 315)

on-the-job training (p. 322)
Patriot Act (p. 316)
pay for performance (or variable pay)
    (p. 319)
pay-for-knowledge plan (p. 319)
performance appraisal (p. 323)
picketing (p. 332)
profit-sharing plan (p. 319)
quid pro quo harassment (p. 316)
realistic job preview (RJP) (p. 317)
recruiting (p. 317)
replacement chart (p. 312)
salary (p. 318)
sexual harassment (p. 316)
strike (p. 332)
strikebreaker (p. 332)
talent management (p. 311)
Title VII of the Civil Rights Act of 1964
    (p. 313)
training (p. 322)
vestibule training (p. 322)
wage reopener clause (p. 331)
wages (p. 318)
work slowdown (p. 332)
workers' compensation insurance
    (p. 319)
workforce diversity (p. 326)

MyLab Intro to Business

To complete the problems with the ✪, go to EOC Discussion Questions in the MyLab.

questions & exercises

QUESTIONS FOR REVIEW

10-1. What are the advantages and disadvantages of internal and external recruiting? Under what circumstances is each more appropriate?

10-2. Why is the formal training of workers so important to most employers? Why don't employers simply let people learn about their jobs as they perform them?

✪**10-3.** What different forms of compensation do firms typically use to attract and keep productive workers?

✪**10-4.** What is a knowledge worker? What strategies do companies use to retain knowledge workers?

QUESTIONS FOR ANALYSIS

✪**10-5.** What are your views on drug testing in the workplace? What would you do if your employer asked you to submit to a drug test?

10-6. Workers at Ford, GM, and Chrysler are represented by the UAW. However, the UAW has been much less successful in its attempts to unionize U.S. workers employed at Toyota, Nissan, and Honda plants in the United States. Why do you think this is so?

10-7. What are the advantages and challenges of having a diverse workforce?

10-8. How much will benefit considerations affect your choice of an employer after graduation? What types of benefits would be most and least appealing to you, and why?

APPLICATION EXERCISES

10-9. Go online and search for at least three companies that are considered great places to work. Describe the compensation, benefits, and perks at each of these companies. Of the three, which is most appealing to you, and why?

10-10. Interview the HR manager at a local company about current hiring processes. Describe how the department recruits employees to apply for jobs, the steps in the selection process, and the orientation program for new employees.

building a business: continuing team exercise

Assignment

Meet with your team members to consider your new business venture and how it relates to the concepts of HRM discussed in this chapter. Develop specific responses to the following:

10-11. As your new venture grows, you will need to hire employees. How will you recruit people to apply for jobs within your organization?

10-12. Ideally, you will be able to select from many applicants for jobs within your company. How will you select the best employee from the pool of applicants?

10-13. How will employees be compensated in your company? How do you think that this compensation system will reflect your company's mission and goals?

10-14. What types of benefits will you offer to employees? Understanding the high cost of benefits, how have you selected these benefits?

10-15. Describe your system for performance appraisal and training. How will you reward good employees? When you have weak employees, how will you change their behavior?

team exercise

THE DOWNSIDE OF DOWNSIZING

The Situation

A moderate-sized consulting company is going through tough times after losing a major contract. As a result, the leadership team is asking managers to make two budget cut proposals for their departments: a 15 percent budget cut that will likely be implemented, and a 30 percent cut that may be implemented depending on the big picture. One of the managers has come to you for advice. She is new to her position and has little experience to draw from. However, it is obvious to her that 90 percent of her budget is personnel and the other 10 percent is overhead and other fixed costs that really can't be cut in the short term. The members of her team are as follows:

- Tony Jones: white male, 10 years with the company; has been turning in above-average performance ratings from his annual reviews for the past two years, even though his actual performance has been suffering due to a divorce and other personal issues, including showing up late for work and calling in sick several times a month.

- Amanda Wiggens: white female; ambitious; 3 years with company; above-average performer; puts in extra time at work; some of her subordinates have complained about her directness and lack of tact, and have even reported angry outbursts; you have informally counseled her in interpersonal communications skills.

- Jorge Gonzalez: Latino, 2 years with the company; he speaks fluent Spanish, has great connections in the Latino business community and has brought in several new clients during the past year; you have rated his work as average due to lack of English communication skills and tardiness.

- Dorothy Henderson: white female, 25 years with company, average performer, filed a sexual harassment complaint against a different member of the leadership team last year which is now in mediation; she is a friend of the company president and is the first person most people talk to when they call the company; she has an immense amount of institutional knowledge and memory, but she comes across as a bit curt on the phone.

- Wanda Jackson: African-American female, 8 years with company; during formal performance reviews you have rated her as outstanding for the past three years; Dorothy Henderson mentioned on promise of anonymity that Jackson was looking for another job and had in fact applied for one with a competing firm; Wanda often works late, even though she is a salaried employee and does not get overtime pay.

- Jerry Loudder: white male, single parent, 5 years with company; gets his work done but has not brought in any new clients and goes home right at five; Jerry has a lot of experience and even though he does not work late, he always hits the deadlines and his work quality is excellent; he often mentors the younger members of the group.

- Martha Strawser: white female, 1 year with company; she is putting her husband through college and appears to have much promise—in fact, some members of the leadership team have mentioned that she may be vice-presidential material once she gains some experience; she holds an MBA and is outgoing and well-connected in the business community.

Team Activity

Assemble a group of four students. Your group has agreed to provide the manager with a recommendation.

ACTION STEPS

10-16. As a group, discuss the underlying legal and ethical issues in this situation. What laws must be considered before making this decision?

10-17. Working individually, prioritize the layoff list. Make notes about your reasoning for each potential layoff.

10-18. Have each team member discuss their recommendation with the group, justifying their decision on the basis of both the ethical and legal considerations.

10-19. Develop a group recommendation for both the 15 percent scenario and the 30 percent scenario.

10-20. Now that you have decided which employee to lay off, develop a set of recommendations on how layoffs should be handled. Be sure to consider how to communicate your decision to the employee being laid off as well as those who remain.

exercising your ethics

OPERATING TACTICALLY

The Situation

Assume that you work as a manager for a medium-sized company that is facing a serious union-organizing campaign. Your boss, who is determined to keep the union out of the workplace, has just given you a list of things to do to thwart the efforts of the organizers. For example, he has suggested each of the following tactics:

- Whenever you learn about a scheduled union meeting, you should schedule a "worker appreciation" event at the same time. He wants you to offer free pizza and to give cash prizes that winners must be present to receive.

- He wants you to look at the most recent performance evaluations of the key union organizers and supporters and to terminate the one with the lowest overall evaluation based on the "need to lower costs."

- He wants you to make an announcement that the firm is seriously considering such new benefits as on-site childcare, flexible work schedules, telecommuting options,

and exercise facilities. Although you know that the firm is indeed looking into these benefits, you also know that, ultimately, your boss will provide far less lavish benefits than he wants you to suggest.

The Dilemma

When you questioned the ethics—and even the legality—of these tactics, your boss explained that he was seriously concerned that a union victory might actually shut down the company's domestic operations altogether, forcing it to move all of its production capacities to lower-cost foreign plants. He concluded by saying that he was really looking out for the employees, even if he had to play hardball to help them.

QUESTIONS TO ADDRESS

10-21. What are the ethical issues in this situation?

10-22. What are the basic arguments for and against extreme measures to fight unionization efforts?

10-23. What do you think most managers would do in this situation? What would you do?

cases

A UNIQUE PARTNERSHIP DRIVES WEGMANS

Continued from page 310

At the beginning of this chapter, you read about Wegmans and its approach to human resource management. Using the information presented in this chapter, you should now be able to respond to these questions.

QUESTIONS FOR DISCUSSION

10-24. If you were an HR executive at Wegmans, would you focus more on *internal recruiting* or on *external recruiting*? Would your strategy for higher-level positions differ from your strategy for lower-level positions? How would current economic conditions influence your strategy?

10-25. As an HR executive at Wegmans, you need to hire a group of new employees as part of your management-trainee program—people who will be put on a track leading, ultimately, to positions as store managers. Briefly outline your program for developing these employees.

10-26. If you were an employee at Wegmans, how would you expect your annual performance appraisal to be conducted? Given the company's customer-relations strategy, which appraisal methods do you think would be most appropriate?

FINDING THE WORK/LIFE BALANCE

SAS Institute is a private tech company headquartered in Cary, North Carolina, that has more than 6,000 employees in the United States and twice that many worldwide. Like most great companies, SAS pays its employees well. This is important—

as a company that helps businesses turn raw data into useful information, their employees are at the core of their success. However, SAS also places a very high value on work/life balance. SAS has a companywide standard that employees don't work more than 37.5 hours per week. Of course, there are times when employees need to put in extra hours, but they are encouraged to take time off soon afterward to recharge. Each employee has a private office (no cubicles or shared work spaces) and is able to take advantage of the on-site hair and nail salons, shoe and jewelry repair shops, and dry-cleaning and tailoring services. Many services are provided for free on-site, such as tax preparation and a health clinic and pharmacy. They even offer a seasonal farmers market, right at Cary headquarters.

SAS Institute is an ideal employer for those with families. Employees' children are welcomed at work, both at the subsidized on-site daycare center and in the cafeteria, which includes kid-friendly items such as octopus-shaped hot dogs on the menu. Employees with school-aged children are encouraged to bring their kids to work with them on the occasional teacher workdays, making the balancing act of parenting and working a little easier. In a recent survey, one employee put it this way: "SAS has provisions to support you at whatever stage of life you are in—child care for your newborn to pre-schooler, resources for dealing with your teenager and college

planning, help with your elderly parent. More importantly, a real sense of community is built when people work together for so long."

Founder and CEO Jim Goodnight believes that it's essential that employees feel trusted and valued. By almost every metric, this has paid off. In the software industry, turnover tends to be about 20 percent per year, as employees hop from one job to the next in hopes of higher pay or better working conditions. This is not the case at SAS, where turnover is just about 4 percent. In a recent survey, more than 95 percent of employees rated SAS as an employer with great challenges, great atmosphere, great rewards, and even great bosses.

QUESTIONS FOR DISCUSSION

10-27. After reading about SAS Institute, what would appeal to you most about working there?

10-28. What trade-offs is SAS making to offer the benefits and culture described?

10-29. What types of policies and benefits do you believe are most supportive of work/life balance?

10-30. What challenges might you face as a manager working in this environment? How could you overcome these challenges?

crafting a business plan

PART 3: PEOPLE IN ORGANIZATIONS

Goal of the Exercise

At this point, your business has an identity and you've described the factors that will affect your business and how you will operate it. Part 3 of the business plan project asks you to think about your employees, the jobs they will be performing, and the ways in which you can lead and motivate them.

Exercise Background: Part 3 of the Business Plan

To complete this part of the plan, you need to refer back to the organizational chart that you created in Part 2. In this part of the business plan exercise, you'll take the different job titles you created in the organizational chart and give thought to the *skills* that employees will need to bring to the job *before* they begin. You'll also consider *training* you'll need to provide *after* they are hired, as well as how you'll compensate your employees. Part 3 of the business plan also asks you to consider how you'll lead your employees and keep them happy and motivated.

Your Assignment

STEP 1
Open the *Business Plan* file you began working on in Parts 1 and 2.

STEP 2
For the purposes of this assignment, you will answer the questions in "Part 3: People in Organizations":

10-31. What do you see as the "corporate culture" of your business? What types of employee behaviors, such as organizational citizenship, will you expect?

   Hint: Will your business demand a casual environment or a more professional environment? Refer to the discussion on employee behavior in Chapter 8 for information on organizational citizenship and other employee behaviors.

10-32. What is your philosophy on leadership? How will you manage your employees day to day?

   Hint: Refer to the discussion on leadership in Chapter 9, to help you formulate your thoughts.

10-33. Looking back at your organizational chart in Part 2, briefly create a job description for each team member.

   Hint: As you learned in this chapter, a job description lists the duties and responsibilities of a job; its working conditions; and the tools, materials, equipment, and information used to perform it. Imagine your business on a typical day. Who is working and what are each person's responsibilities?

10-34. Next, create a job specification for each job, listing the skills, other credentials, and qualifications needed to perform the job effectively.

   Hint: As you write your job specifications, consider what you would write if you were composing an ad for the position. What would the new employee need to bring to the job to qualify for the position?

10-35. What sort of training, if any, will your employees need once they are hired? How will you provide this training?

   Hint: Refer to the discussion of training in this chapter. Will you offer your employees on-the-job training? Off-the-job training? Vestibule training?

10-36. A major factor in retaining skilled workers is a company's compensation system—the total package of rewards it offers employees in return for their labor. Part of this compensation system includes wages or salaries. What wages or salaries will you offer for each job? Why did you decide on that pay rate?

   Hint: Refer to the discussion in this chapter for more information on forms of compensation. You may also want to check out sites such as www.salary.com, which includes a salary wizard you can use to determine how much people with different job titles are making in your area and across the United States.

10-37. As you learned in this chapter, incentive programs are special programs designed to motivate high performance. What incentives will you use to motivate your workforce?

Hint: Be creative and look beyond a simple answer, such as giving pay increases. Ask yourself: Who are my employees and what is important to them? Refer to the discussion in this chapter for more information on the types of incentives you may want to consider.

Note: Once you have answered the questions, save your Word document. You'll be answering additional questions in later chapters.

Writing Assignments

10-38. In many organizations, there are experts who are responsible for job analysis and recruiting. Explain why job analysis should be conducted before recruitment. Assume your organization owns thirty-five casual dining restaurants across the Midwest. It's been many years since the company has looked at its job descriptions for managers. However, due to a recent vacancy, you've been asked to conduct job analysis for the general manager position for each restaurant. Write a job description and job specification for this position. If you were in charge of recruiting, where might you look to find someone to fill this position internally and externally?

10-39. As an upper manager in a large manufacturing company, you have been asked to represent the company during the collective bargaining agreement process with the employees' union. The contract is due for renewal but the company and the union are stuck on the issue of salaries. The CEO (your boss) refuses to allow the company to pay more than the going wage, and he feels that the union is demanding too much. What other kinds of benefits or concessions could you bring to the negotiations? What might happen if the deadlock is not broken, and how would you deal with those repercussions? What are your responsibilities as both a manager and a member of the negotiating team? What are your options?

endnotes

[1] *HR Magazine*, "Nothing Partial About These Benefits," vol. 48, no. 8 by Elayne Robertson Demby, August 1, 2003, see http://www.shrm.org/Publications/hrmagazine/EditorialContent/Pages/0803demby.aspx:; "The Wegmans Way," by Matthew Boyle, January 24, 2005, *Fortune Magazine*, see: http://money.cnn.com/magazines/fortune/fortune_archive/2005/01/24/8234048/; Jon Springer, "Danny Wegman," *Supermarket News*, July 14, 2009, at http://supermarketnews.com, accessed on April 15, 2013; Prospero, Michael A. "Employee Innovator: Wegmans," *Fast Company*, October 2004, at www.fastcompany.com, accessed on April 15, 2011, see http://www.fastcompany.com/51347/employee-innovator-wegmans; Mitchell, Dan. "Wegmans Price War Against Itself," *The Big Money*, November 2, 2009, at www.thebigmoney.com, accessed on April 15, 2013; "100 Best Companies to Work For," *Fortune*, 2011, at http://money.cnn.com, accessed on April 15, 2013; Business Civic Leadership Center, "Wegmans," *2009 Corporate Citizenship Awards* (U.S. Chamber of Commerce, 2009), at www.bclc.uschamber.com, accessed on April 15, 2013; "In 2010, Wegmans Announces Largest Group of Employee Scholarship Recipients Yet," press release, June 16, 2010, at www.wegmans.com,

accessed on April 15, 2013, from http://www.wholefoodsmarket.com/mission-values/core-values/declaration-interdependence.

[2] Wright, Patrick, and McMahan, Gary. "Strategic Human Resources Management: A Review of the Literature," *Journal of Management*, June 1992, pp. 280–319; see also Peter Cappelli, "Talent Management for the Twenty-First Century," *Harvard Business Review*, March 2008, pp. 74–84; and Edward E. Lawler III, "Making Human Capital a Source of Competitive Advantage," *Organizational Dynamics*, January–March 2009, pp. 1–7.

[3] Lepak, David, and Snell, Scott. "Examining the Human Resource Architecture: The Relationships among Human Capital, Employment, and Human Resource Configurations," *Journal of Management*, 2002, vol. 28, no. 4, pp. 517–543. See also Wayne F. Cascio and Herman Aguinis, "Staffing Twenty-First Century Organizations," in James P. Walsh and Arthur P. Brief, *The Academy of Management Annals*, vol. 2 (London: Routledge, 2008), pp. 133–166.

[4] "OSHA Claims Company Knowingly Overexposed Workers to Lead," *Advanced Safety and Health*, January 21, 2011, pp. 35–41.

[5] Breaugh, James A., and Starke, Mary. "Research on Employee Recruiting: So Many Studies, So Many Remaining Questions," *Journal of Management*, 2000, vol. 26, no. 3, pp. 405–434.

[6] "Employee Relations Principles," NUCOR Corporation; "Pain, but No Layoffs at Nucor," *BusinessWeek*, March 26, 2009, at www.businessweek.com, accessed on March 25, 2011; John Byrnes with Michael Arndt, "The Art of Motivation," *BusinessWeek*, May 1, 2006, at www .businessweek.com, accessed on March 26, 2011; "About Us," Nucor website, at www.nucor.com, accessed on April 2, 2011; "Nucor Reports Record Results for 2008," *Reuters*, January 27, 2009, at www.reuters.com, accessed on April 2, 2011; Mayer, Kathy. "Nucor Steel: Pioneering Mill in Crawfordsville Celebrates 20 Years and 30 Million Tons," *AllBusiness*, September 1, 2008, at www.allbusiness.com, accessed on April 3, 2011.

[7] "Some Employers Offer ID Theft Coverage," *USA Today*, September 12, 2005, p. 1B.

[8] Brown, Kenneth B., and Sitzmann, Traci. "Training and Employee Development for Improved Performance," in Zedeck, Sheldon (ed.), *Handbook of Industrial and Organizational Psychology*, vol. 2: *Selecting and Developing Members for the Organization* (Washington, DC: American Psychological Association), pp. 469–504.

[9] DeRouin, Renee, Fritzsche, Barbara, and Salas, Eduardo. "E-Learning in Organizations," *Journal of Management*, 2005, vol. 31, no. 6, pp. 920–940. See Fred Luthans, James B. Avey, and Jaime L. Patera, "Experimental Analysis of a Web-Based Training Intervention to Develop Positive Psychological Capital," *Academy of Management Learning & Education*, 2008, vol. 7, no. 2, pp. 209–221 for a recent illustration.

[10] "'Boeing U': Flying by the Book," *USA Today*, October 6, 1997, pp. 1B, 2B. See also "Is Your Airline Pilot Ready for Surprises?" *Time*, October 14, 2002, p. 72.

[11] "The Secret Sauce at In-N-Out Burger," *BusinessWeek*, April 20, 2009, pp. 68–69; "Despite Cutbacks, Firms Invest in Developing Leaders," *Wall Street Journal*, February 9, 2009, p. B4.

[12] Wildman, Jessica L., Bedwell, Wendy L., Salas, Eduardo, and Smith-Jentsch, Kimberly A. "Performance Measurement at Work: A Multilevel Perspective," in Zedeck, Sheldon (ed.), *Handbook of Industrial and Organizational Psychology*, Vol. 1: *Building and Developing the Organization* (Washington, DC: American Psychological Association, 2010), pp. 303–341.

[13] See Paul Levy and Jane Williams, "The Social Context of Performance Appraisal: A Review and Framework for the Future," *Journal of Management*, 2004, vol. 30, no. 6, pp. 881–905.

[14] See Michael Hammer, "The 7 Deadly Sins of Performance Measurement (and How to Avoid Them)," *MIT Sloan Management Review*, Spring 2007, pp. 19–30.

[15] Yoo, Dan. "How to Fire Employees With Compassion," *Entrepreneur*, at www.entrepreneur.com, accessed May 19, 2015.

[16] "Whatever Happened to … NerdWallet?" PMNTS.com, 2016, http://www.pymnts.com/whatever-happened-to/2016/whatever-happened-to-nerdwallet/, accessed March 27, 2017.

[17] See Angelo S. DeNisi and Avraham N. Kluger, "Feedback Effectiveness: Can 360-Degree Appraisals Be Improved?" *Academy of Management Executive*, 2000, vol. 14, no. 1, pp. 129–139.

[18] Nathan, Barry R., Mohrman, Allan, and Milliman, John. "Interpersonal Relations as a Context for the Effects of Appraisal Interviews on Performance and Satisfaction: A Longitudinal Study," *Academy of Management Journal*, June 1991, pp. 352–369.

[19] "Welcome to Silicon Valley: Perksville, USA," *USA Today*, July 5, 2012, p. 1A.

[20] http://www.bls.gov/opub/cwc/cb20100628ar01p1.htm

[21] U.S. Department of Labor, Bureau of Labor Statistics, at http://www.bls.gov/news.release/union2.nr0.htm, accessed on March 22, 2011.

[22] U.S. Department of Labor, Bureau of Labor Statistics, at http://www.bls.gov/news.release/pdf/wkstp.pdf, accessed on March 22, 2011.

Marketing Processes and
Consumer Behavior

chapter 11

Ouzounova/Splash News/Newscom

As consumers, we are the forces that drive marketing.

But those same marketing campaigns

push us to make

buying decisions without us even knowing it.

After reading this chapter, you should be able to:

11-1 **Explain** the concept of marketing and identify the five forces that constitute the external marketing environment.

11-2 **Explain** the purpose of a marketing plan and identify its main components.

11-3 **Explain** market segmentation and how it is used in target marketing.

11-4 **Discuss** the purpose of marketing research and compare the four marketing research methods.

11-5 **Describe** the consumer buying process and the key factors that influence that process.

11-6 **Discuss** the four categories of organizational markets and the characteristics of business-to-business (B2B) buying behavior.

11-7 **Discuss** the marketing mix as it applies to small business.

Building a Brand With
Social Media

Michelle Phan longed to pursue a career in art so that she could make the life for herself that her parents dreamed of when they emigrated from war-torn Vietnam. But her father racked up gambling debts and then left when Michelle was six, and her stepfather turned out to be overbearing and controlling. Eventually, he left too, leaving Michelle and her mom to scrape out a meager existence in Sarasota, Florida. In 2007, at the age of 19, Michelle Phan was waiting tables at Pacific Rim Sushi and although she'd managed to scrape together enough money for one year of school at the Ringling College of Art and Design, the family was too broke to pay for her second year. She applied for better jobs more in line with her interests, including a makeup artist position at the local Lancôme cosmetics counter, but she was turned down. Despite all this, or maybe because of it, Michelle developed a drive and an inner purpose that led her to persevere.

In her spare time, she started a blog about the life she imagined and a YouTube channel under the screen name RiceBunny, where she projected a confident, charismatic, cool persona. However, her blog was just the start. During that first year at Ringling, Phan used her laptop to record, edit, and post a makeup tutorial video to YouTube—then a brand-new platform just finding its footing. Within a week, it had garnered 40,000 views and demand for more. She created more videos on how to create different looks, from dark and stormy to soft hues appropriate for church. Phan established herself as an authority on beauty and she shared her expertise. "You need interesting content that entertains or informs—preferably both. You want people to look forward to your posts and come back for more. People want to follow you. They want to hear your words and see your vision." Her lack of money to buy makeup didn't limit her ability to create new videos—she scoured the bargain bins at stores, picking up many items for less than a dollar.

Within four years, Phan had become a brand. The name Michelle Phan conveyed an image and position in the market. Google offered her $1 million to create 20 hours of content, and she began creating video content for Lancôme, who contacted her based on her expertise and results. Her video tutorials also led her to start a lifestyle network called ICON and a beauty subscription service called Ipsy. In 2013 she partnered with L'Oreal USA to create her own beauty brand, Em Cosmetics, which she later bought from L'Oreal so that she could have more artistic control.

By 2016, Michelle's YouTube channel had more than 8 million followers and more than a billion views. While many might perceive YouTube as a difficult path to a successful career, Phan believes just the opposite. She explains, "You're in

what's in it for me?

Businesses adapt to their environments in many different ways. One common approach is to use marketing basics in innovative ways to appeal to the forces of the external marketing environment. This chapter discusses these basics along with the marketing plan and components of the marketing mix, as well as target marketing and market segmentation. It also explores key factors that influence consumer and organizational buying processes. By understanding the marketing methods and ideas in this chapter, you will better appreciate the function of marketing professionals in business and also become a more informed consumer.

control of how people perceive you and see you. I can't say the same for traditional media because you have other people who are editing you—producers and other people who have the final say. Your YouTube channel is your own show. I think it's a wonderful platform for anyone who wants to have stronger creative control over their content, their message, their vision, and their branding."[1]

Through hard work, diligence, and a deep understanding of linking consumers to products through the Internet, Phan has established herself as a powerhouse in the beauty and lifestyle industry. She carefully monitors trends in her environment and quickly spots new opportunities. At the same time, she's kept a keen eye on her target market and understands the consumer buying process. Oh, and in 2014 Ringling College of Art and Design awarded her an honorary doctorate. (After studying the content in this chapter, you should be able to answer a set of discussion questions found at the end of the chapter.)

OBJECTIVE 11-1
Explain
the concept of marketing and identify the five forces that constitute the external marketing environment.

What Is Marketing?

As consumers, we are influenced by the marketing activities of people like Michelle Phan and by companies like L'Oreal, Apple, and Pizza Hut that want us to buy their products rather than those of their competitors. Being consumers makes us the essential ingredients in the marketing process. Every day, we express needs for such essentials as food, clothing, and shelter and wants for such nonessentials as entertainment and leisure activities. Our needs and wants are major forces that drive marketing.

Marketing *activities, a set of institutions, and processes for creating, communicating, delivering, and exchanging offerings that have value for customers, clients, partners, and society at large.*

What comes to mind when you think of marketing? Most of us think of marketing as advertisements for products like fast foods, movies, soft drinks, and cars. Marketing, however, actually encompasses a much wider range of activities. The American Marketing Association defines **marketing** as "activities, a set of institutions, and processes for creating, communicating, delivering, and exchanging offerings that have value for customers, clients, partners, and society at large."[2] To see this definition in action, we'll continue this chapter by looking at some marketing basics, including the ways marketers build relationships with customers. We'll then examine forces that constitute the external marketing environment, followed by marketing strategy, the marketing plan, and the components of the marketing mix. We'll then discuss market segmentation and how it is used in target marketing. Next, we'll examine marketing research, followed by a look at key factors that influence the buying processes of consumers and industrial buyers. Finally, we'll consider the marketing mix for small business and then go beyond domestic borders to explore the international marketing mix.

Delivering Value

What causes buyers to purchase one product instead of another? Although our desires for the wide variety of available goods and services may be almost limitless, in most cases our financial resources are not and so we have to be selective. Accordingly, customers usually try to buy products that offer the best value when it comes to meeting their needs and wants.

Value *relative comparison of a product's benefits versus its costs*

Value and Benefits The **value** of a product refers to its comparative benefits versus costs. Benefits, in turn, include not only the functions of the product but also the emotional satisfaction associated with owning, experiencing, or possessing it. For instance, a pair of $40 basketball shoes from Walmart may be perfectly adequate for most recreational players but many people still spend much more for the latest version of Jordan, LeBron, Durant, or Kyrie endorsed shoes because of their style or cache. But every product also has costs, including the sales price, the buyer's time finding the product, and even the emotional costs of making a purchase decision (such as deciding which pair of basketball shoes to buy). A satisfied customer perceives the benefits derived from the purchase to be greater than its costs. Thus, the simple but important ratio for value is derived as follows:

$$Value = \frac{Benefits}{Costs}$$

The marketing strategies of leading firms focus on increasing value for customers. Marketing resources are deployed to add benefits and/or decrease costs of products to provide greater value. To satisfy customers, a company may do the following:

- Develop an entirely new product that performs better (provides greater performance benefits) than existing products.

- Keep a store open longer hours during a busy season (adding the benefit of greater shopping convenience).

- Offer price reductions (the benefit of lower costs).

- Offer information that explains how a product can be used in new ways (the benefit of new uses at no added cost).

Value and Utility To understand how marketing creates value for customers, we need to know the kind of benefits that buyers get from a firm's goods or services. As we discussed in Chapter 7, those benefits provide customers with **utility**, the ability of a product to satisfy a person's wants or needs. Think about the competitive marketing efforts for Microsoft's Xbox series and those for Sony's competing PlayStation game consoles. In both companies, marketing strives to provide four kinds of utility in the following ways:

Utility *ability of a product to satisfy a human want or need*

1 **Form utility.** Marketing has a voice in designing products with features that customers want. Microsoft's Xbox One features Kinect technology (voice- and motion-detecting software) and can record a video of your game. Sony's newest Playstation 4 (PS 4) touts a controller with a six-axis sensor.

Form Utility *providing products with features that customers want*

2 **Time utility.** Marketing creates a time utility by providing products *when* customers will want them. Both Sony and Microsoft create Internet buzz and rumors among gamers by hinting at upcoming release dates without mentioning specifics.

Time Utility *providing products when customers will want them*

3 **Place utility.** Marketing creates a place utility by making products easily accessible—by making products available *where* customers will want them. Xbox One and PS 4 are available online at Amazon.com and at many brick-and-mortar retailers such as Best Buy and Target. Both also offer online networks as well.

Place Utility *providing products where customers will want them*

4 **Possession utility.** Marketing creates a possession utility by transferring product ownership to customers by setting selling prices, setting terms for customer credit payments, if needed, and providing ownership documents. Hints about prices from both companies have fueled rumors: Xbox One sells for around $350, while the PS 4 runs about $400.

Possession Utility *transferring product ownership to customers by setting selling prices, setting terms for customer credit payments, and providing ownership documents*

As you can imagine, marketing responsibilities at Microsoft and Sony are extremely challenging in such a competitive arena, and the stakes are high. Because they determine product features, and the timing, place, and terms of sale that provide utility and add value for customers, marketers must anticipate customers' wants and needs well in advance of actual product launches. And in today's rapidly changing environment, businesses must also be prepared to quickly adapt to fads and shifting wants and needs. Marketing methods for creating utility are described in this and the following two chapters.

Goods, Services, and Ideas

As consumers, we encounter the marketing of tangible goods virtually everywhere we look—on social media and other online sites, on television, in magazines, along the highways and roadsides, on store fronts, in sports arenas, and in our mailboxes.

Marketing actually applies to two types of customers: those who buy consumer goods and those who buy industrial goods. In a department store, a salesperson may ask if you'd like to try a new cologne. On your social media account, a popup ad may promote a new sports drink. A television ad from a pharmaceutical company may proclaim the virtues of its new cold medicine. Your local auto dealer may offer an economy car at a discounted price. These products are all **consumer goods**, tangible goods that you, the consumer, may buy for personal use. Firms that sell goods to consumers for personal consumption are engaged in consumer marketing, also known as business-to-consumer (B2C) marketing.

Marketing also applies to **industrial goods**, physical items used by companies to produce other products. Surgical instruments and bulldozers are industrial goods, as are machine components and parts and raw materials such as integrated circuits, steel beams, coffee beans, and plastic tubing. Firms that sell goods to other companies are engaged in industrial marketing, also known as business-to-business (B2B) marketing.

But marketing techniques are also applied to **services**, products with intangible (nonphysical) features, such as professional advice, timely information for decisions, or arrangements for a vacation. Service marketing, the application of marketing for services, continues to be a major growth area in the United States. Insurance companies, airlines, public accountants, and health clinics all engage in service marketing, both to individuals (consumer markets) and to other companies (industrial markets). Thus, the terms *consumer marketing* and *industrial marketing* include services as well as goods.

Finally, marketers also promote ideas, such as "inspirational values" as seen in "Encouragement, Pass It On," on YouTube and in popular television commercials. Ads in theaters warn us against copyright infringement and piracy. Other marketing campaigns may stress the advantages of avoiding fast foods, texting while driving, or quitting smoking, or they may promote a political party or candidate.

Relationship Marketing and Customer Relationship Management

Although marketing often focuses on single transactions for products, services, or ideas, marketers also take a longer-term perspective. Thus, **relationship marketing** is a type of marketing that emphasizes building lasting relationships with customers and suppliers. Stronger relationships, including stronger economic and social ties, can result in greater long-term satisfaction, customer loyalty, and customer retention.[3] Michelle Phan has used relationship marketing very successfully. Similarly, Starbucks's Rewards attracts return customers with free coffee refills and other extras. Likewise, commercial banks offer economic incentives to encourage longer-lasting relationships. Longtime customers who use a certain number of the bank's products (for example, checking accounts, savings accounts, and loans) accumulate credits toward free or reduced-price products or services, such as free investment advice or reduced checking account fees.

Like many other marketing areas, the ways that marketers go about building relationships with customers have changed dramatically. **Customer relationship management (CRM)** is an organized method that an enterprise uses to build better information connections with clients, so that managers can develop stronger enterprise–client relationships.

The power of online communications coupled with the ability to gather and assemble information on customer preferences allows marketers to better predict what clients will want and buy. Viking Cruises, for instance, communicates with people who have booked future cruises months in advance of departures with e-mails containing onboard restaurant menus and food recipes from countries that vacationers will be visiting. Viking also encourages social networking among booked passengers to establish pre-voyage friendships, which can lead to faster face-to-face acquaintanceships once they board Viking ships.

Consumer Goods *physical products purchased by consumers for personal use*

Industrial Goods *physical products purchased by companies to produce other products*

Services *products having nonphysical features, such as information, expertise, or an activity that can be purchased*

Relationship Marketing *marketing strategy that emphasizes building lasting relationships with customers and suppliers*

Customer Relationship Management (CRM) *organized methods that a firm uses to build better information connections with clients, so that stronger company-client relationships are developed*

Compiling and storing customers' data, known as **data warehousing**, provides the "raw materials" from which marketers can extract information that enables them to find new clients and identify their best customers. Marketers can then inform these priority clients about upcoming new products and post-purchase service reminders. **Data mining** automates the massive analysis of data by using computer software to sift, sort, and search for previously undiscovered clues about what customers look at and react to and how they might be influenced. Marketers use these tools to get a clearer picture about how knowing a client's preferences can satisfy those particular needs, thereby building closer, stronger relationships with those customers.[4]

Toronto-based Fairmont Resort Hotels, for example, first used data mining to rebuild its customer-relations package by finding out what kinds of vacations their customers prefer and then placing ads where they were more likely to reach those customers. When data mining revealed the worldwide destinations of Fairmont customers, it helped determine Fairmont's decision to buy their customers' number-one preference, the Savoy in London.[5] Fairmont's enhanced CRM has attracted new guests and strengthened relationships and loyalty among existing clients through Web-based promotions and incentives. Using profiles of guest information, Fairmont identifies target traveler segments and supplies travelers with personalized price discounts and special hotel services.[6] We'll discuss data warehousing and data mining in more detail in Chapter 14.

The Marketing Environment

Marketing plans and strategies are not determined unilaterally by any business—rather, they are strongly influenced by powerful outside forces. As you see in Figure 11.1, every marketing program must recognize the factors in a company's *external environment*, which is everything outside an organization's boundaries that might affect it. In this section, we'll discuss how these external forces affect the marketing environment in particular.

Political-Legal Environment The **political-legal environment**, both global and domestic, has profound effects on marketing. For example, environmental legislation has determined the destinies of entire industries. The political push for alternative energy sources is creating new markets and products for emerging companies such as India's Suzlon Energy Limited (large wind turbines), wind-powered electric generators by Germany's Nordex AG, and wind farms and power plants by

---

Data Warehousing *the collection, storage, and retrieval of data in electronic files*

Data Mining *the application of electronic technologies for searching, sifting, and reorganizing pools of data to uncover useful information*

Political-Legal Environment *the relationship between business and government, usually in the form of government regulation of business*

FIGURE 11-1 The External Marketing Environment

Spain's Gamesa Corporation. Marketing managers try to maintain favorable political and legal environments in several ways. To gain public support for products and activities, marketers use ad campaigns to raise public awareness of important issues. Companies contribute to political candidates and frequently support the activities of political action committees (PACs) maintained by their respective industries.

Sociocultural Environment *the customs, mores, values, and demographic characteristics of the society in which an organization functions*

Sociocultural Environment

The **sociocultural environment** also impacts marketing. Changing social values force companies to develop and promote new products, such as poultry and meat without antibiotics and growth hormones, for both individual consumers and industrial customers. Just a few years ago, organic foods were available only in specialty food stores such as Whole Foods. Today, in response to a growing demand for healthy foods, Target's Archer Farms product line brings affordable organic food to a much larger audience. Grocers like Kroger and H-E-B also have set aside large areas in their stores where consumers can find organic and/or natural products. In addition, new industrial products reflect changing social values: A growing number of wellness programs are available to companies for improving employees' health. Quest Diagnostics, for example, a B2B company, supplies a "Blueprint for Wellness" service that assesses employee healthcare risks in client companies and recommends programs for reducing those risks. This and other trends reflect the values, beliefs, and ideas that shape society. In similar fashion, businesses strive to distance themselves from people and products that are potentially offensive. For instance, when Donald Trump announced his bid for the presidency of the United States in 2015 he made several controversial remarks about undocumented immigrants from Mexico. In quick response NBC dropped plans to televise the Miss Universe pageant owned by Trump and Macy's discontinued its line of Trump-endorsed men's wear.

Technological Environment *all the ways by which firms create value for their constituents*

Technological Environment

The **technological environment** creates new goods and services. New products make existing products obsolete, and many products change our values and lifestyles. In turn, lifestyle changes often stimulate new products not directly related to the new technologies themselves. Mobile devices, the availability of a vast array of apps, and social media, for example, facilitate business communication just as prepackaged meals provide convenience for busy household cooks. Both kinds of products also free up time for recreation and leisure.

John Locher/AP Images

Marketing strategies are strongly influenced by powerful outside forces. For example, new technologies create new products, such as the cell phone "gas station" shown here. These recharging stations enable customers to recharge their mobile devices just as they would refuel their cars. The screens at the stations also provide marketers with a new way to display ads to waiting customers.

Economic Environment Because economic conditions determine spending patterns by consumers, businesses, and governments, the **economic environment** influences marketing plans for product offerings, pricing, and promotional strategies. Marketers are concerned with such economic variables as inflation, interest rates, and recession. Thus, they monitor the general business cycle and specific economic patterns and projections to anticipate trends in consumer and business spending.

Economic Environment *relevant conditions that exist in the economic system in which a company operates*

Competitive Environment In a **competitive environment**, marketers try to convince buyers that they should purchase their company's products rather than another's. Because both consumers and commercial buyers have limited resources, every dollar spent on one product means one dollar less available for other purchases. Each marketing program, therefore, seeks to make its product the most attractive. Expressed in business terms, a failed program loses the buyer's dollar forever (or at least until it is time for the next purchase decision).

Competitive Environment *the competitive system in which businesses compete*

To promote products effectively, marketers must first understand which of three types of competition they face:

1 **Substitute products** may not look alike or they may seem different from one another, but they can fulfill the same need. For example, your cholesterol level may be controlled with either of two competing products: a physical fitness program or a drug regimen. The fitness program and the drugs compete as substitute products. Similarly, online video streaming services like Netflix provide substitute products for conventional television programming. A Royal Caribbean cruise, a Colorado ski resort, and a Disney theme park provide substitute products for a family looking for a spring break vacation.

Substitute Product *product that is dissimilar from those of competitors, but that can fulfill the same need*

2 **Brand competition** occurs between similar products and is based on buyers' perceptions of the benefits of products offered by particular companies. For online searches, do you turn to Google, Bing, or Dogpile? Brand competition is based on users' perceptions of the benefits offered by each product.

Brand Competition *competitive marketing that appeals to consumer perceptions of benefits of products offered by particular companies*

3 **International competition** matches the products of domestic marketers against those of foreign competitors. As we saw back in Chapter 4, many businesses today compete in global markets. Ford and General Motors (U.S. firms) compete with BMW and Volkswagen (German firms) and Toyota and Nissan (Japanese firms) in every global automobile market. Apple (a U.S. company) competes with Samsung (a Korean company). Sony (a Japanese company) competes with LG (a Korean company). And in each case, these businesses compete in their home countries, the home countries of their international competitors, and in many neutral countries as well. Take Coca-Cola for example. In the United States, Coke clearly promotes itself as a traditional, mainstream American product. In other countries, Coke is also recognized as an American icon. But the company presents itself as more of a global brand than as an American brand. Indeed, Coca-Cola sponsors more than 100 different national Olympic teams around the world.

International Competition *competitive marketing of domestic products against foreign products*

Developing the Marketing Plan

OBJECTIVE 11-2
Explain

the purpose of a marketing plan and identify its main components.

Once marketing managers have a basic understanding of their role and the nature of their competition, their next step is to develop their marketing plan. A marketing manager at a major home appliance manufacturing company explains the concept of *developing the marketing plan* by using the following analogy of planning a trip:

- "First, you decide where you want to go and what you want to happen when you get there. Why take this trip and not others, instead?"
   [Identify the *objective* or *goal* to be achieved.]

- "At some stage, you decide when the trip will happen and how you'll get to the destination."
   [*Plan* for *when* it will happen, and for the *paths* (or *routes*) that will be taken to get there.]

managing in turbulent times

An American Icon

There aren't many people—young, old, rich, or poor—who don't recognize the throaty rumble and iconic look of a Harley-Davidson motorcycle. But it hasn't been an easy ride for the century-old company. There have been challenges, both internal and external, that have tested the company's mettle and its ability to survive. And at the heart of it all, where the rubber meets the road, is marketing.

Founded in 1903 by William Harley and the Davidson brothers, Arthur, Walter, and William, the company made its mark with a signature air-cooled engine that consisted of two cylinders pitched at a 45-degree angle to each other. The rather inefficient and clunky design created a unique, hammering exhaust note that at the time was just considered an annoying side effect of the early attempts at engineering a big motorcycle engine. World War I gave the relatively new company a big financial boost as the military ordered thousands of bikes, and then World War II provided demand for more bikes and a whole new cast of riders—veterans of the war returning home. Despite the bad-boy reputation, Harley riders were mostly ordinary folk who just wanted to feel a bit less ordinary for a while.

In the mid-1960s Harley was making about 15,000 bikes a year and had revenues of about $49 million, but company executives saw the chance to increase market share as the Harley mystique spread. In 1965, in order to raise cash for growth, the owners took the company public. In a quest for increased profits, sporting goods manufacturer AMF bought a controlling interest in Harley and set out on a mission to increase volume significantly, capitalizing on the brand name's

Fadel Senna/Getty Images

growing popularity. By 1973, the company was churning out 37,000 cycles a year and pulling in $122 million, but to do that management cut workers and streamlined the production process, resulting in inferior bikes. Harley owners were still loyal, even though the bikes leaked oil and the stamped metal parts didn't have the same heavy look and feel of the pre-merger bikes, but the consumer public's patience wore thin. When AMF replaced the venerated Harley logo with their own, they lost market share at an alarming pace, paving the way for 13 Harley-Davidson senior executives to buy back the company in 1981 in order to save what was left of the all-American brand.

Unfortunately, Japanese companies had stepped in to the gap. No longer content with selling smaller bikes, they were making 750cc and even larger motorcycles. In 1979 Honda

- "Every trip requires resources, so you identify those resource requirements and compare them against resources that are available."
  [*Evaluate resource* requirements and availabilities.]

- "If available resources are too expensive, then you adjust the trip so it becomes affordable."
  [*Adjust plans* as needed to become *realistic* and *feasible*.]

- "During and after the trip, you assess the successes (what went right) and the drawbacks (what went wrong) and remember them so you can make the next trip even better."
  [Keep notes and data about what happened because *learning* from this experience increases the chances for *greater success on the next*.]

Marketing Plan *detailed strategy for focusing marketing efforts on consumers' needs and wants*

As you will see, our discussion of the marketing plan contains many of these elements. The **marketing plan** identifies the marketing objectives, stating what marketing will accomplish in the future. It also includes a strategy that identifies the specific activities and resources that will be used to meet the needs and desires of customers in the firm's chosen target markets, so as to accomplish the marketing objectives.

First and foremost, marketing plans are future-oriented, showing what will be happening with marketing's upcoming activities. Every well-developed marketing

opened its Marysville, Ohio plant and introduced the Gold Wing, a 1,000cc bike exclusively for the American market. The Gold Wing was as big as a Harley, yet was more comfortable and reliable for long-distance traveling. The entry of Honda Motorcycles into the market chopped Harley's market share from 70 percent to 14 percent. The company had developed a solid reputation for poor quality and questionable reliability. The industry joke at the time was, "If you're buying a Harley, you'd better buy two—one for parts."

Harley management took drastic measures. In 1982 Harley successfully lobbied for high tariffs on foreign bikes, but even as they tried to stop the competition, company executives were trying to mimic them. Harley executives toured Japanese plants to figure out what it was they did so well. What they saw were lean management and just-in-time (JIT) inventory control systems.

So Harley laid off 40 percent of its workforce and cut the pay of remaining employees. It canceled major product development, adopted MAN (materials-as-needed) systems, asked suppliers for price reductions, and shrank its dealer network while cutting dealer margins. The company also ramped up its marketing efforts, most notably by creating the Harley Owners Group (H.O.G.) to sponsor biker rallies, organize charity drives, and offer special promotions to the diverse customer base. Today, H.O.G. has more than a million members in 25 countries. Over half of them regularly attend Harley-Davidson events and the company encourages members to provide direct input into Harley's creative process.

H.O.G was a step in the right direction, and sales, quality, reliability, and reputation improved during the 80s and 90s, but the traditional demographic was over 50 years old, primarily male, and mostly white. That group tends to have disposable income but many already own a bike, and with age comes a necessary slowing of consumption. You can only sell so many bikes to the baby boomers. The effects of this demographic slippage are evident in the company's sales in the new millennium. Harley shipped over 350,000 bikes in 2006, but only 262,000 in 2016, a decrease of almost 30 percent, and even though sales overseas increased, domestic sales slumped and profits have been declining steadily.

But for Harley, this is just another bump in the road. The company is combatting the effects of the changing demographic by trying to connect with a wider customer base. New products like LiveWire (a concept electric motorcycle) and the entry-level Street models are designed to establish a more youthful image in order to pull in new customers—especially millennials, women, and new riders. Recently, in order to encourage the new demographic to try out the product, the company added a series of training courses from certified coaches at select Harley-Davidson dealers and a Jumpstart program where new riders can experience riding one of the big bikes on a stationary support stand. And even though shipments were down in 2016, the company was being strategic, attempting to clear out old inventory to make way for the new. In 2017, Harley-Davidson announced plans to introduce 50 new motorcycles over the next five years. This from a company that shocked investors in 2014 by introducing eight new models—the largest new model launch in the company's history.

plan, as shown in Figure 11.2, begins with objectives or goals that set the stage for everything that follows. **Marketing objectives**, the goals the marketing plan intends to accomplish, are the foundation that guides all the detailed activities in the plan. The marketing objectives themselves, however, exist solely to support the company's overall business mission (at the top in Figure 11.2) and typically focus on maintaining or enhancing the organization's future competitive position in its chosen markets. Suppose, for example, that Starbucks's overall business mission is to be the world's leading retailer of specialty coffee. Two supporting marketing objectives, then, could be (1) a 5 percent increase in its worldwide market share by, say, 2020, and (2) to be the leading retailer (in dollar sales) of specialty coffee in China by 2022.

Marketing Objectives *the things marketing intends to accomplish in its marketing plan*

Marketing Strategy: Planning the Marketing Mix

The marketing team can develop a strategy once it has clarified the marketing objectives. Specifically, **marketing strategy** identifies the planned marketing programs, all the marketing activities that a business will use to achieve its marketing goals, and when those activities will occur. If planned activities are not affordable or feasible, then marketers may need to adjust the activities or goals until realistic

Marketing Strategy *all the marketing programs and activities that will be used to achieve the marketing goals*

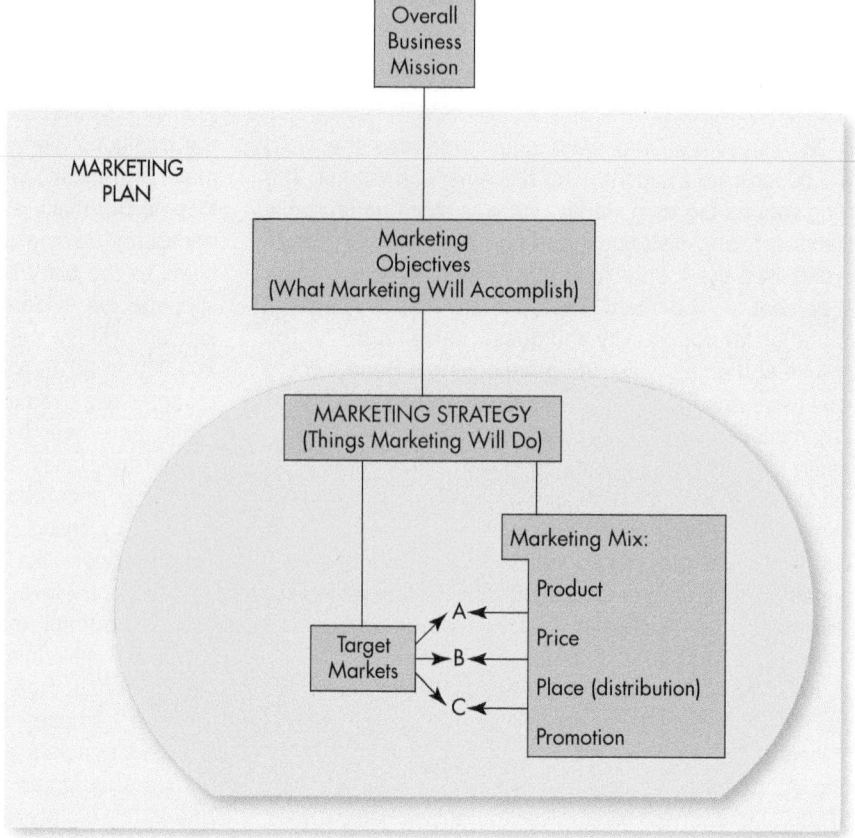

FIGURE 11-2 Components of the Marketing Plan

plans emerge. Finally, because marketing planning is an ongoing process—not just a one-time activity—it can be improved through experience by learning from past successes and mistakes.

Marketing Manager *manager who plans and implements the marketing activities that result in the transfer of products from producer to consumer*

Marketing managers are the people responsible for planning, organizing, leading, and controlling the organization's marketing resources toward supporting and accomplishing the organization's overall mission. To meet these responsibilities, marketing managers rely on mapping out a clear strategy for planning and implementing all the activities that result in the transfer of goods or services to customers. As you can see in Figure 11.2, the marketing strategy focuses on the needs and wants of customers in the company's chosen target markets. Marketing strategy also includes four basic components (often called the *Four Ps*) of the **marketing mix**—*product, pricing, place*, and *promotion*—that marketing managers use to attract customers in target markets. The specific activities for each of the Four Ps are designed differently to best meet the needs of each target market.

Marketing Mix *combination of product, pricing, promotion, and place (distribution) strategies used to market products*

Product *good, service, or idea that is marketed to fill consumers' needs and wants*

Product Differentiation *creation of a product feature or product image that differs enough from existing products to attract customers*

Product Marketing begins with a **product**, a good, a service, or an idea designed to fill a customer's need or want. Producers often promote particular features of products to distinguish them in the marketplace. **Product differentiation** is the creation of a feature or image that makes a product differ enough from existing products to attract customers. For example, in the years since Apple introduced the first iPhone, a succession of newer models evolved with faster, more powerful, and increasingly consumer-friendlier innovations. The iPhone's industry-leading features have attracted an enormous customer following that contributes substantially to Apple's sustained financial success. The design for the newest iPhone, for example, offers more new features than previous models to keep on top in the increasingly competitive smartphone market. The phone is thinner and lighter, and it has a new Retina HD display, improved camera, and faster operating system.

Meanwhile, Samsung surged onto the scene with its competitive Galaxy series. Like Apple, Samsung has introduced several versions of the Galaxy over the years. Popular features have included more powerful and removable batteries, faster download and upload speeds, the popular Android operating system, and numerous additional features. The phone is also dustproof and water-resistant.

Samsung's Galaxy currently has the largest global market share of the smartphone market while Apple is number two. In the U.S. market, however, Apple has a larger share than Samsung. We discuss product development more fully in Chapter 12.

Pricing The **pricing** of a product, selecting the best price at which to sell it, is often a balancing act. On the one hand, prices must be high enough to cover both direct costs (such as the costs of actually manufacturing the product) and indirect costs (such as operating, administrative, research, and marketing costs). On the other hand, prices can't be so high that customers routinely turn to lower-priced competitors. Successful pricing means finding a profitable middle ground between these two extremes.

Pricing *process of determining the best price at which to sell a product*

Both low- and high-price strategies can be effective in different situations. Lower prices, for example, generally lead to more units being sold but lower profits on each unit. Higher prices usually limit the number of units being sold but increase profits per unit. In some cases, though, higher prices may also actually attract customers by signaling that a product is of high quality. We also discuss pricing in more detail in Chapter 12.

Place (Distribution) In the marketing mix, **place** (or **distribution**) refers to *where* and *how* customers get access to the products they buy. When products are created, they must then be made available to customers at some *location* (*place*) such as a retail store, on a digital device, or by direct delivery to the customer. *Distribution* is the set of activities that moves products from producers to customers. Placing a product in the proper outlet, like a retail store, requires decisions about several activities, all of which are concerned with getting the product from the producer to the consumer. Decisions about warehousing and inventory control are distribution decisions, as are decisions about transportation options.

Place (Distribution) *part of the marketing mix concerned with getting products from producers to consumers*

Weng Lei/Imaginechina/AP Images

Rolex has had sustained success as a result of its well-conceived marketing mix. The Swiss company focuses exclusively on high-quality watches (product), sells them for thousands of dollars (price), uses an exclusive network of quality retailers (distribution), and advertises them in interesting ways (promotion).

Firms must also make decisions about the *channels* through which they distribute products. Many manufacturers, for example, sell goods to other companies that, in turn, distribute them to retailers. Others sell directly to major retailers, such as Target and Sears. Still others sell directly to final consumers. We explain distribution decisions further in Chapter 13.

Promotion The most visible component of the marketing mix is no doubt **promotion**, which is a set of techniques for communicating information about products. The most important promotional tools include advertising, personal selling, sales promotions, publicity/public relations, and direct or interactive marketing. Promotion decisions are discussed further in Chapter 13, but we will briefly describe four of the most important promotional tools here.

> **Promotion** *aspect of the marketing mix concerned with the most effective techniques for communicating information about products*

ADVERTISING **Advertising** is any form of paid nonpersonal communication used by an identified sponsor to persuade or inform potential buyers about a product. For example, financial advisory companies that provide investment and securities products reach their customer audience by advertising in *Fortune* magazine and on the *Bloomberg* television network.

> **Advertising** *any form of paid nonpersonal communication used by an identified sponsor to persuade or inform potential buyers about a product*

PERSONAL SELLING Many products (such as insurance, custom-designed clothing, and real estate) are best promoted through **personal selling**, person-to-person sales. Industrial goods and services rely significantly on personal selling. When companies buy from other companies, purchasing agents and others who need technical and detailed information are often referred to the selling company's sales representatives.

> **Personal Selling** *person-to person sales*

SALES PROMOTIONS Historically, relatively inexpensive items have often been marketed through **sales promotions**, which involve one-time direct inducements to buyers. Premiums (usually free gifts), coupons, and package inserts are all sales promotions meant to tempt consumers to buy products. More recently, however, these promotions have expanded into B2B sales and to sales of larger items to consumers through online deals at sources such as Groupon.

> **Sales Promotion** *direct inducements such as premiums, coupons, and package inserts to tempt consumers to buy products*

PUBLIC RELATIONS **Public relations** includes all communication efforts directed at building goodwill. It seeks to build favorable attitudes in the minds of the public toward the organization and its products. The Ronald McDonald House Charities, and its association with McDonald's Corporation, is a well-known example of public relations.

> **Public Relations** *communication efforts directed at building goodwill and favorable attitudes in the minds of the public toward the organization and its products*

Blending It All Together: Integrated Strategy An **integrated marketing strategy** ensures that the Four Ps blend together so that they are compatible with one another and with the company's non-marketing activities. As an example, consider the case of Toyota, the world's largest automaker. Its nearly 30-year auto superiority, even with its massive product recalls a few years ago, stems from a coherent marketing mix that is tightly integrated with its production strategy.

> **Integrated Marketing Strategy** *strategy that blends together the Four Ps of marketing to ensure their compatibility with one another and with the company's nonmarketing activities*

Michael Nagle/Bloomberg/Getty Images

Urban Outfitters is a successful–but sometimes controversial–retailer. The company offers low-priced and unique products targeted at young, urban-oriented consumers. But the firm has also had some public relations problems due in part to some of its more offbeat products.

Offering a relatively small number of different models, Toyota targets auto customers that want high quality, excellent performance reliability, and moderate prices (a good value for the price). With a smaller number of different models than U.S. automakers, fewer components and parts are needed, purchasing costs are lower, and less factory space is required for inventory and assembly in Toyota's lean production system. Lean production's assembly simplicity yields higher quality, the factory's cost savings lead to lower product prices, and speedy production gives shorter delivery times in Toyota's distribution system. Taken together, this integrated strategy is completed when Toyota's advertising communicates its message of consistent industry-high customer satisfaction.

Marketing Strategy: Target Marketing and Market Segmentation

OBJECTIVE 11-3
Explain
market segmentation and how it is used in target marketing.

Marketers have long known that products cannot be all things to all people. The emergence of the marketing concept and the recognition of customers' needs and wants led marketers to think in terms of **target markets**—the particular groups of people or organizations on which a firm's marketing efforts are focused. Selecting target markets is usually the first step in the marketing strategy.

Target Market *the particular group of people or organizations on which a firm's marketing efforts are focused*

Target marketing requires **market segmentation**, dividing a market into categories of customer types or "segments" having similar wants and needs and who can be expected to show interest in the same products. Once they have identified segments, companies may adopt a variety of strategies. Some firms market products by targeting more than one segment. Not that many years ago General Motors tried to offer automobiles for virtually every segment of the market. Its brands included Chevrolet, Buick, Oldsmobile, Pontiac, and Cadillac, as well as specialty products like Saturn, Saab, and Hummer plus assorted SUVs and pick-up trucks. The financial crisis of 2008–2011, though, pushed GM to the brink of financial ruin and caused the company to have to accept a bail-out from the U.S. government. To deal with the crisis GM sold some of its product lines and shut down several others. Today the firm is a much leaner company, targeting fewer marketing segments and earning much higher profits.

Market Segmentation *process of dividing a market into categories of customer types, or "segments," having similar wants and needs and who can be expected to show interest in the same products*

In contrast, some businesses have always focused on a narrower range of products, such as Ferrari's high-priced sports cars, aiming at just one segment. Note that segmentation is a strategy for analyzing consumers, not products. Once marketers identify a target segment, they can begin marketing products for that segment. The process of fixing, adapting, and communicating the nature of the product itself is called **product positioning**.

Product Positioning *process of fixing, adapting, and communicating the nature of a product*

Identifying Market Segments

By definition, members of a market segment must share some common traits that affect their purchasing decisions. In identifying consumer segments, researchers look at several different influences on consumer behavior. We discuss five of the most important variables next.

Geographic Segmentation

Many buying decisions are affected by the places people call home. Urban residents don't need agricultural equipment, and sailboats sell better near large bodies of water than in the mountains. **Geographic variables** are the geographic units, from countries to neighborhoods, that researchers consider in a strategy of **geographic segmentation**. McDonald's restaurants in Germany, in contrast to those in the United States, offer beer on the menu. Pharmacies in Jackson Hole, Wyoming, sell firearms that are forbidden in Chicago. Starbucks is currently focusing on the growing geographic segment in China.

Geographic Variables *geographic units that may be considered in developing a segmentation strategy*

Geographic Segmentation *geographic units, from countries to neighborhoods, that may be considered in identifying different market segments in a segmentation strategy*

table 11.1 Examples of Demographic Variables

Age	Under 5, 5–11, 12–19, 20–34, 35–49, 50–64, 65+
Education	Grade school or less, some high school, graduated high school, some college, college degree, advanced degree
Family Life Cycle	Young single, young married without children, young married with children, older married with children under 18, older married without children under 18, older single, other
Family Size	1, 2–3, 4–5, 6+
Income	Less than $15,000, $15,000–$24,999, $25,000–$50,000, $50,000–$100,000, $100,000–$200,000, more than $200,000
Nationality	African, American, Asian, British, Eastern European, French, German, Irish, Italian, Latin American, Middle Eastern, Scandinavian
Race	American Indian, Asian, African American, Caucasian
Religion	Buddhist, Catholic, Hindu, Jewish, Muslim, Protestant
Gender	Male, Female

Demographic Segmentation

Demographic Segmentation *a segmentation strategy that uses demographic characteristics to identify different market segments*

Demographic Variables *characteristics of populations that may be considered in developing a segmentation strategy*

Demographic segmentation is a strategy used to separate consumers by demographic variables. **Demographic variables** describe populations by identifying traits, such as age, income, gender, ethnic background, marital status, race, religion, and social class, as detailed in Table 11.1. Depending on the marketer's purpose, a demographic segment can be a single classification (for example, ages 20–34) or a combination of categories (ages 20–34, married without children, earning $25,000–$44,999 a year).

For example, Hot Topic started as a California-based chain specializing in clothes, accessories, and jewelry designed to appeal to Generation Y and Millennials, a demographic consisting of U.S. consumers born between the 1980s and 1990s. The theme was pop culture music because it was the biggest influence on the target demographic group's fashion tastes. More recently, Hot Topic has become a national retail chain for clothing, accessories, and entertainment products relating to today's pop culture.

Geo-Demographic Segmentation

Geo-Demographic Segmentation *using a combination of geographic and demographic traits for identifying different market segments in a segmentation strategy*

Geo-Demographic Variables *combination of geographic and demographic traits used in developing a segmentation strategy*

As the name implies, **geo-demographic segmentation** is a combination strategy. **Geo-demographic variables** are a combination of geographic and demographic traits and are becoming the most common segmentation tools. An example would be young urban professional women, well-educated, 25- to 54-year-olds with high-paying professional jobs living in the "downtown" zip codes of major cities. Chico's targets many women in this segment, offering stylish travel clothing well suited to the needs of this subset in the larger population. Segmentation is more effective because the greater number of variables defines the market more precisely.

Psychographic Segmentation

Psychographic Segmentation *a segmentation strategy that uses psychographic characteristics to identify different market segments*

Psychographic Variables *consumer characteristics, such as lifestyles, opinions, interests, and attitudes, that may be considered in developing a segmentation strategy*

Markets can also be separated into a **psychographic segmentation** according to such **psychographic variables** as lifestyles, interests, personalities, and attitudes. For example, Burberry, traditionally promoted as "The Iconic British Luxury Brand" whose raincoats have been a symbol of British tradition since 1856, has in recent years repositioned itself as a global luxury brand like Gucci and Louis Vuitton. The strategy calls for attracting a different type of customer—the top-of-the-line, fashion-conscious individual—who enjoys the prestige of shopping at stores like Neiman Marcus and Bergdorf Goodman. Psychographics are particularly important to marketers because, unlike demographics and geographics, they can be changed by marketing efforts. With the onset of global interdependence and open communications, marketing today is changing some traditional lifestyles and attitudes in nations around the globe. Polish companies, for example, have overcome consumer resistance by promoting the safety and desirability of using credit cards rather than depending on solely using cash.[7]

Behavioral Segmentation

Behavioral segmentation uses **behavioral variables** to market items based on how customers actually behave. These behaviors, in turn, may be caused by a variety of factors. One example is heavy users (customers who buy in bulk, the key to success for Sam's and Costco). Another is what might be called situation buyers (Halloween, for example, is now the second-largest "holiday" in terms of spending). A final example is specific purpose (All Free Clear is a detergent for people who have skin reactions to additives in other detergents).

Behavioral Segmentation a segmentation strategy that uses behavioral variables to identify different market segments

Behavioral Variables behavioral patterns displayed by groups of consumers and that are used in developing a segmentation strategy

Marketing Research

OBJECTIVE 11-4
Discuss
the purpose of marketing research and compare the four marketing research methods.

Unfortunately, no matter how logically or rationally marketing managers approach their work, their decisions and plans may still be less than perfect, but the consequences of their decisions and plans about marketing mix and segmentation strategy can be long lasting. In order to make the best decisions and develop the most effective plans possible marketers try to be customer focused and base their actions on timely information about marketplace trends. **Marketing research**, the study of what customers need and want and how best to meet those needs and wants, is a powerful tool for gaining decision-making information.

Marketing Research the study of what customers need and want and how best to meet those needs and wants

The relationship of research to the overall marketing process is shown in Figure 11.3. Ultimately, its role is to increase competitiveness by clarifying the interactions among a firm's stakeholders (including customers), marketing variables, environmental factors, and marketing decisions. Researchers use several methods to obtain, interpret, and apply information about customers. They determine the kinds of information needed for decisions on marketing strategy, goal setting, and target-market selection. In doing so, they may conduct studies about customer responses to proposed changes in the marketing mix. One researcher, for example, might study response to an experimental paint formula (new product). Another might explore the response to a price reduction (new price) on condominiums. Still a third might check responses to a proposed advertising campaign (new promotion). Marketers also try to learn whether customers will more likely purchase a product in a specialty shop or online (new place).

The importance of selling products in international markets has expanded the role of marketing research. For example, when a company decides to sell goods or services globally, it must decide whether to standardize products across all markets or to specialize by offering different versions for each market. Accordingly, market research's orientation has become increasingly globalized.

The Research Process

Market research can occur at almost any point in a product's life cycle. Typically, then, it's used in developing new products or altering existing products. When Marriott decided to launch its Fairfield Inn & Suites brand several years ago, it sent teams of managers to spend time in other economy hotels across the country to test everything from the thickness of towels to the firmness of mattresses to the size of the rooms. It also conducted numerous focus group interviews with economy-minded travelers to find out what was more and less important to them. After three years of research, the Fairfield brand was successfully launched.

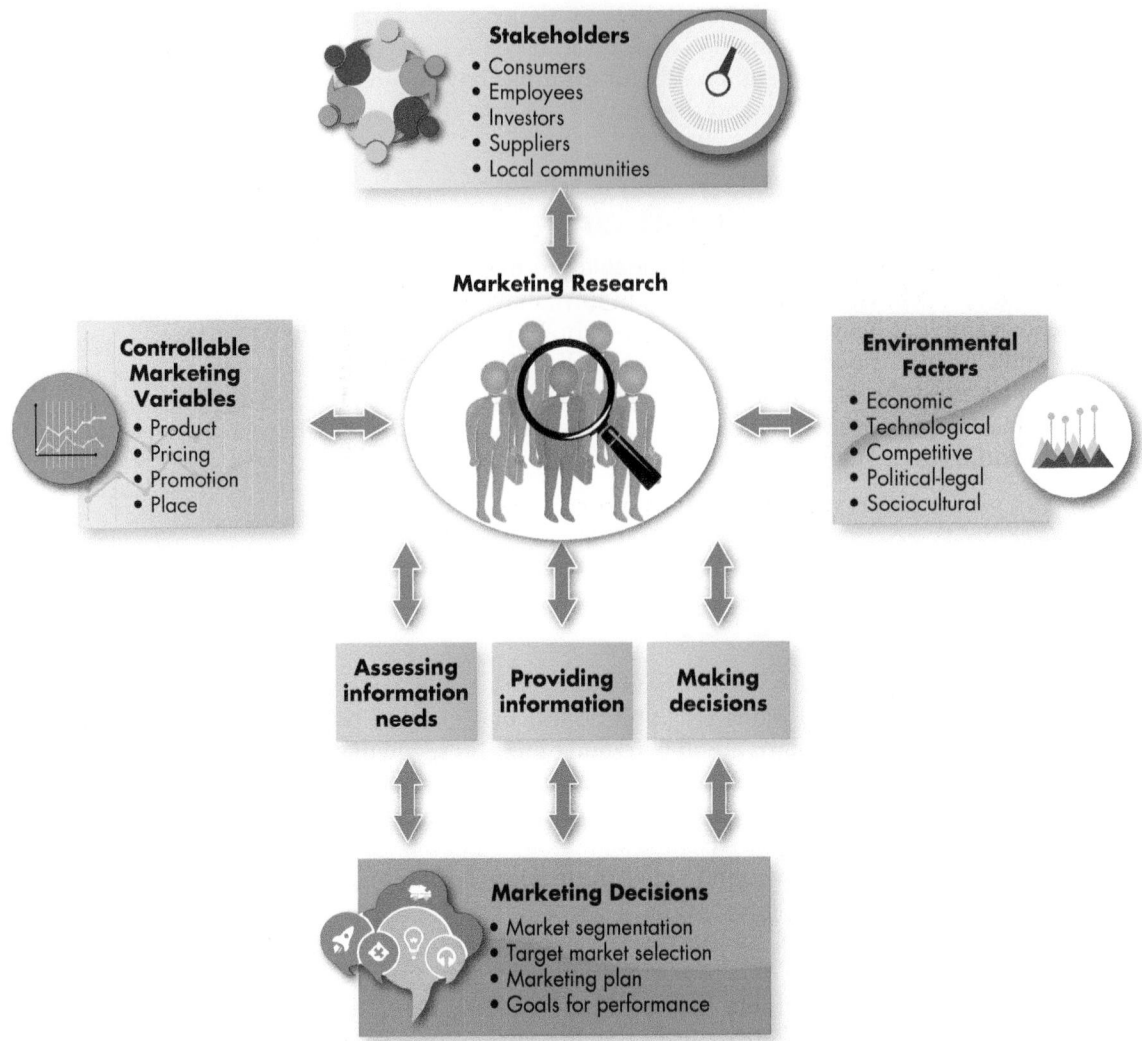

FIGURE 11-3 Market Research and the Marketing Process

Marketing research usually follows five basic steps. But even very effective companies can stumble if their research process is flawed. Consider the classic example of Coca-Cola that we will use to illustrate the five steps in the marketing research process.

1 *Study the current situation.* What is the need and what is being done to meet it? In the mid-1980s, marketing managers at Coca-Cola became alarmed by its declining market share. The company decided to undertake a now-famous (or infamous) marketing study to identify ways to reverse this decline.

2 *Select a research method.* In choosing from a wide range of methods, marketers must consider the effectiveness and costs of different options. Coca-Cola's preliminary information suggested that the taste of Coke was the main source of the problem. In particular, Coca-Cola was losing market share to Pepsi-Cola because customers found Pepsi to taste sweeter. Researchers decided to use taste tests for consumer opinions on a "New Coke" formula that was sweeter than original Coke.

3 *Collect data.* Most research data can be classified into one of two categories. **Secondary data** are already available from previous research. The *Statistical Abstract of the United States*, for instance, provides data collected by the government on geographic and demographic variables. Using secondary data can save time, effort, and money. However, when secondary sources are unavailable or inadequate, researchers must obtain **primary data**, new data from newly

Secondary Data *data that are already available from previous research*

Primary Data *new data that are collected from newly performed research*

Most companies undertake marketing research before launching new products. But even strong marketing research may prove to be inaccurate. For instance, when Google launched Google Glass in 2014 it anticipated huge demand. But slow sales caused the firm to stop distribution in early 2015.

performed research. In Coca-Cola's study, primary data were collected from some 200,000 consumer "tasters" who compared the New Coke versus the taste of the original Coke and Pepsi.

4 *Analyze the data.* Once data are collected they must be analyzed and organized into meaningful information. Analysis of data in the Coke research found that more than one-half of the consumer tasters rated New Coke to be tastier than original Coke and Pepsi.

5 *Prepare a report.* This report should describe the study's methodology and findings. It should also identify solutions and, where appropriate, make recommendations on a course of action. Coca-Cola's resulting recommendation—to replace original Coke with the New Coke—was implemented. As it turned out, the decision was a costly disaster that eventually resulted in restoring original Coke under a new name—Coca-Cola Classic—and then withdrawing New Coke from the market. As it turned out, research flaws had biased the results: (1) Test tasters were not told that if New Coke was launched, then original Coke would no longer be available, and (2) consumers' long-standing attachment to the original Coke brand would be lost when the product was withdrawn from the market.[8]

This Coca-Cola example was a costly learning experience, illustrating that even the most successful companies encounter occasional marketing mistakes. Although Coke's market research ultimately led them down the wrong path, many others, including Marriott Hotels and Resorts, Samsung Electronics, and Procter & Gamble personal care products, have conducted market research campaigns that led to increased market share and a better understanding of their markets.

Research Methods

The success of a research study often depends on the method a research team uses. Consider the following four basic methods of market research:

1 **Observation** involves watching and recording consumer behavior. Today, information technology systems, including live camera feeds and computer recordings, allow marketers to observe consumer preferences rapidly and with great accuracy. Electronic scanners and data files at brick-and-mortar stores, along with data storage of television viewing, phone transactions, and website activity, allow marketers to see each consumer's purchasing history—what products and brands that person prefers over a set period of time.

Observation *research method that obtains data by watching and recording consumer behavior*

finding a better way

The Truth about Your Online Customer Service

One of the basic tenets of marketing is, "find a need, fill a need," and so StellaService Inc. filled a market niche by providing a better way to measure online service, starting from the consumer's perspective with annual customer service ratings. For instance, in 2017, StellaService recognized the Vitamin Shoppe with an Elite Overall Award—a top honor reserved for the best-of-the-best performers across multiple service channels. The Elite Awards annually recognize retailers for best-in-class customer service across phone, e-mail, chat, shipping and returns.

Following its start-up in 2010, StellaService spent two years gathering data on customer satisfaction provided by thousands of online retailers, including such giants as Amazon.com and LLBean.com. Armed with results, co-founders Jordy Leiser and John Ernsberger were able to raise $22 million in venture capital to expand their ability to develop powerful analytics. StellaService measures satisfaction in four service areas— phone support, e-mail support, delivery, returns and refunds— for each retailer. Each area includes from 9 to as many as 25 different measurements. Phone support, for example, considers speed of answering the call and respondent's knowledge of the product among its nine measurements. Delivery measurements include delivery time and product accuracy. Results provide rankings of competitors, from top to bottom, showing where each retailer currently stands relative to competitors in each of the four areas of service. In the category of Sporting Goods, for example, StellaService's report might show phone support rankings among such firms as BassPro.com, Cabelas.com, and DicksSportingGoods.com, along with rankings on delivery, e-mail support, and returns and refunds.

With these measurements, StellaService enables retailers to objectively measure their customer service performance and

Dmitry Kalinovsky/123RF

monitor exactly how their efforts stack up against the competition on an ongoing basis. Knowing that success hinges on the validity and believability of their methods, StellaService uses an independent third-party rating system, and "secret shoppers" (trained employees) use strict and controlled measurement methods as they engage online retailers via e-mails, phone calls, and live chats to purchase, await deliveries, or make returns for refunds. As added assurance for validity, StellaService maintains a "Customer Service Measurement Process Audit" detailing its measurements and procedures for gathering and processing data, with specific steps to assure accuracy and validity, and the company has even gone so far as to hire KPMG, a Big Four auditing and CPA firm, to audit the company's methodologies. Now retailers can base their online marketing and service decisions on independent, objective information. In essence, StellaService is all about increasing the bottom line and helping consumers make better decisions at the same time.[9]

Survey *research method of collecting consumer data using questionnaires, telephone calls, and face-to-face interviews*

2 Sometimes, marketers must go a step further and ask questions. One way to get useful information is by using **surveys**, a method of collecting data in which the researcher interacts with people to gather facts, attitudes, or opinions, either by mailing or e-mailing questionnaires, by telephone calls, or by conducting face-to-face interviews. United Parcel Service (UPS) surveyed customers to find out how to improve service. Clients wanted more interaction with drivers because they can offer practical advice on shipping. As a result, UPS added extra drivers, providing them with more time with customers. Most surveys today are conducted online.

Focus Group *research method using a group of people from a larger population who are asked their attitudes, opinions, and beliefs about a product in an open discussion*

3 In a **focus group**, participants are gathered in one place, presented with an issue or situation, and then asked to discuss it. The researcher takes notes and makes video recordings but provides only a minimal amount of structure. This technique allows researchers to explore issues too complex for questionnaires and can produce creative solutions.

Experimentation *research method using a sample of potential consumers to obtain reactions to test versions of new products or variations of existing products*

4 **Experimentation** compares the responses of the same or similar people under different circumstances. For example, a firm trying to decide whether to include

walnuts in a new candy bar probably wouldn't learn much by asking people what they thought of the idea. However, the company could ask a random sample of people to try the new candy with walnuts and then provide their opinions and a different random sample to try the candy without walnuts and provide their opinions. If the two groups offer different opinions the company will have valuable information about whether or not to include walnuts in its new candy.

Understanding Consumer Behavior

OBJECTIVE 11-5
Describe
the consumer buying process
and the key factors that
influence that process.

Although marketing managers can tell us what features people generally want in a new refrigerator, even if they conduct "perfect" marketing research about refrigerators, they cannot always tell us why people buy particular refrigerators. What preferences are consumers fulfilling? Is there a psychological or sociological explanation for why they purchase one product and not another? These questions and many others are addressed in the study of **consumer behavior**, the decision process by which people buy and consume products.

Consumer Behavior *study of the decision process by which people buy and consume products*

Influences on Consumer Behavior

To understand consumer behavior, marketers draw heavily on such fields as psychology and sociology. The result is a focus on four major influences on consumer behavior: (1) *psychological*, (2) *personal*, (3) *social*, and (3) *cultural*. By identifying which influences are most active in certain circumstances, marketers try to explain consumer choices and predict future buying behavior.

Psychological influences include an individual's motivations, perceptions, ability to learn, and attitudes.

Personal influences include lifestyle, personality, and economic status.

Social influences include family, opinion leaders (people whose opinions are valued by others), and such reference groups as friends, coworkers, and professional associates.

Cultural influences include culture (the way of living that distinguishes one large group from another), subculture (smaller groups with shared values), and social class (the cultural ranking of groups according to such criteria as background, occupation, and income).

Although these factors can have a strong impact on a consumer's choices, their effect on actual purchases is sometimes weak or negligible. Some consumers, for example, exhibit high **brand loyalty**; they regularly purchase products, such as McDonald's foods, because they are satisfied with their performance. Such people, though, are less subject to influence and stick with preferred brands. On the other hand, the clothes you wear, the social network you choose, and the way you decorate your room often reflect social and psychological influences on your consumer behavior.

Psychological Influences *include an individual's motivations, perceptions, ability to learn, and attitudes that marketers use to study buying behavior*

Personal Influences *include lifestyle, personality, and economic status that marketers use to study buying behavior*

Social Influences *include family, opinion leaders (people whose opinions are sought by others), and such reference groups as friends, coworkers, and professional associates that marketers use to study buying behavior*

Cultural Influences *include culture, subculture, and social class influences that marketers use to study buying behavior*

Brand Loyalty *pattern of repeated consumer purchasing based on satisfaction with a product's performance*

The Consumer Buying Process

Students of consumer behavior have constructed various models to help show how consumers decide to buy products. Figure 11.4 presents one such model. At the core of this and similar models is an awareness of the many influences that lead to consumption. Ultimately, marketers use this information to develop marketing plans.

Problem or Need Recognition This process begins when the consumer recognizes a problem or need. Need recognition also occurs when you have a chance to change your buying habits. When you obtain your first job after graduation, for example, your new income may enable you to buy things that were once

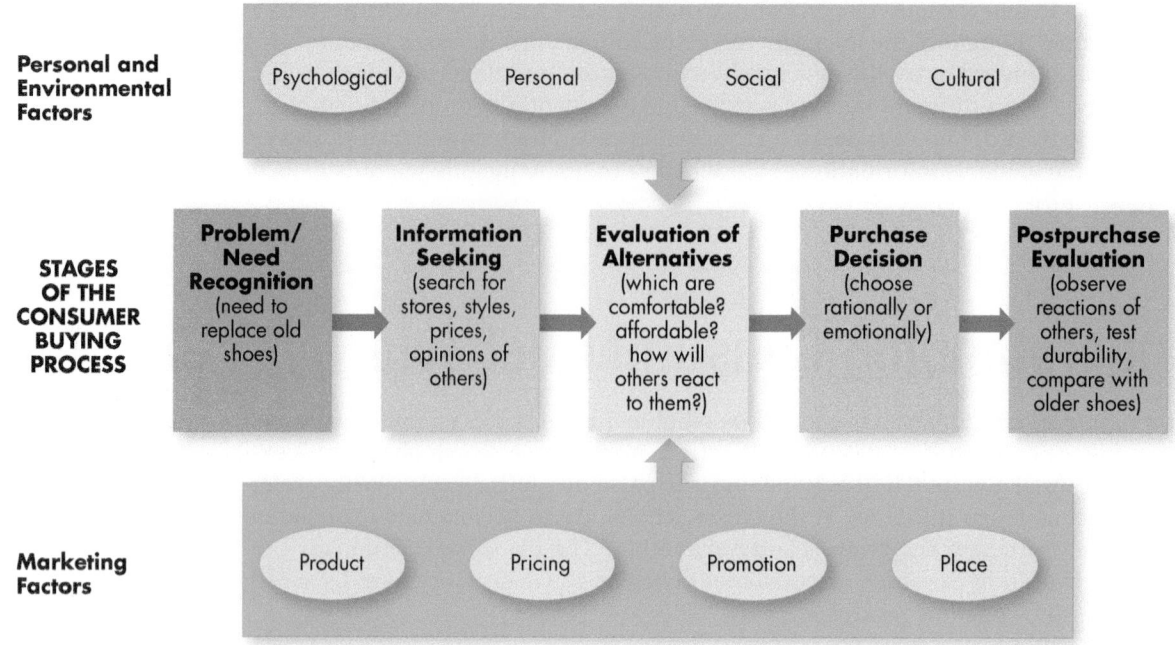

FIGURE 11-4 The Consumer Buying Process

too expensive for you. You may find that you need professional clothing, apartment furnishings, and a car. Bank of America and Citibank cater to such shifts in needs when they market credit cards to college students.

Information Seeking Having recognized a need, consumers then tend to seek information. The search is not always extensive, but before making major purchases, most people seek at least some information from personal sources, public sources, and experiences. Before joining a gym, you may read about your area gyms on yelp.com or you may visit a few gyms in your neighborhood. From this information search, consumers develop an **evoked set** (or **consideration set**), which is the group of products they will consider buying.

Evoked Set (or **consideration set**) *group of products consumers will consider buying as a result of information search*

Evaluation of Alternatives If someone is in the market for skis, they probably have some idea of who makes skis and how they differ. By analyzing product attributes (price, prestige, quality) of the consideration set, consumers compare products before deciding which one best meets their needs.

Purchase Decision Ultimately, in most cases consumers make purchase decisions. "Buy" decisions are based on rational motives, emotional motives, or a combination of the two. **Rational motives** involve the logical evaluation of product attributes: cost, quality, and usefulness. **Emotional motives** involve nonobjective factors and include sociability, imitation of others, and aesthetics. For example, you might buy the same brand of jeans as your friends to feel accepted in a certain group, not because your friends happen to have the "good sense" to prefer durable, reasonably priced jeans.

Rational Motives *reasons for purchasing a product that are based on a logical evaluation of product attributes*

Emotional Motives *reasons for purchasing a product that are based on nonobjective factors*

Postpurchase Evaluation Interestingly, marketing does not stop with the sale of a product; what happens after the sale is also important. Marketers want consumers to be happy after buying products so that they are more likely to buy them again. Because consumers do not want to go through a complex decision process for every purchase, they often repurchase products they have used and liked. Not all consumers are satisfied with their purchases, of course. These buyers are not likely to purchase the same product(s) again and are much more apt to broadcast their poor experiences than are satisfied customers. This is why some companies work so hard to correct problems reported by disgruntled customers.

Organizational Marketing and Buying Behavior

In the consumer market, buying and selling transactions are visible to the public. Equally important, though far less visible, are organizational (or commercial) markets. Marketing to organizations that buy goods and services used in creating and delivering consumer products or public services involves various kinds of markets and buying behaviors different from those in consumer markets.

Business Marketing

Business marketing involves organizational or commercial markets that fall into four B2B categories: (1) services companies, (2) industrial, (3) reseller, and (4) government and institutional markets. Taken together, the B2B markets do more than $25 trillion in business annually—more than double the amount of business conducted in the U.S. consumer market.[10]

Services Market The **services companies market** encompasses the many firms that provide services to the purchasing public. Imagine, for example, the materials and supplies Disney World needs to provide exceptional experiences for visitors. Similar needs exist to operate United Airlines, MTV, and the accounting firm PwC. Everything from veterinary clinics to hospitality services providers to healthcare centers and nursery schools buy materials needed to provide services to customers.

Services Companies Market *firms engaged in the business of providing services to the purchasing public*

Industrial Market The **industrial market** includes businesses that buy goods to be converted into other products or that are used up during production. It includes farmers, manufacturers, and some retailers. For example, piano manufacturer Steinway buys wood, wood stain, metal, and other materials from other companies to make grand pianos. The company also buys office supplies, tools, and factory equipment—items never seen by piano buyers—that are used at its production facilities in New York and Germany.

Industrial Market *organizational market consisting of firms that buy goods that are either converted into products or used during production*

Reseller Market Before products reach consumers, they pass through a **reseller market** consisting of intermediaries, including wholesalers and retailers, that buy and resell finished goods. For example, as a leading distributor of parts and accessories for the pleasure boat market, Coast Distribution System buys lights, steering wheels, and propellers and resells them to marinas and boat-repair shops.

Reseller Market *organizational market consisting of intermediaries that buy and resell finished goods*

Government and Institutional Market In addition to federal and state governments, there are over 89,000 local governments in the United States. In 2016, state and local governments spent over $3 trillion for durable goods, nondurables, services, and construction. The **institutional market** consists of nongovernmental organizations, such as hospitals, churches, museums, and charities, that also use supplies and equipment as well as legal, accounting, and transportation services.

Institutional Market *organizational market consisting of such nongovernmental buyers of goods and services as hospitals, churches, museums, and charitable organizations*

B2B Buying Behavior

In some respects, organizational buying behavior bears little resemblance to consumer buying practices. The primary differences include the buyers' purchasing skills and an emphasis on buyer–seller relationships.

Differences in Buyers Unlike most consumers, organizational buyers purchase in large quantities and are professional, specialized, and well informed. These characteristics of B2B buyers include the following:

- Industrial buyers usually *buy in bulk or large quantities.* Because of this fact, and with so much money at stake, buyers are often experts about the products they buy. On a regular basis, B2B buyers study competing products and alternative suppliers by attending trade shows, by networking with others electronically, by reading trade literature, and by holding technical discussions with sellers' representatives.

- As professionals, B2B buyers *are trained in methods for negotiating purchase terms.* Once buyer–seller agreements have been reached, they also sign formal legal contracts.

- As a rule, industrial buyers *are company specialists in a line of items and are often experts about the products they buy.* As one of several buyers for a large bakery, for example, you may specialize in food ingredients. Another buyer may specialize in baking equipment, while a third may buy office equipment and supplies.

Differences in the Buyer–Seller Relationship Consumer–seller relationships are often impersonal, short-lived, one-time interactions. In contrast, B2B situations often *involve frequent and long-term buyer–seller relationships.* The development of a long-term relationship provides each party with access to the technical strengths of the other as well as the security of knowing what future business activities to expect. Thus, a buyer and a supplier may, for instance, form a design team to create products to benefit both parties. Accordingly, industrial sellers emphasize personal selling by trained representatives who understand the needs of each customer.

Social Media and Marketing

Social Networking *network of communications that flow among people and organizations interacting through an online platform*

Social Networking Media *websites or access channels, such as Facebook, Twitter, LinkedIn, and YouTube, to which consumers go for information and discussions*

Viral Marketing *type of marketing that relies on the Internet to spread information like a "virus" from person to person about products and ideas*

Social networking as used by marketers today refers to communications that flow among people and organizations interacting through an online platform that facilitates building social relations among its users. From a marketing perspective, **social networking media** are the websites or access channels, such as Facebook, Twitter, LinkedIn, and YouTube, to which millions of consumers go for information and discussions before making their purchase decisions.

Viral Marketing and Social Networking **Viral marketing** is a form of marketing that relies on social networking and the Internet to spread information like a "virus" from person to person. The marketing purpose may be to increase brand awareness, to promote new product ideas, or to foster excitement for stimulating sales. Messages about new cars, sports events, movies, and many other goods and services flow via networks among potential customers who pass the information on to others. Using various social network formats—games, contests, chat rooms, blogs, and bulletin boards—marketers encourage potential customers to try out products and tell other people about them. For example, as Disney plans to launch new movies featuring characters from the *Star Wars* mythology and the Marvel universe, it often releases brief sample footage months—or even years—in advance. The hope is that viewers will like what they see and help build anticipation for the new movie well before it actually opens in theaters. Marketers, including such giants as Bank of America, McDonald's, eBay, and Cisco, use **corporate blogs** increasingly for public relations, branding, and otherwise spreading messages that stimulate chat about products in target markets.[11]

Corporate Blogs *comments and opinions published on the Web by or for an organization to promote its activities*

Web-Driven Revenue with Social Networking Although many major consumer companies have their own Facebook pages, small businesses also use social media channels to increase revenues by networking with customers in target markets. A2L Consulting, for example, offers services to law firms, such as jury consulting, pretrial services, courtroom technologies, and litigation graphics, among other litigation services. The company uses multiple social networks, including Google+, YouTube, Pinterest, LinkedIn, and Twitter, to increase Web-driven revenue. With over 15,000 website visits each month, A2L derives considerable revenue from Web traffic. Company representatives credited LinkedIn, from among the social-media networks used by A2L, as the most effective for connecting with this B2B target market. LinkedIn itself now has over 350 million users and adds two new members every second.

How effective can it be? Viral marketing and social networking can lead to consumer awareness faster and with wider reach than traditional media messages—and at a lower cost. It works for two reasons. First, people rely on online media for information that they used to get from newspapers, magazines, and television. Equally important, however, is the interactive element—people become participants in the process of spreading the word by forwarding information to and seeking information from other users.

The continuing growth of social media is changing marketing practices of businesses and consumer behavior, too. Facebook has become the Internet's most-used social media site, with about 1.66 billion active users each month and more than 950 million users each day. Although Facebook is the leader, Twitter is another fast-growing network, ranking number two in size with more than 310 million active users and handling about 525 million tweets each day. These numbers reflect not only the huge size of the social media industry, but also the enormous population of participants that influence and persuade one another to explore new ideas and products, thus becoming both consumers and sellers. The industry's growth is attributed especially to (1) increasing numbers of mobile device users, (2) more participants in the older-than-55 demographic that are using Twitter, and (3) greater global reach to more potential users. As companies gain experience, they are using social media in new ways. In addition to advertising promotions, Kellogg Company uses social media for consumer research and to get new product ideas. Procter & Gamble has learned that viral exposure on Facebook can generate more sales than TV advertising. eBay finds that its sellers and buyers use social media to guide other buyers and sellers to eBay's website. For students of marketing, the social media trend has two clear implications: (1) As consumers using social media, you will receive a growing number of tempting product exposures, and (2) as a user of social media who becomes familiar with its applications and technical operations, you will find a growing number of career opportunities in social media positions.

The International Marketing Mix

Marketing internationally means mounting a strategy to support global business operations. Foreign customers differ from domestic buyers in language, customs, business practices, and consumer behavior. If they go global, marketers must reconsider each element of the marketing mix: product, pricing, place, and promotion.

International Products Some products can be sold abroad with virtually no changes. Coca-Cola and Marlboro are the same in Peoria, Illinois, and Paris, France. In other cases, U.S. firms have had to create products with built-in flexibility, like an electric shaver that is adaptable to either 110- or 220-volt outlets, so travelers can use it in both U.S. and European electrical outlets. Frequently, however, domestic products require a major redesign for buyers in foreign markets. To sell computers in Japan, for example, Apple had to develop a Japanese-language operating system.

International Pricing When pricing for international markets, marketers must consider the higher costs of transporting and selling products abroad. For example, because of the higher costs of buildings, rent, equipment, and imported

Indranil Kishor/Majority World/Photoshot

Before creating an international ad like this Chinese advertisement for Coca-Cola, it is crucial to research what disparities, such as meaning of words, traditions, and taboos, exist between different societies. For example, German manufacturers of backpacks label them as "body bags," not terribly enticing to the U.S. consumer. Can you guess why Gerber baby food is not sold in France? The French translation of Gerber is "to vomit"! Effective marketing does not just involve knowledge of culture abroad, but also requires a general sensitivity to social trends and language.

meat, as well as differences in exchange rates, a McDonald's Big Mac that costs $5.30 in the United States has a price tag of $5.91 in Norway.

International Distribution In some industries, including consumer products and industrial equipment, delays in starting new international distribution networks can be costly, so companies with existing distribution systems often enjoy an advantage. Many companies have avoided time delays by buying existing businesses with already-established distribution and marketing networks. Procter & Gamble, for example, bought Revlon's Max Factor and Betrix cosmetics, both of which have distribution and marketing networks in foreign markets. Distribution methods used in the United States, though, don't always fit in international markets. For example, in Europe, Breathe Right nasal strips are identified as "medicinal" and must be sold in pharmacies.

International Promotion Occasionally, a good ad campaign is a good campaign just about anywhere. Quite often, however, U.S. promotional tactics do not succeed in other countries. Many Europeans believe that a product must be inherently shoddy if a company resorts to any advertising, particularly the U.S. hard-sell variety.

International marketers are ever more aware of cultural differences that can cause negative reactions to improperly advertised products. Some Europeans, for example, are offended by TV commercials that show weapons or violence. On the other hand, some European advertising is more provocative and sexually explicit than would be accepted in some countries. Meanwhile, cigarette commercials that are banned from U.S. television thrive in many Asian and some European markets. Managers must carefully match product promotions to local customs and cultural values to successfully promote sales and avoid offending customers.

Because of the need to adjust the marketing mix, success in international markets is hard won. But whether a firm markets in domestic or international markets, the basic principles of marketing still apply—only their implementation changes.

entrepreneurship and new ventures

Farming Your Niche

By all accounts, seven acres would be a very small farm. But, Rick Crofford, who is employed full-time as an environmental manager for the Virginia Department of Transportation, has a bustling farming operation on the seven acres of former corn-fields that surround his Virginia home. His first foray into farm-ing was blueberries—he has nearly 200 blueberry bushes that produce 10 to 15 pints of fruit each year. However, the blue-berries are labor intensive during harvesting and he's had to install fencing to keep out the deer. He's expanded his berry operation to include 250 strawberry plants and three kinds of raspberries. Crofford has stretched his operation into other crops, including fingerling potatoes. A plot less than an acre yielded 1,000 pounds of four varieties, which average about $2 per pound. Garlic, hot peppers, and broccoli are all grown on the farm with the help of his four children and occasional temporary help. He's funneled all the profits into a college sav-ings plan for his kids.

zigzagmtart/Fotolia

Not far away, Francis Ngoh grows mushrooms and other crops on his 39-acre farm. The West African native came to the United States to earn a degree in engineering at the University of Maryland. Although he held several corporate positions over the years, he has now focused his attention full-time on farm-ing. His main crop is shitake mushrooms, harvesting 3,000 to 4,000 pounds per year, but he also grows asparagus, leeks, garlic, peppers, and greens. Although not yet a certified or-ganic producer, Ngoh has embraced these standards and uses no chemicals. He's also catering to the local Muslim mar-ket with his livestock operation. He slaughters lambs on site according to Islamic tradition, with demand especially high on holy days.

Crofford and Ngoh have been supported in their efforts by finding the right distribution networks, as well as support from the Virginia Cooperative Extension Service. Crofford works ex-tensively with produce wholesaler The Fresh Link. Co-founder Mollie Visosky helps local producers understand the needs of high-end restaurants in the D.C. area, explaining, "We get together with the chefs in January to find out what produce they will want during the next growing season. Then we try to match our growers with crops that they can grow best and make a nice profit." On the other hand, Ngoh has been able to sell his mushrooms and other vegetables to Whole Foods stores as well as a number of other local buyers.

Both Crofford and Ngoh have worked with Jim Haskins from the Virginia Cooperative Extension Service, a program operated jointly by agents from Virginia State University and Virginia Tech. Haskins explains, "I try to identify small produc-ers in our area and give them the technical support to be more successful." This support was key to Mr. Crofford's decision to plant fingerling potatoes, which have a much higher yield than traditional Irish potatoes. Grant funding also helped both farm-ers, providing them with free plants and seeds to get started. In fact, these two have become so successful that Haskins uses them to promote niche farming in the Fauquier County area. And it's likely that this symbiotic relationship is one of the keys to success. Haskins explains, "One of our goals is to increase farm income for small producers. Not only do we need to sus-tain the farm, but we also need to sustain the farmer."[12]

Small Business and the Marketing Mix

OBJECTIVE 11-7
Discuss
the marketing mix as it applies to small business.

Many of today's largest firms were once small businesses. Behind the success of many small firms, in turn, lies a skillful application of the marketing concept and an understanding of each element in the marketing mix.

Small-Business Products

Some new products and firms are doomed at the start because few customers want or need what they have to offer. Many fail to estimate realistic market potential, and some offer new products before they have clear pictures of their target segments.

In contrast, a thorough understanding of what customers want has paid off for many small firms. Take, for example, the case of Little Earth Productions, Inc., a company that makes fashion accessories, such as handbags. Originally, the company merely considered how consumers would use its handbags. But after examining shopping habits, Little Earth Productions redesigned for better in-store display. Because stores can give handbags better visibility by hanging them instead of placing them on floors or low countertops, Little Earth Productions added small handles specifically for that purpose, resulting in increased sales. More recently, Little Earth has been concentrating on accessories for sports fans such as logoed purses, headbands, wallets, and hair accessories.

Small-Business Pricing

Haphazard pricing can sink a firm with a good product. Small-business pricing errors usually result from a failure to estimate operating expenses accurately. The founder of Nomie Baby, makers of spill-proof removable car seat covers for infants, started by setting prices too low. Considering only manufacturing and materials costs, other costs—shipping, storage, designing—were mistakenly ignored and not covered by the original selling price. Thereafter, when start-up prices were increased to cover all costs, sales (fortunately) remained strong. New business owners, afraid to set prices too high, often tend to underprice. Underpricing, in turn, then leads to financial crisis. Failing business owners have often been heard to say, "I didn't realize how much it costs to run the business!" Sometimes, however, firms discover their prices are too low, even when they cover all costs. A computer error at Headsets.com once caused cost-only prices rather than retail prices to be posted for the company's products on the Internet. The CEO was surprised that the erroneous low prices did not create a surge in sales. Instead, steady consumer response indicated that the firm's products were not as price-sensitive as believed, so the company raised original prices once, by 8 percent. Revenue rose as sales continued with little or no change from previous levels.[13] When small businesses set prices by carefully assessing costs and understanding their competitive market, many earn satisfactory profits.

Small-Business Distribution

The ability of many small businesses to attract and retain customers depends partly on the choice of location, especially for new service businesses.

In distribution, as in other aspects of the marketing mix, however, smaller companies may have advantages over larger competitors. A smaller company may be able to address customers' needs more quickly and efficiently with an added personal touch. Everex Systems, Inc. of Fremont, California, designs and sells computers to wholesalers and dealers through a system that the company calls *zero response time*. Because Everex Systems is small and flexible, phone orders can be reviewed every two hours and factory assembly adjusted to match demand.

Small-Business Promotion

Successful small businesses plan for promotional expenses as part of start-up costs. Some hold down costs by using less expensive promotional methods, like publicity in local newspapers and online messaging. Other small businesses identify themselves and their products with associated groups, organizations, and events. Thus, a crafts gallery might partner with a local art league to organize public showings of their combined products.

summary of learning objectives

Explain the concept of marketing and identify the five forces that constitute the external marketing environment. (pp. 346–351)

Marketing is responsible for creating, communicating, and delivering value and satisfaction to customers. With limited financial resources, customers buy products that offer the best value, measured by the relationship between benefits and costs. Marketers must understand customers' wants and needs because they determine product features and the timing, place, and terms of sale that provide utility and add value for customers. A product may be a tangible good, a service, or even an idea. Products may be classified as either consumer products or industrial products when they are marketed to businesses or nonprofit organizations. Although marketing often focuses on single transactions for products, services, or ideas, marketers also take a longer-term perspective by managing customer relationships to benefit the organization and its stakeholders. Customer *relationship marketing* emphasizes building lasting relationships with customers and suppliers. Stronger relationships, including stronger economic and social ties, can result in greater long-term satisfaction, customer loyalty, and customer retention.

Five outside factors make up a company's external environment and influence its marketing programs: (1) The *political and legal environment* includes laws and regulations that may define or constrain business activities, (2) the *sociocultural environment* involves peoples' values, beliefs, and ideas that affect marketing decisions, (3) the *technological environment* includes new technologies that affect existing and new products, (4) the *economic environment* consists of conditions such as inflation, recession, and interest rates that influence organizational and individual spending patterns, and (5) the *competitive environment* is that in which marketers must persuade buyers to purchase their products rather than their competitors'.

Explain the purpose of a marketing plan and identify its main components. (pp. 351–357)

A *marketing plan* is a statement of all the future marketing activities and resources that will be used to meet the desires and needs of customers so that the firm's overall business mission will be accomplished. It begins with objectives or goals setting the stage for everything that follows. *Marketing objectives*—the things marketing intends to accomplish—are the foundation that guides all of the detailed activities in the marketing plan. The marketing objectives focus on maintaining or enhancing the organization's future competitive position in its chosen markets. A marketing strategy can be developed once the marketing objectives have been clarified. *Marketing strategy* identifies the planned marketing programs, including all the marketing activities that will be used for achieving the marketing goals, when those activities will occur, and the contents of its programs. If planned activities are not affordable—requiring more resources than are available—then activities, programs, or goals are adjusted until realistic plans emerge.

Marketing strategy includes four basic components (often called the "Four Ps") of the *marketing mix*—product, pricing, place (distribution), and promotion—that marketing managers use to satisfy customers in target markets. The specific activities for each of the Four Ps are designed differently to best meet the needs of each target market. Marketing begins with a *product*, a good, service, or idea designed to fill a customer's need or want. Conceiving and developing new products is a constant challenge for marketers, who must always consider changing technology, consumer wants and needs, and economic conditions. Producers often promote particular features of products to distinguish them in the marketplace. *Product differentiation* is the creation of a feature or image that makes a product differ enough from existing products to attract consumers. The *pricing* of a product is often a balancing act. Prices must be high enough to support a variety of operating, administrative, research, and marketing costs, but low enough that consumers don't turn to competitors. In the marketing mix, *place* (or distribution) refers to where and how consumers get access to the products they buy. The most visible component of the marketing mix is *promotion*, a set of techniques for communicating information about products. The most important promotional tools include advertising, personal selling, sales promotions, publicity/public relations, and direct or interactive marketing.

OBJECTIVE 11-3

Explain market segmentation and how it is used in target marketing.
(pp. 357–359)

Marketers think in terms of *target markets*—particular groups of people or organizations on which a firm's marketing efforts are focused. Target marketing requires *market segmentation*—dividing a market into categories of customer types or "segments," such as age, geographic location, or level of income. Members of a market segment have similar wants and needs and share some common traits that influence purchasing decisions. Once they identify segments, companies adopt a variety of strategies for attracting customers in one or more of the chosen target segments. Five variables are often used for segmentation: (1) *Geographic variables* are the geographical units that may be considered in developing a segmentation strategy. (2) *Demographic variables* describe populations by identifying such traits as age, income, gender, ethnic background, and marital status. (3) *Geo-demographic variables* combine demographic variables with geographic variables, such as an age category coupled with urban areas. (4) *Psychographic variables* include lifestyles, interests, and attitudes. (5) *Behavioral variables* include categories of behavioral patterns such as online consumers or large-volume buyers. Marketers search for segments showing promise for generating new sales if marketing efforts by other companies have overlooked or misjudged the segment's market potential. Such competitive weaknesses present marketing opportunities for other companies to enter into those segments. Desirable segments with market potential then become candidate target markets and, once chosen, they become part of the marketing strategy where the companion marketing mix is developed.

OBJECTIVE 11-4

Discuss the purpose of marketing research and compare the four marketing research methods. (pp. 359–363)

Effective marketing decisions should be customer based and focused on timely information about trends in the marketplace. *Marketing research* is a tool for gaining such information; it is the study of what customers want and how best to meet those needs. Researchers use several methods to obtain, interpret, and apply information about customers. They determine the kinds of information needed for marketing strategy, goal setting, target-market selection, and developing new or altered products for specific market segments. Marketing research's orientation has become increasingly globalized because of the increasing importance of selling products internationally.

Research success depends on which of four basic research methods is used: (1) *Observation* means watching and recording consumer preferences and behavior. By using live camera feeds, computer tracking, and other electronic technologies, marketers observe and record consumer preferences rapidly and with great accuracy. (2) The heart of any *survey* is a questionnaire on which participants record responses. Surveys can get responses to specific questions quickly and at relatively lower cost. (3) In a *focus group*, people are gathered in one place, presented with an issue or topic, and asked to discuss it. The researcher takes notes, makes video recordings, and encourages open discussion by providing only a minimal amount of structure for the group's discussion. This technique allows researchers to explore issues too complex for questionnaires; it can produce creative ideas and solutions. (4) *Experimentation* compares the responses and behaviors of the same or similar people under different conditions that are of interest to the researcher. Experimentation can be relatively expensive because of costs of obtaining the experimental setting, securing participants, paying participants, and paying those who administer the experiment.

OBJECTIVE 11-5

Describe the consumer buying process and the key factors that influence that process. (pp. 363–365)

In the study of *consumer behavior*, marketers evaluate the decision process by which people buy and consume products. There are four major influences on consumer behavior: (1) *Psychological influences* include an individual's motivations, perceptions, ability to learn, and attitudes. (2) *Personal influences* include lifestyle, personality, and economic status. (3) *Social influences* include family, opinion leaders, and reference groups such as friends, coworkers, and professional associates. (4) *Cultural influences* include culture, subculture, and social class. At times, these influences have a significant impact on buying decisions, although consumers demonstrate high *brand loyalty* at times, regularly purchasing the same products.

Observers of consumer behavior have constructed various models to help marketers understand how consumers decide to purchase products. One model considers five influences that lead to consumption: (1) *Problem or need recognition*: The buying process begins when the consumer recognizes a problem or need. (2) *Information seeking*: Having recognized a need, consumers seek information. The information search leads to an evoked set (or consideration set)—a group of products they will consider buying. (3) *Evaluation of alternatives*: By analyzing product attributes (price, prestige, quality) of the consideration set, consumers compare products to decide which product best meets their needs. (4) *Purchase decision*: "Buy" decisions are based on rational motives, emotional motives, or both. *Rational motives* involve the logical evaluation of product attributes, such as cost, quality, and usefulness. *Emotional motives* involve nonobjective factors and include sociability, imitation of others, and aesthetics. (5) *Postpurchase evaluations*: Consumers continue to form opinions after their purchase. Marketers want consumers to be happy after the consumption of products so that they are more likely to buy them again.

OBJECTIVE 11-6

Discuss the four categories of organizational markets and the characteristics of B2B buying behavior. (pp. 365–369)

The various organizational markets exhibit different buying behaviors from those in consumer markets. Business marketing involves organizational or commercial markets that fall into four B2B categories. (1) The *services companies market* encompasses the many firms that provide services to the purchasing public. Every service company, from pet care to hospitality services to health care and nursery schools, airlines, and more, buys resources needed to provide services to customers. (2) The *industrial market* consists of businesses that buy goods to be converted into other products or that are used during production. It includes farmers, manufacturers, and some retailers. (3) Before some products reach consumers, they pass through a *reseller market* consisting of intermediaries—wholesalers and retailers—that buy finished goods and resell them. (4) The *government and institutional market* includes federal, state, and local governments and nongovernmental buyers—hospitals, churches, museums, and charities—that purchase goods and services needed for serving their clients. Taken together, these four organizational markets do more than two times the business annually as the U.S. consumer markets.

Unlike most consumers, organizational buyers purchase in large quantities and are professional, specialized, and well informed. As professionals, they are trained in methods for negotiating purchase terms. Once buyer–seller agreements have been reached, they also arrange formal contracts. In contrast with consumer–seller relationships that are often one-time interactions, B2B situations involve frequent and enduring buyer–seller relationships that provide each party, buyer and seller, with access to the technical strengths of the other. Thus, a buyer and a supplier may form a design team to create products to benefit both parties. Accordingly, industrial sellers emphasize personal selling by trained representatives who understand the needs of each customer.

OBJECTIVE 11-7

Discuss the marketing mix as it applies to small business. (pp. 369–370)

Each element in the marketing mix can determine success or failure for any *small business*. Many *products* are failures because consumers don't need what they have to offer. A realistic market potential requires getting a clearer picture of what target segments want. Small-business *pricing* errors usually result from a failure to estimate start-up costs and operating expenses accurately. In addition to facilities construction or rental costs, shipping, storage, wages, taxes, utilities, and materials costs also must be considered. By carefully assessing costs, and by learning what customers are willing to pay, prices can be set to earn satisfactory profits. Perhaps the most crucial aspect of *place*, or distribution, is location, especially for services businesses, because locational convenience determines the ability to attract customers. Although *promotion* can be expensive and is essential for small businesses, costs can be reduced by using less expensive promotional methods. Local newspaper articles, online messaging, and television programming cover business events, thus providing free public exposure.

key terms

advertising (p. 356)
behavioral segmentation (p. 359)
behavioral variables (p. 359)
brand competition (p. 351)
brand loyalty (p. 363)
competitive environment (p. 351)
consumer behavior (p. 363)
consumer goods (p. 348)
corporate blogs (p. 366)
cultural influences (p. 363)
customer relationship management
     (CRM) (p. 348)
data mining (p. 349)
data warehousing (p. 349)
demographic segmentation (p. 358)
demographic variables (p. 358)
economic environment (p. 351)
emotional motives (p. 364)
evoked set (or consideration set) (p. 364)
experimentation (p. 362)
focus group (p. 362)
form utility (p. 347)
geographic segmentation (p. 357)
geographic variables (p. 357)
geo-demographic segmentation (p. 358)

geo-demographic variables (p. 358)
industrial goods (p. 348)
industrial market (p. 365)
institutional market (p. 365)
integrated marketing strategy (p. 356)
international competition (p. 351)
market segmentation (p. 357)
marketing (p. 346)
marketing manager (p. 354)
marketing mix (p. 354)
marketing objectives (p. 353)
marketing plan (p. 352)
marketing research (p. 359)
marketing strategy (p. 353)
observation (p. 361)
personal influences (p. 363)
personal selling (p. 356)
place (distribution) (p. 355)
place utility (p. 347)
political-legal environment (p. 349)
possession utility (p. 347)
pricing (p. 355)
primary data (p. 360)
product (p. 354)
product differentiation (p. 354)

product positioning (p. 357)
promotion (p. 356)
psychographic segmentation (p. 358)
psychographic variables (p. 358)
psychological influences (p. 363)
public relations (p. 356)
rational motives (p. 364)
relationship marketing (p. 348)
reseller market (p. 365)
sales promotions (p. 356)
secondary data (p. 360)
services (p. 348)
services companies market (p. 365)
social influences (p. 363)
social networking (p. 366)
social networking media (p. 366)
sociocultural environment (p. 350)
substitute product (p. 351)
surveys (p. 362)
technological environment (p. 350)
time utility (p. 347)
target market (p. 357)
utility (p. 347)
value (p. 346)
viral marketing (p. 366)

MyLab Intro to Business

To complete the problems with the ✪, go to EOC Discussion Questions in the MyLab.

questions & exercises

QUESTIONS FOR REVIEW

11-1. What are the five forces in the external marketing environment?

✪**11-2.** What is the difference between value and utility?

✪**11-3.** What is market segmentation and how is it used in target marketing?

11-4. How does the buying behavior of consumers differ from buyers in organizational markets?

QUESTIONS FOR ANALYSIS

11-5. Select three everyday products (personal fitness training, CDs, dog food, cell phones, coffee, or shoes, for example). Show how these different products might be aimed toward different market segments. Explain how the marketing mix differs for each segment.

11-6. Use the five-step model of rational decision making to describe the process of selecting a college. Does this model reflect the way that you made a decision about attending college? Why, or why not?

✪**11-7.** Imagine being the marketing manager for a large U.S. hotel chain. What factors would you consider as you adapt the marketing mix to the following foreign markets: Mexico City, Dubai, Germany?

11-8. Choose an existing product that could benefit from viral marketing. Once you have identified the product, describe how you would use viral marketing to increase demand for the product.

APPLICATION EXERCISES

11-9. Identify a company with a product that interests you. Consider ways the company could use customer relationship management (CRM) to strengthen relationships with its target market. Specifically, explain your recommendations on how the company can use each of the four basic components of the marketing mix in its CRM efforts.

11-10. The U.S. Census collects an enormous amount of secondary data that is useful in marketing research. Go to the American Fact Finder home page at http://factfinder2.census.gov and collect data about people living in your zip code. Compare your zip code to your state as a whole in terms of factors such as age, race, household size, marital status, and educational attainment. Based on your data, what types of retail establishments would be especially appropriate to your area?

building a business: continuing team exercise

Assignment

Meet with your team members to consider your new business venture and how it relates to the marketing processes and consumer behavior topics in this chapter. Develop specific responses to the following:

11-11. Develop a "Statement of Marketing Objectives" for your company. Justify those marketing objectives by explaining how they contribute to the overall business mission of the company.

11-12. Identify the target market(s) for your business. Who are your customers? Describe the characteristics of customers in your target market(s).

11-13. Discuss how your team is going to identify the existing competitors in your chosen market. Based on the discussion, what are the key elements of your marketing plans that will give you a competitive edge over those competitors?

11-14. Consider, again, the customers in your target market(s). Are they individual consumers, organizations, or a mix of both consumers and organizations? Describe in detail the buying process(es) you expect them to use for purchasing your product(s). Discuss whether the customer buying process should or should not be a concern for your company.

11-15. Develop a preliminary design of the marketing mix for your target market(s). Retain the design for carryover and refinement in the following marketing chapters.

team exercise

HOME AWAY FROM HOME

Although he's been a farmer most of his life, Oliver Douglas is ready to retire and believes the best use of his property is to develop it. Green Hills College, a rapidly growing private college, is right next door. In fact, they share a property line. Many of their students live on campus in dorms, but their growing enrollment has pushed a large percentage of the students off campus. Oliver has made contacts in the county zoning office and has been assured that they are willing to rezone his property for student housing, given the importance of the college to the local economy. Oliver has done his research and has realized that he has several options. He can build dorm-style housing, apartments, townhouses, or even detached homes for students. He does know that he wants to keep the property and manage the housing himself, at least for his lifetime, rather than give the land to the college. He may leave the property to the college in his will, but he will decide that later.

Team Activity

11-16. As a group, describe the characteristics, wants, and needs of the target market.

11-17. In addition to students, who else will have an influence on housing decisions?

11-18. Assign one team member to each of the four housing options: dorm-style housing, apartments, townhouses, and detached homes. Have each group member identify the pros and cons of the type of housing they have been assigned.

11-19. Have each group member share the advantages and disadvantages of the option they have been assigned.

11-20. Considering all the options, which housing option do you think makes the most sense? Come to a group consensus and describe your reasoning.

11-21. Address each element of the marketing mix and describe how it will appeal to the target market.

exercising your ethics

WEIGHING THE ODDS

The Situation

Obesity has become an epidemic in the United States and much of the developed world, and people who are obese are at a significantly greater risk of stroke, heart attack, and diabetes.

Researchers have worked for years to develop a weight-loss product that is safe and effective. Several years ago, researchers identified a naturally occurring compound that was effective in appetite suppression. As the marketing manager for a major dietary supplement company, this was good news and so you convinced your company to invest several hundred thousand dollars in research and development. After several years of testing, the results show that 85 percent of people using the supplement were able to lose at least 20 pounds in the first year of use. In addition, those who continued to take the supplement were able to maintain their weight loss for an additional year. Company executives believe that this drug can bring billions of dollars in revenues in the first year of sales. Because your products are sold over the counter as nutritional supplements rather than as medications, they are not regulated by the Food and Drug Administration.

The Dilemma

You are reviewing the results of the clinical trials and are pleased to see that the product is effective. Just as you are ready to recommend that the company introduce the product to the market, you uncover some upsetting information. A small group of people who took the supplement during testing, actually less than 1 percent, developed a rare neurological disorder. It's not clear that the supplement is the cause of the disorder, but it was not observed in the control group that took a placebo. Because the risk is so small, the risk management team is recommending that the company

go ahead with introducing the supplement and monitor to see if consumers report a similar side effect. Commercialization of this product could make your company profitable and could potentially save thousands of lives by helping consumers lose weight, but you are unsure if this is the right thing to do.

QUESTIONS TO ADDRESS

11-22. How would you characterize the particular ethical issues in this situation?

11-23. From an ethical standpoint, what are the obligations of the marketing manager and the risk control manager regarding the introduction of the product in this situation?

11-24. If you were the marketing manager, how would you handle this situation?

cases

BUILDING A BRAND WITH SOCIAL MEDIA

Continued from page 346

At the beginning of this chapter, you read about Michelle Phan and how she expanded a blog into a beauty and lifestyle empire. Using the information presented in this chapter, you should now be able to answer the following questions.

QUESTIONS FOR DISCUSSION

11-25. What forces in the external environment have created opportunities or challenges for Michelle Phan? Explain.

11-26. How would you describe Michelle's marketing philosophy in terms of her value package, marketing mix, and overall approach?

11-27. Describe the consumer buying process for someone purchasing cosmetic products. Where would videos and a service like Ipsy fit into this process?

11-28. Go to Michelle's YouTube channel https://www.youtube.com/user/MichellePhan. How would you describe her target audience?

WHERE HAS ALL THE MIDDLE GONE?

There aren't many consumer products segments Procter & Gamble has dominated as thoroughly as shaving. With help from powerhouse brands, including Gillette, Mach3, and Fusion, P&G is the global leader for a product that millions of people use daily. In fact, it commands 65 percent of the blades and razors market. However, this core product line is under attack, both from value-focused rivals and from subscription services like Unilever's Dollar Shave Club. Recent competitive wins have whittled P&G's market share down from 70 percent just four years ago.

With its lineup of popular brands such as Folgers, Clairol, Charmin, and Gillette, it is estimated that 98 percent of U.S. households are using at least one P&G product, a position that has grown largely by targeting middle-class consumers. Its products are sold in more than 180 countries, but U.S. consumers provide more than 35 percent of P&G sales and nearly 60 percent of annual profits. However, the company is confronted with a marketing dilemma: annual revenues declined sharply in 2015 and 2106. In fact, fiscal 2016 marked P&G's lowest sales point since 2006.

One problem facing P&G is the shrinkage of middle-class purchasing power, a change that began with the 2008 recession and continues today. Many once-well-off middle-class families are pinched with rising prices for gasoline, food, education, and health care but little or no wage increases, despite the recovering economy. On top of changing economics, preferences also are changing among consumers. Generation Y and Z buyers have been raised on premium brands. Rather than getting their clothes at bargain retailers, younger adults spent their teenage years in clothes from Hollister and Abercrombie & Fitch. As adults, they show a preference for premium brands, even when their incomes are solidly middle class. Based on P&G's research, executives for P&G's North America business expect middle-class downsizing will be a continuing tend. Accordingly, P&G and other companies are rethinking their target markets. The company is now focusing on ten product categories, which include 65 brands, and has reduced its brand portfolio to focus on core categories and fewer brands in order to drive sales growth. In addition, they have increased market research on lower-income households, often using face-to-face interviews to gain in-depth understanding of these consumers. So far, the low-end and the high-end segments each are generally smaller than the former massive middle-class market, which means P&G is splitting its marketing efforts, rather than having just a single larger thrust. As one company official noted, historically they have been good at doing things on a larger scale, but now they are learning how to deal with smaller sales volumes for products in each of two segments. New product development is affected, too, because the high-end segment often involves fewer products with attractive extra features that will sell profitably at higher prices.[14]

QUESTIONS FOR DISCUSSION

11-29. How would you best describe P&G's marketing strategy for the situation presented in this case? Explain why.

11-30. What elements of P&G's external marketing environment, if any, are influencing the company's marketing strategy? Explain your reasoning.

11-31. Why do you suppose P&G's marketing research includes face-to-face interviews for the situation described in this case? Would other forms of marketing research also be useful in this situation? Explain your reasoning.

11-32. Explain the roles of target marketing and market segmentation as they apply in this case.

11-33. In what ways are the components of P&G's marketing mix being affected by the situation described in this case? Give examples to illustrate.

Writing Assignments

11-34. Think of a recent major purchase you have made. Describe the buying process from your viewpoint as a consumer. Now describe that process from the viewpoint of the marketing department. What were the strengths and weaknesses in their approach? What elements of their marketing plan can you glean from your experience as a consumer?

11-35. Compare and contrast business-to-business (B2B) marketing with business-to-consumer marketing. What are the benefits of B2B over retail marketing to consumers? What are the disadvantages and challenges?

endnotes

[1] Michelle Castillo, "YouTube's Leading Ladies," *Adweek* 55, no. 41 (2014), Business Source Premier, EBSCO*host*, accessed May 29, 2015; Glamour, "YouTube Makeup Guru Michelle Phan on Becoming a Beauty Superstar: 'My Only Goal Was to Help My Family,' " September 2013, http://www.glamour.com/lipstick/2013/09/michelle-phan-youtube-beauty-glamour-october-2013; Madeline Stone, "YouTube Superstar Michelle Phan Shares Her Tips for Building a Social Media Brand," *Business Insider*, November 2014, accessed May 29, 2015, http://www.businessinsider.com/social-media-tipsfrom-youtube-star-michelle-phan-2014-11.

[2] American Marketing Association, "Definition of Marketing," at https://www.ama.org/AboutAMA/Pages/Definition-of-Marketing.aspx, accessed on March 20, 2017. Reproduced with the permission of the American Marketing Association.

[3] Philip Kotler and Gary Armstrong, *Principles of Marketing*, 16th ed. (Upper Saddle River, NJ: Prentice Hall, 2016), 7.

[4] "CRM (customer relationship management)," TechTarget.com, at http://searchcrm.techtarget.com/definition/CRM, accessed on March 20, 2017; "Customer Relationship Management," *Wikipedia*, at http://en.wikipedia.org/wiki/Customer_relationship_management, accessed on March 21, 2017.

[5] Poonam Khanna, "Hotel Chain Gets Personal with Customers," *Computing Canada*, April 8, 2005, p. 18.

[6] "Fairmont Hotels & Resorts: Website Development and Enhanced CRM," *accenture*, at http://www.accenture.com/Global/Services/By_Industry/Travel/Client_Successes/FairmontCrm.htm, accessed on December 8, 2010.

[7] "Financial Cards in Poland," Euromonitor International (May 2008), at http://www.euromonitor.com/Consumer_Finance_in_Poland

[8] Scott Smith, "Coca-Cola Lost Millions Because of This Market Research Mistake," Qualtrics (Qualtrics Blog), January 21, 2013, at http://www.qualtrics.com/blog/coca-cola-market-research/

[9] "A World with Better Customer Service—Helping Consumers Find It, and Helping Businesses Achieve It," *StellaService*, at http://www.stellaservice.com/, accessed on March 25, 2013; Dana Mattioli, "Data Firm Attracts Funding," *Wall Street Journal*, February 28, 2013, p. B5; Don Davis, "StellaService Raises $15 Million and Starts Charging for its e-Retail Data," *Internet Retailer*, February 28, 2013, at http://www.internetretailer.com/2013/02/28/stellaservice-raises-15-million-and-starts-charging-data; "Say Goodbye to Fake Reviews," *Inc.* 36, no. 3: 108–110, *Business Source Premier*, EBSCO*host*, accessed May 18, 2017.

[10] "Lists and Structure of Governments," *United States Census Bureau, U.S. Department of Commerce*, at www.census.gov/govs/go, accessed on March 20, 2017.

[11] Judy Strauss, Adel El-Ansary, and Raymond Frost, *E-Marketing*, 5th ed. (Upper Saddle River, NJ: Prentice Hall, 2007); "Ten Corporate Blogs Worth Reading," February 19, 2009, at http://www.blogtrepreneuer.com/2009/02/19/ten-corporate-blogs-worth-reading/

[12] Lyne, David. "Small plots produce nice profits for niche farmers." *Fauquier Now* (Warrenton, VA), September 23, 2012. Accessed May 26, 2015. http://www.fauquiernow.com/index.php/fauquier_news/article/small-plots-produce-nice-profits-for-niche-farmers

[13] Eilene Zimmerman, "Real-Life Lessons in the Delicate Art of Setting Prices," *New York Times*, April 20, 2011, at http://www.nytimes.com/2011/04/21/business/smallbusiness/21sbiz.html?pagewanted=all&_r=0.

[14] Ellen Byron, "As Middle Class Shrinks, P&G Aims High and Low," *Wall Street Journal*, September 12, 2011, pp. A1, A16; Aimee Groth, "The Consumer Hourglass Theory: This Is Why P&G, Saks, and Heinz Are Ignoring the Middle Class," *Business Insider*, September 24, 2011, at http://www.businessinsider.com/hourglass-consumer-theory-pg-citigroup-2011-9.

chapter 12

Developing and Pricing Products

If you want to be number one, know what people

want and how much they want to pay.

Your company's

success may depend on it.

After reading this chapter, you should be able to:

12-1 **Explain** the definition of a product as a value package and classify goods and services.

12-2 **Describe** the new product development process.

12-3 **Describe** the stages of the product life cycle (PLC) and methods for extending a product's life.

12-4 **Identify** the various pricing objectives that govern pricing decisions and describe the price-setting tools used in making these decisions.

12-5 **Discuss** pricing strategies that can be used for different competitive situations and identify the pricing tactics that can be used for setting prices.

The Price of Free College

In early 2017, New York officially became the first U.S. state to cover the cost of public college tuition. The program is limited, at least in the beginning, to students attending State University of New York or City University of New York whose families earn no more than $100,000. The income limit will jump to $110,000 in fall 2018 and $125,000 in 2019. There are some additional requirements on students though. For instance, they have to take 30 credits per year and, upon graduation, have to live and work in New York for the same number of years they received the aid. Even so, Governor Andrew Cuomo's office estimated that about 940,000 families in the state will be eligible when the program is fully implemented. As good as this is in the short run for college students, the resulting price competition may have dramatic negative effects on enrollment in many of the state's private colleges and universities.

According to New York's Commission on Independent Colleges and Universities (CICU), the state is home to more than 100 private non-profit colleges and universities, enrolling about 300,000 students who are residents of New York. Many of these private institutions are small, with less than 2,000 students, so even a small drop in enrollment can have drastic effects on the budget. The CICU projects that public institutions will see an enrollment increase of between 9 and 22 percent, while enrollment in the state's private nonprofit colleges and universities will fall by between 7 and 15 percent.

Private colleges might have to take their evaluation of price beyond tuition discounting. Dr. Kenneth Macur, the president of Medaille College in Buffalo, is encouraging his institution to focus on value, rather than price, saying, "When you're already in a position to compete on value and not on price, then you're in a position to compete." But just like many small, private institutions, Medaille competes for students in part by heavily discounting their tuition, currently by about 50 percent for in-state freshmen, just above the national average tuition discount rate of 48.6 percent for first-time, full-time freshmen, as reported by the National Association of College and University Business Officers.

According to an article in *Inside Higher Education*, Wes Butterfield, vice president overseeing the financial aid services division of the consulting firm Ruffalo Noel Levitz, cautions schools against focusing too much on price. He posits that private colleges and universities need to take a look at their value package, to examine their mission, vision, and values in order to better position themselves in the market. "You have to look at what you do and make sure you are tightening up that aspect of your institution, first and foremost," he said. "Take a look at your programs and make sure you are providing students strong outcomes. That's the easiest and the hardest thing to do in

Auremar/Fotolia

what's in it for me?

Becoming a leading retailer in any market takes a solid understanding of how to develop an attractive product and how best to set prices to achieve profit and market share objectives. This chapter describes what constitutes a good product, identifies important classifications of products, and discusses the activities involved in developing new products. We will also see that any product's marketing success depends on setting prices that appeal to each target audience. By understanding this chapter's methods for pricing, you'll have a clearer picture of how to select pricing that is appropriate for meeting different business objectives, recognize and apply various price-setting tools, and revise pricing strategies and tactics as products move through their life cycles. You'll also be prepared to evaluate a company's product and pricing activities as they relate to its marketing programs and competitive potential.

You might not think about your college education as a "product" or your tuition as a "price" but, in many ways, that's exactly what they are. Just as you exchange money for a new backpack, smartphone, and place to live, so too do you exchange money for the opportunity to attend classes and earn a degree. Some backpacks cost only a few dollars while others cost a lot more, and some may only last a short time while others are designed to last for years. Similarly, degrees from some colleges cost more than degrees from other colleges, and some degrees may result in higher salaries than do other degrees. For their part, college decision makers have to make decisions about what degrees to offer, how much they need to charge for those degrees, and how many students they want to admit. And just like businesses they must market themselves so as to attract the best students. Because of the advent of free tuition for some students, colleges in New York will now have to rethink how they price and market themselves by following the basic rules for developing new products in any industry: Begin by identifying the changing demands of your target audience, develop new or revised products to meet those needs, and set prices to cover your costs. As you will see in this chapter, marketers can meet their goals only by making the right choices in both developing and pricing products.

As we saw in Chapter 11, managers are responsible for developing marketing plans and strategies for meeting customers' needs and wants. We also saw that marketing strategy focuses on the four components (the Four Ps) of the marketing mix: product, price, place, and promotion. Most managers understand, however, that in making strategic marketing decisions it is virtually impossible to focus on one element of the marketing mix (such as product design) without considering the other elements (such as product price) at the same time. In this chapter, we'll look at two of the Four Ps in more detail. We'll start by looking at *product* development and how a company decides what products it will offer to its customers. Next, we'll look at the concept of *pricing* and the price-setting tools used in making pricing decisions. In the next chapter we'll consider the remaining two elements in the marketing mix: *place* (distribution) and *promotion*.

OBJECTIVE 12-1
Explain
the definition of a product as a value package and classify goods and services.

Product Features *tangible and intangible qualities that a company builds into its products*

Value Package *a product is marketed as a bundle of value-adding attributes, including reasonable cost*

some respects, but it allows you to take some of that pressure off of the cost piece."[1]

Highly selective schools are less likely to feel the pinch. It will be the institutions relying on big discounts and financial aid for state students that are going to suffer the most. But it's not just the school that will notice the economic effects. Long-term, the free-tuition program could be millions of dollars of lost economic impact on the local communities as the smaller, private colleges downsize or fold completely. (After studying the content in this chapter, you should be able to answer a set of discussion questions found at the end of the chapter.)

What Is a Product?

In developing the marketing mix for any product, whether goods or services, marketers must consider what customers really want when they purchase products. Only then can these marketers plan strategies effectively. We begin this section where product strategy begins: by understanding that every product is a *value package* that provides benefits to satisfy the needs and wants of customers. Next, we describe the major *classifications of products*, both for consumers and organizations. Finally, we discuss one of the most important decisions faced by any business: its *product mix*.

The Value Package

Whether a product is a physical good, a service, or some combination of the two, customers get value from the various benefits, features, and rewards associated with that product. **Product features** are the qualities, tangible and intangible, that a company builds into its products, such as a 12-horsepower motor on a lawnmower (or the taste and health benefits of a nutrition bar, the styling of a shirt, or the low-price guarantees of a travel website). However, as we discussed previously, to attract buyers, features must also provide benefits; the lawnmower must also be easy to use and cut grass efficiently and effectively. The owner's "pleasure" in knowing that the mower is nearby and ready to use when needed is an intangible reward.

Today's customer regards a product as a bundle of attributes, benefits, and features, which, taken together, marketers call the **value package**. Increasingly, buyers expect to receive products with greater value—with more benefits and features at reasonable costs—so firms must compete on the basis of enhanced value packages. Consider, for example, the possible attributes in a laptop computer value package:

- Easy access to understandable prepurchase information

- Features such as wireless capability

- Attractive color and design

- Useful software packages

- Attractive prices

- Fast, simple online ordering

- Secure credit card purchasing

- Assurance of speedy delivery

- Warranties

- Easy access to technical support

Although the laptop includes physical *features*—processing devices and other hardware—many items in the value package are services or intangibles that, collectively, add value by providing *benefits* that increase the customer's satisfaction. Reliable data processing is certainly a benefit, but so, too, are speedy delivery and easy access to technical support. Today, more and more firms compete on the basis of enhanced value packages. Top-performing companies find that the addition of a simple new service often pleases customers far beyond the cost of providing it. Just making the purchase transaction faster and more convenient, for example, adds value by sparing customers long waits and cumbersome paperwork. Visitors to Walt Disney World can now receive so-called MagicBands before they travel to Florida. When properly configured, these arm bands serve as resort door keys, provide access to the theme parks, help schedule times to visit major attractions without long lines, and can be used for point-of-sale charging. Hence, they serve to increase the value package for visitors by making it easier to plan daily activities.

finding a better way

Snow Wars

"Our goal is to stay in business forever. To do that, we must remain profitable; solve climate change; treat our community well; and operate in a manner that doesn't harm our local environment." This is the commitment from Aspen Skiing Company, one of the most recognized winter sports destinations in the United States.

Aspen as more than just a ski resort dates back to its origin in the 1940s when Walter Paepcke and his wife Elizabeth began to buy land in Aspen with the idea of creating a skiing destination whose purpose would be the "renewal of the inner spirit." Despite its commitment to the environment and the community, however, management can't ignore the bottom line, as they note in the phrase, "we must remain profitable." In order to do that, Aspen has to compete on more than just price, especially in light of their biggest rival, nearby Vail.

Vail recently introduced a wildly successful Epic Pass, which grants unlimited access to its 14 resorts as well as to Arapahoe Basin in Colorado and 30 partner resorts in Europe. Even more recently the Vail Corporation bought Whistler Blackcomb in British Columbia, one of the largest ski resorts in North America. In response, Aspen Skiing Company bought up Mammoth, Steamboat, Winter Park, and Stratton. The two companies may be fierce competitors, but consumers benefit, especially in an industry that has high barriers to entry.

Environmental regulations now pose an enormous barrier to building new ski resorts in North America. The biggest ski areas are on U.S. Forest Service land, which makes them subject to strict regulations governing commercial development. It also takes a long time to build community support. Once you get to that point, it still takes decades and hundreds of millions of dollars to design the ski experience and build the resort. In fact, there hasn't been a new major ski resort opened in the United States since the early 1980s. From an economic

Chelseared/Shutterstock

perspective, these barriers to entry mean less competition, so resorts like Aspen and Vail can afford to raise ticket prices knowing that there's no chance of disruptive competition from a new entrant. Still, they have to compete against each other for a limited number of ticket sales. One way they do this is by staying in tune with what is important to their customers. For instance, Vail's newest member, Whistler Blackcomb, continues to be recognized for its proactive approach to climate change. The resort built a micro-hydro renewable energy project on Fitzsimmons Creek that produces enough electricity to power the entire resort.

Some locals hope that the futility of the price wars will force the resorts to focus less on how many passes they can sell and more on managing crowds and protecting the environment. But even as Vail tries to compete with Aspen's industry-leading environmental programs to lure conscious consumers across the fence, consumers look to see whose season pass will be cheaper, and it all comes back, in essence, to profit.

Classifying Goods and Services

Consumer *person who purchases products for personal use*

Industrial Buyer *a company or other organization that buys products for use in producing other products (goods or services)*

We can classify products according to expected buyers, who fall into two groups: (1) buyers of consumer products and (2) buyers of organizational products. As we saw earlier in Chapter 11, the **consumer** and **industrial buying** processes differ significantly. Similarly, marketing products to consumers is very different from marketing products to companies and other organizations.

Classifying Consumer Products Consumer products are commonly divided into three categories that differ in terms of typical buyer behavior. These categories are outlined in Table 12.1.

Convenience Goods *inexpensive physical goods that are consumed rapidly and regularly*

Convenience Services *inexpensive services that are consumed rapidly and regularly*

Shopping Goods *moderately expensive, infrequently purchased physical goods*

Shopping Services *moderately expensive, infrequently purchased services*

Specialty Goods *expensive, rarely purchased physical goods*

Specialty Services *expensive, rarely purchased services*

1 **Convenience goods** (such as milk and bottled water) and **convenience services** (such as those offered by fast-food restaurants) are consumed rapidly and regularly. They are inexpensive and are purchased often and with little exertion of time and effort.

2 **Shopping goods** (such as appliances and mobile devices) and **shopping services** (such as hotel or airline reservations) are more expensive and are purchased less often than convenience products. Consumers often compare brands, sometimes in different stores and via online searches. They may also evaluate alternatives in terms of style, performance, color, price, and other criteria.

3 **Specialty goods** (such as wedding gowns and tuxedoes) and **specialty services** (such as catering for wedding receptions or healthcare insurance) are extremely important and expensive purchases. Consumers usually decide precisely what they want and are not likely to accept substitutes. They often go from source to source, sometimes spending a great deal of money and time to get exactly what they want.

Classifying Organizational Products Depending on how much they cost and how they will be used, industrial products can also be divided into three categories. These are summarized in Table 12.2.

Production Items *goods or services that are used in the conversion (production) process to make other products*

- **Production items** are goods or services that are used directly in the conversion (production) process, such as petroleum that is converted into gasoline, and passenger demand information that is converted into bus or train services. Most consumer products, including food, clothing, housing, and entertainment services, are created from production items.

table 12.1 Categories of Consumer Products

Category	Description	Examples
Convenience goods and services	• Consumed rapidly and regularly • Inexpensive • Purchased often and with little input of time and effort	• Milk • Bottled water • Fast food
Shopping goods and services	• Purchased less often • More expensive • Consumers may shop around and compare products based on style, performance, color, price, and other criteria.	• Television • Tires • Hotel reservation
Specialty goods and services	• Purchased infrequently • Expensive • Consumer decides on a precise product and will not accept substitutions and spends a good deal of time choosing the "perfect" item.	• Luxury jewelry • Wedding dress • Healthcare insurance

table 12.2 Organizational Products

Category	Description	Examples
Production items	• Goods or services used directly in the production process	• Loads of tea processed into tea bags • Information processing for real-time production • Jet fuel used by airline services
Expense items	• Goods or services that are consumed within a year by firms producing other goods or supplying other services	• Oil and electricity for machines • Building maintenance • Legal services
Capital items	• Permanent (expensive and long-lasting) goods and services • Life expectancy of more than a year • Purchased infrequently so transactions often involve decisions by high-level managers	• Buildings (offices, factories) • Fixed equipment (water towers, baking ovens) • Accessory equipment (information systems, computers, airplanes) • Financial advisory services

- **Expense items** are goods and services that are consumed within a year by organizations producing other goods or supplying other services. The term *expense items* stems from the standard practice of accounting in which expenditures are classified as either (1) expense items or (2) capital items, depending on how quickly they are consumed. Thus, paper used in printers and building maintenance services are expense items if they are expected to be consumed within a year.

Expense Items *industrial products purchased and consumed within a year by firms producing other products*

- **Capital items** are longer-lasting (expensive and sometimes permanent) goods and services. They have expected lives of more than a year and typically last several years. Buildings (offices, factories), fixed equipment (water storage towers, baking ovens), and accessory equipment (information systems, computers, airplanes) are all capital goods. Capital services are those for which long-term commitments are made, such as long-term insurance services, architectural services, and financial advisory services. Because capital items are expensive and long-lasting, they often involve decisions by high-level managers.

Capital Items *expensive, long-lasting, infrequently purchased industrial products, such as a building, or industrial services, such as a long-term agreement for data warehousing services*

The Product Mix

The group of products that a company makes available for sale, whether consumer, industrial, or both, is its **product mix**. E*TRADE, for example, offers online financial investing and trading services, retirement planning, and educational resources. Black & Decker makes toasters, food blenders, electric drills, and a variety of other appliances and tools. 3M makes everything from Post-it Notes to optical systems and more than 1,000 tape products.

Product Mix *the group of products that a firm makes available for sale*

Many companies begin with a single product, such as simple brewed coffee. Over time, they find that the initial product fails to suit every customer shopping for the product type. To meet market demand, they begin to introduce similar products, such as flavored coffees and various coffee bean roasts, designed to reach more customers. For example, Starbucks stores expanded their line of coffees by adding different Italian-style espresso beverages that include mochas, cappuccinos, lattes, and flavored blended crèmes, followed by lighter roasts, different sizes, iced coffees, and so forth. A group of products that are closely related because they function in a similar manner (e.g., flavored coffees) or are sold to the same customer group (e.g., stop-in coffee drinkers) who will use them in similar ways is a **product line**.

Companies sometimes extend their horizons and identify opportunities outside existing product lines. The result, *multiple* (or *diversified*) *product lines*, is evident at ServiceMaster, which was among the first successful home services companies that offered mothproofing and carpet cleaning. The company then

Product Line *group of products that are closely related because they function in a similar manner or are sold to the same customer group who will use them in similar ways*

expanded its product line by adding other closely related services for homeowners: lawn care (TruGreen), pest control (Terminix), and cleaning (Merry Maids). After years of serving *residential customers*, ServiceMaster then added another product line of *business and industry services*, including landscaping and janitorial services, education services (management of support services for schools and institutions, including physical facilities and financial and personnel resources), and healthcare services (management of support services—plant operations, asset management, laundry/linen supply—for long-term care facilities). Multiple product lines increase the chances that a firm can grow rapidly and can help offset the consequences of declining revenues or increased competition in any one product line.

OBJECTIVE 12-2
Describe
the new product development process.

Developing New Products

To expand or diversify product lines—in fact, just to survive—firms must develop and introduce streams of new products. Faced with competition and shifting customer preferences, no firm can count on a single successful product to carry it forever. Even products that have been popular for decades need frequent renewal to keep up with changing technologies and shifting consumer tastes.

Consider one of the best-known brands in the United States, Levi's jeans. Its riveted denim styles were once market leaders, but the company failed to keep pace with changing tastes, fell behind new products from competitors, and lost market share among 14- to 19-year-old males during the 1990s. Approaching the year 2000, at least one industry analyst felt forced to report that Levi's "hasn't had a successful new product in years." Things changed in 2003, on the 130th anniversary of the company's invention of jeans, when Levi's introduced the then-new Signature Brand of casual clothing to mass-channel shoppers, originally available in Walmart stores in the United States. The Signature Brand continues to have a popular following with convenient shopping access online at Google and the websites of Walmart, Kmart, and Meijer. More recently, Levi's expanded to accommodate different body types and styles with Men's 501 CT, which allows men to select a custom color, waist size, and inseam, and Curve ID for women, which has two sets of four options each for waist and seat customization.

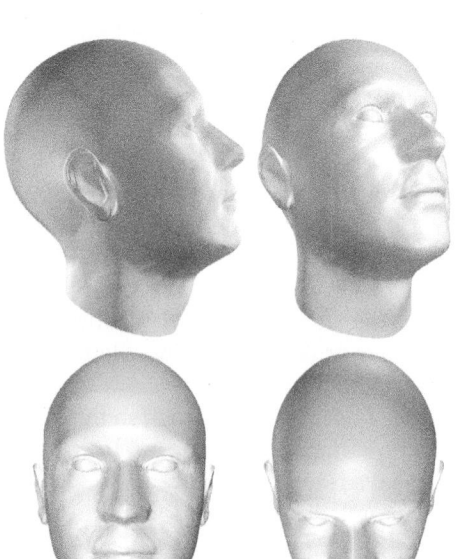

Designers used to create products, such as this head for a human-like toy, by sculpting models out of clay. Now they use "rapid prototyping," a technology that allows several employees to work simultaneously on 3D digital/visual "models" that can be e-mailed to clients for instant review. It now takes days, or just hours, instead of weeks to make an initial sculpture.

Fixer00/Shutterstock

entrepreneurship and new ventures

At a cocktail party in 2011, Michael Dubin met a gentleman who needed to unload a warehouse full of surplus razor blades. Dubin imagined he could mail blades to customers at a fraction of the price of what they were paying currently in the grocery stores, saving just a bit of time, effort, and money. So, on March 6, 2012, at 6 A.M. Pacific time, he published a video that announced Dollar Shave Club to the world. It opens on Dubin at a desk, pitching his razors in one of the most famous viral videos of all time. Although it cost only $4,500 to make, the company took 12,000 orders on that first day of streaming and it's been watched 24 million times since then.

When Dubin launched Dollar Shave Club, Gillette held a 72 percent market share, with Schick a distant second place. Dubin started by undercutting them on razors, but then went on to release a full range of men's grooming products over the years. As a result, he garnered a loyal following. His success paved the way for other small mail-order companies, such as Harry's and ShaveMOB, and by 2015, web sales for men's shaving gear had more than doubled industry-wide, to $263 million. In 2016, Dollar Shave Club had 51 percent of the razor market and Gillette's once-dominant market share had dropped to a meager 21.2 percent. Dollar Shave Club projected more than $250 million in revenue in 2017, up from $6 million just five years earlier.

Katarzyna Bialasiewicz/123RF

In 2017, both Gillette and Schick began to cut prices on all their men's care products in an effort to regain market share, but it may be too little, too late, as Dubin has added a ton of muscle to his company by selling it to Unilever for $1 billion. He's still in charge though, and despite the fact that his initial competitive edge was built on low price, his core philosophy is still one of creating a great customer experience.

The New Product Development Process

For many years, the growing demand for improved health care has stimulated the development of new dietary supplements, heart medicines, and other pharmaceuticals, along with new equipment for diagnosing ailments, surgical procedures, and monitoring patient recovery. However, companies that develop and sell these products face a big challenge. Developing new products can cost well over $100 million, sometimes even more than $1 billion, and can take as long as 8 to 10 years, sometimes longer, to get a new product through the approval process at the U.S. Food and Drug Administration (FDA).

Testing for first FDA approval and then for market acceptance can be the most time-consuming stage of development. For example, for years Merck & Co. has been developing an experimental heart drug called anacetrapib to raise levels of good cholesterol, thereby reducing the risk of heart attack. Merck & Co. has spent years on laboratory research and a lengthy test study, using 1,600 patients, and the results of that study then have to withstand further analysis. If successful, Merck could cash in on the growth of the cholesterol-lowering drug market, with industry estimates of peak sales potential ranging from $3 billion to $10 billion per year. However, getting that far through development requires an immense amount of time, patience, money, and risk of failure.[2]

Product development is a long and expensive process, and like Merck & Co., many firms have research and development (R&D) departments for exploring new product possibilities. Why do they devote so many resources to exploring product possibilities, rejecting many seemingly good ideas along the way? First, high *mortality rates* for new ideas mean that only a few new products reach the market. Second, for many companies, *speed to market* with a product is as important as care in developing it.

Product Mortality Rates

Some experts suggest that it takes 50 new product ideas to generate one product that finally reaches the market. Even then, only a few of these survivors become successful products. Many seemingly great ideas have failed as products. Creating a successful new product has become increasingly difficult—even for the most experienced marketers. Why? The number of new products hitting the market each year has increased dramatically; in 2015 alone, there were 192,000 UFCs and 9,300 new brand launches. In most years, the U.S. consumer packaged goods industry alone launches between 20,000 and 40,000 products (foods, beverages, school supplies, and other nonfood products).[3] At any given time, however, the average North American supermarket carries a total of only about 44,000 different items. Clearly, then, new products have to battle to take shelf space away from existing products. Indeed, about 9 out of 10 new products fail each year because of lack of space or weak customer demand. Those with the best chances are innovative and deliver unique benefits. The single greatest factor in product failure is the lack of significant difference (i.e., the new product is very much like, or imitates, an existing product). Some prominent examples of this are Mr. Pibb (later, Pibb Xtra) versus Dr. Pepper, which although still on the market is a relatively minor competitor, and Burger King's Big King, their answer to the Big Mac.

The more rapidly a product moves from the laboratory to the marketplace, the more likely it is to survive. By introducing new products ahead of competitors, companies establish market leadership. They become entrenched in the market before being challenged by newer competitors. For example, sales of Apple's first iPad surged after its introduction in early 2010, and estimates are that more than 13 million units were sold by year end, for a 75 percent share of the world's tablet PC sales. While nearly every other company in the industry has tried to come out with competing products since 2011, iPad continues to be a global market leader. How important is **speed to market** (or *time compression*) to a firm's success in responding rapidly to customer demand or market changes? One study reports that a product that is only three months late to market (three months behind the leader) loses 12 percent of its lifetime profit potential. After a six-month delay, it will lose 33 percent.

Speed to Market *strategy of introducing new products to respond quickly to customer or market changes*

The Seven-Step Development Process

To increase their chances of developing a successful new product, many firms adopt some version of a seven-step process for developing physical goods. (We will discuss the process for services next.)

1 *Product ideas.* Product development begins with a search for ideas for new products. Ideas typically come from consumers, the sales force, R&D departments, suppliers, or engineering personnel. For the product development example discussed previously in this chapter, Merck & Co.'s research scientists were convinced by 2003 that a pill could be developed to prevent heart attacks.

2 *Screening.* This stage is designed to eliminate ideas that do not mesh with the firm's abilities or objectives. Representatives from marketing, engineering, operations, and finance provide input at this stage. Collaboration among Merck's scientific, marketing, and finance personnel concluded that the protein inhibitor called anacetrapib had reasonable prospects for commercial development.

3 *Concept testing.* Once ideas have been screened, companies use market research to get consumers' input about benefits and prices. Early test results for similar products by other companies indicated that Merck's product concept offered acceptable scientific chances for possible commercialization.

4 *Business analysis.* After gathering consumer opinions, marketers compare production costs and benefits to see whether the product meets minimum profitability goals. Merck's development team concluded that the product could become profitable, with a market potential of up to $10 billion, but revenues would be offset with projected high multiyear development costs.

5 *Prototype development.* Once the firm has determined the potential profitability of a product, engineering, R&D, or design groups produce a prototype. This can be extremely expensive, often requiring the use of three-dimensional computer models followed with expensive equipment to produce the first physical product. Initial development of Merck's anacetrapib required three to five years of laboratory-based chemical and biological science.

6 *Product testing and test marketing.* Applying lessons from the prototype, the company goes into limited production. It then tests the product to see if it meets performance requirements. If it does, it may be sold on a trial basis in limited areas to test consumer reaction. As of 2016, Merck had entered Phase III of continual testing that began in 2011, with some 20,000 patients, and it expects to complete testing by January 2018.

7 *Commercialization.* If test marketing proves positive, the company begins full-scale production and marketing. Because promotional and distribution channels must be established, this stage can be quite expensive. Gradual commercialization, with the firm providing the product to more and more areas over time, prevents undue strain on initial production capabilities. On the other hand, delays in commercialization give other firms the opportunity to bring out competing products. Merck's "go" or "no-go" for commercialization of anacetrapib depends on test results through 2017 and on the emergence of other new products that could upstage Merck's development efforts.

Variations in the Process for Services

The development of services involves many of the same stages. Basically, Steps 2, 3, 4, 6, and 7 are the same. There are, however, important differences in Steps 1 and 5:

1 *Service ideas.* The search for service ideas includes defining the *service value package*, identifying the tangible and intangible features that characterize the service, and stating service specifications. For example, a firm that wants to offer year-end cleaning services to office buildings might commit itself to the following specifications: The building interior will be cleaned with no interference in customer service by midnight, January 5, including carpets swept free of all dust and debris and washbowls and lavatory equipment polished.

Large hotels have detailed process designs for functions such as housekeeping. The designs specify when and how rooms will be cleaned, for example, and include quality indicators that can be used to assess the performance of each housekeeper or housekeeping team.

5   *Service process design.*   Instead of prototype development, services require a three-part *service process design*. (1) *Process selection* identifies each step in the service, including sequence and timing. *Example (partial) process identification:* Office cleanings will be performed December 26–January 5, beginning at 8 P.M. through 5 A.M. Steps: (i) furniture removal from office to hallway; (ii) dust, wash, and dry office walls and fixtures; (iii) power vacuum carpets; (iv) power wet-wash carpets; (v) blow-dry carpets; (vi) return furniture to office; and (vii) final removal of cleaning equipment from client facility begins on January 5, to be completed by midnight. (2) *Worker requirements* state employee behaviors, skills, capabilities, and interactions with customers during the service encounter. *Example (partial) requirements:* One supervisor and 22 workers on 9-hour shifts (1 hour rest break) for 11½ days. Crew supervisor (accessible 24/7) and two lead workers (during work hours) will interact with customer as needed. Workers will (i.) be prebriefed on furniture-moving requirements, carpet characteristics, and safety requirements; (ii.) be skilled in operation of any and all cleaning equipment; and (iii.) respond courteously in encounters with client, referring questions to supervisor or lead workers. (3) *Facility requirements* designate all the equipment that supports service delivery. *Example equipment requirements (partial):* (i.) eight power-dolly transports for moving furniture, (ii.) 50 heavy covers for protecting furniture, (iii.) 10 industrial Class II power wet-washers for carpets, (iv.) 12 industrial-power carpet vacuums, (v.) forty 5-gallon containers Get-it-All scrubbing/sanitizing cleanser, and (vi.) large-haul-capacity truck to transport materials, supplies, and equipment to and from client facility.

OBJECTIVE 12-3
Describe
the stages of the product life cycle (PLC) and methods for extending a product's life.

Product Life Cycle (PLC) *series of stages in a product's commercial life*

Product Life Cycle

When a product reaches the market, it begins the **product life cycle (PLC)**, a series of stages through which it passes during its commercial life. Depending on the product's ability to attract and keep customers, its PLC may be a matter of months, years, or decades. Strong, mature products (such as Clorox bleach and H&R Block tax preparation) have had long productive lives. Some, like Coca-Cola, just seem to go on and on, while others, like VCRs and portable cassette tape players, progress through all four stages fairly quickly, are replaced by products based on newer technologies, and then disappear.

Stages in the PLC

The life cycle for both goods and services is a natural process in which products are born, grow in stature, mature, and finally decline and (potentially) die. Look at the two graphics in Figure 12.1. In Figure 12.1(a), the four phases of the PLC are applied to several products with which you may be familiar:

Introduction. This stage begins when the product reaches the marketplace. Marketers focus on making potential customers aware of the product and its benefits. Extensive development, production, and sales costs generally offset any profits during this first stage.

Growth. If the new product attracts enough customers, sales start to climb rapidly. Marketers may lower price slightly and continue promotional efforts to increase sales. The product starts to earn profits as revenues surpass costs. During this phase other firms may also move rapidly to introduce their own versions of the successful new product.

Maturity. This is typically the longest stage in the PLC for many products, and may last years or even decades. Sales growth peaks, plateaus, and then may start to slowly decline. Although the product earns its highest profit level early in this stage, increased competition eventually forces price-cutting, increasing the costs of advertising and promotional expenditures, and lowering profits. Toward the end of the stage, sales start to fall.

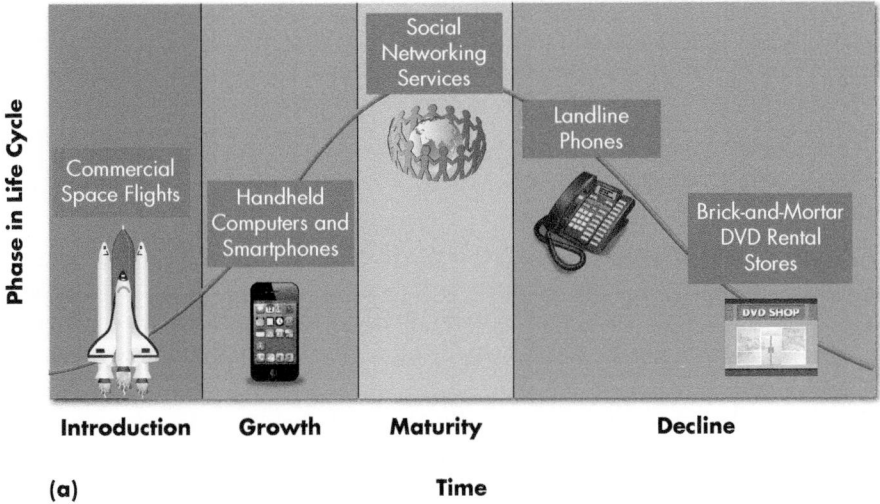

(a)

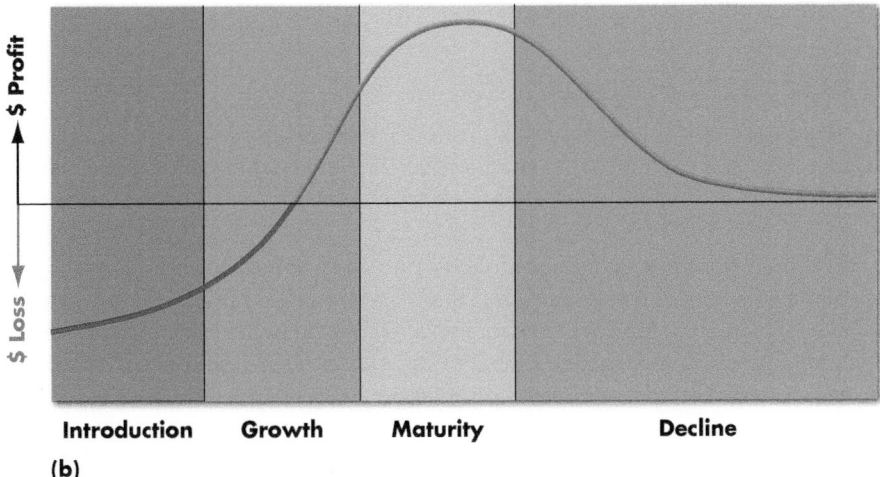

(b)

FIGURE 12.1 Products in the Life Cycle: (a) Phases and (b) Profit (or Loss)

Decline. Sales and profits continue to fall as new products in the introduction stage take away sales. Firms end or reduce promotional support (ads and salespeople), but may let the product linger to provide some profits.

Figure 12.1(b) plots the relationship of the PLC to a product's typical profits (in black) or losses (in red). Although the early stages of the PLC often show financial losses, increased sales for successful products recover previous losses and continue to generate profits until the decline stage. As a result of loss of profits and declining market share, for example, Kodak quit marketing traditional film cameras in the United States in 2004. In 2012, the company announced it would stop making its newer line of digital cameras, too, because of declining profits. For many products, profitable life spans are short. That's why some firms, such as 3M (producer of Post-it Notes and thousands of other products), rely on innovation for constant replenishment of product lines.

Extending Product Life: An Alternative to New Products

Companies try to keep products in the maturity stage as long as they can. At year-end 2012, after 80 years in publication, *Newsweek* magazine mailed its final print issue. At the same time, *Newsweek*'s life was extended by launching its new online-only version. Sales of televisions also have been revitalized through the years by such feature changes as color, portability, stereo capability, enlarged flat-screens, home theater features, streaming capabilities, and other new smart TV features. In fact, companies can extend product life through a number of creative means. Foreign markets, for example, offer three approaches to extending life cycles:

Product Extension *marketing an existing product globally instead of just domestically*

1 In **product extension**, an existing product is marketed globally instead of just domestically. Coca-Cola, Pizza Hut, and Levi's jeans are examples of many product extensions.

Product Adaptation *modifying an existing product for greater appeal in different countries*

2 With **product adaptation**, the product is modified for greater appeal in different countries. In Germany, a McDonald's meal includes beer, and Jeep puts the steering wheel on the right side for sales in South Africa and Japan. Because it involves product changes, this approach is usually more costly than product extension.

Reintroduction *reviving obsolete or older products for new markets*

3 **Reintroduction** means reviving, for new markets, products that are becoming obsolete in older ones. NCR (originally National Cash Register), for instance, reintroduced manually operated cash registers in Latin America. Boeing sells older models of its aircraft in third world countries. Kent & Curwen, a renowned English clothier founded in 1926, has only one store remaining in Britain but opened 95 stores in China. In addition to China, today the retailer has outlets in Japan, London, Tokyo, and Macau.[4]

Identifying Products

As we noted previously, developing a product's features is only part of a marketer's job. Marketers must also identify products so that consumers recognize them. Two important tools for this task are *branding* and *packaging*.

Branding Products Coca-Cola is one of the best-known brands in the world. Some Coke executives claim that if all the company's other assets were obliterated, they could go to lenders and borrow $100 billion on the strength of the brand name alone. Indeed, Interbrand, a global brand-ranking firm, says the Coke brand in 2016 was worth $73.1 billion in terms of revenue generation from its ability to create demand for the product.

Industry observers regard brands as a company's most valuable asset.[5] **Branding** is a process of using names and symbols, like Coca-Cola, the Mercedes tri-star logo,

Branding *process of using symbols to communicate the qualities of a product made by a particular producer*

Coca-Cola has one of the strongest and most recognized brands in the world. Its distinctive lettering is immediately recognized regardless of country or language. From Afghanistan to Zimbabwe, Coca-Cola is a brand that has universal recognition and enormous value.

Nike's "swoosh," Apple's apple silhouette with the bite missing, or McDonald's golden arches, to communicate the qualities of a particular product made by a particular producer. Brands are designed to signal uniform quality—customers who try and like a product can return to it by remembering its name or its logo.

Several benefits result from successful branding, including brand loyalty and **brand awareness**, the brand name that first comes to mind when you consider a particular product category. What company, for example, comes to mind when you need to ship a document a long way on short notice? For many people, UPS has the necessary brand awareness, while for others it may be FedEx.

Table 12.3 shows the 2016 rankings of the top global brands based on estimates of each brand's dollar value. It reflects the earnings boost that each brand delivers—an index of a brand's power to increase sales and earnings, both present and future—and shows how much those future earnings are worth today. Only global brands, those with sales of at least 20 percent outside the home country, are included.

Brand Awareness *extent to which a brand name comes to mind when a consumer considers a particular product category*

GAINING BRAND AWARENESS The expensive, sometimes fierce, struggle for brand recognition is perhaps nowhere more evident than in branding battles among online businesses. Collectively, the top four digital brands, Google (ranked 2nd), Amazon (8th), Facebook (15th), and eBay (32nd), spend billions a year on brand development. Moreover, the mounting costs of establishing a brand identity mean that many more would-be online businesses do and will probably fail.

With its growing importance in nearly every industry, marketers are finding more effective, less expensive ways to gain brand awareness. In addition to using viral marketing and social networking, recent successes have been found with *product placements*.

PRODUCT PLACEMENTS Although a commercial break during a television program usually means a trip to the kitchen, entertainment programming still gets our full attention. And that's when marketers are turning up the promotional juice with **product placement**, a promotional tactic for brand exposure in which characters in television, film, music, magazines, or video games use a real product with a brand visible to viewers.

Product Placement *promotional tactic for brand exposure in which characters in television, film, music, magazines, or video games use a real product with its brand visible to viewers*

Product placements are effective because the message is delivered in an attractive setting that holds the customer's interest. When used in successful films and TV shows, the brand's association with famous performers is an implied celebrity endorsement. The idea is to legitimize the brand in the minds of target customers. In all, more than $5 billion is spent annually on product placements, especially in television, and major companies often have dedicated marketers or hire external experts to assist in product placements. One of the first major success stories was the use of Reese's Pieces in Spielberg's blockbuster movie *E.T.* For years BMW used James Bond movies to introduce new models of exotic cars. In the recent Tom Hanks movie *Sully* characters made a point of staying in Marriott hotels. IKEA shows up in

table 12.3 World's 10 Most Valuable Brands (2016)

Rank	Brand	2016 Brand Value ($billions)
1	Apple	$178.1
2	Google	$133.3
3	Coca-Cola	$73.1
4	Microsoft	$72.8
5	Toyota	$53.6
6	IBM	$52.5
7	Samsung	$51.8
8	Amazon	$50.3
9	Mercedes-Benz	$43.5
10	General Electric	$43.1

Source: "Interbrand Releases 13th Annual Best Global Brands Report," *Interbrand*, at http://www.interbrand.com/en/best-global-brands/2016/downloads.aspx, accessed March 24, 2017.

Deadpool and Audi is used in *Captain America*. In print placements, Hewlett-Packard computers appear in the photo layouts in the IKEA catalog. Television placements are also widespread, including Hyundai in the films *Leverage* and *Burn Notice*, and Junior Mints played a star role when one was dropped into a surgical incision on *Seinfeld*. Characters in the recent HBO mini-series *Big Little Lies* drove Buicks.

Product placements are especially effective for TV because of the popularity of digital video recorders (DVRs). Viewers can use their DVRs to skip commercial breaks in recorded shows, but product placements within the programs are unavoidable.

Ideal product placements show the product in a positive or neutral (or passive) manner, but seldom if ever in a negative light. For instance, in a dramatic fictional story about a plane crash caused by poor maintenance or pilot error the airline will almost always also be fictional—no airline would pay to have its brand portrayed in this manner and most would sue if it were. Further, the product placement will usually be aimed at the same demographic as the target audience of the media where the product is shown. For instance, product placements in *Avengers: The Age of Ultron* included Beats earphones, Adidas sneakers, Under Armor workout gear, and Levis jeans.

Types of Brand Names Just about every product has a brand name. Generally, different types of brand names—*national*, *licensed*, or *private*—increase buyers' awareness of the nature and quality of competing products. When customers are satisfied with a product, marketers try to build brand loyalty among the largest possible segment of repeat buyers.

National Brands *National brands* are produced by, widely distributed by, and carry the name of the manufacturer. These brands (for example, DirecTV, Progressive Insurance, Scotch tape, and Scope mouthwash) are often widely recognized by customers because of consistent national advertising, and they are, therefore, valuable assets. Because the costs of developing a national brand are high, some companies use a national brand on several related products. Procter & Gamble markets Ivory Shampoo, capitalizing on the name of its bar soap and dishwashing liquid. Although cost efficient, doing this can sometimes dilute the original brand names's effectiveness. Coors Light Beer now outsells original Coors Beer.

National Brands *brand-name product produced by, widely distributed by, and carrying the name of a manufacturer*

Licensed Brands We have become used to companies (and even personalities) selling the rights to put their names on products. These are called **licensed brands**. For example, the popularity of auto racing generates millions of dollars in revenues for the NASCAR brand, which licenses its name on car accessories, apparel, headsets, and myriad other items with the names of popular drivers such as Martin, Johnson, Stewart, and Edwards. Harley-Davidson's famous logo, emblazoned on boots, eyewear, gloves, purses, lighters, and watches, brings the motorcycle maker more than $47 million annually. Along with brands such as Coors and Ferrari, licensing for character-based brands, such as Tinker Bell, Mickey Mouse, and other Disney characters, are equally lucrative. Marketers exploit brands because of their public appeal due to the image and status that customers hope to gain by being associated with them.

Licensed Brands *brand-name product for whose name the seller has purchased the right from an organization or individual*

Private Brands When a wholesaler or retailer develops a brand name and has a manufacturer put it on a product, the resulting name is a **private brand** (or **private label**). Macy's, for instance, sells many different products under private brand labels, including Hudson Park, Aqua, Maison Jules, Alfani, Charter Club, Club Room, Home Design, and Studio Silver. Many supermarkets also sell private brand versions of milk, bread, and other food staples.

Private Brand (or Private Label) *brand-name product that a wholesaler or retailer has commissioned from a manufacturer*

Packaging Products With a few exceptions, products need some form of **packaging** to reduce the risk of damage, breakage, or spoilage, and to increase the difficulty of stealing small products. A package also serves as an in-store advertisement that makes the product attractive, displays the brand name, and identifies features

Packaging *physical container in which a product is sold, advertised, or protected*

and benefits. Also, packaging features, such as no-drip bottles of Clorox bleach, add utility for consumers.

Determining Prices

OBJECTIVE 12-4
Identify
the various pricing objectives that govern pricing decisions, and describe the price-setting tools used in making these decisions.

The second major component of the marketing mix is **pricing**, determining what the customer pays and the seller receives in exchange for a product. Setting prices involves understanding how they contribute to achieving the firm's sales objectives. In order to learn more about how prices are determined, we will begin by discussing the objectives that influence a firm's pricing decisions. Then we describe the major tools that companies use to meet those objectives.

Pricing *process of determining what a company will receive in exchange for its products*

Pricing to Meet Business Objectives

Pricing objectives are the goals that sellers hope to achieve in pricing products for sale. Some companies have *profit-maximizing pricing objectives*, others have *market share pricing objectives*, and still others are concerned with pricing for *e-business objectives*. Pricing decisions are also influenced by the need to compete in the marketplace, by social and ethical concerns, and even by corporate image. In recent years we've also seen how prices of financial products, loans, and other borrowing are determined by the government's persuasion and its control of interest rates in times of economic crisis.

Pricing Objectives *the goals that sellers hope to achieve in pricing products for sale*

Profit-Maximizing Objectives The seller's pricing decision is critical for determining the firm's revenue, which is the result of the selling price times the number of units sold.

$$\text{Revenue} = \text{Selling price} \times \text{Units sold}$$

Companies that set prices to maximize profits want to set the selling price to sell the number of units that will generate the highest possible total profits. If a company sets prices too low, it will probably sell more units but may miss out on additional profits on each unit (and may even lose money on each exchange). If a company sets prices too high, it will make a large profit on each item but will sell fewer units. Again, the firm may lose money, and it may also be left with excess inventory because of fewer units sold.

In calculating projected profits, managers weigh sales revenues against costs for materials and labor, as well as capital resources (plant and equipment) and marketing costs (such as maintaining a large sales staff). To use these resources efficiently, many firms set prices to cover costs and achieve a targeted level of return for owners.

Market Share (Market Penetration) Objectives In the long run, a business must make a profit to survive. Because they are often willing to accept minimal profits, or even losses, in the short run to get buyers to try products, companies may initially set low prices for new products to establish **market share** (or **market penetration**), a company's percentage of the total industry sales for a specific product type. Even with established products, market share leadership may outweigh profit as a pricing objective. For brands such as Philadelphia Brand Cream Cheese and iTunes, dominating a market means that consumers are more likely to buy something with which they are familiar. Market domination means continuous sales of more units and higher profits, even at lower unit prices.

Market Share (or **Market Penetration**) *company's percentage of the total industry sales for a specific product type*

Pricing for E-Business Objectives When pricing for online sales, marketers must consider different kinds of costs and different forms of consumer awareness. Many e-businesses reduce both costs and prices because of the Internet's unique marketing capabilities. Because the Web provides a more direct link between producer and customer, buyers often avoid the added costs of wholesalers and retailers.

Another factor is the ease of comparison shopping—obviously, point-and-click shopping can be much more efficient than driving from store to store in search of the best price. Moreover, both consumers and business buyers can get lower prices by joining together online for greater purchasing power. Doctors and employees at Phoenix, Arizona's Arrowhead Health teamed with United Drugs Prescription Benefit Management to set up a new approach for buying generic and name brand drugs at lower costs, thus saving money in the employees' prescription discount program. Two new tools include (1) websites that search for lower-price drug alternatives and (2) a Web portal that serves as a gateway for listing nationwide average retail prices for drugs. The program enables employees and physicians to reduce prescription and benefits claims costs.[6]

Price-Setting Tools

Whatever a company's objectives, managers like to measure the potential impact before deciding on final prices. Two tools used for this purpose are *cost-oriented pricing* and *breakeven analysis*. Although each can be used alone, both are often used because they provide different kinds of information for determining prices that will allow the company to reach its objectives.

Cost-Oriented Pricing *pricing that considers the firm's desire to make a profit and its need to cover operating costs*

Cost-Oriented Pricing **Cost-oriented pricing** considers a firm's desire to make a profit and its need to cover operating costs.

$$\text{Selling price} = \text{Seller's costs} + \text{Profit}$$

A t-shirt store manager would price shirts by calculating the cost of making them available to shoppers. Thus, price would include the costs of store rent, employee wages, utilities, product displays, insurance, and the shirt manufacturer's price.

If the manufacturer's price is $8 per shirt and the store sells shirts for $8, the store won't make any profit. Nor will it make a profit if it sells shirts for $8.50 each, or even $10 or $11. To be profitable, the company must charge enough to cover both product and other costs. Together, these factors determine the **markup**, the amount added to an item's purchase cost to sell it at a profit. In this case, a reasonable markup of $7 more than the purchase cost means a $15 selling price. The following equation calculates the markup percentage and determines what percent of every dollar of revenue is gross profit:

Markup *amount added to an item's purchase cost to sell it at a profit*

$$\text{Markup percentage} = \frac{\text{Markup}}{\text{Sales price}} \times 100\%$$

For our shirt retailer, the markup percentage is 46.7:

$$\text{Markup percentage} = \frac{\$7}{\$15} \times 100\% = 46.7\%$$

Out of every $1.00 taken in, $0.467 will be gross profit. Out of gross profit, of course, the store must still pay rent, utilities, insurance, and all other costs.

For experienced price setters, an even simpler method uses a standard cost-of-goods percentage to determine the markup amount. Many retailers, for example, use 100 percent of cost-of-goods as the standard markup. If the manufacturer's price is $8 per shirt, the markup (100 percent) is also $8, so the selling price is $16.

Variable Cost *cost that changes with the quantity of a product produced and sold*

Fixed Cost *cost that is incurred regardless of the quantity of a product produced and sold*

Breakeven Analysis: Cost-Volume-Profit Relationships

Using cost-oriented pricing, a firm will cover **variable costs**, costs that change with the number of units of a product produced and sold, such as raw materials, sales commissions, and shipping. Firms also need to pay **fixed costs**, such as rent, insurance, and utilities, that must be paid *regardless of the number of units produced and sold*.

Costs, selling price, and the number of units sold determine how many units a company must sell before all costs, both variable and fixed, are covered, and it begins to make a profit. **Breakeven analysis** identifies the sales volume where total costs equal total revenues by assessing costs versus revenues for various sales volumes and showing, at any particular selling price, the amount of loss or profit for each volume of sales.

Breakeven Analysis *identifies the sales volume where total costs equal total revenues by assessing costs versus revenues at various sales volumes and showing, at any particular selling price, the amount of loss or profit for each volume of sales*

If you were the manager of a t-shirt store, how would you determine how many shirts you needed to sell to break even? We know that the *variable cost* of buying each shirt from the manufacturer is $8. This means that the store's annual variable costs depend on how many shirts are sold—the number of shirts sold times the $8 cost for each shirt. Say that *fixed costs* for keeping the store open for one year are $100,000 (no matter how many shirts are sold). At a selling price of $15 each, how many shirts must be sold *so that total revenues exactly cover both* fixed and variable costs? The answer is the breakeven point, which is 14,286 shirts:

$$\text{Breakeven point (in units)} = \frac{\text{Total Fixed Cost}}{\text{Price} - \text{Variable Cost}}$$

$$= \frac{\$100,000}{\$15 - \$8} = 14{,}286 \text{ shirts}$$

The breakeven analysis for this example is shown in Figure 12.2. If the store sells fewer than 14,286 shirts, it loses money for the year. If sales go higher than 14,286, profits grow by $7 for each additional shirt. If the store sells exactly 14,286 shirts, it will cover all its costs but earn zero profit.

Zero profitability at the breakeven point can also be seen by using the profit equation:

$$\text{Profit} = \frac{\text{Total}}{\text{Revene}} - \left(\begin{array}{ccc} \text{Total} & & \text{Total} \\ \text{Fixed} & + & \text{Variable} \\ \text{Cost} & & \text{Cost} \end{array} \right)$$

$$= (14{,}286 \text{ shirts} \times \$15) - (\$100{,}000 \text{ Fixed Cost}$$
$$+ [14{,}286 \text{ shirts} \times \$8 \text{ Variable Cost}])$$
$$\$0 = (\$214{,}290) - (\$100{,}000 + \$114{,}288)$$
$$(\text{rounded to the nearest whole shirt})$$

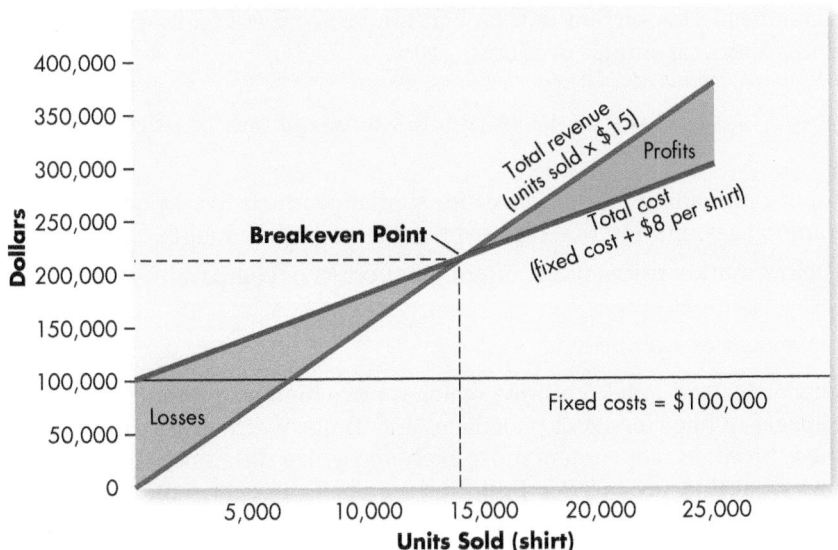

FIGURE 12.2 Breakeven Analysis

Amazon has become a low-price leader for most products. The firm operates a network of warehouses and distribution centers and can package and deliver most products cheaper and faster than its competitors.

<table>
<tr><td>

OBJECTIVE 12-5
Discuss

pricing strategies that can be used for different competitive situations and identify the pricing tactics that can be used for setting prices.

</td></tr>
</table>

Pricing Strategies and Tactics

The pricing tools discussed in the previous section help managers set prices on specific goods. They do not, however, help them decide on pricing philosophies for diverse competitive situations. In this section, we discuss pricing *strategy* (pricing as a planning activity) and some basic pricing *tactics* (ways in which managers implement a firm's pricing strategies).

Pricing Strategies

Pricing is an extremely important element in the marketing mix, as well as a flexible marketing tool; it is certainly easier to change prices than to change products or distribution channels. This section will look at how pricing strategies can result in widely differing prices for similar products.

Pricing Existing Products A firm has three options for pricing existing products:

1 Pricing above prevailing market prices for similar products to take advantage of the common assumption that higher price means higher quality

2 Pricing below market prices while offering a product of comparable quality to higher-priced competitors

3 Pricing at or near market prices

Godiva chocolates and Patek Philippe watches price high by promoting prestige and quality images, while Hershey's chocolates and Timex watches are priced much lower. For these products, consumers most likely recognize differences in the products and know what they are buying. Both Budget and Dollar car-rental companies promote themselves as low-priced alternatives to Hertz and Avis. Since all four companies rent the same kinds of cars, Hertz and Avis generally stress that their customers get greater convenience and better customer service. Pricing below prevailing market price works if a firm offers a product of acceptable quality while keeping costs below those of higher-priced competitors.

Pricing New Products When introducing new products, companies can often choose between higher prices or lower prices. **Price skimming**, setting an initial higher price to cover development and introduction costs and generate a large profit on each item sold, works only if marketers can convince customers that a new product is truly different from existing products and there is no foreseeable major competition on the horizon. Apple's introduction of the iPod is a good example. With no strong competitors entering the market for several years, Apple was able to maintain a high retail price with little discounting, even at Walmart. In contrast, **penetration pricing**, setting an initial low price to establish a new product in the market, seeks to create customer interest and stimulate trial purchases. Penetration strategy is the best strategy when introducing a product that has or expects to have competitors quickly. Gillette uses this strategy on nearly all of its new shaving systems to make sure they receive a high early adoption rate.

> **Price Skimming** *setting an initially high price to cover new product costs and generate a profit*

> **Penetration Pricing** *setting an initially low price to establish a new product in the market*

Start-up firms often use one-price, fixed pricing for launching new products. Carbonite started its online backup service with its strategy of "one-flat-low price," no matter how much space you needed to back up your PC files.[7] Although its pricing strategy changed as the company grew, to date the company has backed up more than 500 billion computer files. When new blockbuster movies are released, most movie theaters charge one price for all showings. After a few weeks, though, when the initial demand has subsided, they may start offering discounted tickets to showings at off-peak times.

Fixed versus Dynamic Pricing for Online Business The digital marketplace has introduced a highly variable pricing system as an alternative to conventional fixed pricing for both consumer and business-to-business (B2B) products. At present, fixed pricing is still the most common option for cybershoppers. Online giant Amazon has maintained this practice as its pricing strategy for its millions of retail items. In contrast, dynamic pricing, like eBay's auction bidding, uses flexibility between buyers and sellers to determine prices.

Another kind of dynamic pricing, the reverse auction, allows sellers to alter prices privately on an individual basis. At Priceline.com, for example, consumers set a price (below the published fixed price) they are willing to pay for airfare (or a rental car or a hotel room). Then an airline can complete the sale by accepting the bid price. For B2B purchases, MediaBids.com uses reverse advertising auctions to sell ad space. A company will notify MediaBids that it is going to spend $1,000 for advertising. Publications then use their ad space as currency to place bids for the advertising dollars. The company can then accept the bid that offers the most ad exposure in the best publication.[8] Budget-conscious companies seeking legal advice are increasingly turning to reverse auctions for lower-cost contracts with law firms as well. Competing law firms, bidding downward in online chat rooms, enter price bids to provide a client company's legal services. Law firms, however, are concerned with reports that about 40 percent of the legal market is being decided in reverse auctions, and the auctions are cutting as much as 15 to 40 percent from traditional legal fees.[9]

Bundling A **bundling strategy** groups several products together to be sold as a single unit, rather than individually. Suppose you have two insurance policies with different companies, one for life insurance and another for auto insurance. You may benefit from bundling—that is, buying both policies as a "package" from just one company. First, your total premium payments may be reduced. In addition, you gain the convenience of communicating with and making monthly payments to just one instead of two companies. The bundling company gains, too, with additional sales of two instead of just one product. CenturyLink, for example, offers a bundle of home phone, Internet, and DirectTV services that is priced below the combined individual prices for the three services.

> **Bundling Strategy** *grouping several products together to be sold as a single unit at a reduced price, rather than individually*

managing in turbulent times

Fair or Foul?

Even though it was its dynamic pricing model that paved the way for its initial success, in the midst of corporate scandal, management shakeups, and lawsuits and investigations by multiple litigants, Uber may be remembered in the future less for innovation and more for complication.

Uber was the brainchild of Travis Kalanick and Garrett Camp in 2008. Stuck in Paris with no cab in sight, in the style of classic entrepreneurs, they started brainstorming ideas to solve their problem. They came up with the idea of a mobile app that could call a nearby car in a short amount of time at a reasonable rate. In a classic model of the laws of supply and demand, Uber would match buyers (who need to get from point A to point B) with sellers (who have a car and are willing to transport buyers). Rather than the fixed-price models that are so common with taxis, Uber would use the market to attract buyers to underserved times and areas. Uber's video explains, "Prices go up to encourage more drivers to go online. The increase in price is proportionate to demand." Uber developed this pricing model after observing consumer demand and driver behavior in Boston in early 2012. Many drivers "clocked off" the system at 1 A.M., just as people were rolling out of bars and restaurants and looking for rides home. Rather than having people wait a long time for a ride because of a limited supply of drivers, Uber decided to reward drivers for staying on the clock after 1 A.M. by providing premium fares. Supply quickly matched demand, and Uber expanded its market and its business.

Soon the problem reversed itself. Where there were once too few cabs to serve customers, now there were too many. In 2015, three cab companies in California sued Uber for predatory pricing, stating that Uber is "pricing its service below cost in order to capture market share and harm competition in the state of California." Reportedly, even though gross bookings are in the billions of dollars, the company is losing money, relying on private investment to keep it afloat. In cities like San Francisco, licensed cab drivers pay anywhere from $125,000 to $250,000 for the official permit, called a medallion, that allows

McClatchy-Tribune/Tribune Content Agency LLC/Alamy Stock Photo

them to transport riders, which contributes to the higher cost of traditional cab fares. So, how does Uber get around the regulations that taxi drivers are bound by? Uber is a ride-sharing app, and the laws governing taxis haven't kept up with the changing technology.

But Uber suffers from internal problems as well as the external problems caused by changing the way people get around. In early 2017, Kalanick was recorded on video berating one of the Uber drivers. A month later, he fired the vice president of engineering, who had not disclosed he was under investigation for sexual harassment during his tenure at his previous employer, Google. A month after that, the company president, Jeff Jones, stepped down and made a series of publicly scathing commentaries on the company culture. In addition, the company is under fire for using a program called Greyball that helps drivers identify and avoid authorities.

Uber, Lyft, and other ride-share companies have created an entirely new product, increasing competition for a needed service, therefore lowering the overall market equilibrium price. However, as with any company, profitability and longevity aren't just a function of being the lowest cost provider. For long-term success, Uber may need to look deeper into its own culture so that it can grow into more than just a cheap ride.

Pricing Tactics

Price Lining *setting a limited number of prices for certain categories of products*

Regardless of its pricing strategy, a company may adopt one or more *pricing tactics*. Companies selling multiple items in a product category often use **price lining**, offering all items in certain categories at a limited number of prices. A department store, for example, might predetermine $175, $250, and $400 as the *price points* for men's suits, so all men's suits would be set at one of these three prices. This practice allows the store to have a suit for all of the different customer segments it hopes to attract. Grocery stores use this strategy as well; for example, in canned goods, they will carry a national brand, a store brand, and a generic brand.

Firms often use psychological pricing tactics to entice customers to buy their products. For instance, this candy store is promoting various products that are priced at one cent below the next dollar amount. The idea is that people may see a price of $4.99 to be meaningfully lower than a price of $5.

Psychological pricing takes advantage of the fact that customers are not completely rational when making buying decisions. One type, **odd-even pricing**, is based on the theory that customers prefer prices that are not stated in even dollar amounts. Thus, customers often regard prices of $1,000, $100, $50, and $10 as significantly higher than $999.95, $99.95, $49.95, and $9.95, respectively. Of course, the price set for a product is not always the price for which it sells. Sellers must often resort to price reductions, or discounts, to stimulate sales. Auto dealers, vacation resorts, airlines, and hotels offer **discount** prices to stimulate demand during off-peak seasons. Hyatt Hotels, like many others, offers commercial room discounts for frequent business users and for large-scale events such as conventions, trade shows, and special events. As you will see in this chapter's ending case, JCPenney created new problems when it stopped discounting in-store prices for retail customers.

Psychological Pricing *pricing tactic that takes advantage of the fact that consumers do not always respond rationally to stated prices*

Odd-Even Pricing *psychological pricing tactic based on the premise that customers prefer prices not stated in even dollar amounts*

Discount *price reduction offered as an incentive to purchase*

International Pricing

When Procter & Gamble (P&G) reviewed its prospects for marketing products in new overseas markets, it encountered an unsettling fact. Because it typically priced products to cover hefty R&D costs, profitably priced items were out of reach for too many global consumers. The solution was, in effect, to reverse the process. Now P&G conducts research to find out what foreign buyers can afford and then develops products that those markets can buy. P&G penetrates markets with lower-priced items and encourages customers to trade up as they become able to afford higher-quality products.

Another strategy calls for increasing foreign market share by pricing products below cost. As a result, a given product is priced lower in a foreign market than in its own country. As we saw in Chapter 4, this practice is called *dumping*, which is illegal in the United States. In 2013, the Coalition of Gulf Shrimp Industries petitioned the U.S. International Trade Commission (ITC) to impose special tariffs on seven countries—China, Ecuador, India, Indonesia, Malaysia, Thailand, and Vietnam—accused of using government subsidies enabling unfair price reductions, or dumping, against the U.S. shrimp industry. If found to be true, international law allows the United States to impose penalties called *countervailing duties* on shrimp coming from those countries as a remedy to balance prices.[10]

summary of learning objectives

Explain the definition of a product as a value package and classify goods and services. (pp. 382–386)

Customers buy products to receive value that satisfies a want or a need. Thus, a successful product is a *value package*, a bundle of attributes that, taken together, provides the right features and offers the right benefits that satisfy customers' wants and needs. *Features* are the qualities, tangible and intangible, that are included with the product. To be satisfying, features must provide *benefits* that allow customers to achieve the end results they want. The value package has services and features that add value by providing benefits that increase the customer's satisfaction.

Products (both goods and services) can be classified according to expected buyers as either *consumer products* or *organizational products*. *Convenience products* are inexpensive consumer goods and services that are consumed rapidly and regularly. *Shopping products* are more expensive and are purchased less often than convenience products. *Specialty products* are extremely important and expensive goods and services. *Organizational products* are classified as either *production items, expense items,* or *capital items*. Production items are goods and services used directly in the production process. *Expense items* are goods or services consumed within a year to produce other products. *Capital items* are expensive and long-lasting goods and services that have expected lives of several years.

The group of products that a company makes available for sale is referred to as its *product mix*. Although many companies start with a single product, they tend to expand into product lines, a group of products that are closely related in function or target market. Companies may develop multiple product lines to serve different types of customers or to meet the needs of existing customers in new ways. Multiple product lines allow a company to grow and can help offset the consequences of slow sales in any one product line.

Describe the new product development process. (pp. 386–390)

To expand and diversify product lines, new products must be developed and introduced. Many firms have research and development (R&D) departments and services development teams for exploring new product possibilities by adopting a basic seven-step process: (1) *Product ideas*: searching for ideas for new products. (2) *Screening*: eliminating all product ideas that do not mesh with the firm's abilities or objectives. (3) *Concept testing*: using market research to get consumers' input about product benefits and prices. (4) *Business analysis*: comparing production costs and benefits to see whether a product meets minimum profitability goals. (5) *Prototype development*: producing a preliminary version of a product. (6) *Product testing and test marketing*: going into limited production, testing the product to see if it meets performance requirements, and, if so, selling it on a limited basis. (7) *Commercialization*: beginning full-scale production and marketing.

For the development of services, there are two important differences in the seven-step model: (1) *Service ideas*: The search for service ideas includes defining the service value package, thus identifying the tangible and intangible features that characterize the service, and stating service specifications. (2) *Service process design:* Instead of prototype development, services require a service process design that identifies each step in the service. The design also identifies worker requirements—employee behaviors, skills, capabilities, and interactions with customers during the service encounter—and facility requirements.

Describe the stages of the product life cycle (PLC) and methods for extending a product's life. (pp. 390–395)

The product life cycle (PLC) for a good or a service product is a series of four stages or phases characterizing the product's profit-producing life. (1) *Introduction*: This stage begins when the product reaches the marketplace. Marketers focus on consumers aware of the product and its benefits. Extensive development, production, and sales costs erase all profits. (2) *Growth*: Sales begin to climb and the product begins to show a profit as marketers decrease prices slightly and continue promotional expenditures. Profits begin as revenues surpass costs. (3) *Maturity*: Typically the longest stage in the PLC, sales growth peaks and then starts to slow. The product's profits are highest early in this stage. As increased competition forces price-cutting, along with more advertising and promotional expenses, profits begin to diminish. (4) *Decline*: Sales and profits continue to fall as new products take away sales. Firms end or reduce promotional support (ads or salespeople are reduced), but modest support allows the product to linger with minimal profits. Eventually the product dies.

Three prominent methods are used for extending the lives of declining or even recently deceased products. (1) In *product extension*, an existing product is marketed globally instead of just domestically. A product that is in the maturity stage or even declining domestically may provide value to customers in other countries. (2) With *product adaptation*, the product is modified to contain changed features that appeal to new customers in different countries. (3) *Reintroduction* means reviving, for new markets, products that are becoming obsolete or have died in older ones.

Marketers must also identify products so that consumers recognize them. Branding is the process of using names and symbols to communicate the qualities of a particular product made by a particular producer. Branding can create brand awareness, in which buyers are aware of a brand, and brand loyalty, in which buyers demonstrate consistent buying behavior. Marketers can use product placement to increase brand awareness and brand loyalty. Product placement occurs when a brand is featured in television, film, magazines, or video games. There are three different kinds of brand names. *National brands* are produced by, widely distributed by, and carry the brand name of the manufacturer. When a company allows another company to use its brand name, that is a *licensed brand*. The final kind of brand name is a *private brand*, which is given to a product by the wholesaler or retailer rather than the manufacturer.

OBJECTIVE 12-4

Identify the various pricing objectives that govern pricing decisions, and describe the price-setting tools used in making these decisions. (pp. 395–398)

In pricing, managers decide what the company will get in exchange for its products. Pricing objectives refer to the goals that producers hope to attain as a result of pricing decisions. Two major pricing objectives are (1) *Pricing to maximize profits*: Set the price to sell the number of units that will generate the highest possible total profits. With prices set too low, the seller misses the chance to make additional profits on each of the many units sold. With prices set too high, a larger profit will be made on each unit, but fewer units will be sold. (2) *Market share objectives*: Pricing is used for establishing market share. The seller is willing to accept minimal profits, even losses, to get buyers to try products. He or she may use pricing to establish market share—a company's percentage of the total market sales for a specific product type.

Managers often prefer to measure the potential impact before deciding on final prices. For this purpose, two basic tools are used: (1) *Cost-oriented pricing* begins by determining total costs for making products available to buyers, including wages, rent, materials, and insurance. Added to those costs is a *markup* for profit to arrive at a selling price. (2) *Breakeven analysis* is used to calculate the **breakeven point**, the number of sales units that must be sold for total revenue to equal total costs (which results in neither a profit nor a loss). To calculate the breakeven point, the company must identify all fixed and variable costs associated with the product. The formula for the breakeven point is the total fixed costs divided by the difference between the sales price and the unit variable cost.

Breakeven Point *sales volume at which the seller's total revenue from sales equals total costs (variable and fixed) with neither profit nor loss*

OBJECTIVE 12-5

Discuss pricing strategies that can be used for different competitive situations and identify the pricing tactics that can be used for setting prices. (pp. 398–402)

Pricing for existing products can be set above, at, or below market prices for similar products. High pricing is often interpreted as meaning higher quality and prestige, and low pricing may attract greater sales volume by keeping costs below those of higher-priced competitors. Pricing strategies for new products include *price skimming*—setting an initially high price to cover costs and generate a profit—that may allow a firm to earn a large profit on each item sold; marketers must convince customers that a product is truly different from existing products. *Penetration pricing*—setting an initially low price to establish a new product in the market— seeks to generate customer interest and stimulate trial purchases. Strategies for e-businesses include dynamic versus fixed pricing. *Dynamic pricing* establishes individual prices by real-time interaction between the seller and each customer on the Internet. *Fixed pricing* is the traditional one-price-for-all arrangement.

Regardless of its pricing strategy, a company can then adopt any of three tactics for setting prices: (1) With *price lining*, any product category (such as lady's shoes) will be set at three or four price levels, and all shoes will be priced at one of those levels. (2) *Psychological pricing* acknowledges that customers are not completely rational when making buying decisions, as with *odd-even pricing* in which customers regard prices such as $10 as being significantly higher than $9.95. (3) *Discount pricing* uses price reductions to stimulate sales.

key terms

brand awareness (p. 393
branding (p. 392)
breakeven analysis (p. 397)
breakeven point (p. 404)
bundling strategy (p. 399)
capital items (p. 385)
consumer (p. 384)
convenience goods (p. 384)
convenience services (p. 384)
cost-oriented pricing (p. 396)
discount (p. 401)
expense items (p. 385)
fixed cost (p. 396)
industrial buyer (p. 384)
licensed brand (p. 394)

market share (or market penetration) (p. 395)
markup (p. 396)
national brand (p. 394)
odd-even pricing (p. 401)
packaging (p. 394)
penetration pricing (p. 399)
price lining (p. 400)
price skimming (p. 399)
pricing (p. 395)
pricing objectives (p. 395)
private brand (private label) (p. 394)
product adaptation (p. 392)
product extension (p. 392)
product features (p. 382)

product life cycle (PLC) (p. 390)
product line (p. 385)
product mix (p. 385)
product placement (p. 393)
production items (p. 384)
psychological pricing (p. 401)
reintroduction (p. 392)
shopping goods (p. 384)
shopping services (p. 384)
specialty goods (p. 384)
specialty services (p. 384)
speed to market (p. 388)
value package (p. 382)
variable cost (p. 396)

MyLab Intro to Business

To complete the problems with the ✪, go to EOC Discussion Questions in the MyLab.

questions & exercises

QUESTIONS FOR REVIEW

12-1. How does breakeven analysis help managers measure the potential impact of prices?

12-2. Discuss the goal of price skimming and penetration pricing.

12-3. What are the various classifications of consumer and industrial products? Give an example of a good and a service for each category other than those discussed in the text.

✪ **12-4.** How is the concept of the value package useful in marketing to consumers and industrial customers?

QUESTIONS FOR ANALYSIS

12-5. Describe the four stages of the product life cycle and the marketing mix that is used in each. Provide at least one example of a product in each stage other than those provided in the text.

12-6. Some companies have very narrow product mixes, producing just one or two products, while others have many different products. What are the advantages of each approach?

12-7. Suppose that a small publisher selling to book distributors has fixed operating costs of $600,000 each year and variable costs of $3.00 per book. How many books must the firm sell to break even if the selling price is $6.00?

12-8. Describe price skimming and penetration pricing. What types of new products would be best suited to price

skimming? What types of products will be most successful with penetration pricing?

APPLICATION EXERCISES

12-9. For this exercise, select a car or truck that interests you and identify the target market. Once you've identified the target market, describe the features of the vehicle that appeal specifically to the target market.

12-10. Select a product and analyze pricing objectives for it. What information would you want if you were to adopt a profit-maximizing objective or a market share objective?

building a business: continuing team exercise

Assignment

Meet with your team members to consider your new business venture and how it relates to the product and pricing topics in this chapter. Develop specific responses to the following:

12-11. Consider the customers in your target market(s). Are they individual consumers, or organizations, or a combination of both? For each of your target markets, identify what customers will expect in the product features and in the value-package features.

12-12. Identify your business's product mix, including its product line(s), if any. How do you justify this product mix rather than others you might have chosen?

12-13. Will your product(s) require new product development, modifications of existing products, or are they fully developed and ready to go? How quickly do you

anticipate your product(s) will be developed and ready for market? How long a life span do you expect for your product(s)?

12-14. Consider various pricing objectives and strategies to use when your product(s) first goes to market. Which pricing objective(s) seems most appropriate for your entry into the market(s)? Identify the pricing strategy(s) that seems best suited for your business. Explain.

12-15. Various pricing tactics, too, are available for planning your business. Describe the pricing tactics you expect to use on opening the business. Explain your choice(s). Might you resort to different pricing tactics as your product(s) moves through various stages in the life cycle(s)? Explain your reasoning.

team exercise

THE PRICE IS RIGHT

You are a member of a team of business students that have organized for the purpose of starting a small business selling mobile phone cases. You have recently established a business relationship with an Indonesian manufacturer that can provide durable and attractive cases at a low cost, and you have secured a kiosk at a local mall that you believe is an excellent location for selling the cases. However, you must decide on a pricing strategy for the phone cases. You have been provided with the following information:

- Your monthly expenses will be rent on the mall kiosk ($2,500) and hourly pay for your four employees. The kiosk will be open 300 hours per month and the hourly cost of an employee (including benefits) is $15/hour. In addition, you have hired a business manager who will handle ordering the inventory, maintaining the accounting records, and scheduling employees. The business manager's monthly salary is $6,000 per month.

- The Indonesian manufacturer of the phone cases has committed to delivering a variety of cases at a cost of $5 per case for the next year in return for a promise that you will order

only from this supplier. There are no other vendors selling these cases within 100 miles and they are expected to be popular.

Team Activity

12-16. Assemble a group of four students and assign each group member to one of the following pricing philosophies:

- Because the future is uncertain, the primary objective of this business venture is to maximize profits.

- There is a considerable amount of competition in the market, so the business wishes to price at a level that will give it a large share of the market.

- The business wishes to establish a premium image for its phone cases.

- The business believes that repeat business is the key to success so it wishes to use penetration pricing.

Have each group member describe the pricing strategy that he or she thinks the business should use for phone cases based on his or her assigned philosophy. Be sure to list the benefits of each approach.

12-17. As a group, develop a consensus about the best pricing philosophy and a rationale for why you have selected this approach.

12-18. Using the information provided in the case, identify the fixed and variable costs.

12-19. Using the amounts calculated in Step 2, calculate the breakeven point at a sales price of $15, $20, $25, and $30.

Based on these answers as well as your assessment about likely monthly sales, decide on the best price for the phone cases.

12-20. What other pricing tactics might you employ at the phone case kiosk to increase sales?

exercising your ethics

DRIVING A LEGITIMATE BARGAIN

The Situation

A firm's marketing methods are sometimes at odds with the consumer's buying process. This exercise illustrates how ethical issues can become entwined with personal selling activities, product pricing, and customer relations.

The Dilemma

In buying his first new car, Matt visited showrooms and websites for every make of SUV. After weeks of reading and test-driving, he settled on a brand-new, well-known Japanese-made vehicle with a manufacturer's suggested retail price of $37,500. The price included accessories and options that Matt considered essential. Because he planned to own the car for at least five years, he was willing to wait for just the right package rather than accept a lesser-equipped car already on the lot. Negotiations with Gary, the sales representative, continued for two weeks. Finally, a sales contract was signed for $33,500, with delivery due no more than two or three months later if the vehicle had to be special-ordered from the factory and earlier if Gary found the exact car when he searched other dealers around the country. On August 30, to secure the terms of the agreement, Matt wrote a check for $1,000 to the dealer.

Matt received a call on September 14 from Angela, Gary's sales manager: "We couldn't get the model you ordered," she reported, "because the new models just came out, but we've got your car, just as you ordered. We've discounted it by the same amount so it's $35,500 to you instead of the MSRP of $39,500." After some argument, he told Angela to send him back everything he had signed plus his $1,000 deposit, claiming that the deal was off.

QUESTIONS TO ADDRESS

12-21. How would you characterize the particular ethical issues in this situation?

12-22. From an ethical standpoint, what are the obligations of the sales representative and the sales manager regarding the pricing of the product in this situation?

12-23. If you were Angela, the sales manager, how would you defend your actions?

12-24. If you were responsible for maintaining good customer relations at the dealership, how would you handle this matter, considering the interests of both the consumer and the business?

cases

SINGING A DIFFERENT TUNE

Continued from page 382

At the beginning of this chapter, you read about the effects of heavy discounting in higher education. Using the information presented in this chapter, you should now be able to answer the following questions:

12-25. How would you describe the value package of your school?

12-26. What is the target market of your college? Do you think it is evolving or is it static?

12-27. If you were a private college administrator in New York or any other state where free tuition threatened your current enrollment, what kinds of responses and reactions could you formulate?

12-28. How do you think your college sets prices, including discounts?

12-29. Based on the answers to the previous questions, develop an overall response strategy for dealing with the issue of free tuition for public institutions.

CHANGING PRICING TACTICS CAN COST A PRETTY PENNEY

For years, iconic retailer JCPenney department stores attracted a loyal following of customers attracted to discounts and promotions, especially with coupons offering deep markdowns on advertised prices. The idea was to stir shoppers' emotions by using eye-catching discounts. Shoppers came to regard in-store specials as an incentive to buy now, feeling they were getting a "good deal." As recently as 2012, JCP ranked 23rd among the top 100 U.S. retailers, although sales fell by nearly 3 percent from the previous year, whereas most others in the top 100 experienced sales increases. Lower revenue, it turns out, was an early sign that the recent change in pricing—replacing coupons and other discounts with its new "everyday low pricing"—was perhaps costing JCPenney its once-loyal customer base.

The dramatic pricing change was headed by CEO Ron Johnson, who for the previous decade had successfully directed Apple's massive retailing operations. Apple's pricing, as contrasted with JCPenney's, more nearly resembles an orientation toward "truth in pricing," where heavy discounting doesn't exist and where, in general, "the price is the price." Johnson brought to JCPenney the notion that customers would appreciate more clarity and consistency in pricing by eliminating heavily discounted sales specials. JCPenney had 590 different sales events in 2011, with special discounts offered at 5 A.M. and on weekends and holidays, and on special clearance days each month. When he arrived at JCPenney, Johnson saw prices that were intentionally inflated or "fake"; management knew that the inflated prices were going to be deeply discounted, sometimes up to 60 percent off, creating the kinds of "specials" that customers had come to expect. So the decision was made to phase out promotional pricing and coupons early in 2012 and change to fixed prices set at 40 to 50 percent below JCPenney's original pre-discounted prices. Women's apparel that formerly was priced first at $60 and then discounted down to $35 was instead now priced firmly at $35 in the new "fair and square" pricing method. The same applied to menswear, children's, and virtually every product in the store.

Consumer reaction wasn't as expected. JCPenney revenues for 2012 were 25 percent below the year before. By early 2013, JCPenney had suffered $13 billion in revenue losses, along with a 50 percent loss in the firm's stock price since Johnson's arrival in 2011. Those attractive discounts that motivated long-time customers were gone, and so was the incentive to shop at JCPenney stores. When customers stopped receiving coupons, they also quit going to JCPenney. While the everyday low prices were clearly lower, consumers no longer had the opportunity for perceived savings when using coupons and other promotions.

Once the financial collapse became unavoidable, CEO Johnson reversed direction early in 2013. In an attempt to rekindle relationships with longtime customers, JCPenney began restoring coupons and the traditional higher prices that could once again be heavily discounted, but the reversal was too little and too late. After just one year of implementing Johnson's risky strategy, it became apparent that downward-spiraling sales and financial losses threatened the company's survival. After his arrival from Apple with much fanfare, and just 17 months on the job, Johnson was fired and replaced with Mike Ullman, the previous CEO.

Ullman returned with a familiar pricing strategy for JCPenney. They propped up list prices as much as 60 percent to allow for deep discounts. One advantage of this strategy is the "price anchoring" effect. A high list price creates a perception that the product is of high quality, even when purchased at a much lower price. While the net result of the increased price and deep discounts was not much different from Johnson's everyday low pricing strategy, Penney's loyal base began to return.[11] It's still an uphill battle though. In mid-2015, Ullman stepped down once again, this time replaced by Marvin Ellison, who had risen through the ranks at Home Depot before being selected for the top job at JCP. Ellison plans to bring on additional product lines, such as appliances, and even though the company turned a profit in 2016 for the first time in six years, he announced plans to close almost 140 under-performing stores across the country.

QUESTIONS FOR DISCUSSION

12-30. Describe the target market for JCPenney and Apple. How are they similar or different? How does the target market influence their pricing strategy?

12-31. How are the products and product lines offered for JCPenney and Apple similar and different? What types of pricing strategies will be most effective for the product strategy of each company?

12-32. Consider the *place* (distribution) where customers go to purchase JCPenney products. Next, consider where Apple customers go to purchase Apple products. How do you suppose differences in the companies' distribution methods may result in differences in their pricing strategies?

12-33. After the demise of everyday low pricing, a pair of earrings once sold at a list price of $200 was marked up to $450. Although the newly revived deep discounts and coupons will considerably lower the actual price to consumers, the actual cost to the average consumer will be higher than $200. Do you think that this is ethical or unethical? Why?

Writing Assignments

12-34. In 2012, Izhar Gafni developed a bicycle built completely from recycled materials. Describe what the product development process and product life cycle might look like for Gafni's cardboard bicycle. What kind of pricing strategies and objectives might he consider as he brings his product to market?

12-35. Companies always face various kinds of decisions for pricing their products in the marketplace. Pricing strategies for existing products, for example, are usually different than for pricing new products. (a) Compare and contrast pricing strategies for existing products versus pricing for new products. (b) Explain how "pricing to maximize profits" differs from "pricing to gain market share." (c) Pricing for products sold online is sometimes different from pricing for traditional face-to-face or in-store transactions. Explain how they may differ.

endnotes

[1] Seltzer, Rick, "A Marketplace in Confusion," Inside Higher Education, April 13, 2017, https://www.insidehighered.com/news/2017/04/13/new-yorks-free-tuition-plan-leaves-private-colleges-uncertain-about-future (Accessed April 16, 2017)

[2] Ron Winslow, "Cholesterol Drug Advances," *The Wall Street Journal*, November 18, 2010, pp. B1–2; "Anacetrapib for the Treatment of Dyslipidemia," *Issues in Emerging Health technologies: Canadian Agency for Drugs and Technologies in Health*, March 2013, at http://www.cadth.ca/media/pdf/EH0007-000Anacetrapib_e.pdf; John Carroll, "Anacetrapib," *FierceBiotech*, October 8, 2012, at http://www.fiercebiotech.com/special-reports/anacetrapib

[3] "New Products," *United States Department of Agriculture: Economic Research Service*, at http://www.ers.usda.gov/topics/food-markets-prices/processing-marketing/new-products.aspx#. UV2FtzemFcI, accessed on March 21, 2017; "Food Marketing System in the U.S.: New Product Introductions," *USDA Economic Research Service*, May 21, 2010, accessed at http://www.ers.usda.gov/Briefing/FoodMarketingSystem/new_product.htm

[4] Kelvin Chan, "Tired Western Brands Find New Life in Asia," Yahoo! News, September 8, 2011, at http://news.yahoo.com/tired-western-brands-life-asia-070448945.html

[5] "Interbrand Releases 16th Annual Best Global Brands Report," *Interbrand*, at http://www.interbrand.com/en/best-global-brands/2012/downloads.aspx, accessed on March 23, 2017.

[6] "Local Arizona Healthcare Companies Join Forces to Create a Unique Prescription Benefit Program for," HR.com, February 3, 2009, at http://www.hr.com/SITEFORUM?&t=/Default/gateway&i=1116423256281&application=story&active=no&ParentID=1119278002800&StoryID=1233685483801&xref=http%3A//www.google.com/url%3Fsa%3Dt%26rct%3Dj%26q%3Dcompanies%2520join%2520forces%2520on%2520internet%2520to%2520reduce%2520drug%2520prices%26source%3Dweb%26cd%3D6%26sqi%3D2%26ved%3D0CFoQFjAF%26url%3Dhttp%253A%252F%252Fwww.hr.com%252Fhr%252Fcommunities%252F_local_arizona_healthcare_companies_join_forces_to_create_a_unique_prescription_benefit_program__eng.html%26ei%3DDwRuFUYSeAbWv4APBz4GACA%26usg%3DAFQjCNHRtbBJU0H9GJtl-zttn4AV9eUi9w

[7] "About Carbonite," at http://www.carbonite.com/en/about/company/our-story

[8] "Reverse Auction," *Encyclopedia of Management. 2009. Encyclopedia.com.* (January 16, 2011), at http://www.encyclopedia.com/doc/1G2-3273100254.html; MediaBids.com, at http://www.mediabids.com/

[9] Patrick G. Lee, "Pricing Tactic Spooks Lawyers," *Wall Street Journal*, August 2, 2011, p. B5.

[10] "Hearing Set In U.S. On Dumping Charges," *SeafoodSource.com*, January 4, 2013, at http://www.seafoodsource.com/newsarticledetail.aspx?id=19025

[11] Sources: Kim Bhasin, "JCPenney Is Raising Prices So That It Can Mark Them Down," *Business Insider*, March 27, 2013, at http://www.businessinsider.com/jcpenney-raising-prices-to-mark-them-down-2013-3; Karen Tally, "Retailers' Discounts Lure Shoppers," *Wall Street Journal*, October 7, 2011, p. B3; Kim Bhasin, "Inside JCPenney: Widespread Fear, Anxiety, and Distrust of Ron Johnson and His New Management Team," *Business Insider*, February 22, 2013, at http://www.businessinsider.com/inside-jcpenney-2013-2; Phil Wahba, "J.C. Penney Overhauls Pricing Strategy as Sales Plummet," *Reuters*, February 27, 2013, at http://www.reuters.com/article/2013/02/28/us-jcpenney-results-idUS-BRE91Q19C20130228; Brad Tuttle, "Why JCPenney's 'No More Coupons' Experiment Is Failing," *Time*, May 17, 2012, at http://business.time.com/2012/05/17/why-jcpenneys-no-more-coupons-experiment-is-failing/; Brad Tuttle, "The Price Is Righter," *Time*, February 13, 2012, at http://www.time.com/time/magazine/article/0,9171,2105961,00.html.; Brad Tuttle, "J. C. Penney's Pricing Is Faker Than Ever," *Time*, 2014, *Business Source Premier*, EBSCO*host* (accessed May 20, 2015).

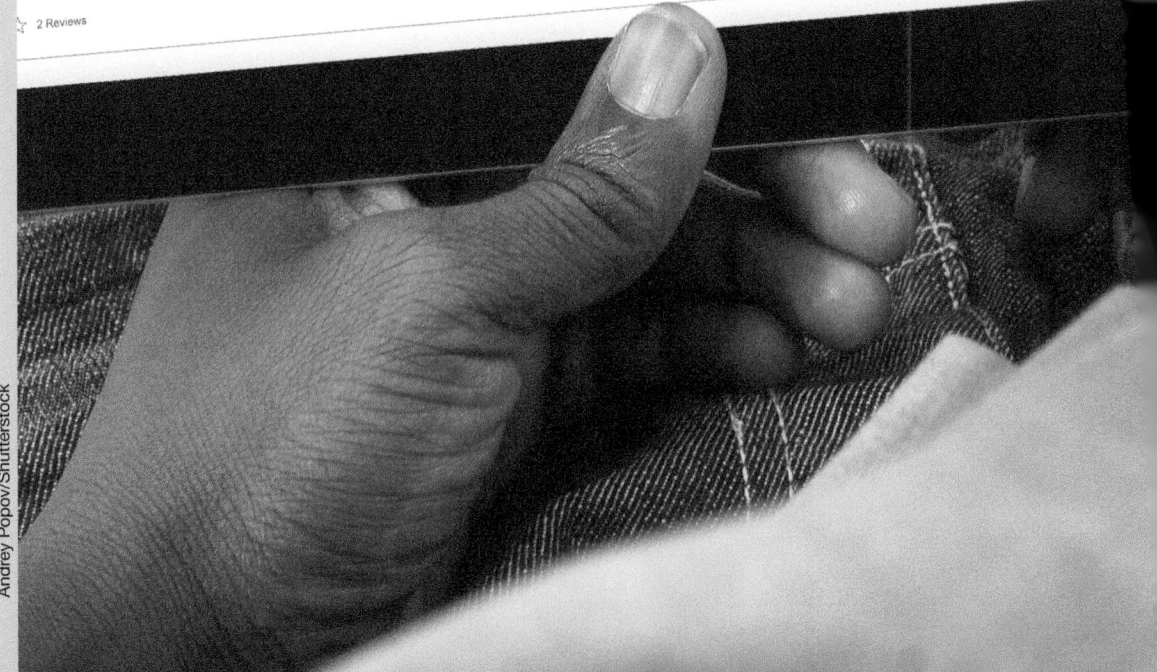

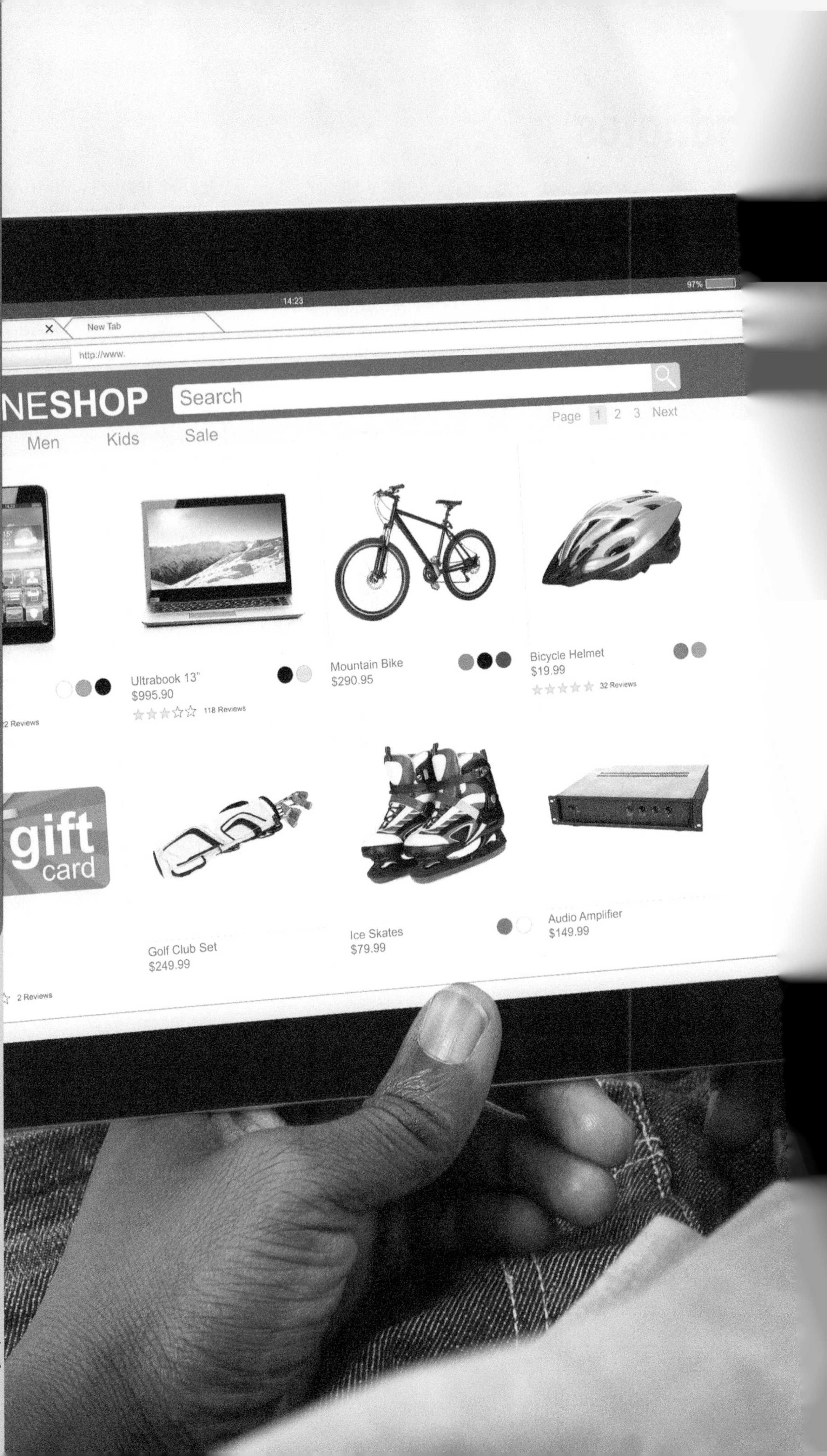

Online commerce brings consumers and businesses together

in ways we could have never imagined. By

collecting   and

studying purchase data, retailers know what

we want even before we do.

After reading this chapter, you should be able to:

13-1 **Explain** the meaning of *distribution mix* and identify the different channels of distribution.

13-2 **Describe** the role of wholesalers and the functions performed by e-intermediaries.

13-3 **Describe** the different types of retailing and explain how online retailers add value for consumers on the Internet.

13-4 **Define** *physical distribution* and describe the major activities in the physical distribution process.

13-5 **Identify** the objectives of promotion and the considerations in selecting a promotional mix, and discuss the various kinds of advertising promotions.

13-6 **Outline** the tasks involved in personal selling and describe the various types of sales promotions.

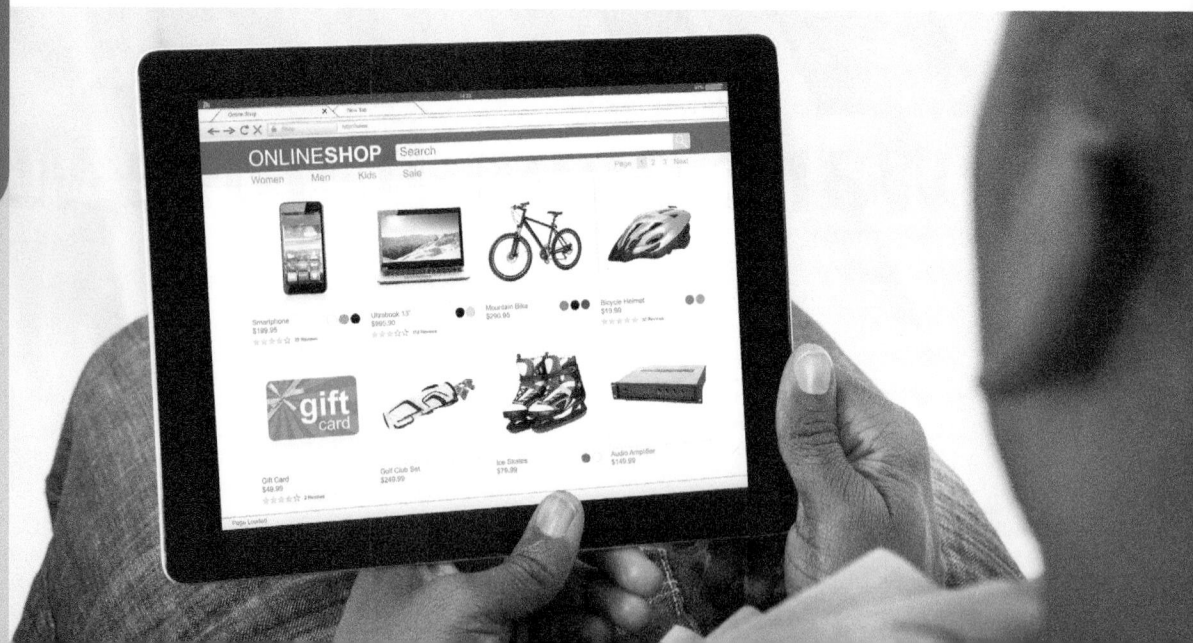

The Changing Landscape of Commerce

In the early days of U.S. commerce, people waited with anticipation for the Sears catalog, and then with even more anticipation for the Wells Fargo wagon to bring their orders.

In 1897, the Sears catalog was almost 800 pages and even had a section offering homes for sale. Pre-cut lumber, doors, windows, and roofing were shipped by rail for the buyer to self-assemble. (Some of these homes are still standing today.) It could take weeks or even months for the order to make its way to Sears, be fulfilled, and shipped back. But even this slow process was a radical improvement over the pre-railroad system of carts and wagons that would supply local stores with a limited array of goods.

Today, we expect to go to a store like Walmart to find just about anything we need in vast supply but, even more importantly, we expect to be able to order online and receive our shipment within days, if not hours. We are accosted by a previously unimaginable array of colors and advertisements. Various studies have shown that message and brand "exposure" can range from 3,000 to 20,000 contacts per day. In addition to traditional ads, those numbers include every time you pass by a label in a grocery store, all the ads in your mailbox whether you see them or not, the label on everything you wear, the condiments in your fridge, the cars on the highway, and every other imaginable brand contact. However, just the fact that you and the message or a brand name or logo are in the same proximity doesn't mean you actually notice it. No one can really process that many exposures. We can't notice, absorb, or even judge the personal merit of 3,000 visual/audio exposures per day, let alone 20,000.

But online vendors have become experts at collecting and collating individual and marketplace buying patterns and tracking individual shopping preferences. Algorithms then predict purchasing patterns and arrange for items to be warehoused within two hours of the final destination. Companies like Stitch Fix deliver clothes based on established personal preferences and then allow the purchaser to return those that don't fit or that are not appealing. Advertising and promotion have changed dramatically as the information age has made targeted marketing possible at a micro-level never before feasible.

E-commerce is changing the physical landscape of the nation as well. Plain, no frills distribution centers in industrial areas are slowly replacing the high-profile, brightly-lit shopping centers that have dominated the urban experience in the past. According to *Business Insider*, in 2017 Macy's announced that it is planning to close 100 stores, Sears rolled out plans for shuttering at least 30 Sears and Kmart stores by April of 2017, and JCPenney announced plans to close 138 stores by the end of the year. Credit Suisse

what's in it for me?

To become a leading retailer in any market takes a solid understanding of how best to distribute and promote products to customers. This chapter describes different types of wholesalers, retailers, and intermediaries, as well as how the online marketplace has changed the nature of how companies do business. By understanding this chapter's methods for distributing and promoting products, you'll have a clearer picture of how to sort out and identify the different kinds of people who are targeted by various companies, products, and advertising campaigns. As an informed consumer, you'll have a better self-awareness of when you are being targeted with promotional activities by businesses. You'll also be prepared to evaluate a company's distribution methods, advertising programs, and competitive potential.

As we saw in Chapter 12, marketing managers are concerned with deciding what products a company will offer to its customers and determining prices for those products. In this chapter, we'll look at the other two of the Four Ps of the marketing mix. We'll start by looking at the concept of *place*, the *distribution mix*, and the different channels and methods of distribution. We'll then look at *promotion* and discuss the factors to consider in selecting a promotional mix. Finally, we'll discuss the tasks involved in personal selling and various types of sales promotions.

released a research report in early 2017 predicting that more than 8,600 brick-and-mortar stores will close their doors by the end of the year.[1]

Companies that want to survive, both those that rely on online sales and those that rely on brick-and-mortar locations, are reaching toward the next level of differentiation. Many products, including cars, are able to be customized online by the consumer, made-to-order and delivered quickly. Amazon and other companies are already experimenting with self-driving delivery vehicles and ways to deliver products before consumers even know they need them, and we can only imagine what is next. 3D printers in every home ready to assemble items to order? Tactile holograms to virtually try on clothes? The next big breakthrough is likely something we haven't even imagined yet. For certain, it is the business students of today who will be creating the shopping experience of the future. After studying the content in this chapter, you should be able to answer a set of discussion questions found at the end of the chapter.

OBJECTIVE 13-1
Explain

the meaning of *distribution mix* and identify the different channels of distribution.

Distribution Mix *combination of distribution channels by which a firm gets its products to end users*

Intermediary *individual or firm that helps to distribute a product*

Wholesaler *intermediary who sells products to other businesses for resale to final consumers*

Retailer *intermediary who sells products directly to consumers*

Distribution Channel *network of interdependent companies through which a product passes from producer to end user*

Direct Channel *distribution channel in which a product travels from producer to consumer without intermediaries*

The Distribution Mix

In addition to a good product mix and effective pricing, the success of any product also depends on its **distribution mix**, the combination of distribution channels by which a firm gets products to end users. In this section, we look at intermediaries and different kinds of distribution channels. Then we discuss some benefits consumers reap from services provided by intermediaries.

Intermediaries and Distribution Channels

Once called *middlemen*, **intermediaries** help to distribute goods, either by moving them or by providing information that stimulates their movement from sellers to customers. **Wholesalers** are intermediaries who sell products to other businesses for resale to final consumers. **Retailers** sell products directly to consumers.

Distribution of Goods and Services A **distribution channel** is the path a product follows from producer to end user. Figure 13.1 shows how four popular distribution channels can be identified according to the channel members involved in getting products to buyers.

CHANNEL 1: DIRECT DISTRIBUTION In a **direct channel**, the product travels from the producer to the consumer or organizational buyer without intermediaries. Avon, Dell, GEICO, and Tupperware, as well as many online companies, use this type of channel. Most business goods, especially those bought in large quantities, are sold directly by the manufacturer to the industrial buyer.

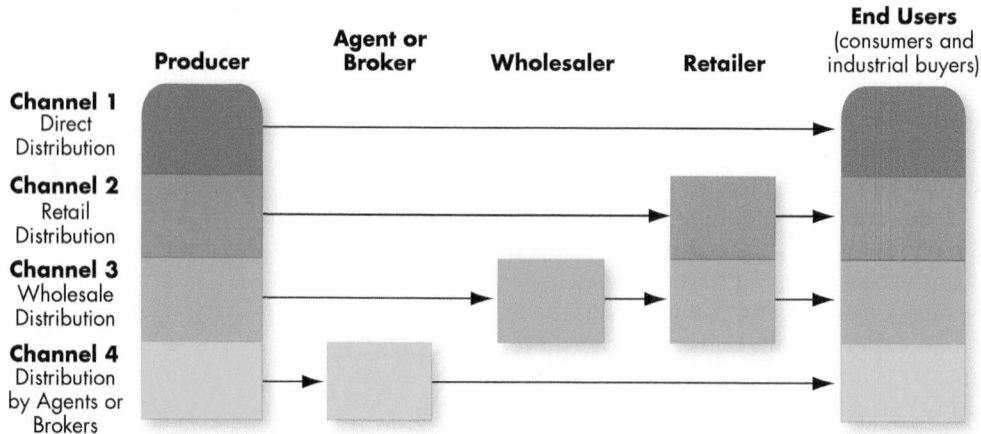

FIGURE 13.1 Channels of Distribution

CHANNEL 2: RETAIL DISTRIBUTION In Channel 2, producers distribute consumer products through retailers. Goodyear, for example, maintains its own network of retail outlets. Levi's has its own outlets but also produces jeans for other retailers. Large outlets, such as Walmart, buy merchandise directly from producers and then resell to customers online and at Walmart retail stores. Consumers can also go online to buy popular products such as book, movie, and music downloads from online retailers. Many industrial buyers, such as businesses buying office supplies from Staples, also rely on this channel.

CHANNEL 3: WHOLESALE DISTRIBUTION Once the most widely used method of non-direct distribution, traditional brick-and-mortar Channel 2 distribution requires a large and costly amount of floor space for storing and displaying merchandise. Wholesalers relieve this space problem by storing merchandise and restocking retailer store displays frequently. With approximately 90 percent of its space used to display merchandise and only 10 percent needed for storage and office facilities, the combination convenience store and gas station's use of wholesalers is an example of Channel 3.

CHANNEL 4: DISTRIBUTION BY AGENTS OR BROKERS Sales agents or brokers represent producers and receive commissions on the goods they sell to consumers or industrial users. **Sales agents**, such as online travel agents, generally deal in the related product lines of a few producers, such as tour companies, to meet the needs of many customers. In industries like real estate and stock exchanges, **brokers** match numerous sellers and buyers as needed to sell properties, often without knowing in advance who they will be.

Sales Agent *independent intermediary who generally deals in the related product lines of a few producers and forms long-term relationships to represent those producers and meet the needs of many customers*

Broker *independent intermediary who matches numerous sellers and buyers as needed, often without knowing in advance who they will be*

The Pros and Cons of Nondirect Distribution One downfall of nondirect distribution is higher prices—the more "stations" in the channel, the more intermediaries making a profit by charging a markup or commission, and the higher the final price. Intermediaries, however, can provide *added value* by providing

At this plant of an electrical components supplier, this employee assembles electrical systems according to a process that meets the requirements for its industrial customers. The finished assemblies are shipped from the plant to customers' facilities, illustrating a direct (producer to customer) channel of distribution.

Keith Dannemiller/Alamy Stock Photo

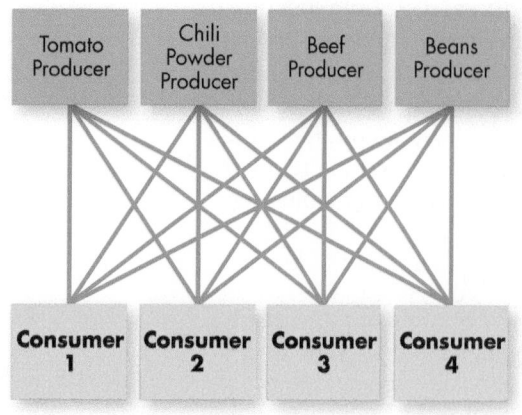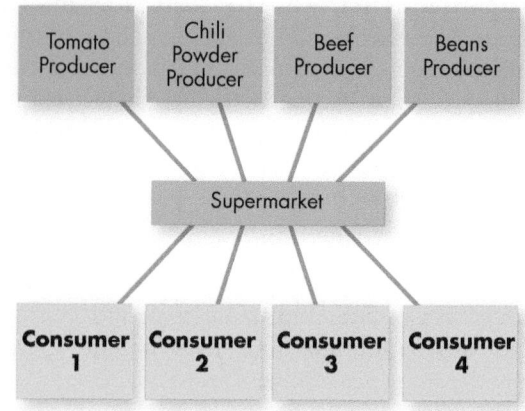

FIGURE 13.2 The Value-Adding Intermediary

time-saving information and making the right quantities of products available where and when consumers need them. Figure 13.2 illustrates the problem of making chili without the benefit of a common intermediary, the supermarket. As a consumer, you would obviously spend a lot more time, money, and energy if you tried to gather all the ingredients from separate producers. In short, intermediaries exist because they provide necessary services that get products efficiently from producers to users.

Distribution Strategies

Selecting an appropriate distribution network is a strategic decision; it determines both the amount and cost of *market coverage* that a product gets, or how many of any kind of intermediary will be used. Generally, strategy depends on the type of product and the degree of market coverage that is most effective in getting it to the greatest number of customers. Marketers strive to make a product accessible in just enough locations to satisfy customers' needs. You can buy milk and bottled water, for instance, in many different retail outlets, but there are very few outlets for buying a new Ferrari. Three strategies, (1) *intensive*, (2) *exclusive*, and (3) *selective distribution*, provide different degrees of market coverage.

Intensive Distribution *strategy by which a product is distributed through as many channels as possible*

- **Intensive distribution** means distributing through as many channels and channel members as possible (both wholesalers and retailers). It is normally used for low-cost consumer goods with widespread appeal, such as candy and magazines. M&M's candies enter the market through many different retail outlets—supermarkets, vending machines, drugstores, online, and so forth.

Exclusive Distribution *strategy by which a manufacturer grants exclusive rights to distribute or sell a product to a limited number of wholesalers or retailers in a given geographic area*

- With **exclusive distribution**, a manufacturer grants the exclusive right to distribute or sell a product to a limited number of wholesalers or retailers, usually in a given geographic area. Such agreements are most common for high-cost prestige products. Rolex watches are sold only by "Official Rolex Jewelers."

Selective Distribution *strategy by which a company uses only wholesalers and retailers who give special attention to specific products in its sales efforts*

- Using **selective distribution**, a producer selects only wholesalers and retailers that will give a product special attention in sales effort, display and promotion advantage, and so forth. Selective distribution is used most often for consumer products such as furniture and appliances. Frigidaire and Whirlpool use selective distribution for appliances to cement relationships with wholesalers who will market Frigidaire and Whirlpool over other brands.

Channel Conflict and Channel Leadership

Manufacturers and services providers (such as Nike, LG Electronics, and Allied Insurance) may distribute through more than one channel, and many retailers (such as Walgreens) are free to strike agreements with as many producers (like the makers of Tylenol, Advil, and Aleve) as capacity permits. In such cases, *channel conflict* may arise. Conflicts are resolved through better coordination, and a key factor in coordinating the activities of organizations is *channel leadership*.

Channel Conflict **Channel conflict** occurs when members of the channel disagree over roles or rewards. John Deere and State Farm would object to their dealers distributing tractors and insurance products of competing brands. Likewise, a manufacturer-owned outlet store runs the risk of alienating other retailers of its products when it discounts the company's products. Conflict may arise if one channel member has more power or is perceived as getting preferential treatment. Before Apple started opening its own retail stores, it distributed its products through many non-Apple retail stores. By opening its own retail outlets, channel conflict was created because the Apple stores substantially reduced sales at stores formerly used to distribute and sell Apple products. Such conflicts, of course, can defeat the purpose of the system by disrupting the flow of goods.

> **Channel Conflict** *conflict arising when the members of a distribution channel disagree over the roles they should play or the rewards they should receive*

Channel Leadership Usually one channel member—the **channel captain**—can determine the roles and rewards of the others. The channel captain is often a manufacturer or an originator of a service. Jewelry artisan Thomas Mann is in such demand that wholesalers and retailers wait years for the chance to distribute his Techno Romantic creations. Mann selects channel members, sets prices, and determines product availability. In other industries, an influential wholesaler or a large retailer such as Walmart may be a channel captain because of large sales volume.

> **Channel Captain** *channel member who is most powerful in determining the roles and rewards of other members*

Wholesaling

OBJECTIVE 13-2
Describe
the role of wholesalers and the functions performed by e-intermediaries.

The roles differ among the various intermediaries in distribution channels. Wholesalers provide a variety of services to buyers of products for resale or business use. In addition to storing and providing an assortment of products, some wholesalers offer delivery, credit, and product information. The range of services depends on the type of intermediary: *merchant wholesaler*, *agent/broker*, or *e-intermediary*.

Merchant Wholesalers

Most wholesalers are independent operations that sell various consumer or business goods produced by a variety of manufacturers. The largest group, **merchant wholesalers**, buys products from manufacturers and sells them to other businesses. They own the goods that they resell and usually provide storage and delivery.

Full-service merchant wholesalers (about 80 percent of all merchant wholesalers) provide value-adding services, including credit, marketing advice, and merchandising services. **Limited-function merchant wholesalers** provide fewer services, sometimes merely storage. Customers are normally small operations that pay cash and pick up their own goods. **Drop shippers** don't even carry inventory or handle products. They take orders from customers, negotiate with producers to supply goods, take title to them, and arrange for shipment. Rack jobbers market consumer goods (mostly nonfood items) directly to retail stores, marking prices and setting up displays in a variety of stores. Procter & Gamble (P&G) uses rack jobbers to distribute products such as its Pamper diapers.

> **Merchant Wholesalers** *independent wholesaler who takes legal possession of goods produced by a variety of manufacturers and then resells them to other organizations*
>
> **Full-Service Merchant Wholesalers** *merchant wholesaler that provides credit, marketing, and merchandising services in addition to traditional buying and selling services*
>
> **Limited-Function Merchant Wholesaler** *merchant wholesaler that provides a limited range of services*
>
> **Drop Shippers** *limited-function merchant wholesaler that receives customer orders, negotiates with producers, takes title to goods, and arranges for shipment to customers*

Agents and Brokers

Agents and brokers, including online e-agents, serve as independent sales representatives for many companies' products. They work on commission, usually about 4 to 5 percent of net sales. Unlike wholesalers, agents and brokers do not own their merchandise. Rather, they serve as sales and merchandising arms for producers or sellers who do not have their own sales forces.

The value of agents and brokers lies in their knowledge of markets and their merchandising expertise. They show sale items to potential buyers and, for retail stores, they provide such services as shelf and display merchandising and advertising layout. They remove open, torn, or dirty packages, arrange products neatly, and generally keep goods attractively displayed. Many supermarket products are handled through brokers.

The E-Intermediary

E-Intermediary *Internet distribution channel member that assists in delivering products to customers or that collects information about various sellers to be presented to consumers, or they help deliver online products to buyers*

The ability of e-commerce to bring together millions of widely dispersed consumers and businesses has changed the types and roles of intermediaries. **E-intermediaries** are online channel members—wholesalers—who perform one or both of two functions: (1) They collect information about sellers and present it to consumers (such as kayak.com) or (2) they help deliver online products to buyers (such as Amazon).

Syndicated Selling *e-commerce practice whereby a website offers other websites commissions for referring customers*

Syndicated Sellers **Syndicated selling** occurs when one website offers another a commission for referring customers. Expedia.com and Dollar Rent A Car illustrate syndicated selling perfectly. With millions of users each month, Expedia.com is a heavily visited travel-services website. Expedia has given Dollar Rent A Car a special banner on its Web page. When Expedia customers click on the banner for a car rental, they are transferred from the Expedia site to the Dollar site. Dollar pays Expedia a fee for each booking that comes through this channel. Although the Expedia intermediary increases the cost of Dollar's supply chain, it adds value for customers. Travelers avoid unnecessary cyberspace searches and are efficiently guided to a car-rental agency.

entrepreneurship and new ventures

Dispensing Hope

On the outskirts of Santiago, Chile, food is expensive and there are limited options. The lack of population density, coupled with low household incomes, has resulted in very few supermarkets. Most residents shop at small stores with narrow product lines and prices up to 40 percent higher than those found in more populated areas. In the hopes of improving the lives of people living in these areas, Algramo, a Santiago-based company, has a unique distribution model. Algramo, whose name means "by the gram," buys products in bulk, keeping their costs low. The company installs high-tech vending machines in local stores and stocks them with beans, lentils, rice, and sugar, as well as other products. They don't charge the storeowner for installing the machine and share the profits from all sales equally with the shopkeeper. In just their first year of operation, Algramo had dispensers in more than 300 locations, serving approximately 36,000 customers.

The company is the brainchild of Chilean student Jose Manuel Moller. He and three friends moved to a small community outside Santiago in hopes of gaining a better understanding of the conditions for residents. While the neighborhood stores are an important meeting place for the community, high prices for food, coupled with low wages, result in most residents struggling to meet their most basic needs. Moller began to see these high prices as a "poverty tax" imposed on the 70 percent of the Chilean population living outside the major cities and he was determined to make a difference. The company estimates that its model has allowed buyers to save up to 40 percent per month

Algramo

on household products, allowing them to use the saved funds to obtain better healthcare or to provide quality educational opportunities for their children. The benefits of Algramo's business model are not limited to the consumer but also extend to shopkeepers. Algramo's vending machines generate profits for small stores that operate on narrow margins, allowing them to stay in business and improve the owners' quality of life. Benefits of the model even extend to the environment—Algramo dispenses its products in reusable containers, reducing the waste associated with disposable packaging.[2]

Shopping Agents **Shopping agents (e-agents)** help online consumers by gathering and sorting information. Although they don't take possession of products, they know which websites and stores to visit, give accurate comparison prices, identify product features, and help consumers complete transactions by presenting information in a usable format—all in an instant. Hotwire.com is a well-known shopping agent for a variety of travel products. When you specify the product—hotels, flights, vacations, cars—Hotwire searches for vendors, does price comparisons, lists prices from low to high, and then transfers you to the websites of different e-stores.

Shopping Agent (e-agent) *e-intermediary (middleman) in the Internet distribution channel that assists users in finding products and prices but does not take possession of products*

Business-to-Business Brokers E-commerce intermediaries provide online value-adding services for business customers. The pricing process between business-to-business (B2B) buyers and sellers of commodities and services can be outsourced, for example, to the online company MediaBids.com. As a pricing broker for advertising services, MediaBids links any large-volume buyer of advertising services with potential suppliers that bid to become the supplier for the industrial customer. Client companies (the buyers of advertising services), such as Biocentric Health Inc., Christian Science Monitor, and Simplicity Sofas, can pay a fixed annual subscription fee and receive networking into MediaBids' auction headquarters, where real-time bids come in from suppliers at remote locations. The website provides current information until the bidding ends with the low-price supplier. In brokering the auction transactions, MediaBids doesn't take possession of any products. As a broker, it brings together timely information and links businesses to one another.

Retailing

OBJECTIVE 13-3
Describe
the different types of retailing and explain how online retailers add value for consumers on the Internet.

There are more than 5 million brick-and-mortar retail establishments in the United States. Many consist only of owners and part-time help. Indeed, more than one-half of the nation's retailers account for less than 10 percent of all retail sales. Retailers also include huge operations, such as Walmart, the world's largest corporate employer, and Home Depot. Although there are large retailers in many other countries—Metro in Germany, Carrefour in France, and Aeon in Japan—most of the world's largest retailers are U.S. businesses.

Types of Brick-and-Mortar Retail Outlets

U.S. retail operations vary widely by type as well as size. They can be classified by their pricing strategies, locations, range of services, or range of product lines. Choosing the right types of retail outlets is a crucial aspect of distribution strategy. This section describes U.S. retail stores by using three classifications: (1) *product-line retailers*, (2) *bargain retailers*, and (3) *convenience stores*.

Product-Line Retailers Retailers featuring broad product lines include **department stores**, which are organized into specialized departments: shoes, furniture, women's petite sizes, and so on. Stores are usually large, handle a wide range of goods, and offer a variety of services, such as credit plans and delivery. Similarly, **supermarkets** are divided into departments of related products: food products, household products, and so forth. They often stress low prices, self-service, and large selections.

In contrast, **specialty stores**, such as Lids, a retailer with more than 1,000 stores selling athletic fashion headwear, are small, serve specific market segments with full product lines in narrow product fields, and often feature knowledgeable salespeople.

Department Store *large product-line retailer characterized by organization into specialized departments*

Supermarket *large product-line retailer offering a variety of food and food-related items in specialized departments*

Specialty Store *retail store carrying one product line or category of related products*

Bargain Retailers **Bargain retailers** carry wide ranges of products at low prices. **Discount houses** began by selling large numbers of items at substantial price reductions to cash-only customers. As name-brand items became more common,

Bargain Retailer *retailer carrying a wide range of products at bargain prices*

Discount House *bargain retailer that generates large sales volume by offering goods at substantial price reductions*

Catalog Showroom *bargain retailer in which customers place orders for catalog items to be picked up at on-premises warehouses*

Factory Outlet *bargain retailer owned by the manufacturer whose products it sells*

Wholesale Club *bargain retailer offering large discounts on brand-name merchandise to customers who have paid annual membership fees*

Convenience Store *retail store offering easy accessibility, extended hours, and fast service*

they offered better product assortments while still transacting cash-only sales in low-rent facilities. As they became more established, they began moving to better locations, improving decor, selling better-quality merchandise at higher prices, and offering services such as credit plans and noncash sales.

Catalog showrooms mail catalogs to attract customers into showrooms to view display samples, place orders, and wait briefly while clerks retrieve orders from attached warehouses. **Factory outlets** are manufacturer-owned stores that avoid wholesalers and retailers by selling merchandise directly from factory to consumer. **Wholesale clubs**, such as Costco, offer large discounts on a wide range of brand-name merchandise to customers who pay annual membership fees.

Convenience Stores **Convenience store** chains, such as 7-Eleven and Circle K stores, stress easily accessible locations, extended store hours, and speedy service. They differ from most bargain retailers in that they carry fewer products and generally charge somewhat higher prices in exchange for the convenience they provide.

finding a better way

The Evolving Way We Pay

In the late 1800s, a saloon keeper in Ohio created a machine that would help account for sales and therefore prevent sales clerks from stealing from the cash drawer. By 1915, nearly 2 million of the cash register machines had been sold to U.S. grocery stores, hotels, department stores, and other retailers and were commonplace until just a few years ago. Today, it's rare to find a traditional cash register as more and more stores are incorporating mobile apps, tablets, and self-checkout lines instead of the labor-intensive and comparatively slow check-out lines. In addition to reducing labor costs, an iPad that includes credit card readers costs $1,500 versus the register's $4,000 price tag, and the financial data information systems are more easily integrated with customer management systems. For instance, a restaurant can place an order, send it to the kitchen for processing, and accept payment from a card reader at the table.

Even the most savvy small business owners used to have some trouble taking credit cards, but now they have access to card readers and apps like Square, PayPal, and a multitude of other online processing tools, many of which integrate with the company's accounting software, making it possible for even a single-person shop to take advantage of a much wider array of payment options.

In addition to convenience, the emergent technologies have made purchases more secure. European banks pioneered the use of difficult-to-copy microchips, and although American banks were slow to adopt the technology, the expense associated with fraudulent charges caused them to reconsider. Apple, ever the innovator, stepped into the authenticated pay arena with Apple Pay. Unlike a traditional credit card that utilizes a fixed 16-digit number, Apple Pay generates a token, a unique, encoded authorization for a purchase. Square and other mobile technologies are now incorporating thumbprint authentication for additional security.

Kali9/E+/Getty Images

Experts have long predicted that retail shopping would inevitably involve no check-out, no cash, and no unwanted waiting, all for a better customer shopping experience. Already, Amazon is leading the way with its beta-version of Amazon Go in Seattle, touting their "Just Walk Out" shopping experience. Using the Amazon Go app, shoppers enter the store, take the products they want, and then leave. Technology embedded in the store detects which products are taken from or returned to the shelves and keeps track of them in a virtual cart. The app then charges the customer's Amazon account and sends a receipt. It might not be too long before cash, checks, and even credit cards are simply museum curiosities like Polaroid cameras and buggy whips.

Nonstore Retailing

Some retailers sell products without brick-and-mortar stores. Certain types of products, such as snack foods, bottled water, and soft drinks, sell well from card- and coin-operated machines. The same can be said for some forms of entertainment (pinball, video games, and billiards) when placed in certain venues (such as movie theater lobbies, bowling alleys, and so forth). Redbox has also been successful in renting DVDs and video games through free-standing kiosks that are essentially vending machines. For all products, global annual sales through vending were almost $200 billion in 2016. Still, vending machine sales make up less than 1 percent of all U.S. retail sales.

Nonstore retailing also includes **direct-response retailing**, in which firms contact customers directly to inform them about products and to solicit sales orders. **Mail order** (or **catalog marketing**) is a popular form of direct-response retailing practiced by Crate and Barrel and Garnet Hill. Less popular in recent years because of do-not-call registries, outbound **telemarketing** uses phone calls to sell directly to consumers. However, telemarketing also includes inbound toll-free calls from customers, a service that most catalog and other retail stores make available. Finally, more than 600 U.S. companies, including Mary Kay cosmetics, use **direct selling** to sell door-to-door or through home-selling parties. Avon Products, one of the world's largest direct sellers, has approximately 5 million door-to-door sales representatives in more than 100 countries.[3]

Direct-Response Retailing *form of nonstore retailing in which firms directly interact with customers to inform them of products and to receive sales orders*

Mail Order (catalog marketing) *form of nonstore retailing in which customers place orders for catalog merchandise received through the mail*

Telemarketing *form of nonstore retailing in which the telephone is used to sell directly to consumers*

Direct Selling *form of nonstore retailing typified by door-to-door sales*

Online Retailing

In 2014, global business-to-consumer (B2C) sales were nearly $2 trillion, and they are projected to exceed the $2 trillion level by 2017.[4] More than 85 percent of the world's online population—more than 1 billion consumers—have made online purchases. iTunes outsells brick-and-mortar music retailers, and Amazon is the world's largest online retailer, selling nationally and internationally with total revenues in 2016 of almost $136 billion. **Online retailing** allows sellers to inform, sell to, and distribute to consumers using online technology. Some of the largest U.S. "e-tailers" are shown in Table 13.1. In addition to large companies, millions of small businesses around the globe have their own websites.

Online Retailing *nonstore retailing in which information about the seller's products and services is connected to consumers' computers, allowing consumers to receive the information and purchase the products in the home*

Electronic Catalogs **E-catalogs** use online displays of products to give millions of retail and business customers instant access to product information. The seller avoids the costs of printing and mail distribution, and once an online catalog

E-Catalog *nonstore retailing in which the Internet is used to display products*

table 13.1 Leading Online Retailers in Selected Consumer Products Categories*

Consumer Product Category	Online Retailer
Mass Merchandise	Amazon.com
Office Supplies	Staples Inc.
Computers and Electronics	Apple Inc.
Video and Audio Entertainment	Netflix Inc.
Home Repair and Improvement	Home Depot
Apparel and Accessories	L.L. Bean Inc.
Home Furnishings and Housewares	Williams-Sonoma Inc.
Toys	Toys "R" Us Inc.
Health and Beauty	Bath & Body Works
Sporting Goods	Cabela's Inc.

*Adapted from "Top 500 Guide," Internet Retailer (2016), at www.internetretailer.com/top500/list/.

is in place there are lower costs in maintaining and updating it. About 90 percent of all catalogs are now online, with digital sales accounting for more than 50 percent of all catalog sales.

Electronic Storefronts and Cybermalls Each seller's website is essentially an **electronic storefront** (or *virtual storefront*) from which shoppers collect information about products and buying opportunities, place orders, and pay for purchases. Producers of large product lines, such as Dell, dedicate storefronts to their own product lines. Other sites, such as Newegg.com, which offers computer and other electronics equipment, are category sellers whose storefronts feature products from many manufacturers.

Search engines such as Google and Dogpile serve as **cybermalls**, collections of virtual storefronts representing diverse products and offering speed, convenience, 24-hour access, and efficient searching. After entering a cybermall, shoppers can navigate by choosing from a list of stores (L.L. Bean, Lids, or Macy's), product listings (sporting goods, women's fashion, or mobile devices), or departments (apparel or bath/beauty).

Interactive and Video Retailing Today, retailers and B2C customers interact with multimedia sites using voice, graphics, animation, film clips, and access to live human advice. Many e-tailers provide real-time sales and customer service that allow customers to enter a live chat room with a service operator who can answer their specific product questions.

Video retailing, a long-established form of interactive marketing, lets viewers shop at home from channels on their TVs. QVC, for example, displays and demonstrates products, allows viewers to phone in or e-mail orders, and is available on Facebook, YouTube, and Twitter. Current generation televisions are available with online capabilities as well, allowing online networking. A television with Wi-Fi network access thus becomes a platform for comfortable at-home online shopping with a large-screen visual display.

Electronic Storefront *commercial website at which customers gather information about products and buying opportunities, place orders, and pay for purchases*

Cybermall *collection of virtual storefronts (business websites) representing a variety of products and product lines on the Internet*

Video Retailing *nonstore retailing to consumers via home television*

Wolfgang Puck products are distributed regularly through QVC and HSN television networks. The chef's name-brand kitchen appliances and cookware are also marketed through such online outlets as eBay and Shopping.com, as well as the QVC and HSN websites.

Physical Distribution

Physical distribution refers to the activities needed to move products from an intermediary or a manufacturer to customers and includes *warehousing* and *transportation operations*. Its purpose is to make goods available when and where customers want them, keep costs low, and provide services to satisfy customers. Because of its importance for customer satisfaction, some firms have adopted distribution as their marketing strategy of choice.

Consider, for example, the pioneering global distribution system of National Semiconductor, one of the world's largest microchip makers. Finished microchips were produced in plants around the world and shipped to hundreds of customers, such as IBM, Toshiba, and Hewlett-Packard, which also ran factories around the globe. Chips originally traveled 20,000 different routes on as many as 12 airlines and sat waiting at one location after another—on factory floors, at customs, in distributors' facilities, and in warehouses—before reaching customers. National streamlined the system by air-freighting chips worldwide from a single center in Singapore. Every activity—storage, sorting, and shipping—was centralized and run by FedEx. By outsourcing the activities, National's distribution costs were reduced, delivery times were cut by half, and sales increased substantially. Acquired in 2011 by Texas Instruments (TI), National Semiconductor and its innovative global distribution system is TI's Silicon Valley Analog division that remains a world leader for producing high-performance analog components.

Warehousing Operations

Storing, or **warehousing**, is a major part of distribution management. In selecting a strategy, managers must keep in mind both the different characteristics and costs of warehousing operations. **Private warehouses** are owned by a single manufacturer, wholesaler, or retailer that deals in mass quantities and needs regular storage. Most are run by large firms that deal in mass quantities and need regular storage. Walmart, for example, maintains its own warehouses to facilitate the movement of products to its retail stores.

Independently owned and operated **public warehouses**, which rent to companies only the space they need, are popular with firms needing storage only during peak periods and with manufacturers who need multiple storage locations to get products to multiple markets.

The digital age has brought with it massive quantities of data that need to be safely stored, preserved, organized, and accessible to users. Many companies, to protect their valuable data resources, rely on remote off-site digital storage services such as ZipCloud for Business as a safety net. Home users, too, use daily online backup services, such as Carbonite and SOS Online Backup, to protect against losing data when their computers crash. In the event of any physical catastrophe—floods, fires, earthquakes—at the client's facility, data can be restored online from the backup system.

Transportation Operations

Physically moving a product creates the highest cost many companies face. In addition to transportation methods, firms must also consider the nature of the product, the distance it must travel, the speed with which it must be received, and customer wants and needs.

Differences in cost among the major transportation modes—trucks, railroads, planes, digital transmission, water carriers, and pipelines—are usually most directly related to delivery speed.

With nearly 2 million drivers and a fleet of 8 million vehicles, trucks haul more than two-thirds of all tonnage carried by all modes of U.S. freight transportation. The advantages of trucks include flexibility for any-distance distribution, fast service, and dependability. Increasing truck traffic, however, raises concerns about highway safety and traffic congestion.

OBJECTIVE 13-4
Define
physical distribution and describe the major activities in the physical distribution process.

Physical Distribution *activities needed to move a product efficiently from manufacturer to consumer*

Warehousing *physical distribution operation concerned with the storage of goods*

Private Warehouse *warehouse owned by and providing storage for a single company*

Public Warehouse *independently owned and operated warehouse that stores goods for many firms*

Chris Salvo/The Image Bank/Getty Images

Specializing in long-haul shipping, US Xpress employs over 3,000 drivers to operate a fleet of 9,000 trucks and 26,000 trailers. Trucks have satellite capabilities, anti-collision radar, vehicle-detection sensors, computers for shifting through 10 speeds, and roomy cabs with sleepers, refrigerators, and microwaves.

Air is the fastest but also the most expensive mode of transportation for physical goods. Air-freight customers benefit from lower inventory costs by eliminating the need to store items that might deteriorate. Shipments of fresh fish, for example, can be picked up by restaurants each day, avoiding the risk of spoilage from packaging and storing.

For downloads of music, software, books, movies, and other digital products, the transportation mode of choice, online transmission, is newer, faster, and less expensive than all other modes. Of course, it is also restricted to products that exist in digital form that can be transmitted over communication channels.

Aside from digital transmission, water is the least expensive mode but, unfortunately, also the slowest. Networks of waterways—oceans, rivers, and lakes—let water carriers reach many areas throughout the world. Boats and barges are used mostly for moving bulky products (such as oil, grain, and gravel). Railroads can economically transport high-volume, heavy, bulky items, such as cars, steel, and coal. However, their delivery routes are limited by fixed, immovable rail tracks. Pipelines are slow and lack flexibility and adaptability, but for specialized products, such as liquids and gases, they provide economical and reliable delivery.

Distribution Through Supply Chains as a Marketing Strategy

Instead of just offering advantages in product features, quality, price, and promotion, many firms have turned to supply chains that depend on distribution as a cornerstone of business strategy. This approach means assessing, improving, and integrating the entire sequence of activities—upstream suppliers, wholesaling, warehousing, transportation, delivery, and follow-up services—involved in getting products to customers.

Since the 1960s, starting with Toyota in Japan, the industrial world has seen the rise of the just-in-time (JIT) inventory system, discussed in Chapter 7. Initially used for quality improvement and cost savings, it was primarily adopted by U.S. manufacturing firms coming by way of Ford Motor Company in the early 1980s. Along with JIT, the past 30 years have seen dramatic improvements in supply chain technology and management, and its adoption by the retail sector. In the 1980s, Walmart decided to build its own distribution system using the best practices of both JIT and supply chains instead of the industry practice of relying on outside freight haulers and wholesalers. Let's look at how this has enabled Walmart to dominate its competition and made it the leading retailer in the world:

Suppose you are shopping at Walmart and decide to pick up a *Mr. Coffee* 8-cup coffeemaker. When you check out, the scanner reads the bar code on the box and Walmart's inventory system is updated instantly, showing that a replacement coffeemaker is needed on the shelf. The replacement comes from "the back" of that store, where the remaining on-hand supply count is reduced in Walmart's information system. Once the back-room supply dwindles to *its* automatic triggering number, Walmart's distribution warehouse receives a digital signal notifying that this store needs more *Mr. Coffee* 8-cup coffeemakers. At the same time, the computer system also notifies the manufacturer that Walmart's distribution warehouse needs a replenishment supply. The manufacturer's suppliers, too, are notified, and so on, continuing upstream with information that enables faster resupply coordination throughout the supply chain. Walmart's data mining system determines the reorder number for every product based on sales (daily, weekly, and even by time of the year). Because of Walmart's constant rapid restocking from upstream sources, its store shelves are resupplied without having to keep large inventories in its warehouses and retail stores, thus reducing inventory costs and providing lower prices.

Walmart's JIT system has allowed it to achieve as low as a two-day turnaround from manufacturer to the store shelf, thus providing cost control and product availability. It maintains lower levels of inventory, meets customer demand, and keeps prices among the lowest in the retail industry. Another retailer that has been able to adopt this method on a similar scale and compete effectively with Walmart (but only in groceries) is the H-E-B Grocery Company's chain of stores in Texas. Its data mining software can evaluate what products are purchased when, and with what other products (so, for example, it knows to have tamales available at Christmas with coupons for enchilada sauce), and uses this information for forecasting upcoming demand.

The Importance of Promotion

OBJECTIVE 13-5
Identify
the objectives of promotion and the considerations in selecting a promotional mix, and discuss the various kinds of advertising promotions.

Promotion refers to techniques for communicating information about products and is part of the *communication mix*, the total message any company sends to customers about its product. Promotional techniques, especially advertising, must communicate the uses, features, and benefits of products, and marketers use an array of tools for this purpose.

Promotion *aspect of the marketing mix concerned with the most effective techniques for communicating information about and selling a product*

Promotional Objectives

The ultimate objective of any promotion is to increase sales. In addition, marketers may use promotion to *communicate information, position products, add value,* and *control sales volume.*

As we saw in Chapter 11, **positioning** is the process of establishing an easily identifiable product image in the minds of consumers by fixing, adapting, and communicating the nature of the product itself. First, a firm must identify which market segments are likely to purchase its product and how its product measures up against competitors. Then, it can focus on promotional choices for differentiating its product and positioning it in the minds of the target audience. As an example, if someone says, "facial tissue," most people respond with ... Kleenex. "The Ultimate Driving Machine" is ... BMW. These ubiquitous associations are indicative of successful positioning.

Positioning *process of establishing an identifiable product image in the minds of consumers*

Promotional mixes are often designed to communicate a product's *value-added benefits* to distinguish it from the competition. Mercedes automobiles and Ritz-Carlton hotels, for example, promote their products as upscale goods and services featuring high quality, style, and performance, all at a higher price.

Promotional Strategies

Once its larger marketing objectives are clear, a firm must develop a promotional strategy to achieve them. Two prominent types of strategies are considered here:

Pull Strategy *promotional strategy designed to appeal directly to consumers who will demand a product from retailers*

- A **pull strategy** appeals directly to consumers who will demand the product from retailers. Pharmaceutical companies use *direct-to-consumer advertising* (DTC) to persuade consumers to aggressively request a product rather than to wait passively until the doctor suggests trying it. "Talk to your doctor about Allegra-D" is just one example of the vast number of television and online ads for prescription drugs, knee replacement systems, and other medical products. The resulting demand by end users stimulates demand for the product from wholesalers and producers.

Push Strategy *promotional strategy designed to encourage wholesalers or retailers to market products to consumers*

- Using a **push strategy**, a firm markets its product to wholesalers and retailers who then persuade customers to buy it. Brunswick Corp., for instance, uses a push strategy to promote Bayliner pleasure boats, directing its promotions at dealers and persuading them to order more inventory. Dealers are then responsible for stimulating demand among boaters at outdoor shows and through other promotions in their market districts.

Many large firms combine pull and push strategies. General Mills, for example, advertises to create consumer demand (pull) for its breakfast cereals, including Lucky Charms, Cheerios, and Count Chocula. At the same time, it pushes wholesalers and retailers to stock and display them.

The Promotional Mix

Promotional Mix *combination of tools used to promote a product*

Five of marketing's most powerful promotional tools are advertising, personal selling, sales promotions, direct or interactive marketing, and publicity and public relations. The best combination of these tools—the best **promotional mix**—depends on many factors. The most important is the target audience. As an example, two generations from now, 25 percent of the U.S. workforce will be Hispanic. With an estimated 52 million Hispanic Americans, the rise in Latinos' disposable income has made them a potent economic force, and marketers are scrambling to redesign and promote products to appeal to them with Spanish-language commercials and ads. Several major cable networks such as HBO and ESPN offer separate Spanish-language channels.

In establishing a promotional mix, marketers match promotional tools with the five stages in the buyer decision process:

1 When consumers first recognize the need to make a purchase, marketers use advertising and publicity, which can reach many people quickly, to make sure buyers are aware of their products.

2 As consumers search for information about available products, advertising and personal selling are important methods to educate them.

3 Personal selling can become vital as consumers compare competing products. Sales representatives can demonstrate product quality, features, benefits, and performance in comparison with competitors' products.

4 When buyers are ready to purchase products, sales promotion can give consumers an incentive to buy. Personal selling can help by bringing products to convenient purchase locations.

5 After making purchases, consumers evaluate products and note (and remember) their strengths and deficiencies. At this stage, advertising and personal selling can remind customers that they made wise purchases.

Figure 13.3 summarizes the effective promotional tools for each stage in the consumer buying process.

Advertising

Advertising *promotional tool consisting of paid, nonpersonal communication used by an identified sponsor to inform an audience about a product*

Advertising is paid, nonpersonal communication by which an identified sponsor informs an audience about a product. In 2016, firms in the United States spent over $210 billion on advertising—almost $30 billion by just 10 companies. Figure 13.4 shows

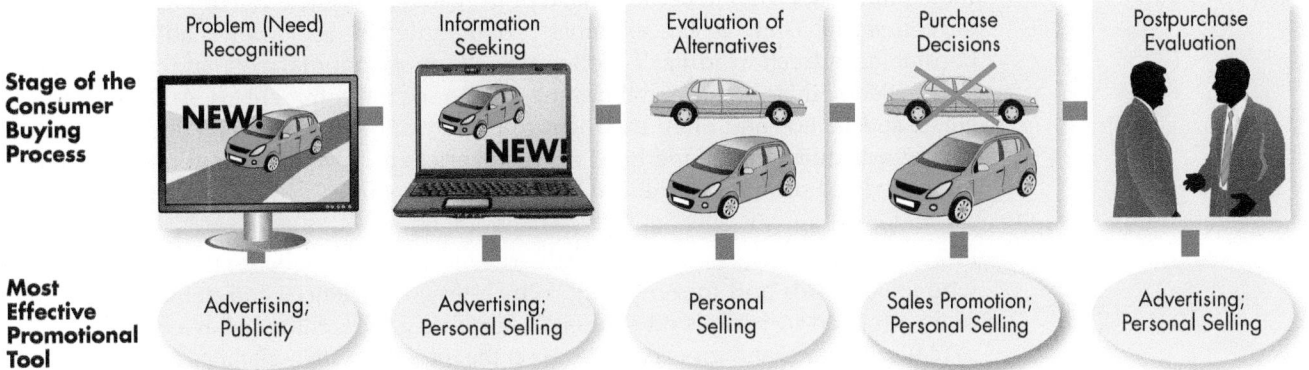

Stage of the Consumer Buying Process	Problem (Need) Recognition	Information Seeking	Evaluation of Alternatives	Purchase Decisions	Postpurchase Evaluation
Most Effective Promotional Tool	Advertising; Publicity	Advertising; Personal Selling	Personal Selling	Sales Promotion; Personal Selling	Advertising; Personal Selling

FIGURE 13.3 The Consumer Buying Process and the Promotional Mix
Source: Multi-Source

U.S. advertising expenditures for the top-spending firms. Let's take a look at the different types of advertising media, noting some of the advantages and limitations of each.

Advertising Media Consumers tend to ignore the bulk of advertising messages that bombard them—they pay attention only to what interests them. Moreover, the advertising process is dynamic, reflecting the changing interests and preferences of both customers and advertisers. One recent customer survey, for example, reports that mail ads are rated as most irritating and boring, and newspaper and magazine ads are least annoying. Yet, although newspaper ads are rated as more informative and useful than some other media, advertisers continue to shift away, using instead

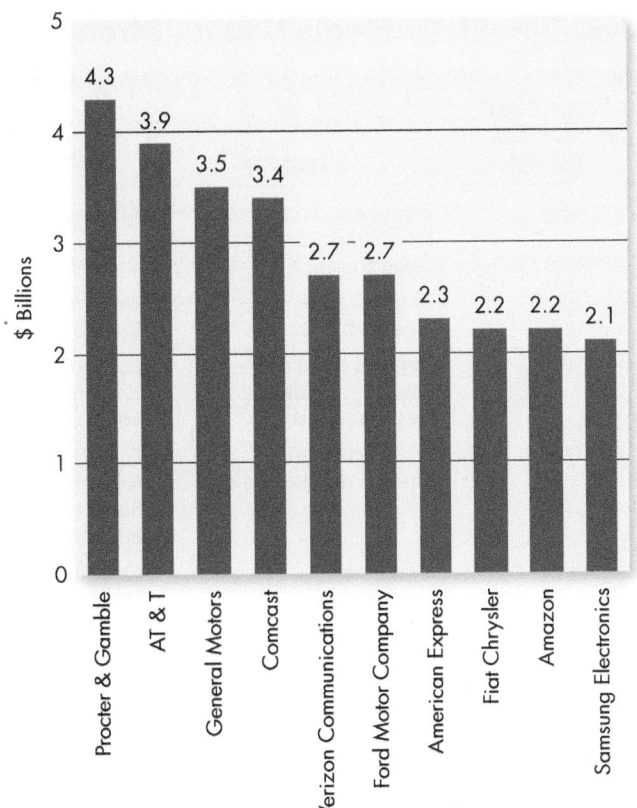

FIGURE 13.4 Top 10 U.S. National Advertisers
Source: Adapted from "Kantar Media Reports U.S. Advertising
Expenditures Increased 3 Percent in 2012," Kantar Media,
March 11, 2013, at http://kantarmediana.com/intelligence/press/
us-advertising-expenditures-increased-3-percent-2012.

more online advertising because newsprint readership (the audience) is dwindling.[5] Of course, in a few instances, most prominently the Superbowl, advertising has become an attraction in itself. Polls track the most popular ads, and some people acknowledge that they watch the game only to see the commercials. Advertisers also create special ads and often use them to promote "big events." Not surprisingly, of course, ads during the Superbowl are also very expensive—$4.5 million was the fee for a single 30-second commercial during the 2017 game.

Real-Time Ad Tracking Advertisers always want better information about who looks at ads and for how long. Which target audiences and demographics are more attracted to various ad contents? Accurate ad-watching behavior of shoppers in malls, theaters, and grocery stores is on the increase with assistance from high-tech real-time surveillance. As passing consumers watch ads on video screens, cameras watch the shoppers, and software analyzes the viewers' demographics and reactions to various ad contents and formats. The makers of the tracking system claim accuracy of up to 90 percent for determining gender, approximate age, and ethnicity. Once perfected, the system might measure your demographics, identify you with a target audience, and then instantly change the presentation to a preferred product and visual format to attract and hold your attention.[6] Marketers must find out, then, who their customers are, to which media they pay attention, what messages appeal to them, and how to get their attention. Thus, marketers use several different **advertising media**, specific communication devices for carrying a seller's message to potential customers. The combination of media through which a company advertises is called its **media mix**. Table 13.2 shows the relative sizes of media usage and their strengths and weaknesses.

Advertising Media *variety of communication devices for carrying a seller's message to potential customers*

Media Mix *combination of advertising media chosen to carry a message about a product*

table 13.2 Total U.S. Media Usage, Strengths, and Weaknesses

Advertising Medium	Percentage* of Advertising Outlays	Strengths	Weaknesses
Television	35%	Program demographics allow for customized ads Large audience	Most expensive
Internet	20%	Targeted audience Measurable success	Nuisance to consumers Easy to ignore
Direct mail	10%	Targeted audience Personal messages Predictable results	Easily discarded Environmentally irresponsible
Newspapers	10%	Broad coverage Ads can be changed daily	Quickly discarded Broad readership limits ability to target specific audience
Radio	8%	Inexpensive Large audience Variety of ready market segmentation	Easy to ignore Message quickly disappears
Magazines	8%	Often reread and shared Variety of ready market segmentation	Require advanced planning Little control over ad placement
Outdoor	3%	Inexpensive Difficult to ignore Repeat exposure	Presents limited information Little control over audience

A combination of additional unmeasured media, such as yellow pages, catalogs, special events, sidewalk handouts, ads on transport vehicles, skywriting, movies, and door-to-door communications, are not included.

*Estimated.

Marketers are also getting increasingly sophisticated by blending their media mix across different platforms. This often comes in the form of marketing partnerships. For example, suppose that you are thinking about taking a trip to New York City. As part of your preliminary planning you check out a new backpack on Amazon, look at airfares on United.com, and compare hotel rates at Marriott.com and Hilton.com. A few hours later you decide to check out what's happening with your friends on Facebook. Scattered among the posts from your friends you are likely to see ads for the same hotels, flights, and backpacks you were checking out earlier. That's because Amazon, United, Hilton, and Marriott each pay Facebook a fee to link your shopping searches back to your Facebook page.

Personal Selling

OBJECTIVE 13-6
Outline
the tasks involved in personal selling and describe the various types of sales promotions.

In the oldest and most expensive form of sales, **personal selling**, a salesperson communicates one-on-one with potential customers to identify their needs and align them with products. Salespeople gain credibility by investing time getting acquainted with potential customers and answering their questions. This professional interaction is especially effective in relationship marketing. It gives the seller a clearer picture of the buyer's business and allows salespeople to provide buyers with value-adding services.

Personal Selling *promotional tool in which a salesperson communicates one-on-one with potential customers*

Personal Selling Situations

Salespeople must consider the ways in which personal sales activities are affected by the differences between consumer and industrial products:

- **Retail selling** is selling a consumer product for the buyer's personal or household use.

Retail Selling *selling a consumer product for the buyer's personal or household use*

- **Industrial selling** is selling products to other businesses, either for the purpose of manufacturing or for resale. Levi's, for instance, sells jeans to Walmart (industrial selling). In turn, consumers purchase Levi's jeans at Walmart stores (retail selling).

Industrial Selling *selling products to other businesses, either for the purpose of manufacturing or for resale*

Each of these situations has distinct characteristics. In retail selling, the buyer usually comes to the seller, whereas the industrial salesperson typically calls on the prospective buyer. An industrial decision usually takes longer than a retail decision because it involves more money, decision makers, and weighing of alternatives. As we saw in Chapter 11, organizational buyers are professional purchasing agents accustomed to dealing with salespeople. Consumers in retail stores, in contrast, may actually be intimidated by salespeople.

Personal Selling Tasks

Salespeople must be adept at performing three basic tasks of personal selling. In **order processing**, a salesperson receives an order and sees to its handling and delivery. Route salespeople, who call on regular customers to check inventories, are often order processors. With the customer's consent, they may decide on the sizes of reorders, fill them directly from their trucks, and even stock shelves. Frito-Lay, Coca-Cola, and many beer distributorships use this approach.

Order Processing *personal-selling task in which salespeople receive orders and see to their handling and delivery*

In other situations, however, when potential customers are not aware that they need or want a product, **creative selling** involves providing information and demonstrating product benefits to persuade buyers to complete a purchase. Creative selling is crucial for industrial products and high-priced consumer products, such as cars, for which buyers comparison shop. Finally, a salesperson may use **missionary selling** to promote a company and its products rather than simply to close a sale. Pharmaceutical companies often use this method to make doctors aware of the

Creative Selling *personal-selling task in which salespeople try to persuade buyers to purchase products by providing information about their benefits*

Missionary Selling *personal-selling task in which salespeople promote their firms and products rather than try to close sales*

company and its products so they will recommend the company's products to others, or so the doctor will prescribe the products to patients. The sale of the product, then, is actually made at the pharmacy. In missionary selling, the goal may be to promote the company's long-term image as much as any given product. Another activity in missionary selling is after-sale technical assistance for complex products. IBM uses after-sale selling to ensure that industrial customers know how to use IBM equipment and services.

managing in turbulent times

The Logic Behind Logistics

The essence of marketing is putting the right product in the right place at the right price at the right time. This is why distribution and logistics are so important.

Distribution is the actual physical movement of goods from manufacturer, to wholesaler, to retailer, and, finally, to the end consumer. In managing distribution, each company has to contemplate the most affordable ways to move goods to its customers. Logistics focuses on the flow of information, which contrasts the physical movement of goods pervasive in distribution. Developing automated inventory systems is a key element of logistics. Many retailers, for instance, sync store computer systems with their own distribution centers or those of suppliers. This electronic integration allows for automated processes for merchandise ordering, distribution center order fulfillment, and transport of goods to the stores.

Knichel Logistics was facing a lack of growth in its Less-than-Truckload, or LTL, division. LTL loads are defined as having a billed weight of less than 10,000 lbs. Knichel couldn't compete on price against larger companies with more volume, but President Kristy Knichel knew that there was demand, saying, "there was a lot more business we could potentially grab. Why aren't we grabbing it and what do we need to do to grab it? We have a huge customer base that we know wanted that service. If we don't offer the service, they are going to go look somewhere else and then potentially we could lose the other modes that we have with that customer as well."

Kristy and her father William founded the company in 2003. Her brother William Jr. and younger sister Casey are actively involved in management, while another sister and her father remain part owners. As a $50 million provider of transportation and logistics, Knichel Logistics is considered a small fish in a highly competitive industry that is undergoing numerous mergers and acquisitions by enormous corporations such as the recent combination of Swift Transportation Co. and Knight Transportation Inc. into a single business called Knight-Swift Transportation Holdings Inc.

But even as the largest logistics and transportation companies are consolidating to gain a competitive advantage, a new breed of logistics and fulfillment operations are forming in the long shadow that Amazon's free shipping is casting across the retail world. Fast-moving fulfillment services like Knichels help

Tamp/ZUMA Press Inc./Alamy Stock Photo

niche retailers compete with Amazon by delivering goods to consumers faster, and by pooling orders from many customers to give smaller retailers the benefits of scale. The fulfillment operators are trying to lower shipping costs, but the real goal for the retailers is to stay in business.

For Knichel, the creative solution to its marketing and growth problem came from an announcement on LinkedIn by a company called BlueGrace requesting proposals from potential franchisees. It took about six months for Knichel Logistics to launch a separate company via the franchising agreement called BlueGrace Logistics Pittsburgh North for its LTL division. By making a strategic, well-planned decision to partner with the franchise, Knichel Logistics is now able to utilize BlueGrace Logistics' Web-based proprietary system and an online customer portal without having to invest the resources into a system of its own, while still keeping autonomy and staff. The big payoff though has been access to BlueGrace's vast carrier network and lower pricing, and the payoff shows in the financial results. As Knichel notes, "At the end of 2016, we saw a 40 percent growth over 2015 and almost 62 percent growth over 2014, our last full year before we became a BlueGrace franchise. And we beat our best year, which was 2013, by almost 17 percent."[7]

Depending on the product and company, sales jobs usually require individuals to perform all three tasks—order processing, creative selling, and missionary selling—to some degree.

The Personal Selling Process

Perhaps the most complex and challenging of these three sales tasks is creative selling. The creative salesperson is responsible for starting and following through on most of the steps in the personal selling process:

- *Prospecting and qualifying.* A salesperson must first have a potential customer, or prospect. **Prospecting** is the process of identifying potential customers. Salespeople find prospects through company personnel records, from social networking on sites such as LinkedIn, and customers, friends, and business associates. In **qualifying**, prospects must be assessed to determine whether they have the authority to buy and the ability to pay.

- *Approaching.* The *approach* refers to the first few minutes of a salesperson's contact with a qualified prospect. Because it affects the salesperson's credibility, the success of later stages depends on the prospect's first impression. A salesperson must, therefore, present a professional appearance and greet prospects in a manner that instills confidence.

- *Presenting and demonstrating.* Next, the salesperson makes a presentation, a full explanation of the product, its features, and its uses. Most important, the presentation links product benefits to the prospect's needs. A presentation may or may not include a demonstration.

- *Handling objections.* No matter what product is for sale, prospects will have some *objections*. At the very least, they may open the door to negotiate for discounts by objecting to price. Objections, however, not only indicate that the buyer is interested but also pinpoint the parts of the presentation that trouble the buyer.

- *Closing.* The most critical part of the selling process is the **closing**, in which the salesperson asks the prospect to buy the product. Successful salespeople recognize the signs that a customer is ready to buy. Prospects who start to figure out monthly payments are clearly indicating readiness to buy. Salespeople should then try to close the sale, either asking directly for the sale or implying a close indirectly. Questions such as "Could you take delivery Tuesday?" and "Why don't we start off with an initial order of 10 cases?" are implied closes. Indirect closes place the burden of rejecting the sale on the prospect, who may find it a little harder to say no.

- *Following up.* Follow-up is a key activity, especially in relationship marketing. For lasting relationships with buyers, good salespeople don't end the sales process with the closing. They want sales to be so successful that customers will buy from them again. Thus, they supply additional services, such as after-sale support that provides convenience and added value. Follow-ups include quick processing of customer orders, on-time delivery, speedy repair service, and timely answers to user questions.

Sales Promotions

Sales promotions are short-term promotional activities designed to encourage consumer buying, industrial sales, or cooperation from distributors. They can increase the likelihood that buyers will try products, enhance product recognition, and increase purchase size and sales revenues.

Successful sales promotions provide potential customers with convenience and accessibility when the decision to buy occurs. If Harley-Davidson holds a one-week motorcycle promotion but you, an interested buyer, have no local dealer and no access to a test ride, the promotion may be useless to you and so you won't buy a

Prospecting *step in the personal selling process in which salespeople identify potential customers*

Qualifying *step in the personal selling process in which salespeople determine whether prospects have the authority to buy and ability to pay*

Closing *step in the personal selling process in which salespeople ask prospective customers to buy products*

Sales Promotion *short-term promotional activity designed to encourage consumer buying, industrial sales, or cooperation from distributors*

Most home sales result from personal selling by a real estate agent to prospective home buyers. Even when people start their search for a home using online search sites they still tend to end up dealing with an individual agent to finalize their purchase.

Bst2012/Fotolia

Coupon *sales-promotion technique in which a certificate is issued entitling the buyer to a reduced price*

Premium *sales-promotion technique in which offers of free or reduced-price items are used to stimulate purchases*

Loyalty Programs *sales promotion technique in which frequent customers are rewarded for making repeat purchases*

Point-of-Sale (POS) Display *sales-promotion technique in which product displays are located in certain areas to stimulate purchase or to provide information on a product*

motorcycle. In contrast, if Tide detergent offers a $1-off coupon that you can save and use on your next trip to the supermarket, the promotion is both convenient and accessible for you.

Most consumers have taken part in a variety of sales promotions such as free *samples* (giveaways), which let customers try products without risk, and **coupon** promotions, which use certificates entitling buyers to discounts to encourage customers to try new products, lure them away from competitors, or induce them to repurchase (buy more of a product). Coupons are available from many sources, including newspapers, in mailings, and at checkout counters when shopping. Online coupon sites such as Coupons.com, CoolSavings.com, and Groupon provide access to printable cost-saving coupons and to some free coupons.

Premiums are free or reduced-price items, such as pencils, coffee mugs, and six-month low-interest credit cards, given to consumers in return for buying a specified product. *Contests* can boost sales by rewarding high-producing distributors and sales representatives with vacation trips to Hawaii or Paris. Consumers, too, may win prizes by entering their cats in the Purina Cat Chow calendar contest, for example, by submitting entry blanks from the backs of cat-food packages.

Loyalty programs reward frequent buyers for making repeat purchases. Oceania Cruises and Tauck (a tour company) offer vacation specials with significant price reductions to loyal customers. Online and mail promotions, for example, may announce two-for-one prices on upcoming cruises and reduced prices for upgrading to more luxurious accommodations. Tour specials may feature reduced airfares, along with free Internet access and shore excursions for repeat customers.

To grab customers' attention in stores, companies use **point-of-sale (POS) displays** at the ends of aisles or near checkout counters to ease finding products and to eliminate competitors from consideration. In addition to physical goods, POS pedestals also provide services, namely information for consumers. Some bank lobbies and physicians' waiting rooms, for example, have interactive kiosks inviting clients to learn more about bank products and educational information about available treatments on consumer-friendly touch-screen displays. For B2B promotions, industries sponsor **trade shows** in which companies rent booths to display and demonstrate products to customers who have a special interest or who are ready to buy.

Direct (or Interactive) Marketing

Direct (or interactive) marketing is one-on-one nonpersonal selling that tries to get consumers to make purchases away from retail stores and, instead, to purchase from home, at work, or using a mobile device. This fast-growing selling method includes nonstore retailers (catalogs, telemarketing, home video shopping), direct mail, direct response advertising (such as infomercials and direct response magazine and newspaper ads), and most important, online connections. When used by B2B businesses, direct marketing is primarily lead generation so a salesperson can close the sale where interest has been shown. In B2C businesses, it has primarily a selling goal. The advantage of direct marketing is that you can target the message to the individual and you can measure the results. For example, Amazon knows when you sign in who you are and what you have purchased in the past and makes recommendations based on your purchase history. And when you select a certain book title or other product, it can suggest additional titles that other buyers of your selection have also purchased and in that way potentially increase sales to you.

The Internet has clearly enhanced traditional direct marketing methods, especially direct mail. By using *permission marketing*, a form of e-mail where the consumer gives a company permission to contact them, a list of customers' e-mails is compiled and they are regularly contacted with special offers and deals based on their past purchases. The e-mail is coming from a company with which the consumer has experience and has agreed to receive their messages, and it contains a direct link to the company's website and the sale item. Companies such as Amazon, Dell, Gap, and Kate Spade are among those who have used this direct marketing method and technology successfully.

Publicity and Public Relations

Publicity is information about a company, a product, or an event transmitted by the general mass media to attract public attention. Although publicity is free, marketers have no control over the content media reporters and writers disseminate, and because it is presented in a news format, consumers often regard it as objective and credible. A classic publicity event occurred in 2005, for example: U.S. fast-food patrons were horrified when a customer said she found a human fingertip in a bowl of Wendy's chili. The publicity nightmare immediately bruised the food chain's reputation and cost about $15 million in lost sales in just six weeks.[8]

In contrast to publicity, **public relations** is company-influenced information that seeks either to build good relations with the public by publicizing the company's charitable contributions, for example, or to deal with unfavorable events. In the Wendy's case, then CEO Jack Schuessler's public relations response was decisive and focused: Protect the brand and tell the truth. That meant there would be no payoff or settlement to keep it out of the news. Instead, Wendy's enlisted the cooperation of the health department and police, did visual inspections, polygraphed employees, publicly announced a hotline for tips, and offered a reward for information, all leading to the conclusion that the reported episode was a hoax. Energetic public relations were an effective promotional tool for clearing the Wendy's name and preserving the company's reputation.[9]

Trade Show *sales-promotion technique in which various members of an industry gather to display, demonstrate, and sell products*

Direct (or Interactive) Marketing *one-on-one nonpersonal selling by nonstore retailers and B2B sellers using direct contact with prospective customers, especially via the Internet*

Publicity *promotional tool in which information about a company, a product, or an event is transmitted by the general mass media to attract public attention*

Public Relations *company-influenced information directed at building goodwill with the public or dealing with unfavorable events*

summary of learning objectives

OBJECTIVE 13-1

Explain the meaning of *distribution mix* and identify the different channels of distribution. (pp. 414–417)

The success of any product depends on its distribution mix: the combination of distribution channels for getting products to end users—consumers and industrial buyers. *Intermediaries* help to distribute a producer's goods by moving them to customers: *Wholesalers* sell products to other businesses, which resell them to final users. *Retailers*, on the other hand, sell products directly to end users. In the simplest of four distribution channels—the *direct channel*—the producer sells directly to the consumer or organizational buyer without intermediaries. In *retail distribution*, producers distribute products through retailers who, in turn, distribute to the consumer or industrial customer. *Wholesale distribution* involves both a wholesaler and then a retailer before the product reaches the end user. In the last type of distribution channel, a sales agent or a broker sells to the consumer or to the industrial customer. A disadvantage of channels with more intermediaries is higher prices because each intermediary charges a markup or commission. However, intermediaries can provide added value by supplying time-saving information and ensuring that products arrive at the right time and place.

In addition to selecting the distribution channel, marketers must select a *market coverage strategy*. *Intensive distribution* means distributing through as many channels and channel members as possible, and *exclusive distribution* occurs when the manufacturer grants the exclusive right to distribute or sell a product to a limited number of wholesalers or retailers, usually for a specific geographic area. Finally, *selective distribution* is a midpoint between intensive and exclusive; it is a strategy in which the producer selects a limited number of wholesalers and retailers to sell its product.

OBJECTIVE 13-2

Describe the role of wholesalers and the functions performed by e-intermediaries. (pp. 417–419)

Wholesalers provide a variety of services—delivery, credit arrangements, and product information—to buyers of products for resale or business use. In buying and reselling products, wholesalers provide storage and marketing advice, and they assist customers by marking prices and setting up displays. Most wholesalers are independent operations that sell goods produced by a variety of manufacturers. The largest group, *merchant wholesalers*, buys products from manufacturers and sells them to other businesses. They own the goods that they resell, store, and deliver. *Agents* and *brokers* work on commission and serve as independent sales representatives for many companies' products. Unlike wholesalers, agents and brokers do not own their merchandise. Rather, they serve as sales and merchandising arms for producers or sellers who do not have their own sales forces.

E-intermediaries are Internet-based channel members—wholesalers—who perform one or both of two functions: (1) they collect information about sellers and present it to consumers or (2) they help deliver online products to buyers. One type of e-intermediary, the *syndicated seller*, is a website that receives commissions for referring online customers to other companies' websites. *Shopping agents* (*e-agents*) help online customers—both industrial customers and consumers—by gathering and sorting information, identifying websites to visit, providing comparison prices, and identifying product features.

OBJECTIVE 13-3

Describe the different types of retailing and explain how online retailers add value for consumers on the Internet. (pp. 419–423)

Retail stores can be organized into three classifications: product-line retailers, bargain retailers, and convenience stores. Product-line retailers include department stores, supermarkets, and specialty stores. *Department stores* have specialized departments for different products. These stores offer a variety of services, such as credit plans and delivery. Similarly, *supermarkets* are divided into departments, and they stress low prices, self-service, and wide selection. In contrast, *specialty stores* are small, offering a full product line in narrow product fields, with knowledgeable sales personnel.

Bargain retailers include discount houses, catalog showrooms, factory outlets, and wholesale clubs. *Catalog showrooms* allow customers to view display samples, place orders, and receive purchases from attached warehouses. *Discount houses* offer a wide variety of products at low prices. *Factory outlets* are manufacturer-owned stores that avoid intermediaries by selling merchandise directly from factory to consumer. *Wholesale clubs* offer large discounts on a wide range of merchandise to customers who pay annual membership fees.

Convenience stores stress easily accessible locations, extended store hours, and speedy service. However, they generally do not feature low prices on most products.

Nonstore retailing includes *direct-response* firms that contact customers to receive sales orders. **Mail order** (or **catalog marketing**) is one form of direct-response retailing, as is outbound *telemarketing* that uses phone calls to sell directly to consumers. Finally, *direct selling* uses door-to-door sales and home-selling parties.

Online retailing provides the convenience of shopping anywhere using the Internet and includes *e-catalogs, electronic storefronts, cybermalls,* and *interactive and video* retailing. *E-catalogs* use online displays of products and product information, thus avoiding mail distribution and printing costs. Each seller's website is an *electronic storefront* where shoppers collect information about products, place orders, and pay for purchases. *Cybermalls* are collections of virtual storefronts where shoppers can navigate from a list of stores or product listings. *Video retailing* lets viewers shop at home from channels on their TVs. For TVs with Internet-ready capabilities, users can relax comfortably at home while shopping online with a large-screen visual display.

OBJECTIVE 13-4

Define *physical distribution* **and describe the major activities in the physical distribution process.** (pp. 423–425)

Physical distribution refers to the activities needed to move products from an intermediary or a manufacturer to customers and includes *warehousing* and *transportation operations*. Its purpose is to make goods available when and where customers want them, keep costs low, and provide services to satisfy customers.

Physical distribution activities include providing customer services, warehousing, and transportation of products. Storing, or *warehousing*, includes *private warehouses*, owned by a single firm that deals in mass quantities and needs regular storage. Independently owned *public warehouses* rent to companies only the space they need, often for storage needs during peak periods. To store digital assets, many companies and home users rely on remote off-site digital storage services to protect against losing data. In the event of physical catastrophe—floods, fires, earthquakes—at the client's facility, data can be restored online from the backup system.

Transportation operations physically move products from suppliers to customers. Differences in cost among the major transportation modes, trucks, railroads, planes, water carriers (boats and barges), digital transmission, and pipelines, are usually most directly related to delivery speed. *Trucks* are the most-used carriers of all modes of U.S. freight transportation. The advantages of trucks include flexibility for any-distance distribution, fast service, and dependability. *Planes* are the fastest and most expensive mode of transportation for physical goods. *Online transmission* of products in digital form is faster and less expensive than all other modes. Aside from digital transmission, transporting by *water carriers* is the least expensive mode, but also the slowest. *Railroads* can economically transport high-volume, heavy, bulky items, such as cars, steel, and coal. However, delivery routes are limited by fixed, immovable rail tracks. *Pipelines* are slow and lack flexibility and adaptability, but for specialized products, like liquids and gases, they provide economical and reliable delivery.

OBJECTIVE 13-5

Identify **the objectives of promotion and the considerations in selecting a promotional mix, and discuss the various kinds of advertising promotions.** (pp. 425–429)

Promotion refers to techniques for communicating information about products and is part of the *communication mix*, the total message any company sends to customers about its products.

Although the ultimate goal of any *promotion* is to increase sales, other goals include communicating information about the company and its products, positioning a product (establishing an identifiable image in the minds of consumers), adding value to distinguish a product from competing products, and controlling sales volume.

Once marketing objectives are clear, a firm must develop a promotional strategy to achieve them. A *pull strategy* appeals directly to consumers who will demand the product from retailers, whereas a *push strategy* occurs when a firm markets its products to wholesalers and retailers who then persuade customers to buy it. In deciding on the appropriate *promotional mix*—the best combination of promotional tools (e.g., advertising, personal selling, sales promotions, direct or interactive marketing, public relations)—marketers must consider the good or service being offered, characteristics of the target audience, the buyer's decision process, and the promotional mix budget. *Advertising* is paid, nonpersonal communication by which an identified sponsor informs an audience about a product. To better understand how consumers respond to ads, marketers use *real-time ad tracking* to find out who their customers are, to which media they pay attention, what messages appeal to them, and how to get their attention. Marketers use several different *advertising media*—specific communication devices for carrying a seller's message to potential customers—each having its advantages and drawbacks. TV is the most-used and most expensive U.S. medium, with the largest audience. The Internet is the fastest-growing medium because it can target specific audiences and its ad success can be measured, but it is also easy to ignore. Outdoor advertising, one of the least-used of major media, is among the least expensive but is limited in the information it presents and exposure time is brief. Other often-used media include newspapers (broad readership), direct mail (for targeted audience), radio (low ad cost), and magazines (often shared and reread). The combination of media through which a company advertises is called its *media mix*.

OBJECTIVE 13-6

Outline the tasks involved in personal selling and describe the various types of sales promotions. (pp. 429–433)

Personal selling is the oldest and most expensive form of promotion. Personal selling tasks include *order processing* (receiving an order and seeing to its handling and delivery), *creative selling* (providing information and demonstrating product benefits to persuade buyers), and *missionary selling* (activities that promote a company and its products). The first step in the personal selling process includes *prospecting* (identify potential customers) and *qualifying* (determining authority to buy and pay). The next step is *approaching* (initial moments of contact with prospect), followed by *presenting* and *demonstrating* (displaying and explaining the product and its use), *handling objections* (overcoming buyer problems), *closing* (asking the prospect to buy the product), and *following up* (supplying after-sales services).

Sales promotions are short-term promotional activities to encourage consumer buying, industrial sales, or cooperation from distributors. They can increase the likelihood that buyers will try products, enhance product recognition, and increase purchase size and sales revenues. Sales promotions include *point-of-sale (POS) displays* to attract consumer attention, help them find products in stores, offices, lobbies, and waiting rooms, and provide product information. *Loyalty programs* reward frequent buyers for past repeat purchases by giving them reduced prices, upgraded products, or other special considerations. Other sales promotions give purchasing incentives, such as *samples* (customers can try products without having to buy them), *coupons* (a certificate for price reduction to encourage customers to try new products, lure them away from competitors, or induce them to buy more of a product), and *premiums* (free or reduced-price rewards for buying products). At *trade shows*, B2B sellers rent booths to display products to industrial customers. *Contests* intend to stimulate sales, with prizes to high-producing intermediaries and consumers who use the seller's products.

The final element of the promotional mix is publicity and public relations. *Publicity* is information about a company, product, or event transmitted by the general mass media to attract public attention. Although publicity is free, marketers have no control over the content media reports ad writers disseminate, and because it is presented in a news format, consumers often regard it as objective and credible. In contrast to publicity, *public relations* is company-influenced information that seeks to build good relations with the public by publicizing the company's charitable contributions or to deal with unfavorable events.

key terms

advertising (p. 426)
advertising media (p. 428)
bargain retailer (p. 419)
broker (p. 415)
catalog showroom (p. 420)
channel captain (p. 417)
channel conflict (p. 417)
closing (p. 431)
convenience store (p. 420)
coupon (p. 432)
creative selling (p. 429)
cybermall (p. 422)
department store (p. 419)
direct (or interactive) marketing (p. 433)
direct channel (p. 414)
direct selling (p. 421)
direct-response retailing (p. 421)
discount house (p. 419)
distribution channel (p. 414)
distribution mix (p. 414)
drop shipper (p. 417)
e-catalog (p. 421)
e-intermediaries (p. 418)

electronic storefront (p. 422)
exclusive distribution (p. 416)
factory outlet (p. 420)
full-service merchant wholesaler (p. 417)
industrial selling (p. 429)
intensive distribution (p. 416)
intermediary (p. 414)
limited-function merchant wholesaler
    (p. 417)
loyalty program (p. 432)
mail order (catalog marketing) (p. 421)
media mix (p. 428)
merchant wholesaler (p. 417)
missionary selling (p. 429)
online retailing (p. 421)
order processing (p. 429)
personal selling (p. 429)
physical distribution (p. 423)
point-of-sale (POS) display (p. 432)
positioning (p. 425)
premium (p. 432)
private warehouse (p. 423)
promotion (p. 425)

promotional mix (p. 426)
prospecting (p. 431)
public relations (p. 433)
public warehouse (p. 423)
publicity (p. 433)
pull strategy (p. 426)
push strategy (p. 426)
qualifying (p. 431)
retail selling (p. 429)
retailer (p. 414)
sales agent (p. 415)
sales promotion (p. 431)
selective distribution (p. 416)
shopping agents (e-agents) (p. 419)
specialty store (p. 419)
supermarket (p. 419)
syndicated selling (p. 418)
telemarketing (p. 421)
trade show (p. 433)
video retailing (p. 422)
warehousing (p. 423)
wholesale club (p. 420)
wholesaler (p. 414)

MyLab Intro to Business

To complete the problems with the ✪, go to EOC Discussion Questions in the MyLab.

questions & exercises

QUESTIONS FOR REVIEW

✪ **13-1.** Describe the types of distribution channels that may be used to get products from manufacturers to end users, and give an example of each.

13-2. What are the three distribution strategies for market coverage? When is each most appropriate?

13-3. Compare each of the major modes of transportation and identify at least one advantage of each.

✪ **13-4.** Select four different kinds of advertising media and compare the advantages and disadvantages of each.

13-5. What are the steps in the personal selling process?

QUESTIONS FOR ANALYSIS

✪ **13-6.** Describe the four forms of non-store retailing. Give examples of products that would be most appropriate for each, and discuss the reasons why that product would do well with that particular form.

13-7. What are the major types of product line and bargain retailers? Identify at least one example of each type.

13-8. Identify the major tools of sales promotion. At which stage of the consumer buying process is each most important? Why?

APPLICATION EXERCISES

13-9. In addition to being a major online retailer, Amazon.com acts as an e-intermediary for many small to medium-sized businesses. Imagine that you are interested in selling refurbished cell phones. Using the information on Amazon's website, how would you become a seller on Amazon? What costs are associated with selling your products through Amazon? If you decided to sell your products through your own website instead, what would be the pros and cons?

13-10. Search for some of the best viral marketing videos of all time and choose one to analyze. What is the product being marketed, and who is the target market? How does the advertisement appeal to the target market? Why do you think this particular video was effective?

building a business: continuing team exercise

Assignment

Meet with your team members to consider your new business venture and how it relates to the marketing issues relating to distributing and promoting products, as discussed in this chapter. Develop specific responses to the following:

13-11. Consider once again the target market(s) for your business. For that target market, develop a "Statement of Promotional Objectives" for your company. What do you intend to accomplish with your chosen promotional objectives?

13-12. Considering your target market, discuss alternative promotional strategies that may be appropriate for your company. What are the pros and cons for each strategy you considered? Which strategy, at the present time, seems more favorable, and why?

13-13. Outline the elements for your promotional mix, including specific promotional tools to be included at the onset (opening) of your company. Rank, in order, the relative importance of each tool in your promotional efforts. How might those rankings change, if at all, after your company is better established?

13-14. Develop a preliminary design of your company's start-up distribution mix, including the reasons for your choices on distribution channels and physical distribution. Explain why (how) your chosen distribution mix is appropriately matched to your target market.

13-15. Estimate the costs required to implement the distribution mix and promotional mix, if those mixes are to be ready-to-go when your company opens for business.

team exercise

MAKING A DIFFERENCE

Team Activity

You and your team are students at Huge University, which has been hit with major budget cuts from state funding agencies as well as increased competition from state supported "free" colleges. The university is interested in expanding the incoming student body in order to offset the decreases in revenues and cost increases, such as increasing expenses for technology and student services. One of the programs the administration has chosen to promote is the Summer Away program. Through this program, students earn Huge college credits while studying in Europe, Asia, Africa, and South America. Over the course of a 10-week summer semester, students will earn 10–12 college credits and will work to improve a community in need through partnerships with programs such as Habitat for Humanity and the United Nations World Food Programme. Your team has been assembled to develop a promotional plan for the program,

with the goal of attracting 150 new students from across the country.

Action Steps

13-16. As a group, develop your promotional objectives. What are the initial objectives of your promotional campaign? Will these change over time?

13-17. What role will each element of the promotional mix play in your promotional plan?

13-18. Develop a one- to two-page recommendation that you could present to the university's leadership team. Remember to address the target audience (e.g., high school students, returning students, transfer students from community colleges, etc.).

13-19. Do you think that the promotional mix will change over time? How might it be different in three years? Be sure to address this in your proposal.

exercising your ethics

THE CHAIN OF RESPONSIBILITY

The Dilemma

A customer bought an expensive vase as wedding gift at a local store and asked that it be shipped to the bride in another state. Several months after the wedding, the buyer became concerned when she had not received a thank-you note from the happy couple. She contacted the bride, who indicated that

she never received the vase. Arguing that the merchandise had not been delivered, the customer requested a refund from the retailer.

However, the store manager uncovered the following facts:

- All shipments from the store were handled by a well-known national delivery firm.
- The delivery firm verified that the package had been delivered to the designated address two days after the sale.

- Normally, the delivery firm does not obtain recipient signatures; deliveries are made to the address of record, regardless of the name on the package.

The gift giver argued that even though the package had been delivered to the right address, it had not been delivered to the named recipient. It turns out that, unbeknownst to the gift giver, the bride and groom had moved. It stood to reason, then, that the gift was in the hands of the new occupant at the couple's former address. The manager informed the gift giver that the store had fulfilled its obligation. The cause of the problem, she explained, was the incorrect address given by the customer. She refused to refund the customer's money and suggested that the customer might want to recover the gift by contacting the stranger who received it at the couple's old address.

QUESTIONS TO ADDRESS

13-20. What are the responsibilities of each party—the customer, the store, and the delivery firm—in this situation?

13-21. From an ethical standpoint, in what ways is the store manager's action right? In what ways is it wrong?

13-22. If you were appointed to settle this matter, what actions would you take?

cases

THE CHANGING LANDSCAPE OF COMMERCE

Continued from page 414

At the beginning of this chapter, you read about the evolution of commerce in the United States, from small mom-and-pop stores to mega-malls and giant box outlets to e-commerce. Using the information presented in this chapter, you should now be able to answer the following questions:

QUESTIONS FOR DISCUSSION

13-23. Why are online retailers taking so much market share from the traditional brick-and-mortar stores?

13-24. Do you think that legacy stores such as Macy's and even Walmart will be able to compete with online stores in the future? How would they have to change in order to be more competitive?

13-25. How have changes in physical distribution changed the marketplace? How has the marketplace changed the distribution networks?

13-26. If everything were available to purchase online, would there still be products and services you would want to buy in person? How can online retailers become more competitive against traditional stores for items that people still prefer to buy in person?

THE LONG TAIL, REVISITED

Back in 2005, the editor of *Wired* Magazine, Chris Anderson, wrote a book called *The Long Tail: Why the Future of Business Is Selling Less of More*. He proposed that, because of the expansion of e-commerce, consumers now had access to an amazing array of products that traditional brick-and-mortar stores would never keep in stock. The term *long tail* refers to the long tapering off portion of the overall demand curve. Without the constraints of physical shelf space and with more access to distribution channels, narrowly-targeted goods and services can be as economically attractive as mainstream fare.

Anderson argued that traditional retail economics dictates that stores only stock the most popular items, because shelf space is expensive, but online retailers, like Amazon, can stock virtually everything, in theory. Amazon's apparent success in generating profits from its endless aisles of products has spurred many competitors to adopt long-tail strategies. However, Amazon doesn't stock all the specialty items itself—instead, Amazon offers a marketplace for long-tail items. In other words, Amazon focuses on directly selling and fulfilling high-demand products and leaves long-tail merchandise for its independent sellers to fulfill. Next time you are shopping on Amazon, take a look for yourself. Search for clothing, electronics, household items, or anything else of interest to you and try to sort out Amazon the store from Amazon the intermediary.

For the consumer, there is a definite up side to the long tail. Products that were previously unavailable in the open market are now available. For instance, a how-to book on breeding and raising gerbils may have been impossible to find before the "endless aisles" of the Internet, but now niche marketers can provide items that are extremely specific and that have an audience that may be scattered geographically. Niche sellers, even though they might be working out of a small home office, know their niche markets better, and they have better access to and relationships with niche suppliers. For Amazon though, allowing third-party sales on its website provides long-tail data that it can then use to directly offer products that have begun to sell well. Essentially, Amazon crowdsources its market research using demographic and sales data provided by the long-tail sellers.

QUESTIONS FOR DISCUSSION

13-27. What kinds of products do you think you would find in Anderson's "long tail"? Give examples.

13-28. Do you think the long tail theory is still applicable? Why, or why not?

13-29. Would you start a niche marketing business? If so, why and how would you market your products or services? If not, why not?

13-30. Do you think it is ethical for companies like Amazon to collect third-party data? How would you feel, and what would you do, if your product suddenly became mainstream and Amazon started carrying it, selling it, and fulfilling those sales? What are the issues? What are the pros and cons?

crafting a business plan

PART 4: PRINCIPLES OF MARKETING

Goal of the Exercise

So far, your business has an identity, you've described the factors that will affect your business, and you've examined your employees, the jobs they'll be performing, and the ways in which you can motivate them. Part 4 of the business plan project asks you to think about marketing's Four Ps—*product, price, place (distribution),* and *promotion*—and how they apply to your business. You'll also examine how you might target your marketing toward a certain group of consumers.

Exercise Background: Part 4 of the Business Plan

In Part 1, you briefly described what your business will do. The first step in Part 4 of the plan is to more fully describe the product (good or service) you are planning to sell. Once you have a clear picture of the product, you'll need to describe how this product will "stand out" in the marketplace—that is, how will it differentiate itself from other products?

In Part 1, you also briefly described who your customers would be. The first step in Part 4 of the plan is to describe your ideal buyer, or target market, in more detail, listing his or her income level, educational level, lifestyle, age, and so forth. This part of the business plan project also asks you to discuss the price of your products, as well as where the buyer can find your product.

Finally, you'll examine how your business will get the attention and interest of the buyer through its *promotional mix*—advertising, personal selling, sales promotions, and publicity and public relations.

This part of the business plan encourages you to be creative. Have fun! Provide as many details as you possibly can because this reflects an understanding of your product and your buyer. Marketing is all about finding a need and filling it. Does your product fill a need in the marketplace?

Your Assignment

STEP 1

Open the saved *Business Plan* file you began working on in Parts 1 to 3.

STEP 2

For the purposes of this assignment, you will answer the following questions in "Part 4: Principles of Marketing":

13-31. Describe your target market in terms of age, education level, income, and other demographic variables.

Hint: Refer to Chapter 11 for more information on the aspects of target marketing and market segmentation that you may want to consider. Be as detailed as possible about who you think your customers will be.

13-32. Describe the features and benefits of your product or service.

Hint: As you learned in Chapter 11, a product is a bundle of attributes—features and benefits. What features does your product have—what does it look like and what does it do? How will the product benefit the buyer?

13-33. How will you make your product stand out in the crowd?

Hint: There are many ways to stand out in the crowd, such as a unique product, outstanding service, or a great location. What makes your great idea special? Does it fill an unmet need in the marketplace? How will you differentiate your product to make sure that it succeeds?

13-34. What pricing strategy will you choose for your product, and what are the reasons for this strategy?

Hint: Refer to Chapter 12 for more information on pricing strategies and tactics. Because your business is new, so is the product. Therefore, you probably want to choose between price skimming and penetration pricing. Which will you choose, and why?

13-35. Where will customers find your product or service? (That is, what issues of the distribution mix should you consider?)

Hint: If your business does not sell its product directly to consumers, what types of retail stores will sell your product? If your product will be sold to another business, which channel of distribution will you use? Refer to this chapter for more information on aspects of distribution you may want to consider.

13-36. How will you advertise to your target market? Why have you chosen these forms of advertisement?

Hint: Marketers use several different advertising media—specific communication devices for carrying a seller's message to potential customers—each having its advantages and drawbacks. Refer to this chapter for a discussion of the types of advertising media you may wish to consider here.

13-37. What other methods of promotion will you use, and why?

Hint: There's more to promotion than simple advertising. Other methods include personal selling, sales promotions, and publicity and public relations. Refer to the discussion of promotion in this chapter for ideas on how to promote your product that go beyond just advertising.

Note: Once you have answered the questions, save your Word document. You'll be answering additional questions in later chapters.

Writing Assignments

13-38. How has the physical distribution of goods changed in the last 20 years? How has this impacted retailers and how have these changes changed the very nature of the marketplace? Is this a global change, or is it localized? Why?

13-39. Marketing promotions refer to methods for communicating information for various purposes about products, including the product's "value-added" benefits. Discuss in an essay why a firm promotes its product's "value-added" benefits. Then, use an example of promoting a service product to illustrate and support your argument. Finally, use an example for promoting a physical good to illustrate and support your argument.

endnotes

1 Peterson, Hayley, "A giant wave of store closures is about to hit the US," Business Insider, December 31, 2016, http://www.businessinsider.com/stores-closing-macys-kohls-walmart-sears-2016-12 (accessed April 23, 2017).

2 "For filling an ignored food gap." *Fast Company*. No 193: 128; *Business Source Premier*, EBSCO*host* (accessed May 20, 2015). "Jose Manuel, Founder and CEO of Algramo, Is the Venture Social Entrepreneur Contender from Chile," Venture.com, n.d. Web. 12 June 2015. https://www.theventure.com/global/en/finalists/algramo

3 *AVON 2016 Annual Report*, at http://investor.avoncompany.com/phoenix.zhtml?c=90402&p=irol-reportsannual

4 "Ecommerce Sales Topped $1 Trillion for the First Time in 2012," *eMarketer*, February 5, 2013, at http://www.emarketer.com/Article/Ecommerce-Sales-Topped-1-Trillion-First-Time-2012/1009649

5 Nat Ives, "Consumers Are Bugged By Many Ads," *Advertising Age*, December 1, 2008, p. 6.

6 "Ads Now Watching Shoppers," *Columbia Daily Tribune* (Associated Press), February 3, 2009, p. 7B.

7 "A creative business solution guides Knichel Logistics to success," Smart Business, April 1, 2017, http://www.sbnonline.com/article/creative-business-model-gives-knichel-logistics-right-answer/3/ (accessed April 23, 2017).

8 Associated Press, "New Arrest in Wendy's Finger Case," *MSNBC.com* (May 19, 2005), at http://www.msnbc.msn.com/id/7844274

9 Ron Insana, "Wendy's Knew from Start Story Was a Hoax," *USA Today* (June 5, 2005), at http://www.usatoday.com/money/companies/management/2005-06-05-insana-wendys_x.htm

PART 5 | MANAGING INFORMATION FOR BETTER BUSINESS DECISIONS

chapter 14

Information Technology (IT) for Business

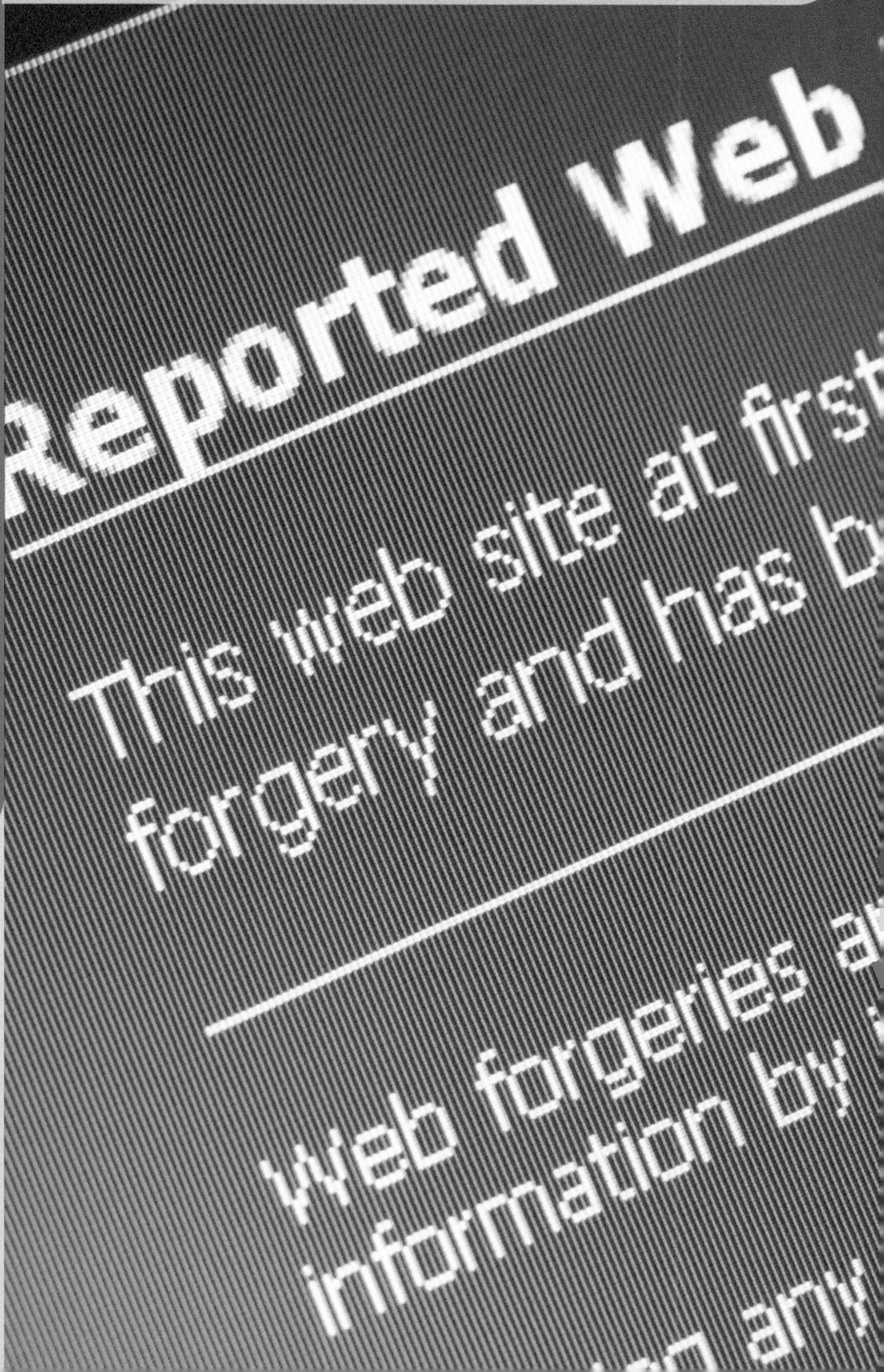

ICP/Incamerastock/Alamy Stock Photo

Engineers alone do not design new products. Customers, marketing strategists, financial experts, **production** managers, and purchasing specialists use **technology** **to** **collaborate** **in** **ways** that seemed impossible just a few years ago.

After reading this chapter, you should be able to:

14-1 **Discuss** the impacts information technology is having on the business world.

14-2 **Identify** the IT resources businesses have at their disposal and how these resources are used.

14-3 **Describe** the role of information systems, the different types of information systems, and how businesses use such systems.

14-4 **Identify** the threats and risks information technology poses to businesses.

14-5 **Describe** the ways in which businesses protect themselves from the threats and risks information technology poses.

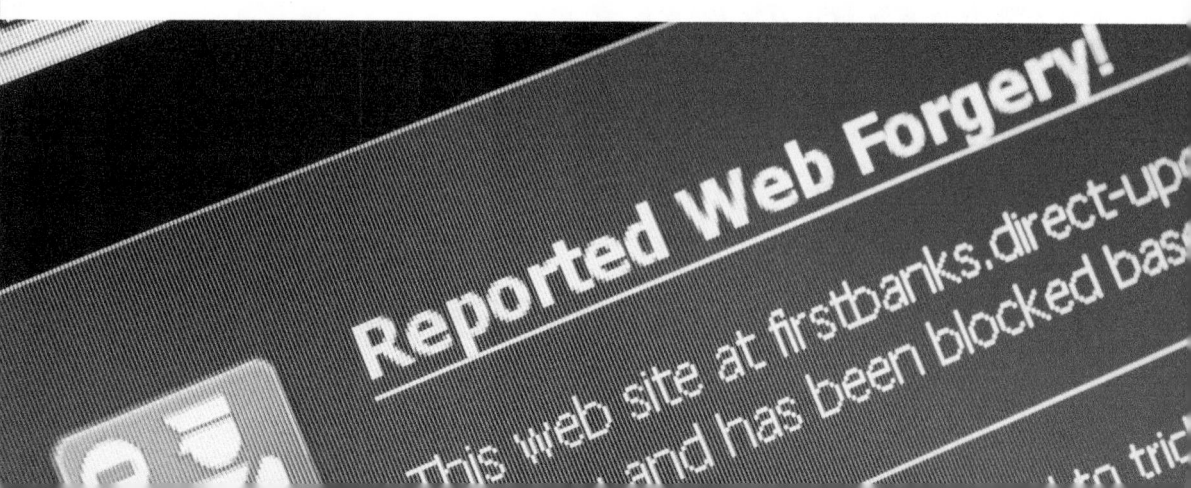

Reported Web Forgery!

This web site at firstbanks.direct-up... and has been blocked bas...

Think Before You Click

"Start a 'work-at-home' job as an "international sales representative" or a 'shipping manager,' with excellent pay. Simply open a new bank account in your name, accept money transfers into the account, then forward the money to our customers at locations around the globe." For the unemployed, under-employed, and dissatisfied workers, an e-mail like this can be quite appealing. Of course, it's unlikely to be legitimate. In this kind of scam, the new "employee" provides anonymous racketeers a safe way to launder stolen or otherwise illegal money. Then, as money transfers arrive, the mule relays them (illegally) to a global network of recipient racketeers.

As these frauds age, they become less and less effective, but the very nature of the Internet creates an almost infinite array of risks. As soon as one scam stops working, con artists are creating ever more sophisticated traps to take their place. For instance, criminals posing as employers contact individuals who have posted their resumes online. They conduct an interview, often electronically, and make the job hunter the offer of a great job. All that's left is collecting a little information, such as the person's Social Security number. Unfortunately, there's really no company and no job, but your Social Security number, as well as other personal information, can be used to apply for credit cards that will never get paid. Before you share information like your Social Security number, be sure to know who is at the other end of an e-mail. Do some research and make sure that the company is legitimate and that the person with whom you are exchanging e-mails is really an employee.

In one popular work-at-home scam, the unsuspecting victim (the new online "employee") cashes checks sent from the "employer" in a foreign country and gets to keep 10 percent of the cash as a payment for service. The remaining 90 percent is sent via Western Union back to the employer. Because the checks are bogus, they bounce, and the victim must repay the full amounts to the bank. Alerting the public to another scam, SC Johnson, the company that makes household products such as Raid, Windex, and Pledge furniture cleaner, warned of phony online job offers for work-at-home customer service jobs falsely using the Johnson name. The scammers say the job pays trainees $20 an hour initially, advancing to $25 after training, but employees must first buy some training software—which, of course, they pay for but never receive.

To protect yourself from cyber criminals when looking for a job, there are a couple of red flags that should alert you that something that's not quite right. These cyber criminals are not human resource professionals, so you may notice spelling or grammatical errors in e-mails. While mistakes can happen, this

what's in it for me?

Protecting against cyber-attacks is an extreme example of the way the Internet and related technologies are reshaping the business landscape. But even the most traditional businesses must change with the times, whether those times are defined by paper and pencil, telephone and fax machine, or digital language translators and smartphones and smartwatches. Indeed, it may seem like the times are changing more rapidly with each passing year, and it is in this context that our discussion of the various kinds of information technology, their functions, and the benefits and risks associated with each assumes particular importance. By understanding the material in this chapter, you'll have a clearer picture of how technology is used by and affects business and how you can use it to your best advantage—as an employee, investor, manager, or a business owner.

is a potential red flag that the communication is not legitimate. Similarly, if an offer seems too good to be true, it probably is. If you're offered a job, but required to pay money up front, there's a good chance that the offer is not legit. Finally, offers that are very time pressured are more likely to be fraudulent. Criminals don't want you to take the time to think through a bad deal and will encourage you to "act now" before this offer goes away.

Obviously, it's not just job hunters who face risks. Text messages saying victims' credit cards have been deactivated lure bank customers into relaying account information to an unknown sender. Internet-based phone users receiving fake caller IDs of real hospitals, government agencies, banks, and other businesses in a now-popular form of telephone phishing that talks victims into revealing personal information. Perhaps most impressive, cyber-thieves are using marketing techniques—most notably "targeting"—to reach specific audiences. Also known as "spear phishing," with targeting, scammers do research to identify wealthy individuals, families, and professional money managers. Victims receive friendly sounding e-mails and social networking contacts containing contaminated attachments that, once opened, infect their computers, exposing bank account and other identity information to scammers. Although computer security devices—spam filters, data encryption, firewalls, and anti-virus software—catch a vast number of intrusions, the threat remains.[1] Recently, Google Docs suffered from an invasion of hackers who were able to use an app to trick users into opening a document from a trusted source that then gave the intruders access to the users' contact lists and possibly other confidential information contained in each person's Google Docs folder. It looked legitimate and although Google took corrective action within hours, much damage had already been done.

Organizations, too, are victims of cyber invasions: Security consultants say that global cyber-attacks originating in China, and known as Night Dragon, have invaded computers of oil companies, stealing information on competitive bidding, financing, and operations practices. Some governments, to save money, are actively scamming others, using hackers to steal technology secrets for leading-edge military equipment, including defense systems of other countries. Organizations of all kinds are finding cyber security more difficult as more and more employees use their personal phones and computers for conducting business. Organizational information, then, is more widely dispersed and increasingly susceptible to intrusion via mobile-phone malware, virus-contaminated applications, and links containing spyware sent from text messages.[2] (After studying the content in this chapter, you should be able to answer a set of discussion questions found at the end of the chapter.)

Information Technology Impacts: A Driver of Changes for Business

OBJECTIVE 14-1
Discuss
the impacts information technology is having on the business world.

Information Technology (IT) *various appliances and devices for creating, storing, exchanging, and using information in diverse modes, including visual images, voice, multimedia, and business data*

The effect of **information technology (IT)** on business cannot be overstated. In fact, IT—the various appliances and devices for creating, storing, exchanging, and using information in diverse modes, including visual images, voice, multimedia, and business data—has altered the very foundations of all organizations, radically changing the way people inside and outside those organizations interact. We see ads everywhere for the latest cell phones, iPads, laptops, tablets, and smartphones, and most of us go online daily without even thinking about what we are doing. E-mail has become a staple in business—and is now seen as a bit old fashioned among many younger people—and even such traditionally "low-tech" businesses as nail salons and garbage collection companies are dependent on online connectivity, computers, and networks. As consumers, we interact with databases of IT networks every time we move money between accounts, order food at McDonald's, or check on the status of a package at UPS.com. Technology and its effects are evident everywhere.

E-commerce (short for *electronic commerce*), the use of online networks and other electronic means for retailing and business-to-business transactions, has created new market relationships around the globe. In this section, we'll look at how businesses are using IT to bolster productivity, improve operations and processes, create new opportunities, and communicate and work in ways not possible until just a few years ago.

E-commerce *use of the Internet and other electronic means for retailing and business-to-business transactions*

Creating Portable Offices: Providing Remote Access to Instant Information

IT devices such as Samsung mobile phones and Apple iPhones, along with IBM wireless Internet access and PC-style office applications, save businesses time and travel expenses by enabling employees, customers, and suppliers to communicate from any location. IT's mobile messaging capabilities mean that geographic separation between the workplace and headquarters is no longer a barrier to getting things done. Employees no longer work only at the office or the factory, nor are all of a company's operations performed at one place—people take their offices with them. When using such devices, off-site employees have continuous access to information, instead of being forced to be at a desk to access their work and work-related data and information. Client project folders, e-mail, and voice messaging are accessible from virtually any location.

Enabling Better Service by Coordinating Remote Deliveries

With access to the Internet, company activities may be geographically scattered but still remain coordinated through a networked system that provides better service for customers. Many businesses, for example, coordinate activities from one centralized location, but their deliveries flow from several remote locations, often at lower cost. When you order furniture—for example, a chair, a sofa, a table, and two lamps—from an online storefront, the chair may come from a warehouse in Philadelphia and the lamps from a manufacturer in California; the sofa and table may be shipped direct from different suppliers in North Carolina. Beginning with the customer's order, activities are coordinated through the company's network, as if the whole

Planetpix/White House Photo/Alamy Stock Photo

Top government leaders like the president and his advisors and colleagues use advanced technology and encrypted systems for secure messaging.

order were being processed at one place. This avoids the expensive in-between step of first shipping all the items to a central location.

Creating Leaner, More Efficient Organizations

Networks and technology are also leading to leaner companies with fewer employees and simpler structures. Because networks enable firms to maintain information linkages among both employees and customers, more work and customer satisfaction can be accomplished with fewer people. Bank customers connect into a 24-hour information system and monitor their accounts without employee assistance. Instructions that once were given to assembly workers by supervisors are now delivered to workstations electronically. IT communications provide better use of employee skills and greater efficiencies from physical resources. For example, truck drivers used to return to a shipping terminal to receive instructions from supervisors on reloading freight for the next delivery. Today, one dispatcher using IT has replaced several supervisors. Instructions to the fleet arrive on electronic screens in trucks on the road so drivers know in advance the next delivery schedule, and satellite navigation services, such as the SiriusXM NavTraffic, alert drivers of traffic incidents ahead so they can reroute to avoid delivery delays.[3]

Enabling Increased Collaboration

Collaboration among internal units and with outside firms is greater when firms use collaboration (collaborative) software and other IT communications devices, which we'll discuss later in this chapter. Companies are learning that complex problems can be better solved through IT-supported collaboration, either with formal teams or spontaneous interaction among people and departments. The design of new products, for example, was once an engineering responsibility; now it is a shared activity using information from customers, along with people in marketing, finance, production, engineering, and purchasing, who collectively determine the best design. For example, the design of Boeing's 787 Dreamliner aircraft is the result of collaboration not just among engineers but also with passengers (who wanted electric outlets to recharge personal digital devices), cabin crews (who wanted more bathrooms and wider aisles), and air-traffic controllers (who wanted larger, safer air brakes).

This Boeing aircraft was the result of collaboration among Boeing engineers, suppliers, and customers.

TonyV3112/Shutterstock

Although the 787 suffered from some initial design flaws, solutions involved a world-wide network of technical collaboration among Boeing engineers, suppliers, customers, and NASA, and now the 787 has become a major business success for Boeing.[4]

Enabling Global Exchange

The global reach of IT enables business collaboration on a scale that was once unheard of. Consider Lockheed Martin's contract for designing and supplying thousands of Joint Strike Fighters in different versions for the United States, Britain, Italy, Denmark, Canada, and Norway. Lockheed can't do the job alone—over the project's 20-year life, more than 1,500 firms will supply everything from radar systems to engines to bolts. In just the start-up phase, Lockheed collaborated with Britain's BAE Systems along with more than 70 U.S. and 18 international subcontractors at some 190 locations, including an Australian manufacturer of aviation communications and a Turkish electronics supplier. In all, 40,000 remote computers are collaborating on the project using Lockheed's online system. Digital collaboration on a massive scale is essential for coordinating design, testing, and construction at this level while avoiding delays, holding down costs, and maintaining quality.[5]

Improving Management Processes

IT has also changed the nature of the management process. The activities and methods of today's manager differ significantly from those that were common just a few years ago. At one time, for instance, upper-level managers didn't concern themselves with all of the detailed information filtering upward from the workplace because it was expensive to gather, the collection and recording process was cumbersome, and information quickly became out of date. Most day-to-day management was delegated to middle and first-line managers.

With digital processing of databases, specialized software, and interactive networks, however, instantaneous information is accessible and useful to all levels of management. For example, consider *enterprise resource planning (ERP)*, which is an information system for organizing and managing a firm's activities across product lines, departments, and geographic locations. The ERP stores real-time information on work status and upcoming transactions and notifies employees when action is required if certain schedules are to be met. It coordinates internal operations with activities of outside suppliers and notifies customers of upcoming deliveries and billings. Consequently, more managers routinely use it for planning and controlling companywide operations. Today, a manager at Hershey Foods, for example, uses ERP to check on the current status of any customer order for Kisses or strawberry Twizzlers, inspect productivity statistics for each workstation, and analyze the delivery performance on any shipment. Managers can better coordinate companywide performance. They can identify departments that are working well together and those that are lagging behind schedule and creating bottlenecks.

Providing Flexibility for Customization

IT advances also create new manufacturing and service capabilities that enable businesses to offer customers greater variety, customizable options, and faster delivery cycles. Whether it's an iPhone app or a Rawlings baseball glove, today's design-it-yourself world is possible through fast, flexible manufacturing using IT networks. At Ponoko.com, you can design and make just about anything, from electronics to furniture. Buyers and materials suppliers, meeting virtually, have rapidly generated thousands of product designs online. The designs can be altered to suit each buyer's tastes. Similarly, at San Francisco–based Timbuk2's website, you can "build your own" custom messenger bag at different price levels with your choice of size, fabric, color combination, accessories, liner material, strap, and even left- or right-hand access.[6] This principle of **mass customization** allows companies to produce in large volumes, and IT allows each item to feature the unique options the customer prefers. With IT, the old standardized assembly line has become quickly adaptable because workers

Mass Customization *principle in which companies produce in large volumes, but each item features the unique options the customer prefers*

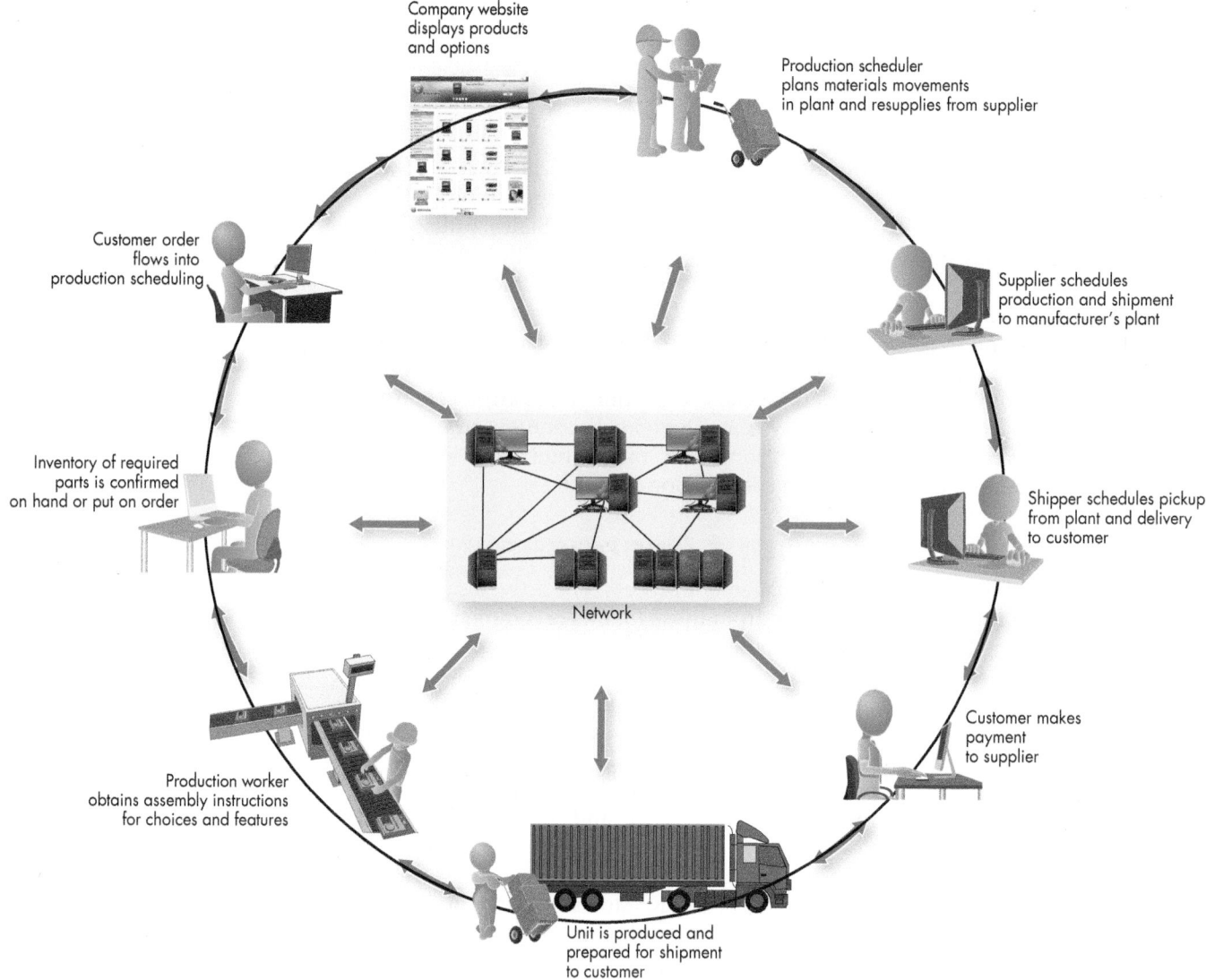

FIGURE 14.1 Networking for Mass Customization of a Physical Product

have instantaneous access to assembly instructions for all the product options, and equipment can be changed quickly for each customer's order.

As shown in Figure 14.1, flexible production and speedy delivery depend on an integrated network of information to coordinate all the activities among customers, manufacturers, suppliers, and shippers.

Service industries, too, including health care, banking, and recreation, are emphasizing greater flexibility for meeting customers' needs. Personalized pet care at HappyPetCare.net, for example, relies on IT for scheduling customized activities—dog walking, pet boarding, pet sitting, house-sitting, pet taxis, and other services. In tourism, at OceaniaCruises.com, passengers have flexibility for selecting personalized onboard services for meals, recreation and entertainment activities, educational classes, and spa treatments. Passengers can also customize their air travel schedules along with personalized pre- and post-cruise land programs.

Providing New Business Opportunities

Not only is IT improving existing businesses, it also is creating entirely new businesses where none existed before. For big businesses, this means developing new products, offering new services, and reaching new clients. Only a few years ago, today's multibillion-dollar behemoth known as Google was a fledgling search engine.

That company now boasts not just a search engine but hundreds of services, including virtual maps, YouTube video, Twitter accounts, Facebook pages, instant messaging, Gmail (Google's e-mail service), and online voicemail and software services such as photo editing, cloud storage, and document creation.

IT-based industries, including computer backup and identity-theft protection, offer valuable services for individuals and business customers. Online backup protects against data loss resulting from hard-drive crashes, fire, flood, and other causes. Carbonite.com and Backblaze.com, for example, provide automatic continuous backup so clients can recover lost data quickly. For guarding against identity theft, firms such as LifeLock.com and IdentityGuard.com protect personal information by alerting clients to various information-theft risks and sending advice on steps for avoiding identity theft.

The IT landscape has also presented home-based businesses with new e-business opportunities. Consider Richard Smith. His love for stamp collecting began at age seven. Now, some 50 years after saving that first stamp, he's turned his hobby into a profitable eBay business. Each day begins at the PC in his home office, scanning eBay's listings for items available and items wanted by sellers and buyers around the world. With more than 6,000 sales transactions to date, Richard maintains a perfect customer rating and has earned more than $4,000 on each of several eBay transactions. Today, thousands of online marketplaces allow entrepreneurs to sell directly to consumers, bypassing conventional retail outlets, and enable business-to-business (B2B) selling and trading with access to a worldwide customer base. To assist start-up businesses, eBay's services network is a ready-made online business model, not just an auction market. Services range from credit financing to protection from fraud and misrepresentation, information security, international currency exchanges, and postsales management. These features enable users to complete sales transactions, deliver merchandise, and get new merchandise for future resale, all from the comfort of their own homes. Many eBay users, like Richard Smith, have carved profitable new careers for themselves with the help of these systems.

Improving the World and Our Lives

Can advancements in IT really make the world a better place? Developments in smartphones, social networking, home entertainment, automobile safety, and other applications have certainly brought enjoyment and convenience to the everyday lives of millions of people around the globe. Extending technology beyond previous model cell phones and PCs, new technologies provide access to endless choices of *apps* (shorthand for *application software*), allowing each user to "build it your way," depending on what you want your device to do and how and where you'll be using it. Apps for computers and smartphones include *programs* for learning languages, music, work, games, traveling, art, and almost any other area of interest. Just two years after its opening, Apple's App Store had supplied more than 40 billion app downloads worldwide to users of Macs, iPhones, iPads, and iPod touches. And that number has continued to grow steadily in the years since.

Social networking, a valuable service for individuals and organizations, is made possible by IT. The many forms of social media—blogs, chats, and networks such as LinkedIn, Twitter, and Facebook—are no longer just playthings for gossips and hobbyists. They're also active tools for getting a job. When the economic meltdown hit in 2009, millions of job seekers turned to online networking—tapping leads from friends, colleagues, and acquaintances—for contacts with companies that might have been hiring. Peers and recruiters are networking using electronic discussion forums and bulletin boards at websites of professional associations and trade groups, technical schools, and alumni organizations. Some social sites provide occupation-specific career coaching and job tips. Scientists connect with Epernicus, top managers use Meet the Boss, and graduate students are connecting with Graduate Junction.[7]

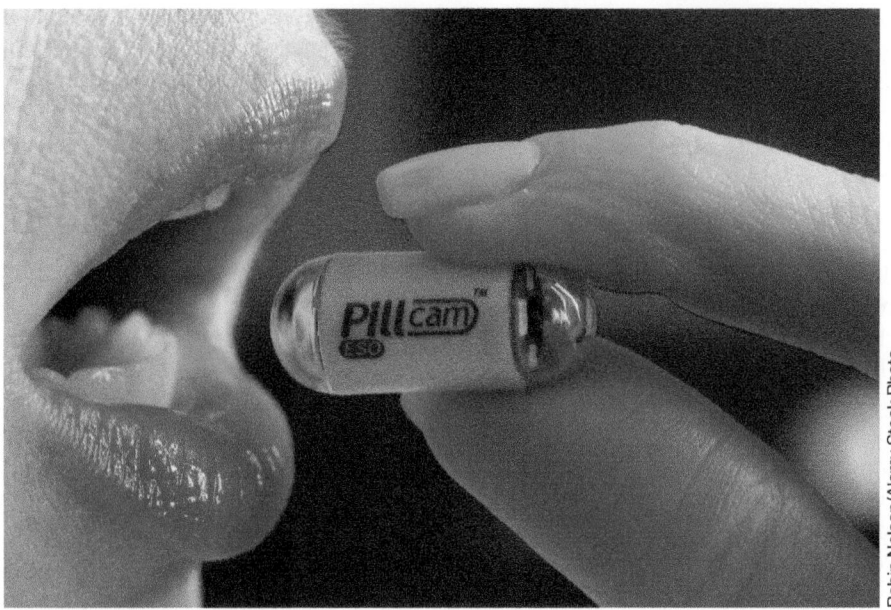

After this capsule is swallowed, the camera inside it can transmit almost 50,000 images during its eight-hour journey through the digestive tract.

Organizations, too, including hospitals and medical equipment companies, have embraced IT advancements to provide better services. For example, when treating combat injuries, surgeons at Walter Reed National Military Medical Center in Bethesda, Maryland, rely on high-tech imaging systems that convert two-dimensional photographs of their patients' anatomies into three-dimensional (3D) physical models for presurgical planning. These 3D mockups of shoulders, femurs, and facial bones give doctors the opportunity to see and feel the anatomy as it will be seen in the operating room, before they even use their scalpels. Meanwhile, pill-sized cameras that patients swallow are providing doctors with images of the insides of the human body, helping them make better diagnoses for such ailments as ulcers and cancer.[8]

OBJECTIVE 14-2
Identify
the IT resources businesses
have at their disposal and how
these resources are used.

IT Building Blocks: Business Resources

Businesses today have a wide variety of IT resources at their disposal. In addition to the Internet and e-mail, these include communications technologies, networks, hardware devices, and software, as shown at technology media sites such as informationweek.com.

The Internet and Other Communication Resources

Internet *gigantic system of interconnected computer networks linked together by voice, electronic, and wireless technologies*

Hypertext Transfer Protocol (HTTP) *communications protocol used for the World Wide Web, in which related pieces of information on separate Web pages are connected using hyperlinks*

World Wide Web *branch of the Internet consisting of interlinked hypertext documents, or Web pages*

The **Internet** is a gigantic global system of interconnected computer networks belonging to millions of collaborating organizations and agencies—government, business, academic, and public—linked together by voice, electronic, and wireless technologies.[9] Computers within the networks are connected by various communications protocols, or standardized coding systems, such as the **hypertext transfer protocol (HTTP)**, which is used for the **World Wide Web**, a branch of the Internet consisting of interlinked hypertext documents, or Web pages. Other protocols serve a variety of purposes, such as sending and receiving e-mail. The World Wide Web and its protocols provide the common language that allows information sharing on the Internet. For most businesses the Internet has replaced the telephone, fax machine, and standard mail as the primary communications tool. The Internet has also spawned a number of other business communications technologies, including *intranets*, *extranets*, *electronic conferencing*, and *VSAT satellite communications*.

Intranets Many organizations have extended Internet technology by maintaining what are essentially internal websites linked throughout the business. These private networks, or **intranets**, are accessible only to employees (and others who may be granted access) and may contain confidential information on benefits programs, a learning library, production management tools, product design resources, and so forth. The Ford Motor Company's intranet is accessible to approximately 200,000 people daily at workstations in Asia, Europe, and the United States. In addition to Ford employees, this intranet is accessible to Ford dealers and suppliers around the world. Sharing information on engineering, distribution, and marketing has reduced the lead time for getting new models into production and has shortened customer delivery times.[10]

Intranet organization's private network of internally linked websites accessible only to employees

Extranets **Extranets** are similar to intranets but allow more outsiders limited access to a firm's internal information network. The most common application allows buyers to enter a system to see which products are available for sale and delivery, thus providing convenient product availability information. Industrial suppliers are often linked into customers' information networks so that they can see planned production schedules and prepare supplies for customers' upcoming operations. The extranet at Nucor Steel, for example, lets customers shop electronically through its storage yards and gives them electronic access to Nucor's planned inventory of industrial steel products. Service industries, too, allow customers access to supplies of available services. For example, tour providers such as Tauck, Globus, and Viking River Cruises rely on major airlines such as Delta to provide flights for tour customers. By connecting into Delta's future flight schedules, tour companies can reserve blocks of flight seats to accommodate tourists.

Extranet system that allows outsiders limited access to a firm's internal information network

Electronic Conferencing **Electronic conferencing** allows groups of people to communicate simultaneously from various locations via e-mail, phone, or video, thereby eliminating travel time and providing immediate contact. One form, called *data conferencing*, allows people in remote locations to work simultaneously on one document. *Video conferencing* allows participants to see one another on digital

Electronic Conferencing IT that allows groups of people to communicate simultaneously from various locations via e-mail, phone, or video

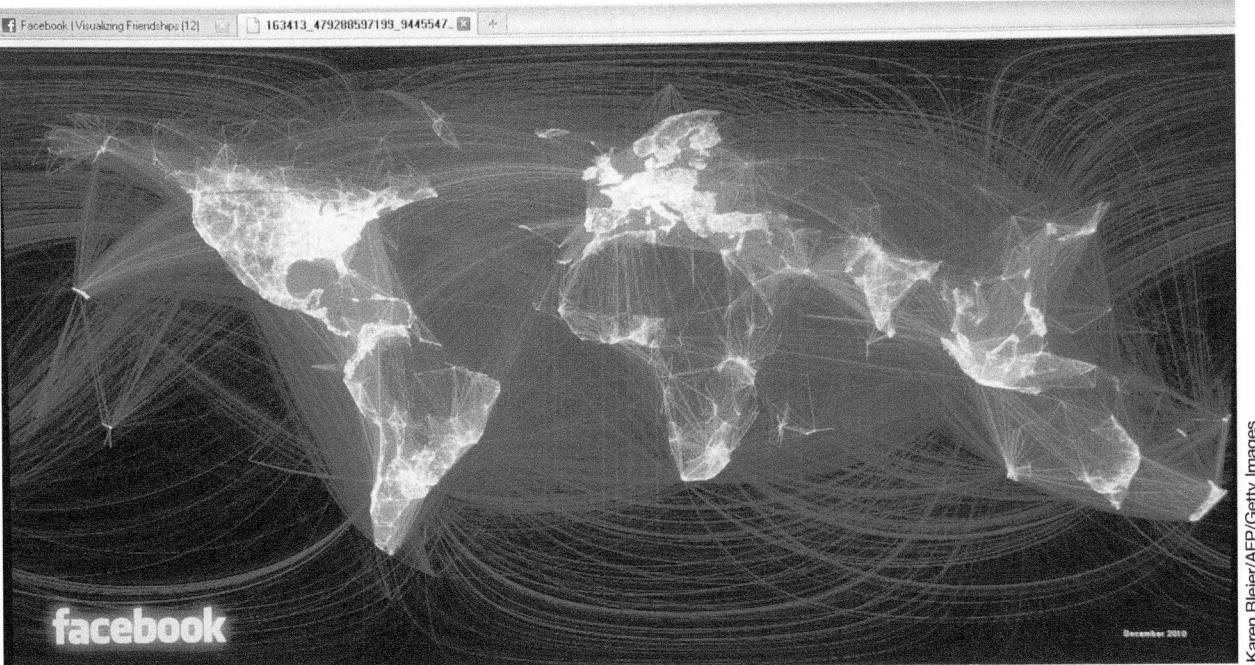

In this map of the Internet, from The Opte Project, each line represents a connection between computers or other network devices.

screens while the conference is in progress. For example, Lockheed Martin's Joint Strike Fighter project, discussed previously, uses online collaboration systems with both voice and video capabilities. Although separated by oceans, partners can communicate as if they were in the same room for redesigning components and production schedules. Electronic conferencing is attractive to many businesses because it eliminates travel and saves time and money.

VSAT Satellite Communications Another Internet technology businesses use to communicate is **VSAT satellite communications**. VSAT (short for *very small aperture terminal*) systems have a transmitter-receiver (*transceiver*) that sits outdoors with a direct line of sight to a satellite. The hub, a ground-station computer at the company's headquarters, sends signals to and receives signals from the satellite, exchanging voice, video, and data transmissions. An advantage of VSAT is privacy. A company that operates its own VSAT system has total control over communications among its facilities, no matter their location, without dependence on other companies. A firm might use VSAT to exchange sales and inventory information, advertising messages, and visual presentations between headquarters and store managers at remote sites. For example, offices in Minneapolis, London, and Boston might communicate with headquarters in New York, sending and receiving information via a satellite, as shown in Figure 14.2.

Networks: System Architecture

A **computer network** is a group of two or more computers linked together, either hardwired or wirelessly, to share data or resources, such as a printer. The most common type of network used in businesses is a **client-server network**. In client-server networks, *clients* are usually the laptop or desktop computers through

VSAT Satellite Communications *network of geographically dispersed transmitter-receivers (transceivers) that send signals to and receive signals from a satellite, exchanging voice, video, and data transmissions*

Computer Network *group of two or more computers linked together by some form of cabling or by wireless technology to share data or resources, such as a printer*

Client-Server Network *common business network in which clients make requests for information or resources and servers provide the services*

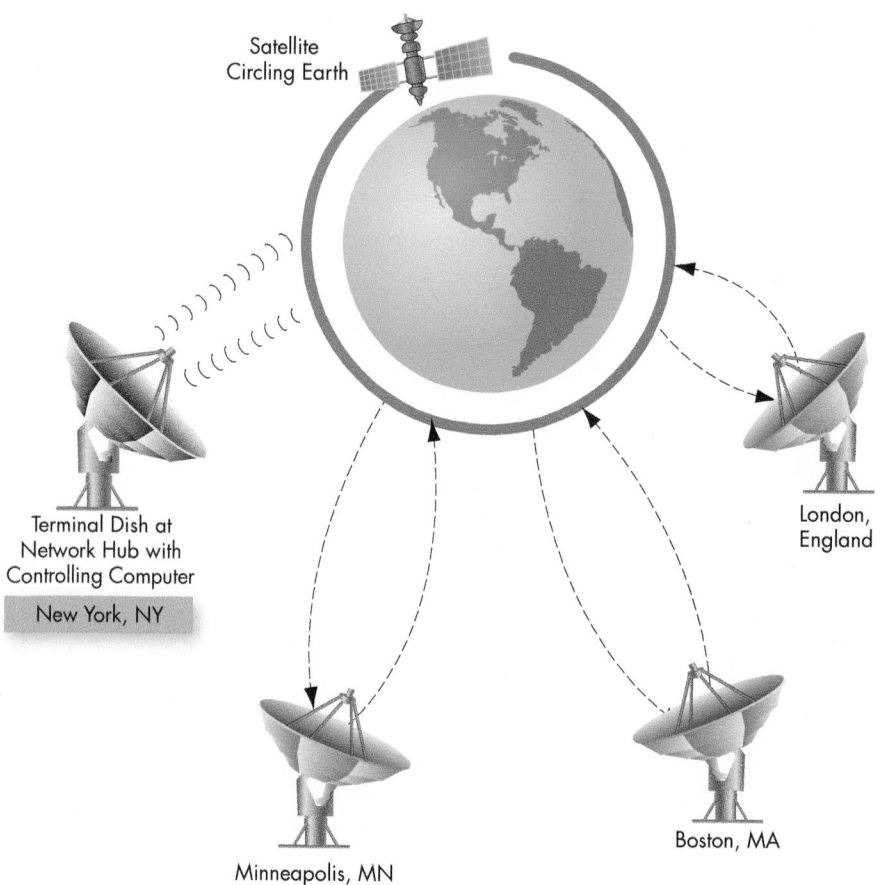

FIGURE 14.2 A VSAT Satellite Communication Network

which users make requests for information or resources. *Servers* are the computers that provide the services shared by users. In big organizations, servers are usually assigned a specific task. For example, in a local university or college network, an *application server* stores the word-processing, spreadsheet, and other programs used by all computers connected to the network. A *print server* controls the printers, stores printing requests from client computers, and routes jobs as the printers become available. An *e-mail server* handles all incoming and outgoing e-mail. With a client-server system, users can share resources and Internet connections—and avoid costly duplication.

Cloud computing modifies traditional networks by adding an externally located component—the "cloud"—that replaces the functions previously performed by application servers. With a cloud, information resources are retrieved via the Internet from a remote storage service, instead of relying on network-connected user-shared servers for storing data and software packages in client-server systems. Data and software resources are accessible through Internet-based devices, including laptops, desktops, tablets, mobile phones, and other devices with access to the Web. The cloud enhances user flexibility, especially for people working remotely, because users can access e-mails and data files from any online location, rather than from one particular location.

Amazon's Simple Storage Service (S3) is an example of a *public* cloud that rents Internet storage space where users can store any amount of data and retrieve it at any time from anywhere on the Web. S3 services have become cost savers for companies by eliminating the need for buying, installing, and maintaining in-house server computers, many of which have excessive unused storage capacity "just in case it's needed in the future." S3 allows you to store and manage your application data, search files online, upgrade software quickly, and then download and share data. In contrast with public clouds, *private* cloud services such as JustCloud and ZipCloud provide an added layer of security by surrounding the user-company's storage with a firewall to ensure against intrusion. Private clouds provide added flexibility for creating customized data storage, automated data integration, and integrated software applications to better meet users' needs. Networks can be classified according to geographic scope and means of connection (either wired or wireless).

Wide Area Networks (WANs) Computers that are linked over long distances—statewide or even nationwide—through long-distance telephone wires, microwave signals, or satellite communications make up what are called **wide area networks (WANs)**. Firms can lease lines from communications vendors or maintain private WANs. Walmart, for example, depends heavily on a private satellite network that links thousands of U.S. and international retail stores to its Bentonville, Arkansas, headquarters.

Wide Area Network (WAN) *computers that are linked over long distances through telephone lines, microwave signals, or satellite communications*

Local Area Networks (LANs) In **local area networks (LANs)**, computers are linked in a smaller area such as an office or a building, using existing telephone wires, fiber-optic, or coaxial cables. For example, a LAN unites hundreds of operators who enter call-in orders at TV's Home Shopping Network facility. The arrangement requires only one computer system with one database and one software system.

Local Area Network (LAN) *computers that are linked in a small area, such as all of a firm's computers within a single building*

Wireless Networks Wireless networks use airborne electronic signals to link network computers and devices. Like wired networks, wireless networks can reach across long distances or exist within a single building or small area. For example, smartphone systems allow users to send and receive transmissions on the **wireless wide area networks (WWANs)** of hundreds of service providers—such as Cellular One (United States), T-Mobile (United States), and Vodafone Italia (Italy)—in more than 90 countries throughout the world. A *firewall* provides privacy protection. We'll discuss firewalls in more detail later in the chapter.

Wireless Wide Area Network (WWAN) *network that uses airborne electronic signals instead of wires to link computers and electronic devices over long distances*

Wi-Fi You probably use—or have at least heard of—"hotspots," millions of locations worldwide, such as coffee shops, hotels, airports, and cities, that provide wireless Internet connections for people on the go. Each hotspot, or **Wi-Fi** (a play on audio recording term *Hi-Fi*) access point, uses its own small network, called a **wireless local area network (wireless LAN or WLAN)**. Although wireless service is free at some hotspots, others charge a fee—a daily or hourly rate—for the convenience of Wi-Fi service.

Wi-Fi *technology using a wireless local area network*

Wireless Local Area Network (Wireless LAN or WLAN) *local area network with wireless access points*

The benefit of Wi-Fi is that its millions of users are not tethered to a wire for accessing the Internet. Employees can wait for a delayed plane in the airport and still be connected to the Internet through their wireless-enabled laptops or other devices. However, as with every technology, Wi-Fi has limitations, including a short range of distance. This means that your laptop's Internet connection can be severed if you move farther than about 300 feet from the hotspot. In addition, thick walls, construction beams, and other obstacles can interfere with the signals sent out by the network. So, although a city may have hundreds of hotspots, your laptop must remain near one to stay connected. *WiMAX* (*Worldwide Interoperability for Microwave Access*), the next step in wireless advancements, improves this distance limitation with its wireless range of up to 30 miles.

"Super Wi-Fi" Network *a powerful Wi-Fi network with extensive reach and strong signals that flow freely through physical objects such as walls*

Proposing a bolder approach for the future, a few years ago the U.S. Federal Communications Commission announced a proposed multiyear project for nationwide **"super Wi-Fi" networks** to be developed by the federal government. More powerful than today's networks, the super Wi-Fi would have further reach, stretching across major metropolitan areas and covering much of the rural countryside as well. Super Wi-Fi's stronger signals would flow more freely, without obstruction, through concrete walls, steel beams, forests, and hills. The proposal would enable users to surf the Internet and make mobile phone calls without paying a monthly cell phone bill or Internet bill.[11] Scientists have also encouraged the government to use the bandwidth from old television frequencies to support super Wi-Fi.

Airlines, too, are expanding Wi-Fi service beyond just domestic flights by providing satellite-based Internet service on long-haul international flights. Japan Airlines offers Wi-Fi on routes between New York and Tokyo, in addition to flights between Tokyo and Los Angeles, Chicago, and Jakarta, Indonesia. Other airlines gearing up for (or already providing) Wi-Fi on long-haul flights include Air France, Delta, and United. Qantas—the Australian airline—discontinued its trial program because of passenger disinterest in international Wi-Fi but has now resumed the service.

Hardware and Software

Any computer network or system needs **hardware**, the physical components, such as keyboards, monitors, system units, and printers. In addition to the laptops and desktop computers, *handheld computers* and mobile devices are also used often in businesses. For example, Target employees roam the store aisles using handheld devices to identify, count, and order items, track deliveries, and update backup stock at distribution centers to keep store shelves replenished with merchandise.

Hardware *physical components of a computer network, such as keyboards, monitors, system units, and printers*

Software *programs that tell the computer how to function, what resources to use, how to use them, and application programs for specific activities*

The other essential in any computer system is **software**: programs that tell the computer how to function. Software includes *system software*, such as Microsoft Windows for PCs, which tells the computer's hardware how to interact with the software, what resources to use, and how to use them. It also includes *application software* (apps) such as Microsoft's Live Messenger and Photo Gallery, which are programs that meet the needs of specific users. Some application programs are used to address such common, long-standing needs as database management and inventory control, whereas others have been developed for a variety of specialized tasks ranging from mapping the oceans' depths to analyzing the anatomical structure of the human body. For example, IBM's Visualization Data Explorer software uses data from field samples to model the underground structure of an oil field. The imagery in the photo, for example, provides engineers with better information on oil location and reduces the risk of their hitting less productive holes.

entrepreneurship and new ventures

Speaking Loud and Clear: The Future of Voice Technology

After he lost the ability to speak in 1985 due to a tracheotomy that saved his life, Stephen Hawking has relied on computers to give his amazing intellect a voice. "The only trouble is [the voice synthesizer] gives me an American accent," he once wrote on his website. For years, programmers have been striving toward a more natural-sounding voice interface to enhance IT systems with vocal output, beyond traditional print or visual output. Vocal technologies, however, continued to sound robotic until 2005, when Matthew Aylett and Nick Wright formed CereProc (short for Cerebral Processing) in Edinburgh, Scotland.[12] From the outset, the firm has been dedicated to creating better synthetic voices with character and emotion that stimulate listeners with natural-sounding messages. Before CereProc, these lofty goals were prohibitive. Speech experts couldn't create text-to-voice software that sounded realistically conversational, varying tone-of-voice and providing various vocal inflections for different situations. Previous software couldn't adapt incoming text (from word processing or from text messages) into natural voice formats. To attack these challenges, CereProc brought together a team of leading speech experts. It also partnered with leading universities and research programs in speech science technology and in developing new applications and markets for voice output.

The company's main product is CereVoice, an advanced text-to-voice technology available on mobile devices, PCs, servers, and headsets, and that has applications in most any company's products for better synthetic voices. Any computer's existing voice system can be replaced with more natural-sounding speech in a choice of accents, including Southern British English, Scottish, and American, that can be sampled with live voice demos at the firm's website.[13] Potential applications are endless—kitchen appliances, alarm systems, traffic controllers, automobile appliances, radio broadcasting, telephone messaging, and movies, to name a few. Although consumers may not see the CereVoice label, they will be hearing its various voices often in their everyday lives.

CereProc's Voice Creation service can create a synthesized imitation of a person's voice, including its tones and inflections. That's how noted film critic, the late Roger Ebert, got his voice back, four years after losing the ability to speak following cancer-related surgery. CereProc's voice engineers used recordings of Ebert's voice from 40 years of past television

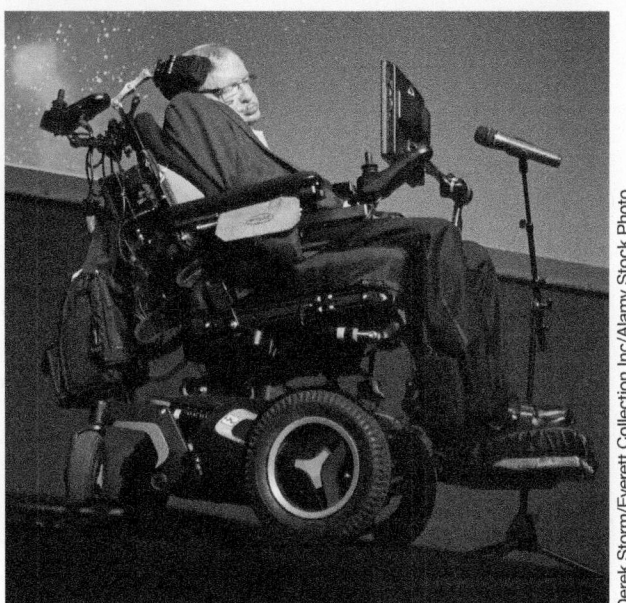

Derek Storm/Everett Collection Inc/Alamy Stock Photo

broadcasts, capturing individual sounds and identifying various voice characteristics. With meticulous care, specialists then pieced them back together into software that mimicked the Pulitzer-Prize winner's earlier voice. Ebert typed his comments into a computer that, in turn, converted the text into words that were spoken in his voice. This first-of-its-kind application made a memorable public appearance on the Oprah show, as Roger enthusiastically demonstrated his voice coming from the computer.[14] Beyond its technical success, this project vividly displays a compassionate side in CereProc's business.

While CereProc has clearly established a niche in the market, many other companies are working on similar technology. Apple has assembled an in-house team, headquartered in Cambridge, Massachusetts, to develop enhanced capabilities in this area, and recently acquired a start-up AI company called VocalIQ for $100 million. Even though Apple is investing heavily in vocal recognition and speech technology, the competition is robust. Google Now, Microsoft's Cortana, and other AI operating systems are breaking new ground daily. As more and more of our cars, appliances, and even houses begin to communicate with us in spoken words, we are seeing that the future is now; voice recognition and voice creation have entered the mainstream of IT capabilities and are rapidly becoming the norm, rather than a curiousity.[15]

Finally *groupware*—software that connects group members for message distribution, electronic meetings, message storing, appointments and schedules, and group writing—allows people to collaborate from their own desktop PCs, even if they're remotely located. It is especially useful when people work together regularly and rely heavily on information sharing. Groupware systems include IBM Lotus software and Micro Focus Groupwise (formerly known as Novell GroupWise).

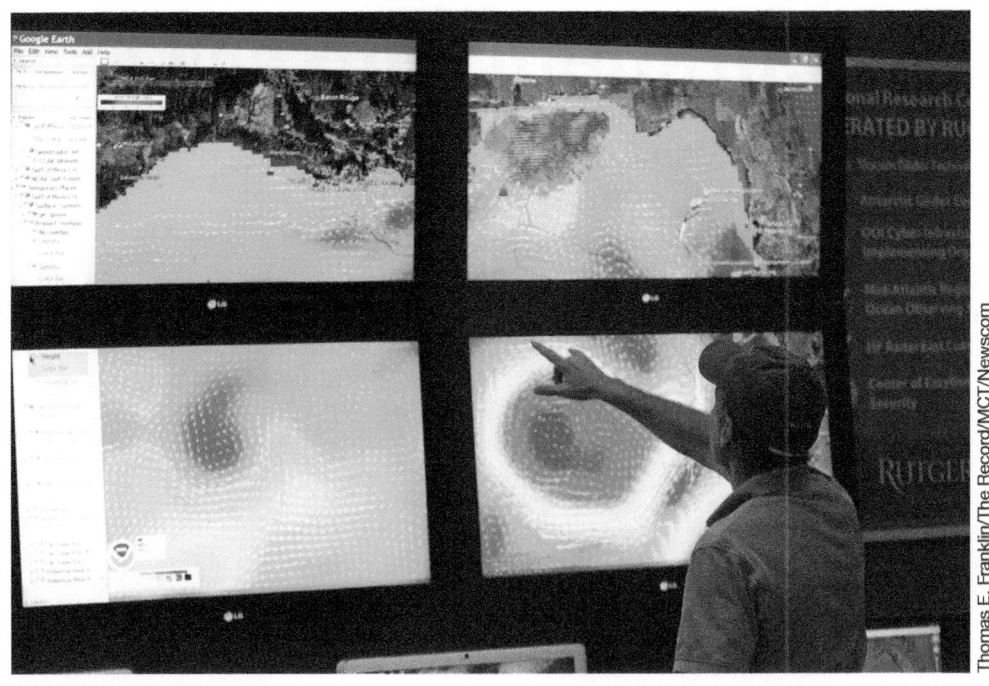

Thomas E. Franklin/The Record/MCT/Newscom

3-D computer modeling software gives engineers a better idea of where oil might be located.

Information Systems: Harnessing the Competitive Power of It

OBJECTIVE 14-3
Describe

the role of information systems, the different types of information systems, and how businesses use such systems.

Information system (IS) *system that uses IT resources to convert data into information and to collect, process, and transmit that information for use in decision making*

Data *raw facts and figures that, by themselves, may not have much meaning*

Information *meaningful, useful interpretation of data*

Information Systems Managers *managers who are responsible for the systems used for gathering, organizing, and distributing information*

Business today relies on information management in ways that no one could have foreseen a decade ago. Managers now treat IT as a basic organizational resource for conducting daily business. At major firms, every activity—designing services, ensuring product delivery and cash flow, and evaluating employee performance—is linked to *information systems*. An **information system (IS)** uses IT resources that enable managers to take **data**, raw facts and figures that, by themselves, may not have much meaning, and turn those data into **information**, the meaningful, useful interpretation of data. Information systems also enable managers to collect, process, and transmit that information for use in decision making.

Walmart is well known for its strategic use of information systems. The nerve center for company operations is a centralized IS in Bentonville, Arkansas. The IS drives costs down and raises efficiency because the same methods and systems are applied for all 11,700-plus stores in 28 countries. Data on the billions of sales transactions—time, date, and place—flow to Bentonville. The IS tracks millions of stock-keeping units (SKUs) weekly, enforces uniform reordering and delivery procedures on its more than 100,000 suppliers, including over 20,000 in China, and regulates the flow of merchandise through its distribution centers and stores.

Beyond the firm's daily operations, information systems are also crucial in planning. Managers routinely use the IS to decide on products and markets for the next 5 to 10 years. The company's vast database enables marketing managers to analyze customer demographics for better marketing, and it is also used for financial planning, materials handling, and electronic funds transfers with suppliers and customers.

Walmart, like most businesses, regards its information as a private resource, an asset that's planned, developed, and protected. Therefore, it's not surprising that they have **information systems managers** who are responsible for the systems used for gathering, organizing, and distributing information, just as they have production, marketing, and finance managers. These managers use many of the IT resources we discussed previously—the Internet, communications technologies, networks, hardware, and software—to sift through information and apply it to their jobs.

Leveraging Information Resources: Data Warehousing and Data Mining

Almost everything you do leaves a trail of information about you. Your preferences in movie rentals, television viewing, online searches, and grocery buying; your phone calls, your credit card charges, your financial status; and personal information about your age, gender, marital status, and even your health are just a few of the items about each of us that are stored in scattered databases. The behavior patterns of millions of users can be traced by analyzing files of information gathered over time from their online activity and in-store purchases.

The collection, storage, and retrieval of such data in electronic files is called **data warehousing**. For managers, the data warehouse can be a gold mine of information about their business. Indeed, Kroger Co., the Ohio-based grocery chain, collects data on customer shopping habits to find ways to gain greater customer loyalty. As part owner of a data-mining firm, Kroger accumulates information from its shopper cards, analyzes the data to uncover shopping patterns, and sends money-saving coupons to regular customers for the specific products they usually buy. Kroger's precision targeting pays off, especially in a sluggish economy. With a rate of coupon usage that is around 50 times the industry average, it's a money saver for Kroger customers and boosts the company's sales, too.[16] To help put this in context, coupons from Kroger's quarterly mailers, uniquely customized for each customer, have a 70 percent redemption rate within six weeks of delivery.

Data Warehousing the collection, storage, and retrieval of data in electronic files

Data Mining After collecting information, managers use **data mining**, the application of advanced statistical analyses and electronic technologies for searching, sifting, and reorganizing pools of data to uncover useful information. Data mining helps managers plan for new products, set prices, and identify trends and shopping patterns. By analyzing what consumers actually do, businesses can determine what subsequent purchases they are likely to make and then send them tailor-made ads. The *Washington Post*, for example, uses data-mining software to analyze census data and target households likely to respond to sales efforts.[17]

Data Mining the application of electronic technologies for searching, sifting, and reorganizing pools of data to uncover useful information

Frank Van Delft/Cultura/Getty Images

Retailers such as Walmart and Sam's Club rely on data warehousing and mining to keep shelves stocked with in-demand merchandise.

managing in turbulent times

Better Care, Lower Costs

Imagine that you are an emergency room doctor and a patient has just come in complaining of chest pains. You know that this could be serious—a heart attack, stroke, or aortic dissection—or perhaps something less dire, such as acid reflux or bruised or broken ribs. You have only minutes to make a quick assessment and connect the patient with the right resources. Well, in addition to the physical exam, the patient's electronic medical record may provide key information to make a quick and accurate diagnosis and treatment plan. Perhaps the patient has had a prior admission for heart-related conditions, or he or she has been prescribed medication for high blood pressure. This information might point the ER team in the direction of quickly ordering tests to identify if a heart attack or other heart-related condition is occurring. On the other hand, if the patient has recently been in a car accident, physicians may try to rule out broken ribs before ordering expensive, and possibly invasive, heart-related testing.

The move to electronic health records is relatively recent, with many doctors and hospitals understandably dragging their feet. Even as more data is collected into electronic health records, producing a wealth of predictive analytics, the health care industry suffers from a pressing problem with data security. In an effort to digitize and integrate while containing costs,

health care professionals often understaff their security systems, leaving doctors and nurses to sort out problems with malware, ransomware, viruses, and other technical problems. In addition, many medical devices have been pressed into service despite known flaws in the systems, and some systems, like Windows XP, that are no longer even supported have known vulnerabilities and yet are pervasive. There is no easy solution in sight, as health care providers strive to keep costs down, and changing technology can be expensive.

Information Linkages with Suppliers The top priority for Walmart's IS—improving in-stock reliability—requires integration of Walmart and suppliers' activities with store sales. That's why Procter & Gamble (P&G), Johnson & Johnson, and other suppliers connect into Walmart's information system to observe up-to-the-minute sales data on individual items, at the individual store level. They can use the system's computer-based tools—spreadsheets, sales forecasting, and even weather information—to forecast sales demand and plan delivery schedules. Coordinated planning avoids excessive inventories, speeds up deliveries, and holds down costs throughout the supply chain while keeping shelves stocked for retail customers.

Types of Information Systems

Employees have a variety of responsibilities and decision-making needs, and a firm's IS may actually be a set of multiple systems that share information while serving different levels of the organization, different departments, or different operations. Because they work on different kinds of problems, managers and their employees have access to the specialized information systems that satisfy their specific information needs.

In addition to different types of users, each business *function*—marketing, human resources, accounting, production, and finance—has special information needs, as do groups working on major projects. Each user group and department, therefore, may need a special information system.

Information Systems for Knowledge Workers As we discussed in Chapter 10, *knowledge workers* are employees for whom information and

Mocart/Shutterstock

The 3-D computer model of this dinosaur is constructed from digital scans of fossilized tissue.

knowledge comprise the core of their work, such as engineers, scientists, and IT specialists who rely on IT to design new products or create new processes. These workers require **knowledge information systems**, which provide resources to create, store, use, and transmit new knowledge for useful applications—for instance, databases to organize and retrieve information, and computational power for data analysis.

Specialized support systems have also increased the productivity of knowledge workers. **Computer-aided design (CAD)** helps knowledge workers—and now many other kinds of people, too, as we saw with consumers designing customized products earlier in this chapter—design products ranging from cell phones to jewelry to auto parts by simulating them and displaying them in 3D graphics. In a more advanced version, known as *rapid prototyping*, the CAD system electronically transfers instructions to a computer-controlled machine that quickly builds a prototype—a physical model—of the newly designed product, such as a toy, an artificial limb for the disabled, or a solar panel. The older method—making handcrafted prototypes from wood, plastic, or clay—is replaced with faster, cheaper prototyping.

CAD is helping archaeological scientists uncover secrets hidden in fossils using 3D computer models of skeletons, organs, and tissues constructed with digital data from computed tomography (CT) scans of dinosaur fossils. From these models, scientists have learned, for example, that the giant apatosaurus's neck curved downward, instead of high in the air as once thought. By seeing how the animals' bones fit together with cartilage, ligaments, and vertebrae, scientists are discovering more about how these prehistoric creatures interacted with their environment.[18]

In a direct offshoot of computer-aided design, **computer-aided manufacturing (CAM)** uses computers to design and control the equipment needed in a manufacturing process. For example, CAM systems can produce digital instructions to control all the machines and robots on a production line, say, as an example, in making jewelry cases. CAM-guided machines cut the materials, move them through the stages of production, and then assemble each stylish case without human physical involvement in production activities. CAD and CAM coupled together (CAD/CAM) are useful to engineers in a manufacturing environment for designing and testing new products and then designing the machines and tools to manufacture those products.

Knowledge Information System *information system that supports knowledge workers by providing resources to create, store, use, and transmit new knowledge for useful applications*

Computer-Aided Design (CAD) *IS with software that helps knowledge workers design products by simulating them and displaying them in three-dimensional graphics*

Computer-Aided Manufacturing (CAM) *IS that uses computers to design and control equipment in a manufacturing process*

Information Systems for Managers Each manager's information activities and IS needs vary according to his or her functional area (accounting or human resources and so forth) and management level. The following are some popular information systems used by managers for different purposes.

MANAGEMENT INFORMATION SYSTEMS **Management information systems (MIS)** support managers by providing reports, schedules, plans, and budgets that can then be used for making both short- and long-term decisions. For example, at Walsworth Publishing Company managers rely on detailed information—current customer orders, staffing schedules, employee attendance, production schedules, equipment status, and materials availability—for moment-to-moment decisions during the day. They require similar information to plan such mid-range activities as employee training, materials movements, and cash flows. They also need to anticipate the status of the jobs and projects assigned to their departments. Many management information systems—cash flow, sales, production scheduling, and shipping—are indispensable for helping managers complete these tasks.

For longer-range decisions involving business strategy, Walsworth managers need information to analyze trends in the publishing industry and overall company performance. They need both external and internal information, current and future, to compare current performance data to data from previous years and to analyze consumer trends and economic forecasts.

DECISION SUPPORT SYSTEMS Managers who face a particular kind of decision repeatedly can get assistance from **decision support systems (DSS)**, interactive systems that create virtual business models and test them with different data to see how they respond. When faced with decisions on plant capacity, for example, Walsworth managers can use a capacity DSS. The manager inputs data on anticipated sales, working capital, and customer-delivery requirements. The data flow into the DSS processor, which then simulates the plant's performance under the proposed data conditions. A proposal to increase facility capacity by, say, 10 percent could be simulated to find costs of operation, percent of customer order fulfillments, and other performance measures that would result due to the expanded capacity. After experimenting with various data conditions, the DSS makes recommendations on the best levels of plant capacity—those that result in best performance—for each future time period.

Management Information System (MIS) *computer system that supports managers by providing information—reports, schedules, plans, and budgets—that can be used for making decisions*

Decision Support System (DSS) *interactive system that creates virtual business models for a particular kind of decision and tests them with different data to see how they respond*

OBJECTIVE 14-4
Identify

the threats and risks information technology poses to businesses.

IT Risks and Threats

Unfortunately, the growth and increased sophistication of information technology have been accompanied by parallel growth in risks and threats to those who use it. These risks and threats range from mild nuisance to theft to outright destruction. Casual IT users everywhere are finding that even social networking and cell phones have a "dark side"—privacy invasion. Facebook postings of personal information about users have been intercepted and misused by intruders. Beacon, the former data-gathering service, caused a public uproar when it published peoples' online purchases publicly on their Facebook newsfeeds. And with cellular technology, some features of Bluetooth connections allow savvy intruders to access a victim's text messages, listen in on live conversations, and even view unwary users' photos.[19]

Businesses, too, are impacted by IT's dark side. Hackers break into computers, stealing personal information about both customers and employees as well as confidential information. And they sometimes go so far as to launch attacks on other computers. Meanwhile, the ease of online information sharing has proven costly for companies who are having an increasingly difficult time protecting their intellectual property, and viruses that crash computers have cost companies many billions annually. In this section, we'll look at these and other IT risks. In the next section, we'll discuss ways in which businesses are protecting themselves from these risks.

Hackers

The term *breaking and entering* once referred to physical intrusion, but today it applies to IT intrusions as well. **Hackers** are cybercriminals who gain unauthorized access to a computer or network, either to steal information, money, or property or to tamper with data. Twitter recently reported that hackers may have intercepted information—names, passwords, e-mail addresses—of some 250,000 of the social media's users. With different motives than the Twitter intruders, Chinese-based hackers, including the Chinese government, are suspected of continuing cyber-attacks into the computer systems of several newspapers, including the *New York Times*, the *Washington Post*, and the *Wall Street Journal*. China-based intruders have been accused of a multiyear campaign to illegally gain corporate secrets and confidential information that can be used to frighten critics from writing unfavorable articles, accusations that the Chinese government has denied.[20] And there were widespread charges that Russian hackers attempted to influence the outcome of the 2016 U.S. presidential election.

Another common hacker activity is to launch *denial of service (DoS) attacks*. DoS attacks flood networks or websites with bogus requests for information and resources, thereby overloading and shutting the networks or websites down. These shutdowns, in turn, prevent legitimate users from accessing them.

Wireless mooching is also a profitable industry for cybercriminals. In just five minutes with a laptop, a reporter working for the *St. Petersburg* (now *Tampa Bay*) *Times* found six unprotected wireless networks that were wide open to outside users.[21] Once inside an unsecured wireless network, hackers can use it to conduct illegal business, such as child pornography or money laundering. When law enforcement officers try to track down these criminals through their Internet usage, they are long gone. However, the innocent but naïve network host has now been potentially exposed to criminal prosecution.

As we saw in this chapter's opening case, hackers, such as the Night Dragon, often break into company networks to steal company or trade secrets. But it's not just hackers who are doing the stealing. Because the chances of getting caught seem slim, some home users continue, illegally, to download unpaid-for movies, music, and other resources from file-swapping networks. A recent study shows that sound piracy costs the United States $12.5 billion and 71,060 jobs annually. However, these losses also showcase what can happen to businesses that fail to adapt to changes in technology. For years the music recording industry was reluctant to embrace online distribution as a revenue path, preferring to prosecute pirates rather than offer them legal online alternatives. On the other hand, Apple has benefitted immensely from its online (download) distribution models, enabling it to become the world's most popular music vendor.[22]

> **Hacker** *cybercriminal who gains unauthorized access to a computer or network, either to steal information, money, or property or to tamper with data*

Identity Theft

Once inside a computer network, hackers are able to commit **identity theft**, such as stealing personal information (for example, an individual's Social Security number and address) to get loans, credit cards, or other monetary benefits by impersonating the victim. Recent studies suggest that as many as 16.6 million victims fall prey to identify theft each year. Indeed, identity theft is among the fastest-growing crimes in the United States.

Clever crooks get information on unsuspecting victims by digging in trash, stealing mail, or using *phishing* or *pharming* schemes to lure online users to bogus websites. For instance, a cybercriminal might send a group of PayPal users an e-mail notifying them of a billing problem with their accounts. If any of these individuals click on what looks like the PayPal Billing Center link in the e-mail,

> **Identity Theft** *unauthorized use of personal information (such as Social Security number and address) to get loans, credit cards, or other monetary benefits by impersonating the victim*

they are transferred to a spoofed (falsified) Web page, modeled after PayPal's. The customer then submits the requested information—credit card number, Social Security number, and PIN—into the hands of the thief. Their accounts are soon empty.

Intellectual Property Theft

Nearly every company faces the dilemma of protecting product plans, new inventions, industrial processes, and other **intellectual property**, something produced by the intellect or mind that has commercial value. Its ownership and right to its use may be protected by patent, copyright, trademark, and other means. But crooks may be able to steal information about intellectual property and create unauthorized duplications.

Computer Viruses, Worms, and Trojan Horses

Another IT risk facing businesses is rogue programmers who disrupt IT operations by contaminating and destroying software, hardware, or data files. *Viruses*, *worms*, and *Trojan horses* are three kinds of malicious programs that, once installed, can shut down any computer system. A *computer virus* exists in a file that attaches itself to a program and migrates from computer to computer as a shared program or as an e-mail attachment. It does not infect the system unless the user opens the contaminated file, and users typically are unaware they are spreading the virus by file sharing. It can, for example, quickly copy itself over and over again, using up all available memory and effectively shutting down a computer.

Worms are a particular kind of virus that travel from computer to computer within networked computer systems, without your needing to open any software to spread the contaminated file. In a matter of days, the notorious Blaster worm infected some 400,000 computer networks, destroying files and even allowing outsiders to take over computers remotely. The worm replicates itself rapidly, sending out thousands of copies to other computers in the network. Traveling through Internet connections and e-mail address books in the network's computers, it absorbs system memory and shuts down network servers, Web servers, and individual computers.

Unlike viruses, a *Trojan horse* does not replicate itself. Instead, it most often comes into the computer, at your request, masquerading as a harmless, legitimate software product or data file. Once installed, however, the damage begins. For instance, it may simply redesign desktop icons (as a "prank") or, more maliciously, delete files and destroy information.

Spyware

As if forced intrusion isn't bad enough, Internet users can also unwittingly invite spies—masquerading as a friendly file available as a giveaway or shared among individual users on their PCs. This so-called **spyware** is downloaded by users who are lured by "free" software. Once installed, it "crawls" around to monitor the host's computer activities, gathering e-mail addresses, credit card numbers, passwords, and other inside information that it transmits back to someone outside the host system. Spyware authors assemble incoming stolen information to create their own "intellectual property" that they then sell to other parties to use for marketing and advertising purposes or for identity theft.[23]

Spam

Spam, junk e-mail sent to a mailing list or a newsgroup (an online discussion group), is a greater nuisance than postal junk mail because the Internet is open to the public, e-mail costs are negligible, and massive mailing lists are accessible through file sharing or by theft. Spam operators send unwanted messages ranging from explicit pornography to hate mail to advertisements, and even destructive computer viruses. In addition to wasting users' time, spam also consumes a network's bandwidth, thereby reducing the amount of data that can be transmitted in a fixed amount of time for useful purposes. U.S. industry experts estimate spam's annual damage in lost time and productivity at between $28 and $66 billion in the United States alone and that it could be as high as $620 billion globally.[24]

Although spammers sometimes gain significant incomes, they also risk anti-spamming prosecution that can be extremely costly. The judge in a lawsuit against Sanford Wallace, who proclaimed himself the "Spam King," issued a judgment for $711 million against Wallace, one of the largest fines ever in an anti-spamming case. He was accused of sending 27 million spam mailings to Facebook, using phishing to get passwords from thousands of Facebook users, and then entering their accounts to post fraudulent information. He was also charged with electronic mail fraud, damage to protected computers, and criminal contempt.[25]

IT Protection Measures

OBJECTIVE 14-5
Describe
the ways in which businesses protect themselves from the threats and risks information technology poses.

Security measures against intrusion and viruses are a constant challenge. Most systems guard against unauthorized access by requiring users to provide confidential login credentials such as user IDs and passwords. Other measures include firewalls, special software, and encryption.

Preventing Unauthorized Access: Firewalls

Firewalls are security systems with special software and/or hardware devices designed to keep computers safe from hackers. A firewall is located where two networks—for example, the Internet and a company's internal network, or intranet—interface. It contains two components for filtering incoming data:

Firewall security system with special software or hardware devices designed to keep computers safe from hackers

- The company's *security policy*—Access rules that identify every type of data that the company doesn't want to pass through the firewall

- A *router*—A table of available routes or paths; a "traffic switch" that determines which route or path on the network to send each piece of data after it is tested against the security policy

Only the information that meets the conditions of the user's security policy is routed through the firewall and permitted to flow between the two networks. Data that fail the access test are blocked and cannot flow between the two networks.

Preventing Identity Theft

Although foolproof prevention is impossible, steps can be taken to avoid being victimized. A visit to the Identity Theft Resource Center (http://www.idtheftcenter.org) is a valuable first step to get information on everything from scam alerts to victim issues to legislation such as the Fair and Accurate Credit Transactions Act (FACTA). FACTA strengthens identity-theft protections by specifying how organizations must destroy information instead of dropping it in a dumpster. When a company disposes of hardcopy documents that contain credit or Social Security information, for instance, they must be shredded, pulverized, or burned, and all digital records (such as those stored in computers and databases) must be permanently removed to keep them out of the hands of intruders.[26]

Preventing Infectious Intrusions: Anti-Virus Software

Anti-Virus Software *product that protects systems by searching incoming e-mails and data files for "signatures" of known viruses and virus-like characteristics*

Combating viruses, worms, Trojan horses, and any other infectious software (collectively known as *malware*) has become a major industry for systems designers and software developers. Installation of any of hundreds of **anti-virus software** products protects systems by searching incoming e-mail and data files for "signatures" of known viruses and virus-like characteristics. Contaminated files are discarded or placed in quarantine for safekeeping. Many viruses take advantage of weaknesses in operating systems, such as Microsoft Windows, to spread and propagate. Software distributors, for their part, are continuously monitoring their own products for potential weaknesses and updating them to thwart malware. Network administrators must make sure that the computers on their systems are using the most up-to-date operating system that includes the latest security protection.

Protecting Electronic Communications: Encryption Software

Encryption System *software that assigns an e-mail message to a unique code number (digital fingerprint) for each computer so only that computer, not others, can open and read the message*

Security for electronic communications is another concern for businesses. Unprotected e-mail can be intercepted, diverted to unintended computers, and opened, revealing the contents to intruders. Protective software is available to guard against those intrusions, adding a layer of security by encoding e-mails so that only intended recipients can open them. An **encryption system** works by scrambling an e-mail message so that it looks like garbled nonsense to anyone who doesn't possess the "key," another part of the software that decodes encrypted e-mails.

Avoiding Spam and Spyware

To help their employees avoid privacy invasion and to improve productivity, businesses often install anti-spyware and spam-filtering software on their systems. Although dozens of anti-spyware products provide protection—software such as Webroot Spy Sweeper and Microsoft Windows Defender—they must be continually updated to keep pace with new spyware techniques.

The federal CAN-SPAM Act of 2003 requires the Federal Trade Commission to shield the public from falsified header information, sexually explicit e-mails that are not so labeled, online spoofing (using trickery to make a message appear as if it came from a trusted source), and hijacking of computers through worms or Trojan horses. Although it cannot be prevented entirely, spam is abated by many Internet service providers (ISPs) that ban the spamming of ISP subscribers. In a now-classic punishment, an ISP in Iowa was awarded $1 billion in a lawsuit against 300 spammers that jammed the ISP system with an astounding 10 million e-mails a day. Anti-spam groups, too, promote the public's awareness of known spammers. The Spamhaus Project (http://www.spamhaus.org), for example, maintains a list of "The 10 Worst Spammers," career spammers that are responsible for most of the world's spam traffic.

Ethical Concerns in IT

It is obvious that IT developments and usage are progressing faster than society's appreciation for the potential consequences, including new ethical concerns. Along with IT's many benefits, its usage is creating previously unanticipated problems for which solutions are needed, yet they don't exist. Ease of access to computers, mobile devices, and the Internet, together with messaging capabilities and social networking, promote widespread public exposure about people's private lives, including

finding a better way

Gleaning Wisdom from the World Wide Web

In 1999, Marc Stiegler wrote a novel called *EarthWeb* based on the premise that the people of Earth were desperately seeking new ways to defeat the systematic attacks of an advanced, mechanical alien foe. The government supplied small computers (like iPads) to the general public in order to devise battle strategies that went beyond the abilities of any single individual. Even though the technology isn't fiction any longer, this was long before any kind of crowdsourcing of ideas was actually possible. The Earth is not under attack, but certainly we've seen the advent of big data, crowdsourcing, and information accessibility. Wikipedia is an example of the collective wisdom of a large group of people, demonstrating both the power and the fallibility of such a system. Errors and omission are rampant, and yet there is an incredible amount of expert information available. Companies like Amazon are using big data, collected from millions of consumers, to drive critical business decisions. Even more recently, the information age has given rise to crowdsourcing companies like Tongal, so-named in honor of polymath Sir Francis Galton, a half-cousin of Charles Darwin, who observed a county fair contest for guessing the weight of an oxen and noted that the average of the crowd's guesses were much closer to the actual weight than any individual guess.

Rawpixel/123RF

Tongal specializes in crowdsourcing creative work, such as instructional videos, marketing materials, and original content for websites for companies such as Gillette (creating 18 authentic "how-to shave" videos for YouTube), General Mills (designing digital ads targeted to the gaming culture), Fiat (a story-based campaign spread across social networks like Facebook, YouTube, and Twitter), and many others. In the summer of 2012, Colgate-Palmolive worked with the Tongal community on a two-month, $17,000 challenge to develop ads for Speed Stick's "Handle It" campaign, and selected one of the resulting submissions for its Super Bowl ad.

Apple encourages users and developers from around the world to create apps that enhance its products. Biologists at the University of Washington used crowdsourcing to map the structure of an AIDS-related virus that had stumped academic and industry experts for more than 15 years. In 2012, Merck offered a $40,000 prize through a crowdsourcing site called Kaggle for innovative ideas in drug development. Competition was intense, with more than 2,900 entries in just 60 days. The winners used a deep learning model originally developed for speech recognition. The artificial neural network they adapted to the problem provided a 17 percent improvement over the industry standard benchmark.

It's not just about groups of people with great ideas. The Web is replete with data being collected all the time from multiple sources that can benefit businesses that are able to compile it into useful information. For instance, the Fashion Institute of Technology in New York City recently began offering a course entitled "Predictive Analytics for Planning and Forecasting: Case Studies with Weatherization." The course teaches business owners how to use big data, including weather predictions, to help to make decisions about when and what clothing to stock.

Despite the success of using big data and crowdsourcing to improve both life and the bottom line, it may have reached a plateau. Businesses, researchers, and even government entities are looking for the next big breakthrough in gleaning wisdom from the Web, and it's likely that the next great innovation is out there, in the crowd.

personal information about how they think and feel. Just how this information should be used, by whom, under what conditions, and with what restrictions, if any, are issues teeming with ethical considerations. Several real-life episodes with ethical implications are shown in Table 14.1. See if you can identify significant ethical issues among the episodes in the table.

table 14.1 Areas for Ethical Concerns in Information Technology and Its Uses

- In a now-classic case of cyber-bullying, a 13-year-old girl hanged herself after being taunted by a hoax message on her MySpace page.
- Secret webcasts of other people's behavior have resulted in embarrassment and even death: A university student, leaving a final message on his Facebook page, jumped from a bridge to his death after other students covertly webcast his sexual activities with another student.
- IT is used increasingly for sending out cries for help. Many college students have posted public messages requesting physical and emotional support. Others, having read those messages, are unsure if they should respond or not.
- Employers and employees struggle about the extent of personal use of the company's IT. Many employees admit they use social networking and personal e-mailing at work, but should they? Many companies say "No," adding that employees should know that the company has access to all e-mails sent, received, and stored on its IT system.
- States are forming database pools, sharing information to check on suspicious prescription drug activities. Data are gathered on purchases at pharmacies, physicians' prescriptions, and police records to identify drug abuse by individuals and companies within states and are being shared across state lines.
- The Department of Homeland Security abandoned one of its major data-mining tools for combating terrorism after questions about its compliance with privacy rules. It was discovered that DHS had tested the data-mining program using information about real people, without ensuring the privacy of that information.
- To save money, IT users retrieve and share intellectual property—movies, articles, books, music, industrial information—with others, ignoring copyright, trademark, and patent protections. Written content is often taken from the Internet, inserted into the user's written work, and represented as the user's own original creation without citing its true source.
- Job seekers are being asked to answer unexpected questions by interviewers: "What is your Facebook username and password?" Some applicants are responding, "No, that's a terrible privacy invasion." Others are revealing the requested information to interviewers.

summary of learning objectives

OBJECTIVE 14-1

Discuss the impacts information technology has had on the business world. (pp. 446–452)

The growth of IT—the various appliances and devices for creating, storing, exchanging, and using information in diverse modes, including visual images, voice, multimedia, and business data—has changed the very structure of business organizations. Its adoption provides new modes of communication, including portable offices using mobile messaging capabilities, resulting in the geographic separation of the workplace from headquarters for many employees. With access to the Internet, company activities may be geographically scattered but still remain coordinated through a networked system that provides better service for customers. Networks and technology are also leading to leaner companies with fewer employees and simpler structures. Because networks enable firms to maintain information linkages among employees and customers, more work and customer satisfaction can be accomplished with fewer people. IT also contributes to greater flexibility in serving customers and enables closer coordination with suppliers. Company activities may be geographically scattered but remain coordinated through a network system that provides better service for customers. Many businesses coordinate activities from one centralized location, but their deliveries flow from several remote locations, often at lower cost. IT's global reach facilitates project collaboration with remote business partners and the formation of new market relationships around the globe. Just as electronic collaboration has changed the way employees interact with each other, IT networks have created new manufacturing flexibility for mass customization, and Internet access has brought new opportunities for small businesses.

OBJECTIVE 14-2

Identify the IT resources businesses have at their disposal and how these resources are used. (pp. 452–458)

The Internet and the World Wide Web serve computers with information and provide communication flows among networks around the world. For many businesses, the Internet has replaced the telephone, fax machine, and standard mail as the primary communications tool. To support internal communications, many companies maintain internal websites—*intranets*—accessible only to employees. Some firms give limited network access to outsiders via *extranets* allowing access to private information among businesses, customers, and suppliers for better planning and coordination of their activities. Electronic conferencing allows simultaneous communication globally among groups from various locations, saving travel time, time for information exchanges, and expenses. *VSAT satellite networks* provide private remote communications for voice, video, and data transmissions.

   Computer networks, including wide area networks and local area networks, enable the sharing of information, hardware, software, and other resources over wired or wireless connections. *Wi-Fi* provides wireless Internet connections through laptops or other devices at "hotspots" or local access points. All computer networks or systems need hardware, the physical components such as keyboards, monitors, and printers. In addition, all systems require *software*, programs that tell the computer how to function. *Application software* includes programs to meet specific user needs, such as groupware with voice and video connections for remote collaboration.

OBJECTIVE 14-3

Describe the role of information systems, the different types of information systems, and how businesses use such systems. (pp. 458–462)

An *information system (IS)* uses IT resources that enable users to create, process, and transmit information for use in decision making. An IS often includes *data warehousing*, a vast collection, storage, and retrieval system, that provides the data resources needed for creating information.

The IS also includes *data-mining* capabilities, the application of technologies for searching, sifting, and reorganizing data, to uncover useful information for planning new products, setting prices, and identifying trends.

The IS is often a set of several systems that share information while serving different levels of an organization, different departments, or different operations. *Knowledge information systems* support knowledge workers—engineers, scientists, and other specialists—by providing resources to create, store, use, and transmit new knowledge they use for specialty applications. Knowledge systems include *computer-aided design (CAD)*, software systems that receive engineering data and convert them into three-dimensional displays, for rapid development of new products. *Computer-aided manufacturing (CAM)* uses computers to design and control the equipment needed in a manufacturing process. *Management information systems (MIS)* support managers by providing reports, schedules, plans, and budgets that can then be used for making decisions at all levels, ranging from detailed daily activities to long-range business strategies. The many uses of information systems include experimenting with *decision support systems (DSS)*, interactive systems that create business models and test them with different data to see how the models respond under diverse business conditions, to test the effectiveness of potential decisions.

OBJECTIVE 14-4

Identify the threats and risks information technology poses to businesses. (pp. 462–465)

IT has attracted abusers that do mischief, with severity ranging from mere nuisance to outright destruction, costing companies millions. Everything from Facebook postings to Bluetooth usage to private computer systems is subject to break-ins and destruction. *Hackers* break into computers, steal personal information and company secrets, tamper with data, and launch attacks on other computers. *Wireless moochers* use victims' networks for illegal activities, exposing the host to criminal prosecution. Once inside a computer network, hackers are able to commit *identity theft*, the unauthorized stealing of personal information to get loans, credit cards, or other monetary benefits by impersonating the victim. Even the ease of information sharing on the Internet poses a threat. It has proven costly for companies who are having a difficult time protecting their *intellectual property*, such as software products, movies, and music. Hackers break into company networks to steal anything of commercial value, including trade secrets, new inventions, and other valuable information that is protected by patent, copyright, or trademark. Another IT risk facing businesses is system shutdown and destruction of software, hardware, or data files by *viruses, worms*, and *Trojan horses* that can shut down a computer system or otherwise disrupt IT operations by contaminating and destroying software, hardware, or data files. After invading a victim's computer, *spyware* gathers inside information and transmits it to outside spies. Masquerading as a friendly file available as a giveaway or shared among individual users on PCs and mobile devices, spyware is downloaded by unsuspecting users. Once installed, it monitors the host's electronic activities, gathers personal information, and transmits stolen information to an outside system. *Spam*, junk e-mail sent to a mailing list or news group, is costly in terms of lost time and productivity by overloading the network's capacity with massive mailings of unwanted messages.

OBJECTIVE 14-5

Describe the ways in which businesses protect themselves from the threats and risks IT poses. (pp. 465–468)

Most systems guard against unauthorized access by requiring users to have protected passwords. In addition, many firms rely on *firewalls*, security systems with special software or hardware devices that intercept would-be intruders, so that only messages that meet the conditions of the company's security policy are permitted to flow through the network. Firms can protect against identity theft by using assistance from advisory sources, such as the Identity Theft Resource Center, and by implementing the identity-theft protection provisions of the federal FACTA rule for maintaining and destroying personal information records. To combat infectious intrusions by viruses, worms, and Trojan horses, *anti-virus software* products search incoming e-mail and data files for "signatures" of known viruses and virus-like characteristics. Contaminated files are discarded or placed in quarantine for safekeeping. Additional intrusion protection is available by installing *anti-spyware* and *spam filtering software*. *Encryption* adds security by encoding, scrambling messages so they look like garbled nonsense to anyone who doesn't possess the key, so that the message can be read only by intended recipients. The federal *CAN-SPAM Act* requires the Federal Trade Commission to shield the public from falsified header information, sexually explicit e-mails that are not so labeled, Internet spoofing (using trickery to make a message appear as if it came from a trusted source), and hijacking of computers through worms or Trojan horses. Although it cannot be prevented entirely, *spam* is abated by many Internet service providers (ISPs) that ban the spamming of ISP subscribers.

key terms

anti-virus software (p. 466)
client-server network (p. 454)
computer-aided design (CAD) (p. 461)
computer-aided manufacturing (CAM) (p. 461)
computer network (p. 454)
data (p. 458)
data mining (p. 459)
data warehousing (p. 459)
decision support system (DSS) (p. 462)
e-commerce (p. 447)
electronic conferencing (p. 453)
encryption system (p. 466)
extranet (p. 453)
firewall (p. 465)

hacker (p. 463)
hardware (p. 456)
hypertext transfer protocol (HTTP) (p. 452)
identity theft (p. 463)
information (p. 458)
information system (IS) (p. 458)
information systems managers (p. 458)
information technology (IT) (p. 446)
intellectual property (p. 464)
Internet (p. 452)
intranet (p. 453)
knowledge information system (p. 461)
local area network (LAN) (p. 455)

management information system (MIS) (p. 462)
mass customization (p. 449)
software (p. 456)
spam (p. 464)
spyware (p. 464)
"super Wi-Fi" network (p. 456)
VSAT satellite communications (p. 454)
wide area network (WAN) (p. 455)
Wi-Fi (p. 456)
wireless local area network (wireless LAN or WLAN) (p. 456)
wireless wide area network (WWAN) (p. 455)
World Wide Web (p. 452)

MyLab Intro to Business

To complete the problems with the ✪, go to EOC Discussion Questions in the MyLab.

questions & exercises

QUESTIONS FOR REVIEW

✪ **14-1.** Compare and contrast an intranet with an extranet.

14-2. How can electronic conferencing increase a company's productivity and efficiency?

14-3. What are the advantages and risks of cloud computing?

14-4. Why should companies be concerned about hackers?

✪ **14-5.** What is *intellectual property*? Provide at least three examples.

QUESTIONS FOR ANALYSIS

14-6. Describe how a company might use data warehousing and data mining in its information system to better plan for new products.

✪ **14-7.** How could an airline use data mining to make better business decisions?

14-8. How do your bank, employer, and e-mail provider protect your personal information from unauthorized use?

APPLICATION EXERCISES

14-9. Consider your daily activities—as a consumer, student, parent, friend, homeowner or renter, car driver, employee, and so forth—and think about the ways that you are involved with IT systems. Make a list of your recent IT encounters and then recall instances in those encounters in which you revealed personal information that could be used to steal your identity. Are some encounters on your list riskier than others? Why, or why not?

14-10. After reading the first section of this chapter, consider how IT has changed the business of higher education. Identify at least three functions, services, or activities that would not have been available even 10 years ago. How do you think that colleges and universities will change in the future because of advances in IT?

building a business: continuing team exercise

Assignment

Meet with your team members to consider your new business venture and how it relates to the information technology topics in this chapter. Develop specific responses to the following:

14-11. In what ways do you expect IT will enable collaboration among your employees? Identify examples of occasions where IT will be useful for providing remote access between employees, and remote access between employees and company data files.

14-12. In what ways will IT be used for collaboration with external stakeholders, such as customers, suppliers, and other constituents? What types of remote interactions do you expect, and what kinds of IT equipment and installations will be needed for those interactions? Discuss how your team is going to identify the IT equipment requirements at this stage of development of your business.

14-13. At what stage of your company's development will you begin planning for its information system(s), if any?

Discuss the technical skills and information-management skills necessary for determining the kind(s) of information system(s) needed for your company's first two years of operation.

14-14. Based on your findings for Question 14-13, where will your company get the skills and resources for IS development and implementation? Have you included the anticipated costs for developing the information systems in your financial plan for year one or will you do so? Explain why, or why not.

14-15. What measures, if any, will you take for protecting against intrusions into your company's IT system? What actions will be taken to prevent unauthorized access to the information of customers, suppliers, and other external constituents? What security measures will be taken to protect non-IT information? Explain.

team exercise

NEW AGE HELP DESK

The Situation

You have been hired to develop and lead a technical support team for a rapidly growing start-up that provides data analysis, business consulting, and targeted marketing to auto dealers. For instance, customers that recently came in for service on an older car would receive trade-in offers suggesting a newer vehicle, as would customers who had purchased more than five years earlier. The company began several years ago when four recent college graduates in Portland, Oregon, spotted a need in the local market and combined their business and technical skills to meet that need. The company quickly grew, adding more than 80 employees in just five years. It now serves dealers in seven West coast cities, and management is seeking to expand into 10 more cities within the next two years, with an ultimate goal of taking the company public within six years. While all of the employees are currently located in the Portland area, the corporate culture has been based on flexible work hours and most of the employees work from home at least one day a week. Because the company has grown organically from that flexible culture, there hasn't been much of a technical support team at the company. An informal network of experts made decisions about which computers to buy, the software they purchased, and their high-speed Internet in the office, and employees depended on friends, family members, or co-workers if they had trouble with their hardware or software.

However, the company's rapid growth has strained this informal network and so management decided to budget three IT professionals for a technical support department,. As the first hire and leader of this nascent department, your first task is to make recommendations for next steps.

QUESTIONS FOR DISCUSSION:

14-16. Many of the company's employees work from home. What benefits can the company and employee expect from allowing employees to do so? Are there some jobs where working from home is not appropriate?

14-17. The company has not had a consistent policy about the technology for those working from home. Should the company provide employees with a computer to use in their home office, or is this a responsibility of the employee? What are the benefits and costs of each?

14-18. How will you provide technical support to employees working from home? Would this be easier if the company provided the employee with a computer? Why, or why not?

14-19. Are there additional data security risks with employees working from home? Describe the potential risks or concerns and how they might be addressed.

14-20. Briefly outline the policies, procedures, and guidelines that your department should propose in your first year on the job.

exercising your ethics

TO READ OR NOT TO READ

The Situation

Companies are able to monitor the ways that their employees use the company e-mail system as well track a history of employees' Internet use while using company resources. This exercise illustrates how ethical issues may arise in tracking and using employee use of digital assets.

The Dilemma

You have recently been promoted to the position of a first-line manager at a local bio-technology company. This is a dream job and you are delighted to have been recognized for your hard work. As you are being oriented to your new job, the human resource (HR) manager explains that the company maintains logs of employee e-mails and tracks all Internet usage on company computers. You were surprised that you had not been informed about this when you were hired, but the HR director has assured you that this is completely legal. The company is concerned that employees may be wasting time on YouTube and other websites while at work, so they believe that there is a business purpose to this program. You will be expected to scan e-mail logs to make sure that employees are not sharing confidential information or trade secrets as well as monitor computer activities.

QUESTIONS TO ADDRESS

14-21. Given the factors in this situation, what, if any, ethical issues exist?

14-22. Do you think that the company is wise to monitor employees in this manner? Why, or why not?

14-23. If you discovered that an employee was spending a lot of time on non-work-related searches, how would you address the issue with the employee?

cases

THINK BEFORE YOU CLICK

Continued from page 446

At the beginning of this chapter, you read about illicit activities of IT pirates and their methods for preying on victims, including both organizations and individuals around the globe. You saw that pirating aims to steal money and other resources by luring vulnerable potential victims with seemingly attractive offers of personal gain. Using the information presented in this chapter, you should now be able to answer the following questions.

QUESTIONS FOR DISCUSSION

14-24. Think about recent spam e-mails and text messages that you have received. What kinds of information were the intruders seeking?

14-25. Were you able to identify the e-mails and messages to be "scams" before opening them, or did you discover their real contents after you opened them? What might have alerted you to the risks?

14-26. In what ways might the "opened" message from a scammer be harmful to you? To your IT devices and systems?

14-27. What steps can you take (or have you taken) to protect against such intrusions? What costs would be involved for gaining that protection?

14-28. Consider the various IT systems you use daily. What kinds of protection do they have to protect against invasion by cyber pirates?

SELLING CUSTOMER SEARCH DATA

In late 2016, Federal Communications Commission (FCC) passed regulations that required Internet service providers (ISPs) to get approval from their customers before they could sell information about what websites they visit to third parties. However, businesses like Amazon, FaceBook, and Google fall under the jurisdiction of the Federal Trade Commission (FTC), not the FCC, and the FTC regulations are more lax than the ones passed by the FCC.

Internet service providers successfully lobbied congress to overturn the FCC regulations, and now ISPs can sell your browsing information.

The ISP lobby argued that they should be subject to the same rules as other Internet-based business that collect, analyze, and disseminate consumer data and then use consumer profiles to target advertising. However, ISPs have an advantage in this market, because they can see all of the websites their customers visit, not just the ones that happen to participate in a particular company's ad network. If you visit a lot of travel sites, for example, your ISP might have software that tells ad networks to show you more ads for airline flights or hotel rooms. Amazon only gathers data while you are logged on to Amazon.com, and even browsers like Google can only collect data while you are in the browser. The ISP has access to all of the browsing history, all of the time.

Proponents of the now-repealed FCC regulations limiting ISP data sharing claim that greater access to customer browsing history comes with a correspondingly higher responsibility to keep that information private, and that even if consumers can "opt-out" in order to keep their data private, most people won't be able to find or understand that provision buried in the fine print of the user agreement.

It's likely that this issue isn't settled and that we'll see more and more action on this front as data becomes the currency of the future.

QUESTIONS FOR DISCUSSION

14-29. How and where do you see your browsing data affecting the ads that you see?

14-30. Do you appreciate the targeted marketing that more and more companies use, or do you feel that it is limiting your options? If so, how?

14-31. As a consumer, how do you feel about your Internet Service Provider selling your browsing data? How do you feel about that as a business owner, marketing manager or entrepreneur? What arguments could you make to Congress either for or against enacting tougher restrictions on data like purchasing patterns, search history, and page visits?

14-32. As part of the marketing department of a consumer products company, how would you use browsing history to help market your products?

14-33. What kinds of measures could you implement in order to protect your privacy? Would you do those things, or do you feel that Internet privacy is an oxymoron?

Writing Assignments

14-34. Organizations of every kind, including governments, not-for-profits, and businesses, have experienced dramatic changes from the implementation and growth of information technology. (a) Describe ways that businesses have been improved by implementing IT. (b) Discuss how employees' activities have been changed with IT. In your discussion, use examples to show how the changes have been beneficial. Show also some ways that IT presents new problems for organizations.

14-35. From current news reports, identify and describe a recent technological threat. Who and what was affected? How was the threat neutralized? How could it have been avoided or minimized?

endnotes

[1] McQueen, M. P. "Cyber-Scams on the Uptick in Downturn," *The Wall Street Journal*, January 29, 2009, pp. D1, D4; Joseph De Avila, "Beware of Facebook 'Friends' Who May Trash Your Laptop," *The Wall Street Journal*, January 29, 2009, pp. D1, D4; Acohido, Byron, and Swartz, Jon. "Data Scams Have Kicked into High Gear as Markets Tumble," *USAToday*, January 28, 2009, at http://www.usatoday.com/tech/news/computersecurity/2009-01-28-hackers-data-scams_N.htm; Wragge, Chris. "FBI Warns of High-Tech Cyber ID Theft," *wcbstv.com*, April 8, 2009, at http://wcbstv.com/local/cyber.criminals.fbi.2.980245.html; Robertson, Jordan. "Bad Economy Helps Web Scammers Recruit 'Mules,'" *ABC News*, December 9, 2008, at http://abcnews.go.com/print?id=6422327. All sources accessed on May 10, 2015.

[2] "Hackers in China Blamed for Cyber-Attacks," *Columbia Daily Tribune*, February 10, 2011, p. 5B, and at http://www.columbiatribune.com/news/2011/feb/10/hackers-in-china-blamed-for-cyber-attacks/?news; Milbourn, Mary Ann. "Beware of Fake Job Offers," *The Orange County Register*, October 12, 2010, at http://economy.ocregister.com/2010/10/12/beware-of-fake-job-offers/42194/; Eppstein, Richard. "Scammers Pop Up During Economic Downturns," *Toledo Biz Insider*, March 4, 2010, at http://www.toledoblade.com/article/20100304/BUSINESS11/100309863/-1/BUSINESS; Warman, Matt. "Viruses on Smart-Phones: Security's New Frontier," *The Telegraph*, February 8, 2011, at http://www.telegraph.co.uk/technology/news/8311214/Viruses-on-smartphones-securitys-new-frontier.html. Accessed on May 10, 2015.

[3] See http://www.siriusxm.com/navtraffic/.

[4] "Appropriator Asks NASA to Help Boeing Fix Dreamliner Problems," January 13, 2013, at http://fattah.house.gov/latest-news/appropriator-asks-nasa-to-help-boeing-fix-dreamliner-problems/. Accessed on May 10, 2015 and April 6, 2017.

[5] "Lockheed Martin Aeronautics: Siemens' PLM Software," *Siemens*, at http://www.plm.automation.siemans.com/en_us/about-us/success/case_s, accessed on June 16, 2009, May 10, 2015, and April 5, 2017.

[6] Northrup, Laura. "Timbuk2 Really, Really Wants You to Be Happy with Their Bags," *The Consumerist*, June 5, 2009, at http://www.consumerist.com/2009/06/timbuk2really-really-wants-you-to-be-happy-with-their-bags.html. Accessed on April 6, 2017.

[7] LaGesse, David. "How to Turn Social Networking into a Job Offer," *U.S. News & World Report*, May 11, 2009, at http://www.usnews.com/money/careers/articles/2009/05/11/how-to-turn-social-networking-into-a-job-offer.html. Accessed on April 6, 2017.

[8] 3D Systems. "3D Systems Helps Walter Reed Army Medical Center Rebuild Lives," at http://www.3dsystems.com/appsolutions/casestudies/walter_reed.asp, accessed on June 15, 2009; Hickey, Hannah. "Camera in a Pill Offers Cheaper, Easier Window on Your Insides," UWNews.org (January 24, 2008), at http://uwnews.org/article.asp?articleid=39292. Accessed on April 6, 2017; see also http://www.wrnmmc.capmed.mil/SitePages/home.aspx.

[9] See http://www.Internetworldstats.com/stats.htm. Accessed on April 6, 2017.

[10] "BAN AMRO Mortgage Group Offers One Fee to Ford Motor Company Employees," *Mortgage Mag*, February 14,

2005, at http://www.mortgagemag.com/n/502_003 .htm; "An Intranet's Life Cycle," *morebusiness.com* (June 16, 1999), at http://www.morebusiness.com/getting_ started/website/d928247851.brc;Ahmed, Sally. "Ford Motor Company—Case Study," *Ezine Articles*, August 18, 2008, at http://ezinearticles.com/?Ford-Motor-Company—Case-Study&id=1420478. Accessed on April 6, 2017.

[11] "Companies Take Sides on Super Wi-Fi," *Columbia Daily Tribune*, February 4, 2013, p. 6B.

[12] Brizius, Glen. "CereProc: An Example of a Technology Finally Fulfilling Its Potential," *Associated Content in Technology*, March 16, 2010, at http://www.associatedcontent.com/ article/2786052/cereproc_an_example_of_a_technology .html?cat=5. Accessed on April 6, 2017.

[13] http://www.cereproc.com/en/products

[14] Sheppard, Alyson. "Giving Roger Ebert a New Voice: Q&A With CereProc," *Popular Mechanics*, March 8, 2010, at http:// www.popularmechanics.com/science/health/ prosthetics/rogerebertvoicetech; Millar, Hayley. "New Voice for Film Critic," *BBC News*, March 3, 2010, at http:// news.bbc.co.uk/2/hi/uk_news/scotland/edinburgh_ and_east/8547645.stm. Accessed on April 6, 2017.

[15] Novet, Jordan. "Apple claims Siri's speech recognition tech is more accurate than Google's," VentureBeat, June 8, 2015, at http://venturebeat.com/2015/06/08/apple-claims-siris-speech-recognition-tech-is-more-accurate-than-googles/.

[16] "Kroger Tailors Ads to Its Customers," *Columbia Daily Tribune*, January 12, 2009, 7B; Pichler, Josh. "dunnhumby: Retailer's Secret Weapon," *Cincinnati.com*, January 31, 2013, at news.cincinnati.com/article/20130130/ BIZ/301190100/dunnhumby-Retailers-secret-weapon?nclick_check=1. Accessed on April 6, 2017.

[17] "Data Mining Examples & Testimonials," at http://www .data-mining-software.com/data_mining_examples.htm, accessed February 24, 2011; Angwin, Julia, and Valentino-DeVries, Jennifer. "New Tracking Frontier: Your License Plates," *Wall Street Journal*, September 29–30, 2012, pp. A1, A13; Troianovski, Anton. "New Wi-Fi Pitch: Tracker," *Wall Street Journal*, June 19, 2012, p. B5. Accessed on April 6, 2017.

[18] Marchant, Jo. "Virtual Fossils Reveal How Ancient Creatures Lived," *NewScientist*, May 27, 2009, at http://www.new-scientist.com/article/mg20227103.500-virtual-fossils-reveal-how-ancient-creatures-lived.html. Accessed on April 6, 2017.

[19] Warman, Matt. "Viruses on Smartphones: Security's New Frontier," *The Telegraph*, February 8, 2011, at http:// www.telegraph.co.uk/technology/news/8311214/ Viruses-on-smartphones-securitys-new-frontier.html; Cheng, Jacqui. "Canadian Group: Facebook 'A Minefield of Privacy Invasion,'" May 30, 2008, at http://arstech-nica.com/tech-policy/news/2008/05/canadian-group-files-complaint-over-facebook-privacy.ars; "Cell Phones a Much Bigger Privacy Risk Than Facebook," *Fox News*, February 20, 2009, at http://www.foxnews.com/ printer_friendly_story/0,3566,497544,00.html. Accessed on April 7, 2017.

[20] Gorman, Siobhan, Barrett, Devlin, and Yadron, Danny. "China Hackers Hit U.S. Media," *Wall Street Journal*, February 1, 2013, pp. B1, B2; "Hackers Hit Twitter, Washington Post," *Columbia Daily Tribune*, February 4, 2013, p. 6B. Accessed on May 10, 2015.

[21] Leary, Alex. "Wi-Fi Cloaks a New Breed of Intruder," *St. Petersburg Times*, July 4, 2005, at http://www.sptimes. com/2005/07/04/State/Wi_Fi_cloaks_a_new_br.shtml. Accessed on April 7, 2017.

[22] Melanson, Donald. "Apple: 16 Billion iTunes Songs Downloaded, 300 Million iPods Sold," *Engadget*, October 4, 2011, at www.engadget.com/2011/10/04/ apple-16-billion-itunes-songs-downloaded-300-million-ipods-sol/; Burgess, Christopher, and Power, Richard. "How to Avoid Intellectual Property Theft," *CIO*, July 10, 2006, at http://www.cio.com/article/22837; "For Students Doing Reports," *RIAA*, at www.riaa.com/faq .php, accessed on February 4, 2013; Sisario, Ben. "AC/ DC Joins iTunes, as Spotify Emerges as Music's New Disrupter," *New York Times*, November 19, 2012, at mediadecoder.blogs.nytimes.com/2012/11/19/acdc-joins-itunes-as-spotify-emerges-as-musics-new-disrupter/. Accessed on April 7, 2017.

[23] See http://www.webopedia.com/TERM/S/spyware.html.

[24] Norman, Donald A. "Got Spam?" MAPI: *Manufacturers Alliance for Productivity and Innovation*, October 20, 2016, at http://www.mapi.net/blog/2016/10/got-spam. Accessed on April 7, 2017.

[25] "'Spam King' Faces Federal Fraud Charges," *Columbia Daily Tribune*, January 21, 2013, accessed at http:// www.columbiatribune.com/wire/spam-king-faces-federal-fraud-charges/article_042ac575-7820-5bb4-bb17-3e425f2f24c0.html#.URE7hPKmFcI. Accessed on April 7, 2017.

[26] Carlson, Brad. "Organizations Face New Records-Destruction Rule," *Idaho Business Review*, July 25, 2005, at http:// www.idahobusiness.net/archive.htm/2005/07/25/ Organizations-face-new-recordsdestruction-rule. Accessed on May 10, 2015.

The Role of Accountants and Accounting Information

chapter 15

Suzanne Plunkett/AP Images

"Crunching numbers" is not enough for today's accountants. They need to **communicate,** think critically, and lead.

After reading this chapter, you should be able to:

15-1 **Explain** the role of accountants and distinguish among the kinds of work done by public accountants, private accountants, management accountants, and forensic accountants.

15-2 **Explain** how the accounting equation is used.

15-3 **Describe** the three basic financial statements and show how they reflect the activity and financial condition of a business.

15-4 **Explain** the key standards and principles for reporting financial statements.

15-5 **Describe** how computing financial ratios can help users get more information from financial statements to determine the financial strengths of a business.

15-6 **Discuss** the role of ethics in accounting.

15-7 **Describe** the purpose of the International Accounting Standards Board and explain why it exists.

CSI: Wall Street

In the 1990s, Dennis Kozlowski built Tyco International, a security systems company (not to be confused with the toy division of Mattel, Inc.), into a multi-billion dollar conglomerate. But many of his deals were based on phone calls or handshakes, and the aftermath of those shaky deals drew the attention of Federal prosecutors, who then discovered that Kozlowski had been living a lavish lifestyle far beyond the means of even his generous salary. He was first indicted on delinquent unpaid sales taxes on his purchases of rare art. Even though that suit was thrown out, the accounting trail led to a larger investigation of his use of Tyco funds for lavish spending on opulent parties and personal assets such as his $30 million Fifth Avenue apartment with a $6,000 shower curtain and a $15,000 umbrella stand. In 2005, Kozlowski was convicted on criminal charges for taking unauthorized bonuses, abusing corporate loan programs, falsifying records, and conspiracy. He went to prison and was released in 2015.

Because of the prevalence of this kind of financial scandal, many companies are showing an urgent and growing interest in investigative accounting, also known as forensic accounting.

Forensic accountants typically begin an investigation of a company by interviewing high-level executives. Team members pursue tips from employees or outsiders and then comb through e-mails, searching for suspicious words and phrases. The combination of interviews and e-mails may lead investigators to specific accounting files or ledger entries. According to Al Vondra, partner in Forensic Services and a Certified Fraud Examiner at PricewaterhouseCoopers, some of the most common fraudulent practices involve hiding revenues and expenses under phony categories, such as "Total Noncurrent Assets" or "Other Current Liabilities." For instance, India's Satyam Computer Services Ltd. founder and former CEO Ramalinga Raju was arrested after admitting he falsified accounts that deceived investors for years. The Indian government's Serious Fraud Investigation Office is searching to identify collaborators who falsely reported more than $1 billion in cash and assets that didn't exist at India's fourth-largest software company.[1]

Although accounting scandals have always existed, they spike upward in economic downturns. Data from the Association of Certified Fraud Examiners (ACFE) indicate that corporate fraud cases began increasing significantly early in the 2008 recession, and worldwide fraud losses reached $3.5 trillion in 2012. At the same time, more than 3,000 fraud-related reports and

what's in it for me?

For many of us, the words and ideas used in accounting can seem like a foreign language, and for that very reason the specialized terminology can be used to mask fraud and corruption. However, accounting terminology is a necessary tool that allows professionals in every industry to analyze growth, understand risk, and communicate detailed ideas about a firm's financial health. This chapter will cover the fundamental concepts of accounting and apply them to familiar business situations. By grasping the basic accounting vocabulary you—as an employee, taxpayer, or owner—will be better able to participate when the conversation turns to the financial matters that constitute so much of a firm's daily operations.

whistle-blowing tips were reported from within U.S. firms. ACFE members believe the increase stems from heavier financial pressures: When employees feel less secure, they may falsify data to show better performance, or they may take greater risks that need to be covered up to show financial success.

The most common kind of fraud is asset theft—stealing cash, falsifying business expenses, forging checks, and stealing noncash assets. The chief financial officer of a Florida tree farm, for example, falsified checks and misused company credit cards to embezzle $10 million, earning a 96-month prison sentence and a $14 million fine.[2] The least-common organizational fraud, and the costliest by far, is financial statement manipulation. In 2012, for example, the financial officer of an energy company was convicted of lying to investors while raising funds for the company's energy projects. Instead, the funds were used for salaries for himself and others. Unsuspecting investors lost some $4.3 million in the scam. The culprit received a 97-month prison sentence.

Fraud also exists among the public at large. Fraudulent insurance claims are on the upswing: A private investigator films an injury victim throwing the neck brace into the back seat of his car after leaving the doctor's office, a homeowner inflates the cost of articles stolen in an alleged burglary, and victims of car wrecks from years past suddenly submit injury claims. Employees, too, are a source of fraud; the U.S. Commerce Department estimates that one-third of business shutdowns are the result of employee theft. Inventory stolen from the firm's warehouse is resold; the company's strategic inside information is stolen and sold to a competitor; and employees receive reimbursement for falsely inflated business expenses.[3]

Because the accounting systems and records—and the accountants that tend to them—are designed to capture all of the financial transactions of the company, it is often those records that lead to fraud detection. But even more significantly, a well-designed accounting system can prevent fraud. And although fraud gets a lot of attention, the day-to-day operational information provided by accountants helps managers create a more profitable business, report results of operations to stakeholders, and manage the long-term health of the company through budgeting, capital acquisition analysis, business segment analysis, and a world of other financial decision-making processes. (After studying the content in this chapter, you should be able to answer a set of discussion questions found at the end of the chapter.)

OBJECTIVE 15-1
Explain
the role of accountants and distinguish among the kinds of work done by public accountants, private accountants, management accountants, and forensic accountants.

Accounting *comprehensive system for collecting, analyzing, and communicating financial information*

Bookkeeping *recording of accounting transactions*

Accounting Information System (AIS) *organized procedure for identifying, measuring, recording, and retaining financial information for use in accounting statements and management reports*

What Is Accounting, and Who Uses Accounting Information?

Accounting is a comprehensive system for collecting, analyzing, and communicating financial information to a firm's owners and employees, to the public, and to various regulatory agencies. To perform these functions, accountants keep records of taxes paid, income received, and expenses incurred, a process historically called **bookkeeping**, and they assess the effects of these transactions on business activities. By sorting and analyzing such transactions, accountants can determine how well a business is being managed and assess its overall financial strength.

Because businesses engage in thousands of transactions, ensuring consistent, dependable financial information is a necessity. This is the job of the **accounting information system (AIS)**, an organized procedure for identifying, measuring, recording, and retaining financial information so that it can be used in accounting statements and management reports. The system includes all of the people, reports, computers, procedures, and resources that are needed to compile financial transactions.[4]

Many different individuals, groups, and other entities use accounting information:

- *Managers* use it to develop goals and plans, set budgets, and make decisions about market opportunities.

- *Employees and unions* use it to plan for and receive compensation and such benefits as health care, vacation time, and retirement pay.

- *Investors and creditors* use it to estimate returns to stockholders, determine growth prospects, and decide whether a firm is a good credit risk.

- *Tax authorities* use it to plan for tax inflows, determine the tax liabilities of individuals and businesses, and ensure that correct amounts are paid on time.

- *Government regulatory agencies* rely on it to fulfill their duties toward the public. The Securities and Exchange Commission (SEC), for example, requires firms to file financial disclosures so that potential investors have valid information about their financial status.

The **controller**, or chief accounting officer, manages a firm's accounting activities by ensuring that the AIS provides the reports and statements needed for planning, decision making, and other management activities. This range of activities requires different types of accounting specialists. In this section, we begin by distinguishing between the two main fields of accounting: *financial* and *managerial*. Then, we discuss the different functions and activities of *certified public accountants, private accountants, management accountants,* and *forensic accountants.*

Controller *person who manages all of a firm's accounting activities (chief accounting officer)*

Financial versus Managerial Accounting

In any company, the two fields of accounting—financial and managerial—can be distinguished by the users they serve: those outside the company and those within.[5]

Financial Accounting A firm's **financial accounting** system is concerned with external information users: consumer groups, unions, stockholders, suppliers, creditors, and government agencies. It prepares reports such as income statements and balance sheets that focus on the activities of the company as a whole rather than on individual departments or divisions.[6]

Financial Accounting *field of accounting concerned with external users of a company's financial information*

Managerial Accounting **Managerial accounting**, on the other hand, serves internal users. Managers at all levels need information to make departmental decisions, monitor projects, and plan future activities. Other employees also need accounting information. Engineers must know certain costs, for example, before making product or operations improvements, purchasing agents use information on materials costs to negotiate terms with suppliers and to set performance goals, and salespeople need historical sales data for each geographic region and for each of its products.

Managerial (Management) Accounting *field of accounting that serves internal users of a company's financial information*

Certified Public Accountants

Public accountants offer accounting services to the public and are distinguished by their independence from the clients they serve. That is to say, they typically work for an accounting firm providing services for outside client firms in which the public accountant has no vested interest, thus avoiding any potential biases in conducting their professional services. Among public accountants, **certified public accountants (CPAs)** are licensed by a state after passing an exam prepared by the American Institute of Certified Public Accountants (AICPA). Preparation for certification begins with majoring in a college program studying the theory, practices, and legal aspects of accounting. In addition to the CPA exam, certification in most states requires some practice, varying up to two years, in a private company or government entity under the direction of a CPA. Once certified, the CPA can perform services beyond those allowed by non-CPAs.[7] Whereas some CPAs work as individual practitioners, many form or join existing partnerships or professional corporations.

Certified Public Accountant (CPA) *accountant licensed by the state and offering services to the public*

The "Big Four" Public Accounting Firms Although thousands of CPA companies of various sizes, ranging from small one-person local operations to large multinationals, operate in the United States, about one-half of their total revenues go to the four biggest CPA firms (listed with their headquarters):

- Deloitte Touche Tohmatsu (United Kingdom)

- Ernst & Young (United Kingdom)

Accountants help monitor and analyze a firm's financial information to make sure that it is accurate and that proper reporting procedures are being followed. Accountants recently uncovered fraudulent activities at Tesco, a large British retailer, resulting in jail time for these three former Tesco executives. All told, accountants discovered that they had inaccurately reported over $400 million in revenues and expenses in order to falsely boost Tesco stock prices.

- PricewaterhouseCoopers, PwC (United Kingdom)

- KPMG (Netherlands)

In addition to prominence in the United States, international operations are important for all four of these companies. They have experienced especially rapid growth in recent years for CPA services in Asia and Latin America. Each of the Big Four firms has more than 150,000 employees worldwide.[8]

CPA Services Virtually all CPA firms, whether large or small, provide auditing, tax, and management services. Larger firms such as Deloitte Touche Tohmatsu and Ernst & Young earn much of their revenue from auditing services, though consulting (management advisory) services constitute a major growth area. Smaller firms earn most of their income from tax and management services.

AUDITING An **audit** examines a company's AIS to determine whether financial reports reliably represent its operations.[9] Organizations must provide audit reports when applying for loans, selling stock, or going through a major restructuring. Independent auditors who do not work for the company must ensure that clients' accounting systems follow **generally accepted accounting principles (GAAP)**, which are formulated by the Financial Accounting Standards Board (FASB) of the AICPA and govern the content and form of financial reports.[10] The auditing of a firm's financial statements is one of the services that can be performed only by a CPA. The SEC is the U.S. government agency that legally enforces accounting and auditing rules and procedures. Ultimately, the CPA performing the audit will certify whether the client's reports comply with GAAP.

TAX SERVICES **Tax services** include assistance not only with tax-return preparation but also with tax planning. A CPA's advice can help a business structure (or restructure) operations and investments and perhaps save millions of dollars in taxes. Staying abreast of tax-law changes is no simple matter. Some critics charge that the changing of tax regulations has become a full-time vocation among some state and federal legislators who add increasingly complicated laws and technical corrections on taxation each year.

MANAGEMENT ADVISORY SERVICES As consultants, some accounting firms also provide **management advisory services** ranging from personal financial planning to planning corporate mergers. Other services include production scheduling, information systems studies, AIS design, and even executive recruitment. The staffs of the

Audit *systematic examination of a company's accounting system to determine whether its financial reports reliably represent its operations*

Generally Accepted Accounting Principles (GAAP) *accounting guidelines that govern the content and form of financial reports*

Tax Services *assistance provided by CPAs for tax preparation and tax planning*

Management Advisory Services *assistance provided by CPA firms in areas such as financial planning, information systems design, and other areas of concern for client firms*

Hannah McKay/PA Images/Alamy Stock Photo

largest CPA firms sometimes include engineers, architects, mathematicians, and psychologists, all of whom are available for consulting.

Noncertified Public Accountants Many accountants don't take the CPA exam; others work in the field while getting ready for it or while meeting requirements for state certification. Many small businesses, individuals, and even larger firms rely on these non-CPAs for income-tax preparation, payroll accounting, and financial-planning services so long as they abide by local and state laws. Non-CPAs often put together financial statements that are used in the firm for internal purposes, based on information provided by management. These statements may include a notification that auditing methods were not used in their preparation.

The CPA Vision Project A continuing talent shortage in accounting has led the profession to rethink its culture and lifestyle.[11] With grassroots participation from CPAs, educators, and industry leaders, the AICPA, through its CPA Vision Project, is redefining the role of the accountant for today's world economy. The Vision Project identifies a unique combination of skills, technology, and knowledge, called **core competencies for accounting**, that will be necessary for the future CPA. The AICPA summarizes the project's core purpose as follows: "CPAs … Making sense of a changing and complex world."[12] As Table 15.1 shows, those skills, which include communication, critical thinking, and leadership, go far beyond the ability to "crunch numbers." They include certain communications skills, along with skills in critical thinking and leadership. Indeed, the CPA Vision Project foresees CPAs who combine specialty skills with a broad-based orientation to communicate more effectively with people in a wide range of business activities.

Core Competencies for Accounting *the combination of skills, technology, and knowledge that will be necessary for the future CPA*

Private Accountants and Management Accountants

To ensure integrity in reporting, CPAs engaged in auditing activities are always independent of the firms they audit. However, many businesses also hire their own salaried employees, **private accountants**, to perform day-to-day activities. These accountants may also be CPAs but cannot engage in the external audit process.

Private Accountant *salaried accountant hired by a business to carry out its day-to-day financial activities*

Private accountants perform numerous jobs. An internal auditor at ConocoPhillips, for example, might fly to the North Sea to confirm the accuracy of oil-flow meters on offshore petroleum drilling platforms. A supervisor responsible for $2 billion in

table 15.1 Emerging Competencies for Success in Accounting

Skills in Strategic Thinking and Critical Problem Solving	The accountant can combine data with reasoning and professional knowledge to recognize and help solve critical problems for better strategic action.
Communications, Interpersonal Skills, and Effective Leadership	The accountant can communicate effectively in various business situations using meaningful communications skills that provide interpersonal effectiveness and leadership.
Dedication to Meeting Customer Needs	The accountant surpasses the competition in understanding each client's unique needs, in meeting those needs, and in visualizing the client's future needs.
Ability to Integrate Diverse Information	The accountant can combine financial and other kinds of information to gain new meaning that provides clients with useful insights and understanding for solving problems.
Proficiency with Information Technology	The accountant can use information technology (IT) in performing services for clients and can identify IT applications that the client can adopt for added value to the business.

Source: Based on "The CPA Vision Project and Beyond," *The American Institute of Certified Public Accountants,* at http://www.aicpa.org/RESEARCH/CPAHORIZONS2025/CPAVISIONPROJECT/Pages/CPAVisionProject.aspx, accessed on April 15, 2017.

monthly payouts to vendors and employees may never leave the executive suite, with duties such as hiring and training, assigning projects, and evaluating performance of accounting personnel. Large businesses employ specialized accountants in such areas as budgeting, financial planning, internal auditing, payroll, and taxation. In small businesses, a single person may handle all accounting tasks.

Although private accountants may be either CPAs or non-CPAs, most are **management accountants** who provide services to support managers in various activities (marketing, production, engineering, and so forth). Many hold the **certified management accountant (CMA)** designation, awarded by the Institute of Management Accountants (IMA), recognizing qualifications of professionals who have passed IMA's experience and examination requirements. With more than 65,000 worldwide members, IMA is dedicated to supporting accounting professionals to create quality internal controls and financial practices in their companies.

Management Accountant private accountant who provides financial services to support managers in various business activities within a firm

Certified Management Accountant (CMA) professional designation awarded by the Institute of Management Accountants (IMA) in recognition of management accounting qualifications

Forensic Accountants

One of the fastest-growing areas in accounting is **forensic accounting**, the use of accounting for legal purposes.[13] Sometimes known as "the private eyes of the corporate culture," forensic accountants must be good detectives. They look behind the corporate façade instead of accepting financial records at face value. In combining investigative skills with accounting, auditing, and the instincts of a detective, they assist in the investigation of business and financial issues that may have application to a court of law. Forensic accountants may be called on by law enforcement agencies, insurance companies, law firms, private individuals, and business firms for both investigative accounting and litigation support in crimes against companies, crimes by companies, and civil disagreements. They may conduct criminal investigations of Internet scams and misuse of government funds. Civil cases often require investigating and quantifying claims of personal injury loss as a result of negligence and analyzing financial issues in matrimonial disputes. Forensic accountants also assist business firms in tracing and recovering lost assets from employee business fraud or theft.

Forensic Accounting the practice of accounting for legal purposes

Investigative Accounting Law enforcement officials may ask a forensic accountant to investigate a trail of financial transactions behind a suspected crime, as in a money-laundering scheme or an investment swindle. The forensic accountant, being familiar with the legal concepts and procedures of the case, would then identify and analyze pertinent financial evidence—documents, bank accounts, phone calls, computer records, and people—and present accounting conclusions and their legal implications. They also develop reports, exhibits, and documents to communicate their findings.

Litigation Support Forensic accountants assist in the application of accounting evidence for judicial proceedings by preparing and preserving evidence for these proceedings. They also assist by presenting visual aids to support trial evidence, by testifying as expert witnesses, and, especially, in determining economic damages in any case before the court. A divorce attorney, for example, may suspect that assets are being understated and request financial analysis by a forensic accountant. A movie producer may need help in determining damages for breach of contract by an actress who quits before a film is completed.

Certified Fraud Examiners One specific area within forensic accounting, the **Certified Fraud Examiner (CFE)** designation, is administered by the ACFE. The CFE's activities focus specifically on fraud-related issues, such as fraud detection, evaluating accounting systems for weaknesses and fraud risks, investigating white-collar crime on behalf of law enforcement agencies, evaluating internal organizational controls for fraud prevention, and expert witnessing. Many CFEs find employment in corporations seeking to prevent fraud from within. The CFE examination covers four areas:

Certified Fraud Examiner (CFE) professional designation administered by the ACFE in recognition of qualifications for a specialty area within forensic accounting

1   *Fraud prevention and deterrence*—Includes why people commit fraud, theories of fraud prevention, and professional code of ethics

2 *Financial transactions*—Examines types of fraudulent financial transactions incurred in accounting records

3 *Fraud investigation*—Pertains to tracing illicit transactions, evaluating deception, and interviewing and taking statements

4 *Legal elements of fraud*—Includes rules of evidence, criminal and civil law, and rights of the accused and accuser

Eligibility to take the exam includes both educational and experience requirements. Although a minimum of a bachelor's degree is required, it does not have to be in accounting or any other specific field of study. Candidates without a bachelor's degree, but with fraud-related professional experience, may substitute two years of experience for each year of academic study. Experience requirements for certification include at least two years in any of several fraud-related areas, such as auditing, criminology, fraud investigation, or law.

managing in turbulent times

Skimming Off the Top

Jennifer Mayberry runs a respectable coffee shop in a small Pacific Northwest town. For years she's dropped her daily receipts off in the night deposit slot at the local Chase Bank, where her friend works, but Jennifer, trusting the banking system, never reconciled her deposit slips to her accounting records. In fact, she never reconciled her checking account to the bank statement. But when her accountants started tallying up revenues for tax reporting, they found a $1,000 discrepancy in the November deposit. That led to the hiring of a forensic accountant who discovered that despite internal controls at the bank, Jennifer's friend had been skimming the cash from the deposits, changing the deposit slips, and then making the smaller deposit into the account. Over the course of 18 months, the friend skimmed $42,828.96. Some simple accounting procedures could have prevented this.[14]

Meanwhile, down in Texas at the Collins Street Bakery, world famous for its delectable fruitcakes, owner Bob McNutt is unraveling a decade of embezzlement. It had started when the head accountant, feeling underpaid, bought himself a new Lexus and paid for it with a company check, covering his tracks by voiding that check in the system and writing another check to a legitimate vendor, which he then never sent. In the bank account, a check cleared for $20,000, and the accounting records showed a payment of $20,000. Since there were no other accountants and the business owner didn't audit the records, no one caught the theft. Soon, the accountant was taking up to $98,000 a month from the bakery and he and his wife were living a lavish lifestyle, explaining it away as the result of an inheritance. No one much questioned the fine cars, vacations, jewelry, country club membership, home remodeling and other obviously expensive purchases. Eventually McNutt, who had been scratching his head now for years trying to figure out how his business, which seemed so outwardly successful, was cash-poor and struggling year after year, examined labor

The Fort Worth Star-Telegram/Ron Jenkins/AP Images

expenses, product expenses, prices, and everything he could think of, but found nothing helpful. But one day, a new hire in the accounting department found a curious voided check in the system. That was the beginning of the end for the thief. As the story unfolded, McNutt found that this one accountant had managed to skim over $17 million from Collins Street Bakery, using an unsophisticated scheme that could have been prevented by a few simple internal control procedures.[15]

Small and medium-sized businesses aren't the only ones who get hit by embezzlers. Cargill Inc. is a global corporation based in Minnesota, and although it's privately held, on the Fortune 500 list it would rank ahead of AT&T. In 2016, one of the accounting managers pled guilty to skimming over $3 million from the company by depositing customer payments into her personal account.[16]

It's not just high-tech scams that these businesses need to watch out for. All three of these instances occurred because the business owners took a relaxed view of the kinds of accounting policies and procedures that protect one of the most valuable assets and easily lifted assets—cash. That's why it pays to become educated in basic financial accounting and human resource management as you move your way up in business.

table 15.2 **Selected Provisions of the Sarbanes-Oxley Act**[17]

- Creates a national Accounting Oversight Board that, among other activities, must establish the ethics standards used by CPA firms in preparing audits
- Requires that auditors retain audit working papers for specified periods of time
- Requires auditor rotation by prohibiting the same person from being the lead auditor for more than five consecutive years
- Requires that the CEO and CFO certify that the company's financial statements are true, fair, and accurate
- Prohibits corporations from extending personal loans to executives and directors
- Requires that the audited company disclose whether it has adopted a code of ethics for its senior financial officers
- Requires that the SEC regularly review each corporation's financial statements
- Prevents employers from retaliating against research analysts who write negative reports
- Imposes criminal penalties on auditors and clients for falsifying, destroying, altering, or concealing records (10 years in prison)
- Imposes a fine or imprisonment (up to 25 years) on any person who defrauds shareholders
- Increases penalties for mail and wire fraud from 5 to 20 years in prison
- Establishes criminal liability for failure of corporate officers to certify financial reports

Federal Restrictions on CPA Services and Financial Reporting: Sarbox

Sarbanes-Oxley Act Of 2002 (Sarbox or Sox) *enactment of federal regulations to restore public trust in accounting practices by imposing new requirements on financial activities in publicly traded corporations*

The financial wrongdoings associated with firms such as ImClone Systems, Tyco, WorldCom (now MCI), Enron, Arthur Andersen, and others have not gone unnoticed in legislative circles. Federal regulations, in particular the **Sarbanes-Oxley Act of 2002 (Sarbox or SOX)**, have been enacted to restore and maintain public trust in corporate accounting practices.

Sarbox restricts the kinds of nonaudit services that CPAs can provide. Under the Sarbox law, for example, a CPA firm can help design a client's financial information system, but not if it also does the client's auditing. Hypothetically, an unscrupulous accounting firm's audit might intentionally overlook a client's false financial statements if, in return, the client rewards the accounting firm with a contract for lucrative nonaccounting services, such as management consulting. This was a core allegation in the Enron-Arthur Andersen scandal. Arthur Andersen, one of the world's largest accounting firms at the time, filed audits that failed to disclose Enron's shaky financial condition that eventually led to the massive energy company's bankruptcy and to Anderson's dissolution. Andersen's auditor gained more money from consulting at Enron than it got for auditing.[18] By prohibiting auditing and nonauditing services to the same client, Sarbox encourages audits that are independent and unbiased.

Sarbox imposes requirements on virtually every financial activity in publicly traded corporations, as well as severe criminal penalties for persons committing or concealing fraud or destroying financial records. CFOs and CEOs, for example, have to pledge that the company's finances are correct and must personally vouch for the methods and internal controls used to get those numbers. Companies have to provide a system that is safe for all employees to anonymously report unethical accounting practices and illegal activities without fear of retaliation. Table 15.2 provides brief descriptions of several of Sarbox's many provisions.

OBJECTIVE 15-2
Explain
how the accounting equation is used.

The Accounting Equation

All accountants rely on record keeping to enter and track transactions. Underlying all record-keeping procedures is the most basic tool of accounting, the **accounting equation**:

$$Assets = Liabilities + Owners' Equity$$

An asset is an economic resource that benefits the firm. Apple's assets include retail outlets and the inventories of Apple products that the stores keep on hand to sell to customers.

After each financial transaction (e.g., payments to suppliers, sales to customers, wages to employees), the accounting equation must be in balance. If it isn't, then an accounting error has occurred. To better understand the importance of this equation, we must understand the terms *assets*, *liabilities*, and *owners' equity*.

Accounting Equation *Assets = Liabilities + Owners' Equity; used by accountants to balance data for the firm's financial transactions at various points in the year*

Assets and Liabilities

An **asset** is any economic resource that is expected to benefit a firm or an individual who owns it. Assets for accounting purposes include land, buildings, equipment, inventories, and payments due the company (accounts receivable). Apple, for example, held total assets amounting to $290,479 million at year end 2016.[19] A **liability**, on the other hand, is a debt that a firm owes to an outside party. The total of Apple's liabilities—all the debt owed to others—was $171,124 million at the end of 2016.

Asset *any economic resource expected to benefit a firm or an individual who owns it*

Liability *debt owed by a firm to an outside organization or individual*

Owners' Equity

You may be familiar with the concept of *equity* that a homeowner has in a house—the amount of money that could be made (or lost) by selling the house and paying off the mortgage. Similarly, **owners' equity** in a business is the amount of money that owners would theoretically receive if they sold all of a company's assets at their presumed value and paid all of its liabilities. Apple's financial reports for 2016 declared shareholders' equity of $119,355 million. At Apple, then, we see that the accounting equation is in balance, as it should be.

Owners' Equity *amount of money that owners would receive if they sold all of a firm's assets and paid all of its liabilities*

$$\text{Assets} = \text{Liabilities} + \text{Owners' Equity}$$
$$\$29.0479 = \$17.1124 + \$11.9355 \text{ billion}$$

We can also rewrite the equation to highlight how owners' equity relates to assets and liabilities.

$$\text{Assets} - \text{Liabilities} = \text{Owners' Equity}$$

Another term for this is *net worth*: the difference between what a firm owns (assets) minus what it owes (liabilities) is its net worth, or owners' equity. If a company's assets exceed its liabilities, owners' equity is *positive*. At Apple, owners' equity is $119,355 million (= $290,479 million − $171,124 million). If the company goes out of business, the owners may receive some cash (a gain) after selling assets and paying off liabilities. However, if liabilities outweigh assets, owners' equity is *negative*; assets are insufficient to pay off all debts, and the firm is bankrupt. If the company goes out of business, the owners will get no cash, and some creditors won't be paid.

Owners' equity is meaningful for both investors and lenders. Before lending money to owners, for example, lenders want to know the amount of owners' equity in a business. A larger owners' equity indicates greater security for lenders. Owners' equity consists of two sources of capital:

1   The amount that the owners originally invested
2   Profits (also owned by the owners) earned by and reinvested in the company

When a company operates profitably, its assets increase faster than its liabilities. Owners' equity, therefore, will increase if profits are retained in the business instead of paid out as dividends to stockholders. Owners' equity also increases if owners invest more of their own money to increase assets. However, owners' equity can shrink if the company operates at a loss or if owners withdraw assets.

entrepreneurship and new ventures

Working With the Accounting Equation

Perhaps you have heard people talking about having equity in their home. A homeowner's equity is simply the difference between what a home is worth (the market value) and the amount owed to the bank. The same could be said of a person's car. If you buy a car for $1,000 and pay cash, your equity is $1,000, but if you pay $50 down and finance the rest, your equity is only $50. You gain equity as you pay the loan down, unless the car loses value faster than you pay the loan. Accounting is based on that equation:

Assets = Liabilities + Owners' Equity.

Dinis Tolipov/123RF

There's one small difference in United States accounting rules, though: For the most part, instead of using the market value of the asset, business accountants use the historical cost.

Generally, the first step in creating a business is to establish the business entity, often by setting up a business bank account. Suppose that you start a woodworking business by filing for a business license with the state and depositing $10,000 into a business bank account. Your business now has $10,000 in assets, the cash that you deposited, no liabilities, and $10,000 in equity. Equity then is the value of the business to the owner—what you would receive if you discontinued operations.

Perhaps you've decided that your best opportunity to make money is to make custom wooden shutters for the windows of historic homes. But, to be able to do this work efficiently, you'll need to buy an expensive piece of equipment costing $20,000. This greatly exceeds your cash, so you take out a loan to purchase the equipment. After this transaction, your business now has two assets—$10,000 in cash and a $20,000 piece of equipment—making your total assets $30,000. On the other side of the accounting equation, you have liabilities of $20,000 and your owners' equity is $10,000, making the total liabilities and owner's equity $30,000, just the same as your total assets.

Imagine that you're lucky enough to receive an order for 10 sets of custom shutters and your profit on this sale is the $20,000 sales price less your cost of $5,000 for wood and other supplies. Once the shutters have been delivered and the bill has been paid, you will have $15,000 in cash, which will be added to your beginning cash balance of $10,000. Your total assets are $45,000, consisting of $25,000 in cash and $20,000 in equipment. On the other side of the equation, your liabilities have remained the same, but your equity has now increased by your profit on your first sale, increasing from $10,000 to $25,000. As a result, your total liabilities and owners' equity is $20,000 in liabilities and $25,000 in equity or $45,000—exactly the same as your total assets.

Finally, after all your hard work, you'd like to treat yourself to a great vacation. You withdraw $8,000 cash from the business, which reduces both your cash and your equity by this amount. As a result, the accounting equation remains in balance, with total assets of $37,000 ($17,000 in cash and $20,000 in equipment) and total liabilities and owner's equity of $40,000 ($20,000 in liabilities and $17,000 in equity). As you can see, the accounting equation provides the framework around which financial information is organized.

Financial Statements

OBJECTIVE 15-3
Describe
the three basic financial statements and show how they reflect the activity and financial condition of a business.

As noted previously, accountants summarize the results of a firm's transactions and issue reports to help managers make informed decisions. Among the most important reports are **financial statements**, which fall into three broad categories: *balance sheets, income statements*, and *statements of cash flows*. Together, these reports indicate the firm's financial health and what affected it. In this section, we discuss these three financial statements as well as the function of the budget as an internal financial statement.

Financial Statement *any of several types of reports summarizing a company's financial status to stakeholders and to aid in managerial decision making*

Balance Sheets

Balance sheets supply detailed information about the items that comprise the accounting equation: *assets, liabilities*, and *owners' equity*. Because they also show a firm's financial condition at one point in time, they are sometimes called *statements of financial position*. Figure 15.1 is a simplified presentation of the balance sheet for Apple, Inc. as of the end of 2016.

Balance Sheet *financial statement that supplies detailed information about a firm's assets, liabilities, and owners' equity*

Assets From an accounting standpoint, most companies have major three types of assets: *current, fixed*, and *intangible*.

CURRENT ASSETS Current assets include cash and assets that can be converted into cash within a year. The act of converting something into cash is called *liquidating*. Assets are normally listed in order of **liquidity**, the ease of converting them into cash. Debts, for example, are usually paid in cash. A company that needs but cannot generate cash—a company that's not "liquid"—may be forced to sell assets at reduced prices or even to go out of business.

Current Asset *asset that can or will be converted into cash within a year*

Liquidity *ease with which an asset can be converted into cash*

Apple, Inc.
Summary of Balance Sheet (condensed)
as of December 31, 2016
(in millions)

Assets		Liabilities and Shareholder's Equity	
Current Assets:		Current liabilities:	
Cash	$21,120	Accounts payable	$35,490
Marketable securities	20,481	Accrued expenses	25,181
Accounts receivable	16,849	Other	19,939
Other	30,928	**Total current liabilities**	**$80,610**
Total current assets	**$89,378**		
		Long-term liabilities:	
Long-term marketable assets:		All long-term debts	$53,463
Total long-term marketable assets	**$164,065**	Other	37,051
		Total long-term liabilities	**$90,514**
Fixed assets:		**Total liabilities**	**$171,124**
Property and equipment, net	$22,471		
Total fixed assets	**$22,471**	Shareholder's equity:	
		Common stock and paid-in capital	$27,416
Intangible assets:		Retained earnings	91,939
Intangible assets	$3,893	**Total shareholder's equity**	**$119,355**
Goodwill	5,116		
Total intangible assets	**$9,009**	**Total liabilities and shareholder's equity**	**$290,479**
Other assets			
Total other assets	**5,556**		
Total assets	**$290,479**		

Apple's balance sheet for year ended December 31, 2016. As clearly indicated, Apple's total assets are equal to its total liabilities and owner's equity.

FIGURE 15.1 Apple's Balance Sheet
Source: Apple, Inc. (2017). 2016 Annual Report. Mountain View, California: Author.

By definition, cash is completely liquid. *Marketable securities* purchased as short-term investments are slightly less liquid but can be sold quickly. These include stocks or bonds of other companies, government securities, and money market certificates. Many companies hold other nonliquid assets such as *merchandise inventory*, the cost of merchandise that's been acquired for sale to customers and is still on hand. Apple keeps very little inventory on hand. For instance, as new iPhones are manufactured they are shipped directly to retailers like AT&T or Verizon and are then carried as inventory on the balance sheets of those companies. However, because Apple generates so much cash it does maintain robust investments in long-term marketable assets.

Fixed Asset *asset with long-term use or value, such as land, buildings, and equipment*

Depreciation *accounting method for distributing the cost of an asset over its useful life*

FIXED ASSETS Fixed assets (such as land, buildings, and equipment) have long-term use or value, but as buildings and equipment wear out or become obsolete, their value decreases. Accountants use **depreciation** to spread the cost of an asset over the years of its useful life. To reflect decreasing value, accountants calculate an asset's useful life in years, divide its worth by that many years, and subtract the resulting amount each year. Every year, therefore, the remaining value (or net value) decreases on the books. In Figure 15.1, Apple shows fixed assets of $22,471 million after depreciation.

Intangible Asset *nonphysical asset, such as a patent or trademark, that has economic value in the form of expected benefit*

Goodwill *amount paid for an existing business above the value of its other assets*

INTANGIBLE ASSETS Although their worth is hard to calculate, **intangible assets** have monetary value in the form of expected benefits, which may include fees paid by others for obtaining rights or privileges—including patents, trademarks, copyrights, and franchises—to your products. **Goodwill** is the amount that a buyer would be expected to pay for an existing business beyond the value of its other assets. A purchased firm, for example, may have a particularly good reputation or location. Apple declares both intangible assets and goodwill in its balance sheet.

Current Liability *debt that must be paid within one year*

Accounts Payable (Payables) *current liability consisting of bills owed to suppliers, plus wages and taxes due within the coming year*

Long-Term Liability *debt that is not due for at least one year*

Liabilities Like assets, liabilities are often separated into different categories. **Current liabilities** are debts that must be paid within one year. These include **accounts payable (payables)**, unpaid bills to suppliers for materials as well as wages and taxes that must be paid in the coming year. Apple has current liabilities of $80,610 million. **Long-term liabilities** are debts that are not due for at least a year. These normally represent borrowed funds on which the company must pay interest. The long-term liabilities of Apple are $90,514 million.

Paid-In Capital *money that is invested in a company by its owners*

Owners' Equity The final section of the balance sheet in Figure 15.1 shows owners' equity (shareholders' equity) broken down into *paid-in capital* and *retained earnings*. When Apple was first formed, it sold a small amount of common stock that provided its first *paid-in capital*. **Paid-in capital** is money invested by owners. Apple's paid-in capital had grown to $27,416 million by year end 2016, and includes proceeds from Apple's initial public offering of stock in 1980 that generated funds that were needed for early business growth.

Retained Earnings *earnings retained by a firm for its use rather than paid out as dividends*

Retained earnings are net profits kept by a firm rather than paid out as dividend payments to stockholders. They accumulate when profits, which can be distributed to shareholders, are kept instead for the company's use. At the close of 2016, Apple had retained earnings of $91,939 million. The total of stockholders' equity—paid-in capital plus retained earnings—was $119,355 million.

The balance sheet for any company, then, is a barometer for its financial condition at one point in time. By comparing the current balance sheet with those of previous years, creditors and owners can better interpret the firm's financial progress and future prospects in terms of changes in its assets, liabilities, and owners' equity.

Income Statements

Income Statement (Profit-and-Loss Statement) *financial statement listing a firm's annual revenues and expenses so that a bottom line shows annual profit or loss*

The **income statement** is sometimes called a **profit-and-loss statement** because its description of revenues and expenses results in a figure showing the firm's annual profit or loss. In other words,

$$\text{Profit (or Loss)} = \text{Revenues} - \text{Expenses}$$

Apple, Inc.
Summary of Income Statement (condensed)
January 1, 2016–December 31, 2016
(in millions)

Revenues (gross sales)		**$233,715**
Cost of revenues	**140,089**	
Gross profit		**$93,626**
Operating expenses:		
Research development	8,067	
Selling, administrative and general	13,044	
Total operating expenses		**$21,111**
Operating income (before taxes)		$72,515
Income taxes*		19,121
Net income		**$53,394**

*approximate

FIGURE 15.2 Apple's Income Statement
Source: Apple, Inc. (2017). 2016 Annual Report. Mountain View, California: Author.

Popularly known as the *bottom line*, profit or loss is probably the most important figure in any business enterprise. Figure 15.2 shows the 2016 income statement for Apple, whose bottom line was $53,394 million in profit. The income statement is divided into four major categories: (1) *revenues*, (2) *cost of revenues*, (3) *operating expenses*, and (4) *net income*. Unlike a balance sheet, which shows the financial condition at a specific *point in time*, an income statement shows the financial results that occurred during a *period of time*, such as a month, quarter, or year.

Revenues When a law firm receives $250 for preparing a will or a supermarket collects $65 from a grocery shopper, both are receiving **revenues**, the funds that flow into a business from the sale of goods or services. In 2016, Apple reported revenues of $233,715 million from the sale of iPhones, iPads, computers, digital music, and other products.

> **Revenues** *funds that flow into a business from the sale of goods or services*

Cost of Revenues (Cost of Goods Sold) In the Apple income statement, the **cost of revenues** section shows the costs of obtaining the revenues from other companies during the year. These are the costs that Apple pays manufacturers for producing its hardware products like phones, tablets, and computers and the licensing fees it pays for the right to distribute music, movies, and so forth. Other costs include expenses arising from the operation of Apple's data centers, including labor, energy, and costs of processing customer transactions. The cost of revenues for Apple in 2016 was $140,089 million.

> **Cost of Revenues** *costs that a company incurs to obtain revenues from other companies*

We should also note that Apple does very little of its own manufacturing—most of its manufacturing is outsourced to low-cost producers in Asia. Traditional manufacturing companies, however, like Ford and Procter & Gamble, use a different reporting category, **cost of goods sold**, which are the costs of obtaining and transforming materials to make physical products sold during the year.

> **Cost of Goods Sold** *costs of obtaining materials for making the products sold by a firm during the year*

GROSS PROFIT Managers are often interested in **gross profit**, a preliminary, quick-to-calculate profit figure that considers just two pieces of data—revenues and cost of revenues (the direct costs of getting those revenues)—from the income statement. To calculate gross profit, simply subtract cost of revenues from revenues obtained by selling the firm's products.

> **Gross Profit** *preliminary, quick-to-calculate profit figure calculated from the firm's revenues minus its cost of revenues (the direct costs of getting the revenues)*

OPERATING EXPENSES In addition to costs directly related to generating revenues, every company has general expenses ranging from office supplies to the CEO's salary. Like cost of revenues and cost of goods sold, **operating expenses** are resources that

> **Operating Expenses** *costs, other than the cost of revenues, incurred in producing a good or service*

must flow out of a company if it is to earn revenues. As shown in Figure 15.2, Apple had operating expenses of $21,111 million in 2016.

Research development expenses are associated with exploring new services and technologies that might be introduced in the future. *Selling expenses* result from activities related to selling goods or services, such as sales-force salaries and advertising expenses. *Administrative and general expenses*, such as management salaries and maintenance costs, are related to the overall management of the company.

Operating Income *gross profit minus operating expenses*

Operating and Net Income **Operating income** compares the gross profit from operations against operating expenses. This calculation for Apple ($93,626 million – $21,111 million) yields an operating income, or income before taxes, of $72,515 million. Subtracting estimated income taxes from operating income ($72,515 million − $19,121 million) yields **net income (net profit or net earnings)**. Apple's net income for 2016 was $53,394 million. The step-by-step detail in an income statement shows how a company obtained its net income for the period, making it easier for shareholders and other stakeholders to evaluate the firm's financial performance.

Net Income (Net Profit or Net Earnings) *gross profit minus operating expenses and income taxes*

Statements of Cash Flows

Some companies prepare only balance sheets and income statements. However, the SEC requires all firms whose stock is publicly traded to issue a third report, the **statement of cash flows**. This statement summarizes yearly cash receipts and cash payments. Because it provides the most detail about how the company generates and uses cash, some investors and creditors consider it one of the most important statements of all. It shows the effects on cash of three aspects of a business: *operating activities*, *investing activities*, and *financing activities*. Apple's (simplified) 2016 statement of cash flows is shown in Figure 15.3.

Statement of Cash Flows *financial statement describing a firm's yearly cash receipts and cash payments*

- *Cash Flows from Operations.* The first set of information presented in the statement concerns primary operating activities: cash transactions involved in buying and selling goods and services. For Apple, it reveals how much of the year's cash balance results from the firm's main line of business, sales of iPhones, iPads, computers, and music. At the beginning of 2016 Apple had $13,844 million of cash

Apple, Inc.
Summary of Cash-flow (condensed)
January 1, 2016–December 31, 2016
(in millions)

Net cash/cash equivalents at beginning of year		$13,844
Net cash provided by operating activities		$53,394
Net cash provided from other sources		
Proceeds from sales of marketable securities	$5,541	
Proceeds from issuance of common stock	543	
Other	289	
Total	$6,373	$73,611
Net cash expended		
Payments for marketable securities	$12,897	
Payments for intangible assets	9,450	
Payments for repurchase of common stock	24,756	
Other	5,388	
Total		$52,491
Net case/cash equivalents at end of year		$21,120

FIGURE 15.3 Apple's Statement of Cash Flows
Source: Apple, Inc. (2017). 2016 Annual Report. Mountain View, California: Author.

on hand. During the year it generated an additional $53,394 million in cash from the sales of its primary product lines.

- **Cash Flows from Investing.** A second set of information in the statement reports net cash used in or provided by investing. It includes cash receipts and payments from buying and selling stocks, bonds, property, equipment, and other productive assets. These sources of cash are not the company's main line of business. Apple generated $5,541 million from sales of marketable securities but also spent $12,897 million on other marketable securities.

- **Cash Flows from Financing.** The third set of information reports net cash from all financing activities. It includes cash inflows from borrowing or issuing stock, as well as outflows for payment of dividends and repayment of borrowed money. Apple's financing activities included $543 million in proceeds from the issuance of common stock but also $24,756 spent on the repurchase of common stock at different times during the year.

- The overall change in cash from all of these sources, as well as a few other minor sources, was an increase in cash from $13,844 million at the beginning of 2016 to $21,120 million at the end of 2016. When creditors and stockholders know how a firm obtained and used funds during the course of a year, it's easier for them to interpret year-to-year changes in the balance sheet and income statement.

The Budget: An Internal Financial Statement

For planning, controlling, and decision making, the most important internal financial statement is the **budget**, a detailed report on estimated receipts and expenditures for a future period of time. Although that period is usually one year, some companies also prepare longer-term projections, most commonly three- or five-year budgets, especially when considering major capital expenditures. The budget differs from the other statements we have discussed in that they are not shared outside the company (hence the "internal financial statement" term).

Budget *detailed statement of estimated receipts and expenditures for a future period of time*

Although the accounting team coordinates the budget process, it needs input from many other managers in the organization about proposed activities and required resources. Figure 15.4 is a sales budget for a hypothetical wholesaler, Perfect Posters. In preparing next year's budget, accounting must obtain from the sales

Perfect Posters, Inc.
555 RIVERVIEW, CHICAGO, IL 60606

Perfect Posters, Inc.
Sales Budget
First Quarter, 2018

	January	February	March	Quarter
Budgeted sales (units)	7,500	6,000	6,500	20,000
Budgeted selling price per unit	$3.50	$3.50	$3.50	$3.50
Budgeted sales revenue	**$26,250**	**$21,000**	**$22,750**	**$70,000**
Expected cash receipts:				
From December sales	$26,210			$26,210
From January sales	17,500	$8,750		26,250
From February sales		14,000	$7,000	21,000
From March sales			15,200	15,200
Total cash receipts:	**$43,710**	**$22,750**	**$22,200**	**$88,660**

FIGURE 15.4 Perfect Posters' Sales Budget

group projections for units to be sold and expected expenses for the coming year. Then, accounting draws up the final budget and, throughout the year, compares the budget to actual expenditures and revenues. Discrepancies signal potential problems and spur action to improve financial performance.

OBJECTIVE 15-4
Explain
the key standards and principles for reporting financial statements.

Reporting Standards and Practices

Accountants follow standard reporting practices and principles when they prepare external reports. The common language dictated by standard practices and spelled out in GAAP is designed to give external users confidence in the accuracy and meaning of financial information. GAAP cover a range of issues, such as when to recognize revenues from operations and how to make full public disclosure of financial information. Without such standards, users of financial statements wouldn't be able to compare information from different companies and would misunderstand—or be led to misconstrue—a company's true financial status. Forensic accountants, such as Al Vondra from the opening case, watch for deviations from GAAP as indicators of possible fraudulent practices.

Revenue Recognition and Activity Timing

Revenue Recognition *formal recording and reporting of revenues at the appropriate time*

The reporting of revenue inflows, and the timing of other transactions, must abide by accounting principles that govern financial statements. **Revenue recognition**, for example, is the formal recording and reporting of revenues at the appropriate time. Although a firm earns revenues continuously as it makes sales, earnings are not reported until the *earnings cycle* is completed. This cycle is complete under two conditions:

1 The sale is complete and the product delivered.
2 The sale price has been collected or is collectible (accounts receivable).

The end of the earnings cycle determines the timing for revenue recognition in a firm's financial statements. Suppose a toy company in January signs a sales contract to supply $1,000 of toys to a retail store with delivery scheduled in February. Although the sale is completed in January, the $1,000 revenue should not then be recognized (that is, not be reported in the firm's financial statements) because the toys have not been delivered and the sale price is not yet collectible, so the earnings cycle is incomplete. Revenues are recorded in the accounting period—February—in which the product is delivered and collectible (or collected). This practice ensures that the statement gives a fair comparison of what was gained (revenues) in return for the resources that were given up (cost of materials, labor, and other production and delivery expenses) for the transaction.

Full Disclosure

Full Disclosure *guideline that financial statements should not include just numbers but should also furnish management's interpretations and explanations of those numbers*

To help users better understand the numbers in a firm's financial statements, GAAP requires that financial statements also include management's interpretations and explanations of those numbers. The idea of requiring input from the manager is known as the **full disclosure** principle. Because they know about events inside the company, managers prepare additional information to explain certain events or transactions or to disclose the circumstances behind certain results.

For example, Borders was once the second-largest bookseller in the United States (behind Barnes and Noble). However, the firm filed for bankruptcy in early 2011 and closed its last store in September of that same year. In its annual reports and financial statements beginning as early as 2008, however, the management of Borders had discussed the competitive and economic risks facing the company. These disclosures noted that consumer spending trends were shifting to online retailers and eBooks and away from in-store purchasing, thus posing growing risks for Borders' cash flows and overall financial condition. Management's discussion noted there could be no assurance that Borders would muster adequate financial resources to remain competitive and, indeed, it soon happened. On filing for bankruptcy, Borders' liabilities of $1.29 billion had surpassed its assets of $1.28 billion.[20] The disclosure information helped investors and other stakeholders make informed decisions about the risks associated with investing in or doing business with Borders. It would have been a far different story had Borders' managers offered deceptively optimistic assessments of the business's future.

Analyzing Financial Statements

OBJECTIVE 15-5
Describe
how computing financial ratios can help users get more information from financial statements to determine the financial strengths of a business.

Financial statements present a lot of information, but how can it be used? How, for example, can statements help investors decide what stock to buy or help lenders decide whether to extend credit? Answers to such questions for various stakeholders— employees, managers, unions, suppliers, the government, customers—can be answered this way: Statements provide data, which can, in turn, reveal trends and be applied to create various *ratios* (comparative numbers). We can then use these trends and ratios to evaluate a firm's financial health, its progress, and its prospects for the future.

Ratios are normally grouped into three major classifications:

1 **Solvency ratios** for estimating short-term and long-term risk
2 **Profitability ratios** for measuring potential earnings
3 **Activity ratios** for evaluating management's use of assets

Depending on the decisions to be made, a user may apply none, some, or all of these ratios.

Solvency Ratio *financial ratio, either short or long term, for estimating the borrower's ability to repay debt*

Profitability Ratio *financial ratio for measuring a firm's potential earnings*

Activity Ratio *financial ratio for evaluating management's efficiency in using a firm's assets*

Solvency Ratios: Borrower's Ability to Repay Debt

What are the chances that a borrower will be able to repay a loan and the interest due? This question is first and foremost in the minds of bank lending officers, managers of pension funds and other investors, suppliers, and the borrowing company's own financial managers. Solvency ratios provide measures of a firm's ability to meet its debt obligations.

The Current Ratio and Short-Term Solvency **Short-term solvency ratios** measure a company's liquidity and its ability to pay immediate debts. The most commonly used of these is the **current ratio** or "banker's ratio." This ratio measures a firm's ability to generate cash to meet current obligations through the normal, orderly process of selling inventories and collecting revenues from customers. It is calculated by dividing current assets by current liabilities. The higher a firm's current ratio, the lower the risk to investors. As a general rule, a current ratio is satisfactory at 2:1 or higher—that is, if current assets more than double current liabilities. A smaller ratio may indicate that a firm will have trouble paying its bills. Of course, a large, successful firm may be able to maintain a lower current ratio.

Short-Term Solvency Ratio *financial ratio for measuring a company's ability to pay immediate debts*

Current Ratio *financial ratio for measuring a company's ability to pay current debts out of current assets*

Long-Term Solvency Stakeholders are also concerned about **long-term solvency**. Has the company been overextended by borrowing so much that it will be unable to repay debts in future years? A firm that can't meet its long-term debt obligations is in danger of collapse or takeover, a risk that makes creditors and investors quite cautious. To evaluate a company's risk of running into this problem, creditors turn to the balance sheet to see the extent to which a firm is financed through borrowed money. Long-term solvency is calculated by dividing **debt** (total liabilities) by owners' equity. The lower a firm's debt, the lower the risk to investors and creditors.

Long-Term Solvency *financial ratio for measuring a company's ability to pay its long-term debt*

Debt *company's total liabilities*

Companies with more debt may find themselves owing so much that they lack the income needed to meet interest payments or to repay borrowed money.

Sometimes, high debt not only can be acceptable but also desirable. Borrowing funds gives a firm **leverage**, the ability to make otherwise unaffordable investments. In *leveraged buyouts*, firms have willingly taken on sometimes huge debts to buy out other companies. If owning the purchased company generates profits above the cost of borrowing the purchase price, leveraging often makes sense. Unfortunately, many buyouts have caused problems because profits fell short of expected levels or because rising interest rates increased payments on the buyer's debt.

Leverage *ability to finance an investment through borrowed funds*

Profitability Ratios: Earnings Power for Owners

It's important to know whether a company is solvent in both the long and the short term, but risk alone is not an adequate basis for investment decisions. Investors also want some indication of the returns they can expect. Evidence of earnings power is available from profitability ratios, such as earnings per share and the price-earnings ratio.

Defined as net income divided by the number of shares of common stock outstanding (that is, in the hands of investors), **earnings per share** determines the size of the dividend that a firm can pay shareholders. As an indicator of a company's wealth potential, investors might use this ratio to decide whether to buy or sell the firm's stock. As the ratio goes up, stock value increases because investors know that the firm can better afford to pay dividends. Naturally, stock loses market value if financial statements report a decline in earnings per share. Another useful profitability ratio is the **price earnings ratio**, most commonly known as the P/E ratio. This ratio is the comparison of a firm's current share price to its current earnings per share.

Earnings Per Share *profitability ratio measuring the net profit that the company earns for each share of outstanding stock*

Price Earnings Ratio *most commonly known as the P/E ratio, this ratio is the comparison of a firm's current share price to its current earnings per share.*

Activity Ratios: How Efficiently Is the Firm Using Its Resources?

The efficiency with which a firm uses resources is linked to profitability. As a potential investor, you want to know which company gets more mileage from its resources. Information obtained from financial statements can be used for *activity ratios* to measure this efficiency. For example, two firms use the same amount of resources or assets to perform a particular activity. If Firm A generates greater profits or sales, it has used its resources more efficiently and so enjoys a better activity ratio. This may apply to any important activity, such as advertising, sales, or inventory management.

Retailers, for example, often focus on inventory turnover ratios. Suppose an appliance retailer expects to sell an average of 30 refrigerators per month over the next year. One strategy would be to order 360 refrigerators to arrive on January 1. This would be a poor strategy, however, for many different reasons: The retailer would need to maintain and pay for a huge warehouse space, there would be increased risk of damage to the refrigerators that will not be sold for several months, and the retailer will have to pay for refrigerators now that will not generate revenue for several months. A better option would be to order fewer refrigerators so that they arrive in smaller quantities but more frequent intervals.

Bringing Ethics into the Accounting Equation

OBJECTIVE 15-6
Discuss
the role of ethics in accounting.

The purpose of ethics in accounting is to maintain public confidence in business institutions, financial markets, and the products and services of the accounting profession. Without ethics, all of accounting's tools and methods would be meaningless because their usefulness depends, ultimately, on veracity in their application.

In addition to the business world's many favorable opportunities and outcomes, there are also instances of misconduct. Amid public reports of unscrupulous activity, ethics remains an area in which one person who is willing to "do the right thing" can make a difference—and people do, every day. The role of ethics in the ground-breaking scandal from several years ago remains a classic example: Refusing to turn a blind eye to unethical accounting around her at Enron, the now-failed giant energy corporation, Lynn Brewer tried to alert people inside about misstatements of the company's assets. When that failed, she, along with colleagues Sherron Watkins and Margaret Ceconi, talked with the U.S. Committee on Energy and Commerce to voice concerns about Enron's condition. To Brewer, maintaining personal and professional integrity was an overriding concern, and she acted accordingly.

AICPA's Code of Professional Conduct

The **code of professional conduct** for public accountants in the United States is maintained and enforced by the AICPA. The institute identifies six ethics-related areas—listed in Table 15.3—with which accountants must comply to maintain certification. Comprehensive details for compliance in each area are spelled out in the AICPA Code of Professional Conduct. The IMA maintains a similar code to provide ethical guidelines for the management accounting profession.

Code of Professional Conduct *code of ethics for CPAs as maintained and enforced by the AICPA*

In reading the AICPA's code, you can see that it forbids misrepresentation and fraud in financial statements. Deception certainly violates the call for exercising moral judgments (in "Responsibilities"), is contrary to the public interest (by deceiving investors), and does not honor the public trust (in "The Public Interest"). Misleading statements destroy the public's confidence in the accounting profession and in business in general. Although the code prohibits such abuses, its success depends, ultimately, on its acceptance and use by the professionals it governs.

table 15.3 Highlights from the Code of Ethics for CPAs

By voluntarily accepting Certified Public Accountant membership, the accountant also accepts self-enforced obligations, listed here, beyond written regulations and laws.

Responsibilities as a Professional	The CPA should exercise their duties with a high level of morality and in a manner that is sensitive to bringing credit to their profession.
Serving the Public Interest	The CPA should demonstrate commitment to the profession by respecting and maintaining the public trust and serving the public honorably.
Maintaining Integrity	The CPA should perform all professional activities with highest regards for integrity, including sincerity and honesty, so as to promote the public's confidence in the profession.
Being Objective and Independent	The CPA should avoid conflicts of interest, and the appearance of conflicts of interest, in performing their professional responsibilities. They should be independent from clients when certifying to the public that the client's statements are true and genuine.
Maintaining Technical and Ethical Standards Through Due Care	The CPA should exercise "due care," through professional improvement, abiding by ethical standards, updating personal competence through continuing accounting education, and improving the quality of services.
Professional Conduct in Providing Services	The CPA in public practice should abide by the meaning and intent of the Code of Professional Conduct when deciding on the kinds of services and the range of actions to be supplied competently and diligently for clients.

Source: Based on "Code of Professional Conduct," *AICPA,* at www.aicpa.org/Research/Standards/CodeofConduct/Pages/sec50.aspx, accessed on April 19, 2017.

table 15.4 Examples of Unethical and Illegal Accounting Actions[21]

Corporation	Accounting Violation
AOL Time Warner	America Online (AOL) inflated ad revenues to keep stock prices high before and after merging with Time Warner.
Freddie Mac	This U.S. government corporation fraudulently misstated $5 billion in earnings.
HCA, Columbia/HCA	Healthcare association and hospital defrauded Medicare, Medicaid, and TRICARE through false cost claims and unlawful billings (paid $1.7 billion in civil penalties, damages, criminal fines, and penalties).
Tyco	CEO Dennis Kozlowski illegally used company funds to buy expensive art for personal possession (he received an 8- to 25-year prison sentence).
Waste Management	Overstated income in financial statements (false and misleading reports) by improperly calculating depreciation and salvage value for equipment.
WorldCom (now MCI)	Hid $3.8 billion in expenses to show an inflated (false) profit instead of loss in an annual income statement.

Violations of Accounting Ethics and GAAP

Unethical and illegal accounting violations have dominated the popular press in recent years. Some of the more notorious cases, listed in Table 15.4, violated the public's trust, ruined retirement plans for tens of thousands of employees, and caused business shutdowns and significant job loss. As you read each case, you should be

finding a better way

Analytics and the Future of Auditing

Following the Stock Market Crash of 1929, the American Institute of Accountants recommended five broad principles of accounting that the committee felt had become most generally accepted by the accounting profession. At the same time, the Federal government created the Securities and Exchange Commission (SEC) in order to regulate financial reports from publicly traded companies. Although the SEC has the legal authority to establish Generally Accepted Accounting Principles (GAAP), as financial transactions became more and more complicated, the SEC and the accounting profession partnered to create the Financial Accounting Standards Board (FASB)—the first full-time accounting standards setting and research board in the world.

In order to enforce the SEC and FASB rules, accounting firms developed audit procedures to apply to company financial statements. As independent auditors, the accounting firms could assure the public that the statements had been prepared in accordance with GAAP. Early audits relied on management assertions, but as they developed, the procedures began to look to more objective evidences, such as visual inspections of inventory and blind confirmations of receivables.

That was the state of auditing for years. Much of the auditing was done using manual procedures, spreadsheets, and some sampling and statistical analysis. But now the audit function is changing rapidly as audit firms are integrating data analytics, machine learning, and other modern technology in audit

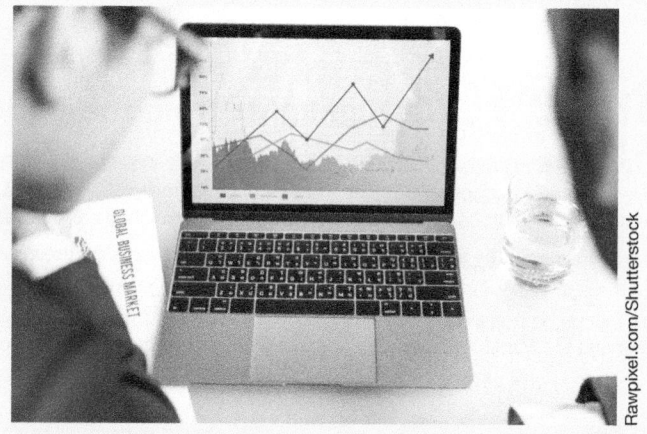

Rawpixel.com/Shutterstock

work, changing the breadth and depth of audits and clients' expectations. In fact, the audit report that has hardly changed since the 1970s may undergo significant revisions within the next few years.

Just as data analytics and big data inform what we buy, what news we read, and even whom we date, it is now becoming a big part of audit work. Data analytics enable auditors to examine 100 percent of a client's transactions; track and analyze trends, as well as anomalies and risks, to identify problematic areas or transactions; and benchmark a company's financial information against others based on industry, geography, size, or other factors. As auditing changes, new risks emerge, but so do new opportunities for tech-savvy auditors.

able to see how its violation relates to the presentation of balance sheets and income statements in this chapter. In each case, adversity would have been prevented if employees had followed the code of professional conduct. In each case, nearly all of the code's six ethics-related areas were violated, and "professionals" willingly participated in unethical behavior. Such unscrupulous behavior was the impetus for Sarbox.

Internationalizing Accounting

Accounting in its earliest forms is known to have existed more than 7,000 years ago in Mesopotamia and Egypt for recording trade transactions and keeping track of resources. With the passage of time, each country or region's accounting practices were refined to meet its needs in commerce while also accommodating local cultural traditions and developments in its laws. Although unique practices served each region well, they later posed problems as international business became prominent. By the late twentieth century, it was apparent that the upsurge in multinational organizations and the global economy demanded more uniformity among accounting practices. The development of "universal" procedures would allow governments and investors in, say, China, Brazil, and Italy to read, interpret, and compare financial statements from all those countries, whereas such comparisons even today are difficult if not sometimes impossible.

International Accounting Standards Board

Established in 2001 and housed at London, England, the **International Accounting Standards Board (IASB)** is an independent, nonprofit organization responsible for developing a set of global accounting standards and for gaining the support and cooperation of the world's various accounting organizations to implement those standards.

International Accounting Standards Board (IASB) *organization responsible for developing a set of global accounting standards and for gaining implementation of those standards*

IASB's 14 board members from various countries are full-time accounting experts with technical and international business experience.[22] Because the board cannot command sovereign nations to accept its recommended standards, its commitment to gaining cooperation around the world is a continuing task. Yet, international acceptance is essential for success. Accordingly, the board's task is a long-term process that requires working with various countries to design proposed standards. As an example, for any IASB proposal to be accepted in the United States, it must first be approved by the U.S.-based FASB and by the U.S. SEC. However, IASB's efforts extend beyond the United States, to all nations. The expected timeline reaches beyond 2015 for convergence of the many local GAAP into one global set of practices.

Why One Set of Global Practices?

Although more than 138 countries have adopted IASB's accounting practices, over 50 others continue to use their national GAAP.[23] U.S.-based global companies such as Google, Caterpillar, and Microsoft may prepare different financial reports using local accounting practices for each country in which they conduct business. They also report the company's overall performance in a set of consolidated statements that combines the financial results of all its global affiliates, using U.S. GAAP. Using different accounting standards, however, can result in vastly different pictures of a firm's financial health. Income statements, balance sheets, and statements of cash flows using local GAAPs versus IASB practices, for example, may contain conflicting information with inconsistencies leading to confusion and misunderstandings among investors and other constituents. To emphasize this point, Hans Hoogervorst, Chairman of the IASB, notes that a company using IASB standards can report balance sheet figures that are twice the size of those using U.S. GAAP accounting standards.[24] Which of the reports tells how well the company is doing? Such inconsistencies in reporting are unacceptable in a global economy and, accordingly, protection against them is a goal of IASB.

Example Areas Targeted for Aligning U.S. GAAP and IASB Among the many differences between the practices of U.S. GAAP and IASB—some reports identify more than 400 such discrepancies—the following examples illustrate some discrepancies and proposals for convergence toward universal standards in financial reporting.

- *In valuing assets* (reported on the balance sheet), U.S. GAAP allows an asset to be written down if for some reason its value decreases. However, the value cannot later be rewritten up, even if it its actual value has increased. IASB standards, in contrast, do allow such write-ups reflecting increased market value, so the reported value of a company's assets can be quite different, depending on the chosen accounting system.[25]

- *In revenue recognition*, when revenues from customers should be recognized (reported), and in what amounts on the income statement, the U.S. GAAP and IASB procedures differ from each other. A current joint proposal, if approved, would remove existing inconsistencies and provide a single standard that recognizes revenue at the time the goods and services are transferred to the customer, and in the amounts that are expected to be received (or are received) from the customer.[26]

- *In devaluing of financial assets*, such as writing down bad loans in the financial crisis, both U.S. GAAP and IASB currently use the same procedure: After a loss occurs (but not until after the fact), the loan's value can be written down in the firm's financial statements, reflecting its lower value. Both groups, however, believe an "expected loss model" that recognizes (and reports) likely loan losses *ahead of time* will provide more timely information for investors and financial planners. A joint proposal for such a procedure has been presented but is still being discussed.[27]

- *In fair value disclosure,* the FASB and IASB jointly propose new standards for improving the comparability of fair value disclosures in financial statements. Unlike dissimilar disclosure practices among many local GAAP, both groups want the reported "fair value" for an asset, a liability, and an item in shareholders' equity to have the same meaning under both FASB and IASB procedures. The disclosure should identify the techniques and inputs used to measure fair value so that users can more clearly assess and compare financial statements.[28]

Timetable for Implementation The U.S. SEC originally targeted 2015 as the earliest date that U.S. companies would be required to use IASB procedures for financial reporting. Some procedures were implemented that year, but others were deferred and/or targeted to be phased in over a period of years. To fully implement any given procedure, IASB must first demonstrate that its standards are developed adequately for use in the U.S. financial reporting system. Doing so includes assuring that investors have developed an understanding of and education in using IASB standards. Accounting education, too, is being updated to prepare U.S. accounting students for IASB, as well as updating practitioners in CPA firms. The AICPA has begun a process of introducing international standards in the CPA examinations. Some of the exam's questions now address some of the areas of difference between U.S. GAAP and International Financial Reporting Standards.

summary of learning objectives

Explain the role of accountants and distinguish among the kinds of work done by public accountants, private accountants, management accountants, and forensic accountants. (pp. 480–486)

The role of accountants is to maintain a comprehensive system for collecting, analyzing, and communicating financial information for use by external constituents and within firms for planning, controlling, and decision making. It measures business performance and translates the results into information for management decisions. The users of accounting information include business managers, employees and unions, investors and creditors, tax authorities, and government regulatory agencies.

The *controller*, or chief accounting officer, manages a firm's accounting activities by ensuring that the *accounting information system* provides the reports and statements needed for planning, decision making, and other management activities. Accounting activities may be either financial or managerial. *Financial accounting* is concerned with external users of information, such as consumer groups, unions, stockholders, and government agencies, and focuses on the entity as a whole. *Managerial accounting*'s focus is internal users, such as managers, engineers, purchasing agents, and salespeople. Managerial accounting focuses on the detailed information needed to make decisions within the organization.

Public accountants offer accounting services to individuals and businesses outside their organization and are distinguished by their independence from the clients they serve. *Certified public accountants (CPAs)* are licensed professionals who provide auditing, tax, and management advisory services for other firms and individuals. Only CPAs can audit a firm's financial statements, and CPAs are always independent of the firms they audit. Many businesses hire their own salaried employees—*private accountants*—to perform internal accounting activities, such as internal auditing, taxation, cost analysis, and budgeting. Among private accountants, *certified management accountants* have passed the profession's experience and examination requirements for proficiency to provide internal accounting services that support managers in various activities (such as marketing, production, and engineering). *Forensic accountants* use accounting for legal purposes by providing investigative and litigation support in crimes against companies, crimes by companies, and civil cases.

Explain how the accounting equation is used. (pp. 486–488)

Accountants use the following equation to balance the data pertaining to financial transactions:

$$\text{Assets} - \text{Liabilities} = \text{Owners' Equity}$$

After each financial transaction (e.g., payments to suppliers, sales to customers, wages to employees), the accounting equation must be in balance. If it isn't, then an accounting error has occurred. An *asset* is any economic resource that is expected to benefit a firm or an individual who owns it. Assets include land, buildings, equipment, inventory, and payments due the company (accounts receivable). A liability is a debt that the firm owes to an outside party. Owners' equity consists of capital from two sources: (1) The amount that the owners originally invested; and (2) profits (also owned by the owners) earned by and reinvested in the company. Owners' equity is meaningful for both investors and lenders. Before lending money to owners, lenders want to know the amount of owners' equity in a business. A larger owners' equity indicates greater security for lenders. As shown from the accounting equation, if assets exceed liabilities, owners' equity is positive; if the firm goes out of business, owners will receive some cash (a gain) after selling assets and paying off liabilities. If liabilities outweigh assets, owners' equity is negative; assets aren't enough to pay off debts. If the company goes under, owners will get no cash and some creditors won't be paid, thus losing their remaining investments in the company.

OBJECTIVE 15-3

Describe the three basic financial statements and show how they reflect the activity and financial condition of a business. (pp. 489–494)

Accounting summarizes the results of a firm's transactions and issues reports—including *financial statements*—to help managers and other stakeholders make informed decisions. The *balance sheet* (sometimes called the *statement of financial position*) supplies detailed information about the accounting equation items—assets, liabilities, and owners' equity—that together are a barometer of the firm's financial condition at a point in time. By comparing the current balance sheet with those of previous years, creditors and owners can better interpret the firm's financial progress and future prospects in terms of changes in assets, liabilities, and owners' equity.

The *income statement* (sometimes called a *profit-and-loss statement*) describes revenues and expenses to show a firm's annual profit or loss during a period of time, such as a year. The information in an income statement shows how a company obtained its net income for the accounting period, making it easier for shareholders and other stakeholders to evaluate the firm's financial health.

A publicly traded firm must issue a *statement of cash flows*, which describes its yearly cash receipts (inflows) and payments (outflows). It shows the effects on cash during the year from three kinds of business activities: (a) cash flows from operations, (b) cash flows from investing, and (c) cash flows from financing. The statement of cash flows then reports the overall change in the company's cash position at the end of the accounting period. When creditors and stockholders know how a firm obtained and used funds during the course of a year, it's easier for them to interpret year-to-year changes in the balance sheet and income statement.

For planning, controlling, and decision making, the most important internal financial statement is the *budget*, a detailed report on estimated receipts and expenditures for a future period of time. Budgets are internal documents and not usually shared outside the company.

OBJECTIVE 15-4

Explain the key standards and principles for reporting financial statements. (pp. 494–495)

Accountants follow standard reporting practices and principles when they prepare financial statements. The common language dictated by standard practices and spelled out in generally accepted accounting principles (GAAP) is designed to give external users confidence in the accuracy and meaning of financial information. Without these standards, users wouldn't be able to compare information from different companies, and they might misunderstand—or be led to misconstrue—a company's true financial status.

Two of the most important standard reporting practices and principles are revenue recognition and full disclosure. *Revenue recognition* refers to the rules associated with the recording and reporting of revenues in financial statements. All firms earn revenues continuously as they make sales, but earnings are not reported until the earnings cycle is completed. This cycle is complete under two conditions: (a) The sale is complete and the product delivered; (b) the sale price has been collected or is collectible (accounts receivable). This practice assures interested parties that the statement gives a fair comparison of what was gained (revenues) for the resources that were given up (cost of materials, labor, and other expenses) for the transaction.

Full disclosure recognizes that a firm's managers have inside knowledge—beyond just the numbers reported in its financial statements—that can explain certain events, transactions, or otherwise disclose the circumstances behind certain results. Full disclosure means that financial statements include management interpretations and explanations to help external users understand the financial information contained in statements.

Describe how computing financial ratios can help users get more information from financial statements to determine the financial strengths of a business. (pp. 495–496)

Financial statements contain data that can be used in *ratios* (comparative numbers) to analyze the financial health of a company in terms of solvency, profitability, and efficiency in performing activities. Ratios can help creditors, investors, and managers assess a firm's current status and check its progress by comparing current with past statements. *Solvency ratios* use balance sheet data to measure the firm's ability to meet (repay) its debts. The most commonly used solvency ratio is known as the current ratio. The *current ratio* measures the ability to meet current (short-term) liabilities out of current assets. It is calculated by dividing current assets by current liabilities. The higher a firm's current ratio, the lower the risk to investors. A smaller ratio may indicate that a firm will have trouble paying its bills. Stakeholders are also concerned about long-term solvency. *Long-term solvency ratios* compare the firm's total liabilities (including long-term debt) against the owners' equity. High indebtedness (a high ratio) can be risky because it requires payment of interest and repayment of borrowed funds that may not be available.

Profitability ratios, such as earnings per share, measure current and potential earnings. Investors are interested in this ratio because it indicates the firm's earnings power and the returns they can expect from their investments. *Activity ratios* reflect management's use of assets by measuring the efficiency with which a firm uses its resources for a particular activity, such as sales, advertising, or inventory management. Sales efficiency, for example, can be measured from income statement data for annual sales revenues as compared with sales expenses. Sales efficiency has increased if the year-to-year growth in sales revenues is larger than the growth in sales expenses.

Discuss the role of ethics in accounting. (pp. 496–499)

The purpose of ethics in accounting is to maintain public confidence in business institutions, financial markets, and the products and services of the accounting profession. Without ethics, all of accounting's tools and methods would be meaningless because their usefulness depends, ultimately, on truthfulness in their application. Accordingly, professional accounting associations such as the AICPA and IMA enforce codes of professional conduct that include ethics-related areas, such as the accountant's responsibilities, the public interest, integrity, and due care. The codes prohibit, among other things, misrepresentation and fraud in financial statements because misleading statements destroy the public's confidence in the accounting profession and in business in general. Although the code prohibits such abuses, its success depends ultimately on its acceptance and use by the professionals it governs.

Describe the purpose of the International Accounting Standards Board and explain why it exists. (pp. 499–500)

The International Accounting Standards Board (IASB) is an independent, nonprofit organization established for the purposes of developing a set of global accounting standards and for gaining the support and cooperation of the world's various accounting organizations to implement those standards. It exists because the upsurge in multinational organizations and the global economy demand more uniformity among accounting practices, so that accounting reports become more understandable across nations and regions. Because the board cannot command sovereign nations to accept its recommended standards, its commitment to gaining cooperation around the world is a continuing task that requires working with various countries to design proposed international standards. Although more than 100 countries have adopted IASB's accounting practices, nearly 40 others, including China, Canada, and the United States, continue to use their national accounting standards that are often not comparable and can result in vastly different pictures of a firm's financial health. The development of "universal" procedures would allow governments and investors everywhere to read, interpret, and compare financial statements from every country, whereas such comparisons even today are difficult if not sometimes impossible. Different accounting standards, such as how assets are valued and how revenues should be recognized, can result in vastly different pictures of a firm's financial health. Income statements, balance sheets, and statements of cash flows using U.S GAAP versus IASB practices may contain conflicting information with inconsistencies leading to confusion and misunderstandings among investors and other constituents. The U.S. SEC targeted 2015 as the earliest date that U.S. companies would be required to use IASB procedures for financial reporting. However, some procedures have been deferred and others are being implemented in phases.

key terms

accounting (or accountancy) (p. 480)
accounting equation (p. 487)
accounting information system (AIS) (p. 480)
accounts payable (payables) (p. 490)
activity ratio (p. 495)
asset (p. 487)
audit (p. 482)
balance sheet (p. 489)
bookkeeping (p. 480)
budget (p. 493)
Certified Fraud Examiner (CFE) (p. 484)
certified management accountant (CMA) (p. 484)
certified public accountant (CPA) (p. 481)
code of professional conduct (p. 497)
controller (p. 481)
core competencies for accounting (p. 483)
cost of goods sold (p. 491)
cost of revenues (p. 491)
current asset (p. 489)
current liability (p. 490)
current ratio (p. 495)

debt (p. 495)
depreciation (p. 490)
earnings per share (p. 496)
financial accounting (p. 481)
financial statement (p. 489)
fixed asset (p. 490)
forensic accounting (p. 484)
full disclosure (p. 494)
generally accepted accounting principles (GAAP) (p. 482)
goodwill (p. 490)
gross profit (p. 491)
income statement (profit-and-loss statement) (p. 490)
intangible asset (p. 490)
International Accounting Standards Board (IASB) (p. 499)
leverage (p. 496)
liability (p. 487)
liquidity (p. 489)
long-term liability (p. 490)
long-term solvency (p. 495)
management accountant (p. 484)

management advisory services (p. 482)
managerial (management) accounting (p. 481)
net income (net profit, net earnings) (p. 492)
operating expenses (p. 491)
operating income (p. 492)
owners' equity (p. 487)
paid-in capital (p. 490)
price earnings ratio (p. 496)
private accountant (p. 483)
profitability ratio (p. 495)
retained earnings (p. 490)
revenue recognition (p. 494)
revenues (p. 491)
Sarbanes-Oxley Act of 2002 (SARBOX or SOX) (p. 486)
short-term solvency ratio (p. 495)
solvency ratio (p. 495)
statement of cash flows (p. 492)
tax services (p. 482)

MyLab Intro to Business

To complete the problems with the ✪, go to EOC Discussion Questions in the MyLab.

questions & exercises

QUESTIONS FOR REVIEW

15-1. Who are the users of accounting information and for what purposes do they use it?

15-2. Identify the three types of services performed by CPAs.

15-3. Explain the ways in which financial accounting differs from managerial accounting.

✪ 15-4. Discuss the activities and services performed by forensic accountants.

✪ 15-5. What are the three basic financial statements, and what major information does each contain?

QUESTIONS FOR ANALYSIS

15-6. If you were planning to invest in a company, which of the three types of financial statements would you most want to see? Why?

15-7. Use the accounting equation to determine your net worth. Identify your assets and liabilities. With this information, how would you increase your net worth in the future?

⭐ **15-8.** Consider possible reasons it is taking so long for IASB's accounting standards to become fully adopted for use in the United States. Using the Internet as your source for information, identify three or more barriers that have deterred implementation of the standards, and explain how (or why) each has (or is) causing implementation delays.

APPLICATION EXERCISES

⭐ **15-9.** Interview an accountant at a local business, nonprofit organization, or government entity. How does the firm use budgets? How does budgeting help managers plan business activities? How does budgeting help them control activities? Give examples.

15-10. Interview the manager of a local retailer, wholesale business, or manufacturing firm about the role of ethics in that company's accounting practices. Is ethics in accounting an important issue to the manager? If the firm has its own private accountants, what measures are taken for ensuring ethical practices internally? What steps, if any, does the company take to maintain ethical relationships in its dealings with CPA firms?

building a business: continuing team exercise

Assignment

Meet with your team members to consider your new business venture and how it relates to the accounting topics in this chapter. Develop specific responses to the following:

15-11. In your first year of operation, who will perform accounting functions inside your company? Will you contract some or all of the work to a public accounting firm?

15-12. Create a list of the types of transactions that your accountant will record, including the purchase and sale of assets as well as revenues and expenses.

15-13. Based on the development of your business to date, create a preliminary or pro-forma income statement for your firm's first year of operation. Be sure it includes listings of relevant terms from the accounting equation.

See if you can estimate anticipated data for each element in the income statement.

15-14. Based on the development of your business to date, create a preliminary or pro-forma balance sheet for your firm's first year of operation. Be sure it includes listings of relevant terms from the accounting equation. See if you can estimate anticipated data for each element in the balance sheet.

15-15. Consider the sources for start-up funds you will need to finance your business. What financial ratios (ratio analysis), if any, are likely to be of interest to lending institutions, personal investors (including yourselves), or other providers of funds? Explain why ratio analysis will be of interest to them, or why it will not be of interest.

team exercise

AN AMERICAN LEGEND

Macy's is an iconic American company, but like many brick-and-mortar retailers, it has been struggling to maintain market share. For this exercise, you and your team need to find the company's most recent financial statements, including the income statement and balance sheet. There are many sources of this data, but one quick source is Morningstar.com. If you enter the company's ticket symbol, "M," in the quote box, you will find a report on the company's stock price as well as a host of other information, such as performance, key ratios and financials. On the financial tab, you can find the income statement and balance sheet for the past five years.

QUESTIONS FOR DISCUSSION

15-16. Looking at Macy's income statement, what has been the trend in sales (total revenue) as well as net income over the past three years?

15-17. As you have learned, gross profit is the difference between sales (or total revenues) and cost of sales (or cost of revenues). Gross profit percentage is calculated by dividing gross profit by sales (or total revenues). What is Macy's gross profit percentage for the last three years? What does this data tell you about Macy's pricing strategy and costs?

15-18. Looking at the balance sheet, what is Macy's current ratio for the three most recent years? What is the significance of these numbers? Have they been improving or getting worse?

15-19. What is the relationship between the price of Macy's stock and earnings? What are the earnings per share for each of the past three years, and what does that number mean to investors?

exercising your ethics

GIVE AND TAKE WITH ACCOUNTING CLIENTS

The Situation

CPAs provide valuable services for their clients, both businesses and individuals. Although it's important to make clients happy, accountants have additional considerations when preparing financial statements and tax returns.

The Dilemma

Aaron Ault is the owner of a small contracting business. In late January 2018, he delivered original expense and income records so that his CPA, Katrina Belinski, could prepare 2017 financial statements and tax returns for Ault's small business firm. Several weeks later, Katrina delivered the completed financial statements and tax return to Ault. Aaron was pleased with the financial statements but realized that he was going to owe a lot of money in taxes. His business is just recovering from tough

times during the recession and he can't afford to pay such a large tax bill. One particularly large job was completed at the end of the year, and Ault has decided that he'd like to record this during the current year. This would result in a much lower taxable income for 2017. However, Ault is disappointed with Belinski, who tells him that she's not able to make this change. Now he's threatening to take his business elsewhere. Belinski is torn because Ault has been a long-time client and she doesn't want to lose his business.

QUESTIONS TO ADDRESS

15-20. What are the ethical issues in this situation?

15-21. What are the basic arguments for and against Aaron Ault's position in this situation? For and against Katrina Belinski's position?

15-22. What do you think that Ault and Belinski should do in this situation?

cases

CSI: WALL STREET

Continued from page 480

At the beginning of this chapter, you read about CFEs and their role in fighting various kinds of fraudulent accounting practices, especially during troubled economic times. Also discussed were examples of fraud by the public at large, along with the resulting financial losses to U.S. businesses. Using the information presented in this chapter, you should now be able to answer the following questions.

QUESTIONS FOR DISCUSSION

15-23. What factors do you think are most important in choosing among various methods to protect against fraud in a firm?

15-24. Suppose you are hoping for a career as a CFE. How do recent trends in fraud provide new opportunities for such a career?

15-25. An external auditor, such as a CPA firm's accountant, may suspect some irregularities in a client firm's accounting practices. In what ways might a CFE be of assistance?

15-26. Consider the anti-fraud training for a company's employees and create an agenda that includes four (or more) topics that should be included in that training, along with descriptions of each.

15-27. What ethical issues, if any, are involved in a decision to investigate a suspected case of fraud in a firm's accounting activities?

FUTURE DIRECTIONS FOR THE MODERN ACCOUNTANT

In the future, while an accountant's knowledge of business aided by analytical and technical skills will be essential, a wider skillset will be necessary to meet market demands in this changing profession. The traditional accountant's role was centered

on analyzing historical financial data, creating financial statements, and providing interpretations of financial data and documents to facilitate business decisions. The expectations for the modern CPAs increasingly call for the more intimate role of leadership in demonstrating financial implications for many additional facets of the business, including its overall operations, strategy, data management, human resources, and technical resources. In consultative roles, accountants are being asked for guidance on broad issues, including business development, evaluating strategic opportunities, assessments of risks and threats, and strategies for using massive databases to identify promising directions for developing new products, improving customer service, and evaluating new lines of business to gain competitive advantage. Beyond just technical expertise, these kinds of participation require thorough knowledge of the client's business and the markets in which they operate.

The following trends have emerged and are contributing to the additional roles of the modern accountant:

- *Fewer restrictions from physical and geographic boundaries*—With increasing globalization, many foreign-based firms are interacting with firms based elsewhere around the world. Coupled with modern technology, accountants and clients in other countries are working together remotely. An accountant based at a company office, or at an office-in-the-home, in Omaha, Nebraska, can provide services to a client located in Singapore.
- *Social media have changed relationships and the way business is conducted*—Modern accountants establish professional relationships through active participation through social media. No longer do CPAs rely on face-to-face interactions at occasional professional meetings. Social media such as LinkedIn provide platforms for at-your-fingertips remote interactions allowing exchanges of information, professional advice, and temporary collaborations among accountants to serve clients in need of particular skill sets. New business opportunities arise, too, when accountants use a social networking presence to establish their business reputations.

- *Effectiveness as a communicator is a must for the accountant*—Communication skills are vital in the modern accountant's role in advising clients on global business trends and strategic perspectives. The accountant's thorough knowledge, to be leveraged into meaningful advice, must be communicated to clients on time, clearly and convincingly, both verbally and in writing. Effectiveness can be critical in a variety of communications contexts, ranging from formal presentations, to ad hoc interactive group meetings, to one-to-one informal conversations, either face to face or remotely.

- *Project management in the accountant's expanded role*—Serving as project manager is becoming commonplace for accountants because they provide guidance on the client's strategy, overall operations, and business development. These broad-based issues typically involve large-scale teams of specialists requiring long-term participation in activities such as financial forecasting, product and process engineering, financial interpretations, cost estimation, and human resources analysis. Success depends on the project manager's ability to decompose the project into manageable tasks, gain acceptance of task assignments, encourage timely reporting by task groups, and merge the project's many steps into coherent conclusions.

It is evident, then, that tomorrow's accountants need to be prepared with more than just traditional skills. They need to know the nature of the client's business and its competitive environment so that they can assist the client in gaining greater competitive advantage.[29]

QUESTIONS FOR DISCUSSION

15-28. In what ways, if any, does the discussion in this case apply to managerial accountants rather than to CPAs? Explain your response.

15-29. In what ways, if any, does the discussion in this case apply to forensic accountants rather than to CPAs? Explain your response.

15-30. Consider the restrictions on CPA services by provisions of the Sarbanes-Oxley Act (Sarbox). In what ways, if any, does this case's description of the modern accountant's activities conflict with Sarbox? Explain your response.

15-31. Ethics has a long-standing role in the accounting profession. Will the emerging role of the modern accountant bring with it a greater emphasis on ethics (as compared with traditional accounting)? Explain.

crafting a business plan

PART 5: MANAGING INFORMATION

Goal of the Exercise

This part of the business plan asks you to think about your business in terms of *information technology needs* and *costs*.

Exercise Background: Part 5 of the Business Plan

In Chapter 14, we discussed the major impact that IT—computers, the Internet, software, and so on—has had on businesses today. This part of the business plan asks you to assess how you will use technology to improve your business. Will you, for example, use a database to keep track of your customers? How will you protect your business from hackers and other IT security risks?

This part of the business plan also asks you to consider the costs of doing business, such as salaries, rent, and utilities. You'll also be asked to complete the following financial statements:

- *Balance Sheet*—The balance sheet is a foundation for financial reporting. This report identifies the valued items of the business (its *assets*) as well as the debts that it owes (its *liabilities*). This information gives the owner and potential investors a "snapshot" into the health of the business.

- *Income Statement (or Profit-and-Loss Statement)*—This is the focus of the financial plan. This document will show you what it takes to be profitable and successful as a business owner for your first year.

Your Assignment

STEP 1

Open the saved *Business Plan* file you began working on in Parts 1 to 4.

STEP 2

For the purposes of this assignment, you will answer the following questions in "Part 5: Managing Information":

15-32. What kinds of IT resources will your business require?

Hint: Think about the employees in your business and what they will need to do their jobs. What computer hardware and software will they need? Will your business need a network and an Internet connection? What type of network? Refer to Chapter 14 for a discussion on IT resources you may want to consider.

15-33. How will you use IT to keep track of your customers and potential customers?

Hint: Many businesses—even small businesses—use databases to keep track of their customers. Will your business require a database? What about other information systems? Refer to Chapter 14 for more information on these topics.

15-34. What are the *costs* of doing business? Equipment, supplies, salaries, rent, utilities, and insurance are just some of these expenses. Estimate what it will cost to do business for one year.

Hint: The *Business Plan Student Template* provides a table for you to insert the costs associated with doing business. Note that these are only estimates—just try your best to include accurate costs for the expenses you think will be a part of doing business.

15-35. How much will you charge for your product? How many products do you believe that you can sell in one year (or how many customers do you think your business can attract)? Multiply the price that you will charge by the number of products that you hope to sell or the amount you hope each customer will spend. This will give you an estimate of your *revenues* for one year.

Hint: You will use the amounts you calculate in the costs and revenues questions in this part of the plan in the accounting statements in the next part, so be as realistic as you can.

15-36. Create a balance sheet and an income statement (profit-and-loss statement) for your business.

Hint: You will have two options for creating these reports. The first option is to use the Microsoft Word versions that are found within the *Business Plan Student Template* itself. The second option is to use the specific Microsoft Excel templates created for each statement, which are found on the book's companion website at www.pearsonhighered.com/ebert. These Excel files are handy to use because they already have the worksheet calculations preset—all you have to do is "plug in" the numbers and the calculations will be performed automatically for you. If you make adjustments to the different values in the Excel worksheets, you'll automatically see how changes to expenses, for example, can improve the "bottom line."

Note: Once you have answered the questions, save your Word document. You'll be answering additional questions in later chapters.

Writing Assignments

15-37. Accounting is a growing profession. What do accountants do? What are the major roles that they play in business? Give an example of the kind of work that each of four different kinds of accountants perform.

15-38. Choose a publicly-traded stock and find the most current audited financial statements and annual report. What information does the annual report contain? How do you know that the reports are accurate and reliable?

endnotes

[1] Lison, Joseph, Sukumar, C. R., and Raghu, K. "Ramalinga Raju Admits to Accounting Fraud, Resigns," *livemint.com*, January 31, 2012, at http://www.livemint.com/Companies/ldmclvNdW3Z6dNayVfZSPI/Ramalinga-Raju-admits-to-accounting-fraud-resigns.html; Piore, Adam. "Fraud Scene Investigator," *Portfolio*, March 10, 2008, at http://www.portfolio.com/careers/job-of-the-week/2008/03/10/Forensic-Accountant-Al-Vondra; Vondra, Albert A. *LinkedIn*, December 12, 2012, at www.linkedin.com/pub/albert-a-vondra/1a/57b/459, accessed on February 14, 2013. Goyal, Kartik, and Sharma, Subramanian. "India Orders Fraud Office Probe into Satyam Computer Accounts," *Bloomberg.com*, January 13, 2009, at http://www.bloomberg.com/apps/news?pid=20601091&refer=india&sid=ayhBmRJs7nh0.

[2] "Examples of Corporate Fraud Investigations—Fiscal Year 2010," *IRS.gov*, at http://www.irs.gov/compliance/enforcement/article/0,,id=213768,00.html; "Examples of Corporate Fraud Investigations—Fiscal Year 2012," IRS.gov, at http://www.irs.gov/uac/Examples-of-Corporate-Fraud-Investigations-Fiscal-Year-2012. All accessed on May 11, 2015.

[3] Schreiber, Russ. "Fighting Fraud: Predictive Analytics & Business Rules Make a Powerful Combination," *Insurance & Technology*, March 19, 2012, at http://www.insurancetech.com/security/fighting-fraud-predictive-analytics-bus/232602826; Stech, Katy. "Fighting Fraud: Link Between Bogus Insurance Claims, Recession is Murky," *The Post and Courier*, August 9, 2010, at http://www.postandcourier.com/news/2010/aug/09/fighting-fraud/; Southerland, Randy. "Recession Pressures May Boost Employee Fraud," *Atlanta Business Chronicle*, August 19, 2010, at http://www.bizjournals.com/atlanta/stories/2010/08/23/focus9.html; "Fraud to Thrive Beyond the Economic Downturn," *Lloyd's*, January 18, 2010, at http://www.lloyds.com/News-and-Insight/News-and-Features/Business-Risk/Business-2010/Fraud_to_thrive_beyond_the_economic_downturn. All accessed on May 11, 2015.

[4] See Marshall B. Romney and Paul John Steinbart, *Accounting Information Systems*, 13th ed. (Upper Saddle River, NJ: Prentice Hall, 2015), Chapter 1.

[5] See Anthony A. Atkinson, Robert S. Kaplan, Ella Mae Matsumura, and S. Mark Young, *Management Accounting*, 5th ed. (Upper Saddle River, NJ: Prentice Hall, 2007), Chapter 1.

[6] See Walter T. Harrison and Charles T. Horngren, *Financial Accounting and Financial Tips*, 7th ed. (Upper Saddle River, NJ: Prentice Hall, 2007), Chapter 1.

[7] "Public Accounting Tips," *LifeTips.com*, at http://accountingjobs.lifetips.com/cat/64430/public-accounting/index.html, accessed on September 13, 2010; "Business Glossary," *AllBusiness.com*, at http://www.allbusiness.com/glossaries/review/4954577-1.html, accessed on April 15, 2017.

[8] Cohn, Michael. "Big Four Firms Saw Big Revenue Increase in 2012," *accountingTODAY for the WebCPA*, January 10, 2013, at http://www.accountingtoday.com/news/Big-Four-Firms-Saw-Big-Revenue-Increase-2012-65309-1.html. All accessed on May 11, 2015.

[9] See Alvin A. Arens, Randal J. Elder, and Mark S. Beasley, *Auditing and Assurance Services: An Integrated Approach*, 13th ed. (Upper Saddle River, NJ: Prentice Hall, 2010), Chapter 1.

[10] See Meg Pollard, Sherry T. Mills, and Walter T. Harrison, *Financial and Managerial Accounting*, Ch. 1–14 (Upper Saddle River, NJ: Prentice Hall, 2008), Chapter 1.

[11] "2012 Talent Shortage Survey," *ManpowerGroup*, at http://www.manpowergroup.us/campaigns/talent-shortage-2012/, accessed February 11, 2013.

[12] "The CPA Vision Project and Beyond," *The American Institute of Certified Public Accountants*, at http://www.aicpa.org/RESEARCH/CPAHORIZONS2025/CPAVISIONPROJECT/Pages/CPAVisionProject.aspx, accessed on April 15, 2017.

[13] Crumbley, D. Larry, Heitger, Lester E., and Smith, G. Stevenson. *Forensic and Investigative Accounting*, 5th ed. (Chicago: CCH, 2011), Chapter 1.

[14] See McConn, Terry, "Ex-Chase Bank teller charged with stealing from Walla Walla business," Walla Walla Union Bulletin, Sept. 2016, http://www.union-bulletin.com/news/courts_and_crime/ex-chase-bank-teller-charged-with-stealing-from-walla-walla/article_0eca4f2e-859b-11e6-baad-c75a9d6d7c00.html. Accessed May 18, 2017.

[15] Vine, Katy "Just Desserts," *Texas Monthly*, January 2016, http://www.texasmonthly.com/articles/just-desserts/ (Accessed May 18, 2017).

[16] United States Department of Justice, Press Release, November 28, 2016, https://www.justice.gov/opa/pr/upstate-new-york-woman-admits-stealing-31-million-cargill-inc. Accessed May 18, 2017.

[17] "Executive Summary of the Sarbanes-Oxley Act of 2002 P.L. 107–204," Conference of State Bank Supervisors, at http://www.csbs.org/legislative/leg-updates/Documents/ExecSummary-SarbanesOxley-2002.pdf; "Sarbanes-Oxley Executive Summary," *Securities Law Update* (Orrick, Herrington & Sutcliffe LLP), August 2002, at http://www.orrick.com/fileupload/144.pdf. All accessed on April 15, 2017.

[18] Rapoport, Michael. "Eyebrows Go Up as Auditors Branch Out," *Wall Street Journal*, December 7, 2012, pages C1, C2.

[19] "Consolidated Balance Sheets," *United States Securities Exchange Commission*, at http://www.sec.gov/Archives/edgar/data/1288776/000119312513028362/d452134d10k.htm#tx452134_23, accessed on April 15, 2017.

[20] "Borders Files for Bankruptcy, to Close 200 Stores," Reuters, February 16, 2011 at http://www.reuters.com/article/2011/02/17/us-borders-idUSTRE71F2P220110217.

[21] Cantoria, Ciel S., edited by Linda Richter. "Unraveling the Details of 10 High-Profile Accounting Scandals," BRIGHT HUB, December 30, 2010, at http://www.brighthub.com/office/finance/articles/101200.aspx; "The Biggest Accounting Scandals of All Time (Photos)," *Huffington Post*, May 17, 2010 at http://www.huffingtonpost.com/2010/03/17/biggest-accounting-scanda_n_502181.html#s74418&title=Madoff_Scandal_; "The Corporate Scandal Sheet," *Citizen Works* (August 2004), at http://www.citizenworks.org/enron/corp-scandal.php; "Largest Health Care Fraud Case in U.S. History Settled," *Department of Justice* (June 26, 2003), at http://www.usdoj.gov/opa/pr/2003/June/03_civ_386.htm; "Kozlowski Is Found Guilty," TheStreet.com, June 17, 2005, at http://www.thestreet.com/story/10228619/1/kozlowski-is-found-guilty.html. All accessed on May 11, 2015.

[22] "IASB and FASB Propose a New Joint Standard for Revenue Recognition," *Financial Accounting Standards Board*, June 24, 2010, at http://www.fasb.org/cs/ContentServer?c=FASBContent_C&pagename=FASB%2FFASBContent_C%2FNewsPage&cid=1176156953088.

[23] "IFRS Overview," *NYSSCPA.ORG*, at http://www.nysscpa.org/ifrs/overview.htm, accessed on April 19, 2017.

[24] "IASB and FASB Propose to Align Balance Sheet Netting Requirements Differences in IFRS and US GAAP Offsetting Requirements to be Eliminated," *FASB: Financial Accounting Standards Board*, (news release) January 28, 2011, at http://www.fasb.org/cs/ContentServer?c=FASBContent_C&pagename=FASB/FASBContent_C/NewsPage&cid=1176158186333. Accessed on May 11, 2015.

[25] Briginshaw, John. "What Will the International Financial Reporting Standards (IFRS) Mean to Businesses and Investors?" *Graziadio Business Review*, 2008, Volume 11, Issue 4, at http://gbr.pepperdine.edu/2010/08/what-will-the-international-financial-reporting-standards-ifrs-mean-to-businesses-and-investors/.

[26] "IASB and FASB Propose a New Joint Standard for Revenue Recognition," Financial *Accounting Standards Board*, June 24, 2010, at http://www.fasb.org/cs/ContentServer?c=FASBContent_C&pagename=FASB%2FFASBContent_C%2FNewsPage&cid=1176156953088.

[27] "IASB and FASB Propose Common Solution for Impairment Accounting," *FASB: Financial Accounting Standards Board*," (news release) January 31, 2011, at http://www.fasb.org/cs/ContentServer?c=FASBContent_C&pagename=FASB/FASBContent_C/NewsPage&cid=1176158192211.

[28] "FASB, IASB Propose Changes in Fair Value Standards," *Insurance Networking News*, June 29, 2010, at http://www.insurancenetworking.com/news/insurance_fair_value_standards_accounting_IASB_FASB_GAAP_IFRS-25136-1.html; "Measurement Uncertainty Analysis Disclosure for Fair Value Measurements," International Accounting Standards Board, June 2010, at http://www.iasb.org/NR/rdonlyres/07855A41-D0A9-4197-ADF9-15A1088E466A/0/EDMeasurementUncertaintyAnalysis0610.pdf. All accessed on May 11, 2015.

[29] Tokc-Wilde, Iwona. "#AAYP 2013: Modern Accountants—People Who Think Differently," *AccountancyAge*, May 1, 2013, at http://www.accountancyage.com/aa/feature/2265153/-aayp-2013-modern-accountants-people-who-think-differently; "Intuit 2020 Report Depicts Future of the Accounting Profession: A New Mindset and Model Required to Thrive in a Connected World," *Intuit Inc.*, February 2, 2011, at http://about.intuit.com/about_intuit/press_room/press_release/articles/2011/Intuit2020ReportDepictsFuture.html; Walker, Rich. "Intuit 2020 Report Depicts Future of the Accounting Profession," *Intuit Accountants News Central*, February 2, 2011, at https://blog.accountants.intuit.com/intuit-news/intuit%C2%AE-2020-report-depicts-future-of-the-accounting-profession/; "Accountants—The Old and the New," *CA Saga*, August 15, 2012, at http://contractaccountants.wordpress.com/2012/08/15/accountants-the-old-and-the-new/; "The Many Hats of a Modern Accountant," *Jobs.net*, May 14, 2013, at http://www.jobs.net/Article/CB-6-Talent-Network-Finance-Ins-The-Many-Hats-of-a-Modern-Accountant/

Understanding Money and the Role of Banking

chapter 16

Making money is more than just dollars and sense.

Technology and a flat world complicate

m a t t e r s ;

businesses need to ask where their money

comes from, who

is using it, and why.

After reading this chapter, you should be able to:

16-1 **Define** *money* and identify the different forms that it takes in the nation's money supply.

16-2 **Describe** the different kinds of financial institutions that compose the U.S. financial system and explain the services they offer.

16-3 **Explain** how financial institutions create money and describe the means by which they are regulated.

16-4 **Discuss** the functions of the Federal Reserve System and describe the tools that it uses to control the money supply.

16-5 **Identify** three important ways in which the money and banking system is changing.

16-6 **Discuss** some of the institutions and activities in international banking and finance.

Chair Yellen

Where Did All the Money Go?

At the beginning of 1923, the newly formed Weimar Republic was in trouble. Germany had borrowed heavily from its own people to finance the war, issuing a series of 5 percent, 10-year bonds that the prior government intended to redeem from the spoils of war. When Germany lost the war, instead of being able to rebuild its economy and redeem the bonds, it was instead forced to pay billions in reparations. But the war had been hard on the country's infrastructure and the people. Both were exhausted and disabled. Without a strong economic presence, the Republic couldn't borrow money to rebuild and make reparations, so the central bank simply printed more money. An almost unlimited supply of cash combined with a severely limited supply of goods and services drove prices up in what economists call hyperinflation. Consumers could not physically carry enough cash to purchase what little food and clothing were available. Ultimately, paper money became virtually worthless. Similar instances of hyperinflation have occurred in Zimbabwe, Hungary, Bolivia, and other countries.

So, printing more money to pay off debt or avoid economic crisis is a bad thing, right? Maybe, or maybe not. In 2008, the U.S. economy hit a crisis point and the country went into a recession. Congress responded by passing the Economic Recovery and Reinvestment Act, pouring borrowed money into the economy in order to stimulate demand, which would then, hopefully, stimulate supply and get the country back on track. So, no new money was created. However, there is another player in this economic game: the Federal Reserve Bank, which is often referred to as simply "the Fed."

Congress created the Federal Reserve System back in 1913 in order to provide a mechanism for stabilizing the economy. After the great depression, Congress created the Federal Open Market Committee within the existing system in order to provide better guidance. Then, in 1977 and 1978, in response to surging inflation, Congress set price stability and full employment as the primary goals of the Fed's monetary policy.

The Fed is set up as an independent government agency, shielded from political pressure but still operating within powers granted by Congress. Each of the seven-member Board of Governors is appointed by the president and confirmed by the Senate, serving staggered 14-year terms that expire in every even-numbered year. The president, with Senate approval, also appoints the Fed chair. The Federal Open Market Committee (FOMC) is the Fed's monetary policy-making body. The FOMC has 12 voting members: all seven members of the Board of Governors plus five of the 12 Reserve Bank presidents. It is this committee that sets monetary policy and is charged with stabilizing inflation and employment. The Fed uses two

what's in it for me?

Dealing in matters of money is vastly more complicated than counting the cash and coins in your pocket or using your smartphone to check your bank balance, especially when technology and globalization come into play. At its core are questions about where money comes from, how national economies depend on it, and the public's trust in its value. This chapter will give you a solid understanding of the different forms of money and how it is created and controlled by different kinds of financial institutions and government regulations.

major strategies to affect the economy: (1) open market operations and (2) the discount rate. In addition, the Fed requires banks to maintain cash reserves, currently 10 percent of deposits. In other words, if you put $1,000 into a savings account, the bank only has to have $100 on hand. It can lend out the other $900.

Here's where things get tricky. Open market operations are the equivalent of printing new money. When times get tough, the Fed can repurchase debt from the public, which results in cash in the banks. The bank only has to keep 10 percent of that cash on hand. As it loans out the rest, it creates more and more money. Imagine that someone borrows the $900 in excess of the required reserves on your deposit, buys a boat, and the boat dealer puts that $900 into a checking account. The bank only needs to keep $90 on hand, and can re-loan the other $810. This is called the money multiplier.

Enter economist and past Federal Reserve Chair Ben Bernanke. In the aftermath of the fiscal crisis of 2008–2009, Bernanke believed that the fiscal stimulus enacted by Congress wasn't enough, and that the country would fall into a further recession without additional intervention. Congress, being a large political body, could only do so much, but the Fed, insulated as it was from political pressure and comprised of economists and bankers, had a mandate to stabilize the economy and the tools to do it. First of all, the Fed lowered the Fed Funds rate to zero, allowing banks to borrow money interest-free. In addition, between 2010 and 2014, the Fed bought over $4.5 trillion in debt from the public, a strategy economists call "Quantitative Easing," which then increased spendable funds, known as M-1, from $1.4 trillion to $3.4 trillion in just 10 years. Even so, this influx of money didn't drive hyperinflation as some critics thought it would. In fact, inflation, which is a leading indicator for economic growth, never reached the Fed's target rate of 2 percent. In retrospect, analysts reason that the hyperinflation experienced by other countries was due more to printing paper money while at the same time experiencing severe limitations in the supply of goods and services, as in the case of war-torn Germany. In the U.S., banks did not loan out all the excess reserves, instead choosing to hoard the newly minted electronic currency, investing it but not putting it into general circulation.

In 2014, then-President Barack Obama appointed Janet Yellen to lead the Federal Reserve Board, succeeding Ben Bernanke. Since taking the lead position, the Fed has raised the Fed funds rate slightly and has ended the quantitative easing. Unemployment has dropped to 4.5 percent and in early 2017 the stock market was seeing healthy increases after years of relative stagnation. It remains to be seen, however, whether Yellen has smooth sailing through her term, which ends in 2018, or if there are still rough waters ahead.[1] (After studying the content in this chapter, you should be able to answer a set of discussion questions found at the end of the chapter.)

OBJECTIVE 16-1
Define
money and identify the different forms that it takes in the nation's money supply.

What Is Money?

If someone asks you how much money you have, do you count the dollar bills and coins in your pockets? Do you include your checking and savings accounts? Do you check your balance in Apple Pay or a similar digital payment option? What about stocks and bonds? Do you count your car? Taken together, the value of all these combined is your personal wealth. Not all of it, however, is "money." This section considers more precisely what *money* is and what it does.

The Characteristics of Money

Money *object that is portable, divisible, durable, and stable, and that serves as a medium of exchange, a store of value, and a measure of worth*

Modern money generally takes the forms of stamped metal or printed paper issued by governments. Theoretically, however, just about anything *portable, divisible, durable,* and *stable* can serve as **money**. To appreciate these qualities, imagine

Cattle are not portable, divisible, durable, or stable, making them an unsuitable medium of exchange in the modern monetized economy.

using something that lacks them—for example, a 1,000-pound cow used as a unit of exchange in ancient agrarian economies:

- *Portability.* Try lugging 1,000 pounds of cow from shop to shop. In contrast, modern currency is light and easy to handle.

- *Divisibility.* How would you divide your cow if you wanted to buy a hat, a book, and a new phone case from three different stores? Is a pound of cow head worth as much as a pound of cow leg? Modern currency is easily divisible into smaller parts with fixed values—for example, a dollar for four quarters or ten dimes, but a cow is much harder to divide.

- *Durability.* Your cow will lose value every day (and eventually die). Modern currency, however, neither dies nor spoils, and if it wears out, it can be replaced. It is also hard to counterfeit—certainly harder than cattle breeding.

- *Stability.* If cows were in short supply, you might be able to make quite a deal for yourself. In the middle of an abundant cow year, however, the market would be flooded with cows, so their value would fall. The value of our paper money also fluctuates, but it is considerably more stable and predictable.

The Functions of Money

Imagine a successful cow rancher who needs a new fence. In a *barter economy*, one in which goods are exchanged directly for another, he or she would have to find someone who is willing to exchange a fence for a cow (or parts of it). If no fence maker wants a cow, the rancher must find someone else—for example, a wagon maker—who does want a cow. Then, the rancher must hope that the fence maker will trade for a new wagon. In a money economy, though, the rancher would sell his or her cow, receive money, and exchange the money for such goods as a new fence.

Money serves three essential functions:

1. *Money is a medium of exchange.* Like the rancher "trading" money for a new fence, money is used to buy and sell things. Without money, we would be bogged down in a system of constant barter.

2. *Money is a store of value.* Pity the rancher whose cow gets sick on Monday and who wants to buy some clothes on the following Saturday, by which time the cow may have died and lost its value. In the form of currency, however, money can be used for future purchases and therefore "stores" its value.

3 *Money is a measure of worth.* Money lets us measure the relative values of goods and services. It acts as a measure of worth because all products can be valued and accounted for in terms of money. For example, the concepts of $1,000 worth of clothes or $500 in labor costs have universal meaning.

We see, then, that money adds convenience and simplicity to our everyday lives, for consumers and businesses alike. Employees, consumers, and businesses use money as the measure of worth for determining wages and for buying and selling products—everything from ice cream to housing rentals. Consumers with cash can make purchases wherever they go because businesses everywhere accept money as a medium for exchange. And because money is stable, businesses and individuals save their money, trusting that its value will be available for future use.

M-1: The Spendable Money Supply

Of course, for money to serve its basic functions, both buyers and sellers must agree on its value. The value of money, in turn, depends in part on its *supply*—how much money is in circulation. All else equal, when the supply of money is high its value drops and when the supply of money is low its value increases. (Note that this pattern is consistent with the principles of supply and demand as discussed in Chapter 1.)

Unfortunately, there is no single measure of the supply of money that all experts accept. The oldest and most basic measure, **M-1**, counts only the most liquid, or spendable, forms of money—cash, checks, and funds in checking accounts.

- Paper money and metal coins are **currency (cash)** issued by the government and widely used for small exchanges. U.S. law requires creditors to accept it in payment of debts.

- A **check** is essentially an order instructing a bank to pay a given sum to a payee. Checks are usually, but not always, accepted because they are valuable only to specified payees and can be exchanged for cash.

- **Checking accounts,** or **demand deposits**, are money because their funds may be withdrawn at any time on demand.

M-1 *measure of the money supply that includes only the most liquid (spendable) forms of money*

Currency (Cash) *government-issued paper money and metal coins*

Check *demand deposit order instructing a bank to pay a given sum to a specified payee*

Checking Account (Demand Deposit) *bank account funds, owned by the depositor, that may be withdrawn at any time by check or cash*

Instead of using a modern monetary system, traders like Muhammed Essa in Quetta, Pakistan, transfer funds through handshakes and code words. The ancient system is called hawala, which means "trust" in Arabic. The worldwide hawala system, though illegal in most countries, moves billions of dollars past regulators annually and is alleged to be the system of choice for terrorists because it leaves no paper trail.

Ton Koene/Alamy Stock Photo

These are all non-interest–bearing or low-interest–bearing forms of money. As of January 2017, M-1 in the United States totaled $3.617 trillion.[2]

M-2: M-1 Plus the Convertible Money Supply

M-2, a second measure of the money supply, is often used for economic planning by businesses and government agencies. **M-2** includes everything in M-1 plus other forms of money that are not quite as liquid, for example, short-term investments that are easily converted to spendable forms, including *time deposits*, *money market mutual funds*, and *savings accounts*. Totaling $13.932 trillion in January 2017, M-2 accounts for most of the nation's money supply.[3] It measures the store of monetary value available for financial transactions by individuals and small businesses. As this overall level increases, more money is available for consumer purchases and business investments. When the supply is tightened, less money is available—financial transactions, spending, and business activity slow down.

Unlike demand deposits, **time deposits**, such as certificates of deposit (CDs), have a fixed term, are intended to be held to maturity, cannot be transferred by check, and pay higher interest rates than checking accounts. Time deposits in M-2 include only accounts of less than $100,000 that can be redeemed on demand, with penalties for early withdrawal. With **money market mutual funds**, investment companies buy a collection of short-term, low-risk financial securities. Ownership of and profits (or losses) from the sale of these securities are shared among the fund's investors.

Figure 16.1 shows how M-1 and M-2 have grown since 1979. For many years, M-1 was the traditional measure of liquid money. Because it was closely related to gross domestic product, it served as a reliable predictor of the nation's real money supply. This situation changed in the early 1980s, with the introduction of new types of investments and the easier transfer of money among investment funds to gain higher interest returns. As a result, most experts today view M-2 as a more reliable measure than M-1.

M-2 *measure of the money supply that includes all the components of M-1 plus the forms of money that can be easily converted into spendable forms*

Time Deposit *bank funds that have a fixed term of time to maturity and cannot be withdrawn earlier or transferred by check*

Money Market Mutual Fund *fund of short-term, low-risk financial securities purchased with the pooled assets of investor-owners*

Credit Cards and Debit Cards: Plastic Money?

The use of credit and debit cards has become so widespread that many people refer to them as "plastic money." Credit cards, however, are not money and, therefore, are not included in M-1 or M-2 when measuring the nation's money supply. Why? Because spending with a credit card creates a debt, but does not move money until later when the debt is paid by cash or check. Debit card transactions, in contrast, transfer money immediately from the consumer's bank account, so they affect the money supply the same way as spending with a check or cash, and are included in M-1. Although consumers enjoy the convenience of credit cards, they may also find that irresponsible use of these cards can be hazardous to their financial health. A discussion of managing the use of credit cards is found in Appendix III: Managing Your Personal Finances.

The U.S. Financial System

Many forms of money depend on the existence of financial institutions that provide money-related services to both individuals and businesses. Just how important are these financial institutions, how do they work, and what are some of the services that they offer? We will explore the answers to these questions in the sections that follow as we explain their role as creators of money and discuss the services they offer in the U.S. banking system.

OBJECTIVE 16-2
Describe
the different kinds of financial institutions that compose the U.S. financial system and explain the services they offer.

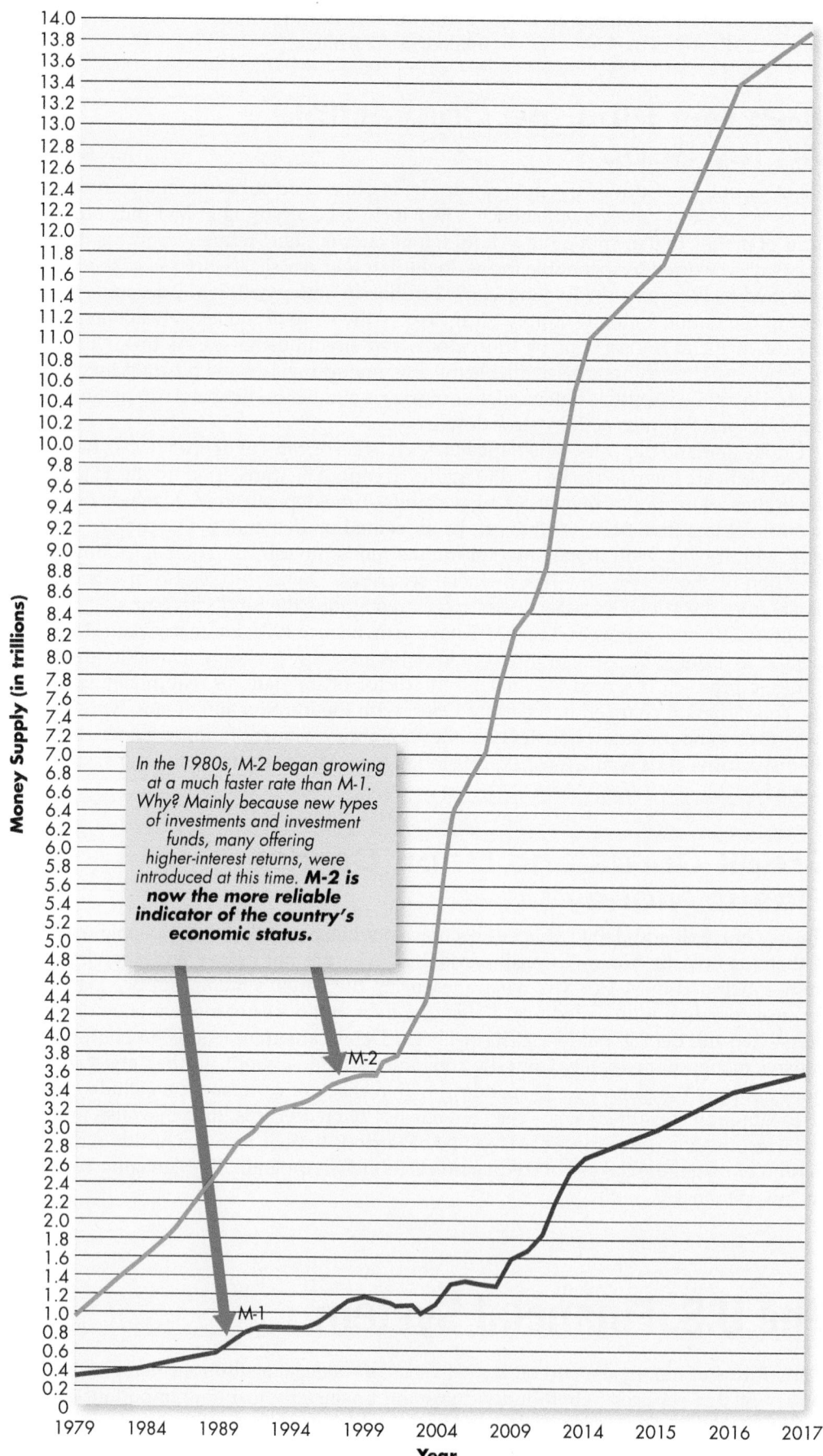

In the 1980s, M-2 began growing at a much faster rate than M-1. Why? Mainly because new types of investments and investment funds, many offering higher-interest returns, were introduced at this time. **M-2 is now the more reliable indicator of the country's economic status.**

FIGURE 16.1 Money Supply Growth

Source: "Money Stock Measures," *Federal Reserve,* at www.federalreserve.gov/releases/h6/current/, accessed on June 1, 2017.

Financial Institutions

The main function of financial institutions is to facilitate the flow of money from users with surpluses to those with deficits by attracting funds into checking and savings accounts. Incoming funds can be loaned to individuals and businesses and perhaps invested in government securities. U.S. consumers have access to more than 90,000 U.S. branches and offices of *commercial banks, savings institutions, credit unions,* and various *nondeposit institutions.*

Commercial Banks Federally insured **commercial banks** accept deposits, make loans, earn profits, and pay interest and dividends. Some 5,600 commercial banks range from the largest institutions headquartered in New York, such as Citigroup, Bank of America, and JPMorgan Chase, to small local banks dotting the rural landscape. Bank liabilities, or holdings owed to others, include checking accounts and savings accounts. U.S. banks hold assets totaling more than $14.8 trillion, consisting of a wide variety of loans to individuals, businesses, farms and ranches, and government entities.[4]

Every bank receives a major portion of its income from interest paid on loans by borrowers. As long as terms and conditions are clearly revealed to borrowers, banks may set their own interest rates, within limits set by each state. Traditionally, banks only offered the lowest rate, or **prime rate**, to their most creditworthy commercial customers. Most commercial loans are set at markups over prime, such as prime + 1, which means 1 percent over the prime rate. To remain competitive with lower-interest foreign banks, U.S. banks offer some commercial loans at rates below prime. Figure 16.2 shows the changes in the prime rate since 2000. Lower rates in 2008–2013 encouraged banks to continue lending in the economic downturn. Indeed, the prime rate stayed around 3.25 percent for several years but edged closer to 4.00 percent in 2017.

Savings Institutions Savings institutions include mutual savings banks and savings and loan associations. They were once called *thrift institutions* because they were established decades ago to promote the idea of saving among the general population and are still referred to by this label by some older Americans.

Savings and Loan Associations Like commercial banks, **savings and loan associations (S&Ls)** accept deposits, make loans, and are owned by investors. Most S&Ls were created to encourage savings habits and provide financing for homes; they did not originally offer checking services. Today, they have ventured into a variety of other loans and services, including checking accounts.

Mutual Savings Banks In a **mutual savings bank**, all depositors are considered owners of the bank. All profits are divided proportionately among depositors,

(margin definitions)

Commercial Bank *company that accepts deposits that it uses to make loans, earn profits, pay interest to depositors, and pay dividends to owners*

Prime Rate *interest rate available to a bank's most creditworthy customers*

Savings and Loan Association (S&L) *financial institution accepting deposits and making loans primarily for home mortgages*

Mutual Savings Bank *financial institution whose depositors are owners sharing in its profits*

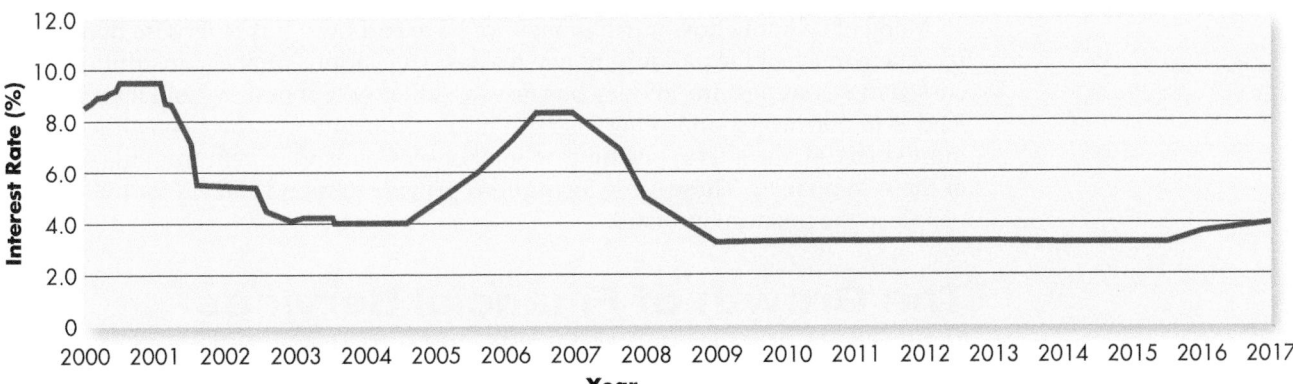

FIGURE 16.2 The Prime Rate

Source: "Prime Interest Rate History," at http://www.fedprimerate.com/wall_street_journal_prime_rate_history.htm, accessed June 1, 2017.

who receive dividends. About 600 U.S. mutual savings banks attract most of their funds in the form of savings deposits, and funds are loaned out in the form of mortgages.

Credit Unions A **credit union** is a nonprofit, cooperative financial institution owned and run by its members. Its purpose is to promote *thrift*, careful management of one's money or resources, and to provide members with a safe place to save and borrow at reasonable rates. Members pool their funds to make loans to one another. Each credit union decides whom it will serve, such as a group of employees of a given organization or from a defined industry, people in a particular community, or members of an association. The credit unions of some universities and the U.S. Navy, for example, are among the nation's 6,900 credit unions.

Credit Union *nonprofit, cooperative financial institution owned and run by its members, usually employees of a particular organization*

Nondeposit Institutions A variety of other organizations take in money, provide interest or other services, and make loans. Unlike commercial banks, these *nondeposit institutions* use inflowing funds for purposes other than earning interest for depositors. Four of the most important are (1) *pension funds*, (2) *insurance companies*, (3) *finance companies*, and (4) *securities investment dealers*.

1 A **pension fund** is a pool of funds that is managed to provide retirement income for its members. *Public pension funds* in the United States include Social Security and the more than $4 trillion in retirement programs for state and local government employees. *Private pension funds*, operated by employers, unions, and other private groups, cover about 36 million people and have total assets of $24.9 trillion, up from $13 trillion during the 2008 recession.[5]

Pension Fund *nondeposit pool of funds managed to provide retirement income for its members*

2 **Insurance companies** accumulate money from premiums charged for coverage. They invest these funds in stocks, real estate, and other assets. Earnings pay for insured losses, such as death benefits, automobile damage, and healthcare expenses.

Insurance Company *nondeposit institution that invests funds collected as premiums charged for insurance coverage*

3 **Finance companies** specialize in making loans to businesses and consumers. HSBC Finance, for example, offers mortgage refinancing and personal loans. *Commercial finance companies* lend to businesses needing capital or long-term funds. *Consumer finance companies* devote most of their resources to providing small noncommercial loans to individuals. Some of these lenders are willing to take on higher-risk borrowers but, in return, charge higher interest rates on their loans.

Finance Company *nondeposit institution that specializes in making loans to businesses and consumers*

4 **Securities investment dealers (brokers)**, such as Merrill Lynch and A. G. Edwards Inc., buy and sell stocks and bonds for client investors. They also invest in securities by buying stocks and bonds for their own accounts in hopes of reselling them later at a profit. These companies hold large sums of money for transfer between buyers and sellers. (We discuss the activities of brokers and investment banking more fully in Chapter 17.)

Securities Investment Dealer (Broker) *financial institution that buys and sells stocks and bonds both for investors and for its own accounts*

Many of us know how much money we have and owe, but otherwise don't realize where much of the nation's money resides. The various financial institutions discussed in this section are "money businesses"—they accept money, hold it for savers, lend it to borrowers, and otherwise use it to earn profits for their constituents. As individuals, many of us at one time or another seek out and benefit from the services of these companies. These same institutions provide jobs and careers for millions of people in the financial industry.

The Growth of Financial Services

The finance business today is highly competitive. No longer is it enough for commercial banks to accept deposits and make loans. Most, for example, also offer bank-issued credit and debit cards, safe-deposit boxes, ATMs, electronic money transfer, online banking, and foreign currency exchange. In addition, many offer pension, trust, international, and brokerage services and financial advice.

Pension and Trust Services
Individual retirement accounts (IRAs) are (typically) tax-deferred pension funds that wage earners and their spouses can set up to supplement other retirement funds. Advantages and drawbacks to various kinds of IRAs—*traditional*, *Roth*, and *education*—are discussed in Appendix III.

Many commercial banks offer **trust services**, the management of funds left in the bank's trust. In return for a fee, the trust department will perform such tasks as making your monthly bill payments and managing your investment portfolio. Trust departments also manage the estates of deceased persons.

International Services
Suppose a U.S. company wants to buy a product from a Chinese supplier. For a fee, it can use one or more of three services offered by its bank:

1 *Currency Exchange:* It can exchange U.S. dollars for Chinese yuan to pay the supplier.

2 *Letters of Credit:* It can pay its bank to issue a **letter of credit**, a promise by the bank to pay the Chinese firm a certain amount if specified conditions are met.

3 *Banker's Acceptances:* It can pay its bank to draw up a **banker's acceptance**, which promises that the bank will pay some specified amount at a future date.

A banker's acceptance requires payment by a particular date. Letters of credit are payable only after certain conditions are met. The Chinese supplier, for example, may not be paid until shipping documents prove that the merchandise has been shipped from China.

Financial Advice and Brokerage Services
Many banks, both large and small, help their customers manage their money. Depending on the customer's situation, the bank, in its role as financial advisor, may recommend different investment opportunities. The recommended mix might include CDs, mutual funds, stocks, and bonds. Many banks also serve as securities intermediaries, using their own stockbrokers to buy and sell securities and their own facilities to hold them.

Electronic Funds Transfer
Electronic funds transfer (EFT) provides for payments and collections by transferring financial information electronically. PayPal and similar services offer online payments and money transfers among businesses and individuals, nationally and internationally, in various currencies, requiring only that recipients have an e-mail address. Consumers using debit cards and mobile devices instead of writing personal checks enjoy EFT's convenience and speed at the checkout. In addition, EFT systems provide automatic payroll deposit, ATM transactions, bill payment, and automatic funds transfer. Such systems can help a businessperson close an important business deal by transferring money from San Francisco to Miami within a few seconds. The U.S. Treasury reports that it costs around $1.03 to issue a check payment, but only $0.105 to issue an EFT payment. The U.S. Social Security system estimates that it has saved more than $1 billion since it began phasing out paper check payments in 2013 and instead started using paperless payments for federal benefits.[6]

Automated teller machines (ATMs) allow customers to withdraw money, make deposits, transfer funds between accounts, and access information on their accounts. There are around 500,000 machines at U.S. banks and other locations. Increasingly, ATMs have become multilingual global fixtures. As Figure 16.3 shows, among the world's more than 2 million ATMs, most are located outside the United States, and many U.S. banks offer international ATM services. China became the world's largest ATM market in 2015.[7]

Individual Retirement Account (IRA) *tax-deferred pension fund that wage earners set up to supplement retirement funds*

Trust Services *management by a bank of an estate, investments, or other assets on behalf of an individual*

Letter of Credit *bank promise, issued for a buyer, to pay a designated firm a certain amount of money if specified conditions are met*

Banker's Acceptance *bank promise, issued for a buyer, to pay a designated firm a specified amount at a future date*

Electronic Funds Transfer (EFT) *communication of fund-transfer information over wire, cable, or microwave*

Automated Teller Machine (ATM) *electronic machine that allows bank customers to conduct account-related activities 24 hours a day, 7 days a week*

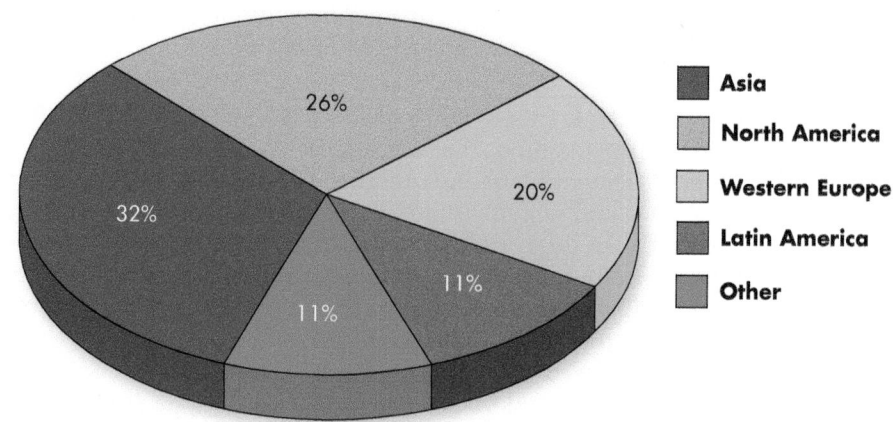

FIGURE 16.3 Global Dispersion of ATMs

managing in turbulent times

Getting Serious with Credit Standards

While banks were trying to avoid drowning in bad loans, borrowers and lenders alike were questioning how the banks got into the 2008–onward financial mess. Many observers today continue to blame subprime mortgage lending. Unlike prime mortgages, subprime loans are made to high-risk borrowers, those with bad credit histories, excessive debt, inadequate income, or other indicators that they will not repay the lender. Also, many of the loans required small or no down-payments, so the borrowers had little equity in the home. In return for these riskier loans, borrowers paid higher interest rates. Subprime mortgages have always been risky, but in 2008, home prices started falling for the first time in decades and unemployment skyrocketed, setting the stage for disaster. Overextended borrowers found they couldn't afford their payments or sell their houses to repay their mortgages, so they just stopped making payments on their loans, forcing banks to foreclose, and that left the banks with unwanted real estate. From 2000–2005, about 6 percent of mortgage loans were uncollectable. Once the bubble burst, delinquencies increased to nearly 30 percent. The chickens had come home to roost.[8]

The subprime crisis was caused by more than just overly relaxed credit standards. One study found that many loan applications listed fraudulent information. Some borrowers, eager to buy the house of their dreams, lied about their income and assets to secure loans. Other misinformation is attributed to mortgage brokers eager to get otherwise unqualified borrowers approved for loans. Some lenders went so far as to have a relative pose as a borrower's fake employer and falsify W-2 forms to gain approval. These problems were compounded further by those within the banking and finance system who knew that rampant fraud was occurring but looked the other way as long as profits kept rolling in.[9]

In response to these predatory lending practices and other unethical actions in the investment and banking arena, Congress

passed an extensive piece of legislation introduced by former Senators Barney Frank and Chris Dodd, and so named the Dodd-Frank Wall Street Reform and Consumer Protection Act. The Act changed the regulatory structure, added new restrictions on lending, required the SEC to implement new rules, and even amended the Federal Reserve Act. In addition, the industry tightened credit standards and lending practices. Federal bank examiners insisted that loan officers use greater caution and judgment to identify creditworthy borrowers. It appears that tighter standards are having a positive effect. For more than a decade before 2008, delinquency rates (the percentage of mortgage borrowers 60 or more days past due) hovered below 3 percent. In the aftermath of the burst of the housing bubble the rate rose to over 11 percent, but it had fallen to 4.77 percent by the end of 2015 and was still falling in 2016.

The stabilization of the housing market and fall in delinquency and foreclosure rates has increased consumer confidence and put the real estate market back on a growth track. However, even with low interest rates on mortgages making the dream of owning a home within the reach of many, the tighter credit standards that emerged out of dishonest and unethical processes in the prior decade and rising home prices can make the dream, for many, unreachable.[10]

How Financial Institutions Create Money and Are Regulated

OBJECTIVE 16-3
Explain
how financial institutions create money and describe the means by which they are regulated.

When individuals make decisions about spending and saving money, they often don't realize they are taking a financial risk. Getting more value for your money requires an awareness of how the value of your money, including savings, changes—and it does change. As the value of money goes down, your purchasing power goes down. Conversely, purchasing power goes up as the value of your money increases. By predicting changes in value, you can time your spending and savings decisions to get the most for your money. Predictions of future values become possible by (1) understanding how money is created and by (2) understanding how the Federal Reserve controls the supply of money. We explore these issues in the following sections.

How Money Is Created

Financial institutions provide a special service to the economy: They create money. They don't actually print bills and mint coins, but by taking in deposits and making loans, they expand the money supply. As Figure 16.4 shows, the money supply expands because banks are allowed to loan out most (although not all) of the money they take in from deposits. If you deposit $100 in your bank and banks are allowed to loan out 90 percent of all their deposits, then your bank will hold $10 in reserve and loan $90 of your money to borrowers. (You still have $100 on deposit.) Meanwhile, a borrower— or the people paid by the borrower—will deposit the $90 loan money in a bank (or banks). The bank will then have another $81 (90 percent of $90) available for new loans. The banks, therefore, have turned your original $100 into $271 ($100 + $90 + $81). The chain continues, with borrowings from one bank becoming deposits in the next.

How Banks Are Regulated

Because commercial banks are essential to the creation of money, the government regulates them to ensure a sound and competitive financial system. Federal and state agencies regulate banks to ensure that the failure of some will not cause the public to lose faith in the banking system itself.

The **Federal Deposit Insurance Corporation (FDIC)** supervises banks and insures deposits in banks and thrift institutions. The FDIC is a government agency created by President Franklin D. Roosevelt to restore public confidence in banks during the Depression era. More than 99 percent of the nation's commercial banks and savings

Federal Deposit Insurance Corporation (FDIC) *federal agency that guarantees the safety of deposits up to $250,000 in the financial institutions that it insures*

Deposit	Money Held in Reserve by Bank	Money to Lend	Total Supply
$100.00	$10.00	$90.00	**$190.00**
90.00	9.00	81.00	**271.00**
81.00	8.10	72.90	**343.90**
72.90	7.29	65.61	**409.51**
65.61	6.56	59.05	**468.56**

FIGURE 16.4 How Banks Create Money

Patti McConville/Alamy Stock Photo

The Federal Deposit Insurance Corporation, or FDIC, protects deposits placed in member banks. Those member banks, in turn, promote the fact that they belong to the FDIC to promote confidence among customers that funds they place on deposit there are safe in the event of a bank failure or other loss. Note, for example, that this bank is promoting its FDIC membership on its front window.

institutions pay fees for membership in the FDIC. In return, the FDIC guarantees the safety of all accounts—checking, savings, and CDs—of every account owner up to the maximum of $250,000. If a bank collapses, or fails, the FDIC promises to pay each depositor for losses up to $250,000 per account. A person with more money can establish accounts in more than one bank to protect sums in excess of $250,000. (A handful of the nation's approximately 5,000 commercial banks are insured by states rather than by the FDIC.) To ensure against multiple bank failures, the FDIC maintains the right to examine the activities and accounts of all member banks.

What happens with banks that fail, such as the nearly 300 U.S. banks that failed in 2009 and 2010? The FDIC becomes responsible for disposing of failed banks. One option is to sell them to other banks that are then responsible for the liabilities of the failed banks. Alternatively, the FDIC can seize the assets of the failed banks and undertake two activities: (1) Pay insurance to depositors and (2) dispose of the banks' assets and settle their debts, all at the lowest cost to the FDIC's insurance deposit fund. The resulting net gain (or loss) is put into (or paid from) the insurance deposit fund. Many banks failed during the recession, costing the FDIC a great deal of money. For example, the fund dwindled from $45 billion in 2008 to $13 billion by the end of 2009. Fortunately, the fund had grown back to $48 billion by the end of 2016. All told, the FDIC now insures around $6.4 trillion in over 600 million accounts at approximately 5,800 institutions. Many other banking activities are regulated by the Federal Reserve System, which is discussed next.

Federal Reserve System (The Fed) *central bank of the United States, which acts as the government's bank, serves member commercial banks, and controls the nation's money supply*

OBJECTIVE 16-4
Discuss
the functions of the Federal Reserve System and describe the tools that it uses to control the money supply.

The Federal Reserve System

Perched atop the U.S. financial system and regulating many aspects of its operation is the **Federal Reserve System (the Fed)**, the nation's central bank, established by Congress in 1913. This section describes the structure of the Fed, its functions, and the tools it uses to control the nation's money supply.

finding a better way

Cultivating a Social Side for Community Banking

Smaller community banks are confronted with vigorous challenges from larger banks that stretch across state lines, competing for local consumers and commercial customers, but the local banks have some advantages. Fidelity Bank, chartered in 1888 by the state of Massachusetts, is an example. With headquarters in Leominster (population 41,000), Fidelity's primary competitive advantage is its commitment to long-term community relationships.

Unlike many smaller banks across the nation, Fidelity remained financially sound through the challenging 2009 economic environment. The bank expanded in 2012 by acquiring depositors from People's United Bank in Leominster and then again in 2015 with the acquisition of Barre Savings and Loan, increasing its assets to over $750 million. In 2016, Fidelity Bank posted a 27 percent increase in deposits, enough to earn recognition as the fastest-growing bank in the state. Its accomplishments, although small from a national bank perspective, speak of its commitment to community. In 2016, Fidelity helped 450 families finance new homes, 62 of which were first-time homeowners, and loaned out in total over $220 million for home improvement projects, college educations, and other consumer and local business loans.

But Fidelity sees itself as more than just a bank. It is a community partner putting customer and community service at the forefront of its mission. For instance, as part of the Barre merger, Fidelity created a $1.5 million community foundation to support nonprofit organizations in the three towns that Barre served: Barre, Paxton, and Princeton.

Fidelity's newest initiative is an even greater giveback to the community called the LifeDesign Community Dividend. Unlike a publicly owned bank that pays dividends to shareholders, Fidelity is mutually owned by the customers. That allows the bank to pay dividends to the community at large. President and COO Chris McCarthy reports, "The LifeDesign Dividend is an integral part of our commitment to help improve the communities we serve. As a community bank, we're very conscious

Kynd/ZUMA Press, Inc./Alamy Stock Photo

of focusing on people, not just profits. When a business does right by people, everybody wins."

Since its founding in 2013, the LifeDesign Community Dividend has distributed more than $1 million in grants. In 2016, the bank paid out $290,000 to community organizations supporting education, health initiatives, youth and senior organizations, cultural centers, and other causes, such as the United Way of North Central Massachusetts, the YWCA Central Massachusetts, the Boys and Girls Club of Fitchburg and Leominster, and many others—over 100 in fact.

Fidelity also promotes a culture of giving within the organization. For instance, employees can donate $5 for the privilege of wearing blue jeans to work every other Friday. The bank matches the donation and then distributes the proceeds to nonprofits. Those distributions amounted to over $11,000 in 2016. And as if that wasn't enough, the official Fidelity ice cream truck visits community events around the region, handing out even more dividends in the form of free ice cream. As the company puts it in its statement of commitment to community, "it is part of our long-term mission to help improve the quality of life of our clients, communities, and employees. We strive to be the most caring bank in the community because we don't just work here, we live, shop, go to school and raise our families here."[11]

The Structure of the Fed

The Fed consists of a board of governors, a group of reserve banks, and member banks. As originally established by the Federal Reserve Act of 1913, the system consisted of 12 relatively autonomous banks and a seven-member committee whose powers were limited to coordinating the activities of those banks. By the 1930s, however, both the structure and function of the Fed had changed dramatically.

The Board of Governors The Fed's board of governors consists of seven members appointed by the U.S. president for overlapping terms of 14 years. The chair of the board serves on major economic advisory committees and works actively

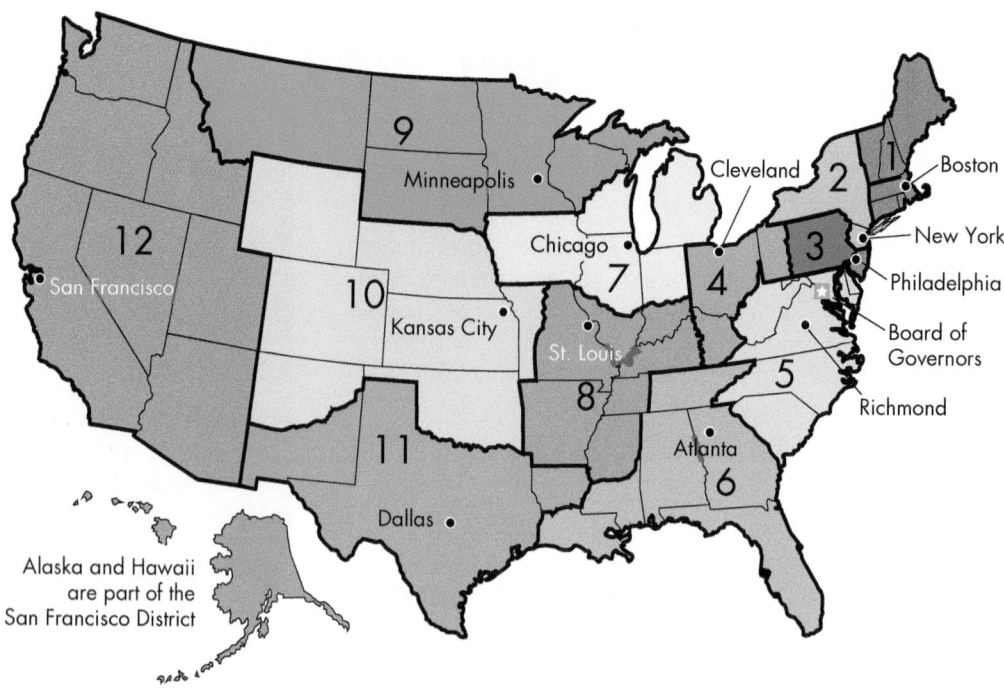

FIGURE 16.5 The Twelve Federal Reserve Districts
Source: http://www.federalreserve.gov/otherfrb.htm, accessed on July 30, 2013.

with the administration to formulate economic policy. The board plays a large role in controlling the money supply. It alone determines the reserve requirements, within statutory limits, for depository institutions. It also works with other members of the Fed to set discount rates and handle the Fed's sale and purchase of government securities.

Reserve Banks   The Fed consists of 12 districts, as shown in Figure 16.5. Each Federal Reserve Bank holds reserve deposits from and sets the discount rate for commercial banks in its geographic region. Reserve banks also play a major role in the nation's check-clearing process.

Open Market Committee   The Federal Open Market Committee is responsible for formulating the Fed's monetary policies to promote economic stability and growth by managing the nation's money supply. Its members include the Board of Governors, the president of the Federal Reserve Bank of New York, and the presidents of four other Reserve Banks, who serve on a rotating basis.

Member Banks   All nationally chartered commercial banks and some state-chartered banks are members of the Fed. The accounts of all member bank depositors are automatically covered by the FDIC (as discussed earlier).

Other Depository Institutions   Although many state-chartered banks, credit unions, and S&Ls do not belong to the Fed, they are subject to its regulations, pay deposit insurance premiums, and are covered by the FDIC or the National Credit Union Administration (NCUA), an independent federal agency that supervises and insures federal credit unions.

The Functions of the Fed

In addition to chartering national banks, the Fed serves as the federal government's bank and the "bankers' bank," regulating a number of banking activities. Most importantly, it controls the money supply.

The Government's Bank The Fed produces the nation's paper currency and decides how many bills to produce and destroy. It also lends money to the government by buying bonds issued by the Treasury Department to help finance the national deficit.

The Bankers' Bank Individual banks that need money can borrow from the Fed and pay interest on the loans. In addition, the Fed provides storage for commercial banks, which are required to keep funds on reserve at a Federal Reserve Bank.

Check Clearing The Fed also clears checks for commercial banks to ensure that cash is deducted from the check writer's bank account and deposited into the check receiver's account. With electronic payments, however, the number of paper checks processed is steadily declining. In 2000, the Fed cleared 60 billion paper checks. By 2015, though, this number had dropped to 15.4 billion paper checks and another 3.6 billion checks cleared as images from mobile apps. Consumers prefer the convenience of debit and credit cards and electronic transactions such as direct deposits and online payments. Even with paper checks, however, the clearing is faster because banks now send the Fed electronic images for presentment, payment, and record keeping (instead of shipping the checks). As a result, the Fed now has just one full-service check-processing site, instead of the 45 locations needed as recently as 2003.[12]

Controlling the Money Supply The Fed is responsible for the implementation of U.S. **monetary policy**, the management of the nation's economic growth by managing the money supply and interest rates. By controlling these two factors, the Fed influences the ability and willingness of banks throughout the country to loan money.

As defined in Chapter 1, *inflation* is a period of widespread price increases throughout an economic system. It occurs if the money supply grows too large. Demand for goods and services increases, and the prices of everything rise. To reduce China's inflationary conditions in 2010–2011, and again in 2013, banking officials decreased the money supply, hoping to slow that nation's economic growth. In contrast, *deflation* occurs when the supply of goods outpaces the supply of money, so demand for goods and services falls. Decreasing prices lead businesses to cut output and also lead to rises in unemployment. The Fed, with its goal of economic stability, uses the money supply to avoid extreme inflation or deflation. Because commercial banks are the main creators of money, much of the Fed's management of the money supply takes the form of regulating the supply of money through commercial banks.

Monetary Policy *management of the nation's economic growth by managing the money supply and interest rates*

The Tools of the Fed

According to the Fed's original charter, its primary duties were to supervise banking and to manage the nation's currency. The duties of the Fed have evolved to include an emphasis on broad economic goals as discussed in Chapter 1, especially growth and stability. The Fed's role in controlling the nation's money supply stems from its role in setting policies to help reach these goals. To control the money supply, the Fed uses *reserve requirements*, *interest rate controls*, and *open-market operations*.

Reserve Requirements The **reserve requirement** is the percentage of its deposits that a bank must hold, in cash or on deposit, with a Federal Reserve Bank. High requirements mean that banks have less money to lend and the money supply is reduced. Conversely, low requirements permit the supply to expand. Because the Fed sets requirements for all depository institutions, it can adjust them to make changes to the overall supply of money in the economy. The Fed's reserve requirements for 2017 depend on the sizes of depositors' accounts. The smallest accounts are exempt (0 percent reserve), for account transactions more than $12.4 million the reserve is 3 percent, and the rate is 10 percent for account transactions greater than $79.5 million.

Reserve Requirement *percentage of its deposits that a bank must hold in cash or on deposit with the Fed*

Discount Rate *interest rate at which member banks can borrow money from the Fed*

Federal Funds Rate (Key Rate) *interest rate at which commercial banks lend reserves to each other, usually overnight*

Interest Rate Controls As the bankers' bank, the Fed loans money to banks. The interest rate on these loans is known as the **discount rate**. If the Fed wants to reduce the money supply, it increases the discount rate, making it more expensive for banks to borrow money and less attractive for them to loan it. Conversely, low rates encourage borrowing and lending and expand the money supply.

More familiar to consumers, the **federal funds rate (or key rate)** reflects the rate at which commercial banks lend reserves overnight to each other. Although the Fed can't actually control this rate, which is determined by the supply and demand of bank reserves, it can control the supply of those reserves to create the desired rate. By instructing its bond traders to buy fewer government bonds, the supply of reserves was decreased, resulting in a series of key rate increases—from a then-historic low of 1 percent in 2004 up to 5.25 percent in 2006—to slow a booming U.S. economy. The Fed then reversed its policy as the economy lost momentum, cutting the target rate gradually down to 0.25 percent in 2008 (to boost the economy during the recession), followed by 0.00–0.25 percent in 2009, and then continuing at 0.00–0.25 percent into 2016 to encourage the economic recovery.[13]

Open-Market Operations *the Fed's sale and purchase of securities in the open market*

Open-Market Operations **Open-market operations** refer to the Fed's sale and purchase of securities (usually U.S. Treasury notes and short-term bonds) in the open market, as directed by the Fed's Open-Market Committee. Open-market operations are particularly effective because they act quickly and predictably on the money supply. The Fed buys government securities from a commercial dealer, whose bank account is credited for the transaction, thus giving that bank more money to lend, so this transaction expands the money supply.

The opposite happens when the Fed sells securities. Selling treasury securities to investors allows the U.S. government to raise money and contract the money supply. These securities may include Treasury bills (T-bills), T-notes, and T-bonds with maturity dates ranging from short-term (a few weeks) to long-term (up to 30 years). Treasury securities are highly liquid because they are actively traded on national securities markets, and traditionally have been considered a risk-free investment because they are backed by the U.S. government.

OBJECTIVE 16-5
Identify
three important ways in which the money and banking system is changing.

The Changing Money and Banking System

The U.S. money and banking system continues to change today. Government emergency intervention aims to stabilize a troubled financial system. Enforcement of antiterrorism regulations deters criminal misuse of the financial system. And with the expansion of banking services, electronic technologies affect how you obtain money and how much interest you pay for it.

Government Intervention for Stabilizing the U.S. Financial System

The financial world was shaken with the 2008 collapse of Lehman Brothers, the leading U.S. investment bank. Lehman's bankruptcy was soon followed by the threat of another giant's demise, as Bear Stearns almost collapsed but was then bought by JPMorgan Chase. But JPMorgan Chase's purchase of Bear Stearns became possible only when the Federal Reserve stepped forward with $26 billion to guarantee potential losses on Bear Stearns's assets. With a goal of stabilizing the fractured financial system, the government continues its unprecedented infusion of funding for U.S. financial institutions.

Government Emergency Investment By mid-2009, the Fed's investments reached nearly $300 billion, mostly in lending programs to commercial banks. Banks used the loans to write off or sell bad mortgages and other hard-to-sell assets, thereby gaining cash for lending to bank customers. Another source of funds, the Troubled Asset Relief Program (TARP), a temporary program under the U.S. Treasury, was included in the government's bailout efforts. TARP support included $15 billion to auto-financing companies at risk of failure and $235 billion in direct investments to some 600 banks to encourage lending. Other government sources provided more than $130 billion to rescue Freddie Mac and Fannie Mae, two government-sponsored enterprises on the verge of financial failure. Freddie Mac and Fannie Mae (also known as FM2) buy home mortgages from the original lenders—for example, from banks—and hold them or resell them. In 2008, FM2 held 80 percent of U.S. home mortgages, many of which turned bad in the collapsed housing market, and many more that continue to default today. FM2 still held some $5 trillion in mortgage assets as of 2013. As a result, critics are questioning whether the government should be involved in the mortgage loan business.[14]

Assurances of Repayment In return for its investments, the government imposes various kinds of assurances. The Fed's loans to banks, for example, are secured by the banks' assets. That is, the Fed holds some of the banks' assets, such as commercial loans, residential mortgages, and asset-backed securities, as collateral until the banks repay the Fed. In return for TARP funds, the U.S. Treasury holds preferred stock (dividend-paying ownership shares) of the banks. The Treasury also holds *warrants*, which give the right to buy shares of the banks' stock in the future at a preset price. In addition to creating the government's precedent-setting part ownership, TARP also imposes stricter executive compensation requirements. In the bailout of FM2, both firms were taken over by the Federal Housing Finance Agency (FHFA) because the failure of either would severely damage global financial markets along with the U.S. economy. FHFA took full control over the two firms' assets and operations.[15]

Anticrime and Antiterrorism Regulations

Enforcement of antiterrorism regulations deters criminal misuse of the financial system. Under provisions of the *Bank Secrecy Act (BSA)*, the U.S. Department of the Treasury imposed a $24 million fine on the New York branch of Jordan-based Arab Bank for failing to implement required monitoring and record-keeping methods to deter funding of crimes. The enforcement of BSA regulations includes tracking and reporting on suspicious transactions, such as a sudden increase in wire transfers or cash transactions exceeding $10,000, to cut off funding of criminal and terrorist activities.[16]

Banks are subject to prosecution when they fail to maintain systems for identifying and reporting suspicious activities that indicate possible drug transactions and money laundering. In violation of the BSA, a Miami, Florida, bank agreed to pay a $55 million penalty to the U.S. government following charges that it did not operate an effective anti-money-laundering program. A Puerto Rico bank was assessed a $21 million penalty for not filing suspicious activity reports when repeated cash deposits were made into one account, often in paper bags in small denominations, totaling $20 million. A California bank was cited for not maintaining an effective anti-money-laundering program when proceeds from cocaine sales were transferred from Mexico for deposit into accounts at the bank. The U.S. Treasury Department, recognizing the rising popularity of virtual currencies and the possibilities of their use in money laundering, recently announced that the federal banking rules also apply to firms that issue exchange money that exists only online and is not issued by any government. This means that online currencies, such as *Bitcoin*, must undertake bookkeeping requirements of the BSA, including reporting of financial transactions exceeding $10,000.[17]

The *USA PATRIOT Act*, passed in 2001 and designed to reduce terrorism risks, requires banks to better know the customer's true identity by obtaining and verifying his or her name, address, date of birth, and Social Security (or tax identification) number. They must also implement a *customer identification program (CIP)* to verify identities, keep records of customer activities, and compare identities of new customers with government terrorist lists. Enforcement resides with examiners from the Department of the Treasury.

The Impact of Electronic Technologies

Banks are among the most enthusiastic adopters of technology to improve efficiency and customer service. Customers of JPMorgan Chase include more than 13 million mobile users, and at Bank of America, more than 100,000 checks each day are deposited remotely by mobile devices.[18] In addition to EFT systems and mobile devices, banks offer access via telephone, TV, and online banking, which allow customers to make around-the-clock transactions. Each business day, trillions of dollars exist in and among banks and other financial institutions in purely electronic form. Each day, the Fed's Fedwire funds transfer system, the world's largest electronic payments system, processes about $5 trillion in transactions for nearly 10,000 financial institutions.

Automated Clearing House (ACH) Network ACH is an electronic funds transfer system that provides interbank clearing of electronic payments for the nation's financial institutions. The ACH network allows businesses, government, and consumers to choose an electronic-over-paper alternative for payments (instead of written checks). The system is green, safe, and efficient.

ACH payments include the following:

- Internet-initiated debit and credit payments by businesses and consumers

- Business-to-business (B2B) electronic payments

- Direct deposit of payroll, Social Security benefits, and tax refunds

- Federal, state, and local tax payments

- E-checks

- Direct payment of consumer bills: mortgages, loans, utility bills, and insurance premiums

- E-commerce payments

In 2015, the ACH system processed over 20 billion payments that were initiated or received by customers at more than 15,000 U.S. businesses and financial institutions. Those payments totaled more than $33 trillion. With the federal government's use of ACH, each direct deposit that replaces a check saves $0.925. With each $1 billion of direct deposits, the federal savings is nearly $1 billion.

The ACH system is governed by NACHA, the Electronic Payments Association, which administers and enforces the association's strict *NACHA Operating Rules* for sound risk management practices. Although NACHA was formed within the American Bankers Association, it later became an independent not-for-profit association that launched the Accredited ACH Professional program and established the system's operating rules.[19]

Check 21: Making the Paper Check Go Away The *Check Clearing for the 21st Century Act (Check 21)*, which became federal law in 2004, allows a receiving bank to make an electronic image of a paper check and electronically send the image to the paying bank for instant payment instead of waiting days for the paper check to wind its way back to the sender. More banks are adopting check image processing (Check 21) and benefitting from its speed and cost efficiency: less paper handling, reduced reliance on physical transportation, faster collection times, and elimination of expensive float. Today, almost 99 percent of the items processed by the Fed are images instead of in paper form. The days of writing a check, mailing it, and having several days to put money in the account to cover it are numbered as a result of faster check clearing.[20]

Blink Credit Card "Blink" technology uses a computer chip that sends radio-frequency signals in place of the magnetic strips that have been embedded in credit cards for the past 30 years. The "contactless" payment system lets consumers wave the card in front of a merchant's terminal at a gas pump or retailer without waiting to swipe and sign. Radio-frequency identification, although new to credit cards, is familiar on toll roads with electronic passes that allow drivers to avoid waiting in line to pay.

Debit Cards Unlike credit cards, **debit cards** do not increase the funds at an individual's disposal but allow users only to transfer money between accounts to make retail purchases. Debit cards are used more than credit cards as payment for U.S. consumer transactions. However, the risk of financial loss is greater for debit cards. Federal law limits the credit card holder's liability to $50 for stolen or fraudulent use. However, a debit cardholder's liability for fraudulent card losses can be higher—ranging up to $500—depending on how quickly the lost card is reported.[21] Many retailers that accept debit cards use **point-of-sale (POS) terminals** to communicate relevant purchase information with a customer's bank. A customer inserts a card, and the bank automatically transfers funds from the customer's account to the store's account.

Debit Card plastic card that allows an individual to transfer money between accounts

Point-of-Sale (POS) Terminal electronic device that transfers funds from the customer's bank account to pay for retail purchases

entrepreneurship and new ventures

Risky Business

When Larry Fink graduated from UCLA's business school in 1976, he went straight to Wall Street and took a job at First Boston as a bond trader. He put in his time, proved himself, and within three years was in charge of what was then a fairly new business segment for First Boston—structuring and trading mortgage-backed securities. Over the years, his hard work and talent led him to fame as one of the architects of the multi-trillion dollar innovative debt-securitization market. The idea was to take all kinds of consumer debt, from credit cards and car loans to mortgages, consolidate them, and then slice them into pieces again and sell the pieces to investors. His uncanny knack for innovation and deal making helped him increase First Boston's bottom line by a billion dollars, and he was on track to be a partner in the firm. Some even said he would one day run the show. He was one of Wall Street's up-and-comers, immersed in the culture of making money. But then, in 1986, predicting that interest rates would rise, Fink took a risky position in the market. Interest rates defied his predictions and his department lost $100 million. Once First Boston's golden boy, overnight he became a pariah.

Being forced out of First Boston turned out to be a turning point for Larry Fink. He was tired of the way Wall Street treated its clients and its traders. Realizing that he'd failed because he wasn't aware of the risks involved, he vowed never to be in that kind of situation again. Coming from that paradigm, he decided to build a company that would invest money for clients and offer sophisticated risk management. From a humble beginning renting a corner office on the Bear-Sterns trading floor, Larry Fink has taken BlackRock from its initial $5 million line of credit to more than $5 trillion in clients' money, more than any asset manager on Earth—even more than Vanguard.

Samuel S/Nchez El Pais Photos/Newscom

Even so, what makes BlackRock even more unique is Aladdin—a state-of-the art computerized risk-management system composed of 5,000 computers managed by a team of engineers, analysts, statisticians, and programmers. Aladdin monitors millions of variables and applies its risk assessments to client's portfolios. In 2000, the company formed BlackRock Solutions, a consulting company, not just for risk avoidance but for advising clients for whom things have already gone wrong.

For Fink though, it's not all about money. In the company's 2013 annual report, Fink wrote "We believe that if our employees seek to act always with integrity, performance follows." From the moment that an employee is hired, BlackRock emphasizes putting the customer first. This means that employees must understand more than just their role in the company, but must be committed to the organization as a whole. For example, a core practice at BlackRock is helping customers to understand risk. As Fink states, performance follows integrity.

Smart Card *credit-card-sized plastic card with an embedded computer chip that can be programmed with electronic money*

Smart Cards A **smart card** has an embedded computer chip that can be programmed with "electronic money." Also known as *electronic purses* or *stored-value cards*, smart cards have existed for more than a decade. They are most popular in gas-pump payments, followed by prepaid phone service, ATMs, self-operated checkouts, vending machines, and automated banking services.[22] Embedded chip technology is also replacing the standard magnetic strips on traditional credit cards and debit cards. This technology provides greater security for both parties during financial transactions.

OBJECTIVE 16-6
Discuss
some of the institutions and activities in international banking and finance.

International Banking and Finance

Electronic technologies permit nearly instantaneous financial transactions around the globe. These business exchanges—the prices asked and paid—are affected by *values of the currencies* among the various nations involved in the transactions. Once agreements are reached, the *international payments process* that moves money between buyers and sellers on different continents is not subject to any worldwide policy system beyond loosely structured agreements among countries.

Currency Values and Exchange Rates

Euros, pesos, yuans, dollars, and yen—money comes in all sizes and stripes. With today's global activities, travelers, shoppers, investors, and businesses often rely on banks to convert their dollars into other currencies. When it comes to choosing one currency over others, the best choice literally changes from day to day. Why? Because every currency's value changes, reflecting global supply and demand—what traders are willing to pay—for one currency relative to others. One index for the value of the U.S. dollar, for example, is the average of its foreign exchange values against the

David Gee 4/Alamy Stock Photo

Exchanges describe the relative value of one currency to another. For instance, if the exchange rate between U.S. dollars and British pounds was 2:1 this would mean that you would need two dollars to "buy" (or exchange for) one pound. Alternatively, one pound could also be exchanged for two dollars. Businesses that handle money exchanges charge a commission on each exchange in order to generate profits for themselves. Alternatively, they may advertise "no commission," but offer less attractive exchange rates. This sign in the Mexico City airport is quoting exchange rates for buying and selling U.S. dollars, euros, pounds, and Canadian dollars relative to the Mexican peso.

currencies of a large group of major U.S. trading partners. The resulting **exchange rate**, the value of one currency compared to the value of another, reveals how much of one currency must be exchanged for another. At any one time, then, some currencies are "strong"—selling at a higher price and worth more—whereas others are "weak." Rates of exchange among currencies are published daily in financial media around the world and at online foreign currency exchange (forex) markets.[23]

Strong Currency or Weak: Which Is Better? Intuitively, it would seem logical to prefer a "strong" currency, right? But in reality, the answer is not so simple and actually depends on how it will be used. Using money for international activities, such as taking a vacation, is really one of those "good news–bad news" situations.

Consider the value of the euro versus the U.S. dollar, as exchange rates fluctuated for those currencies between the ten-year period 2002 and 2012. As a citizen in one of the euro-area countries—for example, France—suppose you were going to take a vacation to the United States in 2002 but, instead, you chose to delay that vacation until 2012. Now, compare your vacation costs if you had gone in 2002 versus 2012, based on currency exchange rates at those times. Each euro in 2012 paid for about $1.45 of the trip (based on currency exchange rates at that time). However, each euro would have covered only $0.87 in 2002 (based on prevailing exchange rates). That's the good news: The stronger euro in 2012 meant more purchasing power against the weaker dollar for French vacationers. It's bad news, though, for French innkeepers because Americans could go elsewhere to avoid expensive European travel that requires $1.45 to pay for each euro of vacation cost, up from only $0.83 to pay per euro ten years previously. Simply put, that $0.83 cup of coffee at a French sidewalk café in 2002 cost $1.45 in 2012. Since 2012, though, the euro has declined in value relative to the dollar and in 2017 was about the same level as in 2002. As a result, it was again less expensive for the French to travel to the United Status.

In terms of trade, the strong euro in 2012 proved to be a stumbling block for Europe's economy, especially for industries that export to non-euro countries with weaker currencies. Prices (in U.S. dollars) had to be increased, for example, on German-made Mercedes and BMW auto exports to the United States to cover the higher euro-based manufacturing costs, causing weaker U.S. demand and sales. Although the weaker dollar hurt many European firms that export products to the United States, others gained by increasing their U.S. investments. When Mercedes-Benz, for example, produces Mercedes M-class autos in Alabama, it pays in weaker dollars for manufacturing them, exports cars to Europe, and sells in euros for windfall profits. On balance, however, many euro-based firms faced sagging sales, with slower revenue growth the result of a strong euro. Again, though, as the euro weakened, those same firms have seen their foreign revenues begin to grow.

Bank Policies Influence Currency Values In managing the money supply and interest rates, the Fed strongly influences the dollar's strength against other currencies. The European Central Bank (ECB) has the same role in the euro zone. The raising of interest rates tends to increase an economic system's currency value, whereas lowering the rate has the opposite effect. Europe's economic recovery is slower than desired when the euro is strong because euro-zone companies are less competitive against global counterparts. Even so, the ECB had refused to weaken the euro by cutting interest rates, even while the euro region was well into the global recession. With lower rates, the supply of euros would increase, and the price of euros would fall, stimulating Europe's economy. But the ECB fears it would also stimulate too much inflation. ECB finally cut interest rates to a record low 0.5 percent in 2015 as the euro region remained in recession. The rate cut was followed by a decrease of 1 percent in the value of the euro on world currency markets.[24]

In contrast, the U.S. Federal Reserve continues with low interest rate policies to stimulate the ailing economy and in doing so contributes to a relatively weak dollar. The weaker dollar makes U.S. goods cheaper and more attractive on the world's markets, thus maintaining or even increasing U.S. export sales. At the same time, the weaker dollar makes foreign imports more expensive, so U.S. consumers can afford fewer imported products, many of which are available only from foreign manufacturers. Some must-have commodities, too, such as petroleum, are priced worldwide in U.S. dollars, so as the dollar's value falls, the price of oil increases because it takes more of those weaker U.S. dollars to buy each barrel.[25] We see, then, some of the ways that banking and banking policies significantly influence currency values.

Compounding the uncertainties facing foreign exchange is Britain's exit from the European Union. Unlike other EU members, Britain never dropped its traditional currency in favor of the euro. But economists, government officials, and business leaders all have a difficult time in predicting how Britain's departure will affect its own international trade, international trade of the EU, and the ripple effects of the major trading partners of both Britain and the EU member nations. Consequently, foreign exchange rates for both the British pound and the euro are likely to fluctuate more than usual over the next few years.

Why care, then, about currency exchange rates? Currencies matter greatly to companies when they buy, sell, and invest with other companies around the globe. Individuals, too, have similar concerns, as when farmers buy grain from Brazil and tractors made in Japan or India, sometimes at higher prices and other times at lower prices, depending on the currency exchange rates of the countries involved. Those exchange rates can be the difference between making a living and losing money during any year. Prices for consumer products, such as electronics by Samsung and autos made in Sweden or Germany, depend on currency exchange rates, too. As an investor looking toward retirement, you may buy an individual retirement account (IRA) in the T. Rowe Price European Stock Fund, or alternatively invest in any of the many other global opportunities for accumulating wealth to meet future needs and dreams. In all of these endeavors, the success or disappointments in your decisions—if and when to buy and to not buy—will be influenced by changes in currency exchange rates. Likewise, as a potential entrepreneur, your business success will be determined, in part, by changes in currency exchange rates.

The International Payments Process

Financial settlements between buyers and sellers in different countries are simplified through services provided by banks. For example, payments from U.S. buyers start at a local bank that converts them from dollars into the seller's currency, such as into euros to be sent to a seller in France. At the same time, payments and currency conversions from separate transactions also are flowing between French businesses and U.S. sellers in the other direction.

If trade between the two countries is in balance—if money inflows and outflows are equal for both countries—then *money does not actually have to flow between the two countries.* If inflows and outflows are not in balance at the U.S. bank (or at the French bank), then a flow of money—either to France or to the United States—is made to cover the difference.

International Bank Structure

There is no worldwide banking system comparable, in terms of policy making and regulatory power, to the system of any industrialized nation. Worldwide banking stability relies on a loose structure of agreements among individual countries or groups of countries.

Two United Nations agencies, the *World Bank* and the *International Monetary Fund*, help to finance international trade. Unlike true banks, the **World Bank** (technically, the International Bank for Reconstruction and Development) provides only a limited scope of services. For instance, it funds national improvements by making loans to build roads, schools, power plants, and hospitals. The resulting improvements eventually enable borrowing countries to increase productive capacity and international trade.

World Bank *UN agency that provides a limited scope of financial services, such as funding improvements in underdeveloped countries*

Another U.N. agency, the **International Monetary Fund (IMF)**, is a group of some 150 nations that have combined resources for the following purposes:

- To promote the stability of exchange rates
- To provide temporary, short-term loans to member countries
- To encourage members to cooperate on international monetary issues
- To encourage development of a system for international payments

The IMF makes loans to nations suffering from temporary negative trade balances. By making it possible for these countries to continue buying products from other countries, the IMF facilitates international trade. The IMF made loans to Greece in 2016 to help support that country's struggling economy. However, some nations have declined IMF funds rather than accept the economic changes that the IMF demands. For example, some developing countries reject the IMF's requirement that they cut back social programs and spending to bring inflation under control.

International Monetary Fund (IMF) *UN agency consisting of about 150 nations that have combined resources to promote stable exchange rates, provide temporary short-term loans, and serve other purposes*

summary of learning objectives

Define *money* **and identify the different forms that it takes in the nation's money supply.** (pp. 514–517)

Modern money takes the form of stamped metal or printed paper issued by governments. However, any item that's *portable*, *divisible*, *durable*, and *stable* satisfies the basic characteristics of money. Money also serves as a *medium of exchange* (it is generally accepted as payment for buying and selling things), a *store of value* (it can be saved and used for future purchases), and a *measure of worth* (it acts as a measure of worth because all products can be valued in terms of money).

A nation's money supply is usually measured in two ways. *M-1*, the spendable money supply, includes the most liquid (or spendable) forms of money: currency (cash), checks, and checking accounts (demand deposits). *M-2* includes M-1 plus other forms of money that are not quite as liquid but are converted easily to spendable forms: time deposits, money market funds, and savings accounts. M-2 is often used for economic planning by businesses and government agencies because it accounts for most of the nation's money supply. M-2 measures the store of monetary value available for consumer purchases and business investments.

Describe **the different kinds of financial institutions that compose the U.S. financial system and explain the services they offer.** (pp. 517–522)

Federally insured commercial banks offer checking accounts and accept deposits that they use to make loans and earn profits for shareholders. Every bank receives a major portion of its income from interest paid on loans by borrowers. As long as terms and conditions are clearly revealed to borrowers, banks may set their own interest rates, within limits set by each state. Traditionally, banks only offered the lowest rate, or *prime rate*, to their most creditworthy commercial customers.

Banks also offer (1) pension services, such as IRAs or other pension options, and trust services in which the bank manages funds on behalf of and in accordance with the wishes of the client that entrusts funds to the bank; (2) international services, including currency exchanges, letters of credit, and banker's acceptances; (3) financial advice by recommending various investment opportunities, and brokerage services in which the bank's stockbrokers can buy and sell securities and hold them in the bank for the client; (4) *electronic funds transfer (EFT)*, payments and collections by transferring financial information electronically; and (5) ATMs for conveniently accessible financial transactions.

Savings institutions, also called thrift institutions, include mutual savings banks and savings and loan associations. *Savings and loan associations (S&Ls)* are owned by shareholders. Most S&Ls were created to encourage savings habits and provide financing for homes. Today, S&Ls accept deposits and make loans and offer many of the same services as commercial banks. In *mutual savings banks*, all depositors are owners of the bank, and all profits are divided among them. *Credit unions* are nonprofit cooperative financial institutions, owned and run by their members, who pool their funds to make loans to one another at reasonable rates. Other organizations called *nondeposit institutions*—pension funds, insurance companies, finance companies, and securities investment dealers—take in money, provide interest or other services, and make loans.

Explain **how financial institutions create money and describe the means by which they are regulated.** (pp. 523–524)

The nation's money supply—the amount of money in circulation—expands because banks and other financial institutions can loan out most of the money they take in from deposits. The loans create additional deposits as follows: Out of a deposit of $100, the bank may hold

$10 in reserve and loan 90 percent—$90—to borrowers. There will still be the original $100 on deposit, and borrowers (of the $90) will also deposit the $90 loans in their banks. Now, the borrowers' banks have $81 of new deposits available for new loans (90 percent of $90). Banks, therefore, have turned the original $100 deposit into $271 ($100 + $90 + $81) of deposits. The chain continues, with borrowings from one bank becoming deposits in the next.

The government regulates all nationally charted commercial banks and most state chartered banks to ensure a sound financial system. Federal and state agencies regulate banks to ensure that the failure of some will not cause the public to lose faith in the banking system. The *Federal Deposit Insurance Corporation (FDIC)* insures deposits and guarantees the safety of all deposits up to $250,000 per account in each bank. To ensure against failures, the FDIC examines the activities and accounts of all member banks and thrift institutions. The FDIC becomes responsible for disposing of failed banks by selling them to other banks or by seizing the assets of failed banks and then (1) paying insurance to depositors and (2) disposing of the failed banks' assets and settling their debts.

OBJECTIVE 16-4

Discuss the functions of the Federal Reserve System and describe the tools that it uses to control the money supply. (pp. 524–528)

The *Federal Reserve System (the Fed)* is the nation's central bank that regulates many aspects of the United States financial system. Although some state-chartered banks, credit unions, and S&Ls do not belong to the Fed, they are subject to its regulations and pay deposit insurance premiums. The Fed consists of a board of governors, a group of reserve banks, and member banks. The Fed's board of governors consists of seven members appointed by the U.S. president for overlapping terms of 14 years. The Fed consists of 12 districts, each with a Federal Reserve Bank. The Fed's Open Market Committee is responsible for formulating the monetary policies to promote economic stability and growth by managing the nation's money supply and interest rates. As the government's bank, the Fed produces currency and lends money to the government by buying bonds issued by the Treasury Department to help finance the national debt. As the bankers' bank, it lends money to member banks, provides storage for funds that commercial banks are required to keep on reserve at a Federal Reserve Bank, and clears checks for commercial banks.

The Fed is responsible for the conduct of U.S. *monetary policy*, the management of the nation's economic growth by managing the money supply and interest rates. Among its tools for controlling the money supply, the Fed specifies *reserve requirements* (the percentage of its deposits that a commercial bank must hold), it sets the *discount rate* at which the Fed lends money to banks, and it conducts *open-market operations* to buy and sell securities in the open market. When the Fed buys securities from a commercial dealer, the dealer's bank account is immediately credited, so that bank has more money to lend and thus the money supply expands and interest rates fall. The opposite happens when the Fed sells securities to investors. Money in the buyer's bank account is reduced, reducing the money supply and increasing interest rates.

OBJECTIVE 16-5

Identify three important ways in which the money and banking system is changing. (pp. 528–532)

The U.S. money and banking system continues to change today. Government emergency intervention aims to stabilize a troubled financial system. Enforcement of antiterrorism regulations deters criminal misuse of the financial system. The Federal Reserve took unprecedented investment actions to stabilize the U.S. financial system following the collapse of major banks in 2008. Commercial banks received massive loans to cover bad mortgages and other toxic assets and to encourage lending to stimulate the sagging economy. The Troubled Asset Relief Program (TARP), a temporary program under the U.S. Treasury, was included in the government's bailout effort, providing billions of dollars to auto-financing companies at risk of failure and billions more to over 600 banks to encourage lending. Other government sources provided funds to rescue Freddie Mac and Fannie Mae, which held vast numbers of defaulted mortgages in the collapsed housing market.

Anticrime and antiterrorism regulations have been enacted to detect and abate use of the financial system for illegal purposes. The Bank Secrecy Act requires financial institutions to deter funding of crimes by tracking and reporting suspicious transactions. The USA PATRIOT Act requires banks to implement a customer identification program to verify identities and compare them with government lists of terrorists.

Banks have adopted new technologies to improve efficiency and customer service. ACH is an electronic funds transfer system that provides interbank clearing of electronic payments for the nation's financial institutions. The ACH network allows businesses, government, and consumers to choose an electronic-over-paper alternative for payments (instead of written checks). In addition to EFT systems and mobile devices, banks offer access through telephone, TV, and Internet banking. *Electronic check clearing* speeds up the check-clearing process, and the "blink" credit card speeds up consumer checkout by replacing magnetic strip cards with contactless cards. *Debit card*s allow the transfer of money from the cardholder's account directly to others' accounts.

OBJECTIVE 16-6

Discuss some of the institutions and activities in international banking and finance. (pp. 532–535)

Changes in currency values and exchange rates reflect global supply and demand—what traders are willing to pay for various currencies. The resulting exchange rate—the value of one currency compared to the value of another—reveals how much of one currency must be exchanged for another. At any one time, then, some currencies are "strong"—selling at a higher price and worth more—whereas others are "weak." In managing the money supply and interest rates, the Fed strongly influences the dollar's strength against other currencies. The European Central Bank (ECB) has the same role in the euro zone. The raising of interest rates tends to increase an economic system's currency value, whereas lowering the rate has the opposite effect.

Country-to-country transactions rely on an international payments process that moves money between buyers and sellers in different nations. If trade between two countries is in balance—if money inflows and outflows are equal for both countries—money does not have to flow between the two countries. If inflows and outflows are not in balance, then a flow of money between them is made to cover the difference.

Because there is no worldwide banking system, global banking stability relies on agreements among countries. Two United Nations agencies help to finance international trade: (1) The *World Bank* funds loans for national improvements so borrowers can increase productive capacity and international trade. (2) The *International Monetary Fund* makes loans to nations suffering from temporary negative trade balances and to provide economic and monetary stability for the borrowing country.

key terms

MyLab Intro to Business

To complete the problems with the ⭐, go to EOC Discussion questions in the MyLab.

questions & exercises

QUESTIONS FOR REVIEW

16-1. Explain the four characteristics of money.

⭐ **16-2.** What are the components of M-1 and M-2?

16-3. Explain the roles of commercial banks, savings and loan associations, credit unions, and nondeposit institutions in the U.S. financial system.

16-4. Describe the structure of the Federal Reserve System.

QUESTIONS FOR ANALYSIS

⭐ **16-5.** As a consumer, when would you favor a strong dollar? What about a weak dollar? Would you consider these factors differently as an employee or employer?

16-6. Should commercial banks be regulated, or should market forces be allowed to determine the kinds of loans and the interest rates for loans and savings deposits? Why?

16-7. Customers who deposit their money in online-only checking and savings accounts can often get higher interest rates than at brick-and-mortar banks. Why do you think that online banks can offer these rates? What might be some drawbacks to online-only banking?

⭐ **16-8.** Start with a $1,000 deposit and assume a reserve requirement of 10 percent. Now calculate the amount of money created by the banking system after five lending cycles.

APPLICATION EXERCISES

16-9. The Federal Reserve Bank maintains historical and current data on exchange rates. You can find detailed historical rates by going to http://www.federalreserve.gov/releases/h10/Hist/. If you used $5,000 to purchase Chinese yuan five years ago, how many yuan would you have received? What would those yuan be worth today? (Use the data on the Fed site to calculate these values and explain your calculations.)

16-10. Interview the manager of a local commercial bank. Identify and list some of the newer regulations that the bank has to comply with, like the Dodd-Frank Act. Does the bank feel that these regulations are just a burden, or do they provide value? How do you feel about the regulations?

building a business: continuing team exercise

Assignment

Meet with your team members to consider your new business venture and how it relates to the money and banking topics in this chapter. Develop specific responses to the following:

16-11. How will your business venture be connected with banks and other financial institutions? In what ways, if any, are such institutions important to your business? Of these relationships, which will be most critical?

16-12. Sales of the product(s) your business offers to customers will depend, in part, on their ability to pay for those products. In what ways, if any, will customers rely on financial institutions for such purchases? Will your company assist customers in connecting with financial institutions to finance their purchases?

16-13. Consider the ways that currency exchange rates will affect your company. Consider also how those rates will affect your customers and their willingness to buy your product(s). Discuss how your team will adjust pricing of your product(s) when the U.S. dollar is strong and when the dollar is weak versus other currencies.

16-14. In what ways will your plans and methods for marketing change, if at all, when the currency values of the U.S. dollar change significantly? Explain.

16-15. Discuss how your team will determine if, and in what ways, your company must comply with the Bank Secrecy Act and the USA Patriot Act in conducting your company's business. Will these acts be a serious concern for your firm? Discuss why, or why not.

team exercise

VIRTUAL BANKING: AN IDEA WHOSE TIME HAS COME?

The Situation

Key Savings and Loan Associations is a multibranch bank located in the Midwest. The company's headquarters is in Indiana and it has more than 35 branches scattered across Illinois, Indiana, Michigan, and Ohio, an area that has, unfortunately, become known as the "Rust Belt." The company has been well managed and profitable for decades, but it is finding it difficult to add new customers or replace ones that leave.

The Dilemma

A member of the bank's board of directors has recommended that the bank consider closing its branch operations and operate as a virtual bank. Its existing customers could maintain their accounts and would have 24-hour access online. Mobile deposit technology will allow customers to deposit checks from their homes and offices. Customers will continue to be able to withdraw cash through ATMs, either those owned by the bank or through the national network. Other banking services would be available online as well, such as car loans and mortgages. Closing the branches will save the company millions of dollars, but it has employees and customers to consider.

Team Activity

Assemble a group of four students and assign each group member to one of the following roles:

- Bill Decker (bank customer)
- Gloria Liu (bank employee)
- Carolyn Kleen (vice president, financial security)
- Karl Marcks (bank stockholder, investor)

Action Steps

16-16. Before hearing any of your group's comments on this situation, and from the perspective of your assigned role, what are the advantages and disadvantages of becoming a virtual bank?

16-17. Join your group and share the advantages and disadvantages of becoming a virtual bank.

16-18. Do you think that going virtual would attract new customers? What types of customers would be most interested in virtual banking?

16-19. What are the potential risks of virtual banking for both the bank and the customer? How can each protect themself?

16-20. What new services might Key Savings and Loan Associations be able to offer if it goes virtual?

exercising your ethics

TELLING THE ETHICAL FROM THE STRICTLY LEGAL

The Situation

When upgrading services for convenience to customers, commercial banks are concerned about setting prices that cover all costs so that, ultimately, they make a profit. This exercise challenges you to evaluate one banking service—ATM transactions—to determine if any ethical issues also should be considered in a bank's pricing decisions.

The Dilemma

A regional commercial bank in the western United States has more than 300 ATMs serving the nearly 400,000 checking and savings accounts of its customers. Bank customers are not charged a fee when they make deposits or withdrawals, just as completing these transactions with a teller in the bank or at a drive-through window is free of charge. In fact, the bank has analyzed the costs associated with each option and has found that deposits and withdrawals are the least expensive option per transaction to the bank. However, in an attempt to cover the costs associated with maintaining the ATM, the bank charges noncustomers a $3 ATM fee. The bank's officers are reexamining their policies on ATM surcharges because of public protests against other banks with similar surcharges in Santa Monica, New York City, and Chicago. Iowa has gone even further, becoming the first state to pass legislation that bans national banks from charging ATM fees for noncustomers. To date, the courts have ruled that the access fees are legal, but some organizations—such as the U.S. Public Interest Research Group (PIRG)—continue to fight publicly against them. In considering its current policies, the western bank's vice president for community relations is concerned about more than mere legalities. She wants to ensure that her company is "being a good citizen and doing the right thing." Any decision on ATM fees will ultimately affect the bank's customers, its image in the community and industry, and its profitability for its owners.

QUESTIONS TO ADDRESS

16-21. From the standpoint of a commercial bank, can you find any economic justification for ATM access fees?

16-22. Based on the scenario described for our bank, do you find any ethical issues in this situation? Or do you find the main issues legal and economic rather than ethical?

16-23. As an officer for this bank, how would you handle this situation?

cases

WHERE DID ALL THE MONEY GO?

Continued from page 514

At the beginning of this chapter, you read about the Fed's role in stabilizing the economy through monetary policy like interest rates, reserve requirements and open market operations,. Using the information presented in this chapter, you should be able to answer the following questions:

16-24. Describe the differences between fiscal policy and monetary policy. What effects do you think each have on the day-to-day operations of a business? Should a business owner be concerned with these kinds of macro-economic issues? If so, why?

16-25. The Fed is supposedly a non-political body. Do you agree with this observation? Do you think it should be, or shouldn't be? Why?

16-26. In 2017, the U.S. government was $20 trillion in debt. Should the government print money to pay off the debt? What effect would such a strategy have on consumers and business?

16-27. Why do economically stressed countries with massive debt have difficulty borrowing outside money needed for economic recovery? Explain.

16-28. If banks are required to keep larger cushions of cash on hand (increased reserve requirements) rather than loaning out that money (as proposed in the Basel III Requirements), in what ways could the U.S. economy be affected?

GLOBAL TRADING PARTNER RESETS ITS ECONOMIC COMPASS

Although Japan may be a small nation, with a population of just 127 million people and relatively limited natural resources, it remains one of the world's economic powers. In the current era of global interdependence, there is no better example of continuing economic relationships—in terms of both trade and capital flows—than that between Japan and the United States. The two countries are both strong industrialized economies that enjoy high standards of living. For example, even though Japan ranked a distant third in the world's gross domestic product (GDP) in 2015 at 4.383 trillion in U.S. dollars, behind the United States ($18 trillion) and China ($11 trillion), its per capita GDP of $35,000 USD in 2015 is closer to that of the U.S. ($56,000) than it is to China ($8,000). Per capita GDP, or GDP per person, is a better measure of the standard of living than overall GDP, and Japan ranks high on the list, even above the European Union. One reason for these rather strange numbers is the fact that the U.S. population at the beginning of 2017 of 325 million people is more than double that of Japan, and our geographic area of 3.8 million square miles is roughly 26 times that of Japan, so we have more capacity to produce goods and services, and more demand. And even though China's overall GDP outdistances Japan's, its per person numbers fall far short.

However, while people in the United States tend to spend more and save less, the Japanese population has a long-standing devotion to saving, resulting at times in a deflationary economy and slow economic growth.

Japan was once the largest source of U.S. imports, but that status has been gradually changing. In 2016, Japan was the fourth-largest supplier (behind Canada, Mexico, and China) of goods imported to the United States—electrical machinery, vehicles, organic chemicals, optic and medical instruments, and agricultural products—amounting to $163 billion. As a trading partner, Japan was the United States' fourth-largest goods export market—including medical instruments, cereals, aircraft, and machinery—amounting to $107 billion. The resulting U.S. trade deficit with Japan was $56 billion.[26]

Its decreasing role in trade with the United States is attributed, among other factors, to Japan's past problems with deflation and the relatively high value of its currency—the yen. Deflationary pressures since the early 1990s stem from the Japanese penchant for saving, rather than spending, together with the Bank of Japan's long-standing monetary policy that limits the supply of money. With limited availability of credit and personal spending, prices tended downward (the opposite of inflation) and purchases were delayed in anticipation of even

lower future prices. Along with diminished profits, employment and incomes suffered, as did the economic expectations of the Japanese people. Meanwhile, the price of the yen in U.S. dollars hit a low of 80 yen per dollar in 2011, down from a range between 200 and 250 in the early 80s. This sounds at first like a favorable trend, but in reality it deterred other countries from purchasing Japan's products—as one dollar buys less and less yen, it also buys less and less products. All of these factors resulted in years of sluggish, and even recessionary, economic performance.

In 2012, Japan took a dramatic step in a new direction with the election of new Prime Minister Shinzo Abe. The Bank of Japan quickly launched a new antideflation program using a more aggressive monetary policy in which the boosting of consumer confidence is a key component for overcoming the deflationary mind-set. The new policy was expected to double the amount of yen held by individuals during the next two years, seeking to increase spending and raise Japan's annual inflation rate to 2 percent. The Japanese central bank injected large amounts of money into the economy using methods similar to those of the U.S. Federal Reserve's "quantitative easing" in an attempt to boost the economy, drive interest rates down to near zero, weaken the yen, and promote Japan's entrepreneurship and competition. In 2013, Japan began to see inflation for the first time in 20 years, but a hike in the national consumption tax halted the economic recovery and by 2014 the country was beginning to experience deflation once again. The Bank of Japan intervened with quantitative easing and stopped the downward slide. Japan continues to battle its deflationary demons, and it looks as if it may be winning, slowly but surely. By the first quarter of 2017, Japan was reporting a 2.2 percent GDP growth rate but only a meager 0.30 percent inflation rate.

Although supporters cite the upside of Shinzo Abe's policies (now called "Abenomics"), others are a bit more cautious in noting some downside risks as well. Critics fear that by weakening the yen, new tensions will arise with other countries that may have to reduce prices of their products to compete against Japan in global markets. It could also mean that imports to Japan from other countries will fall because Japanese consumers will have less purchasing power with a weaker yen.[27]

QUESTIONS FOR DISCUSSION

16-29. What is deflation? How would increasing the money supply in Japan result in an end to deflation?

16-30. The Bank of Japan pumped lots of money into the Japanese economy using tactics similar to the Federal Reserve Bank in the United States. When the Fed wishes to put money into the economy, what tools does it use?

16-31. Consider the ways that Japan's economy would likely be affected by having a strong yen versus a weak yen. Compare and discuss the positive implications and the negative implications for both a strong and a weak yen.

16-32. How will Japan's new monetary policies have an impact on the U.S. economy? Identify and discuss the ways those policies will be felt in the United States.

16-33. Consider Japan's trading status as the fourth-largest source of U.S. imports, and the fourth-largest market for U.S. goods exports. Would you expect that status to change soon relative to other U.S. trading partners such as Canada, China, Germany, and others? Explain.

Writing Assignments

16-34. Research the 2008 financial crisis and the Great Recession that followed. Describe the difference between fiscal and monetary policy by using Congressional actions and Federal Reserve Bank actions as examples. Which was more effective?

16-35. Think about various kinds of financial institutions in the U.S. financial system. (a) Using any three of those institutions, discuss similarities and differences in the services they offer, and the roles they play in the financial system. (b) Explain how financial institutions create money. Give an example.

endnotes

[1] Irwin, Neal. "Quantitative Easing Is Ending. Here's What It Did, in Charts," *New York Times*, October, 2014, https://www.nytimes.com/2014/10/30/upshot/quantitative-easing-is-about-to-end-heres-what-it-did-in-seven-charts.html, (Accessed May 25, 2017).

[2] http://www.federalreserve.gov/releases/h6/current/default.htm, accessed May 1, 2017.

[3] Ibid.

[4] "Economic Research," *Federal Reserve Bank of St. Louis*, at research.stlouisfed.org/fred2/series/USNUM, accessed on May 1, 2017; "Assets and Liabilities of Commercial Banks in the United States," *Board of Governors of the Federal Reserve System*, May 1, 2017, at http://www.federalreserve.gov/releases/h8/current/

[5] http://www.oecd.org/daf/fin/private-pensions/Pension-Markets-in-Focus-2016.pdf, accessed May 1, 2017.

[6] "Electronic Funds Transfer," *Financial Management Service*, at http://fms.treas.gov/eft/index.html, accessed April 20, 2017.

[7] https://www.atmia.com/regions/asia/china-corner/, accessed May 1, 2017.

[8] Sherland, Shane M. "The Past, Present, and Future of Subprime Mortgages," *Finance and Economics Discussion Series, Divisions of Research and Statistics and Monetary Affairs: Federal Reserve Board* (Washington, DC; November 2008); Gerrity, Michael. "MBA Reports Mortgage Loan Delinquencies, Foreclosure Starts Decrease in Q2," *World Property Channel*, August 26, 2010, at http://www.worldpropertychannel.com/us-markets/residential-real-estate-1/real-estate-news-mortgage-bankers-association-national-delinquency-survey-delinquency-rate-for-mortgage-loans-foreclosure-actions-bank-foreclosures-loan-default-rates-3077.php

[9] Bitner, Richard. "Confessions of a Subprime Lender," *Newsweek* (March 12, 2008), at http://www.newsweek.com/id/121512/page/1; Cowen, Tyler. "So We Thought. But Then Again... " *New York Times*, January 13, 2008, at http://www.nytimes.com/2008/01/13/business/13view.html?_r=2&scp=1&sq=Tyler+Cowen&oref=login&oref=slogin; Frank, Robert H. "Don't Blame All Borrowers," *Washington Post* (April 27, 2008), at http://www.washingtonpost.com/wp-dyn/content/article/2008/04/25/AR2008042502783.html

[10] Ely, Bert. "Don't Push Banks to Make Bad Loans," *Wall Street Journal*, February 2, 2009, p. A17; Aversa, Jeannine. "Banks Aren't Budging on Tight Lending Standards," *HuffingtonPost.com*, February 2, 2009, at http://www.huffingtonpost.com/2009/02/02/banks-arent-budging-on-ti_n_163325.html; Simon, Jeremy M. "Lending Standards Keep Tightening, Fed Says," *CreditCards.com*, May 4, 2009, at http://www.creditcards.com/credit-card-news/2009-q1-senior-loan-officers-survey-lending-standards-tighten-1276.php; King, Danny. "Banks Tighten Mortgage Standards for FHA-Insured Loans," *Daily Finance*, November 17, 2010, at http://www.dailyfinance.com/story/credit/banks-tighten-mortgage-standards-for-fha-insured-loans-fico-score/19722792/; Nutting, Rex. "Most Banks Tighten Credit Standards Further, Fed Says," *Market Watch*, May 4, 2009, at http://www.marketwatch.com/story/most-banks-tighten-credit-standards-further; "TransUnion: National Mortgage Loan Delinquency Rate Continues Downward Track in Third Quarter," *Yahoo! Finance*, November 13, 2012, at http://finance.yahoo.com/news/transunion-national-mortgage-loan-delinquency-110000585.html

[11] Fidelity Bank Press Release, May 2017, https://www.fidelitybankonline.com/Our-News/Fidelity-Bank's-LifeDesign-Approach-Results-in-a-B, accessed May 25, 2017.

[12] "Ask Dr. Econ: Is the Fed Still in the Business of Processing Checks?" *Federal Reserve Bank of San Francisco*, 1st Quarter, 2012, at http://www.frbsf.org/education/activities/drecon/2012/Dr-Econ-q1.html, accessed on May 1, 2017; Jacob, Katy, Littman, Daniel, Porter, Richard D., and Rousse, Wade. "Two Cheers for the Monetary Control Act," *Chicago Fed Letter (June 2010, Number 275): The Federal Reserve Bank of Chicago*, at http://www.chicagofed.org/digital_assets/publications/chicago_fed_letter/2010/cfljune2010_275.pdf; Bauer, Paul W., and Gerdes, Geoffrey R. "The Check Is Dead! Long Live the Check! A Check 21 Update," *Federal Reserve Bank of Cleveland*, September 21, 2009, at http://www.clevelandfed.org/research/commentary/2009/0609.cfm; Savage, Jim. "Federal Reserve Banks Complete Check Processing Infrastructure Changes," *Board of Governors of the Federal Reserve System*, March 2, 2010, at http://www

.federalreserve.gov/newsevents/press/other/20100302a.htm

[13] "Open Market Operations," *Board of Governors of the Federal Reserve System*, February 6, 2013, at http://www.federalreserve.gov/monetarypolicy/openmarket.htm#2006

[14] Goldman, David. "CNNMoney.com's Bailout Tracker," *CNNMoney.com*, at http://money.cnn.com/news/storysupplement/economy/bailouttracker/, accessed on April 21, 2011; Griffith, John. "7 Things You Need to Know About Fannie Mae and Freddie Mac," *Center for American Progress*, September 6, 2012, http://www.americanprogress.org/issues/housing/report/2012/09/06/36736/7-things-you-need-to-know-about-fannie-mae-and-freddie-mac/

[15] Crittenden, Michael R. "Regulators See Risk in U.S. Bank Stakes," *Wall Street Journal*, April 24, 2009, at http://online.wsj.com/article/SB124051525463449225.html; Christie, Rebecca. "Treasury May Keep U.S. Bank Stakes After Buyback (Update 3)," *Bloomberg.com*, April 17, 2009, at http://www.bloomberg.com/apps/news?pid=newsarchive&sid=a9F3N8vvrHgY; Goldman, David. "CNNMoney.com's Bailout Tracker," *CNNMoney.com*, April 21, 2011, at http://money.cnn.com/news/story-supplement/economy/bailouttracker/; Jickling, Mark. "Fannie Mae and Freddie Mac in Conservatorship," *CRS Report for* Congress, September 15, 2008, at http://fpc.state.gov/documents/organization/110097.pdf

[16] "U.S. Authorities Fine Arab Bank," *Al Bawaba* (August 18, 2005), p. 1; Osborne, Paul R. "BSA/AML Compliance Provides Opportunity to Improve Security and Enhance Customer Experience," *ABA Bank Compliance*, July/August 2005, p. 4.

[17] Webb, Jason. "American Express Bank Forfeits $55 Million for Bank Secrecy Act Violations," *Associated Content*, August 7, 2007, at http://www.associatedcontent.com/article/339208/american_express_bank_forfeits_55_million.html?cat=17; "Banco Popular de Puerto Rico Enters into Deferred Prosecution Agreement with U.S. Department of Justice," *U.S. Department of Justice*, January 16, 2006, at http://www.usdoj.gov/opa/pr/2003/January/03_crm_024.htm; Union Bank of California Enters into Deferred Prosecution Agreement and Forfeits $21.6 Million to Resolve Bank Secrecy Act Violations," *U.S. Department of Justice*, September 17, 2007, at http://www.usdoj.gov/opa/pr/2007/September/07_crm_726.html; Sparshott, Jeffrey. "Web Money Gets Laundering Rules," *Wall Street Journal*, March 23, 2013, pp. C1, C2.

[18] Sidel, Robin. "Banks Make Smartphone Connection," *Wall Street Journal*, February 12, 2013, pp. C1, C2.

[19] "ACH Payment Volume Exceeds 20.2 Billion for 2011," *NACHA*, April 12, 2012, at https://www.nacha.org/node/1130; "Supporting the Nation's Payment System," *The Federal Reserve Bank of Philadelphia*, April 22, 2011, at http://www.philadelphiafed.org/about-the-fed/who-we-are/payment-system.cfm; "Intro to the ACH Network," *NACHA: The Electronic Payments Association*, at http://nacha.org/c/intro2ach.cfm, accessed on April 22, 2011; "NACHA Reports 18.76 Billion ACH Payments in 2009," *NSF Check Processing*, April 7, 2010, at http://www.nsfcheckprocessing.com/achnetwork.htm

[20] Jacob, Katy, Littman, Daniel, Porter, Richard D., and Rousse, Wade. "Two Cheers for the Monetary Control Act," *Chicago Fed Letter (June 2010, Number 275): The Federal Reserve Bank of Chicago*, at http://www.chicagofed.org/digital_assets/publications/chicago_fed_letter/2010/cfljune2010_275.pdf; Bauer, Paul W., and Gerdes, Geoffrey R. "The Check Is Dead! Long Live the Check! A Check 21 Update," *Federal Reserve Bank of Cleveland*, September 21, 2009, at http://www.clevelandfed.org/research/commentary/2009/0609.cfm; Savage, Jim. "Federal Reserve Banks Complete Check Processing Infrastructure Changes," *Board of Governors of the Federal Reserve System*, March 2, 2010, at http://www.federalreserve.gov/newsevents/press/other/20100302a.htm

[21] Kaste, Martin. "Consumers Opt for Debit Over Credit Cards," *NPR*, June 28, 2009, at http://www.npr.org/templates/story/story.php?storyId=105974724

[22] "About Smart Cards: Introduction: Primer," *Smart Card Alliance*, accessed April 22, 2011, at http://www.smartcardalliance.org/pages/smart-cards-intro-primer

[23] "Summary Measures of the Foreign Exchange Value of the Dollar," *Federal Reserve Statistical Release H:10*, accessed May 1, 2017 at http://www.federalreserve.gov/releases/H10/Summary/

[24] Randow, Jana, and Black, Jeff. "ECB Cuts Interest Rates to Record Low as Recession Lingers," *Bloomberg.com*, May 2, 2013, at http://www.bloomberg.com/news/2013-05-02/ecb-cuts-key-interest-rate-to-record-low-as-recession-lingers.html

[25] Amadeo, Kimberly. "Value of the U.S. Dollar," *About.com*, at http://useconomy.about.com/od/tradepolicy/p/Dollar_Value.htm, accessed on May 1, 2017.

[26] Trade Memo, Office of the United States Trade Representative, https://ustr.gov/countries-regions/japan-korea-apec/japan, accessed May 26, 2017.

[27] "U.S.-Japan Economic Harmonization Initiative," *Office of the United States Trade Representative*, at http://www.ustr.gov/countries-regions/japan-korea-apec/japan, accessed on May 25, 2013; Cooper, William H. "U.S.-Japan Economic Relations: Significance, Prospects, and Policy Options," *Congressional Research Service*, February 20, 2013, at fpc.state.gov/documents/organization/206128.pdf; Mochizuki, Takashi, and Walter, Matthew. "Yen Resumes Its Fall Against the Dollar," *Wall Street Journal*, January 18, 2013, p. C4; Casey, Michael. "Japan's Biggest Export? Deflation," *Market Watch*, May 8, 2013, at http://www.marketwatch.com/story/japans-biggest-export-deflation-2013-05-08; "Japanese Yen," *Wikipedia*, at en.wikipedia.org/wiki/Japanese_yen, accessed on May 22, 2013; Jolly, David. "Japan's Moves to Weaken the Yen Have a Global Effect," *New York Times*, April 8, 2013, at http://www.nytimes.com/2013/04/09/business/global/yen-slides-close-to-level-of-100-to-the-dollar.html?_r=0; Fackler, Martin. "Japan's New Optimism Has Name: Abenomics," *New York Times*, May 20, 2013, at http://www.nytimes.com/2013/05/21/world/asia/hope-in-japan-that-abenomics-may-be-turning-things-around.html?pagewanted=all

Are you lucky enough to make it in the business world? What if luck has nothing to **do with it? How** many wealth-seekers actually find what **they want, and** what are their secrets?

After reading this chapter, you should be able to:

17-1 **Explain** the concept of the time value of money and the principle of compound growth, and discuss the characteristics of common stock.

17-2 **Identify** reasons for investing and the investment opportunities offered by mutual funds and exchange-traded funds.

17-3 **Describe** the role of securities markets and identify the major stock exchanges and stock markets.

17-4 **Describe** the risk–return relationship and discuss the use of diversification and asset allocation for investments.

17-5 **Describe** the various ways that firms raise capital and identify the pros and cons of each method.

17-6 **Identify** the reasons a company might make an initial public offering of its stock, explain how stock value is determined, and discuss the significance of market capitalization.

17-7 **Explain** how securities markets are regulated.

Fire On the Ground

Perhaps you're lucky enough to have visited a Fogo de Chão restaurant—the company had 28 locations in the United States in early 2017, plus two in Mexico and ten in Brazil. Fogo de

Chão is a Brazilian-style steakhouse, or churrascaria, serving a variety of fire-roasted meats, carved at the table by gaucho chefs who have been trained in this southern Brazilian cooking style. Certainly, the roaming chefs serving custom cuts of meat is part of the charm of a Fogo de Chão visit, but it's also part of a unique delivery model that allows the restaurant to control costs by reducing the number of wait staff required. To complement the assortment of meats, diners can visit the extensive buffet, which includes self-service salads, side dishes, and desserts.

This high-end restaurant, which competes head-to-head with Ruth's Chris Steakhouse and The Capital Grille, has humble beginnings. In 1979, two sets of brothers, Jair and Arri Coser and Jorge and Aleixo Ongaratto, opened a churrascaria in a shed with a grass roof in Porto Alegre, Brazil.

The restaurant had a rustic flair, as is suggested in the name Fogo de Chão (for *fire on the ground*). Over the next six years, the company prospered and two additional locations were opened in São Paulo. But a chance encounter with a former president, George H. W. Bush, launched their expansion into the United States. Dining at one of the São Paulo locations in 1995, the former president was so delighted with the food and service that he suggested the brothers expand their operations to the United States. Two weeks later, Jair and Jorge were headed to Texas. "I think about why I came to the United States all the time," says Jair Coser. "I cannot explain it. I had a good life at that time in Brazil. I have my house. I have my family. I have my business. And it was, 'Let's go.'"

In 2005, the Ongaratto brothers sold their interests in the company to the Cosers, who became equal co-owners. To allow for continued expansion, the Cosers brought in GP Investments, one of the largest investment funds in Brazil, the following year, but maintained a controlling interest. In 2012, the Coser brothers decided to liquidate their investments, reportedly selling the company for $426 million to Thomas H. Lee Partners L. P. At that time, the chain was up to 16 U.S. restaurants and seven locations in Brazil.

The new ownership team successfully continued the expansion of the restaurant chain, retaining many of the upper-level managers and bringing in new talent and expertise to shore up accounting and management practices. In 2015, the company went public with an initial public offering of just over 4.4 million shares of stock, raising $88.2 million at a price per share of $20, well above the projected

what's in it for me?

Businesses from all over the world, representing every industry, converge in global financial markets every day, seeking funds that can be used to finance their activities and pay their debts. Individual investors gather as well, in person or—more often—online, looking to make their money "work" for them by buying and selling commodities, stocks, and bonds. The history of Fogo de Chão illustrates each of these activities. This chapter will help you understand the various ways this is possible, whether your goals are short or long term, whether you are motivated by the desire for profit or security, or simply because you enjoy the challenges inherent in successfully raising and investing capital.

selling price range of $16–$18 per share. Thomas H. Lee Partners L. P. retained over 22 million shares for themselves, giving them nearly 80 percent controlling interest in the company. Fogo de Chão used that money to pay down debt, and since then has seen steadily increasing revenues and net income.

Just before Fogo de Chão went public, three other restaurant chains did the same: chicken-wings chain Wingstop Inc. raised $127 million in its IPO, chicken-and-biscuits chain Bojangles' raised $169 million in its IPO, and burger chain Shake Shack Inc. raised $121 million.[1] Shake Shack went public at about $46 per share and within months hit $96 before entering a long slide that led to a mid-2017 price of less than $40. Bojangles', which opened at almost $24 per share, slipped by mid-2017 to less than $18, while Wingstop has bounced between $26 and $33 ever since it went on the market at $30. So, 2016 and early 2017 were rough on the restaurant industry as a whole, and Fogo de Chão, even with a positive earnings report, was no exception. By early 2017 the stock that sizzled at $20 when it first hit the market had dropped in value to less than $15 per share. To be fair, as a full-service restaurant, it doesn't really compare to Wingstop or Shake Shack. With dinner plates ranging from $50–$60, Fogo de Chão competes with the more upscale steakhouses such as Ruth's Chris Steakhouse, Del Frisco's, and The Capital Grille. Nevertheless, the stock price performance has been disappointing.

There's often no one particular reason that a stock will fall or rise in value, but for Fogo de Chão, there are a few factors that investors may be looking at as they consider whether to buy, hold, or sell the stock. For instance, even though paying down debt sounds like a good idea, there are some disadvantages to that strategy, especially for a company-store-owned model. It takes a lot of capital and cash to open new restaurants, and using the IPO proceeds to pay down debt left the company cash poor. Some of the robust sales in 2016 were a collateral effect of the Olympics. In addition, because of the special skills needed to cook gaucho style, Fogo de Chão relies on bringing in chefs from Brazil on L-1B "specialized knowledge" visas, which have been suspended and some even revoked retroactively. So, what does all this point to? As with any investment in a publicly held company, it's actually impossible to accurately predict whether the stock will go up or down. Being a well-informed investor gives you an edge, but as the American business author William Feather once said, "One of the funny things about the stock market is that every time one person buys, another sells, and both think they are astute." (After studying the content in this chapter, you should be able to answer a set of discussion questions found at the end of the chapter.)

OBJECTIVE 17-1
Explain
the concept of the time value of money and the principle of compound growth, and discuss the characteristics of common stock.

Maximizing Capital Growth

Wise investments are the key to growing your money, especially if you are seeking to accumulate capital to start (or grow) your own business or simply as a cushion for a sound financial future. In searching for investment opportunities, a number of concepts come into play for evaluating alternative investments and sorting out the good from the bad. (As we will discuss more fully later in the chapter, a key element to consider is the relationship between potential returns on investments and investment risk.)

The Time Value of Money and Compound Growth

The most-proven "road to wealth" lies in a strategy of saving and investing over a period of years. Only rarely does a "one-in-a-million" opportunity provide a quick fortune. Although the popular "I want it all, and I want it now!" mentality sounds good, it becomes a reality for very few wealth-seekers.

The **time value of money**, perhaps the single most important concept in business finance, recognizes the basic fact that, when it's invested over time, money grows

Time Value of Money *principle that invested money grows, over time, by earning interest or some other form of return*

by earning interest or yielding some other form of return. Time value, in turn, stems from the principle of **compound growth**, the cumulative growth from interest paid to the investor over given time periods. With each additional time period, an investment grows as interest payments accumulate and earn even more interest, thus multiplying the earning capacity of the initial investment.

Compound Growth *compounding of interest over time—with each additional time period, interest returns accumulate and earn more interest*

The Rule of 72 We can better appreciate the concept of the "time value of money" with a practical example based on this question: How long does it take to double an investment? A handy rule of thumb to answer this question is called the "Rule of 72." You can find the number of years needed to double your money by dividing the annual interest rate (in percent) into 72. If, for example, you reinvest annually at 8 percent, you'll double your money in about 9 years:

$$\frac{72}{8} = 9 \text{ years to double the money}$$

By the same reasoning, if you reinvest annually at 4 percent, your money will double in about 18 years.

The Rule of 72 can also calculate how much interest you must get if you want to double your money in a given number of years: Simply divide 72 by the desired number of years. If you have a goal of doubling your money in 10 years, you will need to get 7.2 percent:

$$\frac{72}{10} = 7.2 \text{ percent interest needed to double the money}$$

The lesson for the investor is clear: seek *higher* interest rates because money will double more frequently.

Making Better Use of Your Time Value What if you invested $10,000 at 7 percent interest for one year? You would earn $700 on your $10,000 investment. If you reinvested the principal amount plus the interest you earned during the first year, and then continued to reinvest both the original principal and all interest annually for another four years, you'd end up with $14,025. Now, if you were planning for retirement and reinvested that money at the same interest rate for another 25 years, you could retire with $76,122—almost eight times the amount you started with!

Figure 17.1 illustrates how the returns from an initial investment of $10,000 accumulate substantially over longer periods of time. Notice that the gains for the last 10 years are much greater than for the first 10 years, illustrating the power of compound growth. This is because each year the interest is applied to a larger sum. The figure also illustrates that the accumulations grow even faster at higher interest rates. Even a seemingly small increase in interest rates, from 7 to 8 percent, results in much larger accumulations.

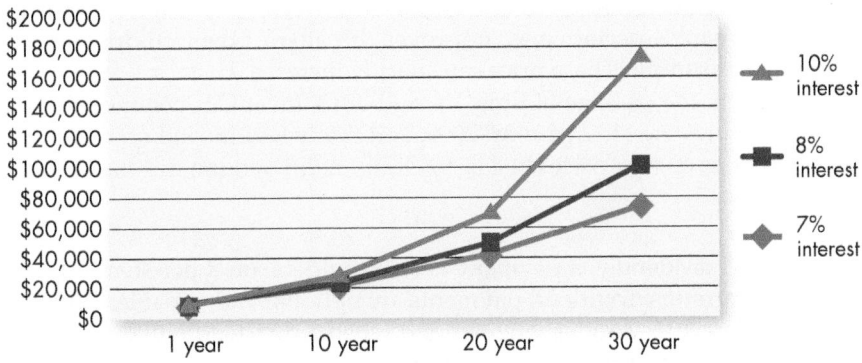

FIGURE 17.1 Amount to Which an Initial $10,000 Investment Grows

As you can see from Figure 17.1, the best way to take advantage of the time value of money is to obtain a high rate of return on your investment. However, various kinds of investments offer opportunities for fulfilling different financial objectives, such as aggressive growth, financial safety, and others, which we discuss later.

Common Stock Investments

Stock *portion of ownership of a corporation*

History has shown that one way to achieve a high rate of return, compared with many other ways, is to invest in the stock market. Consider the average rate of return on the U.S. stock market, as of the beginning of 2012. The 100-year average (1912–2012) was more than 9 percent annually, and the most recent 25-year average return was more than 11.29 percent.[2] A **stock** is a portion of the ownership of a corporation. The corporation's total ownership is divided into small parts called *shares* that can be bought and sold to determine how much of the company (how many shares of stock) is owned by each shareholder. This widespread ownership has become possible because of the availability of different types of stocks and because markets have been established that enable individuals to conveniently buy and sell them.

Common Stock *most basic form of ownership, including voting rights on major issues, in a company*

Although several types of stock exist, so-called "common stock" is the most prominent. A share of **common stock** is the most basic form of ownership in a company. Individuals and other companies purchase a firm's common stock in the hope that it will increase in value and provide dividend income. In addition, each common share has a vote on major issues that are brought before the shareholders.

Stock values are usually expressed in two different ways: as (1) *market value* and (2) *book value*.

Market Value *current price of a share of stock in the stock market*

1 A stock's real value is its **market value**, the current price of a share in the stock market. Market value reflects the amount that buyers are willing to pay for a share of the company's stock.

Book Value *value of a common stock expressed as the firm's owners' equity divided by the number of common shares*

2 The **book value** for a share of common stock is determined as the firm's owners' equity (from the balance sheet) divided by the number of common shares owned by all shareholders. Book value is used as a comparison indicator because the market value for successful companies is usually greater than their book value. Thus, when market price falls to near book value, some profit-seeking investors buy the stock on the principle that it is underpriced and will increase in the future.

Investment Traits of Common Stock Unfortunately, common stocks are among the riskiest of all investments. Uncertainties about the stock market itself can quickly change a given stock's value. Furthermore, when companies have unprofitable years, or when industry or general economic conditions stagnate, they often cannot pay dividends and potential investors become wary of future stock values, so share price drops. U.S. stocks, for example, lost more than half their value in the recession years 2008 and early 2009. More recently, when energy prices plummeted in 2015 most stock prices remained high but the stock prices of oil companies dropped. On the positive side, however, common stocks offer high growth potential; when a company's performance improves (because of the introduction of a hot new product, for example) share price can sharply increase. Historically, stock values generally rise with the passage of time. By mid-2013, most U.S. common stocks had recovered the values they lost in 2008–2009, and many had moved on to new record levels. Similarly, as energy prices began to climb in 2017 so too did the stock prices of oil companies.

Dividend *payment to shareholders, on a per-share basis, out of the company's earnings*

Dividends A **dividend** is a payment to shareholders, on a per-share basis, from the company's earnings. Dividend payments are optional and variable. The corporation's board of directors decides whether and when a dividend will be paid, as well as the amount that is best for the future of the company and its shareholders. Many companies distribute between 30 and 70 percent of their profits to shareholders. The so-called **blue-chip stocks**, those issued by the strongest, well-established, financially sound and respected firms, such as Coca-Cola and ExxonMobil, have historically provided investors steady income through consistent dividend payouts. However, some firms, especially fast-growing companies, do not pay dividends. Instead, they use cash earnings for expanding the company so that future earnings can grow even faster. What's more, any company can have a bad year and decide to reduce or omit dividend payments to stockholders.

We see, then, that success in accumulating capital depends significantly on exploiting the time value of money because compound growth from interest payments across several time periods multiplies the earning capacity of the firm's investments. Investments in common stocks, too, offer the potential for increasing capital growth, but only if the stock provides dividend income and its market value increases.

Investing to Fulfill Financial Objectives

Mutual funds and exchange-traded funds are popular alternatives to stocks because they offer attractive investment opportunities for various financial objectives and often do not require large sums of money for entry. In addition, the simple and easy transaction process makes them very accessible to individual investors.

Mutual funds are created by investment firms such as T. Rowe Price and Vanguard. These firms essentially pool cash investments from individuals and organizations to purchase bundles of stocks, bonds, and other securities. The bundles are expected to appreciate in market value and otherwise produce income for the mutual fund and its investors. Thus, investors, as part owners, expect to receive financial gains as the fund's assets become increasingly valuable. For example, if you invest $1,000 in a mutual fund with assets worth $100,000, you own 1 percent of that fund. Investors in **no-load funds** are not charged sales commissions when they buy into or sell out of funds. Investors in **load funds** generally pay commissions of 2 percent to 8 percent.

Reasons for Investing

It's relatively easy to open a mutual fund account online or by phone. There are numerous funds that meet any chosen financial objective. The funds vary in their investment goals—different funds are designed to appeal to the different motives and goals of investors. Three of the most common objectives are (1) financial stability, (2) conservative growth, and (3) aggressive growth.

- *Stability and Safety.* Funds stressing safety (i.e., the lowest risk) accept only modest growth with little fluctuation in principal value regardless of economic conditions. They include *money market mutual funds* and other funds that preserve the fund holders' capital and reliably pay current income. Typical assets of these funds include lower-risk U.S. corporate bonds, U.S. government bonds, and other similarly safe short-term securities that provide stable income from interest and dividends.

- *Conservative Capital Growth.* Mutual funds that stress preservation of capital and current income but also seek some capital appreciation are called *balanced funds*. Typically, these funds hold a mixture of long-term municipal bonds, corporate bonds, and common stocks with good dividend-paying records for steady income. The common stocks offer potential for market appreciation (higher market value), though there is always the risk of price declines if the general stock market falls.

- *Aggressive Growth.* *Aggressive growth funds* seek maximum long-term capital growth. They sacrifice current income and safety by investing in stocks of new (and even troubled) companies, firms developing new products and technologies, and other higher-risk securities. They are designed for investors who can accept the risk of loss inherent in common stock investing with severe price fluctuations but also the potential for superior returns over time.

Most Mutual Funds Don't Match the Market

Many, but not all, mutual funds are managed by "experts" who select the fund's stocks and other securities that provide the fund's income. Unfortunately, some estimates indicate that up to 80 percent of these managed funds do not perform as well as the average return of the overall stock market as a result of costly management expenses and underperforming stocks.[3] This underperformance disadvantage has resulted in the emergence of passively managed funds, in which the fund manager invests by using a fixed, predetermined strategy that replaces judgmental choices for buying and selling its stock holdings. Those choices are predefined by the strategy, not by the fund manager. The most widespread use of passively managed funds is with index mutual funds, which seek to mimic the holdings and performance of a particular market index. As an example, the widely watched Standard and Poor's 500 Index (S&P 500), which is discussed later, consists of 500 specific common stocks. Any mutual fund company can establish its own index fund by purchasing shares of those same 500 companies, thus matching the market performance of the S&P 500. The selection of which stocks to purchase in an index fund is relatively automatic—it holds many of the same stocks as the market it tracks—and requires little human input, thus reducing management expenses.

Exchange-Traded Funds

Exchange-Traded Fund (ETF) *bundle of stocks or bonds that are in an index that tracks the overall movement of a market, but unlike a mutual fund can be traded like a stock*

As with an index mutual fund, an **exchange-traded fund (ETF)** is a bundle of stocks (or bonds) that are in an index that tracks the overall movement of a market. Unlike a mutual fund, however, an ETF can be traded like a stock. Each share of an ETF rises and falls as market prices change continuously for the market being tracked.

ETFs offer three areas of advantage over mutual funds. First, they can be traded throughout the day like a stock, they have low operating expenses, and they do not require high initial investments. Because they are traded on stock exchanges (hence, "exchange traded"), ETFs can be bought and sold—priced continuously—any time throughout the day. This *intraday trading* means you can time your transaction during the day to buy or sell when (or if) the market reaches a desired price. Mutual fund shares, in contrast, are priced once daily, at the end of the day. Thus, when you buy or sell during the day, you don't find out the share price until after the day has ended.

Second, whereas many mutual funds pass the costs of expensive active management on to shareholders, an ETF is bound by a rule that specifies what stocks will be purchased and when; once the rule is established, little or no active human decisions are involved. The *lower annual operating expenses* mean that, for the buy-and-hold investor, annual fees for ETFs are as low as 0.04 percent of assets; annual fees for mutual funds average 1.4 percent.[4]

Finally, unlike mutual funds, ETFs require no minimum investment, meaning they offer *ease of entry* for investors getting started without much money.[5] On the other hand, because ETFs must be bought and sold through a broker, they require payment of a brokerage commission (transaction fees). Traders who buy and sell frequently can end up paying more in transaction fees, even surpassing a mutual fund's high management expenses.[6]

We see, then, because firms have different financial objectives for investing, they often consider other alternatives, in addition to common stocks, such as mutual funds with varying degrees of safety and stability, funds that seek conservative capital growth, and riskier aggressive growth funds. ETFs are available to those firms that have the time to track moment-to-moment stock market movements for intraday trading. By allowing low minimum investments, ETFs offer ease of entry in addition to low annual operating expenses.

entrepreneurship and new ventures

Find a Need, Fill a Need

On March 17, 2017, Rich and Vicki Fulop's relatively small startup company, Brooklinen, got a $10 million shot in the arm from FirstMark Capital by selling a minority share in the company in what investors call a Series A round.

Rewind just three short years. Rich had been downsized from his job as a finance manager, so he'd taken that opportunity to go back to school with a full scholarship to NYU's Stern School of Business. Vicki had graduated with a law degree but had never taken the bar. Instead, she worked in public relations helping companies build their brands and garner press coverage. Splurging on a much needed vacation stay in a posh hotel, they were enthralled by the luxurious bed linens and wanted to buy a set, but the hotel didn't carry the sheets for sale. So, the Fulops went looking online. What they found was both a challenge and an opportunity. No one seemed to carry quality sheets at an affordable price, and the shopping experience was disappointing. However, the Fulops concluded that there was an unmet need in the market, and they set out to fill it.

Starting with a meager amount of funds from savings and loans from family members, the Fulops set up a website and some initial infrastructure, and then they launched a Kickstarter campaign both to test the water and to raise capital. To their surprise, they raised almost $234,000 in just 30 days, surpassing their $50,000 goal in the first eight.

Using their combined business skills in both finance and marketing, Rich and Vicki kept the company both lean and profitable. By negotiating a manufacturing deal with a company in Israel, where the U.S. has free trade agreements, they were able to cut costs by 22 percent. By November of 2016, Brooklinen was boasting over $20 million in annual sales and a customer base of over 50,000. They're not without competition, though, from retailers like Parachute, Crane & Canopy, and Boll & Branch (another husband and wife startup) that sell high thread count sheets for between $100–$200—expensive, but still a fraction of the price of Frette or Sferra, sheets of equal quality.

Matej Kastelic/Shutterstock

In order to stay competitive and grow, Rich and Vicki needed more capital. Enter FirstMark Capital, a venture capital firm, as the name suggests. FirstMark worked with the Fulops to create an initial private placement of preferred stock, exempting the company from onerous reporting and filing requirements under SEC rules. The Series A preferred stock gives FirstMark some of the security of debt as well as some of the ownership provisions of stock. Usually, series A preferred stock includes some favorable provisions, such as a conversion clause that would allow the investor to trade preferred stock for common stock if the company goes public.

The Fulops, still in control of the company, plan to use the venture capital funds to expand the marketing campaign and grow the team as they increase their offerings to include pillows, duvet covers, candles, and a wide variety of other complementary goods. Will it pay off? For 2017, the company plans to sell more than $50 million in product and to triple the customer base to 150,000. All this from just the germ of an idea on a romantic get-away. As they say in business, the basic building block of success is, "find a need, fill a need." After that, all you need is hard work and lots of money.[7]

The Business of Trading Securities

Stocks, bonds, and mutual funds are known as **securities** because they represent *secured*, or financially valuable, claims on the part of investors. The markets in which stocks and bonds are sold are called **securities markets**. By facilitating the buying and selling of securities, the securities markets provide the capital that companies rely on for survival. Mutual funds, on the other hand, are not bought and sold on securities markets but are managed by financial professionals in the investment companies that create, buy, and sell the funds.

OBJECTIVE 17-3
Describe
the role of securities markets and identify the major stock exchanges and stock markets.

Securities *stocks, bonds, and mutual funds representing secured, or asset-based, claims by investors against issuers*

Securities Markets *markets in which stocks and bonds are sold*

Primary and Secondary Securities Markets

Primary Securities Market *market in which new stocks and bonds are bought and sold by firms and governments*

In **primary securities markets**, new stocks and bonds are bought and sold by firms and governments. New securities are sometimes sold to single buyers or small groups of buyers. These *private placements* are desirable because they allow issuers to keep their plans confidential.

Most new stocks, however, and some bonds are sold on the wider public market. To bring a new security to market, the issuing firm must get approval from the U.S. **Securities and Exchange Commission (SEC)**, the government agency that regulates U.S. securities markets. The firm also relied, traditionally, on the services of an **investment bank**, a financial institution that specialized in issuing and reselling new securities. All that changed, however, in the financial collapse of 2008, when the fall of Lehman Brothers became the largest bankruptcy in U.S. history, Bear Stearns was purchased by JPMorgan Chase, and the two remaining large U.S. investment banks—Morgan Stanley and Goldman Sachs—were allowed to become bank holding companies (much like a commercial bank).[8] Although the companies' structures have changed, they still provide three important investment banking services:

Securities and Exchange Commission (SEC) *government agency that regulates U.S. securities markets*

Investment Bank *financial institution that specializes in issuing and reselling new securities*

1   *Advise* companies on the timing and financial terms of new issues.

2   *Underwrite*—buy and assume liability for—new securities, thus providing the issuing firms with 100 percent of the money (less commission). The inability to resell the securities is a risk that the banks must bear.

3   *Create* distribution networks for moving new securities through groups of other banks and brokers into the hands of individual investors.

Secondary Securities Market *market in which existing (not new) stocks and bonds are sold to the public*

New securities, however, represent only a small portion of traded securities. *Existing* stocks and bonds are sold in the much larger **secondary securities market**, which is handled by such familiar bodies as the New York Stock Exchange and by online trading with electronic communication networks.

Stock Exchanges

Stock Exchange *an organization of individuals to provide an institutional auction setting in which stocks can be bought and sold*

Most of the buying and selling of stocks has historically been handled by organized *stock exchanges*. A **stock exchange** is an organization of individuals coordinated to provide an institutional auction setting in which stocks can be bought and sold.

Founded in 1792 and located at the corner of Wall and Broad Streets in New York City, the New York Stock Exchange sees billions of shares change hands each day.

The Trading Floor Each exchange regulates the places and times at which trading may occur. The most important difference between traditional exchanges and the electronic market is the geographic location of the trading activity. Brokers at an exchange trade face-to-face on the *trading floor* (also referred to as an *outcry market*). The electronic market, on the other hand, conducts trades electronically among thousands of dealers in remote locations around the world.

Trading floors today are equipped with vast arrays of electronic communications equipment for displaying buy and sell orders or confirming completed trades. A variety of news services furnish up-to-the-minute information about world events and business developments. Any change in these factors, then, may be swiftly reflected in share prices.

The Major Stock Exchanges Among the stock exchanges that operate on trading floors in the United States, the New York Stock Exchange is the largest. Today, it faces stiff competition from both the electronic market in the United States and large foreign exchanges, such as those in London and Tokyo.

THE NEW YORK STOCK EXCHANGE For many people, "the stock market" means the *New York Stock Exchange (NYSE)*. Founded in 1792, the NYSE is the model for exchanges worldwide. The merger with Euronext in 2007 formed NYSE Euronext, bringing together marketplaces across Europe and the United States, representing one-third of stock trading worldwide. Only firms meeting certain minimum requirements— earning power, total value of outstanding stock, and number of shareholders—are eligible for listing on the NYSE.[9]

Today's NYSE is a *hybrid market* that uses both floor and electronic trading. When a client places an order through a brokerage house or online, it is transmitted to a broker on the NYSE floor. Floor brokers who want to trade that stock meet together to agree on a trading price based on supply and demand, and the order is executed. Alternatively, buyers can use the NYSE's Direct+ service to automatically execute trades electronically.

GLOBAL STOCK EXCHANGES As recently as 1980, the U.S. market accounted for more than half the value of the world market in traded stocks. Market activities, however, have shifted as the value of shares listed on foreign exchanges continues to grow. Table 17.1 identifies the ten largest exchanges in 2016, the dollar volume of shares that year, and the number of firms listed for trade. While new exchanges are emerging in such diverse settings as Vietnam, Laos, and Rwanda, earlier start-ups are flourishing in cities from Shanghai to Warsaw, and others are merging or partnering in other

table 17.1 Selected Global Stock Exchanges and Markets

Exchange	Trade Volume (2016) (Billions $)	Listings
New York Stock Exchange	$19,223	2,400
NASDAQ	$6,831	3,058
London Stock Exchange	$6,187	3,014
Tokyo Stock Exchange	$4,485	2,292
Shanghai Stock Exchange	$3,986	1,041
Hong Kong Stock Exchanges and Clearing Limited (HKEX)	$3,325	1,866
Euronext	$3,321	1,299
Toronto Stock Exchange	$2,781	1,524
Shenzhen Stock Exchange	$2,285	1,420
Frankfurt Stock Exchange	$1,766	3,769

Source: **www.visualcapitalist.com**, accessed on May 15, 2017.

regions. NYSE Euronext, for example, gained an important presence in the Middle East by joining with Qatar Stock Exchange, which also enabled Qatar to become a stronger international exchange.[10]

National Association of Securities Dealers Automated Quotation (NASDAQ) System *world's oldest electronic stock market consisting of dealers who buy and sell securities over a network of electronic communications*

THE NASDAQ MARKET The National Association of Securities Dealers Automated Quotation (NASDAQ) System, the world's oldest electronic stock market, was established in 1971. Whereas buy and sell orders to the NYSE are gathered on the trading floor, NASDAQ orders are gathered and executed on a digital network connecting 500,000 terminals worldwide. Currently, NASDAQ is working with officials in an increasing number of countries in replacing the trading floors of traditional exchanges with electronic networks like NASDAQ's.

The stocks of some 3,100 companies, both emerging and well known, are traded by NASDAQ. Examples include Marvell, Apple, Microsoft, Intel, and Staples. Although the volume of shares traded surpasses that of the NYSE, the total market value of NASDAQ's U.S. stocks is less than that of the NYSE.

International Consolidation and Cross-Border Ownership

A wave of technological advances, along with regulatory and competitive factors, has propelled the consolidation of stock exchanges and the changeover from physical to digital trading floors across international borders. Electronic communication networks have opened the door to around-the-clock and around-the-globe trading. Every major European stock exchange had gone electronic by the end of the twentieth century, and by 2010 the United States had caught up. Stock exchanges that didn't have a strong enough digital presence have merged or partnered with those having more advanced trading systems. The intensified competition among stock exchanges has brought faster transactions and lower transaction fees for investors.

Nonexchange Trading: Electronic Communication Networks

Electronic Communication Network (ECN) *electronic trading system that brings buyers and sellers together outside traditional stock exchanges*

The SEC authorized the creation of **electronic communication networks (ECNs)** in 1998. These networks are electronic trading systems that bring buyers and sellers together outside traditional stock exchanges by automatically matching buy and sell orders at specified prices. ECNs gained rapid popularity because the trading procedures are fast and efficient, often lowering transaction costs per share to mere pennies. They also allow after-hours trading (after traditional markets have closed for the day) and protect traders' anonymity.[11]

ECNs must register with the SEC as broker-dealers. The ECN then provides service to subscribers—that is, other broker-dealers and institutional investors. Subscribers can view all orders at any time on the system's website to see information on what trades have taken place and at what times. Individual investors must open an account with a subscriber (a broker-dealer) before they can send buy or sell orders to the ECN system.

Individual Investor Trading

More than half of all U.S. citizens have some form of ownership in stocks, bonds, or mutual funds.[12] Many of these investors are novices who rely on the advice of experienced professionals or brokers. Investors who are well informed and experienced, however, often prefer to invest independently without outside guidance.

stock broker *individual or organization that receives and executes buy and sell orders on behalf of outside customers in return for commissions*

STOCK BROKERS Some of the people on the trading floor of stock exchanges are employed by the stock exchange itself. Others are trading stocks for themselves. Many, however, are **stock brokers** who earn commissions by executing buy and sell orders for outside customers. Although they match buyers with sellers, brokers do not own the securities. They earn commissions from the individuals and organizations for whom they place orders.

Discount Brokers As with many other products, brokerage assistance can be purchased at either discount or at full-service prices. Discount brokers, such as E*TRADE and Scottrade, offer well-informed individual investors who know what they want to buy or sell a fast, low-cost way to participate in the market. Buying 200 shares of a $20 stock in 2017 cost the investor a service fee of $7 at Scottrade, and $7.99 to $9.99 at E*Trade. Price differences are obvious even among the discount brokers, but the highest discount price is well below the price of a full-service broker. Sales agents receive fees or salaries, not commissions. Unlike many full-service brokers, many discount brokers do not offer in-depth investment advice or person-to-person sales consultations. They do, however, offer automated online services, such as stock research, industry analysis, and screening for specific types of stocks.

Full-Service Brokers Despite the growth in online investing, full-service brokers remain an important resource, both for new, uninformed investors and for experienced investors who don't have time to keep up with all the latest developments. Full-service brokers, such as Merrill Lynch Wealth Management, offer clients consulting advice in personal financial planning, estate planning, and tax strategies, along with a wider range of investment products. In addition to delivering and interpreting information, financial advisors can point clients toward investments that might otherwise be lost in an avalanche of online financial data.

Online Investing The popularity of digital trading stems from convenient access to online information, fast, no-nonsense transactions, and the opportunity for self-directed investors to manage their own investments while paying low fees for trading.

Online investors buy and sell the stocks of thousands of companies daily. Consequently, keeping track of who owns what at any given time has become extremely complex. As a result, most ownership records are now maintained through what is referred to as **book-entry ownership**. Shares of stock were historically issued as physical paper certificates. But now, though, they are simply recorded in the companies' records (or "books"), thereby eliminating the costs of printing, storing, exchanging, and replacing paper certificates.

Book-Entry Ownership *procedure that holds investors' shares in book-entry form, rather than issuing a physical paper certificate of ownership*

Tracking the Market Using Stock Indexes

For decades, investors have used stock indexes to measure market performance and to predict future movements of stock markets. Although not indicative of the status of individual securities, **market indexes** provide useful summaries of overall price trends, both in specific industries and in the stock market as a whole. Market indexes, for example, reveal *bull* and *bear market* trends. **Bull markets** are periods of rising stock prices, generally lasting 12 months or longer. During bull markets investors are motivated to buy, confident they will realize capital gains. Periods of falling stock prices, usually 20 percent off peak prices, are called **bear markets**. During bear markets investors are motivated to sell, anticipating further falling prices.

As Figure 17.2 shows, the past 37 years have been characterized primarily by bull markets, including the longest in history, from 1981 to the beginning of 2000. In contrast, the period 2000 to 2003 was characterized by a bear market. The period 2007–2009 was the second-worst bear market of all time, exceeded only by that of 1929–1932.[13] The data that characterize such periods are drawn from four leading market indexes: the Dow Jones, Standard & Poor's, NASDAQ Composite, and the Russell 2000 (not shown in Figure 17.2).

Market Index *statistical indicator designed to measure the performance of a large group of stocks or track the price changes of a stock market*

Bull Market *period of rising stock prices, lasting 12 months or longer, featuring investor confidence for future gains and motivation to buy*

Bear Market *period of falling stock prices marked by negative investor sentiments with motivation to sell ahead of anticipated losses*

The Dow The **Dow Jones Industrial Average (DJIA)** is the oldest and most widely cited U.S. market index. It measures the performance of the industrial sector of the U.S. stock markets by focusing on just 30 blue-chip, large-cap companies as reflectors of the economic health of the many similar U.S. firms. The Dow is an average of the

Dow Jones Industrial Average (DJIA) *oldest and most widely cited market index based on the prices of 30 blue-chip, large-cap industrial firms on the NYSE*

finding a better way

Finding a Way to Fund Life After Work

Most firms today offer health benefits and some kind of retirement plan—likely a 401(k)—but even though we may take them for granted as employee perks, both of those benefits are relatively new in the workforce. In fact, prior to 1900, there were only a few companies that offered even a rudimentary pension plan, following the lead of American Express (which was still an express mail company in 1875 when it began offering retirement benefits). The idea behind pension plans when they were first devised was to create a more stable, career-oriented workforce. But back then, people worked until they were physically unable to labor any longer, and life expectancies were relatively short, so the ongoing post-retirement payments of a pension plan were limited.

Two things happened that cemented pension plans into place in American ideology. First, the stock market crash of 1929 and the Great Depression that followed wiped out the life savings of millions of Americans. Gleaning an idea from the private sector, in order to provide security for retirees in the future, Congress passed the Social Security Act of 1935, and Franklin Delano Roosevelt signed it into law, creating the government-sponsored defined benefit retirement plan we know today. Those early pension plans (and Social Security, still) based the payouts on a formula and usually promised a monthly payment for life. Of course, in 1935, the life expectancy was only 60 years, so still the overall liability was limited. Then, in 1942, in an attempt to curtail post-war inflation, Congress passed the Wage and Salary Act that effectively froze wages. However, the freeze didn't apply to fringe benefits like health insurance and retirement benefits, so in order to attract talent, companies began to woo executives with generous benefit packages. As time went by, big unions like the United Auto Workers lobbied for benefits to apply to everyone, not just the highly-compensated employees. In fact, Ford Motor Company didn't offer hourly employees a pension plan until 1950.

Now Pandora's box was open. Life expectancies increased, and workers expected benefits and demanded more. But there was a dark side to the pension promise. In 1963, the Indiana-based car company Studebaker Corp. went bankrupt, and the plan assets were swallowed up in the proceedings, leaving 11,000 workers with no retirement payout. This wasn't the first pension plan failure. In fact, it was one of many, but it is often cited as the tipping point that called Congress into action once more, creating the Employee Retirement Security Act of 1974. This act had some lasting and somewhat unintended consequences.

First, it created the Pension Benefit Guaranty Corporation—a taxpayer-funded pension bailout fund that pays out billions of dollars every year to beneficiaries of failed retirement plans and that is currently running billions of dollars in the red. But there

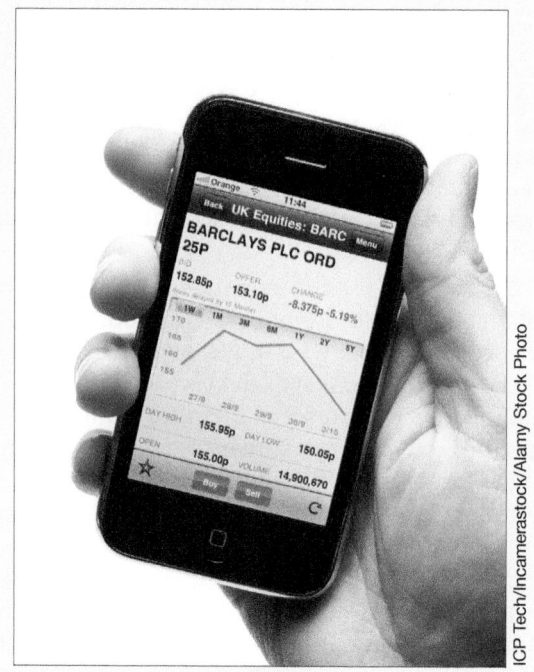

ICP Tech/Incamerastock/Alamy Stock Photo

was also a small provision in the law that created a defined contribution option to augment the traditional defined benefit plan. Earnings from money invested in those plans that qualified under the new law were exempt from tax under section 401(k) of the Internal Revenue Code. The employee could designate a certain amount of pre-tax earnings to go into the fund, and often the employer would match those funds to a certain extent.

Now pension funds are dinosaurs. Employers and shareholders don't like the liability they create, whereas a defined contribution plan, like a 401(k), is usually fully funded. Employees like to know exactly how much they have invested and often take pride in managing the investment mix themselves, within limits. Most participants are offered an array of mutual funds, from high growth to fixed income. Some companies allow the employees to invest in the company stock, but there are drawbacks to that strategy. For instance, at the close of 2000 more than half of the $2.1 billion of assets in the Enron 401(k) retirement plan was invested in Enron stock. When Enron went bankrupt, thousands of employees lost their life savings. For the most part, the PBGC wasn't able to help because it was a defined contribution plan, not really a pension (defined benefit) plan. Lehman Brothers employees and, more recently, Radio Shack employees faced similar upsets. The upshot of all this: Participate in your 401(k) to the maximum amount allowed and let the investments grow tax free, but diversify your investments. The easiest way to do that is to learn all you can about mutual funds and invest your retirement savings balancing risk and return.

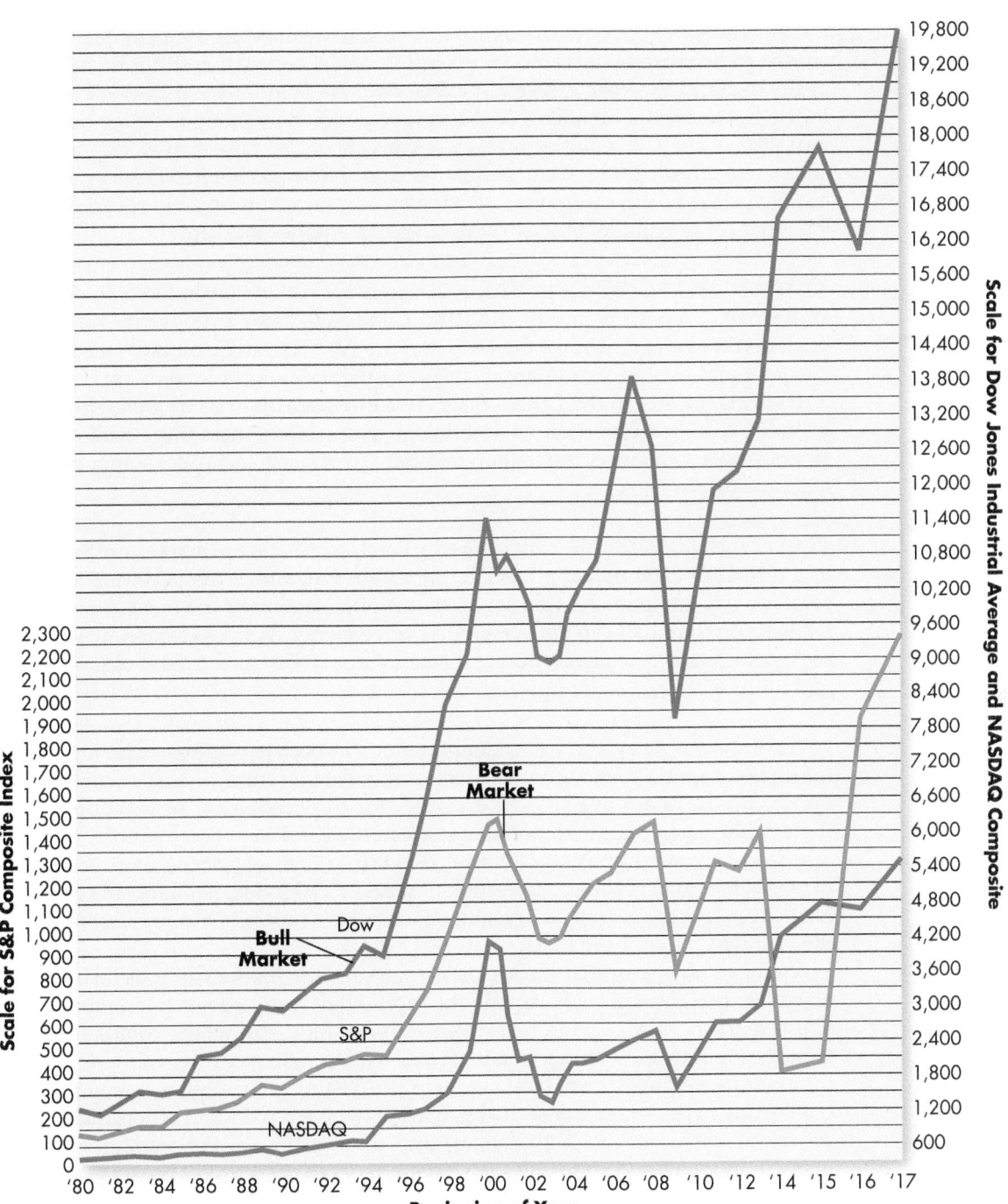

FIGURE 17.2 Bull and Bear Markets
Source: Yahoo! Finance, at http://finance.yahoo.com.

stock prices for these 30 large firms, and traders and investors use it as a traditional barometer of the market's overall movement. Because it includes only 30 of the thousands of companies on the market, the Dow is only an approximation of the overall market's price movements.

Over the last several decades, the Dow has been revised and updated to reflect the changing composition of U.S. companies and industries. Recent modifications occurred in 2008–2009, when three companies were added—Kraft Foods, insurance giant Travelers Companies, and technology titan Cisco Systems—replacing insurance company American International Group, banker Citigroup, and auto icon General Motors. More recently still, after Kraft merged with Heinz in 2015 it was dropped and replaced with Apple.

S&P 500 *market index of U.S. equities based on the performance of 500 large-cap stocks representing various sectors of the overall equities market*

The S&P 500 Even though the 30 firms included in the Dow are carefully chosen to be representative of the overall financial sector, it is still a limited gauge of the overall U.S. stock market. The **S&P 500**, the Standard and Poor's Composite Index, however, is a broader report and is considered by many to be the best single indicator of the U.S. equities market. It consists of 500 large-cap stocks, including companies from various sectors—such as information technology, energy, industrials, financials, health care, consumer staples, and telecommunications—to provide a balanced representation of the overall large-cap equities market.

NASDAQ Composite Index *market index that includes all NASDAQ-listed companies, both domestic and foreign, with a high proportion of technology companies and small-cap stocks*

The NASDAQ Composite Because it considers even more stocks, some Wall Street observers regard the **NASDAQ Composite Index** as one of the most useful of all market indexes. Unlike the Dow and the S&P 500, all NASDAQ-listed companies, not just a selected few, are included in the index for a total of approximately 3,100 firms, mostly in the United States but in other countries as well. However, it includes a high proportion of technology companies, including small-company stocks, and a smaller representation of other sectors—financial, consumer products, and industrials.

Russell 2000 Index *specialty index that uses 2,000 stocks to measure the performance of the smallest U.S. companies*

The Russell 2000 Investors in the U.S. small-cap market are interested in the **Russell 2000 Index**, a specialty index that measures the performance of the smallest U.S. companies based on market capitalization. As the most quoted index focusing on the small-cap portion of the U.S. economy, its stocks represent a range of sectors such as financials, consumer discretionary, health care, technology, materials, and utilities.

Index-Matching ETFs Countless other specialty indexes exist for specific industries, countries, and economic sectors to meet investors' diverse needs. In addition, many ETFs are available to investors for duplicating (or nearly duplicating) the market performance of popular stock-market indexes. For example, one ETF, Standard & Poor's Depositary Receipts (SPDRS, known as *Spiders*), owns a portfolio of stocks that matches the composition of the S&P 500 index. Similarly, the Fidelity® NASDAQ Composite Index® Tracking Stock holds a portfolio of equities for tracking the NASDAQ Composite Index.

We have now seen that the securities markets, the markets in which stocks and bonds are bought and sold, provide the capital that companies rely on for survival. These markets also provide investment opportunities by which companies trade securities to increase a firm's wealth. Firms issuing new securities raise capital with the assistance of investment banking services. Existing securities are traded throughout the day in the secondary securities market (where buyers and sellers make transactions at the major stock exchanges) and through ECNs. For trading securities, many individuals and companies rely on the services of securities brokers, and other self-directed traders use online trading to self-manage their investments. Investors often use stock indexes to measure market performance and to predict future market movements of stock markets. Market indexes reveal bull and bear markets, revealing the risks and opportunities for gaining and losing wealth that are inherent in securities investments.

OBJECTIVE 17-4
Describe
the risk–return relationship and discuss the use of diversification and asset allocation for investments.

The Risk–Return Relationship

Individual investors have different motivations and personal preferences for safety versus risk. That is why, for example, some individuals and firms invest in stocks while others invest only in bonds. Although all investors anticipate receiving future cash flows, some cash flows are more certain than others. Investors generally expect to receive higher returns for higher uncertainty. They do not generally expect large returns for secure, stable investments such as government-insured bonds. The

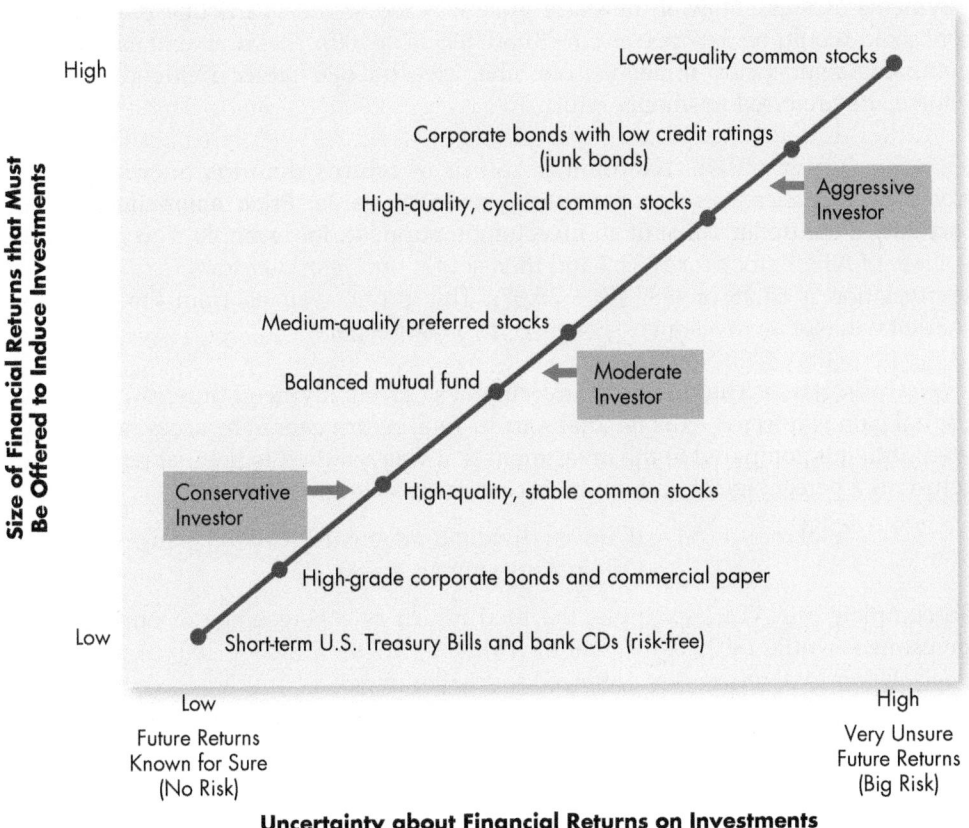

FIGURE 17.3 Potential Financial Returns Rise with Riskier Investments.

investment's time commitment, too, contains an element of risk. While short-term investments are generally considered to be less risky, longer-term investments are subject to future uncertainties in the economy and financial markets. As of mid-2017, the average rate of return on a 1-year U.S. Treasury bill was 0.25 percent, versus 1.51 percent on a 5-year bill, and 2.10 percent on a 10-year bill. Each type of investment, then, has a **risk–return (risk–reward) relationship**: Safer investments tend to offer lower returns, riskier investments tend to offer higher returns (rewards).

Figure 17.3 shows the general risk–return relationship for various financial instruments, along with the types of investors they attract. Thus, conservative investors, who have a low tolerance for risk, will opt for no-risk U.S. Treasury Bills (fully insured by the U.S. government), or even intermediate-term high-grade corporate bonds that rate low in terms of risk on future returns, but also low on the size of expected returns. The reverse is true of aggressive investors who prefer the higher risks and potential returns from long-term junk bonds and common stocks.[14]

Risk–Return (Risk–Reward) Relationship *principle that safer investments tend to offer lower returns whereas riskier investments tend to offer higher returns (rewards)*

Investment Dividends (or Interest), Appreciation, and Total Return

In evaluating potential investments, investors look at returns from dividends (or from interest), returns from price appreciation, and total return.

Dividends The rate of return from dividends paid to shareholders is commonly referred to as the **current dividend yield** (or, in the case of interest from a loan, the **current interest yield**) and is calculated by dividing the yearly dollar amount of dividend income by the investment's current market value. For example, during one recent time period, each share of AT&T stock was receiving annual dividend

Current Dividend Yield and Current Interest Yield *yearly dollar amount of income divided by the investment's current market value, expressed as a percentage*

payments of $1.80. Now, if the share price was $35.67 on a particular day, the current yield would be 5.05 percent or ($1.80/$35.67 × 100). This dividend can then be compared against current yields from other investments. Larger dividend yields, of course, are preferred to smaller returns.

Price Appreciation Another source of returns depends on whether the investment is increasing or decreasing in dollar value. **Price appreciation** is an increase in the dollar value of an investment. Suppose, for example, you purchased a share of AT&T stock for $35.67 and then sold it one year later for $37.45. The price appreciation is $1.78 or ($37.45 − 35.67). This profit, realized from the increased market value of an investment, is known as a **capital gain**.

> **Price Appreciation** *increase in the dollar value of an investment at two points in time (the amount by which the price of a security increases)*

> **Capital Gain** *profit realized from the increased value of an investment*

Total Return The sum of an investment's current dividend (interest) yield and capital gain is referred to as its total return. Total return cannot be accurately evaluated until it is compared to the investment that was required to get that return. Total return as a percentage of investment is calculated as follows:

$$\text{Total return (\%)} = \frac{(\text{Current dividend payment} + \text{Capital gain})}{\text{Original investment}} \times 100.$$

To complete our AT&T example, the total return as a percentage of our one-year investment would be 10.04 percent or [($1.80 + $1.78)/$35.67 × 100]. Again, obviously, larger total returns are preferred to smaller ones.

Fantasy Stock Markets

Enthusiasts of fantasy baseball, football, hockey, and other "hypothetical" games aren't the only people who enjoy competing in fantasy realms. Fantasy stock markets are also popular venues for learning how securities markets work, for trying your hand at various investment strategies, and earning a fantasy fortune (or going broke!). Online games, including free ones such as *Wall Street Survivor* and *How the Market Works*, provide an investment experience that is educational, challenging, and entertaining. Starting with an initial sum of virtual cash with which to manage their own fantasy portfolio of real companies, participants must live with real market results. It's a learn-by-doing experience—using online symbol lookups to enter stock ticker symbols, searching various information sources for research on companies of interest, making buy and sell decisions, and then discovering the financial results as real market prices change for the portfolio holdings. Many students and business practitioners are finding these "games" to be a valuable resource for learning the "how to" of online investing.

Managing Risk with Diversification and Asset Allocation

Investors seldom take an extreme approach—total risk or total risk avoidance—in selecting their investments. Extreme positions tend to lead to extreme results. Instead, most investors select a mixed portfolio of investments—some riskier and some more conservative—that, collectively, provides the overall level of risk and financial returns that feels comfortable. After determining the desired *risk–return* balance, they then achieve it in two ways: through (1) *diversification* and (2) *asset allocation*.

Diversification **Diversification** means buying several different kinds of investments rather than just one. For example, diversification as applied to common stocks means that you invest in stocks of several different companies, companies in different industries, and companies in various countries. The risk of loss is reduced by spreading the total investment across different kinds of stocks because although any one stock price may decline the chances are less that all of them will decline at the same time. For instance, when oil and gas prices drop as they did in 2016, stock prices for oil and gas companies like Shell and Chevron also decline (all else equal) because their revenues go down. However, stock prices for firms that use a lot of oil

> **Diversification** *purchase of several different kinds of investments rather than just one*

and gas fuel, such as UPS, FedEx, and Delta Airlines, might go up (all else equal) because these firms see a drop in their operating expenses.

Even more diversification is gained when assets are spread across a variety of investment alternatives—stocks, bonds, mutual funds, precious metals, real estate, and so on. On the other hand, though, employees who do not have diversified investments and instead have all their retirement funds invested in their firm's stock can lose everything if their company goes bankrupt or invests poorly. The collapse of Enron Corporation in 2001, one of the 10 largest U.S. firms at the time, was a financial disaster for its thousands of its employees because Enron's retirement program was invested solely in Enron common stock. Enron's stock price dropped from near $90 per share to nearly $5, effectively wiping out employees' retirement savings. Putting all their eggs in one basket was an extremely risky position, as they learned the hard way. When their firm's stock took a free fall as a result of a market collapse and resulting scandal, the retirement funds disappeared.

Asset Allocation **Asset allocation** is the proportion (the relative amounts) of funds invested in (or allocated to) each of the investment alternatives. You may decide for example, to allocate 50 percent of your funds to common stocks, 25 percent to a money market mutual fund, and 25 percent to a U.S. Treasury bond mutual fund. Ten years later, with more concern for financial safety as you get closer to retirement, you may decide on a less risky asset allocation of 20 percent, 40 percent, and 40 percent in the same investment categories, respectively. In this example, the portfolio has been changed from moderate-risk to lower-risk investments for the purpose of preserving the investor's accumulated capital. That is, the asset allocation was changed accordingly.

Asset Allocation relative amount of funds invested in (or allocated to) each of several investment alternatives

Performance Differences for Different Portfolios Once an investor has chosen an investment objective with an acceptable risk level, he or she can put the tools of diversification and asset allocation to use in their investor's *portfolio*. A **portfolio** is the combined holdings of all the financial investments—stocks, bonds, mutual funds, real estate—of any company or individual.

Just like investors, investment funds have different investment objectives—ranging from aggressive growth/high risk to stable income/low volatility—and their holdings are diversified accordingly among hundreds of company stocks, corporate bonds, or government bonds that provide the desired orientation. The money in a diversified portfolio is allocated in different proportions among a variety of funds. If all goes according to plan, most of these funds will meet their desired investment objectives and the overall portfolio will increase in value.

Portfolio combined holdings of all the financial investments of any company or individual

A risk–return relationship is inherent in every business investment. Whereas safer investments tend to offer lower returns, riskier investments tend to offer higher returns (rewards). Different types of investments vary along the risk–reward continuum, and most firms strive for a mixture of investments that, overall, provide that firm's desired risk–return posture. Each investment's total financial return is the sum of its capital gain and dividend (interest) yield. After determining the desired risk–return balance, investors use two methods for achieving it: (1) diversification and (2) asset allocation. Diversification means buying several different kinds of investments rather than just one. Asset allocation is the proportion of funds invested in each of the investment alternatives. Diversification and asset allocation, together, are essential to protect against the uncertainties (risks) inherent in any single investment.

Financing the Business Firm

OBJECTIVE 17-5
Describe
the various ways that firms raise capital and identify the pros and cons of each method.

If you invest wisely, and your goal is to start your own firm, you may find yourself in a position to do so. However, that's only the first step in the complicated process of financing a business. Every company needs cash to function. Although a business owner's savings may be enough to get a new venture up and running, ongoing businesses depend on sales revenues to survive. When current sales revenues are insufficient to pay for expenses, firms tap into various other sources of funds, typically starting with the owners' savings (as discussed in Chapter 15, owners usually contribute funds, or paid-in capital, from their own pockets). If a firm needs more money, it can turn to borrowing from banks, soliciting cash from private outside investors, or selling bonds to the public.

Secured Loans for Equipment

Money to purchase new equipment often comes in the form of loans from commercial banks. In a **secured loan (asset-backed loan)**, the borrower guarantees repayment of the loan by pledging the asset as **collateral** to the lender. Suppose a local trucking company needs a $400,000 bank loan to purchase eight dump trucks. The borrower may be required to pledge the trucks plus the company's office building as collateral to the bank. That is, if the borrower defaults, or fails to repay the loan, the bank can take possession of the borrower's pledged assets and sell them to recover the outstanding debt. However, as lenders learned in the 2008 recession, assets from loans defaulted by businesses (and home buyers) may have little or no value.

The amount of money that is loaned and must be repaid is the **loan principal**. However, borrowers must also pay the lender an additional fee, **interest**, for the use of the borrowed funds. The amount of interest owed depends on an **annual percentage rate (APR)** that is agreed on between the lender and borrower. The interest amount is found by multiplying the APR by the loan principal.

Working Capital and Unsecured Loans from Banks

Firms need more than just fixed assets for daily operations. They also need current, liquid assets available to meet short-term operating expenses such as employee wages, utility costs, and marketing expenses. The firm's ability to meet these expenses is measured by its working capital:

$$\text{Working capital} = \text{Current assets} - \text{Current liabilities}$$

Positive working capital means the firm's current assets are large enough to pay off current liabilities (see Chapter 15). Negative working capital means the firm's current liabilities are greater than current assets, so it may need to borrow money from a commercial bank. With an **unsecured loan**, the borrower does not have to put up collateral. In many cases, however, the bank requires the borrower to maintain a *compensating balance*—the borrower must keep a portion of the loan amount on deposit with the bank in a non-interest-bearing account.

Firms with bad credit scores typically cannot get unsecured loans. Because access to such loans requires a good credit history, many firms establish a relationship with a commercial bank and, over time, build a good credit record by consistently repaying loan principal and interest on time. In extreme conditions, however, even a good credit history may not be enough. During the deepening recession back in 2008, the cash shortages at many banks prevented loans to nearly any kind to business customers, thereby slowing down the economy even more. Even after vast injections of cash from TARP and other government sources, banks lagged far behind in supplying loans to meet the working-capital needs of cash-strapped business borrowers.

Even worse, during extreme conditions businesses in good financial standing may still suffer. One Houston-area home builder, for instance, had a $20 million credit line with a consortium of local banks and an outstanding balance of $16 million. On paper, then, the builder was in good standing and still had open credit of $4 million. However, during the 2008 recession and housing market collapse, the bankers reduced the builder's credit line to $10 million as part of an overall credit reduction and informed the builder that he had 60 days to cover the $6 million that he was now "overdrawn." When he was unable to do so, he was forced to declare bankruptcy and eventually went out of business.

Secured Loan (Asset-Backed Loan) *loan to finance an asset, backed by the borrower pledging the asset as collateral to the lender*

Collateral *asset pledged for the fulfillment of repaying a loan*

Loan Principal *amount of money that is loaned and must be repaid*

Interest *fee paid to a lender for the use of borrowed funds; like a rental fee*

Annual Percentage Rate (APR) *one-year rate that is charged for borrowing, expressed as a percentage of the borrowed principal*

Unsecured Loan *loan for which collateral is not required*

Small business entrepreneurs, especially, often underestimate the value of establishing bank credit as a source of funds. Some banks offer financial analysis, cash flow planning, and suggestions based on experiences with other local firms. Some provide loans to small businesses in bad times and work to keep them going. Obtaining credit, therefore, begins with finding a bank that can—and will—support a small firm's financial needs. Once a line of credit is obtained, the small business can seek more liberal credit policies from other businesses. Sometimes, for instance, suppliers give customers longer credit periods—say, 45 or 60 days rather than 30 days—to make payments. Liberal trade credit terms with their suppliers let firms increase short-term funds and avoid additional borrowing from banks.

Obtaining longer-term loans is more difficult for new businesses than for established companies. With unproven repayment ability, start-up firms can expect to pay higher interest rates than older firms. If a new enterprise displays evidence of sound financial planning, however, the U.S. Small Business Administration (SBA, see Chapter 3) may support a guaranteed loan. The presentation of a business plan demonstrates to any lender that the borrower is a good credit risk. The business plan is a document that tells potential lenders why the money is needed, the amount, how the money will be used to improve the company, and when it will be paid back.

Planning for *cash flow requirements* is especially valuable for meeting the small business's financial needs. It also demonstrates to lenders the borrower's prudent use of financial resources. The firm's success or failure may hinge on anticipating those times when either cash will be short or excess cash can be expected. Consider how the owner would compare the expected cash inflows, cash outflows, and net cash position (inflows minus outflows) month by month for Slippery Fish Bait Supply Co., a highly seasonal business. Bait stores (Slippery's customers) buy heavily from Slippery during the spring and summer months. Revenues outpace expenses, leaving surplus funds that can be invested. During the fall and winter, however, expenses exceed revenues. Slippery must borrow funds to keep going until revenues pick up again in the spring. Comparing predicted cash inflows from sales with outflows for expenses will show the firm's expected monthly cash-flow position. Such information can be invaluable for the small-business manager. By anticipating shortfalls, managers can seek funds in advance and minimize their costs. By anticipating excess cash, a manager can plan to put the funds to work in short-term, interest-earning investments.

Angel Investors and Venture Capital

Once a business has been successfully launched, it most likely needs additional capital for growth. Outside individuals who provide such capital are often called **angel investors**. Angel investors help many firms grow rapidly by providing what is known as **venture capital**, private funds from wealthy individuals or companies (see Chapter 3) that seek investment opportunities in new growth companies. In most cases, the growth firm turns to venture capital sources because it has not yet built enough credit history to get a loan from commercial banks or other lending institutions. Peter Thiel supplied an initial $500,000 angel investment in Facebook's early years.

Angel Investors *outside investors who provide new capital for firms in return for a share of equity ownership*

Venture Capital *private funds from wealthy individuals seeking investment opportunities in new growth companies*

In 2016 experts estimated that $25.35 billion was invested in around 71,000 entrepreneurial ventures. Estimates also suggest that there are around 300,000 such investors in the United States. In return for their investment, angel investors typically expect a sizable piece of ownership in the company (up to 50 percent of its equity). They may also want a formal say in how the company is run. If the firm is bought by a larger company or if it sells its stock in a public offering, the angel may receive additional payments.

Sale of Corporate Bonds

Corporations can also raise capital by issuing bonds. A **corporate bond** is a formal pledge (essentially an IOU) obligating the issuer to pay interest periodically and then repay the principal at maturity (a preset future date) to the lender. The federal

Corporate Bond *formal pledge obligating the issuer (the company) to pay interest periodically and repay the principal at maturity*

government also issues bonds to finance projects and meet obligations, as do state and local governments (called *municipal bonds*) for financing the building of schools, roads, sewage disposal systems, and similar projects.

Characteristics of Corporate Bonds

The bondholder (the lender) has no claim to ownership of the company and does not receive dividends. However, interest payments and repayment of principal are financial obligations. Payments to bondholders have priority over dividend payments to stockholders in cases of financial distress.

Each new bond issue has specific terms and conditions spelled out in a **bond indenture**, a legal document identifying the borrower's obligations and the financial returns to lenders. One of the most important details is the **maturity date** (or due date), when the firm must repay the bond's **face value** (also called **par value**, or the amount purchased) to the lender.

Corporate bonds have been traditionally issued to fund outstanding debts and major projects for various lengths of time. Short-term bonds mature less than five years after they are issued. Bonds with 5- to 10-year lives are considered intermediate term, and anything longer than 10 years is considered long term. Longer-term corporate bonds are somewhat riskier than shorter-term bonds because they are exposed to greater unforeseen economic conditions that may potentially lead to default. In general, of course, large companies that have been in existence for decades, such as Ford or General Electric, are not likely to default. At the same time, though, similar firms like Eastman Kodak and Bethlehem Steel went under and defaulted on outstanding long-term corporate bonds in the process.

Default and Bondholders' Claim

A bond is said to be in **default** if the borrower fails to make payment when due to lenders. Bondholders may then file a **bondholders' claim**, a request for court enforcement of the bond's terms of payment. When a financially distressed company cannot pay bondholders, it may seek relief by filing for **bankruptcy**, the court-granted permission not to pay some or all debts. After a restructured General Motors emerged from bankruptcy in 2009, the holders of the old General Motors Corporation's $24 billion in bonds wondered how much payment, if any, they would recover from the financially strapped company. In the 2011 settlement, investors holding bonds in the old GM received stock shares in the new GM that provided a recovery rate of about 40 cents on the dollar of the original bond investment.[15]

Risk Ratings

To aid investors in making purchase decisions, several services measure the default risk of bonds. Table 17.2, for example, shows the rating systems of two well-known services, Moody's and Standard & Poor's. The highest (safest) grades are Aaa and AAA, and the lowest are C and D, representing speculative and highly risky bonds. Low-grade bonds are usually called *junk bonds*. Negative ratings do not necessarily keep issues from being successful. Rather, they raise the interest rates that issuers must offer to attract lenders.

Flawed Ratings Misread Recession Risks

The financial meltdown of 2008 has raised questions about whether any good purpose is being served by credit-rating agencies. Among many other investors, California Public Employees

Bond Indenture *legal document containing complete details of a bond issue*

Maturity Date (Due Date) *future date when repayment of a bond is due from the bond issuer (borrower)*

Face Value (Par Value) *amount of money that the bond buyer (lender) lent the issuer and that the lender will receive on repayment*

Default *failure of a borrower to make payment when due to a lender*

Bondholders' Claim *request for court enforcement of a bond's terms of payment*

Bankruptcy *court-granted permission for a company to not pay some or all debts*

table 17.2 Bond Rating Systems

Rating System	High Grades	Medium Grades (Investment Grades)	Speculative	Poor Grades
Moody's	Aaa, Aa	A, Baa	Ba, B	Caa to C
Standard & Poor's	AAA, AA	A, BBB	BB, B	CCC to D

Retirement Fund (CalPERS), the nation's largest public pension fund, filed a suit against the three top agencies—Moody's, Standard & Poor's, and Fitch—charging losses caused by "wildly inaccurate and unreasonably high" credit ratings. CalPERS officials relied on ratings for investments that proved to be wrong—many failing altogether. Skepticism of agencies' ratings has also increased following the collapse or near-collapse of highly rated giants such as Lehman Brothers, Goldman Sachs, and Citigroup, along with high ratings on billions of dollars of mortgage-backed securities that eventually became toxic. Various lawsuits, including those by the states of Ohio and Connecticut, accused credit rating agencies of reckless assessments that misled investors.[16]

Mortgage-backed securities (MBS) became a trillion-dollar investment industry during the pre-2007 housing market boom. Financial institutions bundled home mortgages into packages and resold them as securities to investors who trusted in the securities' risk ratings given by Moody's, Standard & Poor's, and Fitch. Each MBS is a group of mortgages bundled together to form a debt obligation (a bond) that entitles the holder (the investor) to the cash that flows in from the mortgages. Unknown to investors, some $3 trillion of MBSs contained subprime mortgages—high-risk loans to applicants with bad credit, low income, and low down payments—most of which had received high ratings (AAA) by credit-rating agencies. Misled by flawed risk assessments, investors were left with little or nothing when the highly rated securities turned toxic, causing the collapse of the housing and financial markets.[17]

Mortgage-Backed Security (MBS) *mortgages pooled together to form a debt obligation—a bond—that entitles the holder (investor) to cash that flows in from the bundled mortgages*

Becoming a Public Corporation

OBJECTIVE 17-6
Identify
the reasons a company might make an initial public offering of its stock, explain how stock value is determined, and discuss the significance of market capitalization.

Initial public offerings (IPOs), the first sale of a company's stock to the general public, are a major source of funds that fuel continued growth for many firms and introduce numerous considerations inherent in running a public company. In one of the biggest IPOs in history, Facebook's public offering of common stock in 2012, with an opening price of $38 per share, raised more than $100 billion. In this section, we discuss many of the issues public companies face, such as potential loss of control, fluctuating share prices, how businesses use market capitalization, and how they choose capital sources.

Initial Public Offering (IPO) *first sale of a company's stock to the general public*

Cosmo Condina stock market/Alamy Stock Photo

When firms go public they sell part of their ownership to other investors through a public offering of stock. Monitors such as this one show current prices and overall stock price indicators such as the Dow, S&P, and Nasdaq. Investors then use this information to decide when to buy or sell stock.

Going Public Means Selling Part Ownership of the Company

Private owners lose some control of the company when shares are sold to the public. Common shareholders usually have voting rights in corporate governance, so they elect the board of directors and vote on major issues put forth at the company's annual shareholders' meeting. Anyone owning a large proportion of the company's shares, therefore, gains a powerful position in determining who runs the corporation and how.

Corporate Raider *investor conducting a type of hostile corporate takeover against the wishes of the company*

At an extreme, a **corporate raider**, an investor conducting a type of hostile (unwanted) takeover, buys shares on the open market, attempting to seize control of the company and its assets. The raider then sells off those assets at a profit, perhaps resulting in the company's disappearance. A company is a prime target for raiding when its stock price falls so shares can be cheaply bought, although its assets still have high value.

managing in turbulent times

Winners and Losers

Today's capital markets are larger, faster, and more complex than ever before in history, which means that regulators are constantly trying to catch up with the innovations, changes, and turmoil. For instance, in January 2005 the average speed of a small trade order on the New York Stock Exchange (NYSE) was 10 seconds. By 2015 it was down to less than half a second. This sounds like a good thing, right? Speed and the accompanying technology allow for more trades, quicker reaction times, and more timely data. However, it can also accelerate problems, as it did with the Flash Crash of 2010. On May 6th, stock prices went into a seemingly inexplicable tailspin, falling 10 percent in a matter of minutes, with some blue-chip shares briefly trading at a penny, only to recover most of the lost ground before the end of the trading day. It took the SEC months to figure out what had happened, and in a 100-page report issued in October of that year, SEC staff pointed to unusually high volatility in the market due to a generally unsettled political and economic climate that led to a single, large automated sell order by a mutual fund. Because this automated trade was reacting to trading volume, not price, it executed itself in 20 minutes. Usually, a transaction like that would be spread out over several hours. This is where the High Frequency Traders (HFTs) enter the picture. The computerized version of day traders, the HFTs buy and sell stocks in seconds rather than hours, based on complex algorithms that take into account massive amounts of market data. Sometimes the trades are so fast they seem to happen simultaneously. At one point, experts estimated that up to 70 percent of all stock market trades were attributable to HFT. In the case of the Flash Crash, however, the HFTs at first absorbed the giant sell order by the mutual fund, but soon thereafter began to sell again,

E.J. Baumeister Jr./Alamy Stock Photo

prompting the mutual fund selling program to react, again based on volume, not price. The HFTs and the mutual fund created a feedback loop that momentarily crashed the market. One trillion dollars evaporated in less than 20 minutes, and then the market made a partial recovery. Computer glitches can be less outlandish but still damaging. In 2010 Knight Capital suffered a $460 million trading loss in just under 45 minutes due to a program error.

For business, these issues, along with globalization of markets, increased regulatory oversight, and political unrest, make investing and garnering capital from investors a task not to be taken lightly. A good businessperson, in addition to understanding marketing, accounting, management, and all the other aspects of running a business, must also study the market, be a student of both politics and the economy, and be an alert and active money manager in these fast-moving and technologically sophisticated times.

Stock Valuation

What determines a stock's value after it is offered to the general public? Investors' assessments of the company's management record in past ventures, expectations for competing in the industry, and belief in the public's acceptance of the company's products are among many factors that affect a stock's value, which in turn affect the value of the business. In addition, different investors measure value differently, and their measurements may change according to circumstances. Because of the uncertainties involved in stock prices, investment professionals believe day-to-day prices to be a generally poor indicator of any stock's real value. Instead, a long-run perspective considers the company's overall financial health, past history of results and future forecasts, record for managerial performance, and overall prospects for competing successfully in the coming years. Accordingly, any stock's value today looks beyond the current price and is based on expectations of the financial returns it will provide to shareholders during the long run.

Why Shares Are Different Prices On one specific day in early 2017, the price of Google Inc. was about $562 per share on the NYSE, GE shares traded at about $25.96, Delta Airlines shares were priced at about $48.55, and Berkshire Hathaway shares traded for $216,415.90.

Why such differences? One reason is supply and demand for each company's shares; another is because some corporations want the shares to sell within a particular price range, say between $20 and $80, believing it will attract a larger pool of investors. If the price gets too high, many investors can't afford to buy shares. A company can restore shares to the desired lower range by a **stock split**, a stock dividend paid in additional shares to shareholders. Here's how it works. Suppose company X has 100,000 common shares outstanding that are trading at $100 per share, but the company wants it priced in the $20 to $80 range. X can declare a 2-for-1 stock split, meaning the company gives shareholders one additional share for each share they own. Now X has 200,000 shares outstanding but its financial performance has not changed, so the stock price immediately falls to $50 per share. Every shareholder's investment value, however, is unchanged: they previously owned one share at $100, and now they own two shares at $50 each.

Stock Split *stock dividend paid in additional shares to shareholders, thus increasing the number of outstanding shares*

Comparing Prices of Different Stocks Consider a trading day when PepsiCo's share price was $114.00 and Coca-Cola was $43.90 per share. Does the price difference mean that PepsiCo is a better company than Coca-Cola because its shares are more expensive? Or does it mean that Coke shares are a better value because they can be bought at a lower price than PepsiCo's? In fact, neither of these two reasons is correct. Share prices alone do not provide enough information to determine which is the better investment. Table 17.3 can help us make a better comparison with further information.

First, earnings per share (EPS) are greater for PepsiCo ($4.63 versus $1.42 per share). But since you pay more you also have reason to expect more return. In reality, at the time these data were collected, the return for PepsiCo is actually only slightly higher than for Coke ($4.63 earnings/$114.00 investment = $0.04 Pepsi, versus $1.42 earnings/$43.90 investment = $0.03 Coke): Both companies generated about the same earnings power for each dollar of shareholder investment.

table 17.3 Financial Comparison: Coca-Cola and PepsiCo

	Coca-Cola	PepsiCo
Recent price	$43.90	$114.00
EPS	$1.42	$4.63
Dividend yield	3.37%	2.82%

Now consider annual dividends paid to shareholders. The dividend yield from Coca-Cola was 3.37 percent. That is, the dividend payment amounted to a 3.37 percent return on the shareholder's $43.90 investment, or $1.48 = ($43.90 × 3.37%). PepsiCo's dividend yield was 2.82 percent, so the dividend payment was about $3.21 ($114 × 2.82%). From these limited data it would appear that Coca-Cola might be a slightly better investment than PepsiCo. However, over the last 10 years each firm outperformed the other exactly five times each but never by a very wide margin! Therefore, it is really not clear which of the two companies is the better investment. A more complete evaluation would compare historical performance consistency over a longer period of time, along with a detailed analysis of each firm's prospects for the future.

Market Capitalization

Market Capitalization (Market Cap) *total dollar value of all the company's outstanding shares*

A widely used measure of corporate size and value is known as **market capitalization (market cap)**, the total dollar value of all the company's outstanding shares, calculated as the current stock price multiplied by the number of shares outstanding. As indicated in Table 17.4, the investment industry categorizes firms according to size of capitalization. Investors typically regard larger market caps as less risky, and firms with small market caps (small-cap firms) as being particularly risky investments. Apple has a market cap of approximately $800 billion, making it the largest U.S. company.

Choosing Equity versus Debt Capital

Firms can meet their capital needs through two sources: (1) *debt financing* (from outside the firm) or (2) *equity financing* (putting the owners' capital to work).

Pros and Cons of Debt Financing Long-term borrowing from sources outside the company, **debt financing**, via loans or the sale of corporate bonds is a major component in most U.S. firms' financial planning.

Debt Financing *long-term borrowing from sources outside a company*

LONG-TERM LOANS Long-term loans are attractive for several reasons:

- Because the number of parties involved is limited, loans can often be arranged quickly.

- The firm need not make public disclosure of its business plans or the purpose for which it is acquiring the loan. (In contrast, the issuance of corporate bonds requires such disclosure.)

Long-term loans also have some disadvantages. Borrowers, for example, may have trouble finding lenders to supply large sums. Long-term borrowers may also face restrictions as conditions of the loan. For example, they may have to pledge long-term assets as collateral or agree to take on no more debt until the loan is paid.

CORPORATE BONDS Bonds are attractive when firms need large amounts for long periods of time. The issuing company gains access to large numbers of lenders through nationwide bond markets. On the other hand, bonds entail high administrative and

table 17.4 Corporation Sizes Based on Capitalization

Capitalization Category	Range of Capitalization
Micro-Cap	Below $250 million
Small-Cap	$250 million–$2 billion
Mid-Cap	$2 billion–$10 billion
Large-Cap	Over $10 billion

Tripplaar Kristoffer/SIPA/Newscom

A firm's market capitalization (or market cap) is the number of outstanding shares of stock multiplied by the current price of that stock. General Electric is consistently one of the world's most valuable businesses (that it, it has one of the largest market caps). In 2015 GE's market cap ranged from a high of $274.09 billion to a low of $250.39 billion, with the changes due to fluctuations in its stock price.

selling costs. They may also require stiff interest payments, especially if the issuing company has a poor credit rating. Bonds also impose binding obligations on the firm, in many cases for up to 30 years, to pay bondholders a stipulated sum of annual or semiannual interest, even in times of financial distress. If the company fails to make a bond payment, it goes into default. A classic example is WorldCom (now MCI), which filed for bankruptcy in 2002 when it was the nation's number-two long-distance phone company. With $102 billion in assets, WorldCom's bankruptcy at the time was the largest in U.S. history. Even with those massive assets, however, the firm was crushed by its $41 billion debt, $24 billion of which was in bonds. Facing prospects that the firm would default on upcoming interest payments, many of its creditors began withholding additional money unless loans were secured with WorldCom assets. With more than 1,000 creditors—including Citibank, JPMorgan Chase, and Credit Suisse First Boston—the firm was allowed to operate while in bankruptcy. In 2003, WorldCom changed its name to MCI, before emerging from bankruptcy status in 2004.

Pros and Cons for Equity Financing Although debt financing often has strong appeal, **equity financing**, looking inside the company for long-term funding, is sometimes preferable. Equity financing includes either issuing common stock or retaining the firm's earnings.

Equity Financing *using the owners' funds from inside the company as the source for long-term funding*

THE EXPENSE OF COMMON STOCK The use of equity financing by means of common stock can be expensive because paying dividends is more expensive than paying bond interest. Interest paid to bondholders is a business expense and therefore a tax deduction for the firm. Payments of cash dividends to shareholders are not tax deductible.

RETAINED EARNINGS AS A SOURCE OF CAPITAL As discussed in Chapter 15, *retained earnings* are net profits retained for the firm's use rather than paid out in dividends to stockholders. If a company uses retained earnings as capital, it will not have to borrow money and pay interest. If a firm has a history of reaping profits by reinvesting retained earnings, it may be attractive to some investors. Retaining earnings, however, means smaller dividends for shareholders. This practice may decrease the demand for—and the price of—the company's stock.

We have seen, then, that becoming a public corporation means selling part of the ownership of the business through an initial public offering of stock. Several factors determine the stock's value after that stock is available to the general public. The day-to-day price is a weak indicator of the stock's value, whereas prospects for the firm's future financial health, the performance record of its management, and prospects for competing in the future are considerations that determine the stock's value. Market capitalization, the current stock price multiplied by the number of shares outstanding, is a widely used measure of company size and overall value. A public corporation's continued growth is accompanied by the need for more capital that can be met through two sources: debt financing or equity financing. Borrowing via long-term loans and the issuance of corporate bonds can provide a large supply of funds but also imposes binding obligations on the firm. Likewise, funds can be raised by issuing additional common stock or by increasing retained earnings, but doing so means smaller dividends for shareholders.

OBJECTIVE 17-7
Explain
how securities markets are
regulated.

Regulating Securities Markets

The U.S. government, along with various state agencies, plays a key role in monitoring and regulating the securities industry. Businesses cannot exist in the United States without the public's trust and the public's willingness to participate in business ownership and everyday transactions with companies. Regulation of the U.S. securities markets plays a vital role in maintaining the public's trust in fair and open business ownership.

The Securities and Exchange Commission

The U.S. SEC is the regulation and enforcement agency that oversees the markets' activities, including the ways securities are issued. The SEC was created in 1934 to prevent the kinds of abuses that led to the stock market crash of 1929. The SEC regulates the public offering of new securities by requiring that all companies file a prospectus before proposed offerings commence. To protect investors from fraudulent issues, a **prospectus** contains pertinent information about both the offered security and the issuing company. False statements are subject to criminal penalties.

Prospectus *registration statement filed with the SEC containing information for prospective investors about a security to be offered and the issuing company*

The SEC also enforces laws against **insider trading,** the use of special knowledge about a firm for profit or gain. Suppose, for example, that you work for a pharmaceutical company that is working to develop a major new drug that, if approved for use, will lead to the stock in your company doubling or even tripling in value. You have just seen test results that prove the value of the drug and know that it will now be approved for general use in the next six months. You could tell your friends and family members to buy your company's stock so they can make large sums of money. Doing so, however, would be against the law. In general, it is illegal for an employee of a firm to tell others about an anticipated event that may affect the value of that firm's stock, such as an impending acquisition or a merger, before news of that event is made public. Those in possession of such insider knowledge would have an unfair advantage over other investors.

Insider Trading *illegal practice of using special knowledge about a firm for profit or gain*

Regulations Against Insider Trading

In March 2011, the U.S. Attorney began a criminal trial in New York against Raj Rajaratnam, founder of Galleon Group, on charges that the billionaire fund manager profited from illegal stock tips with a network of financial insiders. Reports indicate the accused gained profits of up to $60 million by using illicit information, confidential company information not available to the public, revealing that stock prices of various companies would be increasing or falling. In conjunction with his arrest

ZUMA Press, Inc./Alamy Stock Photo

Fifty-four-year-old Raj Rajaratnam was sentenced to 11 years in federal prison after being convicted for insider trading.

in 2009, charges were leveled against 26 others in the case—executives and securities traders—19 of whom pleaded guilty. In May 2011, Rajaratnam was convicted on 14 charges and faced possible maximum prison sentences totaling up to 205 years. He was finally sentenced to serve 11 years in prison, the longest ever for an insider-trading violation. In addition to the criminal trial, he faces civil charges brought by the SEC. As a U.S. Attorney stated some years previously, "Insider trading is a crime. Corporate executives are prohibited from enriching themselves while the public remains in the dark about the true financial condition of their companies."[18]

The SEC offers a reward to any person who provides information leading to a civil penalty for illegal insider trading. The courts can render a penalty of up to three times the illegal profit that was gained, and the reward can, at most, be 10 percent of that penalty.

Along with the SEC's enforcement efforts, the stock exchanges and securities firms have adopted self-regulation by participating with the Financial Industry Regulatory Authority (FINRA) in detecting and stopping insider action and violations of other industry regulations. Established in 2003, FINRA's mission is to protect U.S. investors by overseeing the nation's brokerage firms and securities representatives. The major U.S. stock markets are under a contract that allows FINRA to regulate those markets by writing rules, examining securities firms, enforcing the rules, and enforcing federal securities laws as well.

summary of learning objectives

OBJECTIVE 17-1

Explain the concept of the time value of money and the principle of compound growth, and discuss the characteristics of common stock. (pp. 548–551)

The time value of money, perhaps the single most important concept in business finance, recognizes the basic fact that, when it's invested over time, money grows by earning interest or yielding some other form of return. Time value stems from the principle of *compound growth*—the cumulative growth from interest paid to the investor over given time periods. With each additional time period, the investment grows as interest payments accumulate and earn more interest, thus multiplying the earning capacity of the investment.

The "Rule of 72" is a practical example that illustrates the concept of the time value of money. The rule shows the number of years required for an initial investment to double in value, depending on the interest rate received in return for the investment. The rule demonstrates that higher rates of return (interest) result in fewer years required to double the original investment.

A share of *common stock* is the most basic form of ownership in a company. Individuals and organizations purchase a firm's common stock in the hope that it will increase in value and provide dividend income. Each common share has a vote on major issues that are brought before the shareholders. A stock's real value is its *market value*—the current price of a share in the stock market—reflecting the amount buyers are willing to pay for a share of the company's stock. Common stocks are among the riskiest of all investments because uncertainties about the stock market can quickly change the stock's value. *Blue-chip stocks* are issued by the strongest and most well established, financially sound, and respected firms. They have historically provided investors steady income through consistent dividend payouts.

OBJECTIVE 17-2

Identify reasons for investing and the investment opportunities offered by mutual funds and exchange-traded funds. (pp. 551–553)

Mutual funds are attractive investments because different funds are designed to appeal to different financial motives and goals of investors. Three of the most common alternative objectives for investing in mutual funds are stability and safety, conservative capital growth, and aggressive growth. Funds stressing stability and safety seek only modest growth while preserving the fund holders' capital and reliably paying modest current income. Conservative capital growth funds stress preservation of capital and current income but also seek some capital appreciation. Aggressive growth funds seek maximum long-term capital growth.

Unfortunately, many mutual funds do not perform as well as the average return of the overall stock market as a result of costly management expense and underperforming stocks. Index mutual funds, however, closely match the performance of a particular market. An exchange-traded fund (ETF), as with an index mutual fund, is a bundle of stocks (or bonds) that are an index that tracks the overall movement of a market. However, ETFs offer three areas of advantage over mutual funds: They can be traded throughout the day like a stock (whereas a mutual fund cannot be traded like a stock), they have low operating expenses, and they require low initial investments resulting in ease of entry for investors getting started without much money. Because they are traded on stock exchanges (hence, "exchange traded"), ETFs can be bought and sold—priced continuously—any time throughout the day. Mutual fund shares, in contrast, are priced once daily, at the end of the day.

OBJECTIVE 17-3

Describe the role of securities markets and identify the major stock exchanges and stock markets. (pp. 553–560)

The markets in which stocks and bonds are sold are called *securities markets*. By facilitating the buying and selling of securities, the securities markets provide the capital that companies rely on for survival. In *primary securities markets*, new stocks and bonds are bought and sold by firms and governments. Sometimes, new securities are sold to single buyers or small groups of buyers. These private placements are desirable because they allow issuers to keep their business plans confidential. Firms issuing new securities must get approval from the SEC. Issuing firms also usually rely on investment banking services to issue and resell new securities. Investment banks provide several important services. (1) They advise companies on the timing and financial terms of the new issue. (2) The investment bank buys and assumes liability for the new securities, a process referred to as *underwriting*. (3) Investment banks create distribution networks for moving new securities through groups of other financial institutions into the hands of individual investors. In contrast with new securities issues, *existing* stocks and bonds are sold in the much larger *secondary securities market*, consisting largely of *stock exchanges*. A stock exchange is an organization of individuals coordinated to provide an institutional auction setting in which stocks can be bought and sold. Major stock exchanges include the New York Stock Exchange, the NASDAQ market in the United States, and NYSE Euronext, along with various other foreign exchanges such as the London Stock Exchange and the Tokyo Exchange, and online trading with other stock exchanges around the globe.

In 1998, the SEC authorized the creation of *electronic communication networks (ECNs)*, electronic trading systems that bring buyers and sellers together outside traditional stock exchanges by automatically matching buy and sell orders at specified prices. ECNs gained rapid popularity because the trading procedures are fast and efficient, often lowering transaction costs per share to mere pennies. They also allow after-hours trading (after traditional markets have closed for the day) and protect traders' anonymity.

Stock brokers are financial services professionals who earn commissions by executing buy and sell orders for outside customers. As with many other products, brokerage assistance can be purchased at either discount or at full-service prices. Discount brokers, such as E*TRADE and Scottrade, offer well-informed individual investors who know what they want to buy or sell a fast, low-cost way to participate in the market. Full-service brokers, such as Merrill Lynch Wealth Management, offer clients consulting advice in personal financial planning, estate planning, and tax strategies, along with a wider range of investment products.

Although not indicative of the status of individual securities, *market indexes*, such as the Dow Jones Industrial Average and S&P 500, provide useful summaries of overall price trends, both in specific industries and in the stock market as a whole. Market indexes, for example, reveal *bull* and *bear market* trends. *Bull markets* are periods of rising stock prices, generally lasting 12 months or longer; investors are motivated to buy, confident they will realize capital gains. Periods of falling stock prices, usually 20 percent off peak prices, are called *bear markets*; investors are motivated to sell, anticipating further falling prices.

OBJECTIVE 17-4

Describe the risk–return relationship and discuss the use of diversification and asset allocation for investments. (pp. 560–563)

Individual investors have different motivations and personal preferences for safety versus risk. While all investors anticipate receiving future cash flows, some cash flows are more certain than other riskier returns. Investors generally expect to receive higher financial returns for investments having higher uncertainty. They do not expect large returns from secure, stable investments. Each type of investment, then, has a risk–return (risk–reward) relationship. The risk–return relationship is the principle that investors expect to receive higher returns for riskier investments and lower returns for safer investments. Conservative investors who have a low tolerance for risk will seek safer investments with low expected returns. The reverse is true for aggressive investors who prefer taking higher risks with the potential for higher returns.

When evaluating potential investments, investors look at returns from dividends or interest, returns from price appreciation, and total return. The rate of return from dividends paid to shareholders is commonly referred to as the *current dividend* yield. In the case of interest from a loan, the term *interest yield* is used. *Price appreciation* is an increase in the value of an investment over time. *Total* return is the sum of the investment's dividend or interest yields and the *capital gain* from price appreciation.

Diversification and asset allocation are tools for helping investors achieve the desired risk–return balance for an investment portfolio. *Diversification* means buying several different kinds of investments—stocks of different companies, securities of companies in different industries, investments in different countries, combinations of stocks/bonds/real estate/precious metals—to reduce the risk of loss if the value of any one investment should fall. *Asset allocation* is the proportion of overall money invested in each of various investment alternatives so that the overall risks for the portfolio are low, moderate, or high, depending on the investor's objectives and preferences.

OBJECTIVE 17-5

Describe the various ways that firms raise capital and identify the pros and cons of each method. (pp. 563–567)

Every company needs cash to function. Firms often begin with the owner's personal savings. As more money is needed, it is obtained from sales revenues, borrowing from banks, cash from private investors, issuing bonds, or selling stock. Money to purchase new equipment often comes in the form of loans from commercial banks. In a *secured loan (asset-backed loan)* the borrower guarantees repayment of the loan by pledging the asset as *collateral* to the lender. The amount of money that is loaned and must be repaid is the *loan principal*. However, borrowers also pay the lender an additional fee, *interest*, for the use of the borrowed funds. The amount of interest owed depends on an *annual percentage rate (APR)* that is agreed on between the lender and borrower. The interest amount is found by multiplying the APR by the loan principal. With an *unsecured loan*, the borrower does not have to put up collateral. In many cases, however, the bank requires the borrower to maintain a *compensating balance*; the borrower must keep a portion of the loan amount on deposit with the bank in a non-interest-bearing account.

Once a business has been successfully launched, it needs additional capital for growth. Outside individuals who provide such capital are called *angel investors*. Angel investors help many firms grow rapidly by providing what is known as *venture capital*, private funds from wealthy individuals or companies that seek investment opportunities in new growth companies. In most cases, the growth firm turns to venture capital sources because they have not yet built enough credit history to get a loan from commercial banks or other lending institutions.

Corporations can raise capital by issuing bonds. A *corporate bond* is a formal pledge (an IOU) obligating the issuer to pay interest periodically and repay the principal at maturity (a preset future date) to the lender. The federal government also issues bonds to finance projects and meet obligations, as do state and local governments (called *municipal bonds*) for financing the building of schools, roads, and sewage disposal systems.

OBJECTIVE 17-6

Identify the reasons a company might make an initial public offering of its stock, explain how stock value is determined, and discuss the significance of market capitalization. (pp. 567–572)

The initial public offering (IPO)—the first sale of a company's stock to the general public—is a major source of funds for fueling the growth of many firms. IPOs reach far more potential investors, thereby providing access to a larger pool of funds than is available from the owner's personal funds and other private sources. A stock's real value is its market value—the current price of a share in the stock market. Market value reflects the amount that buyers are willing to pay for a share of the company's stock at any given time. However, the valuing of any stock today looks beyond the current price and is based on expectations of the financial returns it will provide to shareholders during the long run. A long-run perspective considers the company's financial health, past history of results and future forecasts, its record for managerial performance, and overall prospects for competing successfully in the coming years. Although supply and demand are a major determiner of a stock's price, another factor is a company's desire that its shares sell within a particular price range, believing it will attract a larger pool of investors. If the stock's market price gets too high, many investors cannot afford to buy shares. A company can restore shares to the desired lower price range by using a stock split in which the company gives shareholders an additional stock holding for each share they own.

The market price per share falls immediately after the split, but with a larger number of shares, every shareholder's investment value is unchanged.

Market capitalization, the total market value of all the company's outstanding shares, is a widely used measure of corporate size and value. Investors leaning toward risk avoidance typically regard larger market-cap firms as less risky, and firms with small market-caps (small-cap firms) as being particularly risky investments. Thus, the persistent demand for large-cap stocks tends to sustain or increase their market values.

Although debt financing often has strong appeal, *equity financing*, looking inside the company for long-term funding, is sometimes preferable. Equity financing includes either issuing common stock or retaining the firm's earnings. The use of equity financing by means of common stock can be expensive because paying dividends is more expensive than paying bond interest. Interest paid to bondholders is a business expense and therefore a tax deduction for the firm. Payments of cash dividends to shareholders are not tax deductible. *Retained earnings* are net profits retained for the firm's use rather than paid out in dividends to stockholders. If a company uses retained earnings as capital, it will not have to borrow money and pay interest. If a firm has a history of reaping profits by reinvesting retained earnings, it may be attractive to some investors. Retained earnings, however, mean smaller dividends for shareholders. This practice may decrease the demand for—and the price of—the company's stock.

OBJECTIVE 17-7

Explain how securities markets are regulated. (pp. 572–573)

The U.S. government, along with various state agencies, plays a key role in monitoring and regulating the securities industry. The U.S. Securities and Exchange Commission (SEC) is the regulation and enforcement agency that oversees the markets' activities. The SEC regulates the public offering of new securities by requiring companies to file *prospectuses* before proposed offerings commence. To protect investors from fraudulent securities issues, the prospectus contains information about the offered security and the issuing company. False statements are subject to criminal penalties.

The SEC also enforces laws against *insider trading*—the use of special knowledge about a firm for profit or gain. An example of illegal insider trading includes an employee of a firm telling others about an anticipated event that may affect the value of that firm's stock, such as an acquisition or a merger, before news of that event is made public. Those in possession of such insider knowledge would have an unfair advantage over other investors. The SEC offers a reward to any person who provides information leading to a civil penalty for illegal insider trading.

Along with the SEC's enforcement, the stock exchanges and securities firms have adopted self-regulation by participating with the Financial Industry Regulatory Authority (FINRA) in detecting and stopping violations of industry regulations. FINRA's mission is to protect U.S. investors by overseeing the nation's brokerage firms and securities representatives. FINRA regulates the U.S. stock markets by writing rules, examining securities firms, enforcing the rules, and enforcing federal securities laws.

key terms

angel investors (p. 565)
annual percentage rate (APR) (p. 564)
asset allocation (p. 563)
bankruptcy (p. 566)
bear market (p. 557)
blue-chip stock (p. 551)
bond indenture (p. 566)
bondholders' claim (p. 566)
book value (p. 550)
book-entry ownership (p. 557)

bull market (p. 557)
capital gain (p. 562)
collateral (p. 564)
common stock (p. 550)
compound growth (p. 549)
corporate bond (p. 565)
corporate raider (p. 568)
current dividend yield and current interest yield (p. 561)
debt financing (p. 570)
default (p. 566)

diversification (p. 562)
dividend (p. 550)
Dow Jones Industrial Average (DJIA) (p. 557)
electronic communication network (ECN) (p. 556)
equity financing (p. 571)
exchange-traded fund (ETF) (p. 552)
face value (par value) (p. 566)
initial public offering (IPO) (p. 567)
insider trading (p. 572)

MyLab Intro to Business

To complete the problems with the ⭐, go to EOC Discussions Questions in the MyLab.

questions & exercises

QUESTIONS FOR REVIEW

17-1. Explain the concept of the *time value of money*.

⭐ **17-2.** Would you rather buy individual stocks or invest in mutual funds? What is the difference, and why would you favor one over the other?

17-3. What is a corporate bond? Why would a company use bonds as a source of financing?

17-4. How does the market value of a stock differ from the book value of a stock?

17-5. How do firms meet their needs through debt financing and equity financing?

QUESTIONS FOR ANALYSIS

17-6. Research several stocks online. You will notice that they continually fluctuate in price. What might be the reason for this? Is a higher-priced stock a better investment than a lower-priced stock? What factors would you consider in purchasing stocks?

⭐ **17-7.** Suppose that you are a business owner and you need new equipment and immediate funds to meet short-term operating expenses. From what sources could you gain the capital you need, and what are some of the characteristics of these sources? Are you limited by your form of doing business, and if so, how?

⭐ **17-8.** Suppose that you are a business owner and you are seeking funds for expansion. From what sources could you gain the capital you need, and what are some of the characteristics of these sources? Are you limited by your form of doing business, and if so, how? How do these kinds of funding sources differ from funding sources for new equipment and short-term operating expenses?

APPLICATION EXERCISES

17-9. Go to http://www.sec.gov and research how a new security is approved by the Securities and Exchange Commission. What is the process involved and how long would it take? Next, contact a financial institution such as Merrill Lynch and request information about its procedures for issuing or reselling new securities. Share this information with your classmates.

17-10. There have been a number of high profile cases in recent years concerning insider trading. Use an online search to find a case involving insider trading. What is insider trading? Who was accused of insider trading and what was his or her relationship to the company? Was he or she convicted of insider trading, and, if so, what was the penalty? Finally, how could the person accused of insider trading have avoided the charges?

building a business: continuing team exercise

Assignment

Meet with your team members to consider your new business venture and how it relates to the finance topics in this chapter. Develop specific responses to the following:

17-11. What role will debt financing play in your business's financial plan? What types of debt financing will you use? Why?

17-12. As your business grows, will you consider bringing in angel investors or venture capital? Why or why not? How would you structure such a transaction?

17-13. Would you consider selling stock to the general public? What advantages would a public sale of stock bring? Are there any downsides to this decision?

17-14. If you decide to sell stock through an initial public offering, what factors will be most important in the valuation of your stock?

17-15. How will the financing of your business change over time?

team exercise

MARKET UPS AND DOWNS

Background Information

Investing in stocks requires an understanding of the various factors that affect stock prices. These factors may be intrinsic to the company itself or part of the external environment.

- Internal factors relate to the company itself, such as an announcement of poor or favorable earnings, earnings that are more or less than expected, major layoffs, labor problems, new products, management issues, and mergers.
- External factors relate to world or national events, such as wars, recessions, weather conditions that affect sales, the Fed's adjustment of interest rates, and employment figures that are higher or lower than expected.

By analyzing these factors, you will often learn a lot about why a stock did well or why it did poorly. Being aware of these influences will help you anticipate future stock movements.

QUESTIONS FOR ANALYSIS

17-16. Choose a company with publicly traded stock that has experienced considerable price fluctuations in the past few years. You may wish to consider companies such as IBM, JPMorgan Chase, AT&T, Amazon.com, United Healthcare, and Apple. Information about stock prices can be found on many websites, including finance.yahoo.com. For example, on the Yahoo! site, you can search for data on a company and then click on Historical Prices to download prices for the past three years.

17-17. Create a graph of the company's stock price over the past three years using Microsoft Excel or other graphing software. Identify dates associated with sharp peaks or valleys in the stock price.

17-18. Use a search engine or your library's online databases to search for articles that might discuss internal or external factors that explain the change in stock price. Write a brief summary explaining why the stock increased or decreased in price during the periods that you have identified.

17-19. Based on your research, what internal and external factors will have the most significant impact on the price of the company's stock in the future?

exercising your ethics

ARE YOU ENDOWED WITH GOOD JUDGMENT?

The Situation

Youth Dreams Charities (YDC) is a not-for-profit, 501(c)(3) organization that assists low-income families in gaining access to educational opportunities. Governance and policy making reside with a board of directors—10 part-time, community-minded volunteers who are entrusted with carrying out YDC's mission—but daily operating decisions are entrusted to a full-time professional manager (the Executive Officer.)

Tuition comes from annual fund-raising activities (a white-tie dance and a seafood carnival) and from financial returns from YDC's $2.1 million endowment, amassed from charitable donations during the past 12 years. For the current year, 23 students received tuition totaling $92,000 paid by YDC. The board's goal is to increase the endowment to $4 million in five years, hoping to increase the amount of scholarships that the organization can provide.

The Dilemma

Based on the finance committee's suggestions, the board is considering a change in YDC's investment policies. The current conservative approach invests the endowment in bonds and public utility stocks, which have consistently yielded a 5 percent annual return. This practice has allowed the endowment to grow modestly (less than 1 percent per year), with the remaining investment proceeds (4 percent) flowing out for tuition. The proposed plan is to move the organization's investment into stocks or mutual funds with a higher rate of return. If the organization is able to generate at least 17.5 percent on its investment over the next 5 years, as well as maintain the current level of financial assistance, the endowment will reach its $4 million goal. Due to a vacancy on the board, there is an even number of board members and they are evenly split, philosophically, between the risk averse and the proponents of faster growth. You have been asked to advise the Executive Director and the board on this issue at their next meeting.

Continued from page 548

QUESTIONS TO ADDRESS

17-20. Why might a conservative versus risky choice be different at a not-for-profit organization than at a for-profit organization?

17-21. What are the ethical issues in this situation?

17-22. What options/alternatives/actions would you recommend to the board?

cases

FIRE ON THE GROUND

At the beginning of this chapter, you read about Fogo de Chão and how the restaurant chain has grown from a single location in Brazil to an international operation. Using the information presented in this chapter, you should be able to answer the following questions:

17-23. When the Coser and Ongaratto brothers started Fogo de Chão, what were their primary sources of financing?

17-24. After the Coser brothers acquired the Ongaratto brothers' shares of the company, they brought in GP Investments, a Brazilian venture capital firm. What are the advantages and disadvantages of using venture capital to build a business venture?

17-25. After the sale of Fogo de Chão to Thomas H. Lee Partners, the board and management team decided to issue an IPO of common stock. What were the goals of the IPO?

17-26. What are the benefits of an IPO as a source of financing? What other options did the company have?

17-27. Would you consider investing in Fogo de Chão? Why, or why not?

17-28. If an investor had bought stock during the IPO, what would that investment be worth today?

TIME TO GOGO?

If you've flown lately, you may be familiar with the in-flight Internet service Gogo. The company's roots go back to 1991, when the company, then called Aircell, developed technology for in-flight phone services. In 2006, the company made a major change in strategy when it secured a 10-year license through the Federal Communications Commission for in-flight Internet services. Industry leaders, including Virgin America, Delta, United, and Frontier, have been offering Gogo in-flight services since 2008. Southwest is the only major airline in the United States not aligned with Gogo, having signed an agreement with a competitor, Row 44.[19]

Gogo realized that international expansion is critical to its long-term plan. Though it can achieve greater saturation of the domestic market by having its equipment installed on more planes, international expansion is the key to turning a profit. The company has begun this effort, signing an agreement with Delta to install its equipment on all 170 planes in Delta's international fleet.

To raise the money needed for a major expansion, Gogo raised $187 million in a June 2013 IPO, underwritten by Wall Street heavy hitters such as Morgan Stanley, JPMorgan, and UBS, hitting the market at $17 per share.[20] The price of the stock fell quickly over the following months, bottoming out at just over $10, but then recovered and hit a high of almost $33 in December. Since then, the stock has steadily declined, but it seems to have hit a floor of about $10.

The enormous technology and operating costs associated with expanding its network have resulted in losses each year and a weak December 31, 2016, balance sheet, with liabilities in excess of assets, $800 million in long-term debt, and a negative equity balance, despite almost $880 million in capital invested. Most of the company's common and preferred stock is still held by company executives and a number of mutual funds and venture capital firms.[21]

The company has made a major investment in improving the speed of its service with the Gogo 2Ku systems installed in 2016. As Gogo moves to penetrate the international market and increase access and speed, investors in Gogo stock could see a huge return on investment. However, there's certainly considerable uncertainty about the future and only time will tell if this risky investment will pay off.[22]

QUESTIONS FOR DISCUSSION

17-29. Given the risk, what would motivate an investor to purchase stock in Gogo?

17-30. Why would Gogo sell stock rather than taking on additional debt financing? Do you think that this was a good decision?

17-31. What role did underwriters, such as Morgan Stanley, JPMorgan, and UBS, play in the IPO?

17-32. Use a Web source, such as Yahoo! Finance or www.nasdaq.com, obtain the current price of Gogo stock. What has happened to the price of the stock over the last six months? What about the last two years?

17-33. Using the data provided from the web source in the previous step, is Gogo a small or large cap stock? How would this affect the risk associated with this investment?

crafting a business plan

PART 6: FINANCIAL ISSUES

Goal of the Exercise

In this final part of the business plan project, you'll consider how you'll finance your business as well as create an executive summary for your plan.

Exercise Background: Part 6 of the Business Plan

In the previous part of the business plan, you discussed the costs of doing business, as well as how much revenue you expect to earn in one year. It's now time to think about how to finance the business. To get a "great idea" off the ground requires money. But how will you get these funds?

You'll then conclude this project by creating an *executive summary*. The purpose of the executive summary is to give the reader a quick snapshot of your proposed business. Although this exercise comes at the end of the project, once you're done writing it, you'll end up placing the executive summary at the *beginning* of your completed business plan.

Your Assignment

STEP 1

Open the saved *Business Plan* file you began working on in Parts 1 to 5.

STEP 2

For the purposes of this assignment, you will answer the following questions, shown in "Part 6: Financial Issues":

17-34. How much money will you need to get your business started?

Hint: Refer back to Part 5 of the plan, where you analyzed the costs involved in running your business. Approximately how much will you need to get your business started?

17-35. How will you finance your business? For example, will you seek out a bank loan? Borrow from friends? Sell stocks or bonds initially or as your business grows?

Hint: Refer to Chapter 17 for information on securities, such as stocks and bonds. Refer also to Appendix I: Financial Risk and Risk Management and Chapter 3 for more information on sources of short-term and long-term funds.

17-36. Now, create an executive summary for your business plan. The executive summary should be brief—no more than two pages long—and should cover the following points:

- The name of your business
- Where your business will be located
- The mission of your business
- The product or service you are selling
- Who your ideal customers are
- How your product or business will stand out from the crowd
- Who the owners of the business are and what experience they have
- An overview of the future prospects for your business and industry

Hint: At this point, you've already answered all of these questions, so what you need to do here is put the ideas together into a "snapshot" format. The executive summary is really a sales pitch—it's the investor's first impression of your idea. Therefore, as with all parts of the plan, write in a clear and professional way.

Congratulations on completing the business plan project!

Writing Assignments

17-37. Suppose you are managing the securities investments for the firm where you work. Several employees have heard hallway conversations about something called a "risk–return relationship" that sounds important, but they are unsure what it means. (a) Write an essay that explains the risk–return relationship and its importance. (b) Discuss the meanings of *diversification* and *asset allocation*. Be sure to explain how they relate to managing investment risk.

17-38. How much money would you recommend a couple save in a qualified retirement plan if they would like to retire at age 68 and they expect to live until the age of 90? What kinds of additional information would you need to determine this? If they are both 35 right now, how much would they have to put into their retirement account every year to have enough to retire on at age 68? State any assumptions you make, such as rate of return and risk tolerance.

endnotes

1 Hall, Cheryl. "Fogo de Chão founder finds success as Texas transplant," *Dallas Morning News*, July 23, 2011, at https://www.dallasnews.com/business/business/2011/07/23/fogo-de-chao-founder-finds-success-as-texas-transplant, accessed June 28, 2015; Linnane, Ciara. "6 things to know about Fogo de Chao ahead of its IPO." *MarketWatch*, June 18, 2015. Accessed June 28, 2015. http://www.marketwatch.com/story/6-things-to-know-about-fogo-de-chao-ahead-of-its-ipo-2015-06-16

2 Whitfield, Craig. "What Returns Should We Expect from the Stock Market?" *Whitfield & Company*, May 15, 2017, at http://www.whitfieldco.com/blog/?p=39

3 "Advantages and Disadvantages of Mutual Funds," *The Motley Fool*, at http://www.fool.com, accessed on May 15, 2017; "Who Pays for Cap and Trade?" *Wall Street Journal*, March 9, 2009, at http://online.wsj.com/article/SB123655590609066021.html

4 "Why Exchange-Traded Funds?" *Yahoo! Finance Exchange-Traded Funds Center*, at http://finance.yahoo.com/etf/education/02, accessed on May 23, 2015; Coombes, Andrea. "Calculating the Costs of an ETF," *Wall Street Journal*, October 23, 2012, at http://online.wsj.com/article/SB1000087239639044402420457804429300857620 4.html

5 Bary, Andrew. "Embracing ETFs," *Barron's*, November 15, 2010, pp. 29–34.

6 Ibid.

7 Crook, Jordan. "Brooklinen tucks in $10M in Series A from FirstMark," Techcrunch.com, March 16, 2017, https://techcrunch.com/2017/03/16/brooklinen-tucks-in-10m-in-series-a-from-firstmark/. Accessed May 31, 2017.

8 "U.S. Investment Banking Era Ends," *UPI.com*, September 22, 2008, at http://www.upi.com/Business_News/2008/09/22/US-Investment-banking-era-ends/UPI-96221222086983/

9 New York Stock Exchange, at http://www.nyse.com, accessed on May 15, 2017.

10 "The State of Qatar Launches 'Qatar Exchange' as it Signs Today Formal Terms of Strategic Partnership with NYSE Euronext," *NYSE News Release*, June 19, 2009, at http://www.nyse.com/press/1245406656784.html

11 "Electronic Communication Network (ECN)," *Investing Answers*, at http://www.investinganswers.com/financial-dictionary/stock-market/electronic-communication-network-ecn-757, accessed on June 4, 2013.

12 "Just 25% Recognize That Most Americans Are Investors," *Rasmussen Reports*, February 11, 2011, at http://www.rasmussenreports.com/public_content/business/general_business/february_2011/just_25_recognize_that_most_americans_are_investors

13 Norwitz, Steven E., ed.. "A Bear Market of Historic Proportions," *T. Rowe Price Report*, Spring 2009, p. 1.

14 Beidelman, Carl. *The Handbook of International Investing* (Chicago, 1987), p. 133.

15 Welch, David. "Old GM Bondholders Getting Shares in New General Motors May Depress Price," *Bloomberg.com*, April 6, 2011, at http://www.bloomberg.com/news/2011-04-06/old-gm-bondholders-getting-shares-in-new-general-motors-may-depress-price.html

[16] Kumar, Ajay. "Can We Trust Moody's, Fitch, Standard & Poor?" *CommodityOnline*, at http://www.commodityonline.com/printnews.php?news_id=15888, accessed on July 22, 2009; Evans, David, and Salas, Caroline. "Flawed Credit Ratings Reap Profits as Regulators Fail (Update 1)," *Bloomberg.com*, April 29, 2009, at http://www.bloomberg.com/apps/news?pid=20670001&sid=au4oIx.judz4; Wayne, Leslie. "Calpers Sues over Ratings of Securities," *New York Times*, July 15, 2009, at http://www.nytimes.com/2009/07/15/business/15calpers.html; Segal, David. "Ohio Sues Rating Firms for Losses in Funds," *New York Times*, November 20, 2009, at http://www.nytimes.com/2009/11/21/business/21ratings.html; Hume, Lynn. "Connecticut AG Sues All Three Rating Agencies, *The Bond Buyer*, July 31, 2008, at http://www.bondbuyer.com/issues/117_145/-292250-1.html

[17] "Mortgage-Backed Securities," *U.S. Securities and Exchange Commission*, June 25, 2007, at http://www.sec.gov/answers/mortgagesecurities.htm; "Mortgage-Backed Security," *riskglossary.com*, at http://www.riskglossary.com/link/mortgage_backed_security.htm, accessed on July 24, 2009.

[18] Reuters. "Rajaratnam Insider Trading Trial Begins," March 9, 2011, *Huffington Post*, at http://www.huffingtonpost.com/2011/03/09/rajaratnam-trial_n_833326.html; U.S. Department of Justice. "Joseph P. Nacchio Indicted by Federal Grand Jury: Former Chief Executive Officer of Qwest Communications Charged with Insider Trading, Selling Over $100 Million Stock," December 20, 2005, at http://lawprofessors.typepad.com/whitecollarcrime_blog/files/nacchio_indictment.pdf

[19] Koenig, David. "IPO Shares of Flight Web Service Gogo Fall." *USA Today*. June 22, 2013, http://www.usatoday.com/story/money/business/2013/06/22/gogo-nasdaq-airlines-wifi/2448083/, accessed on July 16, 2013.

[20] "Gogo—This Recent Public Offering Is Not Going Yet." *Seeking Alpha*. June 28, 2013, http://seekingalpha.com/article/1526942-gogo-this-recent-public-offering-is-not-going-yet, accessed on July 16, 2013.

[21] "GOGO: Summary for Gogo Inc.—Yahoo! Finance." *Yahoo! Finance* July 16, 2013.

[22] Martin, Grant. "Delta Doubles Down on Gogo Inflight Internet With Faster and Broader Service." *Forbes*. February 25, 2015, http://www.forbes.com/sites/grantmartin/2015/02/25/delta-doubles-down-on-gogo-inflight-internet-with-faster-and-broader-service/, accessed on June 24, 2015.

Risk Management

In Chapters 3, 9, and 17 we discussed risk from various perspectives. In this appendix we describe other types of risks that businesses face and discuss some of the ways in which they typically manage them.

Coping with Risk

Businesses constantly face two basic types of **risk**—uncertainty about future events. **Speculative risks,** such as financial investments, involve the possibility of gain or loss. **Pure risks** involve only the possibility of loss or no loss. Designing and distributing a new product, for example, is a speculative risk—the product may fail or it may succeed and earn small or large profits. In contrast, the chance of a warehouse fire is a pure risk.

For a company to survive and prosper, it must manage both types of risk in a cost-effective manner. We can define the process of **risk management** as conserving the firm's earning power and assets by reducing the threat of losses as a result of uncontrollable events. In every company, each manager must be alert for risks to the firm and their impact on profits.

The risk-management process usually involves five steps:

Step 1: Identify Risks and Potential Losses
Managers analyze a firm's risks to identify potential losses.

Step 2: Measure the Frequency and Severity of Losses and Their Impact
To measure the frequency and severity of losses, managers must consider both history and current activities. How often can the firm expect the loss to occur? What is the likely size of the loss in dollars?

Step 3: Evaluate Alternatives and Choose the Techniques that Will Best Handle the Losses
Having identified and measured potential losses, managers are in a better position to decide how to handle them. They generally have four choices:

- A firm opts for **risk avoidance** by declining to enter or by ceasing to participate in a risky activity.

- When avoidance is not practical or desirable, firms can practice **risk control**—the use of loss-prevention techniques to minimize the frequency or severity of losses.

- When losses cannot be avoided or controlled, firms must cope with the consequences. When such losses are manageable and predictable, the firm may decide to cover them out of company funds. The firm is said to assume or retain the financial consequences of the loss; hence, the practice is known as **risk retention.**

- When the potential for large risks cannot be avoided or controlled, managers often opt for **risk transfer** to another firm—namely, an insurance company—to protect itself.

Risk *uncertainty about future events*

Speculative Risk *risk involving the possibility of gain or loss*

Pure Risk *risk involving only the possibility of loss or no loss*

Risk Management *process of conserving the firm's earning power and assets by reducing the threat of losses as a result of uncontrollable events*

Risk Avoidance *practice of avoiding risk by declining or ceasing to participate in an activity*

Risk Control *practice of minimizing the frequency or severity of losses from risky activities*

Risk Retention *practice of covering a firm's losses with its own funds*

Risk Transfer *practice of transferring a firm's risk to another firm*

Step 4: Implement the Risk-Management Program The means of implementing risk-management decisions depend on both the technique chosen and the activity being managed.

- Risk avoidance for certain activities can be implemented by purchasing those activities from outside providers.

- Risk control might be implemented by training employees and designing new work methods and equipment for on-the-job safety.

- For situations in which risk retention is preferred, reserve funds can be set aside from revenues.

- When risk transfer is needed, implementation means selecting an insurance company and buying the appropriate coverage.

Step 5: Monitor Results New types of risks emerge with changes in customers, facilities, employees, and products. Insurance regulations change, and new types of insurance become available. Consequently, managers must continuously monitor a company's risks, re-evaluate the methods used for handling them, and revise them as necessary.

Insurance as Risk Management

Insurance Premium *fee paid to an insurance company by a policyholder for insurance coverage*

Insurance Policy *formal agreement to pay the policyholder a specified amount in the event of certain losses*

Deductible *amount of the loss that the insured must absorb before reimbursement is made*

To deal with some risks, both businesses and individuals may choose to purchase insurance. Insurance is purchased by paying **insurance premiums**—payments to an insurance company to buy a policy and keep it active. In return, the insurance company issues an **insurance policy**—a formal agreement to pay the policyholder a specified amount in the event of certain losses. In some cases, the insured party must also pay a **deductible,** an agreed-on amount of the loss that the insured must absorb before reimbursement is made. Buyers find insurance appealing because they are protected against large, potentially devastating losses in return for a relatively small sum of money.

With insurance, individuals and businesses share risks by contributing to a fund from which those who suffer losses are paid. Insurance companies are willing to accept these risks because they make profits by taking in more premiums than they pay out to cover policyholders' losses. Although many policyholders are paying for protection against the same type of loss, by no means will all of them suffer such a loss.

Insurable Versus Uninsurable Risks Like every business, insurance companies must avoid certain risks. Insurers divide potential sources of loss into *insurable risks* and *uninsurable risks*. They issue policies only for insurable risks. Although there are some exceptions, an insurable risk must meet the following four criteria:

1 *Predictability:* The insurer must be able to use statistical tools to forecast the likelihood of a loss. This forecast also helps insurers determine premiums charged to policyholders.

2 *Casualty:* A loss must result from an *accident*, not from an intentional act by the policyholder. To avoid paying in cases of fraud, insurers may refuse to cover losses when they cannot determine whether policyholders' actions contributed to them.

3 *Unconnectedness:* Potential losses must be random and must occur independently of other losses. No insurer can afford to write insurance when a large percentage of those who are exposed to a particular kind of loss are likely to suffer such a loss. By carefully choosing the risks that it will insure, an insurance company can reduce its chances of a large loss or insolvency.

4 *Verifiability:* Insured losses must be verifiable as to cause, time, place, and amount.

Special Forms of Insurance for Business
Businesses have special insurable concerns—*liability, property, business interruption, key person insurance,* and *business continuation agreements.*

LIABILITY INSURANCE Liability means responsibility for damages in case of accidental or deliberate harm to individuals or property. **Liability insurance** covers losses resulting from damage to people or property when the insured party is judged liable.

A business is liable for any injury to an employee when the injury arises from activities related to the occupation. When workers are permanently or temporarily disabled by job-related accidents or disease, employers are required by law to provide **workers' compensation coverage** for medical expenses, loss of wages, and rehabilitation services.

PROPERTY INSURANCE A firm purchases **property insurance** to cover injuries to itself resulting from physical damage to or loss of real estate or personal property. Property losses may result from fire, lightning, wind, hail, explosion, theft, vandalism, or other destructive forces.

BUSINESS INTERRUPTION INSURANCE In some cases, loss to property is minimal in comparison to loss of income. If a firm is forced to close down for an extended time, it will not be able to generate income. During this time, however, certain expenses—such as taxes, insurance premiums, and salaries for key employees and managers—may continue. To cover such losses, a firm may buy **business interruption insurance.**

KEY PERSON INSURANCE Many businesses choose to protect themselves against loss of the talents and skills of key employees, as well as the recruitment costs to find a replacement and training expenses once a replacement is hired. **Key person insurance** is designed to offset both lost income and additional expenses.

BUSINESS CONTINUATION AGREEMENTS Who takes control of a business when a partner or associate dies? Surviving partners are often faced with the possibility of having to accept an inexperienced heir as a management partner. This contingency can be handled in **business continuation agreements,** whereby owners make plans to buy the ownership interest of a deceased associate from his or her heirs. The value of the ownership interest is determined when the agreement is made. Special policies can also provide survivors with the funds needed to make the purchase.

Liability Insurance *insurance covering losses resulting from damage to people or property when the insured party is judged liable*

Workers' Compensation Coverage *coverage provided by a firm to employees for medical expenses, loss of wages, and rehabilitation costs resulting from job-related injuries or disease*

Property Insurance *insurance covering losses resulting from physical damage to or loss of the insured's real estate or personal property*

Business Interruption Insurance *insurance covering income lost during times when a company is unable to conduct business*

Key Person Insurance *special form of business insurance designed to offset expenses entailed by the loss of key employees*

Business Continuation Agreement *special form of business insurance whereby owners arrange to buy the interests of deceased associates from their heirs*

The Legal Context of Business

In this appendix, we describe the basic tenets of U.S. law and show how these principles work through the court system. We'll also survey a few major areas of business-related law.

The U.S. Legal and Judicial Systems

Laws are the codified rules of behavior enforced by a society. In the United States, laws fall into three broad categories according to their origins: *common, statutory,* and *regulatory.*

Laws *codified rules of behavior enforced by a society*

Types of Law

Law in the United States originated primarily with English common law. U.S. law includes the U.S. Constitution, state constitutions, federal and state statutes, municipal ordinances, administrative agency rules and regulations, executive orders, and court decisions.

Common Law Court decisions follow *precedents*, or the decisions of previous cases. Following precedent lends stability to the law by basing judicial decisions on cases anchored in similar facts. This principle is the keystone of **common law**—the body of decisions handed down by courts ruling on individual cases.

Common Law *body of decisions handed down by courts ruling on individual cases*

Statutory Law Laws created by constitutions or by federal, state, or local legislative acts constitute **statutory law.** Under the U.S. Constitution, federal statutes take precedence over state and local statutes.

Statutory Law *law created by constitution(s) or by federal, state, or local legislative acts*

Regulatory Law Statutory law and common law have long histories. Relatively new is **regulatory (or administrative) law**—law made by the authority of administrative agencies.

Regulatory (Administrative) Law *law made by the authority of administrative agencies*

Although Congress retains control over the scope of agency action, regulations have the force of statutory law once passed. Government regulatory agencies act as a secondary judicial system, determining whether regulations have been violated and then imposing penalties. Much agency activity consists of setting standards for safety or quality and monitoring the compliance of businesses.

Congress has created numerous agencies in response to pressure to address social issues. In some cases, agencies were established in response to public concern about corporate behavior. The activities of these agencies have sometimes forced U.S. firms to consider the public interest almost as routinely as they consider their own financial performance.

Keeping an Eye on Business Today a host of agencies regulate U.S. business practices. Among the most significant are:

- Equal Employment Opportunity Commission (EEOC)
- Environmental Protection Agency (EPA)

- Food and Drug Administration (FDA)
- Federal Trade Commission (FTC)
- Occupational Safety and Health Administration (OSHA)
- Securities and Exchange Commission (SEC)

Trends in Deregulation and Regulation Although government regulation has benefited U.S. business in many ways, it is not without its drawbacks. Managers and business owners complain—with some justification—that government regulations require too much costly paperwork. Many people in both business and government support broader **deregulation**—the elimination of rules that restrict business activity. Deregulation, they argue, is a primary incentive to innovation. Deregulated industries are forced to innovate to survive in competitive industries. Those firms that are already conditioned to compete by being more creative will outperform firms that have been protected by regulatory climates in their home countries.

Over time there are swings between deregulation and then back toward regulation, depending on which political party is in control in Washington as well as prevailing public opinion. Many critics blamed the financial crisis and economic recession of 2008 on the uncontrolled actions of major U.S. banks and called for more regulation to help prevent a future recurrence of the same mistakes. President Barrack Obama responded by increasing regulation of the banking and financial sector. He also increased regulation related to environmental protection in response to concerns about global warming. In the early months of President Donald Trump's administration in 2017, however, many of these regulations were reduced or eliminated altogether.

(margin) **Deregulation** *elimination of rules that restrict business activity*

The U.S. Judicial System

Much of the responsibility for law enforcement falls to the courts. Litigation is a significant part of contemporary life, and we have given our courts a voice in a wide range of issues, some touching personal concerns, some ruling on matters of public policy that affect all our lives.

The Court System There are three levels in the U.S. judicial system—*federal, state,* and *local.* Federal courts hear cases on questions of constitutional law, disputes relating to maritime laws, and violations of federal statutes. They also rule on regulatory actions and on such issues as bankruptcy, postal law, and copyright or patent violation. Both the federal and most state systems embody a three-tiered system of *trial, appellate,* and *supreme courts.*

TRIAL COURTS At the lowest level of the federal court system are the **trial courts,** the general courts that hear cases not specifically assigned to another court. Every state has at least one federal trial court, called a *district court.*

Trial courts also include special courts and administrative agencies. Special courts hear specific types of cases, such as cases involving tax evasion, fraud, international disputes, or claims against the U.S. government. Within their areas of jurisdiction, administrative agencies also make judgments much like those of courts.

Courts in each state deal with the same issues as their federal counterparts. However, they may rule only in areas governed by state law. For example, a state special court would hear a case involving state income tax laws. Local courts in each state system also hear cases on municipal ordinances, local traffic violations, and similar issues.

(margin) **Trial Court** *general court that hears cases not specifically assigned to another court*

APPELLATE COURTS A losing party in a trial court may disagree with the court ruling. If that party can show grounds for review, the case may go before a federal or state **appellate court.** These courts consider questions of law, such as possible errors of legal interpretation made by lower courts. They do not examine questions of fact, however.

(margin) **Appellate Court** *court that reviews case records of trials whose findings have been appealed*

SUPREME COURTS Cases still not resolved at the appellate level can be appealed to the appropriate state supreme courts or to the U.S. Supreme Court. If it believes that an appeal is warranted or that the outcome will set an important precedent, the U.S. Supreme Court also hears cases appealed from state supreme courts.

Business Law

Most legal issues confronted by businesses fall into one of six basic areas: *contract, tort, property, agency, commercial,* or *bankruptcy law*. These areas cover a wide range of business activity.

Contract Law

A **contract** is any agreement between two or more parties that is enforceable in court. As such, it must meet six conditions. If all these conditions are met, one party can seek legal recourse from another if the other party breaches, or violates, the terms of the agreement.

Contract *agreement between two or more parties enforceable in court*

1 *Agreement.* Agreement is the serious, definite, and communicated offer and acceptance of the same terms.

2 *Consent.* A contract is not enforceable if any of the parties has been affected by an honest mistake, fraud, or pressure.

3 *Capacity.* To give real consent, both parties must demonstrate legal **capacity** (competence). A person under legal age (usually 18 or 21) cannot enter into a binding contract.

Capacity *competence required of individual entering into a binding contract*

4 *Consideration.* An agreement is binding only if it exchanges **considerations**— items of value. Note that items of value do not necessarily entail money. Contracts need not be rational, nor must they provide the best possible bargain for both sides. They need only include legally sufficient consideration. The terms are met if both parties receive what the contract details.

Consideration *item of value exchanged between parties to create a valid contract*

5 *Legality.* A contract must be for a lawful purpose and must comply with federal, state, and local laws and regulations.

6 *Proper form.* A contract may be written, oral, or implied from conduct. It must be written, however, if it involves the sale of land or goods worth more than $500. It must also be written if the agreement requires more than a year to fulfill. All changes to written contracts must also be in writing.

Breach of Contract Contract law offers a variety of remedies designed to protect the reasonable expectations of the parties and, in some cases, to compensate them for actions taken to enforce the agreement. As the injured party to a breached contract, any of the following actions might occur:

- You might cancel the contract and refuse to live up to your part of the bargain.

- You might sue for damages up to the amount that you lost as a result of the breach.

- If money cannot repay the damage you suffered, you might demand specific performance, or require the other party to fulfill the original contract.

Tort Law

Tort law applies to most business relationships *not* governed by contracts. A **tort** is a *civil*—that is, noncriminal—injury to people, property, or reputation for which compensation must be paid. Trespass, fraud, defamation, invasion of privacy, and even assault can be torts, as can interference with contractual relations and wrongful use of trade secrets. There are three classifications of torts: *intentional, negligence,* and *product liability*.

Tort *civil injury to people, property, or reputation for which compensation must be paid*

Intentional Tort *tort resulting from the deliberate actions of a party*

Compensatory Damages *monetary payments intended to redress injury actually suffered because of a tort*

Punitive Damages *fines imposed over and above any actual losses suffered by a plaintiff*

Negligence *conduct that falls below legal standards for protecting others against unreasonable risk*

Product Liability *tort in which a company is responsible for injuries caused by its products*

Strict Product Liability *principle that liability can result not from a producer's negligence but from a defect in the product itself*

Intentional Torts **Intentional torts** result from the deliberate actions of another person or organization. To remedy torts, courts will usually impose **compensatory damages**—payments intended to redress an injury actually suffered. They may also impose **punitive damages**—fines that exceed actual losses suffered by plaintiffs and are intended to punish defendants.

Negligence Torts Most suits involve charges of **negligence**—conduct that falls below legal standards for protecting others against unreasonable risk.

Product Liability Torts In cases of **product liability,** a company may be held responsible for injuries caused by its products.

STRICT PRODUCT LIABILITY Since the early 1960s, businesses have faced a number of legal actions based on the relatively new principle of **strict product liability**—the principle that liability can result not from a producer's negligence but from a defect in the product itself. An injured party need only show the following:

1 The product was defective.
2 The defect was the cause of injury.
3 The defect caused the product to be unreasonably dangerous.

Because plaintiffs need not demonstrate negligence or fault, these suits have a good chance of success.

Property Law

Property *anything of value to which a person or business has sole right of ownership*

Tangible Real Property *land and anything attached to it*

Tangible Personal Property *any movable item that can be owned, bought, sold, or leased*

Intangible Personal Property *property that cannot be seen but that exists by virtue of written documentation*

Intellectual Property *property created through a person's creative activities*

Property is anything of value to which a person or business has sole right of ownership. Legally speaking, the right of ownership is itself property.

Within this broad general definition, we can divide property into four categories:

1 **Tangible real property** is land and anything attached to it.
2 **Tangible personal property** is any movable item that can be owned, bought, sold, or leased.
3 **Intangible personal property** cannot be seen but exists by virtue of written documentation.
4 **Intellectual property** is created through a person's creative activities.

Protection of Intellectual Rights The U.S. Constitution grants protection to intellectual property by means of copyrights, trademarks, and patents. Copyrights and patents apply to the tangible expressions of an idea, not to the ideas themselves.

Copyright *exclusive ownership right belonging to the creator of a book, article, design, illustration, photo, film, or musical work*

COPYRIGHTS **Copyrights** give creators exclusive ownership rights to their intellectual property. Copyrights extend to creators for their entire lives and to their estates for 70 years thereafter.

TRADEMARKS Because the development of products is expensive, companies must prevent other firms from using their brand names. Often, they must act to keep competitors from confusing consumers with similar or substitute products. A producer can apply to the U.S. government for a **trademark**—the exclusive legal right to use a brand name.

Trademark *exclusive legal right to use a brand name or symbol*

Trademarks are granted for 20 years and may be renewed indefinitely if a firm continues to protect its brand name. If a firm allows the brand name to lapse into common usage, it may lose protection. Common usage takes effect when a company fails to use the ® symbol to indicate that its brand name is a registered trademark. It also takes effect if a company seeks no action against those who fail to acknowledge its trademark.

Patent *exclusive legal right to use and license a manufactured item or substance, manufacturing process, or object design*

PATENTS **Patents** provide legal monopolies for the use and licensing of manufactured items, manufacturing processes, substances, and designs for objects. A patentable invention must be *novel*, *useful*, and *nonobvious*. Patents are valid for 20 years, with the term running from the date on which the application was *filed*, not the date on which the patent itself was *issued*.

Restrictions on Property Rights

Property rights are not always absolute. For example, rights may be compromised under the following circumstances:

- Utility companies typically have rights called easements, such as the right to run wire over private property or to lay cable or pipe under it.

- Under the principle of **eminent domain,** the government may, on paying owners fair prices, claim private land to expand roads or erect public buildings.

Eminent Domain *principle that the government may claim private land for public use by buying it at a fair price*

Agency Law

The transfer of property often involves agents. An **agent** is a person who acts for and in the name of another party, called the **principal.** Courts have ruled that both a firm's employees and its outside contractors may be regarded as its agents.

Agent *individual or organization acting for and in the name of another party*

Principal *individual or organization authorizing an agent to act on its behalf*

Authority of Agents

Agents have the authority to bind principals to agreements. They receive that authority, however, from the principals themselves; they cannot create their own authority. An agent's authority to bind a principal can be **express, implied,** or **apparent.**

Express Authority *agent's authority, derived from written agreement, to bind a principal to a certain course of action*

Implied Authority *agent's authority, derived from business custom, to bind a principal to a certain course of action*

Responsibilities of Principals

Principals have several responsibilities to their agents. They owe agents reasonable compensation, must reimburse them for related business expenses, and should inform them of risks associated with their business activities. Principals are liable for actions performed by agents *within the scope of their employment*. If agents make untrue claims about products or services, the principal is liable for making amends. Employers are similarly responsible for the actions of employees. Firms are often liable in tort suits because the courts treat employees as agents. Businesses are also increasingly being held accountable for *criminal* acts by employees. Court findings have argued that firms are expected to be aware of workers' negative propensities, to check their employees' backgrounds, and to train and supervise employees properly.

Apparent Authority *agent's authority, based on the principal's compliance, to bind a principal to a certain course of action*

Commercial Law

Managers must be well acquainted with the most general laws affecting commerce. Specifically, they need to be familiar with the provisions of the **Uniform Commercial Code (UCC),** which describes the rights of buyers and sellers in transactions. One key area of coverage by the UCC, contracts, was discussed previously. Another key area is warranties.

A **warranty** is a seller's promise to stand by its products or services if a problem occurs after the sale. Warranties may be express or implied. The seller specifically states the terms of an **express warranty,** whereas an **implied warranty** is dictated by law. Implied warranties embody the principle that a product should (1) fulfill the promises made by advertisements and (2) serve the purpose for which it was manufactured and sold. It is important to note, however, that warranties, unlike most contracts, are easily limited, waived, or disclaimed. Consequently, they are the source of tort action more often, as dissatisfied customers seek redress from producers.

Uniform Commercial Code (UCC) *body of standardized laws governing the rights of buyers and sellers in transactions*

Warranty *seller's promise to stand by its products or services if a problem occurs after the sale*

Express Warranty *a warranty whose terms are specifically stated by the seller*

Implied Warranty *a warranty, dictated by law, based on the principle that products should fulfill advertised promises and serve the purposes for which they are manufactured and sold*

Bankruptcy Law

Both organizations and individuals can seek debt relief by filing for bankruptcy—the court-granted permission not to pay some or all incurred debts. Many individuals and businesses file for bankruptcy each year, and their numbers continue to increase. Three main factors account for the increase in bankruptcy filings:

1 The increased availability of credit
2 The "fresh-start" provisions in current bankruptcy laws
3 The growing acceptance of bankruptcy as a financial tactic

Involuntary Bankruptcy *bankruptcy proceedings initiated by the creditors of an indebted individual or organization*

Voluntary Bankruptcy *bankruptcy proceedings initiated by an indebted individual or organization*

In some cases, creditors force an individual or firm into **involuntary bankruptcy** and press the courts to award them payment of at least part of what they are owed. Far more often, however, a person or business chooses to file for court protection against creditors. In general, individuals and firms whose debts exceed total assets by at least $1,000 may file for **voluntary bankruptcy.**

Business Bankruptcy One of three plans resolves a business bankruptcy:

1 Under a *liquidation plan*, the business ceases to exist. Its assets are sold and the proceeds are used to pay creditors.

2 Under a *repayment plan*, the bankrupt company simply works out a new payment schedule to meet its obligations. The time frame is usually extended, and payments are collected and distributed by a court-appointed trustee.

3 *Reorganization* is the most complex form of business bankruptcy. The company must explain the sources of its financial difficulties and propose a new plan for remaining in business. Reorganization may include a new slate of managers and a new financial strategy. A judge may also reduce the firm's debts to ensure its survival.

Legislation passed since 1994 restricts how long a company can protect itself in bankruptcy while continuing to do business. Critics have charged that many firms have succeeded in operating for long periods of time under bankruptcy protection. During that time, they were able to cut costs and prices, not only competing with an unfair advantage, but also dragging down overall industry profits. The new laws place time limits on various steps in the filing process. The intended effect is to speed the process and prevent assets from being lost to legal fees.

The International Framework of Business Law

International Law *general set of cooperative agreements and guidelines established by countries to govern the actions of individuals, businesses, and nations*

Laws vary from country to country, and many businesses today have international markets, suppliers, and competitors. Managers need a basic understanding of the international framework of business law that affects the ways in which they can do business. Issues such as pollution across borders are matters of **international law**— the general set of cooperative agreements and guidelines established by countries to govern the actions of individuals, businesses, and nations themselves.

International law has several sources. One source is custom and tradition. Among countries that have been trading with one another for centuries, many customs and traditions governing exchanges have gradually evolved into practice. Although some trading practices still follow ancient unwritten agreements, there has been a clear trend in more recent times to approach international trade within a more formal legal framework. Key features of that framework include a variety of formal trade agreements.

Another important source of international law is the formal trade treaties that nations negotiate with one another. Governing entities such as the World Trade Organization and the European Union, for instance, also provide legal frameworks within which participating nations agree to abide.

Managing Your Personal Finances

Dealing with personal finances is a lifelong job involving a crucial choice between two options:

1 Committing to the rational management of your personal finances by controlling them, helping them grow, and therefore enjoying greater personal satisfaction and financial stability

2 Letting the financial chips fall where they may and hoping for the best (which seldom happens) and therefore inviting frustration, disappointment, and financial distress

Personal finance management requires consideration of cash management, financial planning and control, investment alternatives, and risk. Let's start by looking at one key factor in success: the personal financial plan. We'll then discuss the steps in the planning process and show how you can make better decisions to manage your personal finances.

Building Your Financial Plan

Financial planning is the process of looking at your current financial condition, identifying your goals, and anticipating steps toward meeting those goals. Because your goals and finances will change as you get older, your plan should always allow for revision. Figure AIII.1 summarizes a step-by-step approach to personal financial planning.

Financial Planning *process of looking at one's current financial condition, identifying one's goals, and anticipating requirements for meeting those goals*

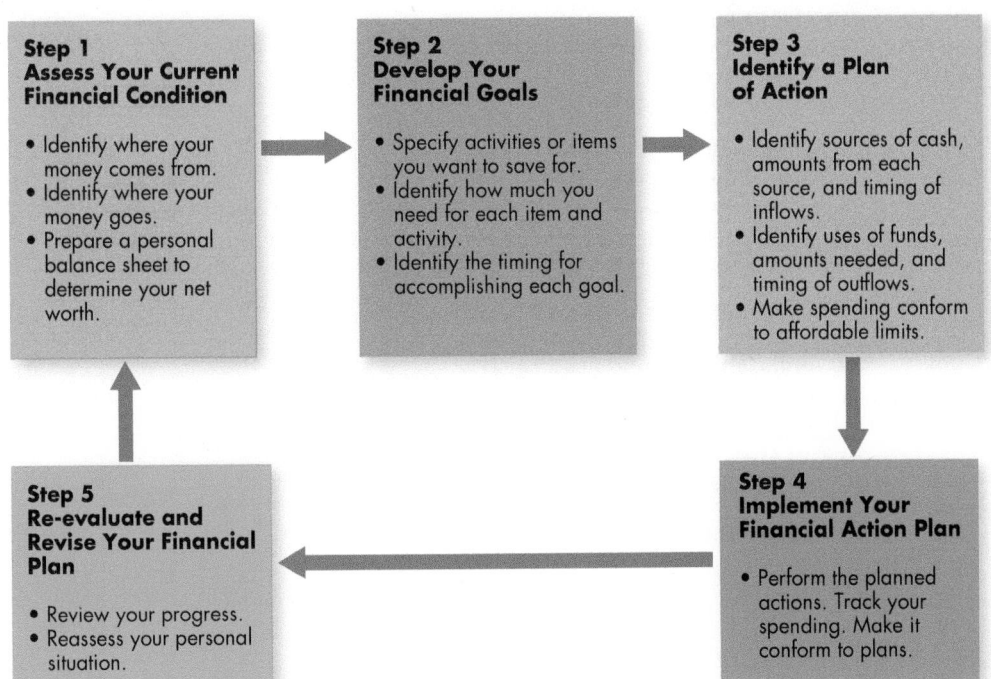

**Step 1
Assess Your Current Financial Condition**

- Identify where your money comes from.
- Identify where your money goes.
- Prepare a personal balance sheet to determine your net worth.

**Step 2
Develop Your Financial Goals**

- Specify activities or items you want to save for.
- Identify how much you need for each item and activity.
- Identify the timing for accomplishing each goal.

**Step 3
Identify a Plan of Action**

- Identify sources of cash, amounts from each source, and timing of inflows.
- Identify uses of funds, amounts needed, and timing of outflows.
- Make spending conform to affordable limits.

**Step 5
Re-evaluate and Revise Your Financial Plan**

- Review your progress.
- Reassess your personal situation.

**Step 4
Implement Your Financial Action Plan**

- Perform the planned actions. Track your spending. Make it conform to plans.

FIGURE AIII.1 Developing a Personal Financial Plan

Assessing Your Current Financial Condition

Personal Net Worth *value of one's total assets minus one's total liabilities (debts)*

The first step in developing a personal financial plan is assessing your current financial position. Your **personal net worth** is the value of all your assets minus all your liabilities (debts) *at the present time.* The worksheet in Figure AIII.2 provides some sample calculations for developing your own personal "balance sheet." Because assets and liabilities change over time, updating your balance sheet not only allows you to monitor changes but also provides more accurate information for realistic budgeting and planning.

Assets: What You Own		Example Numbers	Your Numbers
LIQUID ASSETS:			
1. Cash	$	300	_____
2. Savings	+	3,700	_____
3. Checking	+	1,200	_____
INVESTMENTS:			
4. IRAs	+	12,400	_____
5. Securities	+	500	_____
6. Retirement Plan	+	—	_____
7. Real Estate (other than primary residence)	+	—	
HOUSEHOLD:			
8. Cars (market value)	+	18,000	_____
9. House (market value)	+	—	_____
10. Furniture	+	3,400	_____
11. Personal Property	+	6,600	_____
12. Other assets		—	
13. Total Assets (add lines 1–12)		**= $46,100**	_____
Liabilities (Debt): What You Owe			
CURRENT LIABILITIES:			
14. Credit-card balance	$	1,300	_____
15. Unpaid bills due	+	1,800	_____
16. Alimony and child support	+	—	_____
LONG-TERM LIABILITIES:			
17. Home mortgage	+	—	_____
18. Home equity loan	+	—	_____
19. Car loan	+	4,100	_____
20. Student loan	+	3,600	_____
21. Other liabilities	+	2,400	_____
22. Total Liabilities (add lines 14–21)		**= $13,200**	_____
Net Worth			
23. Total Assets (line 13)		$ 46,100	_____
24. Less: Total Debt (line 22)	−	13,200	_____
25. Results: Net Worth		**= $32,900**	_____

FIGURE AIII.2 Worksheet for Calculating Net Worth

Developing Your Financial Goals

Step 2 involves setting three different types of future goals: *immediate* (within one year), *intermediate* (within five years), and *long-term* (more than five years). The worksheet in Figure AIII.3 will help you establish these goals. By thinking about your finances in three different time frames, you'll be better able to set measurable goals and completion times, or to set priorities for rationing your resources if, at some point, you're not able to pursue all your goals.

Because step 3 (identifying a plan of action) and step 4 (implementing your plan) will affect your assets and liabilities, your balance sheet will change over time. As a result, step 5 (re-evaluating and revising your plan) needs periodic updating.

Name the Goal	Financial Requirement (Amount) for This Goal	Time Frame for Accomplishing Goal	Importance (1 = Highest, 5 = Lowest)
Immediate Goals:			
Live in a better apartment	_____	_____	_____
Establish an emergency cash fund	_____	_____	_____
Pay off credit-card debt	_____	_____	_____
Other	_____	_____	_____
Intermediate Goals:			
Obtain adequate health, life, disability, liability, property insurance	_____	_____	_____
Save for wedding	_____	_____	_____
Save to buy new car	_____	_____	_____
Establish regular savings program (5% of gross income)	_____	_____	_____
Save for college for self	_____	_____	_____
Pay off major outstanding debt	_____	_____	_____
Make major purchase	_____	_____	_____
Save for home remodeling	_____	_____	_____
Save for down payment on a home	_____	_____	_____
Other	_____	_____	_____
Long-Term Goals:			
Pay off home mortgage	_____	_____	_____
Save for college for children	_____	_____	_____
Save for vacation home	_____	_____	_____
Increase personal net worth to $___ in ___ years.	_____	_____	_____
Achieve retirement nest egg of $ __ in ___ years.	_____	_____	_____
Accumulate fund for travel in retirement	_____	_____	_____
Save for long-term care needs	_____	_____	_____
Other	_____	_____	_____

FIGURE AIII.3 Worksheet for Setting Financial Goals

Making Better Use of the Time Value of Money

As discussed in Chapter 17, the value of time with any investment stems from the principle of compound growth, the compounding of interest received over several time periods. With each additional time period, interest receipts accumulate and earn even more interest, thus multiplying the earning capacity of the investment. Whenever you make everyday purchases, you're giving up interest that you could have earned with the same money if you'd invested it instead. From a financial standpoint, "idle" or uninvested money, which could be put to work earning more money, is a wasted resource.

Planning for the "Golden Years"

The sooner you start saving, the greater your financial power will be in the future. This stems from the fact that you will have taken advantage of the time value of money for a longer period of time. Consider coworkers Ellen and Barbara, who are both planning to retire in 25 years, as can be seen in Figure AIII.4.

Over that period, assume that each can expect a 10 percent annual return on investment. (Note: The U.S. stock market averaged more than 10 percent returns for the 75 years before the 2008 recession. However, since the recession ended average returns have not regained the 10 percent level for a sustained period so a more conservative approach may be called for in the future.) Their savings strategies, however, are different: Barbara begins saving immediately, whereas Ellen plans to start later but invest larger sums. Barbara will invest $2,000 annually for each of the

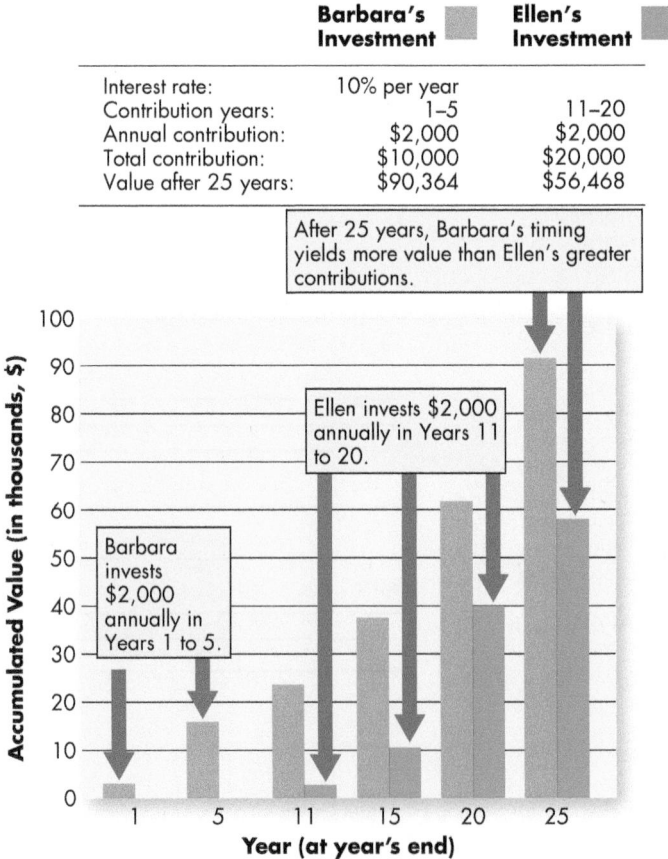

	Barbara's Investment	Ellen's Investment
Interest rate:	10% per year	
Contribution years:	1–5	11–20
Annual contribution:	$2,000	$2,000
Total contribution:	$10,000	$20,000
Value after 25 years:	$90,364	$56,468

After 25 years, Barbara's timing yields more value than Ellen's greater contributions.

Ellen invests $2,000 annually in Years 11 to 20.

Barbara invests $2,000 annually in Years 1 to 5.

FIGURE AIII.4 Compounding Money over Time

next 5 years (years 1 through 5), for a total investment of $10,000. Ellen, meanwhile, wants to live a little larger by spending rather than saving for the next 10 years. Then, for years 11 through 20, she'll start saving $2,000 annually, for a total investment of $20,000. They will both allow annual returns to accumulate until they retire in year 25. Ellen expects to have a larger retirement fund than Barbara because she has contributed twice as much, but she is in for a surprise. Barbara's retirement fund will be much larger—$90,364 versus Ellen's $56,468—even though she invested only half as much. Barbara's advantage lies in the length of her savings program. Her money is invested longer—over a period of 21 to 25 years—with interest compounding over that range of time. Ellen's earnings are compounded over a shorter period—6 to 15 years. Granted, Ellen may have had more fun in years 1 to 10, but Barbara's retirement prospects look brighter.

Other factors that have to be considered are anticipated retirement age and life expectancy. Not that long ago most people considered age 65 to be the "official" retirement age, and many people actually retired earlier than that, some as early as 58. Similarly, the average life expectancy for people born in 1950, the end of the baby boom generation, was around 65 years. Now, however, due to healthier life styles and better health care, life expectancies have been extended to around 78 years and many people work well into their 70s before retiring. As a result of these trends, if a person wants to retire at a relatively early age he or she will need even more retirement savings in anticipation of a longer life. There are numerous online financial planning tools available that help determine projected financial needs based on different retirement periods.

Time Value as a Financial-Planning Tool

A good financial plan takes into account future needs, the sources of funds for meeting those needs, and the time needed to develop those funds. When you begin your financial plan, you can use various time-based tables to take into account the time value of money. Figure AIII.5 shows how much a $1.00 investment will grow over different lengths of time and at different interest rates.

A timetable like this can determine the factor at which your money will multiply over a given period of time and at a given interest rate. It can also help you determine how long and at what interest rate you will need to invest to meet your financial goals. For example, if you wanted to double your money in less than 10 years, you would have to find an interest rate of return of at least 8 percent. The catch is that to obtain a high interest rate, you will have to make riskier investments, such as buying

n	1%	2%	4%	6%	8%	10%
1	1.010	1.020	1.040	1.060	1.080	1.100
2	1.020	1.040	1.082	1.124	1.166	1.210
3	1.030	1.061	1.125	1.191	1.260	1.331
4	1.041	1.082	1.170	1.262	1.360	1.464
5	1.051	1.104	1.217	1.338	1.469	1.611
6	1.062	1.126	1.265	1.419	1.587	1.772
7	1.072	1.149	1.316	1.504	1.714	1.949
8	1.083	1.172	1.369	1.594	1.851	2.144
9	1.094	1.195	1.423	1.689	1.999	2.358
10	1.105	1.219	1.480	1.791	2.159	2.594
15	1.161	1.346	1.801	2.397	3.172	4.177
20	1.220	1.486	2.191	3.207	4.661	6.727
25	1.282	1.641	2.666	4.292	6.848	10.834
30	1.348	1.811	3.243	5.743	10.062	17.449

Note: n = number of time periods; % = various interest rates

FIGURE AIII.5   Timetable for Growing $1.00

stocks. Because higher interest rates carry greater risks, it is unwise to "put all your eggs in one basket." A sound financial plan will include more conservative investments, such as a bank savings account, to mitigate the risks of more speculative investments.

Conserving Money by Controlling It

A major pitfall in any financial plan is the temptation to spend more than you can afford, especially when credit is so easy to get. Because many credit-card issuers target college students and recent graduates with tempting offers appealing to the desire for financial independence, it is important that you arm yourself with a solid understanding of the financial costs entailed by credit cards. The same lessons apply equally to other loans, such as home mortgages, cars, and student financial aid.

Credit Cards: Keys to Satisfaction or Financial Handcuffs?

Although some credit cards don't charge annual fees, all of them charge interest on unpaid (outstanding) balances. Figure AIII.6 reprints part of a page from Bankrate.com's credit-card calculator at www.bankrate.com/brm/calc/MinPayment.asp. Using the table as a guide, suppose you owe $5,000 for credit-card purchases, and your card company requires a minimum monthly payment (minimum payment due [MPD]) of 5 percent of the unpaid balance. The interest rate is 18 percent APR (annual percentage rate) on the outstanding balance.

If you pay only the monthly minimum, it will take you 115 months—more than 9 1/2 years—to pay off your credit-card debt. During this time you will pay $2,096.70 in interest, almost half again the principal balance! Repayment takes so long because you are making only the MPD, which decreases with each monthly payment.

Save Your Money: Lower Interest Rates and Faster Payments

Figure AIII.6 confirms two principles for saving money that you can apply when borrowing from any source, not just credit cards: Look for lower interest rates and make faster repayments.

Seeking Lower Interest Rates Look again at Figure AIII.6 and compare the cost of borrowing $5,000 at 18 percent with the cost of borrowing it at 9 percent. If you assume the same 5-percent minimum monthly payment, a 9-percent APR will save you $1,232.14 in interest during the repayment period—a nearly 59 percent savings.

Balance = $5,000 APR	MPD 3% Months	Costs	MPD 5% Months	Costs	MPD 10% Months	Costs
6%	144	$5,965.56	92	$5,544.58	50	$5,260.74
9%	158	$6,607.24	96	$5,864.56	51	$5,401.63
12%	175	$7,407.50	102	$6,224.26	53	$5,550.32
18%	226	$9,798.89	115	$7,096.70	55	$5,873.86
21%	266	$11,704.63	123	$7,632.92	57	$6,050.28

Note: APR, annual percentage rate; MPD, minimum payment due

FIGURE AIII.6 Paying off Credit-Card Debt

Renting	Buying
• No down payment to get started	• Must make payments for mortgage, property taxes, and insurance
• Flexibility to leave	• Equity builds up over time
• No obligation for upkeep or improvements	• More privacy
• No groundskeeping	• Value of property may increase
• Easy cash-flow planning (a single monthly payment)	• Lower income taxes: mortgage-interest and property tax payments reduce taxable income
• May provide access to recreation and social facilities	• Financial gains from selling house can be exempt from taxes
• Rental conditions may be changed by owner	• Greater control over use of property and improvements
• Timing for repairs controlled by owner	• The home can become a source of cash by refinancing with another mortgage loan or a home-equity loan

FIGURE AIII.7   To Buy or Not to Buy

Making Faster Payments Because money has a time value, lenders charge borrowers according to the length of time for which they borrow it. In general, longer lending periods increase the cost, and shorter periods are cheaper. Using Figure AIII.6, compare the costs of the 5-percent MPD with the faster 10-percent MPD. The faster schedule cuts the repayment period from 115 to 55 months and, at 18 percent APR, reduces interest costs by $1,222.84. Combining both faster repayment and the lower interest rate cuts your total interest cost to $450.30—a savings of $1,695.07 over the amount you'd pay if you made slower repayments at the higher rate.

Declining Asset Value: A Borrower's Regret Financially speaking, nothing's more disappointing than buying an expensive item and then discovering that it's not worth what you paid. For example, if you buy a $5,000 used car with a credit card at 18 percent APR and make only the MPD, as in the preceding example, you'll end up spending a total of $7,407.50 over 9 1/2 years. By that time, however, the car you bought will be worth less than $1,000. Some of this loss in asset value can be avoided through realistic planning and spending—by knowing and staying within your financial means.

Financial Commitments of Home Ownership

Deciding whether to rent or buy a home involves a variety of considerations, including life stage, family needs, career, financial situation, and preferred lifestyle. If you decide to buy, you have to ask yourself what you can afford, and that requires asking yourself questions about your personal financial condition and your capacity for borrowing. Figure AIII.7 summarizes the key considerations in deciding whether to rent or buy.

How Much House Can You Afford?

Buying a home is the biggest investment that most people make. Unfortunately, many make the mistake of buying a house that they can't afford, resulting in unnecessary stress and even devastating financial loss. This happened on a massive scale in the housing downfall that began in 2007 and has still not fully ended. The seeds for destruction sprouted during the years 2000–2007 when millions of optimistic home buyers borrowed beyond their means by getting larger loans than they could afford. With the rising demand for home ownership, housing prices became inflated and borrowers responded by seeking unrealistically larger loans. They implicitly assumed that market prices would continue to rise indefinitely, thereby providing a profitable investment. Borrowers were aided by lenders using loose credit standards, unlike the more conservative time-proven standards that will be presented here, leading to unrealistic repayment requirements. By 2007 the housing market was oversold and the U.S. economy entered a severe recession. With rising unemployment, borrowers were unable to meet monthly payments, especially when interest rates (and thus payments) on loans increased. Consequently, housing vacancies increased and property values plummeted. Borrowers lost their homes and the equity they had built up in them. The depressed housing market did not begin to revive until 2014.

In addition to loan payments, the typical demands of ownership, time and other resources for maintaining and improving a home tend to cut into the money left over for recreation, eating out, taking vacations, and so on. You can reduce the financial pressure by calculating in advance a realistic price range—one that not only lets you buy a house but also lets you live a reasonably pleasant life once you're in it.

Mortgage Loan *loan secured by property (the home) being purchased*

Most people need a loan to buy a house, apartment, or condominium. A **mortgage loan** is secured by the property—the home—being purchased. Because the size of a loan depends on the cost of the property, both borrowers and lenders want to know whether the buyer can afford the house he or she wants. To determine how much you can afford, one time-tested (though somewhat conservative) rule recommends keeping the price below 2 1/2 times your annual income. If your income is $48,000, look for a house priced below $120,000.

Any such calculation, however, will give you only a rough estimate of what you can afford. You should also consider how much money you have for a down payment and how much you can borrow. Lending institutions want to determine a buyer's borrowing capacity, the borrower's ability to meet the *recurring costs* of buying and owning.

PITI Every month, the homeowner must pay **p**rincipal (pay back some of the borrowed money), along with **i**nterest, **t**axes, and homeowner's **i**nsurance, or PITI, for short. As Figure AIII.8 shows, the size of principal and interest payments depends on (1) the mortgage amount, (2) the length of the mortgage loan, and (3) the interest rate.

In evaluating loan applications, lenders use PITI calculations to estimate the buyer's ability to meet monthly payments. To determine how much someone is likely to lend you, calculate 28 percent of your gross monthly income (that is, before taxes and other deductions). If your PITI costs don't exceed that figure, your loan application probably will receive favorable consideration. With a monthly gross income of $4,000, for example, your PITI costs shouldn't exceed $1,120 (28 percent of $4,000). Additional calculations show a house price of $162,382 is the most this borrower can afford. Figure AIII.9 gives a sample calculation, and you should be able to make step-by-step computations by plugging your own numbers into the worksheet.

Other Debt In evaluating financial capacity, lenders also look at any additional outstanding debt, such as loans and credit-card bills. They will generally accept

Interest Rate (%)	Length of Loan				
	3 Years	5 Years	10 Years	20 Years	30 Years
5.0	$299.71	$188.71	$106.07	$66.00	$53.68
6.0	304.22	193.33	111.02	71.64	59.96
6.5	306.49	195.66	113.55	74.56	63.21
7.0	308.77	198.01	116.11	77.53	66.53
8.0	313.36	202.76	121.33	83.65	73.38
9.0	318.00	207.58	126.68	89.98	80.47
10.0	322.67	212.47	132.16	96.51	87.76
11.0	327.39	217.42	137.76	103.22	95.24
12.0	332.14	222.44	143.48	110.11	102.86

FIGURE AIII.8   Monthly Payments on a $10,000 Loan

ASSUMPTIONS:

30-year mortgage
Closing costs (fees for property, survey, credit report, title search,
      title insurance, attorney, interest advance, loan origination) = $5,000
Funds available for closing costs and down payment = $25,000
Interest rate on mortgage = $6\frac{1}{2}$% per year
Estimated real estate taxes = $200 per month
Estimated homeowner's insurance = $20 month

Example Numbers		Your Numbers
1. Monthly income, gross (before taxes or deductions)........$4,000		_____
2. Apply PITI ratio (0.28 x amount on line 1) to determine borrower's payment capacity:		
0.28 x $4,000 = ...$1,120		_____
3. Determine mortgage payment (principal and interest) by subtracting taxes and insurance from PITI (line 2)..–$ 220		_____
4. Result: Maximum mortgage payment (principal and interest)................................. $900		_____
5. Using Figure AIII.8, find the monthly mortgage payment on a $10,000 loan at $6\frac{1}{2}$% interest for 30 years.. $63.21		_____
6. Since each $10,000 loan requires a $63.21 monthly payment, how many $10,000 loans can the borrower afford with the $900 payment capacity? The answer is determined as follows:		
$900.00/$63.21 =		
14.2382 loans of $10,000 each		_____
7. Result: Maximum allowable mortgage loan [calculated as follows]:		
14.2382 loans (from line 6 above)		
x $10,000 per loan = ...**$142,382**		_____
8. Result: Maximum house price borrower can afford using PITI (amount of house that can be bought with available funds):		
From loan...........................$142,382		_____
From down payment............$ 25,000		_____
Less closing cost.................–$ 5,000		_____
...............**$162,382**		_____

FIGURE AIII.9 Worksheet for PITI Calculations

indebtedness (including PITI) up to 36 percent of gross income. Because PITI itself can be up to 28 percent, you might be allowed as little as 8 percent in other long-term debt. With your $4,000 monthly gross income, your total debt should be less than $1,440 ($1,120 for PITI and $320 for other debt). If your total debt exceeds $1,440, you may have to settle for a smaller loan than the one you calculated with the PITI method.

Finally, lenders will also take into account the "quality" of the debt. For instance, suppose you have purchased a car that seems appropriate for your income level and you have a monthly payment of $300 for another 3 years on your car loan. A mortgage lender might not weight that as negatively as multiple high-interest credit card accounts with the same combined monthly payments. Why? The car loan would generally be considered a reasonable financial decision whereas the credit card debt would reflect poor financial decisions. Websites such as http://mortgages.interest .com provide mortgage calculators for testing interest rates, lengths of loans, and other personal financial information.

Cashing Out from Tax Avoidance (Legally)

Personal expenditures always require cash outflows. Some also reduce your tax bill and save you some cash. Individual retirement accounts (IRAs) and some education savings accounts have this effect. (Before you commit any money to these instruments or activities, check with an expert on tax regulations. They change from time to time.)

The IRA Tax Break

Traditional Individual Retirement Account (IRA) *provision allowing individual tax-deferred retirement savings*

With a **traditional individual retirement account (IRA),** you can make an annual tax-deductible savings deposit of up to $5,500, depending on your income level. IRAs are long-term investments, intended to provide income after age 59 1/2. For distant future savings, an IRA boasts immediate cash advantages over a typical savings account because it reduces your current taxable income by the amount of your contribution.

Here's how it works: Assume that you're a qualified employee with a federal income tax rate of 20 percent in year 2018. If you contribute $4,000 to an IRA, you avoid $800 in income taxes (0.20 × $4,000 = $800). Your untaxed contributions and their accumulated earnings will only be taxed later when you withdraw money from your IRA. The tax break is based on the assumption that, after you retire, you're likely to have less total income than you do now and will have to pay less tax on the money withdrawn as income from your IRA.

IRA Risks If you underestimate your future cash requirements and have to withdraw money before you reach 59 1/2, however, you'll probably get hit with a 10-percent penalty. You can, however, make penalty-free withdrawals under certain circumstances—buying a first home, paying college expenses, and paying large medical bills.

The unpredictability of future income tax rates also poses a financial risk. If tax rates increase substantially, future IRA withdrawals could actually be taxed at higher rates, which may offset your original tax savings.

Roth IRA *provision allowing individual retirement savings with tax-free accumulated earnings*

Roth IRA versus Traditional IRA The **Roth IRA** is the reverse of the traditional IRA in that contributions are not tax deductible (you pay taxes on the money before it is placed into the account), withdrawals on initial contribution are not penalized, and withdrawals on accumulated earnings after the age of 59 1/2 are not taxed.

Figure AIII.10 shows the significant advantage of this last feature. Accumulated earnings typically far outweigh the initial contribution, so although you pay an extra $1,285 in front-end taxes, you get $40,732 in additional cash at retirement—and even more if income-tax rates have increased.

IRAs and Education Depending on your income level, you can contribute up to $2,000 annually to a Coverdell Education Savings Account (also known as an *Education IRA*) for each child under age 18. As with the Roth IRA, your initial contribution is not tax deductible, your earnings are tax-free, and you pay no tax on withdrawals to pay for qualified education expenses. However, the Education IRA requires that you use the money by the time your child reaches age 30. Funds that you withdraw but don't use for stipulated education expense are subject to taxation plus a 10-percent penalty.

Protecting Your Net Worth

With careful attention, thoughtful saving and spending, and skillful financial planning (and a little luck), you can build up your net worth over time. Every financial plan should also consider steps for preserving it. One approach involves

Assumptions: Initial contribution and earnings average 10 percent growth annually. Initial contribution and earnings remain invested for 40 years. Income tax rate is 30 percent.		Traditional IRA	Roth IRA
Initial cash contribution to IRA		$3,000	$3,000
Income tax paid initially: $4,285 income x 30% tax rate = $1,285 tax		0	1,285
Total initial cash outlay		**$3,000**	**$4,285**
Accumulated earnings (40 years)		$132,774	$132,774
Initial contribution		+ 3,000	+ 3,000
Total available for distribution after 40 years		= $135,774	= $135,774
Income tax at time of distribution		− $40,732	0
After-tax distribution (cash)		**= $95,042**	**= $135,774**

FIGURE AIII.10 Cash Flows: Roth IRA versus Traditional IRA

the risk–return relationship discussed in Chapter 17. Do you prefer to protect your current assets, or are you willing to risk them in return for greater financial growth? At various life stages and levels of wealth, you should adjust your asset portfolio to conform to your risk and return preferences: conservative, moderate, or aggressive.

Why Buy Life Insurance?

You can think of life insurance as a tool for financial preservation. As explained in Appendix 1, a life insurance policy is a promise to pay beneficiaries after the death of the insured party who paid the insurance company premiums during his or her lifetime.

What Does Life Insurance Do?

Upon the death of the policyholder, life insurance replaces income on which someone else is dependent. The amount of insurance you need depends on how many other people rely on your income. For example, while insurance makes sense for a married parent who is a family's sole source of income, a single college student with no financial dependents needs little or no insurance.

How Much Should I Buy?

The more insurance you buy, the more it's going to cost you. To estimate the amount of coverage you need, begin by adding up all your annual expenses—rent, food, clothing, transportation, schooling, debts to be paid—that you pay for the dependents who'd survive you. Then multiply the total by the number of years that you want the insurance to cover them. Typically, this sum will amount to several times—even 10 to 20 times—your current annual income.

Why Consider Term Insurance?

Term insurance pays a predetermined benefit when death occurs during the stipulated policy term. If the insured outlives the term, the policy loses its value and simply ceases. Term-life premiums are significantly lower than premiums for whole-life insurance.

Unlike term life, *whole-life insurance*, also known as *cash-value insurance*, remains in force as long as premiums are paid. In addition to paying a death benefit, whole life accumulates cash value over time—a form of savings. Paid-in money can be withdrawn; however, whole-life savings earn less interest than most alternative forms of investment.

How Much Does It Cost?

The cost of insurance depends on how much you buy, your life expectancy, and other statistical risk factors. To get the best match between your policy and your personal situation, you should evaluate the terms and conditions of a variety of policies. You can get convenient comparisons on websites such as www.intelliquote .com.

appendix IV

Unions and Labor Management

This appendix is an expansion of material covered in the last section of Chapter 10. After reading it, you should better understand how and why workers organize into labor unions, how unions and businesses relate to each other, and how the collective bargaining process works.

Why Do Workers Unionize?

A **labor union** is a group of individuals working together to achieve shared job-related goals, such as higher pay, shorter working hours, more job security, greater benefits, or better working conditions.[1] **Labor relations** is the process of dealing with employees who are represented by a union.

Labor unions grew in popularity in the United States in the nineteenth and early twentieth centuries. The labor movement was born with the Industrial Revolution, which also gave birth to a factory-based production system that carried with it enormous economic benefits. Job specialization and mass production allowed businesses to create ever-greater quantities of goods at ever-lower costs.

But there was also a dark side to this era. Workers became more dependent on their factory jobs. Eager for greater profits, some owners treated their workers like other raw materials, as resources to be deployed with little or no regard for the individual worker's well-being. Many businesses forced employees to work long hours—60-hour weeks were common, and some workers were routinely forced to work 12 to 16 hours a day. With no minimum-wage laws or other controls, pay was also minimal and safety standards virtually nonexistent. Workers had no job security and received few (if any) benefits. Many companies, especially textile mills, employed large numbers of children at poverty wages. If people complained, nothing prevented employers from firing and replacing them at will.

Unions appeared and ultimately prospered because they constituted a solution to the worker's most serious problem. By uniting the workers, unions forced management to listen to the complaints of all their workers rather than to just the few who were brave (or foolish) enough to speak out. The power of unions, then, comes from collective action. **Collective bargaining** is the process by which union leaders and managers negotiate common terms and conditions of employment for the workers represented by unions. Although collective bargaining does not often occur in small businesses, many midsize and larger businesses must engage in the process.

Labor Union *a group of individuals working together to achieve shared job-related goals, such as higher pay, shorter working hours, more job security, greater benefits, or better working conditions*

Labor Relations *the process of dealing with employees who are represented by a union*

Collective Bargaining *the process by which union leaders and managers negotiate common terms and conditions of employment for the workers represented by unions*

The Evolution of Unionism in the United States

As we discuss the growth—and the more recent decline—of unionism in this section, it is important to remember that the influence of labor unions goes far beyond their membership. For example, many nonunion members have benefited from the improved working conditions won by unions. Union gains often set standards for entire industries, and some organizations make workplace improvements just to discourage their employees from unionizing.

Early Unions

Labor unions grew up with the United States. The earliest formal organizations of U.S. workers appeared during the Revolutionary War. These early organizations were craft unions; each limited itself to representing workers whose common interest was a specific skilled job, and each sought to promote the economic welfare of the skilled craftspeople who made up its membership.

For example, the Federal Society of Journeymen Cordwainers, formed in Philadelphia in 1794, worked to better the pay and working conditions of shoemakers. The Cordwainers was also one of the first unions to encounter legal roadblocks to collective action. When the union struck for higher wages in 1806, the court ruled in favor of employers, who claimed that unions were illegal "combinations" conspiring to restrain trade. The court's ruling applied the *common law conspiracy doctrine*, the principle that the public interest was harmed when two or more people conspired to do something jointly. Unions continued to organize, but for the next four decades, they found it extremely difficult to take action in the face of the conspiracy doctrine.

A milestone in the history of U.S. labor occurred with the formation of the Knights of Labor in 1869. Like previous unions, the Knights began as a craft union. Soon, however, the organization set larger goals for itself. In a drive to organize any workers who were interested in its representation, the Knights expanded to encompass workers in numerous fields (noteworthy exceptions were lawyers, bankers, and bartenders). The Knights was also the first union that actively sought women and blacks as members and was one of the few unions that has ever focused on political lobbying rather than collective bargaining as a means of reaching its goals.

The Knights championed such traditional union issues as better working conditions, campaigning especially for the eight-hour day and the abolition of child labor. At the same time, the union also hoped to achieve a broad range of social goals. Chief among these were such liberal, or reformist, objectives as worker ownership of factories and free public land for those who wished to farm.

These same goals also attracted to the labor movement a variety of radicals and other political reformers, many of whom came in the waves of European immigrants who had begun arriving a few decades previously. Their activities were directed against what they saw as the oppressive nature of the industrial capitalist system, and their tactics did not necessarily reflect the typical strategies of the labor unions. Spurred by a severe depression in 1873, for example, a series of violent labor actions characterized labor-management relations from the mid- to late 1870s. Demonstrators and locked-out strikers blockaded factories, battled strikebreakers in the streets of major cities, and exchanged fire with municipal police, state militia, and armed private agents. Assassinations and bombings led to the trial and execution of anarchists and labor agitators.

However, much of the violence in this period came in direct response to the extraordinary pressures of the depression. Most U.S. laborers were conservative by nature and sought the stability of organizations such as the Knights of Labor. Under the leadership of Terence V. Powderly, the Knights grew to include roughly 700,000 members by the mid-1880s. The union was never successful, however, at increasing the number of skilled workers among its members. In addition, it was weakened by internal disagreements about social goals and outside charges of union violence. By the turn of the century, the Knights had disbanded.

The Emergence of the Major Unions

With its focus on the social welfare of unskilled workers, the Knights of Labor tended to forget that its economic strength lay with its skilled craft workers. As a result of this oversight, many of these workers soon began to look for organizations that would better represent their interests, namely, unions whose primary concern was to improve wages, hours, and working conditions for their members.

The American Federation of Labor Many workers disenchanted with the social agenda of the Knights of Labor found a home in the **American Federation of Labor (AFL).** Made up of craft unions, the AFL was formed in 1886 by Samuel Gompers and other veteran organizers. Unlike the Knights of Labor, the AFL stressed no broad, idealistic legislative or political program. Gompers himself saw the labor union as an integral component, not the inherent enemy, of the capitalist system: "As we get a 25-cents-a-day wage increase," he argued, the process "brings us nearer the time when a greater degree of social justice and fair dealing will obtain among men." The enduring importance of the AFL lies in the fact that it established a solid organizational basis for collective bargaining, economic action, and a pragmatic approach to union-management relations.

> **American Federation of Labor (AFL)** *an association of craft unions formed in 1886 by Samuel Gompers and others; the AFL had no political or social agenda but simply sought to improve working conditions and pay for its members*

The AFL grew rapidly in the early decades of the twentieth century, and by the end of World War I, membership had reached more than 5 million. The 1920s proved difficult for the AFL because increased employer resistance to unions contributed to a steady decline in membership. By 1929, membership had dropped to 3.4 million.

The Great Depression of the 1930s witnessed further membership decline. By 1933, membership stood at just 2.9 million. In the same year, however, newly elected President Franklin D. Roosevelt introduced the nation to the New Deal, a far-reaching program aimed at stimulating the U.S. economy and creating jobs. The New Deal inspired an era of recovery for organized labor. Moreover, as we will see later in this appendix, the New Deal Congress passed a series of laws that made it easier for workers to organize.

The Congress of Industrial Organizations By the mid-1930s, the advent of mass production had significantly increased the demand for semi-skilled workers in the automobile, steel, and mining industries. The AFL, while continuing to grow throughout the 1930s, remained open only to skilled crafts-people. In fact, most AFL leaders opposed **industrial unionism,** the organizing of employees by industry rather than by skill or occupation. When a 1935 convention of AFL unions confirmed this stance, dissident leaders, including John F. Lewis of the United Mine Workers, objected bitterly. Ultimately, the AFL expelled 32 national unions, which in 1938 banded together to form the **Congress of Industrial Organizations (CIO).**

> **Industrial Unionism** *the organizing of employees by industry rather than by skill or occupation*
>
> **Congress of Industrial Organizations (CIO)** *an association of industrial unions formed in 1938 after being expelled from the American Federation of Labor (AFL)*

Soon, the CIO had organized the auto, steel, mining, meatpacking, paper, textile, and electrical industries. By the early 1940s, CIO unions claimed close to 5 million of the slightly more than 10 million unionized U.S. workers. Not surprisingly, the AFL soon abandoned rigid craft unionism and also began to charter industrial unions.

The AFL-CIO Union membership continued to increase during World War II, reaching more than 14 million by the end of the war. However, a series of postwar strikes led Congress to curtail the power of unions. Partly in response to this change, and partly in response to growing conflicts within their ranks, leaders of the AFL and the CIO began merger negotiations. These meetings culminated in the 1955 formation of the AFL-CIO, with a total membership of 15 million. At the same time, organized labor reached its membership zenith, claiming almost 35 percent of the nonfarm workforce.

Today, in addition to lobbying for pro-union issues, the AFL-CIO settles juris-dictional disputes between unions. Remember, however, that the AFL-CIO is not a union itself. Rather, it is a federation of 86 individual unions with about 13 million individual members who belong to various trade or industrial departments (such as building trades, maritime trades, and public employees). The United Food and Commercial Workers is a union, as are the International Brotherhood of Teamsters and the National Education Association.

Unionism Today

While understanding the historical context of labor unions is important, so, too, is appreciating the role of unionism today, especially trends in union membership, union-management relations, and bargaining perspectives. We discuss these topics in the sections that follow.

Trends in Union Membership

Since the mid-1950s, U.S. labor unions have experienced increasing difficulties in attracting new members. Although millions of workers still belong to labor unions, union membership *as a percentage of the total workforce* has continued to decline at a steady rate. In 1977, for example, more than 26 percent of U.S. wage and salary employees belonged to labor unions. Today, that figure is about 14 percent. Moreover, if public employees are excluded from consideration, then only around 11 percent of all private industry wage and salary employees currently belong to labor unions.

Furthermore, just as union membership has continued to decline, so has the percentage of successful union-organizing campaigns. In the years immediately following World War II and continuing through the mid-1960s, most unions routinely won certification elections. In recent years, however, labor unions have been winning certification fewer than 50 percent of the time when workers are called on to vote. By the same token, of course, unions still do win. Meat cutters at a Florida Walmart store recently voted to unionize, the first-ever successful organizing campaign against the retailing giant. "You'll see a lot more attention to Walmart now," exulted one AFL-CIO official. "It's not like Walmart stands out as some unattainable goal."[2]

From most indications, then, the power and significance of U.S. labor unions, although still quite formidable, are also measurably lower than they were just a few decades ago. A number of factors help to explain the decline in union membership.

Composition of the Workforce Union membership was once comprised predominantly of white males in blue-collar jobs. But as most of us know, today's workforce is increasingly composed of women and ethnic minorities. Because these groups have much weaker traditions of union affiliation, their members are less likely to join unions when they enter the workforce. In a related trend, much of the workforce has shifted toward geographic areas in the South and toward occupations in the service sector that have traditionally been less heavily unionized. For instance, Nucor Steel locates its facilities in smaller communities in the southern United States in part because it knows these workers are not prone to unionization.

Anti-Unionization Activities A second reason is more aggressive anti-unionization activity on the part of employers. Although the National Labor Relations Act and other laws specify strict management practices with regard to labor unions, companies are still free to pursue certain strategies that by their very nature tend to minimize employee interest in unionization. Both PepsiCo and Procter & Gamble, for example, now offer no-layoff guarantees for most of their employees, provide competitive wage and benefit packages, and maintain formal grievance systems for all workers. These arrangements were once available only through unions. But because these and other firms offer them independently of any union contract, employees have fewer reasons for unionizing.

Some companies have also worked to create much more employee-friendly work environments and to purposefully treat all employees with respect and dignity. One goal of this approach is to minimize the attractiveness of labor unions for employees. Many Japanese and German automobile manufacturers who have set up shop in the United States have successfully avoided unionization efforts by the United Auto Workers (UAW) by providing job security, higher wages, and a work environment in which employees are allowed to participate and be actively involved in plant management.

Trends in Union-Management Relations

The gradual decline in unionization in the United States has been accompanied by some significant trends in union-management relations. In some sectors of the economy, perhaps most notably the automobile, steel, and shipping industries, labor unions still remain quite strong. In these areas, unions have large memberships and considerable power in negotiating with management. The UAW, for example, is still one of the strongest unions in the United States.

In most sectors, however, unions are clearly in a weakened position, and as a result, many have taken much more conciliatory stances in their relations with management. This situation contrasts sharply with the more adversarial relationship that once dominated labor relations in this country. Increasingly, for instance, unions recognize that they don't have as much power as they once held and that it is in their own best interests, as well as in those of the workers that they represent, to work with management instead of working against it. Ironically, then, union-management relations are in many ways better today than they have been in many years. Admittedly, the improvement is attributable in large part to the weakened power of unions. Even so, however, most experts agree that improved union-management relations have benefited both sides.

Trends in Bargaining Perspectives

Given the trends described in the two previous sections (declining membership and shifts in union-management relationships), we should not be surprised to find changes in bargaining perspectives as well. In the past, most union-management bargaining situations were characterized by union demands for dramatic increases in wages and salaries. A secondary issue was usually increased benefits for members. Now, however, unions often bargain for different benefits, such as job security. Of particular interest in this area is the trend toward relocating jobs to take advantage of lower labor costs in other countries. Unions, of course, want to restrict job movement, whereas companies want to save money by moving facilities—and jobs—to other countries.

As a result of organizational downsizing and several years of relatively low inflation in this country, many unions today find themselves, rather than striving for wage increases, fighting against wage cuts. Similarly, as organizations are more likely to seek lower health care and other benefits, a common goal of union strategy is preserving what's already been won. Unions also place greater emphasis on improved job security. A trend that has become especially important in recent years is toward improved pension programs for employees.

Unions have also begun increasingly to set their sights on preserving jobs for workers in the United States in the face of business efforts to relocate production in some sectors to countries where labor costs are lower. For example, the AFL-CIO has been an outspoken opponent of efforts to normalize trade relations with China, fearing that more businesses might be tempted to move jobs there. General Electric has been targeted for union protests recently because of its strategy to move many of its own jobs—and those of key suppliers—to Mexico.

The Future of Unions

Despite declining membership and some loss of power, labor unions remain a major factor in the U.S. business world. The 86 labor organizations in the AFL-CIO, as well as independent major unions (such as the Teamsters and the National Education Association), still play a major role in U.S. business. Moreover, some unions still wield considerable power, especially in the traditional strongholds of goods-producing industries. Labor and management in some industries, notably airlines and steel, are beginning to favor contracts that establish formal mechanisms for greater worker input into management decisions. Inland Steel, for instance, recently granted its major union the right to name a member to the board of directors. Union officers can also attend executive meetings.

The big question still remains: will unions dwindle in power and perhaps disappear, or can they evolve, survive to face new challenges, and play a new role in U.S. business? They will probably evolve to take on new roles and responsibilities. More and more unions are asking for—and often getting—voices in management. In 1980, for example, as a part of a governemtn-backed and union-supported Chrysler bailout, UAW president Douglas Fraser became the first labor official appointed to the board of directors of a major corporation. Several other companies have since followed suit.

By the same token, unions are increasingly aware that they must cooperate with employers if both are to survive. Critics of unions contend that excessive wage rates won through years of strikes and hard-nosed negotiation are partly to blame for the demise of large employers such as Eastern Airlines. Others argue that excessively tight work rules limit the productivity of businesses in many industries. More often, however, unions are working with organizations to create effective partnerships in which managers and workers share the same goals: profitability, growth, and effectiveness with equitable rewards for everyone.

Contemporary Union Structure

Just as each organization has its own unique structure, each union creates a structure that best serves its own needs. As Figure AIV.1 shows, a general structure characterizes most national and international unions. A major function of unions is to provide service and support to both members and local affiliates. Most of these services are carried out by the types of specialized departments shown in Figure AIV.1. In other unions, departments serve specific employment groups. The Machinists' Union—the International Association of Machinists and Aerospace Workers—has departments for automotive, railroad, and airline workers.

Locals

Local Unions (Locals) *organized at the level of a single company, plant, or small geographic region*

At the same time, most national unions are composed of **local unions (locals),** which are organized at the level of a single company, plant, or small defined geographic region. The functions of these locals vary, depending not only on

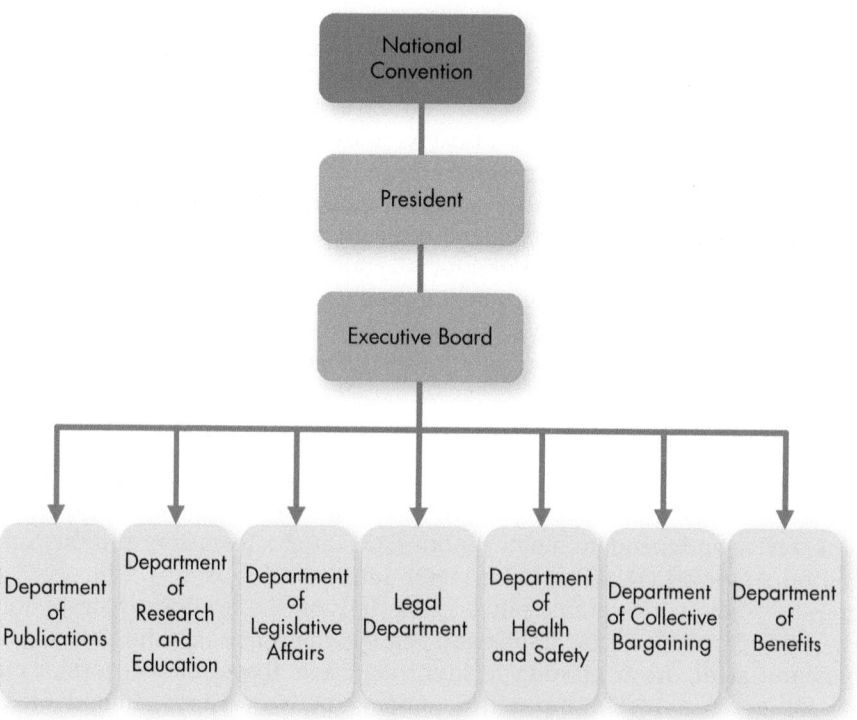

FIGURE AIV.1 Organization of a Large National Union

governance arrangements but also on bargaining patterns in particular industries. Some local unions bargain directly with management regarding wages, hours, and other terms of employment. Many local unions are also active in disciplining members for violations of contract standards and in pressing management to respond to worker complaints. Local unions also serve as grassroots bases for union political activities, registering voters and getting them out to vote on election day.

Each department or unit represented at the local level elects a **shop steward,** a regular employee who acts as a liaison between union members and supervisors. For example, if workers have a grievance, they take it to the steward, who tries to resolve the problem with the supervisor. If the local is large, the union might hire a full-time **business agent** (or business representative) to play the same role.

Within a given union, the main governing bodies are the national union (or international union when members come from more than one country) and its officers. Among their other duties, national and international unions charter local affiliates and establish general standards of conduct and procedures for local operations. For example, they set dues assessments, arrange for the election of local officers, sanction strikes, and provide guidance in the collective bargaining process. Many national unions also engage in a variety of political activities, such as lobbying. They may also help coordinate organizing efforts and establish education programs.

Given the magnitude of their efforts, it is little wonder that unions often take on many of the same characteristics as the companies for which their members work. For example, almost all large unions have full-time administrators, formal organizational structures (see Figure AIV.1), goals and strategic plans, and so forth. James P. Hoffa, current president of the International Brotherhood of Teamsters, earns an annual salary of $309,000 and oversees a large full-time staff.[3] Because of their size, power, and importance, Congress has passed numerous laws to govern union activities. It is to these laws that we now turn our attention.

Shop Steward *a regular employee who acts as a liaison between union members and supervisors*

Business Agent or Business Representative *a full-time employee hired to act as a liaison between union members and supervisors if a local union is large*

Laws Governing Labor-Management Relations

Like almost every other aspect of labor-management relations today, the process of unionizing workers is governed by numerous laws, administrative interpretations, and judicial decisions. In fact, the growth and decline of unionism in the United States can be traced by following the history of labor laws.

For the first 150 years of U.S. independence, workers were judged to have little legal right to organize. Indeed, interpretation of the 1890 Sherman Antitrust Act classified labor unions as monopolies, thus making them illegal. During the first 30 years of the twentieth century, however, social activism and turmoil in the labor force changed the landscape of U.S. labor relations.

The Major Labor Laws

Five major federal laws, all enacted between 1932 and 1959, laid the groundwork for all the rules, regulations, and judicial decisions governing union activity in the United States. A number of more recent laws have dealt with specific groups and specific issues. In general, these laws have been passed with a goal of maintaining a reasonable balance of power between business and labor such that neither side gains an unreasonable advantage over the other.

Norris-LaGuardia Act During the 1930s, labor leaders finally persuaded lawmakers that the legal environment discriminated against the collective efforts of workers to improve working conditions. Legislators responded with the **Norris-LaGuardia Act** in 1932. This act imposed severe limitations on the ability of the courts to issue injunctions prohibiting certain union activities, including strikes.

Norris-LaGuardia Act *act that imposed severe limitations on the ability of the courts to issue injunctions prohibiting certain union activities, including strikes*

Yellow-Dog Contracts *requirements that workers state that they did not belong to and would not join a union*

Norris-LaGuardia also outlawed **yellow-dog contracts,** requirements that workers state that they did not belong to and would not join a union.

National Labor Relations (Wagner) Act In 1935 Congress passed the **National Labor Relations Act** (also called the Wagner Act), which is the cornerstone of contemporary labor relations law. This act put labor unions on a more equal footing with management in terms of the rights of employees to organize and bargain:

National Labor Relations Act or Wagner Act *act that put labor unions on a more equal footing with management in terms of the rights of employees to organize and bargain*

- It gave most workers the right to form unions, bargain collectively, and engage in group activities (such as strikes) to reach their goals.

- It forced employers to bargain with duly elected union leaders and prohibited employer practices that unjustly restrict employees' rights (e.g., discriminating against union members in hiring, promoting, and firing).

National Labor Relations Board (NLRB) *established by the Wagner Act to administer its provisions*

The Wagner Act also established the **National Labor Relations Board (NLRB)** to administer its provisions. Today, the NLRB administers virtually all labor law in this country. For example, it determines the appropriate unit for conducting bargaining at any workplace. The NLRB also oversees most of the elections held by employees to determine whether they will be represented by particular unions. It decides who is eligible to vote and who will be covered by bargaining agreements once they have been reached.

Fair Labor Standards Act *addressed issues of minimum wages and maximum work hours*

Fair Labor Standards Act Enacted in 1938, the **Fair Labor Standards Act** addressed issues of minimum wages and maximum work hours:

- It set a minimum wage (originally $.25 an hour) to be paid to workers. The federal minimum wage has been increased many times since 1938 and now stands at $7.25 per hour (several states have higher minimum wages).

- It set a maximum number of hours for the workweek, initially 44 hours per week, later 40 hours.

- It mandated time-and-a-half pay for those who worked beyond the legally stipulated number of hours.

- It outlawed child labor.

Taft-Hartley Act Supported by the Norris-LaGuardia, Wagner, and Fair Labor Standards Acts, organized labor eventually grew into a powerful political and economic force. But a series of disruptive strikes in the immediate post–World War II years turned public opinion against unions. Inconvenienced by strikes and the resulting shortages of goods and services, the public became openly critical of unions and pressured the government to take action. Congress responded by passing the Labor-Management Relations Act (more commonly known as the Taft-Hartley Act) in 1947.

UNFAIR AND ILLEGAL UNION PRACTICES The Taft-Hartley Act defined certain union practices as unfair and illegal. For example, it prohibited such practices as featherbedding (requiring extra workers solely to provide more jobs) and refusing to bargain in good faith. It also generally forbade the **closed shop,** a workplace in which only workers already belonging to a union may be hired by an employer. Instead, Taft-Hartley promoted open shops by allowing states to enact **right-to-work laws.** Such laws prohibit both union shops and agency shops, thus making it illegal to require union membership as a condition of employment. A **union shop** requires employees to join a union within a specified period after being hired. An **agency shop** requires employees to pay union fees even if they choose not to join. To date, 28 states have enacted right-to-work laws (West Virginia has also passed Right-to-Work legislation but it is currently being appealed in court). These states are shown in Figure AIV.2.

Closed Shop *a workplace in which only workers already belonging to a union may be hired by an employer*

Right-to-Work Laws *such laws prohibit both union shops and agency shops, thus making it illegal to require union membership as a condition of employment*

Union Shop *requires employees to join a union within a specified period after being hired*

Agency Shop *requires employees to pay union fees even if they choose not to join*

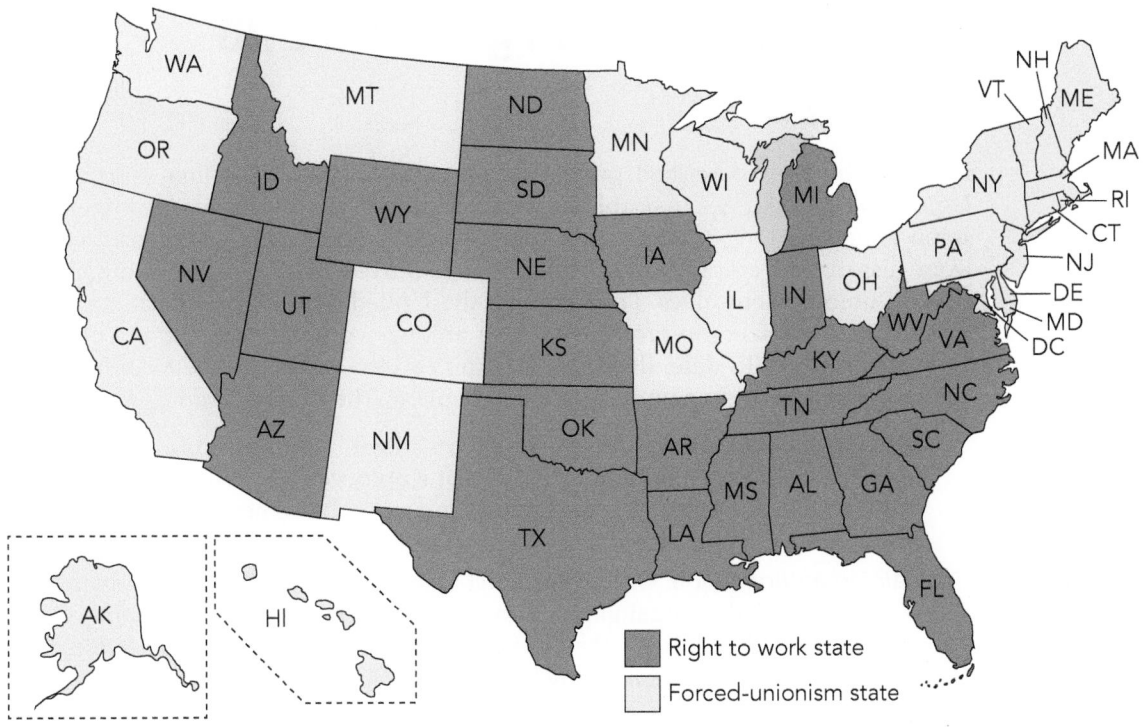

FIGURE AIV.2 Right-to-Work States

Legend:
- Right to work state
- Forced-unionism state

INJUNCTIONS AND COOLING-OFF PERIODS Passed in the wake of crippling strikes in the steel industry, the Taft-Hartley act also established procedures for resolving any strike deemed to pose a national emergency. Initially, the concept of national emergency was broadly interpreted. For example, virtually any large company could claim that a strike was doing irreparable harm to its financial base and that the nation's economy would be harmed if workers were not forced back to their jobs.

Today, however, the courts use a more precise definition of national emergency. For example, a strike must affect a whole industry or most of it. Similarly, the use of Taft-Hartley is more restrictive. Now the president may request an injunction requiring that workers restrain from striking for 60 days. During this cooling-off period, labor and management must try to resolve their differences.

ENFORCED RESOLUTION If differences are not resolved during the cooling-off period, the injunction may be extended for another 20 days. During this period, employees must vote, in a secret ballot election, on whether to accept or reject the employer's latest offer. If they accept the offer, the threat of strike is ended and the contract signed. If they do not accept the offer, the president reports to Congress and the workers may either be forced back to work under threat of criminal action or fired and replaced by nonunion employees. Presidential intervention has been invoked only 35 times since Taft-Hartley was passed.

Landrum-Griffin Act The National Labor Relations Act was further amended by the **Landrum-Griffin Act** in 1959. Officially titled the **Labor-Management Reporting and Disclosure Act**, this law resulted from congressional hearings that revealed unethical, illegal, and undemocratic union practices. The act thus imposed regulations on internal union procedures:

Landrum-Griffin Act or Labor-Management Reporting and Disclosure Act *amendment to the National Labor Relations Act that imposed regulations on internal union procedures*

- It required the election of national union leaders at least once every five years.

- It gave union members the right to participate in various union affairs.

- It required unions to file annual financial disclosure statements with the Department of Labor.

How Unions Are Organized and Certified

Many of the laws described previously address the issue of union certification. Figure AIV.3 illustrates a simplified version of this process. First, there must be some interest among workers in having a union. Sometimes this interest comes from dissatisfied employees; sometimes it is stirred by professional organizers sent by unions themselves. For example, the United Auto Workers has for years dispatched organizers to promote interest among workers at the Honda plant in Marysville, Ohio. To date, they have had no success in Marysville or in Smyrna, Tennessee, where Nissan built its major U.S. plant. The process unfolds as follows:

1 *Defining the bargaining unit.* Interested organizers start by asking the NLRB to define the **bargaining unit**, the group of employees who will be represented by the union. For instance, a bargaining unit might be all nonmanagement employees in an organization or all electrical workers at a certain plant.

2 *Gaining authorization.* Organizers must then get 30 percent of the eligible workers within the bargaining unit to sign authorization cards requesting a certification election. If less than 30 percent of the workers want an election, the process ends and no election is held.

3 *Conducting an election.* If the required number of signatures is obtained, however, the organizers petition the NLRB to conduct the election. The NLRB then holds a secret ballot election. If a simple majority of those voting approves the certification, the union becomes the official bargaining agent of eligible employees. If a majority fails to approve certification, the process ends and an election cannot be called again for at least one year.

Unions are not necessarily permanent fixtures in a workplace, and if conditions warrant, a union may be *decertified*. For example, workers may become disenchanted with a union and may even feel that they are being hurt by its presence. They may believe that management is trying to be cooperative while the union is refusing to negotiate in good faith.

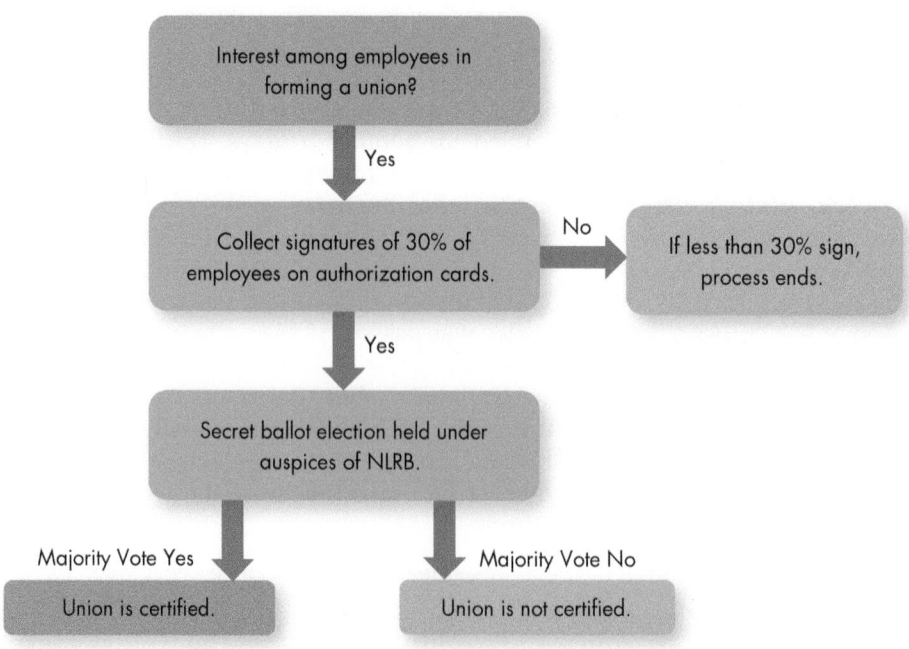

FIGURE AIV.3 Certifying a Labor Union

Decertification requires two conditions:

1 The union must have served the unit as its official bargaining agent for at least one year.

2 There must be no labor contract currently in effect.

If these conditions are met, employees or their representatives can solicit signatures on decertification cards. If 30 percent of the employees in the unit sign, the NLRB conducts a decertification election. If a majority of those voting favor decertification, the union is removed as the unit's official bargaining agent. Following decertification, a new election cannot be requested for at least one year.

Collective Bargaining

When a union has been legally certified, it assumes the role of official bargaining agent for the workers whom it represents. Collective bargaining is an ongoing process involving both the drafting and the administering of the terms of a labor contract.

Reaching Agreement on Contract Terms

The collective bargaining process begins when the union is recognized as the exclusive negotiator for its members. The bargaining cycle itself begins when union leaders meet with management representatives to agree on a contract. By law, both parties must sit down at the bargaining table and negotiate in good faith.

When each side has presented its demands, sessions focus on identifying the *bargaining zone*. The process is shown in Figure AIV.4. For example, although an employer may initially offer no pay raise, it may expect to grant a raise of up to 6 percent. Likewise, the union may initially *demand* a 10-percent pay raise while *expecting* to accept a raise as low as 4 percent. The bargaining zone, then, is a raise between 4 and 6 percent. Ideally, some compromise is reached between these levels and the new agreement submitted for a ratification vote by union membership.

Sometimes, this process goes quite smoothly. At other times, however, the two sides cannot—or will not—agree. The speed and ease with which such an impasse is resolved depend in part on the nature of the contract issues, the willingness of each side to use certain tactics, and the prospects for mediation or arbitration.

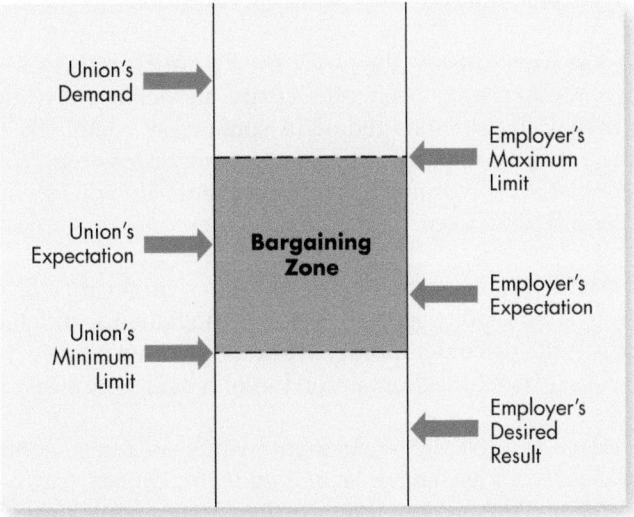

FIGURE AIV.4 The Bargaining Zone

Contract Issues

The labor contract itself can address an array of different issues. Most of these concern demands that unions make on behalf of their members. In this section, we will survey the categories of issues that are typically most important to union negotiators: *compensation*, *benefits*, and *job security*. Although few issues covered in a labor contract are company sponsored, we will also describe the kinds of *management rights* that are negotiated in most bargaining agreements.

First, note that bargaining items generally fall into two categories:

- *Mandatory items* are matters over which both parties must negotiate if either wants to. This category includes wages, working hours, and benefits.

- *Permissive items* may be negotiated if both parties agree. A union demand for veto power over the promotion of managerial personnel would be a permissive bargaining item.

Illegal items may not be brought to the table by either party. A management demand for a nonstrike clause, for example, would be an illegal item.

Compensation The most common issue is compensation. One aspect of compensation is current wages. Obviously, unions generally want their employees to earn higher wages and try to convince management to raise hourly wages for all or some employees.

Of equal concern to unions is future compensation, wage rates to be paid during subsequent years of the contract. One common tool for securing wage increases is a **cost-of-living adjustment (COLA).** Most COLA clauses tie future raises to the *consumer price index*, a government statistic that reflects changes in consumer purchasing power. The premise is that as the CPI increases by a specified amount during a given period of time, wages will automatically be increased. Almost half of all labor contracts today include COLA clauses.

Wage reopener clauses are now included in almost 10 percent of all labor contracts. Such a clause allows wage rates to be negotiated at preset times during the life of the contract. For example, a union might be uncomfortable with a long-term contract based solely on COLA wage increases. A long-term agreement might be more acceptable, however, if management agrees to renegotiate wages every two years.

Benefits Employee benefits are also an important component in most labor contracts. Unions typically want employers to pay all or most of the costs of insurance for employees. Other benefits commonly addressed during negotiations include retirement benefits, paid holidays, and working conditions.

Job Security Nevertheless, the UAW's top priority in its most recent negotiations with U.S. automakers has been job security, an increasingly important agenda item in many bargaining sessions today. In some cases, demands for job security entail the promise that a company not move to another location. In others, the contract may dictate that if the workforce is reduced, seniority will be used to determine which employees lose their jobs.

Other Union Issues Other possible issues might include such things as working hours, overtime policies, rest period arrangements, differential pay plans for shift employees, the use of temporary workers, grievance procedures, and allowable union activities (dues collection, union bulletin boards, and so forth).

Management Rights Management wants as much control as possible over hiring policies, work assignments, and so forth. Unions, meanwhile, often try to limit management rights by specifying hiring, assignment, and other policies. At a Chrysler plant in Detroit, for example, one recent contract stipulated that three

Cost-of-Living Adjustment (COLA) *labor contract clause tying future raises to changes in consumer purchasing power*

Wage Reopener Clauses *allow wage rates to be negotiated at preset times during the life of the contract*

workers were needed to change fuses in robotic equipment, a machinist to open the robotic fuse panel, an electrician to actually change the fuse, and a supervisor to oversee the process. As in this case, contracts often bar workers in one job category from performing work that falls in the domain of another. Unions try to secure jobs by defining as many different categories as possible (the Chrysler plant had more than 100). Of course, management resists the practice, which limits flexibility and makes it difficult to reassign workers.

When Bargaining Fails

An impasse occurs when, after a series of bargaining sessions, management and labor have failed to agree on a new contract or a contract to replace an agreement that is about to expire. Although it is generally agreed that both parties suffer when an impasse is reached and action is taken, each side can use several tactics to support its cause until the impasse is resolved.

Union Tactics When their demands are not met, unions may bring a variety of tactics to the bargaining table. Chief among these is the strike, which may be supported by *pickets*, *boycotts*, or both.

THE STRIKE A **strike** occurs when employees temporarily walk off the job and refuse to work. Most strikes in the United States are **economic strikes,** triggered by stalemates over mandatory bargaining items, including such noneconomic issues as working hours. For example, the Teamsters union struck United Parcel Service (UPS) a few years ago over several noneconomic issues. Specifically, the union wanted the firm to transform many of its temporary and part-time jobs into permanent and full-time jobs. Strikers returned to work only when UPS agreed to create 10,000 new jobs. The Teamsters also struck Union Pacific Corp. in 2013. And union members at the Lockheed-Martin plant in Fort Worth, Texas, staged a two-week strike in 2014. Reflected the president of the union local: "I think our people gained a lot of respect for taking a stand. We had a good strike."

Still, there are far fewer strikes today than there were in previous years. For example, there were 222 strikes in the United States in 1960 involving a total of 896,000 workers. In 1970, 2,468,000 workers took part in 381 strikes. But in 1990, there were only 44 strikes involving 185,000 workers. Since 1990, the largest number of major strikes in one year was 45 in 1994. There were only 15 major strikes in 2016.[4] The largest of these occurred when 40,000 Verizon workers walked off their jobs for six weeks until new contract terms were reached.

Not all strikes are legal. Sympathy strikes (also called secondary strikes), which occur when one union strikes in sympathy with action initiated by another, may violate the sympathetic union's contract. Wildcat strikes, strikes unauthorized by the union that occur during the life of a contract, deprive strikers of their status as employees and thus of the protection of the national labor law.

OTHER LABOR ACTIONS To support a strike, a union faced with an impasse has recourse to additional legal activities:

- In **picketing**, workers stand or march at the entrance to the employer's facility with signs explaining their reasons for striking.

- A **boycott** occurs when union members agree not to buy the products of a targeted employer. Workers may also urge consumers to boycott the firm's products.

- Another alternative to striking is a work **slowdown**. Instead of striking, workers perform their jobs but at a much slower pace than normal. A variation is the sickout, during which large numbers of workers call in sick. Pilots at American Airlines engaged in a massive "sickout" a few years ago, causing the airline to cancel thousands of flights before a judge ordered them back to work.[5]

Strike *occurs when employees temporarily walk off the job and refuse to work*

Economic Strikes *strikes triggered by stalemates over mandatory bargaining items, including such noneconomic issues as working hours*

Management Tactics Like workers, management can respond forcefully to an impasse:

Lockouts *occur when employers deny employees access to the workplace*

- **Lockouts** occur when employers deny employees access to the workplace. Lockouts are illegal if they are used as offensive weapons to give management a bargaining advantage. However, they are legal if management has a legitimate business need (for instance, avoiding a buildup of perishable inventory). Although rare today, ABC once locked out its off-camera employees because they staged an unannounced one-day strike during a critical broadcasting period.[6] Likewise, NFL players were locked out during contract negotiations in 2011 and the referees were locked out during contract negotiations in 2012.

Strikebreakers *temporary or permanent replacements*

A firm can also hire temporary or permanent replacements called **strikebreakers.** (The NFL employed temporary referees during the 2012 lockout.) However, the law forbids the permanent replacement of workers who strike because of unfair practices. In some cases, an employer can also obtain legal injunctions that either prohibit workers from striking or prohibit a union from interfering with its efforts to use replacement workers.

Mediation and Arbitration Rather than wield these often unpleasant weapons against one another, labor and management can agree to call in a third party to help resolve the dispute:

Mediation *a neutral third party (the mediator) can advise, but cannot impose a settlement on the other parties*

- In **mediation,** the neutral third party (the mediator) can advise, but cannot impose a settlement on the other parties.

Voluntary Arbitration *a neutral third party (the arbitrator) dictates a settlement between the two sides, who have agreed to submit to outside judgment*

- In **voluntary arbitration,** the neutral third party (the arbitrator) dictates a settlement between the two sides, who have agreed to submit to outside judgment.

Compulsory Arbitration *used to settle disputes between the government and public employees such as firefighters and police officers*

- In some cases, arbitration is legally required to settle bargaining disputes. **Compulsory arbitration** is used to settle disputes between the government and public employees such as firefighters and police officers.

Administering a Labor Agreement

Once a labor agreement has been reached, its details are written into the form of a contract legally enforceable in the courts. Labor contracts almost always have precise agreements as to how the agreement will be enforced. In some cases, of course, enforcement is quite clear. If the two sides agree that the company will increase wages by 2 percent per year over the next three years according to a prescribed schedule, then there is little opportunity for disagreement. Wage increases can be mathematically calculated and union members will see the effects in their paychecks. But other provisions may be much more prone to misinterpretation and different perceptions.

Suppose, for example, that a labor contract specifies the process for allocating overtime assignments. Such strategies are often complex, and the employer may have to take into account a variety of factors, such as seniority, previous overtime allocations, the hours or days in which the overtime work is needed, and so forth. Now suppose that a factory supervisor is trying to follow the labor contract and offers overtime to a specific employee. This employee, however, indicates that before accepting, it may be necessary to check with his or her spouse to make sure that child care responsibilities can be rearranged. The supervisor, however, may feel the pressure of a deadline and award the overtime opportunity to a second employee. If the first employee objects to this course of action, then he or she may file a complaint with the union.

When such differences of opinion arise, the union member takes the complaint to the shop steward. The shop steward may advise the employee that the supervisor handled things properly, but there are other appeal mechanisms, and the employee, even if refuted by the shop steward, still has channels for appeal.

Of course, if the shop steward agrees with the employee, the shop steward may follow prescribed methods for pursuing the complaint. The prescribed methods might include talking with the supervisor to get the other side of the story and then provide for lines of appeal on up the hierarchy of both the union and the company. In some cases, mediation or arbitration may be called into play, as may other efforts to resolve the dispute. The overtime, for example, may be reassigned to the first employee. Or the overtime may remain with the second employee while the first employee is also paid.

Let's return for a moment to the agreement reached by the Teamsters and United Parcel Service that we described previously. After the agreement was reached, the union became concerned that UPS was not moving quickly enough to create the new jobs to which it had agreed two years earlier. The union submitted its complaint to arbitration and won. UPS was given a specific timetable for adding the new jobs as agreed.[7]

endnotes

[1] Lipsky, David, and Donn, Clifford. *Collective Bargaining in American Industry* (Lexington, MA: Lexington Books, 1981). See also John Fossum, *Labor Relations: Development, Structure, Process*, 12th Ed. (Homewood, Illinois, Irwin Management, 2016).

[2] Koenig, David. "Labor Unions Say Recent Victories Signal a Comeback," Associated Press news release published in *The Bryan-College Station Eagle*, June 11, 2013, pp. E1, E6.

[3] Dwyer, Paula. "Hoffa at Halftime," *Business Week*, June 26, 2000, pp. 156–160.

[4] https://www.bls.gov/wsp/, accessed on May 21, 2017.

[5] Amour, Stephanie. "Will Fine Divide or Solidify Pilots?" *USA Today*, February 15, 1999, p. 1B.

[6] Amour, Stephanie. "ABC Locks Out Striking Employees," *USA Today*, November 3, 1998, p. B1.

[7] Dwyer, Paula. "Hoffa at Halftime," pp. 156–160.

glossary

A

Absenteeism when an employee does not show up for work

Absolute Advantage the ability to produce something more efficiently than any other country can

Accommodative Stance approach to social responsibility by which a company, if specifically asked to do so, exceeds legal minimums in its commitments to groups and individuals in its social environment

Accountability obligation employees have to their manager for the successful completion of an assigned task

Accounting comprehensive system for collecting, analyzing, and communicating financial information

Accounting Equation Assets = Liabilities Owners' Equity; used by accountants to balance data for the firm's financial transactions at various points in the year

Accounting Information System (AIS) organized procedure for identifying, measuring, recording, and retaining financial information for use in accounting statements and management reports

Accounts Payable (Payables) current liability consisting of bills owed to suppliers, plus wages and taxes due within the coming year

Acquisition the purchase of one company by another

Activity Ratio financial ratio for evaluating management's efficiency in using a firm's assets

Adverse Impact when minorities and women meet or pass the requirement for a job at a rate less than 80 percent of the rate of majority group members

Advertising any form of paid nonpersonal communication used by an identified sponsor to persuade or inform potential buyers about a product

Advertising Media variety of communication devices for carrying a seller's message to potential customers

Advertising promotional tool consisting of paid, nonpersonal communication used by an identified sponsor to inform an audience about a product

Affect a person's feelings toward something

Affirmative Action intentionally seeking and hiring employees from groups that are underrepresented in the organization

Affirmative Action Plan written statement of how the organization intends to actively recruit, hire, and develop members of relevant protected classes

Age Discrimination in Employment Act outlaws discrimination against people older than 40 years

Agency Shop requires employees to pay union fees even if they choose not to join

Agent individual or organization acting for and in the name of another party

Aggregate Output the total quantity of goods and services produced by an economic system during a given period

American Federation of Labor (AFL) an association of craft unions formed in 1886 by Samuel Gompers and others; the AFL had no political or social agenda but simply sought to improve working conditions and pay for its members

Americans with Disabilities Act forbids discrimination on the basis of disabilities and requires employers to provide reasonable accommodations for disabled employees

Angel Investors outside investors who provide new capital for firms in return for a share of equity ownership

Annual Percentage Rate (APR) one-year rate that is charged for borrowing, expressed as a percentage of the borrowed principal

Anti-Virus Software product that protects systems by searching incoming e-mails and data files for "signatures" of known viruses and virus-like characteristics

Apparent Authority agent's authority, based on the principal's compliance, to bind a principal to a certain course of action

Appellate Court court that reviews case records of trials whose findings have been appealed

Arbitration method of resolving a labor dispute in which both parties agree to submit to the judgment of a neutral party

Assembly Line Layout a same-steps layout in which a product moves step by step through a plant on conveyor belts or other equipment until it is completed

Asset Allocation relative amount of funds invested in (or allocated to) each of several investment alternatives

Asset any economic resource expected to benefit a firm or an individual who owns it

Association of Southeast Asian Nations (ASEAN) organization for economic, political, social, and cultural cooperation among Southeast Asian nations

Attitudes a person's beliefs and feelings about specific ideas, situations, or people

Audit systematic examination of a company's accounting system to determine whether its financial reports reliably represent its operations

Authoritarianism the extent to which a person believes that power and status differences are appropriate within hierarchical social systems such as organizations

Authority power to make the decisions necessary to complete a task

Automated Teller Machine (ATM) electronic machine that allows bank customers to conduct account-related activities 24 hours a day, 7 days a week

B

Balance of Payments flow of all money into or out of a country

Balance of Trade economic value of all products a country exports minus the economic value of all products it imports

Balance Sheet financial statement that supplies detailed information about a firm's assets, liabilities, and owners' equity

Banker's Acceptance bank promise, issued for a buyer, to pay a designated firm a specified amount at a future date

Bankruptcy court-granted permission for a company to not pay some or all debts

Bargain Retailer retailer carrying a wide range of products at bargain prices

Bear Market period of falling stock prices marked by negative investor sentiments with motivation to sell ahead of anticipated losses

Behavioral Approach to Leadership focused on determining what behaviors are employed by leaders

Behavioral Segmentation a segmentation strategy that uses behavioral variables to identify different market segments

Behavioral Variables behavioral patterns displayed by groups of consumers and that are used in developing a segmentation strategy

Benefits compensation other than wages and salaries

"Big Five" Personality Traits five fundamental personality traits especially relevant to organizations

Blue-Chip Stock common stock issued by a well-established and respected company with a sound financial history and a stable pattern of dividend payouts

Board of Directors governing body of a corporation that reports to its shareholders and delegates power to run its day-to-day operations while remaining responsible for sustaining its assets

Bond Indenture legal document containing complete details of a bond issue

Bondholders' Claim request for court enforcement of a bond's terms of payment

Bonus individual performance incentive in the form of a special payment made over and above the employee's salary

Book Value value of a common stock expressed as the firm's owners' equity divided by the number of common shares

Book-Entry Ownership procedure that holds investors' shares in book-entry form, rather than issuing a physical paper certificate of ownership

Bookkeeping recording of accounting transactions

Boycott labor action in which workers refuse to buy the products of a targeted employer

Branch Office foreign office set up by an international or multinational firm

Brand Awareness extent to which a brand name comes to mind when a consumer considers a particular product category

Brand Competition competitive marketing that appeals to consumer perceptions of benefits of products offered by particular companies

Brand Loyalty pattern of repeated consumer purchasing based on satisfaction with a product's performance

Branding process of using symbols to communicate the qualities of a product made by a particular producer

Breakeven Analysis identifies the sales volume where total costs equal total revenues by assessing costs versus revenues at various sales volumes and showing, at any particular selling price, the amount of loss or profit for each volume of sales

Breakeven Point sales volume at which the seller's total revenue from sales equals total costs (variable and fixed) with neither profit nor loss

Broker independent intermediary who matches numerous sellers and buyers as needed, often without knowing in advance who they will be

Budget detailed statement of estimated receipts and expenditures for a future period of time

Bull Market period of rising stock prices, lasting 12 months or longer, featuring investor confidence for future gains and motivation to buy

Bundling Strategy grouping several products together to be sold as a single unit at a reduced price, rather than individually

Business organization that provides goods or services to earn profits

Business (or Competitive) Strategy strategy, at the business-unit or product-line level, focusing on improving a firm's competitive position

Business Agent or Business Representative a full-time employee hired to act as a liaison between union members and supervisors if a local union is large

Business Continuation Agreement special form of business insurance whereby owners arrange to buy the interests of deceased associates from their heirs

Business Cycle short-term pattern of economic expansions and contractions

Business Ethics ethical or unethical behaviors by employees in the context of their jobs

Business Interruption Insurance insurance covering income lost during times when a company is unable to conduct business

Business Plan document in which the entrepreneur summarizes his or her business strategy for the proposed new venture and how that strategy will be implemented

Business Practice Law law or regulation governing business practices in given countries

Business Process Reengineering rethinking and radical redesign of business processes to improve performance, quality, and productivity

C

Cafeteria Benefits Plan benefit plan that sets limits on benefits per employee, each of whom may choose from a variety of alternative benefits

Capacity (production) amount of a product that a company can produce under normal conditions

Capacity (legal) competence required of individual entering into a binding contract

Capital funds needed to create and operate a business enterprise

Capital Gain profit realized from the increased value of an investment

Capital Items expensive, long-lasting, infrequently purchased industrial products, such as a building, or industrial services, such as a long-term agreement for data warehousing services

Capitalism system that sanctions the private ownership of the factors of production and encourages entrepreneurship by offering profits as an incentive

Cartel association of producers whose purpose is to control supply and prices

Catalog Showroom bargain retailer in which customers place orders for catalog items to be picked up at on-premises warehouses

Centralized Organization organization in which most decision-making authority is held by upper-level management

Certified Fraud Examiner (CFE) professional designation administered by the ACFE in recognition of qualifications for a specialty area within forensic accounting

Certified Management Accountant (CMA) professional designation awarded by the Institute of Management Accountants (IMA) in recognition of management accounting qualifications

Certified Public Accountant (CPA) accountant licensed by the state and offering services to the public

Chain of Command reporting relationships within a company

Channel Captain channel member who is most powerful in determining the roles and rewards of other members

Channel Conflict conflict arising when the members of a distribution channel disagree over the roles they should play or the rewards they should receive

Charismatic Leadership type of influence based on the leader's personal charisma

Check demand deposit order instructing a bank to pay a given sum to a specified payee

Checking Account (Demand Deposit) bank account funds, owned by the depositor, that may be withdrawn at any time by check or cash

Chief Executive Officer (CEO) the top manager of an organization

Civil Rights Act of 1991 amended the original Civil Rights Act

Classical Theory of Motivation theory holding that workers are motivated solely by money

Client-Server Network common business network in which clients make requests for information or resources and servers provide the services

Closed Shop a workplace in which only workers already belonging to a union may be hired by an employer

Closely Held (or Private) Corporation corporation whose stock is held by only a few people and is not available for sale to the general public

Closing step in the personal selling process in which salespeople ask prospective customers to buy products

Coalition an informal alliance of individuals or groups formed to achieve a common goal

Code of Professional Conduct code of ethics for CPAs as maintained and enforced by the AICPA

Coercive Power the power to force compliance by means of psychological, emotional, or physical threat

Cognition the knowledge a person presumes to have about something

Cognitive Dissonance when two sets of cognitions or perceptions are contradictory or incongruent

Collateral asset pledged for the fulfillment of repaying a loan

Collective Bargaining process by which labor and management negotiate conditions of employment for union-represented workers

Collusion illegal agreement between two or more companies to commit a wrongful act

Commercial Bank company that accepts deposits that it uses to make loans, earn profits, pay interest to depositors, and pay dividends to owners

Committee and Team Authority authority granted to committees or teams involved in a firm's daily operations

Common Law body of decisions handed down by courts ruling on individual cases

Common Stock most basic form of ownership, including voting rights on major issues, in a company

Communism political system in which the government owns and operates all factors of production

Comparative Advantage the ability to produce some products more efficiently than others

Compensation System total package of rewards that organizations provide to individuals in return for their labor

Compensatory Damages monetary payments intended to redress injury actually suffered because of a tort

Competition vying among businesses for the same resources or customers

Competitive Environment the competitive system in which businesses compete

Competitive Product Analysis process by which a company analyzes a competitor's products to identify desirable improvements

Compound Growth compounding of interest over time—with each additional time period, interest returns accumulate and earn more interest

Compulsory Arbitration used to settle disputes between the government and public employees such as firefighters and police officers

Computer Network group of two or more computers linked together by some form of cabling or by wireless technology to share data or resources, such as a printer

Computer-Aided Design (CAD) IS with software that helps knowledge workers design products by simulating them and displaying them in three-dimensional graphics

Computer-Aided Manufacturing (CAM) IS that uses computers to design and control equipment in a manufacturing process

Conceptual Skills abilities to think in the abstract, diagnose and analyze different situations, and see beyond the present situation

Congress of Industrial Organizations (CIO) an association of industrial unions formed in 1938 after being expelled from the American Federation of Labor (AFL)

Consideration item of value exchanged between parties to create a valid contract

Consistency dimension of quality that refers to sameness of product quality from unit to unit

Consumer person who purchases products for personal use

Consumer Behavior study of the decision process by which people buy and consume products

Consumer Goods physical products purchased by consumers for personal use

Consumer Price Index (CPI) a measure of the prices of typical products purchased by consumers living in urban areas

Consumerism form of social activism dedicated to protecting the rights of consumers in their dealings with businesses

Contingency Planning identifying aspects of a business or its environment that might entail changes in strategy

Contingent Worker employee hired on something other than a full-time basis to supplement an organization's permanent workforce

Contract agreement between two or more parties enforceable in court

Controller person who manages all of a firm's accounting activities (chief accounting officer)

Controlling management process of monitoring an organization's performance to ensure that it is meeting its goals

Convenience Goods inexpensive physical goods that are consumed rapidly and regularly

Convenience Services inexpensive services that are consumed rapidly and regularly

Convenience Store retail store offering easy accessibility, extended hours, and fast service

Cooperatives form of ownership in which a group of sole proprietorships or partnerships agree to work together for common benefits

Copyright exclusive ownership right belonging to the creator of a book, article, design, illustration, photo, film, or musical work

Core Competencies for Accounting the combination of skills, technology, and knowledge that will be necessary for the future CPA

Corporate Blogs comments and opinions published on the Web by or for an organization to promote its activities

Corporate Bond formal pledge obligating the issuer (the company) to pay interest periodically and repay the principal at maturity

Corporate Culture the shared experiences, stories, beliefs, and norms that characterize an organization

Corporate Governance roles of shareholders, directors, and other managers in corporate decision making and accountability

Corporate Raider investor conducting a type of hostile corporate takeover against the wishes of the company

Corporate Social Audit systematic analysis of a firm's success in using funds earmarked for meeting its social responsibility goals

Corporate Strategy strategy for determining the firm's overall attitude toward growth and the way it will manage its businesses or product lines

Corporation business that is legally considered an entity separate from its owners and is liable for its own debts; owners' liability extends to the limits of their investments

Cost of Goods Sold costs of obtaining materials for making the products sold by a firm during the year

Cost of Revenues costs that a company incurs to obtain revenues from other companies

Cost-of-Living Adjustment (COLA) labor contract clause tying future raises to changes in consumer purchasing power

Cost-Oriented Pricing pricing that considers the firm's desire to make a profit and its need to cover operating costs

Counterproductive Behaviors behaviors that detract from organizational performance

Coupon sales-promotion technique in which a certificate is issued entitling the buyer to a reduced price

Creative Selling personal-selling task in which salespeople try to persuade buyers to purchase products by providing information about their benefits

Credit Union nonprofit, cooperative financial institution owned and run by its members, usually employees of a particular organization

Crisis Management organization's methods for dealing with emergencies

Cultural Influences include culture, subculture, and social class influences that marketers use to study buying behavior

Currency (Cash) government-issued paper money and metal coins

Current Asset asset that can or will be converted into cash within a year

Current Dividend Yield and Current Interest Yield yearly dollar amount of income divided by the investment's current market value, expressed as a percentage

Current Liability debt that must be paid within one year

Current Ratio financial ratio for measuring a company's ability to pay current debts out of current assets

Customer Departmentalization dividing an organization to offer products and meet needs for identifiable customer groups

Customer Relationship Management (CRM) organized methods that a firm uses to build better information connections with clients, so that stronger company-client relationships are developed

Cybermall collection of virtual storefronts (business websites) representing a variety of products and product lines on the Internet

D

Data raw facts and figures that, by themselves, may not have much meaning

Data Mining the application of electronic technologies for searching, sifting, and reorganizing pools of data to uncover useful information

Data Warehousing the collection, storage, and retrieval of data in electronic files

Debit Card plastic card that allows an individual to transfer money between accounts

Debt company's total liabilities

Debt Financing long-term borrowing from sources outside a company

Decentralized Organization organization in which a great deal of decision-making authority is delegated to levels of management at points below the top

Decision Making choosing one alternative from among several options

Decision Support System (DSS) interactive system that creates virtual business models for a particular kind of decision and tests them with different data to see how they respond

Decision Tree Approach approach to leadership that provides decision rules for deciding how much participation to allow

Decisional Roles a category of managerial roles, including entrepreneur, disturbance handler, resource allocator, and negotiator

Decision-Making Process recognizing and defining the nature of a decision situation, identifying alternatives, choosing the "best" alternative, and putting it into practice

Decision-Making Skills skills in defining problems and selecting the best courses of action

Deductible amount of the loss that the insured must absorb before reimbursement is made

Default failure of a borrower to make payment when due to a lender

Defensive Stance approach to social responsibility by which a company meets only minimum legal requirements in its commitments to groups and individuals in its social environment

Delegation process through which a manager allocates work to subordinates

Demand the willingness and ability of buyers to purchase a good or service

Demand and Supply Schedule assessment of the relationships among different levels of demand and supply at different price levels

Demand Curve graph showing how many units of a product will be demanded (bought) at different prices

Demographic Segmentation a segmentation strategy that uses demographic characteristics to identify different market segments

Demographic Variables characteristics of populations that may be considered in developing a segmentation strategy

Department Store large product-line retailer characterized by organization into specialized departments

Departmentalization process of grouping jobs into logical units

Depreciation accounting method for distributing the cost of an asset over its useful life

Depression a prolonged and deep recession

Deregulation elimination of rules that restrict business activity

Detailed Schedule schedule showing daily work assignments with start and stop times for assigned jobs

Development usually refers to teaching managers and professionals the skills needed for both present and future jobs

Direct (or Interactive) Marketing one-on-one nonpersonal selling by nonstore retailers and B2B sellers using direct contact with prospective customers, especially via the Internet

Direct Channel distribution channel in which a product travels from producer to consumer without intermediaries

Direct Selling form of nonstore retailing typified by door-to-door sales

Direct-Response Retailing form of nonstore retailing in which firms directly interact with customers to inform them of products and to receive sales orders

Discount price reduction offered as an incentive to purchase

Discount House bargain retailer that generates large sales volume by offering goods at substantial price reductions

Discount Rate interest rate at which member banks can borrow money from the Fed

Distribution Channel network of interdependent companies through which a product passes from producer to end user

Distribution Mix combination of distribution channels by which a firm gets its products to end users

Diversification purchase of several different kinds of investments rather than just one

Divestiture strategy whereby a firm sells one or more of its business units

Dividend payment to shareholders, on a per-share basis, out of the company's earnings

Division department that resembles a separate business in that it produces and markets its own products

Divisional Structure organizational structure in which corporate divisions operate as autonomous businesses under the larger corporate umbrella

Domestic Business Environment the environment in which a firm conducts its operations and derives its revenues

Double Taxation situation in which taxes may be payable both by a corporation on its profits and by shareholders on dividend incomes

Dow Jones Industrial Average (DJIA) oldest and most widely cited market index based on the prices of 30 blue-chip, large-cap industrial firms on the NYSE

Drop Shippers limited-function merchant wholesaler that receives customer orders, negotiates with producers, takes title to goods, and arranges for shipment to customers

Dumping practice of selling a product abroad for less than the cost of production

E

Earnings Per Share profitability ratio measuring the net profit that the company earns for each share of outstanding stock

E-Catalog nonstore retailing in which the Internet is used to display products

E-commerce use of the Internet and other electronic means for retailing and business-to-business transactions

Economic Environment relevant conditions that exist in the economic system in which a company operates

Economic Indicators statistics that help assess the performance of an economy

Economic Strikes strikes triggered by stalemates over mandatory bargaining items, including such noneconomic issues as working hours

Economic System a nation's system for allocating its resources among its citizens

E-Intermediary Internet distribution channel member that assists in delivering products to customers or that collects information about various sellers to be presented to consumers, or they help deliver online products to buyers

Electronic Communication Network (ECN) electronic trading system that brings buyers and sellers together outside traditional stock exchanges

Electronic Conferencing IT that allows groups of people to communicate simultaneously from various locations via e-mail, phone, or video

Electronic Funds Transfer (EFT) communication of fund-transfer information over wire, cable, or microwave

Electronic Storefront commercial website at which customers gather information about products and buying opportunities, place orders, and pay for purchases

Embargo government order banning exportation or importation of a particular product or all products to or from a particular country

Eminent Domain principle that the government may claim private land for public use by buying it at a fair price

Emotional Intelligence (Emotional Quotient, EQ) the extent to which people are self-aware, can manage their emotions, can motivate themselves, express empathy for others, and possess social skills

Emotional Motives reasons for purchasing a product that are based on nonobjective factors

Employee Behavior the pattern of actions by the members of an organization that directly or indirectly influences the organization's effectiveness

Employee Information System (Skills Inventory) computerized system containing information on each employee's education, skills, work experiences, and career aspirations

Employee Retirement Income Security Act (ERISA) of 1974 ensures the financial security of pension funds by regulating how they can be invested

Employee Stock Ownership Plan (ESOP) arrangement in which a corporation holds its own stock in trust for its employees, who gradually receive ownership of the stock and control its voting rights

Employee-Focused Leader Behavior leader behavior focusing on satisfaction, motivation, and well-being of employees

Employment at Will principle, increasingly modified by legislation and judicial decision, that organizations should be able to retain or dismiss employees at their discretion

Encryption System software that assigns an e-mail message to a unique code number (digital fingerprint) for each computer so only that computer, not others, can open and read the message

Entrepreneur individual who accepts the risks and opportunities involved in creating and operating a new business venture

Entrepreneurship the process of seeking businesses opportunities under conditions of risk

Environmental Analysis process of scanning the business environment for threats and opportunities

Equal Employment Opportunity Commission (EEOC) federal agency enforcing several discrimination-related laws

Equal Employment Opportunity legally mandated nondiscrimination in employment on the basis of race, creed, sex, or national origin

Equal Pay Act of 1963 requires that men and women be paid the same amount for doing the same job

Equity Financing using the owners' funds from inside the company as the source for long-term funding

Equity Theory theory of motivation holding that people evaluate their treatment by the organization relative to the treatment of others

Escalation of Commitment condition in which a decision maker becomes so committed to a course of action that she or he stays with it even when it appears to have been wrong

Established Market one in which many firms compete according to relatively well-defined criteria

Ethical Behavior behavior conforming to generally accepted social norms concerning beneficial and harmful actions

Ethical Compliance the extent to which the members of the organization follow basic ethical (and legal) standards of behavior

Ethical Leadership leader behaviors that reflect high ethical standards

Ethics beliefs about what is right and wrong or good and bad in actions that affect others

Euro a common currency shared among most of the members of the EU (excluding Denmark, Sweden, and the United Kingdom)

European Union (EU) agreement among major European nations to eliminate or make uniform most trade barriers affecting group members

Evoked Set (or Consideration Set) group of products consumers will consider buying as a result of information search

Exchange Rate rate at which the currency of one nation can be exchanged for the currency of another nation

Exchange-Traded Fund (ETF) bundle of stocks or bonds that are in an index that tracks the overall movement of a market, but unlike a mutual fund can be traded like a stock

Exclusive Distribution strategy by which a manufacturer grants exclusive rights to distribute or sell a product to a limited number of wholesalers or retailers in a given geographic area

Expectancy Theory theory of motivation holding that people are motivated to work toward rewards that they want and that they believe they have a reasonable chance of obtaining

Expense Items industrial products purchased and consumed within a year by firms producing other products

Experimentation research method using a sample of potential consumers to obtain reactions to test versions of new products or variations of existing products

Expert Power power derived from information or expertise

Export product made or grown domestically but shipped and sold abroad

Exporter firm that distributes and sells products to one or more foreign countries

Express Authority agent's authority, derived from written agreement, to bind a principal to a certain course of action

Express Warranty a warranty whose terms are specifically stated by the seller

External Environment everything outside an organization's boundaries that might affect it

External Recruiting attracting persons outside the organization to apply for jobs

Extranet system that allows outsiders limited access to a firm's internal information network

F

Face Value (Par Value) amount of money that the bond buyer (lender) lent the issuer and that the lender will receive on repayment

Factors of Production resources used in the production of goods and services—labor, capital, entrepreneurs, physical resources, and information resources

Factory Outlet bargain retailer owned by the manufacturer whose products it sells

Fair Labor Standards Act sets a minimum wage and requires the payment of overtime rates for work in excess of 40 hours per week

Family and Medical Leave Act (FMLA) of 1993 requires employers to provide up to 12 weeks of unpaid leave for family and medical emergencies

Federal Deposit Insurance Corporation (FDIC) federal agency that guarantees the safety of deposits up to $250,000 in the financial institutions that it insures

Federal Funds Rate (Key Rate) interest rate at which commercial banks lend reserves to each other, usually overnight

Federal Reserve System (The Fed) central bank of the United States, which acts as the government's bank, serves member commercial banks, and controls the nation's money supply

Finance Company nondeposit institution that specializes in making loans to businesses and consumers

Financial Accounting field of accounting concerned with external users of a company's financial information

Financial Planning process of looking at one's current financial condition, identifying one's goals, and anticipating requirements for meeting those goals

Financial Statement any of several types of reports summarizing a company's financial status to stakeholders and to aid in managerial decision making

Firewall security system with special software or hardware devices designed to keep computers safe from hackers

First-Line Manager manager responsible for supervising the work of employees

First-Mover Advantage any advantage that comes to a firm because it exploits an opportunity before any other firm does

Fiscal Policies policies used by a government regarding how it collects and spends revenue

Fixed Asset asset with long-term use or value, such as land, buildings, and equipment

Fixed Cost cost that is incurred regardless of the quantity of a product produced and sold

Fixed-Position Layout labor, equipment, materials, and other resources are brought to the geographic location where all production work is done

Flat Organizational Structure characteristic of decentralized companies with relatively few layers of management

Flextime Programs method of increasing job satisfaction by allowing workers to adjust work schedules on a daily or weekly basis

Focus Group research method using a group of people from a larger population who are asked their attitudes, opinions, and beliefs about a product in an open discussion

Follow-Up operations control activity for ensuring that production decisions are being implemented

Foreign Direct Investment (FDI) arrangement in which a firm buys or establishes tangible assets in another country

Forensic Accounting the practice of accounting for legal purposes

Form Utility providing products with features that customers want

Franchise arrangement in which a buyer (franchisee) purchases the right to sell the good or service of the seller (franchiser)

Full Disclosure guideline that financial statements should not include just numbers but should also furnish management's interpretations and explanations of those numbers

Full-Service Merchant Wholesalers merchant wholesaler that provides credit, marketing, and merchandising services in addition to traditional buying and selling services

Functional Departmentalization dividing an organization according to groups' functions or activities

Functional Strategy strategy by which managers in specific areas decide how best to achieve corporate goals through productivity

Functional Structure organization structure in which authority is determined by the relationships between group functions and activities

G

Gainsharing Plan incentive plan that rewards groups for productivity improvements

Gantt Chart production schedule that breaks down large projects into steps to be performed and specifies the time required to perform each step

GDP per Capita gross domestic product divided by total population

General (or Active) Partner partner who actively manages a firm and who has unlimited liability for its debts

General Agreement on Tariffs and Trade (GATT) international trade agreement to encourage the multilateral reduction or elimination of trade barriers

General Partnership business with two or more owners who share in both the operation of the firm and the financial responsibility for its debts

Generally Accepted Accounting Principles (GAAP) accounting guidelines that govern the content and form of financial reports

Geo-Demographic Segmentation using a combination of geographic and demographic traits for identifying different market segments in a segmentation strategy

Geo-Demographic Variables combination of geographic and demographic traits used in developing a segmentation strategy

Geographic Departmentalization dividing an organization according to the areas of the country or the world served by a business

Geographic Segmentation geographic units, from countries to neighborhoods, that may be considered in identifying different market segments in a segmentation strategy

Geographic Variables geographic units that may be considered in developing a segmentation strategy

Global Business Environment the international forces that affect a business

Globalization process by which the world economy is becoming a single interdependent system

Goal objective that a business hopes and plans to achieve

Goal Orientation the manner in which people are motivated to work toward different kinds of goals

Goods Operations (or Goods Production) activities producing tangible products, such as radios, newspapers, buses, and textbooks

Goodwill amount paid for an existing business above the value of its other assets

Grapevine informal communication network that runs through an organization

Gross Domestic Product (GDP) total value of all goods and services produced within a given period by a national economy through domestic factors of production

Gross National Product (GNP) total value of all goods and services produced by a national economy within a given period regardless of where the factors of production are located

Gross Profit preliminary, quick-to-calculate profit figure calculated from the firm's revenues minus its cost of revenues (the direct costs of getting the revenues)

H

Hacker cybercriminal who gains unauthorized access to a computer or network, either to steal information, money, or property or to tamper with data

Hardware physical components of a computer network, such as keyboards, monitors, system units, and printers

Hawthorne Effect tendency for productivity to increase when workers believe they are receiving special attention from management

Hierarchy of Human Needs Model theory of motivation describing five levels of human needs and arguing that basic needs must be fulfilled before people work to satisfy higher-level needs

High-Contact System level of customer contact in which the customer is part of the system during service delivery

Hostile Work Environment form of sexual harassment deriving from off-color jokes, lewd comments, and so forth

Human Capital reflects the organization's investment in attracting, retaining, and motivating an effective workforce

Human Relations Skills skills in understanding and getting along with people

Human Resource Management (HRM) set of organizational activities directed at attracting, developing, and maintaining an effective workforce

Human Resources (HR) the people comprising an organization's workforce

Hypertext Transfer Protocol (HTTP) communications protocol used for the World Wide Web, in which related pieces of information on separate Web pages are connected using hyperlinks

I

Identity Theft unauthorized use of personal information (such as Social Security number and address) to get loans, credit cards, or other monetary benefits by impersonating the victim

Implied Authority agent's authority, derived from business custom, to bind a principal to a certain course of action

Implied Warranty a warranty, dictated by law, based on the principle that products should fulfill advertised promises and serve the purposes for which they are manufactured and sold

Import product made or grown abroad but sold domestically

Importer firm that buys products in foreign markets and then imports them for resale in its home country

Incentive Program special compensation program designed to motivate high performance

Income Statement (Profit-and-Loss Statement) financial statement listing a firm's annual revenues and expenses so that a bottom line shows annual profit or loss

Independent Agent foreign individual or organization that agrees to represent an exporter's interests

Individual Differences personal attributes that vary from one person to another

Individual Retirement Account (IRA) tax-deferred pension fund that wage earners set up to supplement retirement funds

Industrial Buyer a company or other organization that buys products for use in producing other products (goods or services)

Industrial Goods physical products purchased by companies to produce other products

Industrial Market organizational market consisting of firms that buy goods that are either converted into products or used during production

Industrial Selling selling products to other businesses, either for the purpose of manufacturing or for resale

Industrial Unionism the organizing of employees by industry rather than by skill or occupation

Inflation occurs when widespread price increases occur throughout an economic system

Informal Organization network, unrelated to the firm's formal authority structure, of everyday social interactions among company employees

Information meaningful, useful interpretation of data

Information Resources data and other information used by businesses

Information System (IS) system that uses IT resources to convert data into information and to collect, process, and transmit that information for use in decision making

Information Systems Managers managers who are responsible for the systems used for gathering, organizing, and distributing information

Information Technology (IT) various appliances and devices for creating, storing, exchanging, and using information in diverse modes, including visual images, voice, multimedia, and business data

Informational Roles a category of managerial roles, including monitor, disseminator, and spokesperson

Initial Public Offering (IPO) first sale of a company's stock to the general public

Insider Trading illegal practice of using special knowledge about a firm for profit or gain

Institutional Investor large investor, such as a mutual fund or a pension fund, that purchases large blocks of corporate stock

Institutional Market organizational market consisting of such nongovernmental buyers of goods and services as hospitals, churches, museums, and charitable organizations

Insurance Company nondeposit institution that invests funds collected as premiums charged for insurance coverage

Insurance Policy formal agreement to pay the policyholder a specified amount in the event of certain losses

Insurance Premium fee paid to an insurance company by a policyholder for insurance coverage

Intangible Asset nonphysical asset, such as a patent or trademark, that has economic value in the form of expected benefit

Intangible Personal Property property that cannot be seen but that exists by virtue of written documentation

Integrated Marketing Strategy strategy that blends together the Four Ps of marketing to ensure their compatibility with one another and with the company's nonmarketing activities

Intellectual Property property created through a person's creative activities

Intensive Distribution strategy by which a product is distributed through as many channels as possible

Intention part of an attitude that guides a person's behavior

Intentional Tort tort resulting from the deliberate actions of a party

Interest fee paid to a lender for the use of borrowed funds; like a rental fee

Intermediary individual or firm that helps to distribute a product

Intermediate Goal goal set for a period of one to five years into the future

Internal Recruiting considering present employees as candidates for openings

International Accounting Standards Board (IASB) organization responsible for developing a set of global accounting standards and for gaining implementation of those standards

International Competition competitive marketing of domestic products against foreign products

International Firm firm that conducts a significant portion of its business in foreign countries

International Law general set of cooperative agreements and guidelines established by countries to govern the actions of individuals, businesses, and nations

International Monetary Fund (IMF) UN agency consisting of about 150 nations that have combined resources to promote stable exchange rates, provide temporary short-term loans, and serve other purposes

International Organizational Structures approaches to organizational structure developed in response to the need to manufacture, purchase, and sell in global markets

Internet gigantic system of interconnected computer networks linked together by voice, electronic, and wireless technologies

Interpersonal Roles a category of managerial roles, including figurehead, leader, and liaison

Intranet organization's private network of internally linked websites accessible only to employees

Intrapreneuring process of creating and maintaining the innovation and flexibility of a small-business environment within the confines of a large organization

Intuition an innate belief about something, often without conscious consideration

Inventory Control process of receiving, storing, handling, and counting of all raw materials, partly finished goods, and finished goods

Investment Bank financial institution that specializes in issuing and reselling new securities

Involuntary Bankruptcy bankruptcy proceedings initiated by the creditors of an indebted individual or organization

ISO 14000 certification program attesting to the fact that a factory, laboratory, or office has improved its environmental performance

ISO 9000 program certifying that a factory, laboratory, or office has met the quality management standards set by the International Organization for Standardization

J

Job Analysis systematic analysis of jobs within an organization

Job Description description of the duties and responsibilities of a job, its working conditions, and the tools, materials, equipment, and information used to perform it

Job Enrichment method of increasing job satisfaction by adding one or more motivating factors to job activities

Job Redesign method of increasing job satisfaction by designing a more satisfactory fit between workers and their jobs

Job Satisfaction degree of enjoyment that people derive from performing their jobs

Job Specialization the process of identifying the specific jobs that need to be done and designating the people who will perform them

Job Specification description of the skills, abilities, and other credentials and qualifications required by a job

Joint Venture strategic alliance in which the collaboration involves joint ownership of the new venture

Just-in-Time (JIT) Production type of lean production system that brings together all materials at the precise time they are required at each production stage

K

Key Person Insurance special form of business insurance designed to offset expenses entailed by the loss of key employees

Knowledge Information System information system that supports knowledge workers by providing resources to create, store, use, and transmit new knowledge for useful applications

Knowledge Workers employees who are of value because of the knowledge they possess

L

Labor (Human Resources) physical and mental capabilities of people as they contribute to economic production

Labor Relations process of dealing with employees who are represented by a union

Labor Union a group of individuals working together to achieve shared job-related goals, such as higher pay, shorter working hours, more job security, greater benefits, or better working conditions

Labor-Management Relations Act (also known as the **Taft-Hartley Act**) passed to limit union power

Landrum-Griffin Act or Labor-Management Reporting and Disclosure Act amendment to the National Labor Relations Act that imposed regulations on internal union procedures

Law of Demand principle that buyers will purchase (demand) more of a product as its price drops and less as its price increases

Law of Supply principle that producers will offer (supply) more of a product for sale as its price rises and less as its price drops

Laws codified rules of behavior enforced by a society

Leader–Member Exchange (LMX) Model approach to leadership that stresses the importance of variable relationships between supervisors and each of their subordinates

Leadership the processes and behaviors used by someone, such as a manager, to motivate, inspire, and influence the behaviors of others

Leadership Neutralizers factors that may render leader behaviors ineffective

Leadership Substitutes individual, task, and organizational characteristics that tend to outweigh the need for a leader to initiate or direct employee performance

Leading management process of guiding and motivating employees to meet an organization's objectives

Lean Production System production system designed for smooth production flows that avoid inefficiencies, eliminate unnecessary inventories, and continuously improve production processes

Legal Compliance the extent to which the organization conforms to local, state, federal, and international laws

Legitimate Power power granted through the organizational hierarchy

Letter of Credit bank promise, issued for a buyer, to pay a designated firm a certain amount of money if specified conditions are met

Leverage ability to finance an investment through borrowed funds

Liability debt owed by a firm to an outside organization or individual

Liability Insurance insurance covering losses resulting from damage to people or property when the insured party is judged liable

Licensed Brands brand-name product for whose name the seller has purchased the right from an organization of individual

Licensing Arrangement arrangement in which firms choose foreign individuals or organizations to manufacture or market their products in another country

Limited Liability Corporation (LLC) hybrid of a publicly held corporation and a partnership in which owners are taxed as partners but enjoy the benefits of limited liability

Limited Liability legal principle holding investors liable for a firm's debts only to the limits of their personal investments in it

Limited Partner partner who does not share in a firm's management and is liable for its debts only to the limits of said partner's investment

Limited Partnership type of partnership consisting of limited partners and a general (or managing) partner

Limited-Function Merchant Wholesaler merchant wholesaler that provides a limited range of services

Line Authority organizational structure in which authority flows in a direct chain of command from the top of the company to the bottom

Line Department department directly linked to the production and sales of a specific product

Liquidity ease with which an asset can be converted into cash

Load Fund mutual fund in which investors are charged sales commissions when they buy in or sell out

Loan Principal amount of money that is loaned and must be repaid

Lobbying the use of persons or groups to formally represent an organization or group of organizations before political bodies

Local Area Network (LAN) computers that are linked in a small area, such as all of a firm's computers within a single building

Local Content Law law requiring that products sold in a particular country be at least partly made there

Local Unions (Locals) organized at the level of a single company, plant, or small geographic region

Lockout management tactic whereby workers are denied access to the employer's workplace

Locus of Control the extent to which people believe that their behavior has a real effect on what happens to them

Long-Term Goal goal set for an extended time, typically five years or more into the future

Long-Term Liability debt that is not due for at least one year

Low-Contact System level of customer contact in which the customer need not be part of the system to receive the service

Loyalty Programs sales promotion technique in which frequent customers are rewarded for making repeat purchases

M

M-1 measure of the money supply that includes only the most liquid (spendable) forms of money

M-2 measure of the money supply that includes all the components of M-1 plus the forms of money that can be easily converted into spendable forms

Machiavellianism used to describe behavior directed at gaining power and controlling the behavior of others

Mail Order (catalog marketing) form of nonstore retailing in which customers place orders for catalog merchandise received through the mail

Make-to-Order Operations activities for one-of-a-kind or custom-made production

Make-to-Stock Operations activities for producing standardized products for mass consumption

Management process of planning, organizing, leading, and controlling an organization's resources to achieve its goals

Management Accountant private accountant who provides financial services to support managers in various business activities within a firm

Management Advisory Services assistance provided by CPA firms in areas such as financial planning, information systems design, and other areas of concern for client firms

Management by Objectives (MBO) set of procedures involving both managers and subordinates in setting goals and evaluating progress

Management Information System (MIS) computer system that supports managers by providing information—reports, schedules, plans, and budgets—that can be used for making decisions

Manager someone whose primary work responsibilities are a part of the management process

Managerial (Management) Accounting field of accounting that serves internal users of a company's financial information

Managerial Ethics standards of behavior that guide individual managers in their work

Market mechanism for exchange between buyers and sellers of a particular good or service

Market Capitalization (Market Cap) total dollar value of all the company's outstanding shares

Market Economy economy in which individuals control production and allocation decisions through supply and demand

Market Index statistical indicator designed to measure the performance of a large group of stocks or track the price changes of a stock market

Market Price (Equilibrium Price) profit-maximizing price at which the quantity of goods demanded and the quantity of goods supplied are equal

Market Segmentation process of dividing a market into categories of customer types, or "segments" having similar wants and needs and who can be expected to show interest in the same products

Market Share (or Market Penetration) company's percentage of the total industry sales for a specific product type

Market Value current price of a share of stock in the stock market

Marketing activities, a set of institutions, and processes for creating, communicating, delivering, and exchanging offerings that have value for customers, clients, partners, and society at large.

Marketing Manager manager who plans and implements the marketing activities that result in the transfer of products from producer to consumer

Marketing Mix combination of product, pricing, promotion, and place (distribution) strategies used to market products

Marketing Objectives the things marketing intends to accomplish in its marketing plan

Marketing Plan detailed strategy for focusing marketing efforts on consumers' needs and wants

Marketing Research the study of what customers need and want and how best to meet those needs and wants

Marketing Strategy all the marketing programs and activities that will be used to achieve the marketing goals

Markup amount added to an item's purchase cost to sell it at a profit

Mass Customization principle in which companies produce in large volumes, but each item features the unique options the customer prefers

Master Limited Partnership form of ownership that sells shares to investors who receive profits and that pays taxes on income from profits

Master Operations Schedule schedule showing which products will be produced, and when, in upcoming time periods

Materials Management process of planning, organizing, and controlling the flow of materials from sources of supply through distribution of finished goods

Matrix Structure organizational structure created by superimposing one form of structure onto another

Maturity Date (Due Date) future date when repayment of a bond is due from the bond issuer (borrower)

Media Mix combination of advertising media chosen to carry a message about a product

Mediation a conflict resolution method used in labor disputes in which a neutral third party (the mediator) suggests, but cannot impose, a resolution to the other parties

Merchant Wholesalers independent wholesaler who takes legal possession of goods produced by a variety of manufacturers and then resells them to other organizations

Merger the union of two corporations to form a new corporation

Merit Salary System individual incentive linking compensation to performance in nonsales jobs

Middle Manager manager responsible for implementing the strategies and working toward the goals set by top managers

Mission Statement organization's statement of how it will achieve its purpose in the environment in which it conducts its business

Missionary Selling personal-selling task in which salespeople promote their firms and products rather than try to close sales

Mixed Market Economy economic system featuring characteristics of both planned and market economies

Monetary Policies policies used by a government to control the size of its money supply

Monetary Policy management of the nation's economic growth by managing the money supply and interest rates

Money object that is portable, divisible, durable, and stable, and that serves as a medium of exchange, a store of value, and a measure of worth

Money Market Mutual Fund fund of short-term, low-risk financial securities purchased with the pooled assets of investor-owners

Monopolistic Competition market or industry characterized by numerous buyers and relatively numerous sellers trying to differentiate their products from those of competitors

Monopoly market or industry in which there is only one producer that can therefore set the prices of its products

Mortgage Loan loan secured by property (the home) being purchased

Mortgage-Backed Security (MBS) mortgages pooled together to form a debt obligation—a bond—that entitles the holder (investor) to cash that flows in from the bundled mortgages

Motivation the set of forces that cause people to behave in certain ways

Multinational (or Transnational) Corporation form of corporation spanning national boundaries

Multinational Firm firm that designs, produces, and markets products in many nations

Mutual Fund company that pools cash investments from individuals and organizations to purchase a portfolio of stocks, bonds, and other securities

Mutual Savings Bank financial institution whose depositors are owners sharing in its profits

Myers-Briggs Type Indicator (MBTI) a popular questionnaire that some organizations use to assess personality types

N

NASDAQ Composite Index market index that includes all NASDAQ-listed companies, both domestic and foreign, with a high proportion of technology companies and small-cap stocks

National Association of Securities Dealers Automated Quotation (NASDAQ) System world's oldest electronic stock market consisting of dealers who buy and sell securities over a network of electronic communications

National Brands brand-name product produced by, widely distributed by, and carrying the name of a manufacturer

National Competitive Advantage international competitive advantage stemming from a combination of factor conditions, demand conditions, related and supporting industries, and firm strategies, structures, and rivalries

National Debt the amount of money the government owes its creditors

National Labor Relations Act (also known as the **Wagner Act**) sets up a procedure for employees to vote on whether to have a union

National Labor Relations Board (NLRB) established by the Wagner Act to administer its provisions

Natural Monopoly industry in which one company can most efficiently supply all needed goods or services

Need for Achievement an individual's desire to accomplish a goal or task as effectively as possible

Need for Affiliation an individual's desire for human companionship

Need for Power the desire to control one's environment, including financial, material, informational, and human resources

Negligence conduct that falls below legal standards for protecting others against unreasonable risk

Net Income (Net Profit or Net Earnings) gross profit minus operating expenses and income taxes

Niche a segment of a market that is not currently being exploited

No-Load Fund mutual fund in which investors pay no commissions when they buy in or sell out

Nominal GDP GDP measured in current dollars or with all components valued at current prices

Nonprogrammed Decision decision that is relatively unstructured and that occurs with low frequency

Norris-LaGuardia Act act that imposed severe limitations on the ability of the courts to issue injunctions prohibiting certain union activities, including strikes

North American Free Trade Agreement (NAFTA) agreement to gradually eliminate tariffs and other trade barriers among the United States, Canada, and Mexico

O

Observation research method that obtains data by watching and recording consumer behavior

Obstructionist Stance approach to social responsibility that involves doing as little as possible and may involve attempts to deny or cover up violations

Occupational Safety and Health Act (OSHA) of 1970 federal law setting and enforcing guidelines for protecting workers from unsafe conditions and potential health hazards in the workplace

Odd-Even Pricing psychological pricing tactic based on the premise that customers prefer prices not stated in even dollar amounts

Officers top management team of a corporation

Offshoring the practice of outsourcing to foreign countries

Oligopoly market or industry characterized by a handful of (generally large) sellers with the power to influence the prices of their products

Online Retailing nonstore retailing in which information about the seller's products and services is connected to consumers' computers, allowing consumers to receive the information and purchase the products in the home

On-the-Job Training training, sometimes informal, conducted while an employee is at work

Open-Market Operations the Fed's sale and purchase of securities in the open market

Operating Expenses costs, other than the cost of revenues, incurred in producing a good or service

Operating Income gross profit minus operating expenses

Operational Plan plan setting short-term targets for daily, weekly, or monthly performance

Operations (or Production) activities involved in making products—goods and services—for customers

Operations (Production) Management systematic direction and control of the activities that transform resources into finished products that create value for and provide benefits to customers

Operations (Production) Managers managers responsible for ensuring that operations activities create value and provide benefits to customers.

Operations Capability (Production Capability) special ability that production does especially well to outperform the competition

Operations Control process of monitoring production performance by comparing results with plans and taking corrective action when needed

Operations Process set of methods and technologies used to produce a good or a service

Order Processing personal-selling task in which salespeople receive orders and see to their handling and delivery

Organization Chart diagram depicting a company's structure and showing employees where they fit into its operations

Organizational Analysis process of analyzing a firm's strengths and weaknesses

Organizational Citizenship positive behaviors that do not directly contribute to the bottom line

Organizational Commitment an individual's identification with the organization and its mission

Organizational Stakeholders those groups, individuals, and organizations that are directly affected by the practices of an organization and who therefore have a stake in its performance

Organizational Structure specification of the jobs to be done within an organization and the ways in which they relate to one another

Organizing management process of determining how best to arrange an organization's resources and activities into a coherent structure

Outsourcing replacing internal processes by paying suppliers and distributors to perform business processes or to provide needed materials or services

Owners' Equity amount of money that owners would receive if they sold all of a firm's assets and paid all of its liabilities

P

Packaging physical container in which a product is sold, advertised, or protected

Paid-In Capital money that is invested in a company by its owners

Participative Management and Empowerment method of increasing job satisfaction by giving employees a voice in the management of their jobs and the company

Patent exclusive legal right to use and license a manufactured item or substance, manufacturing process, or object design

Path–Goal Theory theory of leadership that is a direct extension of the expectancy theory of motivation

Patriot Act legislation that increased U.S. government's power to investigate and prosecute suspected terrorists

Pay for Performance (or Variable Pay) individual incentive that rewards a manager for especially productive output

Pay-for-Knowledge Plan incentive plan to encourage employees to learn new skills or become proficient at different jobs

Penetration Pricing setting an initially low price to establish a new product in the market

Pension Fund nondeposit pool of funds managed to provide retirement income for its members

Perfect Competition market or industry characterized by numerous small firms producing an identical product

Performance dimension of quality that refers to how well a product does what it is supposed to do

Performance Appraisal evaluation of an employee's job performance to determine the degree to which the employee is performing effectively

Performance Behaviors the total set of work-related behaviors that the organization expects employees to display

Personal Influences include lifestyle, personality, and economic status that marketers use to study buying behavior

Personal Net Worth value of one's total assets minus one's total liabilities (debts)

Personal Selling promotional tool in which a salesperson communicates one-on-one with potential customers

Personality the relatively stable set of psychological attributes that distinguish one person from another

Person-Job Fit the extent to which a person's contributions and the organization's inducements match one another

PERT Chart production schedule specifying the sequence of activities, time requirements, and critical path for performing the steps in a project

Philanthropic Giving the awarding of funds or gifts to charities or other worthy causes

Physical Distribution activities needed to move a product efficiently from manufacturer to consumer

Physical Resources tangible items that organizations use in the conduct of their businesses

Picketing labor action in which workers publicize their grievances at the entrance to an employer's facility

Place (Distribution) part of the marketing mix concerned with getting products from producers to consumers

Place Utility providing products where customers will want them

Planned Economy economy that relies on a centralized government to control all or most factors of production and to make all or most production and allocation decisions

Planning management process of determining what an organization needs to do and how best to get it done

Point-of-Sale (POS) Display sales-promotion technique in which product displays are located in certain areas to stimulate purchase or to provide information on a product

Point-of-Sale (POS) Terminal electronic device that transfers funds from the customer's bank account to pay for retail purchases

Political Action Committees (PACs) special organizations created to solicit money and then distribute it to political candidates

Political-Legal Environment the relationship between business and government, usually in the form of government regulation of business

Portfolio combined holdings of all the financial investments of any company or individual

Positioning process of establishing an identifiable product image in the minds of consumers

Positive Reinforcement reward that follows desired behaviors

Possession Utility transferring product ownership to customers by setting selling prices, setting terms for customer credit payments, and providing ownership documents

Power the ability to affect the behavior of others

Power Orientation the beliefs that people in a culture hold about the appropriateness of power and authority differences in hierarchies such as business organizations

Premium sales-promotion technique in which offers of free or reduced-price items are used to stimulate purchases

Price Appreciation increase in the dollar value of an investment at two points in time (the amount by which the price of a security increases)

Price Earnings Ratio most commonly known as the P/E ratio, this ratio is the comparison of a firm's current share price to its current earnings per share.

Price Lining setting a limited number of prices for certain categories of products

Price Skimming setting an initially high price to cover new product costs and generate a profit

Pricing process of determining the best price at which to sell a product

Pricing Objectives the goals that sellers hope to achieve in pricing products for sale

Primary Data new data that are collected from newly performed research

Primary Securities Market market in which new stocks and bonds are bought and sold by firms and governments

Prime Rate interest rate available to a bank's most creditworthy customers

Principal individual or organization authorizing an agent to act on its behalf

Private Accountant salaried accountant hired by a business to carry out its day-to-day financial activities

Private Brand (or Private Label) brand-name product that a wholesaler or retailer has commissioned from a manufacturer

Private Enterprise economic system that allows individuals to pursue their own interests without undue governmental restriction

Private Warehouse warehouse owned by and providing storage for a single company

Privatization process of converting government enterprises into privately owned companies

Proactive Stance approach to social responsibility by which a company actively seeks opportunities to contribute to the well-being of groups and individuals in its social environment

Process Departmentalization dividing an organization according to production processes used to create a good or service

Process Layout (Custom-Product Layout) physical arrangement of production activities that groups equipment and people according to function

Product good, service, or idea that is marketed to fill consumers' needs and wants

Product Adaptation modifying an existing product for greater appeal in different countries

Product Departmentalization dividing an organization according to specific products or services being created

Product Differentiation creation of a product feature or product image that differs enough from existing products to attract customers

Product Extension marketing an existing product globally instead of just domestically

Product Features tangible and intangible qualities that a company builds into its products

Product Layout (Same-Steps Layout) physical arrangement of production steps designed to make one type of product in a fixed sequence of activities according to its production requirements

Product Liability tort in which a company is responsible for injuries caused by its products

Product Life Cycle (PLC) series of stages in a product's commercial life

Product Line group of products that are closely related because they function in a similar manner or are sold to the same customer group who will use them in similar ways

Product Mix the group of products that a firm makes available for sale

Product Placement promotional tactic for brand exposure in which characters in television, film, music, magazines, or video games use a real product with its brand visible to viewers

Product Positioning process of fixing, adapting, and communicating the nature of a product

Production Items goods or services that are used in the conversion (production) process to make other products

Productivity the amount of output produced compared with the amount of resources used to produce that output

Professional Corporation form of ownership allowing professionals to take advantage of corporate benefits while granting them limited business liability and unlimited professional liability

Profit Center separate company unit responsible for its own costs and profits

Profitability Ratio financial ratio for measuring a firm's potential earnings

Profits difference between a business's revenues and its expenses

Profit-Sharing Plan incentive plan for distributing bonuses to employees when company profits rise above a certain level

Programmed Decision decision that is relatively structured or recurs with some frequency (or both)

Promotion aspect of the marketing mix concerned with the most effective techniques for communicating information about products

Promotional Mix combination of tools used to promote a product

Property anything of value to which a person or business has sole right of ownership

Property Insurance insurance covering losses resulting from physical damage to or loss of the insured's real estate or personal property

Prospecting step in the personal selling process in which salespeople identify potential customers

Prospectus registration statement filed with the SEC, containing information for prospective investors about a security to be offered and the issuing company

Protectionism practice of protecting domestic business against foreign competition

Psychographic Segmentation a segmentation strategy that uses psychographic characteristics to identify different market segments

Psychographic Variables consumer characteristics, such as lifestyles, opinions, interests, and attitudes, that may be considered in developing a segmentation strategy

Psychological Contract set of expectations held by an employee concerning what he or she will contribute to an organization (referred to as *contributions*) and what the organization will in return provide the employee (referred to as *inducements*)

Psychological Influences include an individual's motivations, perceptions, ability to learn, and attitudes that marketers use to study buying behavior

Psychological Pricing pricing tactic that takes advantage of the fact that consumers do not always respond rationally to stated prices

Public Relations communication efforts directed at building goodwill and favorable attitudes in the minds of the public toward the organization and its products

Public Warehouse independently owned and operated warehouse that stores goods for many firms

Publicity promotional tool in which information about a company, a product, or an event is transmitted by the general mass media to attract public attention

Publicly Held (or **Public**) **Corporation** corporation whose stock is widely held and available for sale to the general public

Pull Strategy promotional strategy designed to appeal directly to consumers who will demand a product from retailers

Punishment unpleasant consequences of an undesirable behavior

Punitive Damages fines imposed over and above any actual losses suffered by a plaintiff

Purchasing acquisition of the materials and services that a firm needs to produce its products

Purchasing Power Parity the principle that exchange rates are set so that the prices of similar products in different countries are about the same

Pure Risk risk involving only the possibility of loss or no loss

Push Strategy promotional strategy designed to encourage wholesalers or retailers to market products to consumers

Q

Qualifying step in the personal selling process in which salespeople determine whether prospects have the authority to buy and ability to pay

Quality combination of "characteristics of a product or service that bear on its ability to satisfy stated or implied needs"

Quality Control action of ensuring that operations produce products that meet specific quality standards

Quality Improvement Team total quality management tool in which collaborative groups of employees from various work areas work together to improve quality by solving common shared production problems

Quality Ownership principle of total quality management that holds that quality belongs to each person who creates it while performing a job

Quid Pro Quo Harassment form of sexual harassment in which sexual favors are requested in return for job-related benefits

Quota restriction on the number of products of a certain type that can be imported into a country

R

Rational Motives reasons for purchasing a product that are based on a logical evaluation of product attributes

Real GDP GDP adjusted to account for changes in currency values and price changes

Realistic Job Preview (RJP) providing the applicant with a real picture of what it would be like performing the job the organization is trying to fill

Recession a period during which aggregate output, as measured by GDP, declines

Recruiting process of attracting qualified persons to apply for jobs an organization is seeking to fill

Referent Power power based on identification, imitation, loyalty, or charisma

Regulation the establishment of laws and rules that dictate what organizations can and cannot do

Regulatory (Administrative) Law law made by the authority of administrative agencies

Reintroduction reviving obsolete or older products for new markets

Relationship Marketing marketing strategy that emphasizes building lasting relationships with customers and suppliers

Replacement Chart list of each management position, who occupies it, how long that person will likely stay in the job, and who is qualified as a replacement

Reseller Market organizational market consisting of intermediaries that buy and resell finished goods

Reserve Requirement percentage of its deposits that a bank must hold in cash or on deposit with the Fed

Responsibility duty to perform an assigned task

Retail Selling selling a consumer product for the buyer's personal or household use

Retailer intermediary who sells products directly to consumers

Retained Earnings earnings retained by a firm for its use rather than paid out as dividends

Revenue Recognition formal recording and reporting of revenues at the appropriate time

Revenues funds that flow into a business from the sale of goods or services

Reward Power the power to give or withhold rewards

Right-to-Work Laws such laws prohibit both union shops and agency shops, thus making it illegal to require union membership as a condition of employment

Risk uncertainty about future events

Risk Avoidance practice of avoiding risk by declining or ceasing to participate in an activity

Risk Control practice of minimizing the frequency or severity of losses from risky activities

Risk Management process of conserving the firm's earning power and assets by reducing the threat of losses as a result of uncontrollable events

Risk Propensity the degree to which a person is willing to take chances and make risky decisions

Risk Retention practice of covering a firm's losses with its own funds

Risk Transfer practice of transferring a firm's risk to another firm

Risk–Return (Risk–Reward) Relationship principle that safer investments tend to offer lower returns whereas riskier investments tend to offer higher returns (rewards)

Roth IRA provision allowing individual retirement savings with tax-free accumulated earnings

Russell 2000 Index specialty index that uses 2,000 stocks to measure the performance of the smallest U.S. companies

S

S Corporation hybrid of a closely held corporation and a partnership, organized and operated like a corporation but treated as a partnership for tax purposes

S&P 500 market index of U.S. equities based on the performance of 500 large-cap stocks representing various sectors of the overall equities market

Salary compensation in the form of money paid for discharging the responsibilities of a job

Sales Agent independent intermediary who generally deals in the related product lines of a few producers and forms long-term relationships to represent those producers and meet the needs of many customers

Sales Promotion short-term promotional activity designed to encourage consumer buying, industrial sales, or cooperation from distributors

Sarbanes-Oxley Act of 2002 (Sarbox or Sox) enactment of federal regulations to restore public trust in accounting practices by imposing new requirements on financial activities in publicly traded corporations

Savings and Loan Association (S&L) financial institution accepting deposits and making loans primarily for home mortgages

Secondary Data data that are already available from previous research

Secondary Securities Market market in which existing (not new) stocks and bonds are sold to the public

Secured Loan (Asset-Backed Loan) loan to finance an asset, backed by the borrower pledging the asset as collateral to the lender

Securities stocks, bonds, and mutual funds representing secured, or asset-based, claims by investors against issuers

Securities and Exchange Commission (SEC) government agency that regulates U.S. securities markets

Securities Investment Dealer (Broker) financial institution that buys and sells stocks and bonds both for investors and for its own accounts

Securities Markets markets in which stocks and bonds are sold

Selective Distribution strategy by which a company uses only wholesalers and retailers who give special attention to specific products in its sales efforts

Self-Efficacy a person's belief about his or her capabilities to perform a task

Self-Esteem the extent to which a person believes that he or she is a worthwhile and deserving individual

Service Operations (or Service Production) activities producing intangible and tangible products, such as entertainment, transportation, and education

Services products having nonphysical features, such as information, expertise, or an activity that can be purchased

Services Companies Market firms engaged in the business of providing services to the purchasing public

Sexual Harassment making unwelcome sexual advances in the workplace

Shop Steward a regular employee who acts as a liaison between union members and supervisors

Shopping Agent (e-agent) e-intermediary (middleman) in the Internet distribution channel that assists users in finding products and prices but does not take possession of products

Shopping Goods moderately expensive, infrequently purchased physical goods

Shopping Services moderately expensive, infrequently purchased services

Shortage situation in which quantity demanded exceeds quantity supplied

Short-Term Goal goal set for the near future

Short-Term Solvency Ratio financial ratio for measuring a company's ability to pay immediate debts

Situational Approach to Leadership assumes that appropriate leader behavior varies from one situation to another

Small Business independently owned business that has relatively little influence in its market

Small Business Administration (SBA) government agency charged with assisting small businesses

Small Business Development Center (SBDC) SBA program designed to consolidate information from various disciplines and make it available to small businesses

Small Business Investment Company (SBIC) government-regulated investment company that borrows money from the SBA to invest in or lend to a small business

Smart Card credit-card-sized plastic card with an embedded computer chip that can be programmed with electronic money

Social Influences include family, opinion leaders (people whose opinions are sought by others), and such reference groups as friends, coworkers, and professional associates that marketers use to study buying behavior

Social Learning learning that occurs when people observe the behaviors of others, recognize their consequences, and alter their own behavior as a result

Social Networking Media websites or access channels, such as Facebook, Twitter, LinkedIn, and YouTube, to which consumers go for information and discussions

Social Networking network of communications that flow among people and organizations interacting through an online platform

Social Orientation a person's beliefs about the relative importance of the individual versus groups to which that person belongs

Social Responsibility the attempt of a business to balance its commitments to groups and individuals in its environment, including customers, other businesses, employees, investors, and local communities

Socialism planned economic system in which the government owns and operates only selected major sources of production

Sociocultural Environment the customs, mores, values, and demographic characteristics of the society in which an organization functions

Software programs that tell the computer how to function, what resources to use, how to use them, and application programs for specific activities

Sole Proprietorship business owned and usually operated by one person who is responsible for all of its debts

Solvency Ratio financial ratio, either short or long term, for estimating the borrower's ability to repay debt

Spam junk e-mail sent to a mailing list or a newsgroup

Span of Control number of people supervised by one manager

Specialty Goods expensive, rarely purchased physical goods

Specialty Services expensive, rarely purchased services

Specialty Store retail store carrying one product line or category of related products

Speculative Risk risk involving the possibility of gain or loss

Speed to Market strategy of introducing new products to respond quickly to customer or market changes

Spin-off strategy of setting up one or more corporate units as new, independent corporations

Spyware program unknowingly downloaded by users that monitors their computer activities, gathering e-mail addresses, credit card numbers, and other information that it transmits to someone outside the host system

Stability condition in which the amount of money available in an economic system and the quantity of goods and services produced in it are growing at about the same rate

Stabilization Policy government economic policy intended to smooth out fluctuations in output and unemployment and to stabilize prices

Staff Authority authority based on expertise that usually involves counseling and advising line managers

Staff Members advisers and counselors who help line departments in making decisions but who do not have the authority to make final decisions

Staff Schedule assigned working times in upcoming days for each employee on each work shift

Standard of Living the total quantity and quality of goods and services people can purchase with the currency used in their economic system

State of Certainty when the decision maker knows with reasonable certainty what the alternatives are and what conditions are associated with each alternative

State of Risk when the availability of each alternative and its potential payoffs and costs are all associated with probability estimates

State of Uncertainty when the decision maker does not know all the alternatives, the risks associated with each, or the likely consequences of each alternative

Statement of Cash Flows financial statement describing a firm's yearly cash receipts and cash payments

Statutory Law law created by constitution(s) or by federal, state, or local legislative acts

Stock portion of ownership of a corporation

Stock Broker individual or organization that receives and executes buy and sell orders on behalf of outside customers in return for commissions

Stock Exchange an organization of individuals to provide an institutional auction setting in which stocks can be bought and sold

Stock Split stock dividend paid in additional shares to shareholders, thus increasing the number of outstanding shares

Stockholder (or Shareholder) owner of shares of stock in a corporation

Strategic Alliance strategy in which two or more organizations collaborate on a project for mutual gain

Strategic Goal goal derived directly from a firm's mission statement

Strategic Leadership leader's ability to understand the complexities of both the organization and its environment and to lead change in the organization so as to enhance its competitiveness

Strategic Management process of helping an organization maintain an effective alignment with its environment

Strategic Plan plan reflecting decisions about resource allocations, company priorities, and steps needed to meet strategic goals

Strategy broad set of organizational plans for implementing the decisions made for achieving organizational goals

Strategy Formulation creation of a broad program for defining and meeting an organization's goals

Strict Product Liability principle that liability can result not from a producer's negligence but from a defect in the product itself

Strike labor action in which employees temporarily walk off the job and refuse to work

Strikebreaker worker hired as a permanent or temporary replacement for a striking employee

Subsidy government payment to help a domestic business compete with foreign firms

Substitute Product product that is dissimilar from those of competitors, but that can fulfill the same need

Supermarket large product-line retailer offering a variety of food and food-related items in specialized departments

"Super Wi-Fi" Network a powerful Wi-Fi network with extensive reach and strong signals that flow freely through physical objects such as walls

Supplier Selection process of finding and choosing suppliers from whom to buy

Supply the willingness and ability of producers to offer a good or service for sale

Supply Chain (or Value Chain) flow of information, materials, and services that starts with raw-materials suppliers and continues adding value through other stages in the network of firms until the product reaches the end customer

Supply Chain Management (SCM) principle of looking at the supply chain as a whole to improve the overall flow through the system

Supply Curve graph showing how many units of a product will be supplied (offered for sale) at different prices

Surplus situation in which quantity supplied exceeds quantity demanded

Survey research method of collecting consumer data using questionnaires, telephone calls, and face-to-face interviews

SWOT Analysis identification and analysis of organizational strengths and weaknesses and environmental opportunities and threats as part of strategy formulation

Syndicated Selling e-commerce practice whereby a website offers other websites commissions for referring customers

T

Tactical Plan generally short-term plan concerned with implementing specific aspects of a company's strategic plans

Talent Management the view that the people in an organization represent a portfolio of valuable talents that can be effectively managed and tapped in ways best targeted to organizational success

Tall Organizational Structures characteristic of centralized companies with multiple layers of management

Tangible Personal Property any movable item that can be owned, bought, sold, or leased

Tangible Real Property land and anything attached to it

Target Market the particular group of people or organizations on which a firm's marketing efforts are focused

Tariff tax levied on imported products

Task-Focused Leader Behavior leader behavior focusing on how tasks should be performed to meet certain goals and to achieve certain performance standards

Tax Services assistance provided by CPAs for tax preparation and tax planning

Technical Skills skills needed to perform specialized tasks

Technological Environment all the ways by which firms create value for their constituents

Telecommuting (or teleworking) form of flextime that allows people to perform some or all of a job away from standard office settings

Telemarketing form of nonstore retailing in which the telephone is used to sell directly to consumers

Tender Offer offer to buy shares made by a prospective buyer directly to a target corporation's shareholders, who then make individual decisions about whether to sell

Theory X theory of motivation holding that people are naturally lazy and uncooperative

Theory Y theory of motivation holding that people are naturally energetic, growth-oriented, self-motivated, and interested in being productive

360-Degree Feedback performance appraisal technique in which managers are evaluated by everyone around them—their boss, their peers, and their subordinates

Time Deposit bank funds that have a fixed term of time to maturity and cannot be withdrawn earlier or transferred by check

Time Management Skills skills associated with the productive use of time

Time Orientation the extent to which members of a culture adopt a long-term versus a short-term outlook on work, life, and other elements of society

Time Utility providing products when customers will want them

Time Value of Money principle that invested money grows, over time, by earning interest or some other form of return

Title VII of the Civil Rights Act of 1964 forbids discrimination in all areas of the employment relationship

Top Manager manager responsible for a firm's overall performance and effectiveness

Tort civil injury to people, property, or reputation for which compensation must be paid

Total Quality Management (TQM) all activities involved in getting high-quality goods and services into the marketplace

Trade Deficit situation in which a country's imports exceed its exports, creating a negative balance of trade

Trade Show sales-promotion technique in which various members of an industry gather to display, demonstrate, and sell products

Trade Surplus situation in which a country's exports exceed its imports, creating a positive balance of trade

Trademark exclusive legal right to use a brand name or symbol

Traditional Individual Retirement Account (IRA) provision allowing individual tax-deferred retirement savings

Training usually refers to teaching operational or technical employees how to do the job for which they were hired

Trait Approach to Leadership focused on identifying the essential traits that distinguished leaders

Transactional Leadership comparable to management, it involves routine, regimented activities

Transformational Leadership the set of abilities that allows a leader to recognize the need for change, to create a vision to guide that change, and to execute the change effectively

Transportation activities in transporting resources to the producer and finished goods to customers

Trial Court general court that hears cases not specifically assigned to another court

Trust Services management by a bank of an estate, investments, or other assets on behalf of an individual

Turnover annual percentage of an organization's workforce that leaves and must be replaced

Two-Factor Theory theory of motivation holding that job satisfaction depends on two factors, hygiene and motivation

U

Uncertainty Orientation the feeling individuals have regarding uncertain and ambiguous situations

Unemployment the level of joblessness among people actively seeking work in an economic system

Unethical Behavior behavior that does not conform to generally accepted social norms concerning beneficial and harmful actions

Uniform Commercial Code (UCC) body of standardized laws governing the rights of buyers and sellers in transactions

Union Shop requires employees to join a union within a specified period after being hired

Unlimited Liability legal principle holding owners responsible for paying off all debts of a business

Unsecured Loan loan for which collateral is not required

Utility ability of a product to satisfy a human want or need

V

Value relative comparison of a product's benefits versus its costs

Value Package a product is marketed as a bundle of value-adding attributes, including reasonable cost

Value-Added Analysis process of evaluating all work activities, materials flows, and paperwork to determine the value that they add for customers

Variable Cost cost that changes with the quantity of a product produced and sold

Venture Capital private funds from wealthy individuals seeking investment opportunities in new growth companies

Venture Capital Company group of small investors who invest money in companies with rapid growth potential

Vestibule Training off-the-job training conducted in a simulated environment

Video Retailing nonstore retailing to consumers via home television

Viral Marketing type of marketing that relies on the Internet to spread information like a "virus" from person to person about products and ideas

Virtual Leadership leadership in settings where leaders and followers interact electronically rather than in face-to-face settings

Voluntary Arbitration a neutral third party (the arbitrator) dictates a settlement between the two sides, who have agreed to submit to outside judgment

Voluntary Bankruptcy bankruptcy proceedings initiated by an indebted individual or organization

VSAT Satellite Communications network of geographically dispersed transmitter-receivers (transceivers) that send signals to and receive signals from a satellite, exchanging voice, video, and data transmissions

W

Wage Reopener Clauses allow wage rates to be negotiated at preset times during the life of the contract

Wages compensation in the form of money paid for time worked

Warehousing storage of incoming materials for production and finished goods for distribution to customers

Warranty seller's promise to stand by its products or services if a problem occurs after the sale

Whistle-Blower employee who detects and tries to put an end to a company's unethical, illegal, or socially irresponsible actions by publicizing them

Wholesale Club bargain retailer offering large discounts on brand-name merchandise to customers who have paid annual membership fees

Wholesaler intermediary who sells products to other businesses for resale to final consumers

Wide Area Network (WAN) computers that are linked over long distances through telephone lines, microwave signals, or satellite communications

Wi-Fi technology using a wireless local area network

Wireless Local Area Network (Wireless LAN or WLAN) local area network with wireless access points for PC users

Wireless Wide Area Network (WWAN) network that uses airborne electronic signals instead of wires to link computers and electronic devices over long distances

Work Sharing (or Job Sharing) method of increasing job satisfaction by allowing two or more people to share a single full-time job

Work Slowdown labor action in which workers perform jobs at a slower than normal pace

Work Team groups of operating employees who are empowered to plan and organize their own work and to perform that work with a minimum of supervision

Workers' Compensation Coverage coverage provided by a firm to employees for medical expenses, loss of wages, and rehabilitation costs resulting from job-related injuries or disease

Workers' Compensation Insurance legally required insurance for compensating workers injured on the job

Workforce Diversity the range of workers' attitudes, values, beliefs, and behaviors that differ by gender, race, age, ethnicity, physical ability, and other relevant characteristics

World Bank UN agency that provides a limited scope of financial services, such as funding improvements in underdeveloped countries

World Trade Organization (WTO) organization through which member nations negotiate trading agreements and resolve disputes about trade policies and practices

World Wide Web branch of the Internet consisting of interlinked hypertext documents, or Web pages

Y

Yellow-Dog Contracts requirements that workers state that they did not belong to and would not join a union

Index

Disseminator, manager's role as, 153
Dissonance reduction, 253
Distribution channels, 355–356
  agents, 415
  brokers, 415
  channel conflict, 416–417
  channel leadership, 416, 417
  defined, 414
  direct, 414
  nondirect, 415–416
  physical distribution, 423–425
  retail, 414–415, 419–422
  wholesale, 414, 415, 417, 420
Distribution mix, 355–356, 414–417
  defined, 414
  intermediaries in, 414
  international, 368
  small business, 369, 370
Distribution strategies, 416
District sales manager, 151
Disturbance handler, manager's role as, 153
Diversification, 562–563
  related, 158
  unrelated, 158
Diversified product lines, 385
Diversity
  distribution of labor force by race, 327
  talent development and recruiting, 328
  workforce, 326
Divestiture, 97, 98
Dividends, 97, 550–551, 561–562
Divine Chocolate, 40, 68
Division, 188–189
Divisional structure, 188–189
Division controller, 151
Division manager, 149, 150
DJIA. *See* Dow Jones Industrial Average
Dodd, Chris, 522
Dodd-Frank Wall Street Reform and Consumer
    Protection Act, 522
Dole, 130
Dollar Rent-A-Car, 398, 418
Dollar Shave Club, 387
Domestic business environment, 8–9
Donovan, Daniel, 63
Dorsey, Jack, 14
DoS. *See* Denial of service attacks
DoubleClick, 143
Double taxation, 94
Douglas, Oliver, 375
Dow Jones Industrial Average (DJIA), 557–559
Dream Dinners, 215
Drop shipper, 417
Drug tests in employee selection, 318
DSS. *See* Decision support system
DTC. *See* Direct-to-consumer advertising
Dubin, Michael, 387
Due date, 566

Duke Energy, 164
Dumping, 131, 401
Duncan, David, 63
Dunn, Kally, 245
DuPont, 49
Dynamic pricing, 399, 400

E

E-agents, 419
Early behavioral theory
  Hawthorne effect, 257
  hierarchy of human needs model, 258
  human resources model, 257–258
  need for achievement, 259–260
  need for affiliation, 260
  need for power, 260
  two-factor theory, 258–259
Earnings cycle, 494
Earnings per share, 496
EarthWeb (Steigler), 467
Ease of entry, 552
Eastwood, Clint, 287
eBay, 260, 367, 393, 399, 422
Ebert, Roger, 457
E-business
  pricing objectives, 395–396
  pricing strategies, 399
E-catalog, 421, 422
ECB. *See* European Central Bank
ECN. *See* Electronic communication network
E-commerce, 10, 87, 447
Economic agents, ethical behavior toward, 42
Economic differences as international trade barriers, 129
Economic environment, 8, 10–11, 351
Economic growth, 21–24, 80
Economic indicators
  aggregate output, 21
  defined, 21
  of economic growth, 20–24
  of economic stability, 25–27
  GDP per capita, 22
  gross domestic product, 21
  gross national product, 21
  productivity, 23–24
  purchasing power parity, 23
  real GDP, 22–23
  real growth rate, 22
Economic Recovery Act (2009), 26
Economic Recovery and Reinvestment Act, 513
Economic stability. *See* Stability
Economic strike, 619
Economic systems, 11–16
  balance of trade, 24
  capital, 12
  defined, 11
  entrepreneurs, 12
  factors of production in, 11–13